4th Edition
# 1995 North American
# Coins & Prices

## A GUIDE TO U.S., CANADIAN, AND MEXICAN COINS

edited by
David C. Harper
Editor of WORLD COIN NEWS
and BANK NOTE REPORTER

Published by

**krause
publications**

700 E. State Street • Iola, WI  54990-0001
Telephone: 715/445-2214

Please call or write for our free catalog of numismatic publications. Our toll-free number to
place an order or obtain a free catalog is 800-258-0929 or please use our regular business
telephone 715-445-2214 for editorial comment
and further information.

Library of Congress Catalog Number: 91-76402
ISBN: 0-87341-315-6

Printed in the United States of America

# Contents

# Preface

Providing coin collectors with accurate, independently produced pricing information on collectible coins has become a trademark of Krause Publications in its 40 years of publishing. We employ a full-time staff of market analysts who monitor auction results, trading on electronic networks connecting dealers across the United States, and trading at major coin shows.

This information is compiled by our analysts, and they determine what price most accurately reflects the trading that has occurred for each date and mintmark in each grade listed in *North American Coins & Prices*. By studying this information and referring back to it repeatedly, a collector can arm himself with the necessary knowledge to go out in the market and make wise purchasing decisions in adding pieces to his collection.

U.S. coins are perhaps the most popularly collected issues in the world. This is attributable in part to the popularity of coin collecting in the United States, but collectors in many other countries also covet collectible U.S. coins. After collecting U.S. coins for a while, many collectors in the United States branch out into issues of Canada and Mexico. These coins also enjoy a popular following in their countries of origin.

Thus, *North American Coins & Prices* brings together pricing information on all three of these countries. But this book also takes the price-guide concept a step further by providing information on the nuts and bolts of collecting coins: acquiring coins, grading them, organizing them into a collection, storing them properly, and much more. Novice collectors can gain the necessary knowledge to collect coins enjoyably; veterans can pick up some pointers to add to their knowledge.

# 1

# "A small beginning"

## The U.S. Mint grew from a modest start

**By Robert R. Van Ryzin**

It was a "small beginning" but a significant one. In July 1792, a site for the new U.S. Mint not yet having been secured, 1,500 silver half dismes were struck on a small screw press nestled in the cellar of a Philadelphia building owned by sawmaker John Harper. Though some have since categorized these early emissions of the fledgling U.S. Mint as patterns, it is clear that first President George Washington — who is said to have deposited the silver from which the coins were struck — considered this small batch of half dismes the first official U.S. coins.

It is true that this limited coinage, the first since passage of the act establishing the Mint on April 2, 1792, pales by comparison to modern U.S. Mint presses. Today's machines can churn out up to 750 coins a minute, striking as many as four coins at a time and boasting yearly mintages in the billions. But it is also true that these first small pieces — struck from silver and stamped with a plump Liberty on the obverse and a scrawny eagle in flight on the reverse — have tremendous historical importance.

For within what Washington would declare in his 1792 address to Congress as a "small beginning" were the seeds of a monetary system that has lasted more than 200 years and has become the study and admiration of many.

## Before the U.S. Mint

Collectors today can trace much of the nation's development and learn of its struggles and growth through its coinage: from a cumbersome system first proposed by Robert Morris, a Revolutionary War financier and first superintendent of finance, to the refinements tendered by Thomas Jefferson and Alexander Hamilton, which firmly placed the nation on an easily understood decimal system of coinage.

At first there was little coinage in circulation, except for foreign coins that arrived through trade or in the purses of the first settlers. Despite a dire need for coinage in the Colonies, Great Britain considered it a royal right and granted franchises sparingly. Much of the Colonial economy, therefore, revolved around barter, with food staples, crops, and goods serving as currency. Indian waupum or bead money also was used, first in the fur trade and later as a form of money for Colonial use.

Copper pieces were produced around 1616 for Sommer Islands (now Bermuda), but coinage within the American Colonies apparently didn't begin until 1652, when John Hull struck silver threepence, sixpence and shillings under authority of the General Court of Massachusetts. This coinage continued, with design changes (willow, oak and pine trees), through 1682. Most of the coins were dated 1652, apparently to avoid problems with England.

In 1658 Cecil Calvert, second Lord Baltimore, commissioned coins to be struck in England for use in Maryland. Other authorized and unauthorized coinages — including those of Mark Newby, John Holt, William Wood, and Dr. Samuel Higley — all became part of the landscape of circulating coins. In the 1780s this hodgepodge of coinage was augmented by influxes of counterfeit British halfpence and various state coinages.

In terms of the latter, the Articles of Confederation had granted individual states the right to produce copper coins. Many states found this to be appealing, and merchants in the mid-1780s traded copper coins of Vermont, Connecticut, Massachusetts, New Jersey, and New York. Not all were legal issues; various entrepreneurs used this as an invitation to strike imitation state coppers and British halfpence. Mutilated and worn foreign coins also circulated in abundance. Included among these were coins of Portugal, Great Britain and France, with the large majority of the silver arriving from Spain.

The accounting system used by the states was derived from the British system of pounds, shillings and pence. Each state was allowed to set its own rates at which foreign gold and silver coins would trade in relation to the British pound.

In 1782 Robert Morris, newly named superintendent of finance, was appointed to head a committee to determine the values and weights of the gold and silver coins in circulation. Asked simply to draw up a table of values, Morris took the opportunity to propose the establishment of a federal mint. In his Jan. 15, 1782, report (largely prepared by his assistant, Gouverneur Morris), Morris noted that the exchange rates between the states were complicated.

He observed that a farmer in New Hampshire would be hard-pressed if asked to determine the value of a bushel of wheat in South Carolina. Morris recorded that an amount of wheat worth four shillings in his home state of New Hampshire would be worth 21 shillings and eightpence under the

Robert Morris devised
a complicated plan for
a national coinage
based on a common
denominator of 1,440.

accounting system used in South Carolina.

Morris claimed these difficulties plagued not only farmers, but that "they are perplexing to most Men and troublesome to all." Morris further pressed for the adoption of an American coin to solve the problems of the need for small change and debased foreign coinages in circulation.

In essence, what he was advocating was a monometallic system based on silver. He said that gold and silver had fluctuated throughout history. Because these fluctuations resulted in the more valuable metal leaving the country, any nation that adopted a bimetallic coinage was doomed to have its gold or silver coins disappear from circulation.

Gouverneur Morris calculated the rate at which the Spanish dollar traded to the British pound in the various states. Leaving out South Carolina, because it threw off his calculations, Gouverneur Morris arrived at a common denominator of 1,440. Robert Morris, therefore, recommended a unit of value of 1/1,440, equivalent to a quarter grain of silver. He suggested the striking of a silver 100-unit coin, or cent; a silver 500-unit coin, or quint; a silver 1,000-unit coin, or mark; and two copper coins, one of eight units and the other of five units.

On Feb. 21, 1782, the Grand Committee of Congress approved the proposal and directed Morris to press forward and report with a plan to establish a mint. Morris had already done so. Apparently feeling confident that Congress would like his coinage ideas, Morris (as shown by his diary) began efforts at the physical establishment prior to his January 1782 report. He had already engaged Benjamin Dudley to acquire necessary equipment for the mint and hoped to have sample coins available to submit with his original report to Congress.

Things went awry, however.

By Dec. 12, 1782, 10 months after Congress had approved his plan, Morris still could not show any samples of his coins. He was forced, ironically, to suggest that Congress draw up a table of rates for foreign coins to be used until his report was ready. It was not until April 2, 1783, that Morris was able to note in his diary that the first of his pattern coins were being struck.

"I sent for Mr. Dudley who delivered me a piece of Silver Coin," he wrote, "being the first that has been struck as an American Coin."

He also recorded that he had urged Dudley to go ahead with production of the silver patterns.

It wasn't until April 23, 1783, that Morris was able to send his Nova Constellatio patterns to Congress and suggest that he was ready to report on establishing a mint. Apparently nothing came of Morris' efforts. Several committees looked into the matter, but nothing was accomplished. Dudley was eventually discharged as Morris' hopes dimmed.

Thomas Jefferson was the next to offer a major plan. Jefferson liked the idea of a decimal system of coinage, but disliked Morris' basic unit of value. As chairman of the Currency Committee, Jefferson reviewed Morris' plan and formulated his own ideas.

To test public reaction, Jefferson gave his "Notes on Coinage" to *The Providence Gazette, and Country Journal,* which published his plan in its July 24, 1784, issue. Jefferson disagreed with Morris' suggestion for a 1/1,440 unit of value and instead proposed a decimal coinage based on the dollar, with the lowest unit of account being the mil, or 1/1,000.

"The most easy ratio of multiplication and division is that by ten," Jefferson wrote. "Every one knows the facility of Decimal Arithmetic."

Jefferson argued that although Morris' unit would have eliminated the unwanted fraction that occurred when merchants converted British farthings to dollars, this was of little significance. After all, the original idea of establishing a mint was to get rid of foreign currencies.

Morris' unit, Jefferson said, was too cumbersome for use in normal business transactions. According to Jefferson, under Morris' plan a horse valued at 80 Spanish dollars would require a notation of six figures and would be shown as 115,200 units.

Jefferson's coinage plan suggested the striking of a dollar, or unit; half dollar, or five-tenths; a double tenth, or fifth of a dollar, equivalent to a pistereen; a tenth, equivalent to a Spanish bit; and a one-fifth copper coin, relating to the British farthing. He also wanted a gold coin of $10, corresponding to the British double guinea; and a copper one-hundredth coin, relating to the British halfpence.

In reference to his coinage denominations, Jefferson said, it was important that the coins "coincide in value with some of the known coins so nearly, that the people may by quick reference in the mind, estimate their value."

Thomas Jefferson pro-
posed that the United
States adopt a decimal
system of coinage.

More than a year, however, passed without any further action on his
plan or that proposed by Morris. In a letter to William Grayson, a member
of the Continental Congress, Washington expressed concern for the establishment of a national coinage system, terming it "indispensibly necessary." Washington also complained of the coinage in circulation: "A man
must travel with a pair of scales in his pocket, or run the risk of receiving
gold at one-fourth less than it counts."

## A plan at last

On May 13, 1785, the 13-member Grand Committee, to whom Jefferson's plan had been submitted, filed its report, generally favoring Jefferson's coinage system. The committee did, however, make slight alterations,
including the elimination of the gold $10 coin, the addition of a gold $5
coin, and the dropping of Jefferson's double tenth, which it replaced with a
quarter dollar. The committee also added a coin equal to 1/200 of a dollar (half cent). On July 6, 1785, Congress unanimously approved the Grand
Committee's plan. It failed, however, to set a standard weight for the silver
dollar or to order plans drawn up for a mint. These two factors led to new
proposals.

On April 8, 1786, the Board of Treasury, which had been reinstated after Morris' resignation as superintendent of finance two years prior, tendered three distinct coinage proposals based on varying weights and bimetallic ratios for the silver dollar. The first of these three plans (the one passed by Congress on Aug. 8, 1786) required the silver dollar to contain 375.64 grains of pure silver. The board's proposal varied from earlier coinage plans in that it advocated a higher bimetallic ratio of 15.256-to-1 and differing charges to depositors for coining of gold and silver. It called for minting of gold $5 and $10 coins, and silver denominations of the dime, double dime, half dollar, and dollar. In copper were a cent and half cent. The proposal came during the peak of state coinages and influxes of debased coppers, which, as the board reported, were being "Imported into or manufactured in the Several States."

Concerned over the need to control state coinages and foreign coppers, the board suggested that, within nine months of passage of its proposal, the legal-tender status of all foreign coppers be repealed and that values be set at which the state coppers would circulate. The board obviously expected immediate action and ordered a supply of copper that was being stored in Boston to be brought to New York in the hope that it might soon be coined. Their hopes, however, rested on the positive and quick action of Congress, something that hadn't occurred with the other proposals and would not occur this time.

Opposition to the mint was beginning to surface. Several members of Congress expressed their belief that the supply of foreign gold and silver coins in circulation was sufficient to preclude any need for a mint. They also argued that the problem with debased coppers could be solved by contracting with private individuals to strike the nation's cents and half cents.

Several proposals were offered for a contract coinage. On April 21, 1787, the board accepted a proposal by James Jarvis to strike 300 tons of copper coin at the federal standard. Jarvis, however, delivered slightly less than 9,000 pounds of his contract. The contract was voided the following year for his failure to meet scheduled delivery times, but helped to delay further action on a mint. Concerted action on a coinage system and a mint would wait until the formation of the new government.

Alexander Hamilton, named in September 1789 to head the new Treasury, offered three different methods by which the new nation could achieve economic stability, including the funding of the national debt, establishment of the Bank of North America, and the founding of the U.S. Mint. On Jan. 21, 1791, Hamilton submitted to Congress a "Report on the Establishment of a Mint." It was compiled through his study of European economic theories and the earlier works of Morris and Jefferson, along with the 1786 report of the Board of Treasury.

Hamilton agreed with Jefferson that the dollar seemed to be best suited to serve as the basic unit, but believed it necessary to establish a proper weight and fineness for the new coin. To do so, Hamilton had several Spanish coins assayed to determine the fine weight of the Spanish dollar. He also watched the rate at which Spanish dollars traded for fine gold (24 3/4 grains per dollar) on the world market.

From his assays and observations he determined that the Spanish dollar contained 371 grains of silver. He then multiplied 24 3/4 by 15 (the gold value of silver times his suggested bimetallic ratio) and arrived at 371 1/4 as the proper fine silver weight for the new silver dollar.

In regard to his findings, Hamilton admitted that Morris had made similar assays and had arrived at a weight of 373 grains for the Spanish dollar. Hamilton attributed the discrepancy to the differing equipment used in making the assays. He failed, however, to observe that silver coins were traded in the world market at actual weight rather than the weight at time of issue. The Spanish dollar contained 376 grains of pure silver when new, 4 3/4 grains more than Hamilton's proposed silver dollar.

Hamilton also wanted a bimetallic ratio of 15-to-1, in contrast to the Board of Treasury's 15.6-to-1 ratio. Hamilton said his ratio was closer to Great Britain's, which would be important for trade, and Holland's, which would be important for repaying loans from that country.

His report suggested the striking of a gold $10; gold dollar; silver dollar; silver tenth, or disme; and copper one-hundredth and half-hundredth. Hamilton felt the last of these, the half cent, was necessary because it would enable merchants to lower their prices, which would help the poor.

Congress passed the act establishing the U.S. Mint in April 1792. It reinstated several coin denominations left out by Hamilton and dropped his gold dollar. In gold, the act authorized a $10 coin, or "eagle"; a $5 coin, or "half eagle"; and a $2.50 coin, or "quarter eagle". In silver were to be a dollar, half dollar, quarter dollar, disme, and half disme, and in copper a cent and half cent.

Though it established a sound system of U.S. coinage, the act failed to address the problem of foreign coins in circulation. It was amended in February 1793 to cancel their legal-tender status within three years of the Mint's opening.

# Coinage begins

Coinage totals at the first mint were understandably low. Skilled coiners, assayers and others who could handle the mint's daily operations were in short supply in the United States. Also in want were adequate equipment and supplies of metal for coinage. Much of the former had to be built or imported. Much of the latter was also imported or salvaged from various domestic sources, including previously struck tokens and coins, and scrap metal.

Coinage began in earnest in 1793 with the striking of half cents and cents at the new mint located at Seventh Street between Market and Arch streets in Philadelphia. Silver coinage followed in 1794, with half dimes, half dollars and dollars. Gold coinage did not begin until 1795 with the minting of the first $5 and $10 coins. Silver dimes and quarters and gold $2.50

Production at the first U.S. mint, in Philadelphia, was minuscule by today's standards.

coins did not appear until 1796.

Under the bimetallic system of coinage by which gold and silver served as equal representations of the unit of value, much of the success and failure of the nation's coinage to enter and remain in circulation revolved around the supply and valuation of precious metals. One need only to gain a cursory knowledge of such movements to understand what role precious metals played in development of U.S. coinage. That role, to a large extent, determined why some coins today are rare and why some passed down from generation to generation are still plentiful and of lower value to collectors.

From the Mint's beginning, slight miscalculations in the proper weight for the silver dollar and a proper bimetallic ratio led gold and silver to disappear from circulation. The U.S. silver dollar traded at par with Spanish and Mexican dollars, but because the U.S. coin was lighter, it was doomed to export.

A depositor at the first mint could make a profit at the mint's expense by sending the coins to the West Indies. There they could be traded at par for the heavier Spanish or Mexican eight reales, which were then shipped back to the United States for recoinage. As a result, few early silver dollars entered domestic circulation; most failed to escape the melting pots.

Gold fared no better. Calculations of the bimetallic ratio by which silver traded for gold on the world market were also askew at first and were always subject to fluctuations. Gold coins either disappeared quickly after minting or never entered circulation, languishing in bank vaults. These problems led President Jefferson to halt coinage of the gold $10 and silver dollar.

The gold $10 reappeared in 1838 at a new, lower-weight standard. The silver dollar, not coined for circulation since 1803, returned in 1836 with a limited mintage. Full-scale coinage waited until 1840.

Nor was the coining of copper an easy matter for the first mint. Severe shortages of the metal led the Mint to explore various avenues of obtaining sufficient supplies for striking cents and half cents.

Witness, for example, the half-cent issues of 1795 and 1797 struck over privately issued tokens of the New York firm of Talbot, Allum & Lee because of a shortage of copper for the federal issue. Rising copper prices and continued shortages forced the Mint to lower the cent's weight from 208 grains to 168 grains in 1795.

By that same year Congress had begun to investigate the Mint. Complaints about high costs and low production had been raised. Suggestions that a contract coinage might be more suitable for the new nation surfaced again, despite bad experiences with previous attempts.

The Mint survived this and another investigation, but the problems of fluctuating metal supplies continued to plague the nation. In 1798, because of the coinage shortage, the legal-tender status of foreign coins was restored. Several more extensions were given during the 1800s, ending with the withdrawal of legal-tender status for Spanish coins in 1857.

In the 1830s great influxes of silver from foreign mints raised the value of gold in relation to silver, which made it necessary for the Mint to lower the standard weight of all gold coins in 1834. It also led to the melting of great numbers of gold coins of the old specifications.

By the 1850s discovery of gold in California had again made silver the dearer metal. All silver quickly disappeared from circulation. Congress reacted in 1853 by lowering the weight of the silver half dime, dime, quarter, and half dollar, hoping to keep silver in circulation. A new gold coin of $20 value was introduced to absorb a great amount of the gold from Western mines.

Not long after, silver was discovered in Nevada. By the mid-1870s the various mines that made up what was known as the Comstock Lode (after its colorful early proprietor, Henry P. Comstock) had hit the mother lode. Large supplies of silver from the Comstock, combined with European demonetization, caused a severe drop in its value, which continued through the close of the 19th century.

It was believed that the introduction of a heavier, 420-grain silver dollar in 1873, known as the Trade dollar, would create a market for much of the Comstock silver, bolster its price, and at the same time wrest control from Great Britain of lucrative trade with the Orient. It didn't. Large numbers of Trade dollars eventually flooded back into the United States, where they were, ironically, accepted only at a discount to the lesser-weight Morgan dollars.

The latter had been introduced in 1878 as a panacea to the severe economic problems following the Civil War. Those who proudly carried the banner of free silver contended that by taking the rich output of the Comstock mines and turning it into silver dollars, a cheaper, more plentiful form of money would become available. In its wake, they believed, would be a much needed economic recovery.

The Free Silver Movement gained its greatest support during the late 19th century when William Jennings Bryan attempted to gain the White House on a plank largely based on restoration of the free and unlimited coinage of the standard 412.5-grain silver dollar. He failed. Silver failed. Shortly thereafter the United States officially adopted a gold standard.

Silver continued to be a primary coinage metal until 1964, when rising prices led the Mint to remove it from the dime and quarter. Mintage of the silver dollar had ended in 1935. The half dollar continued to be coined through 1969 with a 40-percent-silver composition. It, too, was then debased.

Gold coinage ended in 1933 and exists today only in commemorative issues and American Eagle bullion coins with fictive face values. A clad composition of copper and nickel is now the primary coinage metal. Even the cent is no longer all copper; a copper-coated zinc composition has been used since 1982.

Precious-metal supplies were also linked to the opening of additional mints, which served the parent facility in Philadelphia. The impact of gold discoveries in the 1820s in the southern Appalachian Mountains was directly tied to the construction of branch mints in Dahlonega, Ga., and Charlotte, N.C., in 1838. These new mints struck only gold coins. New Orleans also became the site of a branch mint in the same year as Dahlonega and Charlotte. It took in some of the outflow of gold from Southern mines, but also struck silver coins.

Discovery of gold in California in the late 1840s created a gold rush, and from it sprang a great western migration. Private issues of gold coinage, often of debased quality, were prevalent, and the cost of shipping the metal eastward for coinage at Philadelphia was high. A call for an official branch mint was soon heard and heeded in 1852 with the authorization of the San Francisco Mint, which began taking deposits in 1854.

The discovery of silver in the Comstock Lode led to yet another mint. Located only a short distance via Virginia & Truckee Railroad from the fabulous Comstock Lode, the Carson City Mint began receiving bullion in early 1870. It struck only silver coins during its tenure.

Denver, also located in a mineral-rich region, became the site of an assay office in 1863 when the government purchased the Clark, Gruber & Co. private mint. It became a U.S. branch mint in 1906. In addition to the Denver and Philadelphia mints, San Francisco and a newly upgraded facility in West Point, N.Y., continue to serve as U.S. mints, but the others have left behind a rich legacy.

The collector taking a more extended journey into the history of U.S. coinage can find plenty of interesting tales — some as tall as the day is long and others factually based — all of which are part of the rich and ever-changing panoply of U.S. coinage history. There are stories of denominations that failed, great discoveries, great rarities, great collectors, and, for those with an artistic bent, a rich field of pattern coins to be explored and a wealth of much-heralded designs by famous sculptors such as Augustus Saint-Gaudens, Adolph Weinman, James Earle Fraser, and others.

For those who are drawn to the hobby by the allure of age-old relics of days gone by, or by coins handed down through the family, or even by dreams of great wealth, coin collecting has much to offer. The history of the U.S. Mint, with its small but ever so important beginning, is the starting point.

# 2

# Making money
## How coins are manufactured

**By Alan Herbert**

Just as printing is the process by which paper money is made, so is minting the method of manufacturing coins. The two are often confused by the public, but they are completely different.

The history of minting goes back several centuries before the birth of Christ. The Lydians are credited with making the first crude coins in the Middle East about 700 B.C., although the Chinese and Koreans trace their coinage back even further.

Some early coins were cast. That process continued in China into the 1900s, but only for low-value pieces. Here again the average person often assumes that all coins are cast, but as you will see, only a tiny fraction of a percent are — or were — actually made that way.

The methods developed by the Greeks and Romans centered on making dies that could be hammered by hand into the surface of a lump of metal, flattening it and impressing a design. Hammered coinage continued until after the end of the Middle Ages, about 1500. After that the first machines that could strike coins were invented. Today their successors can pound out 750 or more coins a minute.

From the early days when the fixed die was driven into a stump or a hole drilled in a rock, through fixing it in an anvil (the fixed die is still called the anvil die), to today's modern coin presses, the process is much the same. Force is applied to devices that impress or apply a design to a piece of material, which is transformed into a coin.

Early dies were made of wood. Then came copper, bronze, and finally iron as technology advanced. Today dies are made from exotic steels with special qualities that make them ideal for striking coins.

The history of coinage is fascinating. Interwoven into it are several familiar names: Leonardo da Vinci is credited with inventing one of the first coin presses. James Watt, English inventor of the steam engine, was the first to incorporate steam power to drive the coin presses that earlier had depended on horses or human arms.

Whether the power comes from a hand holding a hammer or a mechanical ram, and whether it comes from above, below, or the side, the process is called "striking" a coin. Modern coin presses use a variety of methods in applying brute force to a piece of metal to turn it into a coin.

Another fable that traces to casting coins is the common belief that coins are made from liquid metal or at the least are red hot when they are struck. Neither is true. A coin's design is formed by the pressure that causes the metal to cold-flow into the pattern that you see on the coins in your pocket.

There are three basic parts of the minting process: (1) the making of the planchet, which is divided into the selection and processing of the metal and the preparation of the planchets, (2) the making of the dies, and (3) the use of the dies to strike the planchets. To help you remember these three parts, think of "P", "D" and "S" for planchet, die and striking.

# Choosing a metal

Many different metals have and are being used for coins. The most popular coinage metals are those commonly found and relatively cheap, so they can be used for striking low-value coins. Precious metals — like silver, gold and platinum — are still used for commemorative coins.

A good coinage metal requires certain properties. The metal must be soft enough to be easily worked yet hard enough to withstand the wear and tear of a thousand pockets, a hundred thousand transactions. Few metals have all the right properties, so coin metals usually are an alloy, or mixture of two or more metals.

Copper is a favorite coin metal, either by itself or in an alloy. Zinc, nickel, iron, and aluminum are also found in coins struck by the United States and other countries. Silver and gold have to be alloyed with some metal, usually copper, to be hard enough to withstand commercial life. The so-called "pure" coins of silver or gold are known as "bullion coins," bought and sold primarily for their precious-metal content.

The metals chosen for a coin are melted and mixed together, and either poured into ingots or blocks, or extruded from furnaces that continuously cast a long strip of the metal. The ingots are passed several times between the big rolls in a rolling mill to reduce the ingot to the thickness of the blanks needed.

Once the strip is rolled to the correct thickness, it is sent to a blanking press. A gang of blunt-end punches are driven through the sheet, producing a dozen or more blanks with each stroke. The rough blanks are then ready to be processed.

Strips of coin metal stand ready to be cut into "blanks."

A binful of blanks are ready for the coin press.

# Making the "blanks"

The piece of metal (occasionally some other material, so it isn't always metal) that becomes a coin is known as a "blank." This is a usually round, flat piece that usually has been punched or cut from a sheet or strip of coin metal.

Before a blank can become a coin it has to be processed, cleaned, softened, and given what is known as an "upset edge" — a raised ridge or rim around both sides. The blank then becomes a "planchet" and is ready to be struck into a coin by the dies.

First they go through what looks like a monstrous cement mixer. A huge cylinder revolves slowly as the planchets are fed in at one end and spiral their way through. This is an annealing oven, which heats the planchets to soften them. When they come out the end, they fall into a bath where they are cleaned with a diluted acid or soap solution.

As the final step, they go through the upsetting mill, the machine that puts the raised rim on the blank and turns it into a planchet, ready to be struck. In a different department the process of making the dies used to strike the coins has already begun.

# Preparing the dies

For those who haven't studied metallurgy, the concept of hard metal flowing about is pretty hard to swallow, but this is actually what happens. It is basically the same process as the one used in an auto plant to turn a flat sheet of steel into a fender with multiple curves and sharp bends. The cold metal is moved about by the pressure applied.

To make the metal move into the desired design, there has to be a die. Actually there has to be two dies, because one of the laws of physics is that for every action there has to be an equal and opposite reaction. You cannot hold a piece of metal in midair and strike one side of it. Instead you make two dies, fix one, and drive the other one against it — with a piece of metal in between to accept the design from each die.

A die is a piece of hard metal, like steel, with a design on its face that helps to form a mirror image on the struck coin. Early dies were made by hand. Engravers used hand tools to laboriously cut each letter, each digit, and each owl or eagle or whatever design was being used into the face of the die. Notice that this is "into" the surface of the die. Each part of the die design is a hole or cavity of varying shape and depth.

This is because we want a mirror image on the coin, but we want it raised, or in "relief." To make a relief image on a coin, the image on the die has to be into the face of the die, or "incuse." Of course, if we want an incuse image on the coin, such as the gold $2.50 and $5 coins of 1908-1929, the design on the die face would have to be in relief.

To fully understand this, take a coin from your pocket and a piece of aluminum foil. Press the foil down over the coin design and rub it with an

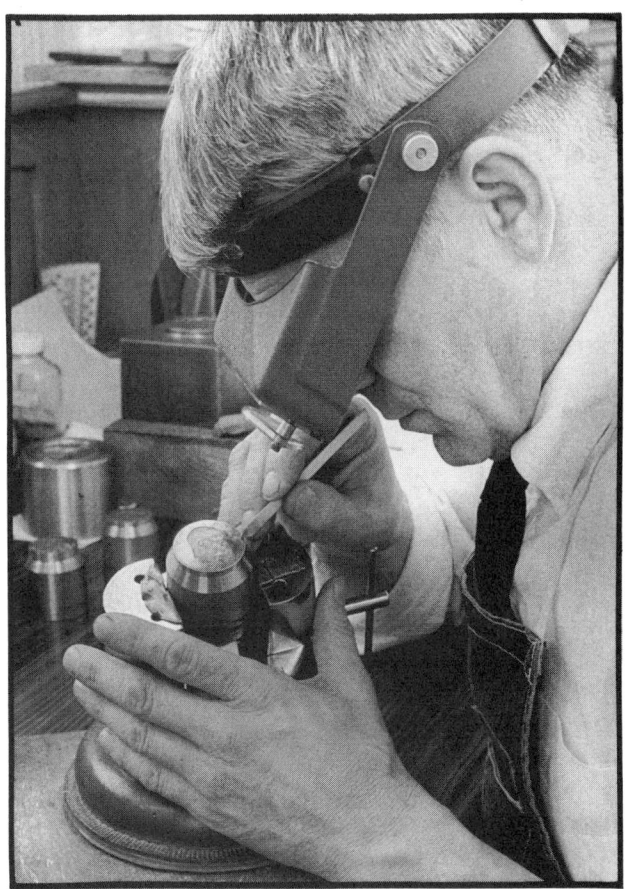

An engraver at the U.S. Mint puts the finishing touches on a die.

eraser. When you take the foil off and look at the side that was in contact with the coin, you have a perfect copy of a die. Everywhere there is a relief design on the coin there is an incuse design on your foil "die."

A galvano goes on the reducing lathe.

# From sketchbook to coin

The design process begins with an artist's sketch. This is translated into a three-dimensional relief design that is hand-carved from plaster or, in recent years, from a form of plastic.

The plaster or plastic design is then transformed into a "galvano," which is an exact copy of the design that has been plated with a thin layer of copper. This is used as a template or pattern in a reducing lathe, which cuts the design into a die blank.

This die becomes the master die, from which all of the following steps descend. The process can be reversed so that the design will be cut in relief, forming a tool called a "hub," which is simply a piece of steel with the design in relief, exactly the same as the relief design on the intended coin.

To make working dies, pieces of special steel are prepared, with one end shaped with a slight cone. The die blank is softened by heating it. Then the hub is forced into the face of the die, forming the incuse, mirror-image design in the face of the die.

The process usually has to be repeated because the die metal will harden from the pressure. The die is removed, softened, and returned to the hubbing press for a second impression from the hub. As you can imagine, it takes several hundred tons per square inch to force the hub into the die. Logically, this process is called "hubbing" a die.

The advantage of hubbing a die is that thousands of working dies can be made from a single hub, each one for all practical purposes as identical as the proverbial peas in a pod. This enables, for example, U.S. mints to strike billions of one-cent coins each year, each with the identical design.

Die making has come a long way from the early days when it took a skilled engraver a full day to carve a single letter into a die. The use of punches with the digits, letters or even parts of the design on the end reduced the amount of time required for the process. Today, thanks to the use of hubs, a complete die can be finished in a matter of hours.

# Striking the coin

Yesterday's die might strike only a few hundred coins. Today it is not unusual for a die to strike well over a million coins.

The coin press used to strike modern coins is a complicated piece of equipment that consists basically of a feed system to place the planchets in position for the stroke of the hammer die to form a coin. This process takes only a fraction of a second, so the press has to operate precisely to spew out the hundreds of coins that are struck every minute.

The end of the early hammered coinage came with the introduction of the collar, which often is called the "third" die. The collar is nothing more than a steel plate with a hole in it. This hole is the exact diameter of the intended coin and often is lined with carbide to prolong its life. It surrounds the lower, or fixed, die. Its sole purpose is to contain the coin metal

Rows of modern coin presses at the Philadelphia Mint turn out billions of coins a year.

A hopper is full of shiny new one-cent coins ready for shipment.

to keep it from spreading sideways under the force of the strike.

If the intended coin has serrations, or "reeds," on the edge, then the collar has the matching design. The strike forces the coin metal against the serrations in the collar, forming the reeded edge at the same time that the two dies form the front and back, or obverse and reverse, of the coin.

Lettered-edge coins are produced usually by running the planchets through an edge-lettering die, or by using a segmented collar that is forced against the edge of the planchet during the strike by hydraulic pressure.

Several hundred tons were required to drive a hub into a die. Not as much but still significant amounts of force are needed to strike coins. A cent, for example, requires about 30 tons per square inch. One of the silver dollars took 150 tons. The other denominations fall in between.

Modern coin presses apply pressure in a variety of ways. A ram, carrying the moving or "hammer" die, is forced against the planchet. Most commonly this is with the mechanical advantage of a "knuckle" or connected pieces to which pressure is applied from the side. When the joint straightens — like straightening your finger — the ram at the end of the piece is driven into the planchet.

Once the strike is complete, at the final impact of the die pair, the coin has been produced. It is officially a coin now, and it's complete and ready to be spent.

# The making of proof coins

While the high-speed coining presses are turning out billions of coins for commerce, there are other presses working at much slower speeds to produce collector coins, such as "proof" coins.

Proof coins started out as special presentation pieces. They were and still are struck on specially prepared planchets with specially prepared dies. Today the definition of a proof coin also requires that it be struck two or more times.

To make a proof coin, the planchets go through much the same process, but with some special care and some extra steps. Currently all proof versions of circulating U.S. coins are struck at the San Francisco Mint, but some of the proof commemorative coins have been struck at the other mints, including West Point.

After the proof blanks are punched from the strip, they go through the annealing oven, but on a conveyor belt rather than being tumbled in the revolving drum. After cleaning and upsetting they go into a huge vibrating machine where they are mixed with steel pellets that look like tiny footballs. The movement of the steel pellets against the planchets burnishes, or smooths, the surface so any scratches and gouges the planchets pick up during processing are smoothed over.

Proof dies get an extra polishing before the hubbing process. Like all other dies, they are made at Philadelphia and shipped to the branch mints.

When the proof dies arrive at San Francisco, they are worked on by a team of specialists who use diamond dust and other polishing agents to turn the fields of the proof dies into mirrorlike surfaces. The incuse design is sandblasted to make the surface rough, producing what is known as a "frosted" design.

Because collectors like the frosted proofs, the design is periodically swabbed with acid to keep the surface rough and increase the number of frosted proofs from each die. This is a relatively recent improvement, so frosted examples of earlier proofs are considerably scarcer.

The presses that strike proof coins usually are hand-operated rather than automatic. Some of the newer presses use equipment such as vacuum suction devices to pick up the planchets, place them in the coining chamber, and then remove the struck coins. This avoids handling the pieces any more than necessary.

On a hand-operated press, the operator takes a freshly washed and dried planchet and, using tongs, places it in the collar. The ram with the die descends two or more times before the finished coin is removed from the collar and carefully stored in a box for transport to storage or the packaging line. After each strike the operator wipes the dies to make sure that lint or other particles don't stick to the dies and damage the coins as they are struck.

Proof dies are used for only a short time before being discarded. Maximum die life is usually less than 10,000 coins, varying with the size of the coin and the alloy being struck.

# Keeping up with demand

The minting process has come a long way from the first metal pellets that are barely recognizable as coins. Companies that manufacture equipment used in the world's mints are constantly researching to develop new methods of producing coins.

The purpose is to strike coins at as low a cost as possible and still retain the desired beauty in the design. Modern machines and new methods help the mints keep up with demand for coins.

The important point to remember is that the coins in your pocket are made no differently from the coins in the pocket of an English schoolchild or a Spanish police officer or an Italian opera singer. Mints around the world use the same methods, same equipment, and same common coin metals, with few if any variations from the basic methods. The minting process was shrouded in secrecy for centuries, but now has become common knowledge.

For the collector, knowing exactly how coins are minted can be some of the most valuable knowledge that can be learned. It often will make the difference between accepting a coin as a valuable addition to a collection or spotting it as a fake, counterfeit, or altered coin.

Because of the improvements in the making of coins, collecting the rare misstrikes and defective coins that escape quality control has become an important segment of the numismatic hobby. For a detailed description of over 400 categories of minting varieties, see the "U.S. Minting Varieties and Errors" section in this book.

# 3

# The thrill of the hunt

## *How to acquire coins for your collection*

### By Al Doyle

Among the many pleasures coin collecting offers is the satisfaction of acquiring that long-sought piece that fills an important hole in a set or completes a collection. Many collectors say half the fun of pursuing the hobby is the thrill of the hunt — trying to find that needed coin in the condition desired and for a good price. Following are the main sources from which collectors acquire coins.

## Circulation finds

Once the most popular method of building a collection, hunting through pocket change has declined substantially since 1965, when silver dimes and quarters were replaced by clad (base-metal) coinage.

Most collectors from 1935 into the 1960s got started in numismatics by searching through circulating coinage. It was worth the effort, as scarce and interesting coins such as the 1909-S "VDB" and 1914-D Lincoln cents, Liberty and Buffalo nickels, 1916-D and 1921 Mercury dimes, and Barber and Standing Liberty quarters were often found. Hobbyists who searched bank rolls and bags obtained at face value had no downside risk, and entire date collections of Lincoln cents were obtained in this manner.

Other denominations were also pursued in the treasure hunt. One Midwestern dealer found dozens of 1939-D Jefferson nickels (worth $1 to $30 each at the time, depending on condition) by searching through change obtained from parking meters of a nearby city. Another well-known numismatist put together a complete date and mintmark set of Walking Liberty half dollars in one afternoon by searching through coins obtained at his bank. Needless to say, those days are gone forever.

What is available to pocket-change searchers today? Even the pre-1959

It's still possible to find collectible coins by searching large quantities of change, such as rolls.

cents, with the wheat-ears reverse, are rare sights, but some interesting coins remain undiscovered.

Jefferson nickels can provide plenty of collecting enjoyment for virtually no financial commitment. A recent sampling of five rolls (200 coins, or $10) turned up 58 different date and mintmark combinations. Some of the highlights were a 1938-S (mintage 4.1 million) in grade fine, a 1947 in very fine, and a 1953-S. Looking through Jeffersons on a regular basis should lead to building the better part of a date and mintmark set.

Half dollars are the other relatively untapped area in modern coinage. The 40-percent-silver pieces of 1965 to 1969 can sometimes be found in bank rolls. Half dollars seldom circulate, which means that older coins may be gathering dust in your local bank vault at this very moment.

Collecting Lincoln cents with the memorial reverse, from 1959 to date, makes an excellent starter set. Many of the dates can be found in circulation.

What else might turn up in pocket change? Modern proofs enter circulation from time to time, and foreign coins are found occasionally. Canadian and U.S. coins frequently cross their respective borders.

Collectors of error coins sometimes find unusual pieces in circulation. What may be scorned as a reject by the average person is a valuable item to the error and variety specialist.

Start examining your pocket change. It's an inexpensive and pleasant way to get involved in the coin hobby.

## Coin shops

Most medium-sized or larger cities and suburbs have at least one coin shop within driving distance, and a surprising number of small towns also boast of having a store that caters to local numismatists. Living in or near a metropolitan area is an advantage for the coin-shop enthusiast. For example, more than 15 dealers live in or near Cincinnati, and southern California and the New York area are home to hundreds of numismatic firms.

In some ways, a coin shop is similar to a small museum. All kinds of items from early coppers to gold coinage and other collectibles such as paper currency, stock certificates, and historic curiosities can be seen. A visit to a well-stocked shop is a visual treat.

It is likely that some of those coins in the display cases will appeal to you, and that means some comparison shopping and determining the value of your favorite coin are desirable. Prices do fluctuate, although collector-oriented coins tend to maintain steadier values than coins sought by investors.

If you are a casual collector, consider a subscription to *Coins* magazine. A monthly publication, *Coins* offers articles on a wide range of topics as well as a Coin Value Guide of retail prices for U.S. coins in most grades.

Serious collectors and others who want more frequent information will find *Numismatic News* to be a timely source of knowledge. Published weekly, the *News* includes coverage of recent market trends and reports from major coin conventions. *World Coin News* is published every other week and covers non-U.S. issues. All three publications also carry display advertisements from dozens of coin dealers.

Prices are determined by supply and demand as well as the grade, or state of preservation. Grading is often described as a subjective art rather than an exact science, and it does take some study and experience to become a competent grader (see Chapter 4).

Numismatic education is a never-ending process. Getting to know an experienced dealer who is enthusiastic about his product will certainly increase your knowledge of coins. Most shops carry a wide assortment of items, but dealers (like anyone else) have their personal favorites. If you find a dealer who is especially knowledgeable about a certain series, it could be to your advantage to do business with him or her if that also happens to be your favorite area too.

Strangely enough, doing business with a dealer who does not share your particular interest could work in your favor. Learning about collectible coins is a massive undertaking, and no one knows everything. Collectors of large cents and Bust half dollars are willing to pay substantial premiums for coins that have minor differences from other specimens struck during the same year, and specialists in those areas frequently "cherrypick" rare varieties that are offered at common-date prices.

Never be embarrassed to ask questions about coins or the dealer's experience in the hobby. As the old saying goes, "There is no such thing as a dumb question." A question asked at the right time could save you plenty of grief and money.

# Mail order

This is one area that generates a fair amount of emotion among collectors. Many hobbyists swear by the convenience of shopping at home; others

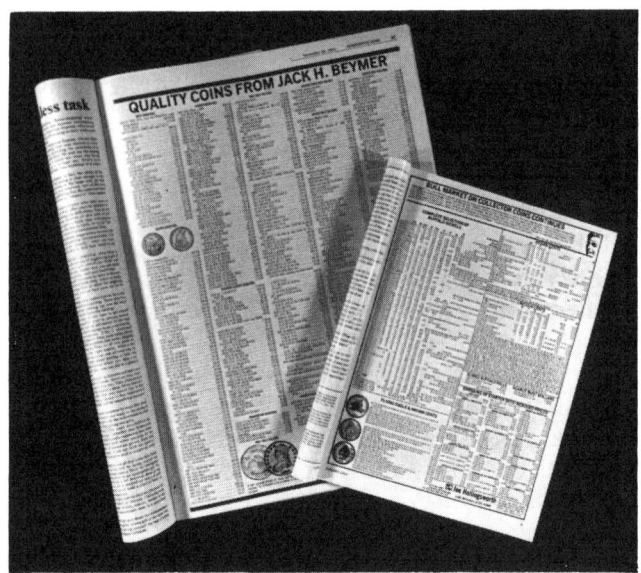

Advertisements in numismatic publications provide the convenience of shopping at home.

swear at mail-order firms that send overgraded and overpriced coins. Common sense and the same guidelines that apply to shopping for any other item should be used in selecting a mail-order coin dealer.

Look for someone who has a fair amount of experience in coins as well as enthusiasm for the hobby. Reputable dealers are willing to answer questions about their numismatic backgrounds and business practices. Word of mouth is often said to be one of the most effective forms of advertising, and it pays to ask other collectors about their favorite mail-order companies.

If several people agree that a firm provides accurately graded coins at fair prices, chances are excellent that you will also be a satisfied customer. How do you avoid being cheated? Collectors can be their own worst enemies and are often victimized by their own greed.

Take a coin that has a retail value in the $100 range in a particular grade. If that same coin is advertised at the same grade for $49.95, the savvy collector should immediately become suspicious. When a coin is offered at a price far under the going rate, remember these two sayings: "If it sounds too good to be true, it usually is," and "there is no Santa Claus in numismatics."

A dealer will generally pay $70 to $80 to acquire a popular coin with a retail value of $100. With that in mind, how can someone offer the same coin in the same grade at far less than wholesale cost? Wouldn't it be much easier to sell those coins to other dealers at a higher price and save on advertising expenses?

Obviously, the "underpriced" coins are not the same quality as their properly graded counterparts. It pays to keep up with current prices and grading standards. It is possible to find good deals at less than full retail cost, but don't expect to purchase decent coins for half price.

Does that mean all coins sold at real market prices are properly graded? Don't get complacent; overgraded coins are sometimes sold at full retail. But not everyone who sells an overgraded coin is intentionally fraudulent.

Grading standards are not carved in stone, which means that one person's MS-63 can be someone else's MS-64. Even though most dealers are extremely knowledgeable about coins, they can be fooled at times. The altered coin that a dealer bought as problem-free may be passed on to a collector in good faith, with no intention of deceit.

There is one important means of protection for consumers who buy through the mail: the return policy. Reputable firms allow buyers to return any unsatisfactory item for a full refund. The time allowed for returns varies widely from three working days to a month, but seven to ten days seems to be the most popular policy among mail-order dealers.

Most dealers list "terms of sale" in their ads. Always look for them and read them before placing your order.

If you don't like coins received through the mail for any reason, send them back within the alloted time for a full refund. Companies might extend the deadline by a day or two if you call and ask for extra time.

What happens if you don't receive a refund or cannot satisfactorily resolve a problem with a mail-order dealer? There are several options:

The first step is to file a written complaint with the advertising department of any publication in which the dealer advertises. Include copies of invoices and other documentation. The publication cannot act on verbal complaints.

Written complaints can also be filed with a local or state chapter of the Better Business Bureau as well as any hobby-related organizations (the American Numismatic Association, Professional Numismatists Guild, and so on) in which the dealer holds membership. If you do business with a reputable dealer, it is unlikely that you will ever have to endure such a drawn-out complaint process, but be ready to take the proper steps if necessary.

For those who live in rural areas or prefer to shop at home, buying coins through the mail can be a rewarding experience and a convenient way to build a collection.

# Coin shows

Dozens of shows are held every weekend across the nation. These events range from simple one-day shows with 10 to 20 tables to nationally known events such as the annual American Numismatic Association convention, Florida United Numismatists convention, the three-times-a-year shows held in Long Beach, Calif., and the Central States Numismatic Society convention.

Admission to club-sponsored shows is usually free. Commercially sponsored shows oftentimes charge a small admission fee.

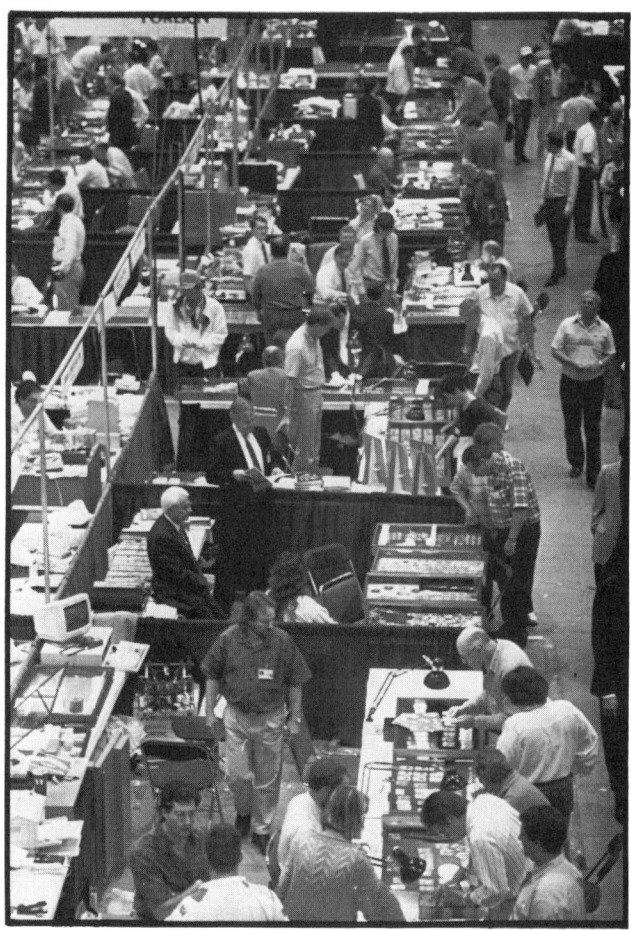

Shows big and small
are held across the
nation every weekend.

Somewhere between the show at the local VFW hall and Long Beach are state and regional conventions. Often sponsored by a club, these shows will have 40 to 150 dealer tables as compared to the 400 to 600 tables at a major convention. Tables at local and some regional conventions are often manned by part-time, or "vest pocket," dealers. Smaller shows tend to feature less expensive items; the larger shows will have a greater variety of scarce and expensive coins in addition to the more affordable pieces.

Major conventions will have a stunning array of merchandise ranging from coins of ancient Greece to major U.S. rarities. Even if you can't afford the expensive items, it doesn't cost anything to stroll the aisles and see some historic coins.

The big-ticket items are just part of the action at regional and major shows. A large assortment of affordable coins are available, and prices are often lower than at coin shops.

Dealers buy and sell thousands of coins among themselves at shows, and new purchases can often be had for a small markup. Good buys can sometimes be found later in the show when dealers are preparing to return home. A reasonable offer will often result in a new addition to your collection.

Speaking of offers, negotiating and dickering are as much a part of coin shows as silver dollars, but be reasonable. Tossing out an offer of $50 on a $200 coin is not shrewd; it's insulting.

If you make an offer on a coin and it is accepted, the coin is yours. Backing out of a deal is considered bad form. The coin business tends to be informal, and verbal offers carry serious weight. Your word is your bond on the bourse floor.

Purchases at a coin show do not carry a return policy. Unlike a mail-order transaction, you have ample opportunity to carefully examine the coin firsthand before making a financial commitment.

Why attend a show when you can acquire coins through the mail or from a local shop? There are many reasons to give the show circuit a try:

Conventions are an educational experience. Touring the bourse floor and talking to dealers and other collectors will increase your knowledge of numismatics, but there are other learning opportunities as well.

Many shows offer educational forums featuring speakers and presentations on various topics. These seminars cover everything from little-known specialties to advice on obtaining the best buys in a particular area of numismatics.

Exhibits will also add to your knowledge. Most medium-sized and major shows reserve a section of the bourse for collectors to display some of their holdings and compete for awards based on the educational value of their exhibit. The exhibit section offers an excellent opportunity to view something new and different.

You might be motivated to put together an exhibit yourself after a visit to a show. Keep in mind that it does not require a major collection to create a decent exhibit. Some of the most interesting displays incorporate low-priced coins and other collectibles.

Shows are excellent places to search for key-date coins and other material that may not be in stock at your local shop. Dealers do much of their shopping at shows, which should tell you something about the opportunities at a good-sized convention.

Want to introduce a friend or relative to coin collecting? Take them to a show and let them look around. Chances are excellent that the newcomer will become a fellow collector.

Looking for something different to collect? Paper money, world coins, tokens, medals, and medieval coins are often found at shows. You could find a new area of interest, and shows provide collectors with a chance to meet dealers and well-known hobbyists from across the country.

Have a game plan when you attend a show. Decide beforehand what you want to buy and how much money you plan to spend. Buying whatever looks nice will soon deplete your funds.

Coin shows offer something for everyone, so consider bringing the family. Jewelry (usually for much less than jewelry-store prices), baseball cards, antiques, and arts and crafts are also sometimes found at bourse tables.

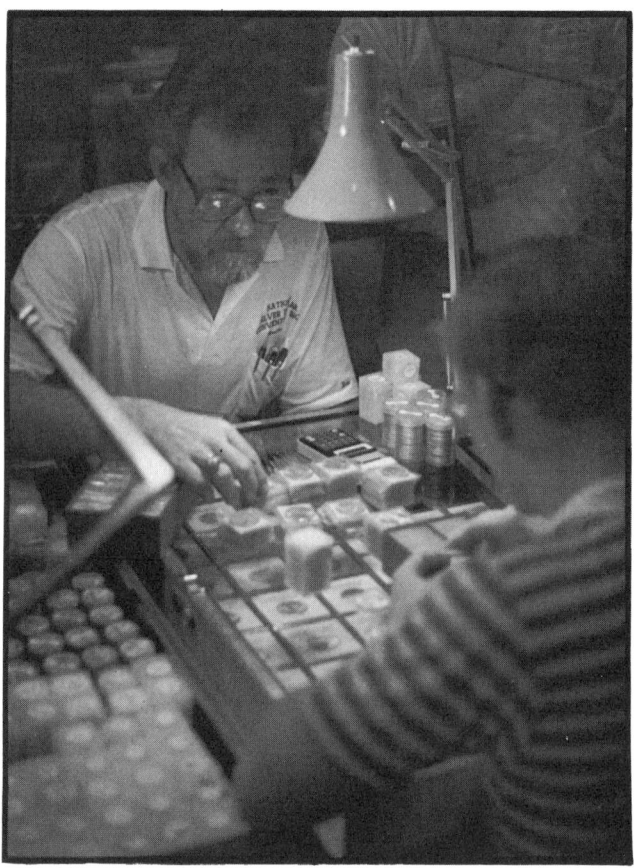

**It's OK to bargain with a dealer at a show or shop, but collectors should be reasonable with their offers.**

One final note on coin-show etiquette: If you don't agree with a dealer's prices or grading, do not tell him that you can buy the same coin for less at another table or call him a crook. Just move on to the next table, and enjoy the rest of the show.

Information on upcoming shows in your area can be found in *Coins* and *Numismatic News*. Shows that feature a significant number of world coins are also listed in *World Coin News*. Coin-show advertising sometimes appears in local newspapers during the week prior to a show or in the paper's free listings of community events.

# Auctions

As in other collectible fields, auctions play an important role in the coin business. Prices realized at major auctions can indicate where the coin market is headed, as price fluctuations are a fact of life in numismatics. Important collections with major rarities are usually sold at auction.

However, affordable coins are often sold along with the heart-stopping pieces. A typical sale for a major auction firm will contain 1,000 to 4,000 lots, and most of those coins are not of the headline-grabbing variety.

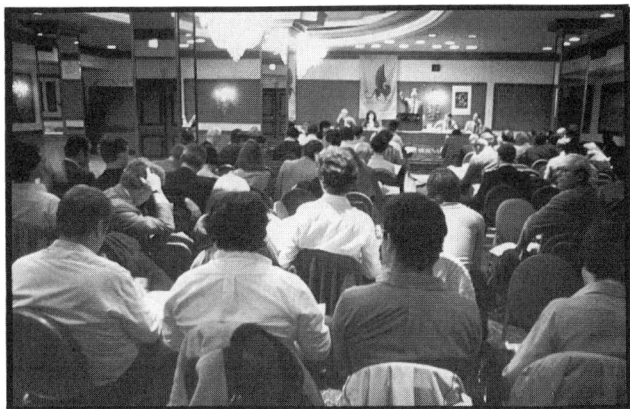

A collector doesn't have to actually attend an auction to participate in it.

The vast number of coins offered at a typical coin auction can work in favor of the collector who has a limited budget. Typical low- to medium-priced coins are often overlooked, as dealers and collectors focus on the trophy items. That may allow you to pick up some coins at reasonable prices.

How can you participate in an auction that is being held thousands of miles from your home? Catalogs are produced by auction companies for each sale, and mail bids are encouraged.

A typical auction catalog is illustrated with black and white as well as color photos of hundreds of coins. Descriptions of each lot give you an idea of the appearance of any coins that might be of interest.

If you are located near an auction site, it pays to examine your potential purchases at the pre-auction viewing session. The process is simple: Just visit the auction location (usually a major hotel or convention center) prior to the sale. The auction company sets up a room where the lots can be viewed. Long rows of tables with good lighting are provided. All you have to do is tell one of the attendants the lot numbers of the coins you want to view.

You can place written bids before you leave the premises, but it might pay to hang around for the auction and bid on coins in person. The action can be fast and furious at a major auction. Bidding increments of thousands of dollars are the rule when an expensive coin is being sold. It's an unforgettable sight to watch five or six serious competitors run up the price on a truly rare coin.

Keep several things in mind before you get involved in buying through auctions:

■ You are legally responsible to honor all winning bids placed, so plan accordingly. It is unlikely that you will win every coin on which you bid, but placing too many bids could be hazardous to your financial health.

■ Return policies vary among the major firms. Generally, floor bidders (those who personally attend the sale) do not have return privileges, as it is assumed that an adequate opportunity was provided to examine coins during the pre-auction viewing session.

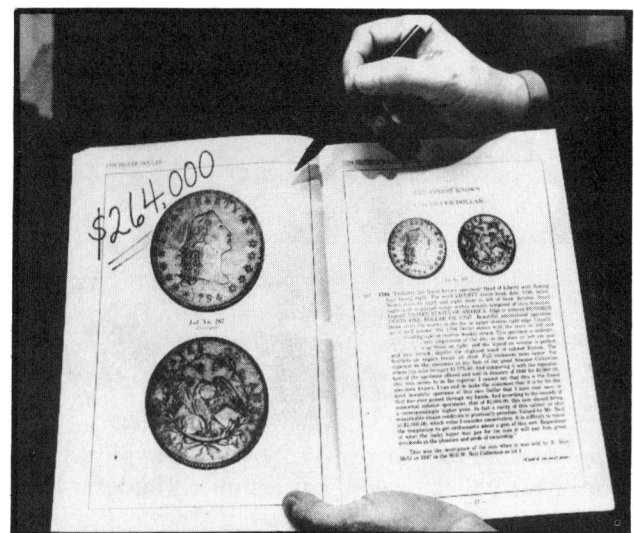

An auction catalog describes each lot offered.

One auction house does not allow any returns by mail bidders on certified coins, which are independently graded and encapsulated in a protective holder by an outside grading service. However, return privileges are the rule for all coins graded by the auction company's staff.

■ Winning bids are generally subject to a 10 percent premium, or buyer's fee. If you successfully bid $300 on a coin, your final cost will be $330 plus postage and handling. Consider the buyer's fee when deciding on bids.

Getting started in buying through auctions requires a catalog of an upcoming sale. Typically priced at $10 to $25, auction catalogs can be excellent buys even if you don't participate in the sale, as they provide a wealth of numismatic information.

Following are the four major U.S. auction houses:

■ Auctions by Bowers and Merena, P.O. Box 1224, Wolfeboro, NH 03894.

■ Heritage Numismatic Auctions, Heritage Plaza, Highland Park Village, Dallas, TX 75205.

■ Stack's, 123 W. 57th St., New York, NY 10019.

■ Superior Galleries, 9478 W. Olympic Blvd., Beverly Hills, CA 90212.

Smaller auctions will allow you to test the bidding process before you compete at a major sale. Local firms concentrate on less expensive coins, and a typical sale for these companies ranges from 250 to 1,000 lots. Catalogs are less elaborate, but they are also inexpensive. Prices range from free to $3, and mail bids are accepted.

Among the dozens of local companies that conduct coin auctions are the following:

■ Michael Aron, P.O. Box 4388, San Clemente, CA 92674.

■ Connecticut Numismatic Auctions, P.O. Box 471, Plantsville, CT 06479.

■ D'Atri Auction, 2405 Essington Road, Suite 124, Joliet, IL 60435.

■ Sonny Henry's Auction Service, 1510 Illinois Ave., Mendota, IL 61342.

■ Bruce Hickman and Associates, 800 W. Rand Road, Arlington Heights, IL 60004.

■ Mel's Auction, P.O. Box 1103, Fowlerville, MI 48836.

## Where to write for more information

*Coins Magazine:* 700 E. State St., Iola, WI 54990.

*Numismatic News:* 700 E. State St., Iola, WI 54990.

*World Coin News:* 700 E. State St., Iola, WI 54990.

**American Numismatic Association:** 818 N. Cascade Ave., Colorado Springs, CO 80903-3279.

# 4

# The grading factor
## *How to classify a coin's condition*

**By Arlyn G. Sieber**

Grading is one of the most important factors in buying and selling coins as collectibles. Unfortunately, it's also one of the most controversial. Since the early days of coin collecting in the United States, buying through the mail has been a convenient way for collectors to acquire coins. As a result, there has always been a need in numismatics for a concise way to classify the amount of wear on a coin and its condition in general.

## A look back

In September 1888, Dr. George Heath, a physician in Monroe, Mich., published a four-page pamphlet titled *The American Numismatist*. Publication of subsequent issues led to the founding of the American Numismatic Association, and *The Numismatist*, as it's known today, is the association's official journal. Heath's first issues were largely devoted to selling world coins from his collection. There were no formal grades listed with the coins and their prices, but the following statement by Heath indicates that condition was a consideration for early collectors:

"The coins are in above average condition," Heath wrote, "and so confident am I that they will give satisfaction, that I agree to refund the money in any unsatisfactory sales on the return of the coins."

As coin collecting became more popular and *The Numismatist* started accepting paid advertising from others, grading became more formal. The February 1892 issue listed seven "classes" for the condition of coins (from worst to best): mutilated, poor, fair, good, fine, uncirculated, and proof. Through the years, the hobby has struggled with developing a grading sys-

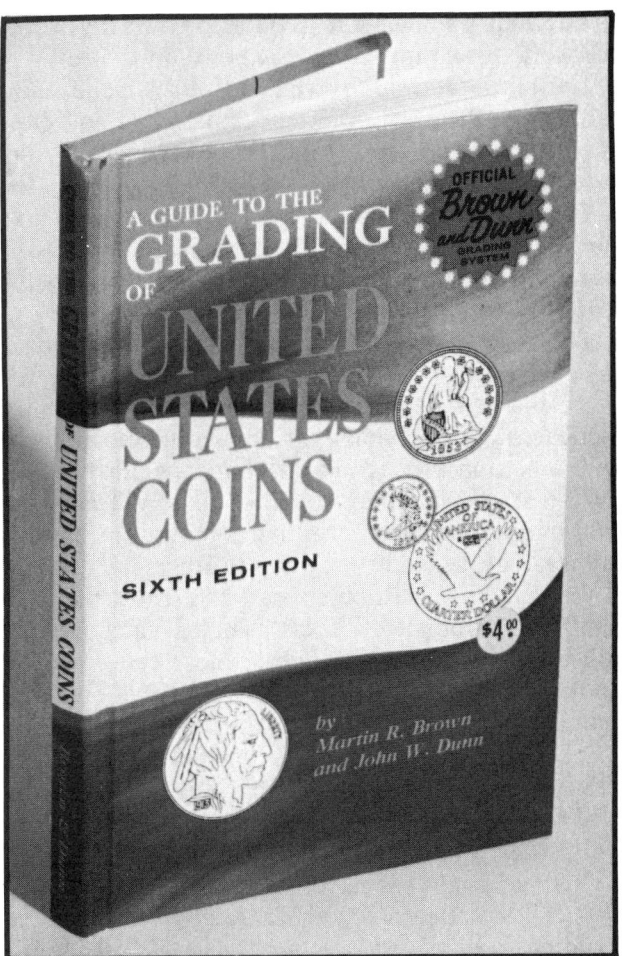

The first formal grading guide was Brown and Dunn's *A Guide to the Grading of United States Coins.*

tem that would be accepted by all and could apply to all coins. The hobby's growth was accompanied by a desire for more grades, or classifications, to more precisely define a coin's condition. The desire for more precision, however, was at odds with the basic concept of grading: to provide a *concise* method for classifying a coin's condition.

For example, even the conservatively few classifications of 1892 included fudge factors.

"To give flexibility to this classification," *The Numismatist* said, "such modification of fine, good and fair, as 'extremely,' 'very,' 'almost,' etc. are used to express slight variations from the general condition."

The debate over grading continued for decades in *The Numismatist*. A number of articles and letters prodded the ANA to write grading guidelines and endorse them as the association's official standards. Some submitted specific suggestions for terminology and accompanying standards for each grade. But grading remained a process of "instinct" gained through years of collecting or dealing experience.

A formal grading guide in book form finally appeared in 1958, but it was the work of two individuals rather than the ANA. *A Guide to the Grading of United States Coins* by Martin R. Brown and John W. Dunn was a breakthrough in the great grading debate. Now collectors had a reference that gave them specific guidelines for specific coins and could be studied and restudied at home.

The first editions of Brown and Dunn carried text only, no illustrations. For the fourth edition, in 1964, publication was assumed by Whitman Publishing Co. of Racine, Wis., and line drawings were added to illustrate the text.

The fourth edition listed six principal categories for circulated coins (from worst to best): good, very good, fine, very fine, extremely fine, and about uncirculated. But again, the desire for more precise categories was evidenced. In the book's introduction, Brown and Dunn wrote, "Dealers will sometimes advertise coins that are graded G-VG, VG-F, F-VF, VF-XF. Or the description may be ABT. G. or VG plus, etc. This means that the coin in question more than meets minimum standards for the lower grade but is not quite good enough for the higher grade."

When the fifth edition appeared, in 1969, the "New B & D Grading System" was introduced. The six principal categories for circulated coins were still intact, but variances within those categories were now designated by up to four letters: "A", "B", "C" or "D". For example, an EF-A coin was "almost about uncirculated." An EF-B was "normal extra fine" within the B & D standards. EF-C had a "normal extra fine" obverse, but the reverse was "obviously not as nice as obverse due to poor strike or excessive wear." EF-D had a "normal extra fine" reverse but a problem obverse.

But that wasn't the end. Brown and Dunn further listed 29 problem points that could appear on a coin — from No. 1 for an "edge bump" to No. 29 for "attempted re-engraving outside of the Mint." The number could be followed by the letter "O" or "R" to designate whether the problem appeared on the obverse or reverse and a Roman numeral corresponding to a clock face to designate where the problem appears on the obverse or reverse. For example, a coin described as "VG-B-9-O-X" would grade "VG-B"; the 9 designated a "single rim nick"; the "O" indicated the nick was on the obverse; and the "X" indicated it appeared at the 10 o'clock position, or upper left, of the obverse.

The authors' goal was noble — to create the perfect grading system. They again, however, fell victim to the age-old grading-system problem: Precision comes at the expense of brevity. Dealer Kurt Krueger wrote in the January 1976 issue of *The Numismatist*, ". . . under the new B & D system, the numismatist must contend with a minimum of 43,152 different grading combinations! Accuracy is apparent, but simplicity has been lost." As a result, the "new B & D system" never caught on in the marketplace.

The 1970s saw two important grading guides make their debut. The first was *Photograde* by James F. Ruddy. As the title implies, Ruddy uses photographs instead of line drawings to show how coins look in the various circulated grades. Simplicity is also a virtue of Ruddy's book. Only seven

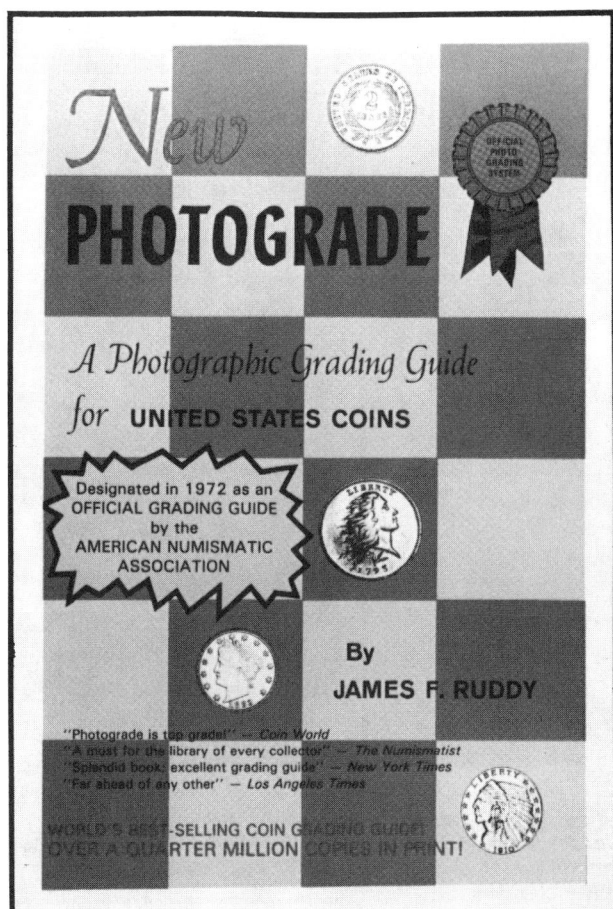

*Photograde* was the first widely accepted grading guide to use photos to illustrate the amount of wear on cir-culated coins.

circulated grades are listed (about good, good, very good, fine, very fine, extremely fine, and about uncirculated), and the designations stop there.

In 1977 the longtime call for the ANA to issue grading standards was met with the release of *Official A.N.A. Grading Standards for United States Coins*. Like Brown and Dunn, the first editions of the ANA guide used line drawings to illustrate coins in various states of wear. But instead of using adjectival descriptions, the ANA guide adopted a numerical system for designating grades.

The numerical designations were based on a system used by Dr. William H. Sheldon in his book *Early American Cents*, first published in 1949. He used a scale of 1 to 70 to designate the grades of large cents.

"On this scale," Sheldon wrote, "1 means that the coin is identifiable and not mutilated — no more than that. A 70-coin is one in flawless Mint State, exactly as it left the dies, with perfect mint color and without a blemish or nick."

(Sheldon's scale also had its pragmatic side. At the time, a No. 2 large cent was worth about twice a No. 1 coin; a No. 4 was worth about twice a

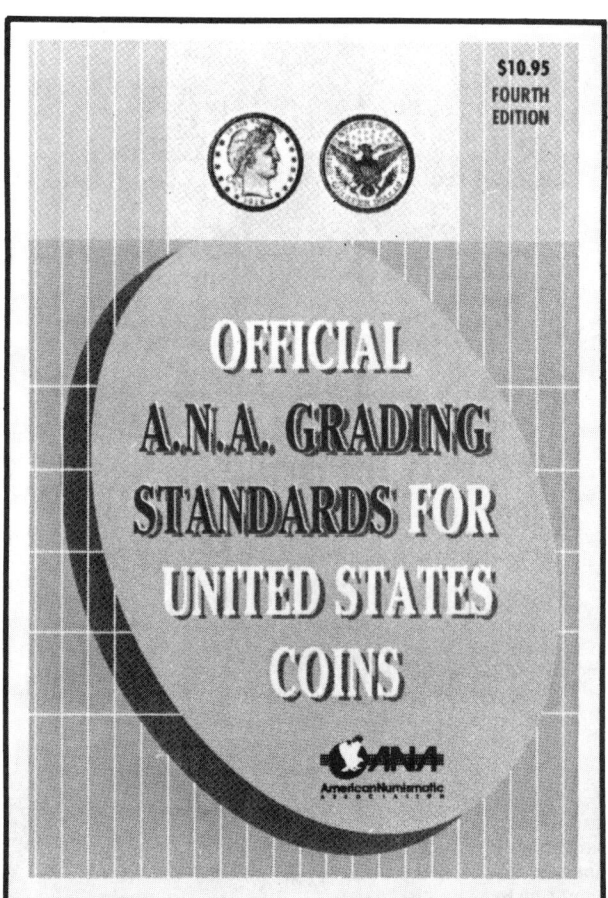

*Official A.N.A. Grading
Standards for United
States Coins* is now in
its fourth edition.

No. 2, and so on up the scale.)

With the first edition of its grading guide, the ANA adopted the 70-point scale for grading all U.S. coins. It designated 10 categories of circulated grades: AG-3, G-4, VG-8, F-12, VF-20, VF-30, EF-40, EF-45, AU-50, and AU-55. The third edition, released in 1987, replaced the line drawings with photographs, and another circulated grade was added: AU-58. A fourth edition was released in 1991.

## Grading circulated U.S. coins

Dealers today generally use either the ANA guide or *Photograde* when grading circulated coins for their inventories. (Brown and Dunn is now out of print.) Many local coin shops sell both books. Advertisers in *Numismatic News*, *Coins*, and *Coin Prices* must indicate which standards they are using in grading their coins. If the standards are not listed, they must conform to ANA standards.

Following are some general guidelines, accompanied by photos, for grading circulated U.S. coins. Grading even circulated pieces can be subjective, particularly when attempting to draw the fine line between, for example, AU-55 and AU-58. Two longtime collectors or dealers can disagree in such a case.

But by studying some combination of the following guidelines, the ANA guide, and *Photograde*, and by looking at a lot of coins at shops and shows, collectors can gain enough grading knowledge to buy circulated coins confidently from dealers and other collectors. The more you study, the more knowledge and confidence you will gain. When you decide which series of coins you want to collect, focus on the guidelines for that particular series. Read them, reread them, and then refer back to them again and again.

# AU-50

Indian cent

Lincoln cent

Buffalo nickel

Jefferson nickel

Mercury dime

Standing Liberty quarter

Washington quarter

Walking Liberty half dollar

Morgan dollar

Barber coins

**AU-50 (about uncirculated):** Just a slight trace of wear, the result of brief exposure to circulation or light rubbing from mishandling, may be evident on the elevated design areas. These imperfections may appear as scratches or dull spots, along with bag marks or edge nicks. At least half of the original mint luster generally is still evident.

# XF-40

**Indian cent**

**Lincoln cent**

**Buffalo nickel**

**Jefferson nickel**

**Mercury dime**

**Standing Liberty quarter**

**Washington quarter**

**Walking Liberty half dollar**

**Morgan dollar**

**Barber coins**

**XF-40 (extremely fine):** The coin must show only slight evidence of wear on the highest points of the design, particularly in the hair lines of the portrait on the obverse. The same may be said for the eagle's feathers and wreath leaves on the reverse of most U.S. coins. A trace of mint luster may still show in protected areas of the coin's surface.

# VF-20

**Indian cent**

**Lincoln cent**

**Buffalo nickel**

**Jefferson nickel**

**Mercury dime**

**Standing Liberty quarter**

**Washington quarter**                    **Walking Liberty half dollar**

**Morgan dollar**                          **Barber coins**

**VF-20 (very fine):** The coin will show light wear at the fine points in the design, though they may remain sharp overall. Although the details may be slightly smoothed, all lettering and major features must remain sharp.

Indian cent: All letters in "Liberty" are complete but worn. Headdress shows considerable flatness, with flat spots on the tips of the feathers.

Lincoln cent: Hair, cheek, jaw, and bow-tie details will be worn but clearly separated, and wheat stalks on the reverse will be full with no weak spots.

Buffalo nickel: High spots on hair braid and cheek will be flat but show some detail, and a full horn will remain on the buffalo.

Jefferson nickel: Well over half of the major hair detail will remain, and the pillars on Monticello will remain well defined, with the triangular roof partially visible.

Mercury dime: Hair braid will show some detail, and three-quarters of the detail will remain in the feathers. The two diagonal bands on the fasces will show completely but will be worn smooth at the middle, with the vertical lines sharp.

Standing Liberty quarter: Rounded contour of Liberty's right leg will be flattened, as will the high point of the shield.

Washington quarter: There will be considerable wear on the hair curls, with feathers on the right and left of the eagle's breast showing clearly.

Walking Liberty half dollar: All lines of the skirt will show but will be worn on the high points. Over half the feathers on the eagle will show.

Morgan dollar: Two-thirds of the hairlines from the forehead to the ear must show. Ear should be well defined. Feathers on the eagle's breast may be worn smooth.

Barber coins: All seven letters of "Liberty" on the headband must stand out sharply. Head wreath will be well outlined from top to bottom.

# F-12

Indian cent

Lincoln cent

Buffalo nickel

Jefferson nickel

Mercury dime

Standing Liberty quarter

Washington quarter

Walking Liberty half dollar

Morgan dollar

Barber coins

**F-12 (fine):** Coins show evidence of moderate to considerable but generally even wear on all high points, though all elements of the design and lettering remain bold. Where the word "Liberty" appears in a headband, it must be fully visible. On 20th century coins, the rim must be fully raised and sharp.

# VG-8

**Indian cent**

**Lincoln cent**

**Buffalo nickel**

**Jefferson nickel**

**Mercury dime**

**Standing Liberty quarter**

Washington quarter

Walking Liberty half dollar

Morgan dollar

Barber coins

**VG-8 (very good):** The coin will show considerable wear, with most detail points worn nearly smooth. Where the word "Liberty" appears in a headband, at least three letters must show. On 20th century coins, the rim will start to merge with the lettering.

# G-4

**Indian cent**

**Lincoln cent**

**Buffalo nickel**

**Jefferson nickel**

**Mercury dime**

**Standing Liberty quarter**

Washington quarter

Walking Liberty half dollar

Morgan dollar

Barber coins

**G-4 (good):** Only the basic design remains distinguishable in outline form, with all points of detail worn smooth. The word "Liberty" has disappeared, and the rims are almost merging with the lettering.

**About good or fair:** The coin will be identifiable by date and mint but otherwise badly worn, with only parts of the lettering showing. Such coins are of value only as fillers in a collection until a better example of the date and mintmark can be obtained. The only exceptions would be rare coins.

## Grading uncirculated U.S. coins

The subjectivity of grading and the trend toward more classifications becomes more acute when venturing into uncirculated, or mint-state, coins. A minute difference between one or two grade points can mean a difference in value of hundreds or even thousands of dollars. In addition, the standards are more difficult to articulate in writing and illustrate through drawings or photographs. Thus, the possibilities for differences of opinion on one or two grade points increase in uncirculated coins.

Coins graded and encapsulated by a third-party grading service are nicknamed "slabs." The Professional Coin Grading Service graded this Saint-Gaudens gold $20 coin.

Back in Dr. George Heath's day and continuing through the 1960s, a coin was either uncirculated or it wasn't. Little distinction was made between uncirculated coins of varying condition, largely because there was little if any difference in value. When *Numismatic News* introduced its value guide in 1962 (the forerunner of today's Coin Market section in the *News*), it listed only one grade of uncirculated for Morgan dollars.

But as collectible coins increased in value and buyers of uncirculated coins became more picky, distinctions within grade uncirculated started to surface. In 1975 *Numismatic News* still listed only one uncirculated grade in Coin Market, but added this note: "Uncirculated and proof specimens in especially choice condition will also command proportionately higher premiums than these listed."

The first edition of the ANA guide listed two grades of uncirculated, MS-60 and MS-65, in addition to the theoretical but non-existent MS-70 (a flawless coin). MS-60 was described as "typical uncirculated" and MS-65 as "choice uncirculated." *Numismatic News* adopted both designations for Coin Market. In 1981, when the second edition of the ANA grading guide was released, MS-67 and MS-63 were added. In 1985 *Numismatic News* started listing six grades of uncirculated for Morgan dollars: MS-60, MS-63, MS-65, MS-65+, and MS-63 prooflike.

Then in 1986, a new entity appeared that has changed the nature of grading and trading uncirculated coins ever since. A group of dealers led by David Hall of Newport Beach, Calif., formed the Professional Coin Grading Service. For a fee, collectors could submit a coin through an authorized PCGS dealer and receive back a professional opinion of its grade.

The concept was not new; the ANA had operated an authentication service since 1972 and a grading service since 1979. A collector or dealer could submit a coin directly to the service and receive a certificate giving the service's opinion on authenticity and grade. The grading service was the source of near constant debate among dealers and ANA officials. Dealers charged that ANA graders were too young and inexperienced, and

**The Numismatic Guaranty Corp. is another major grading service.**

that their grading was inconsistent.

Grading stability was a problem throughout the coin business in the early 1980s, not just with the ANA service. Standards among uncirculated grades would tighten during a bear market and loosen during a bull market. As a result, a coin graded MS-65 in a bull market may have commanded only MS-63 during a bear market.

PCGS created several innovations in the grading business in response to these problems:

1. Coins could be submitted through PCGS-authorized dealers only.

2. Each coin would be graded by at least three members of a panel of "top graders," all prominent dealers in the business. (Since then, however, PCGS does not allow its graders to also deal in coins.)

3. After grading, the coin would be encapsulated in an inert, hard-plastic holder with a serial number and the grade indicated on the holder.

4. PCGS-member dealers pledged to make a market in PCGS-graded coins and honor the grades assigned.

5. In one of the most far-reaching moves, PCGS said it would use all 11 increments of uncirculated on the 70-point numerical scale: MS-60, MS-61, MS-62, MS-63, MS-64, MS-65, MS-66, MS-67, MS-68, MS-69, and MS-70.

The evolution of more uncirculated grades had reached another milestone.

Purists bemoaned the entombment of classic coins in the plastic holders and denounced the 11 uncirculated grades as implausible. Nevertheless, PCGS was an immediate commercial success. The plastic holders were nicknamed "slabs," and dealers couldn't get coins through the system fast enough.

In subsequent years, a number of similar services have appeared. Among them, one of the original PCGS "top graders," John Albanese, left PCGS to found the Numismatic Guaranty Corp. The ANA grading service succumbed to "slab mania" and introduced its own encapsulated product.

Although there are still several other reputable grading services, PCGS

An NGC worker places
a coin in its holder after
it has been graded.

and NGC dominate market share. In 1990 the ANA sold its grading service to a private company. The association continues to authenticate coins.

How should a collector approach the buying and grading of uncirculated coins? Collecting uncirculated coins worth thousands of dollars implies a higher level of numismatic expertise by the buyer. Those buyers without that level of expertise should cut their teeth on more inexpensive coins, just as today's experienced collectors did. Inexperienced collectors can start toward that level by studying the guidelines for mint-state coins in the ANA grading guide and looking at lots of coins at shows and shops.

Study the condition and eye appeal of a coin and compare it to other coins of the same series. Then compare prices. Do the more expensive coins look better? If so, why? Start to make your own judgments concerning relationships between condition and value.

According to numismatic legend, a collector walked up to a crusty old dealer at a show one time and asked the dealer to grade a coin the collector had with him. The dealer looked at the coin and said, "I grade it a hundred dollars." Such is the bottom line to coin grading.

# Grading U.S. proof coins

Because proof coins are struck by a special process (see Chapter 2), they receive their own grading designation. A coin does not start out being a proof and then become mint state if it becomes worn. Once a proof coin, always a proof coin.

In the ANA system, proof grades use the same numbers as circulated and uncirculated grades, and the amount of wear on the coin corresponds to those grades. But the number is preceded by the word "proof." For example, Proof-65, Proof-55, Proof-45, and so on. In addition, the ANA says a proof coin with many marks, scratches or other defects should be called an "impaired proof."

# Grading world coins

The state of grading non-U.S. issues is similar to U.S. coin grading before Brown and Dunn. There is no detailed, illustrated guide that covers the enormous scope and variety of world coins; collectors and dealers rely on their experience in the field and knowledge of the marketplace.

The *Standard Catalog of World Coins* gives the following guidelines for grading world coins, which apply to the Canadian and Mexican value listings in this book:

In grading world coins, there are two elements to look for: (1) overall wear and (2) loss of design details, such as strands of hair, feathers on eagles, designs on coats of arms, and so on. Grade each coin by the weaker of the two sides. Age, rarity or type of coin should not be considered in grading.

Grade by the amount of overall wear and loss of detail evident in the main design on each side. On coins with a moderately small design element that is prone to early wear, grade by that design alone.

In the marketplace, adjectival grades are still used for Mexican coins. The numerical system for Canadian coins is now commonplace:

**Uncirculated, MS-60:** No visible signs of wear or handling, even under a 30X microscope. Bag marks may be present.

**Almost uncirculated, AU-50:** All detail will be visible. There will be wear on only the highest point of the coin. There will often be half or more of the original mint luster present.

**Extremely fine, XF-40:** About 95 percent of the original detail will be visible. Or, on a coin with a design that has no inner detail to wear down, there will be light wear over nearly the entire coin. If a small design is used as the grading area, about 90 percent of the original detail will be visible. This latter rule stems from the logic that a smaller amount of detail needs to be present because a small area is being used to grade the whole coin.

**Very fine, VF-20:** About 75 percent of the original detail will be visible. Or, on a coin with no inner detail, there will be moderate wear over the entire coin. Corners of letters and numbers may be weak. A small grading area will have about 60 percent of the original detail.

**Fine, F-12:** About 50 percent of the original detail will be visible. Or, on a coin with no inner detail, there will be fairly heavy wear over the entire coin. Sides of letters will be weak. A typically uncleaned coin will often appear dirty or dull. A small grading area will have just under 50 percent of the original detail.

**Very good, VG-8:** About 25 percent of the original detail will be visible. There will be heavy wear on the entire coin.

**Good, G-4:** Design will be clearly outlined but with substantial wear. Some of the larger detail may be visible. The rim may have a few weak spots of wear.

**About good, AG-3:** Typically only a silhouette of a large design will be visible. The rim will be worn down into the letters, if any.

## Where to write for more information

*Official A.N.A. Grading Standards for United States Coins:* Whitman Coin Products M.S. 438R, Western Publishing Co., Inc., 1220 Mound Ave., Racine, WI 53404.

*Photograde:* Bowers and Merena Galleries Inc., Books Department, Box 1224, Wolfeboro, NH 03894.

**Professional Coin Grading Service:** P.O. Box 9458, Newport Beach, CA 92658.

**Numismatic Guaranty Corp.:** P.O. Box 1776, Parsippany, NJ 07054.

**American Numismatic Association Authentication Bureau:** 818 N. Cascade Ave., Colorado Springs, CO 80903-3279.

# 5

# Get a map

## *How to organize a collection*

**By David C. Harper**

Do you have a jar full of old coins? Did a favorite relative give you a few silver dollars over the years? Or did you just come across something unusual that you set aside?

All three circumstances make good beginnings for collecting coins. It may surprise you, but this is how just about everybody starts in the hobby. It is a rare collector who decides to start down the hobby road without first having come into a few coins one way or another.

What these random groupings lack is organization. It is organization that makes a collection. But think about it another way: Organization is the map that tells you where you can go in coin collecting and how you can get there.

Have you ever been at a large fair or a huge office building and seen the maps that say "you are here"? Did you ever consider that, over time, thousands of other people have stood on the same spot? This is true in numismatics also. Figuratively, you are standing on the same spot on which the writers of this book stood at some point in their lives.

At a fair, the map helps you consider various ways of seeing all the sights. In coin collecting, too, there are different ways to organize a collection. The method you choose helps you see the hobby sights you want to see.

It should be something that suits you. Remember, do what you want to do. See what you want to see. But don't be afraid to make a mistake; there aren't any. Just as one can easily retrace steps at a fair, one can turn around and head in another direction in the coin-collecting hobby. Besides, when you start off for any given point, often you see something along the way that was unplanned but more interesting. That's numismatics.

There are two major ways to organize a collection: by type, and by date and mintmark. These approaches work in basically the same fashion for coins of the United States, Canada and Mexico. Naturally, there are differences. But to establish the concepts, let's focus first on U.S. coins.

# United States

Let's take collecting by type first. Look at your jar of coins, or take the change out of your pocket. You find Abraham Lincoln and the Lincoln Memorial on current cents. You find Thomas Jefferson and his home, Monticello, on the nickel. Franklin D. Roosevelt and a torch share the dime. George Washington and an eagle appear on the quarter. John F. Kennedy and the presidential seal are featured on the half dollar.

Each design is called a "type." If you took one of each and put the five coins in a holder, you would have a type set of the coins that are currently being produced for circulation by the U.S. Mint.

With just these five coins, you can study various metallic compositions. You can evaluate their states of preservation and assign a grade to each. You can learn about the artists who designed the coins, and you can learn of the times in which these designs were created.

As you might have guessed, many different coin types have been used in the United States over the years. You may remember seeing some of them circulating. These designs reflect the hopes and aspirations of people over time. Putting all of them together forms a wonderful numismatic mosaic of American history.

George Washington did not mandate that his image appear on the quarter. Quite the contrary. He would have been horrified. When he was president, he headed off those individuals in Congress who thought the leader of the country should have his image on its coins. Washington said it smacked of monarchy and would have nothing of it.

Almost a century and a half later, during the bicentennial of Washington's birth in 1932, a nation searching for its roots during troubled economic times decided that it needed his portrait on its coins as a reminder of his great accomplishments and as reassurance that this nation was the same place it had been in more prosperous days.

In its broadest definition, collecting coins by type requires that you obtain an example of every design that was struck by the U.S. Mint since it was founded in 1792. That's a tall order. You would be looking for denominations like the half cent, two-cent piece, three-cent piece, and 20-cent piece, which have not been produced in over a century. You would be looking for gold coins ranging in face value from $1 to $50.

But even more important than odd-sounding denominations or high face values is the question of rarity. Some of the pieces in this two-century type set are rare and expensive. That's why type collectors often divide the challenge into more digestible units.

Type collecting can be divided into 18th, 19th and 20th century units. Starting type collectors can focus on 20th century coin designs, which are easily obtainable. The fun and satisfaction of putting the 20th century set together then creates the momentum to continue backward in time.

In the process of putting a 20th century type set together, one is also learning how to grade, learning hobby jargon, and discovering how to obtain coins from dealers, the U.S. Mint, and other collectors. All of this knowledge is then refined as the collector increases the challenge to himself.

This book is designed to help. How many dollar types were struck in the 20th century? Turn to the U.S. price-guide section and check it out. We see the Morgan dollar, Peace dollar, Eisenhower dollar, and Anthony dollar. Hobbyists could also add the Ike dollar with the Bicentennial design of 1976 and the silver American Eagle bullion coin struck since 1986. One can also find out their approximate retail prices from the listings.

The beauty of type collecting is that one can choose the most inexpensive example of each type. There is no need to select a 1903-O Morgan when the 1921 will do just as well. With the 20th century type set, hobbyists can dodge some truly big-league prices.

As a collector's hobby confidence grows, he can tailor goals to fit his desires. He can take the road less traveled if that is what suits him. Type sets can be divided by denomination. You can choose two centuries of one-cent coins. You can take just obsolete denominations or copper, silver or gold denominations.

You can even collect by size. Perhaps you would like to collect all coin types larger than 30 millimeters or all coins smaller than 20 millimeters. Many find this freedom of choice stimulating.

Type collecting has proven itself to be enduringly popular over the years. It provides a maximum amount of design variety while allowing collectors to set their own level of challenge.

The second popular method of collecting is by date and mintmark. What this means, quite simply, is that a collector picks a given type — Jefferson nickels, for example — and then goes after an example of every year, every mintmark, and every type of manufacture that was used with the Jefferson design.

Looking at this method of collecting brings up the subject of mintmarks. The "U.S. Mint" is about as specific as most non-collectors get in describing the government agency that provides everyday coins. Behind that label are the various production facilities that actually do the work.

In two centuries of U.S. coinage, there have been eight such facilities. Four are still in operation. Those eight in alphabetical order are Carson City, Nev., which used a "CC" mintmark to identify its work; Charlotte, N.C. ("C"); Dahlonega, Ga. ("D"); Denver (also uses a "D," but it opened long after the Dahlonega Mint closed, so there was never any confusion); New Orleans ("O"); Philadelphia (because it was the primary mint, it used no mintmark for much of its history, but currently uses a "P"); San Francisco ("S"); and West Point, N.Y. ("W").

A basic type set of 20th century dollar coins would consist of (from top), a Morgan type, Peace type, Eisenhower type, and Anthony type.

A person contemplating the collecting of Jefferson nickels by date and mintmark will find that three mints produced them: San Francisco, Denver and Philadelphia. Because the first two are branch mints serving smaller populations, their output has tended over time to be smaller than that of Philadelphia. This fact, repeated in other series, has helped give mintmarks quite an allure to collectors. It provides one of the major attractions in collecting coins by date and mintmark.

The key date for Jeffersons is the 1950-D when using mintages as a guide. In that year, production was just 2.6 million pieces. Because collectors of the time were aware of the coin's low mintage, many examples were saved. As a result, prices are reasonable.

Jefferson nickels have been produced at the (from top) Philadelphia, Denver and San Francisco mints. Note the Denver and San Francisco mintmarks to the right of Monticello.

The wartime nickels of 1942-45 marked the first time a "P" mint-mark, for Philadelphia, was used.

The Depression-era 1939-D comes in as the most valuable regular-issue Jefferson nickel despite a mintage of 3.5 million — almost 1 million more than the 1950-D. The reason: Fewer were saved for later generations of coin collectors.

Date and mintmark collecting teaches hobbyists to use mintage figures as a guide but to take them with a grain of salt. Rarity, after all, is determined by the number of surviving coins, not the number initially created.

The Jefferson series is a good one to collect by date and mintmark, because the mintmarks have moved around, grown in size, and expanded in number.

When the series was first introduced, the Jefferson nickel was produced at the three mints previously mentioned. In 1942, because of a diversion of certain metals to wartime use, the coin's alloy of 75 percent copper and 25 percent nickel was changed. The new alloy was 35 percent silver, 56 percent copper, and 9 percent manganese.

To denote the change, the mintmarks were moved and greatly enlarged. The pre-1942 mintmarks were small and located to the right of Monticello; the wartime mintmarks were enlarged and placed over the dome. What's more, for the first time in American history, the Philadelphia Mint used a mintmark ("P").

The war's end restored the alloy and mintmarks to their previous status. The "P" disappeared. This lasted until the 1960s, when a national coin shortage saw all mintmarks removed for three years (1965-1967) and then returned, but in a different location. Mintmarks were placed on the obverse, to the right of Jefferson's portrait near the date in 1968. In 1980 the "P" came back in a smaller form and is still used.

Another consideration arises with date and mintmark collecting: Should the hobbyist include proof coins in the set? This can be argued both ways. Suffice to say that anyone who has the desire to add proof coins to the set will have a larger one. It is not necessary nor is it discouraged.

Some of the first proof coins to carry mintmarks were Jefferson nickels. When proof coins were made in 1968 after lapsing from 1965 to 1967, pro-duction occurred at San Francisco instead of Philadelphia. The "S" mint-mark was placed on the proof coins of that year, including the Jefferson nickel, to denote the change. Since that time, mintmarks used on proof

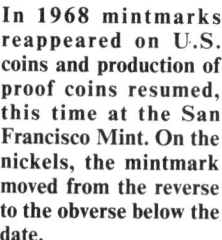

In 1968 mintmarks reappeared on U.S. coins and production of proof coins resumed, this time at the San Francisco Mint. On the nickels, the mintmark moved from the reverse to the obverse below the date.

examples of various denominations have included the "P", "D", "S", and "W".

For all of the mintmark history that is embodied in the Jefferson series, prices are reasonable. For a first attempt at collecting coins by date and mintmark, it provides excellent background for going on to the more expensive and difficult types. After all, if you are ever going to get used to the proper handling of a coin, it is far better to experiment on a low-cost coin than a high-value rarity.

As one progresses in date and mintmark collecting and type collecting, it is important to remember that all of the coins should be of similar states of preservation. Sets look slapdash if one coin is VG and another is MS-65 and still another is VF. Take a look at the prices of all the coins in the series before you get too far, figure out what you can afford, and then stick to that grade or range of grades.

Sure, there is a time-honored practice of filling a spot with any old example until a better one comes along. That is how we got the term "filler." But if you get a few placeholders, don't stop there. By assembling a set of uniform quality, you end up with a more aesthetically pleasing collection.

The date and mintmark method used to be the overwhelmingly dominant form of collecting. It still has many adherents. Give it a try if you think it sounds right for you.

Before we leave the discussion of collecting U.S. coins, it should be pointed out that the two major methods of organizing a collection are simply guidelines. They are no hard-and-fast rules that must be followed without question. Collecting should be satisfying to the hobbyist. It should never be just one more item in the daily grind. Take the elements of these collecting approaches that you like or invent your own.

It should also be pointed out that U.S. coinage history does not start with 1792 nor do all of the coins struck since that time conform precisely to the two major organizational approaches. But these two areas are good places to start.

There are coins and tokens from the American Colonial period (1607-1776) that are just as fascinating and collectible as regular U.S. Mint issues. There are federal issues struck before the Mint was actually established. See the Colonial price-guide section in this book.

There are special coins called commemoratives, which have been struck by the U.S. Mint since 1892 to celebrate some aspect of American history or a contemporary event. They are not intended for circulation. There was a long interruption between 1954 and 1982, but currently numerous commemoratives are being offered for sale directly to collectors by the Mint.

Collecting commemoratives has always been considered something separate from collecting regular U.S. coinage. It is, however, organized the same way. Commemoratives can be collected by date and mintmark or by type.

Current commemoratives can be purchased from the U.S. Mint. To get on its mailing list, write U.S. Mint, Customer Service Center, 10001 Aerospace Drive, Lanham MD 20706. Once on the list, hobbyists will get the various solicitations for not only commemoratives, but regular proof sets and mint sets and American Eagle bullion coinage.

Buying coins from the Mint can be considered a hobby pursuit in its own right. Some collectors let the Mint organize their holdings for them. They buy complete sets and put them away. They never buy anything from anywhere else.

Admittedly, this is a passive form of collecting, but there are individuals around the world who enjoy collecting at this level without ever really going any deeper. They like acquiring every new issue as it comes off the Mint's presses.

Once done, there is a certain knowledge that one has all the examples of the current year. Obviously, too, collectors by date and mintmark of the current types would have to buy the new coins each year, but, of course, they do not stop there.

Varieties and errors make up another area. Under this heading come the coins the Mint did not intend to make. There are all kinds of errors. Many of them are inexpensive. Check out the U.S. Minting Varieties and Errors section in the price guide. If you want to pursue it further, there are specialty books that deal with the topic in more detail.

# Canada

Starting point for the national coinage of Canada is popularly fixed at 1858. In that year a large cent was first produced for use in Upper and Lower Canada (Ontario and Quebec). These pieces were intended to supplant local copper coinage, which in turn had been attempts to give various regions a medium of exchange.

What was circulating in Canada at the time was a hodgepodge of world issues. The large cent predates a unified national government by nine years, but it is considered the beginning of national issues nevertheless.

There are many similarities between the United States and Canada and their respective monetary systems. Both continent-sized nations thought in terms of taming the frontier, new settlements, and growth. Both came to use the dollar as the unit of account because of the pervasiveness of the Spanish milled dollar in trade. For each, the dollar divides into 100 cents.

Canadian coins have depicted (from top) Queen Victoria, King Edward VII, King George V, King George VI, and Queen Elizabeth II.

However, Canada had a far longer colonial history. Many of its residents resisted the tide that carried the United States to independence and worked to preserve their loyalties to the British crown. As a result, Canada was firmly a part of the British Empire. So even today with its constitution (the British North America Act transferred from Westminster to Ottawa in 1982), parliamentary democracy, and a national consciousness perhaps best symbolized by the maple leaf, Canada retains a loyalty to the crown in the person of Queen Elizabeth II of the United Kingdom. Canada is a member of the British Commonwealth of Nations.

The effect of this on coins is obvious. Current issues carry the queen's effigy. How Canada got its coins in the past was also influenced. The fledgling U.S. government set about creating its own mint as one of its earliest goals, despite that better-quality pieces could be purchased abroad at lower cost. Canada found that ties to mints located in England were logical and comfortable.

The Royal Canadian Mint was not established until 1908, when it was called the Ottawa branch of the British Royal Mint, and it was not given its present name until 1931. Both events are within living memory. Canadian coins, therefore, have a unique mixture of qualities. They are tantalizingly familiar to U.S. citizens yet distinctly different.

The coinage of a monarchy brings its own logic to the organization of a collection. Type collecting is delineated by the monarch. United Canada has had six. The first was Queen Victoria, whose image appeared on those large cents of 1858. Her reign began in 1837 and lasted until 1901.

She was followed by Edward VII, 1901-1910; George V, 1910-1936; Edward VIII, 1936; George VI, 1936-1952; and Queen Elizabeth II, 1952-present. All but Edward VIII had coins struck for circulation in Canada. The collectible monarchs, therefore, number five, but the longer reigns inspired changes of portraits over time to show the aging process at work. Legends also changed. When George VI ceased being emperor of India, Canada's coins were modified to recognize the change.

Like U.S. coins, sizes and alloys were altered to meet new demands placed on the coinage. However, the separateness of each nation might best be summed up this way: Though the United States abolished its large cent in 1857, Canada's was just getting under way in 1858. The United States put an end to the silver dollar in 1935, the very year Canada finally got its series going.

And Canada, the nickel-mining giant, used a small-sized silver five-cent coin until 1921, almost 50 years after the half dime was abolished in the United States. But whereas the Civil War was the major cause of the emergence of modern U.S. coinage as specified by the Coinage Act of 1873, World War I influenced the alterations that made Canada's coins what they are today.

It might be assumed that change in the monarch also signaled a change in the reverse designs of the various denominations. A check of the Canadian price guide section shows this is not necessarily the case. Current designs paired with Queen Elizabeth II basically date back to the beginning of her father's reign. The familiar maple-leaf cent, beaver five-cent piece, schooner 10-cent, caribou 25-cent, and coat-of-arms 50-cent have been running for over 50 years. Significant changes were made to the 50-cent coin in 1959, but the reverse design remains the coat of arms.

So where does that leave type collectors? It puts them in a situation similar to categorizing the various eagles on U.S. coins. They can be universalists and accept the broadest definitions of type, or they can narrow the bands to whatever degree suits them best.

By checking the price-guide section, date and mintmark collectors will quickly note that their method of organization more or less turns into collecting by date. Though currently there are three mints in Canada — Hull, Quebec; Ottawa, Ontario; and Winnipeg, Manitoba — they don't use mintmarks. Historically, few mintmarks were employed.

Ottawa used a "C" on gold sovereigns of 1908-1919 and on some exported colonial issues. The private Heaton Mint in Birmingham, England, used an "H" on coins it supplied to Canada from 1871 to 1907.

But the coins supplied to Canada by the British Royal Mint and later by its Ottawa branch did not carry any identifying mark. Collectors who confine their activities to the more recent issues need never think about a mintmark.

It would be easy to slant a presentation on Canadian issues to stress similarities or differences to U.S. issues. One should remember that the monetary structures of each evolved independently, but each was always having an impact on the other.

Common events, such as World War II, had a similar impact. For example, the Canadian five-cent coin changed in much the same way as the U.S. nickel. In Canada, nickel was removed and replaced first by a tombac (brass) alloy and then by chromium-plated steel. Peace brought with it a return to the prewar composition.

To see an example of differences between the United States and Canada, take the Canadian approach to the worldwide trend of removing silver from coinage. Canada made its move in 1968, three years after the United States. Instead of choosing a copper-nickel alloy as a substitute for silver, Canada looked to its own vast natural resources and employed pure nickel.

Canada also seems more comfortable with its coinage than the United States. Whereas the United States often feared confusion and counterfeiting from making the least little changes in its coins, Canada has long embraced coinage to communicate national events, celebrations and culture. Its silver-dollar series actually began as a celebration of George V's 25 years on the throne.

Succeeding years saw additional commemorative $1 designs interspersed with the regular voyageur design. When the centennial of national confederation was observed in 1967, all of the denominations were altered for one year. The United States only reluctantly tried out the idea on three of its denominations for the nation's Bicentennial.

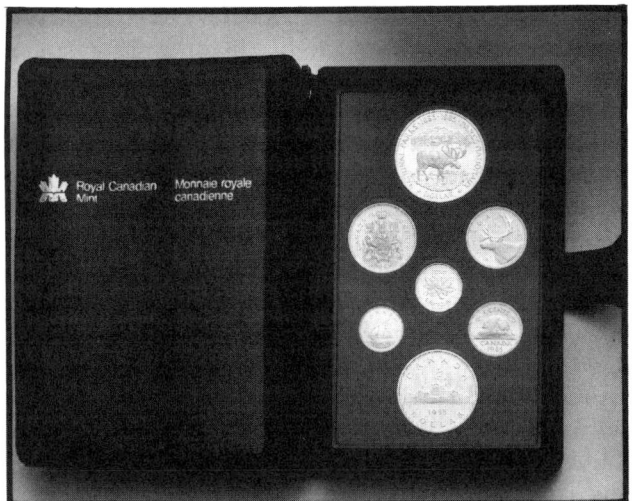

Like the U.S. Mint, the Royal Canadian Mint offers sets of coins in a variety of finishes to the collector market.

Ultimately, Canada began an annual commemorative dollar series in 1971. It issued coins for the 1976 Montreal Olympic Games and again in 1988 for the Calgary Olympic Games. Bullion coins were created to market its gold, silver and platinum output. A commemorative series of gold $100 coins was also undertaken. Canada, too, issues special proof, prooflike and specimen sets, similar to the United States.

Hobbyists who would like to be informed of new issues should write Royal Canadian Mint, P.O. Box 473, Station "A," Ottawa, Ontario K1N 1A1, Canada. The mint also maintains special toll-free lines. In the United States, hobbyists may telephone the Royal Canadian Mint at 1-800-268-6468. In Canada the number is 1-800-267-1871. You can get on the mailing list by using these numbers and you can buy currently available coins.

When collecting Canada, another thing to remember is the importance varieties play in the nation's various series. Certainly, a type collector has no need to dwell on this information, but the date and mintmark collector may puzzle over the many extra identifying abbreviations in the price guide for certain coins. These varieties should not be confused with the U.S. variety-and-error category.

Here the varieties are not mistakes; they are deliberately created and issued variations of the standard design. We see voyageur dollars on which the number of water lines changes. Other dollars count the number of beads.

These differences are minor. Though they were deliberately done to meet varying mint needs, they were not intended to be set apart in the public mind. The hobby, however, likes to look at things under a microscope.

Some varieties were indeed intended to be deliberately and noticeably different. An example of this occurs with 1947-dated issues. A maple leaf was placed on the 1947-dated cent through 50-cent issues. This indicated the coin was struck after George VI lost his title of emperor of India, as proclaimed in the Latin legend, but that the design had not yet been altered to reflect this. All of these varieties are considered integral parts of the Canadian series, and they are listed as such.

Do not construe any of this to mean there is no collecting of varieties and errors of the type common in the United States. There is. Collecting Royal Canadian Mint mistakes is just as active, just as interesting, and just as rewarding. After all, mint errors are universal. The methods of manufacture are the same. So the mistakes can be classified in the same manner.

Canada's numismatic listings also include items from various provinces issued before they were part of the confederation. The largest portion of this section is devoted to Newfoundland, because it retained a separate status far longer than the other provinces — until 1949 in fact.

Advice given to collectors of U.S. coins also applies to collectors of Canadian coins: Do what interests you. Do what you can afford. Create sets of uniform grade.

The rules of rarity transcend national boundaries. The only thing to keep in mind is the relative size of the collecting population. Because Canada has only a tenth of the U.S. population, it stands to reason that the number of collectors in that nation is but a fraction of the U.S. number. A mintage that seems to indicate scarcity for a U.S. coin, therefore, could indicate something quite common in Canada.

Don't forget that mintage is just a guide. The same factors that caused loss of available specimens or preserved unusually large quantities were at work in Canada, too.

# Mexico

Coinage produced in Mexico dates to the establishment of a mint in Mexico City in 1536, over 250 years before a federal mint was set up in the United States and more than 300 years before Canada circulated its own coins. The output of those extra centuries alone would make organizing a Mexican coin collection more challenging than a collection of U.S. or Canadian coins. But there are numerous other factors involved.

You say you like the kings and queens on Canada's coins? Mexico has kings, too — nearly 300 years' worth, plus a couple of emperors. You say the ideals of liberty embodied by the great men and women on U.S. coins is more your cup of tea? Mexico's coins also feature men and women committed to liberty.

In addition, Mexico is the crossroads of civilizations and empires. The great pyramid-building society of southern Mexico and Central America met its end at the hands of the Spanish conquistadors led initially by Hernando Cortez. The great Aztec empire was looted and overturned in 1519-1521 in the name of Spain.

The great natural resources of the area then supported successive Spanish kings in their grand dreams of dominating Europe. Through the doors

One thousand of these equaled one new peso as 1993 began. The new peso is worth about 33 cents.

of the Mexico City Mint and later facilities scattered about the country passed legendary quantities of silver. Even today the country ranks at the top of the list of silver producers.

But while Spain could dominate Mexico for a long time, the basic ideals of liberty and human dignity eventually motivated the people to throw off the foreign yoke. Unfortunately, victory was often neither complete nor wisely led. And in more recent years, the scourge of inflation has exacted a high toll on the currency itself. The numismatic consequences of a long history punctuated by periods of turmoil are an abundance of denominations, metals and types.

It is tempting for a would-be collector of Mexican coins to forget about anything that happened in the country prior to its monetary reform of 1905. By starting at that point, a hobbyist can happily overlook anything other than a decimal monetary system in which 100 centavos equal 1 peso. That system is as modern as any. The coins' striking quality is high. Legends are easy to read and understand, and the variety of issues is wide but not overwhelming.

There always is a certain logic to begin the collecting of any country with recent issues. The costs of learning are minimized, and as one becomes comfortable, a level of confidence can be built up sufficient to prompt diving further into the past.

The issues of 1905 to date also more easily fit into the mold of type collecting and collecting by date and mintmark. To take type collecting, for example, let's look at the peso. In 1905 it was a silver-dollar-sized coin with a silver-dollar-sized quantity of bullion in it, 0.786 ounces. In 1918 it was reduced to 0.4663 ounces; in 1920, 0.3856 ounces; in 1947, 0.2250 ounces; 1950, 0.1285 ounces; 1957, 0.0514 ounces; and in 1970 silver was eliminated completely in favor of a copper-nickel alloy.

At almost every one of those steps, the design changed, too. After sinking to 3,300 to the U.S. dollar, monetary reform dropped three zeroes at the start of 1993. The new peso, equal to 1,000 old pesos, is three to the dollar.

By beginning with 1905, a date and mintmark collector misses out on issues of the various branch mints that were located around the country. Regular issues were all struck in Mexico City. Yearly output was reasonably regular for the various denominations, so date sets are extensive.

There have been rumblings since the early 1980s that Mexico would

Mexico also strikes commemorative coins for the collector market. They are available through private firms in the United States.

abandon the peso because of its greatly reduced value. The government, however, has been working hard to retain it. So far it has succeeded.

One thing the government cannot do, however, is turn the clock back to a time when the fractional denominations of 1, 2, 5, 10, 20, 25, and 50 centavos had sufficient face value to circulate. However, it is stimulating to assemble sets because they offer a range of rarities. They are neither so expensive that it would prevent a collector from acquiring them at some point, but neither are they so common that you can walk into a shop, write a check, and come away with all of the 20th century sets complete. Check out the price guide section and see.

Gold in the post-1905 era is basically so much bullion. There are some scarcer pieces and some strikingly beautiful designs, such as the centenario, a gold 50-peso coin containing 1.2 ounces of bullion. It was first struck in 1921 to mark 100 years of independence. Because Mexico actively restruck its gold coins, however, it is virtually impossible to tell an original issue from the newer version.

The result is a retail price structure based on metallic content. Gold, however, does not conjure up the images that silver does. Silver is the magic word for Mexico. That, of course, means the peso.

The modern Mexico City Mint also strikes commemoratives and collector sets from time to time. These are generally marketed to collectors through private firms, details of which are published in hobby newspapers like *World Coin News*. Mexico, like the United States and Canada, also issues gold and silver bullion coins.

These also are marketed through arrangements with private firms. Interestingly, Mexico's many gold-coin restrikes were the bullion coins of their day. They had the advantage of ready identification, and they were legally tradable according to gold-coin regulations that existed in the United States from 1933 through 1974.

It is appropriate that we conclude discussion of the modern period on the concept of bullion, because bullion is at the root of Mexico's numismatic history. That is a period to which we now turn.

When Cortez toppled the Aztec Empire, for a time the wealth returning to Spain was merely that taken by the victors from the vanquished. But the business of permanently administering a vast area in the name of the Spanish king, exploiting its natural resources, and funneling the proceeds to Spain quite soon involved the establishment of a mint in Mexico City. This was undertaken in 1536, just 15 years after the end of Aztec dominion.

At first, the authorized coins were low denominations: silver quarter, half, 1, 2, 3, and 4 reales, and copper 2 and 4 maravedis. To understand their face values and how they related to each other, let's take the common reference point of a silver dollar. The silver dollar is 8 reales, and you might recognize the nickname for the denomination of "piece of eight" from pirate lore. The eighth part, the silver real, was divided into 34 copper maravedis. That means the 8 reales was worth 272 copper maravedis.

The copper coinage was hated and soon abolished, not to reappear until 1814. The silver coins were fine as far as they went. When the mines of Mexico began producing undreamed of quantities of metal, however, it was the 8 reales that took center stage. This occurred after 1572. The piece of eight became the standard form for shipping silver back to Spain.

Mexico City's output was prodigious. Minting standards were crude. All denominations produced are called "cobs," because they are basically little more than irregular-looking lumps of metal on which bits and pieces of design can be seen. The only constant was weight, fineness, and the appearance of assayer's initials (which guaranteed the weight and fineness). Not showing those initials was cause for severe punishment.

Designs showed the arms of the monarch on one side, a cross on the other, appropriate legends, and an indication of denomination. The period of cob issues lasted until 1732. Rulers of the period start with Charles and Johanna, 1516-1556; Philip II, 1556-1598; Philip III, 1598-1621; Philip IV, 1621-1665; Charles II, 1665-1700; Philip V, 1700-1724 and 1724-1746; and Luis I, 1724.

Modern mint machinery began turning out coins in 1732. Quality was similar to today. The arms design was continued. It was not until 1772 that the monarch's portrait began appearing. The honor of this numismatic debut belongs to Charles III. Kings of this period are Ferdinand VI, 1746-1759; Charles III, 1760-1788; Charles IV, 1788-1808; and Ferdinand VII, 1808-1821. The *Standard Catalog of Mexican Coins* by Colin R. Bruce II and Dr. George W. Vogt is recommended to those who want to study this period in greater depth.

The revolutionary period begins in 1810, when a parish priest, Miguel Hidalgo y Costilla, issued the call for independence. The first attempts to achieve this were violently suppressed. Hidalgo was executed, but independence did come in 1821.

With revolt against central authority came a dispersal of the right to strike coins. Mexico City continued as the major facility, but other operations began. The list of these over the next century is lengthy. Mintmarks and assayer initials proliferated.

The old colonial coinage standard survived the period. The 8 reales and its parts carried on. A slight reduction in bullion content had been ordered by the king in 1760, but otherwise things continued as they were. Gold was coined during the colonial period beginning in 1679 based on an 8-escudo piece, which divided into eighths just like the 8 reales. Gold, however, was not as important as silver.

Mexico's first emperor came shortly after independence. He was a leader in the struggle that set Mexico free from Spain. Augustin de Iturbide, originally an officer in the service of Spain, was proclaimed emperor in 1822. He abdicated in 1823 and was executed in 1824.

The second emperor had a reign almost as short as the first. Maximilian I, emperor only because he had a French army to secure the throne, reigned from 1863 to 1867. He was shot by a firing squad when the French left.

He is remembered numismatically because he decided to decimalize the coinage. The centavo and peso were born. Soon afterward, the republic was re-established. Further monetary changes were minor thereafter until 1905.

Collectors focusing on Mexico can devote much time to the study of the quasi-official issues of rebels during the periods of instability. They can look at hacienda tokens, which were issued by large farms or ranches that employed hundreds or thousands of people. Or they can pick whichever period in Mexico's history that fascinates them most. Whatever collectors of Mexico eventually settle on, they will find it rewarding.

# Where to write for more information

*World Coin News:* 700 E. State St., Iola, WI 54990.

# 6

# Caring for coins

## *How to store and preserve your collection*

### By Alan Herbert

From the day you acquire your first collectible coin, you have to consider where and how to store your collection. Often a shoebox or a small cardboard or plastic box of some kind will be the principal storage point as you start to gather coins, even before they can be considered a collection. Sooner or later you will outgrow that first box and need to think seriously about what to do with your coins to protect and preserve them.

All too often security takes precedence over preservation. We're more worried that the kids will dip into the coins for candy or ice cream or that burglars will somehow learn about your "valuable" collection and pay a visit. It often isn't until years later when you suddenly notice that your once beautiful coins are now dingy and dull, with spots and fingerprints all over them, that preservation becomes a primary consideration.

Learning good storage habits should be one of the first things to do right along with acquiring those first coins. There are a multitude of storage products on the market that are intended for more or less specific situations, so learning which to use and how to use them is vital to the health of your collection. Most if not all of the products mentioned here should be available at your nearest coin shop or hobby store.

## Safe storage methods

The common impulse is to use what's available around the house; never allow that impulse to control your collecting. Plastic wrap, aluminum foil, cardboard, stationery envelopes, and other common household products are not designed for coin storage and never should be used for your collec-

Two-by-two cardboard holders are a common form of short-term, inexpensive coin storage.

Many dealers sell coins in 2-by-2 plastic "flips," but they should not be used for long-term storage.

tion. The same goes for soaps and cleansers found around the home.

There are specific products that have been designed, tested and found safe to use for coins. These are the media your collection deserves. The slight added expense will pay a thousand dividends years from now when you sell your collection or pass it on to your heirs.

The most common storage media are 2-inch by 2-inch cardboard holders with Mylar windows, 2-by-2 plastic "flips," coin tubes, hard-plastic holders, coin boards, and coin albums.

The 2-by-2 cardboard holders are the cheapest and most commonly used storage method. They are usually folded and stapled around the coin. They are intended for short-term general storage. They are not airtight or watertight, and staples driven too close to the coin can ruin it.

The 2-by-2 plastic flips come in good and bad varieties. The old, usually soft flips are made of plastics that contain polyvinylchloride, a chemical found in many plastics. Over time it breaks down into substances that put a green slime on your coins, which attacks the surface and ruins them.

The good flips are made of Mylar, but they are brittle and prone to splitting. So they should not be used to mail coins or when the coins are moved about frequently. Mylar flips, too, are for short-term general storage.

Coin tubes are often used for bulk storage, but there is a proper technique to placing the coins in the tube.

Often you will find coins in PVC holders when you buy them from a dealer. Remove them immediately and put them in some better storage medium.

Coin tubes come in clear and cloudy, or translucent, plastic. These are made of an inert plastic that will not harm your coins. Tubes are intended for bulk, medium- to long-term storage, with one caution: Use care when inserting the coins. Merely dropping one coin onto another in a tube can damage both coins. The best technique is to make a stack or pile of the coins, then slide the pile carefully into the tube while holding it at an angle.

Hard-plastic holders are the elite items for storing your collection. There are a number of varieties, some of which come in three parts that are screwed together. Some come in two pieces that fit together. Some of these are airtight and watertight. They are more expensive, but they deserve to be used for any really valuable coins in your collection.

Coins processed by the third-party grading services come in hard-plastic holders, most of which are at least semiairtight. The hard-plastic holders used by the U.S. Mint for proof sets since 1968 are not airtight, so coins should be watched carefully for signs of problems. In recent years these holders have been improved, but you should check your proof sets periodically.

Any stored coins should be checked regularly, at least twice a year. Check coins for signs of spotting or discoloration. Check the storage media for any signs of deterioration, rust, mildew, or other problems.

The older mint sets and proof sets — issued from 1955 to 1964 — come in soft-plastic envelopes that are not intended for long-term storage. Coins

**Hard-plastic holders are the top of the line in coin storage.**

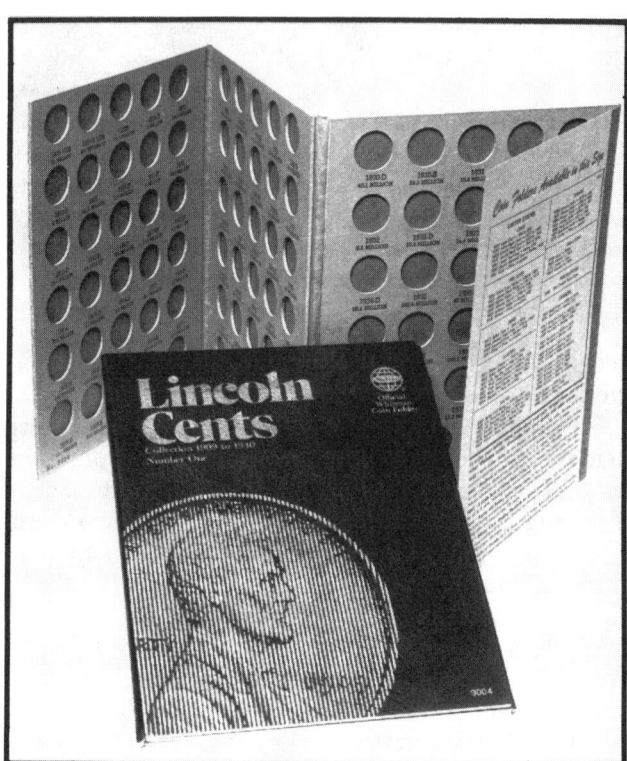

**Coin folders are a low-cost and attractive way to store inexpensive circulated coins.**

in these envelopes should be put in better storage media for the long term. In recent years the Mint has switched to an inert, stiffer plastic for the mint sets. This plastic is safe.

A coin folder is frequently the first piece of equipment the beginning collector buys. It is simply a piece of cardboard with holes to hold the coins. The holder folds up for storage. It is intended for inexpensive circulated coins only.

They give no protection from contamination or fingerprints. Worn coins will often fall out of the holes, which leads some novice collectors to tape the coins in the album. This is another example of misuse of a household

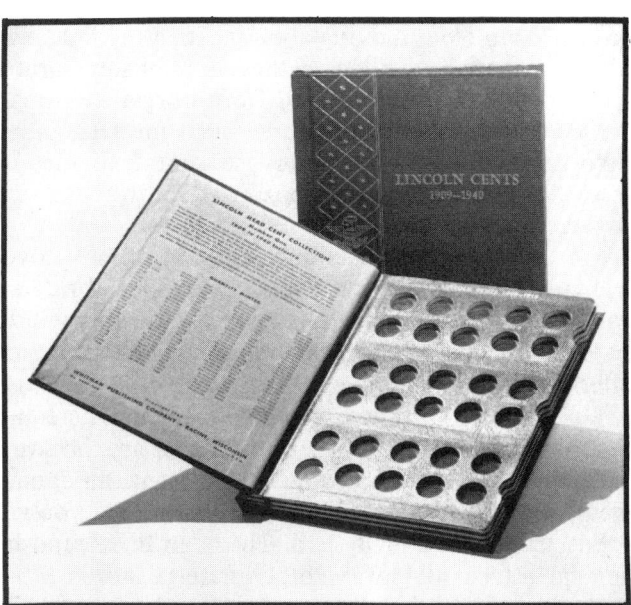

Coin albums also pro-
vide attractive storage
for inexpensive circu-
lated coins.

product; tape can permanently damage a coin's surface.

Pride of ownership and the desire to show off a collection are the moving forces behind the sale of thousands of coin albums. They should also be used for inexpensive circulated coins only, with a couple of exceptions.

Some albums are merely coin boards mounted between covers. Others have pages with sliding plastic strips on both sides of the page so both sides of the coin can be seen.

The open-face albums are subject to fingerprints and contamination. Sneezing on your coins can do as much damage as gouging them with a knife. The slides will rub on your coins, damaging the high points of the design over time. These two types of albums should never be used for expensive uncirculated or proof coins, although they are fine for circulated coins that you want to display.

Fairly new on the market are albums designed for coins in inert, airtight holders. This allows you to display your coins and still keep them safe from handling and contact with the atmosphere.

One more storage medium that deserves mention is the clear-plastic notebook page that has pockets for 2-by-2 holders or flips. Here again there are good and bad. Most old pocket sheets contain PVC, so they cannot be used to hold coins in non-airtight holders because the gases will migrate into the holders and damage the coins. The newer Mylar pages are brittle but will not generate damaging gases or liquids.

When buying storage media, make sure the dealer guarantees that his products are safe for coins. Many of the old albums, flips and pocket pages are still around, especially at flea markets. If you are in doubt, don't buy.

There are also thin, two-piece, inert plastic holders that many collectors use to protect coins put in flips or 2-by-2 cardboard holders, especially to protect them from moving about against the holder and getting scratched. They are virtually airtight, so they do offer some protection.

Coins need to be protected from burglars. A box under the bed or in the closet offers no protection. If you must keep coins at home, a good, fireproof safe is a must. Otherwise, rent a safe-deposit box at a bank, but read the fine print on your box contract to make sure a coin collection is covered.

Most homeowner's insurance policies will not cover a coin collection or will cover only a fraction of its value. Special riders are expensive, but if you keep most of your coins at the bank, this will cut costs. For details, consult your insurance agent. The American Numismatic Association also offers collection insurance.

Where to store coins is often a problem. The commonest solution is to put them in the attic or basement. Those are the two worst places for your collection. Attics are notoriously hot. Heat can damage almost any storage media, and if there is the slightest hint of PVC, you've got trouble.

Basements are equally bad. They can flood, and humidity is high. Mildew can attack holders and other material stored with your coins.

So what's left? Ideally coins should be treated like a family member. They should be stored in some part of the house where temperature and humidity are relatively constant year round. If it's comfortable for you, it's probably much more comfortable for your coins than the basement or attic.

Protecting coins from humidity is always a good idea, even in areas where it is not a major health problem. For your coins, too much dampness can become a serious problem, often before you realize it. A good solution is to get several good-sized packets of silica gel and store them with your coins in your safe or a container of some kind that will isolate them from the general climate in the home.

# To clean or not to clean

Before you store your coins, you should be aware that coins are like dishes: They should never be put away dirty. Ah, but you've probably already heard or read that you should never clean a coin. If you haven't, I'll say it now: Never clean a coin.

OK, so there are exceptions, but be careful of those exceptions and for good reason. Ignoring the exceptions can be excruciatingly and embarrassingly expensive.

Coins get dirty, just like anything else. The impulse is to shine them up — polish them to a brilliance that will dazzle the viewer. If you've already succumbed to the temptation to clean even a single coin, stand up, kick yourself, then sit back down and read on. The one exception is loose dirt, grease, oil, or something similar, and there are even exceptions to that rule.

Use a neutral solvent to dissolve the grease and oils that usually coat uncirculated coins as they come from the mint. Follow the instructions on the container exactly, and if the directions say to use the product outdoors, they mean it.

For circulated coins, lighter fluid will often dissolve the accumulated "gunk" that sticks to them, but I don't recommend it for uncirculated coins, especially copper alloy coins. Air dry the coins; don't rub or wipe them. Even the softest cloth or paper towel can pick up sharp-edged particles that will ruin a coin's surface. Proof coins are clean when they are packaged, so this should not be necessary and should be done only as a last resort if they have somehow picked up oil in handling.

Using dips, household cleansers, metal polish, and even soap can permanently damage a coin. Avoid acid-based cleaners at all costs. They work by eating away the coin's surface to remove the embedded dirt or discoloration. Cleaning a coin with any of these products will sharply reduce its collectible value. To put it simply, collectors do not want cleaned coins, so they are heavily discounted.

One of the reasons for this is that once a coin has been cleaned, it will discolor much more quickly, requiring fresh cleaning. Each time it is cleaned, the surface is further dulled, reducing the coin's appeal and reducing its value.

Obviously this advice applies especially to uncirculated and proof coins, but it applies to any coin that is or has the potential to become valuable. But if you clean it, its career ends right there.

There are products specifically designed for removing the green PVC slime from coins. They do not contain acid, so they are safe. They will stop but cannot reverse the damage that the PVC has already done to the coin. Read the label, and use exactly as directed.

I frequently am asked about ultrasonic cleaners. They fall under the same heading as the various cleaning products I've described. In other words, the apparatus should not be used for uncirculated, proof, or other valuable coins. If you do use one, do one coin at a time so there is no chance for the vibration to rub two coins together. Change or filter the cleaning solution frequently to keep abrasive particles from coming in contact with the vibrating coin.

Like anything else, cleaning can be carried to an extreme, so I'll give you one horror story of just such a mistake: Years ago I had a collector fly several hundred miles to bring his collection for me to sell for him. When he laid out the coins on the table, I was shocked to discover that the hundreds of coins had all been harshly cleaned.

When I questioned him he calmly recounted that he had decided that the coins needed cleaning, so he dumped them all into a rock tumbler and left it on for several hours. It ruined all his coins, reducing them to face value. With his passion for cleanliness he had destroyed several thousand dollars worth of collectible value, plus air fare, a rental car, and a motel bill.

The key to a long-term collection that might appreciate in value is to learn what not to do to your coins and what care they need to survive years of waiting in the wings. Learning to protect your coins with the best available storage methods and media is a key first step toward enjoying your collection for years to come.

## Where to write for more information

**American Numismatic Association:** 818 N. Cascade Ave., Colorado Springs, CO 80903-3279.

# 7

# The profit motive

## *Some comments on coins as investments*

### By Robert E. Wilhite

When gold and silver bullion prices reached all-time highs in 1980, prices for many U.S. gold and silver coins hit record highs too. Double-digit inflation prompted many investors to seek refuge in tangible assets. Companies touting coins as investments popped up all over. Many of those investors, however, became disenchanted when coin prices crashed along with precious-metals prices just a few months later.

Also, as mentioned in Chapter 4, grading standards for uncirculated coins were loose during the boom but tightened during the bust in these pre-slab days. Investors who bought coins billed as MS-65 or higher during the boom tried to sell during the bust and oftentimes were offered only MS-63 or lower money.

The investment aspect of coins was not new in 1980. Articles in early coin publications often addressed the subject. Those collectors who fancy themselves as traditionalists generally scorn the thought of coins as investments. To them, the reasons to collect coins are the joy and educational benefits of pursuing a hobby.

In reality, though, few collectors purchase coins with the expectation that they will go down in value. There is no guarantee that their coins will increase in value, but collectors who do their homework before buying help their chances. They check the value guides — such as those appearing in *Numismatic News*, *Coins* and *Coin Prices* — and shop their local dealers, shows and advertisements in the aforementioned publications to try to get the best value for their money.

There are many financial success stories in numismatics, as evidenced by auction results. Some common themes keep reappearing in profiles of the people whose collections have provided major sales: These people collected coins over a long time — 10, 20, 30 years or more — and they knew their stuff. They knew what was rare and what was common, and they knew the going rates for each. They formed collections of coins; they didn't just accumulate a mishmash of pieces.

Many had an advantage from the beginning: They were wealthy and could afford some of the top rarities. But their methods carry lessons for collectors of all means.

The financial failure stories also have common themes: There are coin sellers who operate on the fringe of numismatics and prey upon people who know nothing about coins. A slick salesman calls on the telephone and overstates the rarity of the coins he has for sale. He sells them for several times what they could be purchased for from a mainstream numismatic dealer. Several years later the buyer takes them to a mainstream dealer and finds out his coins are worth a fraction of what he paid for them. A person who studies coins and the market for them before jumping in, however, avoids such a scenario.

The value guide for U.S. coins in this book includes charts showing the price performance of selected key dates. As can be seen, coins are subject to price fluctuations just like any investment that carries risk. Some coins experienced a great increase in value in the early 1980s and then dropped toward the middle of the decade. Others have been less volatile, showing little if any fluctuation over the time studied.

Generally the volatile areas are the more popularly collected coins in high grades — series like Morgan dollars, Walking Liberty half dollars, and some gold coins. The less volatile areas usually have a smaller universe of collectors — series like the early silver and copper coins, and obsolete denominations (3 cents and 20 cents, for example).

In the latter case, the rarity of these coins sometimes works against them. To have a successful promotion, a dealer selling coins as investments needs a certain quantity to fill all his orders. The earlier issues are usually not available in the quantities needed for a profitable promotion. Demand for these earlier issues comes mostly from a relatively small but avid group of collectors, and as a result, they're less subject to sharp price fluctuations.

In 1979 *Numismatic News* began publishing a weekly Coin Market Index. The index charts the composite performance of the market's more expensive coins, similar to the stock market's Dow Jones industrial average. It provides a means for comparing the state of the market at various points in the index's 15-year history.

A chart of the index from 1979 through 1994 shows a number of peaks and valleys in the market. After its inception in May 1979, the index jumped over 4,000 points to 6,062 on July 5, 1980, during the precious metals boom. It then crashed to 3,540 on Sept. 11, 1982. Over the next six years the index enjoyed a steady climb to 6,311 on Sept. 27, 1988.

Shortly thereafter, several Wall Street investment firms announced that they would offer limited partnerships that invested in coins. This set off speculation that coins would increase in value because of the new demand. The index climbed to an all-time high of 10,190 on June 18, 1989, but

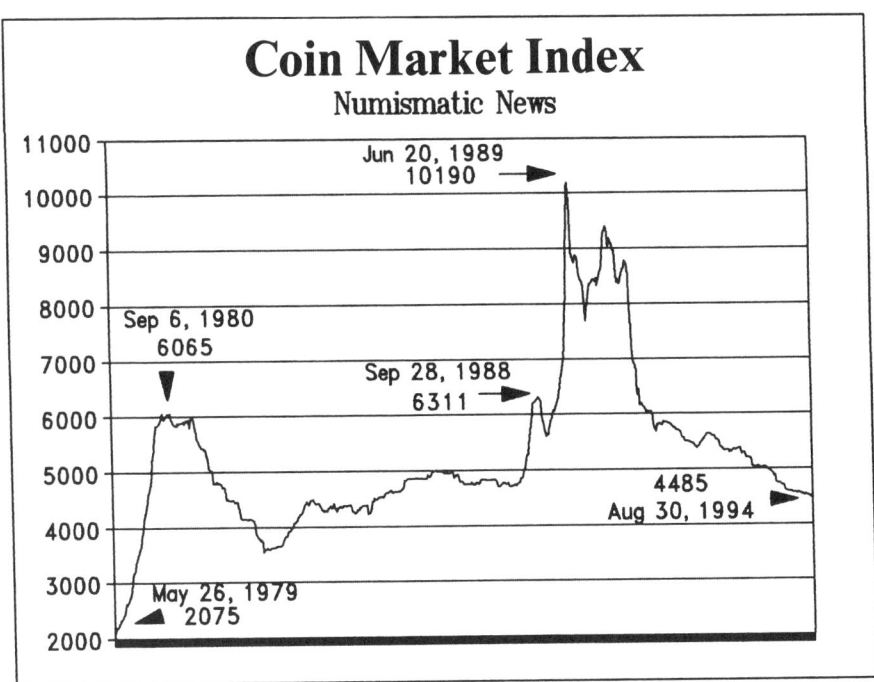

# Coin Market Index
## Numismatic News

Jun 20, 1989
10190 →

Sep 6, 1980
6065

Sep 28, 1988
6311 →

4485
Aug 30, 1994 ►

May 26, 1979
▲ 2075

when the demand did not turn out to be great enough to support the widespread speculation, the index crashed to 6,160 on Dec. 18, 1990. It enjoyed a bit of a spurt in early 1991, before dropping steadily to close the year at 5482. The index recovered slightly in the first two quarters of 1992, but by August 1994 its descent took it to 4485.

The lesson the index teaches is, to be a successful coin investor, think like a collector. That means forming a "set" of coins (see Chapter 5) and holding for the long term — 10, 15, 20 years or more. Those who bought high-grade coins at the June 18, 1989, peak are hurting right now, but maybe they won't be in 10 years. Those who bought in May 1979 and didn't sell on June 18, 1989, probably wish they had, but they're still ahead of prices from 15 years ago.

There is no guarantee that high-grade coins will continue to increase in value over time, but market history shows that the odds favor those collectors who stick it out for the long term. Remember, too, that the index is slanted toward high-grade coins. Because the index is down, it does not mean that every coin decreased in value. In fact, as high-grade investment coins experienced a slump in 1991, some traditional collectible series — such as Indian cents, Lincoln cents, and Buffalo nickels — saw a resurgence of trading activity.

Whether your motivation for buying collectible coins is purely investment or purely collecting pleasure or somewhere in between, keep good records of your purchases. You'll need them after you sell your coins for figuring your gain or loss on your taxes. Record the date of purchase, seller, and purchase price. To make sure your records are adequate, consult a certified public accountant.

Also, advise your heirs on the disposal of your collection in the event of your death. Make sure they know where your records stored, approximately how much your collection is worth, and possible purchasers of your coins.

# 8

# Join the club

*Coin collecting has lots of organizations*

**By David C. Harper**

More than 150 years ago, Alexis de Tocqueville noted in his *Democracy in America* the penchant of people in the United States to create and voluntarily join public groups for a multitude of purposes. This urge to join carries over into coin collecting.

Whether it be a national organization or local coin club, groups have been organized in the United States, Canada and Mexico to help collectors enhance their hobby knowledge and enjoyment. They serve as clearing-houses for new information, maintain libraries, and bring collectors together in meetings to share their hobby experiences with each other. Clubs are so well defined that collectors can find one to serve any activity level and any degree of personal interaction with other collectors.

At the extreme, you can join a national organization by mail, spend a hobby lifetime utilizing its services, and yet never leave the privacy and comfort of home. At the other end, some areas offer such a multitude of clubs that you can find a meeting to attend on many nights of the week.

There are many ways to find a club. Some hobbyists inquire at the local coin shop to identify the organization nearest them. *Numismatic News* publishes news about clubs. Also, watch your local newspaper for listings of community events.

How does a collector match his needs with an appropriate club? The closest thing to a one-stop shopping place for an answer is the American Numismatic Association.

It is the United States' national coin-collecting organization and was granted a perpetual charter by Congress with a mission of education. It can be reached at 818 N. Cascade Ave., Colorado Springs, CO 80903-3279. It offers a wide array of personal hobby services, and its benefits cross national boundaries. In fact, when it was founded in 1891, it was expected that Canadians and Mexicans would be just as likely to join as U.S. citizens.

The most obvious benefit to an ANA member is a subscription to *The Numismatist*, the association's monthly magazine. In it you find news, historical features, membership information, and advertisements placed by dealers who are ready to fill every collector's want list.

More than 30,000 titles are available in the ANA library, and you don't have to walk into the ANA building to check them out. Any member anywhere can do that by mail. The ANA has called upon renowned numismatic authorities to create a correspondence course, which distills into 29 separate readings information that has taken many people a lifetime to learn. There are ANA educational seminars held in Colorado Springs and other sites across the United States.

The ANA sponsors two conventions annually. The early spring convention is usually held in March at locations across the country, selected and announced well in advance. The summer convention, which is so huge that it's billed as the "World's Fair of Money," is a tradition that dates back almost to the organization's founding.

Members also are offered a variety of optional services, ranging from coin-collection insurance to credit cards and car rental discounts. And if you do go to Colorado Springs, the ANA maintains its Money Museum at its headquarters. In it are some of the rarest and most famous coins in history.

Joining the ANA is easy. The membership fee is $32 the first year and $26 thereafter. Members over 65 years old get a $4 discount, and junior members (those under 18) are charged $11.

Beyond simply belonging to the ANA, though, are the doors that open to members. If you want to find a regional, state or local club, you can get help from the ANA. The important thing to remember is that you set your own level of involvement. If your profession is so hectic that you don't need another meeting to go to, the ANA is the place for you. If your hours are so regular that joining in the fun and camaraderie of a local club is just what you are looking for, the ANA can help you find that, too.

And just because the American Numismatic Association has "American" in its name, it doesn't mean that members are focused only on U.S. coins. Far from it. It is more accurate to say that if a coin was struck at any time anywhere in the world in the last 2,600 years, there are ANA members who collect it.

The ANA, if it connotes any exclusivity at all, is basically a regional designation based on where its members live. The farther one gets from the United States, the longer correspondence takes and the greater the possibility of a language barrier between the ANA staff and a potential member. It is therefore not surprising to find that the 31,000 members are predominantly located in the United States.

The Canadian Numismatic Association dates to 1950. It publishes *The Canadian Numismatic Journal*, published 11 times a year, and it also sponsors an annual summer convention. Membership is considerably smaller than the ANA's, in line with the population difference between the United States and Canada. Membership fee is $30 a year. The mailing address is Executive Secretary, Canadian Numismatic Association, P.O. Box 226, Barrie, Ontario L4M 4T2, Canada.

The Sociedad Numismatica de Mexico A.C. was established in 1952. Basically, it oversees a convention in Mexico City once a year. It may be contacted through its U.S. representative at P.O. Box B, Tekonsha, MI 49092.

That covers the national hobby umbrella groups. There are many more organizations of a national character that have somewhat narrower purposes. Among these is the American Numismatic Society in New York City. It is older than the ANA, having been established in 1858. It also maintains a superb museum of U.S. and world coins, and a world-class library. Emphasis in the ANS is on scholarly research.

Numismatics would be nothing if it were not for its research pioneers. If that is what appeals to you, you can write the ANS at Broadway and 155th St., New York, NY 10032, for information regarding its structure and various classes of membership.

Other national organizations focus on specific collectible areas, such as Seated Liberty coinage or tokens and medals. These are popular and active. Many are member organizations of the ANA and hold meetings in conjunction with the ANA's conventions.

Coin dealers have organizations of their own. The Professional Numismatists Guild Inc. maintains high standards of membership qualification and conduct. Members are a who's who of the commercial sector of the hobby. All are ready to serve you in furthering your collecting goals. For a membership roster, contact Robert Brueggeman, Executive Director, 3950 Concordia Lane, Fallbrook, CA 92028.

This brief review merely puts you on the threshold of the organized numismatic world. It is up to you to open that door or walk away. Over the years, many collectors have found membership to be the most rewarding aspect of the hobby. They have benefited from working with others with a common interest to further their own knowledge and advance their collecting goals in an environment of mutual support and friendship.

# 9
# Changes are coming
## *Cent, $1 bill may disappear*
### By Christopher Batio

People and politicians always seem to be calling for change — change in the economy, change in the government and change in society.

For coin collectors, two kinds of change could directly affect us. The first would be to put new designs on the same old denominations, cent through dollar on coins, and dollar through $100 on paper.

The second would be to abolish some part of the money we currently use and replace it with something else, or in the case of the cent, perhaps do without the denomination entirely.

Personal preferences most directly influence the first kind of change. Do you like George Washington on the quarter, or would he perhaps be better placed on the dollar coin?

Economic pressures and changing national circumstances are the primary influences on the second. What is the rate of inflation? What do vending machines need? Is there a counterfeiting problem?

That the current U.S. coin and paper money designs have endured for as long as they have is a tribute to their creators. They were a credit to their times. Times change. Ultimately, U.S. coins and paper money will have to change with them. That has been the experience in Canada and in Mexico. Change has been slow in coming to the United States, but the path blazed by the United States' northern neighbor ultimately may be the path we follow.

Let's look at recent history. Coin collectors have for years called for new portraits on our circulating coins. Under U.S. law there are only two ways that the design of our coins can be changed: by vote of Congress, or by direct action of the Treasury secretary once a coin design is at least 25 years old.

Currently, there are five circulating designs that could be altered through direct action by Treasury Secretary Lloyd Bentsen:

■ The Lincoln cent, whose obverse designed by Victor D. Brenner dates to 1909. The reverse by Frank Gasparro was introduced in 1959.

■ The Jefferson nickel, which was designed by Felix Schlag in 1938.

■ The Roosevelt dime, designed by John R. Sinnock and introduced into circulation during 1946, just one year after President Franklin Delano Roosevelt's death.

■ The Washington quarter introduced in 1932 from a John Flanagan design. It was originally intended to be a one-year circulating commemorative for the 200th anniversary of Washington's birth.

■ The Kennedy half dollar, introduced in 1964, with obverse designed by

Gilroy Roberts and reverse by Frank Gasparro. The coin was intended to memorialize President John F. Kennedy, who had been assassinated Nov. 22, 1963, in Dallas.

Even though Bentsen has made no moves indicating he will change the coin designs, getting him to exercise this power is still theoretically the best chance collectors have of getting new designs any time soon. This is because the Congress has been continually deadlocked on the subject since redesign first surfaced as a renewed possibility in 1987.

The scenario usually went this way . . . A bill to redesign the nation's circulating coins was introduced. Collectors enthusiastically supported it and after much testimony at a hearing, the Senate passed the proposal, but the House of Representatives ultimately balked and the bill died. Collectors felt the excitement of Senate approval about a dozen times over five years, only to be disappointed by the House.

Though coin redesign never was a partisan issue, legislative gridlock occurred anyway.

Rather than getting new designs on our current denominations, it seems we may be closer to getting a new dollar coin.

Even though the Susan B. Anthony dollar, which was struck from 1979 to 1981, has proved to be more successful than conventional wisdom admits (the Treasury's stockpile has been reduced to about 350 million, which means about 500 million Anthony coins have entered circulation), the Canadian and Australian experiences with introducing dollar coins have shown that if a U.S. dollar coin is to be successful it will have to be significantly distinguishable from lesser-value coins. That may mean striking it from a gold-colored metal and maybe giving it a plain edge. A multi-sided planchet could also be used for this purpose.

Another factor in ensuring the success of any new dollar coin that might be introduced is the need to withdraw the $1 note from service. All countries that have successfully introduced a high-denomination circulating coin have done away with the corresponding bank note.

According to a March 1993 study by the General Accounting Office, the United States could save nearly $400 million per year by using a $1 coin rather than a bank note These savings would mainly arise from seigniorage (the profit that accrues to the government from the difference between a coin's face value and the low cost of striking it) and the fact that a coin lasts 30 years in circulation, compared with just 18 months for a $1 bill.

And if the savings involved in issuing a dollar coin aren't enough, the government may soon be forced to eliminate the $1 bill for the simple reason that the Bureau of Engraving and Printing may not have enough printing capacity to continue making them under certain circumstances. This is because American bank notes, especially the $100 note, are now being counterfeited at an unprecedented rate on printing presses in the Middle East and one-at-a-time on color laser copiers here at home.

The far greater threat is from the Middle Eastern notes, which are of such quality that only the most technologically advanced methods can detect them. Their presence in Europe in large numbers was first reported in *Bank*

*Note Reporter* in February 1992.

Since then, several members of Congress — especially Rep. Henry B. Gonzalez, who chairs the House Banking Committee — have urged the Treasury Department to make substantial changes in our bank notes to make them less vulnerable to counterfeiting, and a proposal to completely overhaul the design of the $100 bill was introduced in May 1994 by Sen. Patrick Leahy of Vermont.

If this is done (by the time you are reading this it may already have happened), the Bureau of Engraving and Printing will have to quickly replace the entire inventory of $100 bills in circulation here and abroad. That daunting task will strain its note-printing capacity to the breaking point and will very likely force the Treasury Department to suspend production of $1 bills and introduce a new $1 coin, or rev up the coin presses and once again produce Anthony dollars.

If the U.S. government is forced to introduce a new dollar coin, the next crisis that could arise is whether the U.S. Mint can strike these coins, plus the half dollars, quarters, dimes, nickels and cents that are needed. The only solution may be to eliminate the cent altogether — a controversial decision because some people insist that eliminating the cent would lead to inflation. On the other hand, many people say the cent is a thing of the past that has almost no buying power and is viewed by many as a nuisance. What other monetary unit is thrown or given away with such frequency?

Another change that has affected the American economy, as well as those in Canada and Mexico, is the growing trend toward electronic banking. According to the American Banker's Association, 6,000 financial institutions in the United States currently issue debit or credit cards.

These plastic cards carry information on a magnetic strip that is designed to provide access to a revolving credit line, money in a savings account or both. Their proliferation as an everyday economic tool has lessened the role that cash plays in our lives, especially for major purchases. This will only increase as the century winds to a close.

In addition, their increased use — combined with the myriad designs and types available — will open up more and more opportunities for collectors of credit cards, debit cards and phone cards.

Technological progress may influence our money in another way. As computers and laser copiers make it easier to copy existing bank notes, the money in our pockets may not only look different, it could feel different too. During the last few years, several countries have been experimenting with plastic bank notes. These notes were originally designed to be a more durable alternative to paper money, which deteriorates quickly in hot, humid climates.

Today, Australia is the biggest issuer of plastic notes for circulation. The trend to plastic notes is slow, but growing. Other nations, including Indonesia, Singapore and Haiti, have issued commemorative notes in plastic. Beyond their durability, a nice side effect of these notes is that they are harder to counterfeit. Only time will tell whether plastic is the wave of the future. If it is, plastic U.S. folding money might become common in the 21st century.

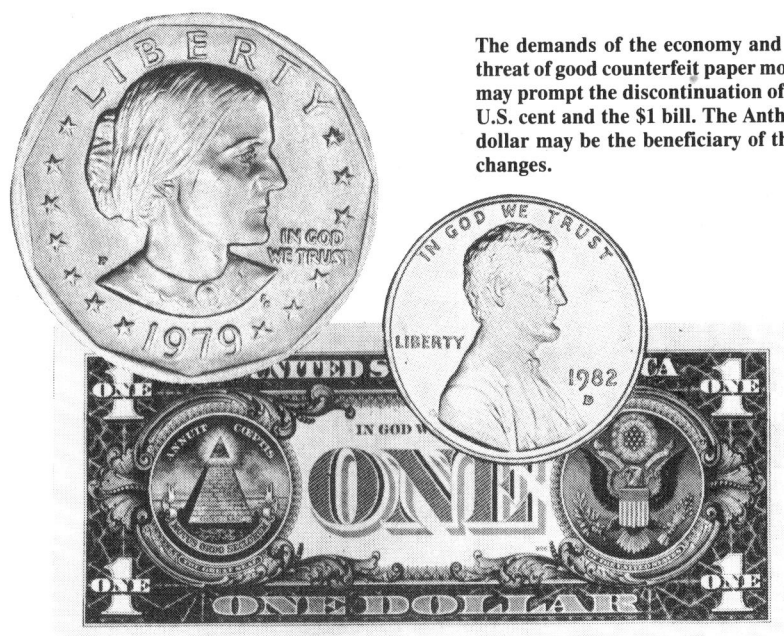

The demands of the economy and the threat of good counterfeit paper money may prompt the discontinuation of the U.S. cent and the $1 bill. The Anthony dollar may be the beneficiary of these changes.

Another new fashion in monetary instruments is bi-metallism — producing coins of one metal surrounded by a ring made of an entirely different metal. For example, in 1988 France began producing a 10-franc coin with an aluminum-bronze ring surrounding a stainless steel center. Mexico began issuing similar coins in 1992 after it implemented a monetary reform that revalued all coins (1 new peso=1,000 old pesos).

The bi-metallic coins have a distinct look that sets them apart from the older Mexican coins they replaced. The 1-, 2- and 5-new peso coins have an "white" stainless steel ring surrounding a "golden" aluminum-bronze center.

With bi-metallism, Mexico also reintroduced silver to circulating coinage. The 10-, 20- and 50-new peso coins both have an aluminum-bronze ring surrounding a sterling silver center. How effectively these coins are circulating, we do not know; but the 10 and 20 new pesos (worth about $3 and $6, respectively) and the base-metal coins are meant to be business strikes.

Meanwhile in Canada, current coinage trends mirror many of the issues just now being raised in the United States. Canada has already eliminated its $1 bill and now strikes an aureate nickel 11-sided dollar coin. It has discussed eliminating its cent and has invigorated Canadian coin design with the circulating commemoratives of the "Canada 125" program.

So what is left for us to look for? Will we ever have the cashless society that so many techno-visionaries and science-fiction writers have imagined? The answer is probably no, at least not as long as there are numismatists around. But one thing is certain, the cash of tomorrow will probably look very different from today's coins and bank notes. Take care to collect today's coins while it is still easy to do so.

# 10

# End of U.S. silver coins

## *Coinage Act of 1965 changed America*

**By Eric von Klinger**

The advent of U.S. clad coinage 30 years ago was greeted by collectors with an air of inevitability coupled with dismay at the debasement.

"The sandwich coins will still buy you a sandwich at the corner delicatessen, but they are in all physical properties a greater disappointment than the sandwich might be," Walter Breen wrote in *Coins* Magazine.

U.S. conversion from 90 percent silver to clad metal coinage was approached reluctantly but was finally accomplished in short order.

After World War II, the price of silver began advancing, but so slowly that few Americans anticipated a time when they would no longer have the precious metal jingling in their pocket change.

About mid-1962 more people began redeeming their Silver Certificates in silver dollars. In a year, 50 million coins left the Treasury, leaving 65 million. By the end of 1963, another 35 million were withdrawn. On March 25, 1964, with only about three million of the coins on hand, and those determined to be worth a numismatic premium, the Treasury Department halted release of the coins.

In mid-1963, with the price of silver pointing to a time soon when it would have to be reduced or eliminated in coinage, the Treasury Department had begun to study alternatives.

Even so, calls were heard for new silver dollars to be coined. In one of his last acts in office, President John F. Kennedy called for Congress to approve the new coinage.

In April 1964 hearings on the measure before the Senate Banking and Currency Committee, Sen. Mike Mansfield, D-Mont., declared that he liked the "clink and clank" of the big coin. Sen. Len B. Jordan, R-Idaho, said, "I was a full-grown man before I came in contact with a paper dollar, because silver dollars were the medium of exchange out West, and I grew to like them and I still do."

President Lyndon B. Johnson signed legislation Aug. 3, 1964, for the production of 45 million new silver dollars.

Others, seeing demand and price rising, tried to make a case for somehow retaining at least some silver in the coinage.

"We have always had silver in our coinage; and although the value of the coins is not dependent on their silver content, silver has had a stabilizing effect and has given confidence in our money," Sen. Wallace F. Bennett, R-Utah, told the American Mining Congress convention Sept. 16, 1964.

The January 1965 issue of *The Numismatist* carried the conclusion of Dr. Vladimir Clain-Stefanelli, co-curator of the Smithsonian Institution numismatic collection, that silver should be abandoned — in an orderly way, but promptly. In the same issue, the Silver Committee of the American Mining Congress called for reducing the silver content of coins to 50 percent, arguing that only such an alloy could avert a great changeover and dislocation in the vending machine business.

In May 1965, the findings of the Treasury study group were reported.

"The conclusion of the Treasury Staff Study of Silver and Coinage that there is not a sufficient supply of silver to warrant the retention by the United States of its traditional silver coinage is supported by an independent study, commissioned by the Treasury, of the Battelle Memorial Institute, also being made public at this time, and by other inquiries into this subject," it stated.

Battelle, a think tank in Columbus, Ohio, had turned in its report Feb. 12, 1965. It recommended the composition that finally resulted: layers of cupronickel (75 percent copper, 25 percent nickel) bonded to a layer of pure copper. "In the event that some unforeseen problem should disqualify" this material, it recommended homogeneous cupronickel.

For the sake of "tradition and prestige," Battelle offered politically face-saving ways to retain some silver in the coinage. The half dollar could be reduced to 40 percent silver content by bonding layers of glittering 80 percent silver to a layer of lesser silver alloy, it suggested. Or, it stated, all three coins from dime to half could be made 15 percent silver by bonding layers of a successful Swedish coinage material (40 percent silver, 50 percent copper, 5 percent nickel, 5 percent zinc) to a layer of silver-bearing copper alloy.

In either case, this reduced silver coinage could be sustained for only about 10 years, Battelle projected.

President Johnson directed on May 15, 1965, that minting of the new silver dollars proceed. After the Denver Mint produced 316,076 Peace dollars (dated 1964), the Treasury Department announced May 25 that the presidential order was being "deferred" pending further consideration. Officially, all these 1964-D dollars were melted, but rumors persist that one or more went into hiding. If a 1964-D silver dollar ever does turn up in collector hands, the Treasury Department says it will seize it.

On June 3, 1965, Johnson submitted legislation to Congress incorporating the recommendations of Battelle and the Treasury study. The half dollar would be of the overall 40 percent silver clad material. The White House announcement referred to the half as "the silver standard bearer of the new coinage" and emphasized the continuity in size and design of the new coins.

"It is possible," Johnson said in his message to Congress, "that implementation of the new coinage legislation . . . will actually make feasible the minting of additional silver dollars in the future."

The legislation permitted continued minting of silver coins alongside those of the new material; expressly declared the clad metal pieces to be legal tender; authorized the secretary of the Treasury to prohibit "the exportation, melting, or treating of coins of the United States"; and authorized the Treasury Department to contract for provision of the clad metal. The Mint would not have its own cladding mill until 1969.

Amendments were offered in both the Senate and the House of Representatives to make the half dollar of the same copper-nickel clad composition, but these failed. Congress did add provisions to prohibit coining of silver dollars for five years and to ban mintmarks for the same period. (This last provision was to discourage hoarding by coin collectors; it was repealed in 1967, and 1968-dated coins had mintmarks.)

The final act also officially designated the new pieces "clad coins" and defined the term. But *Coins* Magazine noted, "Clad coinage will be the official terminology for the new issues; sandwich coinage will be the public's description."

The president signed the measure into law July 23, 1965. Contracts to supply clad strip were signed July 28. Production of clad quarter dollars began Aug. 23; dimes, Dec. 6; half dollars, Dec. 30. The quarters first entered commerce Nov. 1, 1965; the dimes and half dollars, in March 1966.

"The Mint built up a substantial inventory in each denomination before releasing them to the banking system, thus assuring regional distribution throughout the country at the same time," Mint Director Eva Adams wrote in her annual report.

The first public showing of the new coins was at the 91st annual convention of the American Bankers Association, Oct. 3-6, 1965 in Chicago.

The clad coins of 1965 stand as a sort of numismatic Berlin Wall dividing past from present. All of the old silver coins disappeared from circulation.

Round-the-clock security was given the exhibit case, which contained three of each denomination (displaying obverse, reverse and edge) alongside their silver counterparts.

"The Treasury still has very large stocks of silver — nearly 900 million ounces — and is authorized by the Coinage Act of 1965 to use these stocks to keep the price of silver below the point at which it would become profitable to melt the silver coinage for its silver content," the Nov. 22, 1965, issue of *Numismatic News* noted.

Silver coin production continued into 1966. The date was frozen at 1964 on these silver dimes, quarters and halves so collectors cannot distinguish them from the coins actually made in 1964. The first clad dimes and quarters were dated 1965 and the first 40 percent silver half dollar was also dated 1965.

On May 18, 1967, the Treasury Department invoked its authority to ban the melting or exportation of silver coins. But people continued saving them, and illegal melting went on as surely as bathtub gin was made during Prohibition days. On May 12, 1969, the ban was lifted.

By 1970 silver coins had virtually disappeared from circulation. This changed collector habits forever. Even the 40 percent silver half dollars were minted only for mint and proof sets that year. On Dec. 31, 1970, President Richard Nixon signed legislation changing the composition of the half to copper-nickel clad metal.

Silver was gone from U.S. coinage struck for circulation, after 177 years. The Coinage Act of 1965 had altered the lives of all Americans.

# 11

# 21st century coin picks

## *A dozen to put away now*

### By David C. Harper

"If only I had saved those!" is a frequent lament by people who are reacquainted with the coins of their youth. The high price tags of some previously common coins get them to thinking about what might have been.

The passage of time does tend to reward those who give thoughtful consideration to what the next generation of collectors might want. In that light, here is a selection of a dozen coins that have a good chance of being worth more in the year 2020 than they are now.

There is a certain logic behind the selections. If hobby trends don't follow it, then all bets are off. The selections are heavily influenced by the assumption that average collectors like you and me are going to dominate the hobby in the year 2020, much as they did in the 1950s and 1960s. These hobbyists are not going to bet their next new car against some so-called coin investment. They are going to work steadily on their collections and buy coins that cost less than a king's ransom. In fact, these collectors will spend in one year on all the coins they buy much less than a king's ransom. That's how the hobby used to be and that is where it will return.

These collectors will sacrifice a bit of quality for their lower-priced coins, but they will not give up eye appeal entirely. They just will not spend their time and vast sums of money chasing uncirculated coins that are so well preserved that only a couple of others exist in similar high grade for each date and mintmark.

That tendency to pay any price for quality that started in the 1970s and built to an incredible peak in 1989, especially in silver dollars, will not exist in 2020. A pleasing XF-40 or AU-55 set of coins, carefully matched, will be the generally agreed upon goal. After all, what is more fun, spending 10 years putting together a beautiful set of XF-40 Barber quarters, or spending the cost of the entire set for a single high-grade uncirculated silver dollar? I think the hobby is going to be focusing on the sets.

Those who might be inclined to quibble need only look at the 80% and 90% price declines from 1989 to 1994 that hit so many top quality uncirculated silver dollars. If that occurrence doesn't shout "spend your money on something else," it is hard to know what would.

Nobody wants to lose money. Buyers of those high-priced silver dollars certainly didn't, but they got caught up in the speculative fever of chasing those few coins that were nearly perfect, much as 17th century Dutch specu-

**Every collector should own a large cent. This coin has always enjoyed wide appeal among collectors and interest is rising. The 1855 date in XF-40 condition can still be purchased for $45. That is very little more than the price of a common date.**

lators were looking for the perfect tulip bulb.

In coins, as well as other things, there is safety in numbers. If you know a lot of other people are collecting something, you can be assured that when the time comes to sell your collection, those other people will be keenly interested in your coins. What do you think happens when you have a silver dollar that population reports compiled by the commercial grading services say is one of only 10 or 20 such coins? The resale market for the silver dollar, obviously, doesn't include many people.

This said, let's get into the specifics. They are the most fun, anyway. Here are a dozen items to pick up for the 21st century:

**1855 Braided Hair large cent**, XF-40. Everybody should own at least one large cent. Large cent collectors are a determined and growing group. Even if everybody else quit, large cent collectors would still be collecting. They would probably also enjoy having the hobby to themselves. Mintage of this date is 1,574,829. Price is $45. This is almost the common coin price for a scarcer coin.

**1909 Liberty Head nickel**, XF-40. Current retail price is $17. Common dates sell for $15. This particular date has a mintage of 11,590,526. Common dates run in the 20 million to 40 million range. This isn't the coin that is going to buy your vacation dream home, but it should gain a firmer individual identity and, with that improved identity, it will move further ahead of the common dates.

**1931-S Buffalo nickel**, XF-40, current price $12.50. I believe the Buffalo nickel will always be an American classic. There are enough of them around that many people can aspire to own them, yet they are scarce enough to be always a little hard to get. The 1931-S has a mintage of just 1.2 million pieces, and the price has been kept down in recent years by the existence of a hoard. As soon as these are dispersed, you are going to have quite a winner here. Besides, for $12.50, what can you lose?

**1849 Seated Liberty half dime**, XF-40. Price $45. This coin is tiny. That's a

**The Buffalo nickel is an American classic. As long as there are collectors, this series will be avidly sought. The 1931-S in XF-40 condition is a candidate for price appreciation over the next 25 years. At $12.50 each, the price seems very reasonable.**

liability in a hobby where large and flashy equates to the big bucks. However, this is one of the oddest denominations in American history. Every collector should own one. If everyone tries to buy a Seated Liberty half dime, this date will benefit more. Mintage is 1,309,000.

**1915-S Barber quarter**, XF-40, price $80. The mintage on this beauty is just 704,000 pieces. The price of the most common XF-40 Barber quarter is $72, so for eight bucks you are stepping up to a coin that adds a scarcity kicker. The Barber series will stand the test of time, too. By 2020, the collecting fads of the 20th century will be distant memories, but Barbers will be honored.

**1872 Seated Liberty half dollar**, XF-40. The $63 price of this coin means it is considered common, but with a mintage of just 881,550, collectors of the 21st century are going to be more acutely aware of the appeal of such classic series as the Seated Liberty halves. They are not the great rarities of the caliber of the Flowing Hair type, but they aren't available just anywhere now, nor will they be in the future.

**1939-S Walking Liberty half dollar**, XF-40. The great silver boom of 1980 greatly distorted the value of the various scarce dates in this series. When silver was $50 per ounce and each half dollar had a melt value of $18, nobody paid any attention to the small scarcity premiums that had existed before. These premiums will be back in 2020. Mintage is 2,552,000. Retail price is $12.50. Again, what can you lose? If silver should go back to $50, you will be able to sell at a profit regardless.

**1955 Franklin half dollar**, MS-60. With a mintage of 2,876,381 and a price of $8.50, this looks tempting. It was once considered a somewhat scarce coin. Its current price reflects a small shade of difference between it and the more common 1956 and 1957 pieces, but the gap isn't wide. It should be much bigger than it is; perhaps by 2020 that will be recognized.

**1860-O Seated Liberty silver dollar**, XF-40. Price is $275. If you want to collect large silver coins, the Seated Liberty series is the place to be. If you

**Common Liberty Head nickels sell for $15 in XF-40 condition. The 1909, with a mintage that is less than half of the common dates, is priced at $17. It wouldn't take much new interest in the coin to cause that narrow pricing gap to widen considerably.**

want to put together a type set, because this is the cheapest date, this is the coin to own. Either way, it is unlikely that collectors will lose interest in it. After the great decline of Morgan and Peace uncirculated dollars, collectors will feel more comfortable owning a high-grade, but somewhat circulated, coin. Mintage is only 515,000.

**1973-S 40% silver Eisenhower dollar**, proof, nicknamed brown Ike from the color of the box it was packaged in. OK, I am a sucker for modern coins. I just can't believe the key date of the Eisenhower series, the coin I paid $10 for at the time of issue, will stay at the current $18 over the next quarter century. Mintage is 1,005,617. Fifteen years ago this coin was well over $100. By 2020 it will be 47 years old.

**1986-D Statue of Liberty half dollar**, uncirculated. It would probably be wise not to wade into the pool of modern U.S. commemoratives. The U.S. Mint has been cranking them out faster than the hobby can absorb them. The result has been a large decline in prices. This particular coin is priced at $3.20. With a mintage of 928,008, the price seems cheap. It may not be, but a 1,000% profit over the next 25 years would still put the coin at only $37.40, affordable to just about everyone. Surely someone will be collecting these in 2020.

**The 1981 U.S. mint set.** This is another case where it just looks too cheap to last. The 1981 mint set contains the only 1981-dated Anthony dollars struck — and there are three of them — one each from Philadelphia, Denver and San Francisco. Face value of all the coins in the set is $4.82. The price is $8.50. Mintage is 2,908,145.

There you have it. A dozen items to put away for 2020. If you buy them all, and can get them for the current retail price as published in this book, your total cost would be $588.20. Unfortunately, as with every list, if more than a few people try to purchase the items on it, retail prices will be boosted, because only the most modern pieces have large numbers currently available — but that's part of the fun.

# Glossary of coin terms

**Adjustment marks:** Marks made by use of a file to correct the weight of overweight coinage planchets prior to striking. Adjusting the weight of planchets was a common practice at the first U.S. mint in Philadelphia and was often carried out by women hired to weigh planchets and do any necessary filing.

**Altered coin:** A coin that has been changed after it left the mint. Such changes are often to the date or mintmark of a common coin in an attempt to increase its value by passing to an unsuspecting buyer as a rare date or mint.

**Alloy:** A metal or mixture of metals added to the primary metal in the coinage composition, often as a means of facilitating hardness during striking. For example, most U.S. silver coins contain an alloy of 10-percent copper.

**Anneal:** To heat in order to soften. In the minting process planchets are annealed prior to striking.

**Authentication**: The act of determining whether a coin, medal, token or other related item is a genuine product of the issuing authority.

**Bag marks:** Scrapes and impairments to a coin's surface obtained after minting by contact with other coins. The term originates from the storage of coins in bags, but such marks can occur as coins leave the presses and enter hoppers. A larger coin is more susceptible to marks, which affect its grade and, therefore, its value.

**Base metal:** A metal with low intrinsic value.

**Beading**: A form of design around the edge of a coin. Beading once served a functional purpose of deterring clipping or shaving parts of the metal by those looking to make a profit and then return the debased coin to circulation.

**Blank**: Often used in reference to the coinage planchet or disc of metal from which the actual coin is struck. Planchets or blanks are punched out of a sheet of metal by what is known as a blanking press.

**Business strike:** A coin produced for circulation.

Beading

**Cast copy:** A copy of a coin or medal made by a casting process in which molds are used to produce the finished product. Casting imparts a different surface texture to the finished product than striking and often leaves traces of a seam where the molds came together.

**Center dot:** A raised dot at the center of a coin caused by use of a compass to aid the engraver in the circular positioning of die devices, such as stars, letters and dates. Center dots are prevalent on early U.S. coinage.

Chop mark

**Chop mark:** A mark used by Oriental merchants as a means of guaranteeing the silver content of coins paid out. The merchants' chop marks, or stamped insignia, often obliterated the original design of the host coin. U.S. Trade dollars, struck from 1873 through 1878 and intended for use in trade with China, are sometimes found bearing multiple marks.

**Clash marks**: Marks impressed in the coinage dies when they come together without a planchet between them. Such marks will affect coins struck subsequently by causing portions of the obverse design to appear in raised form on the reverse, and vice versa.

**Clipping**: The practice of shaving or cutting small pieces of metal from a coin in circulation. Clipping was prevalent in Colonial times as a means of surreptitiously extracting precious metal from a coin before placing it back into circulation. The introduction of beading and a raised border helped to alleviate the problem.

**Coin alignment:** U.S. coins are normally struck with an alignment by which, when a coin is held by the top and bottom edge and rotated from side-to-side, the reverse will appear upside down.

**Collar**: A ring-shaped die between which the obverse and reverse coinage dies are held during striking. The collar contains the outward flow during striking and can be used to produce edge reeding.

**Commemorative:** A coin issued to honor a special event or person. U.S. commemoratives are generally produced for sale to collectors and are not placed in circulation.

**Copy:** A replica of an original issue. Copies often vary in quality and metallic composition to the original. Since passage of the Hobby Protection Act (Public Law 93-167) of Nov. 29, 1973, it has been illegal to produce or import copies of coins or other numismatic items that are not clearly and permanently marked with the word "Copy."

**Counterfeit:** A coin or medal or other numismatic item made fraudulently, either for entry into circulation or sale to collectors.

**Denticles**: The toothlike pattern found around a coin's obverse or reverse border.

**Die**: A cylindrical piece of metal containing an incuse image that imparts a raised image when stamped into a planchet.

**Die crack:** A crack that develops in a coinage die after extensive usage, or if the die is defective or is used to strike harder metals. Die cracks, which often run through border lettering, appear as raised lines on the finished coin.

**Device:** The principal design element.

**Double eagle:** Name adopted by the Act of March 3, 1849, for the gold coin valued at 20 units or $20.

Rim

Field

Mintmark

Exergue

Obverse

Legend

Reverse

**Eagle:** Name adopted by the Coinage Act of 1792 for a gold coin valued at 10 units or $10.

**Edge:** The cylindrical surface of a coin between the two sides. The edge can be plain, reeded, ornamented, or lettered.

**Electrotype:** A copy of a coin, medal or token made by electroplating.

**Exergue:** The lower segment of a coin, below the main design, generally separated by a line and often containing the date, designer initials and mintmark.

**Face value:** The nominal legal-tender value assigned to a given coin by the governing authority.

**Fasces:** A Roman symbol of authority consisting of a bound bundle of rods and an ax.

**Field:** The flat area of a coin's obverse or reverse, devoid of devices or inscriptions.

**Galvano:** A reproduction of a proposed design from an artist's original model produced in plaster or other substance and then electroplated with metal. The galvano is then used in a reducing lathe to make a die or hub.

**Glory:** A heraldic term for stars, rays or other devices placed as if in the sky or luminous.

**Grading:** The largely subjective practice of providing a numerical or adjectival ranking of the condition of a coin, token or medal. The grade is often a major determinant of value.

**Gresham's law:** The name for the observation made by Sir Thomas Gresham, 16th century English financier, that when two coins with the same face value but different intrinsic values are in circulation at the same time, the one with the lesser intrinsic value will remain in circulation while the other is hoarded.

**Half eagle:** Name adopted by the Coinage Act of 1792 for a gold coin valued at five units or $5.

**Hub:** A piece of die steel showing the coinage devices in relief. The hub is used to produce a die that, in contrast, has the relief details incuse. The die is then used to produce the final coin, which looks much the same as the hub. Hubs may be reused to make new dies.

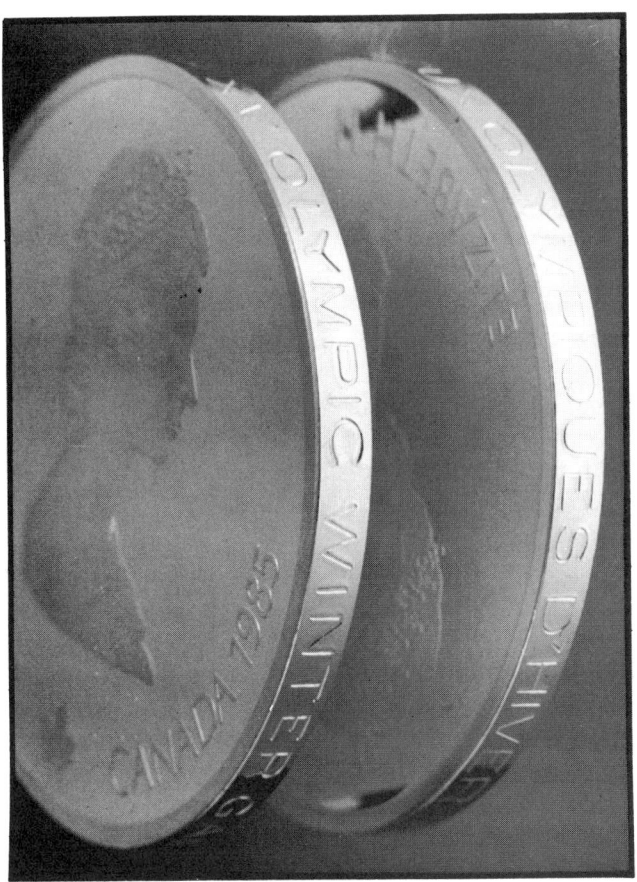

These Canadian Olympic commemoratives have lettered edges.

**Legend:** A coin's principal lettering, generally shown along its outer perimeter.

**Lettered edge:** Incuse or raised lettering on a coin's edge.

**Matte proof:** A proof coin on which the surface is granular or dull. On U.S. coins this type of surface was used on proofs of the early 20th century. The process has since been abandoned.

**Magician's coin:** A term sometimes used to describe a coin with two heads or two tails. Such a coin is impossible in normal production, and all are products made outside the Mint as novelty pieces.

**Medal:** Made to commemorate an event or person. Medals differ from coins in that a medal is not legal tender and, in general, is not produced with the intent of circulating as money.

A medal usually commemorates an event but has no monetary value. It can be issued by a private entity or a government.

**Medal alignment:** Medals are generally struck with the coinage dies facing the same direction during striking. When held by the top and bottom edge and rotated from side-to-side, a piece struck in this manner will show both the obverse and reverse right side up.

**Mintage:** The total number of coins struck during a given time frame, generally one year.

**Mintmark:** A letter or other marking on a coin's surface to identify the mint at which the coin was struck.

**Mule:** The combination of two coinage dies not intended for use together.

**Numismatics:** The science, study or collecting of coins, tokens, medals, paper money, and related items.

**Obverse:** The front or "heads" side of a coin, medal or token.

**Overdate:** Variety produced when one or more digits of the date are re-engraved over an old date on a die at the Mint, generally to save on dies or correct an error. Portions of the old date can still be seen under the new one.

**Overmintmark:** Variety created at the Mint when a different mintmark is punched over an already existing mintmark, generally done to make a coinage die already punched for one mint usable at another. Portions of the old mintmark can still be seen under the new one.

**Overstrike:** A coin, token or medal struck over another coin, token or medal.

**Pattern:** A trial strike of a proposed coin design, issued by the Mint or authorized agent of a governing authority. Patterns can be in a variety of metals, thicknesses and sizes.

**This U.S. Trade dollar has a reeded edge.**

**Phrygian cap:** A close-fitting, egg-shell-shaped hat placed on the head of a freed slave when Rome was in its ascendancy. Hung from a pole, it was a popular symbol of freedom during the French Revolution and in 18th century United States.

**Planchet:** A disc of metal or other material on which the image of the dies are impressed, resulting in a finished coin. Also sometimes called a blank.

**Proof:** A coin struck twice or more from specially polished dies and polished planchets. Modern proofs are prepared with a mirror finish. Early 20th century proofs were prepared with a matte surface.

**Prooflike:** A prooflike coin exhibits some of the characteristics of a proof despite having been struck by regular production processes. Many Morgan dollars are found with prooflike surfaces. The field will have a mirror background similar to that of a proof, and design details are frosted like some proofs.

**Quarter eagle:** Name adopted by the Coinage Act of 1792 for a gold coin valued at 2.5 units or $2.50.

**Reeding:** Serrated (toothlike) ornamentation applied to the coin's edge during striking.

**Relief:** The portion of a design raised above the surface of a coin, medal or token.

A token is issued by a private entity and can be redeemed for its face value in trade or service.

**Restrike:** A coin, medal or token produced from original dies at a later date, often with the purpose of sale to collectors.

**Reverse:** The backside or "tails" side of a coin, medal or token, opposite from the principal figure of the design or obverse.

**Rim:** The raised area bordering the edge and surrounding the field.

**Series:** The complete group of coins of the same denomination and design and representing all issuing mints.

**Token:** A privately issued piece, generally in metal, with a represented value in trade or offer of service. Tokens are also produced for advertising purposes.

**Type coin:** A coin from a given series representing the basic design. A type coin is collected as an example of a particular design rather than for its date and mintmark.

**Variety:** Any coin noticeably different in dies from another of the same design, date and mint. Overdates and overmintmarks are examples of varieties.

**Wire edge:** Created when coinage metal flows between the coinage die and collar, producing a thin flange of coin metal at the outside edge or edges of a coin.

# PRICING SECTION

# Introduction to pricing

The following value guide is divided into six sections:

1. Colonial coins, issued prior to the establishment of the United States.
2. U.S. issues of 1792.
3. U.S. issues of 1793-present.
4. U.S. minting varieties and errors.
5. Canadian coins.
6. Mexican coins.

### Value listings

Values listed in the following price guide are average retail prices. These are the approximate prices collectors can expect to pay when purchasing coins from dealers. They are not offers to buy or sell. The pricing section should be considered a guide only; actual selling prices will vary.

The values were compiled by Krause Publications' independent staff of market analysts. They derived the values listed by monitoring auction results, business on electronic dealer trading networks, and business at major shows, and in consultation with a panel of dealers. For rare coins, when only a few specimens of a particular date and mintmark are known, a confirmed transaction may occur only once every several years. In those instances, the most recent auction result is listed.

### Grading

Values are listed for coins in various states of preservation, or grades. Standards used in determining grades for U.S. coins are those set by the American Numismatic Association. See Chapter 4 for more on grading.

### Dates and mintmarks

The dates listed are the individual dates that appear on each coin. The letter that follows the date is the mintmark and indicates where the coin was struck: "C" — Charlotte, N.C. (1838-1861); "CC" — Carson City, Nev. (1870-1893); "D" — Dahlonega, Ga. (1838-1861), and Denver (1906-present); "O" — New Orleans (1838-1909); "P" — Philadelphia (1793-present); "S" — San Francisco (1854-present); and "W" — West Point, N.Y. (1984-present). Coins without mintmarks were struck at Philadelphia.

A slash mark in a date indicates an overdate. This means a new date was engraved on a die over an old date. For example, if the date is listed as "1899/8," an 1898 die had a 9 engraved over the last 8 in the date. Portions of the old numeral are still visible on the coin.

A slash mark in a mintmark listing indicates an overmintmark (example: "1922-P/D"). The same process as above occurred, but this time a new mintmark was engraved over an old.

See the "U.S. Minting Varieties and Errors" section for more information on overdates and overmintmarks.

## Price charts
Pricing data for the selected charts in the U.S. section were taken from the January issues of "Coin Prices" for the years indicated.

## Mexican coin mintages
Quantities minted of each date are indicated when that information is available, generally stated in millions and rounded off to the nearest 10,000 pieces. The following mintage conversion formulas are used:

10,000,000 — 10,000.
1,000,000 — 1.000.
100,000 — .100.
10,000 — .010.
9,999 — 9,999.
1,000 — 1,000.
842 — 842 pcs. (pieces).
27 — 27 pcs.

## Precious-metal content
Throughout this book precious-metal content is indicated in troy ounces. One troy ounce equals 480 grains, or 31.103 grams.

## Abbreviations
**AGW.** Actual gold weight.

**APW.** Actual platinum weight.

**ASW.** Actual silver weight.

**BV.** Bullion value. This indicates the coin's current value is based on the amount of its precious-metal content and the current price for that metal.

**Est.** Indicates the exact mintage is not known and the figure listed is an estimate.

**G.** Grams.

**Inc. Abv.** Indicates the mintage for the date and mintmark listed is included in the previous listing.

**KM#.** In the Canadian and Mexican price sections, indicates "Krause-Mishler number." This sequential cataloging numbering system originated with the "Standard Catalog of World Coins" by Chester L. Krause and Clifford Mishler, and provides collectors with a means for identifying world issues.

**Leg.** Legend.

**Mkt value.** Market value.

**MM.** Millimeters.

**Obv.** Obverse.

**P/L.** Indicates "prooflike," a type of finish used on some Canadian coins.

**Rev.** Reverse.

**Spec.** Indicates "specimen," a type of finish used on some Canadian coins.

# Colonial coins

## Massachusetts

### "New England" Coinage

**NE/III THREEPENCE**

| Date | |
|---|---|
| (1652) | Only two examples known |

**NE/VI SIXPENCE**

| (1652) | Garrett 75,000. | Only seven examples known |
|---|---|---|

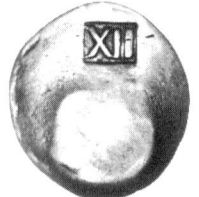

**NE/XII SHILLING**

| Date | AG | Good | VG | Fine | VF |
|---|---|---|---|---|---|
| (1652) | 1250. | 3500. | 5500. | 11,000. | 25,000. |

## Willow Tree Coinage

### THREEPENCE

| 1652 | Only three examples known |
|---|---|

### SIXPENCE

| 1652 | 3500. | 7500. | 10,000. | 15,000. | 20,000. |
|---|---|---|---|---|---|

## SHILLING

| Date | AG | Good | VG | Fine | VF |
|------|------|--------|--------|--------|--------|
| 1652 | 4000. | 10,000. | 12,500. | 18,000. | 25,000. |

# Oak Tree Coinage

## TWOPENCE

| | AG | Good | VG | Fine | VF |
|------|------|--------|--------|--------|--------|
| 1662 | 150.00 | 300.00 | 500.00 | 715.00 | 1250. |

## THREEPENCE

| | AG | Good | VG | Fine | VF |
|------|------|--------|--------|--------|--------|
| 1652 (two types of legends) | 200.00 | 400.00 | 600.00 | 950.00 | 1800. |

## SIXPENCE

| | AG | Good | VG | Fine | VF |
|------|------|--------|--------|--------|--------|
| 1652 (three types of legends) | 200.00 | 400.00 | 600.00 | 1000. | 2100. |

## SHILLING

| | AG | Good | VG | Fine | VF |
|------|------|--------|--------|--------|--------|
| 1652 (two types of legends) | 175.00 | 300.00 | 500.00 | 725.00 | 1500. |

# Pine Tree Coinage

## THREEPENCE

| Date | AG | Good | VG | Fine | VF |
|---|---|---|---|---|---|
| 1652 tree w/o berries | 150.00 | 320.00 | 400.00 | 550.00 | 950.00 |

| | AG | Good | VG | Fine | VF |
|---|---|---|---|---|---|
| 1652 tree w/berries (two types of legends) | 180.00 | 360.00 | 450.00 | 600.00 | 1000. |

## SIXPENCE

| | AG | Good | VG | Fine | VF |
|---|---|---|---|---|---|
| 1652 tree w/o berries ("Spiney Tree") | 525.00 | 900.00 | 1400. | 1800. | 2650. |

| | AG | Good | VG | Fine | VF |
|---|---|---|---|---|---|
| 1652 tree w/berries | 150.00 | 300.00 | 450.00 | 650.00 | 1100. |

## SHILLING, Large Planchet

| | AG | Good | VG | Fine | VF |
|---|---|---|---|---|---|
| 1652 (many varieties; some very rare) | 160.00 | 350.00 | 550.00 | 850.00 | 1600. |

### Small Planchet, Large Dies
1652 (struck w/large dies. All examples are thought to be contemporary fabrications.)

### Small Planchet, Small Dies

| Date | AG | Good | VG | Fine | VF |
|---|---|---|---|---|---|
| 1652 (many varieties; some very rare) | 150.00 | 220.00 | 320.00 | 550.00 | 1150. |

# Maryland

## Lord Baltimore's Coinage

### PENNY (Denarium)

| Date | AG | Good | VG | Fine | VF |
|---|---|---|---|---|---|
| (1659) | | | | Only four examples known | |

### FOURPENCE (Groat)

| Date | Good | VG | Fine | VF | XF |
|---|---|---|---|---|---|
| (1659) large bust and shield | 1000. | 1750. | 3250. | 4500. | 6500. |
| (1659) small bust and shield | Norweb 26,400. | | | | Unique |

### SIXPENCE

| | Good | VG | Fine | VF | XF |
|---|---|---|---|---|---|
| (1659) small bust | 800.00 | 1250. | 2000. | 3500. | 5000. |

Known in two other rare small bust varieties, plus two rare large bust varieties.

## SHILLING

| Date | AG | Good | VG | Fine | VF |
|------|-----|------|-----|------|-----|
| (1659) varieties, one very rare | 900.00 | 1500. | 2500. | 4000. | 5500. |

# New Jersey

## St. Patrick or Mark Newby Coinage

## FARTHING

| Date | AG | Good | VG | Fine | VF |
|------|-----|------|-----|------|-----|
| (1682) also rare varieties | 20.00 | 40.00 | 60.00 | 100.00 | 225.00 |
| (1682) struck of silver | 300.00 | 500.00 | 1000. | 1450. | 2250. |

## HALFPENNY

| Date | | | | | |
|------|-----|------|-----|------|-----|
| (1682) | 50.00 | 80.00 | 120.00 | 200.00 | 375.00 |

# Coinage of William Wood

## "Rosa Americana" Coinage

## HALFPENNY

| Date | Good | VG | Fine | VF | XF |
|------|------|-----|------|-----|-----|
| 1722 D.G. REX | 40.00 | 70.00 | 100.00 | 220.00 | 450.00 |

| Date | Good | VG | Fine | VF | XF |
|---|---|---|---|---|---|
| 1722 DIE GRATIA REX (Several varieties) | 30.00 | 60.00 | 85.00 | 150.00 | 300.00 |

| | | | | | |
|---|---|---|---|---|---|
| 1722 VTILE DVLCI | — | — | 1045. | — | — |

| | | | | | |
|---|---|---|---|---|---|
| 1723 Crowned Rose | 35.00 | 65.00 | 90.00 | 170.00 | 350.00 |

| | | | | | |
|---|---|---|---|---|---|
| 1723 Uncrowned Rose | — | — | 660.00 | — | — |

## PENNY

| | | | | | |
|---|---|---|---|---|---|
| 1722 UTILE DULCI (Several Varieties) | 30.00 | 50.00 | 85.00 | 135.00 | 250.00 |

| Date | Good | VG | Fine | VF | XF |
|---|---|---|---|---|---|
| 1722 VTILE DVLCI (Several Varieties) | 30.00 | 50.00 | 90.00 | 150.00 | 275.00 |

Also known in two rare pattern types w/long hair ribbons, one w/V's for U's on obverse.

| | Good | VG | Fine | VF | XF |
|---|---|---|---|---|---|
| 1723 (several varieties) | 30.00 | 50.00 | 100.00 | 150.00 | 275.00 |

1724 (Pattern)                                                    Only two examples known

(1724) undated          Norweb 2,035.                            Only five examples known
1727 Pattern, George II                                          Only two examples known

## TWOPENCE

| | Good | VG | Fine | VF | XF |
|---|---|---|---|---|---|
| (1722) Undated, motto w/scroll | 60.00 | 100.00 | 190.00 | 300.00 | 450.00 |

| Date | Good | VG | Fine | VF | XF |
|------|------|-----|------|-----|-----|
| (1722) w/o scroll | | | | Only three examples known | |
| 1722 dated, period after REX | 40.00 | 60.00 | 90.00 | 165.00 | 370.00 |
| 1722 w/o period | 40.00 | 60.00 | 90.00 | 165.00 | 370.00 |
| 1723 (several varieties) | 30.00 | 50.00 | 80.00 | 150.00 | 275.00 |
| 1724 Patterns; two types | ex-Garrett 5,775. | | | Both extremely rare | |

| Date | Good | VG | Fine | VF | XF |
|---|---|---|---|---|---|
| 1733 Pattern | Norweb 19,800. | | | Only four examples known | |

# Hibernia Coinage

## FARTHING

| | Good | VG | Fine | VF | XF |
|---|---|---|---|---|---|
| 1722 Pattern | 50.00 | 125.00 | 220.00 | 325.00 | 700.00 |
| 1723 D:G:REX. (1722 obverse) | 40.00 | 60.00 | 90.00 | 150.00 | 300.00 |

| | Good | VG | Fine | VF | XF |
|---|---|---|---|---|---|
| 1723 DEI. GRATIA. REX. | 20.00 | 40.00 | 65.00 | 100.00 | 170.00 |
| 1723 Silver | — | — | — | 800.00 | 1600. |
| 1723 Silver | — | — | — | Proof | 2700. |
| 1724 | 25.00 | 45.00 | 75.00 | 125.00 | 200.00 |

## HALFPENNY

| | Good | VG | Fine | VF | XF |
|---|---|---|---|---|---|
| 1722 harp left, head right | 15.00 | 35.00 | 55.00 | 115.00 | 210.00 |

| | Good | VG | Fine | VF | XF |
|---|---|---|---|---|---|
| 1722 harp left, head right (pattern) | — | — | 1800. | 2350. | 3200. |

| Date | Good | VG | Fine | VF | XF |
|---|---|---|---|---|---|
| 1722 harp right | 15.00 | 30.00 | 55.00 | 115.00 | 210.00 |
| 1722 legend DEII error | 90.00 | 180.00 | 300.00 | 500.00 | 750.00 |
| 1723/22 three varieties | 20.00 | 40.00 | 90.00 | 150.00 | 250.00 |

| | | | | | |
|---|---|---|---|---|---|
| 1723 many varieties | 15.00 | 25.00 | 40.00 | 80.00 | 150.00 |
| 1723 large head, rare, generally mint state only. Probably a pattern. | | | | | Rare |

| | | | | | |
|---|---|---|---|---|---|
| 1724 varieties | 15.00 | 25.00 | 50.00 | 110.00 | 220.00 |
| 1724 continuous legend over head | 65.00 | 150.00 | 300.00 | 475.00 | 750.00 |

# Pitt tokens

## FARTHING

| 1766 | — | — | 1250. | 2500. | 4750. |
|---|---|---|---|---|---|

## HALFPENNY

| 1766 | 60.00 | 100.00 | 200.00 | 375.00 | 900.00 |
|---|---|---|---|---|---|

# States of the Confederation

## Connecticut

| Date | Good | VG | Fine | VF | XF |
|------|------|----|------|-----|-----|
| 1785 bust right | 30.00 | 50.00 | 70.00 | 150.00 | 375.00 |

| | | | | | |
|------|------|----|------|-----|-----|
| 1785 African head | 45.00 | 65.00 | 175.00 | 350.00 | 1200. |

| | | | | | |
|------|------|----|------|-----|-----|
| 1785 bust left | 120.00 | 160.00 | 250.00 | 385.00 | 725.00 |

### Small Mailed Bust Right

| | | | | | |
|------|------|----|------|-----|-----|
| 1786 ETLIB INDE | 35.00 | 55.00 | 85.00 | 160.00 | 400.00 |
| 1786 INDE ET LIB | 55.00 | 75.00 | 115.00 | 225.00 | 450.00 |

| Date | Good | VG | Fine | VF | XF |
|---|---|---|---|---|---|
| 1786 large mailed bust right | 45.00 | 85.00 | 155.00 | 325.00 | 750.00 |
| 1786 Mailed bust left | 30.00 | 50.00 | 90.00 | 175.00 | 450.00 |
| 1786 Hercules head | 40.00 | 75.00 | 120.00 | 250.00 | 500.00 |
| 1786 draped bust | 35.00 | 65.00 | 115.00 | 225.00 | 500.00 |
| 1787 small head, ETLIB INDE | 40.00 | 90.00 | 150.00 | 275.00 | 550.00 |
| 1787 small head, INDE ET LIB | 125.00 | 165.00 | 245.00 | 375.00 | 650.00 |
| 1787 medium bust, two rev. legend types | 80.00 | 140.00 | 200.00 | 325.00 | 575.00 |

| Date | Good | VG | Fine | VF | XF |
|---|---|---|---|---|---|
| 1787 Muttonhead variety | 50.00 | 120.00 | 250.00 | 600.00 | 1400. |

(Extremely rare with legend: INDE ET LIB)

| | Good | VG | Fine | VF | XF |
|---|---|---|---|---|---|
| 1787 Mailed bust left | 25.00 | 45.00 | 90.00 | 150.00 | 300.00 |
| 1787 Perfect date, legend: IN DE ET | 65.00 | 85.00 | 125.00 | 225.00 | 550.00 |

| | Good | VG | Fine | VF | XF |
|---|---|---|---|---|---|
| 1787 Laughing head | 25.00 | 40.00 | 65.00 | 150.00 | 450.00 |
| 1787 Horned bust | 25.00 | 40.00 | 65.00 | 150.00 | 450.00 |
| 1787/8 IND ET LIB | 40.00 | 75.00 | 130.00 | 250.00 | 600.00 |
| 1787/1887 INDE ET LIB | 30.00 | 50.00 | 90.00 | 180.00 | 475.00 |
| 1787 CONNECT/INDE ET LIB | 37.50 | 60.00 | 115.00 | 200.00 | 525.00 |

Also two additional scarce reverse legend types.

| | Good | VG | Fine | VF | XF |
|---|---|---|---|---|---|
| 1787 Draped bust, many varieties | 20.00 | 40.00 | 80.00 | 135.00 | 275.00 |
| 1787 AUCIORI variety | 25.00 | 45.00 | 90.00 | 180.00 | 475.00 |
| 1787 AUCTOPI variety | 30.00 | 50.00 | 100.00 | 200.00 | 500.00 |
| 1787 AUCTOBI variety | 30.00 | 50.00 | 90.00 | 165.00 | 450.00 |
| 1787 CONNFC variety | 20.00 | 40.00 | 85.00 | 150.00 | 425.00 |
| 1787 CONNLC variety | 30.00 | 60.00 | 120.00 | 250.00 | 550.00 |
| 1787 FNDE variety | 25.00 | 45.00 | 90.00 | 160.00 | 450.00 |
| 1787 ETLIR variety | 25.00 | 45.00 | 90.00 | 160.00 | 450.00 |
| 1787 ETIIB variety | 30.00 | 50.00 | 100.00 | 180.00 | 475.00 |

| Date | Good | VG | Fine | VF | XF |
|------|------|-----|------|-----|-----|
| 1788 mailed bust right | 25.00 | 45.00 | 80.00 | 175.00 | 375.00 |
| 1788 small mailed bust right | 125.00 | 250.00 | 500.00 | 1000. | 2400. |

| | Good | VG | Fine | VF | XF |
|------|------|-----|------|-----|-----|
| 1788 mailed bust left | 25.00 | 50.00 | 100.00 | 200.00 | 475.00 |

| Date | Good | VG | Fine | VF | XF |
|------|------|-----|------|-----|-----|
| 1788 legend: CONNLC | 25.00 | 40.00 | 65.00 | 150.00 | 350.00 |
| 1788 draped bust left, INDE ET LIB | 20.00 | 35.00 | 55.00 | 115.00 | 265.00 |
| 1788 similar, INDLET LIB | 30.00 | 55.00 | 75.00 | 135.00 | 285.00 |
| 1788 similar, CONNLC/INDE ET LIB | 35.00 | 60.00 | 90.00 | 160.00 | 375.00 |
| 1788 similar, CONNLC/INDL ET LIB | 35.00 | 60.00 | 90.00 | 160.00 | 375.00 |

# Massachusetts

## HALFPENNY

| | | |
|---|---|---|
| 1776 | Garrett 40,000. | Unique |

## PENNY

| Date | Good | VG | Fine | VF | XF |
|------|------|-----|------|-----|-----|
| 1776 | | | | | Unique |

## HALF CENT

| | Good | VG | Fine | VF | XF |
|------|------|-----|------|-----|-----|
| 1787 (varieties-some rare) | 45.00 | 60.00 | 95.00 | 250.00 | 500.00 |
| 1788 (two varieties-one rare) | 50.00 | 90.00 | 130.00 | 300.00 | 575.00 |

## CENT

| | Good | VG | Fine | VF | XF |
|------|------|-----|------|------|------|
| 1787 arrows in right talon | Garrett 5500. | | | | Rare |
| 1787 arrows in left talon | 35.00 | 60.00 | 90.00 | 220.00 | 475.00 |

| Date | Good | VG | Fine | VF | XF |
|---|---|---|---|---|---|
| 1787 "Horned Eagle" die break | 40.00 | 65.00 | 110.00 | 250.00 | 475.00 |

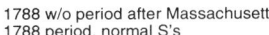

| | | | | | |
|---|---|---|---|---|---|
| 1788 w/o period after Massachusetts | 40.00 | 65.00 | 115.00 | 275.00 | 525.00 |
| 1788 period, normal S's | 35.00 | 60.00 | 90.00 | 250.00 | 475.00 |

| | | | | | |
|---|---|---|---|---|---|
| 1788 period, S's like 8's | 35.00 | 60.00 | 90.00 | 250.00 | 475.00 |

# New Hampshire

| | | |
|---|---|---|
| 1776 | Garrett 13,000. | Extremely Rare |

# New Jersey

| Date | Good | VG | Fine | VF | XF |
|------|------|-----|------|-----|-----|
| (1786) Washington obverse | | Garrett 50,000. Steinberg 12,650. | | Only three examples known | |

| | | | | | |
|------|------|-----|------|-----|-----|
| 1786 Eagle obv. | | Garrett 37,500. | | Unique | |
| 1786 Wash. obv., eagle rev. | | | | Only two examples known | |

| | | | | | |
|------|------|-----|------|-----|-----|
| 1786 Immunis Columbia obv. | | Rescigno AU 33,000. Steinberg VF 11,000. | | Extremely Rare | |

| | | | | | |
|------|------|-----|------|-----|-----|
| 1786 Immunis Columbia/eagle | | | | Only three examples known | |

| | | | | | |
|------|------|-----|------|-----|-----|
| 1786 date below draw bar | | Garrett 52,000. | | Extremely Rare | |

| Date | Good | VG | Fine | VF | XF |
|---|---|---|---|---|---|
| 1786 large horse head, date below plow, no coulter on plow | 125.00 | 250.00 | 425.00 | 950.00 | 3200. |
| 1786 narrow shield, straight beam | 35.00 | 55.00 | 110.00 | 265.00 | 900.00 |
| 1786 wide shield, curved beam (varieties) | 45.00 | 65.00 | 120.00 | 275.00 | 900.00 |
| 1786 bridle variety (die break) (other rev. varieties) | 45.00 | 70.00 | 125.00 | 285.00 | 925.00 |
| 1787 small planchet, plain shield (varieties) | 30.00 | 50.00 | 90.00 | 160.00 | 375.00 |
| 1787 small planchet, shield heavily outlined | 30.00 | 50.00 | 90.00 | 160.00 | 375.00 |
| 1787 "serpent head" variety | 45.00 | 70.00 | 125.00 | 265.00 | 675.00 |
| 1787 large planchet, plain shield (varieties) | 30.00 | 50.00 | 90.00 | 175.00 | 450.00 |

| Date | Good | VG | Fine | VF | XF |
|---|---|---|---|---|---|
| 1787 "PLURIBS" variety | 60.00 | 120.00 | 170.00 | 425.00 | 675.00 |
| 1788 horse's head right (varieties) | 30.00 | 60.00 | 100.00 | 200.00 | 500.00 |

| | | | | | |
|---|---|---|---|---|---|
| 1788 fox before rev. legend (varieties) | 60.00 | 120.00 | 180.00 | 450.00 | 1000. |

| | | | | | |
|---|---|---|---|---|---|
| 1788 horse's head left (varieties) | 135.00 | 225.00 | 400.00 | 800.00 | 1650. |

# New York

| Date | Good | VG | Fine | VF | XF |
|---|---|---|---|---|---|
| 1786 NON VI VIRTUTE VICI | 1800. | 2800. | 3750. | 5850. | 10,000. |

| | | | | | |
|---|---|---|---|---|---|
| 1787 obv. eagle on globe faces right | 650.00 | 950.00 | 1750. | 4000. | 9000. |

| Date | Good | VG | Fine | VF | XF |
|---|---|---|---|---|---|
| 1787 Obv.: Eagle on globe faces left | 600.00 | 925.00 | 1500. | 3750. | 8800. |

| 1787 Rev.: Large eagle, arrows in right talon | Norweb 18,700. | | | | Only two examples known |

| 1787 George Clinton | 3500. | 4500. | 7500. | 19,500. | — |

| 1787 Indian/N.Y. arms | 1750. | 3250. | 5000. | 10,500. | 20,900. |

| 1787 Indian/eagle on globe | 2250. | 5000. | 9750. | 20,000. | 30,000. |

| Date | Good | VG | Fine | VF | XF |
|---|---|---|---|---|---|
| 1787 IMMUNIS COLUMBIA | 200.00 | 325.00 | 450.00 | 750.00 | 2250. |

| | | | | | |
|---|---|---|---|---|---|
| 1787 NOVA EBORAC/Rev: Figure seated right | 65.00 | 100.00 | 200.00 | 300.00 | 700.00 |

| | | | | | |
|---|---|---|---|---|---|
| 1787 Rev: Figure seated left | 50.00 | 85.00 | 170.00 | 275.00 | 550.00 |

| | | | | | |
|---|---|---|---|---|---|
| 1787 NOVA EBORAC/Obv: Small head, star above. | 600.00 | 1750. | 3000. | 4500. | 6500. |

| | | | | | |
|---|---|---|---|---|---|
| 1787 NOVA EBORAC/Obv: Large head, two quatrefoils left | 300.00 | 400.00 | 650.00 | 1150. | 2450. |

# Machin's Mill Coppers

| Date | Good | VG | Fine | VF | XF |
|------|------|-----|------|-----|-----|
| | 40.00 | 80.00 | 150.00 | 200.00 | 750.00 |

Crude, lightweight imitations of the British Halfpenny were struck at Machin's Mill in large quantities bearing the obverse legends: GEORGIVS II REX, GEORGIVS III REX, and GEORGIUS III REX, with the BRITANNIA reverse, and dates of: 1747, 1771, 1772, 1774, 1775, 1776, 1777, 1778, 1784, 1785, 1786, 1787 and 1788. Other dates may exist. There are many different mulings. These pieces, which have plain crosses in the shield of Britannia, are not to be confused with the very common British made imitations, which usually have outlined crosses in the shield. Some varieties are very rare.

# Vermont

| | Good | VG | Fine | VF | XF |
|------|------|-----|------|-----|-----|
| (1785) IMMUNE COLUMBIA | 1750. | 2650. | 3750. | — | — |
| 1785 VERMONTIS | 150.00 | 200.00 | 300.00 | 750.00 | 2000. |
| 1785 VERMONTS | 100.00 | 175.00 | 275.00 | 550.00 | 1800. |
| 1786 VERMONTENSIUM | 75.00 | 150.00 | 275.00 | 750.00 | 1900. |

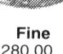

| Date | Good | VG | Fine | VF | XF |
|---|---|---|---|---|---|
| 1786 AUCTORI:VERMON:/baby head | 100.00 | 180.00 | 280.00 | 800.00 | 3200. |

| 1786 VERMON:AUCTORI:/head left | 70.00 | 160.00 | 260.00 | 475.00 | 1500. |
| 1787 bust left | | | | | Extremely Rare |

| 1787 bust right, several varieties | 45.00 | 85.00 | 175.00 | 400.00 | 1200. |

| 1787 BRITANNIA mule | 40.00 | 60.00 | 120.00 | 280.00 | 800.00 |

| 1788 Rev: INDE ET LIB, several varieties | 45.00 | 75.00 | 180.00 | 400.00 | 1000. |
| 1788 "C" backwards in AUCTORI | | | | | Extremely Rare |
| 1788 ET LIB INDE | 120.00 | 225.00 | 350.00 | 700.00 | — |
| 1788 GEORGE III REX mule | 120.00 | 275.00 | 400.00 | 850.00 | 1750. |

# Federal issues
# of the confederation

## Continental dollar

| Date | VG | Fine | VF | XF | Unc |
|------|-----|------|-----|-----|-----|
| 1776 CURRENCY, Pewter | 1600. | 2450. | 2850. | 5250. | 7000. |
| 1776 CURRENCY, EG FECIT, Pewter | 1500. | 2250. | 2750. | 5000. | 6500. |
| 1776 CURRENCY, EG FECIT, Silver | | | | Only two examples known | |
| 1776 CURRENCY, Pewter | | | | Extremely rare | |
| 1776 CURRENCY, Pewter, floral cross | | Norweb 50,600. | | Two recorded | |

| | VG | Fine | VF | XF | Unc |
|------|-----|------|-----|-----|-----|
| 1776 CURENCY, Pewter | 1500. | 2250. | 2750. | 5000. | 6500. |
| 1776 CURENCY, Brass (2 varieties) | — | — | 12,000. | 15,500. | — |
| 1776 CURENCY, Silver | | Romano 99,000. | | | Unique |

## Nova Constellatio coppers

 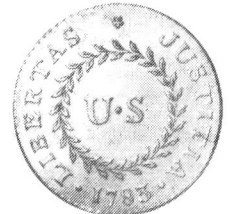

| Date | Good | VG | Fine | VF | XF |
|------|------|-----|------|-----|-----|
| 1783 CONSTELLATIO, pointed rays, small US | 25.00 | 50.00 | 75.00 | 170.00 | 400.00 |

| Date | Good | VG | Fine | VF | XF |
|---|---|---|---|---|---|
| 1783 CONSTELLATIO, pointed rays, large US | 25.00 | 50.00 | 75.00 | 170.00 | 400.00 |

 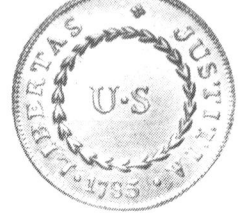

| 1783 CONSTELATIO, blunt rays | 28.00 | 55.00 | 100.00 | 225.00 | 475.00 |

| 1785 CONSTELLATIO, blunt rays | 28.00 | 55.00 | 100.00 | 200.00 | 425.00 |

| 1785 CONSTELLATIO, pointed rays | 35.00 | 75.00 | 150.00 | 260.00 | 500.00 |
| 1786 Similar, contemporary circulating counterfeit | | | | | Extremely Rare |

## Nova Constellatio silver

### BIT - 100

| Date | Good | VG | Fine | VF | XF |
|---|---|---|---|---|---|
| 1783 leaf edge | | | Garrett 97,500. | | 2 known |
| 1783 plain edge | | Stack's auction, May 1991, 72,500 | | | Unique |

## QUINT - 500

| Date | Good | VG | Fine | VF | XF |
|------|------|-----|------|-----|-----|
| 1783 Type 1 | | | Garrett 165,000. | | Unique |

| 1783 Type 2 | | | Garrett 55,000. | | Unique |

## MARK - 1000

| 1783 | | | Garrett 190,000. | | Unique |

# Immune Columbia coppers

| Date | Good | VG | Fine | VF | XF |
|------|------|-----|------|-----|-----|
| 1785 CONSTELLATIO, Copper | — | — | — | — | 13,750. |
| 1785 CONSTELLATIO, Silver | — | — | — | — | 17,600. |

| 1785 CONSTELLATIO, Copper, extra star in border | | | Caldwell 4675. | — | — |

| Date | Good | VG | Fine | VF | XF |
|---|---|---|---|---|---|
| 1785 CONSTELATIO, Copper, blunt rays | Norweb 22,000. | | | Only two examples known | |
| 1785 CONSTELATIO, Gold | | | | Unique | |

| | Good | VG | Fine | VF | XF |
|---|---|---|---|---|---|
| 1785 George III obv. | 1250. | 1850. | 2250. | 5000. | 9000. |
| 1785 Vermon obv. | 1000. | 1650. | 2000. | 4750. | 8500. |

# Confederatio coppers

| Date | Good | VG | Fine | VF | XF |
|---|---|---|---|---|---|
| 1785 small circle of stars | — | — | — | 8800. | 16,500. |

| | |
|---|---|
| 1785 large circle of stars | Extremely Rare |

**NOTE:** The Confederatio dies were struck in combination with thirteen other dies of the period. All surviving examples of these combinations are extremely rare.

# Fugio cents

| Date | Good | VG | Fine | VF | XF |
|---|---|---|---|---|---|
| 1787 club rays, round ends | 50.00 | 100.00 | 220.00 | 450.00 | 900.00 |
| 1787 club rays, concave ends | 500.00 | 1000. | 2000. | 4000. | — |
| 1787 similar, FUCIO error | 550.00 | 1200. | 2250. | 4850. | — |

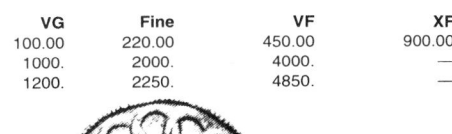

| | Good | VG | Fine | VF | XF |
|---|---|---|---|---|---|
| 1787 pointed rays, UNITED above, STATES below | 200.00 | 500.00 | 900.00 | 1350. | 3000. |
| 1787 similar, UNITED STATES, at sides of ring | 40.00 | 65.00 | 115.00 | 175.00 | 400.00 |
| 1787 similar, STATES UNITED at sides of ring | 45.00 | 90.00 | 140.00 | 220.00 | 500.00 |
| 1787 similar, 8-pointed stars on ring | 60.00 | 100.00 | 150.00 | 275.00 | 550.00 |
| 1787 similar, raised rims on ring, large lettering in center | 65.00 | 120.00 | 185.00 | 400.00 | 750.00 |
| 1787 Obv: No cinquefoils. Cross after date. Rev: UNITED STATES | 100.00 | 200.00 | 425.00 | 575.00 | 950.00 |
| 1787 Same obv., Rev: STATES UNITED | 125.00 | 225.00 | 450.00 | 650.00 | 1250. |
| 1787 Same obv. Rev: Raised rims on ring | — | — | — | 2600. | — |

| | | |
|---|---|---|
| 1787 Same obv. Rev. w/rays and AMERICAN CONGRESS | Norweb 63,800. | Extremely Rare |

| | | |
|---|---|---|
| New Haven Restrikes (1858) Brass | | Unc 350.00 |
| Copper | | 350.00 |
| Silver | | 950.00 |
| Gold | Norweb 1430. (holed) | Only two examples known |

# Colonial tokens

## New Yorke token

| Date | Good | VG | Fine | VF | XF |
|------|------|----|------|-----|-----|
| C.1700 Brass | 1250. | 2750. | 4000. | 6500. | — |
| White Metal | | | | Only four examples known | |

## American plantations 1/24th-real

| Date | Good | VG | Fine | VF | XF |
|------|------|----|------|-----|-----|
| (1688) leg: ET HIB REX | 125.00 | 165.00 | 220.00 | 300.00 | 425.00 |
| (1828) restrike, two obv. dies | | | | | |
|   rider's head left of "B" in leg. | 70.00 | 100.00 | 150.00 | 225.00 | 325.00 |
| (1688) rev, horizontal 4 | 325.00 | 400.00 | 475.00 | 550.00 | 1150. |
| (1688) leg: ET HB REX | | | | | Unc 6000. |
| (1688) rev, Arms of Scotland left, Ireland right | | | | | |
| | 750.00 | 1250. | 2000. | 2500. | — |

## Elephant tokens

| Date | Good | VG | Fine | VF | XF |
|------|------|----|------|-----|-----|
| (1664) thick planchet | 80.00 | 100.00 | 150.00 | 300.00 | 550.00 |
| (1664) thin planchet | 100.00 | 150.00 | 225.00 | 450.00 | 850.00 |
| (1664) diagonals tie shield | 140.00 | 175.00 | 300.00 | 550.00 | 1000. |
| (1664) sword right side of shield | | | Norweb 1320. | Only three examples known | |

| | Good | VG | Fine | VF | XF |
|------|------|----|------|-----|-----|
| (1684) leg: LON DON | 300.00 | 500.00 | 1000. | 1450. | 2300. |

| Date | Good | VG | Fine | VF | XF |
|------|------|-----|------|-----|-----|
| 1694 NEW ENGLAND | | | Norweb 25,300. | Only two examples known | |

| | | | | | |
|------|------|-----|------|-----|-----|
| 1694 CAROLINA (PROPRIETERS) | | | Norweb 35,200. | Only five examples known | |

| | Good | VG | Fine | VF | XF |
|------|------|-----|------|-----|-----|
| 1694 CAROLINA (PROPRIETORS, O over E) | 1000. | 1600. | 2500. | 5000. | 10,000. |
| | Norweb 17,600. | | | | |

## Gloucester token

| Date | Good | VG | Fine | VF | XF |
|------|------|-----|------|-----|-----|
| (1714) | Garrett 36,000. | | | Only two examples known | |

## Higley or Granby coppers

| Date | Good | VG | Fine | VF | XF |
|------|------|-----|------|-----|-----|
| 1737 THE VALVE OF THREE PENCE/ CONNECTICVT | | | | | Garrett 16,000. |
| 1737 THE VALVE OF THREE PENCE/ I AM GOOD COPPER | ex-Norweb 6875. | | | Only two examples known | |

| Date | Good | VG | Fine | VF | XF |
|---|---|---|---|---|---|
| 1737 VALUE ME AS YOU PLEASE/I AM GOOD COPPER | | | | Garrett 8000. | |
| 1737 Similar except leg: VALVE | | | | Only two examples known | |

| | | | | | |
|---|---|---|---|---|---|
| (1737) Broad axe rev. | | | | Garrett 45,000. | |
| 1739 Similar | Oechsner 9900. | | | Only five examples known | |
| | Steinberg (holed) 4400. | | | | |

| | | | | | |
|---|---|---|---|---|---|
| (1737) THE WHEELE GOES ROUND/ J CUT MY WAY THROUGH | Roper 60,500. | | | Unique | |

## Hibernia-Voce Populi coppers

### FARTHING

| | Good | VG | Fine | VF | XF |
|---|---|---|---|---|---|
| 1760 large letters | 100.00 | 200.00 | 300.00 | 525.00 | 1150. |
| 1760 small letters | | Norweb 5940. | | | Extremely Rare |

### HALFPENNY

| | Good | VG | Fine | VF | XF |
|---|---|---|---|---|---|
| 1700 date is error | ex-Roper 575. Norweb 577.50 | | | | Extremely Rare |
| 1760 varieties | 30.00 | 50.00 | 90.00 | 125.00 | 265.00 |

| Date | Good | VG | Fine | VF | XF |
|------|------|-----|------|-----|-----|
| 1760 leg. VOOE POPULI | 35.00 | 60.00 | 110.00 | 150.00 | 350.00 |

## Virginia halfpenny

| Date | VG | Fine | VF | XF | Unc |
|------|-----|------|-----|-----|------|
| 1773 small 7's in date, struck on Irish halfpenny planchets | | | | Proof | 3500. |
| 1773 period after GEORGIVS varieties w/7 to 8 strings in harp | 25.00 | 50.00 | 100.00 | 150.00 | 350.00 |
| 1773 w/o period after GEORGIVS Varieties w/6,7 or 8 strings in harp | 30.00 | 60.00 | 120.00 | 185.00 | 465.00 |

**NOTE:** 1773 w/o period 8 harp strings, dot on cross variety Unc.

ex-Steinberg 2600.

1774 so-called "Shilling" Silver Proofs

Garrett 23,000. Only six examples known

# Early American tokens

## Rhode Island ship tokens

| Date | Good | VG | Fine | VF | XF |
|------|------|-----|------|-----|-----|
| 1779 w/o wreath below ship, Brass or Copper | 150.00 | 250.00 | 425.00 | 850.00 | 1450. |
| 1779 w/o wreath below ship, Pewter | — | — | 800.00 | 1650. | 3700. |

| Date | Good | VG | Fine | VF | XF |
|------|------|-----|------|-----|-----|
| 1779 wreath below ship, Brass or Copper | 200.00 | 325.00 | 575.00 | 900.00 | 1500. |
| 1779 wreath below ship, Pewter | — | — | 850.00 | 1750. | 3750. |
| 1779 "VLUGTENDE" below ship, Brass | | | Garrett 16,000. | | Unique |

# North American token

| Date | VG | Fine | VF | XF | Unc |
|------|-----|------|-----|------|------|
| 1781 Halfpenny | 20.00 | 50.00 | 120.00 | 375.00 | 700.00 |

# Chalmers' silver tokens

## THREEPENCE

| Date | Good | VG | Fine | VF | XF |
|------|------|-----|------|-----|------|
| 1783 | 500.00 | 900.00 | 1250. | 1850. | 3500. |

## SIXPENCE

| Date | Good | VG | Fine | VF | XF |
|------|------|-----|------|-----|------|
| 1783 small date (unique in trial piece exists.) | 700.00 | 1500. | 2200. | 4750. | 12,000. |
| 1783 large date | 500.00 | 1000. | 1800. | 2800. | 9000. |

## SHILLING

| Date | Good | VG | Fine | VF | XF |
|------|------|-----|------|-----|------|
| 1783 birds w/long worm | 325.00 | 475.00 | 850.00 | 1600. | 2700. |
| 1783 birds w/short worm | 225.00 | 400.00 | 750.00 | 1500. | 2400. |

| Date | Good | VG | Fine | VF | XF |
|------|------|-----|------|-----|------|
| 1783 rings and stars rev. | Garrett 75,000. | | | Only four examples known | |

# Bar "cent"

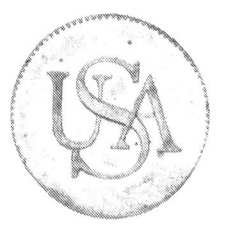

| Date | Good | VG | Fine | VF | XF |
|------|------|------|------|------|------|
| (1785) | 150.00 | 275.00 | 650.00 | 1000. | 1850. |

# Auctori Plebis token

| Date | Good | VG | Fine | VF | XF |
|------|------|------|------|------|------|
| 1787 | 35.00 | 50.00 | 100.00 | 150.00 | 325.00 |

# Brasher's doubloon

| Date | Good | VG | Fine | VF | XF |
|------|------|------|------|------|------|
| 1787 E.B. on wing | Garrett 725,000. | | | Only six examples known | |

| 1787 EB on breast | Garrett 625,000. | | | Unique | |

# Mott token

| Date | Good | VG | Fine | VF | XF |
|------|------|----|------|----|----|
| 1789 thin planchet | 60.00 | 120.00 | 200.00 | 325.00 | 650.00 |
| 1789 thick planchet (weight generally about 170 grs.) | 50.00 | 100.00 | 150.00 | 275.00 | 475.00 |
| 1789 fully engrailed edge | 85.00 | 160.00 | 325.00 | 600.00 | 1200. |

(Specimens of the above struck with perfect dies are scarcer and generally command higher prices.)

# Albany church penny

| Date | VG | Fine | VF | XF | Unc |
|------|----|------|----|----|----|
| (1790) w/o "D" above CHURCH | 2500. | 5500. | 11,500. | | Five known |
| (1790) w/"D" above CHURCH | 2000. | 3000. | 6500. | — | Rare |

# Standish Barry threepence

| Date | Good | VG | Fine | VF | XF |
|------|------|----|------|----|----|
| 1790 | 1200. | 1850. | 2750. | 4500. | 9000. |

# Kentucky token

| Date | VG | Fine | VF | XF | Unc |
|------|----|------|----|----|----|
| (c.1793) plain edge | 40.00 | 60.00 | 75.00 | 200.00 | 400.00 |
| Engrailed edge | 125.00 | 200.00 | 300.00 | 600.00 | 1450. |
| Lettered edge | 45.00 | 65.00 | 85.00 | 250.00 | 550.00 |
| PAYABLE AT BEDWORTH | — | — | — | 1980. | Unique |
| PAYABLE AT LANCASTER | 40.00 | 60.00 | 75.00 | 200.00 | 400.00 |
| PAYABLE AT I.FIELDING | | | | | Unique |
| PAYABLE AT W. PARKERS | — | — | 1800. | — | Unique |
| Branch w/two leaves on edge | | | | | Unique |

# Talbot, Allum & Lee cents

**With NEW YORK above ship**

| Date | Good | VG | Fine | VF | XF |
|---|---|---|---|---|---|
| 1794 edge: PAYABLE AT THE STORE OF | 40.00 | 65.00 | 125.00 | 225.00 | 550.00 |
| 1794 edge: plain | | | | Only three examples known | |

(Size of ampersand varies on obv. and rev. dies.)

**Without NEW YORK**

| | Good | VG | Fine | VF | XF |
|---|---|---|---|---|---|
| 1794 edge: PAYABLE AT THE STORE OF | 300.00 | 600.00 | 900.00 | 1850. | 3500. |

| Date | VG | Fine | VF | XF | Unc |
|---|---|---|---|---|---|
| 1795 edge: WE PROMISE TO PAY THE BEARER ONE CENT | 25.00 | 50.00 | 120.00 | 210.00 | 525.00 |
| 1795 edge: CURRENT EVERYWHERE | | | | | Unique |
| 1795 edge: olive leaf | | Norweb 4400. | | | Unique |
| 1795 plain edge | | | | | Two known |
| 1795 edge: Cambridge Bedford Huntingdon.X.X. | | | Norweb 3960. | | Unique |

# Franklin press token

| Date | VG | Fine | VF | XF | Unc |
|---|---|---|---|---|---|
| 1794 plain edge | 60.00 | 90.00 | 175.00 | 300.00 | 650.00 |

# Myddelton tokens

| Date | VG | Fine | VF | XF | Unc |
|---|---|---|---|---|---|
| 1796 Copper | | | | Proof | 6500. |
| 1796 Silver | | | | Proof | 5000. |

# Copper Company of Upper Canada

| Date | VG | Fine | VF | XF | Unc |
|---|---|---|---|---|---|
| 1796 Copper/Copper Company rev. | | | | Proof | 2650. |

# Castorland "Half Dollar"

| Date | Good | VG | Fine | VF | XF |
|---|---|---|---|---|---|
| 1796 Silver, reeded edge | | | | | 3500. |
| 1796 Copper, reeded edge | Only three examples known | | | | 1600. |
| 1796 Brass, reeded edge | | | | | Unique |
| 1796 Copper, plain edge, thin planchet | Norweb 467.50 | | | | Unique |
| 1796 Silver, same dies, reeded edge, thin planchet restrick | | | | Proof | 250.00 |
| 1796 Silver, same but ARGENT on plain edge | | | | Proof | 60.00 |
| 1796 Copper, same restrike on thin planchet | | | | Proof | 175.00 |
| 1796 Copper, same but CUIVRE on plain edge | | | | Proof | 40.00 |

Modern restrikes with large and small lettering on the rev. have been produced in Gold, Silver, Copper and Bronze. Original dies distinguished by wavy die breaks about the upper right corner of pot on the rev.

# New York Theatre token

| Date | VG | Fine | VF | XF | Unc |
|---|---|---|---|---|---|
| (c.1796) | 250.00 | 850.00 | 1750. | 2750. | 6000. |

# Washington pieces

| Date | Good | VG | Fine | VF | XF |
|---|---|---|---|---|---|
| 1783 GEORGIVS TRIUMPHO | 35.00 | 50.00 | 115.00 | 225.00 | 600.00 |

| | | | | | |
|---|---|---|---|---|---|
| 1783 large military bust, several varieties | 12.00 | 20.00 | 40.00 | 85.00 | 190.00 |
| 1783 small military bust, plain edge | 18.00 | 25.00 | 45.00 | 100.00 | 210.00 |
| **NOTE:** One Proof is known. Value $12,500. | | | | | |
| 1783 similar, engrailed edge | 30.00 | 45.00 | 65.00 | 125.00 | 275.00 |

| | | | | | |
|---|---|---|---|---|---|
| 1783 draped bust, no button on drapery, small letter | 15.00 | 30.00 | 50.00 | 85.00 | 200.00 |
| 1783 draped bust, button on drapery, large letter | 25.00 | 40.00 | 80.00 | 150.00 | 265.00 |
| 1783 similar, copper restrike, large modern lettering, plain edge | | | | Proof | 500.00 |
| 1783 similar but engrailed edge | | | | Proof | 300.00 |
| 1783 similar, bronzed | | | | Proof | 250.00 |
| 1783 similar, Silver | | | | Proof | 1000. |
| 1783 similar, Gold | | | | Only two examples known | |

| Date | Good | VG | Fine | VF | XF |
|---|---|---|---|---|---|
| 1783 UNITY STATES | 15.00 | 30.00 | 50.00 | 100.00 | 200.00 |
| (1783) double head cent | 15.00 | 30.00 | 50.00 | 100.00 | 200.00 |
| 1784 ugly head | Roper 14,850. | | | | 3 known Copper, 1 White Metal |
| 1791 LIVERPOOL HALFPENNY | 450.00 | 550.00 | 750.00 | — | — |
| 1791 small eagle cent | 60.00 | 125.00 | 250.00 | 375.00 | 950.00 |

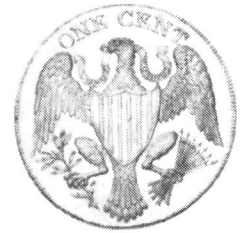

| Date | VG | Fine | VF | XF | Unc |
|------|------|------|------|------|------|
| 1791 large eagle cent | 60.00 | 125.00 | 250.00 | 375.00 | 950.00 |

| Date | Good | VG | Fine | VF | XF |
|------|------|------|------|------|------|
| 1792 "Half Dollar" Copper, lettered edge | Roper 2860. | | | Only two examples known | |
| 1792 similar, plain edge | | | | Only three examples known | |
| 1792 similar, Silver, lettered edge | Roper 35,200. | | | Rare | |
| 1792 similar, plain edge | | | | Rare | |
| 1792 similar, Gold | | | | Unique | |

| Date | VG | Fine | VF | XF | Unc |
|------|------|------|------|------|------|
| 1792 WASHINGTON PRESIDENT | Steinberg 12,650. | | | | |
| cent, plain edge | 1450. | 3250. | 5000. | 7500. | — |
| | Garrett 15,500. | | | | |
| 1792 similar, lettered edge est. | 2250. | 4500. | 7500. | 12,500. | — |

| Date | Good | VG | Fine | VF | XF |
|------|------|------|------|------|------|
| (1792) BORN VIRGINIA, varieties | 450.00 | 850.00 | 1350. | 2250. | 6500. |
| Silver, lettered edge | | | | Only two examples known | |
| Silver, plain edge | Roper 16,500. | | | Only four examples known | |
| Mule, heraldic eagle 1792 half dollar rev. | | | | Only three examples known | |

| Date | Good | VG | Fine | VF | XF |
|---|---|---|---|---|---|
| 1792 Half dollar, Silver, small eagle, plain edge   Garrett 24,500. | | Roper 17,050. | | Levinson 6160. | Rare |
| 1792 Half Dollar, similar, circle and squares, ornamented edge | | | | Only five examples known | |
| 1792 half dollar, similar, Copper | | Garrett 34,000. | | Roper 24,200. | Rare |
| 1792 half dollar, Copper, plain edge | 1450. | 2000. | 3500. | — | — |
| | | Garrett 32,000. | | | |
| 1792 Half Dollar, Silver, twin olive leaves on edge | | | | | Unique |

| | | | | | |
|---|---|---|---|---|---|
| 1792 Half Dollar, Silver, large heraldic eagle | | Garrett 16,500. | | | Unique |

| | | | | | |
|---|---|---|---|---|---|
| 1792 Roman head cent | | | | Proof | 11,000. |

| | Good | VG | Fine | VF | XF |
|---|---|---|---|---|---|
| 1793 Ship Halfpenny, lettered edge | 30.00 | 60.00 | 100.00 | 200.00 | 500.00 |
| 1793 Ship Halfpenny, plain edge | | | | | Extremely Rare |

| Date | VG | Fine | VF | XF | Unc |
|---|---|---|---|---|---|
| 1795 "Grate" Halfpenny, large coat buttons, reeded edge | 30.00 | 60.00 | 110.00 | 220.00 | 525.00 |
| 1795 similar, lettered edge | 180.00 | 250.00 | 320.00 | 650.00 | 1200. |
| 1795 similar, small coat buttons, reeded edge | 60.00 | 100.00 | 150.00 | 300.00 | 750.00 |

| | VG | Fine | VF | XF | Unc |
|---|---|---|---|---|---|
| 1795 LIBERTY AND SECURITY Halfpenny, plain edge | 60.00 | 100.00 | 180.00 | 350.00 | 490.00 |
| 1795 similar, edge lettered: PAYABLE AT LONDON etc. | 30.00 | 50.00 | 85.00 | 135.00 | 325.00 |
| 1795 similar, edge lettered: BIRMINGHAM etc. | 35.00 | 55.00 | 95.00 | 145.00 | 425.00 |
| 1795 similar, edge lettered: AN ASYLUM etc. | 50.00 | 80.00 | 150.00 | 325.00 | 650.00 |
| 1795 similar, edge lettered: PAYABLE AT LIVERPOOL etc. | | | | | Unique |
| 1795 similar, edge lettered: PAYABLE AT LONDON-LIVERPOOL | | | | | Unique |

| | VG | Fine | VF | XF | Unc |
|---|---|---|---|---|---|
| (1795) LIBERTY AND SECURITY penny, lettered edge | 60.00 | 120.00 | 200.00 | 450.00 | 1100. Extremely Rare |
| (1795) similar, plain edge | | | | | |
| (1795) similar, engine turned borders | | ex-Garrett 2750. | | | Very Rare |
| 1795 similar to halfpenny w/date on rev. | | Roper 6600. | | | Very Rare |

| Date | VG | Fine | VF | XF | Unc |
|---|---|---|---|---|---|
| (c.1795) small success medal, plain or reeded edge | 60.00 | 90.00 | 135.00 | 245.00 | 500.00 |
| (c.1795) large success medal, plain or reeded edge | 60.00 | 90.00 | 135.00 | 245.00 | 480.00 |

| | VG | Fine | VF | XF | Unc |
|---|---|---|---|---|---|
| (1795) NORTH WALES Halfpenny, plain edge | 75.00 | 115.00 | 185.00 | 450.00 | 1250. |
| (1795) similar, lettered edge | 325.00 | 450.00 | 725.00 | 1400. | 2950. |
| (1795) four stars at bottom of rev. | 600.00 | 1250. | 2250. | 4000. | — |

# Issues of 1792

## HALF DISME

| Date | Good | Fine | VF |
|---|---|---|---|
| 1792 | 1,000 | 3,000 | 5,000 |
| 1792 copper, (Unique) | 2,000 | 3,500 | 6,000 |

## DISME

| | |
|---|---|
| 1792 silver | 3 known |
| 1792 Copper, (2 reeded edge, about 10 plain right | Garrett 54,000 |

## SILVER-CENTER CENT

| | |
|---|---|
| 1792 Silver center (about 8 known) | Norweb, MS-60,143,000 |
| 1792 no silver center (copper or billon, 4 known | Norweb, EF-40, 35,200 |

## BIRCH CENT

| | |
|---|---|
| 1792 Copper known with plain and two types of lettered edges, about 15 known combined | Garrett 200,000 |
| 1792 "G.W.Pt." on reverse below wreath tie white metal, unique | Garrett 90,000 |

## WRIGHT QUARTER

| Date | Good | Fine | VF |
|---|---|---|---|
| 1792 Copper, reeded edge (2 known) | | | |
| 1792 White metal, die trial | | Garrett | 12,000 |

# Half cents

## Liberty Cap

### Head facing left

**Designer:** Adam Eckfeldt. **Size:** 22 millimeters. **Weight:** 6.74 grams. **Composition:** 100% copper.

| Date | Mintage | G-4 | VG-8 | F-12 | VF-20 | XF-40 | MS-60 |
|------|---------|-----|------|------|-------|-------|-------|
| 1793 | 35,334 | 1600. | 2250. | 4500. | 6500. | 11,000. | — |

### Head facing right

**Designers:** Robert Scot (1794) and John Smith Gardner (1795). **Size:** 23.5 millimeters. **Weight:** 6.74 grams (1794-1795) and 5.44 grams (1795-1797). **Composition:** 100% copper. **Notes:** The "lettered edge" varieties have "Two Hundred for a Dollar" inscribed around the edge. The "pole" varieties have a pole, upon which the cap is hanging, resting on Liberty's shoulder. The "punctuated date" varieties have a comma after the 1 in the date. The 1797 "1 above 1" variety has a second 1 above the 1 in the date.

| Date | Mintage | G-4 | VG-8 | F-12 | VF-20 | XF-40 | MS-60 |
|------|---------|-----|------|------|-------|-------|-------|
| 1794 | 81,600 | 265. | 375. | 750. | 1400. | 2450. | — |
| 1795 lettered edge, pole | 25,600 | 245. | 350. | 550. | 1000. | 1900. | — |
| 1795 plain edge, no pole | 109,000 | 225. | 285. | 540. | 915. | 1700. | — |
| 1795 lettered edge, punctuated date | Inc. Ab. | 245. | 350. | 550. | 1000. | 2100. | — |
| 1795 plain edge, punctuated date | Inc. Ab. | 240. | 335. | 535. | 900. | 1800. | — |
| 1796 pole | 5,090 | 5500. | 6900. | 9500. | 12,500. | 20,000. | — |
| 1796 no pole | 1,390 | — | — | — | Rare | | — |
| 1797 pl. edge | 119,215 | 265. | 375. | 575. | 1000. | 1900. | — |
| 1797 let. edge | Inc. Ab. | 1000. | 1600. | 2500. | 5000. | — | — |
| 1797 1 above 1 | Inc. Ab. | 225. | 285. | 540. | 915. | 1700. | — |

# Draped Bust

  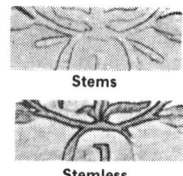

Stems

Stemless

**Designer:** Robert Scot. **Size:** 23.5 millimeters. **Weight:** 5.44 grams. **Composition:** 100% copper. **Notes:** The wreath on the reverse was redesigned slightly in 1802, resulting in "reverse of 1800" and "reverse of 1802" varieties. The "stems" varieties have stems extending from the wreath above and on both sides of the fraction on the reverse. On the "crosslet 4" variety, a serif appears at the far right of the crossbar on the 4 in the date. The "spiked chin" variety appears to have a spike extending from Liberty's chin, the result of a damaged die. Varieties of the 1805 strikes are distinguished by the size of the 5 in the date. Varieties of the 1806 strikes are distinguished by the size of the 6 in the date.

| Date | Mintage | G-4 | VG-8 | F-12 | VF-20 | XF-40 | MS-60 |
|---|---|---|---|---|---|---|---|
| 1800 | 211,530 | 30.00 | 42.50 | 65.00 | 150. | 325. | — |
| 1802/0 rev. 1800 | 14,366 | 5000. | 8500. | 12,000. | — | — | — |
| 1802/0 rev. 1802 | Inc. Ab. | 440. | 975. | 2350. | 4000. | 9800. | — |
| 1803 | 97,900 | 33.00 | 44.00 | 65.00 | 125. | 325. | — |
| 1804 plain 4, stemless wreath | 1,055,312 | 28.00 | 32.00 | 44.00 | 63.00 | 140. | 1050. |
| 1804 plain 4, stems | Inc. Ab. | 30.00 | 40.00 | 52.00 | 75.00 | 175. | 1050. |
| 1804 crosslet 4, stemless | Inc. Ab. | 30.00 | 40.00 | 52.00 | 75.00 | 175. | 1050. |
| 1804 crosslet 4, stems | Inc. Ab. | 30.00 | 40.00 | 52.00 | 75.00 | 175. | 1050. |
| 1804 spiked chin | Inc.Ab. | 28.00 | 32.00 | 44.00 | 63.00 | 175. | 1050. |
| 1805 small 5, stemless | 814,464 | 29.00 | 37.00 | 50.00 | 77.00 | 200. | — |
| 1805 small 5, stems | Inc. Ab. | 475. | 995. | 2250. | 3000. | 3800. | — |
| 1805 large 5, stems | Inc. Ab. | 29.00 | 37.00 | 50.00 | 77.00 | 200. | — |
| 1806 small 6, stems | 356,000 | 185. | 295. | 450. | 775. | 1650. | — |
| 1806 small 6, stemless | Inc. Ab. | 28.00 | 32.00 | 44.00 | 63.00 | 185. | 1040. |
| 1806 large 6, stems | Inc. Ab. | 28.00 | 32.00 | 44.00 | 63.00 | 185. | — |
| 1807 | 476,000 | 28.00 | 32.00 | 50.00 | 77.00 | 325. | 1500. |
| 1808/7 | 400,000 | 60.00 | 105. | 200. | 625. | — | — |
| 1808 | Inc. Ab. | 29.00 | 37.00 | 50.00 | 77.00 | 330. | 1050. |

# Classic Head

**Designer:** John Reich. **Size:** 23.5 millimeters. **Weight:** 5.44 grams. **Composition:** 100% copper. **Notes:** Restrikes listed were produced privately in the mid-1800s. The two varieties of the 1831 restrikes are distinguished by the size of the berries in the wreath on the reverse. The 1828 strikes have either 12 or 13 stars on the obverse.

| Date | Mintage | G-4 | VG-8 | F-12 | VF-20 | XF-40 | MS-60 |
|---|---|---|---|---|---|---|---|
| 1809/6 | 1,154,572 | 26.00 | 32.00 | 36.00 | 56.00 | 80.00 | 500. |
| 1809 | Inc. Ab. | 21.00 | 30.00 | 36.00 | 53.00 | 75.00 | 475. |
| 1810 | 215,000 | 31.00 | 36.00 | 45.00 | 105. | 200. | 1750. |
| 1811 | 63,140 | 80.00 | 175. | 550. | 1100. | 1950. | — |

# 1825 Half Cent
## Grade F-12

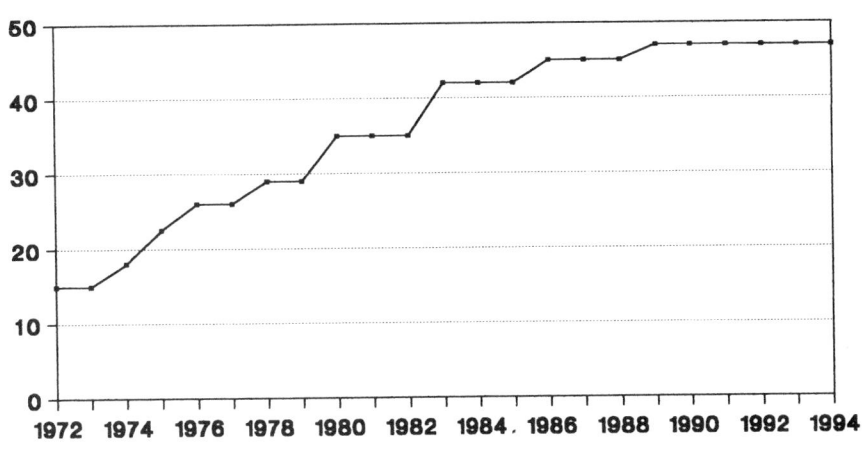

**⬝— Retail Price**

Source: COIN PRICES

| Date | Mintage | G-4 | VG-8 | F-12 | VF-20 | XF-40 | MS-60 |
|------|---------|-----|------|------|-------|-------|-------|
| 1811 restrike, reverse of 1802, uncirculated | | | | | | — | 6500. |
| 1825 | 63,000 | 33.00 | 39.00 | 47.00 | 67.00 | 225. | 1000. |
| 1826 | 234,000 | 28.00 | 35.00 | 40.00 | 56.00 | 110. | 675. |
| 1828 13 stars | 606,000 | 21.00 | 30.00 | 35.00 | 44.00 | 57.00 | 220. |
| 1828 12 stars | Inc. Ab. | 25.00 | 35.00 | 40.00 | 56.00 | 80.00 | 500. |
| 1829 | 487,000 | 25.00 | 32.00 | 35.00 | 46.00 | 69.00 | 600. |
| 1831 original | 2,200 | — | — | — | 4000. | 5000. | 7500. |
| 1831 restrike, lg. berries, reverse of 1836, proof | | | | | | — | 6000. |
| 1831 restrike, sm. berries, reverse of 1852, proof | | | | | | — | 7000. |
| 1832 | 154,000 | 21.00 | 30.00 | 35.00 | 44.00 | 57.00 | 220. |
| 1833 | 120,000 | 21.00 | 30.00 | 35.00 | 44.00 | 57.00 | 220. |
| 1834 | 141,000 | 21.00 | 30.00 | 35.00 | 44.00 | 57.00 | 220. |
| 1835 | 398,000 | 21.00 | 30.00 | 35.00 | 44.00 | 57.00 | 220. |
| 1836 original | — | — | | Proof only | — | — | 6500. |
| 1836 restrike, reverse of 1852, proof only | | | | | | — | 6500. |

# Coronet

**Designer:** Christian Gobrecht. **Size:** 23 millimeters. **Weight:** 5.44 grams. **Composition:** 100% copper. **Notes:** 1840-1848 strikes, both originals and restrikes, are known in proof only; mintages are unknown. The small-date varieties of the 1849, both originals and restrikes, are known in proof only. Restrikes were produced clandestinely by Philadelphia Mint personnel in the mid-1800s.

| Date | Mintage | G-4 | VG-8 | F-12 | VF-20 | XF-40 | MS-60 | Prf-60 |
|---|---|---|---|---|---|---|---|---|
| 1840 original | — | — | — | | Proof only | — | — | 3800. |
| 1840 restrike | — | — | — | | Proof only | — | — | 3200. |
| 1841 original | — | — | — | | Proof only | — | — | 3800. |
| 1841 restrike | — | — | — | | Proof only | — | — | 3000. |
| 1842 original | — | — | — | | Proof only | — | — | 3800. |
| 1842 restrike | — | — | — | | Proof only | — | — | 3200. |
| 1843 original | — | — | — | | Proof only | — | — | 3800. |
| 1843 restrike | — | — | — | | Proof only | — | — | 3200. |
| 1844 original | — | — | — | | Proof only | — | — | 3800. |
| 1844 restrike | — | — | — | | Proof only | — | — | 3200. |
| 1845 original | — | — | — | | Proof only | — | — | 3800. |
| 1845 restrike | — | — | — | | Proof only | — | — | 3200. |
| 1846 original | — | — | — | | Proof only | — | — | 3800. |
| 1846 restrike | — | — | — | | Proof only | — | — | 3200. |
| 1847 original | — | — | — | | Proof only | — | — | 3800. |
| 1847 restrike | — | — | — | | Proof only | — | — | 3200. |
| 1848 original | — | — | — | | Proof only | — | — | 3800. |
| 1848 restrike | — | — | — | | Proof only | — | — | 3200. |
| 1849 original, small date | | — | — | | Proof only | — | — | 3800. |
| 1849 restrike small date | | — | | | Proof only | — | — | 3200. |

| Date | Mintage | G-4 | VG-8 | F-12 | VF-20 | XF-40 | MS-60 |
|---|---|---|---|---|---|---|---|
| 1849 lg. date | 39,864 | 39.00 | 43.00 | 50.00 | 58.00 | 80.00 | 400. |
| 1850 | 39,812 | 36.00 | 40.00 | 48.00 | 55.00 | 80.00 | 400. |
| 1851 | 147,672 | 27.00 | 34.00 | 43.00 | 50.00 | 63.00 | 185. |
| 1852 | — | — | — | | Proof only | — | 4250. |
| 1853 | 129,694 | 27.00 | 34.00 | 43.00 | 50.00 | 63.00 | 170. |
| 1854 | 55,358 | 29.00 | 37.00 | 44.00 | 52.00 | 75.00 | 175. |
| 1855 | 56,500 | 29.00 | 37.00 | 44.00 | 52.00 | 75.00 | 170. |
| 1856 | 40,430 | 35.00 | 39.00 | 50.00 | 60.00 | 85.00 | 275. |
| 1857 | 35,180 | 50.00 | 55.00 | 65.00 | 80.00 | 110. | 275. |

# Large cents

## Flowing Hair

### Chain reverse

**Designer:** Henry Voigt. **Size:** 26-27 millimeters. **Weight:** 13.48 grams. **Composition:** 100% copper.

| Date | Mintage | G-4 | VG-8 | F-12 | VF-20 | XF-40 | MS-60 |
|---|---|---|---|---|---|---|---|
| 1793 chain | 36,103 | 2500. | 4850. | 6650. | 9750. | 25,000 | — |

### Wreath reverse

**Designer:** Adam Eckfeldt. **Size:** 26-28 millimeters. **Weight:** 13.48 grams. **Composition:** 100% copper.

| Date | Mintage | G-4 | VG-8 | F-12 | VF-20 | XF-40 | MS-60 |
|---|---|---|---|---|---|---|---|
| 1793 wreath | 63,353 | 975. | 1450. | 1950. | 3750. | 6950. | — |

# Liberty Cap

**Designers:** Joseph Wright (1793-1795) and John Smith Gardner (1795-1796). **Size:** 29 millimeters. **Weight:** 13.48 grams (1793-1795) and 10.89 grams (1795-1796). **Notes:** The heavier pieces were struck on thicker planchets. The Liberty design on the obverse was revised slightly in 1794, but the 1793 design was used on some 1794 strikes. The 1795 "lettered edge" variety has "One Hundred for a Dollar" and a leaf inscribed on the edge.

| Date | Mintage | G-4 | VG-8 | F-12 | VF-20 | XF-40 | MS-60 |
|------|---------|-----|------|------|-------|-------|-------|
| 1793 cap | 11,056 | 1850. | 2800. | 4500. | 6000. | — | — |
| 1794 | 918,521 | 165. | 250. | 440. | 825. | 1450. | — |
| 1794 head '93 | Inc. Ab. | 325. | 500. | 1100. | 2000. | — | — |
| 1795 | 501,500 | 160. | 200. | 415. | 725. | 1400. | — |
| 1795 lettered edge, "One Cent" high in wreath | | | | | | | |
| | 37,000 | 180. | 275. | 450. | 750. | 1375. | — |
| 1796 Lib. Cap | 109,825 | 175. | 260. | 415. | 900. | 1650. | — |

# Draped Bust

**Designer:** Robert Scot. **Size:** 29 millimeters. **Weight:** 10.98 grams. **Composition:** 100% copper. **Notes:** The "stemless" variety does not have stems extending from the wreath above and on both sides of the fraction on the reverse. The 1801 "3 errors" variety has the fraction on the reverse reading "1/000", has only one stem extending from the wreath above and on both sides of the fraction on the reverse, and "United" in "United States of America" appears as "Iinited."

| Date | Mintage | G-4 | VG-8 | F-12 | VF-20 | XF-40 | MS-60 |
|------|---------|-----|------|------|-------|-------|-------|
| 1796 | 363,375 | 70.00 | 90.00 | 165. | 335. | 750. | — |
| 1797 | 897,510 | 40.00 | 60.00 | 125. | 325. | 750. | — |
| 1797 stemless | Inc. Ab. | 60.00 | 100. | 200. | 1500. | 2250. | — |
| 1798 | 1,841,745 | 30.00 | 50.00 | 125. | 325. | 700. | — |
| 1798/97 | Inc. Ab. | 70.00 | 115. | 185. | 450. | 800. | — |
| 1799 | 42,540 | 900. | 1650. | 4000. | 5900. | — | — |
| 1800 | 2,822,175 | 37.00 | 45.00 | 110. | 425. | 700. | — |
| 1801 | 1,362,837 | 37.00 | 45.00 | 110. | 375. | 690. | — |
| 1801 3 errors | Inc. Ab. | 37.00 | 65.00 | 170. | 425. | 700. | — |
| 1802 | 3,435,100 | 35.00 | 42.00 | 95.00 | 285. | 700. | 2000. |
| 1803 | 2,471,353 | 35.00 | 42.00 | 95.00 | 285. | 665. | 2000. |
| 1804 | 756,838 | 600. | 1000. | 1800. | 3250. | 5000. | — |
| 1805 | 941,116 | 35.00 | 42.00 | 100. | 290. | 665. | — |
| 1806 | 348,000 | 40.00 | 65.00 | 125. | 475. | 750. | — |
| 1807 | 727,221 | 30.00 | 42.00 | 120. | 350. | 665. | — |

# 1804 Cent
## Grade F-12

—•— **Retail Price**

**Source: COIN PRICES**

# Classic Head

**Designer:** John Reich. **Size:** 29 millimeters. **Weight:** 10.89 grams. **Composition:** 100% copper.

| Date | Mintage | G-4 | VG-8 | F-12 | VF-20 | XF-40 | MS-60 |
|------|---------|-----|------|------|-------|-------|-------|
| 1808 | 1,109,000 | 33.00 | 65.00 | 195. | 510. | 1075. | 3150. |
| 1809 | 222,867 | 70.00 | 135. | 250. | 800. | 1500. | — |
| 1810 | 1,458,500 | 32.00 | 65.00 | 190. | 500. | 1075. | 3150. |
| 1811 | 218,025 | 65.00 | 105. | 250. | 695. | 1070. | — |
| 1812 | 1,075,500 | 33.00 | 65.00 | 190. | 510. | 1075. | 3150. |
| 1813 | 418,000 | 45.00 | 72.00 | 200. | 600. | 1200. | — |
| 1814 | 357,830 | 32.00 | 65.00 | 190. | 530. | 1100. | 3150. |

# Coronet

**Designer:** Robert Scot. **Size:** 28-29 millimeters. **Weight:** 10.89 grams. **Composition:** 100% copper. **Notes:** The 1817 strikes have either 13 or 15 stars on the obverse.

| Date | Mintage | G-4 | VG-8 | F-12 | VF-20 | XF-40 | MS-60 |
|------|---------|-----|------|------|-------|-------|-------|
| 1816 | 2,820,982 | 12.50 | 17.00 | 30.00 | 70.00 | 120. | 300. |
| 1817 13 stars | 3,948,400 | 11.00 | 13.00 | 21.00 | 40.00 | 100. | 225. |
| 1817 15 stars | Inc. Ab. | 12.00 | 20.00 | 30.00 | 60.00 | 155. | 450. |
| 1818 | 3,167,000 | 10.00 | 13.00 | 21.00 | 40.00 | 100. | 350. |
| 1819 | 2,671,000 | 11.00 | 13.00 | 21.00 | 40.00 | 100. | 315. |
| 1820 | 4,407,550 | 11.00 | 13.00 | 21.00 | 40.00 | 100. | 225. |
| 1821 | 389,000 | 17.50 | 30.00 | 45.00 | 100. | 250. | — |
| 1822 | 2,072,339 | 11.00 | 15.00 | 24.00 | 46.00 | 135. | 350. |
| 1823 | Inc. 1824 | 30.00 | 55.00 | 90.00 | 235. | 650. | — |
| 1823/22 | Inc. 1824 | 27.00 | 45.00 | 65.00 | 175. | 350. | 1750. |
| 1824 | 1,262,000 | 11.50 | 16.00 | 28.00 | 60.00 | 80.00 | 575. |
| 1824/22 | Inc. Ab. | 20.00 | 95.00 | 220. | 295. | — | 1500. |
| 1825 | 1,461,100 | 10.50 | 14.00 | 24.00 | 55.00 | 150. | 350. |
| 1826 | 1,517,425 | 10.50 | 14.00 | 24.00 | 50.00 | 130. | 600. |
| 1826/25 | Inc. Ab. | 18.00 | 30.00 | 60.00 | 115. | 250. | 800. |
| 1827 | 2,357,732 | 10.50 | 12.50 | 20.00 | 45.00 | 115. | 600. |
| 1828 | 2,260,624 | 10.00 | 12.50 | 20.00 | 50.00 | 115. | 300. |
| 1829 | 1,414,500 | 11.00 | 13.00 | 21.00 | 45.00 | 120. | 350. |
| 1830 | 1,711,500 | 11.00 | 13.00 | 20.00 | 40.00 | 110. | 325. |
| 1831 | 3,359,260 | 10.00 | 11.00 | 20.00 | 35.00 | 100. | 325. |
| 1832 | 2,362,000 | 10.00 | 11.00 | 20.00 | 40.00 | 100. | 325. |
| 1833 | 2,739,000 | 10.00 | 11.00 | 20.00 | 35.00 | 100. | 325. |
| 1834 | 1,855,100 | 10.00 | 11.00 | 20.00 | 40.00 | 100. | 350. |
| 1835 | 3,878,400 | 10.00 | 11.00 | 20.00 | 40.00 | 100. | 325. |
| 1836 | 2,111,000 | 10.00 | 11.00 | 20.00 | 40.00 | 95.00 | 300. |

# Braided Hair

**Designer:** Christian Gobrecht. **Size:** 27.5 millimeters. **Weight:** 10.89 grams. **Composition:** 100% copper. **Notes:** 1840 and 1842 strikes have either small or large dates, with little difference in value. 1855 and 1856 strikes have either slanting or upright 5s in the date, with little difference in value. A slightly larger Liberty head and larger reverse lettering were used beginning in 1843. One 1843 variety uses the old obverse with the new reverse.

| Date | Mintage | G-4 | VG-8 | F-12 | VF-20 | XF-40 | MS-60 |
|------|---------|-----|------|------|-------|-------|-------|
| 1837 | 5,558,300 | 9.50 | 10.50 | 16.50 | 33.00 | 90.00 | 300. |
| 1838 | 6,370,200 | 9.50 | 10.50 | 16.50 | 33.00 | 80.00 | 225. |
| 1839 | 3,128,661 | 9.50 | 10.50 | 16.50 | 42.00 | 100. | 350. |
| 1839/36 | Inc. Ab. | 175. | 350. | 750. | 1500. | — | — |
| 1840 | 2,462,700 | 9.50 | 10.50 | 11.50 | 19.00 | 58.00 | 265. |
| 1841 | 1,597,367 | 10.00 | 12.00 | 15.00 | 23.00 | 68.00 | 300. |
| 1842 | 2,383,390 | 9.50 | 10.50 | 11.50 | 18.00 | 55.00 | 265. |
| 1843 | 2,425,342 | 9.50 | 10.50 | 17.00 | 25.00 | 65.00 | 225. |
| 1843 obverse 1842 with reverse of 1844 | | | | | | | |
| | Inc. Ab. | 10.00 | 13.00 | 19.00 | 38.00 | 80.00 | 350. |

| Date | Mintage | G-4 | VG-8 | F-12 | VF-20 | XF-40 | MS-60 |
|------|---------|-----|------|------|-------|-------|-------|
| 1844 | 2,398,752 | 9.75 | 10.50 | 12.00 | 17.00 | 49.00 | 160. |
| 1844/81 | Inc. Ab. | 12.00 | 20.00 | 28.00 | 60.00 | 130. | 450. |
| 1845 | 3,894,804 | 9.50 | 10.50 | 12.00 | 14.00 | 40.00 | 160. |
| 1846 | 4,120,800 | 9.50 | 10.50 | 12.00 | 14.00 | 40.00 | 160. |
| 1847 | 6,183,669 | 9.50 | 10.50 | 12.00 | 14.00 | 40.00 | 160. |
| 1848 | 6,415,799 | 9.50 | 10.50 | 12.00 | 14.00 | 40.00 | 160. |
| 1849 | 4,178,500 | 9.50 | 10.50 | 12.00 | 14.00 | 40.00 | 160. |
| 1850 | 4,426,844 | 9.50 | 10.50 | 12.00 | 14.00 | 40.00 | 160. |
| 1851 | 9,889,707 | 9.50 | 10.50 | 12.00 | 14.00 | 40.00 | 160. |
| 1851/81 | Inc. Ab. | 10.00 | 12.50 | 18.00 | 35.00 | 95.00 | 400. |
| 1852 | 5,063,094 | 9.50 | 10.50 | 12.00 | 14.00 | 40.00 | 160. |
| 1853 | 6,641,131 | 9.50 | 10.50 | 12.00 | 14.00 | 40.00 | 160. |
| 1854 | 4,236,156 | 9.50 | 10.50 | 12.00 | 14.00 | 40.00 | 160. |
| 1855 | 1,574,829 | 9.75 | 11.00 | 14.00 | 17.00 | 45.00 | 170. |
| 1856 | 2,690,463 | 9.50 | 10.50 | 12.00 | 14.00 | 40.00 | 160. |
| 1857 | 333,456 | 25.00 | 28.00 | 35.00 | 55.00 | 85.00 | 300. |

# Small cents

## Flying Eagle

Large letters; "AM" connected          Small letters; "AM" separated

**Designer:** James B. Longacre. **Size:** 19 millimeters. **Weight:** 4.67 grams. **Composition:** 88% copper, 12% nickel. **Notes:** On the large-letter variety of 1858, the "A" and "M" in "America" are connected at their bases; on the small-letter variety, the two letters are separated.

| Date | Mintage | G-4 | VG-8 | F-12 | VF-20 | XF-40 | AU-50 | MS-60 | MS-65 | Prf-65 |
|------|---------|-----|------|------|-------|-------|-------|-------|-------|--------|
| 1856 | Est. 1,000 | 3500. | 3900. | 4500. | 5100. | 5400. | 5600. | 6300. | 20,000. | 21,000. |
| 1857 | 17,450,000 | 16.50 | 19.00 | 24.00 | 36.00 | 88.00 | 165. | 225. | 2500. | 16,750. |
| 1858 LL | 24,600,000 | 17.50 | 20.00 | 25.00 | 40.00 | 105. | 165. | 265. | 2500. | 15,000. |
| 1858 SL | Inc. Ab. | 17.50 | 20.00 | 25.00 | 40.00 | 105. | 165. | 265. | 2500. | 13,000. |

## Indian Head

1859          1860-1909          1864 "L"

### Copper-nickel composition

**Designer:** James B. Longacre. **Size:** 19 millimeters. **Weight:** 4.67 grams. **Composition:** 88% copper, 12% nickel.

| Date | Mintage | G-4 | VG-8 | F-12 | VF-20 | XF-40 | AU-50 | MS-60 | MS-65 | Prf-65 |
|------|---------|-----|------|------|-------|-------|-------|-------|-------|--------|
| 1859 | 36,400,000 | 7.50 | 8.00 | 11.00 | 31.00 | 75.00 | 160. | 180. | 2050. | 4900. |
| 1860 | 20,566,000 | 5.00 | 7.00 | 9.50 | 15.00 | 42.00 | 75.00 | 140. | 650. | 2400. |
| 1861 | 10,100,000 | 16.00 | 20.00 | 24.00 | 38.00 | 75.00 | 155. | 200. | 875. | 2400. |
| 1862 | 28,075,000 | 3.75 | 5.00 | 5.50 | 11.00 | 25.00 | 49.00 | 100. | 650. | 1750. |
| 1863 | 49,840,000 | 3.00 | 4.00 | 5.50 | 11.00 | 22.00 | 45.00 | 55.00 | 600. | 1750. |
| 1864 | 13,740,000 | 15.00 | 18.00 | 21.00 | 26.00 | 42.00 | 77.00 | 140. | 900. | 2300. |

# 1857 Cent
## Grade XF-40

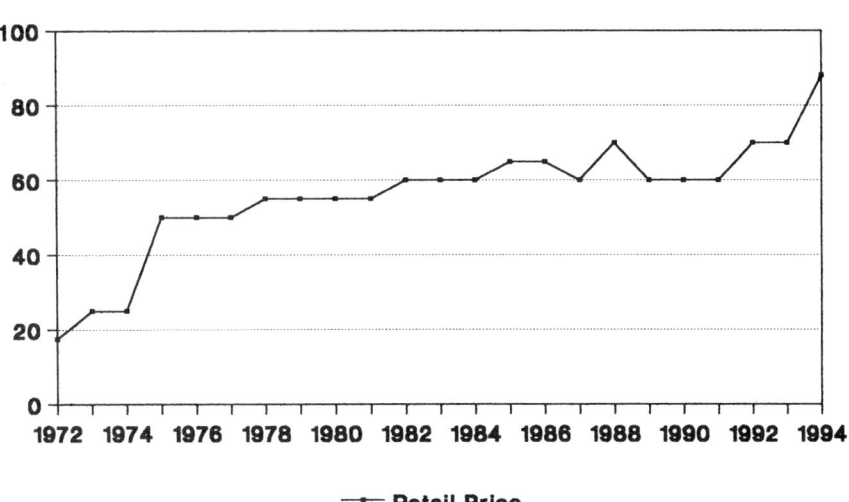

**―•― Retail Price**

Source: COIN PRICES

## Bronze composition

**Weight:** 3.11 grams. **Composition:** 95% copper, 5% tin and zinc. **Notes:** The 1864 "L" variety has the designer's initial in Liberty's hair to the right of her neck.

| Date | Mintage | G-4 | VG-8 | F-12 | VF-20 | XF-40 | AU-50 | MS-60 | MS-65 | Prf-65 |
|------|---------|-----|------|------|-------|-------|-------|-------|-------|--------|
| 1864 | 39,233,714 | 5.50 | 6.50 | 10.00 | 22.00 | 37.00 | 50.00 | 77.00 | 350. | 2800. |
| 1864 L | Inc. Ab. | 35.00 | 48.00 | 70.00 | 115. | 190. | 225. | 315. | 1150. | 44,000. |
| 1865 | 35,429,286 | 5.25 | 7.00 | 9.50 | 19.50 | 30.00 | 42.00 | 77.00 | 315. | 900. |
| 1866 | 9,826,500 | 29.00 | 33.00 | 45.00 | 77.00 | 135. | 180. | 240. | 900. | 725. |
| 1867 | 9,821,000 | 29.00 | 33.00 | 45.00 | 94.00 | 135. | 195. | 250. | 770. | 850. |
| 1868 | 10,266,500 | 29.00 | 33.00 | 45.00 | 77.00 | 125. | 175. | 240. | 900. | 675. |
| 1869/8 | 6,420,000 | 110. | 160. | 195. | 310. | 400. | 525. | 625. | 2100. | — |
| 1869 | Inc. Ab. | 40.00 | 65.00 | 160. | 235. | 275. | 350. | 420. | 1250. | 875. |
| 1870 | 5,275,000 | 34.00 | 40.00 | 140. | 220. | 295. | 350. | 470. | 1000. | 875. |
| 1871 | 3,929,500 | 38.00 | 70.00 | 170. | 280. | 310. | 385. | 455. | 1250. | 1050. |
| 1872 | 4,042,000 | 56.00 | 95.00 | 225. | 280. | 350. | 420. | 525. | 1675. | 1400. |
| 1873 | 11,676,500 | 12.00 | 15.50 | 30.00 | 39.00 | 91.00 | 120. | 170. | 595. | 610. |
| 1874 | 14,187,500 | 12.00 | 15.50 | 25.00 | 39.00 | 85.00 | 120. | 170. | 500. | 550. |
| 1875 | 13,528,000 | 12.00 | 15.50 | 23.00 | 39.00 | 77.00 | 115. | 170. | 560. | 700. |
| 1876 | 7,944,000 | 23.00 | 30.00 | 37.00 | 55.00 | 105. | 135. | 190. | 630. | 560. |
| 1877 | 852,500 | 310. | 345. | 490. | 675. | 1350. | 1900. | 2200. | 4750. | 4150. |
| 1878 | 5,799,850 | 23.00 | 30.00 | 35.00 | 55.00 | 95.00 | 125. | 190. | 595. | 525. |
| 1879 | 16,231,200 | 4.50 | 5.00 | 7.00 | 14.00 | 30.00 | 40.00 | 63.00 | 385. | 525. |
| 1880 | 38,964,955 | 2.75 | 3.50 | 5.50 | 7.50 | 20.00 | 30.00 | 63.00 | 350. | 500. |
| 1881 | 39,211,575 | 2.75 | 3.75 | 5.50 | 7.50 | 18.50 | 25.00 | 35.00 | 280. | 500. |
| 1882 | 38,581,100 | 2.75 | 3.75 | 5.50 | 7.50 | 16.00 | 25.00 | 39.00 | 280. | 500. |
| 1883 | 45,589,109 | 2.00 | 3.75 | 5.50 | 7.50 | 16.00 | 25.00 | 35.00 | 280. | 525. |
| 1884 | 23,261,742 | 2.75 | 4.00 | 6.00 | 10.00 | 20.00 | 30.00 | 50.00 | 335. | 500. |
| 1885 | 11,765,384 | 3.95 | 6.50 | 9.75 | 19.50 | 48.00 | 65.00 | 100. | 490. | 500. |
| 1886 | 17,654,290 | 3.00 | 5.00 | 10.00 | 27.00 | 58.00 | 75.00 | 105. | 490. | 500. |
| 1887 | 45,226,483 | 1.35 | 1.80 | 3.00 | 4.95 | 13.50 | 25.00 | 35.00 | 245. | 500. |
| 1888 | 37,494,414 | 1.35 | 1.80 | 3.00 | 4.95 | 13.50 | 25.00 | 35.00 | 350. | 500. |
| 1889 | 48,869,361 | 1.35 | 1.65 | 2.75 | 4.50 | 12.00 | 25.00 | 35.00 | 250. | 520. |
| 1890 | 57,182,854 | 1.35 | 1.65 | 2.50 | 4.50 | 10.00 | 23.00 | 35.00 | 250. | 520. |
| 1891 | 47,072,350 | 1.35 | 1.65 | 2.50 | 4.50 | 10.00 | 23.00 | 35.00 | 250. | 500. |
| 1892 | 37,649,832 | 1.35 | 1.65 | 2.50 | 4.50 | 10.00 | 23.00 | 35.00 | 250. | 530. |
| 1893 | 46,642,195 | 1.35 | 1.65 | 2.50 | 4.50 | 10.00 | 23.00 | 35.00 | 250. | 650. |
| 1894 | 16,752,132 | 1.75 | 3.00 | 6.50 | 10.00 | 18.00 | 32.00 | 49.00 | 375. | 650. |
| 1895 | 38,343,636 | 1.25 | 1.75 | 2.50 | 4.00 | 10.00 | 19.00 | 30.00 | 165. | 530. |

# 1864-L Cent
## Grade F-12

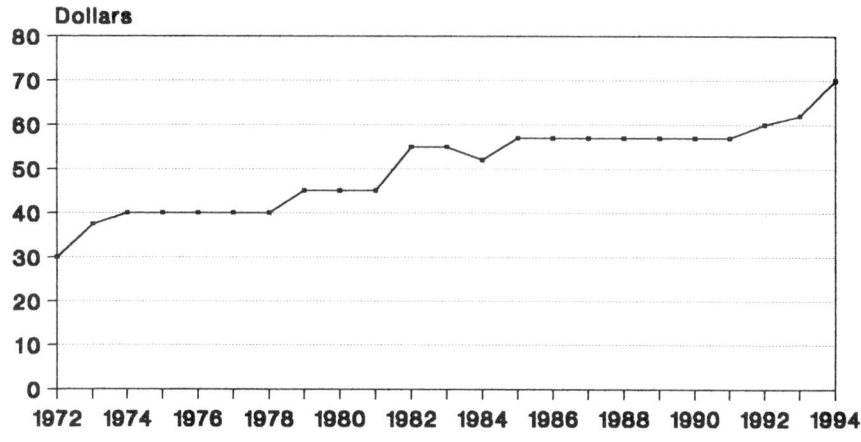

**Dollars**

—•— **Retail Price**

**Source: COIN PRICES**

| Date | Mintage | G-4 | VG-8 | F-12 | VF-20 | XF-40 | AU-50 | MS-60 | MS-65 | Prf-65 |
|------|---------|-----|------|------|-------|-------|-------|-------|-------|--------|
| 1896 | 39,057,293 | 1.30 | 1.75 | 2.50 | 4.00 | 10.00 | 17.00 | 30.00 | 160. | 540. |
| 1897 | 50,466,330 | 1.30 | 1.75 | 2.50 | 4.00 | 10.00 | 17.00 | 30.00 | 160. | 475. |
| 1898 | 49,823,079 | 1.30 | 1.75 | 2.50 | 4.00 | 10.00 | 17.00 | 30.00 | 160. | 475. |
| 1899 | 53,600,031 | 1.30 | 1.50 | 2.00 | 3.50 | 9.50 | 17.00 | 30.00 | 160. | 475. |
| 1900 | 66,833,764 | 1.30 | 1.50 | 2.25 | 3.50 | 9.50 | 15.00 | 22.00 | 145. | 350. |
| 1901 | 79,611,143 | 1.25 | 1.40 | 1.75 | 2.75 | 7.50 | 15.00 | 22.00 | 145. | 350. |
| 1902 | 87,376,722 | 1.25 | 1.40 | 1.75 | 2.75 | 7.50 | 15.00 | 22.00 | 145. | 350. |
| 1903 | 85,094,493 | 1.25 | 1.40 | 1.75 | 2.75 | 7.50 | 15.00 | 22.00 | 145. | 350. |
| 1904 | 61,328,015 | 1.25 | 1.40 | 1.75 | 2.75 | 7.50 | 15.00 | 22.00 | 145. | 350. |
| 1905 | 80,719,163 | 1.25 | 1.40 | 1.75 | 2.75 | 7.50 | 15.00 | 22.00 | 145. | 350. |
| 1906 | 96,022,255 | 1.25 | 1.40 | 1.75 | 2.75 | 7.50 | 15.00 | 22.00 | 145. | 350. |
| 1907 | 108,138,618 | 1.25 | 1.40 | 1.75 | 2.75 | 7.50 | 15.00 | 22.00 | 145. | 350. |
| 1908 | 32,327,987 | 1.25 | 1.40 | 2.00 | 3.00 | 7.50 | 15.00 | 22.00 | 145. | 350. |
| 1908S | 1,115,000 | 25.00 | 28.00 | 30.00 | 40.00 | 84.00 | 135. | 225. | 595. | — |
| 1909 | 14,370,645 | 1.60 | 2.00 | 2.65 | 4.50 | 9.00 | 19.00 | 31.00 | 145. | 450. |
| 1909S | 309,000 | 195. | 215. | 230. | 245. | 325. | 390. | 500. | 975. | — |

# Lincoln

"V.D.B."

## Wheat reverse, bronze composition

**Designer:** Victor D. Brenner. **Size:** 19 millimeters. **Weight:** 3.11 grams. **Composition:** 95% copper, 5% tin and zinc. **Notes:** The 1909 "V.D.B." varieties have the designer's initials inscribed at the 6 o'clock position on the reverse. Later in 1909 the initials were removed until 1918, when they were placed on the obverse.

# 1914-D Cent
## Grade F-12

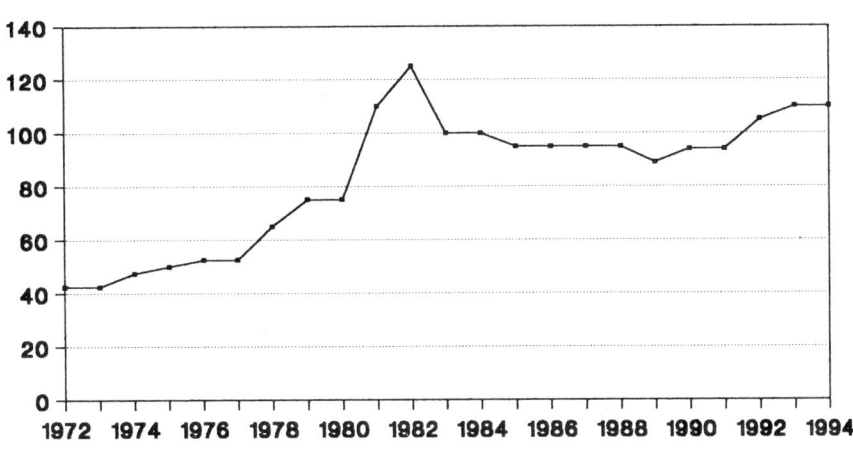

—■— **Retail Price**

**Source: COIN PRICES**

| Date | Mintage | G-4 | VG-8 | F-12 | VF-20 | XF-40 | AU-50 | MS-60 | MS-65 | Prf-65 |
|------|---------|-----|------|------|-------|-------|-------|-------|-------|--------|
| 1909 | 72,702,618 | .50 | .55 | .85 | 1.35 | 2.25 | 5.50 | 15.00 | 80.00 | 460. |
| 1909VDB | 27,995,000 | 2.10 | 2.30 | 2.40 | 2.75 | 3.00 | 6.00 | 10.00 | 45.00 | 2800. |
| 1909S | 1,825,000 | 42.00 | 46.00 | 53.00 | 63.00 | 95.00 | 120. | 155. | 250. | — |
| 1909SVDB | 484,000 | 350. | 400. | 475. | 520. | 575. | 615. | 715. | 1900. | — |
| 1910 | 146,801,218 | .15 | .20 | .25 | .60 | 2.50 | 4.90 | 14.00 | 63.00 | 450. |
| 1910S | 6,045,000 | 7.00 | 7.75 | 8.50 | 12.00 | 23.00 | 53.00 | 75.00 | 195. | — |
| 1911 | 101,177,787 | .25 | .30 | .50 | 1.95 | 5.25 | 7.00 | 18.00 | 135. | 450. |
| 1911D | 12,672,000 | 4.25 | 5.50 | 6.75 | 11.50 | 32.00 | 50.00 | 77.00 | 700. | — |
| 1911S | 4,026,000 | 17.00 | 20.00 | 22.00 | 24.00 | 43.00 | 65.00 | 140. | 800. | — |
| 1912 | 68,153,060 | .65 | .85 | 1.85 | 3.90 | 10.00 | 15.00 | 25.00 | 160. | 450. |
| 1912D | 10,411,000 | 4.00 | 5.00 | 6.00 | 15.00 | 39.50 | 54.00 | 120. | 840. | — |
| 1912S | 4,431,000 | 12.00 | 12.75 | 14.25 | 17.25 | 40.00 | 53.00 | 100. | 975. | — |
| 1913 | 76,532,352 | .45 | .50 | 1.25 | 3.50 | 9.50 | 11.00 | 23.00 | 220. | 450. |
| 1913D | 15,804,000 | 2.00 | 2.50 | 3.00 | 7.00 | 24.00 | 40.00 | 84.00 | 745. | — |
| 1913S | 6,101,000 | 5.75 | 6.25 | 7.75 | 12.00 | 30.00 | 51.00 | 110. | 1250. | — |
| 1914 | 75,238,432 | .35 | .40 | 1.50 | 3.75 | 10.00 | 18.50 | 40.00 | 155. | 450. |
| 1914D | 1,193,000 | 84.00 | 91.00 | 110. | 175. | 420. | 595. | 840. | 4300. | — |
| 1914S | 4,137,000 | 9.75 | 10.75 | 12.00 | 19.75 | 40.00 | 66.00 | 190. | 3900. | — |
| 1915 | 29,092,120 | 1.10 | 1.35 | 3.90 | 10.75 | 41.00 | 60.00 | 84.00 | 365. | 450. |
| 1915D | 22,050,000 | 1.00 | 1.25 | 2.20 | 3.50 | 10.00 | 22.00 | 49.00 | 390. | — |
| 1915S | 4,833,000 | 7.00 | 8.50 | 9.00 | 11.50 | 31.00 | 46.00 | 105. | 1550. | — |
| 1916 | 131,833,677 | .15 | .20 | .45 | 1.50 | 4.50 | 5.00 | 11.00 | 85.00 | 665. |
| 1916D | 35,956,000 | .25 | .35 | 1.25 | 2.50 | 9.50 | 16.00 | 53.00 | 980. | — |
| 1916S | 22,510,000 | .60 | 1.00 | 1.50 | 2.50 | 9.00 | 17.00 | 63.00 | 3650. | — |
| 1917 | 196,429,785 | .10 | .15 | .35 | .75 | 2.75 | 5.00 | 11.00 | 120. | — |
| 1917D | 55,120,000 | .30 | .40 | 1.00 | 2.20 | 7.50 | 13.50 | 56.00 | 560. | — |
| 1917S | 32,620,000 | .45 | .55 | .80 | 2.20 | 6.75 | 15.00 | 58.00 | 1325. | — |
| 1918 | 288,104,634 | .10 | .15 | .35 | .60 | 2.50 | 4.50 | 11.00 | 100. | — |
| 1918D | 47,830,000 | .30 | .35 | 1.00 | 2.00 | 7.00 | 13.00 | 53.00 | 800. | — |
| 1918S | 34,680,000 | .45 | .50 | .80 | 2.00 | 6.50 | 16.00 | 59.00 | 2800. | — |
| 1919 | 392,021,000 | .10 | .15 | .20 | .50 | 2.00 | 5.00 | 8.50 | 56.00 | — |
| 1919D | 57,154,000 | .20 | .30 | .60 | 2.20 | 7.50 | 11.00 | 45.00 | 560. | — |
| 1919S | 139,760,000 | .10 | .25 | .50 | .85 | 2.00 | 6.00 | 30.00 | 910. | — |
| 1920 | 310,165,000 | .10 | .15 | .20 | .45 | 2.50 | 4.00 | 9.75 | 63.00 | — |
| 1920D | 49,280,000 | .20 | .35 | .75 | 2.00 | 8.00 | 11.00 | 53.00 | 595. | — |
| 1920S | 46,220,000 | .20 | .30 | .40 | 1.25 | 4.00 | 14.00 | 85.00 | 2800. | — |
| 1921 | 39,157,000 | .25 | .35 | .60 | 2.00 | 5.75 | 10.00 | 39.00 | 125. | — |
| 1921S | 15,274,000 | .75 | .85 | 1.50 | 3.50 | 12.00 | 50.00 | 100. | 2500. | — |
| 1922D | 7,160,000 | 5.85 | 6.75 | 8.00 | 9.50 | 17.00 | 42.00 | 70.00 | 490. | — |
| 1922 | Inc. Ab. | 265. | 275. | 370. | 575. | 2100. | 3200. | 5600. | 23,500. | — |
| 1923 | 74,723,000 | .20 | .30 | .35 | 1.80 | 2.50 | 4.00 | 9.75 | 140. | — |

| Date | Mintage | G-4 | VG-8 | F-12 | VF-20 | XF-40 | AU-50 | MS-60 | MS-65 | Prf-65 |
|---|---|---|---|---|---|---|---|---|---|---|
| 1923S | 8,700,000 | 1.70 | 1.90 | 3.00 | 5.00 | 20.00 | 70.00 | 190. | 2450. | — |
| 1924 | 75,178,000 | .20 | .25 | .30 | 1.50 | 5.75 | 7.00 | 22.00 | 155. | — |
| 1924D | 2,520,000 | 9.25 | 10.50 | 11.50 | 19.00 | 48.00 | 100. | 235. | 2800. | — |
| 1924S | 11,696,000 | .75 | 1.10 | 1.50 | 3.75 | 16.00 | 28.00 | 120. | 2500. | — |
| 1925 | 139,949,000 | .10 | .15 | .20 | .85 | 2.50 | 4.50 | 8.50 | 59.00 | — |
| 1925D | 22,580,000 | .40 | .45 | .70 | 2.90 | 7.50 | 12.00 | 47.00 | 775. | — |
| 1925S | 26,380,000 | .30 | .35 | .45 | 1.25 | 6.75 | 14.00 | 61.00 | 2500. | — |
| 1926 | 157,088,000 | .10 | .15 | .20 | .85 | 2.00 | 3.50 | 7.00 | 35.00 | — |
| 1926D | 28,020,000 | .30 | .35 | .65 | 1.75 | 4.00 | 10.00 | 45.00 | 1050. | — |
| 1926S | 4,550,000 | 3.50 | 3.75 | 4.00 | 4.75 | 11.00 | 50.00 | 100. | 3000. | — |
| 1927 | 144,440,000 | .10 | .15 | .25 | .85 | 2.00 | 3.75 | 7.25 | 70.00 | — |
| 1927D | 27,170,000 | .25 | .30 | .45 | 1.00 | 3.25 | 9.50 | 35.00 | 800. | — |
| 1927S | 14,276,000 | .60 | .70 | 1.60 | 3.00 | 9.50 | 16.00 | 65.00 | 1200. | — |
| 1928 | 134,116,000 | .10 | .15 | .20 | .80 | 2.00 | 3.75 | 7.00 | 56.00 | — |
| 1928D | 31,170,000 | .25 | .30 | .35 | .75 | 2.25 | 6.00 | 20.00 | 295. | — |
| 1928S | 17,266,000 | .45 | .50 | .70 | 1.75 | 3.50 | 10.00 | 48.00 | 630. | — |
| 1929 | 185,262,000 | .15 | .20 | .25 | .80 | 1.50 | 3.75 | 5.50 | 70.00 | — |
| 1929D | 41,730,000 | .15 | .20 | .25 | .45 | 2.00 | 5.00 | 16.00 | 115. | — |
| 1929S | 50,148,000 | .15 | .20 | .25 | 1.00 | 2.25 | 3.75 | 7.75 | 140. | — |
| 1930 | 157,415,000 | .15 | .20 | .30 | .45 | 1.50 | 2.50 | 4.25 | 23.00 | — |
| 1930D | 40,100,000 | .15 | .20 | .30 | .50 | 1.75 | 5.75 | 12.00 | 67.00 | — |
| 1930S | 24,286,000 | .20 | .25 | .35 | .70 | 1.60 | 3.00 | 6.00 | 49.00 | — |
| 1931 | 19,396,000 | .40 | .50 | .65 | 1.00 | 2.50 | 6.00 | 16.50 | 91.00 | — |
| 1931D | 4,480,000 | 2.85 | 2.95 | 3.50 | 4.00 | 7.00 | 28.00 | 45.00 | 330. | — |
| 1931S | 866,000 | 34.00 | 34.50 | 37.00 | 39.00 | 42.00 | 49.00 | 59.00 | 245. | — |
| 1932 | 9,062,000 | 1.95 | 2.10 | 2.15 | 2.25 | 3.50 | 9.00 | 19.00 | 53.00 | — |
| 1932D | 10,500,000 | .90 | 1.00 | 1.10 | 1.35 | 3.75 | 8.00 | 14.00 | 53.00 | — |
| 1933 | 14,360,000 | 1.15 | 1.25 | 1.50 | 1.80 | 3.75 | 8.00 | 16.00 | 59.00 | — |
| 1933D | 6,200,000 | 2.00 | 2.10 | 2.25 | 2.50 | 4.50 | 11.00 | 17.00 | 35.00 | — |
| 1934 | 219,080,000 | — | .10 | .15 | .20 | .75 | 1.50 | 3.00 | 15.00 | — |
| 1934D | 28,446,000 | .10 | .15 | .20 | .25 | 2.00 | 6.50 | 18.00 | 35.00 | — |
| 1935 | 245,338,000 | — | .10 | .15 | .20 | .75 | 1.00 | 1.50 | 7.75 | — |
| 1935D | 47,000,000 | — | .10 | .15 | .20 | .75 | 3.00 | 4.50 | 15.00 | — |
| 1935S | 38,702,000 | — | .20 | .25 | .30 | 2.25 | 5.00 | 10.00 | 42.00 | — |
| 1936 | 309,637,569 | — | .10 | .15 | .20 | .75 | 1.00 | 1.50 | 6.25 | 800. |
| 1936D | 40,620,000 | — | .10 | .15 | .25 | .75 | 1.50 | 1.75 | 9.00 | — |
| 1936S | 29,130,000 | .10 | .15 | .25 | .30 | .75 | 1.75 | 2.25 | 10.00 | — |
| 1937 | 309,179,320 | — | .10 | .15 | .20 | .70 | .90 | 1.00 | 6.25 | 140. |
| 1937D | 50,430,000 | — | .10 | .15 | .25 | .70 | 1.00 | 1.90 | 7.70 | — |
| 1937S | 34,500,000 | — | .10 | .15 | .25 | .60 | 1.50 | 1.75 | 10.50 | — |
| 1938 | 156,696,734 | — | .10 | .15 | .20 | .50 | 1.00 | 1.60 | 7.00 | 95.00 |
| 1938D | 20,010,000 | .15 | .15 | .25 | .30 | .75 | 1.50 | 2.00 | 9.00 | — |
| 1938S | 15,180,000 | .30 | .35 | .45 | .60 | .80 | 1.25 | 1.80 | 11.00 | — |
| 1939 | 316,479,520 | — | .10 | .15 | .20 | .25 | .40 | .65 | 4.25 | 75.00 |
| 1939D | 15,160,000 | .35 | .40 | .50 | .60 | .85 | 1.90 | 2.25 | 12.50 | — |
| 1939S | 52,070,000 | — | .15 | .20 | .25 | .45 | .90 | 1.15 | 15.00 | — |
| 1940 | 586,825,872 | — | — | .15 | .20 | .25 | .40 | .85 | 4.25 | 75.00 |
| 1940D | 81,390,000 | — | .10 | .15 | .20 | .25 | .50 | .90 | 5.25 | — |
| 1940S | 112,940,000 | — | .10 | .15 | .20 | .25 | .75 | 1.00 | 7.00 | — |
| 1941 | 887,039,100 | — | — | — | — | .15 | .30 | .85 | 4.25 | 70.00 |
| 1941D | 128,700,000 | — | — | — | .10 | .15 | 1.00 | 1.75 | 8.50 | — |
| 1941S | 92,360,000 | — | — | — | .10 | .15 | 1.25 | 2.00 | 9.00 | — |
| 1942 | 657,828,600 | — | — | — | — | .15 | .25 | .50 | 2.75 | 77.00 |
| 1942D | 206,698,000 | — | — | — | .10 | .15 | .25 | .50 | 4.25 | — |
| 1942S | 85,590,000 | — | — | — | .15 | .25 | 1.50 | 4.00 | 24.00 | — |

## Steel composition

**Weight:** 2.7 grams. **Composition:** steel coated with zinc.

| Date | Mintage | G-4 | VG-8 | F-12 | VF-20 | XF-40 | AU-50 | MS-60 | MS-65 | Prf-65 |
|---|---|---|---|---|---|---|---|---|---|---|
| 1943 | 684,628,670 | — | — | — | — | .40 | .60 | .70 | 2.80 | — |
| 1943D | 217,660,000 | — | — | — | — | .45 | .65 | 1.00 | 5.00 | — |
| 1943S | 191,550,000 | — | — | — | — | .45 | .70 | 1.50 | 8.50 | — |

## Copper-zinc composition

**Weight:** 3.11 grams. **Composition:** 95% copper, 5% zinc. **Notes:** The 1955 "doubled die" has distinct doubling of the date and lettering on the obverse.

| Date | Mintage | XF-40 | MS-60 | Prf-65 | Date | Mintage | XF-40 | MS-60 | Prf-65 |
|---|---|---|---|---|---|---|---|---|---|
| 1944 | 1,435,400,000 | .10 | .40 | — | 1946S | 198,100,000 | .15 | .50 | — |
| 1944D | 430,578,000 | .10 | .45 | — | 1947 | 190,555,000 | .15 | 1.00 | — |
| 1944D/S | — | 150. | 375. | — | 1947D | 194,750,000 | .10 | .40 | — |
| 1944S | 282,760,000 | .15 | .45 | — | 1947S | 99,000,000 | .15 | .45 | — |
| 1945 | 1,040,515,000 | .10 | .50 | — | 1948 | 317,570,000 | .10 | .50 | — |
| 1945D | 226,268,000 | .10 | .70 | — | 1948D | 172,637,000 | .10 | .45 | — |
| 1945S | 181,770,000 | .15 | .45 | — | 1948S | 81,735,000 | .15 | .50 | — |
| 1946 | 991,655,000 | .10 | .30 | — | 1949 | 217,775,000 | .10 | .40 | — |
| 1946D | 315,690,000 | .10 | .45 | — | 1949D | 153,132,000 | .10 | .40 | — |

| Date | Mintage | XF-40 | MS-60 | Prf-65 |
|---|---|---|---|---|
| 1949S | 64,290,000 | .20 | 1.00 | — |
| 1950 | 272,686,386 | .10 | .50 | 35.00 |
| 1950D | 334,950,000 | .10 | .50 | — |
| 1950S | 118,505,000 | .15 | .80 | — |
| 1951 | 295,633,500 | .10 | .90 | 35.00 |
| 1951D | 625,355,000 | .10 | .50 | — |
| 1951S | 136,010,000 | .15 | .75 | — |
| 1952 | 186,856,980 | .10 | .50 | 30.00 |
| 1952D | 746,130,000 | .10 | .50 | — |
| 1952S | 137,800,004 | .15 | .75 | — |
| 1953 | 256,883,800 | .10 | .50 | 19.00 |
| 1953D | 700,515,000 | .10 | .50 | — |
| 1953S | 181,835,000 | .15 | .45 | — |
| 1954 | 71,873,350 | .15 | .75 | 10.00 |
| 1954D | 251,552,500 | .10 | .25 | — |
| 1954S | 96,190,000 | .15 | .35 | — |
| 1955 | 330,958,000 | .10 | .20 | 8.00 |
| 1955 doubled die | — | 440. | 700. | — |
| 1955D | 563,257,500 | .10 | .20 | — |
| 1955S | 44,610,000 | .25 | .60 | — |
| 1956 | 421,414,384 | — | .15 | 2.25 |
| 1956D | 1,098,201,100 | — | .15 | — |
| 1957 | 283,787,952 | — | .15 | 1.40 |
| 1957D | 1,051,342,000 | — | .15 | — |
| 1958 | 253,400,652 | — | .15 | 1.75 |
| 1958D | 800,953,300 | — | .15 | — |

## Lincoln Memorial reverse

**Reverse designer:** Frank Gasparro. **Weight:** 3.11 grams (1959-82) and 2.5 grams (1982-present). **Composition:** 95% copper, 5% tin and zinc (1959-62); 95% copper, 5% zinc (1962-82); and 97.6% zinc, 2.4% copper (1982-present). **Notes:** The dates were modified in 1960, 1970 and 1982, resulting in large-date and small-date varieties for those years. The 1972 "doubled die" shows doubling of "In God We Trust." The 1979-S Type II proof has a clearer mintmark than the Type I proof. Some 1982 cents have the predominantly copper composition; others have the predominantly zinc composition. They can be distinguished by weight. The 1983 "doubled die reverse" shows doubling of "United States of America." The 1984 "doubled die" shows doubling of Lincoln's ear on the obverse.

| Date | Mintage | XF-40 | MS-65 | Prf-65 |
|---|---|---|---|---|
| 1959 | 610,864,291 | — | .20 | 1.00 |
| 1959D | 1,279,760,000 | — | .20 | — |
| 1960 small date | 588,096,602 | 1.50 | 4.50 | 15.00 |
| 1960 large date | Inc. Ab. | — | .15 | .95 |
| 1960D small date | 1,580,884,000 | — | .25 | — |
| 1960D large date | Inc. Ab. | — | .15 | — |
| 1961 | 756,373,244 | — | .15 | .60 |
| 1961D | 1,753,266,700 | — | .15 | — |
| 1962 | 609,263,019 | — | .15 | .60 |
| 1962D | 1,793,148,400 | — | .15 | — |
| 1963 | 757,185,645 | — | .15 | .60 |
| 1963D | 1,774,020,400 | — | .15 | — |
| 1964 | 2,652,525,762 | — | .15 | .60 |
| 1964D | 3,799,071,500 | — | .15 | — |
| 1965 | 1,497,224,900 | — | .15 | — |
| 1966 | 2,188,147,783 | — | .15 | — |
| 1967 | 3,048,667,100 | — | .15 | — |
| 1968 | 1,707,880,970 | — | .15 | — |
| 1968D | 2,886,269,600 | — | .15 | — |
| 1968S | 261,311,510 | — | .15 | .85 |
| 1969 | 1,136,910,000 | — | .25 | — |
| 1969D | 4,002,832,200 | — | .15 | — |
| 1969S | 547,309,631 | — | .15 | .85 |
| 1970 | 1,898,315,000 | — | .15 | — |
| 1970D | 2,891,438,900 | — | .15 | — |
| 1970S | 693,192,814 | — | .15 | .85 |
| 1970S small date | — | — | 45.00 | .80 |
| 1971 | 1,919,490,000 | — | .25 | — |
| 1971D | 2,911,045,600 | — | .25 | — |
| 1971S | 528,354,192 | — | .15 | .85 |
| 1972 | 2,933,255,000 | — | .15 | — |
| 1972 doubled die | — | 120. | 300. | — |
| 1972D | 2,665,071,400 | — | .15 | — |
| 1972S | 380,200,104 | — | .15 | .90 |
| 1973 | 3,728,245,000 | — | .10 | — |
| 1973D | 3,549,576,588 | — | .10 | — |
| 1973S | 319,937,634 | — | .15 | .80 |
| 1974 | 4,232,140,523 | — | .10 | — |
| 1974D | 4,235,098,000 | — | .10 | — |
| 1974S | 412,039,228 | — | .15 | .80 |
| 1975 | 5,451,476,142 | — | .10 | — |
| 1975D | 4,505,245,300 | — | .10 | — |
| 1975S | (2,845,450) | — | — | 4.50 |
| 1976 | 4,674,292,426 | — | .10 | — |
| 1976D | 4,221,592,455 | — | .10 | — |
| 1976S | (4,149,730) | — | — | 3.00 |
| 1977 | 4,469,930,000 | — | .10 | — |
| 1977D | 4,149,062,300 | — | .10 | — |
| 1977S | (3,251,152) | — | — | 1.95 |
| 1978 | 5,558,605,000 | — | .10 | — |
| 1978D | 4,280,233,400 | — | .10 | — |
| 1978S | (3,127,781) | — | — | 1.90 |
| 1979 | 6,018,515,000 | — | .10 | — |
| 1979D | 4,139,357,254 | — | .10 | — |
| 1979S T-I | (3,677,175) | — | — | 2.00 |
| 1979S T-II | (Inc. Ab.) | — | — | 2.20 |
| 1980 | 7,414,705,000 | — | .10 | — |
| 1980D | 5,140,098,660 | — | .10 | — |
| 1980S | (3,554,806) | — | — | 1.35 |
| 1981 | 7,491,750,000 | — | .10 | — |
| 1981D | 5,373,235,677 | — | .10 | — |
| 1981S T-I | (4,063,083) | — | — | 1.00 |
| 1981S T-II | (Inc. Ab.) | — | — | 28.00 |
| 1982 copper large date | 10,712,525,000 | — | .10 | — |
| 1982 copper small date | | — | .15 | — |
| 1982 zinc large date | | — | .35 | — |
| 1982 zinc small date | | — | .75 | — |
| 1982D copper large date | 6,012,979,368 | — | .10 | — |
| 1982D zinc large date | | — | .20 | — |
| 1982D zinc small date | | — | .10 | — |
| 1982S | (3,857,479) | — | .10 | 2.25 |
| 1983 | 7,752,355,000 | — | .10 | — |
| 1983 doubled die rev. | — | | 195. | — |
| 1983D | 6,467,199,428 | — | .10 | — |
| 1983S | (3,279,126) | — | — | 3.50 |
| 1984 | 8,151,079,000 | — | .10 | — |
| 1984 doubled die | — | | 130. | — |
| 1984D | 5,569,238,906 | — | .25 | — |
| 1984S | (3,065,110) | — | — | 4.50 |
| 1985 | 5,648,489,887 | — | .10 | — |
| 1985D | 5,287,399,926 | — | .10 | — |
| 1985S | (3,362,821) | — | — | 3.00 |
| 1986 | 4,491,395,493 | — | .15 | — |
| 1986D | 4,442,866,698 | — | .10 | — |
| 1986S | (3,010,497) | — | — | 8.00 |
| 1987 | 4,682,466,931 | — | .10 | — |
| 1987D | 4,879,389,514 | — | .10 | — |
| 1987S | (4,227,728) | — | — | 3.95 |

PRICING SECTION

**1955 doubled die**

**1972 doubled die**

**1983 doubled die**

**Small date**

**Large date**

**Large date**

**Small date**

**Large date**

**Small date**

| Date | Mintage | XF-40 | MS-65 | Prf-65 | Date | Mintage | XF-40 | MS-65 | Prf-65 |
|------|---------|-------|-------|--------|------|---------|-------|-------|--------|
| 1988 | 6,092,810,000 | — | .10 | — | 1991D | — | — | .10 | — |
| 1988D | 5,253,740,443 | — | .10 | — | 1991S | Proof only | — | — | 9.00 |
| 1988S | (3,262,948) | — | — | 4.50 | 1992 | — | — | .10 | — |
| 1989 | 7,261,535,000 | — | .10 | — | 1992D | — | — | .10 | — |
| 1989D | 5,345,467,111 | — | .10 | — | 1992S | Proof only | — | — | 7.00 |
| 1989S | (3,220,194) | — | — | 4.50 | 1993 | — | — | — | — |
| 1990 | 6,851,765,000 | — | .10 | — | 1993D | — | — | — | — |
| 1990D | 4,922,894,533 | — | .10 | — | 1993S | Proof only | — | — | 6.00 |
| 1990S | Proof only | — | — | 8.00 | 1994 | — | — | .10 | — |
| 1990 no S | — | — | — | 1850. | 1994D | — | — | .10 | — |
| 1991 | — | — | .10 | — | 1994S | Proof only | — | — | 7.00 |

# Two-cent

Small motto

Large motto

**Designer:** James B. Longacre. **Size:** 23 millimeters. **Weight:** 6.22 grams. **Composition:** 95% copper, 5% tin and zinc. **Notes:** The motto "In God We Trust" was modified in 1864, resulting in small-motto and large-motto varieties for that year.

| Date | Mintage | G-4 | VG-8 | F-12 | VF-20 | XF-40 | AU-50 | MS-60 | MS-65 | Prf-65 |
|------|---------|-----|------|------|-------|-------|-------|-------|-------|--------|
| 1864 SM | 19,847,500. | 60.00 | 75.00 | 100. | 135. | 230. | 325. | 550. | 1700. | 30,000. |
| 1864 LM | Inc. Ab. | 7.00 | 11.00 | 19.50 | 21.00 | 27.00 | 45.00 | 95.00 | 400. | 900. |
| 1865 | 13,640,000 | 7.00 | 11.00 | 19.50 | 21.00 | 27.00 | 45.00 | 95.00 | 400. | 900. |
| 1866 | 3,177,000 | 7.00 | 11.00 | 19.50 | 21.00 | 27.00 | 45.00 | 95.00 | 510. | 900. |
| 1867 | 2,938,750 | 7.00 | 11.00 | 19.50 | 21.00 | 27.00 | 60.00 | 110. | 450. | 900. |
| 1868 | 2,803,750 | 7.00 | 11.00 | 19.50 | 24.00 | 33.00 | 65.00 | 145. | 450. | 900. |
| 1869 | 1,546,000 | 8.50 | 11.00 | 19.50 | 22.00 | 36.00 | 75.00 | 135. | 465. | 900. |
| 1870 | 861,250 | 8.00 | 12.00 | 18.50 | 32.50 | 57.00 | 90.00 | 210. | 630. | 900. |
| 1871 | 721,250 | 10.00 | 15.00 | 22.00 | 40.00 | 75.00 | 120. | 235. | 690. | 900. |
| 1872 | 65,000 | 75.00 | 120. | 170. | 250. | 375. | 490. | 775. | 2750. | 900. |
| 1873 | Est. 1100 | — | — | Proof only | | — | — | — | — | 2000. |
| | | Impaired proof | | 900. | 930. | 960. | 990. | — | — | — |

# Silver three-cent

## Type I

**Designer:** James B. Longacre. **Size:** 14 millimeters. **Weight:** 0.8 grams. **Composition:** 75% silver (0.0193 ounces), 25% copper. **Notes:** The Type I design has no outlines in the star.

| Date | Mintage | G-4 | VG-8 | F-12 | VF-20 | XF-40 | AU-50 | MS-60 | MS-65 | Prf-65 |
|------|---------|-----|------|------|-------|-------|-------|-------|-------|--------|
| 1851 | 5,447,400 | 13.50 | 15.00 | 20.00 | 25.00 | 65.00 | 120. | 145. | 1350. | — |
| 1851O | 720,000 | 18.00 | 22.00 | 35.00 | 54.00 | 130. | 225. | 375. | 1850. | — |
| 1852 | 18,663,500 | 13.50 | 15.00 | 20.00 | 25.00 | 60.00 | 120. | 145. | 1350. | — |
| 1853 | 11,400,000 | 13.50 | 15.00 | 20.00 | 25.00 | 50.00 | 130. | 145. | 1350. | — |

## Type II

**Weight:** 0.75 grams. **Composition:** 90% silver (0.0218 ounces), 10% copper. **Notes:** The Type II design has three lines outlining the star.

# 1851-O Silver Three-Cent
## Grade XF-40

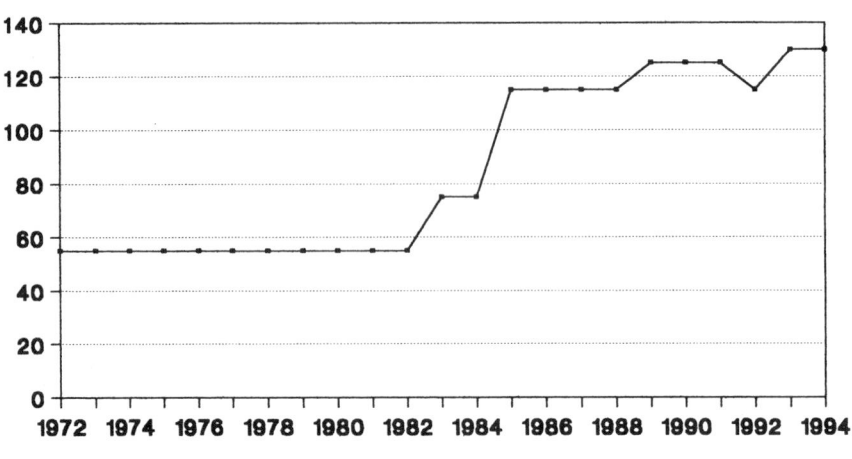

—•— **Retail Price**

**Source: CQIN PRICES**

| Date | Mintage | G-4 | VG-8 | F-12 | VF-20 | XF-40 | AU-50 | MS-60 | MS-65 | Prf-65 |
|------|---------|-----|------|------|-------|-------|-------|-------|-------|--------|
| 1854 | 671,000 | 13.50 | 17.00 | 25.00 | 38.00 | 110. | 230. | 280. | 4500. | 25,000. |
| 1855 | 139,000 | 21.00 | 29.00 | 49.00 | 85.00 | 165. | 250. | 440. | 12,000. | 15,000. |
| 1856 | 1,458,000 | 14.00 | 18.00 | 25.00 | 40.00 | 95.00 | 210. | 215. | 6700. | — |
| 1857 | 1,042,000 | 13.50 | 17.00 | 22.00 | 35.00 | 85.00 | 225. | 280. | 4500. | 9750. |
| 1858 | 1,604,000 | 13.50 | 17.00 | 25.00 | 40.00 | 95.00 | 210. | 215. | 4500. | 7000. |

**Type III**

**Notes:** The Type III design has two lines outlining the star.

| Date | Mintage | G-4 | VG-8 | F-12 | VF-20 | XF-40 | AU-50 | MS-60 | MS-65 | Prf-65 |
|------|---------|-----|------|------|-------|-------|-------|-------|-------|--------|
| 1859 | 365,000 | 13.50 | 17.00 | 22.00 | 32.00 | 55.00 | 125. | 150. | 1050. | 2250. |
| 1860 | 287,000 | 17.00 | 20.00 | 25.00 | 32.00 | 55.00 | 125. | 150. | 1050. | 7500. |
| 1861 | 498,000 | 14.00 | 18.00 | 24.00 | 32.00 | 68.00 | 125. | 150. | 1050. | 2250. |
| 1862 | 343,550 | 17.00 | 20.00 | 25.00 | 32.00 | 55.00 | 125. | 150. | 1050. | 2500. |
| 1863 | 21,460 | 200. | 225. | 280. | 315. | 350. | 375. | 565. | 2750. | 1500. |
| 1864 | 12,470 | 250. | 275. | 325. | 375. | 425. | 465. | 565. | 2150. | 1500. |
| 1865 | 8,500 | 260. | 300. | 350. | 375. | 400. | 450. | 565. | 3125. | 1500. |
| 1866 | 22,725 | 225. | 250. | 280. | 325. | 375. | 450. | 600. | 2650. | 1500. |
| 1867 | 4,625 | 285. | 325. | 350. | 375. | 400. | 485. | 625. | 4100. | 1500. |
| 1868 | 4,100 | 285. | 325. | 350. | 375. | 400. | 440. | 625. | 4800. | 1500. |
| 1869 | 5,100 | 285. | 325. | 350. | 375. | 460. | 525. | 625. | 4550. | 1500. |
| 1870 | 4,000 | 285. | 325. | 350. | 375. | 400. | 440. | 625. | 4600. | 1625. |
| 1871 | 4,360 | 285. | 325. | 350. | 375. | 400. | 440. | 565. | 2150. | 1500. |
| 1872 | 1,950 | 325. | 375. | 450. | 550. | 650. | 750. | 950. | 6400. | 1500. |
| 1873 | 600 | — | — | Proof only | | — | — | — | — | 1750. |
| | | Impaired proof | | 750. | 850. | 950. | 1200. | — | — | — |

# Nickel three-cent

**Designer:** James B. Longacre. **Size:** 17.9 millimeters. **Weight:** 1.94 grams. **Composition:** 75% copper, 25% nickel.

| Date | Mintage | G-4 | VG-8 | F-12 | VF-20 | XF-40 | AU-50 | MS-60 | MS-65 | Prf-65 |
|------|---------|-----|------|------|-------|-------|-------|-------|-------|--------|
| 1865 | 11,382,000 | 7.00 | 7.25 | 7.75 | 8.50 | 15.00 | 37.50 | 95.00 | 750. | 1700. |
| 1866 | 4,801,000 | 7.00 | 7.25 | 7.75 | 8.50 | 15.00 | 37.50 | 95.00 | 750. | 1250. |
| 1867 | 3,915,000 | 7.00 | 7.25 | 7.75 | 8.50 | 15.00 | 37.50 | 95.00 | 750. | 1025. |
| 1868 | 3,252,000 | 7.00 | 7.25 | 7.75 | 8.50 | 15.00 | 37.50 | 95.00 | 750. | 1025. |
| 1869 | 1,604,000 | 7.00 | 7.25 | 7.75 | 8.50 | 15.00 | 40.00 | 95.00 | 750. | 900. |
| 1870 | 1,335,000 | 7.00 | 7.75 | 8.50 | 10.00 | 16.00 | 42.00 | 100. | 750. | 1000. |
| 1871 | 604,000 | 7.00 | 7.75 | 8.75 | 11.00 | 18.00 | 45.00 | 100. | 750. | 550. |
| 1872 | 862,000 | 7.00 | 7.50 | 8.50 | 10.00 | 17.00 | 43.00 | 100. | 1250. | 875. |
| 1873 | 1,173,000 | 7.00 | 7.25 | 7.75 | 8.50 | 16.00 | 42.00 | 100. | 2400. | 900. |
| 1874 | 790,000 | 7.00 | 7.50 | 8.50 | 10.00 | 17.00 | 43.00 | 110. | 2000. | 875. |
| 1875 | 228,000 | 8.00 | 9.00 | 11.50 | 16.00 | 25.00 | 63.00 | 160. | 750. | 1300. |
| 1876 | 162,000 | 11.00 | 14.00 | 17.00 | 24.00 | 38.00 | 100. | 175. | 2150. | 550. |
| 1877 | Est. 900 | — | — | Proof only | 900. | — | — | — | — | 1400. |
|  |  | Impaired proof | | 875. | | 950. | 975. | | | |
| 1878 | 2,350 | — | — | Proof only | 400. | — | — | — | — | 700. |
|  |  | Impaired proof | | 375. | | 425. | 450. | | | |
| 1879 | 41,200 | 45.00 | 50.00 | 60.00 | 70.00 | 80.00 | 120. | 240. | 750. | 650. |
| 1880 | 24,955 | 63.00 | 70.00 | 90.00 | 105. | 130. | 150. | 265. | 750. | 650. |
| 1881 | 1,080,575 | 7.00 | 7.25 | 7.50 | 8.00 | 14.00 | 38.00 | 95.00 | 750. | 600. |
| 1882 | 25,300 | 63.00 | 70.00 | 84.00 | 95.00 | 110. | 145. | 250. | 1000. | 650. |
| 1883 | 10,609 | 125. | 145. | 175. | 200. | 240. | 270. | 375. | 2900. | 650. |
| 1884 | 5,642 | 290. | 330. | 350. | 380. | 425. | 450. | 550. | 4800. | 650. |
| 1885 | 4,790 | 350. | 380. | 425. | 460. | 500. | 600. | 725. | 1950. | 675. |
| 1886 | 4,290 | — | — | Proof only | | — | — | — | — | 650. |
|  |  | Impaired proof | | — | — | — | — | | | |
| 1887/6 | 7,961 | — | — | Proof only | | — | — | — | — | 625. |
|  |  | Impaired proof | | — | — | — | — | | | |
| 1887 | Inc. Ab. | 240. | 250. | 275. | 300. | 325. | 425. | 500. | 1175. | 700. |
| 1888 | 41,083 | 35.00 | 40.00 | 45.00 | 50.00 | 70.00 | 110. | 270. | 750. | 650. |
| 1889 | 21,561 | 63.00 | 70.00 | 90.00 | 105. | 125. | 150. | 260. | 750. | 650. |

# Half dimes

## Flowing Hair

**Designer:** Robert Scot. **Size:** 16.5 millimeters. **Weight:** 1.35 grams. **Composition:** 89.24% silver (0.0388 ounces), 10.76% copper.

| Date | Mintage | G-4 | VG-8 | F-12 | VF-20 | XF-40 | MS-60 |
|------|---------|-----|------|------|-------|-------|-------|
| 1794 | 86,416 | 850. | 1050. | 1450. | 2000. | 3450. | 8500. |
| 1795 | Inc. Ab. | 600. | 750. | 1000. | 1400. | 2650. | 5050. |

# Draped Bust

## Small-eagle reverse

**Designer:** Robert Scot. **Size:** 16.5 millimeters. **Weight:** 1.35 grams. **Composition:** 89.24% silver (0.0388 ounces), 10.76% copper. **Notes:** Some 1796 strikes have "Liberty" spelled as "Libekty." The 1797 strikes have either 13, 15 or 16 stars on the obverse.

| Date | Mintage | G-4 | VG-8 | F-12 | VF-20 | XF-40 | MS-60 |
|------|---------|-----|------|------|-------|-------|-------|
| 1796 | 10,230 | 825. | 1150 | 1550. | 2600. | 4150. | 5650. |
| 1796 "Liberty" | Inc. Ab. | 825. | 1150. | 1550. | 2600. | 4150. | — |
| 1796/5 | Inc. Ab. | 1025. | 1750. | 2000. | 3350. | 5450. | 9000. |
| 1797 13 stars | 44,527 | 1100. | 1425. | 1850. | 3100. | 5150. | 11,500. |
| 1797 15 stars | Inc. Ab. | 775. | 950. | 1250. | 2000. | 3650. | 5650. |
| 1797 16 stars | Inc. Ab. | 800. | 1000. | 1300. | 2150. | 3350. | 5650. |

## Heraldic-eagle reverse

**Notes:** Some 1800 strikes have "Liberty" spelled as "Liberty."

| Date | Mintage | G-4 | VG-8 | F-12 | VF-20 | XF-40 | MS-60 |
|------|---------|-----|------|------|-------|-------|-------|
| 1800 | 24,000 | 500. | 625. | 800. | 1250. | 2450. | 5050. |
| 1800 "Libekty" | Inc. Ab. | 550. | 675. | 875. | 1375. | 2575. | 5050. |
| 1801 | 33,910 | 575. | 700. | 925. | 1500. | 2650. | 10,000. |
| 1802 | 13,010 | 9500. | 13,500. | 20,000. | 35,000. | 60,000. | — |
| 1803 | 37,850 | 500. | 625. | 800. | 1250. | 2450. | 5050. |
| 1805 | 15,600 | 600. | 750. | 975. | 1550. | 2750. | — |

# Liberty Cap

**Designer:** William Kneass. **Size:** 15.5 millimeters. **Weight:** 1.35 grams. **Composition:** 89.24% silver (0.0388 ounces), 10.76% copper. **Notes:** Design modifications in 1835, 1836 and 1837 resulted in variety combinations with large and small dates, and large and small "5C." inscriptions on the reverse.

| Date | Mintage | G-4 | VG-8 | F-12 | VF-20 | XF-40 | AU-50 | MS-60 | MS-65 |
|------|---------|-----|------|------|-------|-------|-------|-------|-------|
| 1829 | 1,230,000 | 12.00 | 18.00 | 25.00 | 60.00 | 125. | 225. | 290. | 3000. |
| 1830 | 1,240,000 | 12.00 | 18.00 | 25.00 | 60.00 | 125. | 225. | 290. | 3000. |
| 1831 | 1,242,700 | 12.00 | 18.00 | 25.00 | 60.00 | 125. | 225. | 290. | 3000. |
| 1832 | 965,000 | 12.00 | 18.00 | 25.00 | 60.00 | 125. | 300. | 450. | 7000. |
| 1833 | 1,370,000 | 12.00 | 18.00 | 25.00 | 60.00 | 125. | 230. | 325. | 3500. |
| 1834 | 1,480,000 | 12.00 | 18.00 | 25.00 | 60.00 | 125. | 230. | 290. | 3000. |
| 1835 large date, large "5C." | 2,760,000 | 12.00 | 18.00 | 25.00 | 60.00 | 110. | 250. | 290. | 3000. |
| 1835 large date, small "5C." | Inc. Ab. | 12.00 | 18.00 | 25.00 | 60.00 | 125. | 230. | 290. | 3000. |

# 1802 Half Dime
## Grade F-12

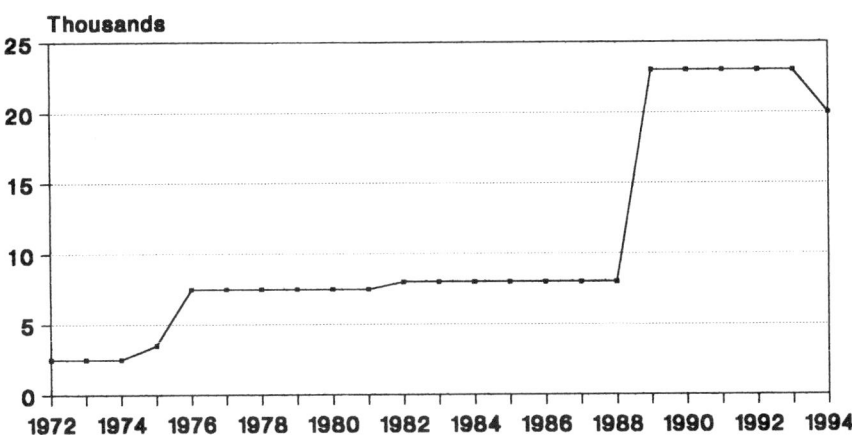

**Thousands**

—•— **Retail Price**

**Source: COIN PRICES**

| Date | Mintage | G-4 | VG-8 | F-12 | VF-20 | XF-40 | AU-50 | MS-60 | MS-65 |
|---|---|---|---|---|---|---|---|---|---|
| 1835 small date, large "5C." | | | | | | | | | |
| | Inc. Ab. | 12.00 | 18.00 | 25.00 | 60.00 | 125. | 225. | 290. | 3000. |
| 1835 small date, small "5C." | | | | | | | | | |
| | Inc. Ab. | 12.00 | 18.00 | 25.00 | 60.00 | 125. | 225. | 290. | 3000. |
| 1836 large "5C." | | | | | | | | | |
| | 1,900,000 | 12.00 | 18.00 | 25.00 | 60.00 | 125. | 225. | 290. | 3000. |
| 1836 small "5C." | | | | | | | | | |
| | Inc. Ab. | 12.00 | 18.00 | 25.00 | 60.00 | 125. | 225. | 290. | 3000. |
| 1837 large "5C." | | | | | | | | | |
| | 2,276,000 | 12.00 | 18.00 | 25.00 | 60.00 | 125. | 225. | 290. | 3000. |
| 1837 small "5C." | | | | | | | | | |
| | Inc. Ab. | 25.00 | 40.00 | 60.00 | 105. | 150. | 350. | 1250. | 8500. |

# Seated Liberty

## No stars around rim

**Designer:** Christian Gobrecht. **Size:** 15.5 millimeters. **Weight:** 1.34 grams. **Composition:** 90% silver (0.0388 ounces), 10% copper. **Notes:** A design modification in 1837 resulted in small-date and large-date varieties for that year.

| Date | Mintage | G-4 | VG-8 | F-12 | VF-20 | XF-40 | AU-50 | MS-60 | MS-65 |
|---|---|---|---|---|---|---|---|---|---|
| 1837 sm. date | Inc. Ab. | 25.00 | 35.00 | 53.00 | 100. | 210. | 375. | 590. | 4500. |
| 1837 lg. date | Inc. Ab. | 25.00 | 35.00 | 53.00 | 100. | 210. | 375. | 590. | 4500. |
| 1838O | 70,000 | 70.00 | 110. | 225. | 400. | 750. | 2500. | — | — |

PRICING SECTION

# 1846 Half Dime
## Grade XF-40

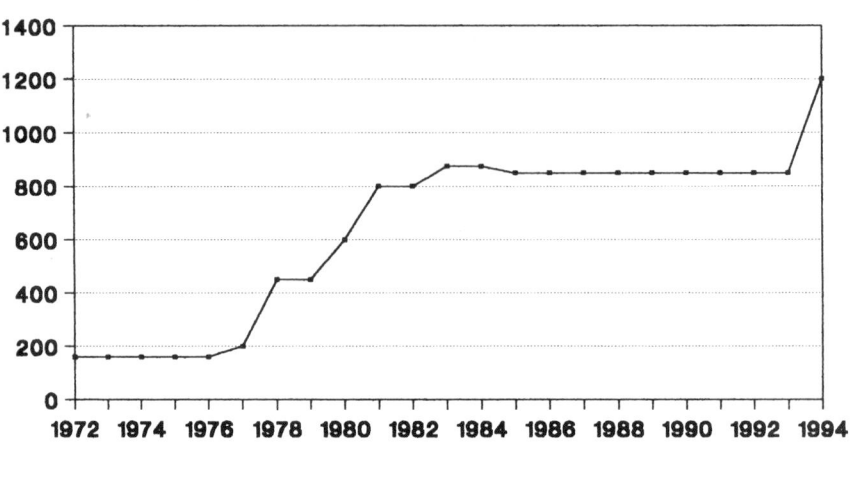

— Retail Price

Source: COIN PRICES

## Stars around rim

**Notes:** The two varieties of 1838 are distinguished by the size of the stars on the obverse. The 1839-O with reverse of 1838-O was struck from rusted reverse dies. The result is a bumpy surface on this variety's reverse.

| Date | Mintage | G-4 | VG-8 | F-12 | VF-20 | XF-40 | AU-50 | MS-60 | MS-65 |
|---|---|---|---|---|---|---|---|---|---|
| 1838 lg.stars | 2,255,000 | 5.00 | 6.25 | 10.00 | 25.00 | 65.00 | 135. | 250. | 2100. |
| 1838 sm.stars | Inc. Ab. | 20.00 | 30.00 | 50.00 | 125. | 225. | 285. | 750. | 10,500. |
| 1839 | 1,069,150 | 8.00 | 10.00 | 13.00 | 29.00 | 70.00 | 170. | 250. | 2100. |
| 1839O | 1,034,039 | 9.00 | 12.00 | 16.00 | 31.00 | 75.00 | 200. | 400. | 2100. |
| 1839O rev. 1838O | — | 375. | 575. | 750. | 1200. | 2250. | 3500. | — | — |
| 1840 | 1,344,085 | 5.00 | 6.25 | 13.00 | 21.00 | 65.00 | 135. | 450. | 2100. |
| 1840O | 935,000 | 10.00 | 13.00 | 18.00 | 35.00 | 85.00 | 200. | 600. | 10,500. |

## Drapery added to Liberty

**Notes:** In 1840 drapery was added to Liberty's left elbow. Varieties for the 1848 Philadelphia strikes are distinguished by the size of the numerals in the date.

| Date | Mintage | G-4 | VG-8 | F-12 | VF-20 | XF-40 | AU-50 | MS-60 | MS-65 |
|---|---|---|---|---|---|---|---|---|---|
| 1840 | Inc. Ab. | 20.00 | 32.50 | 50.00 | 75.00 | 150. | 250. | 700. | 6500. |
| 1840O | Inc. Ab. | 30.00 | 50.00 | 80.00 | 125. | 325. | 950. | — | — |
| 1841 | 1,150,000 | 5.00 | 6.25 | 8.75 | 22.00 | 55.00 | 95.00 | 160. | 1750. |
| 1841O | 815,000 | 10.00 | 15.00 | 22.50 | 40.00 | 85.00 | 200. | 650. | — |
| 1842 | 815,000 | 5.00 | 6.25 | 8.75 | 22.00 | 55.00 | 95.00 | 160. | 1750. |
| 1842O | 350,000 | 28.00 | 40.00 | 65.00 | 225. | 700. | 1800. | — | — |
| 1843 | 1,165,000 | 5.00 | 6.25 | 8.75 | 18.00 | 41.00 | 95.00 | 160. | 1750. |
| 1844 | 430,000 | 6.50 | 8.50 | 11.00 | 24.00 | 60.00 | 110. | 225. | 2450. |
| 1844O | 220,000 | 60.00 | 85.00 | 195. | 350. | 950. | 2800. | — | 15,000. |
| 1845 | 1,564,000 | 5.00 | 6.25 | 8.75 | 22.00 | 44.00 | 95.00 | 160. | 1750. |
| 1845/1845 | Inc. Ab. | 8.00 | 11.00 | 15.00 | 30.00 | 75.00 | 200. | 225. | 5000. |
| 1846 | 27,000 | 150. | 200. | 350. | 550. | 1200. | 2850. | — | — |
| 1847 | 1,274,000 | 6.00 | 7.00 | 8.00 | 18.00 | 55.00 | 95.00 | 225. | 2450. |
| 1848 med. date | 668,000 | 7.00 | 8.50 | 11.00 | 32.00 | 60.00 | 125. | 225. | 2450. |
| 1848 lg. date | Inc. Ab. | 15.00 | 20.00 | 30.00 | 50.00 | 125. | 300. | 425. | 2450. |
| 1848O | 600,000 | 12.00 | 17.50 | 25.00 | 42.50 | 90.00 | 225. | 600. | 5000. |
| 1849/8 | 1,309,000 | 12.00 | 17.50 | 25.00 | 45.00 | 100. | 180. | 500. | 5000. |
| 1849/6 | Inc. Ab. | 10.00 | 14.00 | 20.00 | 35.00 | 75.00 | 175. | 425. | 5000. |
| 1849 | Inc. Ab. | 6.00 | 8.00 | 11.00 | 18.00 | 45.00 | 95.00 | 600. | 5000. |
| 1849O | 140,000 | 22.00 | 40.00 | 75.00 | 200. | 450. | 800. | 1200. | 16,000. |
| 1850 | 955,000 | 5.00 | 6.25 | 8.75 | 18.00 | 41.00 | 175. | 250. | 2750. |
| 1850O | 690,000 | 11.00 | 16.00 | 22.50 | 50.00 | 100. | 350. | 800. | 4000. |
| 1851 | 781,000 | 5.00 | 6.25 | 8.75 | 18.00 | 50.00 | 115. | 300. | 2450. |
| 1851O | 860,000 | 10.00 | 15.00 | 25.00 | 35.00 | 75.00 | 165. | 800. | 2450. |
| 1852 | 1,000,500 | 6.00 | 7.00 | 12.50 | 18.00 | 41.00 | 115. | 160. | 1750. |
| 1852O | 260,000 | 30.00 | 48.00 | 70.00 | 125. | 265. | 800. | — | 11,000. |
| 1853 | 135,000 | 25.00 | 38.00 | 55.00 | 85.00 | 185. | 350. | 500. | 8500. |
| 1853O | 160,000 | 135. | 190. | 275. | 450. | 1000. | 3000. | — | — |

## Arrows at date

**Weight:** 1.24 grams. **Composition:** 90% silver (0.0362 ounces), 10% copper.

| Date | Mintage | G-4 | VG-8 | F-12 | VF-20 | XF-40 | AU-50 | MS-60 | MS-65 | Prf-65 |
|---|---|---|---|---|---|---|---|---|---|---|
| 1853 | 13,210,020 | 5.00 | 6.25 | 8.75 | 17.00 | 50.00 | 100. | 160. | 2450. | 20,000. |
| 1853O | 2,200,000 | 6.00 | 8.00 | 11.00 | 24.00 | 60.00 | 125. | 325. | — | — |
| 1854 | 5,740,000 | 5.00 | 6.50 | 8.75 | 17.00 | 50.00 | 135. | 250. | 4550. | 20,000. |
| 1854O | 1,560,000 | 7.00 | 9.00 | 12.00 | 20.00 | 55.00 | 175. | 700. | — | — |
| 1855 | 1,750,000 | 5.50 | 7.00 | 12.00 | 20.00 | 55.00 | 135. | 250. | 5000. | 20,000. |
| 1855O | 600,000 | 12.00 | 17.00 | 25.00 | 55.00 | 125. | 275. | 1000. | — | — |

## Arrows at date removed

**Notes:** On the 1858/inverted date variety, the date was engraved into the die upside down and then re-engraved right side up. Another 1858 variety has the date doubled.

| Date | Mintage | G-4 | VG-8 | F-12 | VF-20 | XF-40 | AU-50 | MS-60 | MS-65 | Prf-65 |
|---|---|---|---|---|---|---|---|---|---|---|
| 1856 | 4,880,000 | 5.00 | 6.25 | 9.00 | 18.00 | 41.00 | 95.00 | 225. | 1750. | 22,500. |
| 1856O | 1,100,000 | 8.00 | 10.00 | 12.00 | 27.00 | 70.00 | 200. | 600. | — | — |
| 1857 | 7,280,000 | 5.00 | 6.25 | 8.75 | 15.00 | 45.00 | 95.00 | 225. | 1750. | 5000. |
| 1857O | 1,380,000 | 7.00 | 9.00 | 11.00 | 25.00 | 65.00 | 200. | 450. | — | — |
| 1858 | 3,500,000 | 5.00 | 6.25 | 8.75 | 18.00 | 45.00 | 85.00 | 160. | 1750. | 9000. |
| 1858 inverted date | | | | | | | | | | |
| | Inc. Ab. | 30.00 | 40.00 | 65.00 | 115. | 200. | 350. | 700. | — | — |
| 1858 doubled date | | | | | | | | | | |
| | Inc. Ab. | 35.00 | 50.00 | 90.00 | 140. | 240. | 500. | 1200. | — | — |
| 1858O | 1,660,000 | 7.00 | 9.00 | 12.00 | 26.00 | 65.00 | 190. | 265. | — | — |
| 1859 | 340,000 | 9.00 | 12.00 | 15.00 | 33.00 | 85.00 | 175. | 250. | 3000. | 5000. |
| 1859O | 560,000 | 8.00 | 10.00 | 13.00 | 30.00 | 80.00 | 175. | 350. | — | — |

## Transitional patterns

**Notes:** These non-circulation pieces were struck as experiments in transferring the legend "United States of America" from the reverse to the obverse.

| Date | Mintage | G-4 | VG-8 | F-12 | VF-20 | XF-40 | AU-50 | MS-60 | MS-65 | Prf-65 |
|------|---------|-----|------|------|-------|-------|-------|-------|-------|--------|
| 1859 obverse of 1859, reverse 1860 | | | | | | — | — | — | — | 17,500. |
| 1860 obverse of 1859, reverse 1860 | | | | | | — | — | 4000. | 8500. | — |

## Obverse legend

**Notes:** In 1860 the legend "United States of America" replaced the stars on the obverse.

| Date | Mintage | G-4 | VG-8 | F-12 | VF-20 | XF-40 | AU-50 | MS-60 | MS-65 | Prf-65 |
|------|---------|-----|------|------|-------|-------|-------|-------|-------|--------|
| 1860 | 799,000 | 6.00 | 7.50 | 12.50 | 25.00 | 40.00 | 70.00 | 140. | 1300. | 2150. |
| 1860O | 1,060,000 | 8.00 | 10.00 | 15.00 | 25.00 | 40.00 | 85.00 | 350. | 3550. | — |
| 1861 | 3,361,000 | 5.00 | 6.25 | 8.00 | 14.00 | 28.00 | 57.00 | 140. | 1300. | 1850. |
| 1861/0 | Inc. Ab. | 20.00 | 30.00 | 50.00 | 90.00 | 150. | 500. | 800. | — | — |
| 1862 | 1,492,550 | 5.00 | 6.25 | 8.00 | 16.00 | 30.00 | 57.00 | 140. | 1300. | 1850. |
| 1863 | 18,460 | 135. | 165. | 200. | 260. | 375. | 500. | 800. | 3250. | 3500. |
| 1863S | 100,000 | 15.00 | 23.00 | 35.00 | 65.00 | 125. | 250. | 900. | — | — |
| 1864 | 48,470 | 225. | 290. | 350. | 450. | 625. | 700. | 950. | 4500. | 3500. |
| 1864S | 90,000 | 22.50 | 34.00 | 50.00 | 80.00 | 200. | 425. | 1000. | — | — |
| 1865 | 13,500 | 200. | 250. | 325. | 425. | 500. | 800. | 1300. | 4700. | 3500. |
| 1865S | 120,000 | 12.50 | 18.00 | 25.00 | 50.00 | 100. | 300. | 975. | — | — |
| 1866 | 10,725 | 185. | 225. | 285. | 375. | 475. | 600. | 1000. | 4700. | 3500. |
| 1866S | 120,000 | 12.50 | 18.00 | 25.00 | 50.00 | 100. | 300. | 950. | 6000. | — |
| 1867 | 8,625 | 350. | 400. | 475. | 550. | 625. | 800. | 1300. | 4700. | 3500. |
| 1867S | 120,000 | 12.50 | 18.00 | 25.00 | 55.00 | 100. | 300. | 900. | — | — |
| 1868 | 89,200 | 30.00 | 60.00 | 95.00 | 135. | 195. | 300. | 600. | 5000. | 3500. |
| 1868S | 280,000 | 10.00 | 14.00 | 20.00 | 33.00 | 60.00 | 150. | 325. | — | — |
| 1869 | 208,600 | 6.50 | 8.00 | 20.00 | 30.00 | 50.00 | 175. | 475. | 4900. | 3500. |
| 1869S | 230,000 | 10.00 | 14.00 | 20.00 | 33.00 | 60.00 | 150. | 500. | — | — |
| 1870 | 536,600 | 6.00 | 7.50 | 9.00 | 17.00 | 35.00 | 125. | 275. | 4400. | 1850. |
| 1870S | Unique, Superior Galleries, July 1986, B.U., $253,000. | | | | | | | | | |
| 1871 | 1,873,960 | 5.00 | 6.25 | 8.00 | 14.00 | 28.00 | 65.00 | 160. | 4400. | 1850. |
| 1871S | 161,000 | 16.00 | 22.00 | 30.00 | 45.00 | 85.00 | 135. | 350. | 3800. | — |
| 1872 | 2,947,950 | 5.00 | 6.25 | 8.00 | 13.00 | 25.00 | 65.00 | 160. | 4400. | 1850. |
| 1872S mint mark in wreath | 837,000 | 5.00 | 6.50 | 8.00 | 15.00 | 30.00 | 65.00 | 165. | 4400. | — |
| 1872S mint mark below wreath | Inc. Ab. | 5.00 | 6.50 | 8.00 | 15.00 | 30.00 | 65.00 | 160. | 2400. | — |
| 1873 | 712,600 | 8.00 | 10.00 | 12.50 | 18.00 | 32.00 | 85.00 | 200. | 4450. | 3500. |
| 1873S | 324,000 | 8.00 | 10.00 | 14.00 | 22.00 | 45.00 | 65.00 | 200. | 4000. | — |

# Nickel five-cent

# Shield

With rays          Without rays

**Designer:** James B. Longacre. **Size:** 20.5 millimeters. **Weight:** 5 grams. **Composition:** 75% copper, 25% nickel. **Notes:** In 1867 the rays between the stars on the reverse were eliminated, resulting in varieties with and without rays for that year.

| Date | Mintage | G-4 | VG-8 | F-12 | VF-20 | XF-40 | AU-50 | MS-60 | MS-65 | Prf-65 |
|---|---|---|---|---|---|---|---|---|---|---|
| 1866 | 14,742,500 | 11.00 | 13.00 | 20.00 | 31.00 | 95.00 | 140. | 215. | 2350. | 3550. |
| 1867 with rays | | | | | | | | | | |
| | 2,019,000 | 13.00 | 16.00 | 25.00 | 50.00 | 125. | 250. | 290. | 4200. | 37,500. |
| 1867 without rays | | | | | | | | | | |
| | 28,890,500 | 7.00 | 9.50 | 10.00 | 14.00 | 26.00 | 56.00 | 100. | 600. | 1200. |
| 1868 | 28,817,000 | 7.00 | 9.50 | 10.00 | 14.00 | 26.00 | 50.00 | 100. | 600. | 1150. |
| 1869 | 16,395,000 | 7.00 | 9.50 | 10.00 | 14.00 | 31.00 | 52.00 | 100. | 600. | 940. |
| 1870 | 4,806,000 | 9.50 | 10.00 | 11.00 | 17.50 | 45.00 | 56.00 | 100. | 1050. | 1200. |
| 1871 | 561,000 | 25.00 | 30.00 | 45.00 | 75.00 | 95.00 | 160. | 270. | 1550. | 1000. |
| 1872 | 6,036,000 | 9.50 | 10.00 | 11.00 | 17.50 | 40.00 | 70.00 | 115. | 780. | 825. |
| 1873 | 4,550,000 | 9.50 | 10.00 | 12.00 | 19.00 | 34.00 | 65.00 | 125. | 780. | 1000. |
| 1874 | 3,538,000 | 10.00 | 11.50 | 12.50 | 19.00 | 38.00 | 70.00 | 125. | 1100. | 700. |
| 1875 | 2,097,000 | 10.00 | 12.50 | 17.50 | 40.00 | 65.00 | 85.00 | 150. | 2600. | 1125. |
| 1876 | 2,530,000 | 10.00 | 12.00 | 16.50 | 32.00 | 55.00 | 90.00 | 125. | 1250. | 1000. |
| 1877 | Est. 900 | — | — | Proof only | — | — | — | — | — | 1875. |
| | | | Impaired proof | — | 1000. | 1050. | 1100. | — | — | — |
| 1878 | 2,350 | — | — | Proof only | — | — | — | — | — | 1000. |
| | | | Impaired proof | 550. | 600. | 650. | 675. | — | — | — |
| 1879 | 29,100 | 240. | 280. | 330. | 415. | 480. | 550. | 625. | 2000. | 825. |
| 1880 | 19,995 | 265. | 325. | 350. | 400. | 550. | 600. | 650. | 4000. | 1000. |
| 1881 | 72,375 | 150. | 180. | 250. | 300. | 400. | 430. | 530. | 1250. | 700. |
| 1882 | 11,476,600 | 8.75 | 9.50 | 11.00 | 16.00 | 30.00 | 50.00 | 100. | 600. | 700. |
| 1883 | 1,456,919 | 12.00 | 14.00 | 17.50 | 22.50 | 32.50 | 60.00 | 100. | 600. | 700. |
| 1883/2 | — | — | 50.00 | 75.00 | 180. | 225. | 275. | 325. | 3000. | — |

# Liberty

With "Cents"    No "Cents"

**Designer:** Charles E. Barber. **Size:** 21.2 millimeters. **Weight:** 5 grams. **Composition:** 75% copper, 25% nickel. **Notes:** In 1883 the word "Cents" was added to the reverse, resulting in varieties with "Cents" and without "Cents" for that year.

| Date | Mintage | G-4 | VG-8 | F-12 | VF-20 | XF-40 | AU-50 | MS-60 | MS-65 | Prf-65 |
|---|---|---|---|---|---|---|---|---|---|---|
| 1883 NC | 5,479,519 | 2.60 | 3.25 | 3.60 | 5.00 | 6.75 | 11.50 | 32.00 | 400. | 850. |
| 1883 WC | 16,032,983 | 5.00 | 7.00 | 12.00 | 20.00 | 36.00 | 68.00 | 94.00 | 600. | 550. |
| 1884 | 11,273,942 | 7.00 | 9.00 | 13.00 | 22.00 | 42.00 | 68.00 | 120. | 775. | 500. |
| 1885 | 1,476,490 | 180. | 250. | 315. | 390. | 600. | 650. | 850. | 1800. | 875. |
| 1886 | 3,330,290 | 44.00 | 56.00 | 115. | 175. | 220. | 325. | 470. | 1900. | 700. |
| 1887 | 15,263,652 | 5.40 | 6.25 | 11.00 | 14.00 | 29.00 | 60.00 | 90.00 | 700. | 500. |
| 1888 | 10,720,483 | 7.50 | 9.00 | 14.00 | 23.00 | 40.00 | 80.00 | 115. | 675. | 500. |
| 1889 | 15,881,361 | 3.75 | 5.00 | 9.25 | 13.50 | 29.00 | 60.00 | 94.00 | 650. | 500. |
| 1890 | 16,259,272 | 4.25 | 5.50 | 11.00 | 17.00 | 31.00 | 66.00 | 100. | 825. | 500. |
| 1891 | 16,834,350 | 3.50 | 4.50 | 9.50 | 13.00 | 28.00 | 60.00 | 94.00 | 725. | 500. |
| 1892 | 11,699,642 | 3.50 | 4.00 | 9.50 | 14.50 | 31.00 | 66.00 | 100. | 690. | 500. |
| 1893 | 13,370,195 | 3.50 | 4.00 | 10.00 | 14.50 | 28.00 | 60.00 | 95.00 | 775. | 500. |
| 1894 | 5,413,132 | 5.25 | 7.00 | 26.00 | 56.00 | 120. | 150. | 170. | 1100. | 500. |
| 1895 | 9,979,884 | 2.25 | 2.75 | 7.00 | 12.00 | 28.00 | 60.00 | 87.00 | 1075. | 780. |
| 1896 | 8,842,920 | 3.00 | 4.00 | 9.50 | 15.00 | 32.00 | 69.00 | 94.00 | 1075. | 500. |
| 1897 | 20,428,735 | 1.50 | 2.00 | 3.75 | 6.50 | 19.00 | 55.00 | 80.00 | 950. | 500. |
| 1898 | 12,532,087 | 1.50 | 2.00 | 4.50 | 6.50 | 20.00 | 57.00 | 80.00 | 600. | 500. |
| 1899 | 26,029,031 | 1.00 | 1.20 | 4.00 | 5.50 | 16.00 | 50.00 | 80.00 | 600. | 500. |
| 1900 | 27,255,995 | 1.00 | 1.15 | 3.75 | 5.00 | 15.00 | 41.00 | 70.00 | 550. | 500. |
| 1901 | 26,480,213 | 1.00 | 1.15 | 3.75 | 5.00 | 15.00 | 41.00 | 70.00 | 550. | 500. |
| 1902 | 31,480,579 | 1.00 | 1.15 | 3.75 | 5.00 | 15.00 | 41.00 | 70.00 | 550. | 500. |
| 1903 | 28,006,725 | 1.00 | 1.15 | 3.75 | 5.00 | 15.00 | 41.00 | 70.00 | 550. | 500. |
| 1904 | 21,404,984 | 1.00 | 1.15 | 3.75 | 5.00 | 15.00 | 41.00 | 70.00 | 550. | 725. |
| 1905 | 29,827,276 | 1.00 | 1.15 | 3.75 | 5.00 | 15.00 | 41.00 | 70.00 | 550. | 500. |
| 1906 | 38,613,725 | 1.00 | 1.15 | 3.75 | 5.00 | 15.00 | 41.00 | 70.00 | 550. | 500. |
| 1907 | 39,214,800 | 1.00 | 1.15 | 3.75 | 5.00 | 15.00 | 41.00 | 70.00 | 550. | 500. |
| 1908 | 22,686,177 | 1.00 | 1.15 | 3.75 | 5.00 | 15.00 | 41.00 | 70.00 | 775. | 500. |
| 1909 | 11,590,526 | 1.00 | 1.30 | 5.00 | 6.00 | 17.00 | 60.00 | 80.00 | 725. | 500. |
| 1910 | 30,169,353 | 1.00 | 1.15 | 3.75 | 5.00 | 15.00 | 41.00 | 70.00 | 550. | 500. |
| 1911 | 39,559,372 | 1.00 | 1.15 | 3.75 | 5.00 | 15.00 | 41.00 | 70.00 | 550. | 500. |
| 1912 | 26,236,714 | 1.00 | 1.15 | 3.75 | 5.00 | 15.00 | 41.00 | 70.00 | 550. | 500. |
| 1912D | 8,474,000 | 1.00 | 1.15 | 4.25 | 7.50 | 36.00 | 95.00 | 145. | 800. | — |
| 1912S | 238,000 | 38.00 | 41.00 | 65.00 | 220. | 400. | 530. | 595. | 2300. | — |

1913 Only 5 known, Hawn Sale, Oct. 1993, Prf, $962,500.

# 1884 Nickel Five-Cent
## Grade F-12

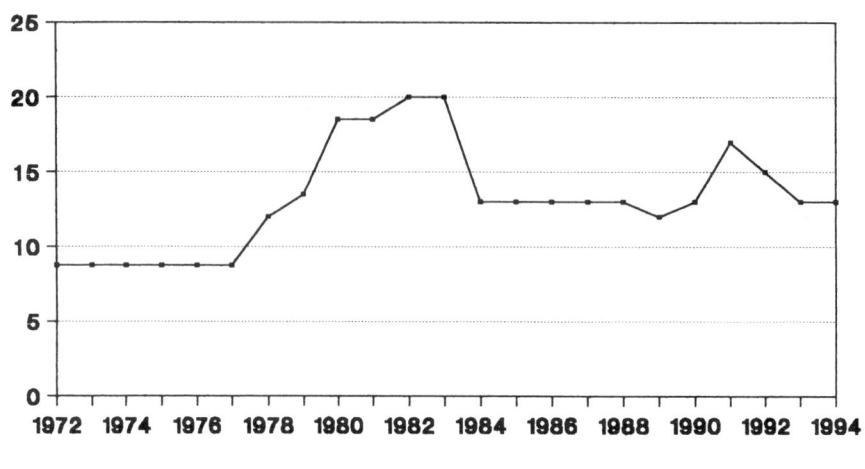

─●── Retail Price

Source: COIN PRICES

# Buffalo

## Mound type

**Designer:** James Earle Fraser. **Size:** 21.2 millimeters. **Weight:** 5 grams. **Composition:** 75% copper, 25% nickel.

| Date | Mintage | G-4 | VG-8 | F-12 | VF-20 | XF-40 | AU-50 | MS-60 | MS-65 | Prf-65 |
|------|---------|-----|------|------|-------|-------|-------|-------|-------|--------|
| 1913 | 30,993,520 | 5.00 | 5.75 | 6.00 | 8.00 | 12.00 | 21.00 | 35.00 | 100. | 2200. |
| 1913D | 5,337,000 | 8.00 | 9.50 | 11.00 | 14.00 | 25.00 | 41.00 | 56.00 | 240. | — |
| 1913S | 2,105,000 | 11.00 | 12.50 | 17.00 | 25.00 | 41.00 | 53.00 | 63.00 | 800. | — |

## Line type

**Notes:** In 1913 the reverse design was modified so the ground under the buffalo was represented as a line rather than a mound. On the 1937-D 3-legged variety, the buffalo's right front leg is missing, the result of a damaged die.

# 1921-S Nickel Five-Cent
## Grade F-12

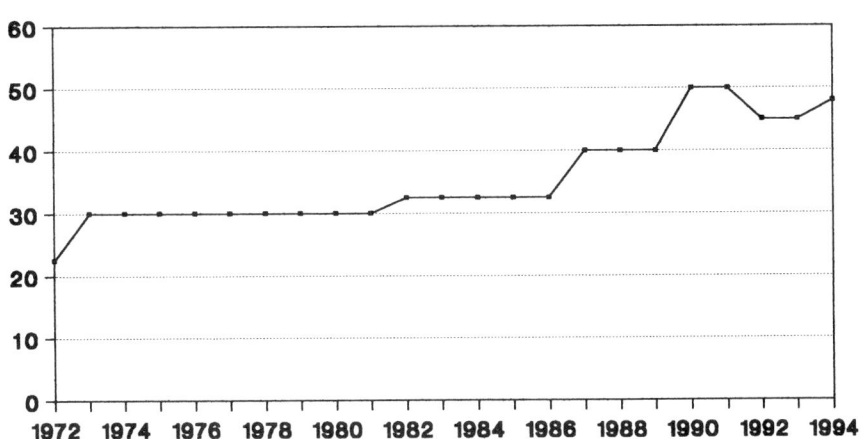

**—•— Retail Price**

**Source: COIN PRICES**

| Date | Mintage | G-4 | VG-8 | F-12 | VF-20 | XF-40 | AU-50 | MS-60 | MS-65 | Prf-65 |
|---|---|---|---|---|---|---|---|---|---|---|
| 1913 | 29,858,700 | 5.00 | 5.75 | 7.00 | 9.00 | 13.50 | 20.00 | 29.00 | 400. | 1350. |
| 1913D | 4,156,000 | 34.00 | 40.00 | 50.00 | 62.00 | 70.00 | 115. | 170. | 1100. | — |
| 1913S | 1,209,000 | 84.00 | 100. | 140. | 160. | 195. | 280. | 335. | 2800. | — |
| 1914 | 20,665,738 | 5.60 | 6.30 | 7.50 | 9.50 | 17.00 | 27.00 | 45.00 | 400. | 1100. |
| 1914D | 3,912,000 | 32.00 | 42.00 | 50.00 | 67.00 | 105. | 140. | 210. | 1365. | — |
| 1914S | 3,470,000 | 6.00 | 7.00 | 11.00 | 18.00 | 35.00 | 50.00 | 110. | 2700. | — |
| 1915 | 20,987,270 | 3.15 | 3.50 | 5.60 | 7.50 | 13.50 | 26.00 | 45.00 | 335. | 1100. |
| 1915D | 7,569,500 | 7.50 | 11.50 | 20.00 | 38.00 | 55.00 | 75.00 | 170. | 2725. | — |
| 1915S | 1,505,000 | 12.00 | 18.00 | 29.00 | 63.00 | 125. | 210. | 420. | 2700. | — |
| 1916 | 63,498,066 | 1.25 | 1.75 | 2.50 | 3.75 | 4.90 | 15.00 | 38.00 | 325. | 2000. |
| 1916/16 | Inc. Ab. | 1500. | 3350. | 5300. | 8400. | 11,000. | 14,000. | 16,000. | 70,000. | — |
| 1916D | 13,333,000 | 6.00 | 8.50 | 11.50 | 25.00 | 50.00 | 75.00 | 140. | 3200. | — |
| 1916S | 11,860,000 | 4.00 | 5.50 | 9.00 | 19.00 | 48.00 | 74.00 | 155. | 2950. | — |
| 1917 | 51,424,029 | 1.25 | 2.00 | 3.00 | 6.00 | 11.00 | 26.00 | 42.00 | 525. | — |
| 1917D | 9,910,800 | 6.00 | 9.00 | 18.00 | 45.00 | 90.00 | 120. | 275. | 3000. | — |
| 1917S | 4,193,000 | 5.25 | 8.75 | 18.00 | 45.00 | 105. | 195. | 280. | 2950. | — |
| 1918 | 32,086,314 | 1.50 | 2.25 | 3.50 | 5.60 | 18.00 | 35.00 | 56.00 | 1650. | — |

**1918/17-D**

| Date | Mintage | G-4 | VG-8 | F-12 | VF-20 | XF-40 | AU-50 | MS-60 | MS-65 | Prf-65 |
|---|---|---|---|---|---|---|---|---|---|---|
| 1918/17D | 8,362,314 | 385. | 500. | 800. | 2275. | 4000. | 5950. | 12,000. | 100,000. | — |
| 1918D | Inc. Ab. | 5.00 | 7.00 | 16.00 | 67.00 | 160. | 245. | 330. | 3425. | — |
| 1918S | 4,882,000 | 4.00 | 5.25 | 13.00 | 59.00 | 160. | 210. | 280. | 10,500. | — |
| 1919 | 60,868,000 | 1.25 | 1.60 | 2.00 | 4.00 | 10.00 | 22.00 | 42.00 | 450. | — |
| 1919D | 8,006,000 | 6.50 | 11.00 | 22.00 | 75.00 | 170. | 265. | 500. | 3700. | — |
| 1919S | 7,521,000 | 4.50 | 7.00 | 15.00 | 65.00 | 160. | 250. | 435. | 8250. | — |
| 1920 | 63,093,000 | 1.15 | 1.50 | 2.00 | 3.00 | 10.00 | 24.00 | 45.00 | 765. | — |
| 1920D | 9,418,000 | 5.00 | 7.00 | 14.00 | 70.00 | 210. | 280. | 420. | 5300. | — |
| 1920S | 9,689,000 | 2.75 | 4.75 | 9.00 | 49.00 | 150. | 195. | 365. | 13,500. | — |

| Date | Mintage | G-4 | VG-8 | F-12 | VF-20 | XF-40 | AU-50 | MS-60 | MS-65 | Prf-65 |
|------|---------|-----|------|------|-------|-------|-------|-------|-------|--------|
| 1921 | 10,663,000 | 1.75 | 2.50 | 3.50 | 6.00 | 20.00 | 42.00 | 87.00 | 615. | — |
| 1921S | 1,557,000 | 17.50 | 25.00 | 48.00 | 315. | 700. | 875. | 1050. | 4400. | — |
| 1923 | 35,715,000 | 1.15 | 1.50 | 2.00 | 4.00 | 6.75 | 17.00 | 35.00 | 540. | — |
| 1923S | 6,142,000 | 2.50 | 4.00 | 10.00 | 85.00 | 190. | 230. | 310. | 8950. | — |
| 1924 | 21,620,000 | 1.15 | 1.50 | 2.00 | 5.50 | 8.75 | 28.00 | 49.00 | 550. | — |
| 1924D | 5,258,000 | 3.00 | 4.75 | 9.50 | 57.00 | 150. | 220. | 280. | 3125. | — |
| 1924S | 1,437,000 | 6.50 | 9.50 | 38.00 | 425. | 1075. | 1250. | 1825. | 4700. | — |
| 1925 | 35,565,100 | .90 | 1.35 | 2.00 | 4.00 | 7.00 | 21.00 | 31.00 | 345. | — |
| 1925D | 4,450,000 | 5.50 | 7.50 | 19.50 | 60.00 | 165. | 200. | 350. | 3775. | — |
| 1925S | 6,256,000 | 2.50 | 4.50 | 11.50 | 53.00 | 140. | 225. | 390. | 25,000. | — |
| 1926 | 44,693,000 | .70 | .95 | 1.50 | 2.50 | 7.00 | 17.00 | 28.00 | 160. | — |
| 1926D | 5,638,000 | 4.00 | 7.50 | 20.00 | 63.00 | 120. | 160. | 210. | 2700. | — |
| 1926S | 970,000 | 7.25 | 10.00 | 27.00 | 300. | 850. | 1085. | 2725. | 21,000. | — |
| 1927 | 37,981,000 | .70 | .95 | 1.50 | 2.50 | 7.00 | 18.00 | 25.00 | 245. | — |
| 1927D | 5,730,000 | 1.75 | 2.75 | 6.00 | 11.00 | 39.00 | 65.00 | 140. | 2675. | — |
| 1927S | 3,430,000 | 1.25 | 2.00 | 3.75 | 18.00 | 65.00 | 105. | 450. | 14,000. | — |
| 1928 | 23,411,000 | .65 | .90 | 1.50 | 2.50 | 5.50 | 18.00 | 27.00 | 390. | — |
| 1928D | 6,436,000 | 1.50 | 2.00 | 2.75 | 4.50 | 14.00 | 25.00 | 31.00 | 1100. | — |
| 1928S | 6,936,000 | .85 | 1.35 | 2.25 | 3.15 | 10.00 | 30.00 | 175. | 3850. | — |
| 1929 | 36,446,000 | .65 | .90 | 1.50 | 2.50 | 8.00 | 15.00 | 25.00 | 315. | — |
| 1929D | 8,370,000 | 1.25 | 1.75 | 2.50 | 6.00 | 12.50 | 28.00 | 42.00 | 1275. | — |
| 1929S | 7,754,000 | .70 | .95 | 1.50 | 2.75 | 10.00 | 21.00 | 36.00 | 450. | — |
| 1930 | 22,849,000 | .60 | .80 | 1.25 | 2.25 | 6.00 | 15.00 | 23.00 | 115. | — |
| 1930S | 5,435,000 | .65 | .85 | 1.25 | 2.75 | 9.50 | 25.00 | 34.00 | 575. | — |
| 1931S | 1,200,000 | 3.75 | 4.25 | 4.75 | 5.50 | 12.50 | 28.00 | 38.00 | 260. | — |
| 1934 | 20,213,003 | .65 | .70 | .85 | 1.40 | 6.00 | 13.00 | 21.00 | 345. | — |
| 1934D | 7,480,000 | .65 | .95 | 1.50 | 3.50 | 5.50 | 18.00 | 36.00 | 1500. | — |
| 1935 | 58,264,000 | .50 | .55 | .65 | 1.25 | 4.00 | 8.50 | 18.00 | 97.00 | — |
| 1935D | 12,092,000 | .60 | .90 | 1.45 | 3.50 | 8.50 | 21.00 | 27.00 | 475. | — |
| 1935S | 10,300,000 | .50 | .55 | .65 | 1.75 | 5.50 | 13.00 | 24.00 | 210. | — |
| 1936 | 119,001,420 | .50 | .55 | .65 | 1.25 | 3.50 | 7.50 | 14.00 | 77.00 | 1000. |
| 1936D | 24,814,000 | .50 | .55 | .75 | 1.95 | 4.00 | 10.50 | 17.50 | 91.00 | — |
| 1936S | 14,930,000 | .50 | .55 | .65 | 1.40 | 4.00 | 12.00 | 16.00 | 83.00 | — |
| 1937 | 79,485,769 | .50 | .55 | .65 | 1.25 | 3.50 | 7.00 | 13.00 | 35.00 | 800. |
| 1937D | 17,826,000 | .50 | .55 | .65 | 1.40 | 4.00 | 9.00 | 14.00 | 45.00 | — |
| 1937D 3 Leg. | Inc. Ab. | 150. | 225. | 295. | 325. | 490. | 750. | 1375. | 13,300. | — |

**1937-D three-legged**

| Date | Mintage | G-4 | VG-8 | F-12 | VF-20 | XF-40 | AU-50 | MS-60 | MS-65 | Prf-65 |
|------|---------|-----|------|------|-------|-------|-------|-------|-------|--------|
| 1937S | 5,635,000 | .50 | .55 | .65 | 1.40 | 4.00 | 9.00 | 14.00 | 63.00 | — |
| 1938 | 7,020,000 | .50 | .55 | .65 | 1.50 | 4.00 | 8.50 | 13.00 | 32.00 | — |
| 1938 D/D | — | 2.25 | 4.25 | 5.75 | 8.00 | 11.00 | 13.50 | 16.00 | 90.00 | — |
| 1938D/S | Inc. Ab. | 6.00 | 7.50 | 9.00 | 11.00 | 15.00 | 21.00 | 35.00 | 150. | — |

# Jefferson

## Prewar composition

**Designer:** Felix Schlag. **Size:** 21.2 millimeters. **Weight:** 5 grams. **Composition:** 75% copper, 25% nickel. **Notes:** Some 1939 strikes have doubling of the word "Monticello" on the reverse.

| Date | Mintage | G-4 | VG-8 | F-12 | VF-20 | XF-40 | MS-60 | MS-65 | Prf-65 |
|---|---|---|---|---|---|---|---|---|---|
| 1938 | 19,515,365 | — | .40 | .50 | 1.00 | 1.50 | 3.50 | 7.00 | 45.00 |
| 1938D | 5,376,000 | .60 | .90 | 1.00 | 1.25 | 1.75 | 4.25 | 7.00 | — |
| 1938S | 4,105,000 | 1.00 | 1.25 | 1.50 | 1.75 | 2.00 | 3.75 | 7.50 | — |
| 1939 | 120,627,535 | — | — | .15 | .15 | .30 | 1.75 | 2.00 | 40.00 |
| Doubled Monticello | | | 7.50 | 10.00 | 25.00 | 50.00 | 200. | — | — |
| 1939D | 3,514,000 | 2.50 | 3.00 | 3.50 | 4.50 | 7.25 | 28.00 | 40.00 | — |
| 1939S | 6,630,000 | .40 | .45 | .60 | 1.00 | 2.50 | 15.00 | 30.00 | — |
| 1940 | 176,499,158 | — | — | — | — | .25 | 1.00 | 1.25 | 45.00 |
| 1940D | 43,540,000 | — | — | .15 | .30 | .40 | 2.50 | 2.75 | — |
| 1940S | 39,690,000 | — | — | .15 | .20 | .50 | 2.75 | 3.50 | — |
| 1941 | 203,283,720 | — | — | — | — | .20 | .85 | 1.10 | 35.00 |
| 1941D | 53,432,000 | — | — | .15 | .25 | .35 | 2.50 | 4.00 | — |
| 1941S | 43,445,000 | — | — | .15 | .25 | .40 | 3.75 | 5.75 | — |
| 1942 | 49,818,600 | — | — | — | — | .40 | 3.75 | 6.00 | 25.00 |
| 1942D | 13,938,000 | — | .30 | .40 | .60 | 2.00 | 19.00 | 35.00 | — |

## Wartime composition

**Composition:** 56% copper, 35% silver (0.0563 ounces), 9% manganese. **Notes:** Wartime-composition nickels have a large mintmark above Monticello on the reverse.

| Date | Mintage | G-4 | VG-8 | F-12 | VF-20 | XF-40 | MS-60 | MS-65 | Prf-65 |
|---|---|---|---|---|---|---|---|---|---|
| 1942P | 57,900,600 | .40 | .65 | .85 | 1.00 | 1.75 | 8.00 | 20.00 | 110. |
| 1942S | 32,900,000 | .40 | .70 | 1.00 | 1.10 | 1.75 | 9.00 | 15.00 | — |
| 1943P | 271,165,000 | .30 | .50 | .85 | 1.00 | 1.50 | 4.00 | 6.50 | — |
| 1943/2P | Inc. Ab. | 20.00 | 30.00 | 45.00 | 60.00 | 90.00 | 250. | 575. | — |
| 1943D | 15,294,000 | .55 | .90 | 1.10 | 1.50 | 1.75 | 2.75 | 5.50 | — |
| 1943S | 104,060,000 | .40 | .65 | .85 | 1.00 | 1.50 | 3.50 | 5.75 | — |
| 1944P | 119,150,000 | .30 | .50 | .85 | 1.00 | 1.50 | 3.50 | 6.00 | — |
| 1944D | 32,309,000 | .40 | .65 | .85 | 1.00 | 1.75 | 9.00 | 12.00 | — |
| 1944S | 21,640,000 | .45 | .85 | .95 | 1.25 | 2.00 | 5.50 | 15.00 | — |
| 1945P | 119,408,100 | .30 | .50 | .85 | 1.00 | 1.75 | 4.00 | 7.50 | — |
| 1945D | 37,158,000 | .40 | .65 | .85 | 1.00 | 1.25 | 3.25 | 6.50 | — |
| 1945S | 58,939,000 | .30 | .50 | .70 | .80 | .90 | 2.25 | 7.50 | — |

## Prewar composition resumed

**Notes:** The 1979-S Type II proof has a clearer mintmark than the Type I.

| Date | Mintage | G-4 | VG-8 | F-12 | VF-20 | XF-40 | MS-60 | MS-65 | Prf-65 |
|---|---|---|---|---|---|---|---|---|---|
| 1946 | 161,116,000 | — | — | — | .15 | .20 | .40 | .60 | — |
| 1946D | 45,292,200 | — | — | — | .25 | .35 | .75 | .95 | — |
| 1946S | 13,560,000 | — | — | — | .30 | .40 | .60 | .70 | — |
| 1947 | 95,000,000 | — | — | — | .15 | .20 | .40 | .55 | — |
| 1947D | 37,822,000 | — | — | — | .20 | .30 | .65 | .75 | — |
| 1947S | 24,720,000 | — | — | — | .15 | .20 | .55 | .65 | — |
| 1948 | 89,348,000 | — | — | — | .15 | .20 | .35 | .55 | — |
| 1948D | 44,734,000 | — | — | — | .25 | .35 | 1.00 | 1.25 | — |
| 1948S | 11,300,000 | — | — | — | .25 | .50 | 1.00 | 1.25 | — |
| 1949 | 60,652,000 | — | — | — | .20 | .25 | .75 | 1.25 | — |
| 1949D | 36,498,000 | — | — | — | .30 | .40 | 1.00 | 1.25 | — |
| 1949D/S | Inc. Ab. | — | — | 20.00 | 40.00 | 65.00 | 165. | 350. | — |
| 1949S | 9,716,000 | — | .25 | .35 | .45 | 1.50 | 2.00 | 2.50 | — |
| 1950 | 9,847,386 | — | .25 | .45 | .50 | .75 | 1.90 | 2.25 | 35.00 |
| 1950D | 2,630,030 | — | 5.00 | 5.00 | 5.25 | 5.50 | 6.50 | 9.00 | — |
| 1951 | 28,609,500 | — | — | — | .40 | .50 | 1.00 | 1.50 | 32.00 |
| 1951D | 20,460,000 | — | .25 | .30 | .40 | .50 | 1.25 | 1.50 | — |
| 1951S | 7,776,000 | — | .30 | .40 | .50 | .75 | 1.75 | 4.00 | — |
| 1952 | 64,069,980 | — | — | — | .15 | .20 | .85 | 1.25 | 28.00 |
| 1952D | 30,638,000 | — | — | — | .20 | .35 | 1.00 | 1.75 | — |
| 1952S | 20,572,000 | — | — | — | .15 | .20 | .65 | .90 | — |
| 1953 | 46,772,800 | — | — | — | .15 | .25 | .35 | .45 | 27.00 |
| 1953D | 59,878,600 | — | — | — | .15 | .20 | .30 | .40 | — |
| 1953S | 19,210,900 | — | — | — | .15 | .20 | .40 | .50 | — |
| 1954 | 47,917,350 | — | — | — | — | — | .20 | .30 | 18.00 |
| 1954D | 117,136,560 | — | — | — | — | — | .30 | .40 | — |
| 1954S | 29,384,000 | — | — | — | — | .15 | .35 | .45 | — |
| 1954S/D | Inc. Ab. | — | — | 3.50 | 6.50 | 9.50 | 22.00 | 65.00 | — |
| 1955 | 8,266,200 | — | .25 | .35 | .40 | .45 | .75 | 1.25 | 11.00 |
| 1955D | 74,464,100 | — | — | — | — | — | .20 | .30 | — |
| 1955D/S | Inc. Ab. | — | — | 3.00 | 7.00 | 12.00 | 35.00 | 69.00 | 69.00 |
| 1956 | 35,885,384 | — | — | — | — | — | .25 | .35 | 2.50 |

**PRICING SECTION**

| Date | Mintage | G-4 | VG-8 | F-12 | VF-20 | XF-40 | MS-60 | MS-65 | Prf-65 |
|------|---------|-----|------|------|-------|-------|-------|-------|--------|
| 1956D | 67,222,940 | — | — | — | — | — | .20 | .35 | — |
| 1957 | 39,655,952 | — | — | — | — | — | .25 | .35 | 1.25 |
| 1957D | 136,828,900 | — | — | — | — | — | .20 | .40 | — |
| 1958 | 17,963,652 | — | — | — | .15 | .20 | .30 | .55 | 2.00 |
| 1958D | 168,249,120 | — | — | — | — | — | .20 | .35 | — |

| Date | Mintage | MS-65 | Prf-65 | Date | Mintage | MS-65 | Prf-65 |
|------|---------|-------|--------|------|---------|-------|--------|
| 1959 | 28,397,291 | .35 | .80 | 1979D | 325,867,672 | .15 | — |
| 1959D | 160,738,240 | .25 | — | 1979S T-I | Proof only | — | .75 |
| 1960 | 57,107,602 | .25 | .60 | 1979S T-II | Proof only | — | 1.45 |
| 1960D | 192,582,180 | .25 | — | 1980P | 593,004,000 | .15 | — |
| 1961 | 76,668,244 | .25 | .40 | 1980D | 502,323,448 | .15 | — |
| 1961D | 229,342,760 | .25 | — | 1980S | Proof only | — | .65 |
| 1962 | 100,602,019 | .25 | .40 | 1981P | 657,504,000 | .15 | — |
| 1962D | 280,195,720 | .25 | — | 1981D | 364,801,843 | .15 | — |
| 1963 | 178,851,645 | .25 | .40 | 1981S T-I | Proof only | — | .65 |
| 1963D | 276,829,460 | .25 | — | 1981S T-II | Proof only | — | 1.75 |
| 1964 | 1,028,622,762 | .25 | .40 | 1982P | 292,355,000 | .55 | — |
| 1964D | 1,787,297,160 | .25 | — | 1982D | 373,726,544 | 1.75 | — |
| 1965 | 136,131,380 | .25 | — | 1982S | Proof only | — | 1.25 |
| 1966 | 156,208,283 | .25 | — | 1983P | 561,615,000 | .70 | — |
| 1967 | 107,325,800 | .25 | — | 1983D | 536,726,276 | .75 | — |
| 1968 | None minted | — | — | 1983S | Proof only | — | 1.50 |
| 1968D | 91,227,880 | .25 | — | 1984P | 746,769,000 | .20 | — |
| 1968S | 103,437,510 | .25 | .50 | 1984D | 517,675,146 | .20 | — |
| 1969 | None minted | — | — | 1984S | Proof only | — | 2.50 |
| 1969D | 202,807,500 | .25 | — | 1985P | 647,114,962 | .20 | — |
| 1969S | 123,099,631 | .25 | .50 | 1985D | 459,747,446 | .20 | — |
| 1970 | None minted | — | — | 1985S | Proof only | — | 1.75 |
| 1970D | 515,485,380 | .25 | — | 1986P | 536,883,483 | .25 | — |
| 1970S | 241,464,814 | .25 | .50 | 1986D | 361,819,140 | .80 | — |
| 1971 | 106,884,000 | .60 | — | 1986S | Proof only | — | 4.50 |
| 1971D | 316,144,800 | .25 | — | 1987P | 371,499,481 | .15 | — |
| 1971S | Proof only | — | 1.25 | 1987D | 410,590,604 | .15 | — |
| 1972 | 202,036,000 | .25 | — | 1987S | Proof only | — | 1.50 |
| 1972D | 351,694,600 | .20 | — | 1988P | 771,360,000 | .15 | — |
| 1972S | Proof only | — | 1.10 | 1988D | 663,771,652 | .15 | — |
| 1973 | 384,396,000 | .15 | — | 1988S | Proof only | — | 2.50 |
| 1973D | 261,405,000 | .15 | — | 1989P | 898,812,000 | .15 | — |
| 1973S | Proof only | — | 1.00 | 1989D | 570,842,474 | .15 | — |
| 1974 | 601,752,000 | .15 | — | 1989S | Proof only | — | 2.00 |
| 1974D | 277,373,000 | .20 | — | 1990P | 661,636,000 | .15 | — |
| 1974S | Proof only | — | 1.00 | 1990D | 663,938,503 | .15 | — |
| 1975 | 181,772,000 | .35 | — | 1990S | Proof only | — | 3.50 |
| 1975D | 401,875,300 | .15 | — | 1991P | — | .15 | — |
| 1975S | Proof only | — | 1.00 | 1991D | — | .15 | — |
| 1976 | 367,124,000 | .15 | — | 1991S | Proof only | — | 3.00 |
| 1976D | 563,964,147 | .15 | — | 1992P | — | .15 | — |
| 1976S | Proof only | — | 1.00 | 1992D | — | .15 | — |
| 1977 | 585,376,000 | .15 | — | 1992S | Proof only | — | 2.50 |
| 1977D | 297,313,460 | .35 | — | 1993P | — | .15 | — |
| 1977S | Proof only | — | .55 | 1993D | — | .15 | — |
| 1978 | 391,308,000 | .15 | — | 1993S | Proof only | — | 2.00 |
| 1978D | 313,092,780 | .15 | — | 1994P | — | .15 | — |
| 1978S | Proof only | — | .55 | 1994D | — | .15 | — |
| 1979 | 463,188,000 | .15 | — | 1994S | Proof only | — | 3.50 |

# Dimes

## Draped Bust

**Small-eagle reverse**

**Designer:** Robert Scot. **Size:** 19 millimeters. **Weight:** 2.7 grams. **Composition:** 89.24% silver (0.0775 ounces), 10.76% copper. **Notes:** The 1797 strikes have either 13 or 16 stars on the obverse.

| Date | Mintage | G-4 | VG-8 | F-12 | VF-20 | XF-40 | MS-60 |
|------|---------|-----|------|------|-------|-------|-------|
| 1796 | 22,135 | 1050. | 1600. | 1900. | 3100. | 5000. | 7000. |
| 1797 13 stars | 25,261 | 1150. | 1750. | 2100. | 3450. | 5500. | 7500. |
| 1797 16 stars | Inc. Ab. | 1050. | 1600. | 1900. | 3250. | 5250. | 7000. |

### Heraldic-eagle reverse

**Notes:** The 1798 overdates have either 13 or 16 stars on the obverse. Varieties of the regular 1798 strikes are distinguished by the size of the 8 in the date. The 1804 strikes have either 13 or 14 stars on the obverse. The 1805 strikes have either 4 or 5 berries on the olive branch held by the eagle.

| Date | Mintage | G-4 | VG-8 | F-12 | VF-20 | XF-40 | MS-60 |
|------|---------|-----|------|------|-------|-------|-------|
| 1798 | 27,550 | 450. | 560. | 750. | 1125. | 1975. | 6000. |
| 1798/97 13 stars | Inc. Ab. | 1650. | 2600. | 4100. | 6100. | 7500. | — |
| 1798/97 16 stars | Inc. Ab. | 475. | 650. | 950. | 1800. | 2775. | 6000. |
| 1798 small 8 | Inc. Ab. | 850. | 1200. | 1650. | 2800. | 4400. | — |
| 1800 | 21,760 | 450. | 560. | 750. | 1125. | 1975. | 5400. |
| 1801 | 34,640 | 450. | 560. | 750. | 1150. | 2100. | — |
| 1802 | 10,975 | 660. | 975. | 1400. | 2650. | 4850. | — |
| 1803 | 33,040 | 450. | 560. | 750. | 1125. | 1975. | 5500. |
| 1804 13 stars | 8,265 | 925. | 1275. | 2100. | 4400. | 7500. | — |
| 1804 14 stars | Inc. Ab. | 1200. | 1700. | 2350. | 4750. | 8000. | — |
| 1805 4 berries | 120,780 | 425. | 525. | 725. | 950. | 1800. | 4050. |
| 1805 5 berries | Inc. Ab. | 550. | 650. | 975. | 1200. | 1850. | 4200. |
| 1807 | 165,000 | 425. | 525. | 725. | 975. | 1800. | 4050. |

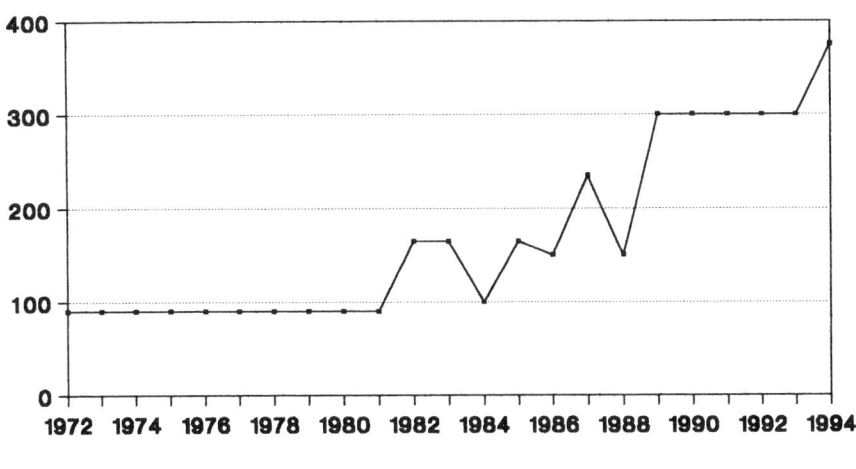

# 1809 Dime
## Grade F-12

Retail Price

Source: COIN PRICES

# Liberty Cap

**Designer:** John Reich. **Size:** 18.8 millimeters. **Weight:** 2.7 grams. **Composition:** 89.24% silver (0.0775 ounces), 10.76% copper. **Notes:** Varieties of the 1814, 1821 and 1828 strikes are distinguished by the size of the numerals in the dates. The 1820 varieties are distinguished by the size of the 0 in the date. The 1823 overdates have either large "E's" or small "E's" in "United States of America" on the reverse.

| Date | Mintage | G-4 | VG-8 | F-12 | VF-20 | XF-40 | AU-50 | MS-60 | MS-65 |
|---|---|---|---|---|---|---|---|---|---|
| 1809 | 51,065 | 100. | 200. | 375. | 585. | 875. | 1250. | 4200. | 22,500. |
| 1811/9 | 65,180 | 55.00 | 90.00 | 165. | 275. | 575. | 1050. | 4000. | 22,500. |
| 1814 sm. dt. | 421,500 | 40.00 | 60.00 | 90.00 | 185. | 450. | 700. | 800. | 11,500. |
| 1814 lg. dt. | Inc.Ab. | 17.50 | 26.00 | 44.00 | 115. | 350. | 625. | 800. | 11,500. |
| 1820 lg. O | 942,587 | 17.00 | 24.00 | 35.00 | 105. | 330. | 625. | 800. | 11,500. |
| 1820 sm. O | Inc.Ab. | 17.00 | 24.00 | 35.00 | 105. | 330. | 625. | 800. | 11,500. |
| 1821 lg. dt. | 1,186,512 | 16.00 | 23.00 | 38.00 | 105. | 330. | 625. | 800. | 11,500. |
| 1821 sm. dt. | Inc.Ab. | 18.50 | 25.00 | 45.00 | 125. | 370. | 625. | 800. | 11,500. |
| 1822 | 100,000 | 300. | 450. | 800. | 1250. | 2500. | 4450. | 6000. | — |
| 1823/22 lg.E's | 440,000 | 15.00 | 20.00 | 33.00 | 95.00 | 300. | 625. | 800. | 11,500. |
| 1823/22 sm.E's | Inc.Ab. | 17.50 | 25.00 | 45.00 | 125. | 380. | 625. | 800. | 11,500. |
| 1824/22 | Undetermined | 30.00 | 40.00 | 60.00 | 165. | 450. | 1100. | 2500. | — |
| 1825 | 510,000 | 15.00 | 22.00 | 35.00 | 95.00 | 300. | 775. | 1000. | 11,500. |
| 1827 | 1,215,000 | 15.00 | 22.00 | 35.00 | 95.00 | 300. | 775. | 1000. | 11,500. |
| 1828 lg.dt. | 125,000 | 30.00 | 40.00 | 60.00 | 165. | 500. | 875. | 2200. | — |

## Reduced size

**Size:** 18.5 millimeters. **Notes:** The three varieties of 1829 strikes and two varieties of 1830 strikes are distinguished by the size of "10C." on the reverse. On the 1833 "high 3" variety, the last 3 in the date is higher than the first 3. The two varieties of the 1834 strikes are distinguished by the size of the 4 in the date.

| Date | Mintage | G-4 | VG-8 | F-12 | VF-20 | XF-40 | AU-50 | MS-60 | MS-65 |
|---|---|---|---|---|---|---|---|---|---|
| 1828 sm.dt. | Inc. Ab. | 20.00 | 35.00 | 50.00 | 125. | 325. | 515. | 1400. | — |
| 1829 lg.10C. | 770,000 | 20.00 | 28.00 | 38.00 | 75.00 | 275. | 475. | 625. | 8000. |
| 1829 med.10C. | Inc. Ab. | 17.50 | 25.00 | 35.00 | 85.00 | 265. | 425. | 625. | 8000. |
| 1829 sm.10C. | Inc.Ab. | 14.00 | 17.00 | 22.00 | 60.00 | 185. | 415. | 625. | 8000. |
| 1830 lg.10C. | 510,000 | 14.00 | 17.00 | 22.00 | 60.00 | 185. | 415. | 625. | 8000. |
| 1830 sm.10C. | Inc. Ab. | 15.00 | 19.00 | 25.00 | 63.00 | 200. | 415. | 625. | 8000. |
| 1830/29 | Inc. Ab. | 20.00 | 33.00 | 50.00 | 90.00 | 260. | 550. | 1040. | — |
| 1831 | 771,350 | 14.00 | 17.00 | 22.00 | 60.00 | 185. | 350. | 600. | 7000. |
| 1832 | 522,500 | 14.00 | 17.00 | 22.00 | 60.00 | 185. | 350. | 600. | 7000. |
| 1833 | 485,000 | 14.00 | 17.00 | 22.00 | 60.00 | 185. | 350. | 600. | 7000. |
| 1834 lg. 4 | 635,000 | 14.00 | 17.00 | 22.00 | 60.00 | 185. | 350. | 600. | 7000. |
| 1835 | 1,410,000 | 14.00 | 17.00 | 22.00 | 60.00 | 185. | 350. | 600. | 9100. |
| 1836 | 1,190,000 | 14.00 | 17.00 | 22.00 | 60.00 | 185. | 350. | 600. | 7000. |
| 1837 | 1,042,000 | 14.00 | 17.00 | 22.00 | 60.00 | 185. | 350. | 625. | 7000. |

# Seated Liberty

## No stars

**Designer:** Christian Gobrecht. **Size:** 17.9 millimeters. **Weight:** 2.67 grams. **Composition:** 90% silver (0.0773 ounces), 10% copper. **Notes:** The two 1837 varieties are distinguished by the size of the numerals in the date.

| Date | Mintage | G-4 | VG-8 | F-12 | VF-20 | XF-40 | AU-50 | MS-60 | MS-65 |
|------|---------|-----|------|------|-------|-------|-------|-------|-------|
| 1837 sm.date | Inc. Ab. | 29.00 | 40.00 | 75.00 | 275. | 550. | 750. | 1100. | 6500. |
| 1837 lg.date | Inc. Ab. | 29.00 | 40.00 | 75.00 | 275. | 550. | 850. | 1100. | 6500. |
| 1838O | 406,034 | 40.00 | 55.00 | 90.00 | 325. | 650. | 1000. | 3500. | 21,000. |

## Stars around rim

**Notes:** The two 1838 varieties are distinguished by the size of the stars on the obverse. The 1838 "partial drapery" variety has drapery on Liberty's left elbow. The 1839-O with reverse of 1838-O variety was struck from rusted dies. This variety has a bumpy surface on the reverse.

| Date | Mintage | G-4 | VG-8 | F-12 | VF-20 | XF-40 | AU-50 | MS-60 | MS-65 |
|------|---------|-----|------|------|-------|-------|-------|-------|-------|
| 1838 sm.stars | 1,992,500 | 20.00 | 30.00 | 45.00 | 75.00 | 175. | 425. | 1400. | — |
| 1838 lg.stars | Inc. Ab. | 9.00 | 11.00 | 15.00 | 25.00 | 60.00 | 170. | 575. | 8500. |
| 1838 partial drapery | | | | | | | | | |
| | Inc. Ab. | 20.00 | 25.00 | 45.00 | 85.00 | 175. | 300. | 1200. | — |
| 1839 | 1,053,115 | 8.00 | 11.00 | 15.00 | 35.00 | 70.00 | 170. | 265. | 3000. |
| 1839O | 1,323,000 | 7.00 | 12.00 | 20.00 | 40.00 | 85.00 | 300. | 950. | — |
| 1839O rev. 1838O | — | 125. | 185. | 275. | 475. | 625. | — | — | — |
| 1840 | 1,358,580 | 8.00 | 11.00 | 15.00 | 25.00 | 60.00 | 170. | 265. | 3000. |
| 1840O | 1,175,000 | 8.00 | 15.00 | 20.00 | 40.00 | 85.00 | 250. | 1500. | — |

## Drapery added to Liberty

**Notes:** In 1840 drapery was added to Liberty's left elbow.

| Date | Mintage | G-4 | VG-8 | F-12 | VF-20 | XF-40 | AU-50 | MS-60 | MS-65 |
|------|---------|-----|------|------|-------|-------|-------|-------|-------|
| 1840 | Inc. Ab. | 25.00 | 45.00 | 85.00 | 135. | 275. | 1000. | — | — |
| 1841 | 1,622,500 | 6.00 | 7.50 | 10.00 | 17.00 | 45.00 | 175. | 260. | 2500. |
| 1841O | 2,007,500 | 8.00 | 11.00 | 15.00 | 28.00 | 60.00 | 250. | 1500. | — |
| 1842 | 1,887,500 | 6.00 | 7.50 | 10.00 | 17.00 | 45.00 | 175. | 260. | 2500. |
| 1842O | 2,020,000 | 8.00 | 11.00 | 15.00 | 40.00 | 120. | 750. | 2300. | — |
| 1843 | 1,370,000 | 6.00 | 8.00 | 10.00 | 17.00 | 45.00 | 175. | 260. | 2500. |
| 1843/1843 | — | 15.00 | 20.00 | 30.00 | 70.00 | 125. | 200. | 400. | — |
| 1843O | 150,000 | 35.00 | 65.00 | 125. | 275. | 700. | 2000. | — | — |
| 1844 | 72,500 | 125. | 175. | 225. | 400. | 900. | 1850. | 3000. | — |
| 1845 | 1,755,000 | 6.00 | 7.50 | 10.00 | 19.00 | 45.00 | 120. | 260. | 2500. |
| 1845/1845 | Inc. Ab. | 10.00 | 15.00 | 25.00 | 45.00 | 135. | — | — | — |
| 1845O | 230,000 | 19.00 | 35.00 | 60.00 | 165. | 475. | 1200. | — | — |
| 1846 | 31,300 | 95.00 | 125. | 150. | 300. | 850. | 2000. | — | — |
| 1847 | 245,000 | 13.50 | 20.00 | 30.00 | 60.00 | 125. | 350. | 950. | — |
| 1848 | 451,500 | 9.00 | 12.00 | 17.00 | 30.00 | 65.00 | 165. | 750. | 7050. |
| 1849 | 839,000 | 7.00 | 9.50 | 11.00 | 18.00 | 50.00 | 125. | 500. | 7050. |

| Date | Mintage | G-4 | VG-8 | F-12 | VF-20 | XF-40 | AU-50 | MS-60 | MS-65 |
|------|---------|-----|------|------|-------|-------|-------|-------|-------|
| 1849O | 300,000 | 10.00 | 18.00 | 30.00 | 85.00 | 175. | 1200. | — | — |
| 1850 | 1,931,500 | 6.00 | 7.00 | 9.00 | 25.00 | 60.00 | 120. | 260. | 2500. |
| 1850O | 510,000 | 10.00 | 14.00 | 28.00 | 60.00 | 135. | 400. | 1250. | — |
| 1851 | 1,026,500 | 6.00 | 7.00 | 9.00 | 19.00 | 60.00 | 120. | 325. | — |
| 1851O | 400,000 | 10.00 | 15.00 | 30.00 | 75.00 | 150. | 450. | 1500. | — |
| 1852 | 1,535,500 | 6.00 | 7.00 | 9.00 | 15.00 | 50.00 | 120. | 290. | 2500. |
| 1852O | 430,000 | 14.00 | 22.00 | 30.00 | 85.00 | 175. | 425. | 1800. | — |
| 1853 | 95,000 | 65.00 | 85.00 | 100. | 180. | 300. | 450. | 800. | — |

## Arrows at date

**Weight:** 2.49 grams. **Composition:** 90% silver (0.0721 ounces), 10% copper.

| Date | Mintage | G-4 | VG-8 | F-12 | VF-20 | XF-40 | AU-50 | MS-60 | MS-65 | Prf-65 |
|------|---------|-----|------|------|-------|-------|-------|-------|-------|--------|
| 1853 | 12,078,010 | 5.40 | 6.25 | 7.50 | 14.00 | 45.00 | 125. | 330. | 3800. | 38,000. |
| 1853O | 1,100,000 | 6.00 | 7.00 | 10.00 | 40.00 | 110. | 400. | 900. | — | — |
| 1854 | 4,470,000 | 5.75 | 6.25 | 7.50 | 14.00 | 45.00 | 125. | 330. | 3800. | 38,000. |
| 1854O | 1,770,000 | 5.50 | 6.50 | 9.00 | 25.00 | 75.00 | 175. | 600. | — | — |
| 1855 | 2,075,000 | 5.40 | 6.25 | 7.50 | 15.00 | 48.00 | 170. | 350. | 3800. | 38,000. |

## Arrows at date removed

**Notes:** The two 1856 varieties are distinguished by the size of the numerals in the date.

| Date | Mintage | G-4 | VG-8 | F-12 | VF-20 | XF-40 | AU-50 | MS-60 | MS-65 | Prf-65 |
|------|---------|-----|------|------|-------|-------|-------|-------|-------|--------|
| 1856 small date | | | | | | | | | | |
|  | 5,780,000 | 5.40 | 6.50 | 8.25 | 12.50 | 32.00 | 115. | 250. | 7050. | 38,000. |
| 1856 large date | | | | | | | | | | |
|  | Inc. Ab. | 10.00 | 12.00 | 15.00 | 25.00 | 65.00 | 175. | 475. | — | — |
| 1856O | 1,180,000 | 7.00 | 9.00 | 12.00 | 25.00 | 70.00 | 200. | 500. | — | — |
| 1856S | 70,000 | 100. | 165. | 225. | 425. | 800. | 1500. | — | — | — |
| 1857 | 5,580,000 | 5.40 | 6.25 | 8.25 | 12.50 | 32.00 | 100. | 260. | 2500. | 4000. |
| 1857O | 1,540,000 | 6.00 | 7.25 | 9.00 | 18.00 | 50.00 | 200. | 350. | — | — |
| 1858 | 1,540,000 | 5.40 | 6.25 | 8.25 | 17.50 | 40.00 | 115. | 260. | 2500. | 4000. |
| 1858O | 290,000 | 15.00 | 19.00 | 35.00 | 60.00 | 125. | 275. | 800. | — | — |
| 1858S | 60,000 | 80.00 | 125. | 175. | 290. | 600. | 1100. | 1800. | — | — |
| 1859 | 430,000 | 6.00 | 7.00 | 12.00 | 25.00 | 50.00 | 140. | 350. | — | 4000. |
| 1859O | 480,000 | 7.50 | 9.50 | 12.50 | 25.00 | 70.00 | 225. | 550. | — | — |
| 1859S | 60,000 | 100. | 130. | 225. | 400. | 900. | 2000. | — | — | — |
| 1860S | 140,000 | 28.00 | 36.00 | 48.00 | 100. | 225. | 800. | — | — | — |

## Transitional patterns

**Notes:** These non-circulation strikes were struck as experiments in transferring the legend "United States of America" from the reverse to the obverse.

| Date | Mintage | G-4 | VG-8 | F-12 | VF-20 | XF-40 | AU-50 | MS-60 | MS-65 | Prf-65 |
|------|---------|-----|------|------|-------|-------|-------|-------|-------|--------|
| 1859 obverse of 1859, reverse of 1860 | | | | — | — | — | — | — | 25,000. |

# 1866-S Dime
## Grade F-12

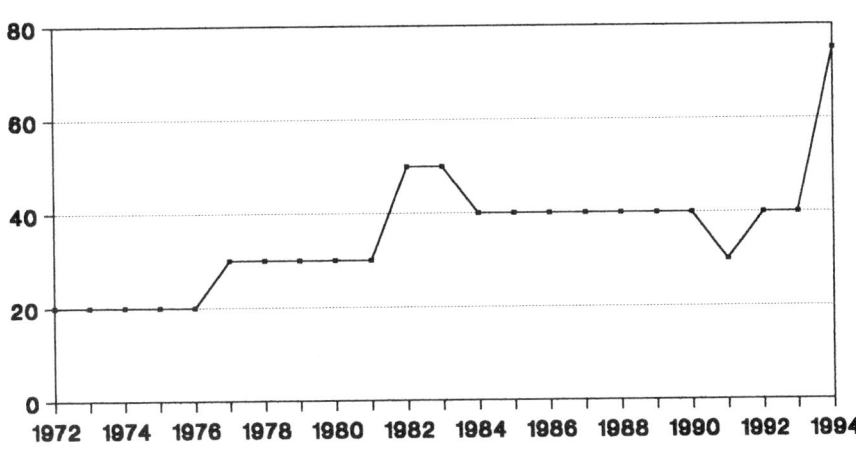

—•— **Retail Price**

**Source: COIN PRICES**

### Obverse legend

**Notes:** In 1860 the legend "United States of America" replaced the stars on the obverse. The 1873 "closed-3" and "open-3" varieties are distinguished by the amount of space between the upper left and lower left serifs of the 3 in the date.

| Date | Mintage | G-4 | VG-8 | F-12 | VF-20 | XF-40 | AU-50 | MS-60 | MS-65 | Prf-65 |
|------|---------|-----|------|------|-------|-------|-------|-------|-------|--------|
| 1860 | 607,000 | 6.00 | 7.50 | 12.00 | 18.00 | 40.00 | 85.00 | 200. | — | 1400. |
| 1860O | 40,000 | 300. | 475. | 800. | 1350. | 2500. | 4200. | 6000. | — | — |
| 1861 | 1,884,000 | 4.50 | 5.50 | 7.00 | 12.00 | 28.00 | 65.00 | 125. | — | 1400. |
| 1861S | 172,500 | 35.00 | 70.00 | 125. | 225. | 375. | 900. | — | — | — |
| 1862 | 847,550 | 5.50 | 7.00 | 8.50 | 14.00 | 35.00 | 65.00 | 150. | — | 1400. |
| 1862S | 180,750 | 30.00 | 52.00 | 85.00 | 140. | 300. | 700. | — | — | — |
| 1863 | 14,460 | 250. | 375. | 500. | 600. | 750. | 900. | 1200. | — | 1400. |
| 1863S | 157,500 | 30.00 | 35.00 | 55.00 | 90.00 | 200. | 400. | 1200. | — | — |
| 1864 | 11,470 | 250. | 325. | 400. | 500. | 600. | 775. | 1650. | — | 1400. |
| 1864S | 230,000 | 19.00 | 27.00 | 37.00 | 80.00 | 140. | 325. | 1200. | — | — |
| 1865 | 10,500 | 275. | 350. | 450. | 550. | 675. | 1050. | 1250. | — | 1400. |
| 1865S | 175,000 | 22.00 | 29.00 | 47.00 | 85.00 | 185. | 700. | — | — | — |
| 1866 | 8,725 | 300. | 375. | 575. | 675. | 800. | 1200. | 1800. | — | 4400. |
| 1866S | 135,000 | 35.00 | 45.00 | 75.00 | 110. | 200. | 400. | 1500. | — | — |
| 1867 | 6,625 | 350. | 450. | 600. | 700. | 850. | 1350. | 1800. | — | 4400. |
| 1867S | 140,000 | 30.00 | 40.00 | 70.00 | 95.00 | 195. | 385. | 1200. | — | — |
| 1868 | 464,000 | 10.00 | 12.00 | 20.00 | 31.00 | 70.00 | 175. | 300. | — | 1400. |
| 1868S | 260,000 | 12.00 | 17.00 | 27.00 | 55.00 | 115. | 285. | 600. | — | — |
| 1869 | 256,600 | 12.00 | 16.00 | 30.00 | 55.00 | 115. | 200. | 600. | — | 1400. |
| 1869S | 450,000 | 12.00 | 14.00 | 18.00 | 38.00 | 85.00 | 150. | 400. | — | — |
| 1870 | 471,000 | 9.75 | 11.00 | 15.00 | 32.00 | 70.00 | 135. | 300. | — | 1400. |
| 1870S | 50,000 | 215. | 280. | 375. | 450. | 575. | 850. | 2000. | — | — |
| 1871 | 907,710 | 7.75 | 9.00 | 11.00 | 21.00 | 42.00 | 130. | 300. | — | 1400. |
| 1871CC | 20,100 | 675. | 850. | 1300. | 2000. | 3200. | 5000. | — | — | — |

| Date | Mintage | G-4 | VG-8 | F-12 | VF-20 | XF-40 | AU-50 | MS-60 | MS-65 | Prf-65 |
|------|---------|-----|------|------|-------|-------|-------|-------|-------|--------|
| 1871S | 320,000 | 13.00 | 20.00 | 30.00 | 75.00 | 135. | 350. | 900. | — | — |
| 1872 | 2,396,450 | 6.50 | 8.00 | 10.00 | 18.00 | 31.00 | 95.00 | 175. | — | 1400. |
| 1872CC | 35,480 | 350. | 500. | 850. | 1200. | 2500. | 4000. | — | — | — |
| 1872S | 190,000 | 29.00 | 43.00 | 70.00 | 125. | 215. | 450. | 1100. | — | — |
| 1873 closed 3 | 1,568,600 | 7.00 | 8.50 | 10.00 | 18.00 | 50.00 | 100. | 200. | — | 1400. |
| 1873 open 3 | Inc. Ab. | 15.00 | 18.00 | 30.00 | 48.00 | 100. | 225. | 650. | — | — |
| 1873CC | 12,400 | — | — | | Unique | — | — | — | — | — |

## Arrows at date

**Weight:** 2.5 grams. **Composition:** 90% silver (0.0724 ounces), 10% copper.

| Date | Mintage | G-4 | VG-8 | F-12 | VF-20 | XF-40 | AU-50 | MS-60 | MS-65 | Prf-65 |
|------|---------|-----|------|------|-------|-------|-------|-------|-------|--------|
| 1873 | 2,378,500 | 8.00 | 13.00 | 25.00 | 50.00 | 150. | 350. | 500. | 6000. | 6000. |
| 1873CC | 18,791 | 650. | 850. | 1300. | 2500. | 3500. | 6000. | — | — | — |
| 1873S | 455,000 | 10.00 | 16.00 | 17.00 | 60.00 | 180. | 320. | 1500. | — | — |
| 1874 | 2,940,700 | 8.00 | 13.00 | 17.50 | 50.00 | 150. | 315. | 500. | 6000. | 6000. |
| 1874CC | 10,817 | 1500. | 2200. | 3500. | 5500. | 11,000. | — | — | — | — |
| 1874S | 240,000 | 20.00 | 30.00 | 55.00 | 100. | 250. | 450. | 1500. | — | — |

## Arrows at date removed

**Notes:** On the 1876-CC doubled-obverse variety, doubling appears in the words ''of America'' in the legend.

| Date | Mintage | G-4 | VG-8 | F-12 | VF-20 | XF-40 | AU-50 | MS-60 | MS-65 | Prf-65 |
|------|---------|-----|------|------|-------|-------|-------|-------|-------|--------|
| 1875 | 10,350,700 | 5.50 | 6.50 | 7.50 | 11.00 | 22.00 | 60.00 | 125. | 2250. | 4600. |
| 1875CC mint mark in wreath | 4,645,000 | 6.50 | 8.00 | 11.00 | 18.00 | 30.00 | 90.00 | 160. | 2700. | — |
| 1875CC mint mark under wreath | Inc. Ab. | 7.00 | 9.00 | 13.00 | 25.00 | 50.00 | 165. | 235. | 3000. | — |
| 1875S mint mark in wreath | 9,070,000 | 8.00 | 12.00 | 17.00 | 25.00 | 45.00 | 125. | 225. | 3100. | — |
| 1875S mint mark under wreath | Inc. Ab. | 5.50 | 6.25 | 7.50 | 11.50 | 22.00 | 60.00 | 110. | 1150. | — |
| 1876 | 11,461,150 | 5.50 | 6.25 | 7.50 | 11.00 | 24.00 | 60.00 | 110. | 1150. | 1250. |
| 1876CC | 8,270,000 | 5.50 | 6.50 | 7.50 | 18.00 | 30.00 | 60.00 | 175. | — | — |
| 1876CC (doubled obverse) | Inc. Ab. | 15.00 | 25.00 | 40.00 | 125. | 250. | 400. | 700. | — | — |
| 1876S | 10,420,000 | 5.50 | 6.50 | 12.50 | 20.00 | 35.00 | 60.00 | 110. | 1150. | — |
| 1877 | 7,310,510 | 5.50 | 6.25 | 8.50 | 13.00 | 23.00 | 60.00 | 110. | 1150. | 1250. |
| 1877CC | 7,700,000 | 5.50 | 6.50 | 9.00 | 18.00 | 30.00 | 75.00 | 175. | — | — |
| 1877S | 2,340,000 | 7.75 | 9.00 | 12.00 | 20.00 | 39.00 | 90.00 | 150. | — | — |
| 1878 | 1,678,800 | 5.50 | 6.50 | 10.00 | 18.00 | 30.00 | 60.00 | 110. | 1150. | 1250. |
| 1878CC | 200,000 | 40.00 | 55.00 | 90.00 | 145. | 250. | 450. | 775. | 3900. | — |
| 1879 | 15,100 | 165. | 200. | 250. | 275. | 350. | 400 | 600. | 4300. | 4400. |
| 1880 | 37,335 | 100. | 125. | 165. | 210. | 250. | 325. | 450. | 4300. | 4400. |
| 1881 | 24,975 | 125. | 150. | 180. | 230. | 325. | 425. | 650. | 4300. | 4400. |
| 1882 | 3,911,100 | 5.40 | 6.25 | 7.50 | 11.00 | 22.00 | 60.00 | 110. | 1150. | 1200. |
| 1883 | 7,675,712 | 5.50 | 6.25 | 7.50 | 11.00 | 24.00 | 60.00 | 110. | 1150. | 1250. |
| 1884 | 3,366,380 | 5.50 | 6.25 | 7.50 | 11.00 | 22.00 | 60.00 | 110. | 1150. | 1250. |
| 1884S | 564,969 | 14.00 | 17.00 | 29.00 | 43.00 | 80.00 | 175. | 500. | — | — |
| 1885 | 2,533,427 | 5.50 | 6.25 | 7.50 | 11.00 | 22.00 | 60.00 | 110. | 1150. | 1250. |
| 1885S | 43,690 | 300. | 450. | 600. | 1100. | 1500. | 2500. | 3000. | — | — |
| 1886 | 6,377,570 | 5.50 | 6.25 | 7.50 | 11.00 | 22.00 | 60.00 | 110. | 1150. | 1250. |
| 1886S | 206,524 | 30.00 | 40.00 | 57.00 | 80.00 | 115. | 225. | 600. | — | — |
| 1887 | 11,283,939 | 5.50 | 6.25 | 7.50 | 11.00 | 22.00 | 60.00 | 110. | 1150. | 1250. |
| 1887S | 4,454,450 | 5.50 | 6.25 | 7.50 | 11.00 | 22.00 | 60.00 | 110. | 1150. | — |
| 1888 | 5,496,487 | 5.50 | 6.25 | 7.50 | 11.00 | 22.00 | 60.00 | 110. | 1150. | 1250. |
| 1888S | 1,720,000 | 6.00 | 6.75 | 9.50 | 14.00 | 35.00 | 95.00 | 200. | — | — |
| 1889 | 7,380,711 | 5.50 | 6.25 | 7.50 | 11.00 | 22.00 | 60.00 | 110. | 1150. | 1250. |

| Date | Mintage | G-4 | VG-8 | F-12 | VF-20 | XF-40 | AU-50 | MS-60 | MS-65 | Prf-65 |
|------|---------|-----|------|------|-------|-------|-------|-------|-------|--------|
| 1889S | 972,678 | 14.00 | 17.00 | 23.00 | 40.00 | 75.00 | 150. | 475. | 4500. | — |
| 1890 | 9,911,541 | 5.50 | 6.25 | 7.50 | 11.00 | 22.00 | 60.00 | 110. | 1150. | 1250. |
| 1890S | 1,423,076 | 8.00 | 10.00 | 18.00 | 32.00 | 70.00 | 135. | 400. | 4900. | — |
| 1890S/S | Inc. Ab. | 100. | 120. | 150. | 185. | 275. | 450. | — | — | — |
| 1891 | 15,310,600 | 5.50 | 6.25 | 7.50 | 11.00 | 22.00 | 60.00 | 110. | 1150. | 1250. |
| 1891O | 4,540,000 | 5.50 | 6.50 | 7.75 | 11.50 | 22.00 | 70.00 | 475. | 2250. | — |
| 1891O/horz. O | | | | | | | | | | |
| | Inc. Ab. | 100. | 120. | 150. | 185. | 275. | 400. | — | — | — |
| 1891S | 3,196,116 | 5.50 | 6.25 | 7.50 | 12.00 | 28.00 | 70.00 | 500. | 4400. | — |

# Barber

**Designer:** Charles E. Barber. **Size:** 17.9 millimeters. **Weight:** 2.5 grams. **Composition:** 90% silver (0.0724 ounces), 10% copper.

| Date | Mintage | G-4 | VG-8 | F-12 | VF-20 | XF-40 | AU-50 | MS-60 | MS-65 | Prf-65 |
|------|---------|-----|------|------|-------|-------|-------|-------|-------|--------|
| 1892 | 12,121,245 | 2.60 | 4.90 | 14.00 | 19.50 | 25.00 | 60.00 | 100. | 630. | 1450. |
| 1892O | 3,841,700 | 5.25 | 8.00 | 23.50 | 32.00 | 35.00 | 59.00 | 145. | 1200. | — |
| 1892S | 990,710 | 33.00 | 58.00 | 135. | 175. | 190. | 200. | 360. | 3600. | — |
| 1893 | 3,340,792 | 5.50 | 9.50 | 14.00 | 20.00 | 40.00 | 65.00 | 145. | 630. | 1450. |
| 1893O | 1,760,000 | 15.00 | 26.00 | 95.00 | 110. | 120. | 135. | 260. | 3600. | — |
| 1893S | 2,491,401 | 6.50 | 13.50 | 21.00 | 30.00 | 39.00 | 110. | 230. | 2400. | — |
| 1894 | 1,330,972 | 8.00 | 15.00 | 91.00 | 110. | 120. | f30. | 250. | 1175. | 1450. |
| 1894O | 720,000 | 32.00 | 65.00 | 165. | 210. | 290. | 600. | 945. | 8300. | — |
| 1894S | 24 | | | Stacks Sale, Jan. 1990, Ch. Proof $275,000. | | | | — | — | — |
| 1895 | 690,880 | 65.00 | 85.00 | 305. | 400. | 430. | 525. | 610. | 2400. | 2000. |
| 1895O | 440,000 | 170. | 265. | 675. | 950. | 1825. | 1950. | 2200. | 10,000. | — |
| 1895S | 1,120,000 | 19.50 | 29.00 | 105. | 145. | 150. | 180. | 390. | 6200. | — |
| 1896 | 2,000,762 | 6.50 | 14.00 | 39.00 | 56.00 | 58.00 | 85.00 | 165. | 1560. | 1450. |
| 1896O | 610,000 | 43.00 | 75.00 | 215. | 280. | 350. | 550. | 725. | 6000. | — |
| 1896S | 575,056 | 41.00 | 62.00 | 195. | 250. | 300. | 410. | 585. | 3600. | — |
| 1897 | 10,869,264 | 1.30 | 2.60 | 5.85 | 8.50 | 23.00 | 68.00 | 115. | 630. | 1450. |
| 1897O | 666,000 | 36.00 | 57.00 | 230. | 285. | 325. | 520. | 725. | 5400. | — |
| 1897S | 1,342,844 | 8.00 | 17.00 | 70.00 | 83.00 | 90.00 | 195. | 325. | 4800. | — |
| 1898 | 16,320,735 | 1.50 | 1.70 | 6.00 | 9.00 | 20.00 | 50.00 | 100. | 630. | 1450. |
| 1898O | 2,130,000 | 11.00 | 42.00 | 75.00 | 95.00 | 125. | 165. | 425. | 4300. | — |
| 1898S | 1,702,507 | 3.90 | 7.75 | 18.00 | 31.00 | 35.00 | 100. | 325. | 5300. | — |
| 1899 | 19,580,846 | 1.30 | 1.65 | 5.85 | 8.50 | 20.00 | 60.00 | 100. | 630. | 1450. |
| 1899O | 2,650,000 | 8.00 | 30.00 | 60.00 | 80.00 | 110. | 200. | 360. | 5750. | — |
| 1899S | 1,867,493 | 4.00 | 8.00 | 11.00 | 18.00 | 32.00 | 85.00 | 295. | 3500. | — |
| 1900 | 17,600,912 | 1.35 | 2.50 | 6.00 | 8.50 | 20.00 | 45.00 | 100. | 900. | 1450. |
| 1900O | 2,010,000 | 5.25 | 11.00 | 78.00 | 105. | 155. | 260. | 625. | 6000. | — |
| 1900S | 5,168,270 | 2.50 | 2.90 | 8.50 | 11.00 | 23.00 | 72.00 | 155. | 1920. | — |
| 1901 | 18,860,478 | 1.30 | 1.65 | 5.25 | 7.75 | 20.00 | 45.00 | 100. | 1170. | 1450. |
| 1901O | 5,620,000 | 2.25 | 3.50 | 12.00 | 18.00 | 42.00 | 115. | 360. | 2900. | — |
| 1901S | 593,022 | 35.00 | 53.00 | 250. | 325. | 370. | 585. | 825. | 4750. | — |
| 1902 | 21,380,777 | 1.30 | 1.65 | 3.90 | 6.75 | 21.00 | 45.00 | 100. | 630. | 1450. |
| 1902O | 4,500,000 | 2.35 | 4.00 | 11.00 | 20.00 | 35.00 | 105. | 325. | 3350. | — |
| 1902S | 2,070,000 | 4.00 | 8.00 | 41.00 | 58.00 | 71.00 | 130. | 325. | 4080. | — |
| 1903 | 19,500,755 | 1.30 | 1.65 | 3.90 | 7.15 | 20.00 | 45.00 | 100. | 1100. | 1450. |
| 1903O | 8,180,000 | 2.00 | 2.75 | 8.75 | 13.00 | 26.00 | 91.00 | 240. | 5050. | — |
| 1903S | 613,300 | 30.00 | 47.00 | 310. | 450. | 700. | 750. | 1075. | 4550. | — |
| 1904 | 14,601,027 | 1.30 | 1.65 | 5.25 | 9.00 | 20.00 | 45.00 | 125. | 3250. | 1450. |
| 1904S | 800,000 | 21.00 | 36.00 | 110. | 155. | 230. | 420. | 525. | 4600. | — |
| 1905 | 14,552,350 | 1.30 | 1.65 | 3.90 | 6.50 | 21.00 | 60.00 | 100. | 630. | 1450. |
| 1905O | 3,400,000 | 2.25 | 4.50 | 28.00 | 39.00 | 45.00 | 105. | 230. | 2900. | — |
| 1905S | 6,855,199 | 2.10 | 3.00 | 6.50 | 17.00 | 33.00 | 75.00 | 200. | 1150. | — |
| 1906 | 19,958,406 | 1.30 | 1.45 | 3.00 | 6.50 | 21.00 | 45.00 | 100. | 630. | 1450. |
| 1906D | 4,060,000 | 2.10 | 3.00 | 6.50 | 11.00 | 25.00 | 80.00 | 150. | 2200. | — |
| 1906O | 2,610,000 | 3.50 | 5.50 | 41.00 | 57.00 | 63.00 | 120. | 210. | 1250. | — |
| 1906S | 3,136,640 | 1.60 | 3.50 | 11.00 | 16.00 | 33.00 | 91.00 | 215. | 1350. | — |
| 1907 | 22,220,575 | 1.30 | 1.55 | 3.00 | 6.50 | 21.00 | 46.00 | 100. | 630. | 1450. |
| 1907D | 4,080,000 | 1.45 | 2.60 | 7.50 | 10.00 | 30.00 | 85.00 | 260. | 4150. | — |
| 1907O | 5,058,000 | 1.45 | 2.60 | 30.00 | 41.00 | 46.00 | 72.00 | 220. | 1625. | — |
| 1907S | 3,178,470 | 1.90 | 3.90 | 7.75 | 13.00 | 35.00 | 100. | 325. | 3100. | — |
| 1908 | 10,600,545 | 1.45 | 1.55 | 3.00 | 6.50 | 21.00 | 45.00 | 100. | 630. | 1450. |
| 1908D | 7,490,000 | 1.30 | 1.80 | 5.50 | 9.50 | 25.00 | 55.00 | 140. | 1550. | — |
| 1908O | 1,789,000 | 2.30 | 4.50 | 39.00 | 52.00 | 57.00 | 125. | 250. | 2275. | — |
| 1908S | 3,220,000 | 1.65 | 2.60 | 7.50 | 12.00 | 26.00 | 91.00 | 260. | 2300. | — |
| 1909 | 10,240,650 | 1.45 | 1.65 | 3.00 | 6.50 | 21.00 | 45.00 | 100. | 630. | 1700. |
| 1909D | 954,000 | 2.95 | 7.00 | 58.00 | 77.00 | 81.00 | 150. | 390. | 2750. | — |

# 1901-S Dime
## Grade F-12

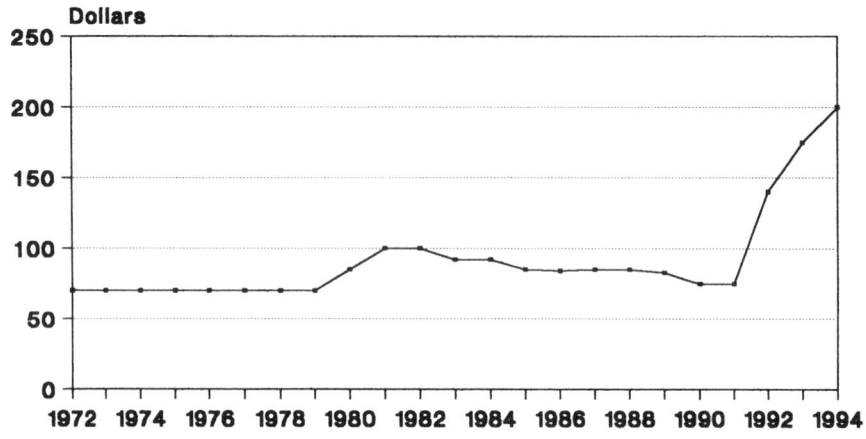

**Dollars**

——— **Retail Price**

**Source: COIN PRICES**

| Date | Mintage | G-4 | VG-8 | F-12 | VF-20 | XF-40 | AU-50 | MS-60 | MS-65 | Prf-65 |
|------|---------|-----|------|------|-------|-------|-------|-------|-------|--------|
| 1909O | 2,287,000 | 1.65 | 3.40 | 7.80 | 15.00 | 27.00 | 91.00 | 180. | 1400. | — |
| 1909S | 1,000,000 | 3.00 | 7.50 | 78.00 | 100. | 135. | 280. | 470. | 3600. | — |
| 1910 | 11,520,551 | 1.45 | 1.55 | 6.50 | 10.50 | 22.00 | 46.00 | 100. | 630. | 1450. |
| 1910D | 3,490,000 | 1.65 | 3.25 | 7.50 | 11.00 | 37.00 | 91.00 | 195. | 2400. | — |
| 1910S | 1,240,000 | 1.65 | 4.50 | 49.00 | 62.00 | 69.00 | 150. | 350. | 1975. | — |
| 1911 | 18,870,543 | 1.30 | 1.45 | 3.00 | 6.50 | 19.50 | 45.00 | 100. | 630. | 1700. |
| 1911D | 11,209,000 | 1.30 | 1.45 | 3.90 | 7.00 | 21.50 | 47.00 | 100. | 630. | — |
| 1911S | 3,520,000 | 1.65 | 3.00 | 7.00 | 11.00 | 26.00 | 85.00 | 145. | 840. | — |
| 1912 | 19,350,700 | 1.30 | 1.45 | 3.00 | 6.50 | 21.00 | 47.00 | 100. | 630. | 1700. |
| 1912D | 11,760,000 | 1.30 | 1.45 | 4.00 | 6.75 | 21.00 | 47.00 | 100. | 850. | — |
| 1912S | 3,420,000 | 1.30 | 1.80 | 5.25 | 7.50 | 23.00 | 72.00 | 150. | 1200. | — |
| 1913 | 19,760,622 | 1.30 | 1.45 | 2.80 | 6.50 | 21.00 | 47.00 | 100. | 660. | 1450. |
| 1913S | 510,000 | 8.00 | 12.00 | 65.00 | 110. | 175. | 295. | 360. | 1325. | — |
| 1914 | 17,360,655 | 1.30 | 1.45 | 2.80 | 6.50 | 21.00 | 47.00 | 100. | 630. | 1700. |
| 1914D | 11,908,000 | 1.30 | 1.45 | 4.00 | 6.75 | 21.00 | 47.00 | 100. | 630. | — |
| 1914S | 2,100,000 | 1.95 | 2.25 | 5.00 | 10.00 | 26.00 | 72.00 | 145. | 1200. | — |
| 1915 | 5,620,450 | 1.30 | 1.45 | 3.90 | 7.00 | 21.00 | 47.00 | 100. | 850. | 2000. |
| 1915S | 960,000 | 1.75 | 3.50 | 22.00 | 39.00 | 43.00 | 125. | 235. | 2300. | — |
| 1916 | 18,490,000 | 1.30 | 1.45 | 5.00 | 6.75 | 21.00 | 47.00 | 100. | 630. | — |
| 1916S | 5,820,000 | 1.30 | 1.45 | 4.00 | 6.50 | 21.00 | 47.00 | 100. | 780. | — |

# Mercury

**Designer:** Adolph A. Weinman. **Size:** 17.9 millimeters. **Weight:** 2.5 grams. **Composition:** 90% silver (0.0724 ounces), 10% copper. **Notes:** "-65FSB" values are for coins with fully split and rounded horizontal bands around the fasces on the reverse. The 1945-S "micro" variety has a smaller mintmark than the normal variety.

# 1916-D Dime
## Grade F-12

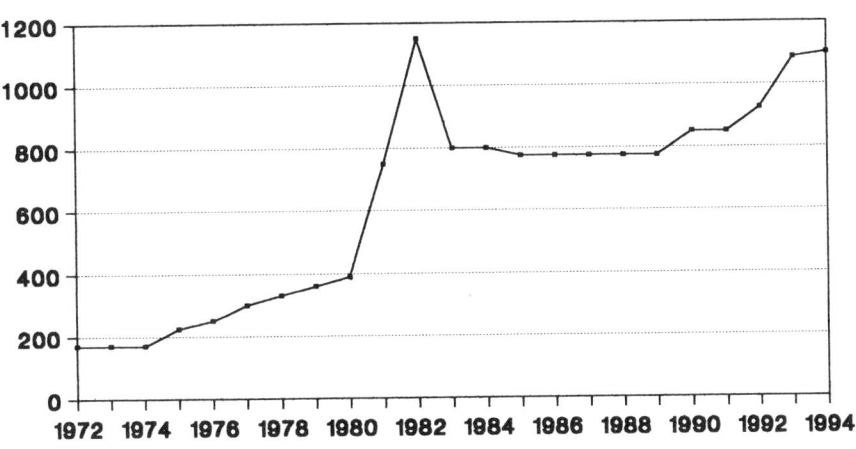

—•— Retail Price

Source: COIN PRICES

| Date | Mintage | G-4 | VG-8 | F-12 | VF-20 | XF-40 | MS-60 | MS-65 | -65FSB | Prf-65 |
|------|---------|-----|------|------|-------|-------|-------|-------|--------|--------|
| 1916 | 22,180,080 | 2.25 | 3.50 | 4.75 | 7.25 | 11.00 | 25.00 | 90.00 | 110. | — |
| 1916D | 264,000 | 435. | 665. | 1100. | 1900. | 2700. | 4550. | 11,750. | 14,500. | — |
| 1916S | 10,450,000 | 3.50 | 4.50 | 5.75 | 9.75 | 16.50 | 34.00 | 195. | 450. | — |
| 1917 | 55,230,000 | 1.00 | 2.10 | 2.75 | 5.50 | 8.00 | 28.00 | 150. | 340. | — |
| 1917D | 9,402,000 | 3.50 | 5.25 | 8.00 | 16.00 | 38.00 | 125. | 1825. | 5700. | — |
| 1917S | 27,330,000 | 1.25 | 2.35 | 3.25 | 6.00 | 9.50 | 49.00 | 585. | 1690. | — |
| 1918 | 26,680,000 | 1.25 | 3.00 | 4.25 | 11.00 | 25.00 | 70.00 | 390. | 675. | — |
| 1918D | 22,674,800 | 2.25 | 3.00 | 4.00 | 9.50 | 23.00 | 105. | 680. | 9750. | — |
| 1918S | 19,300,000 | 2.00 | 2.50 | 3.50 | 6.50 | 14.00 | 85.00 | 975. | 5850. | — |
| 1919 | 35,740,000 | 1.00 | 2.25 | 3.25 | 5.50 | 8.00 | 35.00 | 360. | 550. | — |
| 1919D | 9,939,000 | 3.00 | 4.25 | 6.00 | 15.00 | 39.00 | 140. | 1800. | 5600. | — |
| 1919S | 8,850,000 | 2.50 | 3.60 | 5.00 | 13.00 | 29.00 | 175. | 1100. | 4350. | — |
| 1920 | 59,030,000 | 1.00 | 2.10 | 2.75 | 5.00 | 7.00 | 27.00 | 230. | 365. | — |
| 1920D | 19,171,000 | 2.25 | 3.25 | 4.25 | 7.00 | 15.00 | 100. | 1250. | 3050. | — |
| 1920S | 13,820,000 | 2.00 | 2.80 | 4.00 | 6.50 | 13.50 | 70.00 | 1175. | 4875. | — |
| 1921 | 1,230,000 | 19.50 | 30.00 | 70.00 | 175. | 425. | 1050. | 2900. | 4000. | — |
| 1921D | 1,080,000 | 30.00 | 41.00 | 110. | 220. | 500. | 1150. | 2850. | 4550. | — |
| 1923 | 50,130,000 | 1.00 | 2.10 | 2.75 | 4.25 | 7.00 | 25.00 | 115. | 195. | — |
| 1923S | 6,440,000 | 2.25 | 3.50 | 4.25 | 9.50 | 29.00 | 135. | 1500. | 4000. | — |
| 1924 | 24,010,000 | 1.00 | 2.10 | 2.75 | 5.00 | 9.00 | 38.00 | 170. | 480. | — |
| 1924D | 6,810,000 | 2.25 | 3.25 | 5.50 | 10.00 | 29.00 | 155. | 1275. | 3300. | — |
| 1924S | 7,120,000 | 2.00 | 3.00 | 4.00 | 8.00 | 29.00 | 155. | 1550. | 6050. | — |
| 1925 | 25,610,000 | 1.00 | 2.10 | 2.75 | 4.25 | 7.50 | 28.00 | 195. | 535. | |
| 1925D | 5,117,000 | 4.00 | 5.75 | 8.50 | 25.00 | 85.00 | 260. | 1700. | 5300. | — |
| 1925S | 5,850,000 | 2.00 | 2.80 | 4.00 | 8.00 | 30.00 | 140. | 2200. | 4250. | — |
| 1926 | 32,160,000 | 1.00 | 1.85 | 2.25 | 4.25 | 6.50 | 28.00 | 235. | 560. | — |
| 1926D | 6,828,000 | 1.95 | 3.00 | 4.00 | 7.50 | 15.00 | 70.00 | 550. | 2400. | — |
| 1926S | 1,520,000 | 5.50 | 9.50 | 15.00 | 34.00 | 190. | 770. | 3000. | 4950. | — |
| 1927 | 28,080,000 | 1.00 | 1.80 | 2.25 | 4.25 | 6.50 | 21.00 | 180. | 325. | — |
| 1927D | 4,812,000 | 2.75 | 3.75 | 5.00 | 12.00 | 42.00 | 175. | 1200. | 4950. | — |
| 1927S | 4,770,000 | 1.90 | 2.65 | 3.75 | 5.50 | 11.00 | 125. | 1050. | 4550. | — |
| 1928 | 19,480,000 | 1.00 | 1.80 | 2.25 | 4.25 | 6.50 | 21.00 | 115. | 250. | — |
| 1928D | 4,161,000 | 3.00 | 4.25 | 6.00 | 15.00 | 30.00 | 135. | 910. | 2500. | — |
| 1928S | 7,400,000 | 1.75 | 2.35 | 3.25 | 5.00 | 12.00 | 70.00 | 495. | 1500. | — |
| 1929 | 25,970,000 | 1.00 | 1.80 | 2.35 | 3.75 | 5.00 | 19.50 | 58.00 | 180. | — |
| 1929D | 5,034,000 | 2.65 | 3.60 | 5.00 | 8.00 | 12.00 | 28.00 | 85.00 | 130. | — |
| 1929S | 4,730,000 | 1.65 | 1.90 | 2.25 | 4.25 | 5.50 | 34.00 | 120. | 310. | — |
| 1930 | 6,770,000 | 1.50 | 1.80 | 2.25 | 4.25 | 5.50 | 22.00 | 130. | 275. | — |
| 1930S | 1,843,000 | 3.50 | 4.25 | 5.00 | 7.50 | 13.00 | 70.00 | 135. | 260. | — |
| 1931 | 3,150,000 | 2.00 | 2.75 | 3.50 | 5.00 | 11.00 | 35.00 | 155. | 440. | — |
| 1931D | 1,260,000 | 5.50 | 7.50 | 11.00 | 18.00 | 30.00 | 77.00 | 210. | 290. | — |
| 1931S | 1,800,000 | 3.50 | 4.00 | 5.00 | 7.50 | 13.00 | 63.00 | 210. | 1300. | — |

PRICING SECTION

| Date | Mintage | G-4 | VG-8 | F-12 | VF-20 | XF-40 | MS-60 | MS-65 | -65FSB | Prf-65 |
|---|---|---|---|---|---|---|---|---|---|---|
| 1934 | 24,080,000 | 1.00 | 1.45 | 1.75 | 3.00 | 5.00 | 15.00 | 32.00 | 52.00 | — |
| 1934D | 6,772,000 | 1.80 | 2.10 | 2.75 | 4.00 | 8.00 | 32.00 | 62.00 | 220. | — |
| 1935 | 58,830,000 | 1.00 | 1.20 | 1.50 | 2.15 | 4.25 | 11.00 | 30.00 | 36.00 | — |
| 1935D | 10,477,000 | 1.75 | 2.00 | 3.00 | 4.75 | 9.25 | 32.00 | 60.00 | 310. | — |
| 1935S | 15,840,000 | 1.35 | 1.50 | 1.75 | 3.00 | 5.50 | 24.00 | 33.00 | 145. | — |
| 1936 | 87,504,130 | 1.00 | 1.25 | 1.50 | 2.25 | 3.50 | 8.50 | 24.00 | 36.00 | 875. |
| 1936D | 16,132,000 | 1.25 | 1.50 | 2.00 | 3.25 | 6.75 | 22.00 | 42.00 | 130. | — |
| 1936S | 9,210,000 | 1.25 | 1.50 | 1.75 | 2.75 | 4.75 | 17.00 | 28.00 | 30.00 | — |
| 1937 | 56,865,756 | 1.00 | 1.25 | 1.50 | 2.00 | 3.25 | 10.00 | 24.00 | 36.00 | 300. |
| 1937D | 14,146,000 | 1.25 | 1.50 | 1.90 | 3.00 | 5.50 | 21.00 | 41.00 | 52.00 | — |
| 1937S | 9,740,000 | 1.25 | 1.50 | 1.90 | 3.00 | 5.50 | 18.00 | 31.00 | 85.00 | — |
| 1938 | 22,198,728 | 1.00 | 1.25 | 1.50 | 2.25 | 3.50 | 14.00 | 23.00 | 36.00 | 215. |
| 1938D | 5,537,000 | 1.75 | 2.00 | 2.25 | 3.75 | 6.00 | 15.00 | 26.00 | 36.00 | — |
| 1938S | 8,090,000 | 1.35 | 1.55 | 1.85 | 2.35 | 3.75 | 15.00 | 29.00 | 46.00 | — |
| 1939 | 67,749,321 | 1.00 | 1.25 | 1.50 | 2.00 | 3.25 | 10.00 | 25.00 | 72.00 | 210. |
| 1939D | 24,394,000 | 1.25 | 1.45 | 1.75 | 2.25 | 3.50 | 12.50 | 24.00 | 36.00 | — |
| 1939S | 10,540,000 | 1.55 | 1.75 | 2.00 | 2.50 | 4.25 | 24.00 | 35.00 | 340. | — |
| 1940 | 65,361,827 | .80 | .90 | 1.00 | 1.10 | 2.50 | 6.50 | 23.00 | 33.00 | 185. |
| 1940D | 21,198,000 | .80 | .90 | 1.00 | 1.10 | 1.50 | 8.50 | 23.00 | 33.00 | — |
| 1940S | 21,560,000 | .80 | .90 | 1.00 | 1.10 | 1.50 | 8.50 | 23.00 | 43.00 | — |
| 1941 | 175,106,557 | .80 | .90 | 1.00 | 1.10 | 1.50 | 5.50 | 19.00 | 23.00 | 180. |
| 1941D | 45,634,000 | .80 | .90 | 1.00 | 1.10 | 1.50 | 8.00 | 21.00 | 23.00 | — |
| 1941S | 43,090,000 | .80 | .90 | 1.00 | 1.10 | 1.50 | 10.00 | 19.00 | 30.00 | — |

Fully split bands

1942/41

1942/41-D

| Date | Mintage | G-4 | VG-8 | F-12 | VF-20 | XF-40 | MS-60 | MS-65 | -65FSB | Prf-65 |
|---|---|---|---|---|---|---|---|---|---|---|
| 1942 | 205,432,329 | .80 | .90 | 1.00 | 1.10 | 1.50 | 5.50 | 20.00 | 36.00 | 180. |
| 1942/41 | Inc. Ab. | 155. | 180. | 230. | 250. | 310. | 1600. | 6500. | 9350. | — |
| 1942D | 60,740,000 | .80 | .90 | 1.00 | 1.10 | 1.50 | 8.50 | 23.00 | 30.00 | — |
| 1942/41D | Inc. Ab. | 165. | 190. | 240. | 260. | 400. | 1400. | 5000. | 7300. | — |
| 1942S | 49,300,000 | .80 | .90 | 1.00 | 1.10 | 1.50 | 10.00 | 23.00 | 61.00 | — |
| 1943 | 191,710,000 | .80 | .90 | 1.00 | 1.10 | 1.50 | 6.50 | 19.00 | 23.00 | — |
| 1943D | 71,949,000 | .80 | .90 | 1.00 | 1.10 | 1.50 | 8.50 | 24.00 | 26.00 | — |
| 1943S | 60,400,000 | .80 | .90 | 1.00 | 1.10 | 1.50 | 10.00 | 20.00 | 32.00 | — |
| 1944 | 231,410,000 | .80 | .90 | 1.00 | 1.10 | 1.50 | 5.50 | 20.00 | 39.00 | — |
| 1944D | 62,224,000 | .80 | .90 | 1.00 | 1.10 | 1.50 | 8.50 | 20.00 | 27.00 | — |
| 1944S | 49,490,000 | .80 | .90 | 1.00 | 1.10 | 1.50 | 10.00 | 20.00 | 30.00 | — |
| 1945 | 159,130,000 | .80 | .90 | 1.00 | 1.10 | 1.50 | 5.50 | 22.00 | 3125. | — |
| 1945D | 40,245,000 | .80 | .90 | 1.00 | 1.10 | 1.50 | 8.00 | 20.00 | 29.00 | — |
| 1945S | 41,920,000 | .80 | .90 | 1.00 | 1.10 | 1.50 | 8.50 | 20.00 | 58.00 | — |
| 1945S micro | Inc. Ab. | 1.50 | 1.65 | 1.85 | 3.00 | 4.25 | 17.00 | 52.00 | 450. | — |

# Roosevelt

Reverse mintmark
(1946-64)

Obverse mintmark
(1968-present)

## Silver composition

**Designer:** John R. Sinnock. **Size:** 17.9 millimeters. **Weight:** 2.5 grams. **Composition:** 90% silver (0.0724 ounces), 10% copper.

| Date | Mintage | G-4 | VG-8 | F-12 | VF-20 | XF-40 | AU-50 | MS-60 | MS-65 | Prf-65 |
|------|---------|-----|------|------|-------|-------|-------|-------|-------|--------|
| 1946 | 225,250,000 | — | — | — | .65 | .80 | .95 | 1.05 | 2.50 | — |
| 1946D | 61,043,500 | — | — | — | .65 | .80 | 1.10 | 1.25 | 4.50 | — |
| 1946S | 27,900,000 | — | — | — | .65 | .80 | 1.10 | 2.00 | 5.25 | — |
| 1947 | 121,520,000 | — | — | — | .65 | .80 | .95 | 1.00 | 4.75 | — |
| 1947D | 46,835,000 | — | — | — | .65 | .95 | 1.20 | 1.40 | 10.00 | — |
| 1947S | 34,840,000 | — | — | — | .65 | .95 | 1.10 | 1.35 | 5.50 | — |
| 1948 | 74,950,000 | — | — | — | .65 | .95 | 1.10 | 1.75 | 11.00 | — |
| 1948D | 52,841,000 | — | — | — | .65 | 1.20 | 1.50 | 2.00 | 10.00 | — |
| 1948S | 35,520,000 | — | — | — | .65 | .95 | 1.10 | 1.35 | 9.00 | — |
| 1949 | 30,940,000 | — | — | — | 1.00 | 1.50 | 4.50 | 6.00 | 29.00 | — |
| 1949D | 26,034,000 | — | — | .60 | .80 | 1.25 | 2.00 | 3.50 | 12.50 | — |
| 1949S | 13,510,000 | — | 1.00 | 1.25 | 1.50 | 2.75 | 7.50 | 9.00 | 55.00 | — |
| 1950 | 50,181,500 | — | — | — | .65 | .95 | 1.10 | 1.35 | 4.60 | 25.00 |
| 1950D | 46,803,000 | — | — | — | .65 | .80 | .95 | 1.00 | 4.60 | — |
| 1950S | 20,440,000 | — | .85 | 1.00 | 1.10 | 1.25 | 5.00 | 7.00 | 35.00 | — |
| 1951 | 102,937,602 | — | — | — | .65 | .85 | 1.00 | 1.10 | 3.30 | 23.00 |
| 1951D | 56,529,000 | — | — | — | .60 | .80 | .95 | 1.00 | 3.50 | — |
| 1951S | 31,630,000 | — | — | .95 | 1.00 | 1.05 | 2.75 | 3.25 | 24.00 | — |
| 1952 | 99,122,073 | — | — | — | .65 | .95 | 1.10 | 1.20 | 3.30 | 23.00 |
| 1952D | 122,100,000 | — | — | — | .65 | .80 | .95 | 1.00 | 3.80 | — |
| 1952S | 44,419,500 | — | — | .95 | 1.00 | 1.05 | 1.10 | 1.35 | 7.00 | — |
| 1953 | 53,618,920 | — | — | — | .65 | .90 | 1.00 | 1.10 | 3.60 | 20.00 |
| 1953D | 136,433,000 | — | — | — | .65 | .80 | .95 | 1.00 | 3.50 | — |
| 1953S | 39,180,000 | — | — | — | .65 | .95 | 1.10 | 1.35 | 2.25 | — |
| 1954 | 114,243,503 | — | — | — | .65 | .75 | .90 | .95 | 2.15 | 10.00 |
| 1954D | 106,397,000 | — | — | — | .65 | .80 | .95 | 1.00 | 2.15 | — |
| 1954S | 22,860,000 | — | — | — | .65 | .75 | .80 | .90 | 2.20 | — |
| 1955 | 12,828,381 | — | — | — | .65 | .75 | .80 | .90 | 3.00 | 7.50 |
| 1955D | 13,959,000 | — | — | — | .65 | .75 | .80 | .90 | 2.25 | — |
| 1955S | 18,510,000 | — | — | — | .65 | .75 | .80 | .90 | 2.00 | — |
| 1956 | 109,309,384 | — | — | — | .60 | .70 | .80 | .90 | 2.00 | 2.50 |
| 1956D | 108,015,100 | — | — | — | .60 | .70 | .80 | .90 | 1.65 | — |
| 1957 | 161,407,952 | — | — | — | .60 | .70 | .80 | .90 | 1.60 | 1.50 |
| 1957D | 113,354,330 | — | — | — | .60 | .70 | .80 | .90 | 3.00 | — |
| 1958 | 32,785,652 | — | — | — | .60 | .70 | .80 | .90 | 1.80 | 2.00 |
| 1958D | 136,564,600 | — | — | — | .60 | .70 | .80 | .90 | 1.50 | — |
| 1959 | 86,929,291 | — | — | — | .60 | .70 | .80 | .90 | 1.50 | 1.50 |
| 1959D | 164,919,790 | — | — | — | .60 | .70 | .80 | .90 | 1.35 | — |
| 1960 | 72,081,602 | — | — | — | .60 | .70 | .80 | .90 | 1.40 | 1.40 |
| 1960D | 200,160,400 | — | — | — | .60 | .70 | .80 | .90 | 1.35 | — |
| 1961 | 96,758,244 | — | — | — | .60 | .70 | .80 | .90 | 1.35 | 1.10 |
| 1961D | 209,146,550 | — | — | — | .60 | .70 | .80 | .90 | 1.35 | — |
| 1962 | 75,668,019 | — | — | — | .60 | .70 | .80 | .90 | 1.35 | 1.10 |
| 1962D | 334,948,380 | — | — | — | .60 | .70 | .80 | .90 | 1.35 | — |
| 1963 | 126,725,645 | — | — | — | .60 | .70 | .80 | .90 | 1.35 | 1.10 |
| 1963D | 421,476,530 | — | — | — | .60 | .70 | .80 | .90 | 1.35 | — |
| 1964 | 933,310,762 | — | — | — | .60 | .70 | .80 | .90 | 1.35 | 1.00 |
| 1964D | 1,357,517,180 | — | — | — | .60 | .70 | .80 | .90 | 1.35 | — |

## Clad composition

**Weight:** 2.27 grams. **Composition:** clad layers of 75% copper and 25% nickel, bonded to a pure-copper core. **Notes:** The 1979-S Type II proof has a clearer mintmark than the Type I. On the 1982 no-mintmark variety, the mintmark was inadvertently left off.

| Date | Mintage | G-4 | F-12 | VF-20 | XF-40 | AU-50 | MS-60 | MS-65 | Prf-65 |
|------|---------|-----|------|-------|-------|-------|-------|-------|--------|
| 1965 | 1,652,140,570 | — | — | — | — | — | — | .40 | — |
| 1966 | 1,382,734,540 | — | — | — | — | — | — | .30 | — |
| 1967 | 2,244,007,320 | — | — | — | — | — | — | .30 | — |
| 1968 | 424,470,000 | — | — | — | — | — | — | .25 | — |
| 1968D | 480,748,280 | — | — | — | — | — | — | .25 | — |
| 1968S | Proof only | — | — | — | — | — | — | — | .65 |
| 1969 | 145,790,000 | — | — | — | — | — | — | .45 | — |
| 1969D | 563,323,870 | — | — | — | — | — | — | .40 | — |
| 1969S | Proof only | — | — | — | — | — | — | — | .65 |
| 1970 | 345,570,000 | — | — | — | — | — | — | .30 | — |
| 1970D | 754,942,100 | — | — | — | — | — | — | .30 | — |
| 1970S | Proof only | — | — | — | — | — | — | — | .65 |
| 1971 | 162,690,000 | — | — | — | — | — | — | .35 | — |
| 1971D | 377,914,240 | — | — | — | — | — | — | .35 | — |
| 1971S | Proof only | — | — | — | — | — | — | — | .80 |
| 1972 | 431,540,000 | — | — | — | — | — | — | .30 | — |
| 1972D | 330,290,000 | — | — | — | — | — | — | .25 | — |
| 1972S | Proof only | — | — | — | — | — | — | — | .80 |
| 1973 | 315,670,000 | — | — | — | — | — | — | .25 | — |
| 1973D | 455,032,426 | — | — | — | — | — | — | .20 | — |
| 1973S | Proof only | — | — | — | — | — | — | — | .60 |
| 1974 | 470,248,000 | — | — | — | — | — | — | .20 | — |
| 1974D | 571,083,000 | — | — | — | — | — | — | .20 | — |
| 1974S | Proof only | — | — | — | — | — | — | — | .75 |
| 1975 | 585,673,900 | — | — | — | — | — | — | .30 | — |
| 1975D | 313,705,300 | — | — | — | — | — | — | .25 | — |
| 1975S | Proof only | — | — | — | — | — | — | — | .60 |
| 1976 | 568,760,000 | — | — | — | — | — | — | .35 | — |

**PRICING SECTION**

| Date | Mintage | G-4 | F-12 | VF-20 | XF-40 | AU-50 | MS-60 | MS-65 | Prf-65 |
|---|---|---|---|---|---|---|---|---|---|
| 1976D | 695,222,774 | — | — | — | — | — | — | .35 | — |
| 1976S | Proof only | — | — | — | — | — | — | — | .75 |
| 1977 | 796,930,000 | — | — | — | — | — | — | .20 | — |
| 1977D | 376,607,228 | — | — | — | — | — | — | .25 | — |
| 1977S | Proof only | — | — | — | — | — | — | — | .60 |
| 1978 | 663,980,000 | — | — | — | — | — | — | .20 | — |
| 1978D | 282,847,540 | — | — | — | — | — | — | .20 | — |
| 1978S | Proof only | — | — | — | — | — | — | — | .60 |
| 1979 | 315,440,000 | — | — | — | — | — | — | .20 | — |
| 1979D | 390,921,184 | — | — | — | — | — | — | .20 | — |
| 1979S T-I | Proof only | — | — | — | — | — | — | — | .55 |
| 1979S T-II | Proof only | — | — | — | — | — | — | — | 1.25 |
| 1980P | 735,170,000 | — | — | — | — | — | — | .20 | — |
| 1980D | 719,354,321 | — | — | — | — | — | — | .20 | — |
| 1980S | Proof only | — | — | — | — | — | — | — | .50 |
| 1981P | 676,650,000 | — | — | — | — | — | — | .20 | — |
| 1981D | 712,284,143 | — | — | — | — | — | — | .20 | — |
| 1981S T-I | Proof only | — | — | — | — | — | — | — | .50 |
| 1981S T-II | Proof only | — | — | — | — | — | — | — | 4.00 |
| 1982P | 519,475,000 | — | — | — | — | — | — | 1.10 | — |
| 1982 no mint mark | | — | — | — | — | 85.00 | 95.00 | 175. | — |
| 1982D | 542,713,584 | — | — | — | — | — | — | .30 | — |
| 1982S | Proof only | — | — | — | — | — | — | — | .65 |
| 1983P | 647,025,000 | — | — | — | — | — | — | .75 | — |
| 1983D | 730,129,224 | — | — | — | — | — | — | .70 | — |
| 1983S | Proof only | — | — | — | — | — | — | — | 1.10 |
| 1984P | 856,669,000 | — | — | — | — | — | — | .25 | — |
| 1984D | 704,803,976 | — | — | — | — | — | — | .35 | — |
| 1984S | Proof only | — | — | — | — | — | — | — | 1.60 |
| 1985P | 705,200,962 | — | — | — | — | — | — | .35 | — |
| 1985D | 587,979,970 | — | — | — | — | — | — | .30 | — |
| 1985S | Proof only | — | — | — | — | — | — | — | 1.10 |
| 1986P | 682,649,693 | — | — | — | — | — | — | .35 | — |
| 1986D | 473,326,970 | — | — | — | — | — | — | .35 | — |
| 1986S | Proof only | — | — | — | — | — | — | — | 2.00 |
| 1987P | 762,709,481 | — | — | — | — | — | — | .20 | — |
| 1987D | 653,203,402 | — | — | — | — | — | — | .20 | — |
| 1987S | Proof only | — | — | — | — | — | — | — | 1.25 |
| 1988P | 1,030,550,000 | — | — | — | — | — | — | .20 | — |
| 1988D | 962,385,488 | — | — | — | — | — | — | .20 | — |
| 1988S | Proof only | — | — | — | — | — | — | — | 1.50 |
| 1989P | 1,298,400,000 | — | — | — | — | — | — | .20 | — |
| 1989D | 896,535,597 | — | — | — | — | — | — | .20 | — |
| 1989S | Proof only | — | — | — | — | — | — | — | 1.45 |
| 1990P | 1,034,340,000 | — | — | — | — | — | — | .20 | — |
| 1990D | 839,995,824 | — | — | — | — | — | — | .20 | — |
| 1990S | Proof only | — | — | — | — | — | — | — | 2.50 |
| 1991P | — | — | — | — | — | — | — | .20 | — |
| 1991D | — | — | — | — | — | — | — | .20 | — |
| 1991S | Proof only | — | — | — | — | — | — | — | 2.75 |
| 1992P | — | — | — | — | — | — | — | .20 | — |
| 1992D | — | — | — | — | — | — | — | .20 | — |
| 1992S | Proof only | — | — | — | — | — | — | — | 1.80 |
| 1993P | — | — | — | — | — | — | — | .20 | — |
| 1993D | — | — | — | — | — | — | — | .20 | — |
| 1993S | Proof only | — | — | — | — | — | — | — | 1.80 |
| 1994P | — | — | — | — | — | — | — | .20 | — |
| 1994D | — | — | — | — | — | — | — | .20 | — |
| 1994S | Proof only | — | — | — | — | — | — | — | 3.50 |

# 20-cent

**Designer:** William Barber. **Size:** 22 millimeters. **Weight:** 5 grams. **Composition:** 90% silver (0.1447 ounces), 10% copper.

| Date | Mintage | G-4 | VG-8 | F-12 | VF-20 | XF-40 | AU-50 | MS-60 | MS-65 | Prf-65 |
|---|---|---|---|---|---|---|---|---|---|---|
| 1875 | 39,700 | 60.00 | 70.00 | 90.00 | 145. | 240. | 400. | 1300. | 8400. | 9500. |
| 1875S | 1,155,000 | 50.00 | 55.00 | 75.00 | 115. | 170. | 380. | 500. | 5000. | — |
| 1875CC | 133,290 | 60.00 | 70.00 | 90.00 | 155. | 275. | 525. | 1450. | 9500. | — |
| 1876 | 15,900 | 100. | 120. | 150. | 215. | 350. | 600. | 1500. | 9500. | 6000. |
| 1876CC | 10,000 | | | | Norweb Sale, Oct. 1987, MS-64, $69,300. | | | — | — | — |
| 1877 | 510 | — | | Proof only | — | — | — | — | — | 23,000. |
| Impaired proof | | | | — | 1850. | 2100. | 2450. | — | — | — |
| 1878 | 600 | — | | Proof only | — | — | — | — | — | 23,000. |
| Impaired proof | | | | — | 1175. | 1575. | 2000. | — | — | — |

# 1876 20-Cent
## Grade F-12

— Retail Price

Source: COIN PRICES

# 1804 Quarter
## Grade XF-40

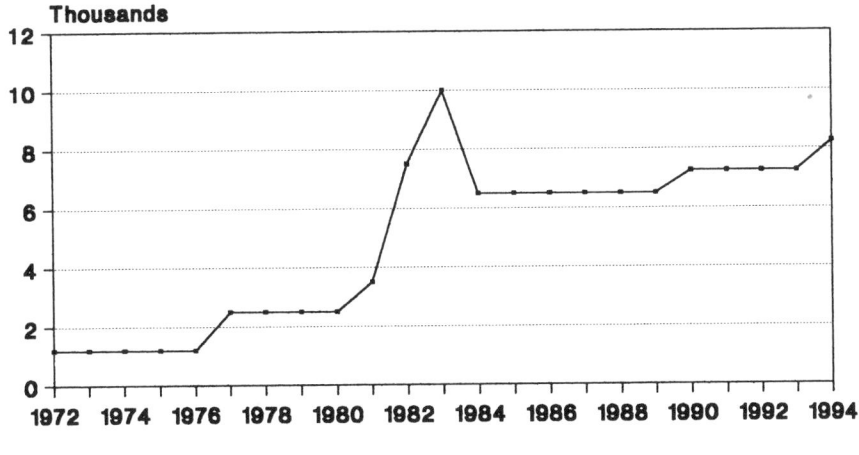

— Retail Price

Source: COIN PRICES

# Quarters

## Draped Bust

### Small-eagle reverse

**Designer:** Robert Scot. **Size:** 27.5 millimeters. **Weight:** 6.74 grams. **Composition:** 89.24% silver (0.1935 ounces), 10.76% copper.

| Date | Mintage | G-4 | VG-8 | F-12 | VF-20 | XF-40 | AU-50 | MS-60 | MS-65 |
|------|---------|-----|------|------|-------|-------|-------|-------|-------|
| 1796 | 6,146 | 4350. | 6000. | 9150. | 14,000. | 17,000. | 19,000. | 28,000. | 125,000. |

### Heraldic-eagle reverse

| Date | Mintage | G-4 | VG-8 | F-12 | VF-20 | XF-40 | AU-50 | MS-60 | MS-65 |
|------|---------|-----|------|------|-------|-------|-------|-------|-------|
| 1804 | 6,738 | 1000. | 1475. | 2350. | 4000. | 8250. | 16,500. | 22,000. | 116,000. |
| 1805 | 121,394 | 210. | 300. | 450. | 850. | 2200. | 4150. | 4400. | 46,500. |
| 1806 | 206,124 | 225. | 285. | 425. | 800. | 2150. | 4150. | 4400. | 46,500. |
| 1806/5 | Inc. Ab. | 225. | 315. | 465. | 875. | 2250. | 4150. | 4400. | 46,500. |
| 1807 | 220,643 | 210. | 300. | 450. | 850. | 2200. | 4150. | 5650. | 46,500. |

## Liberty Cap

**Designer:** John Reich. **Size:** 27 millimeters. **Weight:** 6.74 grams. **Composition:** 89.24% silver (0.1935 ounces), 10.76% copper. **Notes:** Varieties of the 1819 strikes are distinguished by the size of the 9 in the date. Varieties of the 1820 strikes are distinguished by the size of the 0 in the date. One 1822 variety and one 1828 variety have "25" engraved over "50" in the denomination. The 1827 restrikes were produced privately using dies sold as scrap by the U.S. Mint.

| Date | Mintage | G-4 | VG-8 | F-12 | VF-20 | XF-40 | AU-50 | MS-60 | MS-65 |
|------|---------|-----|------|------|-------|-------|-------|-------|-------|
| 1815 | 89,235 | 60.00 | 80.00 | 110. | 335. | 850. | 2000. | 3100. | 22,000. |
| 1818 | 361,174 | 39.00 | 50.00 | 90.00 | 275. | 725. | 1300. | 1550. | 12,500. |
| 1818/15 | Inc. Ab. | 65.00 | 80.00 | 110. | 315. | 800. | 2000. | 3100. | 22,000. |
| 1819 sm.9 | 144,000 | 55.00 | 70.00 | 100. | 300. | 775. | 1350. | 1550. | 12,500. |
| 1819 lg.9 | Inc. Ab. | 55.00 | 70.00 | 100. | 300. | 775. | 1350. | 1550. | 12,500. |
| 1820 sm.O | 127,444 | 60.00 | 75.00 | 110. | 315. | 800. | 1500. | 3000. | 12,500. |
| 1820 lg.O | Inc. Ab. | 50.00 | 65.00 | 100. | 275. | 725. | 1300. | 1550. | 12,500. |
| 1821 | 216,851 | 50.00 | 65.00 | 100. | 275. | 725. | 1300. | 1550. | 12,500. |
| 1822 | 64,080 | 75.00 | 90.00 | 130. | 400. | 975. | 1400. | 1550. | 12,500. |
| 1822 25/50C. | I.A. | 2500. | 3500. | 4750. | 6500. | 8750. | 10,000. | 15,000. | 25,000. |
| 1823/22 | 17,800 | 8250. | 12,000. | 17,500. | 24,500. | 31,500. | — | — | — |
| | | | | Superior, Aug. 1990, proof, $62,500. | | | | | |
| 1824/2 | Unrecorded | 100. | 140. | 200. | 575. | 1250. | 1400. | 1800. | 12,500. |
| 1825/22 | 168,000 | 100. | 140. | 200. | 575. | 1250. | 1500. | 1900. | 12,500. |
| 1825/23 | Inc. Ab. | 50.00 | 65.00 | 100. | 275. | 725. | 1500. | 1900. | 12,500. |
| 1825/24 | Inc. Ab. | 50.00 | 65.00 | 100. | 275. | 725. | 1500. | 1900. | 12,500. |
| 1827 original | 4,000 | | | | Superior, Aug. 1990, proof, $42,000. | | | | — |
| 1827 restrike | I.A. | | | | Superior, Aug. 1990, proof, $23,000. | | | — | — |
| 1828 | 102,000 | 50.00 | 65.00 | 95.00 | 275. | 775. | 1500. | 1900. | 12,500. |
| 1828 25/50C. | I.A. | 150. | 200. | 300. | 650. | 1350. | 2000. | 3100. | — |

## No motto

**Designer:** William Kneass. **Size:** 24.3 millimeters. **Notes:** In 1831 the motto "E Pluribus Unum" was removed from the reverse. Varieties of the 1831 strikes are distinguished by the size of the lettering on the reverse.

| Date | Mintage | G-4 | VG-8 | F-12 | VF-20 | XF-40 | AU-50 | MS-60 | MS-65 |
|------|---------|-----|------|------|-------|-------|-------|-------|-------|
| 1831 small letters | 398,000 | 45.00 | 50.00 | 60.00 | 90.00 | 240. | 750. | 900. | 13,000. |
| 1831 lg.let. | Inc. Ab. | 45.00 | 50.00 | 60.00 | 90.00 | 240. | 750. | 900. | 13,000. |
| 1832 | 320,000 | 45.00 | 50.00 | 60.00 | 90.00 | 240. | 750. | 900. | 13,000. |
| 1833 | 156,000 | 48.00 | 54.00 | 65.00 | 100. | 265. | 800. | 1000. | 17,000. |
| 1834 | 286,000 | 45.00 | 50.00 | 60.00 | 90.00 | 240. | 750. | 900. | 13,000. |
| 1835 | 1,952,000 | 45.00 | 50.00 | 60.00 | 90.00 | 240. | 750. | 900. | 13,000. |
| 1836 | 472,000 | 45.00 | 50.00 | 60.00 | 90.00 | 240. | 750. | 900. | 13,000. |
| 1837 | 252,400 | 45.00 | 50.00 | 60.00 | 90.00 | 240. | 750. | 900. | 13,000. |
| 1838 | 832,000 | 45.00 | 50.00 | 60.00 | 90.00 | 240. | 750. | 900. | 13,000. |

# Seated Liberty

## No drapery

**Designer:** Christian Gobrecht. **Size:** 24.3 millimeters. **Weight:** 6.68 grams. **Composition:** 90% silver (0.1934 ounces), 10% copper.

| Date | Mintage | G-4 | VG-8 | F-12 | VF-20 | XF-40 | AU-50 | MS-60 | MS-65 |
|------|---------|-----|------|------|-------|-------|-------|-------|-------|
| 1838 | Inc. Ab. | 11.00 | 15.00 | 26.00 | 55.00 | 195. | 475. | 900. | — |
| 1839 | 491,146 | 9.50 | 15.00 | 24.00 | 52.00 | 195. | 450. | 900. | 25,000. |
| 1840O | 425,200 | 9.50 | 15.00 | 28.00 | 60.00 | 300. | 400. | 900. | 25,000. |

## Drapery added to Liberty

**Notes:** In 1840 drapery was added to Liberty's left elbow. Two varieties for 1842 and 1842-O are distinguished by the size of the numerals in the date. 1852 obverse dies were used to strike the 1853 no-arrows variety, with the 2 being recut to form a 3.

| Date | Mintage | G-4 | VG-8 | F-12 | VF-20 | XF-40 | AU-50 | MS-60 | MS-65 |
|------|---------|-----|------|------|-------|-------|-------|-------|-------|
| 1840 | 188,127 | 28.00 | 35.00 | 50.00 | 75.00 | 180. | 350. | 750. | — |
| 1840O | Inc. Ab. | 20.00 | 30.00 | 50.00 | 110. | 185. | 500. | 1150. | — |
| 1841 | 120,000 | 45.00 | 60.00 | 80.00 | 120. | 225. | — | 800. | — |
| 1841O | 452,000 | 12.50 | 24.00 | 40.00 | 70.00 | 150. | — | 800. | — |
| 1842 sm. dt. | 88,000 | | | | Stacks, Jan. 1989, proof, $22,000. | | | | — |
| 1842 lg. dt. | Inc. Ab. | 85.00 | 115. | 150. | 225. | 425. | 875. | 2700. | — |
| 1842O sm. dt. | 769,000 | 375. | 500. | 850. | 1550. | 3250. | — | — | — |
| 1842O lg. dt. | Inc. Ab. | 10.00 | 16.00 | 30.00 | 60.00 | 165. | 650. | — | — |
| 1843 | 645,600 | 9.50 | 15.00 | 18.00 | 40.00 | 80.00 | — | 290. | 3500. |
| 1843O | 968,000 | 15.00 | 27.00 | 45.00 | 100. | 200. | — | — | — |
| 1844 | 421,200 | 12.50 | 16.00 | 20.00 | 43.00 | 80.00 | 185. | 290. | 3500. |
| 1844O | 740,000 | 12.50 | 21.00 | 38.00 | 55.00 | 125. | 375. | 1200. | — |
| 1845 | 922,000 | 9.50 | 15.00 | 25.00 | 40.00 | 75.00 | 185. | 450. | 3500. |
| 1846 | 510,000 | 12.50 | 20.00 | 35.00 | 65.00 | 115. | 245. | 485. | 3500. |
| 1847 | 734,000 | 9.50 | 12.50 | 25.00 | 45.00 | 75.00 | 190. | 425. | 3500. |
| 1847O | 368,000 | 22.00 | 40.00 | 80.00 | 110. | 225. | 675. | 725. | — |
| 1848 | 146,000 | 30.00 | 42.00 | 70.00 | 130. | 210. | 425. | 1175. | — |
| 1849 | 340,000 | 12.00 | 20.00 | 40.00 | 70.00 | 100. | 375. | 1000. | — |
| 1849O | Unrecorded | 350. | 545. | 900. | 1500. | 3000. | 7000. | — | — |
| 1850 | 190,800 | 23.00 | 45.00 | 55.00 | 85.00 | 150. | 325. | 1000. | — |
| 1850O | 412,000 | 17.50 | 30.00 | 40.00 | 80.00 | 175. | 585. | 1100. | — |
| 1851 | 160,000 | 30.00 | 50.00 | 75.00 | 135. | 225. | 400. | 1000. | — |
| 1851O | 88,000 | 175. | 265. | 325. | 575. | 1000. | 2600. | — | — |
| 1852 | 177,060 | 35.00 | 45.00 | 75.00 | 110. | 185. | 400. | 900. | — |
| 1852O | 96,000 | 165. | 255. | 300. | 550. | 900. | 2500. | — | — |
| 1853 recut date | 44,200 | 225. | 275. | 375. | 525. | 750. | 1500. | 3250. | — |

## Arrows at date, reverse rays

**Weight:** 6.22 grams. **Composition:** 90% silver (0.18 ounces), 10% copper.

| Date | Mintage | G-4 | VG-8 | F-12 | VF-20 | XF-40 | AU-50 | MS-60 | MS-65 | Prf-65 |
|------|---------|-----|------|------|-------|-------|-------|-------|-------|--------|
| 1853 rays | | | | | | | | | | |
| | 15,210,020 | 7.25 | 14.00 | 20.00 | 40.00 | 165. | 350. | 900. | 17,500. | — |
| 1853/4 | Inc. Ab. | 30.00 | 65.00 | 100. | 165. | 300. | 800. | 2000. | — | — |
| 1853O rays | | | | | | | | | | |
| | 1,332,000 | 10.00 | 26.00 | 30.00 | 75.00 | 250. | 1250. | 3000. | — | — |

**Reverse rays removed**

**Notes:** The 1854-O "huge O" variety has an oversized mintmark.

| Date | Mintage | G-4 | VG-8 | F-12 | VF-20 | XF-40 | AU-50 | MS-60 | MS-65 | Prf-65 |
|------|---------|-----|------|------|-------|-------|-------|-------|-------|--------|
| 1854 | 12,380,000 | 7.50 | 14.00 | 21.00 | 32.00 | 165. | 285. | 410. | 8500. | 15,000. |
| 1854O | 1,484,000 | 9.00 | 17.00 | 28.00 | 45.00 | 145. | 325. | 1500. | — | — |
| 1854O huge O | | | | | | | | | | |
| | Inc. Ab. | 90.00 | 145. | 200. | 275. | 475. | — | — | — | — |
| 1855 | 2,857,000 | 7.50 | 12.50 | 18.00 | 24.00 | 65.00 | 285. | 410. | 8500. | 15,000. |
| 1855O | 176,000 | 30.00 | 45.00 | 90.00 | 245. | 500. | — | 1850. | — | — |
| 1855S | 396,400 | 25.00 | 45.00 | 65.00 | 145. | 325. | — | 1750. | — | — |

**Arrows at date removed**

# 1856-S Quarter
## Grade F-12

—•— **Retail Price**

**Source: COIN PRICES**

| Date | Mintage | G-4 | VG-8 | F-12 | VF-20 | XF-40 | AU-50 | MS-60 | MS-65 | Prf-65 |
|------|---------|-----|------|------|-------|-------|-------|-------|-------|--------|
| 1856 | 7,264,000 | 7.50 | 12.50 | 23.00 | 32.00 | 58.00 | 145. | 325. | 3500. | 15,000. |
| 1856O | 968,000 | 12.00 | 16.00 | 26.00 | 40.00 | 110. | 375. | 850. | — | — |
| 1856S | 286,000 | 35.00 | 55.00 | 75.00 | 175. | 425. | 1050. | — | — | — |
| 1856S/S | Inc. Ab. | 45.00 | 70.00 | 125. | 265. | 750. | — | — | — | — |
| 1857 | 9,644,000 | 7.50 | 12.50 | 17.50 | 28.00 | 50.00 | 145. | 290. | 3500. | 15,000. |
| 1857O | 1,180,000 | 13.00 | 17.00 | 27.00 | 40.00 | 80.00 | 275. | 900. | — | — |
| 1857S | 82,000 | 75.00 | 100. | 140. | 235. | 450. | 975. | — | — | — |
| 1858 | 7,368,000 | 7.50 | 12.50 | 21.00 | 28.00 | 50.00 | 190. | 290. | 3500. | 11,500. |
| 1858O | 520,000 | 10.00 | 17.00 | 30.00 | 45.00 | 85.00 | 300. | 900. | — | — |
| 1858S | 121,000 | 45.00 | 70.00 | 120. | 200. | 475. | 1650. | — | — | — |
| 1859 | 1,344,000 | 11.00 | 15.00 | 23.00 | 30.00 | 63.00 | 190. | 700. | — | 7000. |
| 1859O | 260,000 | 18.00 | 25.00 | 35.00 | 50.00 | 90.00 | 450. | 900. | — | — |
| 1859S | 80,000 | 90.00 | 125. | 175. | 275. | 575. | 7000. | — | — | — |
| 1860 | 805,400 | 9.50 | 13.00 | 23.00 | 30.00 | 64.00 | 155. | 900. | 11,500. | 3500. |
| 1860O | 388,000 | 11.00 | 19.00 | 35.00 | 50.00 | 95.00 | 225. | 925. | — | — |
| 1860S | 56,000 | 145. | 225. | 350. | 625. | 2750. | 9000. | — | — | — |
| 1861 | 4,854,600 | 7.50 | 12.50 | 17.50 | 28.00 | 45.00 | 190. | 290. | 3500. | 3500. |
| 1861S | 96,000 | 60.00 | 80.00 | 135. | 240. | 500. | 3750. | — | — | — |
| 1862 | 932,550 | 8.00 | 12.50 | 18.00 | 35.00 | 60.00 | 175. | 290. | 3500. | 3500. |
| 1862S | 67,000 | 55.00 | 70.00 | 125. | 225. | 450. | 1250. | 2750. | — | — |
| 1863 | 192,060 | 25.00 | 35.00 | 50.00 | 75.00 | 150. | 300. | 750. | — | 7000. |
| 1864 | 94,070 | 50.00 | 60.00 | 90.00 | 125. | 245. | 400. | 900. | 11,500. | 7000. |
| 1864S | 20,000 | 185. | 325. | 425. | 850. | 1700. | 3000. | — | — | — |
| 1865 | 59,300 | 55.00 | 70.00 | 95.00 | 120. | 250. | 375. | 875. | 11,500. | 7000. |
| 1865S | 41,000 | 70.00 | 100. | 135. | 225. | 450. | 1250. | 2000. | — | — |
| 1866 | — | Unique | | — | — | — | — | — | — | — |

## Motto above eagle

**Notes:** In 1866 the motto "In God We Trust" was added to the reverse. The 1873 closed-3 and open-3 varieties are distinguished by the amount of space between the upper left and lower left serifs in the 3.

| Date | Mintage | G-4 | VG-8 | F-12 | VF-20 | XF-40 | AU-50 | MS-60 | MS-65 | Prf-65 |
|------|---------|-----|------|------|-------|-------|-------|-------|-------|--------|
| 1866 | 17,525 | 225. | 285. | 375. | 425. | 615. | 1100. | 2000. | — | 6750. |
| 1866S | 28,000 | 185. | 260. | 400. | 650. | 1250. | 1800. | — | — | — |
| 1867 | 20,625 | 175. | 200. | 240. | 325. | 475. | — | 1300. | — | 6750. |
| 1867S | 48,000 | 145. | 200. | 275. | 375. | 625. | 1750. | 3000. | — | — |
| 1868 | 30,000 | 105. | 155. | 200. | 255. | 375. | 525. | 1200. | — | 6750. |
| 1868S | 96,000 | 50.00 | 70.00 | 110. | 195. | 425. | 1100. | 2300. | — | — |
| 1869 | 16,600 | 200. | 260. | 325. | 425. | 550. | 950. | 1400. | — | 6750. |
| 1869S | 76,000 | 60.00 | 95.00 | 150. | 240. | 400. | 1275. | — | — | — |
| 1870 | 87,400 | 40.00 | 48.00 | 80.00 | 135. | 250. | 325. | 1000. | — | 6550. |
| 1870CC | 8,340 | 1500. | 3250. | 4750. | 8000. | 12,500. | — | — | — | — |
| 1871 | 119,160 | 30.00 | 40.00 | 55.00 | 115. | 185. | — | 1000. | — | 6550. |
| 1871CC | 10,890 | 1250. | 2250. | 3250. | 5250. | 8000. | 15,000. | — | — | — |
| 1871S | 30,900 | 240. | 300. | 400. | 575. | 825. | — | 3000. | — | — |
| 1872 | 182,950 | 30.00 | 40.00 | 50.00 | 100. | 155. | — | 1000. | — | 4050. |
| 1872CC | 22,850 | 375. | 525. | 900. | 1750. | 3000. | 4000. | — | — | — |
| 1872S | 83,000 | 400. | 525. | 1050. | 1700. | 2850. | — | 4700. | — | — |
| 1873 clsd.3 | 212,600 | 140. | 200. | 300. | 425. | 625. | 750. | — | — | 8000. |
| 1873 open 3 | Inc. Ab. | 30.00 | 35.00 | 50.00 | 90.00 | 145. | 325. | 750. | — | — |
| 1873CC | 4,000 | RARCOA, Aug. 1990, MS-65, $310,000. | | | | | | — | — | — |

## Arrows at date

**Weight:** 6.25 grams. **Composition:** 90% silver (0.1809 ounces), 10% copper.

| Date | Mintage | G-4 | VG-8 | F-12 | VF-20 | XF-40 | AU-50 | MS-60 | MS-65 | Prf-65 |
|------|---------|-----|------|------|-------|-------|-------|-------|-------|--------|
| 1873 | 1,271,700 | 10.00 | 15.00 | 28.00 | 50.00 | 190. | 380. | 650. | 4500. | 5500. |
| 1873CC | 12,462 | 1350. | 2350. | 3450. | 6500. | 9500. | — | — | — | — |
| 1873S | 156,000 | 25.00 | 35.00 | 70.00 | 145. | 275. | 600. | 1100. | — | — |
| 1874 | 471,900 | 17.50 | 30.00 | 45.00 | 75.00 | 200. | 400. | 750. | 4500. | 5500. |
| 1874S | 392,000 | 18.50 | 28.00 | 40.00 | 110. | 195. | 400. | 700. | — | — |

### Arrows at date removed

**Notes:** The 1876-CC fine-reeding variety has a more finely reeded edge.

| Date | Mintage | G-4 | VG-8 | F-12 | VF-20 | XF-40 | AU-50 | MS-60 | MS-65 | Prf-65 |
|------|---------|-----|------|------|-------|-------|-------|-------|-------|--------|
| 1875 | 4,293,500 | 7.50 | 12.50 | 19.50 | 28.00 | 60.00 | 115. | 350. | 4100. | 2100. |
| 1875CC | 140,000 | 50.00 | 80.00 | 145. | 250. | 400. | 700. | 1400. | — | — |
| 1875S | 680,000 | 22.00 | 30.00 | 50.00 | 80.00 | 165. | 300. | 575. | — | — |
| 1876 | 17,817,150 | 7.50 | 12.50 | 19.50 | 28.00 | 55.00 | 115. | 350. | 4100. | 2100. |
| 1876CC | 4,944,000 | 9.00 | 15.00 | 22.50 | 35.00 | 70.00 | 200. | 350. | 3900. | — |
| 1876CC fine reeding |  |  |  |  |  |  |  |  |  |  |
| Inc. Ab. | | 9.00 | 15.00 | 22.00 | 35.00 | 70.00 | 210. | 375. | — | — |
| 1876S | 8,596,000 | 7.50 | 12.50 | 19.50 | 28.00 | 70.00 | 115. | 220. | 1950. | — |
| 1877 | 10,911,710 | 7.50 | 12.50 | 19.50 | 28.00 | 55.00 | 115. | 220. | 1950. | 2100. |
| 1877CC | 4,192,000 | 7.50 | 15.00 | 25.00 | 35.00 | 70.00 | 200. | 375. | — | — |
| 1877S | 8,996,000 | 6.75 | 12.00 | 19.50 | 28.00 | 55.00 | 115. | 220. | 1950. | — |
| 1877S/horizontal S |  |  |  |  |  |  |  |  |  |  |
| Inc. Ab. | | 25.00 | 48.00 | 65.00 | 100. | 225. | 375. | 650. | — | — |
| 1878 | 2,260,800 | 9.00 | 14.00 | 25.00 | 40.00 | 65.00 | 165. | 360. | 4100. | 2100. |
| 1878CC | 996,000 | 16.00 | 25.00 | 38.00 | 55.00 | 100. | 215. | 425. | 4100. | — |
| 1878S | 140,000 | 75.00 | 140. | 185. | 250. | 425. | 800. | 1500. | — | — |
| 1879 | 14,700 | 135. | 160. | 200. | 250. | 325. | 400. | 525. | — | 2100. |
| 1880 | 14,955 | 145. | 160. | 200. | 250. | 325. | 400. | 525. | — | 2100. |
| 1881 | 12,975 | 135. | 160. | 200. | 250. | 325. | 400. | 525. | — | 2100. |
| 1882 | 16,300 | 150. | 175. | 210. | 265. | 335. | 450. | 600. | — | 2100. |
| 1883 | 15,439 | 155. | 180. | 210. | 265. | 335. | 450. | 600. | — | 2100. |
| 1884 | 8,875 | 180. | 220. | 270. | 350. | 425. | 475. | 650. | — | 2100. |
| 1885 | 14,530 | 145. | 170. | 200. | 250. | 325. | 400. | 600. | — | 2100. |
| 1886 | 5,886 | 300. | 345. | 400. | 540. | 675. | 850. | 1000. | — | 2100. |
| 1887 | 10,710 | 210. | 220. | 250. | 315. | 400. | 475. | 650. | — | 2100. |
| 1888 | 10,833 | 150. | 180. | 210. | 260. | 325. | 475. | 600. | — | 2100. |
| 1888S | 1,216,000 | 8.00 | 14.00 | 22.00 | 30.00 | 65.00 | 135. | 220. | 1950. | 2100. |
| 1889 | 12,711 | 160. | 190. | 220. | 275. | 340. | 450. | 600. | — | 2100. |
| 1890 | 80,590 | 50.00 | 55.00 | 80.00 | 110. | 185. | 275. | 400. | — | 2100. |
| 1891 | 3,920,600 | 6.75 | 12.50 | 20.00 | 30.00 | 55.00 | 150. | 220. | 1950. | 2100. |
| 1891O | 68,000 | 125. | 165. | 225. | 425. | 600. | — | — | — | — |
| 1891S | 2,216,000 | 6.75 | 12.00 | 20.00 | 33.00 | 60.00 | 135. | 350. | 4400. | — |

# Barber

**Designer:** Charles E. Barber. **Size:** 24.3 millimeters. **Weight:** 6.25 grams. **Composition:** 90% silver (0.1809 ounces), 10% copper.

| Date | Mintage | G-4 | VG-8 | F-12 | VF-20 | XF-40 | AU-50 | MS-60 | MS-65 | Prf-65 |
|------|---------|-----|------|------|-------|-------|-------|-------|-------|--------|
| 1892 | 8,237,245 | 2.50 | 4.00 | 14.00 | 35.00 | 72.00 | 120. | 205. | 1900. | 1850. |
| 1892O | 2,640,000 | 4.00 | 7.50 | 15.00 | 47.00 | 85.00 | 155. | 250. | 2100. | — |

PRICING SECTION

| Date | Mintage | G-4 | VG-8 | F-12 | VF-20 | XF-40 | AU-50 | MS-60 | MS-65 | Prf-65 |
|------|---------|-----|------|------|-------|-------|-------|-------|-------|--------|
| 1892S | 964,079 | 18.00 | 26.00 | 33.00 | 49.00 | 110. | 285. | 375. | 7500. | — |
| 1893 | 5,484,838 | 3.00 | 4.00 | 14.00 | 30.00 | 75.00 | 130. | 205. | 1900. | 1850. |
| 1893O | 3,396,000 | 3.50 | 5.50 | 22.00 | 50.00 | 85.00 | 160. | 245. | 2900. | — |
| 1893S | 1,454,535 | 5.00 | 9.00 | 28.00 | 40.00 | 90.00 | 245. | 380. | 6700. | — |
| 1894 | 3,432,972 | 2.75 | 5.50 | 22.00 | 35.00 | 78.00 | 125. | 205. | 2050. | 1850. |
| 1894O | 2,852,000 | 4.00 | 10.00 | 30.00 | 42.00 | 72.00 | 180. | 325. | 6300. | — |
| 1894S | 2,648,821 | 4.00 | 10.00 | 30.00 | 48.00 | 90.00 | 175. | 325. | 6700. | — |
| 1895 | 4,440,880 | 2.75 | 6.00 | 20.00 | 35.00 | 75.00 | 125. | 205. | 4900. | 1850. |
| 1895O | 2,816,000 | 3.75 | 5.75 | 17.00 | 32.00 | 80.00 | 200. | 340. | 3100. | — |
| 1895S | 1,764,681 | 4.00 | 9.00 | 24.00 | 38.00 | 80.00 | 210. | 345. | 6000. | — |
| 1896 | 3,874,762 | 2.75 | 4.00 | 14.00 | 26.00 | 75.00 | 125. | 210. | 2650. | 1850. |
| 1896O | 1,484,000 | 3.75 | 8.75 | 38.00 | 180. | 320. | 580. | 800. | 8500. | — |
| 1896S | 188,039 | 210. | 375. | 600. | 825. | 1600. | 2600. | 3250. | 24,500. | — |
| 1897 | 8,140,731 | 3.50 | 6.00 | 22.00 | 35.00 | 72.00 | 125. | 205. | 2100. | 1850. |
| 1897O | 1,414,800 | 9.50 | 15.00 | 70.00 | 165. | 310. | 550. | 725. | 5100. | — |
| 1897S | 542,229 | 11.00 | 22.00 | 60.00 | 135. | 235. | 525. | 660. | 6800. | — |
| 1898 | 11,100,735 | 2.00 | 7.75 | 19.00 | 35.00 | 72.00 | 125. | 225. | 2050. | 1850. |
| 1898O | 1,868,000 | 4.00 | 15.00 | 35.00 | 60.00 | 135. | 350. | 460. | 7900. | — |
| 1898S | 1,020,592 | 3.75 | 7.75 | 19.00 | 35.00 | 89.00 | 165. | 345. | 3700. | — |
| 1899 | 12,624,846 | 2.00 | 7.75 | 13.00 | 26.00 | 74.00 | 125. | 205. | 2000. | 2200. |
| 1899O | 2,644,000 | 5.00 | 14.00 | 30.00 | 52.00 | 100. | 265. | 350. | 6300. | — |
| 1899S | 708,000 | 6.75 | 15.00 | 35.00 | 80.00 | 105. | 180. | 345. | 3600. | — |
| 1900 | 10,016,912 | 2.10 | 5.50 | 18.00 | 35.00 | 70.00 | 125. | 205. | 2000. | 2200. |
| 1900O | 3,416,000 | 4.50 | 8.00 | 34.00 | 60.00 | 110. | 225. | 375. | 4100. | — |
| 1900S | 1,858,585 | 4.25 | 6.50 | 16.00 | 39.00 | 77.00 | 150. | 300. | 5600. | — |
| 1901 | 8,892,813 | 2.75 | 3.10 | 14.00 | 35.00 | 73.00 | 125. | 205. | 2300. | 1900. |
| 1901O | 1,612,000 | 14.00 | 34.00 | 60.00 | 150. | 260. | 560. | 700. | 7400. | — |
| 1901S | 72,664 | 1250. | 2100. | 3000. | 4500. | 5700. | 7100. | 9000. | 48,000. | — |
| 1902 | 12,197,744 | 2.00 | 2.75 | 14.00 | 26.00 | 72.00 | 125. | 190. | 2000. | 2275. |
| 1902O | 4,748,000 | 3.75 | 5.00 | 20.00 | 52.00 | 86.00 | 180. | 360. | 5800. | — |
| 1902S | 1,524,612 | 6.00 | 11.50 | 21.00 | 57.00 | 115. | 190. | 375. | 4400. | — |
| 1903 | 9,670,064 | 2.20 | 3.00 | 14.00 | 35.00 | 74.00 | 125. | 205. | 2500. | 1850. |
| 1903O | 3,500,000 | 3.75 | 12.00 | 29.00 | 52.00 | 97.00 | 200. | 275. | 7500. | — |
| 1903S | 1,036,000 | 7.00 | 11.50 | 23.00 | 42.00 | 85.00 | 220. | 340. | 3400. | — |
| 1904 | 9,588,813 | 2.20 | 3.00 | 18.00 | 35.00 | 72.00 | 125. | 205. | 2400. | 1850. |
| 1904O | 2,456,000 | 4.50 | 6.75 | 30.00 | 67.00 | 160. | 325. | 650. | 3250. | — |
| 1905 | 4,968,250 | 2.75 | 3.25 | 17.00 | 34.00 | 72.00 | 125. | 205. | 2200. | 1850. |
| 1905O | 1,230,000 | 4.50 | 7.00 | 25.00 | 52.00 | 125. | 275. | 360. | 6100. | — |
| 1905S | 1,884,000 | 4.50 | 7.00 | 15.00 | 44.00 | 95.00 | 185. | 280. | 6700. | — |
| 1906 | 3,656,435 | 2.75 | 3.50 | 15.00 | 35.00 | 72.00 | 130. | 205. | 1700. | 1850. |
| 1906D | 3,280,000 | 2.60 | 4.50 | 23.00 | 39.00 | 75.00 | 150. | 210. | 5400. | — |

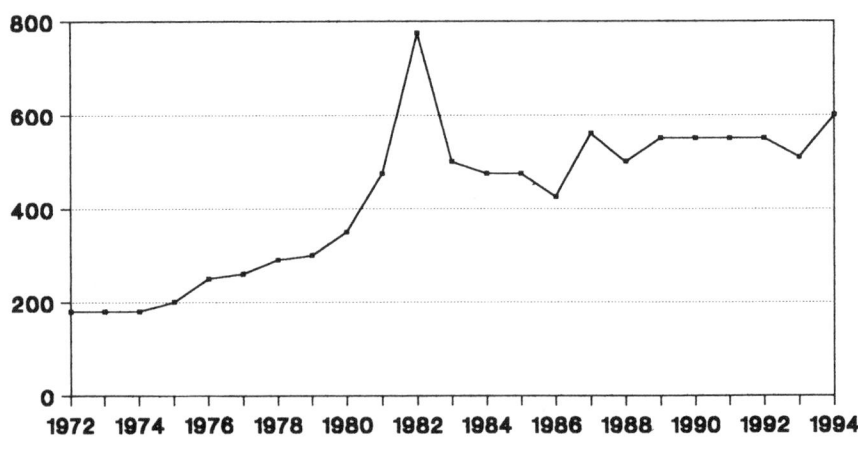

# 1896-S Quarter
## Grade F-12

—•— Retail Price

Source: COIN PRICES

# 1913-S Quarter
## Grade XF-40

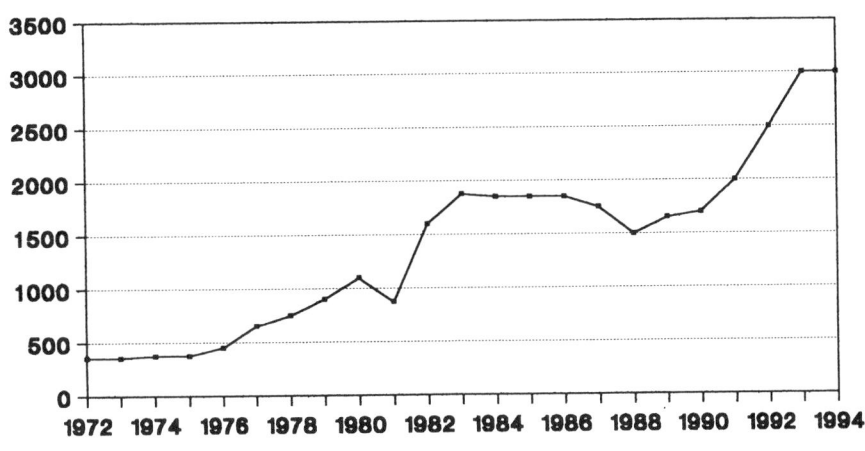

—•— **Retail Price**

**Source: COIN PRICES**

| Date | Mintage | G-4 | VG-8 | F-12 | VF-20 | XF-40 | AU-50 | MS-60 | MS-65 | Prf-65 |
|------|---------|-----|------|------|-------|-------|-------|-------|-------|--------|
| 1906O | 2,056,000 | 2.75 | 4.50 | 29.00 | 47.00 | 80.00 | 180. | 250. | 2000. | — |
| 1907 | 7,192,575 | 2.10 | 2.75 | 14.00 | 34.00 | 72.00 | 125. | 205. | 2000. | 1850. |
| 1907D | 2,484,000 | 2.60 | 4.00 | 16.00 | 40.00 | 82.00 | 170. | 275. | 4100. | — |
| 1907O | 4,560,000 | 2.40 | 3.25 | 14.00 | 39.00 | 77.00 | 140. | 225. | 4000. | — |
| 1907S | 1,360,000 | 3.50 | 4.50 | 28.00 | 60.00 | 100. | 200. | 340. | 5600. | — |
| 1908 | 4,232,545 | 2.20 | 3.00 | 14.00 | 26.00 | 72.00 | 125. | 205. | 2150. | 4050. |
| 1908D | 5,788,000 | 2.50 | 3.25 | 14.00 | 26.00 | 72.00 | 130. | 225. | 2400. | — |
| 1908O | 6,244,000 | 2.50 | 3.25 | 19.00 | 32.00 | 85.00 | 130. | 205. | 2100. | — |
| 1908S | 784,000 | 7.00 | 11.50 | 48.00 | 120. | 215. | 365. | 625. | 8000. | — |
| 1909 | 9,268,650 | 2.00 | 2.75 | 13.00 | 32.00 | 72.00 | 125. | 205. | 1900. | 1850. |
| 1909D | 5,114,000 | 2.50 | 3.00 | 13.50 | 32.00 | 72.00 | 155. | 225. | 2450. | — |
| 1909O | 712,000 | 7.00 | 13.00 | 38.00 | 88.00 | 180. | 335. | 625. | 12,500. | — |
| 1909S | 1,348,000 | 2.60 | 4.25 | 15.00 | 28.00 | 72.00 | 170. | 260. | 2500. | — |
| 1910 | 2,244,551 | 2.60 | 3.00 | 17.00 | 30.00 | 72.00 | 130. | 200. | 2050. | 1850. |
| 1910D | 1,500,000 | 2.75 | 4.00 | 16.00 | 33.00 | 80.00 | 160. | 265. | 3000. | — |
| 1911 | 3,720,543 | 2.10 | 3.00 | 14.00 | 26.00 | 72.00 | 125. | 205. | 1900. | 1850. |
| 1911D | 933,600 | 3.00 | 11.00 | 70.00 | 175. | 260. | 425. | 550. | 7200. | — |
| 1911S | 988,000 | 2.75 | 3.75 | 16.50 | 30.00 | 88.00 | 195. | 280. | 1600. | — |
| 1912 | 4,400,700 | 2.10 | 2.75 | 13.00 | 25.00 | 72.00 | 125. | 205. | 1900. | 1850. |
| 1912S | 708,000 | 3.00 | 4.00 | 19.00 | 33.00 | 72.00 | 190. | 325. | 2450. | — |
| 1913 | 484,613 | 8.00 | 20.00 | 45.00 | 110. | 400. | 600. | 1000. | 5500. | 2500. |
| 1913D | 1,450,800 | 2.75 | 4.00 | 15.00 | 30.00 | 82.00 | 150. | 260. | 2300. | — |
| 1913S | 40,000 | 325. | 475. | 1400. | 2450. | 3000. | 3500. | 4300. | 10,000. | — |
| 1914 | 6,244,610 | 2.00 | 2.10 | 13.00 | 25.00 | 72.00 | 125. | 205. | 1900. | 2200. |
| 1914D | 3,046,000 | 2.00 | 3.00 | 14.00 | 26.00 | 72.00 | 125. | 205. | 1900. | — |
| 1914S | 264,000 | 55.00 | 90.00 | 135. | 180. | 325. | 535. | 800. | 4700. | — |
| 1915 | 3,480,450 | 2.10 | 3.00 | 14.50 | 27.00 | 72.00 | 125. | 205. | 2000. | 2500. |
| 1915D | 3,694,000 | 2.10 | 2.75 | 13.50 | 26.00 | 72.00 | 125. | 205. | 1900. | — |
| 1915S | 704,000 | 4.00 | 5.00 | 17.00 | 35.00 | 80.00 | 190. | 285. | 2300. | — |
| 1916 | 1,788,000 | 2.10 | 3.00 | 14.50 | 27.00 | 72.00 | 125. | 205. | 1900. | — |
| 1916D | 6,540,800 | 2.00 | 2.60 | 13.00 | 25.00 | 72.00 | 125. | 205. | 1900. | — |

# Standing Liberty

## Type I

**Designer:** Hermon A. MacNeil. **Size:** 24.3 millimeters. **Weight:** 6.25 grams. **Composition:** 90% silver (0.1809 ounces), 10% copper. **Notes:** "MS-65FH" values are for coins that have full detail on Liberty's head.

| Date | Mintage | G-4 | VG-8 | F-12 | VF-20 | XF-40 | AU-50 | MS-60 | MS-65 | -65FH |
|---|---|---|---|---|---|---|---|---|---|---|
| 1916 | 52,000 | 900. | 1250. | 1500. | 2150. | 2700. | 3300. | 4250. | 13,500. | 21,000. |
| 1917 | 8,792,000 | 8.00 | 10.00 | 14.00 | 32.00 | 62.00 | 110. | 160. | 600. | 800. |
| 1917D | 1,509,200 | 12.00 | 14.00 | 25.00 | 60.00 | 90.00 | 120. | 215. | 1170. | 1875. |
| 1917S | 1,952,000 | 12.00 | 14.50 | 20.00 | 65.00 | 130. | 195. | 200. | 1425. | 2200. |

## Type II

**Notes:** In 1917 the obverse design was modified to cover Liberty's bare right breast. On the reverse, three stars were added below the eagle.

| Date | Mintage | G-4 | VG-8 | F-12 | VF-20 | XF-40 | AU-50 | MS-60 | MS-65 | -65FH |
|---|---|---|---|---|---|---|---|---|---|---|
| 1917 | 13,880,000 | 11.00 | 13.00 | 16.00 | 22.00 | 48.00 | 80.00 | 125. | 475. | 1050. |
| 1917D | 6,224,400 | 16.00 | 21.00 | 49.00 | 65.00 | 95.00 | 110. | 175. | 1300. | 4000. |
| 1917S | 5,522,000 | 15.00 | 20.00 | 35.00 | 70.00 | 80.00 | 115. | 160. | 1100. | 3350. |
| 1918 | 14,240,000 | 12.00 | 15.00 | 21.00 | 33.00 | 53.00 | 73.00 | 125. | 500. | 1250. |
| 1918D | 7,380,000 | 19.00 | 25.00 | 44.00 | 60.00 | 90.00 | 140. | 180. | 1550. | 5600. |
| 1918S | 11,072,000 | 13.00 | 16.00 | 24.00 | 30.00 | 45.00 | 85.00 | 165. | 1700. | 15,000. |
| 1918/17S | Inc.Ab. | 950. | 1200. | 1625. | 2200. | 4000. | 8100. | 9400. | 52,000. | 78,000. |
| 1919 | 11,324,000 | 22.00 | 29.00 | 45.00 | 55.00 | 70.00 | 90.00 | 135. | 490. | 1000. |
| 1919D | 1,944,000 | 40.00 | 63.00 | 115. | 175. | 250. | 330. | 425. | 2600. | 19,500. |
| 1919S | 1,836,000 | 38.00 | 58.00 | 95.00 | 200. | 375. | 525. | 650. | 3500. | 17,000. |
| 1920 | 27,860,000 | 13.00 | 15.00 | 19.00 | 24.00 | 35.00 | 60.00 | 125. | 500. | 1300. |
| 1920D | 3,586,400 | 20.00 | 30.00 | 60.00 | 80.00 | 100. | 150. | 200. | 2000. | 6250. |
| 1920S | 6,380,000 | 14.00 | 17.00 | 25.00 | 35.00 | 55.00 | 80.00 | 180. | 2600. | 18,000. |
| 1921 | 1,916,000 | 60.00 | 80.00 | 110. | 185. | 230. | 315. | 400. | 1975. | 3500. |
| 1923 | 9,716,000 | 12.00 | 14.00 | 22.00 | 26.00 | 33.00 | 60.00 | 125. | 400. | 1575. |
| 1923S | 1,360,000 | 85.00 | 140. | 175. | 295. | 375. | 450. | 550. | 1875. | 3900. |
| 1924 | 10,920,000 | 13.00 | 15.00 | 19.00 | 23.00 | 45.00 | 60.00 | 125. | 470. | 1200. |
| 1924D | 3,112,000 | 21.00 | 30.00 | 50.00 | 68.00 | 95.00 | 120. | 150. | 470. | 6250. |
| 1924S | 2,860,000 | 15.00 | 18.00 | 21.00 | 27.00 | 77.00 | 165. | 220. | 1950. | 5200. |
| 1925 | 12,280,000 | 2.25 | 3.00 | 5.00 | 14.00 | 25.00 | 50.00 | 125. | 495. | 950. |
| 1926 | 11,316,000 | 2.25 | 3.00 | 5.00 | 14.00 | 32.00 | 65.00 | 125. | 495. | 1375. |
| 1926D | 1,716,000 | 5.50 | 7.00 | 11.00 | 18.50 | 40.00 | 72.00 | 125. | 495. | 12,250. |
| 1926S | 2,700,000 | 3.50 | 4.25 | 10.00 | 19.00 | 90.00 | 200. | 300. | 2500. | 12,500. |
| 1927 | 11,912,000 | 2.25 | 3.00 | 5.00 | 14.00 | 25.00 | 60.00 | 125. | 475. | 1100. |
| 1927D | 976,400 | 5.50 | 7.00 | 15.00 | 40.00 | 72.00 | 120. | 135. | 500. | 3500. |
| 1927S | 396,000 | 7.00 | 10.00 | 55.00 | 150. | 1050. | 2400. | 3450. | 10,000. | 20,000. |
| 1928 | 6,336,000 | 2.25 | 3.00 | 5.00 | 14.00 | 25.00 | 50.00 | 125. | 525. | 1250. |
| 1928D | 1,627,600 | 4.00 | 5.00 | 8.00 | 18.00 | 34.00 | 63.00 | 135. | 475. | 4350. |
| 1928S | 2,644,000 | 2.50 | 3.25 | 5.50 | 16.00 | 33.00 | 68.00 | 135. | 450. | 700. |
| 1929 | 11,140,000 | 2.25 | 3.00 | 4.50 | 13.00 | 30.00 | 50.00 | 125. | 475. | 700. |
| 1929D | 1,358,000 | 4.00 | 5.00 | 6.50 | 18.00 | 30.00 | 70.00 | 135. | 475. | 4700. |
| 1929S | 1,764,000 | 2.40 | 2.75 | 5.25 | 13.50 | 32.00 | 52.00 | 130. | 450. | 700. |
| 1930 | 5,632,000 | 2.25 | 2.75 | 5.00 | 13.00 | 30.00 | 60.00 | 125. | 475. | 700. |
| 1930S | 1,556,000 | 2.40 | 3.25 | 5.25 | 13.50 | 26.00 | 53.00 | 130. | 475. | 700. |

# Washington

**Reverse mintmark
(1932-1964)**

## Silver composition

**Designer:** John Flanagan. **Size:** 24.3 millimeters. **Weight:** 6.25 grams. **Composition:** 90% silver (0.1809 ounces), 10% copper.

| Date | Mintage | G-4 | VG-8 | F-12 | VF-20 | XF-40 | AU-50 | MS-60 | MS-65 | Prf-65 |
|------|---------|-----|------|------|-------|-------|-------|-------|-------|--------|
| 1932 | 5,404,000 | 3.00 | 3.25 | 4.50 | 6.75 | 9.00 | 14.00 | 28.00 | 185. | — |
| 1932D | 436,800 | 34.00 | 38.00 | 45.00 | 65.00 | 150. | 265. | 400. | 5000. | — |
| 1932S | 408,000 | 28.00 | 30.00 | 35.00 | 45.00 | 60.00 | 95.00 | 260. | 3600. | — |
| 1934 | 31,912,052 | 2.00 | 3.00 | 3.75 | 4.50 | 5.75 | 11.00 | 21.00 | 91.00 | — |
| 1934D | 3,527,200 | 3.25 | 4.00 | 6.00 | 7.00 | 10.00 | 33.00 | 100. | 960. | — |
| 1935 | 32,484,000 | 2.00 | 3.00 | 3.75 | 4.50 | 5.75 | 11.00 | 20.00 | 84.00 | — |
| 1935D | 5,780,000 | 2.40 | 4.00 | 6.00 | 7.00 | 10.00 | 39.00 | 112. | 310. | — |
| 1935S | 5,660,000 | 2.40 | 3.00 | 4.50 | 5.00 | 7.50 | 18.00 | 53.00 | 190. | — |
| 1936 | 41,303,837 | 2.00 | 3.00 | 4.00 | 4.50 | 6.00 | 11.00 | 17.00 | 74.00 | 875. |
| 1936D | 5,374,000 | 2.80 | 3.50 | 4.00 | 14.00 | 30.00 | 93.00 | 310. | 910. | — |
| 1936S | 3,828,000 | 2.80 | 3.00 | 4.00 | 7.00 | 10.00 | 24.00 | 56.00 | 110. | — |
| 1937 | 19,701,542 | 2.00 | 3.00 | 4.00 | 5.75 | 7.50 | 11.75 | 23.00 | 85.00 | 580. |
| 1937D | 7,189,600 | 2.75 | 3.00 | 4.00 | 7.00 | 9.00 | 14.00 | 38.00 | 105. | — |
| 1937S | 1,652,000 | 3.50 | 4.00 | 4.50 | 12.00 | 20.00 | 46.00 | 95.00 | 175. | — |
| 1938 | 9,480,045 | 2.80 | 3.00 | 4.50 | 7.50 | 12.00 | 24.00 | 49.00 | 100. | 450. |
| 1938S | 2,832,000 | 2.80 | 3.00 | 4.50 | 7.50 | 11.00 | 22.00 | 51.00 | 125. | — |
| 1939 | 33,548,795 | 2.00 | 3.00 | 3.75 | 4.25 | 5.50 | 10.50 | 14.00 | 49.00. | 400. |
| 1939D | 7,092,000 | 2.40 | 3.00 | 3.75 | 4.50 | 7.50 | 13.00 | 29.00 | 77.00 | — |

# 1932-D Quarter
## Grade F-12

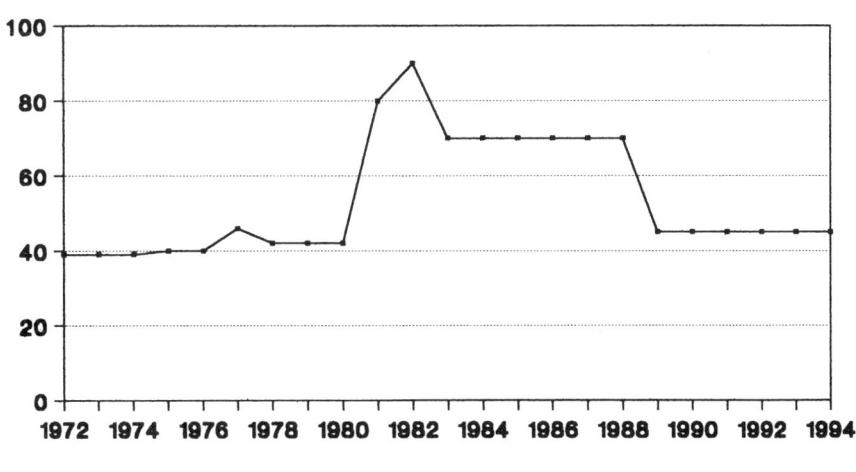

**Retail Price**

**Source: COIN PRICES**

| Date | Mintage | G-4 | VG-8 | F-12 | VF-20 | XF-40 | AU-50 | MS-60 | MS-65 | Prf-65 |
|------|---------|-----|------|------|-------|-------|-------|-------|-------|--------|
| 1939S | 2,628,000 | 3.00 | 3.50 | 5.00 | 6.00 | 10.00 | 26.00 | 59.00 | 130. | — |
| 1940 | 35,715,246 | 2.00 | 3.00 | 3.75 | 4.00 | 4.50 | 8.25 | 10.00 | 42.00 | 170. |
| 1940D | 2,797,600 | 3.25 | 3.50 | 7.00 | 10.00 | 15.50 | 28.00 | 62.00 | 110. | — |
| 1940S | 8,244,000 | 2.40 | 3.00 | 3.75 | 4.25 | 5.50 | 9.00 | 16.00 | 35.00 | — |
| 1941 | 79,047,287 | — | — | 1.50 | 2.00 | 3.25 | 4.50 | 7.50 | 23.00 | 100. |
| 1941D | 16,714,800 | — | — | 1.50 | 2.00 | 3.25 | 6.50 | 18.00 | 34.00 | — |
| 1941S | 16,080,000 | — | — | 1.50 | 2.00 | 3.25 | 6.50 | 15.00 | 70.00 | — |
| 1942 | 102,117,123 | — | — | 1.50 | 2.00 | 3.25 | 4.00 | 6.50 | 23.00 | 100. |
| 1942D | 17,487,200 | — | — | 1.50 | 2.00 | 3.25 | 5.00 | 10.00 | 29.00 | — |
| 1942S | 19,384,000 | — | — | 1.50 | 2.00 | 4.50 | 14.00 | 50.00 | 125. | — |
| 1943 | 99,700,000 | — | — | 1.50 | 2.00 | 2.25 | 2.75 | 5.00 | 23.00 | — |
| 1943D | 16,095,600 | — | — | 1.50 | 2.00 | 3.25 | 7.50 | 14.00 | 30.00 | — |
| 1943S | 21,700,000 | — | — | 1.50 | 2.00 | 5.50 | 11.50 | 29.00 | 39.00 | — |
| 1944 | 104,956,000 | — | — | 1.50 | 2.00 | 3.25 | 3.75 | 4.50 | 16.00 | — |
| 1944D | 14,600,800 | — | — | 1.50 | 2.00 | 3.25 | 5.00 | 9.00 | 21.00 | — |
| 1944S | 12,560,000 | — | — | 1.50 | 2.00 | 3.25 | 5.50 | 9.00 | 26.00 | — |
| 1945 | 74,372,000 | — | — | 1.50 | 2.00 | 3.25 | 4.00 | 5.00 | 14.00 | — |
| 1945D | 12,341,600 | — | — | 1.50 | 2.00 | 3.25 | 5.00 | 7.50 | 22.00 | — |
| 1945S | 17,004,001 | — | — | 1.50 | 2.00 | 3.25 | 4.50 | 6.00 | 18.00 | — |
| 1946 | 53,436,000 | — | — | 1.50 | 2.00 | 2.25 | 2.50 | 4.75 | 15.00 | — |
| 1946D | 9,072,800 | — | — | 1.50 | 2.00 | 2.25 | 2.75 | 4.00 | 12.00 | — |
| 1946S | 4,204,000 | — | — | 1.50 | 2.00 | 2.25 | 2.50 | 4.00 | 19.00 | — |
| 1947 | 22,556,000 | — | — | 1.50 | 2.00 | 3.00 | 3.75 | 6.50 | 12.00. | — |
| 1947D | 15,338,400 | — | — | 1.50 | 2.00 | 3.00 | 4.25 | 5.50 | 14.00 | — |
| 1947S | 5,532,000 | — | — | 1.50 | 2.00 | 2.25 | 2.50 | 5.00 | 16.50 | — |
| 1948 | 35,196,000 | — | — | 1.50 | 2.00 | 2.25 | 2.50 | 4.00 | 10.00 | — |
| 1948D | 16,766,800 | — | — | 1.50 | 2.00 | 2.25 | 2.50 | 5.00 | 12.00 | — |
| 1948S | 15,960,000 | — | — | 1.50 | 2.00 | 3.25 | 3.60 | 5.00 | 12.50 | — |
| 1949 | 9,312,000 | — | — | 1.50 | 2.00 | 3.50 | 9.00 | 19.00 | 25.00 | — |
| 1949D | 10,068,400 | — | — | 1.50 | 2.50 | 4.00 | 7.00 | 8.75 | 20.00 | — |
| 1950 | 24,971,512 | — | — | 1.50 | 2.50 | 3.00 | 3.75 | 5.00 | 8.00 | 55.00 |
| 1950D | 21,075,600 | — | — | 1.50 | 2.50 | 2.75 | 3.00 | 4.50 | 8.00 | — |
| 1950D/S | Inc. Ab. | 21.00 | 25.00 | 30.00 | 60.00 | 140. | 215. | 260. | 515. | — |
| 1950S | 10,284,004 | — | — | 1.50 | 3.00 | 3.25 | 5.75 | 7.25 | 13.50 | — |
| 1950S/D | Inc. Ab. | 21.00 | 25.00 | 30.00 | 60.00 | 170. | 315. | 460. | 625. | — |
| 1951 | 43,505,602 | — | — | 1.25 | 1.75 | 2.00 | 2.25 | 4.75 | 6.00 | 34.00 |
| 1951D | 35,354,800 | — | — | 1.25 | 1.75 | 2.00 | 2.25 | 3.25 | 5.50 | — |
| 1951S | 9,048,000 | — | — | 1.25 | 1.75 | 4.25 | 8.25 | 12.75 | 18.50 | — |
| 1952 | 38,862,073 | — | — | 1.25 | 1.75 | 2.00 | 2.25 | 3.00 | 5.50 | 30.00 |
| 1952D | 49,795,200 | — | — | 1.25 | 1.75 | 2.00 | 1.95 | 3.25 | 6.00 | — |
| 1952S | 13,707,800 | — | — | 1.25 | 2.00 | 2.50 | 5.25 | 8.50 | 11.50 | — |
| 1953 | 18,664,920 | — | — | 1.25 | 1.75 | 2.00 | 2.50 | 3.25 | 5.25 | 20.00 |
| 1953D | 56,112,400 | — | — | — | 1.25 | 1.50 | 1.75 | 2.25 | 5.25 | — |
| 1953S | 14,016,000 | — | — | 1.25 | 1.75 | 2.25 | 2.75 | 4.00 | 6.50 | — |
| 1954 | 54,645,503 | — | — | — | — | 1.25 | 1.50 | 2.00 | 4.75 | 12.00 |
| 1954D | 42,305,500 | — | — | — | 1.50 | 1.75 | 2.00 | 2.00 | 4.50 | — |
| 1954S | 11,834,722 | — | — | — | 1.50 | 1.75 | 2.00 | 2.00 | 5.25 | — |
| 1955 | 18,558,381 | — | — | — | 1.50 | 1.75 | 2.00 | 2.00 | 6.00 | 12.00 |
| 1955D | 3,182,400 | — | — | — | 1.50 | 2.00 | 2.25 | 2.50 | 7.50 | — |
| 1956 | 44,813,384 | — | — | — | 1.25 | 1.75 | 2.00 | 2.00 | 4.00 | 6.50 |
| 1956D | 32,334,500 | — | — | — | 1.25 | 2.00 | 2.50 | 2.75 | 4.00 | — |
| 1957 | 47,779,952 | — | — | — | — | 1.25 | 2.00 | 2.75 | 6.50 | 3.50 |
| 1957D | 77,924,160 | — | — | — | — | 1.25 | 1.75 | 2.00 | 4.50 | — |
| 1958 | 7,235,652 | — | — | — | — | 1.25 | 2.00 | 2.50 | 6.50 | 6.00 |
| 1958D | 78,124,900 | — | — | — | — | 1.25 | 1.75 | 2.00 | 4.50 | — |
| 1959 | 25,533,291 | — | — | — | — | 1.25 | 1.75 | 2.00 | 4.00 | 4.25 |
| 1959D | 62,054,232 | — | — | — | — | 1.25 | 1.75 | 2.00 | 4.00 | — |
| 1960 | 30,855,602 | — | — | — | — | 1.25 | 1.75 | 2.75 | 5.00 | 3.75 |
| 1960D | 63,000,324 | — | — | — | — | 1.25 | 1.75 | 2.00 | 4.00 | — |
| 1961 | 40,064,244 | — | — | — | — | 1.25 | 1.50 | 1.75 | 4.00 | 3.50 |
| 1961D | 83,656,928 | — | — | — | — | 1.25 | 1.50 | 1.75 | 4.00 | — |
| 1962 | 39,374,019 | — | — | — | — | 1.25 | 1.50 | 1.75 | 4.00 | 3.50 |
| 1962D | 127,554,756 | — | — | — | — | 1.25 | 1.50 | 1.75 | 4.00 | — |
| 1963 | 77,391,645 | — | — | — | — | 1.25 | 1.50 | 1.75 | 3.75 | 3.50 |
| 1963D | 135,288,184 | — | — | — | — | 1.25 | 1.50 | 1.75 | 3.75 | — |
| 1964 | 564,341,347 | — | — | — | — | 1.25 | 1.50 | 1.75 | 3.75 | 3.50 |
| 1964D | 704,135,528 | — | — | — | — | 1.25 | 1.50 | 1.75 | 3.75 | — |

## Clad composition

**Weight:** 5.67 grams. **Composition:** clad layers of 75% copper and 25% nickel bonded to a pure-copper core.

| Date | Mintage | MS-65 | Prf-65 | Date | Mintage | MS-65 | Prf-65 |
|------|---------|-------|--------|------|---------|-------|--------|
| 1965 | 1,819,717,540 | .80 | — | 1971 | 109,284,000 | .50 | — |
| 1966 | 821,101,500 | .80 | — | 1971D | 258,634,428 | .50 | — |
| 1967 | 1,524,031,848 | 1.00 | — | 1971S | Proof only | — | .95 |
| 1968 | 220,731,500 | .80 | — | 1972 | 215,048,000 | .40 | — |
| 1968D | 101,534,000 | 1.00 | — | 1972D | 311,067,732 | .40 | — |
| 1968S | Proof only | — | 1.25 | 1972S | Proof only | — | .95 |
| 1969 | 176,212,000 | 1.00 | — | 1973 | 346,924,000 | .40 | — |
| 1969D | 114,372,000 | 1.25 | — | 1973D | 232,977,400 | .40 | — |
| 1969S | Proof only | — | 1.00 | 1973S | Proof only | — | .95 |
| 1970 | 136,420,000 | .50 | — | 1974 | 801,456,000 | .40 | — |
| 1970D | 417,341,364 | .50 | — | 1974D | 353,160,300 | .40 | — |
| 1970S | Proof only | — | .95 | 1974S | Proof only | — | .95 |

**Obverse mintmark
(1968-present)**

## Bicentennial reverse, clad composition

**Reverse designer:** Jack L. Ahr.

| Date | Mintage | G-4 | VG-8 | F-12 | VF-20 | XF-40 | MS-60 | MS-65 | Prf-65 |
|------|---------|-----|------|------|-------|-------|-------|-------|--------|
| 1976 | 809,784,016 | — | — | — | — | — | — | .60 | — |
| 1976D | 860,118,839 | — | — | — | — | — | — | .60 | — |
| 1976S | — | — | — | — | — | — | — | — | .90 |

## Bicentennial reverse, silver composition

**Weight:** 5.75 grams. **Composition:** clad layers of 80% silver and 20% copper bonded to a core of 20.9% silver and 79.1% copper (0.0739 total ounces of silver).

| Date | Mintage | G-4 | VG-8 | F-12 | VF-20 | XF-40 | MS-60 | MS-65 | Prf-65 |
|------|---------|-----|------|------|-------|-------|-------|-------|--------|
| 1976S silver | 11,000,000 | — | — | — | — | — | — | 1.10 | 1.95 |

## Regular design resumed, clad composition

**Notes:** The 1979-S Type II proof has a clearer mintmark than the Type I.

| Date | Mintage | MS-65 | Prf-65 | Date | Mintage | MS-65 | Prf-65 |
|------|---------|-------|--------|------|---------|-------|--------|
| 1977 | 468,556,000 | .40 | — | 1985S | Proof only | — | 1.25 |
| 1977D | 258,898,212 | .45 | — | 1986P | 551,199,333 | 4.00 | — |
| 1977S | Proof only | — | .95 | 1986D | 504,298,660 | 2.75 | — |
| 1978 | 521,452,000 | .40 | — | 1986S | Proof only | — | 2.00 |
| 1978D | 287,373,152 | .40 | — | 1987P | 582,499,481 | .50 | — |
| 1978S | Proof only | — | .95 | 1987D | 655,594,696 | .50 | — |
| 1979 | 515,708,000 | .50 | — | 1987S | Proof only | — | 1.10 |
| 1979D | 489,789,780 | .50 | — | 1988P | 562,052,000 | 1.50 | — |
| 1979S T-I | Proof only | — | .95 | 1988D | 596,810,688 | .60 | — |
| 1979S T-II | Proof only | — | 1.45 | 1988S | Proof only | — | 1.25 |
| 1980P | 635,832,000 | .50 | — | 1989P | 512,868,000 | .50 | — |
| 1980D | 518,327,487 | .50 | — | 1989D | 896,535,597 | .50 | — |
| 1980S | Proof only | — | .95 | 1989S | Proof only | — | 1.35 |
| 1981P | 601,716,000 | .50 | — | 1990P | 613,792,000 | .50 | — |
| 1981D | 575,722,833 | .50 | — | 1990D | 927,638,181 | .50 | — |
| 1981S T-I | Proof only | — | .95 | 1990S | Proof only | — | 2.75 |
| 1981S T-II | Proof only | — | 3.00 | 1991P | — | .50 | — |
| 1982P | 500,931,000 | 5.25 | — | 1991D | — | .50 | — |
| 1982D | 480,042,788 | 1.00 | — | 1991S | Proof only | — | 2.95 |
| 1982S | Proof only | — | 2.25 | 1992P | — | .50 | — |
| 1983P | 673,535,000 | 5.75 | — | 1992D | — | .50 | — |
| 1983D | 617,806,446 | 6.00 | — | 1992S | Proof only | — | 2.40 |
| 1983S | Proof only | — | 1.75 | 1993P | — | .50 | — |
| 1984P | 676,545,000 | .85 | — | 1993D | — | .50 | — |
| 1984D | 546,483,064 | 2.00 | — | 1993S | Proof only | — | 1.75 |
| 1984S | Proof only | — | 1.60 | 1994P | — | .50 | — |
| 1985P | 775,818,962 | 2.50 | — | 1994D | — | .50 | — |
| 1985D | 519,962,888 | 3.25 | — | 1994S | Proof only | — | 3.50 |

# Half dollars

## Flowing Hair

**Designer:** Robert Scot. **Size:** 32.5 millimeters. **Weight:** 13.48 grams. **Composition:** 89.24% silver (0.3869 ounces), 10.76% copper. **Notes:** The 1795 "recut date" variety had the date cut into the dies twice, so both sets of numbers are visible on the coin. The 1795 "3 leaves" variety has three leaves under each of the eagle's wings on the reverse.

| Date | Mintage | G-4 | VG-8 | F-12 | VF-20 | XF-40 | MS-60 |
|------|---------|-----|------|------|-------|-------|-------|
| 1794 | 23,464 | 1150. | 1950. | 2950. | 4000. | 9500. | — |
| 1795 | 299,680 | 450. | 625. | 950. | 2150. | 5500. | 9500. |
| 1795 recut date | Inc. Ab. | 500. | 700. | 1000. | 2275. | 7000. | 9500. |
| 1795 3 leaves | Inc. Ab. | 1850. | 2500. | 3300. | 5850. | 9500. | — |

# 1797 Half Dollar
## Grade F-12

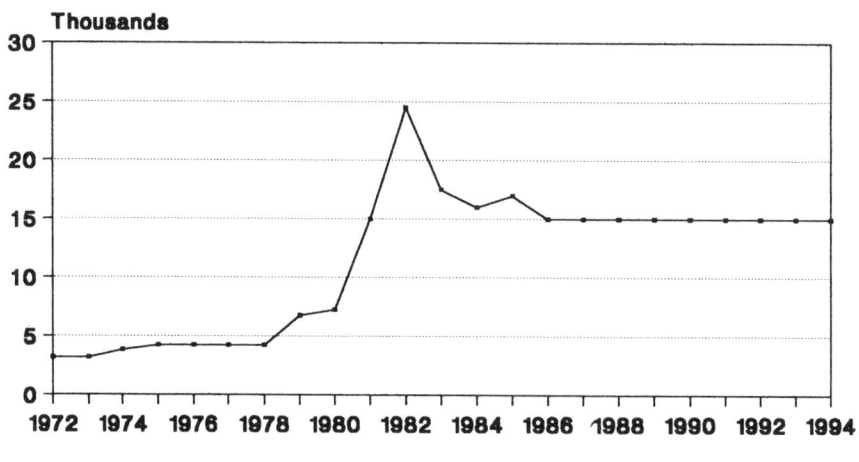

Retail Price

**Source: COIN PRICES**

# Draped Bust

## Small-eagle reverse

**Designer:** Robert Scot. **Size:** 32.5 millimeters. **Weight:** 13.48 grams. **Composition:** 89.24% silver (0.3869 ounces), 10.76% copper. **Notes:** The 1796 strikes have either 15 or 16 stars on the obverse.

| Date | Mintage | G-4 | VG-8 | F-12 | VF-20 | XF-40 | MS-60 |
|------|---------|-----|------|------|-------|-------|-------|
| 1796 15 stars | 3,918 | 10,000. | 12,000. | 15,000. | 27,000. | 39,000. | — |
| 1796 16 stars | Inc. Ab. | 10,000. | 12,000. | 15,000. | 27,000. | 39,000. | — |
| 1797 | Inc. Ab. | 10,000. | 12,000. | 15,000. | 27,000. | 39,000. | — |

## Heraldic-eagle reverse

**Notes:** The two varieties of the 1803 strikes are distinguished by the size of the 3 in the date. The several varieties of the 1806 strikes are distinguished by the style of 6 in the date, size of the stars on the obverse, and whether the stem of the olive branch held by the reverse eagle extends through the claw.

| Date | Mintage | G-4 | VG-8 | F-12 | VF-20 | XF-40 | MS-60 |
|------|---------|-----|------|------|-------|-------|-------|
| 1801 | 30,289 | 190. | 285. | 500. | 800. | 1850. | 9500. |
| 1802 | 29,890 | 175. | 240. | 440. | 750. | 1575. | 8750. |
| 1803 sm. 3 | 188,234 | 150. | 170. | 285. | 450. | 1000. | 6300. |
| 1803 lg. 3 | Inc. Ab. | 140. | 150. | 225. | 380. | 750. | 5700. |
| 1805 | 211,722 | 140. | 150. | 225. | 350. | 800. | 5700. |
| 1805/4 | Inc. Ab. | 150. | 250. | 475. | 600. | 1200. | 8750. |
| 1806 round top 6, large stars | 839,576 | 125. | 150. | 210. | 325. | 625. | 5400. |
| 1806 round top 6, small stars | Inc. Ab. | 125. | 150. | 210. | 325. | 625. | 5400. |
| 1806 pointed top 6, stem not through claw | Inc. Ab. | 125. | 150. | 210. | 325. | 625. | 5400. |
| 1806 pointed top 6, stem through claw | Inc. Ab. | 125. | 150. | 210. | 325. | 625. | 5400. |
| 1806/5 | Inc. Ab. | 125. | 150. | 210. | 450. | 775. | 5400. |
| 1806/inverted 6 | Inc. Ab. | 175. | 225. | 535. | 875. | 1175. | 9250. |
| 1807 | 301,076 | 125. | 150. | 210. | 285. | 625. | 5400. |

# Liberty Cap

**Designer:** John Reich. **Size:** 32.5 millimeters. **Weight:** 13.48 grams. **Composition:** 89.24% silver (0.3869 ounces), 10.76% copper. **Notes:** There are three varieties of the 1807 strikes. Two are distinguished by the size of the stars on the obverse. The third was struck from a reverse die that had a 5 cut over a 2 in the "50C." denomination. Two varieties of the 1811 are distinguished by the size of the 8 in the date. A third has a period between the 8 and second 1 in the date. One variety of the 1817 has a period between the 1 and 7 in the date. Two varieties of the 1819/18 overdate are distinguished by the size of the 9 in the date. Two varieties of the 1820 are distinguished by the size of the date. On the 1823 varieties, the "broken 3" appears to be almost separated in the middle of the 3 in the date; the "patched 3" has the error repaired; the "ugly 3" has portions of its detail missing. The 1827 "curled-2" and "square-2" varieties are distinguished by the numeral's base — either curled or square. Among the 1828 varieties, "knobbed 2" and "no knob" refers to whether the upper left serif of the digit is rounded. The 1830 varieties are distinguished by the size of the 0 in the date. The four 1834 varieties are distinguished by the sizes of the stars, date and letters in the inscriptions. The 1836 "50/00" variety was struck from a reverse die that had "50" recut over "00" in the denomination.

| Date | Mintage | G-4 | VG-8 | F-12 | VF-20 | XF-40 | AU-50 | MS-60 | MS-65 |
|------|---------|-----|------|------|-------|-------|-------|-------|-------|
| 1807 sm. stars | 750,500 | 55.00 | 100. | 175. | 300. | 625. | 2000. | 3200. | — |
| 1807 lg. stars | Inc. Ab. | 50.00 | 65.00 | 150. | 285. | 625. | 2000. | 3200. | — |
| 1807 50/20 C. | Inc. Ab. | 45.00 | 60.00 | 75.00 | 140. | 350. | 1500. | 2900. | — |
| 1808 | 1,368,600 | 37.50 | 42.50 | 53.00 | 90.00 | 185. | 450. | 1000. | — |
| 1808/7 | Inc. Ab. | 40.00 | 50.00 | 60.00 | 125. | 200. | 500. | 1500. | — |
| 1809 | 1,405,810 | 36.00 | 42.50 | 55.00 | 100. | 440. | 600. | 1000. | — |
| 1810 | 1,276,276 | 34.50 | 38.00 | 46.00 | 100. | 225. | 500. | 1000. | — |
| 1811 sm. 8 | 1,203,644 | 32.00 | 37.50 | 45.00 | 70.00 | 145. | 450. | 750. | — |
| 1811 lg. 8 | Inc. Ab. | 32.50 | 37.00 | 50.00 | 85.00 | 165. | 450. | 750. | — |
| 1811 dt. 18.11 | Inc. Ab. | 35.00 | 40.00 | 60.00 | 95.00 | 185. | 500. | 1400. | — |
| 1812 | 1,628,059 | 32.50 | 37.50 | 45.00 | 100. | 180. | 325. | 700. | — |
| 1812/11 | Inc. Ab. | 42.50 | 50.00 | 80.00 | 115. | 225. | 700. | 2150. | — |
| 1813 | 1,241,903 | 32.50 | 37.50 | 45.00 | 95.00 | 225. | 350. | 875. | — |
| 1814 | 1,039,075 | 34.50 | 38.00 | 47.00 | 70.00 | 145. | 500. | 1800. | — |
| 1814/13 | Inc. Ab. | 42.50 | 52.50 | 69.00 | 100. | 200. | 350. | 900. | — |
| 1815/12 | 47,150 | 750. | 1000. | 1350. | 1875. | 2800. | 3600. | 4500. | — |
| 1817 | 1,215,567 | 31.50 | 33.00 | 40.00 | 65.00 | 135. | 250. | 700. | — |
| 1817/13 | Inc. Ab. | 80.00 | 135. | 185. | 325. | 500. | 975. | 1100. | — |
| 1817/14 | | | | | 5 pieces known | | — | | — |
| 1817 dt. 181.7 | Inc. Ab. | 37.00 | 47.00 | 70.00 | 115. | 195. | 395. | 700. | — |
| 1818 | 1,960,322 | 31.50 | 33.00 | 40.00 | 70.00 | 135. | 250. | 700. | — |
| 1818/17 | Inc. Ab. | 31.50 | 33.00 | 40.00 | 70.00 | 135. | 250. | 700. | — |
| 1819 | 2,208,000 | 31.50 | 33.00 | 40.00 | 70.00 | 135. | 250. | 700. | — |
| 1819/18 sm. 9 | Inc. Ab. | 31.50 | 33.00 | 40.00 | 70.00 | 135. | 250. | 700. | — |
| 1819/18 lg. 9 | Inc. Ab. | 31.50 | 33.00 | 40.00 | 70.00 | 135. | 250. | 700. | — |
| 1820 sm. dt. | 751,122 | 39.00 | 49.00 | 67.00 | 135. | 210. | 300. | 700. | — |
| 1820 lg. dt. | Inc. Ab. | 39.00 | 50.00 | 67.00 | 135. | 210. | 300. | 700. | — |
| 1820/19 | Inc. Ab. | 37.00 | 49.00 | 75.00 | 130. | 225. | 275. | 700. | — |
| 1821 | 1,305,797 | 33.00 | 35.00 | 40.00 | 70.00 | 135. | 250. | 700. | — |
| 1822 | 1,559,573 | 32.00 | 34.00 | 40.00 | 65.00 | 135. | 250. | 700. | — |
| 1822/1 | Inc. Ab. | 50.00 | 69.00 | 110. | 185. | 300. | 475. | 1100. | — |
| 1823 | 1,694,200 | 31.50 | 33.00 | 40.00 | 65.00 | 135. | 250. | 700. | — |
| 1823 broken 3 | Inc. Ab. | 37.00 | 52.00 | 84.00 | 115. | 220. | 400. | 700. | — |
| 1823 patched 3 | Inc. Ab. | 37.00 | 50.00 | 75.00 | 95.00 | 195. | 325. | 700. | — |
| 1823 ugly 3 | Inc. Ab. | 35.00 | 40.00 | 65.00 | 95.00 | 185. | 265. | 700. | — |
| 1824 | 3,504,954 | 31.00 | 33.00 | 40.00 | 50.00 | 95.00 | 250. | 700. | — |
| 1824/21 | Inc. Ab. | 35.00 | 40.00 | 58.00 | 95.00 | 185. | 250. | 700. | — |
| 1824/various dates | | | | | | | | | |
| | Inc. Ab. | 31.50 | 33.00 | 40.00 | 65.00 | 145. | 250. | 700. | — |
| 1825 | 2,943,166 | 31.50 | 33.00 | 40.00 | 50.00 | 95.00 | 250. | 700. | — |
| 1826 | 4,004,180 | 31.50 | 33.00 | 40.00 | 50.00 | 95.00 | 250. | 700. | — |
| 1827 curled 2 | 5,493,400 | 33.00 | 36.00 | 42.50 | 85.00 | 150. | 250. | 700. | — |
| 1827 square 2 | Inc. Ab. | 31.50 | 33.00 | 40.00 | 50.00 | 95.00 | 250. | 700. | — |
| 1827/6 | Inc. Ab. | 35.00 | 40.00 | 60.00 | 90.00 | 145. | 265. | 1100. | — |
| 1828 curled base 2, no knob | | | | | | | | | |
| | 3,075,200 | 30.00 | 33.00 | 37.50 | 50.00 | 95.00 | 250. | 700. | 6000. |
| 1828 curled base 2, knobbed 2 | | | | | | | | | |
| | Inc. Ab. | 35.00 | 45.00 | 60.00 | 85.00 | 150. | 350. | 750. | — |
| 1828 small 8s, square base 2, large letters | | | | | | | | | |
| | Inc. Ab. | 27.50 | 32.00 | 34.00 | 43.00 | 90.00 | 250. | 700. | 15,500. |
| 1828 small 8s, square base 2, small letters | | | | | | | | | |
| | Inc. Ab. | 27.50 | 32.00 | 65.00 | 125. | 250. | 350. | 750. | — |

| Date | Mintage | G-4 | VG-8 | F-12 | VF-20 | XF-40 | AU-50 | MS-60 | MS-65 |
|------|---------|-----|------|------|-------|-------|-------|-------|-------|
| 1828 large 8s, square base 2 | | | | | | | | | |
| | Inc. Ab. | 27.50 | 32.00 | 34.00 | 43.00 | 90.00 | 250. | 700. | — |
| 1829 | 3,712,156 | 27.50 | 32.00 | 34.00 | 43.00 | 90.00 | 250. | 700. | — |
| 1829/27 | Inc. Ab. | 35.00 | 40.00 | 60.00 | 85.00 | 165. | 250. | 800. | — |
| 1830 small 0 in date | | | | | | | | | |
| | 4,764,800 | 27.50 | 32.00 | 34.00 | 43.00 | 89.00 | 250. | 700. | 6000. |
| 1830 large 0 in date | | | | | | | | | |
| | Inc. Ab. | 27.50 | 32.00 | 34.00 | 43.00 | 89.00 | 250. | 700. | 6000. |
| 1831 | 5,873,660 | 27.50 | 32.00 | 34.00 | 43.00 | 89.00 | 250. | 700. | 6000. |
| 1832 sm. lt. | 4,797,000 | 27.50 | 32.00 | 34.00 | 43.00 | 89.00 | 250. | 700. | 6000. |
| 1832 lg. let. | Inc. Ab. | 30.00 | 38.00 | 45.00 | 65.00 | 195. | 495. | 1250. | 8500. |
| 1833 | 5,206,000 | 27.50 | 32.00 | 34.00 | 43.00 | 89.00 | 250. | 700. | 6000. |
| 1834 small date, large stars, small letters | | | | | | | | | |
| | 6,412,004 | 27.50 | 32.00 | 34.00 | 43.00 | 89.00 | 250. | 700. | 6000. |
| 1834 small date, small stars, small letters | | | | | | | | | |
| | Inc. Ab. | 27.50 | 32.00 | 34.00 | 43.00 | 89.00 | 250. | 700. | 6000. |
| 1834 large date, small letters | | | | | | | | | |
| | Inc. Ab. | 27.50 | 32.00 | 34.00 | 43.00 | 89.00 | 250. | 700. | 6000. |
| 1834 large date, large letters | | | | | | | | | |
| | Inc. Ab. | 27.50 | 32.00 | 34.00 | 43.00 | 89.00 | 250. | 700. | 6000. |
| 1835 | 5,352,006 | 27.50 | 32.00 | 34.00 | 43.00 | 89.00 | 250. | 700. | 6000. |
| 1836 | 6,545,000 | 27.50 | 32.00 | 34.00 | 43.00 | 89.00 | 250. | 700. | 6000. |
| 1836 50/00 | Inc. Ab. | 50.00 | 60.00 | 80.00 | 160. | 225. | 475. | 1100. | — |

### Reeded edge, "50 Cents" on reverse

**Designer:** Christian Gobrecht. **Size:** 30 millimeters. **Weight:** 13.36 grams. **Composition:** 90% silver (0.3867 ounces). 10% copper.

| Date | Mintage | G-4 | VG-8 | F-12 | VF-20 | XF-40 | AU-50 | MS-60 | MS-65 |
|------|---------|-----|------|------|-------|-------|-------|-------|-------|
| 1836 | 1,200 | 750. | 900. | 1150. | 1275. | 1750. | 3000. | 5000. | — |
| 1837 | 3,629,820 | 32.00 | 40.00 | 50.00 | 85.00 | 150. | 365. | 750. | 13,500. |

### "Half Dol." on reverse

| Date | Mintage | G-4 | VG-8 | F-12 | VF-20 | XF-40 | AU-50 | MS-60 | MS-65 |
|------|---------|-----|------|------|-------|-------|-------|-------|-------|
| 1838 | 3,546,000 | 32.00 | 38.00 | 41.00 | 60.00 | 125. | 475. | 1200. | 8500. |
| 1838O | Est. 20 | | | | | Auction '82, MS-63, $47,000. | | | — |
| 1839 | 3,334,560 | 32.00 | 38.00 | 41.00 | 60.00 | 125. | 365. | 750. | 8500. |
| 1839O | 178,976 | 105. | 140. | 185. | 300. | 500. | — | 3250. | — |

# Seated Liberty

**Designer:** Christian Gobrecht. **Size:** 30.6 millimeters. **Weight:** 13.36 grams. **Composition:** 90% silver (0.3867 ounces), 10% copper. **Notes:** Some 1839 strikes have drapery extending from Liberty's left elbow. One variety of the 1840 strikes has smaller lettering; another used the old reverse of 1838. Varieties of 1842 and 1846 are distinguished by the size of the numerals in the date.

| Date | Mintage | G-4 | VG-8 | F-12 | VF-20 | XF-40 | AU-50 | MS-60 | MS-65 |
|------|---------|-----|------|------|-------|-------|-------|-------|-------|
| 1839 no drapery from elbow | | | | | | | | | |
| | Inc. Ab. | 38.00 | 65.00 | 110. | 250. | 725. | 1500. | 2350. | 107 K |
| 1839 drapery | Inc. Ab. | 20.00 | 28.00 | 40.00 | 70.00 | 115. | 265. | 450. | — |

| Date | Mintage | G-4 | VG-8 | F-12 | VF-20 | XF-40 | AU-50 | MS-60 | MS-65 |
|------|---------|-----|------|------|-------|-------|-------|-------|-------|
| 1840 sm. let. | 1,435,008 | 16.50 | 20.00 | 30.00 | 60.00 | 110. | 350. | 575. | 8250. |
| 1840 rev. 1838 | Inc. Ab. | 105. | 130. | 215. | 300. | 500. | 1200. | 2500. | — |
| 1840O | 855,100 | 17.00 | 23.00 | 34.00 | 70.00 | 125. | 300. | 585. | — |
| 1841 | 310,000 | 35.00 | 45.00 | 80.00 | 140. | 265. | 425. | 1300. | — |
| 1841O | 401,000 | 17.00 | 25.00 | 45.00 | 85.00 | 150. | 240. | 875. | — |
| 1842 sm. date | 2,012,764 | 27.00 | 32.00 | 40.00 | 75.00 | 125. | 325. | 1300. | 12,000. |
| 1842 lg. date | Inc. Ab. | 16.00 | 21.00 | 33.00 | 50.00 | 75.00 | 120. | 1250. | 12,000. |
| 1842O sm. date | 957,000 | 500. | 800. | 1400. | 2250. | 4000. | — | — | — |
| 1842O lg. date | Inc. Ab. | 17.00 | 23.00 | 34.00 | 65.00 | 135. | 285. | 500. | — |
| 1843 | 3,844,000 | 16.00 | 21.00 | 30.00 | 50.00 | 80.00 | 180. | 410. | 5500. |
| 1843O | 2,268,000 | 16.00 | 21.00 | 30.00 | 55.00 | 90.00 | 250. | 550. | — |
| 1844 | 1,766,000 | 16.00 | 21.00 | 30.00 | 50.00 | 85.00 | 180. | 410. | 5500. |
| 1844O | 2,005,000 | 16.00 | 21.00 | 36.00 | 55.00 | 80.00 | 195. | 525. | — |
| 1844/1844O | Inc. Ab. | 350. | 650. | 975. | 1375. | 2700. | — | — | — |
| 1845 | 589,000 | 30.00 | 40.00 | 50.00 | 90.00 | 170. | 340. | 900. | — |
| 1845O | 2,094,000 | 16.00 | 21.00 | 30.00 | 42.00 | 100. | 240. | 550. | — |
| 1845O no drapery | | | | | | | | | |
| | Inc. Ab. | 25.00 | 30.00 | 50.00 | 90.00 | 150. | 375. | 750. | — |
| 1846 med. dt. | 2,210,000 | 16.00 | 20.00 | 28.00 | 40.00 | 70.00 | 175. | 500. | 9000. |
| 1846 tall dt. | Inc. Ab. | 22.00 | 30.00 | 60.00 | 80.00 | 125. | 250. | 650. | 12,000. |
| 1846/horizontal 6 | | | | | | | | | |
| | Inc. Ab. | 140. | 185. | 250. | 375. | 550. | 1000. | 2500. | — |
| 1846O med.dt. | 2,304,000 | 16.00 | 18.00 | 28.00 | 38.00 | 100. | 225. | 550. | 12,000. |
| 1846O tall dt. | Inc. Ab. | 125. | 245. | 325. | 500. | 950. | 2000. | 3600. | — |
| 1847/1846 | 1,156,000 | 1900. | 2900. | 3200. | 4250. | 5750. | — | — | — |
| 1847 | Inc. Ab. | 20.00 | 30.00 | 45.00 | 60.00 | 90.00 | 190. | 480. | 9000. |
| 1847O | 2,584,000 | 15.00 | 25.00 | 35.00 | 50.00 | 95.00 | 250. | 640. | 7000. |
| 1848 | 580,000 | 30.00 | 50.00 | 75.00 | 135. | 240. | 475. | 1400. | 9000. |
| 1848O | 3,180,000 | 18.00 | 25.00 | 40.00 | 50.00 | 95.00 | 285. | 750. | 9000. |
| 1849 | 1,252,000 | 22.00 | 35.00 | 50.00 | 85.00 | 150. | 365. | 1250. | 9000. |
| 1849O | 2,310,000 | 15.00 | 25.00 | 40.00 | 60.00 | 115. | 250. | 650. | 9000. |
| 1850 | 227,000 | 200. | 250. | 340. | 375. | 500. | 875. | 1500. | — |

# 1855-S Half Dollar
## Grade XF-40

Source: COIN PRICES

| Date | Mintage | G-4 | VG-8 | F-12 | VF-20 | XF-40 | AU-50 | MS-60 | MS-65 |
|------|---------|-----|------|------|-------|-------|-------|-------|-------|
| 1850O | 2,456,000 | 15.00 | 25.00 | 40.00 | 55.00 | 115. | 250. | 650. | 9000. |
| 1851 | 200,750 | 250. | 300. | 375. | 465. | 600. | 800. | 1800. | — |
| 1851O | 402,000 | 37.00 | 45.00 | 57.00 | 90.00 | 175. | 300. | 610. | 9000. |
| 1852 | 77,130 | 300. | 350. | 425. | 525. | 650. | 800. | 1450. | — |
| 1852O | 144,000 | 50.00 | 80.00 | 125. | 250. | 425. | 800. | 1850. | — |
| 1853O | Unrecorded | | | Garrett Sale, 1979, VF, $40,000. | | | | | |

## Arrows at date, reverse rays

**Weight:** 12.44 grams. **Composition:** 90% silver (0.36 ounces), 10% copper.

| Date | Mintage | G-4 | VG-8 | F-12 | VF-20 | XF-40 | AU-50 | MS-60 | MS-65 | Prf-65 |
|------|---------|-----|------|------|-------|-------|-------|-------|-------|--------|
| 1853 rays on reverse | 3,532,708 | 16.50 | 30.00 | 45.50 | 90.00 | 250. | 505. | 1700. | 21,500. | — |
| 1853O rays on reverse | 1,328,000 | 19.00 | 30.00 | 45.50 | 100. | 290. | 700. | 2100. | 21,500. | — |

## Reverse rays removed

| Date | Mintage | G-4 | VG-8 | F-12 | VF-20 | XF-40 | AU-50 | MS-60 | MS-65 | Prf-65 |
|------|---------|-----|------|------|-------|-------|-------|-------|-------|--------|
| 1854 | 2,982,000 | 15.00 | 20.00 | 29.00 | 50.00 | 100. | 270. | 675. | 10,000. | — |
| 1854O | 5,240,000 | 15.00 | 20.00 | 29.00 | 50.00 | 100. | 265. | 500. | 10,000. | — |
| 1855 | 759,500 | 23.00 | 30.00 | 40.00 | 60.00 | 150. | 325. | 1200. | 10,000. | 22,500. |
| 1855/4 | Inc. Ab. | 35.00 | 60.00 | 80.00 | 125. | 225. | 400. | 1500. | — | — |
| 1855O | 3,688,000 | 15.00 | 20.00 | 29.00 | 50.00 | 100. | 270. | 650. | 10,000. | — |
| 1855S | 129,950 | 300. | 425. | 650. | 1300. | 2650. | 6000. | — | — | — |

 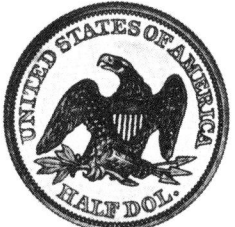

## Arrows at date removed

| Date | Mintage | G-4 | VG-8 | F-12 | VF-20 | XF-40 | AU-50 | MS-60 | MS-65 | Prf-65 |
|------|---------|-----|------|------|-------|-------|-------|-------|-------|--------|
| 1856 | 938,000 | 18.00 | 25.00 | 32.00 | 47.50 | 90.00 | 150. | 410. | 6500. | 12,500. |
| 1856O | 2,658,000 | 15.00 | 21.00 | 28.00 | 45.00 | 82.00 | 150. | 450. | 12,500. | — |
| 1856S | 211,000 | 40.00 | 50.00 | 95.00 | 200. | 375. | 1250. | 2500. | 19,000. | — |
| 1857 | 1,988,000 | 15.00 | 18.00 | 28.00 | 45.00 | 82.00 | 150. | 410. | 5500. | 12,500. |
| 1857O | 818,000 | 18.00 | 21.00 | 25.00 | 55.00 | 100. | 250. | 850. | 12,500. | — |
| 1857S | 158,000 | 50.00 | 65.00 | 110. | 225. | 450. | 800. | 2400. | 19,000. | — |
| 1858 | 4,226,000 | 15.00 | 18.00 | 35.00 | 60.00 | 80.00 | 150. | 410. | 6500. | 12,500. |
| 1858O | 7,294,000 | 14.00 | 17.00 | 35.00 | 45.00 | 70.00 | 150. | 450. | 12,500. | — |

| Date | Mintage | G-4 | VG-8 | F-12 | VF-20 | XF-40 | AU-50 | MS-60 | MS-65 | Prf-65 |
|------|---------|-----|------|------|-------|-------|-------|-------|-------|--------|
| 1858S | 476,000 | 20.00 | 30.00 | 48.00 | 90.00 | 175. | 400. | 950. | 12,500. | — |
| 1859 | 748,000 | 16.50 | 27.00 | 42.00 | 55.00 | 90.00 | 200. | 650. | 6600. | 5500. |
| 1859O | 2,834,000 | 15.00 | 25.00 | 40.00 | 50.00 | 85.00 | 150. | 450. | 6500. | — |
| 1859S | 566,000 | 20.00 | 28.00 | 45.00 | 70.00 | 150. | 200. | 750. | 12,500. | — |
| 1860 | 303,700 | 18.00 | 21.00 | 35.00 | 70.00 | 120. | 350. | 1000. | 6500. | 5500. |
| 1860O | 1,290,000 | 15.00 | 18.00 | 35.00 | 45.00 | 63.00 | 150. | 450. | 5500. | — |
| 1860S | 472,000 | 18.00 | 30.00 | 50.00 | 70.00 | 130. | 175. | 850. | 12,500. | — |
| 1861 | 2,888,400 | 15.00 | 25.00 | 35.00 | 45.00 | 70.00 | 150. | 410. | 5500. | 5500. |
| 1861O | 2,532,633 | 15.00 | 25.00 | 40.00 | 50.00 | 70.00 | 150. | 450. | 5500. | — |
| 1861S | 939,500 | 17.00 | 20.00 | 35.00 | 45.00 | 70.00 | 150. | 975. | 9500. | — |
| 1862 | 253,550 | 24.00 | 32.00 | 50.00 | 80.00 | 150. | 225. | 750. | 5500. | 5500. |
| 1862S | 1,352,000 | 16.00 | 27.00 | 35.00 | 60.00 | 90.00 | 175. | 450. | 9000. | — |
| 1863 | 503,660 | 18.00 | 25.00 | 40.00 | 70.00 | 130. | 250. | 750. | 5500. | 5500. |
| 1863S | 916,000 | 16.00 | 25.00 | 35.00 | 45.00 | 80.00 | 150. | 410. | 9000. | — |
| 1864 | 379,570 | 24.00 | 32.00 | 55.00 | 85.00 | 160. | 200. | 750. | 5500. | 5500. |
| 1864S | 658,000 | 16.50 | 20.00 | 40.00 | 50.00 | 85.00 | 165. | 450. | 9000. | — |
| 1865 | 511,900 | 18.00 | 23.00 | 40.00 | 60.00 | 110. | 240. | 750. | 4200. | 5500. |
| 1865S | 675,000 | 17.00 | 21.00 | 30.00 | 50.00 | 75.00 | 160. | 450. | 9000: | — |
| 1866 | — | — | — | — | Proof, unique | | — | — | — | — |
| 1866S | 60,000 | 75.00 | 110. | 165. | 275. | 475. | 1500. | 5000. | — | — |

## Motto above eagle

**Notes:** In 1866 the motto "In God We Trust" was added to the reverse. The "closed-3" and "open-3" varieties are distinguished by the amount of space between the upper left and lower left serifs of the 3.

| Date | Mintage | G-4 | VG-8 | F-12 | VF-20 | XF-40 | AU-50 | MS-60 | MS-65 | Prf-65 |
|------|---------|-----|------|------|-------|-------|-------|-------|-------|--------|
| 1866 | 745,625 | 15.00 | 24.00 | 29.00 | 40.00 | 80.00 | 145. | 350. | 4800. | 3750. |
| 1866S | 994,000 | 15.00 | 24.00 | 29.00 | 39.00 | 75.00 | 145. | 350. | 5000. | — |
| 1867 | 449,925 | 16.00 | 27.00 | 45.00 | 80.00 | 145. | 240. | 350. | 4800. | 3750. |
| 1867S | 1,196,000 | 15.00 | 24.00 | 29.00 | 39.00 | 75.00 | 145. | 350. | 7000. | — |
| 1868 | 418,200 | 30.00 | 40.00 | 55.00 | 120. | 200. | 300. | 525. | 7100. | 3750. |
| 1868S | 1,160,000 | 15.00 | 24.00 | 29.00 | 39.00 | 95.00 | 165. | 350. | 4600. | — |
| 1869 | 795,900 | 15.00 | 24.00 | 29.00 | 39.00 | 80.00 | 160. | 385. | 4600. | 3750. |
| 1869S | 656,000 | 15.00 | 27.00 | 35.00 | 50.00 | 80.00 | 160. | 600. | 7000. | — |
| 1870 | 634,900 | 17.00 | 27.00 | 35.00 | 60.00 | 95.00 | 160. | 475. | 7000. | 3750. |
| 1870CC | 54,617 | 500. | 850. | 1300. | 2350. | 4200. | — | — | — | — |
| 1870S | 1,004,000 | 15.00 | 24.00 | 40.00 | 60.00 | 110. | 275. | 575. | 7000. | — |
| 1871 | 1,204,560 | 16.00 | 24.00 | 29.00 | 39.00 | 70.00 | 145. | 350. | 7000. | 3750. |
| 1871CC | 153,950 | 135. | 180. | 295. | 425. | 875. | 2000. | 3500. | 9150. | — |
| 1871S | 2,178,000 | 15.00 | 24.00 | 29.00 | 39.00 | 63.00 | 145. | 400. | 7000. | — |
| 1872 | 881,550 | 15.00 | 24.00 | 29.00 | 39.00 | 63.00 | 145. | 430. | 4500. | 3750. |
| 1872CC | 272,000 | 70.00 | 110. | 150. | 300. | 650. | 1700. | 2500. | 8800. | — |
| 1872S | 580,000 | 23.00 | 28.00 | 55.00 | 85.00 | 170. | 375. | 975. | 7000. | — |
| 1873 closed 3 | 801,800 | 15.00 | 24.00 | 38.00 | 70.00 | 100. | 235. | 500. | 4500. | 3750. |
| 1873 open 3 | Inc. Ab. | 2650. | 3350. | 4750. | 6500. | 9250. | — | — | — | — |
| 1873CC | 122,500 | 110. | 130. | 240. | 400. | 800. | 1300. | 4100. | 9000. | 3750. |

1873S no arrows, 5,000 minted, no specimens known to survive.

## Arrows at date

**Weight:** 12.5 grams. **Composition:** 90% silver (0.3618 ounces), 10% copper.

| Date | Mintage | G-4 | VG-8 | F-12 | VF-20 | XF-40 | AU-50 | MS-60 | MS-65 | Prf-65 |
|------|---------|-----|------|------|-------|-------|-------|-------|-------|--------|
| 1873 | 1,815,700 | 16.50 | 25.00 | 36.00 | 80.00 | 225. | 535. | 950. | 21,500. | 9000. |
| 1873CC | 214,560 | 100. | 120. | 225. | 400. | 800. | 1250. | 4500. | — | — |
| 1873S | 233,000 | 45.00 | 60.00 | 90.00 | 195. | 400. | 725. | 1600. | 21,500. | — |
| 1874 | 2,360,300 | 16.50 | 25.00 | 36.00 | 80.00 | 225. | 535. | 950. | 21,500. | 9000. |
| 1874CC | 59,000 | 200. | 300. | 450. | 750. | 1150. | 2300. | 4500. | 21,500. | — |
| 1874S | 394,000 | 25.00 | 30.00 | 55.00 | 125. | 275. | 575. | 1700. | 21,500. | — |

### Arrows at date removed

| Date | Mintage | G-4 | VG-8 | F-12 | VF-20 | XF-40 | AU-50 | MS-60 | MS-65 | Prf-65 |
|------|---------|-----|------|------|-------|-------|-------|-------|-------|--------|
| 1875 | 6,027,500 | 15.00 | 24.00 | 29.00 | 37.00 | 60.00 | 120. | 425. | 3500. | 2550. |
| 1875CC | 1,008,000 | 17.00 | 33.00 | 40.00 | 60.00 | 120. | 300. | 540. | 5450. | — |
| 1875S | 3,200,000 | 15.00 | 24.00 | 29.00 | 37.00 | 60.00 | 120. | 340. | 2900. | — |
| 1876 | 8,419,150 | 15.00 | 24.00 | 32.00 | 40.00 | 60.00 | 135. | 340. | 5300. | 3750. |
| 1876CC | 1,956,000 | 17.00 | 30.00 | 35.00 | 55.00 | 100. | 275. | 560. | 4200. | — |
| 1876S | 4,528,000 | 15.00 | 24.00 | 32.00 | 40.00 | 63.00 | 145. | 340. | 2900. | — |
| 1877 | 8,304,510 | 15.00 | 24.00 | 29.00 | 45.00 | 63.00 | 145. | 340. | 2900. | 3750. |
| 1877CC | 1,420,000 | 17.00 | 33.00 | 35.00 | 60.00 | 95.00 | 275. | 630. | 3250. | — |
| 1877S | 5,356,000 | 15.00 | 24.00 | 29.00 | 37.00 | 65.00 | 145. | 340. | 2900. | — |
| 1878 | 1,378,400 | 20.00 | 28.00 | 36.00 | 50.00 | 115. | 170. | 425. | 3650. | 2550. |
| 1878CC | 62,000 | 250. | 300. | 425. | 800. | 1350. | 2300. | 4000. | — | — |
| 1878S | 12,000 | 6750. | 8000. | 10,000. | 13,000. | 17,500. | 20,000. | 25,000. | — | — |
| 1879 | 5,900 | 200. | 220. | 290. | 350. | 400. | 475. | 700. | 2900. | 2550. |
| 1880 | 9,755 | 190. | 210. | 240. | 310. | 375. | 475. | 700. | 2900. | 2550. |
| 1881 | 10,975 | 170. | 195. | 240. | 300. | 365. | 465. | 700. | 2900. | 2550. |

# 1878-S Half Dollar
## Grade F-12

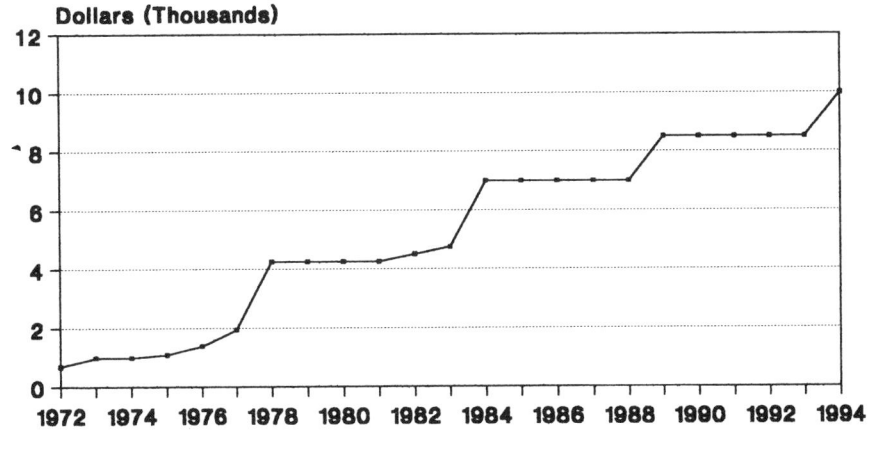

Retail Price

Source: COIN PRICES

| Date | Mintage | G-4 | VG-8 | F-12 | VF-20 | XF-40 | AU-50 | MS-60 | MS-65 | Prf-65 |
|------|---------|-----|------|------|-------|-------|-------|-------|-------|--------|
| 1882 | 5,500 | 210. | 230. | 290. | 365. | 440. | 500. | 800. | 3600. | 2550. |
| 1883 | 9,039 | 180. | 210. | 240. | 290. | 375. | 475. | 750. | 2900. | 2550. |
| 1884 | 5,275 | 225. | 285. | 330. | 395. | 450. | 550. | 800. | 2900. | 2550. |
| 1885 | 6,130 | 215. | 235. | 300. | 360. | 435. | 525. | 800. | 2900. | 2550. |
| 1886 | 5,886 | 260. | 325. | 410. | 450. | 495. | 600. | 850. | 4800. | 2550. |
| 1887 | 5,710 | 325. | 385. | 450. | 550. | 650. | 750. | 900. | 2900. | 2550. |
| 1888 | 12,833 | 175. | 200. | 235. | 300. | 375. | 425. | 700. | 2900. | 2550. |
| 1889 | 12,711 | 175. | 200. | 235. | 300. | 375. | 425. | 700. | 2900. | 2550. |
| 1890 | 12,590 | 175. | 200. | 235. | 300. | 375. | 425. | 700. | 3250. | 2550. |
| 1891 | 200,600 | 40.00 | 50.00 | 60.00 | 90.00 | 140. | 290. | 500. | 3250. | 2550. |

# Barber

**Designer:** Charles E. Barber. **Size:** 30.6 millimeters. **Weight:** 12.5 grams. **Composition:** 90% silver (0.3618 ounces), 10% copper.

| Date | Mintage | G-4 | VG-8 | F-12 | VF-20 | XF-40 | AU-50 | MS-60 | MS-65 | Prf-65 |
|------|---------|-----|------|------|-------|-------|-------|-------|-------|--------|
| 1892 | 935,245 | 18.00 | 25.00 | 43.00 | 84.00 | 180. | 310. | 400. | 2350. | 2500. |
| 1892O | 390,000 | 78.00 | 130. | 190. | 290. | 415. | 475. | 845. | 5225. | — |
| 1892S | 1,029,028 | 110. | 130. | 180. | 280. | 390. | 585. | 850. | 5225. | — |
| 1893 | 1,826,792 | 13.00 | 17.00 | 42.00 | 75.00 | 150. | 340. | 500. | 3775. | 2500. |
| 1893O | 1,389,000 | 17.00 | 26.00 | 52.00 | 115. | 260. | 370. | 490. | 9600. | — |
| 1893S | 740,000 | 57.00 | 74.00 | 130. | 260. | 385. | 520. | 1100. | 12,000. | — |
| 1894 | 1,148,972 | 14.00 | 27.00 | 55.00 | 87.00 | 210. | 350. | 520. | 3300. | 2500. |
| 1894O | 2,138,000 | 9.00 | 15.50 | 51.00 | 91.00 | 250. | 370. | 500. | 4500. | — |
| 1894S | 4,048,690 | 7.50 | 13.00 | 45.00 | 71.00 | 200. | 340. | 440. | 9600. | — |
| 1895 | 1,835,218 | 7.50 | 13.00 | 43.00 | 78.00 | 165. | 325. | 535. | 3400. | 2500. |
| 1895O | 1,766,000 | 8.00 | 17.00 | 47.00 | 85.00 | 220. | 360. | 535. | 6000. | — |
| 1895S | 1,108,086 | 14.00 | 23.00 | 56.00 | 100. | 250. | 360. | 500. | 7800. | — |
| 1896 | 950,762 | 17.00 | 18.00 | 45.00 | 80.00 | 190. | 325. | 500. | 5400. | 3400. |
| 1896O | 924,000 | 17.00 | 22.00 | 74.00 | 145. | 345. | 620. | 1100. | 12,000. | — |
| 1896S | 1,140,948 | 56.00 | 67.00 | 100. | 180. | 350. | 550. | 1100. | 10,250. | — |
| 1897 | 2,480,731 | 6.50 | 7.50 | 26.00 | 61.00 | 135. | 310. | 425. | 3300. | 2500. |
| 1897O | 632,000 | 45.00 | 65.00 | 275. | 400. | 845. | 1175. | 1500. | 4700. | — |
| 1897S | 933,900 | 85.00 | 95.00 | 250. | 410. | 650. | 975. | 1200. | 7600. | — |
| 1898 | 2,956,735 | 6.50 | 7.50 | 25.00 | 57.00 | 135. | 300. | 425. | 2300. | 2500. |
| 1898O | 874,000 | 13.00 | 22.00 | 74.00 | 160. | 350. | 495. | 715. | 8400. | — |
| 1898S | 2,358,550 | 7.75 | 14.00 | 38.00 | 73.00 | 200. | 350. | 600. | 9000. | — |
| 1899 | 5,538,846 | 4.75 | 7.50 | 26.00 | 61.00 | 135. | 300. | 425. | 3300. | 3900. |
| 1899O | 1,724,000 | 7.25 | 11.00 | 43.00 | 85.00 | 210. | 360. | 550. | 6100. | — |
| 1899S | 1,686,411 | 7.00 | 12.00 | 42.00 | 78.00 | 180. | 340. | 535. | 6600. | — |
| 1900 | 4,762,912 | 5.25 | 7.50 | 26.00 | 61.00 | 135. | 300. | 425. | 3250. | 2500. |
| 1900O | 2,744,000 | 7.00 | 10.00 | 39.00 | 85.00 | 240. | 360. | 685. | 14,500. | — |
| 1900S | 2,560,322 | 7.00 | 10.00 | 36.00 | 91.00 | 180. | 325. | 520. | 9600. | — |
| 1901 | 4,268,813 | 5.25 | 7.50 | 26.00 | 61.00 | 135. | 300. | 425. | 4200. | 3250. |
| 1901O | 1,124,000 | 7.00 | 12.00 | 47.00 | 105. | 270. | 450. | 1250. | 14,500. | — |
| 1901S | 847,044 | 12.00 | 18.00 | 94.00 | 195. | 500. | 880. | 1400. | 12,500. | — |
| 1902 | 4,922,777 | 5.25 | 7.50 | 26.00 | 61.00 | 135. | 300. | 425. | 3400. | 2900. |
| 1902O | 2,526,000 | 6.50 | 10.00 | 40.00 | 72.00 | 180. | 350. | 650. | 9900. | — |
| 1902S | 1,460,670 | 6.50 | 10.00 | 40.00 | 80.00 | 200. | 360. | 540. | 5500. | — |
| 1903 | 2,278,755 | 5.25 | 7.75 | 32.00 | 65.00 | 130. | 325. | 480. | 8000. | 3125. |
| 1903O | 2,100,000 | 5.50 | 10.00 | 39.00 | 72.00 | 180. | 350. | 570. | 9000. | — |
| 1903S | 1,920,772 | 6.00 | 11.00 | 39.00 | 74.00 | 210. | 365. | 540. | 5900. | — |
| 1904 | 2,992,670 | 5.25 | 7.50 | 28.00 | 61.00 | 135. | 300. | 425. | 4200. | 3400. |
| 1904O | 1,117,600 | 8.25 | 13.00 | 49.00 | 110. | 300. | 500. | 1000. | 9600. | — |
| 1904S | 553,038 | 11.00 | 22.00 | 110. | 290. | 570. | 910. | 1525. | 14,000. | — |
| 1905 | 662,727 | 9.00 | 11.00 | 45.00 | 78.00 | 215. | 375. | 540. | 5400. | 3125. |
| 1905O | 505,000 | 9.50 | 18.00 | 61.00 | 130. | 225. | 415. | 680. | 6000. | — |
| 1905S | 2,494,000 | 5.25 | 8.00 | 34.00 | 72.00 | 190. | 345. | 515. | 9000. | — |
| 1906 | 2,638,675 | 5.25 | 7.75 | 25.00 | 62.00 | 130. | 300. | 425. | 3400. | 2500. |
| 1906D | 4,028,000 | 5.25 | 8.25 | 27.00 | 61.00 | 140. | 350. | 425. | 4100. | — |
| 1906O | 2,446,000 | 5.25 | 8.00 | 32.00 | 66.00 | 190. | 300. | 540. | 5400. | — |
| 1906S | 1,740,154 | 5.50 | 11.00 | 40.00 | 63.00 | 180. | 300. | 525. | 5650. | — |
| 1907 | 2,598,575 | 5.25 | 7.50 | 25.00 | 61.00 | 135. | 300. | 425. | 2300. | 3250. |
| 1907D | 3,856,000 | 5.25 | 8.00 | 27.00 | 61.00 | 150. | 300. | 425. | 2300. | — |
| 1907O | 3,946,000 | 5.25 | 8.00 | 27.00 | 61.00 | 145. | 300. | 490. | 3400. | — |
| 1907S | 1,250,000 | 5.25 | 9.75 | 57.00 | 97.00 | 290. | 450. | 775. | 12,000. | — |
| 1908 | 1,354,545 | 5.25 | 8.50 | 25.00 | 65.00 | 150. | 310. | 425. | 3600. | 3250. |
| 1908D | 3,280,000 | 5.25 | 8.00 | 30.00 | 65.00 | 155. | 310. | 480. | 2300. | — |
| 1908O | 5,360,000 | 5.25 | 8.00 | 27.00 | 61.00 | 140. | 310. | 480. | 2300. | — |

| Date | Mintage | G-4 | VG-8 | F-12 | VF-20 | XF-40 | AU-50 | MS-60 | MS-65 | Prf-65 |
|------|---------|-----|------|------|-------|-------|-------|-------|-------|--------|
| 1908S | 1,644,828 | 5.50 | 10.50 | 36.00 | 72.00 | 180. | 340. | 680. | 5200. | — |
| 1909 | 2,368,650 | 5.25 | 8.00 | 25.00 | 61.00 | 135. | 300. | 425. | 2300. | 3200. |
| 1909O | 925,400 | 7.75 | 10.00 | 39.00 | 84.00 | 260. | 475. | 700. | 4750. | — |
| 1909S | 1,764,000 | 5.25 | 8.50 | 26.00 | 71.00 | 175. | 330. | 520. | 3350. | — |
| 1910 | 418,551 | 8.00 | 13.00 | 55.00 | 110. | 260. | 415. | 585. | 3850. | 3450. |
| 1910S | 1,948,000 | 5.25 | 8.00 | 27.00 | 66.00 | 165. | 325. | 585. | 4300. | — |
| 1911 | 1,406,543 | 5.25 | 8.00 | 25.00 | 62.00 | 140. | 300. | 425. | 2300. | 2500. |
| 1911D | 695,080 | 6.00 | 10.00 | 32.00 | 70.00 | 175. | 310. | 500. | 2300. | — |
| 1911S | 1,272,000 | 5.25 | 8.00 | 30.00 | 66.00 | 165. | 320. | 550. | 6500. | — |
| 1912 | 1,550,700 | 5.25 | 8.00 | 25.00 | 61.00 | 150. | 320. | 440. | 3700. | 3200. |
| 1912D | 2,300,800 | 5.25 | 8.00 | 25.00 | 61.00 | 135. | 300. | 425. | 2400. | — |
| 1912S | 1,370,000 | 5.25 | 8.00 | 25.00 | 61.00 | 155. | 320. | 500. | 5000. | — |
| 1913 | 188,627 | 15.00 | 21.00 | 80.00 | 175. | 325. | 650. | 910. | 3600. | 3000. |
| 1913D | 534,000 | 6.00 | 9.00 | 31.00 | 66.00 | 175. | 320. | 495. | 4550. | — |
| 1913S | 604,000 | 6.50 | 10.00 | 39.00 | 78.00 | 190. | 370. | 585. | 4000. | — |
| 1914 | 124,610 | 18.00 | 28.00 | 150. | 295. | 450. | 750. | 950. | 11,000. | 3575. |
| 1914S | 992,000 | 6.00 | 3400. | 30.00 | 65.00 | 175. | 345. | 500. | 3400. | — |
| 1915 | 138,450 | 16.00 | 22.00 | 80.00 | 200. | 350. | 685. | 975. | 4300. | 3250. |
| 1915D | 1,170,400 | 5.25 | 7.50 | 25.00 | 61.00 | 135. | 300. | 425. | 2300. | — |
| 1915S | 1,604,000 | 5.25 | 7.50 | 25.00 | 64.00 | 135. | 300. | 490. | 2300. | — |

# Walking Liberty

Obverse mintmark

## Mintmark on obverse

**Designer:** Adolph A. Weinman. **Size:** 30.6 millimeters. **Weight:** 12.5 grams. **Composition:** 90% silver (0.3618 ounces), 10% copper.

| Date | Mintage | G-4 | VG-8 | F-12 | VF-20 | XF-40 | AU-50 | MS-60 | MS-65 | Prf-65 |
|------|---------|-----|------|------|-------|-------|-------|-------|-------|--------|
| 1916 | 608,800 | 19.00 | 25.00 | 55.00 | 120. | 160. | 210. | 275. | 1425. | — |
| 1916D | 1,014,400 | 11.00 | 17.00 | 30.00 | 70.00 | 135. | 175. | 260. | 2100. | — |
| 1916S | 508,000 | 55.00 | 68.00 | 115. | 280. | 510. | 645. | 800. | 4750. | — |
| 1917D | 765,400 | 11.50 | 15.00 | 30.00 | 84.00 | 150. | 210. | 430. | 6300. | — |
| 1917S | 952,000 | 12.50 | 20.00 | 48.00 | 235. | 595. | 975. | 1750. | 11,000. | — |

Reverse mintmark

## Mintmark on reverse

| Date | Mintage | G-4 | VG-8 | F-12 | VF-20 | XF-40 | AU-50 | MS-60 | MS-65 | Prf-65 |
|------|---------|-----|------|------|-------|-------|-------|-------|-------|--------|
| 1917 | 12,292,000 | 4.00 | 8.00 | 10.50 | 20.00 | 35.00 | 63.00 | 85.00 | 970. | — |
| 1917D | 1,940,000 | 8.50 | 11.00 | 19.00 | 50.00 | 140. | 310. | 675. | 15,500. | — |
| 1917S | 5,554,000 | 5.00 | 8.00 | 13.50 | 25.00 | 48.00 | 105. | 280. | 9600. | — |
| 1918 | 6,634,000 | 4.00 | 9.00 | 17.00 | 45.00 | 130. | 250. | 410. | 3500. | — |
| 1918D | 3,853,040 | 6.00 | 9.50 | 18.00 | 51.00 | 140. | 315. | 750. | 22,750. | — |
| 1918S | 10,282,000 | 4.00 | 8.00 | 14.00 | 27.00 | 49.00 | 120. | 330. | 12,500. | — |
| 1919 | 962,000 | 10.50 | 14.00 | 30.00 | 140. | 375. | 560. | 915. | 4800. | — |
| 1919D | 1,165,000 | 9.50 | 12.00 | 32.00 | 165. | 450. | 900. | 2300. | 40,000. | — |
| 1919S | 1,552,000 | 10.00 | 13.50 | 25.00 | 135. | 600. | 1600. | 2100. | 9750. | — |
| 1920 | 6,372,000 | 4.00 | 8.00 | 13.00 | 23.00 | 53.00 | 91.00 | 220. | 6750. | — |
| 1920D | 1,551,000 | 8.50 | 10.00 | 25.00 | 125. | 315. | 665. | 1040. | 9000. | — |
| 1920S | 4,624,000 | 6.00 | 8.00 | 14.00 | 42.00 | 150. | 350. | 590. | 7800. | — |
| 1921 | 246,000 | 50.00 | 80.00 | 180. | 525. | 1350. | 2300. | 3150. | 11,000. | — |
| 1921D | 208,000 | 77.00 | 100. | 240. | 650. | 1900. | 2800. | 2950. | 11,000. | — |
| 1921S | 548,000 | 19.00 | 24.00 | 60.00 | 525. | 3900. | 6700. | 8550. | 32,500. | — |
| 1923S | 2,178,000 | 7.00 | 10.00 | 18.00 | 65.00 | 250. | 525. | 1060. | 12,250. | — |
| 1927S | 2,392,000 | 4.00 | 7.00 | 11.00 | 35.00 | 95.00 | 245. | 610. | 8850. | — |

PRICING SECTION

# 1923-S Half Dollar
## Grade XF-40

-•- **Retail Price**

**Source: COIN PRICES**

| Date | Mintage | G-4 | VG-8 | F-12 | VF-20 | XF-40 | AU-50 | MS-60 | MS-65 | Prf-65 |
|------|---------|-----|------|------|-------|-------|-------|-------|-------|--------|
| 1928S | 1,940,000 | 4.00 | 7.00 | 12.50 | 42.00 | 115. | 290. | 620. | 4950. | — |
| 1929D | 1,001,200 | 6.25 | 7.50 | 10.50 | 19.00 | 70.00 | 155. | 245. | 2200. | — |
| 1929S | 1,902,000 | 4.00 | 6.75 | 10.00 | 16.00 | 64.00 | 155. | 300. | 2300. | — |
| 1933S | 1,786,000 | 5.50 | 8.50 | 10.00 | 11.50 | 45.00 | 155. | 450. | 3375. | — |
| 1934 | 6,964,000 | 2.50 | 2.75 | 3.50 | 4.50 | 11.00 | 26.50 | 48.00 | 410. | — |
| 1934D | 2,361,400 | 3.25 | 4.00 | 5.50 | 7.50 | 25.00 | 56.00 | 97.00 | 1235. | — |
| 1934S | 3,652,000 | 3.00 | 3.50 | 4.50 | 6.00 | 25.00 | 70.00 | 215. | 2600. | — |
| 1935 | 9,162,000 | 2.50 | 2.75 | 3.50 | 4.50 | 9.00 | 19.50 | 44.00 | 290. | — |
| 1935D | 3,003,800 | 3.25 | 4.00 | 5.50 | 7.50 | 25.00 | 56.00 | 105. | 1250. | — |
| 1935S | 3,854,000 | 3.10 | 3.50 | 4.50 | 5.50 | 25.00 | 68.00 | 110. | 2000. | — |
| 1936 | 12,617,901 | 2.50 | 2.75 | 3.50 | 4.50 | 9.00 | 19.50 | 39.00 | 145. | 2500. |
| 1936D | 4,252,400 | 2.95 | 3.50 | 4.50 | 5.50 | 17.00 | 47.00 | 71.00 | 325. | — |
| 1936S | 3,884,000 | 3.00 | 3.50 | 4.50 | 5.50 | 17.00 | 45.00 | 110. | 535. | — |
| 1937 | 9,527,728 | 2.50 | 2.75 | 3.50 | 4.50 | 9.00 | 19.50 | 36.00 | 175. | 850. |
| 1937D | 1,676,000 | 6.00 | 7.00 | 8.75 | 10.50 | 28.00 | 125. | 150. | 490. | — |
| 1937S | 2,090,000 | 5.00 | 6.00 | 7.25 | 8.00 | 16.50 | 56.00 | 110. | 540. | — |
| 1938 | 4,118,152 | 3.00 | 3.50 | 4.50 | 6.50 | 11.00 | 42.00 | 65.00 | 220. | 580. |
| 1938D | 491,600 | 18.00 | 20.00 | 28.00 | 45.00 | 110. | 260. | 390. | 980. | — |
| 1939 | 6,820,808 | 2.50 | 2.75 | 3.50 | 4.50 | 10.00 | 22.00 | 40.00 | 150. | 525. |
| 1939D | 4,267,800 | 3.00 | 3.50 | 4.50 | 5.50 | 10.50 | 24.00 | 39.00 | 155. | — |
| 1939S | 2,552,000 | 4.50 | 4.75 | 6.00 | 8.75 | 12.50 | 39.00 | 91.00 | 235. | — |
| 1940 | 9,167,279 | 2.45 | 3.50 | 4.00 | 5.50 | 9.00 | 14.00 | 32.00 | 115. | 450. |
| 1940S | 4,550,000 | 2.45 | 3.50 | 4.00 | 5.50 | 10.00 | 21.00 | 32.00 | 400. | — |
| 1941 | 24,207,412 | 2.45 | 2.65 | 3.50 | 4.50 | 7.00 | 7.75 | 32.00 | 110. | 435. |
| 1941D | 11,248,400 | 2.45 | 2.65 | 3.50 | 4.50 | 6.00 | 12.50 | 32.00 | 125. | — |
| 1941S | 8,098,000 | 2.60 | 2.80 | 3.75 | 4.75 | 7.00 | 28.00 | 84.00 | 975. | — |
| 1942 | 47,839,120 | 2.45 | 2.65 | 3.50 | 4.50 | 5.50 | 7.75 | 32.00 | 105. | 435. |
| 1942D | 10,973,800 | 2.45 | 2.65 | 3.50 | 4.50 | 6.00 | 16.00 | 39.00 | 195. | — |
| 1942S | 12,708,000 | 2.45 | 2.65 | 3.50 | 4.75 | 7.00 | 21.00 | 34.00 | 400. | — |
| 1943 | 53,190,000 | 2.45 | 2.65 | 3.50 | 4.50 | 5.50 | 7.75 | 32.00 | 110. | — |
| 1943D | 11,346,000 | 2.45 | 2.65 | 3.50 | 4.50 | 6.00 | 20.00 | 41.00 | 190. | — |
| 1943S | 13,450,000 | 2.45 | 2.65 | 3.75 | 4.75 | 6.00 | 21.00 | 34.00 | 370. | — |
| 1944 | 28,206,000 | 2.45 | 2.65 | 3.50 | 4.50 | 5.50 | 7.75 | 32.00 | 110. | — |
| 1944D | 9,769,000 | 2.45 | 2.65 | 3.50 | 4.50 | 6.00 | 18.00 | 36.00 | 125. | — |
| 1944S | 8,904,000 | 2.45 | 2.65 | 3.50 | 4.75 | 6.25 | 20.00 | 34.00 | 550. | — |
| 1945 | 31,502,000 | 2.45 | 2.65 | 3.50 | 4.50 | 5.50 | 7.75 | 32.00 | 110. | — |
| 1945D | 9,966,800 | 2.45 | 2.65 | 3.50 | 4.50 | 6.00 | 14.00 | 34.00 | 110. | — |
| 1945S | 10,156,000 | 2.45 | 2.65 | 3.50 | 4.75 | 6.00 | 17.00 | 34.00 | 170. | — |
| 1946 | 12,118,000 | 2.45 | 2.65 | 3.50 | 4.50 | 5.50 | 12.50 | 32.00 | 135. | — |
| 1946D | 2,151,000 | 4.50 | 4.75 | 6.00 | 8.75 | 9.50 | 17.00 | 34.00 | 105. | — |
| 1946S | 3,724,000 | 2.60 | 2.80 | 3.50 | 5.00 | 5.50 | 14.00 | 34.00 | 110. | — |
| 1947 | 4,094,000 | 2.60 | 2.80 | 3.50 | 5.00 | 7.00 | 17.00 | 34.00 | 130. | — |
| 1947D | 3,900,600 | 2.60 | 2.80 | 3.50 | 5.00 | 7.00 | 17.00 | 34.00 | 120. | — |

# 1953 Half Dollar
## Grade MS-60

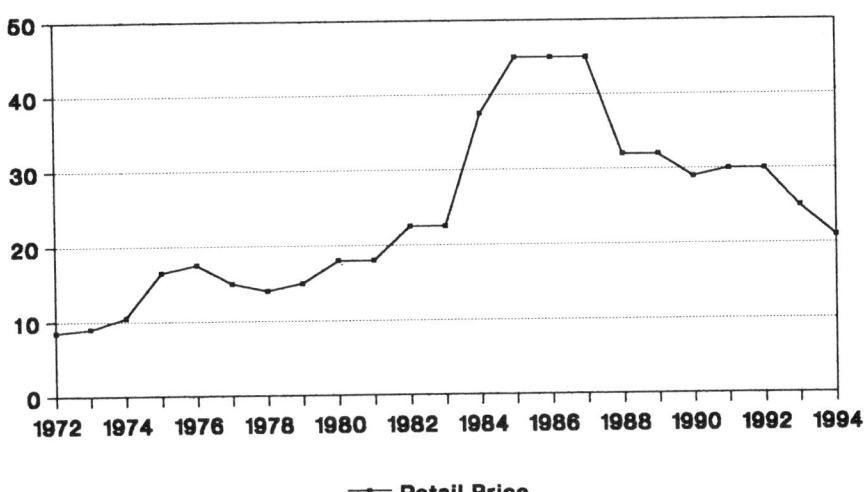

Retail Price

Source: COIN PRICES

# Franklin

**Designer:** John R. Sinnock. **Size:** 30.6 millimeters. **Weight:** 12.5 grams. **Composition:** 90% silver (0.3618 ounces), 10% copper. **Notes:** "MS-65FBL" values are for coins with full lines across the bell on the reverse.

| Date | Mintage | G-4 | VG-8 | F-12 | VF-20 | XF-40 | AU-50 | MS-60 | MS-65 | -65FBL | Prf-65 |
|------|---------|-----|------|------|-------|-------|-------|-------|-------|--------|--------|
| 1948 | 3,006,814 | — | 3.50 | 4.00 | 4.50 | 9.00 | 10.00 | 19.50 | 63.00 | — | — |
| 1948D | 4,028,600 | — | 3.50 | 4.00 | 4.50 | 8.00 | 9.00 | 10.00 | 200. | — | — |
| 1949 | 5,614,000 | — | 3.50 | 4.00 | 6.00 | 11.00 | 15.00 | 49.00 | 90.00 | 250. | — |
| 1949D | 4,120,600 | — | 3.50 | 4.00 | 6.00 | 12.00 | 19.00 | 43.00 | 825. | — | — |
| 1949S | 3,744,000 | — | 3.75 | 4.75 | 6.00 | 10.00 | 30.00 | 60.00 | 140. | 450. | — |
| 1950 | 7,793,509 | — | — | 4.00 | 4.50 | 9.00 | 12.00 | 37.50 | 95.00 | — | 275. |
| 1950D | 8,031,600 | — | — | 4.00 | 4.50 | 9.00 | 10.00 | 25.00 | 485. | — | — |
| 1951 | 16,859,602 | — | — | 4.00 | 4.50 | 7.00 | 8.00 | 14.00 | 80.00 | — | 200. |
| 1951D | 9,475,200 | — | — | 3.50 | 4.25 | 5.00 | 12.50 | 35.00 | 195. | — | — |
| 1951S | 13,696,000 | — | — | 3.50 | 4.25 | 5.00 | 20.00 | 31.00 | 72.00 | 360. | — |
| 1952 | 21,274,073 | — | — | 3.50 | 4.25 | 5.00 | 6.00 | 9.50 | 65.00 | — | 135. |
| 1952D | 25,395,600 | — | — | 3.00 | 3.50 | 4.50 | 5.00 | 8.50 | 190. | — | — |
| 1952S | 5,526,000 | — | — | 3.50 | 4.25 | 4.75 | 12.00 | 37.50 | 56.00 | 400. | — |
| 1953 | 2,796,920 | 3.75 | 4.00 | 4.25 | 5.00 | 6.00 | 10.00 | 21.00 | 135. | — | 70.00 |
| 1953D | 20,900,400 | — | — | 3.00 | 3.50 | 4.00 | 8.00 | 8.75 | 215. | — | — |
| 1953S | 4,148,000 | — | — | 3.50 | 4.25 | 4.75 | 10.00 | 18.00 | 51.00 | 700. | — |
| 1954 | 13,421,503 | — | — | 3.00 | 3.50 | 4.75 | 5.50 | 6.00 | 64.00 | — | 55.00 |
| 1954D | 25,445,580 | — | — | 3.00 | 3.00 | 4.00 | 5.00 | 6.00 | 165. | — | — |

| Date | Mintage | G-4 | VG-8 | F-12 | VF-20 | XF-40 | AU-50 | MS-60 | MS-65 | -65FBL | Prf-65 |
|------|---------|-----|------|------|-------|-------|-------|-------|-------|--------|--------|
| 1954S | 4,993,400 | — | — | 3.50 | 4.25 | 4.75 | 6.50 | 7.50 | 50.00 | 165. | — |
| 1955 | 2,876,381 | 4.50 | 5.00 | 6.50 | 7.00 | 7.50 | 8.00 | 8.50 | 50.00 | — | 40.00 |
| 1956 | 4,701,384 | — | — | 3.50 | 4.00 | 4.50 | 5.50 | 7.25 | 44.00 | — | 15.00 |
| 1957 | 6,361,952 | — | — | 3.50 | 4.00 | 4.50 | 5.00 | 7.25 | 44.00 | — | 13.00 |
| 1957D | 19,966,850 | — | — | — | — | 2.75 | 3.00 | 6.25 | 45.00 | — | — |
| 1958 | 4,917,652 | — | — | 2.75 | 3.00 | 3.50 | 3.75 | 5.25 | 44.00 | — | 13.00 |
| 1958D | 23,962,412 | — | — | — | 2.50 | 2.75 | 3.00 | 4.25 | 44.00 | — | — |
| 1959 | 4,917,652 | — | — | — | 2.50 | 2.75 | 3.00 | 5.25 | 160. | — | 12.00 |
| 1959D | 13,053,750 | — | — | — | 2.50 | 2.75 | 3.00 | 5.50 | 180. | — | — |
| 1960 | 7,715,602 | — | — | — | 2.50 | 2.75 | 3.00 | 4.50 | 165. | — | 12.00 |
| 1960D | 18,215,812 | — | — | — | 2.50 | 2.75 | 3.00 | 5.25 | 500. | — | — |
| 1961 | 11,318,244 | — | — | — | 2.50 | 2.75 | 3.00 | 4.50 | 250. | — | 8.50 |
| 1961D | 20,276,442 | — | — | — | 2.50 | 2.75 | 3.00 | 4.50 | 525. | — | — |
| 1962 | 12,932,019 | — | — | — | 2.50 | 2.75 | 3.00 | 4.50 | 215. | — | 8.50 |
| 1962D | 35,473,281 | — | — | — | 2.50 | 2.75 | 3.50 | 4.50 | 475. | — | — |
| 1963 | 25,239,645 | — | — | — | 2.50 | 2.75 | 3.00 | 3.25 | 90.00 | — | 8.50 |
| 1963D | 67,069,292 | — | — | — | 2.50 | 2.60 | 2.75 | 3.25 | 90.00 | — | — |

# Kennedy

**Reverse mintmark (1964)**

**Obverse mintmark (1968-present)**

## 90% silver composition

**Designers:** Gilroy Roberts and Frank Gasparro. **Size:** 30.6 millimeters. **Weight:** 12.5 grams. **Composition:** 90% silver (0.3618 ounces), 10% copper.

| Date | Mintage | G-4 | VG-8 | F-12 | VF-20 | XF-40 | MS-60 | MS-65 | Prf-65 |
|------|---------|-----|------|------|-------|-------|-------|-------|--------|
| 1964 | 277,254,766 | — | — | — | — | — | 2.75 | 3.50 | 8.00 |
| 1964D | 156,205,446 | — | — | — | — | — | 2.75 | 3.50 | — |

## 40% silver composition

**Weight:** 11.5 grams. **Composition:** clad layers of 80% silver and 20% copper bonded to a core of 20.9% silver and 79.1% copper (0.148 total ounces of silver).

| Date | Mintage | G-4 | VG-8 | F-12 | VF-20 | XF-40 | MS-60 | MS-65 | Prf-65 |
|------|---------|-----|------|------|-------|-------|-------|-------|--------|
| 1965 | 65,879,366 | — | — | — | — | — | 1.25 | 2.50 | — |
| 1966 | 108,984,932 | — | — | — | — | — | 1.20 | 2.40 | — |
| 1967 | 295,046,978 | — | — | — | — | — | 1.00 | 2.25 | — |
| 1968D | 246,951,930 | — | — | — | — | — | 1.00 | 2.25 | — |
| 1968S | 3,041,506 | — | — | — | — | Proof only | — | 3.50 |
| 1969D | 129,881,800 | — | — | — | — | — | 1.00 | 2.00 | — |
| 1969S | 2,934,631 | — | — | — | — | — | — | — | 3.50 |
| 1970D | 2,150,000 | — | — | — | — | — | 12.00 | 15.00 | — |
| 1970S | 2,632,810 | — | — | — | — | Proof only | — | 7.50 |

## Clad composition

**Weight:** 11.34 grams. **Composition:** clad layers of 75% copper and 25% nickel bonded to a pure-copper core.

| Date | Mintage | G-4 | VG-8 | F-12 | VF-20 | XF-40 | MS-60 | MS-65 | Prf-65 |
|------|---------|-----|------|------|-------|-------|-------|-------|--------|
| 1971 | 155,640,000 | — | — | — | — | — | 1.50 | 2.50 | — |
| 1971D | 302,097,424 | — | — | — | — | — | 1.00 | 1.50 | — |
| 1971S | 3,244,183 | — | — | — | — | — | Proof only | — | 2.75 |
| 1972 | 153,180,000 | — | — | — | — | — | 2.00 | 2.50 | — |
| 1972D | 141,890,000 | — | — | — | — | — | 2.00 | 2.50 | — |
| 1972S | 3,267,667 | — | — | — | — | — | Proof only | — | 2.50 |
| 1972S | 3,267,667 | — | — | — | — | — | Proof only | — | 2.50 |
| 1973 | 64,964,000 | — | — | — | — | — | 1.35 | 2.50 | — |
| 1973D | 83,171,400 | — | — | — | — | — | — | 2.50 | — |
| 1973S | Proof only | — | — | — | — | — | — | — | 1.75 |
| 1974 | 201,596,000 | — | — | — | — | — | 1.00 | 2.00 | — |
| 1974D | 79,066,300 | — | — | — | — | — | 1.20 | 2.00 | — |
| 1974S | Proof only | — | — | — | — | — | — | — | 1.75 |

## Bicentennial design, clad composition

Reverse designer: Seth Huntington.

| Date | Mintage | G-4 | VG-8 | F-12 | VF-20 | XF-40 | MS-60 | MS-65 | Prf-65 |
|------|---------|-----|------|------|-------|-------|-------|-------|--------|
| 1976 | 234,308,000 | — | — | — | — | — | 1.00 | 1.50 | — |
| 1976D | 287,565,248 | — | — | — | — | — | 1.00 | 1.50 | — |
| 1976S | — | — | — | — | — | — | — | — | 1.25 |

## Bicentennial design, silver composition

Weight: 11.5 grams. Composition: 40% silver (0.148 ounces), 60% copper.

| Date | Mintage | G-4 | VG-8 | F-12 | VF-20 | XF-40 | MS-60 | MS-65 | Prf-65 |
|------|---------|-----|------|------|-------|-------|-------|-------|--------|
| 1976S silver | 11,000,000 | — | — | — | — | — | — | 6.00 | 5.75 |

## Regular design resumed, clad composition

Notes: 1979-S Type II proof has a clearer mintmark than the Type I.

| Date | Mintage | G-4 | VG-8 | F-12 | VF-20 | XF-40 | MS-60 | MS-65 | Prf-65 |
|------|---------|-----|------|------|-------|-------|-------|-------|--------|
| 1977 | 43,598,000 | — | — | — | — | — | 2.60 | 2.50 | — |
| 1977D | 31,449,106 | — | — | — | — | — | 2.60 | 2.50 | — |
| 1977S | Proof only | — | — | — | — | — | — | — | 1.75 |
| 1978 | 14,350,000 | — | — | — | — | — | 1.25 | 2.50 | — |
| 1978D | 13,765,799 | — | — | — | — | — | 1.00 | 2.50 | — |
| 1978S | Proof only | — | — | — | — | — | — | — | 1.75 |
| 1979 | 68,312,000 | — | — | — | — | — | — | 1.50 | — |
| 1979D | 15,815,422 | — | — | — | — | — | — | 1.25 | — |
| 1979S T-I | Proof only | — | — | — | — | — | — | — | 2.00 |
| 1979S T-II | Proof only | — | — | — | — | — | — | — | 14.00 |
| 1980P | 44,134,000 | — | — | — | — | — | — | 1.75 | — |
| 1980D | 33,456,449 | — | — | — | — | — | — | 2.00 | — |
| 1980S | Proof only | — | — | — | — | — | — | — | 1.25 |
| 1981P | 29,544,000 | — | — | — | — | — | — | 2.00 | — |
| 1981D | 27,839,533 | — | — | — | — | — | — | 2.00 | — |
| 1981S T-I | Proof only | — | — | — | — | — | — | — | 1.25 |
| 1981S T-II | Proof only | — | — | — | — | — | — | — | 14.50 |
| 1982P | 10,819,000 | — | — | — | — | — | — | 1.50 | — |
| 1982D | 13,140,102 | — | — | — | — | — | — | 1.50 | — |
| 1982S | Proof only | — | — | — | — | — | — | — | 3.50 |
| 1983P | 34,139,000 | — | — | — | — | — | — | 1.50 | — |
| 1983D | 32,472,244 | — | — | — | — | — | — | 1.50 | — |
| 1983S | Proof only | — | — | — | — | — | — | — | 3.00 |
| 1984P | 26,029,000 | — | — | — | — | — | — | 1.50 | — |
| 1984D | 26,262,158 | — | — | — | — | — | — | 1.50 | — |
| 1984S | Proof only | — | — | — | — | — | — | — | 6.50 |
| 1985P | 18,706,962 | — | — | — | — | — | — | 1.50 | — |
| 1985D | 19,814,034 | — | — | — | — | — | — | 1.25 | — |
| 1985S | Proof only | — | — | — | — | — | — | — | 4.50 |
| 1986P | 13,107,633 | — | — | — | — | — | — | 2.00 | — |
| 1986D | 15,336,145 | — | — | — | — | — | — | 1.50 | — |

| Date | Mintage | G-4 | VG-8 | F-12 | VF-20 | XF-40 | MS-60 | MS-65 | Prf-65 |
|---|---|---|---|---|---|---|---|---|---|
| 1986S | Proof only | — | — | — | — | — | — | — | 15.00 |
| 1987P | 2,890,758 | — | — | — | — | — | — | 3.00 | — |
| 1987D | 2,890,758 | — | — | — | — | — | — | 3.00 | — |
| 1987S | Proof only | — | — | — | — | — | — | — | 3.50 |
| 1988P | 13,626,000 | — | — | — | — | — | — | 2.50 | — |
| 1988D | 12,000,096 | — | — | — | — | — | — | 2.50 | — |
| 1988S | Proof only | — | — | — | — | — | — | — | 7.25 |
| 1989P | 24,542,000 | — | — | — | — | — | — | 2.50 | — |
| 1989D | 23,000,216 | — | — | — | — | — | — | 2.50 | — |
| 1989S | Proof only | — | — | — | — | — | — | — | 3.50 |
| 1990P | 22,780,000 | — | — | — | — | — | — | 1.50 | — |
| 1990D | 20,096,242 | — | — | — | — | — | — | 1.50 | — |
| 1990S | Proof only | — | — | — | — | — | — | — | 6.50 |
| 1991P | — | — | — | — | — | — | — | 1.50 | — |
| 1991D | — | — | — | — | — | — | — | 1.50 | — |
| 1991S | Proof only | — | — | — | — | — | — | — | 8.50 |
| 1992P | — | — | — | — | — | — | — | 1.00 | — |
| 1992D | — | — | — | — | — | — | — | 1.00 | — |
| 1992S | Proof only | — | — | — | — | — | — | — | 7.00 |
| 1993P | — | — | — | — | — | — | — | 1.00 | — |
| 1993D | — | — | — | — | — | — | — | 1.00 | — |
| 1993S | Proof only | — | — | — | — | — | — | — | 6.00 |
| 1994P | — | — | — | — | — | — | — | 1.00 | — |
| 1994D | — | — | — | — | — | — | — | 1.00 | — |
| 1994S | Proof only | — | — | — | — | — | — | — | 7.00 |

# Silver dollars
## Flowing Hair

**Designer:** Robert Scot. **Size:** 39-40 millimeters. **Weight:** 26.96 grams. **Composition:** 89.24% silver (0.7737 ounces), 10.76% copper. **Notes:** The two 1795 varieties have either two or three leaves under each of the eagle's wings on the reverse.

| Date | Mintage | G-4 | VG-8 | F-12 | VF-20 | XF-40 | MS-60 |
|---|---|---|---|---|---|---|---|
| 1794 | 1,758 | 10,000. | 13,500. | 18,500. | 27,500. | 42,500. | — |
| 1795 2 leaves | 203,033 | 800. | 900. | 1500. | 2300. | 4950. | 40,000. |
| 1795 3 leaves | Inc. Ab. | 800. | 900. | 1500. | 2300. | 4950. | 40,000. |

# Draped Bust

**Small eagle**

**Designer:** Robert Scot. **Size:** 39-40 millimeters. **Weight:** 26.96 grams. **Composition:** 89.24% silver (0.7737 ounces), 10.76% copper. **Notes:** The 1796 varieties are distinguished by the size of the numerals in the date and letters in "United States of America." The 1797 varieties are distinguished by the number of stars to the left and right of the word "Liberty" and by the size of the letters in "United States of America." The 1798 varieties have either 13 or 15 stars on the obverse.

| Date | Mintage | G-4 | VG-8 | F-12 | VF-20 | XF-40 | MS-60 |
|---|---|---|---|---|---|---|---|
| 1795 | Inc. Ab. | 600. | 800. | 1070. | 1825. | 3750. | 17,000. |
| 1796 small date, small letters | 72,920 | 625. | 800. | 1150. | 1950. | 3650. | 15,500. |
| 1796 small date, large letters | Inc. Ab. | 625. | 775. | 1070. | 1825. | 3550. | 15,500. |
| 1796 large date, small letters | Inc. Ab. | 575. | 765. | 1070. | 1825. | 3550. | 15,500. |
| 1797 9 stars left, 7 stars right, small letters | 7,776 | 1500. | 2000. | 2750. | 4500. | 8450. | 22,000. |
| 1797 9 stars left, 7 stars right, large letters | Inc. Ab. | 585. | 775. | 1070. | 1825. | 3550. | 15,500. |
| 1797 10 stars left, 6 stars right | Inc. Ab. | 585. | 775. | 1070. | 1825. | 3550. | 15,500. |
| 1798 13 stars | 327,536 | 900. | 1150. | 1450. | 2400. | 4500. | 18,000. |
| 1798 15 stars | Inc. Ab. | 1100. | 1600. | 2100. | 3150. | 6900. | 18,000. |

**Heraldic eagle**

# 1794 Silver Dollar
## Grade XF-40

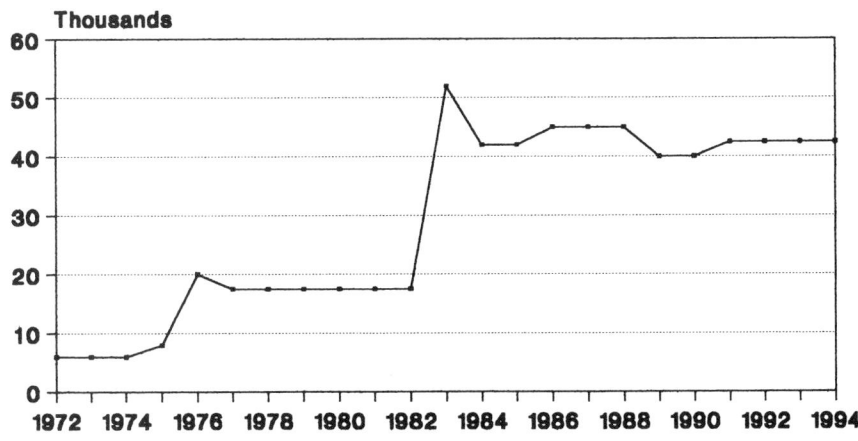

**Thousands**

—•— **Retail Price**

**Source: COIN PRICES**

**Notes:** The 1798 "knob 9" variety has a serif on the lower left of the 9 in the date. The 1798 varieties are distinguished by the number of arrows held by the eagle on the reverse and the number of berries in the olive branch. On the 1798 "high 8" variety, the 8 in the date is higher than the other numerals. The 1799 varieties are distinguished by the number and positioning of the stars on the obverse and by the size of the berries in the olive branch on the reverse. On the 1799 "irregular date" variety, the first 9 in the date is smaller than the other numerals. Some varieties of the 1800 strikes had letters in the legend cut twice into the dies; as the dies became worn, the letters were touched up. On the 1800 "very wide date, low 8" variety, the spacing between the numerals in the date is wider than other varieties, and the 8 is lower than the other numerals. The 1800 "small berries" variety refers to the size of the berries in the olive branch on the reverse. The 1800 "12 arrows" and "10 arrows" varieties refer to the number of arrows held by the eagle. The 1800 "Americai" variety appears to have the faint outline of an "I" after "America" in the reverse legend. The "close" and "wide" varieties of 1802 refer to the amount of space between the numerals in the date. For the 1802 "perfect date" varieties, all numerals in the date are of the same size. The 1803 large-3 and small-3 varieties are distinguished by the size of the 3 in the date.

| Date | Mintage | G-4 | VG-8 | F-12 | VF-20 | XF-40 | MS-60 |
|---|---|---|---|---|---|---|---|
| 1798 knob 9 | Inc. Ab. | 375. | 450. | 575. | 850. | 1675. | 9000. |
| 1798 10 arrows | Inc. Ab. | 355. | 415. | 525. | 700. | 1300. | 9000. |
| 1798 4 berries | Inc. Ab. | 355. | 415. | 525. | 700. | 1300. | 9000. |
| 1798 5 berries, 12 arrows | | | | | | | |
| | Inc. Ab. | 355. | 415. | 525. | 700. | 1300. | 9000. |
| 1798 high 8 | Inc. Ab. | 355. | 415. | 525. | 700. | 1300. | 9000. |
| 1798 13 arrows | Inc. Ab. | 355. | 415. | 525. | 700. | 1300. | 9000. |
| 1799/98 13 star reverse | | | | | | | |
| | 423,515 | 355. | 415. | 525. | 700. | 1300. | 15,000. |
| 1799/98 15 star reverse | | | | | | | |
| | Inc. Ab. | 400. | 500. | 850. | 1150. | 2000. | 15,000. |
| 1799 irregular date, 13 star reverse | | | | | | | |
| | Inc. Ab. | 355. | 415. | 525. | 690. | 1250. | 9000. |
| 1799 irregular date, 15 star reverse | | | | | | | |
| | Inc. Ab. | 355. | 415. | 525. | 690. | 1250. | 9000. |
| 1799 perfect date, 7 and 6 star obverse, no berries | | | | | | | |
| | Inc. Ab. | 355. | 415. | 525. | 690. | 1250. | 9000. |
| 1799 perfect date, 7 and 6 star obverse, small berries | | | | | | | |
| | Inc. Ab. | 355. | 415. | 525. | 690. | 1250. | 9000. |
| 1799 perfect date, 7 and 6 star obverse, medium large | | | | | | | |
| berries | Inc. Ab. | 355. | 415. | 525. | 690. | 1250. | 9000. |
| 1799 perfect date, 7 and 6 star obverse, extra large | | | | | | | |
| berries | Inc. Ab. | 355. | 415. | 525. | 690. | 1250. | 9000. |
| 1799 8 stars left, 5 stars right on obverse | | | | | | | |
| | Inc. Ab. | 425. | 500. | 800. | 1100. | 2000. | 9000. |
| 1800 "R" in "Liberty" double cut | | | | | | | |
| | 220,920 | 355. | 415. | 525. | 690. | 1300. | 9000. |
| 1800 first "T" in "States" double cut | | | | | | | |
| | Inc. Ab. | 355. | 415. | 525. | 690. | 1300. | 9000. |
| 1800 both letters double cut | | | | | | | |
| | Inc. Ab. | 355. | 415. | 525. | 690. | 1300. | 9000. |
| 1800 "T" in "United" double cut | | | | | | | |
| | Inc. Ab. | 355. | 415. | 525. | 690. | 1300. | 9000. |
| 1800 very wide date, low 8 | | | | | | | |
| | Inc. Ab. | 355. | 415. | 525. | 690. | 1300. | 9000. |
| 1800 sm. berries | Inc. Ab. | 355. | 415. | 525. | 690. | 1300. | 9000. |
| 1800 dot date | Inc. Ab. | 355. | 415. | 525. | 690. | 1300. | 9000. |
| 1800 12 arrows | Inc. Ab. | 355. | 415. | 525. | 690. | 1300. | 9000. |
| 1800 10 arrows | Inc. Ab. | 355. | 415. | 525. | 690. | 1300. | 9000. |
| 1800 "Americai" | Inc. Ab. | 360. | 415. | 525. | 800. | 1500. | 9000. |
| 1801 | 54,454 | 375. | 450. | 600. | 850. | 1900. | 9000. |
| 1801 | Unrecorded | | Proof restrike, rare | | | | |
| 1802/1 close | Inc. Ab. | 360. | 425. | 550. | 850. | 1600. | 9000. |
| 1802/1 wide | Inc. Ab. | 360. | 425. | 550. | 850. | 1600. | 9000. |
| 1802 close, perfect date | | | | | | | |
| | Inc. Ab. | 375. | 450. | 600. | 875. | 1650. | 9000. |
| 1802 wide, perfect date | | | | | | | |
| | Inc. Ab. | 375. | 450. | 600. | 875. | 1650. | 9000. |
| 1802 | Unrecorded | | Proof restrike, rare | | | | |
| 1803 lg. 3 | 85,634 | 360. | 425. | 600. | 850. | 1575. | 9000. |
| 1803 sm. 3 | Inc. Ab. | 375. | 450. | 650. | 900. | 1700. | 9000. |
| 1803 | Unrecorded | | Proof restrike, rare | | | | |
| 1804 | 15 known | | 3 varieties | | | | |
| | | | Hawn Sale, Oct. 1993, AU-55, $522,500. | | | | — |

# Gobrecht

**Designer:** Christian Gobrecht. **Size:** 38.1 millimeters. **Weight:** 26.73 grams. **Composition:** 90% silver (0.7736 ounces), 10% copper. **Notes:** Several obverse and reverse combinations exist, as described. Restrikes were produced by the U.S. Mint between 1855 and 1860.

| Date | Mintage | VF-20 | XF-40 | AU-50 | Prf-60 |
|---|---|---|---|---|---|
| 1836 "C. Gobrecht F." below base. Rev: eagle flying left amid stars. Plain edge. | — | → | — | — | — |
| 1836 Obv: same as above. Rev: eagle flying in plain field. Plain edge. | — | — | — | — | — |

| Date | Mintage | VF-20 | XF-40 | AU-50 | Prf-60 |
|------|---------|-------|-------|-------|--------|
| 1836 "C. Gobrecht F." on base. Rev: eagle flying left amid stars. Plain edge. | — | 2500. | 3750. | 4750. | 7500. |
| 1836 Same as above, reeded edge. | — | — | — | — | — |
| 1836 Obv: same as above. Rev: eagle flying in plain field. Plain edge. | — | — | — | — | 10,000. |

Obverse stars

Reverse stars

| Date | Mintage | VF-20 | XF-40 | AU-50 | Prf-60 |
|------|---------|-------|-------|-------|--------|
| 1838 Similar obv., designer's name omitted, stars added around border. Rev: eagle flying left in plain field. Reeded edge. | — | 3000. | 4500. | — | 7500. |
| 1838 Same as above. Plain edge. Restrikes only. | 3 known | — | — | — | — |
| 1838 Obv: same as above. Rev: eagle flying left amid stars. Plain edge. Restrikes only. | 2 known | — | — | — | — |
| 1839 Obv: same as above. Rev: eagle in plain field. Reeded edge. Also known with plain edge and plain edge with eagle amid stars. | — | — | 3750. | — | 15,000. |

# Seated Liberty

## No motto

**Designer:** Christian Gobrecht. **Size:** 38.1 millimeters. **Weight:** 26.73 grams. **Composition:** 90% silver (0.7736 ounces), 10% copper.

| Date | Mintage | G-4 | VG-8 | F-12 | VF-20 | XF-40 | AU-50 | MS-60 | MS-65 | Prf-65 |
|------|---------|-----|------|------|-------|-------|-------|-------|-------|--------|
| 1840 | 61,005 | 130. | 160. | 225. | 300. | 475. | 750. | 1600. | — | — |
| 1841 | 173,000 | 100. | 130. | 180. | 220. | 375. | 575. | 1300. | 24,000. | — |
| 1842 | 184,618 | 90.00 | 120. | 160. | 200. | 300. | 550. | 1100. | 24,000. | — |
| 1843 | 165,100 | 90.00 | 120. | 160. | 200. | 300. | 550. | 1400. | 24,000. | — |
| 1844 | 20,000 | 200. | 250. | 300. | 425. | 575. | 800. | 2000. | — | — |
| 1845 | 24,500 | 150. | 200. | 250. | 350. | 500. | 750. | 3000. | — | — |
| 1846 | 110,600 | 90.00 | 120. | 160. | 200. | 275. | 500. | 1400. | 24,000. | — |
| 1846O | 59,000 | 110. | 140. | 190. | 325. | 700. | 2000. | 4000. | — | — |
| 1847 | 140,750 | 90.00 | 120. | 160. | 200. | 300. | 650. | 850. | 24,000. | — |
| 1848 | 15,000 | 225. | 250. | 400. | 550. | 800. | 1400. | 2050. | — | — |
| 1849 | 62,600 | 110. | 140. | 190. | 240. | 350. | 700. | 1600. | — | — |
| 1850 | 7,500 | 400. | 450. | 600. | 800. | 1300. | 2600. | 3500. | — | — |
| 1850O | 40,000 | 200. | 260. | 350. | 650. | 1400. | 3200. | 5000. | — | — |
| 1851 | 1,300 | — | — | 8000. | 9500. | 13,500. | 16,500. | — | — | — |
| 1852 | 1,100 | — | — | 6000. | 7500. | 11,500. | 15,000. | — | — | — |
| 1853 | 46,110 | 160. | 190. | 240. | 375. | 575. | 800. | 1300. | — | — |

| Date | Mintage | G-4 | VG-8 | F-12 | VF-20 | XF-40 | AU-50 | MS-60 | MS-65 | Prf-65 |
|------|---------|-----|------|------|-------|-------|-------|-------|-------|--------|
| 1854 | 33,140 | 900. | 1200. | 1500. | 2000. | 3000. | 4200. | 7000. | — | — |
| 1855 | 26,000 | 750. | 1000. | 1300. | 1900. | 2650. | 4500. | 9000. | — | — |
| 1856 | 63,500 | 250. | 350. | 450. | 600. | 800. | 1300. | 2000. | — | — |
| 1857 | 94,000 | 250. | 350. | 450. | 650. | 900. | 1400. | 1800. | — | — |
| 1858 | Est. 200 | — | — | — | Proof only | — | — | — | — | — |
|  | Impaired Proof | — | — | — | 4200. | 5500. | 6250. | — | — | — |
| 1859 | 256,500 | 200. | 250. | 350. | 450. | 700. | 1000. | 2500. | 24,000. | 13,500. |
| 1859O | 360,000 | 85.00 | 100. | 155. | 195. | 275. | 500. | 850. | 24,000. | — |
| 1859S | 20,000 | 200. | 275. | 385. | 600. | 1350. | 3000. | — | — | — |
| 1860 | 218,930 | 140. | 180. | 230. | 300. | 475. | 925. | 1300. | 24,000. | 13,500. |
| 1860O | 515,000 | 85.00 | 100. | 155. | 195. | 275. | 500. | 850. | 24,000. | — |
| 1861 | 78,500 | 335. | 450. | 575. | 800. | 1000. | 1400. | 2000. | — | 13,500. |
| 1862 | 12,090 | 320. | 425. | 550. | 750. | 975. | 1450. | 2200. | — | 13,500. |
| 1863 | 27,660 | 240. | 290. | 350. | 500. | 625. | 1100. | 1800. | — | 13,500. |
| 1864 | 31,170 | 175. | 210. | 260. | 350. | 550. | 950. | 2000. | — | 13,500. |
| 1865 | 47,000 | 175. | 210. | 250. | 400. | 625. | 1100. | 1800. | — | 13,500. |
| 1866 | 2 known without motto | | | | | | | | | |

## Motto added on reverse

**Notes:** In 1866 the motto "In God We Trust" was added to the reverse above the eagle.

| Date | Mintage | G-4 | VG-8 | F-12 | VF-20 | XF-40 | AU-50 | MS-60 | MS-65 | Prf-65 |
|------|---------|-----|------|------|-------|-------|-------|-------|-------|--------|
| 1866 | 49,625 | 150. | 200. | 250. | 350. | 550. | 900. | 1600. | 28,500. | 10,000. |
| 1867 | 47,525 | 170. | 250. | 300. | 450. | 675. | 1000. | 1800. | 28,500. | 10,000. |
| 1868 | 162,700 | 140. | 190. | 225. | 350. | 525. | 900. | 2000. | 28,500. | 10,000. |
| 1869 | 424,300 | 115. | 150. | 200. | 325. | 500. | 800. | 2000. | 28,500. | 10,000. |
| 1870 | 416,000 | 100. | 135. | 175. | 225. | 325. | 600. | 1500. | 28,500. | 10,000. |
| 1870CC | 12,462 | 200. | 245. | 325. | 500. | 975. | 2250. | 4250. | — | — |
| 1870S | Unrecorded | | | | Stacks, Nov. 1989, VF, $77,000. | | | | — | — |
| 1871 | 1,074,760 | 85.00 | 95.00 | 165. | 200. | 315. | 550. | 1150. | 28,500. | 10,000. |
| 1871CC | 1,376 | 1650. | 2350. | 3200. | 5000. | 8500. | 15,000. | — | — | — |
| 1872 | 1,106,450 | 85.00 | 95.00 | 165. | 200. | 315. | 550. | 1250. | 28,500. | 10,000. |
| 1872CC | 3,150 | 900. | 1250. | 1600. | 2150. | 3750. | 6500. | 15,000. | — | — |
| 1872S | 9,000 | 150. | 225. | 400. | 575. | 1100. | 3000. | 10,000. | — | — |
| 1873 | 293,600 | 130. | 150. | 200. | 250. | 350. | 600. | 1350. | 28,500. | 10,000. |
| 1873CC | 2,300 | 2450. | 3500. | 5000. | 8500. | 14,000. | 25,000. | 40,000. | — | — |
| 1873S | 700 | | | None known to exist | | | | — | — | — |

# Trade

**Designer:** William Barber. **Size:** 38.1 millimeters. **Weight:** 27.22 grams. **Composition:** 90% silver (0.7878 ounces), 10% copper.

# 1875 Trade Dollar
## Grade F-12

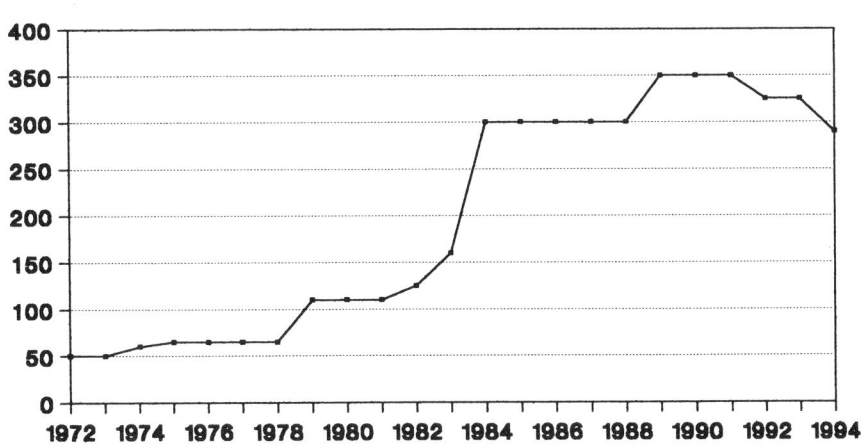

**──•── Retail Price**

**Source: COIN PRICES**

| Date | Mintage | G-4 | VG-8 | F-12 | VF-20 | XF-40 | AU-50 | MS-60 | MS-65 | Prf-65 |
|------|---------|-----|------|------|-------|-------|-------|-------|-------|--------|
| 1873 | 397,500 | 90.00 | 105. | 125. | 165. | 250. | 325. | 1000. | 19,000. | 12,000. |
| 1873CC | 124,500 | 150. | 175. | 225. | 275. | 425. | 675. | 1500. | 19,000. | — |
| 1873S | 703,000 | 130. | 145. | 160. | 180. | 260. | 350. | 1200. | 12,000. | — |
| 1874 | 987,800 | 80.00 | 90.00 | 125. | 165. | 225. | 325. | 700. | 7500. | 12,000. |
| 1874CC | 1,373,200 | 80.00 | 90.00 | 105. | 165. | 240. | 350. | 1000. | 17,000. | — |
| 1874S | 2,549,000 | 70.00 | 80.00 | 95.00 | 120. | 165. | 250. | 675. | 7500. | — |
| 1875 | 218,900 | 200. | 225. | 290. | 365. | 550. | 800. | 1850. | 19,000. | 6500. |
| 1875CC | 1,573,700 | 80.00 | 90.00 | 105. | 130. | 200. | 375. | 900. | 18,500. | — |
| 1875S | 4,487,000 | 60.00 | 70.00 | 85.00 | 100. | 120. | 210. | 500. | 7500. | — |
| 1875S/CC | Inc.Ab. | 275. | 325. | 400. | 500. | 750. | 1000. | 1500. | — | — |
| 1876 | 456,150 | 70.00 | 80.00 | 100. | 125. | 165. | 400. | 675. | 7500. | 6500. |
| 1876CC | 509,000 | 110.00 | 125.00 | 150. | 200. | 325. | 400. | 900. | 13,000. | — |
| 1876S | 5,227,000 | 60.00 | 70.00 | 85.00 | 100. | 120. | 210. | 480. | 7500. | — |
| 1877 | 3,039,710 | 60.00 | 70.00 | 85.00 | 105. | 130. | 210. | 525. | 7500. | 19,000. |
| 1877CC | 534,000 | 110. | 125. | 150. | 200. | 325. | 500. | 1200. | 13,000. | — |
| 1877S | 9,519,000 | 60.00 | 70.00 | 85.00 | 100. | 120. | 210. | 480. | 7500. | — |
| 1878 | 900 | | | Proof only | | | — | | — | 22,000. |
| | Impaired Proof | — | — | 1000. | 1150. | 1500. | — | — | — | |
| 1878CC | 97,000 | 425. | 525. | 675. | 850. | 1350. | 2100. | 5500. | — | — |
| 1878S | 4,162,000 | 60.00 | 70.00 | 85.00 | 100. | 120. | 210. | 480. | 7500. | — |
| 1879 | 1,541 | | | Proof only | | | — | | — | 22,000. |
| | Impaired Proof | — | — | | 900. | 950. | 1100. | — | — | — |
| 1880 | 1,987 | | | Proof only | | | — | | — | 19,500. |
| | Impaired Proof | — | — | | 900. | 950. | 1100. | — | — | — |
| 1881 | 960 | | | Proof only | | | — | | — | 20,000. |
| | Impaired Proof | — | — | | 950. | 1000. | 1250. | — | — | — |
| 1882 | 1,097 | | | Proof only | | | — | | — | 20,000. |
| | Impaired Proof | — | — | | 950. | 1000. | 1250. | — | — | — |
| 1883 | 979 | | | Proof only | | | — | | — | 20,000. |
| | Impaired Proof | — | — | | 950. | 1000. | 1250. | — | — | — |
| 1884 | 10 | | | Proof only | | Superior, Aug. 1990, $75,000. | | | | | — |
| 1885 | 5 | | | Proof only, Stack's, Jan. 1989, $104,500. | | | | | | — |

PRICING SECTION

# 1889-O Silver Dollar
## Grade F-12

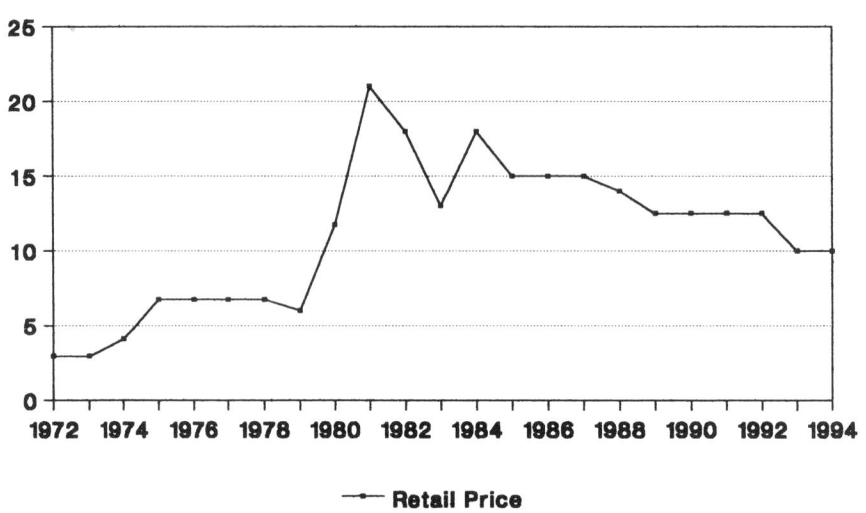

-•- **Retail Price**

**Source: COIN PRICES**

# Morgan

Reverse of 1879              7 over 8 tail feathers

**Designer:** George T. Morgan. **Size:** 38.1 millimeters. **Weight:** 26.73 grams. **Composition:** 90% silver (0.7736 ounces), 10% copper. **Notes:** "65DMPL" values are for coins grading MS-65 with deep-mirror prooflike surfaces. The 1878 "8 tail feathers" and "7 tail feathers" varieties are distinguished by the number of feathers in the eagle's tail. On the "reverse of 1878" varieties, the top of the top feather in the arrows held by the eagle is straight across and the eagle's breast is concave. On the "reverse of 1878 varieties," the top of the top feather in the arrows held by the eagle is slanted and the eagle's breast is convex. The 1890-CC "tail-bar variety" has a bar extending from the arrow feathers to the wreath on the reverse, the result of a die gouge.

| Date | Mintage | G-4 | VG-8 | F-12 | VF-20 | XF-40 | AU-50 | MS-60 | MS-63 | MS-64 | MS-65 | Prf-65 |
|---|---|---|---|---|---|---|---|---|---|---|---|---|
| 1878 8 tail feathers | | | | | | | | | | | | |
| | 750,000 | 7.00 | 10.00 | 12.50 | 14.00 | 18.00 | 29.00 | 43.00 | 60.00 | 170. | 900. | 5850. |
| 1878 7 tail feathers, reverse of 1878 | | | | | | | | | | | | |
| | Inc. Ab. | 7.00 | 9.50 | 10.00 | 11.50 | 12.50 | 19.00 | 25.00 | 45.00 | 105. | 800. | 7800. |
| 1878 7 tail feathers, reverse of 1879 | | | | | | | | | | | | |
| | Inc. Ab. | 7.00 | 11.00 | 12.50 | 15.00 | 17.50 | 28.00 | 31.00 | 110. | 320. | 1650. | — |
| 1878 7 over 8 tail feathers | | | | | | | | | | | | |
| | 9,759,550 | 7.00 | 12.50 | 15.00 | 19.00 | 28.00 | 42.00 | 63.00 | 100. | 350. | 1600. | — |
| 1878CC | 2,212,000 | 12.50 | 19.00 | 23.00 | 27.00 | 33.00 | 46.00 | 70.00 | 90.00 | 200. | 900. | — |
| 1878S | 9,744,000 | 7.00 | 9.00 | 9.50 | 11.50 | 12.50 | 15.00 | 20.00 | 31.00 | 45.00 | 250. | — |
| 1879 | 14,807,100 | 7.00 | 9.00 | 9.50 | 10.00 | 11.00 | 14.00 | 20.00 | 42.00 | 100. | 650. | 4000. |
| 1879CC | 756,000 | 17.00 | 32.00 | 48.00 | 100. | 275. | 700. | 1300. | 2200. | 3850. | 14,000. | — |
| 1879O | 2,887,000 | 7.00 | 9.00 | 9.50 | 10.00 | 11.50 | 17.50 | 39.00 | 160. | 450. | 2250. | — |
| 1879S reverse of 1878 | | | | | | | | | | | | |
| | 9,110,000 | 7.00 | 11.50 | 12.50 | 15.00 | 19.00 | 30.00 | 91.00 | 280. | 1100. | 5000. | — |
| 1879S reverse of 1879 | | | | | | | | | | | | |
| | 9,110,000 | 7.00 | 9.00 | 10.00 | 11.00 | 12.00 | 14.00 | 18.00 | 29.00 | 42.00 | 110. | — |
| 1880 | 12,601,335 | 7.00 | 9.00 | 9.50 | 10.00 | 11.00 | 12.50 | 22.00 | 31.00 | 110. | 750. | 4000. |
| 1880CC reverse of 1878 | | | | | | | | | | | | |
| | 591,000 | 25.00 | 33.00 | 53.00 | 60.00 | 91.00 | 125. | 145. | 240. | 500. | 1250. | — |
| 1880CC reverse of 1879 | | | | | | | | | | | | |
| | 591,000 | 25.00 | 33.00 | 53.00 | 60.00 | 88.00 | 120. | 140. | 170. | 220. | 550. | — |
| 1880O | 5,305,000 | 7.00 | 9.00 | 9.50 | 10.00 | 11.00 | 22.00 | 38.00 | 330. | 1400. | 16,500. | — |
| 1880S | 8,900,000 | 7.00 | 9.00 | 9.50 | 10.00 | 11.00 | 14.00 | 18.00 | 29.00 | 42.00 | 110. | — |
| 1881 | 9,163,975 | 7.00 | 8.50 | 9.50 | 10.00 | 11.00 | 14.00 | 21.00 | 32.00 | 90.00 | 750. | 4000. |
| 1881CC | 296,000 | 50.00 | 72.00 | 100. | 125. | 130. | 140. | 170. | 180. | 210. | 350. | — |
| 1881O | 5,708,000 | 7.00 | 9.00 | 9.50 | 10.00 | 11.00 | 12.50 | 18.00 | 32.00 | 130. | 950. | — |
| 1881S | 12,760,000 | 7.00 | 9.00 | 10.00 | 11.00 | 12.00 | 13.00 | 18.00 | 29.00 | 42.00 | 110. | — |
| 1882 | 11,101,100 | 7.00 | 9.00 | 9.50 | 10.00 | 11.00 | 12.50 | 20.00 | 29.00 | 55.00 | 400. | 4000. |
| 1882CC | 1,133,000 | 14.00 | 26.00 | 30.00 | 36.00 | 44.00 | 51.00 | 57.00 | 70.00 | 80.00 | 200. | — |
| 1882O | 6,090,000 | 7.00 | 9.00 | 9.50 | 10.00 | 11.50 | 12.50 | 20.00 | 38.00 | 70.00 | 800. | — |
| 1882S | 9,250,000 | 7.00 | 9.00 | 10.00 | 11.00 | 12.00 | 15.00 | 20.00 | 28.00 | 43.00 | 110. | — |
| 1883 | 12,291,039 | 7.00 | 9.00 | 9.50 | 10.00 | 11.00 | 12.50 | 20.00 | 38.00 | 48.00 | 130. | 4000. |
| 1883CC | 1,204,000 | 14.00 | 26.00 | 29.00 | 36.00 | 44.00 | 50.00 | 55.00 | 63.00 | 75.00 | 180. | — |
| 1883O | 8,725,000 | 7.00 | 9.00 | 9.50 | 10.00 | 11.00 | 12.00 | 15.00 | 29.00 | 46.00 | 110. | — |
| 1883S | 6,250,000 | 7.00 | 10.00 | 11.50 | 14.00 | 19.00 | 95.00 | 315. | 1200. | 2900. | 20,000. | — |
| 1884 | 14,070,875 | 7.00 | 9.00 | 9.50 | 10.00 | 11.00 | 14.00 | 17.00 | 38.00 | 45.00 | 250. | 4000. |
| 1884CC | 1,136,000 | 38.00 | 47.00 | 50.00 | 52.00 | 53.00 | 54.00 | 56.00 | 70.00 | 80.00 | 150. | — |
| 1884O | 9,730,000 | 7.00 | 8.50 | 9.50 | 10.00 | 11.00 | 12.00 | 17.00 | 29.00 | 42.00 | 110. | — |
| 1884S | 3,200,000 | 7.50 | 10.00 | 11.50 | 14.00 | 28.00 | 220. | 3900. | 19,000. | 47,000. | 107,000. | — |
| 1885 | 17,787,767 | 7.00 | 9.00 | 9.50 | 10.00 | 11.00 | 12.00 | 15.00 | 31.00 | 43.00 | 120. | 4000. |
| 1885CC | 228,000 | 150. | 160. | 170. | 175. | 180. | 185. | 190. | 205. | 240. | 450. | — |
| 1885O | 9,185,000 | 7.00 | 9.00 | 9.50 | 10.00 | 11.00 | 12.00 | 17.00 | 29.00 | 42.00 | 110. | — |
| 1885S | 1,497,000 | 7.50 | 10.00 | 14.00 | 16.50 | 20.00 | 44.00 | 88.00 | 160. | 410. | 1300. | — |
| 1886 | 19,963,886 | 7.00 | 9.00 | 9.50 | 10.00 | 11.00 | 12.00 | 15.00 | 29.00 | 42.00 | 110. | 4000.' |
| 1886O | 10,710,000 | 7.00 | 9.50 | 11.50 | 12.50 | 16.50 | 49.00 | 205. | 1800. | 5500. | 38,000. | — |
| 1886S | 750,000 | 11.00 | 12.50 | 15.00 | 20.00 | 45.00 | 50.00 | 105. | 225. | 550. | 1750. | — |
| 1887 | 20,290,710 | 7.00 | 9.00 | 9.50 | 10.00 | 11.00 | 12.00 | 15.00 | 31.00 | 43.00 | 120. | 4000. |
| 1887O | 11,550,000 | 7.00 | 9.00 | 9.50 | 10.00 | 12.50 | 20.00 | •34.00 | 105. | 400. | 4300. | — |
| 1887S | 1,771,000 | 7.00 | 10.00 | 12.50 | 14.00 | 17.50 | 31.00 | 60.00 | 160. | 500. | 2850. | — |
| 1888 | 19,183,833 | 7.00 | 9.00 | 9.50 | 10.00 | 11.00 | 12.00 | 15.00 | 29.00 | 48.00 | 190. | 4400. |
| 1888O | 12,150,000 | 7.00 | 9.00 | 9.50 | 10.00 | 11.50 | 14.00 | 18.00 | 34.00 | 53.00 | 500. | — |
| 1888S | 657,000 | 8.50 | 12.50 | 20.00 | 24.00 | 30.00 | 50.00 | 100. | 240. | 600. | 2100. | — |
| 1889 | 21,726,811 | 7.00 | 9.00 | 9.00 | 9.50 | 10.00 | 11.50 | 15.00 | 35.00 | 45.00 | 350. | 4000. |
| 1889CC | 350,000 | 95.00 | 150. | 175. | 285. | 725. | 3100. | 6600. | 11,500. | 24,000. | 94,500. | — |
| 1889O | 11,875,000 | 7.00 | 9.00 | 10.00 | 11.00 | 15.00 | 30.00 | 70.00 | 230. | 550. | 3650. | — |
| 1889S | 111320. | 900. | 12.50 | 20.00 | 22.00 | 25.00 | 48.00 | 83.00 | 180. | 320. | 950. | — |
| 1890 | 16,802,590 | 7.00 | 9.00 | 9.50 | 10.00 | 11.50 | 12.50 | 18.00 | 38.00 | 200. | 2400. | 4000. |
| 1890CC | 2,309,041 | 12.50 | 19.00 | 23.00 | 29.00 | 40.00 | 82.00 | 180. | 380. | 650. | 3500. | — |
| 1890CC tail bar | | | | | | | | | | | | |
| | Inc. Ab. | 12.50 | 19.00 | 23.00 | 29.00 | 40.00 | 82.00 | 180. | 380. | 650. | 3500. | — |
| 1890O | 10,701,000 | 7.00 | 9.00 | 9.50 | 10.00 | 12.50 | 20.00 | 31.00 | 60.00 | 180. | 1650. | — |
| 1890S | 8,230,373 | 7.00 | 9.00 | 9.50 | 11.00 | 13.00 | 22.00 | 35.00 | 53.00 | 160. | 700. | — |
| 1891 | 8,694,206 | 7.00 | 9.00 | 10.00 | 12.00 | 14.00 | 22.00 | 45.00 | 135. | 650. | 4500. | 4000. |
| 1891CC | 1,618,000 | 15.00 | 22.00 | 27.00 | 32.00 | 40.00 | 82.00 | 160. | 280. | 550. | 2150. | — |
| 1891O | 7,954,529 | 8.50 | 9.00 | 10.00 | 12.50 | 17.50 | 30.00 | 70.00 | 240. | 650. | 5500. | — |
| 1891S | 5,296,000 | 8.50 | 9.00 | 9.50 | 11.00 | 12.50 | 21.00 | 38.00 | 59.00 | 220. | 900. | — |
| 1892 | 1,037,245 | 8.00 | 12.50 | 13.50 | 15.00 | 17.50 | 50.00 | 126. | 300. | 600. | 2350. | 4000. |
| 1892CC | 1,352,000 | 18.00 | 26.00 | 39.00 | 45.00 | 82.00 | 175. | 300. | 700. | 1100. | 3400. | — |
| 1892O | 2,744,000 | 7.00 | 11.50 | 12.50 | 15.00 | 16.50 | 44.00 | 83.00 | 225. | 500. | 4500. | — |
| 1892S | 1,200,000 | 12.00 | 13.00 | 16.00 | 34.00 | 105. | 2450. | 10,000. | 19,000. | 28,500. | 50,500. | — |
| 1893 | 378,792 | 29.00 | 44.00 | 48.00 | 54.00 | 68.00 | 145. | 280. | 650. | 1100. | 5000. | 4000. |
| 1893CC | 677,000 | 30.00 | 48.00 | 72.00 | 115. | 410. | 725. | 1070. | 2250. | 4400. | 33,000. | — |
| 1893O | 300,000 | 55.00 | 78.00 | 83.00 | 90.00 | 150. | 365. | 1250. | 4050. | 13,500. | 82,000. | — |
| 1893S | 100,000 | 380. | 610. | 875. | 1100. | 3000. | 12,500. | 27,500. | 46,000. | 63,000. | 170,000 | — |
| 1894 | 110,972 | 135. | 185. | 225. | 250. | 290. | 515. | 800. | 2400. | 3650. | 10,500. | 4100. |
| 1894O | 1,723,000 | 8.00 | 15.00 | 19.00 | 24.00 | 27.00 | 115. | 600. | 2300. | 4400. | 24,000. | — |
| 1894S | 1,260,000 | 11.50 | 15.00 | 22.00 | 33.00 | 77.00 | 155. | 300. | 690. | 1100. | 3400. | — |
| 1895 | 12,880 | Proof only | | 6250. | 9500. | 12,000. | 13,000. | — | — | — | — | 26,000. |
| 1895O | 450,000 | 46.00 | 91.00 | 95.00 | 105. | 165. | 695. | 8800. | 19,500. | 29,000. | 82,000. | — |
| 1895S | 400,000 | 90.00 | 115. | 145. | 190. | 360. | 565. | 1100. | 2750. | 3750. | 17,500. | — |
| 1896 | 9,967,762 | 7.00 | 9.00 | 9.50 | 10.00 | 11.00 | 12.50 | 20.00 | 29.00 | 48.00 | 200. | 4000. |
| 1896O | 4,900,000 | 7.00 | 9.00 | 11.00 | 12.00 | 15.00 | 88.00 | 720. | 5550. | 19,500. | 35,500. | — |
| 1896S | 5,000,000 | 8.00 | 10.00 | 17.50 | 35.00 | 115. | 300. | 640. | 1150. | 2150. | 5500. | — |
| 1897 | 2,822,731 | 7.00 | 9.00 | 9.50 | 10.00 | 11.00 | 12.50 | 17.00 | 31.00 | 46.00 | 250. | 4800. |

**PRICING SECTION**

# 1897-O Silver Dollar
## Grade MS-60

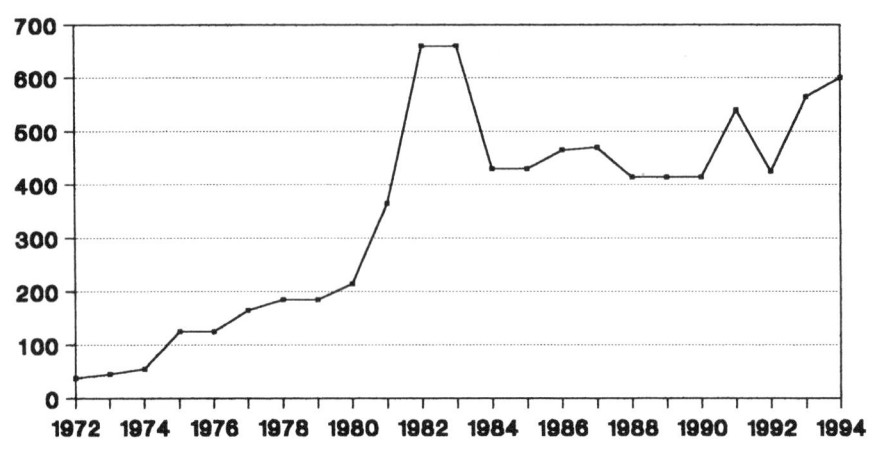

—•— Retail Price

Source: COIN PRICES

| Date | Mintage | G-4 | VG-8 | F-12 | VF-20 | XF-40 | AU-50 | MS-60 | MS-63 | MS-64 | MS-65 | Prf-65 |
|------|---------|-----|------|------|-------|-------|-------|-------|-------|-------|-------|--------|
| 1897O | 4,004,000 | 7.00 | 9.00 | 10.00 | 11.50 | 15.00 | 70.00 | 600. | 2550. | 12,000. | 23,500. | — |
| 1897S | 5,825,000 | 7.00 | 9.00 | 10.00 | 11.00 | 13.00 | 20.00 | 35.00 | 46.00 | 80.00 | 450. | — |
| 1898 | 5,884,735 | 7.00 | 9.00 | 9.50 | 10.00 | 11.00 | 12.00 | 15.00 | 29.00 | 50.00 | 200. | 4000. |
| 1898O | 4,440,000 | 8.00 | 10.00 | 11.00 | 12.00 | 13.00 | 14.00 | 17.00 | 29.00 | 43.00 | 120. | — |
| 1898S | 4,102,000 | 7.00 | 11.50 | 12.50 | 16.50 | 24.00 | 50.00 | 110. | 215. | 450. | 1050. | — |
| 1899 | 330,846 | 15.00 | 19.00 | 26.00 | 30.00 | 40.00 | 56.00 | 76.00 | 100. | 180. | 600. | 5850. |
| 1899O | 12,290,000 | 7.00 | 9.00 | 9.50 | 10.00 | 11.00 | 12.00 | 15.00 | 29.00 | 56.00 | 110. | — |
| 1899S | 2,562,000 | 7.00 | 11.50 | 12.50 | 17.50 | 25.00 | 56.00 | 105. | 225. | 500. | 1100. | — |
| 1900 | 8,880,938 | 7.00 | 8.50 | 9.00 | 9.50 | 10.00 | 11.50 | 15.00 | 32.00 | 45.00 | 200. | 4000. |
| 1900O | 12,590,000 | 7.00 | 8.00 | 9.00 | 10.00 | 12.00 | 13.00 | 18.00 | 32.00 | 45.00 | 110. | — |
| 1900O/CC | 1490. | 11.00 | 16.50 | 19.00 | 22.00 | 27.00 | 75.00 | 170. | 300. | 490. | 1050. | — |
| 1900S | 3,540,000 | 7.00 | 10.00 | 12.50 | 16.50 | 25.00 | 44.00 | 91.00 | 175. | 350. | 1400. | — |
| 1901 | 6,962,813 | 8.00 | 14.00 | 16.50 | 25.00 | 38.00 | 155. | 1350. | 7500. | 26,500. | 126,000. | 5850. |
| 1901O | 13,320,000 | 7.00 | 9.00 | 9.50 | 10.00 | 11.00 | 12.50 | 18.00 | 29.00 | 48.00 | 200. | — |
| 1901S | 2,284,000 | 7.50 | 12.50 | 15.00 | 21.00 | 38.00 | 95.00 | 215. | 390. | 700. | 2450. | — |
| 1902 | 7,994,777 | 7.00 | 9.50 | 10.00 | 11.00 | 12.00 | 22.00 | 38.00 | 70.00 | 110. | 500. | 4000. |
| 1902O | 8,636,000 | 7.00 | 9.00 | 9.50 | 10.00 | 11.00 | 12.00 | 15.00 | 34.00 | 48.00 | 140. | — |
| 1902S | 1,530,000 | 13.00 | 17.00 | 30.00 | 44.00 | 57.00 | 88.00 | 140. | 250. | 500. | 2100. | — |
| 1903 | 4,652,755 | 7.00 | 12.50 | 14.00 | 15.00 | 16.50 | 19.00 | 29.00 | 42.00 | 60.00 | 200. | 4000. |
| 1903O | 4,450,000 | 100. | 110. | 120. | 125. | 130. | 135. | 145. | 160. | 180. | 350. | — |
| 1903S | 1,241,000 | 10.00 | 15.00 | 19.00 | 56.00 | 215. | 785. | 1900. | 3450. | 3900. | 5300. | — |
| 1904 | 2,788,650 | 7.00 | 9.50 | 10.00 | 11.50 | 15.00 | 30.00 | 57.00 | 160. | 540. | 2600. | 4000. |
| 1904O | 3,720,000 | 7.00 | 9.00 | 9.50 | 10.00 | 11.00 | 12.00 | 15.00 | 29.00 | 43.00 | 130. | — |
| 1904S | 2,304,000 | 9.00 | 12.50 | 16.50 | 32.00 | 150. | 480. | 800. | 1500. | 2250. | 5000. | — |
| 1921 | 44,690,000 | 6.50 | 7.00 | 7.50 | 8.00 | 8.50 | 9.00 | 10.00 | 22.00 | 32.00 | 100. | — |
| 1921D | 20,345,000 | 6.50 | 7.00 | 7.50 | 8.00 | 9.00 | 11.00 | 22.00 | 29.00 | 50.00 | 350. | — |
| 1921S | 21,695,000 | 6.50 | 7.00 | 7.50 | 8.00 | 9.00 | 11.00 | 24.00 | 35.00 | 125. | 1000. | — |

# 1903-O Silver Dollar
## Grade MS-60

—•— Retail Price

Source: COIN PRICES

# 1921 Silver Dollar
## Grade MS-60

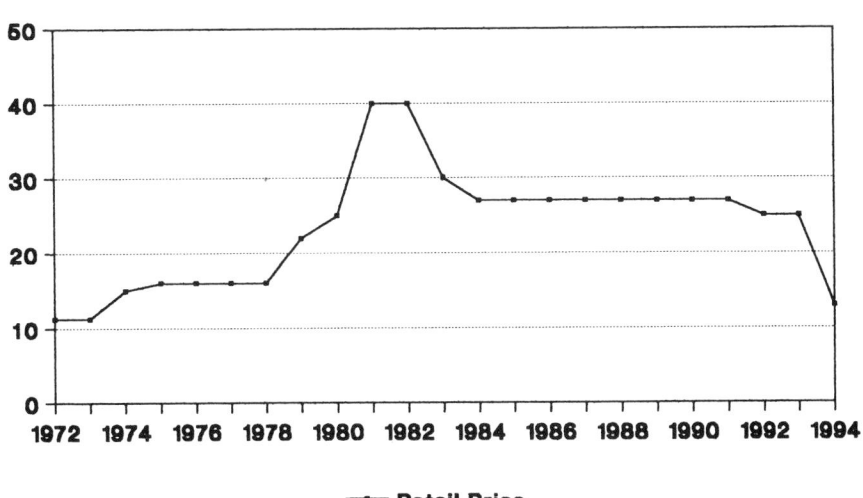

—•— Retail Price

Source: COIN PRICES

PRICING SECTION

# Peace

**Designer:** Anthony de Francisci. **Size:** 38.1 millimeters. **Weight:** 26.73 grams. **Composition:** 90% silver (0.7736 ounces), 10% copper.

| Date | Mintage | G-4 | VG-8 | F-12 | VF-20 | XF-40 | AU-50 | MS-60 | MS-63 | MS-64 | MS-65 |
|------|---------|-----|------|------|-------|-------|-------|-------|-------|-------|-------|
| 1921 | 1,006,473 | 15.00 | 20.00 | 25.00 | 34.00 | 41.00 | 75.00 | 120. | 225. | 400. | 1750. |
| 1922 | 51,737,000 | 6.50 | 7.00 | 7.50 | 8.00 | 9.00 | 10.00 | 11.00 | 20.00 | 40.00 | 150. |
| 1922D | 15,063,000 | 6.50 | 7.00 | 7.50 | 8.00 | 9.00 | 10.00 | 17.00 | 30.00 | 55.00 | 400. |
| 1922S | 17,475,000 | 6.50 | 7.00 | 7.50 | 8.00 | 9.00 | 10.00 | 20.00 | 40.00 | 285. | 1600. |
| 1923 | 30,800,000 | 6.50 | 7.00 | 7.50 | 8.00 | 9.00 | 10.00 | 11.00 | 20.00 | 40.00 | 150. |
| 1923D | 6,811,000 | 6.50 | 7.00 | 7.50 | 8.00 | 9.00 | 14.00 | 25.00 | 65.00 | 200. | 1400. |
| 1923S | 19,020,000 | 6.50 | 7.00 | 7.50 | 8.00 | 9.00 | 10.00 | 20.00 | 75.00 | 300. | 4000. |
| 1924 | 11,811,000 | 6.50 | 7.00 | 7.50 | 8.00 | 9.00 | 10.00 | 11.00 | 21.00 | 40.00 | 200. |
| 1924S | 1,728,000 | 7.00 | 8.50 | 9.50 | 11.50 | 15.00 | 47.00 | 140. | 390. | 1000. | 4000. |
| 1925 | 10,198,000 | 6.50 | 7.00 | 7.50 | 8.00 | 9.00 | 10.00 | 150. | 20.00 | 40.00 | 150. |
| 1925S | 1,610,000 | 6.50 | 7.00 | 7.50 | 10.00 | 12.50 | 26.00 | 50.00 | 90.00 | 550. | 6500. |
| 1926 | 1,939,000 | 6.50 | 7.00 | 7.50 | 9.00 | 11.00 | 15.00 | 20.00 | 25.00 | 50.00 | 450. |
| 1926D | 2,348,700 | 6.50 | 7.00 | 7.50 | 9.00 | 11.50 | 25.00 | 48.00 | 100. | 180. | 700. |
| 1926S | 6,980,000 | 6.50 | 7.00 | 7.50 | 9.00 | 11.50 | 16.00 | 27.00 | 35.00 | 160. | 1000. |

# 1927-S Silver Dollar
## Grade MS-60

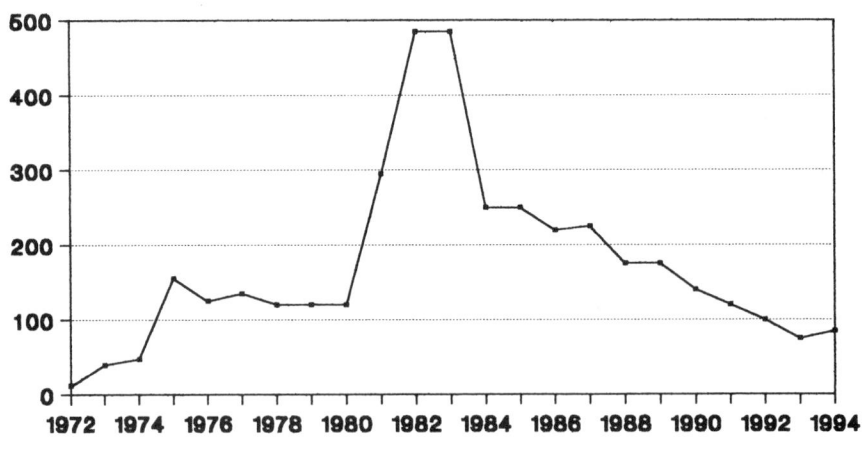

—•— **Retail Price**

**Source: COIN PRICES**

| Date | Mintage | G-4 | VG-8 | F-12 | VF-20 | XF-40 | AU-50 | MS-60 | MS-63 | MS-64 | MS-65 |
|------|---------|-----|------|------|-------|-------|-------|-------|-------|-------|-------|
| 1927 | 848,000 | 8.00 | 12.50 | 14.00 | 16.50 | 21.00 | 30.00 | 45.00 | 85.00 | 300. | 2150. |
| 1927D | 1,268,900 | 7.50 | 11.50 | 12.50 | 14.00 | 20.00 | 69.00 | 100. | 150. | 600. | 3600. |
| 1927S | 866,000 | 9.00 | 11.50 | 12.50 | 14.00 | 19.00 | 55.00 | 85.00 | 155. | 700. | 4000. |
| 1928 | 360,649 | 65.00 | 90.00 | 95.00 | 100. | 110. | 140. | 160. | 240. | 500. | 2250. |
| 1928S | 1,632,000 | 6.50 | 10.00 | 11.50 | 12.50 | 15.00 | 38.00 | 65.00 | 280. | 1000. | 10,000. |
| 1934 | 954,057 | 8.00 | 12.50 | 14.00 | 15.00 | 20.00 | 32.00 | 55.00 | 100. | 200. | 1050. |
| 1934D | 1,569,500 | 6.50 | 11.50 | 12.50 | 14.00 | 17.50 | 32.00 | 75.00 | 155. | 500. | 1300. |
| 1934S | 1,011,000 | 8.00 | 11.50 | 14.00 | 38.00 | 150. | 440. | 1000. | 2300. | 2900. | 5000. |
| 1935 | 1,576,000 | 6.50 | 9.00 | 10.00 | 11.50 | 15.00 | 22.00 | 38.00 | 70.00 | 155. | 600. |
| 1935S | 1,964,000 | 6.50 | 9.00 | 10.00 | 12.50 | 16.50 | 60.00 | 105. | 250. | 300. | 800. |

# Clad dollars

## Eisenhower

**Designer:** Frank Gasparro. **Size:** 38.1 millimeters. **Weight:** 24.59 grams (silver issues) and 22.68 grams (copper-nickel issues). **Clad composition:** 75% copper and 25% nickel bonded to a pure copper core. **Silver clad composition:** clad layers of 80% silver and 20% copper bonded to a core of 20.9% silver and 79.1% copper (0.3161 total ounces of silver).

| Date | Mintage | (Proof) | MS-65 | Prf-65 |
|------|---------|---------|-------|--------|
| 1971 | 47,799,000 | — | 2.50 | — |
| 1971D | 68,587,424 | — | 1.70 | — |
| 1971S silver | 6,868,530 | (4,265,234) | 3.50 | 3.50 |
| 1972 | 75,890,000 | — | 1.60 | — |
| 1972D | 92,548,511 | — | 1.60 | — |
| 1972S silver | 2,193,056 | (1,811,631) | 3.50 | 4.00 |
| 1973 | 2,000,056 | — | 4.25 | — |
| 1973D | 2,000,000 | — | 3.80 | — |
| 1973S silver | 1,833,140 | (1,005,617) | 3.50 | 18.00 |
| 1973S clad | — | 2,769,624 | — | 3.80 |
| 1974 | 27,366,000 | — | 1.60 | — |
| 1974D | 35,466,000 | — | 1.70 | — |
| 1974S silver | 1,720,000 | (1,306,579) | 3.60 | 5.50 |
| 1974S clad | — | (2,617,350) | — | 3.50 |

**Type I Bicentennial reverse**     **Type II Bicentennial reverse**

## Bicentennial design

**Reverse designer:** Dennis R. Williams. **Notes:** In 1976 the lettering on the reverse was changed to thinner letters, resulting in Type I and Type II varieties for that year.

| Date | Mintage | (Proof) | MS-65 | Prf-65 |
|---|---|---|---|---|
| 1976 Type I | 117,337,000 | — | 2.50 | — |
| 1976 Type II | Inc. Ab. | — | 1.60 | — |
| 1976D Type I | 103,228,274 | — | 1.80 | — |
| 1976D Type II | Inc. Ab. | — | 1.60 | — |
| 1976S cld Type I | — | (2,909,369) | — | 3.80 |
| 1976S cld Type II | — | (4,149,730) | — | 3.80 |
| 1976S silver | 11,000,000 | (4,000,000) | 6.00 | 7.90 |

## Regular design resumed

| Date | Mintage | (Proof) | MS-65 | Prf-65 |
|---|---|---|---|---|
| 1977 | 12,596,000 | — | 1.60 | — |
| 1977D | 32,983,006 | — | 1.60 | — |
| 1977S clad | — | (3,251,152) | — | 2.85 |
| 1978 | 25,702,000 | — | 1.60 | — |
| 1978D | 33,012,890 | — | 1.60 | — |
| 1978S clad | — | (3,127,788) | — | 3.15 |

# Anthony

**Designer:** Frank Gasparro. **Size:** 26.5 millimeters. **Weight:** 8.1 grams. **Composition:** clad layers of 75% copper and 25% nickel bonded to a pure copper core. **Notes:** The 1979-S and 1981-S Type II coins have a clearer mintmark than the Type I varieties for those years.

| Date | Mintage | MS-65 | Date | Mintage | MS-65 |
|---|---|---|---|---|---|
| 1979P | 360,222,000 | 1.40 | 1980S | 20,422,000 | 1.45 |
| 1979D | 288,015,744 | 1.40 | 1980S Prf. | 3,547,030 | 4.00 |
| 1979S | 109,576,000 | 1.40 | 1981P | 3,000,000 | 2.50 |
| 1979S Prf. Type I | 3,677,175 | 3.20 | 1981D | 3,250,000 | 2.40 |
| 1979S Prf. Type II | — | 58.00 | 1981S | 3,492,000 | 2.25 |
| 1980P | 27,610,000 | 1.45 | 1981S Prf.Type I | 4,063,083 | 6.00 |
| 1980D | 41,628,708 | 1.45 | 1981S Prf. Type II | — | 86.00 |

# Type coins

**Notes:** Values listed are for the most common dates of each design type in grades MS-64 and proof-64. The -64 grade is relatively new. Except for Morgan dollars, Peace dollars and commemoratives, there is little history among other issues to support MS-64 and proof-64 values, other than as type coins. Among copper coins, the "red" and "brown" designations refer to coins that still retain their original color (red) and those that have toned over time (brown).

| Description | MS-64 | Proof-64 |
|---|---|---|
| Draped Bust half cents (red & brown) | 4150. | — |
| Classic Head half cents (red & brown) | 600. | — |
| Braided Hair half cents (red & brown) | 650. | — |
| Draped Bust large cents (red & brown) | 9500. | — |
| Classic Head large cents (red & brown) | 11,500. | — |
| Coronet large cents (red & brown) | 800. | — |
| Braided Hair large cents (red & brown) | 350. | — |
| Flying Eagle cents | 700. | 4550. |
| Indian Head cents, 1859 copper-nickel | 700. | 2450. |
| Indian Head cents, 1860-1864 copper-nickel | 250. | 850. |
| Indian Head cents, bronze (red & brown) | 45.00 | 175. |
| Two-cent (red & brown) | 190. | 550. |
| Nickel three-cent | 290. | 400. |
| Silver three-cent, Type I | 400. | — |
| Silver three-cent, Type II | 1100. | 3500. |
| Silver three-cent, Type III | 450. | 650. |
| Flowing Hair half dimes | 12,500. | — |
| Draped Bust half dimes, small eagle | 22,500. | — |
| Draped Bust half dimes, heraldic eagle | 16,500. | — |
| Liberty Cap half dimes | 1050. | — |
| Seated Liberty half dimes, no stars | 1900. | — |
| Seated Liberty half dimes, no drapery | 700. | — |
| Seated Liberty half dimes, stars around rim | 650. | 1900. |
| Seated Liberty half dimes, with arrows | 900. | — |
| Seated Liberty half dimes, obverse legend | 450. | 750. |
| Shield nickels, with rays | 650. | 2350. |
| Shield nickels, no rays | 300. | 400. |
| Liberty nickels, no "Cents" | 90.00 | 400. |
| Liberty nickels, with "Cents" | 150. | 300. |
| Buffalo nickels, Type I | 70.00 | 1300. |
| Buffalo nickels, Type II | — | 900. |
| Jefferson nickels, wartime | — | 100. |
| Draped Bust dimes, small eagle | 16,500. | — |
| Draped Bust dimes, heraldic eagle | 13,000. | — |
| Liberty Cap dimes, 1809-1827 (large size) | 3000. | — |
| Liberty Cap dimes, 1828-1837 (reduced size) | 2350. | — |
| Seated Liberty dimes, no stars | 3400. | — |
| Seated Liberty dimes, no drapery | 1250. | — |
| Seated Liberty dimes, stars around rim | 1150. | 1850. |
| Seated Liberty dimes, 1853-1855 with arrows | 1850. | 19,000. |
| Seated Liberty dimes, obverse legend | 350. | 650. |
| Seated Liberty dimes, 1873-1874 with arrows | 2500. | 1650. |
| Barber dimes | 200. | 650. |
| Mercury dimes | — | 155. |
| Twenty-cent | 1900. | 2750. |
| Draped Bust quarters, heraldic eagle | 20,000. | — |
| Liberty Cap quarters, 1815-1828 (large size) | 5500. | — |
| Liberty Cap quarters, 1831-1838 (reduced size) | 4050. | — |
| Seated Liberty quarters, no drapery | 7000. | — |
| Seated Liberty quarters, no motto | 1150. | 2000. |
| Seated Liberty quarters, arrows and rays | 4500. | — |
| Seated Liberty quarters, 1854-1855, with arrows | 4050. | — |
| Seated Liberty quarters, with motto | 750. | 1050. |
| Seated Liberty quarters, 1873-1874, with arrows | 2250. | 2850. |
| Barber quarters | 550. | 950. |
| Standing Liberty quarters, Type I, full head | 380. | — |
| Standing Liberty quarters, Type II | 215. | — |
| Standing Liberty quarters, Type II, full head | 350. | — |
| Flowing Hair half dollars | 94,500. | — |
| Draped Bust half dollars, heraldic eagle | 22,500. | — |
| Liberty Cap half dollars | 2650. | — |
| Liberty Cap half dollars, reeded edge | 4000. | — |
| Seated Liberty half dollars, no drapery | 44,000. | — |
| Seated Liberty half dollars, no motto | 2000. | 1900. |
| Seated Liberty half dollars, arrows and rays | 5500. | — |
| Seated Liberty half dollars, 1854-1855, with arrows | 2550. | — |
| Seated Liberty half dollars, with motto | 1050. | 1100. |
| Seated Liberty half dollars, 1873-1874, with arrows | 5000. | 3150. |
| Barber half dollars | 1150. | 1300. |
| Walking Liberty half dollars | — | 380. |
| Draped Bust dollars, small eagle | 88,000. | — |
| Draped Bust dollars, heraldic eagle | 27,500. | — |
| Seated Liberty dollars, no motto | 6000. | 6000. |
| Seated Liberty dollars, with motto | 5500. | 5000. |
| Morgan dollars | — | 2350. |
| Trade dollars | 2750. | 3150. |

# Gold dollars
## Liberty Head

**Designer:** James B. Longacre. **Size:** 13 millimeters. **Weight:** 1.672 grams. **Composition:** 90% gold (0.0484 ounces), 10% copper. **Notes:** On the "closed wreath" varieties of 1849, the wreath on the reverse extends closer to the numeral 1.

| Date | Mintage | F-12 | VF-20 | XF-40 | AU-50 | MS-60 |
|------|---------|------|-------|-------|-------|-------|
| 1849 open wreath | 688,567 | 120. | 145. | 160. | 200. | 500. |
| 1849 closed wreath | Inc. Ab. | 120. | 145. | 160. | 200. | 500. |
| 1849C closed wreath | 11,634 | 285. | 475. | 875. | 2200. | 4200. |
| 1849C open wreath | Inc. Ab. | | | Extremely Rare | | — |
| 1849D open wreath | 21,588 | 285. | 410. | 750. | 1250. | 2900. |
| 1849O open wreath | 215,000 | 135. | 165. | 210. | 440. | 910. |
| 1850 | 481,953 | 115. | 150. | 170. | 190. | 420. |
| 1850C | 6,966 | 390. | 585. | 975. | 2200. | 6200. |
| 1850D | 8,382 | 350. | 550. | 1150. | 1950. | 6000. |
| 1850O | 14,000 | 195. | 260. | 370. | 775. | 2700. |
| 1851 | 3,317,671 | 115. | 150. | 170. | 190. | 420. |
| 1851C | 41,267 | 275. | 450. | 650. | 1150. | 2300. |
| 1851D | 9,882 | 275. | 425. | 775. | 1500. | 3800. |
| 1851O | 290,000 | 150. | 175. | 195. | 250. | 690. |
| 1852 | 2,045,351 | 115. | 150. | 170. | 190. | 420. |
| 1852C | 9,434 | 275. | 390. | 775. | 1300. | 3200. |
| 1852D | 6,360 | 325. | 700. | 1375. | 2000. | 5700. |
| 1852O | 140,000 | 140. | 165. | 195. | 300. | 1050. |
| 1853 | 4,076,051 | 115. | 150. | 170. | 190. | 420. |
| 1853C | 11,515 | 240. | 490. | 1000. | 1650. | 5200. |
| 1853D | 6,583 | 340. | 700. | 1075. | 2300. | 6500. |
| 1853O | 290,000 | 140. | 160. | 195. | 220. | 585. |
| 1854 | 736,709 | 115. | 150. | 170. | 190. | 420. |
| 1854D | 2,935 | 550. | 890. | 1850. | 6500. | 14,500. |
| 1854S | 14,632 | 260. | 315. | 440. | 725. | 1800. |

# Small Indian Head

**Designer:** James B. Longacre. **Size:** 15 millimeters. **Weight:** 1.672 grams. **Composition:** 90% gold (0.0484 ounces), 10% copper.

| Date | Mintage | F-12 | VF-20 | XF-40 | AU-50 | MS-60 |
|------|---------|------|-------|-------|-------|-------|
| 1854 | 902,736 | 210. | 290. | 520. | 750. | 3000. |
| 1855 | 758,269 | 210. | 290. | 520. | 750. | 3000. |
| 1855C | 9,803 | 675. | 975. | 2350. | 5150. | 10,000. |
| 1855D | 1,811 | 1400. | 2300. | 4700. | 9500. | 19,500. |
| 1855O | 55,000 | 370. | 575. | 800. | 1500. | 7700. |
| 1856S | 24,600 | 390. | 650. | 1250. | 2500. | 8000. |

# Large Indian Head

**Designer:** James B. Longacre. **Size:** 15 millimeters. **Weight:** 1.672 grams. **Composition:** 90% gold (0.0484 ounces), 10% copper. **Notes:** The 1856 varieties are distinguished by whether the 5 in the date is slanted or upright. The 1873 varieties are distinguished by the amount of space between the upper left and lower left serifs in the 3.

| Date | Mintage | F-12 | VF-20 | XF-40 | AU-50 | MS-60 | Prf-65 |
|---|---|---|---|---|---|---|---|
| 1856 upright 5 | 1,762,936 | 130. | 160. | 180. | 325. | 585. | — |
| 1856 slanted 5 | Inc. Ab. | 120. | 140. | 170. | 190. | 370. | — |
| 1856D | 1,460 | 2600. | 3900. | 7000. | 12,250. | 22,500. | — |
| 1857 | 774,789 | 120. | 140. | 170. | 190. | 375. | — |
| 1857C | 13,280 | 350. | 575. | 1150. | 2850. | 9750. | — |
| 1857D | 3,533 | 285. | 850. | 1800. | 3800. | 11,000. | — |
| 1857S | 10,000 | 285. | 525. | 750. | 1950. | 8550. | — |
| 1858 | 117,995 | 120. | 140. | 170. | 190. | 375. | 19,000. |
| 1858D | 3,477 | 390. | 775. | 1300. | 2600. | 7500. | — |
| 1858S | 10,000 | 300. | 400. | 625. | 1800. | 6500. | — |
| 1859 | 168,244 | 120. | 140. | 160. | 190. | 425. | 12,000. |
| 1859C | 5,235 | 300. | 490. | 1250. | 2600. | 10,500. | — |
| 1859D | 4,952 | 475. | 875. | 1400. | 2700. | 7500. | — |
| 1859S | 15,000 | 260. | 310. | 550. | 1950. | 7000. | — |
| 1860 | 36,668 | 120. | 140. | 170. | 190. | 375. | 12,000. |
| 1860D | 1,566 | 2300. | 2750. | 4700. | 7700. | 25,000. | — |
| 1860S | 13,000 | 200. | 325. | 400. | 800. | 2850. | — |
| 1861 | 527,499 | 120. | 140. | 170. | 190. | 375. | 18,000. |
| 1861D | Unrecorded | 4900. | 6800. | 13,500. | 19,500. | 39,500. | — |
| 1862 | 1,361,390 | 120. | 140. | 170. | 190. | 375. | 12,000. |
| 1863 | 6,250 | 360. | 450. | 875. | 1900. | 4400. | 12,000. |
| 1864 | 5,950 | 285. | 370. | 475. | 750. | 1500. | 12,000. |
| 1865 | 3,725 | 285. | 370. | 585. | 850. | 1600. | 12,000. |
| 1866 | 7,130 | 290. | 380. | 450. | 700. | 1200. | 12,000. |
| 1867 | 5,250 | 345. | 440. | 550. | 750. | 1200. | 12,000. |
| 1868 | 10,525 | 260. | 295. | 400. | 585. | 1200. | 12,000. |
| 1869 | 5,925 | 325. | 360. | 520. | 800. | 1300. | 12,000. |
| 1870 | 6,335 | 260. | 285. | 425. | 520. | 1050. | 12,000. |
| 1870S | 3,000 | 350. | 475. | 800. | 1400. | 3000. | — |
| 1871 | 3,930 | 260. | 285. | 440. | 525. | 750. | 18,000. |
| 1872 | 3,530 | 285. | 315. | 480. | 575. | 900. | 18,000. |
| 1873 closed 3 | 125,125 | 325. | 425. | 850. | 1200. | 3250. | 18,000. |
| 1873 open 3 | Inc. Ab. | 120. | 140. | 170. | 190. | 425. | — |
| 1874 | 198,820 | 120. | 140. | 170. | 190. | 425. | 19,000. |
| 1875 | 420 | 1800. | 2500. | 4200. | 5900. | 9100. | 45,000. |
| 1876 | 3,245 | 220. | 250. | 360. | 475. | 890. | 12,000. |
| 1877 | 3,920 | 150. | 175. | 350. | 480. | 760. | 24,000. |
| 1878 | 3,020 | 180. | 215. | 365. | 470. | 795. | 12,000. |
| 1879 | 3,030 | 165. | 190. | 300. | 400. | 550. | 12,000. |
| 1880 | 1,636 | 145. | 160. | 200. | 235. | 450. | 12,000. |
| 1881 | 7,707 | 145. | 160. | 200. | 235. | 450. | 12,000. |
| 1882 | 5,125 | 160. | 175. | 210. | 235. | 450. | 12,000. |
| 1883 | 11,007 | 145. | 165. | 200. | 235. | 450. | 12,000. |
| 1884 | 6,236 | 140. | 160. | 190. | 230. | 450. | 12,000. |
| 1885 | 12,261 | 145. | 160. | 200. | 235. | 450. | 12,000. |
| 1886 | 6,016 | 145. | 165. | 200. | 235. | 450. | 12,000. |
| 1887 | 8,543 | 145. | 165. | 200. | 235. | 450. | 12,000. |
| 1888 | 16,580 | 145. | 165. | 200. | 235. | 450. | 12,000. |
| 1889 | 30,729 | 145. | 165. | 200. | 235. | 365. | 12,000. |

# Gold $2.50 (Quarter Eagle)

## Liberty Cap

**Designer:** Robert Scot. **Size:** 20 millimeters. **Weight:** 4.37 grams. **Composition:** 91.67% gold (0.1289 ounces), 8.33% copper. **Notes:** The 1796 "no-stars" variety does not have stars on the obverse. The 1804 varieties are distinguished by the number of stars on the obverse.

| Date | Mintage | F-12 | VF-20 | XF-40 | MS-60 |
|------|---------|------|-------|-------|-------|
| 1796 no stars | 963 | 9500. | 21,000. | 31,000. | 100,000. |
| 1796 stars | 432 | 7500. | 9000. | 14,000. | 85,000. |
| 1797 | 427 | 7500. | 9500. | 14,500. | 52,000. |
| 1798 | 1,094 | 2800. | 4000. | 6250. | 28,000. |
| 1802/1 | 3,035 | 2800. | 3750. | 5000. | 14,500. |
| 1804 13-star reverse | 3,327 | 13,000. | 18,500. | 30,000. | — |
| 1804 14-star reverse | Inc. Ab. | 2800. | 3750. | 5750. | 16,000. |
| 1805 | 1,781 | 2800. | 3750. | 5400. | 18,500. |
| 1806/4 | 1,616 | 2800. | 3750. | 5000. | 14,500. |
| 1806/5 | Inc. Ab. | 4750. | 6500. | 12,500. | — |
| 1807 | 6,812 | 2800. | 3500. | 4500. | 14,500. |

# Turban Head

**Designer:** John Reich. **Sizes:** 20 millimeters (1808), 18.5 millimeters (1821-1827), and 18.2 millimeters (1829-1834). **Weight:** 4.37 grams. **Composition:** 91.67% gold (0.1289 ounces), 8.33% copper.

| Date | Mintage | F-12 | VF-20 | XF-40 | MS-60 |
|------|---------|------|-------|-------|-------|
| 1808 | 2,710 | 9000. | 12,500. | 22,000. | 45,000. |
| 1821 | 6,448 | 3250. | 4000. | 5750. | 14,000. |
| 1824/21 | 2,600 | 3250. | 4000. | 5000. | 10,500. |
| 1825 | 4,434 | 3250. | 4000. | 5750. | 10,500. |
| 1826/25 | 760 | 3500. | 5500. | 7500. | 19,000. |
| 1827 | 2,800 | 3250. | 4000. | 6300. | 14,000. |
| 1829 | 3,403 | 3250. | 3750. | 4500. | 8500. |
| 1830 | 4,540 | 3250. | 3750. | 4500. | 8500. |
| 1831 | 4,520 | 3250. | 3750. | 4500. | 8500. |
| 1832 | 4,400 | 3250. | 3750. | 4500. | 8500. |
| 1833 | 4,160 | 3250. | 3750. | 4500. | 8500. |
| 1834 | 4,000 | 6750. | 10,000. | 16,500. | 37,000. |

# Classic Head

**Designer:** William Kneass. **Size:** 18.2 millimeters. **Weight:** 4.18 grams. **Composition:** 89.92% gold (0.1209 ounces), 10.08% copper.

| Date | Mintage | VF-20 | XF-40 | AU-50 | MS-60 | MS-65 |
|------|---------|-------|-------|-------|-------|-------|
| 1834 | 112,234 | 300. | 550. | 1100. | 3000. | 37,000. |
| 1835 | 131,402 | 265. | 500. | 900. | 2850. | 37,000. |
| 1836 | 547,986 | 255. | 500. | 900. | 2850. | 37,000. |
| 1837 | 45,080 | 265. | 500. | 900. | 2850. | 37,000. |
| 1838 | 47,030 | 265. | 500. | 900. | 2850. | 37,000. |
| 1838C | 7,880 | 1000. | 2300. | 5200. | 19,500. | — |
| 1839 | 27,021 | 265. | 500. | 1800. | 6000. | 37,000. |
| 1839C | 18,140 | 550. | 1800. | 3500. | 13,600. | — |
| 1839D | 13,674 | 950. | 2750. | 5750. | 18,000. | — |
| 1839O | 17,781 | 500. | 1250. | 2600. | 6500. | 55,000. |

# Coronet Head

**Designer:** Christian Gobrecht. **Size:** 18 millimeters. **Weight:** 4.18 grams. **Composition:** 90% gold (0.121 ounces), 10% copper. **Notes:** Varieties for 1843 are distinguished by the size of the numerals in the date. One 1848 variety has "Cal." inscribed on the reverse, indicating it was made from California gold. The 1873 "closed-3" and "open-3" varieties are distinguished by the amount of space between the upper left and lower left serifs in the 3 in the date.

| Date | Mintage | F-12 | VF-20 | XF-40 | AU-50 | MS-60 | Prf-65 |
|---|---|---|---|---|---|---|---|
| 1840 | 18,859 | 180. | 245. | 700. | 1625. | 3600. | — |
| 1840C | 12,822 | 325. | 600. | 1250. | 4000. | 12,000. | — |
| 1840D | 3,532 | 500. | 2000. | 4100. | 9500. | — | — |
| 1840O | 33,580 | 225. | 250. | 900. | 1800. | 7500. | — |
| 1841 | — | — | — | 30,000. | 85,000. | — | — |
| 1841C | 10,281 | 275. | 475. | 1150. | 3250. | 16,000. | — |
| 1841D | 4,164 | 800. | 1375. | 2900. | 7500. | 15,500. | — |
| 1842 | 2,823 | 350. | 850. | 3000. | 6250. | 14,500. | — |
| 1842C | 6,729 | 525. | 1200. | 2600. | 5000. | 14,500. | — |
| 1842D | 4,643 | 800. | 1500. | 2900. | 9500. | 16,000. | — |
| 1842O | 19,800 | 375. | 375. | 1125. | 2900. | 12,000. | — |
| 1843 | 100,546 | 200. | 225. | 250. | 375. | 750. | — |
| 1843C sm. dt. | 26,064 | 750. | 2500. | 4900. | 10,000. | 24,000. | — |
| 1843C lg. dt. | Inc. Ab. | 300. | 525. | 900. | 2850. | 8000. | — |
| 1843D | 36,209 | 300. | 650. | 1100. | 2500. | 7500. | — |
| 1843O sm. dt. | 288,002 | 200. | 225. | 325. | 450. | 1150. | — |
| 1843O lg. dt. | 76,000 | 250. | 350. | 450. | 1000. | 2000. | — |
| 1844 | 6,784 | 200. | 400. | 850. | 2500. | 8000. | — |
| 1844C | 11,622 | 325. | 675. | 1550. | 6500. | 16,000. | — |
| 1844D | 17,332 | 325. | 625. | 1200. | 2700. | 6500. | — |
| 1845 | 91,051 | 200. | 275. | 325. | 500. | 1100. | — |
| 1845D | 19,460 | 325. | 650. | 1700. | 2500. | 8500. | — |
| 1845O | 4,000 | 750. | 1500. | 2400. | 6000. | 14,000. | — |
| 1846 | 21,598 | 300. | 400. | 725. | 2400. | 7250. | — |
| 1846C | 4,808 | 275. | 1000. | 2000. | 5000. | 14,000. | — |
| 1846D | 19,303 | 350. | 750. | 1200. | 2600. | 7750. | — |
| 1846O | 66,000 | 200. | 300. | 525. | 1600. | 5000. | — |
| 1847 | 29,814 | 200. | 275. | 400. | 1100. | 3800. | — |
| 1847C | 23,226 | 300. | 600. | 1150. | 2300. | 7450. | — |
| 1847D | 15,784 | 300. | 600. | 1250. | 2750. | 7500. | — |
| 1847O | 124,000 | 200. | 275. | 425. | 1150. | 3500. | — |
| 1848 | 7,497 | 350. | 625. | 1000. | 3500. | 8200. | — |

**1848 "Cal."**

| Date | Mintage | F-12 | VF-20 | XF-40 | AU-50 | MS-60 | Prf-65 |
|---|---|---|---|---|---|---|---|
| 1848 "Cal." | 1,389 | 5000. | 8000. | 14,000. | 17,000. | 30,000. | — |
| 1848C | 16,788 | 300. | 750. | 1500. | 3200. | 9000. | — |
| 1848D | 13,771 | 350. | 600. | 1325. | 2350. | 8000. | — |
| 1849 | 23,294 | 300. | 500. | 650. | 1400. | 3600. | — |
| 1849C | 10,220 | 325. | 600. | 1400. | 4750. | 19,000. | — |
| 1849D | 10,945 | 400. | 700. | 1550. | 3150. | 13,000. | — |
| 1850 | 252,923 | 175. | 200. | 225. | 300. | 900. | — |
| 1850C | 9,148 | 275. | 600. | 1400. | 3250. | 14,000. | — |
| 1850D | 12,148 | 275. | 700. | 1200. | 2850. | 14,000. | — |
| 1850O | 84,000 | 200. | 300. | 575. | 1400. | 4400. | — |
| 1851 | 1,372,748 | 135. | 150. | 185. | 235. | 300. | — |
| 1851C | 14,923 | 375. | 675. | 1400. | 3650. | 12,500. | — |
| 1851D | 11,264 | 275. | 650. | 1300. | 3450. | 12,000. | — |
| 1851O | 148,000 | 200. | 250. | 350. | 1200. | 4750. | — |
| 1852 | 1,159,681 | 135. | 150. | 185. | 235. | 350. | — |
| 1852C | 9,772 | 350. | 625. | 1550. | 4000. | 17,000. | — |
| 1852D | 4,078 | 450. | 850. | 2400. | 6500. | 18,000. | — |
| 1852O | 140,000 | 200. | 250. | 300. | 975. | 1700. | — |
| 1853 | 1,404,668 | 175. | 185. | 210. | 250. | 450. | — |
| 1853D | 3,178 | 500. | 1350. | 2650. | 5000. | 16,000. | — |
| 1854 | 596,258 | 175. | 185. | 210. | 250. | 425. | — |
| 1854C | 7,295 | 250. | 625. | 1650. | 4100. | 14,000. | — |
| 1854D | 1,760 | 1400. | 2700. | 5000. | 8000. | 18,000. | — |
| 1854O | 153,000 | 200. | 250. | 300. | 650. | 1700. | — |
| 1854S | 246 | 18,000. | 40,000. | 65,000. | 95,000. | — | — |
| 1855 | 235,480 | 175. | 185. | 210. | 275. | 600. | — |

| Date | Mintage | F-12 | VF-20 | XF-40 | AU-50 | MS-60 | Prf-65 |
|---|---|---|---|---|---|---|---|
| 1855C | 3,677 | 500. | 1300. | 2850. | 4800. | 17,000. | — |
| 1855D | 1,123 | 2500. | 3750. | 7500. | 14,000. | 23,000. | — |
| 1856 | 384,240 | 175. | 185. | 200. | 225. | 275. | 32,000. |
| 1856C | 7,913 | 500. | 850. | 2000. | 4500. | 13,500. | — |
| 1856D | 874 | 4500. | 7250. | 13,000. | 23,000. | 45,000. | — |
| 1856O | 21,100 | 200. | 250. | 715. | 2250. | 7000. | — |
| 1856S | 71,120 | 200. | 250. | 435. | 1050. | 7000. | — |
| 1857 | 214,130 | 175. | 185. | 210. | 250. | 390. | — |
| 1857D | 2,364 | 565. | 1500. | 3000. | 4000. | 10,000. | — |
| 1857O | 34,000 | 200. | 250. | 350. | 1650. | 6000. | — |
| 1857S | 69,200 | 200. | 325. | 500. | 1600. | 5000. | — |
| 1858 | 47,377 | 200. | 250. | 300. | 400. | 2000. | 20,000. |
| 1858C | 9,056 | 265. | 600. | 1300. | 3000. | 9000. | — |
| 1859 | 39,444 | 200. | 250. | 300. | 720. | 1350. | 20,000. |
| 1859D | 2,244 | 600. | 1350. | 2300. | 7000. | 23,000. | — |
| 1859S | 15,200 | 200. | 300. | 1200. | 4000. | 6250. | — |
| 1860 | 22,675 | 200. | 250. | 300. | 600. | 1250. | 20,000. |
| 1860C | 7,469 | 350. | 750. | 2250. | 6000. | 19,500. | — |
| 1860S | 35,600 | 200. | 250. | 700. | 1800. | 5000. | — |
| 1861 | 1,283,878 | 150. | 175. | 200. | 225. | 350. | 20,000. |
| 1861S | 24,000 | 200. | 400. | 1700. | 3400. | 5500. | — |
| 1862 | 98,543 | 200. | 250. | 300. | 550. | 1450. | 20,000. |
| 1862/1 | Inc. Ab. | — | 850. | 1900. | 5750. | 13,500. | — |
| 1862S | 8,000 | 650. | 950. | 2500. | 5950. | 15,500. | — |
| 1863 | 30 | | | | RARCOA, Aug. 1990, proof only, $80,000. | | |
| 1863S | 10,800 | 300. | 465. | 1700. | 3000. | 6600. | — |
| 1864 | 2,874 | 2000. | 5400. | 11,500. | 24,000. | 42,000. | 20,000. |
| 1865 | 1,545 | 1550. | 4325. | 9600. | 17,000. | 32,000. | 37,500. |
| 1865S | 23,376 | 200. | 225. | 630. | 2000. | 4500. | — |
| 1866 | 3,110 | 550. | 1200. | 5000. | 11,000. | 20,000. | 20,000. |
| 1866S | 38,960 | 200. | 300. | 975. | 2600. | 8400. | — |
| 1867 | 3,250 | 225. | 360. | 840. | 1700. | 5500. | 20,000. |
| 1867S | 28,000 | 200. | 250. | 875. | 2400. | 5000. | — |
| 1868 | 3,625 | 200. | 300. | 500. | 1000. | 3000. | 20,000. |
| 1868S | 34,000 | 200. | 250. | 500. | 1500. | 5000. | — |
| 1869 | 4,345 | 200. | 250. | 500. | 850. | 4800. | 20,000. |
| 1869S | 29,500 | 200. | 250. | 600. | 1200. | 4500. | — |
| 1870 | 4,555 | 210. | 275. | 550. | 1000. | 3800. | 20,000. |
| 1870S | 16,000 | 200. | 285. | 350. | 1300. | 5500. | — |
| 1871 | 5,350 | 210. | 275. | 350. | 900. | 2400. | 20,000. |
| 1871S | 22,000 | 225. | 285. | 350. | 800. | 3000. | — |
| 1872 | 3,030 | 225. | 360. | 825. | 2000. | 8000. | 20,000. |
| 1872S | 18,000 | 225. | 285. | 500. | 1375. | 4300. | — |
| 1873 closed 3 | 178,025 | 200. | 250. | 300. | 475. | 1300. | 20,000. |
| 1873 open 3 | Inc. Ab. | 175. | 200. | 225. | 250. | 325. | — |
| 1873S | 27,000 | 200. | 250. | 575. | 1100. | 4000. | — |
| 1874 | 3,940 | 200. | 250. | 500. | 1000. | 3700. | 20,000. |
| 1875 | 420 | 1500. | 3600. | 5250. | 9000. | 16,000. | 32,000. |
| 1875S | 11,600 | 200. | 250. | 400. | 800. | 4500. | — |
| 1876 | 4,221 | 210. | 300. | 750. | 1600. | 6500. | 20,000. |
| 1876S | 5,000 | 210. | 250. | 800. | 1800. | 6000. | — |
| 1877 | 1,652 | 325. | 450. | 800. | 1700. | 3500. | 48,000. |
| 1877S | 35,400 | 125. | 180. | 210. | 250. | 850. | — |
| 1878 | 286,260 | 125. | 150. | 160. | 180. | 245. | 18,000. |
| 1878S | 178,000 | 125. | 150. | 160. | 210. | 425. | — |
| 1879 | 88,990 | 125. | 150. | 160. | 180. | 270. | 18,000. |
| 1879S | 43,500 | 125. | 150. | 160. | 1000. | 2500. | — |
| 1880 | 2,996 | 215. | 250. | 350. | 600. | 1500. | 20,000. |
| 1881 | 691 | 700. | 1350. | 4500. | 7500. | 14,500. | 20,000. |
| 1882 | 4,067 | 125. | 225. | 300. | 350. | 1200. | 18,000. |
| 1883 | 2,002 | 125. | 225. | 400. | 1000. | 2700. | 20,000. |
| 1884 | 2,023 | 125. | 225. | 400. | 500. | 2000. | 32,000. |
| 1885 | 887 | 500. | 800. | 1700. | 3000. | 7500. | 32,000. |
| 1886 | 4,088 | 125. | 210. | 300. | 550. | 1400. | 18,000. |
| 1887 | 6,282 | 125. | 190. | 225. | 500. | 1300. | 18,000. |
| 1888 | 16,098 | 125. | 190. | 225. | 300. | 525. | 18,000. |
| 1889 | 17,648 | 125. | 190. | 250. | 275. | 450. | 18,000. |
| 1890 | 8,813 | 125. | 190. | 280. | 295. | 475. | 18,000. |
| 1891 | 11,040 | 125. | 190. | 250. | 275. | 450. | 18,000. |
| 1892 | 2,545 | 135. | 195. | 200. | 325. | 950. | 18,000. |
| 1893 | 30,106 | 125. | 150. | 200. | 260. | 300. | 18,000. |
| 1894 | 4,122 | 125. | 150. | 200. | 325. | 850. | 18,000. |
| 1895 | 6,199 | 125. | 150. | 200. | 270. | 425. | 18,000. |
| 1896 | 19,202 | 125. | 150. | 160. | 180. | 245. | 18,000. |
| 1897 | 29,904 | 125. | 150. | 160. | 180. | 245. | 18,000. |
| 1898 | 24,165 | 125. | 150. | 160. | 180. | 245. | 18,000. |
| 1899 | 27,350 | 125. | 150. | 160. | 180. | 245. | 18,000. |
| 1900 | 67,205 | 125. | 150. | 160. | 180. | 245. | 18,000. |
| 1901 | 91,322 | 125. | 150. | 160. | 180. | 245. | 18,000. |
| 1902 | 133,733 | 125. | 150. | 160. | 180. | 245. | 16,000. |
| 1903 | 201,257 | 125. | 150. | 160. | 180. | 245. | 16,000. |
| 1904 | 160,960 | 125. | 150. | 160. | 180. | 245. | 16,000. |
| 1905 | 217,944 | 125. | 150. | 160. | 180. | 245. | 16,000. |
| 1906 | 176,490 | 125. | 150. | 160. | 180. | 245. | 16,000. |
| 1907 | 336,448 | 125. | 150. | 160. | 180. | 245. | 16,000. |

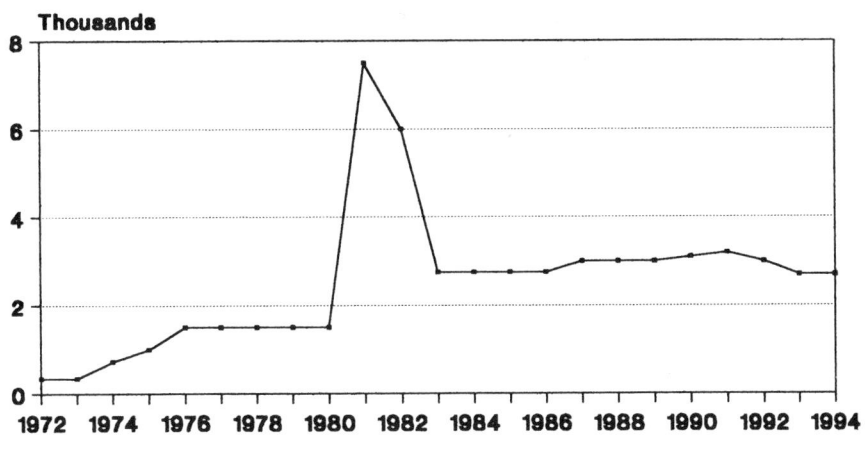

# 1911-D Gold $2.50
## Grade MS-60

**Thousands**

Chart showing Retail Price from 1972 to 1994

← **Retail Price**

**Source: COIN PRICES**

# Indian Head

**Designer:** Bela Lyon Pratt. **Size:** 18 millimeters. **Weight:** 4.18 grams. **Composition:** 90% gold (0.121 ounces), 10% copper.

| Date | Mintage | VF-20 | XF-40 | AU-50 | MS-60 | MS-63 | MS-65 | Prf-65 |
|------|---------|-------|-------|-------|-------|-------|-------|--------|
| 1908 | 565,057 | 135. | 155. | 175. | 260. | 1050. | 6000. | 14,400. |
| 1909 | 441,899 | 135. | 155. | 175. | 310. | 1150. | 6600. | 19,000. |
| 1910 | 492,682 | 135. | 155. | 175. | 295. | 1250. | 8400. | 15,000. |
| 1911 | 704,191 | 135. | 155. | 175. | 290. | 1150. | 9100. | 14,400. |
| 1911D | 55,680 | 700. | 950. | 1150. | 2700. | 6400. | 30,000. | — |
| 1912 | 616,197 | 135. | 160. | 180. | 300. | 1200. | 12,250. | 15,000. |
| 1913 | 722,165 | 135. | 155. | 175. | 265. | 1200. | 10,250. | 14,400. |
| 1914 | 240,117 | 140. | 160. | 190. | 550. | 2800. | 19,000. | 15,500. |
| 1914D | 448,000 | 135. | 155. | 175. | 350. | 1900. | 19,000. | — |
| 1915 | 606,100 | 135. | 155. | 175. | 265. | 1200. | 6000. | 15,000 |
| 1925D | 578,000 | 135. | 155. | 175. | 220. | 1050. | 6350. | — |
| 1926 | 446,000 | 135. | 155. | 175. | 220. | 1050. | 6000. | — |
| 1927 | 388,000 | 135. | 155. | 175. | 220. | 1050. | 6500. | — |
| 1928 | 416,000 | 135. | 155. | 175. | 220. | 1050. | 6700. | — |
| 1929 | 532,000 | 135. | 155. | 175. | 220. | 1050. | 9250. | — |

# Gold $3

**Designer:** James B. Longacre. **Size:** 20.5 millimeters. **Weight:** 5.015 grams. **Composition:** 90% gold (0.1452 ounces), 10% copper. **Notes:** The 1873 "closed-3" and "open-3" varieties are distinguished by the amount of space between the upper left and lower left serifs of the 3 in the date.

| Date | Mintage | F-12 | VF-20 | XF-40 | AU-50 | MS-60 | Prf-65 |
|------|---------|------|-------|-------|-------|-------|--------|
| 1854 | 138,618 | 365. | 505. | 650. | 850. | 2050. | 35,000. |
| 1854D | 1,120 | — | 6500. | 12,000. | 23,500. | 60,000. | — |
| 1854O | 24,000 | 365. | 600. | 950. | 3000. | 8200. | — |
| 1855 | 50,555 | 365. | 505. | 650. | 850. | 2500. | — |
| 1855S | 6,600 | 550. | 900. | 2000. | 5000. | 12,750. | — |
| 1856 | 26,010 | 365. | 535. | 690. | 1200. | 2700. | — |
| 1856S | 34,500 | 500. | 760. | 1200. | 2000. | 7000. | — |
| 1857 | 20,891 | 365. | 535. | 690. | 1100. | 3000. | 35,000. |
| 1857S | 14,000 | 510. | 760. | 1800. | 4000. | 10,000. | — |
| 1858 | 2,133 | 550. | 800. | 1450. | 2300. | 5000. | 35,000. |
| 1859 | 15,638 | 365. | 505. | 725. | 1150. | 2700. | 35,000. |
| 1860 | 7,155 | 550. | 760. | 850. | 1200. | 2900. | 35,000. |
| 1860S | 7,000 | 525. | 760. | 2500. | 5500. | 12,500. | — |
| 1861 | 6,072 | 550. | 760. | 1100. | 2100. | 4000. | 35,000. |
| 1862 | 5,785 | 525. | 760. | 1100. | 2100. | 4000. | 35,000. |
| 1863 | 5,039 | 600. | 760. | 1125. | 2400. | 4000. | 35,000. |
| 1864 | 2,680 | 600. | 760. | 1150. | 2400. | 4000. | 35,000. |
| 1865 | 1,165 | 700. | 800. | 1600. | 6000. | 14,000. | 35,000. |
| 1866 | 4,030 | 525. | 760. | 1500. | 2400. | 4200. | 35,000. |
| 1867 | 2,650 | 575. | 800. | 1150. | 2400. | 4200. | 35,000. |
| 1868 | 4,875 | 525. | 760. | 1100. | 2400. | 3900. | 35,000. |
| 1869 | 2,525 | 575. | 760. | 1100. | 2500. | 4200. | 35,000. |
| 1870 | 3,535 | 525. | 760. | 1100. | 2400. | 4200. | 35,000. |
| 1870S | Unique | | | Private Sale, 1992 XF-40 $1,500,000. | | | |
| 1871 | 1,330 | 550. | 880. | 1200. | 2600. | 3900. | 35,000. |
| 1872 | 2,030 | 525. | 800. | 1200. | 2200. | 3500. | 35,000. |
| 1873 open 3 | 25 | | | Proof only | — | | — |
| 1873 closed 3 | Unknown | — | 4000. | 6500. | 10,000. | 23,000. | — |
| 1874 | 41,820 | 365. | 525. | 800. | 1300. | 3000. | 35,000. |
| 1875 | 20 | | | Proof only | | | |
| | | | | RARCOA, Aug. 1990, proof, $159,000. | | | |
| 1876 | 45 | | | 14,000. | 18,000. | | 90,000. |
| 1877 | 1,488 | 600. | 900. | 3000. | 5000. | 6700. | 35,000. |
| 1878 | 82,324 | 365. | 500. | 1000. | 1300. | 3000. | 30,000. |
| 1879 | 3,030 | 550. | 800. | 1400. | 2400. | 3900. | 30,000. |
| 1880 | 1,036 | 550. | 900. | 1400. | 2600. | 3900. | 30,000. |
| 1881 | 554 | 900. | 1600. | 2500. | 3900. | 5500. | 32,000. |
| 1882 | 1,576 | 550. | 1000. | 1500. | 2500. | 4000. | 30,000. |
| 1883 | 989 | 550. | 1000. | 1500. | 2600. | 4400. | 32,000. |
| 1884 | 1,106 | 550. | 1000. | 2000. | 3000. | 4000. | 30,000. |
| 1885 | 910 | 550. | 1000. | 1700. | 2700. | 4000. | 32,000. |
| 1886 | 1,142 | 550. | 1000. | 1600. | 3000. | 4400. | 30,000. |
| 1887 | 6,160 | 525. | 800. | 1200. | 2100. | 3100. | 30,000. |
| 1888 | 5,291 | 525. | 800. | 1200. | 2100. | 3100. | 30,000. |
| 1889 | 2,429 | 525. | 800. | 1200. | 2100. | 3100. | 30,000. |

# Gold $4 (Stella)

Flowing Hair                    Coiled Hair

**Designers:** Charles E. Barber (Flowing Hair type) and George T. Morgan (Coiled Hair type). **Notes:** These are patterns, rather than coins struck for circulation. Examples in other metals also exist; values listed here are only for those struck in gold.

| Date | Type | Mintage | VF-20 | XF-40 | AU-50 | Prf-65 |
|------|------|---------|-------|-------|-------|--------|
| 1879 | Flowing Hair | 415 | — | — | — | 90,000. |
| Impaired Proofs | | — | 10,000. | 13,500. | 33,000. | — |
| 1879 | Coiled Hair | 10 | — | — | — | 500,000. |
| 1880 | Flowing Hair | 15 | — | — | — | 225,000. |
| 1880 | Coiled Hair | 10 | — | — | — | 500,000. |

# Gold $5
# (Half Eagle)

## Liberty Cap

Small eagle                    Heraldic eagle

**Designer:** Robert Scot. **Size:** 25 millimeters. **Weight:** 8.75 grams. **Composition:** 91.67% gold (0.258 ounces), 8.33% copper. **Notes:** From 1795 through 1798, varieties exist with either a "small eagle" or a "large (heraldic) eagle" on the reverse. After 1798, only the heraldic eagle was used. Two 1797 varieties are distinguished by the number of stars on the obverse. 1798 varieties are distinguished by the size of the 8 in the date and the number of stars on the reverse. 1804 varieties are distinguished by the size of the 8 in the date. 1806 varieties are distinguished by whether the top of the 6 has a serif.

| Date | Mintage | F-12 | VF-20 | XF-40 | MS-60 |
|------|---------|------|-------|-------|-------|
| 1795 sm. eagle | 8,707 | 5250. | 7250. | 9250. | 31,500. |
| 1795 lg. eagle | Inc. Ab. | 6900. | 10,000. | 15,000. | 48,000. |
| 1796/95 small eagle | 6,196 | 6000. | 9100. | 14,000. | — |
| 1797/95 large eagle | 3,609 | 5000. | 7000. | 9600. | 30,000. |
| 1797 15 stars, small eagle | Inc. Ab. | 7500. | 10,000. | 18,500. | 45,000. |
| 1797 16 stars, small eagle | Inc. Ab. | 7000. | 9000. | 17,500. | 55,000. |
| 1798 sm.eagle | 7 known | — | — | 45,000. | — |
| 1798 large eagle, small 8 | 24,867 | 1500. | 1850. | 3700. | 10,500. |
| 1798 large eagle, large 8, 13-star reverse | Inc. Ab. | 1200. | 1850. | 3000. | 7300. |
| 1798 large eagle, large 8, 14-star reverse | Inc. Ab. | 1600. | 2300. | 4300. | 24,000. |
| 1799 | 7,451 | 1300. | 1600. | 3000. | 12,500. |
| 1800 | 37,628 | 1150. | 1550. | 2150. | 6000. |
| 1802/1 | 53,176 | 1150. | 1550. | 2000. | 6000. |
| 1803/2 | 33,506 | 1150. | 1550. | 2000. | 6000. |
| 1804 sm. 8 | 30,475 | 1150. | 1550. | 2000. | 6000. |
| 1804 lg. 8 | Inc. Ab. | 1150. | 1550. | 2000. | 6000. |
| 1805 | 33,183 | 1150. | 1550. | 2000. | 6000. |
| 1806 pointed 6 | 64,093 | 1150. | 1550. | 2200. | 10,000. |
| 1806 round 6 | Inc. Ab. | 1150. | 1550. | 2000. | 6000. |
| 1807 | 32,488 | 1150. | 1550. | 2000. | 6000. |

# Turban Head

## Capped draped bust

**Designer:** John Reich. **Size:** 25 millimeters. **Weight:** 8.75 grams. **Composition:** 91.67% gold (0.258 ounces), 8.33% copper. **Notes:** The 1810 varieties are distinguished by the size of the numerals in the date and the size of the 5 in the "5D." on the reverse. The 1811 varieties are distinguished by the size of the 5 in the "5D." on the reverse.

| Date | Mintage | F-12 | VF-20 | XF-40 | MS-60 |
|---|---|---|---|---|---|
| 1807 | 51,605 | 1250. | 1650. | 2150. | 6000. |
| 1808 | 55,578 | 1250. | 1650. | 2150. | 6000. |
| 1808/7 | Inc. Ab. | 1400. | 1550. | 2400. | 9500. |
| 1809/8 | 33,875 | 1250. | 1500. | 2150. | 6000. |
| 1810 small date, small 5 | 100,287 | | 6500. | 12,000. | — |
| 1810 small date, large 5 | | | | | |
| | Inc. Ab. | 1300. | 1650. | 2400. | 6000. |
| 1810 large date, small 5 | | | | | |
| | Inc. Ab. | 3750. | 4750. | 7500. | 24,000. |
| 1810 large date, large 5 | | | | | |
| | Inc. Ab. | 1250. | 1400. | 2000. | 6000. |
| 1811 small 5 | 99,581 | 1250. | 1400. | 2000. | 5500. |
| 1811 large 5 | Inc. Ab. | 1150. | 1350. | 2000. | 6500. |
| 1812 | 58,087 | 1000. | 1350. | 2000. | 6250. |

## Capped head

**Notes:** 1820 varieties are distinguished by whether the 2 in the date has a curved base or square base, and by the size of the letters in the reverse inscriptions. 1832 varieties are distinguished by whether the 2 in the date has a curved base or square base and by the number of stars on the reverse. 1834 varieties are distinguished by whether the 4 has a serif at its far right.

| Date | Mintage | F-12 | VF-20 | XF-40 | MS-60 |
|---|---|---|---|---|---|
| 1813 | 95,428 | 1300. | 1500. | 2250. | 6600. |
| 1814/13 | 15,454 | 1600. | 2000. | 4000. | 10,000. |
| 1815 | 635 | | | Private sale Jan. 1994, MS-61, $150,000. | |
| 1818 | 48,588 | 1500. | 1900. | 2850. | 8500. |
| 1819 | 51,723 | — | — | 40,000. | — |
| 1820 curved base 2, small letters | | | | | |
| | 263,806 | 1500. | 1900. | 4500. | 16,000. |
| 1820 curved base 2, large letters | | | | | |
| | Inc. Ab. | 1500. | 1900. | 4500. | 40,000. |
| 1820 sq. base 2 | Inc. Ab. | 1500. | 1900. | 3100. | 8500. |
| 1821 | 34,641 | 2200. | 3850. | 7300. | 23,000. |
| 1822 | (3 known) 17,796 | | | Private Sale 1993, VF-30, $1,000,000. | |
| 1823 | 14,485 | 1600. | 2000. | 3700. | 14,500. |
| 1824 | 17,340 | 2200. | 3500. | 8800. | — |
| 1825/21 | 29,060 | 3250. | 5000. | 6500. | 20,000. |
| 1825/24 | Inc. Ab. | | | Bowers & Merena, Mar. 1989, XF, $148,500. | |
| 1826 | 18,069 | 2750. | 6000. | 7100. | 25,000. |
| 1827 | 24,913 | — | — | — | 32,500. |
| 1828/7 | 28,029 | | | Bowers & Merena, Jun. 1989, XF, $20,900. | |
| 1828 | Inc. Ab. | — | — | 30,000. | — |
| 1829 lg. dt. | 57,442 | | | Superior, July 1985, MS-65, $104,500. | |
| 1829 sm. dt. | Inc. Ab. | | | Private Sale, 1992 (XF-45), $89,000. | |
| 1830 sm. "5D." | 126,351 | 3500. | 5000. | 6500. | 15,000. |
| 1830 lg. "5D." | Inc. Ab. | 3500. | 5000. | 7000. | 16,500. |
| 1831 | 140,594 | 3500. | 5100. | 6500. | 16,500. |
| 1832 curved base 2, 12-stars | 157,487 | — | Rare | — | — |

| Date | Mintage | F-12 | VF-20 | XF-40 | MS-60 |
|------|---------|------|-------|-------|-------|
| 1832 square base 2, 13 stars | Inc. Ab. | 4000. | 6500. | 8750. | 21,000. |
| 1833 | 193,630 | 3500. | 5000. | 6250. | 15,500. |
| 1834 plain 4 | 50,141 | 3500. | 5000. | 6250. | 16,000. |
| 1834 crosslet 4 | Inc. Ab. | 4000. | 6000. | 8250. | ·26,500. |

# Classic Head

**Designer:** William Kneass. **Size:** 22.5 millimeters. **Weight:** 8.36 grams. **Composition:** 89.92% gold (0.2418 ounces), 10.08% copper. **Notes:** 1834 varieties are distinguished by whether the 4 has a serif at its far right.

| Date | Mintage | VF-20 | XF-40 | AU-50 | MS-60 | MS-65 |
|------|---------|-------|-------|-------|-------|-------|
| 1834 plain 4 | 658,028 | 300. | 500. | 850. | 2950. | 90,000. |
| 1834 crosslet 4 | Inc. Ab. | 1150. | 2375. | 5250. | 15,000. | — |
| 1835 | 371,534 | 300. | 500. | 900. | 2900. | 62,000. |
| 1836 | 553,147 | 300. | 500. | 850. | 2900. | 62,000. |
| 1837 | 207,121 | 325. | 525. | 925. | 3500. | 62,000. |
| 1838 | 286,588 | 300. | 500. | 900. | 3250. | 62,000. |
| 1838C | 17,179 | 1550. | 4250. | 9500. | 20,000. | — |
| 1838D | 20,583 | 1450. | 3500. | 7000. | 15,000. | — |

# Coronet Head

## No motto

**Designer:** Christian Gobrecht. **Size:** 21.6 millimeters. **Weight:** 8.359 grams. **Composition:** 90% gold (0.242 ounces), 10% copper. **Notes:** Varieties for the 1842 Philadelphia strikes are distinguished by the size of the letters in the reverse inscriptions. Varieties for the 1842-C and -D strikes are distinguished by the size of the numerals in the date. Varieties for the 1843-O strikes are distinguished by the size of the letters in the reverse inscriptions.

| Date | Mintage | F-12 | VF-20 | XF-40 | MS-60 | Prf-65 |
|------|---------|------|-------|-------|-------|--------|
| 1839 | 118,143 | 200. | 250. | 435. | 3500. | — |
| 1839/8 curved date | Inc. Ab. | 200. | 300. | 600. | 1750. | — |
| 1839C | 17,205 | 450. | 950. | 2000. | 20,000. | — |
| 1839D | 18,939 | 400. | 800. | 1700. | 11,000. | — |
| 1840 | 137,382 | 190. | 225. | 350. | 4100. | — |
| 1840C | 18,992 | 400. | 700. | 1650. | 15,500. | — |
| 1840D | 22,896 | 400. | 700. | 1500. | 11,000. | — |
| 1840O | 40,120 | 200. | 325. | 700. | 7500. | — |
| 1841 | 15,833 | 200. | 375. | 1200. | 7500. | — |
| 1841C | 21,467 | 300. | 675. | 1450. | 12,000. | — |
| 1841D | 30,495 | 325. | 600. | 1250. | 12,000. | — |
| 1841O | 50 | | 2 known | — | | — |
| 1842 sm. let. | 27,578 | 150. | 300. | 1300. | 10,000. | — |
| 1842 lg. let. | Inc. Ab. | 350. | 700. | 2000. | 11,500. | — |
| 1842C sm. dt. | 28,184 | 1750. | 3500. | 12,250. | — | — |
| 1842C lg. dt. | Inc. Ab. | 350. | 750. | 1500. | 17,500. | — |
| 1842D sm. dt. | 59,608 | 350. | 650. | 1250. | 12,000. | — |
| 1842D lg. dt. | Inc. Ab. | 1250. | 2250. | 6000. | 18,000. | — |
| 1842O | 16,400 | 350. | 1000. | 5000. | 24,000. | — |
| 1843 | 611,205 | 150. | 180. | 210. | 2200. | — |
| 1843C | 44,201 | 350. | 600. | 1400. | 13,000. | — |
| 1843D | 98,452 | 350. | 550. | 1000. | 8000.· | — |
| 1843O sm. let. | 19,075 | 325. | 550. | 1400. | 11,000. | — |
| 1843O lg. let. | 82,000 | 200. | 325. | 900. | 15,000. | — |
| 1844 | 340,330 | 150. | 180. | 250. | 2100. | — |

PRICING SECTION

# 1852-C Gold $5
## Grade MS-60

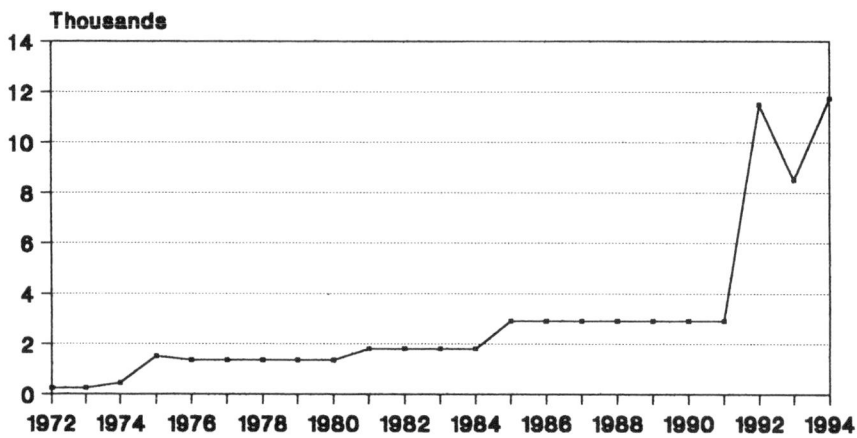

— Retail Price

Source: COIN PRICES

| Date | Mintage | F-12 | VF-20 | XF-40 | MS-60 | Prf-65 |
|------|---------|------|-------|-------|-------|--------|
| 1844C | 23,631 | 300. | 725. | 2700. | 13,500. | — |
| 1844D | 88,982 | 375. | 550. | 1050. | 10,000. | — |
| 1844O | 364,600 | 200. | 225. | 600. | 5000. | — |
| 1845 | 417,099 | 150. | 180. | 210. | 2750. | — |
| 1845D | 90,629 | 360. | 850. | 1850. | 11,000. | — |
| 1845O | 41,000 | 200. | 350. | 1100. | 9500. | — |
| 1846 | 395,942 | 150. | 180. | 210. | 3000. | — |
| 1846C | 12,995 | 425. | 900. | 2500. | 17,500. | — |
| 1846D | 80,294 | 400. | 550. | 1350. | 9250. | — |
| 1846O | 58,000 | 200. | 350. | 1450. | 12,750. | — |
| 1847 | 915,981 | 150. | 180. | 210. | 1550. | — |
| 1847C | 84,151 | 375. | 575. | 1450. | 16,500. | — |
| 1847D | 64,405 | 400. | 500. | 1100. | 9000. | — |
| 1847O | 12,000 | 475. | 2300. | 10,500. | 29,000. | — |
| 1848 | 260,775 | 150. | 180. | 250. | 2500. | — |
| 1848C | 64,472 | 400. | 650. | 1600. | 15,000. | — |
| 1848D | 47,465 | 400. | 500. | 1500. | 13,000. | — |
| 1849 | 133,070 | 150. | 180. | 300. | 2700. | — |
| 1849C | 64,823 | 350. | 500. | 1100. | 11,500. | — |
| 1849D | 39,036 | 350. | 700. | 1350. | 11,500. | — |
| 1850 | 64,491 | 200. | 350. | 875. | 5700. | — |
| 1850C | 63,591 | 325. | 550. | 1100. | 13,000. | — |
| 1850D | 43,984 | 350. | 500. | 1500. | 18,000. | — |
| 1851 | 377,505 | 150. | 180. | 265. | 2800. | — |
| 1851C | 49,176 | 325. | 600. | 1100. | 11,000. | — |
| 1851D | 62,710 | 350. | 525. | 1375. | 11,500. | — |
| 1851O | 41,000 | 325. | 650. | 1500. | — | — |
| 1852 | 573,901 | 150. | 180. | 210. | 1850. | — |
| 1852C | 72,574 | 350. | 550. | 1100. | 11,750. | — |
| 1852D | 91,584 | 350. | 500. | 1000. | 9000. | — |
| 1853 | 305,770 | 150. | 180. | 210. | 2250. | — |
| 1853C | 65,571 | 350. | 525. | 1000. | 12,000. | — |
| 1853D | 89,678 | 350. | 500. | 900. | 9000. | — |
| 1854 | 160,675 | 160. | 200. | 500. | 3000. | — |
| 1854C | 39,283 | 400. | 600. | 1600. | 14,500. | — |
| 1854D | 56,413 | 350. | 500. | 1000. | 9250. | — |
| 1854O | 46,000 | 250. | 300. | 500. | 6800. | — |
| 1854S | 268 | Bowers & Ruddy, Oct. 1982, AU-55, $170,000. | | | | — |
| 1855 | 117,098 | 160. | 200. | 250. | 2400. | — |
| 1855C | 39,788 | 350. | 625. | 1750. | 13,500. | — |
| 1855D | 22,432 | 400. | 600. | 1500. | 16,000. | — |

| Date | Mintage | F-12 | VF-20 | XF-40 | MS-60 | Prf-65 |
|---|---|---|---|---|---|---|
| 1855O | 11,100 | 350. | 700. | 2900. | 16,500. | — |
| 1855S | 61,000 | 200. | 425. | 1100. | 10,000. | — |
| 1856 | 197,990 | 175. | 310. | 340. | 3500. | — |
| 1856C | 28,457 | 350. | 600. | 1300. | 12,000. | — |
| 1856D | 19,786 | 400. | 600. | 1300. | 7800. | — |
| 1856O | 10,000 | 400. | 800. | 2800. | — | — |
| 1856S | 105,100 | 190. | 300. | 800. | — | — |
| 1857 | 98,188 | 160. | 200. | 250. | 3000. | — |
| 1857C | 31,360 | 300. | 600. | 1300. | 8000. | — |
| 1857D | 17,046 | 300. | 600. | 1250. | 8000. | — |
| 1857O | 13,000 | 300. | 700. | 2000. | — | — |
| 1857S | 87,000 | 200. | 300. | 700. | 7000. | — |
| 1858 | 15,136 | 200. | 275. | 800. | 5250. | 70,000. |
| 1858C | 38,856 | 375. | 800. | 1250. | 11,000. | — |
| 1858D | 15,362 | 300. | 600. | 1200. | 12,000. | — |
| 1858S | 18,600 | 350. | 650. | 2600. | — | — |
| 1859 | 16,814 | 200. | 275. | 600. | 6500. | — |
| 1859C | 31,847 | 300. | 525. | 1400. | 13,000. | — |
| 1859D | 10,366 | 400. | 725. | 2000. | 11,500. | — |
| 1859S | 13,220 | 450. | 1250. | 4750. | — | — |
| 1860. | 19,825 | 200. | 300. | 600. | 6500. | — |
| 1860C | 14,813 | 350. | 800. | 2000. | 11,500. | — |
| 1860D | 14,635 | 300. | 800. | 1800. | 13,500. | — |
| 1860S | 21,200 | 450. | 1200. | 2800. | 18,500. | — |
| 1861 | 688,150 | 150. | 175. | 210. | 1900. | — |
| 1861C | 6,879 | 700. | 1500. | 3400. | 25,000. | — |
| 1861D | 1,597 | 2500. | 4000. | 7000. | — | — |
| 1861S | 18,000 | 450. | 1100. | 4500. | — | — |
| 1862 | 4,465 | 450. | 750. | 2500. | — | — |
| 1862S | 9,500 | 1400. | 4500. | 10,500. | — | — |
| 1863 | 2,472 | 500. | 1150. | 3450. | — | — |
| 1863S | 17,000 | 425. | 1200. | 4750. | — | — |
| 1864 | 4,220 | 400. | 600. | 2100. | 11,500. | — |
| 1864S | 3,888 | 2200. | 6750. | 15,000. | — | — |
| 1865 | 1,295 | 600. | 1200. | 3150. | — | — |
| 1865S | 27,612 | 425. | 1200. | 3600. | — | — |
| 1866S | 9,000 | 600. | 1600. | 6000. | — | — |

## With motto

**Notes:** In 1866 the motto "In God We Trust" was added above the eagle on the reverse. The 1873 "closed-3" and "open-3" varieties are distinguished by the amount of space between the upper left and lower left serifs of the 3 in the date.

| Date | Mintage | VF-20 | XF-40 | AU-50 | MS-60 | MS-65 | Prf-65 |
|---|---|---|---|---|---|---|---|
| 1866 | 6,730 | 725. | 1800. | 4400. | 12,500. | — | 35,000. |
| 1866S | 34,920 | 1350. | 4500. | 8500. | 18,500. | — | — |
| 1867 | 6,920 | 550. | 2500. | 4000. | 8000. | — | 35,000. |
| 1867S | 29,000 | 1600. | 5000. | 10,000. | — | — | — |
| 1868 | 5,725 | 650. | 1800. | 4000. | 10,000. | — | 35,000. |
| 1868S | 52,000 | 500. | 2400. | 7200. | — | — | — |
| 1869 | 1,785 | 875. | 2300. | 5000. | — | — | 35,000. |
| 1869S | 31,000 | 375. | 2400. | 9750. | — | — | — |
| 1870 | 4,035 | 700. | 2800. | 4500. | — | — | 35,000. |
| 1870CC | 7,675 | 4400. | 9500. | 20,000. | — | — | — |
| 1870S | 17,000 | 1200. | 4000. | 11,500. | — | — | — |
| 1871 | 3,230 | 875. | 2150. | 6500. | — | — | 35,000. |
| 1871CC | 20,770 | 975. | 3000. | 13,000. | — | — | — |
| 1871S | 25,000 | 550. | 2000. | 6000. | 17,500. | — | — |
| 1872 | 1,690 | 750. | 2000. | 4700. | 15,000. | — | 35,000. |
| 1872CC | 16,980 | 850. | 3500. | 14,000. | — | — | — |
| 1872S | 36,400 | 525. | 1850. | 7000. | — | — | — |
| 1873 closed 3 | 49,305 | 225. | 250. | 625. | 2800. | — | 35,000. |
| 1873 open 3 | 63,200 | 225. | 250. | 625. | 2800. | — | — |
| 1873CC | 7,416 | 2200. | 6500. | 15,500. | — | — | — |
| 1873S | 31,000 | 875. | 2700. | — | — | — | — |
| 1874 | 3,508 | 625. | 2200. | 5000. | — | — | 35,000. |
| 1874CC | 21,198 | 675. | 1750. | 5500. | 12,000. | — | — |
| 1874S | 16,000 | 725. | 3750. | 9000. | — | — | — |
| 1875 | 220 | 45,000. | 55,000. | 96,000. | — | — | 110,000. |
| 1875CC | 11,828 | 1500. | 5400. | 13,000. | — | — | — |

| Date | Mintage | VF-20 | XF-40 | AU-50 | MS-60 | MS-65 | Prf-65 |
|------|---------|-------|-------|-------|-------|-------|--------|
| 1875S | 9,000 | 950. | 3300. | — | — | — | — |
| 1876 | 1,477 | 1000. | 2600. | 5300. | 15,500. | — | 35,000. |
| 1876CC | 6,887 | 1500. | 5750. | 9500. | — | — | — |
| 1876S | 4,000 | 1700. | 5000. | 12,750. | — | — | — |
| 1877 | 1,152 | 800. | 2400. | 4500. | 12,000. | — | 35,000. |
| 1877CC | 8,680 | 1000. | 3300. | 8000. | — | — | — |
| 1877S | 26,700 | 325. | 900. | 3600. | — | — | — |
| 1878 | 131,740 | 120. | 225. | 250. | 1000. | — | 35,000. |
| 1878CC | 9,054 | 3500. | 9000. | 20,000. | — | — | — |
| 1878S | 144,700 | 175. | 275. | 475. | 1200. | — | — |
| 1879 | 301,950 | 120. | 175. | 250. | 525. | — | 20,000. |
| 1879CC | 17,281 | 350. | 1300. | 3000. | — | — | — |
| 1879S | 426,200 | 200. | 275. | 325. | 975. | — | — |
| 1880 | 3,166,436 | 120. | 145. | 175. | 250. | — | 20,000. |
| 1880CC | 51,017 | 350. | 875. | 2000. | 7500. | — | — |
| 1880S | 1,348,900 | 120. | 145. | 175. | 190. | — | — |
| 1881 | 5,708,802 | 120. | 145. | 175. | 195. | 7000. | 20,000. |
| 1881/80 | Inc. Ab. | 350. | 700. | 1800. | 4050. | — | — |
| 1881CC | 13,886 | 500. | 1500. | 4150. | 9000. | — | — |
| 1881S | 969,000 | 120. | 145. | 175. | 190. | — | — |
| 1882 | 2,514,568 | 120. | 175. | 195. | 250. | 7000. | 20,000. |
| 1882CC | 82,817 | 375. | 650. | 1500. | 5000. | — | — |
| 1882S | 969,000 | 120. | 145. | 175. | 190. | — | — |
| 1883 | 233,461 | 120. | 175. | 200. | 550. | 7000. | 20,000. |
| 1883CC | 12,958 | 375. | 800. | 3500. | 12,000. | — | — |
| 1883S | 83,200 | 195. | 225. | 330. | 1150. | — | — |
| 1884 | 191,078 | 150. | 175. | 260. | 1250. | — | 20,000. |
| 1884CC | 16,402 | 450. | 825. | 4250. | — | — | — |
| 1884S | 177,000 | 200. | 275. | 325. | 775. | — | — |
| 1885 | 601,506 | 120. | 145. | 160. | 190. | — | 20,000. |
| 1885S | 1,211,500 | 120. | 175. | 190. | 225. | 7000. | — |
| 1886 | 388,432 | 150. | 185. | 225. | 375. | — | 20,000. |
| 1886S | 3,268,000 | 120. | 165. | 175. | 225. | — | — |
| 1887 | 87 | | Proof only | — | — | — | 100,000. |
| 1887S | 1,912,000 | 120. | 175. | 185. | 240. | — | — |
| 1888 | 18,296 | 175. | 250. | 300. | 2000. | — | 20,000. |
| 1888S | 293,900 | 190. | 275. | 800. | 2800. | — | — |
| 1889 | 7,565 | 400. | 700. | 1500. | — | — | 20,000. |
| 1890 | 4,328 | 250. | 400. | 1500. | 3500. | — | 20,000. |
| 1890CC | 53,800 | 300. | 400. | 550. | 1250. | — | — |
| 1891 | 61,413 | 120. | 235. | 250. | 775. | 7500. | 20,000. |
| 1891CC | 208,000 | 250. | 375. | 500. | 850. | — | — |
| 1892 | 753,572 | 120. | 145. | 180. | 220. | — | 20,000. |
| 1892CC | 82,968 | 300. | 600. | 700. | 1550. | — | — |
| 1892O | 10,000 | 600. | 1250. | 2250. | 4700. | — | — |
| 1892S | 298,400 | 175. | 225. | 325. | 2500. | — | — |
| 1893 | 1,528,197 | 120. | 175. | 195. | 225. | 5000. | 20,000. |
| 1893CC | 60,000 | 300. | 400. | 625. | 2000. | — | — |
| 1893O | 110,000 | 200. | 300. | 400. | 2000. | — | — |
| 1893S | 224,000 | 175. | 200. | 325. | 600. | 7500. | — |
| 1894 | 957,955 | 120. | 175. | 195. | 300. | 5000. | 20,000. |
| 1894O | 16,600 | 195. | 350. | 475. | 2000. | — | — |
| 1894S | 55,900 | 275. | 350. | 850. | 3750. | 7500. | — |
| 1895 | 1,345,936 | 120. | 145. | 160. | 190. | 5000. | 20,000. |
| 1895S | 112,000 | 250. | 375. | 1000. | 5000. | 26,000. | — |
| 1896 | 59,063 | 160. | 185. | 225. | 350. | 7500. | 20,000. |
| 1896S | 155,400 | 225. | 275. | 600. | 2100. | — | — |
| 1897 | 867,883 | 120. | 145. | 160. | 190. | 5000. | 20,000. |
| 1897S | 354,000 | 165. | 250. | 525. | 1800. | — | — |
| 1898 | 633,495 | 120. | 145. | 160. | 190. | 5000. | 20,000. |
| 1898S | 1,397,400 | 120. | 145. | 175. | 300. | 5000. | — |
| 1899 | 1,710,729 | 120. | 145. | 160. | 190. | 5000. | 20,000. |
| 1899S | 1,545,000 | 120. | 145. | 160. | 190. | 5000. | — |
| 1900 | 1,405,730 | 120. | 145. | 160. | 190. | 5000. | 20,000. |
| 1900S | 329,000 | 165. | 200. | 300. | 700. | 5000. | — |
| 1901 | 616,040 | 120. | 145. | 160. | 190. | 5000. | 12,500. |
| 1901S | 3,648,000 | 120. | 145. | 160. | 190. | 5000. | — |
| 1902 | 172,562 | 120. | 145. | 160. | 190. | 5000. | 12,500. |
| 1902S | 939,000 | 120. | 145. | 160. | 190. | 5000. | — |
| 1903 | 227,024 | 120. | 145. | 160. | 190. | 5000. | 15,000. |
| 1903S | 1,855,000 | 120. | 145. | 160. | 190. | 5000. | — |
| 1904 | 392,136 | 120. | 145. | 160. | 190. | 5000. | 12,500. |
| 1904S | 97,000 | 180. | 225. | 300. | 800. | 11,000. | — |
| 1905 | 302,308 | 120. | 145. | 160. | 190. | 7200. | 12,500. |
| 1905S | 880,700 | 120. | 175. | 260. | 900. | 5000. | — |
| 1906 | 348,820 | 120. | 145. | 160. | 190. | 5000. | 12,500. |
| 1906D | 320,000 | 120. | 145. | 160. | 190. | 5000. | — |
| 1906S | 598,000 | 120. | 145. | 185. | 275. | 5000. | — |
| 1907 | 626,192 | 120. | 145. | 160. | 190. | 5000. | 20,000. |
| 1907D | 888,000 | 120. | 145. | 160. | 190. | 5000. | — |
| 1908 | 421,874 | 120. | 145. | 160. | 190. | 5000. | — |

# Indian Head

**Designer:** Bela Lyon Pratt. **Size:** 21.6 millimeters. **Weight:** 8.359 grams. **Composition:** 90% gold (0.242 ounces), 10% copper.

| Date | Mintage | VF-20 | XF-40 | AU-50 | MS-60 | MS-63 | MS-65 | Prf-65 |
|------|---------|-------|-------|-------|-------|-------|-------|--------|
| 1908 | 578,012 | 195. | 225. | 240. | 300. | 2500. | 14,500. | 22,000. |
| 1908D | 148,000 | 195. | 225. | 240. | 300. | 3400. | 26,500. | — |
| 1908S | 82,000 | 225. | 450. | 540. | 1850. | 3700. | 20,000. | — |
| 1909 | 627,138 | 195. | 225. | 240. | 445. | 3400. | 19,500. | 26,500. |
| 1909D | 3,423,560 | 195. | 225. | 240. | 300. | 2500. | 20,500. | — |
| 1909O | 34,200 | 600. | 900. | 1600. | 6900. | 30,000. | 120,000. | — |
| 1909S | 297,200 | 215. | 230. | 275. | 1175. | 6600. | 42,000. | — |
| 1910 | 604,250 | 195. | 225. | 240. | 300. | 3700. | 30.000. | 24,000. |
| 1910D | 193,600 | 195. | 225. | 240. | 510. | 4800. | 36,000. | — |
| 1910S | 770,200 | 195. | 225. | 240. | 1800. | 7200. | 42,000. | — |
| 1911 | 915,139 | 195. | 225. | 240. | 300. | 3400. | 24,000. | 25,000. |
| 1911D | 72,500 | 350. | 500. | 600. | 5600. | 19,000. | 68,500. | — |
| 1911S | 1,416,000 | 195. | 235. | 250. | 840. | 6000. | 42,000. | — |
| 1912 | 790,144 | 195. | 225. | 240. | 300. | 3400. | 21,500. | 24,000. |
| 1912S | 392,000 | 215. | 235. | 250. | 1550. | 8500. | 42,000. | — |
| 1913 | 916,099 | 195. | 225. | 240. | 300. | 3400. | 21,000. | 25,000. |
| 1913S | 408,000 | 250. | 300. | 350. | 2650. | 15,000. | 66,000. | — |
| 1914 | 247,125 | 195. | 225. | 240. | 300. | 3400. | 23,500. | 25,000. |
| 1914D | 247,000 | 195. | 225. | 240. | 300. | 3700. | 48,000. | — |
| 1914S | 263,000 | 215. | 230. | 255. | 1050. | 7550. | 47,000. | — |
| 1915 | 588,075 | 195. | 225. | 240. | 300. | 3400. | 23,500. | 33,000. |
| 1915S | 164,000 | 300. | 325. | 425. | 2650. | 8700. | 66,000. | — |
| 1916S | 240,000 | 195. | 225. | 265. | 660. | 4700. | 30,000. | — |
| 1929 | 662,000 | 2000. | 3500. | 4850. | 6000. | 9250. | 45,500. | — |

# Gold $10 (Eagle)

## Liberty Cap

### Small eagle

**Designer:** Robert Scot. **Size:** 33 millimeters. **Weight:** 17.5 grams. **Composition:** 91.67% gold (0.5159 ounces), 8.33% copper.

| Date | Mintage | F-12 | VF-20 | XF-40 | MS-60 |
|------|---------|------|-------|-------|-------|
| 1795 13 leaves | 5,583 | 6000. | 8500. | 11,000. | 39,500. |
| 1795 9 leaves | Inc. Ab. | 17,000. | 30,000. | 50,000. | — |
| 1796 | 4,146 | 6000. | 8500. | 11,000. | 50,000. |
| 1797 sm. eagle | 3,615 | 6000. | 10,250. | 35,000. | — |

### Heraldic eagle

**Notes:** The 1798/97 varieties are distinguished by the positioning of the stars on the obverse.

| Date | Mintage | F-12 | VF-20 | XF-40 | MS-60 |
|------|---------|------|-------|-------|-------|
| 1797 lg. eagle | 10,940 | 2500. | 3500. | 5000. | 14,000. |
| 1798/97, 9 stars left, 4 right | 900 | 4500. | 8000. | 20,000. | 70,000. |
| 1798/97, 7 stars left, 6 right | 842 | 15,000. | 27,500. | 57,500. | — |
| 1799 | 37,449 | 2400. | 3000. | 4500. | 11,000. |
| 1800 | 5,999 | 2400. | 3250. | 5000. | 13,750. |
| 1801 | 44,344 | 2400. | 3000. | 4000. | 11,000. |
| 1803 | 15,017 | 2600. | 3250. | 4000. | 11,000. |
| 1804 | 3,757 | 3750. | 4200. | 8500. | 32,500. |

# Coronet Head

### Old-style head, no motto

**Designer:** Christian Gobrecht. **Size:** 27 millimeters. **Weight:** 16.718 grams. **Composition:** 90% gold (0.4839 ounces), 10% copper.

| Date | Mintage | F-12 | VF-20 | XF-40 | MS-60 | Prf-65 |
|------|---------|------|-------|-------|-------|--------|
| 1838 | 7,200 | 550. | 900. | 2750. | 26,000. | — |
| 1839 lg. lts. | 38,248 | 450. | 800. | 1700. | 16,000. | — |

### New-style head, no motto

**Notes:** The 1842 varieties are distinguished by the size of the numerals in the date.

| Date | Mintage | F-12 | VF-20 | XF-40 | MS-60 | Prf-65 |
|------|---------|------|-------|-------|-------|--------|
| 1839 sm. lts. | Inc. Ab. | 700. | 1600. | 4000. | — | — |
| 1840 | 47,338 | 380. | 425. | 750. | 13,000. | — |
| 1841 | 63,131 | 380. | 415. | 650. | 14,000. | — |
| 1841O | 2,500 | 850. | 2000. | 7000. | — | — |
| 1842 sm. dt. | 81,507 | 380. | 425. | 700. | — | — |
| 1842 lg. dt. | Inc. Ab. | 380. | 415. | 750. | 13,500. | — |
| 1842O | 27,400 | 250. | 285. | 700. | 12,500. | — |
| 1843 | 75,462 | 380. | 415. | 700. | 7500. | — |
| 1843O | 175,162 | 380. | 415. | 600. | 7750. | — |
| 1844 | 6,361 | 475. | 1300. | 3600. | — | — |
| 1844O | 118,700 | 380. | 425. | 600. | 11,000. | — |
| 1845 | 26,153 | 380. | 750. | 2100. | — | — |
| 1845O | 47,500 | 350. | 425. | 800. | 12,500. | — |
| 1846 | 20,095 | 500. | 900. | 2850. | — | — |
| 1846O | 81,780 | 350. | 600. | 1400. | — | — |
| 1847 | 862,258 | 240. | 265. | 325. | 5250. | — |
| 1847O | 571,500 | 250. | 290. | 400. | 5000. | — |
| 1848 | 145,484 | 300. | 350. | 400. | 5500. | — |
| 1848O | 38,850 | 400. | 600. | 1400. | — | — |
| 1849 | 653,618 | 240. | 265. | 300. | 3850. | — |
| 1849O | 23,900 | 500. | 800. | 3600. | — | — |
| 1850 | 291,451 | 240. | 265. | 300. | 3850. | — |
| 1850O | 57,500 | 350. | 400. | 600. | — | — |
| 1851 | 176,328 | 300. | 325. | 525. | 9500. | — |
| 1851O | 263,000 | 280. | 300. | 550. | — | — |
| 1852 | 263,106 | 330. | 425. | 525. | 3850. | — |
| 1852O | 18,000 | 500. | 700. | 2600. | — | — |
| 1853 | 201,253 | 240. | 265. | 300. | 3850. | — |
| 1853O | 51,000 | 350. | 400. | 575. | — | — |
| 1854 | 54,250 | 350. | 400. | 700. | — | — |
| 1854O sm. dt. | 52,500 | 225. | 400. | 1250. | 12,000. | — |
| 1854O lg. dt. | Inc. Ab. | 375. | 600. | 2250. | — | — |
| 1854S | 123,826 | 280. | 300. | 575. | 11,000. | — |
| 1855 | 121,701 | 240. | 265. | 300. | 3850. | — |
| 1855O | 18,000 | 350. | 600. | 2000. | — | — |
| 1855S | 9,000 | 850. | 1900. | 4250. | — | — |
| 1856 | 60,490 | 300. | 330. | 360. | 4800. | — |
| 1856O | 14,500 | 400. | 600. | 2900. | — | — |
| 1856S | 68,000 | 330. | 380. | 625. | 10,000. | — |
| 1857 | 16,606 | 330. | 380. | 1000. | — | — |
| 1857O | 5,500 | 700. | 1000. | 3000. | — | — |
| 1857S | 26,000 | 380. | 525. | 800. | 7750. | — |
| 1858 | 2,521 | 2500. | 5000. | 11,000. | — | — |
| 1858O | 20,000 | 330. | 380. | 850. | 12,000. | — |

# 1853 Gold $10
## Grade XF-40

—•— Retail Price

Source: COIN PRICES

PRICING SECTION

| Date | Mintage | F-12 | VF-20 | XF-40 | MS-60 | Prf-65 |
|------|---------|------|-------|-------|-------|--------|
| 1858S | 11,800 | 750. | 2150. | 7000. | — | — |
| 1859 | 16,093 | 330. | 380. | 1000. | — | — |
| 1859O | 2,300 | 1275. | 3500. | 9000. | — | — |
| 1859S | 7,000 | 900. | 2500. | 7400. | — | — |
| 1860 | 15,105 | 330. | 380. | 1000. | 12,500. | — |
| 1860O | 11,100 | 400. | 575. | 2100. | 17,000. | — |
| 1860S | 5,000 | 750. | 2700. | 9000. | — | — |
| 1861 | 113,233 | 280. | 325. | 375. | 8000. | — |
| 1861S | 15,500 | 675. | 1900. | 4750. | — | — |
| 1862 | 10,995 | 350. | 475. | 1350. | — | — |
| 1862S | 12,500 | 700. | 1950. | 5000. | — | — |
| 1863 | 1,248 | 2000. | 3650. | 11,000. | 50,000. | — |
| 1863S | 10,000 | 725. | 1700. | 6500. | — | — |
| 1864 | 3,580 | 800. | 1900. | 4900. | — | — |
| 1864S | 2,500 | 2750. | 5800. | 11,500. | — | — |
| 1865 | 4,005 | 750. | 2150. | 5250. | — | — |
| 1865S | 16,700 | 1450. | 5000. | 20,000. | — | — |
| 1865S/inverted 186 | — | — | 2500. | 7500. | — | — |
| 1866S | 8,500 | 1300. | 3000. | 6500. | — | — |

### New-style head, with motto

**Notes:** In 1866 the motto "In God We Trust" was added above the eagle on the reverse. The 1873 "closed-3" and "open-3" varieties are distinguished by the amount of space between the upper left and lower left serifs of the 3 in the date.

| Date | Mintage | VF-20 | XF-40 | AU-50 | MS-60 | MS-65 | Prf-65 |
|------|---------|-------|-------|-------|-------|-------|--------|
| 1866 | 3,780 | 750. | 3000. | 6750. | — | — | 60,000. |
| 1866S | 11,500 | 1750. | 3900. | 9500. | — | — | — |
| 1867 | 3,140 | 1750. | 4500. | 10,500. | — | — | 60,000. |
| 1867S | 9,000 | 2600. | 8500. | 20,000. | — | — | — |
| 1868 | 10,655 | 600. | 1800. | 5750. | 15,000. | — | 60,000. |
| 1868S | 13,500 | 1600. | 5000. | 20,000. | — | — | — |
| 1869 | 1,855 | 1750. | 5000. | 11,500. | — | — | 65,000. |
| 1869S | 6,430 | 1800. | 5000. | 11,500. | — | — | — |
| 1870 | 4,025 | 750. | 1450. | 5000. | — | — | 60,000. |
| 1870CC | 5,908 | 7000. | 19,000. | 32,500. | — | — | — |
| 1870S | 8,000 | 2000. | 7500. | 14,000. | — | — | — |
| 1871 | 1,820 | 1600. | 4000. | 8750. | 3500. | — | 60,000. |
| 1871CC | 8,085 | 2250. | 6000. | 15,000. | — | — | — |
| 1871S | 16,500 | 1750. | 4700. | 8000. | — | — | — |
| 1872 | 1,650 | 3000. | 8000. | 18,000. | — | — | 60,000. |
| 1872CC | 4,600 | 2500. | 10,000. | 25,000. | — | — | — |
| 1872S | 17,300 | 900. | 2000. | 8500. | — | — | — |
| 1873 closed 3 | 825 | 4200. | 14,000. | 28,000. | — | — | 60,000. |
| 1873CC | 4,543 | 2700. | 12,000. | 27,000. | — | — | — |
| 1873S | 12,000 | 1600. | 5000. | 9000. | — | — | — |
| 1874 | 53,160 | 300. | 350. | 550. | 2450. | — | 60,000. |
| 1874CC | 16,767 | 875. | 5000. | 10,500. | — | — | — |
| 1874S | 10,000 | 1700. | 5000. | 14,250. | — | — | — |
| 1875 | 120 | Akers, Aug. 1990, proof, $115,000. | | | | | — |
| 1875CC | 7,715 | 2500. | 15,000. | 35,000. | — | — | — |
| 1876 | 732 | 3000. | 11,000. | 20,000. | — | — | 50,000. |
| 1876CC | 4,696 | 3000. | 10,000. | 19,000. | — | — | — |
| 1876S | 5,000 | 2100. | 4000. | 12,000. | — | — | — |
| 1877 | 817 | 3500. | 9000. | 16,000. | — | — | 40,000. |
| 1877CC | 3,332 | 2400. | 6000. | 13,000. | — | — | — |
| 1877S | 17,000 | 600. | 2200. | 7500. | — | — | — |
| 1878 | 73,800 | 290. | 350. | 450. | 2550. | — | 50,000. |
| 1878CC | 3,244 | 3500. | 11,750. | 27,000. | — | — | — |
| 1878S | 26,100 | 650. | 2000. | 10,000. | — | — | — |
| 1879 | 384,770 | 285. | 300. | 375. | 850. | — | 40,000. |
| 1879CC | 1,762 | 5000. | 12,500. | 26,000. | — | — | — |
| 1879O | 1,500 | 2200. | 7700. | 17,000. | — | — | — |
| 1879S | 224,000 | 310. | 360. | 425. | 1700. | — | — |
| 1880 | 1,644,876 | 265. | 280. | 285. | 400. | — | 40,000. |
| 1880CC | 11,190 | 425. | 675. | 2200. | 8500. | — | — |
| 1880O | 9,200 | 400. | 950. | 3000. | 7500. | — | — |
| 1880S | 506,250 | 265. | 285. | 325. | 600. | — | — |
| 1881 | 3,877,260 | 265. | 285. | 310. | 350. | — | 40,000. |
| 1881CC | 24,015 | 400. | 550. | 1300. | 7500. | — | — |
| 1881O | 8,350 | 400. | 875. | 3000. | 8000. | — | — |

| Date | Mintage | VF-20 | XF-40 | AU-50 | MS-60 | MS-65 | Prf-65 |
|------|--------:|------:|------:|------:|------:|------:|-------:|
| 1881S | 970,000 | 265. | 280. | 300. | 450. | 6500. | — |
| 1882 | 2,324,480 | 265. | 280. | 285. | 325. | 6500. | 40,000. |
| 1882CC | 6,764 | 475. | 1800. | 5250. | 10,000. | — | — |
| 1882O | 10,820 | 400. | 850. | 2500. | 5000. | — | — |
| 1882S | 132,000 | 265. | 280. | 300. | 1100. | 13,500. | — |
| 1883 | 208,740 | 275. | 285. | 325. | 450. | 6500. | 40,000. |
| 1883CC | 12,000 | 400. | 850. | 3000. | 9250. | — | — |
| 1883O | 800 | 3200. | 8500. | 17,000. | 37,500. | — | — |
| 1883S | 38,000 | 295. | 375. | 450. | 1350. | 13,500. | — |
| 1884 | 76,905 | 265. | 285. | 400. | 1850. | 13,500. | 86,000. |
| 1884CC | 9,925 | 525. | 1300. | 4000. | 10,000. | — | — |
| 1884S | 124,250 | 265. | 280. | 400. | 1300. | 6500. | — |
| 1885 | 253,527 | 265. | 280. | 300. | 775. | 6500. | 40,000. |
| 1885S | 228,000 | 265. | 280. | 360. | 600. | 6500. | — |
| 1886 | 236,160 | 280. | 300. | 400. | 1100. | 6500. | 40,000. |
| 1886S | 826,000 | 265. | 280. | 295. | 340. | 6500. | — |
| 1887 | 53,680 | 310. | 300. | 475. | 1800. | 50,000. | 40,000. |
| 1887S | 817,000 | 265. | 280. | 300. | 425. | 6500. | — |
| 1888 | 132,996 | 300. | 325. | 365. | 1500. | 50,000. | 40,000. |
| 1888O | 21,335 | 265. | 285. | 350. | 750. | — | — |
| 1888S | 648,700 | 265. | 285. | 300. | 500. | 6500. | — |
| 1889 | 4,485 | 400. | 500. | 1000. | 3750. | — | 40,000. |
| 1889S | 425,400 | 265. | 280. | 285. | 375. | 6500. | — |
| 1890 | 58,043 | 300. | 315. | 425. | 2250. | 13,500. | 40,000. |
| 1890CC | 17,500 | 375. | 450. | 600. | 2000. | — | — |
| 1891 | 91,868 | 265. | 280. | 300. | 450. | 13,500. | 40,000. |
| 1891CC | 103,732 | 300. | 350. | 550. | 1000. | — | — |
| 1892 | 797,552 | 285. | 280. | 295. | 325. | 6500. | 40,000. |
| 1892CC | 40,000 | 375. | 550. | 1000. | 4000. | — | — |
| 1892O | 28,688 | 285. | 300. | 325. | 600. | — | — |
| 1892S | 115,500 | 300. | 310. | 350. | 750. | 13,500. | — |
| 1893 | 1,840,895 | 265. | 280. | 300. | 350. | 5000. | 40,000. |
| 1893CC | 14,000 | 380. | 600. | 1075. | 2700. | — | — |
| 1893O | 17,000 | 265. | 280. | 350. | 675. | — | — |
| 1893S | 141,350 | 300. | 310. | 350. | 800. | 13,500. | — |
| 1894 | 2,470,778 | 265. | 280. | 295. | 360. | 5000. | 40,000. |
| 1894O | 107,500 | 265. | 280. | 375. | 2000. | 13,500. | — |
| 1894S | 25,000 | 300. | 475. | 1200. | 4500. | 13,500. | — |
| 1895 | 567,826 | 265. | 280. | 295. | 325. | 6500. | 40,000. |
| 1895O | 98,000 | 265. | 300. | 325. | 650. | 13,500. | — |
| 1895S | 49,000 | 265. | 400. | 1250. | 4000. | 40,000. | — |
| 1896 | 76,348 | 265. | 280. | 295. | 350. | 6500. | 40,000. |
| 1896S | 123,750 | 265. | 350. | 1000. | 6750. | — | — |
| 1897 | 1,000,159 | 265. | 280. | 295. | 325. | 5000. | 40,000. |
| 1897O | 42,500 | 265. | 300. | 375. | 850. | 11,000. | — |
| 1897S | 234,750 | 265. | 325. | 500. | 2000. | 6500. | — |
| 1898 | 812,197 | 265. | 280. | 295. | 325. | 6500. | 40,000. |
| 1898S | 473,600 | 265. | 280. | 350. | 525. | 6500. | — |
| 1899 | 1,262,305 | 265. | 280. | 295. | 325. | 5000. | 40,000. |
| 1899O | 37,047 | 300. | 315. | 375. | 950. | 13,500. | — |
| 1899S | 841,000 | 265. | 300. | 325. | 475. | 6500. | — |
| 1900 | 293,960 | 265. | 280. | 295. | 325. | 6500. | 40,000. |
| 1900S | 81,000 | 300. | 330. | 400. | 1600. | 12,500. | — |
| 1901 | 1,718,825 | 265. | 280. | 295. | 325. | 4500. | 40,000. |
| 1901O | 72,041 | 300. | 325. | 350. | 675. | 13,500. | — |
| 1901S | 2,812,750 | 265. | 280. | 295. | 300. | 4500. | — |
| 1902 | 82,513 | 265. | 280. | 295. | 350. | 12,500. | 40,000. |
| 1902S | 469,500 | 265. | 280. | 295. | 350. | 6500. | — |
| 1903 | 125,926 | 265. | 280. | 295. | 350. | 6500. | 40,000. |
| 1903O | 112,771 | 265. | 290. | 325. | 565. | 6500. | — |
| 1903S | 538,000 | 265. | 300. | 340. | 375. | 6500. | — |
| 1904 | 162,038 | 265. | 280. | 295. | 325. | 6500. | 40,000. |
| 1904O | 108,950 | 265. | 300. | 350. | 575. | 6500. | — |
| 1905 | 201,078 | 265. | 280. | 295. | 325. | 6500. | 40,000. |
| 1905S | 369,250 | 265. | 350. | 425. | 4000. | 6500. | — |
| 1906 | 165,497 | 265. | 280. | 295. | 325. | 6500. | 40,000. |
| 1906D | 981,000 | 265. | 280. | 295. | 325. | 6500. | — |
| 1906O | 86,895 | 265. | 310. | 350. | 750. | 13,500. | — |
| 1906S | 457,000 | 280. | 300. | 325. | 675. | 6500. | — |
| 1907 | 1,203,973 | 265. | 280. | 295. | 325. | 5000. | 40,000. |
| 1907D | 1,030,000 | 265. | 280. | 295. | 325. | 5000. | — |
| 1907S | 210,500 | 275. | 325. | 400. | 1000. | 6500. | — |

# Indian Head

## No motto

**Designer:** Augustus Saint-Gaudens. **Size:** 27 millimeters. **Weight:** 16.718 grams. **Composition:** 90% gold (0.4839 ounces), 10% copper. **Notes:** 1907 varieties are distinguished by whether the edge is rolled or wired, and whether the legend "E Pluribus Unum" has periods between each word.

| Date | Mintage | VF-20 | XF-40 | AU-50 | MS-60 | MS-63 | MS-65 | Prf-65 |
|---|---|---|---|---|---|---|---|---|
| 1907 wire edge, periods before & after leg. | | | | | | | | |
| | 500 | — | 4500. | — | 7800. | 12,000. | 39,000. | 60,000. |
| 1907 same, without stars on edge | | | | | | | | |
| | | — | Unique | — | — | — | — | — |
| 1907 rolled edge, periods | | | | | | | | |
| | 42 | — | — | — | 21,500. | 34,000. | 60,000. | — |
| 1907 without periods | | | | | | | | |
| | 239,406 | 425. | 450. | 500. | 625. | 2200. | 9000. | — |
| 1908 without motto | | | | | | | | |
| | 33,500 | 535. | 585. | 600. | 900. | 3350. | 12,000. | — |
| 1908D without motto | | | | | | | | |
| | 210,000 | 400. | 425. | 500. | 720. | 4100. | 36,000. | — |

# 1933 Gold $10
## Grade MS-60

- Retail Price

Source: COIN PRICES

### With motto

**Notes:** In 1908 the motto "In God We Trust" was added on the reverse to the left of the eagle.

| Date | Mintage | VF-20 | XF-40 | AU-50 | MS-60 | MS-63 | MS-65 | Prf-65 |
|---|---|---|---|---|---|---|---|---|
| 1908 | 341,486 | 375. | 390. | 400. | 420. | 1700. | 7550. | 35,000. |
| 1908D | 836,500 | 375. | 400. | 525. | 710. | 3500. | 24,000. | — |
| 1908S | 59,850 | 400. | 535. | 700. | 2500. | 6600. | 34,000. | — |
| 1909 | 184,863 | 360. | 390. | 400. | 480. | 2450. | 15,500. | 39,000. |
| 1909D | 121,540 | 400. | 440. | 500. | 975. | 11,000. | 42,000. | — |
| 1909S | 292,350 | 375. | 425. | 475. | 840. | 2650. | 14,500. | — |
| 1910 | 318,704 | 380. | 390. | 400. | 430. | 1600. | 7550. | 35,000. |
| 1910D | 2,356,640 | 360. | 390. | 400. | 445. | 1600. | 7800. | — |
| 1910S | 811,000 | 475. | 500. | 550. | 1050. | 4100. | 48,000. | — |
| 1911 | 505,595 | 360. | 375. | 400. | 430. | 2300. | 7200. | 35,000. |
| 1911D | 30,100 | 400. | 550. | 750. | 4800. | 12,500. | 90,000. | — |
| 1911S | 51,000 | 350. | 450. | 600. | 1500. | 3250. | 9100. | — |
| 1912 | 405,083 | 350. | 390. | 400. | 435. | 1600. | 8400. | 35,000. |
| 1912S | 300,000 | 350. | 400. | 510. | 900. | 2500. | 46,000. | — |
| 1913 | 442,071 | 350. | 375. | 400. | 430. | 1100. | 8400. | 35,000. |
| 1913S | 66,000 | 550. | 650. | 780. | 5150. | 25,000. | 162,000. | — |
| 1914 | 151,050 | 320. | 350. | 360. | 395. | 1800. | 10,500. | 35,000. |
| 1914D | 343,500 | 320. | 360. | 370. | 400. | 1700. | 10,500. | — |
| 1914S | 208,000 | 350. | 375. | 500. | 635. | 3700. | 39,500. | — |
| 1915 | 351,075 | 320. | 360. | 380. | 480. | 1700. | 7450. | 42,000. |
| 1915S | 59,000 | 350. | 500. | 575. | 2700. | 8800. | 73,000. | — |
| 1916S | 138,500 | 375. | 475. | 535. | 725. | 3500. | 18,500. | — |
| 1920S | 126,500 | 6500. | 7500. | 8000. | 15,000. | 33,000. | 120,000. | — |
| 1926 | 1,014,000 | 380. | 390. | 400. | 445. | 1600. | 6700. | — |
| 1930S | 96,000 | 3500. | 5000. | 7500. | 8300. | 12,500. | 51,000. | — |
| 1932 | 4,463,000 | 380. | 390. | 400. | 445. | 1600. | 6000. | — |
| 1933 | 312,500 | — | — | — | 57,000. | 87,000. | 450,000. | — |

# Gold $20 (Double Eagle)

## Coronet Head

### "Twenty D.," no motto

**Designer:** James B. Longacre. **Size:** 34 millimeters. **Weight:** 33.436 grams. **Composition:** 90% gold (0.9677 ounces), 10% copper. **Notes:** In 1861 the reverse was redesigned by Anthony C. Paquet, but it was withdrawn soon after its release. The letters in the inscriptions on the Paquet-reverse variety are taller than those on the regular reverse.

| Date | Mintage | VF-20 | XF-40 | AU-50 | MS-60 | MS-65 | Prf-65 |
|---|---|---|---|---|---|---|---|
| 1849 | 1 | | Unique, in Smithsonion collection | | | — | — |
| 1850 | 1,170,261 | 530. | 625. | 1000. | 4100. | — | — |
| 1850O | 141,000 | 600. | 1100. | 3000. | 7500. | — | — |
| 1851 | 2,087,155 | 490. | 525. | 650. | 2750. | — | — |
| 1851O | 315,000 | 600. | 750. | 1700. | 11,500. | — | — |
| 1852 | 2,053,026 | 500. | 525. | 675. | 2200. | — | — |
| 1852O | 190,000 | 600. | 750. | 2400. | 12,000. | — | — |
| 1853 | 1,261,326 | 490. | 600. | 800. | 5500. | — | — |
| 1853O | 71,000 | 625. | 1000. | 3400. | 7500. | — | — |
| 1854 | 757,899 | 500. | 625. | 950. | 6500. | — | — |
| 1854O | 3,250 | 13,500. | 30,000. | 60,000. | — | — | — |
| 1854S | 141,468 | 550. | 650. | 1000. | 4750. | 28,000. | — |
| 1855 | 364,666 | 550. | 575. | 1000. | 9000. | 28,000. | — |
| 1855O | 8,000 | 3000. | 6000. | 14,750. | — | — | — |
| 1855S | 879,675 | 500. | 575. | 1200. | 8750. | — | — |
| 1856 | 329,878 | 500. | 575. | 1000. | 8750. | — | — |
| 1856O | 2,250 | 15,000. | 30,000. | 60,000. | — | — | — |
| 1856S | 1,189,750 | 500. | 575. | 850. | 5800. | — | — |
| 1857 | 439,375 | 500. | 565. | 825. | 5000. | — | — |
| 1857O | 30,000 | 800. | 1600. | 4500. | — | — | — |
| 1857S | 970,500 | 500. | 575. | 850. | 6000. | — | — |
| 1858 | 211,714 | 550. | 700. | 1850. | 6500. | — | — |
| 1858O | 35,250 | 1000. | 1750. | 6000. | 8000. | — | — |
| 1858S | 846,710 | 500. | 575. | 925. | 8500. | — | — |
| 1859 | 43,597 | 900. | 2250. | 8000. | 30,000. | — | — |
| 1859O | 9,100 | 2750. | 6750. | 15,000. | — | — | — |
| 1859S | 636,445 | 500. | 600. | 1000. | 6750. | — | — |
| 1860 | 577,670 | 500. | 600. | 800. | 6500. | — | — |
| 1860O | 6,600 | 3000. | 6250. | 14,000. | — | — | — |
| 1860S | 544,950 | 500. | 600. | 1450. | 7250. | — | — |
| 1861 | 2,976,453 | 500. | 520. | 700. | 2750. | — | — |

**Paquet reverse**

| Date | Mintage | VF-20 | XF-40 | AU-50 | MS-60 | MS-65 | Prf-65 |
|---|---|---|---|---|---|---|---|
| 1861 Paquet rev. | Inc. Ab. | | | | | | |
| | | Bowers & Merena, Nov. 1988, MS-67, $660,000. | | | | | — |
| 1861O | 17,741 | 1750. | 3750. | 7000. | — | — | — |
| 1861S | 768,000 | 550. | 650. | 1500. | 7500. | — | — |
| 1861S Paquet rev. | Inc. Ab. | 4500. | 9750. | 20,000. | — | — | — |
| 1862 | 92,133 | 725. | 1600. | 3750. | 14,750. | — | — |
| 1862S | 854,173 | 550. | 775. | 1700. | 8000. | — | — |
| 1863 | 142,790 | 550. | 900. | 1800. | 12,500. | — | — |
| 1863S | 966,570 | 490. | 600. | 1400. | 6750. | — | — |
| 1864 | 204,285 | 550. | 700. | 2000. | 10,500. | — | — |
| 1864S | 793,660 | 550. | 825. | 2800. | 10,000. | — | — |
| 1865 | 351,200 | 475. | 600. | 1050. | 7000. | — | — |
| 1865S | 1,042,500 | 490. | 545. | 1400. | 8000. | — | — |
| 1866S | Inc. Below | 1350. | 3750. | 7750. | — | — | — |

**"Twenty D.," with motto**

**Notes:** In 1866 the motto "In God We Trust" was added to the reverse above the eagle. The 1873 "closed-3" and "open-3" varieties are distinguished by the amount of space between the upper left and lower left serif in the 3 in the date.

| Date | Mintage | VF-20 | XF-40 | AU-50 | MS-60 | MS-65 | Prf-65 |
|------|---------|-------|-------|-------|-------|-------|--------|
| 1866 | 698,775 | 485. | 625. | 1500. | 8000. | — | — |
| 1866S | 842,250 | 500. | 800. | 2600. | — | — | — |
| 1867 | 251,065 | 485. | 500. | 750. | 1500. | — | — |
| 1867S | 920,750 | 485. | 625. | 1675. | 13,250. | — | — |
| 1868 | 98,600 | 550. | 900. | 2450. | 7500. | — | — |
| 1868S | 837,500 | 485. | 725. | 1900. | 10,250. | — | — |
| 1869 | 175,155 | 485. | 750. | 2200. | 6000. | 44,000. | — |
| 1869S | 686,750 | 485. | 600. | 1750. | 6250. | — | — |
| 1870 | 155,185 | 500. | 1000. | 2700. | — | — | — |
| 1870CC | 3,789 | 35,000. | 65,000. | 80,000. | 125,000. | — | — |
| 1870S | 982,000 | 485. | 550. | 775. | 6000. | — | — |
| 1871 | 80,150 | 700. | 1100. | 2250. | 6500. | — | — |
| 1871CC | 17,387 | 1850. | 4500. | 10,500. | 35,000. | — | — |
| 1871S | 928,000 | 485. | 550. | 850. | 5500. | — | — |
| 1872 | 251,880 | 485. | 500. | 700. | 4000. | — | — |
| 1872CC | 26,900 | 1100. | 1650. | 6100. | 14,000. | — | — |
| 1872S | 780,000 | 485. | 525. | 675. | 2500. | — | — |
| 1873 closed 3 | Est. 208,925 | 600. | 825. | 1700. | 15,000. | — | — |
| 1873 open 3 | Est. 1,500,900 | 480. | 490. | 515. | 625. | — | — |
| 1873CC | 22,410 | 950. | 1600. | 4500. | 16,000. | — | — |
| 1873S | 1,040,600 | 485. | 525. | 575. | 1950. | — | — |
| 1874 | 366,800 | 475. | 550. | 825. | 1900. | — | — |
| 1874CC | 115,085 | 550. | 700. | 2350. | 11,500. | — | — |
| 1874S | 1,214,000 | 485. | 500. | 650. | 2200. | — | — |
| 1875 | 295,740 | 490. | 525. | 550. | 975. | — | — |
| 1875CC | 111,151 | 525. | 650. | 750. | 2400. | — | — |
| 1875S | 1,230,000 | 485. | 490. | 550. | 1100. | — | — |
| 1876 | 583,905 | 485. | 490. | 525. | 950. | — | — |
| 1876CC | 138,441 | 525. | 725. | 1150. | 7500. | — | — |
| 1876S | 1,597,000 | 485. | 490. | 515. | 1100. | — | — |

## "Twenty Dollars"

**Notes:** In 1877 the denomination on the reverse was changed to read "Twenty Dollars" instead of "Twenty D."

| Date | Mintage | VF-20 | XF-40 | AU-50 | MS-60 | MS-65 | Prf-65 |
|------|---------|-------|-------|-------|-------|-------|--------|
| 1877 | 397,670 | 485. | 510. | 550. | 875. | — | — |
| 1877CC | 42,565 | 600. | 850. | 1800. | — | — | — |
| 1877S | 1,735,000 | 480. | 500. | 575. | 1000. | — | — |
| 1878 | 543,645 | 480. | 500. | 550. | 750. | — | — |
| 1878CC | 13,180 | 750. | 2000. | 5250. | 18,000. | — | — |
| 1878S | 1,739,000 | 480. | 500. | 525. | 1500. | — | — |
| 1879 | 207,630 | 500. | 525. | 575. | 1650. | — | — |
| 1879CC | 10,708 | 850. | 2500. | 6500. | — | — | — |
| 1879O | 2,325 | 3250. | 4250. | 14,500. | 45,000. | — | — |
| 1879S | 1,223,800 | 480. | 490. | 550. | 1650. | — | — |
| 1880 | 51,456 | 485. | 510. | 850. | — | — | — |
| 1880S | 836,000 | 500. | 575. | 750. | — | — | — |
| 1881 | 2,260 | 3500. | 7500. | 16,500. | 45,000. | — | — |
| 1881S | 727,000 | 480. | 550. | 700. | — | — | — |
| 1882 | 630 | 8000. | 15,000. | 30,000. | 50,000. | — | — |
| 1882CC | 39,140 | 675. | 775. | 1150. | 4400. | — | — |
| 1882S | 1,125,000 | 480. | 490. | 510. | 1000. | — | — |
| 1883 | 92 | — | — | — | — | — | — |
| 1883CC | 59,962 | 600. | 625. | 1000. | 4700. | — | — |
| 1883S | 1,189,000 | 480. | 490. | 505. | 725. | — | — |
| 1884 | 71 | | | Stacks, Nov. 1989, proof, $71,500. | | — | — |
| 1884CC | 81,139 | 525. | 800. | 950. | 2900. | — | — |
| 1884S | 916,000 | 480. | 490. | 505. | 600. | — | — |
| 1885 | 828 | 6500. | 8750. | 18,500. | 42,500. | — | — |
| 1885CC | 9,450 | 1000. | 1800. | 4000. | 12,000. | — | — |
| 1885S | 683,500 | 480. | 525. | 550. | 650. | — | — |
| 1886 | 1,106 | 8000. | 12,500. | 25,000. | 32,000. | — | — |
| 1887 | 121 | — | — | — | — | — | 65,000. |
| 1887S | 283,000 | 500. | 525. | 550. | 1000. | — | — |
| 1888 | 226,266 | 480. | 525. | 550. | 1100. | — | — |
| 1888S | 859,600 | 485. | 525. | 550. | 650. | — | — |
| 1889 | 44,111 | 650. | 700. | 750. | 1175. | — | — |

# 1907-S Gold $20
## Grade VF-20

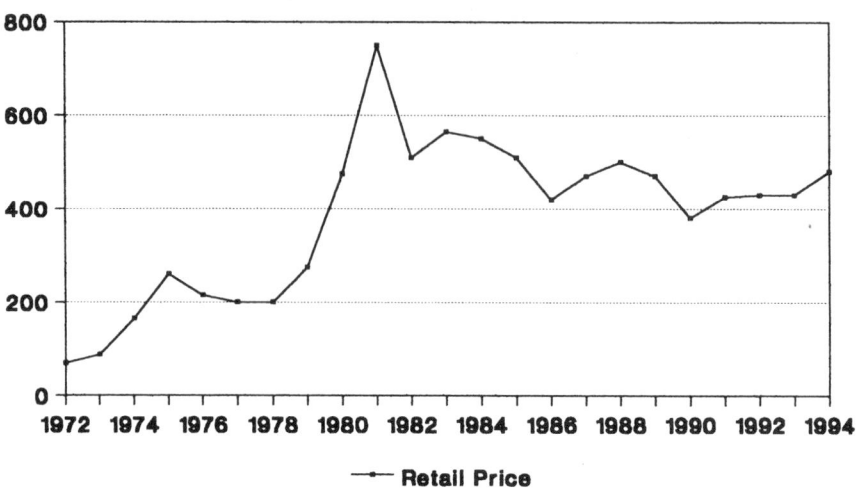

—•— Retail Price

**Source: COIN PRICES**

| Date | Mintage | VF-20 | XF-40 | AU-50 | MS-60 | MS-65 | Prf-65 |
|------|---------|-------|-------|-------|-------|-------|--------|
| 1889CC | 30,945 | 650. | 700. | 1200. | 3500. | — | — |
| 1889S | 774,700 | 480. | 525. | 550. | 700. | — | — |
| 1890 | 75,995 | 600. | 675. | 700. | 1000. | — | — |
| 1890CC | 91,209 | 675. | 725. | 950. | 4250. | — | — |
| 1890S | 802,750 | 480. | 525. | 550. | 1400. | — | — |
| 1891 | 1,442 | 3100. | 4250. | 8250. | 27,000. | — | — |
| 1891CC | 5,000 | 1900. | 2900. | 5500. | 18,000. | — | — |
| 1891S | 1,288,125 | 480. | 490. | 505. | 600. | — | — |
| 1892 | 4,523 | 1200. | 1750. | 2750. | 7000. | — | — |
| 1892CC | 27,265 | 675. | 850. | 1550. | 5750. | — | — |
| 1892S | 930,150 | 480. | 490. | 505. | 565. | — | — |
| 1893 | 344,339 | 480. | 500. | 525. | 600. | — | — |
| 1893CC | 18,402 | 675. | 925. | 1300. | 2800. | — | — |
| 1893S | 996,175 | 480. | 490. | 525. | 590. | — | — |
| 1894 | 1,368,990 | 480. | 490. | 505. | 565. | — | — |
| 1894S | 1,048,550 | 480. | 490. | 525. | 600. | — | — |
| 1895 | 1,114,656 | 480. | 490. | 505. | 520. | — | — |
| 1895S | 1,143,500 | 440. | 445. | 525. | 600. | 7200. | — |
| 1896 | 792,663 | 480. | 490. | 505. | 565. | — | — |
| 1896S | 1,403,925 | 480. | 490. | 505. | 565. | — | — |
| 1897 | 1,383,261 | 480. | 490. | 505. | 565. | — | — |
| 1897S | 1,470,250 | 480. | 500. | 525. | 565. | — | — |
| 1898 | 170,470 | 480. | 490. | 505. | 800. | — | — |
| 1898S | 2,575,175 | 480. | 490. | 505. | 565. | 7100. | — |
| 1899 | 1,669,384 | 480. | 490. | 505. | 565. | 7100. | — |
| 1899S | 2,010,300 | 480. | 490. | 505. | 580. | — | — |
| 1900 | 1,874,584 | 480. | 490. | 505. | 565. | 7100. | — |
| 1900S | 2,459,500 | 480. | 490. | 505. | 600. | 7200. | — |
| 1901 | 111,526 | 480. | 490. | 505. | 600. | 7000. | — |
| 1901S | 1,596,000 | 480. | 490. | 505. | 565. | — | — |
| 1902 | 31,254 | 550. | 600. | 700. | 1025. | 7200. | — |
| 1902S | 1,753,625 | 480. | 490. | 505. | 565. | — | — |
| 1903 | 287,428 | 480. | 490. | 505. | 565. | 7000. | — |
| 1903S | 954,000 | 480. | 490. | 505. | 565. | 7200. | — |
| 1904 | 6,256,797 | 480. | 490. | 505. | 565. | 4000. | — |
| 1904S | 5,134,175 | 480. | 490. | 505. | 565. | 7000. | — |
| 1905 | 59,011 | 525. | 550. | 575. | 1475. | — | — |
| 1905S | 1,813,000 | 480. | 490. | 505. | 565. | — | — |
| 1906 | 69,690 | 600. | 640. | 800. | 1000. | 7000. | — |
| 1906D | 620,250 | 480. | 490. | 505. | 565. | — | — |
| 1906S | 2,065,750 | 480. | 490. | 505. | 565. | — | — |
| 1907 | 1,451,864 | 480. | 490. | 505. | 565. | 7200. | — |
| 1907D | 842,250 | 480. | 490. | 505. | 565. | 7000. | — |
| 1907S | 2,165,800 | 480. | 490. | 505. | 565. | — | — |

# 1908-D Gold $20
## Grade MS-60

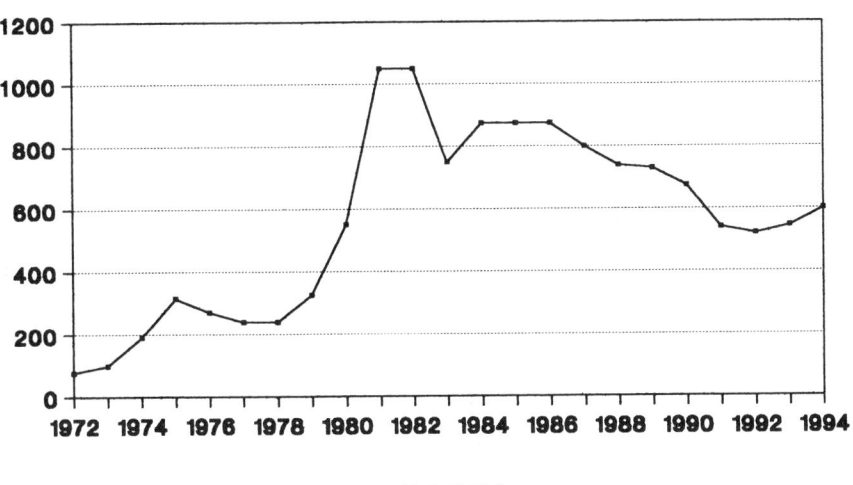

—•— **Retail Price**

**Source: COIN PRICES**

# Saint-Gaudens

### No motto

**Designer:** Augustus Saint-Gaudens. **Size:** 34 millimeters. **Weight:** 33.436 grams. **Composition:** 90% gold (0.9677 ounces), 10% copper. **Notes:** The "Roman numerals" varieties for 1907 use Roman numerals for the date instead of Arabic numerals. The lettered-edge varieties have "E Pluribus Unum" on the edge, with stars between the words.

| Date | Mintage | VF-20 | XF-40 | AU-50 | MS-60 | MS-63 | MS-65 | Prf-65 |
|------|---------|-------|-------|-------|-------|-------|-------|--------|
| 1907 extremely high relief, plain edge | | | | | | | | |
| | — | | Unique | — | — | — | — | — |
| 1907 extremely high relief, lettered edge | | | | | | | | |
| | Unrecorded | | | Prf-68 Private sale 1990 $1,500,000. | | | — | — |
| 1907 high relief, Roman numerals, plain edge | | | | | | | | |
| | | | Unique - AU-55 $150,000. | | — | — | — | — |
| 1907 high relief, Roman numerals, wire rim | | | | | | | | |
| | 11,250 | 2500. | 3600. | 4000. | 6400. | 11,000. | 30,000. | — |
| 1907 high relief, Roman numerals, flat rim | | | | | | | | |
| | Inc. Ab. | 3000. | 4000. | 4500. | 6500. | 12,500. | 35,000. | — |
| 1907 large letters on edge | | | | | | Unique | — | — |
| 1907 small letters on edge | | | | | | | | |
| | 361,667 | 495. | 515. | 535. | 610. | 950. | 4550. | — |
| 1908 | 4,271,551 | 495. | 505. | 525. | 585. | 700. | 1650. | — |
| 1908D | 663,750 | 495. | 505. | 520. | 600. | 1100. | 10,750. | — |

## With motto

**Notes:** In 1908 the motto "In God We Trust" was added at the bottom of the reverse.

| Date | Mintage | VF-20 | XF-40 | AU-50 | MS-60 | MS-63 | MS-65 | Prf-65 |
|---|---|---|---|---|---|---|---|---|
| 1908 | 156,359 | 495. | 505. | 550. | 600. | 1800. | 13,250. | 41,000. |
| 1908D | 349,500 | 495. | 505. | 550. | 585. | 1125. | 3650. | — |
| 1908S | 22,000 | 800. | 1150. | 1350. | 3000. | 9600. | 27,500. | — |
| 1909/8 | 161,282 | 500. | 465. | 600. | 2000. | 6850. | 48,000. | — |
| 1909 | Inc. Ab. | 495. | 505. | 550. | 875. | 10,000. | 38,500. | 45,000. |
| 1909D | 52,500 | 575. | 600. | 650. | 1325. | 3250. | 36,000. | — |
| 1909S | 2,774,925 | 495. | 505. | 510. | 585. | 645. | 4800. | — |
| 1910 | 482,167 | 495. | 505. | 520. | 585. | 880. | 7900. | 50,000. |
| 1910D | 429,000 | 495. | 505. | 520. | 575. | 870. | 4550. | — |
| 1910S | 2,128,250 | 495. | 505. | 520. | 575. | 1100. | 14,000. | — |
| 1911 | 197,350 | 495. | 505. | 520. | 585. | 2300. | 11,000. | 41,000. |
| 1911D | 846,500 | 495. | 505. | 520. | 575. | 645. | 2050. | — |
| 1911S | 775,750 | 495. | 505. | 520. | 595. | 875. | 7200. | — |
| 1912 | 149,824 | 495. | 505. | 520. | 600. | 2750. | 13,250. | 41,000. |
| 1913 | 168,838 | 495. | 515. | 525. | 600. | 4150. | 18,000. | 41,000. |
| 1913D | 393,500 | 495. | 505. | 520. | 595. | 1000. | 6000. | — |
| 1913S | 34,000 | 495. | 520. | 560. | 1150. | 5600. | 27,500. | — |
| 1914 | 95,320 | 500. | 525. | 550. | 680. | 2700. | 11,000. | 41,000. |
| 1914D | 453,000 | 495. | 505. | 520. | 575. | 800. | 3750. | — |
| 1914S | 1,498,000 | 495. | 505. | 520. | 575. | 800. | 3500. | — |
| 1915 | 152,050 | 495. | 505. | 530. | 630. | 2700. | 14,000. | 56,000. |
| 1915S | 567,500 | 495. | 505. | 520. | 575. | 800. | 2150. | — |
| 1916S | 796,000 | 495. | 505. | 525. | 625. | 800. | 2050. | — |
| 1920 | 228,250 | 495. | 505. | 520. | 575. | 1400. | 15,500. | — |
| 1920S | 558,000 | 4500. | 6000. | 7200. | 18,000. | 39,500. | 96,000. | — |
| 1921 | 528,500 | 7200. | 9550. | 15,000. | 30,000. | 60,000. | 144,000. | — |
| 1922 | 1,375,500 | 495. | 505. | 520. | 575. | 800. | 6000. | — |
| 1922S | 2,658,000 | 500. | 525. | 600. | 740. | 1825. | 24,000. | — |
| 1923 | 566,000 | 495. | 505. | 520. | 575. | 800. | 7200. | — |
| 1923D | 1,702,250 | 495. | 505. | 520. | 575. | 800. | 1700. | — |
| 1924 | 4,323,500 | 495. | 505. | 520. | 575. | 775. | 1550. | — |
| 1924D | 3,049,500 | 700. | 1150. | 1350. | 2100. | 5200. | 48,000. | — |
| 1924S | 2,927,500 | 700. | 800. | 975. | 1700. | 4350. | 42,000. | — |
| 1925 | 2,831,750 | 495. | 505. | 520. | 575. | 645. | 1250. | — |
| 1925D | 2,938,500 | 875. | 1100. | 1300. | 2250. | 6500. | 45,000. | — |
| 1925S | 3,776,500 | 875. | 950. | 1200. | 4700. | 24,000. | 60,000. | — |
| 1926 | 816,750 | 495. | 505. | 520. | 575. | 800. | 1750. | — |
| 1926D | 481,000 | 1800. | 2500. | 4500. | 8500. | 35,000. | 60,000. | — |
| 1926S | 2,041,500 | 700. | 950. | 1100. | 1900. | 3500. | 38,000. | — |
| 1927 | 2,946,750 | 495. | 505. | 520. | 575. | 645. | 1250. | — |
| 1927D | 180,000 | — | — | 150,000. | 265,000. | — | 522,500. | — |
| 1927S | 3,107,000 | 2000. | 4500. | 5500. | 10,500. | 26,000. | 100,000. | — |
| 1928 | 8,816,000 | 495. | 505. | 520. | 575. | 645. | 1250. | — |
| 1929 | 1,779,750 | 4000. | 7000. | 10,000. | 15,000. | 19,000. | 57,000. | — |
| 1930S | 74,000 | 6000. | 9000. | 13,000. | 22,500. | 36,000. | 72,000. | — |
| 1931 | 2,938,250 | 4250. | 8500. | 10,000. | 15,000. | 24,000. | 66,000. | — |
| 1931D | 106,500 | 5500. | 7500. | 9500. | 15,000. | 21,500. | 60,000. | — |
| 1932 | 1,101,750 | 7000. | 9500. | 12,000. | 14,500. | 20,000. | 54,000. | — |
| 1933 | 445,500 | | | | None placed in circulation | | — | — |

# Proof sets

**Notes:** Proof sets have been sold off and on by the U.S. Mint since 1858. Listings here are for sets from what is commonly called the modern era, since 1936. Values for earlier individual proof coins are included in the regular date listings. Sets were not offered in years not listed. Since 1968, proof versions of circulating U.S. coins have been produced at the San Francisco Mint; before that they were produced at the Philadelphia Mint. In 1942 the five-cent coin was struck in two compositions. Some proof sets for that year contain only one type (five-coin set); others contain both types. Two types of packaging were used in 1955: a box and sealed Pliofilm packets. The 1960 large-date and small-date sets are distinguished by the size of the date on the cent. Some 1968 sets are missing the mintmark on the dime, the result of an error in the preparation of an obverse die. The 1970 large-date and small-date sets are distinguished by the size of the date on the cent. Some 1970 sets are missing the mintmark on the dime, the result of an error in the preparation of an obverse die. Some 1971 sets are missing the mintmark on the five-cent piece, the result of an error in the preparation of an obverse die. The 1976 three-piece set contains the quarter, half dollar and dollar with the Bicentennial designs. The 1979 and 1981 Type II sets have clearer mintmarks than the Type I sets for those years. Some 1983 sets are missing the mintmark on the dime, the result of an error in the preparation of an obverse die. Prestige sets contain the five regular-issue coins plus a commemorative silver dollar from that year: 1983, Olympics; 1984, Olympics; 1986, Statue of Liberty; 1987, Constitution Bicentennial; 1988, Olympics; 1989, Congress Bicentennial; 1990, Eisenhower; and 1991, Mount Rushmore. The 1992 prestige set contains the Olympic silver dollar and half dollar from that year.

| Date | Sets Sold | Issue Price | Value |
|---|---|---|---|
| 1936 | 3,837 | 1.89 | 3350. |
| 1937 | 5,542 | 1.89 | 2100. |
| 1938 | 8,045 | 1.89 | 950. |
| 1939 | 8,795 | 1.89 | 970. |
| 1940 | 11,246 | 1.89 | 760. |
| 1941 | 15,287 | 1.89 | 620. |
| 1942 6 coins | 21,120 | 1.89 | 620. |
| 1942 5 coins | Inc. Ab. | 1.89 | 600. |
| 1950 | 51,386 | 2.10 | 405. |
| 1951 | 57,500 | 2.10 | 285. |
| 1952 | 81,980 | 2.10 | 160. |
| 1953 | 128,800 | 2.10 | 120. |
| 1954 | 233,300 | 2.10 | 76.00 |
| 1955 box | 378,200 | 2.10 | 64.00 |
| 1955 flat pack | Inc. Ab. | 2.10 | 57.00 |
| 1956 | 669,384 | 2.10 | 25.00 |
| 1957 | 1,247,952 | 2.10 | 13.00 |
| 1958 | 875,652 | 2.10 | 19.00 |
| 1959 | 1,149,291 | 2.10 | 15.00 |
| 1960 large date | 1,691,602 | 2.10 | 11.00 |
| 1960 small date | Inc. Ab. | 2.10 | 19.50 |
| 1961 | 3,028,244 | 2.10 | 7.50 |
| 1962 | 3,218,019 | 2.10 | 7.50 |
| 1963 | 3,075,645 | 2.10 | 7.50 |
| 1964 | 3,950,762 | 2.10 | 8.50 |
| 1968S | 3,041,509 | 5.00 | 5.00 |
| 1968 S no mint mark dime | — | 5.00 | 7950. |
| 1969S | 2,934,631 | 5.00 | 4.50 |
| 1970S no mint mark dime | Est. 2,200 | 5.00 | 620. |
| 1971S | 3,224,138 | 5.00 | 3.80 |
| 1971S no mint mark nickel | Est. 1,655 | 5.00 | 850. |

| Date | Sets Sold | Issue Price | Value |
|---|---|---|---|
| 1972S | 3,267,667 | 5.00 | 4.40 |
| 1973S | 2,769,624 | 7.00 | 6.00 |
| 1974S | 2,617,350 | 7.00 | 5.00 |
| 1975S | 2,909,369 | 7.00 | 7.00 |
| 1976S 3 coins | 3,998,621 | 12.00 | 14.00 |
| 1976S | 4,149,730 | 7.00 | 10.00 |
| 1977S | 3,251,152 | 9.00 | 5.70 |
| 1978S | 3,127,788 | 9.00 | 6.50 |
| 1979S Type I | 3,677,175 | 9.00 | 7.50 |
| 1979S Type II | Inc.Ab. | 9.00 | 70.00 |
| 1980S | 3,547,030 | 10.00 | 6.95 |
| 1981S Type I | 4,063,083 | 11.00 | 8.35 |
| 1981S Type II | — | 11.00 | 165. |
| 1982S | 3,857,479 | 11.00 | 5.00 |
| 1983S Prestige set | 140,361 | 59.00 | 113. |
| 1983S | 3,138,765 | 11.00 | 5.50 |
| 1983S no mint mark dime | — | 11.00 | 470. |
| 1984S Prestige set | 316,680 | 59.00 | 28.00 |
| 1984S | 2,748,430 | 11.00 | 11.50 |
| 1985S | 3,362,821 | 11.00 | 7.50 |
| 1986S Prestige set | 599,317 | 48.50 | 27.00 |
| 1986S | 2,411,180 | 11.00 | 18.50 |
| 1987S | 3,972,233 | 11.00 | 5.00 |
| 1987S Prestige set | 435,495 | 45.00 | 20.00 |
| 1988S | 3,031,287 | 11.00 | 10.00 |
| 1988S Prestige set | 231,661 | 45.00 | 24.00 |
| 1989S | 3,009,107 | 11.00 | 9.00 |
| 1989S Prestige set | 211,087 | 45.00 | 31.00 |
| 1990S | 2,793,433 | 11.00 | 21.50 |
| 1990S no S 1¢ | 3,555 | 11.00 | 1350. |
| 1990S Prestige set | 506,126 | 45.00 | 27.00 |
| 1990S no S 1¢ Prestige set | — | 45.00 | 1350. |
| 1991S | 2,610,833 | 11.00 | 32.00 |
| 1991S Prestige set | 256,954 | 59.00 | 57.00 |
| 1992S | 2,675,618 | 12.50 | 22.00 |
| 1992S Prestige set | 183,285 | 59.00 | 59.00 |
| 1992S Silver | 1,009,585 | 21.00 | 28.00 |
| 1992S Silver premier | 308,055 | 37.00 | 28.00 |
| 1993S | — | 12.50 | 18.00 |
| 1993S Prestige set | — | 57.00 | 57.00 |
| 1993S Silver | — | 21.00 | 20.00 |
| 1993S Silver premier | — | 37.00 | 25.00 |
| 1994S | — | 12.50 | 15.00 |
| 1994S Prestige Set | — | — | 57.00 |
| 1994S Silver | — | — | 21.00 |
| 1994S Silver premier | — | — | 28.00 |

# 1952 Proof Set
## Issue Price: $2.10

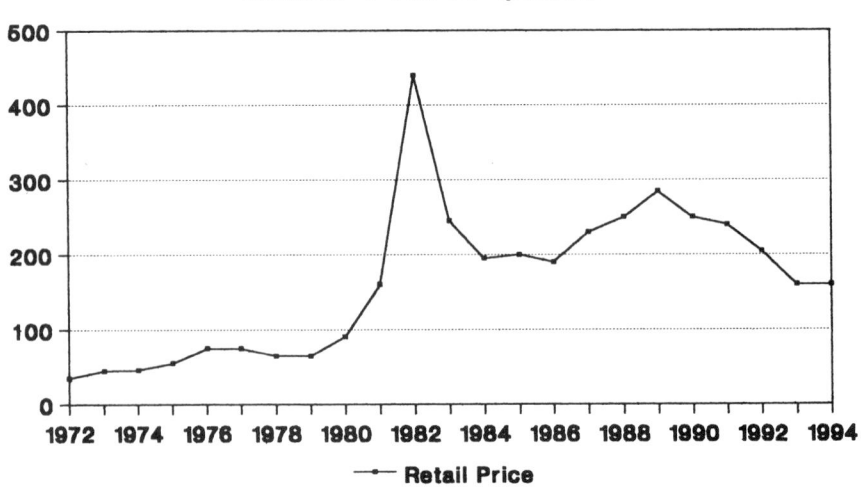

— Retail Price

Source: COIN PRICES

# Mint sets

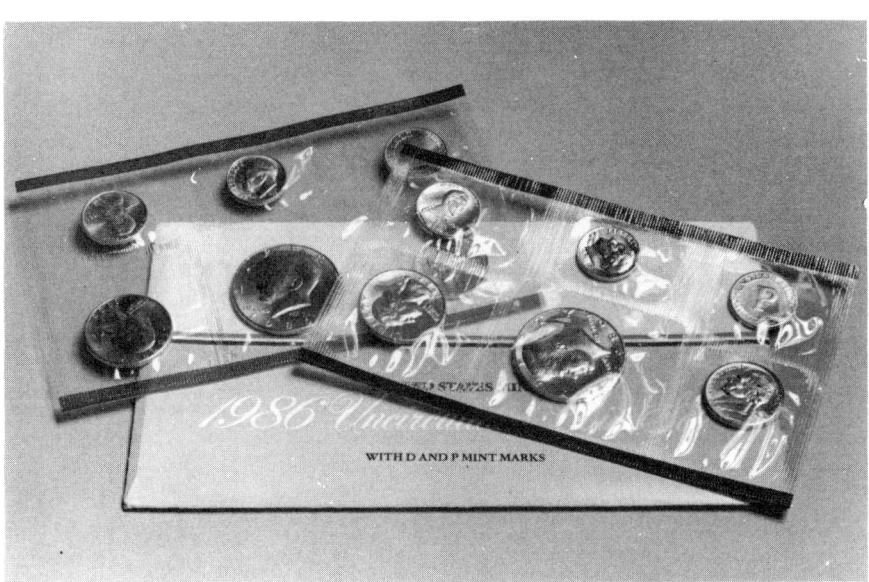

**Notes:** Mint, or uncirculated, sets contain one uncirculated coin of each denomination from each mint produced for circulation that year. Values listed here are only for those sets packaged and marketed by the U.S. Mint. Sets were not offered in years not listed. In years when the Mint did not offer the sets, some private companies packaged and marketed uncirculated sets. Mint sets from 1947 through 1958 contain two examples of each coin mounted in cardboard holders, which caused the coins to tarnish. Beginning in 1959, the sets have been packaged in sealed Pliofilm packets and include only one specimen of each non-commemorative coin authorized for that year. Listings for 1965, 1966 and 1967 are for "special mint sets," which were of higher quality than regular mint sets and were prooflike. The 1965 sets were packaged in Pliofilm; the '66 and '67 sets in plastic cases. The 1970 large-date and small-date varieties are distinguished by the size of the date on the cent. The 1976 three-piece set contains the quarter, half dollar and dollar with the Bicentennial design. The 1971 and 1972 sets do not include a dollar coin; the 1979 set does not include an S-mintmarked dollar.

| Date | Sets Sold | Issue Price | Value |
|---|---|---|---|
| 1947 | Est. 5,000 | 4.87 | 610. |
| 1948 | Est. 6,000 | 4.92 | 225. |
| 1949 | Est. 5,200 | 5.45 | 530. |
| 1950 | None issued | — | — |
| 1951 | 8,654 | 6.75 | 390. |
| 1952 | 11,499 | 6.14 | 280. |
| 1953 | 15,538 | 6.14 | 225. |
| 1954 | 25,599 | 6.19 | 105. |
| 1955 | 49,656 | 3.57 | 70.00 |
| 1956 | 45,475 | 3.34 | 57.00 |
| 1957 | 32,324 | 4.40 | 95.00 |
| 1958 | 50,314 | 4.43 | 90.00 |
| 1959 | 187,000 | 2.40 | 15.00 |
| 1960 | 260,485 | 2.40 | 14.00 |
| 1961 | 223,704 | 2.40 | 14.00 |
| 1962 | 385,285 | 2.40 | 10.50 |
| 1963 | 606,612 | 2.40 | 9.00 |
| 1964 | 1,008,108 | 2.40 | 10.00 |
| 1965 SMS* | 2,360,000 | 4.00 | 3.90 |
| 1966 SMS* | 2,261,583 | 4.00 | 4.60 |
| 1967 SMS* | 1,863,344 | 4.00 | 6.70 |
| 1968 | 2,105,128 | 2.50 | 3.35 |
| 1969 | 1,817,392 | 2.50 | 3.90 |
| 1970 large date | 2,038,134 | 2.50 | 11.00 |
| 1970 small date | Inc. Ab. | 2.50 | 39.00 |
| 1971 | 2,193,396 | 3.50 | 2.95 |
| 1972 | 2,750,000 | 3.50 | 2.80 |
| 1973 | 1,767,691 | 6.00 | 7.50 |
| 1974 | 1,975,981 | 6.00 | 6.15 |
| 1975 | 1,921,488 | 6.00 | 6.00 |
| 1976 3 coins | 4,908,319 | 9.00 | 10.00 |
| 1976 | 1,892,513 | 6.00 | 6.60 |

| Date | Sets Sold | Issue Price | Value |
|------|-----------|-------------|-------|
| 1977 | 2,006,869 | 7.00 | 5.90 |
| 1978 | 2,162,609 | 7.00 | 5.60 |
| 1979 | 2,526,000 | 8.00 | 5.35 |
| 1980 | 2,815,066 | 9.00 | 6.75 |
| 1981 | 2,908,145 | 11.00 | 8.50 |
| 1982 & 1983 | None issued | — | — |
| 1984 | 1,832,857 | 7.00 | 4.50 |
| 1985 | 1,710,571 | 7.00 | 5.00 |
| 1986 | 1,153,536 | 7.00 | 17.50 |
| 1987 | 2,890,758 | 7.00 | 5.90 |
| 1988 | 1,646,204 | 7.00 | 3.65 |
| 1989 | 1,987,915 | 7.00 | 3.10 |
| 1990 | 1,809,184 | 7.00 | 5.05 |
| 1991 | 1,352,101 | 7.00 | 6.85 |
| 1992 | — | 7.00 | 9.40 |
| 1993 | 1,500,098 | 7.00 | 10.00 |
| 1994 | — | 7.00 | 10.00 |

# Uncirculated rolls

**Notes:** Listings are for rolls containing uncirculated coins. Large-date and small-date varieties for 1960 and 1970 apply to the one-cent coins.

| Date | Cents | Nickels | Dimes | Quarters | Halves |
|------|-------|---------|-------|----------|--------|
| 1934 | 230. | 1765. | 1250. | 1100. | 1550. |
| 1934D | 900. | 3400. | 3400. | 5550. | — |
| 1934S | — | — | — | — | — |
| 1935 | 100. | 1000. | 850. | 855. | 1200. |
| 1935D | 210. | 2150. | 3300. | 5650. | 4050. |
| 1935S | 500. | 1450. | 1650. | 4550. | 6300. |
| 1936 | 69.00 | 750. | 650. | 750. | 1135. |
| 1936D | 155. | 900. | 2000. | — | 2250. |
| 1936S | 125. | 1000. | 1150. | 3650. | 3300. |
| 1937 | 50.00 | 500. | 650. | 750. | 1200. |
| 1937D | 80.00 | 750. | 1250. | 1500. | 3900. |
| 1937S | 105. | 750. | 1325. | 5400. | 3150. |
| 1938 | 69.00 | 101. | 1010. | 2140. | 1750. |
| 1938D | 100. | 140. | 1050. | — | — |
| 1938D Buffalo | — | 500. | — | — | — |
| 1938S | 50.00 | 125. | 1400. | 2455. | — |
| 1939 | 38.00 | 57.00 | 700. | 565. | 1250. |
| 1939D | 105. | 1610. | 550. | 1050. | 1300. |
| 1939S | 67.00 | 665. | 1550. | 2585. | 2250. |
| 1940 | 38.00 | 25.00 | 380. | 440. | 950. |
| 1940D | 32.00 | 76.00 | 650. | 2250. | — |
| 1940S | 32.00 | 107. | 600. | 600. | 1200. |
| 1941 | 53.00 | 31.00 | 350. | 210. | 850. |
| 1941D | 105. | 98.00 | 650. | 800. | 1150. |
| 1941S | 115. | 145. | 400. | 950. | 3500. |
| 1942 | 22.50 | 151. | 250. | 205. | 800. |
| 1942P | — | 285. | — | — | — |
| 1942D | 15.50 | 755. | 550. | 500. | 1250. |
| 1942S | 180. | 250. | 750. | 3000. | 1450. |
| 1943 | 30.00 | 140. | 250. | 140. | 750. |
| 1943D | 43.00 | 120. | 450. | 600. | 1650. |
| 1943S | 90.00 | 140. | 750. | 1200. | 1300. |
| 1944 | 14.00 | 140. | 250. | 100. | 800. |
| 1944D | 21.50 | 315. | 400. | 280. | 1100. |
| 1944S | 9.50 | 160. | 415. | 285. | 1200. |
| 1945 | 21.00 | 160. | 225. | 75.00 | 750. |
| 1945D | 9.00 | 125. | 300. | 260. | 1000. |
| 1945S | 6.50 | 85.00 | 300. | 170. | 1050. |
| 1946 | 10.50 | 17.50 | 28.00 | 145. | 1000. |
| 1946D | 9.00 | 19.00 | 35.00 | 100. | 800. |
| 1946S | 10.00 | 11.50 | 55.00 | 100. | 1000. |
| 1947 | 43.00 | 40.50 | 55.00 | 205. | 1000. |
| 1947D | 8.20 | 21.50 | 100. | 140. | 900. |
| 1947S | 25.00 | 15.50 | 85.00 | 100. | — |
| 1948 | 17.50 | 11.50 | 175. | 110. | 365. |
| 1948D | 10.50 | 51.50 | 140. | 120. | 285. |
| 1948S | 19.00 | 19.00 | 90.00 | 140. | — |
| 1949 | 19.00 | 20.00 | 550. | 650. | 900. |
| 1949D | 19.00 | 27.50 | 205. | 270. | 800. |
| 1949S | 44.00 | 39.00 | 925. | — | 1100. |
| 1950 | 26.50 | 24.00 | 90.00 | 90.00 | 550. |
| 1950D | 29.00 | 195. | 65.00 | 100. | 505. |
| 1950S | 28.50 | — | 485. | 210. | — |
| 1951 | 25.00 | 44.00 | 55.00 | 100. | 315. |
| 1951D | 10.00 | 31.50 | 60.00 | 90.00 | 700. |
| 1951S | 28.00 | 78.00 | 240. | 550. | 500. |
| 1952 | 18.50 | 29.00 | 75.00 | 90.00 | 230. |
| 1952D | 7.60 | 38.00 | 35.00 | 85.00 | 160. |
| 1952S | 73.00 | 20.00 | 225. | 330. | 895. |
| 1953 | 3.50 | 5.00 | 50.00 | 75.00 | 280. |
| 1953D | 3.50 | 5.40 | 29.00 | 50.00 | 160. |
| 1953S | 10.00 | 14.00 | 25.00 | 85.00 | 265. |

| Date | Cents | Nickels | Dimes | Quarters | Halves |
|------|-------|---------|-------|----------|--------|
| 1954 | 5.50 | 5.00 | 25.00 | 50.00 | 110. |
| 1954D | 3.50 | 6.30 | 25.00 | 50.00 | 110. |
| 1954S | 2.50 | 5.00 | 30.00 | 55.00 | 135. |
| 1955 | 4.15 | 9.50 | 30.00 | 50.00 | 150. |
| 1955D | 2.80 | 5.20 | 28.00 | 55.00 | — |
| 1955S | 12.50 | — | 27.00 | — | — |
| 1956 | 2.40 | 3.30 | 28.00 | 55.00 | 90.00 |
| 1956D | 1.90 | 3.15 | 25.00 | 55.00 | — |
| 1957 | 1.25 | 3.80 | 27.00 | 50.00 | 110. |
| 1957D | 1.45 | 3.00 | 25.00 | 50.00 | 100. |
| 1958 | 1.25 | 2.95 | 25.00 | 55.00 | 75.00 |
| 1958D | .75 | 3.00 | 25.00 | 50.00 | 70.00 |
| 1959 | .85 | 2.85 | 25.00 | 50.00 | 105. |
| 1959D | .75 | 2.85 | 25.00 | 50.00 | 105. |
| 1960 lg. dt. | .70 | 2.85 | 25.00 | 50.00 | 75.00 |
| 1960 sm. dt. | 56.50 | — | — | — | — |
| 1960D lg. dt. | .85 | 2.85 | 25.00 | 50.00 | 105. |
| 1960D sm. dt. | .85 | — | — | — | — |
| 1961 | .90 | 3.00 | 25.00 | 49.00 | 85.00 |
| 1961D | .75 | 2.95 | 25.00 | 50.00 | 85.00 |
| 1962 | .75 | 2.85 | 25.00 | 49.00 | 65.00 |
| 1962D | .75 | 3.45 | 25.00 | 49.00 | 65.00 |
| 1963 | .75 | 2.85 | 25.00 | 50.00 | 55.00 |
| 1963D | .75 | 2.85 | 24.50 | 49.00 | 55.00 |
| 1964 | .85 | 4.15 | 24.50 | 49.00 | 49.00 |
| 1964D | .85 | 4.15 | 24.50 | 49.00 | 49.00 |
| 1965 | 1.00 | 3.30 | 7.50 | 21.00 | 21.00 |
| 1966 | 1.75 | 2.85 | 8.00 | 21.00 | 21.00 |
| 1967 | .85 | 3.80 | 7.50 | 21.00 | 19.50 |
| 1968 | 1.70 | — | 7.90 | 22.50 | — |
| 1968D | 1.25 | 3.50 | 7.60 | 28.50 | 21.00 |
| 1968S | .70 | 3.80 | — | — | — |
| 1969 | 4.00 | — | 27.50 | 25.00 | — |
| 1969D | .90 | 5.00 | 12.00 | 25.00 | 21.00 |
| 1969S | 1.25 | 5.00 | — | — | — |
| 1970 | 3.50 | — | 9.00 | 19.00 | — |
| 1970D | 1.00 | 3.15 | 9.00 | 17.50 | 195. |
| 1970S | 1.10 | 3.50 | — | — | — |
| 1970S sm. dt. | 1510. | — | — | — | — |
| 1971 | 5.50 | 14.00 | 11.50 | 26.50 | 15.50 |
| 1971D | 4.50 | 4.55 | 9.00 | 35.00 | 15.50 |
| 1971S | 4.15 | — | — | — | — |
| 1972 | 1.05 | 4.15 | 9.00 | 14.00 | 19.00 |
| 1972D | 1.00 | 5.00 | 9.50 | 19.50 | 17.50 |
| 1972S | .70 | — | — | — | — |
| 1973 | 1.05 | 3.80 | 8.00 | 19.50 | 19.50 |
| 1973D | .90 | 3.50 | 8.50 | 19.50 | 16.00 |
| 1973S | 1.00 | — | — | — | — |
| 1974 | .70 | 3.80 | 9.00 | 16.00 | 16.00 |
| 1974D | .85 | 5.40 | 8.00 | 22.50 | 16.00 |
| 1974S | 1.10 | — | — | — | — |
| 1975 | 1.00 | 10.00 | 10.50 | — | — |
| 1975D | 1.00 | 6.30 | 9.50 | — | — |
| 1976 | .90 | 11.35 | 15.00 | 19.00 | 16.00 |
| 1976D | 3.15 | 9.45 | 14.00 | 19.00 | 16.00 |
| 1977 | .75 | 3.80 | 7.50 | 15.50 | 20.00 |
| 1977D | .90 | 5.65 | 7.90 | 15.50 | 20.00 |
| 1978 | 1.05 | 3.55 | 8.50 | 19.50 | 20.00 |
| 1978D | 1.00 | 4.15 | 9.50 | 15.50 | 19.50 |
| 1979 | 1.25 | 3.45 | 7.90 | 19.50 | 17.50 |
| 1979D | .85 | 4.90 | 7.90 | 19.50 | 17.50 |
| 1980 | 1.00 | 4.15 | 8.25 | 14.00 | 16.00 |
| 1980D | 1.00 | 3.30 | 7.50 | 14.00 | 16.00 |
| 1981 | .75 | 3.50 | 7.50 | 15.50 | 21.00 |
| 1981D | .90 | 3.50 | 7.00 | 15.50 | 24.00 |
| 1982 | .85 | 20.00 | 55.00 | 155. | 24.00 |
| 1982D | .90 | 44.00 | 12.50 | 20.00 | 28.50 |
| 1983 | 1.25 | 26.50 | 31.50 | 210. | 22.50 |
| 1983D | 1.40 | 29.00 | 31.50 | 165. | 19.00 |
| 1984 | 2.00 | 5.00 | 14.00 | 30.00 | 19.50 |
| 1984D | 9.15 | 5.65 | 14.50 | 70.00 | 17.50 |
| 1985 | 2.40 | 6.65 | 13.00 | 90.00 | 21.50 |
| 1985D | 2.00 | 6.50 | 11.50 | 110. | 19.50 |
| 1986 | 5.20 | 6.00 | 15.50 | 105. | 28.50 |
| 1986D | 2.20 | 29.00 | 14.50 | 80.00 | 25.00 |
| 1987 | 2.75 | 4.00 | 7.50 | 16.00 | 50.00 |
| 1987D | 1.40 | 4.00 | 7.50 | 15.50 | 50.00 |
| 1988 | 1.65 | 3.45 | 9.00 | 59.00 | 16.00 |
| 1988D | 1.90 | 3.80 | 8.20 | 17.50 | 19.00 |
| 1989 | .90 | 3.15 | 7.00 | 19.50 | 16.00 |
| 1990 | .95 | 3.15 | 7.20 | 17.00 | 14.00 |
| 1990D | 1.15 | 3.50 | 7.20 | 14.00 | 15.50 |
| 1991 | .95 | 3.50 | 8.20 | 14.50 | 14.00 |
| 1991D | .75 | 3.50 | 8.20 | 14.00 | 15.50 |
| 1992 | 1.00 | 4.15 | 7.50 | 19.50 | 14.00 |
| 1992D | .75 | 3.50 | 7.50 | 15.50 | 15.50 |
| 1993 | 1.00 | 4.15 | 7.50 | 19.50 | 14.00 |
| 1993D | .75 | 3.50 | 7.50 | 15.50 | 15.50 |
| 1994 | 1.00 | 4.15 | 7.50 | 19.50 | 16.00 |
| 1994D | .75 | 3.50 | 7.50 | 15.50 | 15.50 |

# Commemoratives, 1892-1954

## Quarter

**Designer:** Charles E. Barber. **Size:** 24.3 millimeters. **Weight:** 6.25 grams. **Composition:** 90% silver (0.1809 ounces), 10% copper.

| Date | Event | Mintage | AU-50 | MS-60 | MS-63 | MS-64 | MS-65 |
|------|-------|---------|-------|-------|-------|-------|-------|
| 1893 | Isabella (25¢) | 24,214 | 215. | 325. | 600. | 950. | 2000. |

## Half dollars

**Designers:** Alabama: Laura G. Fraser. Albany: Gertrude K. Lathrop. Arkansas: Edward E. Burr. Bay Bridge: Jacques Schnier. Boone: Augustus Lukeman. Bridgeport: Henry Kreis. California Jubilee: Jo Mora. Cincinnati: Constance Ortmayer. Cleveland-Great Lakes: Brenda Putnam. Columbia: A. Wolfe Davidson. Columbian Expo: Olin L. Warner. Connecticut: Henry Kreis. Delaware: Carl L. Schmitz. Elgin: Trygve Rovelstad. Gettysburg: Frank Vittor. Grant: Laura G. Fraser. Hawaiian: Juliette M. Fraser. Hudson: Chester Beach. Huguenot-Walloon: George T. Morgan. Lincoln-Illinois: George T. Morgan. Iowa: Adam Pietz. Lexington-Concord: Chester Beach. Long Island: Howard K. Weinman. Lynchburg: Charles Keck. Maine: Anthony de Francisci. Maryland: Hans Schuler. Missouri: Robert Aitken. Monroe: Chester Beach. New Rochelle: Gertrude K. Lathrop. Norfolk: William M. and Marjorie E. Simpson. Oregon: James E. and Laura G. Fraser. Panama-Pacific: Charles E. Barber (obverse) and George T. Morgan (reverse). Pilgrim: Cyrus E. Dallin. Rhode Island: Arthur G. Carey and John H. Benson. Roanoke: William M. Simpson. Robinson-Arkansas: Henry Kreis (obverse) and Edward E. Burr. San Diego: Robert Aitken. Sesquicentennial: John F. Lewis. Spanish Trail: L.W. Hoffecker. Stone Mountain: Gutzon Borglum. Texas: Pompeo Coppini. Fort Vancouver: Laura G. Fraser. Vermont: Charles Keck. Booker T. Washington: Isaac S. Hathaway. Washington-Carver: Isaac S. Hathaway. Wisconsin: David Parsons. York County: Walter H. Rich. **Size:** 30.6 millimeters. **Weight:** 12.5 grams. **Composition:** 90% silver (0.3618 ounces), 10% copper. **Notes:** Values for "PDS sets" contain one example each from the Philadelphia, Denver and San Francisco mints. "Type coin" values are for the most inexpensive single coin available from the date and mintmark combinations listed. The Alabama half-dollar varieties are distinguished by whether "2x2" appears on the obverse behind the head. The Grant half-dollar varieties are distinguished by whether a star appears above the word "Grant" on the obverse. The Missouri half-dollar varieties are distinguished by whether "2 ☆ 2" appears on the obverse to the left of the head.

2x2

| Date | Event | Mintage | AU-50 | MS-60 | MS-63 | MS-64 | MS-65 |
|------|-------|---------|-------|-------|-------|-------|-------|
| 1921 | Alabama 2X2 | 6,006 | 140. | 275. | 655. | 1100. | 3400. |
| 1921 | Alabama | 59,038 | 60.00 | 195. | 580. | 1000. | 3400. |

| Date | Event | Mintage | AU-50 | MS-60 | MS-63 | MS-64 | MS-65 |
|------|-------|---------|-------|-------|-------|-------|-------|
| 1936 | Albany | 17,671 | 210. | 215. | 235. | 325. | 575. |

| Date | Event | Mintage | AU-50 | MS-60 | MS-63 | MS-64 | MS-65 |
|------|-------|---------|-------|-------|-------|-------|-------|
| 1937 | Antietam | 18,028 | 400. | 410. | 445. | 495. | 660. |

| Date | Event | Mintage | AU-50 | MS-60 | MS-63 | MS-64 | MS-65 |
|------|-------|---------|-------|-------|-------|-------|-------|
| 1935 | Arkansas PDS set | 5,505 | — | 245. | 255. | 340. | 1300. |
| 1936 | Arkansas PDS set | 9,660 | — | 245. | 255. | 340. | 1450. |
| 1937 | Arkansas PDS set | 5,505 | — | 245. | 290. | 350. | 1650. |
| 1938 | Arkansas PDS set | 3,155 | — | 365. | 425. | 680. | 2300. |
| 1939 | Arkansas PDS set | 2,104 | — | 730. | 800. | 1100. | 2800. |
|  | Arkansas type coin | — | 73.00 | 80.00 | 85.00 | 110. | 380. |

See also Robinson-Arkansas

| Date | Event | Mintage | AU-50 | MS-60 | MS-63 | MS-64 | MS-65 |
|------|-------|---------|-------|-------|-------|-------|-------|
| 1936 | Bay Bridge | 71,424 | 92.00 | 95.00 | 120. | 180. | 400. |

"1934" added to
1935-1938 issues

| Date | Event | Mintage | AU-50 | MS-60 | MS-63 | MS-64 | MS-65 |
|------|-------|---------|-------|-------|-------|-------|-------|
| 1934 | Boone | 10,007 | 92.00 | 97.00 | 105. | 115. | 180. |
| 1935 | Boone PDS set w/1934 | 5,005 | — | 545. | 970. | 400. | 1800. |
| 1935 | Boone PDS set | 2,003 | — | 255. | 275. | 340. | 545. |
| 1936 | Boone PDS set | 5,005 | — | 255. | 275. | 340. | 545. |
| 1937 | Boone PDS set | 2,506 | — | 580. | 655. | 750. | 1150. |
| 1938 | Boone PDS set | 2,100 | — | 825. | 910. | 1100. | 1900. |
|  | Boone type coin | — | 73.00 | 85.00 | 90.00 | 95.00 | 180. |

| Date | Event | Mintage | AU-50 | MS-60 | MS-63 | MS-64 | MS-65 |
|------|-------|---------|-------|-------|-------|-------|-------|
| 1936 | Bridgeport | 25,015 | 95.00 | 105. | 115. | 140. | 425. |

| Date | Event | Mintage | AU-50 | MS-60 | MS-63 | MS-64 | MS-65 |
|------|-------|---------|-------|-------|-------|-------|-------|
| 1925S | California Jubilee | 86,594 | 85.00 | 110. | 235. | 385. | 900. |

| Date | Event | Mintage | AU-50 | MS-60 | MS-63 | MS-64 | MS-65 |
|------|-------|---------|-------|-------|-------|-------|-------|
| 1936 | Cincinnati PDS set | 5,005 | — | 765. | 835. | 1050. | 2650. |
| 1936 | Cincinnati type coin | — | 245. | 255. | 275. | 340. | 700. |

| Date | Event | Mintage | AU-50 | MS-60 | MS-63 | MS-64 | MS-65 |
|------|-------|---------|-------|-------|-------|-------|-------|
| 1936 | Cleveland - Great Lakes | 50,030 | 55.00 | 61.00 | 66.00 | 110. | 305. |

| Date | Event | Mintage | AU-50 | MS-60 | MS-63 | MS-64 | MS-65 |
|------|-------|---------|-------|-------|-------|-------|-------|
| 1936 | Columbia PDS set | 9,007 | — | 560. | 620. | 700. | 790. |
| 1936 | Columbia type coin | — | 175. | 195. | 210. | 225. | 255. |

# 1892 Columbian Expo Half
## Grade MS-60

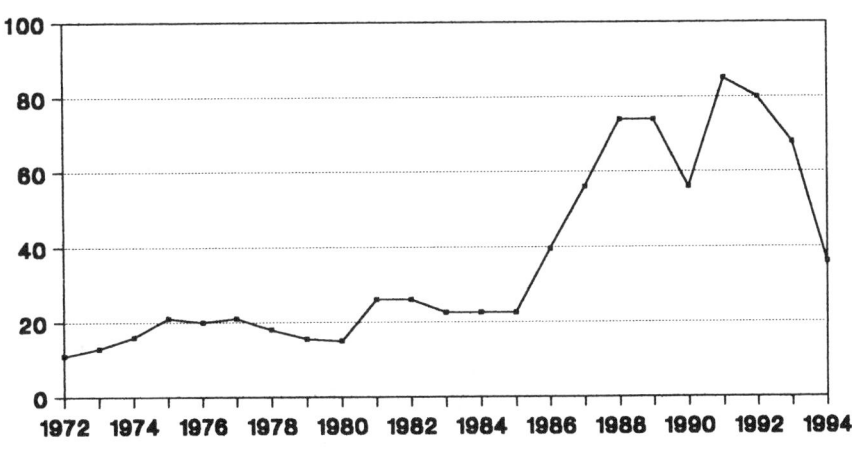

—•— **Retail Price**

**Source: COIN PRICES**

| Date | Event | Mintage | AU-50 | MS-60 | MS-63 | MS-64 | MS-65 |
|------|-------|---------|-------|-------|-------|-------|-------|
| 1892 | Columbian Expo | 950,000 | 11.00 | 32.00 | 85.00 | 265. | 700. |
| 1893 | Columbian Expo | 1,550,405 | 11.00 | 34.00 | 95.00 | 255. | 900. |

| Date | Event | Mintage | AU-50 | MS-60 | MS-63 | MS-64 | MS-65 |
|------|-------|---------|-------|-------|-------|-------|-------|
| 1935 | Connecticut | 25,018 | 160. | 195. | 215. | 340. | 700. |

| Date | Event | Mintage | AU-50 | MS-60 | MS-63 | MS-64 | MS-65 |
|------|-------|---------|-------|-------|-------|-------|-------|
| 1936 | Delaware | 20,993 | 190. | 215. | 245. | 290. | 550. |

| Date | Event | Mintage | AU-50 | MS-60 | MS-63 | MS-64 | MS-65 |
|------|-------|---------|-------|-------|-------|-------|-------|
| 1936 | Elgin | 20,015 | 180. | 205. | 215. | 245. | 275. |

| Date | Event | Mintage | AU-50 | MS-60 | MS-63 | MS-64 | MS-65 |
|------|-------|---------|-------|-------|-------|-------|-------|
| 1936 | Gettysburg | 26,928 | 210. | 225. | 265. | 350. | 700. |

  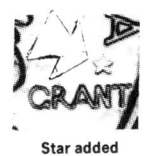

Star added

| Date | Event | Mintage | AU-50 | MS-60 | MS-63 | MS-64 | MS-65 |
|------|-------|---------|-------|-------|-------|-------|-------|
| 1922 | Grant with star | 4,256 | 535. | 885. | 2250. | 3150. | 8500. |
| 1922 | Grant | 67,405 | 68.00 | 80.00 | 215. | 400. | 950. |

| Date | Event | Mintage | AU-50 | MS-60 | MS-63 | MS-64 | MS-65 |
|------|-------|---------|-------|-------|-------|-------|-------|
| 1928 | Hawaiian | 10,008 | 825. | 1095. | 1800. | 2500. | 5250. |

| Date | Event | Mintage | AU-50 | MS-60 | MS-63 | MS-64 | MS-65 |
|------|-------|---------|-------|-------|-------|-------|-------|
| 1935 | Hudson | 10,008 | 400. | 460. | 500. | 730. | 1450. |

| Date | Event | Mintage | AU-50 | MS-60 | MS-63 | MS-64 | MS-65 |
|------|-------|---------|-------|-------|-------|-------|-------|
| 1924 | Huguenot-Walloon | 142,080 | 63.00 | 85.00 | 100. | 195. | 750. |

| Date | Event | Mintage | AU-50 | MS-60 | MS-63 | MS-64 | MS-65 |
|------|-------|---------|-------|-------|-------|-------|-------|
| 1918 | Lincoln-Illinois | 100,058 | 68.00 | 80.00 | 90.00 | 215. | 600. |

| Date | Event | Mintage | AU-50 | MS-60 | MS-63 | MS-64 | MS-65 |
|------|-------|---------|-------|-------|-------|-------|-------|
| 1946 | Iowa | 100,057 | 68.00 | 73.00 | 80.00 | 90.00 | 100. |

| Date | Event | Mintage | AU-50 | MS-60 | MS-63 | MS-64 | MS-65 |
|------|-------|---------|-------|-------|-------|-------|-------|
| 1925 | Lexington-Concord | 162,013 | 58.00 | 68.00 | 95.00 | 195. | 1100. |

| Date | Event | Mintage | AU-50 | MS-60 | MS-63 | MS-64 | MS-65 |
|------|-------|---------|-------|-------|-------|-------|-------|
| 1936 | Long Island | 81,826 | 61.00 | 68.00 | 73.00 | 110. | 500. |

| Date | Event | Mintage | AU-50 | MS-60 | MS-63 | MS-64 | MS-65 |
|------|-------|---------|-------|-------|-------|-------|-------|
| 1936 | Lynchburg | 20,013 | 140. | 155. | 180. | 275. | 425. |

| Date | Event | Mintage | AU-50 | MS-60 | MS-63 | MS-64 | MS-65 |
|------|-------|---------|-------|-------|-------|-------|-------|
| 1920 | Maine | 50,028 | 61.00 | 85.00 | 160. | 340. | 800. |

| Date | Event | Mintage | AU-50 | MS-60 | MS-63 | MS-64 | MS-65 |
|------|-------|---------|-------|-------|-------|-------|-------|
| 1934 | Maryland | 25,015 | 120. | 140. | 150. | 205. | 450. |

2 ☆ 4

| Date | Event | Mintage | AU-50 | MS-60 | MS-63 | MS-64 | MS-65 |
|------|-------|---------|-------|-------|-------|-------|-------|
| 1921 | Missouri 2 ◗ 4 | 5,000 | 245. | 380. | 765. | 1200. | 7000. |
| 1921 | Missouri | 15,428 | 180. | 330. | 675. | 1100. | 7000. |

| Date | Event | Mintage | AU-50 | MS-60 | MS-63 | MS-64 | MS-65 |
|------|-------|---------|-------|-------|-------|-------|-------|
| 1923S | Monroe | 274,077 | 38.00 | 43.00 | 95.00 | 390. | 2750. |

| Date | Event | Mintage | AU-50 | MS-60 | MS-63 | MS-64 | MS-65 |
|------|-------|---------|-------|-------|-------|-------|-------|
| 1938 | New Rochelle | 15,266 | 275. | 295. | 330. | 350. | 475. |

| Date | Event | Mintage | AU-50 | MS-60 | MS-63 | MS-64 | MS-65 |
|------|-------|---------|-------|-------|-------|-------|-------|
| 1936 | Norfolk | 16,936 | 385. | 400. | 420. | 450. | 465. |

# 1926 Oregon Trail Half Dollar
## Grade MS-60

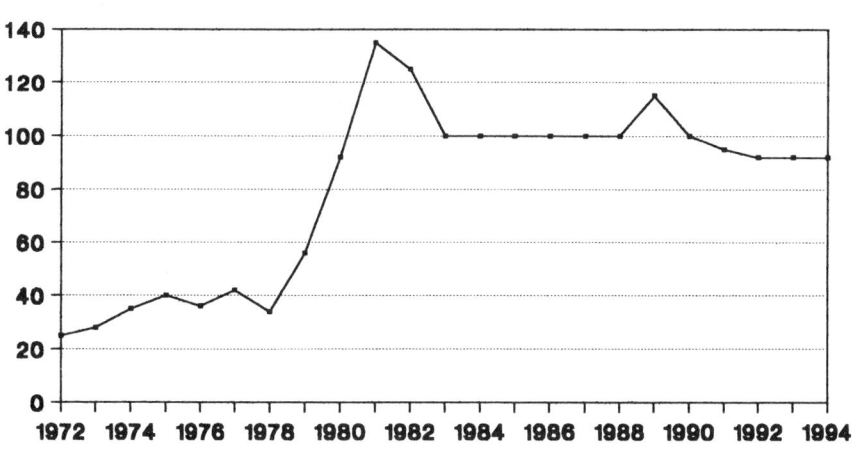

—•— **Retail Price**

**Source: COIN PRICES**

| Date | Event | Mintage | AU-50 | MS-60 | MS-63 | MS-64 | MS-65 |
|------|-------|---------|-------|-------|-------|-------|-------|
| 1926 | Oregon | 47,955 | 85.00 | 92.00 | 135. | 180. | 250. |
| 1926S | Oregon | 83,055 | 85.00 | 92.00 | 135. | 180. | 250. |
| 1928 | Oregon | 6,028 | 165. | 175. | 190. | 275. | 450. |
| 1933D | Oregon | 5,008 | 290. | 305. | 325. | 385. | 465. |
| 1934D | Oregon | 7,006 | 155. | 170. | 210. | 230. | 370. |
| 1936 | Oregon | 10,006 | 120. | 150. | 155. | 190. | 255. |
| 1936S | Oregon | 5,006 | 155. | 170. | 195. | 265. | 365. |
| 1937D | Oregon | 12,008 | 110. | 130. | 155. | 205. | 305. |
| 1938 | Oregon PDS set | 6,005 | — | 670. | 680. | 765. | 900. |
| 1939 | Oregon PDS set | 3,004 | — | 970. | 1300. | 1650. | 2050. |
| | Oregon type coin | — | 92.00 | 97.00 | 135. | 180. | 245. |

| Date | Event | Mintage | AU-50 | MS-60 | MS-63 | MS-64 | MS-65 |
|------|-------|---------|-------|-------|-------|-------|-------|
| 1915S | Panama - Pacific | 27,134 | 195. | 295. | 695. | 1300. | 2750. |

| Date | Event | Mintage | AU-50 | MS-60 | MS-63 | MS-64 | MS-65 |
|------|-------|---------|-------|-------|-------|-------|-------|
| 1920 | Pilgrim | 152,112 | 68.00 | 73.00 | 81.00 | 170. | 700. |
| 1921 | Pilgrim | 20,053 | 81.00 | 97.00 | 170. | 305. | 1050. |

| Date | Event | Mintage | AU-50 | MS-60 | MS-63 | MS-64 | MS-65 |
|------|-------|---------|-------|-------|-------|-------|-------|
| 1936 | Rhode Island PDS set | 15,010 | — | 215. | 235. | 385. | 1150. |
| 1936 | Rhode Island type coin | — | 68.00 | 73.00 | 80.00 | 130. | 385. |

| Date | Event | Mintage | AU-50 | MS-60 | MS-63 | MS-64 | MS-65 |
|------|-------|---------|-------|-------|-------|-------|-------|
| 1937 | Roanoke | 29,030 | 195. | 205. | 215. | 255. | 265. |

| Date | Event | Mintage | AU-50 | MS-60 | MS-63 | MS-64 | MS-65 |
|------|-------|---------|-------|-------|-------|-------|-------|
| 1936 | Robinson-Arkansas | 25,265 | 68.00 | 80.00 | 90.00 | 120. | 425. |
|      |       | (See also Arkansas) |  |  |  |  |  |

| Date | Event | Mintage | AU-50 | MS-60 | MS-63 | MS-64 | MS-65 |
|------|-------|---------|-------|-------|-------|-------|-------|
| 1935S | San Diego | 70,132 | 61.00 | 73.00 | 80.00 | 95.00 | 115. |
| 1936D | San Diego | 30,092 | 61.00 | 73.00 | 80.00 | 90.00 | 140. |

| Date | Event | Mintage | AU-50 | MS-60 | MS-63 | MS-64 | MS-65 |
|------|-------|---------|-------|-------|-------|-------|-------|
| 1926 | Sesquicentennial | 141,120 | 68.00 | 73.00 | 160. | 520. | 5500. |

| Date | Event | Mintage | AU-50 | MS-60 | MS-63 | MS-64 | MS-65 |
|------|-------|---------|-------|-------|-------|-------|-------|
| 1935 | Spanish Trail | 10,008 | 670. | 790. | 825. | 865. | 1100. |

| Date | Event | Mintage | AU-50 | MS-60 | MS-63 | MS-64 | MS-65 |
|------|-------|---------|-------|-------|-------|-------|-------|
| 1925 | Stone Mountain | 1,314,709 | 34.00 | 41.00 | 51.00 | 90.00 | 210. |

| Date | Event | Mintage | AU-50 | MS-60 | MS-63 | MS-64 | MS-65 |
|------|-------|---------|-------|-------|-------|-------|-------|
| 1934 | Texas | 61,463 | 80.00 | 95.00 | 100. | 110. | 155. |
| 1935 | Texas PDS set | 9,994 | — | 290. | 310. | 340. | 475. |
| 1936 | Texas PDS set | 8,911 | — | 290. | 310. | 340. | 475. |
| 1937 | Texas PDS set | 6,571 | — | 330. | 365. | 425. | 475. |
| 1938 | Texas PDS set | 3,775 | — | 545. | 850. | 1015. | 1300. |
|  | Texas type coins | — | 80.00 | 95.00 | 100. | 110. | 155. |

| Date | Event | Mintage | AU-50 | MS-60 | MS-63 | MS-64 | MS-65 |
|------|-------|---------|-------|-------|-------|-------|-------|
| 1925 | Fort Vancouver | 14,994 | 205. | 275. | 400. | 545. | 1150. |

| Date | Event | Mintage | AU-50 | MS-60 | MS-63 | MS-64 | MS-65 |
|------|-------|---------|-------|-------|-------|-------|-------|
| 1927 | Vermont | 28,142 | 120. | 155. | 210. | 380. | 1050. |

| Date | Event | Mintage | AU-50 | MS-60 | MS-63 | MS-64 | MS-65 |
|------|-------|---------|-------|-------|-------|-------|-------|
| 1946 | B.T. Washington PDS set | 200,113 | — | 36.00 | 49.00 | 68.00 | 150. |
| 1947 | B.T. Washington PDS set | 100,017 | — | 45.00 | 73.00 | 110. | 275. |
| 1948 | B.T. Washington PDS set | 8,005 | — | 92.00 | 105. | 170. | 180. |
| 1949 | B.T. Washington PDS set | 6,004 | — | 205. | 215. | 235. | 270. |
| 1950 | B.T. Washington PDS set | 6,004 | — | 95.00 | 110. | 150. | 160. |
| 1951 | B.T. Washington PDS set | 7,004 | — | 120. | 135. | 155. | 160. |
|      | B.T. Washington type coin | — | 10.00 | 12.00 | 16.00 | 23.00 | 35.00 |

| Date | Event | Mintage | AU-50 | MS-60 | MS-63 | MS-64 | MS-65 |
|------|-------|---------|-------|-------|-------|-------|-------|
| 1951 | Washington-Carver PDS set | 10,004 | — | 93.00 | 110. | 115. | 495. |
| 1952 | Washington-Carver PDS set | 8,006 | — | 93.00 | 110. | 130. | 275. |
| 1953 | Washington-Carver PDS set | 8,003 | — | 93.00 | 110. | 135. | 485. |
| 1954 | Washington-Carver PDS set | 12,006 | — | 80.00 | 85.00 | 97.00 | 440. |
|      | Washington-Carver type coin | — | 10.00 | 12.00 | 20.00 | 23.00 | 60.00 |

| Date | Event | Mintage | AU-50 | MS-60 | MS-63 | MS-64 | MS-65 |
|------|-------|---------|-------|-------|-------|-------|-------|
| 1936 | Wisconsin | 25,015 | 170. | 175. | 190. | 210. | 245. |

 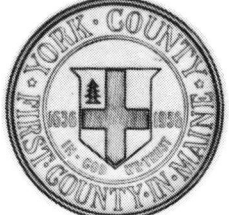

| Date | Event | Mintage | AU-50 | MS-60 | MS-63 | MS-64 | MS-65 |
|------|-------|---------|-------|-------|-------|-------|-------|
| 1936 | York County | 25,015 | 170. | 180. | 190. | 195. | 215. |

# Silver dollar

**Designer:** Charles E. Barber. **Size:** 38.1 millimeters. **Weight:** 26.73 grams. **Composition:** 90% silver (0.7736 ounces), 10% copper.

| Date | Event | Mintage | AU-50 | MS-60 | MS-63 | MS-64 | MS-65 |
|------|-------|---------|-------|-------|-------|-------|-------|
| 1900 | Lafayette ($1) | 36,026 | 275. | 545. | 1750. | 3200. | 8500. |

# Gold dollars

**Designers:** Louisiana: Charles E. Barber. Lewis and Clark Expo: Charles E. Barber. Panama-Pacific Expo: Charles Keck. McKinley Memorial: Charles E. Barber (obverse) and George T. Morgan (reverse). Grant: Laura G. Fraser. **Size:** 15 millimeters. **Weight:** 1.672 grams. **Composition:** 90% gold (0.0484 ounces), 10% copper. **Notes:** The Grant gold-dollar varieties are distinguished by whether a star appears on the obverse above the word "Grant."

Jefferson                    McKinley

| Date | Event | Mintage | AU-50 | MS-60 | MS-63 | MS-64 | MS-65 |
|------|-------|---------|-------|-------|-------|-------|-------|
| 1903 | Louisiana, Jefferson | 17,500 | 325. | 405. | 950. | 1700. | 2700. |
| 1903 | Louisiana, McKinley | 17,500 | 330. | 385. | 1000. | 1550. | 2450. |

| Date | Event | Mintage | AU-50 | MS-60 | MS-63 | MS-64 | MS-65 |
|------|-------|---------|-------|-------|-------|-------|-------|
| 1904 | Lewis and Clark Expo | 10,025 | 395. | 800. | 2300. | 3750. | 6500. |
| 1905 | Lewis and Clark Expo | 10,041 | 495. | 850. | 3100. | 5950. | 16,000. |

| Date | Event | Mintage | AU-50 | MS-60 | MS-63 | MS-64 | MS-65 |
|------|-------|---------|-------|-------|-------|-------|-------|
| 1915S | Panama-Pacific Expo | 15,000 | 320. | 435. | 950. | 1500. | 2500. |

| Date | Event | Mintage | AU-50 | MS-60 | MS-63 | MS-64 | MS-65 |
|------|-------|---------|-------|-------|-------|-------|-------|
| 1916 | McKinley Memorial | 9,977 | 320. | 435. | 900. | 1300. | 2350. |
| 1917 | McKinley Memorial | 10,000 | 325. | 440. | 1350. | 2000. | 3300. |

**With star**

| Date | Event | Mintage | AU-50 | MS-60 | MS-63 | MS-64 | MS-65 |
|------|-------|---------|-------|-------|-------|-------|-------|
| 1922 | Grant Memorial w/o star | 5,016 | 950. | 1400. | 1800. | 2100. | 2950. |
| 1922 | Grant Memorial w/star | 5,000 | 1100. | 1550. | 1850. | 2200. | 2650. |

# Gold $2.50

**Designers:** Panama-Pacific Expo: Charles E. Barber (obverse) and George T. Morgan (reverse). Sesquicentennial: John R. Sinnock. **Size:** 18 millimeters. **Weight:** 4.18 grams. **Composition:** 90% gold (0.121 ounces), 10% copper.

| Date | Event | Mintage | AU-50 | MS-60 | MS-63 | MS-64 | MS-65 |
|------|-------|---------|-------|-------|-------|-------|-------|
| 1915S | Panama Pacific Expo. | 6,749 | 1025. | 1350. | 2750. | 3750. | 4500. |

| Date | Event | Mintage | AU-50 | MS-60 | MS-63 | MS-64 | MS-65 |
|------|-------|---------|-------|-------|-------|-------|-------|
| 1926 | Philadelphia Sesquicentennial | 46,019 | 295. | 350. | 700. | 1200. | 7500. |

# Gold $50

**Designer:** Robert Aitken. **Size:** 44 millimeters. **Weight:** 83.59 grams. **Composition:** 90% gold (2.42 ounces), 10% copper.

| Date | Event | Mintage | AU-50 | MS-60 | MS-63 | MS-64 | MS-65 |
|------|-------|---------|-------|-------|-------|-------|-------|
| 1915S | Panama-Pacific Expo, round | 483 | 21,000. | 23,500. | 35,000. | 44,500. | 99,500. |
| 1915S | Panama-Pacific Expo, octagon | 645 | 18,500. | 21,000. | 28,500. | 44,500. | 88,000. |

# Commemoratives 1982-present

## Silver half dollar

**Designer:** Elizabeth Jones. **Size:** 30.6 millimeters. **Weight:** 12.5 grams. **Composition:** 90% silver (0.3618 ounces), 10% copper.

| Date | Mintage | (Proof) | MS-65 | Prf-65 |
|------|---------|---------|-------|--------|
| 1982D Geo. Washington | 2,210,458 | — | 4.10 | — |
| 1982S Geo. Washington | — | (4,894,044) | — | 4.20 |

## Clad half dollars

**Designers:** Statue of Liberty: Edgar Steever (obverse) and Sherl Joseph Winter (reverse). Congress: Patricia Lewis Verani (obverse) and William Woodward (reverse). Mount Rushmore: Marcel Jovine (obverse) and James Ferrell (reverse). 1992 Olympics: William C. Cousins (obverse) and Steven M. Bieda (reverse). **Size:** 30.6 millimeters. **Weight:** 11.34 grams. **Composition:** clad layers of 75% copper and 25% nickel bonded to a pure-copper core.

| Date | Mintage | (Proof) | MS-65 | Prf-65 |
|------|---------|---------|-------|--------|
| 1986D Statue of Liberty | 928,008 | — | 3.20 | — |
| 1986S Statue of Liberty | — | (6,925,627) | — | 3.20 |

| Date | Mintage | (Proof) | MS-65 | Prf-65 |
|------|---------|---------|-------|--------|
| 1989D Congress | 163,753 | — | 13.00 | — |
| 1989S Congress | 767,897 | — | — | 7.00 |

| Date | Mintage | (Proof) | MS-65 | Prf-65 |
|---|---|---|---|---|
| 1991D Mt. Rushmore | 172,754 | — | 11.00 | — |
| 1991S Mt. Rushmore | 753,257 | — | — | 12.00 |

| Date | Mintage | (Proof) | MS-65 | Prf-65 |
|---|---|---|---|---|
| 1992P Olympic | 161,607 | — | 6.30 | — |
| 1992S Olympic | — | (519,645) | — | 9.00 |

| Date | Mintage | (Proof) | MS-65 | Prf-65 |
|---|---|---|---|---|
| 1992D Columbus | 135,702 | — | 10.00 | — |
| 1992S Columbus | — | (390,154) | — | 10.00 |

| Date | Mintage | (Proof) | MS-65 | Prf-65 |
|---|---|---|---|---|
| 1993W Madison/Bill of Rights | — | — | 10.00 | — |
| 1993S Madison/Bill of Rights | — | — | — | 9.00 |

| Date | Mintage | (Proof) | MS-65 | Prf-65 |
|---|---|---|---|---|
| 1993P World War II | — | — | 10.00 | 10.00 |

| Date | Mintage | (Proof) | MS-65 | Prf-65 |
|---|---|---|---|---|
| 1994 World Cup Soccer | — | — | — | — |
| 1994 World Cup Soccer | — | — | — | — |

# Silver dollars

**Designers:** 1983 Olympics: Elizabeth Jones. 1984 Olympics: Robert Graham. Statue of Liberty: John Mercanti. Constitution: Patricia Lewis Verani. 1988 Olympics: Patricia Lewis Verani (obverse) and Sherl Joseph Winter (reverse). Congress: William Woodward. Eisenhower: John Mercanti (obverse) and Marcel Jovine (reverse). Mount Rushmore: Marika Somogyi (obverse) and Frank Gasparro (reverse). Korean War: John Mercanti (obverse) and James Ferrell (reverse). United Service Organizations: Robert Lamb (obverse) and John Mercanti (reverse). 1992 Olympics: John R. Deecken (obverse) and Marcel Jovine (reverse). **Size:** 38.1 millimeters. **Weight:** 26.73 grams. **Composition:** 90% silver (0.76 ounces), 10% copper.

| Date | Mintage | (Proof) | MS-65 | Prf-65 |
|---|---|---|---|---|
| 1983P Olympic | 294,543 | — | 9.00 | — |
| 1983D Olympic | 174,014 | — | 24.00 | — |
| 1983S Olympic | 174,014 | (1,577,025) | 21.00 | 10.00 |

| Date | Mintage | (Proof) | MS-65 | Prf-65 |
|---|---|---|---|---|
| 1984P Olympic | 217,954 | — | 15.00 | — |
| 1984D Olympic | 116,675 | — | 40.00 | — |
| 1984S Olympic | 116,675 | (1,801,210) | 42.00 | 11.00 |

| Date | Mintage | (Proof) | MS-65 | Prf-65 |
|---|---|---|---|---|
| 1986P Statue of Liberty | 723,635 | — | 9.00 | — |
| 1986S Statue of Liberty | — | (6,414,638) | — | 9.00 |

 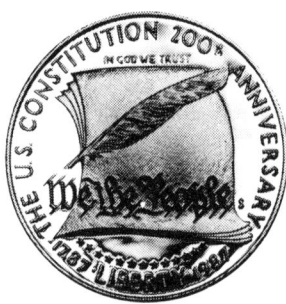

| Date | Mintage | (Proof) | MS-65 | Prf-65 |
|---|---|---|---|---|
| 1987P Constitution | 451,629 | — | 10.00 | — |
| 1987S Constitution | — | (2,747,116) | — | 9.00 |

| Date | Mintage | (Proof) | MS-65 | Prf-65 |
|---|---|---|---|---|
| 1988D Olympic | 191,368 | — | 20.00 | — |
| 1988S Olympic | — | (1,359,366) | — | 8.00 |

| Date | Mintage | (Proof) | MS-65 | Prf-65 |
|------|---------|---------|-------|--------|
| 1989D Congress | 135,203 | — | 20.00 | — |
| 1989S Congress | — | (762,198) | — | 14.00 |

| Date | Mintage | (Proof) | MS-65 | Prf-65 |
|------|---------|---------|-------|--------|
| 1990W Eisenhower | 241,669 | — | 20.00 | — |
| 1990P Eisenhower | — | (638,335) | — | 11.00 |

| Date | Mintage | (Proof) | MS-65 | Prf-65 |
|------|---------|---------|-------|--------|
| 1991P Mt. Rushmore | 133,139 | — | 35.00 | — |
| 1991S Mt. Rushmore | — | (738,419) | — | 26.00 |

| Date | Mintage | (Proof) | MS-65 | Prf-65 |
|------|---------|---------|-------|--------|
| 1991D Korean War | 213,049 | — | 16.00 | — |
| 1991P Korean War | — | (618,488) | — | 15.00 |

| Date | Mintage | (Proof) | MS-65 | Prf-65 |
|------|---------|---------|-------|--------|
| 1991D USO | 124,958 | — | 38.00 | — |
| 1991S USO | — | (321,275) | — | 25.00 |

| Date | Mintage | (Proof) | MS-65 | Prf-65 |
|------|---------|---------|-------|--------|
| 1992D Olympic | 187,552 | — | 26.00 | — |
| 1992S Olympic | — | (504,505) | — | 28.00 |

| Date | Mintage | (Proof) | MS-65 | Prf-65 |
|------|---------|---------|-------|--------|
| 1992D White House | 123,803 | — | 64.00 | — |
| 1992W White House | — | (375,851) | — | 69.00 |

| Date | Mintage | (Proof) | MS-65 | Prf-65 |
|------|---------|---------|-------|--------|
| 1992D Columbus | 106,949 | — | 32.00 | — |
| 1992P Columbus | — | (385,241) | — | 29.00 |

| Date | Mintage | (Proof) | MS-65 | Prf-65 |
|------|---------|---------|-------|--------|
| 1993D Madison/Bill of Rights | — | — | 26.00 | — |
| 1993S Madison/Bill of Rights | — | — | — | 20.00 |

| Date | Mintage | (Proof) | MS-65 | Prf-65 |
|------|---------|---------|-------|--------|
| 1993D World War II | — | — | 31.00 | — |
| 1993W World War II | — | — | — | 37.00 |

| Date | Mintage | (Proof) | MS-65 | Prf-65 |
|------|---------|---------|-------|--------|
| 1994 World Cup Soccer | — | — | — | — |
| 1994 World Cup Soccer | — | — | — | — |

# Gold $5

**Designers:** Statue of Liberty: Elizabeth Jones. Constitution: Marcel Jovine. 1988 Olympics: Elizabeth Jones (obverse) and Marcel Jovine (reverse). Congress: John Mercanti. Mount Rushmore: John Mercanti (obverse) and Robert Lamb (reverse). 1992 Olympics: James C. Sharpe (obverse) and James M. Peed (reverse). **Size:** 21.5 millimeters. **Weight:** 90% gold (0.24 ounces), 10% alloy.

| Date | Mintage | (Proof) | MS-65 | Prf-65 |
|------|---------|---------|-------|--------|
| 1986W Statue of Liberty | 95,248 | (404,013) | 124. | 124. |

| Date | Mintage | (Proof) | MS-65 | Prf-65 |
|------|---------|---------|-------|--------|
| 1987W Constitution | 214,225 | (651,659) | 122. | 122. |

| Date | Mintage | (Proof) | MS-65 | Prf-65 |
|---|---|---|---|---|
| 1988W Olympic | 62,913 | (281,456) | 122. | 122. |

| Date | Mintage | (Proof) | MS-65 | Prf-65 |
|---|---|---|---|---|
| 1989W Congress | 46,899 | (164,690) | 120. | 120. |

| Date | Mintage | (Proof) | MS-65 | Prf-65 |
|---|---|---|---|---|
| 1991W Mt. Rushmore | 31,959 | (111,991) | 125. | 125. |

| Date | Mintage | (Proof) | MS-65 | Prf-65 |
|---|---|---|---|---|
| 1992W Olympic | 27,732 | (77,313) | 135. | 135. |

| Date | Mintage | (Proof) | MS-65 | Prf-65 |
|---|---|---|---|---|
| 1992W Columbus | 24,329 | (79,730) | 190. | 210. |

| Date | Mintage | (Proof) | MS-65 | Prf-65 |
|---|---|---|---|---|
| 1993W Madison/Bill of Rights | — | — | 175. | 170. |

| Date | Mintage | (Proof) | MS-65 | Prf-65 |
|---|---|---|---|---|
| 1993W World War II | — | — | 150. | 155. |

| Date | Mintage | (Proof) | MS-65 | Prf-65 |
|---|---|---|---|---|
| 1994 World Cup Soccer | — | — | — | — |
| 1994 World Cup Soccer | — | — | — | — |

# Gold $10

| Date | Mintage | (Proof) | MS-65 | Prf-65 |
|---|---|---|---|---|
| 1984W Olympic | 75,886 | (381,085) | 243. | 243. |
| 1984P Olympic | 33,309 | — | — | 280. |
| 1984D Olympic | 34,533 | — | — | 276. |
| 1984S Olympic | 48,551 | — | — | 246. |

# Sets

## Olympic

| Date | Price |
|---|---|
| 1983 & 1984 proof dollars. | 16.00 |

| Date | Price |
|---|---|
| 1983 collectors set1983 PDS uncirculated dollars. | 32.00 |
| 1984 collectors set1984 PDS uncirculated dollars. | 60.00 |
| 1983 & 1984 gold and silver uncirculated set. One 1983 and one 1984 uncirculated dollar and one 1984 uncirculated gold $10. | 245. |
| 1983 & 1984 gold and silver proof set. One 1983 and one 1984 proof dollar and one 1984 proof gold $10. | 240. |
| 1983 & 1984 6 coin set. One 1983 and one 1984 uncirculated and proof dollar. One uncirculated and one proof gold $10. | 490. |
| 1988 2 coin set: uncirculated silver dollar and gold $5. | 130. |
| 1988 2 coin set: proof silver dollar and gold $5. | 120. |
| 1988 4 coin set: 1 each of proof and uncirculated issues. | 250. |
| 1992 2 coin set: uncirculated half dollar and silver dollar. | 30.00 |
| 1992 2 coin set: proof half dollar and silver dollar. | 34.00 |
| 1992 3 coin set: uncirculated half dollar, silver dollar and gold $5. | 165. |
| 1992 3 coin set: proof half dollar, silver dollar and gold $5. | 165. |
| 1992 6 coin set: 1 each of proof and uncirculated issues. | 295. |

# Statue of Liberty

| Date | Price |
|---|---|
| 1986 2 coin set: uncirculated silver dollar and clad half dollar. | 12.00 |
| 1986 2 coin set: proof silver dollar and clad half dollar. | 12.00 |
| 1986 3 coin set: uncirculated silver dollar, clad half dollar and gold $5. | 130. |
| 1986 3 coin set: proof silver dollar, clad half dollar and gold $5. | 130. |
| 1986 6 coin set: 1 each of the proof and uncirculated issues. | 255. |

# Constitution

| Date | Price |
|---|---|
| 1987 2 coin set: uncirculated silver dollar and gold $5. | 125. |
| 1987 2 coin set: proof silver dollar and gold $5. | 125. |
| 1987 4 coin set: 1 each of the proof and uncirculated issues. | 240. |

# Congress

| Date | Price |
|---|---|
| 1989 2 coin set: uncirculated silver dollar and clad half dollar. | 33.00 |
| 1989 2 coin set: proof silver dollar and clad half dollar. | 20.00 |
| 1989 3 coin set: uncirculated silver dollar, clad half and gold $5. | 145. |
| 1989 3 coin set: proof silver dollar, clad half and gold $5. | 135. |
| 1989 6 coin set: 1 each of the proof and uncirculated issues. | 255. |

# Mt. Rushmore

| Date | Price |
|---|---|
| 1991 2 coin set: uncirculated half dollar and silver dollar. | 40.00 |
| 1991 2 coin set: proof half dollar and silver dollar. | 35.00 |
| 1991 3 coin set: uncirculated half dollar, silver dollar and gold $5. | 165. |
| 1991 3 coin set: proof half dollar, silver dollar and gold $5. | 150. |
| 1991 6 coin set: 1 each of proof and uncirculated issues. | 295. |

# Columbus Quincentenary

| Date | Price |
|---|---|
| 1992 2 coin set: uncirculated half dollar and silver dollar. | 30.00 |
| 1992 2 coin set: proof half dollar and silver dollar. | 30.00 |
| 1992 3 coin set: uncirculated half dollar, silver dollar and gold $5. | 210. |
| 1992 3 coin set: proof half dollar, silver dollar and gold $5. | 200. |
| 1992 6 coin set: 1 each of proof and uncirculated issues. | 420. |

# Madison/Bill of Rights

| Date | Price |
|---|---|
| 1993 2 coin set: uncirculated half dollar and silver dollar. | 25.00 |
| 1993 2 coin set: proof half dollar and silver dollar. | 20.00 |
| 1993 3 coin set: uncirculated half dollar, silver dollar and gold $5. | 205. |
| 1993 3 coin set: proof half dollar, silver dollar and gold $5. | 175. |
| 1993 6 coin set: 1 each of proof and uncirculated issues. | 385. |

# World War II

| Date | Price |
|---|---|
| 1993 2 coin set: uncirculated half dollar and silver dollar. | 30.00 |
| 1993 2 coin set: proof half dollar and silver dollar. | 35.00 |
| 1993 3 coin set: uncirculated half dollar, silver dollar and gold $5. | 195. |
| 1993 3 coin set: proof half dollar, silver dollar and gold $5. | 200. |
| 1993 6 coin set: 1 each of proof and uncirculated issues. | 385. |

# American Eagle bullion coins

**Notes:** American Eagle bullion coins are traded for their precious-metal content and compete with similar coins from other countries. Values for the non-proof issues will fluctuate with gold and silver prices.

## Silver

### One-ounce

**Designers:** Adolph A. Weinman (obverse) and John Mercanti (reverse). **Size:** 40.6 millimeters. **Weight:** 31.103 grams. **Composition:** 99.93% silver (0.999 ounces), 0.07% copper.

Prices based on $5.30 spot silver.

| Date | Mintage | Unc | Prf. |
|---|---|---|---|
| 1986 | 5,393,005 | 11.25 | — |
| 1986S | 1,446,778 | — | 20.00 |
| 1987 | 11,442,335 | 7.50 | — |
| 1987S | 904,732 | — | 20.00 |
| 1988 | 5,004,500 | 7.70 | — |
| 1988S | 557,370 | — | 74.00 |
| 1989 | 5,203,327 | 7.70 | — |
| 1989S | 617,694 | — | 20.00 |
| 1990 | 5,840,210 | 7.50 | — |
| 1990S | 695,510 | — | 28.00 |
| 1991 | 7,191,066 | 7.50 | — |
| 1991S | 511,924 | — | 25.00 |
| 1992 | 5,540,068 | 7.50 | — |
| 1992S | 498,552 | — | 24.00 |
| 1993 | — | 7.50 | — |
| 1993P | — | — | 31.00 |
| 1994 | — | 7.50 | — |
| 1994P | — | — | — |

## Gold

Arabic numeral date     Roman numeral date

### Tenth-ounce

**Designers:** Augustus Saint-Gaudens (obverse) and Miley Busiek (reverse). **Size:** 16.5 millimeters. **Weight:** 3.393 grams. **Composition:** 91.67% gold (0.1 ounces), 5.33% copper, 3% silver.

Prices based on $387.10 spot gold.

| Date | Mintage | Unc | Prf. |
|------|---------|-----|------|
| 1986 | 912,609 | 51.10 | — |
| 1987 | 580,266 | 51.10 | — |
| 1988 | 159,500 | 65.00 | — |
| 1988P | 143,881 | — | 54.00 |
| 1989 | 264,790 | 54.00 | — |
| 1989P | 82,924 | — | 60.00 |
| 1990 | 210,210 | 51.10 | — |
| 1990P | 99,349 | — | 54.00 |
| 1991 | 165,200 | 51.10 | — |
| 1991P | 70,344 | — | 54.00 |
| 1992 | 209,300 | 51.10 | — |
| 1992P | 64,902 | — | 62.00 |
| 1993 | — | 51.10 | — |
| 1993P | — | — | 74.00 |
| 1994 | — | 51.10 | — |
| 1994P | — | — | — |

Arabic numeral date          Roman numeral date

## Quarter-ounce

**Size:** 22 millimeters. **Weight:** 8.483 grams. **Composition:** 91.67% gold (0.25 ounces), 5.33% copper, 3% silver.

| Date | Mintage | Unc | Prf. |
|------|---------|-----|------|
| 1986 | 726,031 | 109.25 | — |
| 1987 | 269,255 | 109.25 | — |
| 1988 | 49,000 | 109.25 | — |
| 1988P | 98,028 | — | 124. |
| 1989 | 81,789 | 125. | — |
| 1989P | 53,593 | — | 130. |
| 1990 | 41,000 | 109.25 | — |
| 1990P | 62,674 | — | 130. |
| 1991 | 36,100 | 130. | — |
| 1991P | 50,839 | — | 136. |
| 1992P | 46,290 | — | 142. |
| 1993 | — | 109.25 | — |
| 1993P | — | — | 170. |
| 1994 | — | — | — |
| 1994P | — | — | — |

Arabic numeral date          Roman numeral date

## Half-ounce

**Size:** 27 millimeters. **Weight:** 16.966 grams. **Composition:** 91.67% gold (0.5 ounces), 5.33% copper, 3% silver.

| Date | Mintage | Unc | Prf. |
|------|---------|-----|------|
| 1986 | 599,566 | 223. | — |
| 1987 | 131,255 | 223. | — |
| 1987P | 143,398 | — | 241. |
| 1988 | 45,000 | 223. | — |
| 1988P | 76,528 | — | 253. |
| 1989 | 44,829 | 223. | — |
| 1989P | 44,264 | — | 259. |
| 1990 | 31,000 | 550. | — |
| 1990P | 51,636 | — | 270. |
| 1991 | 24,100 | 425. | — |
| 1991P | 53,125 | — | 265. |
| 1992 | 54,404 | 290. | — |
| 1992P | 40,982 | — | 265. |
| 1993 | — | 223. | — |
| 1993P | — | — | 288. |
| 1994 | — | 223. | — |
| 1994P | — | — | — |

Arabic numeral date

Roman numeral date

## One-ounce

**Size:** 32.7 millimeters. **Weight:** 33.931 grams. **Composition:** 91.67% gold (1 ounce), 5.33% copper, 3% silver.

Prices based on $385.90 gold.

| Date | Mintage | Unc | Prf. |
|------|---------|-----|------|
| 1986 | 1,362,650 | 409.40 | — |
| 1986W | 446,290 | — | 481. |
| 1987 | 1,045,500 | 409.40. | — |
| 1987W | 147,498 | — | 482. |
| 1988 | 465,000 | 409.40 | — |
| 1988W | 87,133 | — | 505. |
| 1989 | 415,790 | 409.40 | — |
| 1989W | 53,960 | — | 505. |
| 1990 | 373,210 | 409.40 | — |
| 1990W | 62,401 | — | 505. |
| 1991 | 243,100 | 409.40 | — |
| 1991W | 50,411 | — | 505. |
| 1992 | 275,000 | 409.40 | — |
| 1992W | 44,835 | — | 496. |
| 1993 | — | 409.40 | — |
| 1993W | — | — | 599. |
| 1994 | — | 409.40 | — |
| 1994W | — | — | — |

# U.S. minting varieties and errors

## Introduction

The cataloging system used here for varieties and errors, compiled by Alan Herbert, began as the "PDS system," for "planchet," "die" and "striking," the three main divisions of the minting process. Two more divisions covering collectible modifications after the strike and alterations and damage have since been added.

The PDS system groups varieties of like cause. It can also be applied to foreign coins, with several classes added specifically to cover certain foreign minting processes.

Prices for U.S. coins listed here do not directly apply to foreign coins, but they can be used as a guide to the relative rarity of many foreign minting varieties. The prices quoted are the values for a common date and mint of the variety. In some instances, such as hubbing varieties, coins grading higher than MS-60 will bring a premium over the quoted prices.

The values quoted on the following pages are intended as a guide only; the ultimate price is determined by a willing buyer and seller. All prices are for grade uncirculated (MS-60), with a 20 percent to 50 percent or greater reduction for lesser grades.

## Quick check index

### If you have a coin and are not sure where to look for the possible variety:

If your coin shows doubling, check II-A, II-B, II-C, II-G, II-H, III-A, III-C-7, III-E, III-H-1, IV-D, or ejection doubling.

If part of the coin is missing, check I-B, I-C, or I-D.

If there is a raised line of coin metal, check II-D, II-G.

If there is a raised area of coin metal, check I-F, II-E, or II-F.

If the coin is out of round and too thin, check III-D.

If the coin appears to be the wrong metal, check I-A, I-E, I-G, and III-D.

If the die appears to have been damaged, check II-E, II-G, II-H. (Damage to the coin itself usually is not a minting variety.)

If the coin shows incomplete or missing design, check I-B-3, I-B-5, I-D, II-A, II-E, III-A, III-C, and III-D.

If only part of the planchet was struck, check II-E, II-G, III-A, III-B, III-C, III-E, III-F, III-G.

If something was struck into the coin, check III-B and III-C.

If something has happened to the coin's edge, check II-D-6, II-E-9 and 10, III-A-2, III-F, and III-H.

If your coin shows other than the normal design, check II-A or II-C.

If a layer of the coin metal is missing or a clad layer is missing, check I-D.

If you have an unstruck planchet, check I-H.

If your coin is a restrike, check IV-D.

If your coin has a counterstamp, additional engraving or apparent official modifications, check IV-A, IV-B, and IV-C.

Do not depend on the naked eye to examine your coins. Always use a magnifying lens. Circulation damage, wear, and alterations frequently can be mistaken for legitimate minting varieties.

# Division I: Planchet varieties

These varieties and errors occur in the manufacture of the planchet on which the coin is struck and includes classes resulting from faulty metallurgy, mechanical damage, faulty processing or equipment, or human malfunction prior to the actual coin striking.

### I-A: Improper alloy mix

Includes classes I-A-1, improper mix; and I-A-2, slag. Values for I-A-1 run from a few cents to a couple of dollars, depending on the denomination. Values for I-A-2 will run from several dollars on up, depending on the denomination and size of the slag area.

### I-B: Damaged and defective planchets

This section involves planchets that are damaged, broken, or otherwise defective as a result of the production process. It does not include coins damaged after minting. Included are 23 classes, among them: I-B-1, defective planchets; I-B-2, mechanical damage; I-B-3, rolled thin; I-B-4, rolled thick; I-B-5, tapered; I-B-6, incomplete cladding; I-B-7, weld area planchet; I-B-8, unpunched center hole; I-B-9, uncentered center hole; I-B-10, clad stock missing clad layer; I-B-11, clad stock missing both clad layers; I-B-12, multiple punched center hole; I-B-13, incomplete punched center hole; I-B-14, wrong size or shape center hole; I-B-15, improperly prepared proof planchet; I-B-16, bubbled plating; I-B-17, broken planchet before strike; I-B-18, broken planchet after strike; I-B-19, improper annealing; I-B-20, unplated planchets; I-B-21, faulty upset planchet edge; I-B-22, rolled-in metal; I-B-23, included gas bubbles. (Values for I-B-20 cent planchets may range above $100.)

**Defective planchet**

**Tapered planchet**

| | Defective<br>I-B-1 | Rolled<br>Thin<br>I-B-3 | Rolled<br>Thick<br>I-B-4 | Tapered<br>I-B-5 |
|---|---|---|---|---|
| Indian cent 1859-1909 | 10. | 10. | 50. | 10. |
| Lincoln cent 1909-1942 | 5. | 5. | 15. | 5. |
| Lincoln cent 1943 | 15. | 25. | — | — |
| Lincoln cent 1944-1958 | 5. | 5. | 15. | 5. |
| Lincoln cent 1959-1982 | 3. | 10. | 15. | 3. |
| Lincoln cent 1976 | 5. | 10. | 20. | 5. |
| Lincoln cent 1982- | 5. | 25. | 35. | 10. |
| Buffalo nickel 1913-1938 | 20. | — | — | — |
| Jefferson nickel 1938- | 15. | — | 20. | — |
| Jefferson nickel 1942-1945 | 10. | — | 50. | — |
| Jefferson nickel 1976 | 25. | — | 50. | — |
| Mercury dime 1916-1945 | 35. | — | 75. | — |
| Roosevelt dime 1946-1964 | 25. | — | 50. | — |
| Roosevelt dime 1965- | 15. | — | 25. | — |
| Roosevelt dime 1976 | 25. | — | 50. | — |
| Washington quarter 1932-64 | 50. | Rare | 100. | — |
| Washington quarter 1965- | 20. | 10. | Rare | — |
| Washington quarter 1976 | 50. | Rare | 100. | — |
| Franklin half 1948-1963 | 50. up | — | Rare | — |
| Kennedy half 1964 | 50. up | — | Rare | — |
| Kennedy half 1965-1970 | 25. up | — | Rare | — |
| Kennedy half 1971- | 20. up | — | Rare | — |
| Kennedy half 1976 | 100. up | — | Rare | — |
| Proof coins | 25. up | Rare | Rare | Rare |

## I-C: Clipped planchets

Sixteen classes are listed in this section. Clips occur as the blanking-press punches overlap into areas of the coin-metal strip that have already been punched out, or where the end of the strip is broken or ragged, or over an incomplete punch.

The classes are I-C-1, curved clip to 5 percent; I-C-2, curved clip 6 percent to 10 percent or double clip; I-C-3, curved 11 percent to 25 percent; I-C-4, curved 26 percent to 60 percent; I-C-5, triple clip; I-C-6, multiple clip; I-C-7, incomplete punch; I-C-8, oval clip; I-C-9, crescent clip, 61 percent or larger; I-C-10, straight clip; I-C-11, ragged clip; I-C-12, outside corner clip; I-C-13, overlapping clips; I-C-14, inside corner clip; I-C-15, disc clip; and I-C-16, incomplete straight clip.

**5 percent**

**50 percent**

**Ragged-edge clip**

**Multiple**

**Incomplete punch**

| | Curved to 5% | Curved to 10% | Curved to 25% | Curved to 60% | Triple Clip | Multiple Clip | Incomp Punch | Oval Clip | Crescent Clip 61%+ | Straight Clip | Ragged Clip |
|---|---|---|---|---|---|---|---|---|---|---|---|
| | I-C-1 | I-C-2 | I-C-3 | I-C-4 | I-C-5 | I-C-6 | I-C-7 | I-C-8 | I-C-9 | I-C-10 | I-C-11 |
| Indian cent 1859-1909 | 10. up | 15. up | 25. up | 50. up | 35. up | 50. up | — | — | — | — | 50. |
| Lincoln cent 1909-1942 | 5. | 10. | 15. | 25. up | 15. up | 25. up | 20. | 50. | 50. | 5. | 10. |
| Lincoln cent 1943 | 5. | 10. | 35. | 50. up | 15. | 50. up | 100. | 150. | — | 25. | 50. |
| Lincoln cent 1944-1958 | 3. | 8. | 12. | 25. up | 5. | 15. up | 15. | 50. | 40. | 5. | 10. |
| Lincoln cent 1959-1982 | 2. | 5. | 10. | 25. up | 5. | 15. up | 15. | 45. | 35. | 5. | 10. |
| Lincoln cent 1982- | 1. | 7. | 15. | 50. up | 15. | 50. up | 35. | 150. | — | 25. | — |
| Buffalo nickel 1913-1938 | 5. up | 15. up | 25. up | 100. up | 50. up | 100. up | 35. | 75. | — | 25. | — |
| Jefferson nickel 1938- | 2. | 5. | 10. | 50. up | 10. up | 50. up | 25. | 50. | 35. | 5. | 10. |
| Jefferson nickel 1942-1945 | 5. | 10. | 15. | 150. up | 25. up | 100. up | 35. | 75. | 50. | 15. | 20. |
| Mercury dime 1916-1945 | 10 | 25. | 40. | 75. up | 30. | 75. up | 35. | — | — | 15. | 25. |
| Roosevelt dime 1946-1964 | 2. | 3. | 5. | 75. up | 15. | 50. up | 30. | Rare | 75. | 10. | 15. |
| Roosevelt dime 1965- | 1. | 2. | 3. | 50. up | 10. | 35. up | 25. | 100. | 60. | 5. | 10. |
| Roosevelt dime 1976 · | 2. | 3. | 5. | 75. up | 15. | 50. up | 30.: | Rare | 75. | 10. | 15. |
| Washington quarter 1932-64 | 5. | 8. | 10. | 100. up | 15. | 75. up | 35. | 60. | — | 10. | 15. |
| Washington quarter 1965- | 2. | 3. | 5. | 50. up | 10. | 35. up | 25. | 50. | — | 5. | 10. |
| Washington quarter 1976 | 5. | 8. | 10. up | 50. up | 15. | 75. up | 50. | 100. | — | 15. | 25. |
| Franklin half 1948-1963 | 10. | 15. | 40. | — | 50. | — | — | — | — | 50. | 75. |
| Kennedy half 1964 | 10. | 15. | 25. | — | 50. | — | — | — | — | 50. | 75. |
| Kennedy half 1965-1970 | 10. | 15. | 20. | — | 25. | 50. | 50. | — | — | 35. | 50. |
| Kennedy half 1971- | 5. | 10. | 15. | — | 20. | 40. | 40. | — | — | 30. | 40. |
| Kennedy half 1976- | 50. | 20. | 30. | — | 100. | — | — | — | — | 50. | 75. |
| Morgan dollar 1878-1921 | 35. | 75. | 125. | — | — | — | — | — | — | — | — |
| Peace dollar 1921-1935 | 30. | 65. | 110. | — | — | — | — | — | — | — | — |
| Ike dollar (clad) 1971-78 | 15. | 50. | 100. | — | 200. | 500. up | — | — | 1750. | 50. | 100. |
| Ike dollar (silver) 1971-1975 | Rare to unknown in all classes | | | | | | | | | | |
| Ike dollar (clad) 1976 | Rare | | | | | | | | | | |
| Ike dollar (silver) 1976 | Rare to unknown in all classes | | | | | | | | | | |
| Anthony dollar 1979-81 | 25. | 50. up | 175. up | 250. | Rare | — | — | — | — | 20. | 35. |
| Commemoratives | Rare | | | | | | | | | | |
| Proof coins | $25 to $200 cent to half dollar | | | | | | | | | | |

## I-D: Laminations and split planchets

There are 11 classes in this section, covering planchets that split, or crack parallel to the flat surfaces, or have chunks of metal rolled into the surface. I-D-10 (unstruck clad layer) ranges from $10 for a dime to $100 for a clad Eisenhower dollar. I-D-12 (broken planchet before strike) and I-D-13 (broken planchet after strike) are valued according to the size and coin.

The classes are I-D-1, lamination crack or up to 25 percent of surface missing; I-D-2, large lamination, over 25 percent missing; I-D-3, split unstruck planchet, rolled in metal; I-D-4, split before strike; I-D-5, split after strike; I-D-6, missing clad layer; I-D-7, both clad layers missing; I-D-8, struck clad layer, split off before strike; I-D-9, struck clad layer, split off after strike; I-D-10, unstruck clad layer; I-D-11, hinged split.

| Split planchet | Layer peeled off | Metal split away | Lamination crack |
|---|---|---|---|

| | Lamination Crack or -25% of Surface Missing I-D-1 | Large Lamination +25% of Surface Missing I-D-2 | Rolled in Metal I-D-3 | Split Before Strike I-D-4 | Split After Strike I-D-5 | Missing Clad Layer I-D-6 | Missing Both Clad Layers I-D-7 | Struck & Split Before Strike I-D-8 | Struck & Split After Strike I-D-9 | Hinged Split Planchet I-D-11 |
|---|---|---|---|---|---|---|---|---|---|---|
| Lincoln cent 1909-1942 | 1. | 5. | 2. | 5. | 3. | — | — | — | — | 30. |
| Lincoln cent 1943 | 5. | 15. | 10. | 50. | 35. | — | — | — | — | 100. |
| Lincoln cent 1944-1958 | 1. | 5. | 2. | 5. | 3. | — | — | — | — | 25. |
| Lincoln cent 1959-1982 | 1. | 3. | 1. | 3. | 3. | — | — | — | — | 20. |
| Lincoln cent 1982- | — | — | — | 10. | 15. | N/A | N/A | N/A | N/A | 50. |
| Buffalo nickel 1913-1938 | — | — | — | 35. | 35. | — | — | — | — | 50. |
| Jefferson nickel 1938- | 3. | 10. | 5. | 15. | 10. | — | — | — | — | 35. |
| Jefferson nickel 1942-1945 | Common | 5. | 5. | 5. | 5. | — | — | — | — | 25. |
| Mercury dime 1916-1945 | 15. | 50. | 15. | — | — | — | — | — | — | — |
| Roosevelt dime 1946-1964 | 10. | 35. | 10. | — | — | — | — | — | — | 50. |
| Roosevelt dime 1965- | 3. | 10. | 5. | — | — | 20. | 35. | 25. | 35. | 45. |
| Washington quarter 1932-64 | 15. | 50. | 10. | 50. | 50. | — | — | — | — | 75. |
| Washington quarter 1965- | 10. | 25. | 10. | — | — | 25. | 50. | 50. | 35. | 60. |
| Washington quarter 1976 | 25. | 50. | 25. | — | — | 50. | 75. | 75. | 60. | 100. |
| Walking Liberty 1916-47 | — | — | — | 150. | 125. | — | — | — | — | — |
| Franklin half 1948-1963 | 20. | 50. up | 50. up | 125. | 100. | — | — | — | — | — |
| Kennedy half 1964 | 20. | 50. up | 50. up | 100. | 75. | — | — | — | — | 150. |
| Kennedy half 1965-1970 | 15. | 35. up | 35. up | 75. | 50. | 125. | 200. | 150. | 100. | 125. |
| Kennedy half 1971- | 10. | 25. up | 25. up | 50. | 35. | 100. | 200. | 125. | 75. | 100. |
| Kennedy half 1976 | 20. | 50. up | 50. up | 100. | 75. | 150. | 300. | 200. | 150. | 200. |
| Morgan dollar 1878-1921 | 50. up | 100. up | 50. up | 275. | 175. | — | — | — | — | — |
| Peace dollar 1921-1935 | 50. up | 100. up | 50. up | 275. | 175. | — | — | — | — | — |
| Ike dollar (clad) 1971-78 | 35. up | 75. up | 35. up | 250. | 150. | 500. | RARE | 500. | 400. | — |
| Ike dollar (silver) 1971-1975 | | | | | | | | | | Rare in all classes |
| Ike Dollar (clad) 1976 | | | | | | | | | | Rare in all classes |
| Ike Dollar (silver) 1976 | | | | | | | | | | Rare to unknown in all classes |
| SBA dollar 1979-81 | | | | | | | | | | Rare in all classes |
| Commemoratives | | | | | | | | | | Rare to unknown in all classes |
| Proof coins | | | | | | | | | | Rare in all classes |
| Gold coins | | | | | | | | | | Rare in all classes |

### I-E: Wrong-stock planchets

This section consists of planchets that were punched from strip intended for a different denomination, series, or for coins of another country. The classes are I-E-1, dime stock; I-E-2, quarter stock; I-E-3, half-dollar stock; I-E-4, dollar stock; I-E-5, foreign stock; and I-E-6, token or medal stock. I-E-7, punched from spoiled planchets (wrong thickness); I-E-8, punched from spoiled planchets (correct thickness); I-E-9, punched from tokens (wrong thickness); I-E-10, purchased planchets; I-E-11, half-cent stock; I-E-12, cent stock; I-E-13, experimental and pattern stock; I-E-14, proof stock; I-E-15, two-cent stock; I-E-16, silver three-cent stock; I-E-17, nickel three-cent stock; I-E-18, half-dime stock; I-E-19, 20-cent stock; I-E-20, clad stock; I-E-21, adjusted specifications; I-E-22, punched from trial strike; I-E-23, plated stock.

| | Dime Stock | Quarter Stock | Half Dollar Stock |
|---|---|---|---|
| | I-E-1 | I-E-2 | I-E-3 |
| Mercury dime 1916-1945 | — | $200. | — |
| Roosevelt dime 1946-1964 | — | 100. | — |
| Roosevelt dime 1965- | — | 75. | — |
| Washington quarter 1932-64 | 100. | — | — |
| Washington quarter 1965- | 10. | — | 125. |

**Quarter on dime stock**

### I-F: Extra metal

As planchets are punched from the strip, they can pick up extra metal that adheres to the punch press. This is found only in the rim area as a raised spur on the planchet or as an "island" on the rim on the struck coin. It cannot project above the normal surface of the coin, like a die break.

The classes are I-F-1, on Type I planchet; I-F-2, on Type II planchet; and I-F-3, on a struck coin.

| | I-F-1 | I-F-2 | I-F-3 |
|---|---|---|---|
| Cent 1909-1988 | 50. | 25. | 15. |
| Nickel 1938-1988 | 60. | 50. | 20. |
| Dime 1946-1988 | 75. | 70. | 35. |

### I-G: Sintered planchet

Color is not a minting variety. Many coins with a golden color are incorrectly described as the result of a "copper wash." The real cause is a thin coating of bronze or brass powder adhering to the planchets in the annealing drum. A thicker layer is classed as a sintered planchet. Although it is quite rare, it usually has a value of less than $50.

## I-H: Unstruck planchets

Coin planchets may bypass parts of the processing and escape into circulation. The Type I-H-1 planchets are flat with sharp edges; the Type I-H-2 planchets have a slightly raised rim on both sides. Type I planchets are often difficult to authenticate. The classes are I-H-1, Type I planchet; I-H-2, Type II (upset edge) planchet.

| | Type I I-H-1 | Type II I-H-2 | | Type I I-H-1 | Type II I-H-2 |
|---|---|---|---|---|---|
| Half cent 1793-1857 | 50. | 125. | Quarter 1796-1836 | 200. | 200. |
| Large cent 1793-1857 | 15. | 65. | Quarter 1837-1852 | 200. | 200. |
| Small cent 1856-1864 | 250. | 250. | Quarter 1853-1873 | 200. | 200. |
| Indian cent 1854-1909 | — | 120. | Quarter 1873-1964 | 60. | 50. |
| Lincoln cent 1909-1982 | 1.25 | 0.50 | Quarter 1965- | 2. | 3. |
| Lincoln cent 1943 | — | 15. | Half dollar 1794-1836 | 250. | 250. |
| Lincoln cent 1982- | 5. | 5. | Half dollar 1837-1852 | 250. | 250. |
| Two-cent 1864-1873 | 150. | 160. | Half dollar 1853-1873 | 250. | 250. |
| Three-cent (nickel) 1865-89 | 200. | 200. | Half dollar 1873-1964 | 240. | 160. |
| Three-cent (silver) 1851-73 | 200. | 200. | Half dollar 1965-1970 | 110. | 330. |
| Nickel 1866- | 3. | 2. | Half dollar 1971- | 2. | 4. |
| Nickel 1942-1945 (silver) | 235. | 210. | Silver dollar 1794-1803 | 500. | 500. |
| Half dime 1794-1873 | 150. | 300. | Silver dollar 1840-1935 | 240. | 160. |
| Dime 1798-1837 | 200. | 200. | Trade dollar 1873-1885 | | Rare |
| Dime 1837-1853 | 150. | 150. | Ike dollar (clad) 1971-78 | 35. | 40. |
| Dime 1853-1873 | 200. | 200. | Ike dollar (silver) 1971-1976 | 200. | 250. |
| Dime 1873-1964 | 10. | 10. | Anthony dollar 1979-81 | 125. | 130. |
| Roosevelt dime 1965- | 1. | 2. | | | |
| Twenty cent 1875-1878 | | Rare | | | |

Note: The market is flooded with many denominations of clad Type I and steel-cent Type I planchets.

## I-I: Coin metal strip

The remains of the coin metal strip from which the planchets have been punched sometimes leave the mint as scrap and is acquired by collectors. A section of strip with punched holes (I-I-1) or a piece of chopped-up strip (I-I-2) are considered collectible. The sections are worth $5-$100. The chopped pieces are valued from a few cents to a few dollars, depending on the size of the piece and the metal.

| | I-1 |
|---|---|
| Cent planchet strip | 15. up |
| Steel cent strip | 10. up |
| Nickel strip | 15. up |
| Clad dime strip | 20. up |
| Clad quarter strip | 35. up |
| Clad half-dollar strip | 100. up |

# Division II: Die varieties

This division contains all the classes that deal with variations in the die itself, which result in a change in the intended design as a result of accident, intent, alteration, or other change in the die. Every class in this division repeats exactly on every coin struck by the given die.

## II-A: Engraving varieties

With 37 classes, this is the largest section of the entire PDS system. II-A-1, overdates, are covered in the regular price charts, as are II-A-3, small dates. Other examples, however, are so scattered through the coinage that it would be impossible to accurately price them except on a case-by-case basis.

The other classes are II-A-2, repunched dates; II-A-4, large date; II-A-5, small over large date; II-A-6, large over small; II-A-7, misspelled engraving; II-A-8, one letter over another; II-A-9, wrong number (other than date); II-A-10, one number over another (other than date); II-A-11, missing designer's initials; II-A-12, recutting; II-A-13, repunched numbers (other than date); II-A-14, repunched letter (other than mintmark); II-A-15, repunched design; II-A-16, modified design; II-A-17, normal design; II-A-18, design mistakes; II-A-19, broken punch; II-A-20, incomplete die; II-A-21, pattern; II-A-22, abnormal reeding; II-A-23, plugged die; II-A-24, wrong-size letters or numbers; II-A-25, letter over number; II-A-26, number over letter; II-A-27, trial design; II-A-28, numbered dies; II-A-29, expedient punch; II-A-30, misplaced device punch; II-A-31, layout marks; II-A-32, worn punch; II-A-33, misaligned punch; II-A-34, style overpunch; II-A-35, one design over another; II-A-36, wrong date; II-A-37, canceled die; and II-A-38, reducing-lathe doubling.

## II-B: Hubbing varieties

This section includes seven classes of hub doubling, plus three more forms of hubbing varieties, all directly connected to the hub, which is the tool used to press the coin design into the face of the die. Each class of hub doubling is from a different cause, described by the title of the class. At the latest count, over 1,200 doubled dies have been reported among U.S. coinage, the most famous occurring on some cents of 1955 and 1972.

The classes are II-B-1, rotated hub doubling; II-B-2, distorted hub; II-B-3, design hub; II-B-4, offset hub; II-B-5, pivoted hub; II-B-6, distended hub; II-B-7, modified hub; II-B-8, hub cracks; II-B-9, hub breaks; II-B-10, worn or damaged hub; and II-B-11, tilted hub.

Rotated hub doubling

Hub break

| | II-B-1 | II-B-2 | II-B-3 | II-B-4 | II-B-5 | II-B-6 | II-B-7 | II-B-9 |
|---|---|---|---|---|---|---|---|---|
| Flying Eagle cent 1856-58 | 750. | 550. | 600. | — | — | — | — | — |
| Indian cent 1873 | — | — | 500. | — | — | — | — | — |
| Lincoln cent 1909 "VDB" | — | — | 125. | — | — | — | — | — |
| Lincoln cent 1917 | — | — | — | — | 175. | — | — | — |
| Lincoln cent 1936 | — | — | 8. | 250. | 100. | 4. | — | — |
| Lincoln cent 1941 | 150. | — | — | 150. | 25. | 4. | — | — |
| Lincoln cent 1955 | 775. | 250. | — | — | — | 3. | — | — |

| | II-B-1 | II-B-2 | II-B-3 | II-B-4 | II-B-5 | II-B-6 | II-B-7 | II-B-9 |
|---|---|---|---|---|---|---|---|---|
| Lincoln cent 1960-P&D Lg/Sm, Sm/Lg | — | — | 150. | — | — | 4. | — | — |
| Lincoln cent 1964 | — | 4. | — | — | 150. | — | — | — |
| Lincoln cent 1964 Pr | 15. | — | — | — | 35. | — | — | — |
| Lincoln cent 1969-S | 5500. | — | — | — | — | — | — | — |
| Lincoln cent 1970-S | 750. | — | 5. | — | — | — | 35. | — |
| Lincoln cent 1970-S Pr | 250. | — | — | — | — | 300. | — | — |
| Lincoln cent 1971 | 75. | 75. | — | — | — | — | — | — |
| Lincoln cent 1971-S Pr | — | 750. | — | — | — | — | — | — |
| Lincoln cent 1972 | 2.-225. | — | 5. | — | — | — | — | — |
| Lincoln cent 1972-D | 25. | — | — | — | — | — | — | — |
| Lincoln cent 1972-S Pr | 300. | 10. | — | — | — | — | — | — |
| Lincoln cent 1980 | — | — | 100. | — | — | — | — | — |
| Lincoln cent 1983 | — | — | — | 175. | — | — | — | — |
| Lincoln cent 1984 | — | — | — | 90. | — | — | — | — |
| Lincoln cent 1987-D | — | 50. | — | — | — | — | — | — |
| Two-cent 1864-1873 | — | 275. | 500. | 350. | 350. | — | — | — |
| Three-cent 1864-1871 | — | — | 325. | — | 300. | — | — | — |
| Shield nickel 1866-1883 | — | — | 75.-425. | — | — | — | — | — |
| Buffalo nickel 1916/1916 | — | — | — | — | 9000. | — | — | — |
| Buffalo nickel 1918/1917-D | — | — | 8500. | — | — | — | — | — |
| Jefferson nickel 1938 LD/SD | — | — | 150. | — | — | — | — | — |
| Jefferson nickel 1939 | — | 200. | 150. | — | — | 40. | 15. | — |
| Jefferson nickel 1943/1942 | — | — | 250. | — | — | — | — | — |
| Half dime 1861 | — | — | — | — | 550. | — | — | — |
| Mercury dime 1942/1941 | — | — | 1025. | — | — | — | — | — |
| Mercury dime 1942/2/1941-D | — | — | 1175. | — | — | — | — | — |
| Roosevelt dime 1970 | — | 100. | — | — | — | — | — | — |
| Twenty-cent 1876-CC | — | — | 69,300. | — | — | — | — | — |
| Standing Liberty quarter 1918/1917-S | — | — | 8750. | — | — | — | — | — |
| Washington quarter 1934 | 15.-350. | — | — | — | — | — | — | — |
| Washington quarter 1936 | 625. | — | — | — | — | — | — | — |
| Washington quarter 1942-D | — | — | 350. | — | — | — | — | — |
| Washington quarter 1943-S | — | — | 250. | — | — | — | — | — |
| Washington quarter 1945 | 250. | — | — | — | — | — | — | — |
| Washington quarter 1968-S Pr | 200. | — | — | — | — | — | — | — |
| Washington quarter 1976-D | 450. | — | — | — | — | — | — | — |
| Walking Liberty half 1942 | — | 125. | — | — | — | — | — | — |
| Walking Liberty half 1946 | — | 150. | — | — | — | — | — | — |
| Kennedy half 1964-P&D | 10.-25. | 10.-75. | 10. | — | — | — | — | — |
| Morgan dollar 1878 7/8 TF | — | — | 63. | — | — | — | — | — |
| Morgan dollar 1878-CC | — | 175. | — | — | — | — | — | — |
| Morgan dollar 1901 | — | — | — | 700. | — | — | — | — |
| Ike dollar 1976-PDS | — | — | 20. | — | — | — | — | — |
| Anthony dollar 1979 | — | 25. | 25. | — | — | — | — | — |

Note: More than one die may exist for a given date. Prices for coins grading above MS-60 will be considerably higher.

## II-C: Mintmark varieties

Mintmarks are punched into the die by hand. Variations resulting from mistakes in the punching are listed in this section. Unless exceptionally mispunched, values are usually estimated at 150 percent of numismatic value. Slightly tilted or displaced mintmarks have no value.

The classes are II-C-1, double punched; II-C-2, triple; II-C-3, quadruple; II-C-4, vertical/horizontal; II-C-5, vertical/upside down; II-C-6, overmintmark (such as D/S); II-C-7, small; II-C-8, large; II-C-9, large over small; II-C-10, missing; II-C-11, small over large; II-C-12, displaced; II-C-13, modified; II-C-14, tilted (45 degrees or more) mintmark; II-C-15, separated punches; II-C-16, normal mintmark; II-C-17, broken punch; II-C-18, mintmark touching design.

**Double**          **Triple**

| | II-C-1 | II-C-2 | II-C-4 | II-C-5 | II-C-6 | II-C-9 | II-C-10 | II-C-13 | II-C-15 |
|---|---|---|---|---|---|---|---|---|---|
| Indian cent 1908-S | 225. | — | — | — | — | — | — | — | — |
| Lincoln cent 1909-S V/H | — | — | 275. | — | — | — | — | — | — |
| Lincoln cent 1922 | — | — | — | — | — | — | 4000. | — | — |
| Lincoln cent 1944-D D/S | — | — | — | — | 375. | — | — | — | — |
| Lincoln cent 1956-D | — | — | — | — | — | — | — | — | 35. |
| Lincoln cent 1960-D V/H | — | — | 3. | — | — | — | — | — | — |
| Lincoln cent 1961-D V/H | — | — | 2. | — | — | — | — | — | — |
| Lincoln cent 1985-D | 10. | — | — | — | — | — | — | — | — |
| Buffalo nickel 1935-D D/D/D | — | 135. | — | — | — | — | — | — | — |
| Buffalo nickel 1937-D D/S | — | — | — | — | 35. | — | — | — | — |
| Buffalo nickel 1938-D D/D/D/S | — | — | — | — | 35. | — | — | — | — |
| Jefferson nickel 1942-D D/D/HD | — | — | 30. | — | — | — | — | — | — |
| Jefferson nickel 1949-D D/S | — | — | — | — | 330. | — | — | — | — |
| Jefferson nickel 1954-S S/D | — | — | — | — | 31. | — | — | — | — |
| Jefferson nickel 1955-D D/S | — | — | — | — | 15.-30. (10 dies) | — | — | — | — |
| Jefferson nickel 1971-(S) Pr | — | — | — | — | — | — | 1055. | — | — |
| Seated Liberty dime 1890-S Lg/Sm | — | — | — | — | — | 650. | — | — | — |
| Seated Liberty dime 1891-O V/H | — | — | 600. | — | — | — | — | — | — |
| Roosevelt dime 1968-(S) Pr | — | — | — | — | — | — | 8900. | — | — |
| Roosevelt dime 1970-(S) Pr | — | — | — | — | — | — | 780. | — | — |
| Roosevelt dime 1975-(S) Pr | — | — | — | — | — | Two | known | — | — |
| Roosevelt dime 1982-(P) | — | — | — | — | — | — | 200. | — | — |
| Roosevelt dime 1983-(S) Pr | — | — | — | — | — | — | 675. | — | — |
| Roosevelt dime 1985-P P&P | — | — | — | — | — | — | — | — | 150. |
| Seated Liberty quarter 1856-S Lg/Sm | — | — | — | — | — | 740. | — | — | — |
| Seated Liberty quarter 1877-S V/H | — | — | 550. | — | — | — | — | — | — |
| Washington quarter 1950-D D/S | — | — | — | — | 335. | — | — | — | — |
| Washington quarter 1950-S S/D | — | — | — | — | 520. | — | — | — | — |
| Washington quarter 1956-D V/UD | — | — | — | 30. | — | — | — | — | — |
| Seated Liberty half 1855-O V/H | — | — | 1175. | — | — | — | — | — | — |
| Trade dollar 1875-S S/S/CC | — | — | — | — | 1500. | — | — | — | — |
| Morgan dollar 1879-O V/H | — | — | 1200. | — | — | — | — | — | — |
| Morgan dollar 1879-CC Lg/Sm | — | — | — | — | — | 4850. | — | 130. | — |
| Morgan dollar 1900-O O/CC | — | — | — | — | 115. (8 dies) | — | — | 230. | — |

1979-S proof set (Variety II mintmark, all 6 coins) II-C-13 .......... 73.
1981-S Proof Set (Variety II mintmark, all 6 coins) II-C-13 .......... 295.

Note: More than 2,000 dies are known with mintmark varieties in most denominations and series. Those listed are some of the more valuable examples. Values are usually estimated at 150 percent of normal numismatic value for the grade, more for exceptional specimens. Prices for grades above MS-60 are substantially higher.

## II-D: Die cracks

Cracks in the surface of the die allow coin metal to squeeze in, resulting in raised, irregular lines above the coin's normal surface. These are one of the commonest forms of die damage, making them easily collectible.

The classes are II-D-1, single die crack; II-D-2, multiple; II-D-3, head to rim (Lincoln cent); II-D-4, split die; II-D-5, rim to rim; and II-D-6, collar crack.

## II-E: Die breaks

Breaks in the surface of the die allow coin metal to squeeze into the resulting holes, causing raised, irregular areas above the coin's normal surface. Die chips and small die breaks are nearly as common as die

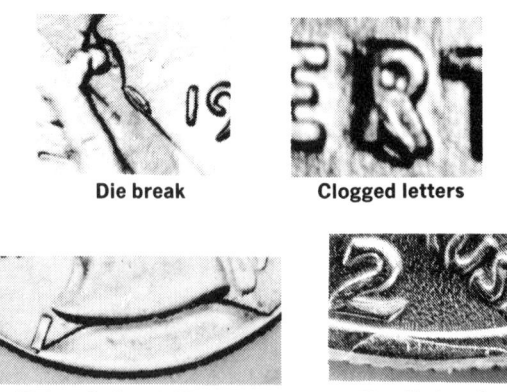

Die break                    Clogged letters

Major die break ("cud")          Rim die break

cracks, but major die breaks ("cuds"), which extend in from the coin's edge, are quite rare on the larger coins. If the broken piece of the die is retained, the resulting design will be above or below the level of the rest of the surface.

The classes are II-E-1, die chip; II-E-2, small die break; II-E-3, large die break; II-E-4, rim die break; II-E-5, major die break; II-E-6, retained broken die; II-E-7, laminated die; II-E-8, split or chipped chrome plating; II-E-9, collar break; II-E-10, broken letter on edge die; II-E-11, missing letter on edge die; II-E-12, retained center broken die; and II-E-13, bar next to rim.

## II-F: "BIE" varieties

A series of small die breaks or die chips in the letters of "Liberty," mostly on the wheat-reverse Lincoln cent, is actively collected. The 'name results from the resemblance to an "I" between the "B" and "E"

BIE error

on many of the dies, but they are found between all of the letters in different cases. Well over 1,500 dies are known and cataloged. Values range from 10 cents for common examples in circulated grades to $75 for the more scarce varieties in top grade.

## II-G: Die dents, gouges, scratches, and polished dies

The die is subject to all sorts of damage, which will show on the struck coin. Any dent, gouge, pit, or scratch in the die will result in a matching raised area on the coin. This damage is repaired by polishing the die, resulting in removal or doubling of the design. All of these classes are quite common and have no value unless they are exceptional examples.

**Scratches**

**Gouge**        **Dent**

This section is divided into eight classes: II-G-1, dents; II-G-2, gouges or damaged die; II-G-3, scratches; II-G-4, polished die; II-G-5, polishing doubling (inside); II-G-6, polishing doubling (outside); II-G-7, worn or deformed die; II-G-8, pitted or rusted die.

### II-H: Die clashes, collar clashes, and design transfer

Die clashes occur when the dies hit each other, damaging the faces of the dies. The opposing design is thus transferred to the die and struck coin.

A collar clash results from the die hitting the collar, damaging the rim area of the die, which shows on the struck coin.

Design transfer ("ghost" images) result from deformation of the die from constant use. Only extreme examples have any value, as these are common forms of damage to the die. Heavy die and collar clashes will bring from a few cents to several dollars, depending on the coin's denomination.

### II-I: Progressions

When additional changes occur in a die, the resulting variety is classed as a "progression." Up to a dozen or more stages of a given die pair may be traced by additional die breaks, die cracks, die substitutions, and so on. Values depend on the initial class of the variety, bringing a small premium for additional stages of the same die pair.

# Division III: Striking varieties

Once the planchets have been prepared and the dies made, the planchets are struck by a pair of dies and become a coin. In this division are listed the misstrikes resulting from human or mechanical malfunction in the striking process. These are one-of-a-kind varieties, but there may be

PRICING SECTION

many similar coins that fall in a given class. Multiples and combinations of classes must be considered on a case-by-case basis.

## III-A: Die-adjustment strikes

As the dies are adjusted in the coin press, variations in the strike occur until the press is properly set up. These coins are normally scrapped, but on occasion reach circulation. The classes are III-A-1, die-adjustment strike; III-A-2, edge strike; III-A-3, weak strike; III-A-4, strong strike; III-A-5, jam strike; III-A-6, die trial; and III-A-7, edge die-adjustment strike.

| | Die Adjustment Strike III-A-1 | Edge Strike III-A-2 | Weak Strike III-A-3 | Strong Strike III-A-4 | Jam Strike III-A-5 |
|---|---|---|---|---|---|
| Indian cent 1859-1909 | 150. | — | — | — | — |
| Lincoln cent 1909-1942 | 50. | — | — | — | — |
| Lincoln cent 1943 | 150. | — | — | — | — |
| Lincoln cent 1944-1958 | 35. | — | — | — | — |
| Lincoln cent 1959-1982 | 25. | — | — | — | — |
| Lincoln cent 1976 | 35. | — | — | — | — |
| Lincoln cent 1982- | 35. | — | — | — | — |
| Buffalo nickel 1913-1938 | Unknown | — | — | — | — |
| Jefferson nickel 1938- | 25. | — | — | — | — |
| Jefferson nickel 1942-1945 | 50. | — | — | — | — |
| Jefferson nickel 1976 | 35. | — | — | — | — |
| Mercury dime 1916-1945 | 100. | — | — | — | — |
| Roosevelt dime 1946-1964 | 50. | — | — | — | — |
| Roosevelt dime 1965- | 35. | — | — | — | — |
| Roosevelt dime 1976 | 50. | — | — | — | — |
| Washington quarter 1932-64 | 125. | — | — | — | — |
| Washington quarter 1965- | 75. | — | — | — | — |
| Washington quarter 1976 | 150. | — | — | — | — |
| Franklin half 1948-1963 | 275. | — | — | — | — |
| Kennedy half 1964 | 250. | — | — | — | — |
| Kennedy half 1965-1970 | 200. | — | — | — | — |
| Kennedy half 1971- | 150. | — | — | — | — |
| Kennedy half 1976 | 350. | — | — | — | — |
| Morgan dollar 1878-1921 | Rare | — | — | — | — |
| Peace dollar 1921-1935 | Rare | — | — | — | — |
| Ike dollar 1971-78 | 300. | — | — | — | — |
| Ike dollar 1976 | 500. | — | — | — | — |
| Anthony dollar 1979-81 | 150. | — | — | — | — |
| Commemoratives | Rare | — | — | — | — |

## III-B: Indented, brockage, and counter-brockage strikes

Indented and uniface strikes involve an extra unstruck planchet between one of the dies and the planchet being struck. Brockage strikes involve a struck coin between one of the dies and the planchet, and a counter-brockage requires a brockage coin between one of the dies and the planchet.

A cap or capped-die strike results when a coin sticks to the die and is squeezed around it in the shape of a bottle cap. There are 18 classes in this section with variations on the planchet and coin relationship.

The classes are III-B-1, indented; III-B-2, uniface; III-B-3, indent of smaller planchet; III-B-4, partial brockage; III-B-5, full brockage; III-B-6, brockage of smaller coin; III-B-7, partial counter-brockage; III-B-8, full counter-brockage; III-B-9, brockage-counter-brockage; III-B-10, cap; III-B-11, indented second strike; III-B-12, brockage second strike; III-B-13, counter-brockage second strike; III-B-14, multiple brockage; III-B-15, reverse (die) cap; and III-B-16, edge counter-brockage; III-B-17, indent of feed finger; III-B-18, brockage of struck fragment.

| III-B-1 | III-B-8 | III-B-10 |

| | Indented Strike | Full Brockage | Full Counter Brockage | Cap (Capped Die) |
|---|---|---|---|---|
| | III-B-1 | III-B-5 | III-B-8 | III-B-10 |
| Indian cent 1859-1909 | 75. | 150. | 300. | 1600. |
| Lincoln cent 1909-1942 | 15. | 20. | 125. | 325. |
| Lincoln cent 1943 | 30. | 75. | 200. | Rare |
| Lincoln cent 1944-1958 | 10. | 20. | 100. | 300. |
| Lincoln cent 1959-1982 | 5. | 15. | 75. | 275. |
| Lincoln cent 1976 | 10. | 20. | 100. | 300. |
| Lincoln cent 1982- | 10. | 20. | 100. | Rare |
| Buffalo nickel 1913-1938 | 50. | 75. | 125. | Rare |
| Jefferson nickel 1938- | 35. | 50. | 100. | 300. |
| Jefferson nickel 1942-1945 | 50. | 75. | 150. | Rare |
| Jefferson nickel 1976 | 50. | 75. | 150. | Rare |
| Mercury dime 1916-1945 | 35. | 50. | 100. | 300. up |
| Roosevelt dime 1946-1964 | 25. | 35. | 60. | 250. |
| Roosevelt dime 1965- | 20. | 30. | 50. | 200. |
| Roosevelt dime 1976 | 25. | 35. | 60. | 250. |
| Washington quarter 1932-64 | 40. | 60. | 125. | Rare |
| Washington quarter 1965- | 25. | 50. | 100. | 250. |
| Washington quarter 1976 | 50. | 100. | 200. | Rare |
| Franklin half 1948-1963 | 125. | 500. | Rare | Rare |
| Kennedy half 1964 | 125. | 450. | Rare | Rare |
| Kennedy half 1965-1970 | 100. | 350. | Rare | Rare |
| Kennedy half 1971- | 75. | 250. | Rare | Rare |
| Kennedy half 1976 | 125. | 500. | Rare | Rare |
| Morgan dollar 1878-1921 | Rare in all classes | | | |
| Peace dollar 1921-1935 | Rare in all classes | | | |
| Ike dollar 1971-78 | 200. | Rare | — | 3500. |
| Ike dollar 1976 | Rare in all classes | | | |
| Anthony dollar 1979-81 | 25. | 100. | — | — |
| Proof coins | Rare in all classes | | | |

## III-C: Struck through abnormal objects

Just about anything can get between the die and planchet, and be struck into the coin's surface, leaving a distinctive indentation, such as the pattern of the weave of cloth. The object must be retained to identify certain classes, such as struck in wrong metal.

| Cloth scrap | Filled die | Dropped letter |

The classes are III-C-1, struck through cloth; III-C-2, wire; III-C-3, thread; III-C-4, filled die; III-C-5, dropped filling; III-C-6, wrong-metal fragments; III-C-7, struck coin fragments; III-C-8, rim burr; III-C-9, miscellaneous objects; and III-C-10, unstruck planchet fragments.

| | Struck Through Cloth III-C-1 | Wire III-C-2 | Dropped Filling III-C-5 | Struck Coin Fragment III-C-7 |
|---|---|---|---|---|
| Indian cent 1859-1909 | 50. | 50. | 20. | 75. up |
| Lincoln cent 1909-1942 | 35. | 35. | 15. | 50. up |
| Lincoln cent 1943 | — | 75. | 25. | 100. up |
| Lincoln cent 1944-1958 | 25. | 50. | 10. | 35. up |
| Lincoln cent 1959-1982 | 20. | 50. | 10. | 25. up |
| Lincoln cent 1982- | 25. | 60. | 15. | 35. up |
| Buffalo nickel 1913-1938 | 60. | 100. | 10. | 50. up |
| Jefferson nickel 1938- | 50. | 75. | 10. | 40. up |
| Jefferson nickel 1942-1945 | 60. | 100. | 15. | 50. up |
| Mercury dime 1916-1945 | 60. | 60. | 15. | 50. up |
| Roosevelt dime 1946-1964 | 50. | 50. | 15. | 50. up |
| Roosevelt dime 1965- | 35. | 35. | 10. | 35. up |
| Roosevelt dime 1976 | 45. | 45. | 15. | 45. up |
| Washington quarter 1932-64 | 75. | 50. | 15. | 50. up |
| Washington quarter 1965- | 45. | 35. | 10. | 35. up |
| Washington quarter 1976 | 100. | 75. | 25. | 100. up |
| Franklin half 1948-1963 | 75. | 75. | 25. | 100. up |
| Kennedy half 1964 | 75. | 75. | 25. | 100. up |
| Kennedy half 1965-1970 | 60. | 60. | 20. | 100. up |
| Kennedy half 1971- | 50. | 50. | 15. | 75. up |
| Kennedy half 1976 | | | | Rare in all classes |
| Morgan dollar 1878-1921 | | | | Rare in all classes |
| Peace dollar 1921-1935 | | | | Rare in all classes |
| Ike dollar 1971-78 | | | | Rare in all classes |
| Ike dollar 1976 | | | | Rare in all classes |
| Anthony dollar 1979-81 | | | | Scarce to rare in all classes |

Note: Some 1987, 1988 and 1989 quarters are found without mintmarks, classed as III-C-4, filled die. Values depend on market conditions. Filled dies have value only on current, uncirculated coins.

## III-D: Struck on abnormal objects

This section contains coins struck on the wrong planchet, objects similar to a planchet, pieces of scrap and junk metal, two or more planchets stuck together, planchets that do not have the normal upset edge, and even on medal planchets. Anything the same size or smaller than a normal planchet can get into the dies and be struck.

**Cent on dime planchet**

**Half dollar on dime planchet**

**Half dollar on quarter planchet**

The classes are III-D-1, wrong metal on a cent planchet; III-D-2, on a nickel planchet; III-D-3, on a dime planchet; III-D-4, quarter planchet; III-D-5, half-dollar planchet; III-D-6, gold planchet; III-D-7, U.S. coin on foreign planchet; III-D-8, foreign coin on U.S. planchet; III-D-9, wrong-series planchet; III-D-10, scrap coin metal; III-D-11, junk non-coin metal; III-D-12, false planchet; III-D-13, bonded planchets; III-D-14, dollar planchet; III-D-15, medal planchet; III-D-16, Type I planchet; III-D-17, foreign coin on wrong foreign planchet; III-D-18, large planchet; III-D-19, hard planchet; III-D-20, small planchet; III-D-21, official samples; III-D-22, planchet fragment or lamination; and III-D-23, half-cent planchet.

| | III-D-1 | III-D-2 | III-D-3 | III-D-4 | III-D-5 | III-D-6 | III-D-7 | III-D-8 |
|---|---|---|---|---|---|---|---|---|
| Flying Eagle cent 1856-58 | — | — | 2000. | — | — | — | — | — |
| Indian cent 1859-1909 | — | — | 1200. | — | — | — | — | — |
| Lincoln cent 1909-1942 | — | — | 375. up | — | — | — | 100. | — |
| Lincoln cent 1943 (PD&S) | — | — | 375. (On bronze $30,000) | — | — | — | 2500. | — |
| Lincoln cent 1944-1958 | — | — | 150.-450. | — | — | — | 100. | 2000. |
| Lincoln cent 1959-1982 | — | — | 125.-450. | — | — | — | 100. | 100. |
| Lincoln cent 1976 | — | — | 150. | — | — | — | 100. | 100. |
| Lincoln cent 1982- | — | — | 150. | — | — | — | 100. | 100. |
| Two-cent 1864-1873 | 800. | 700. | 1300. | — | — | — | — | — |
| Shield nickel 1866-1883 | — | 900. | Rare | — | — | — | — | — |
| Liberty nickel 1883-1912 | 650. | — | Rare | — | — | — | — | 250. |
| Buffalo nickel 1913-1938 | 550. | — | Rare | — | — | — | — | — |
| Jefferson nickel 1938- | 35.-500. | — | 45.-550. | — | — | — | 100. | — |
| Jefferson nickel 1942-1945 | 350.-850. | — | 250.-400. | — | — | — | — | — |
| Jefferson nickel 1976 | 65. | — | 100. | — | — | — | 125. | — |
| Roosevelt dime 1965- | — | — | — | — | — | — | 400. | — |
| Roosevelt dime 1976 | — | — | — | — | — | — | 1000. | — |
| Barber quarter 1892-1916 | 1200. | 1200. | Rare | — | — | — | — | — |
| Standing Liberty 1916-30 | 800. | 900. | Unknown | — | — | — | — | — |
| Washington quarter 1932-64 | 100. | 55.-300. | 100.-500. | — | — | — | 300. | 275. |
| Washington quarter 1965- | 50. | 35.-90. | 50.-150. | — | — | — | 200. | 150. |
| Washington quarter 1976 | — | 250. | 350. | — | — | — | — | — |
| Barber half 1891-1915 | Rare in all classes | | | | | | | |
| Walking Liberty half 1916-47 | Rare in all classes | | | | | | | |
| Franklin half 1948-1963 | 450. | 500. | 600. | 300. | — | — | 250. | — |
| Kennedy half 1964 | 400. | 450. | 500. | 250. | — | — | 250. | — |
| Kennedy half 1965-1970 | 350. | 400. | 400. | 200. | — | — | 250. | — |
| Kennedy half 1971- | 300. | 350. | 300. | 100. | — | — | 250. | 400. |
| Kennedy half 1976 | Rare | Rare | Rare | 375. | — | — | — | — |
| Ike dollar 1971-78 | Rare in all classes | | | | | | | |
| Ike dollar 1976 | Rare in all classes | | | | | | | |
| Anthony dollar 1979-81 | Rare | Rare | Rare | 300. | — | — | — | — |
| Proof coins | Rare to unknown in all classes | | | | | | | |

### III-E: Double strikes

Only coins that receive two or more strikes fall in this section. Both sides of the coin are affected. Unless some object interferes, an equal area of both sides of the coin will be equally doubled. The exception is the second strike with a loose die, which will double only one side of a coin, but is a rare form occurring only on proofs.

A similar effect is flat-field doubling from die chatter, also only on proofs, which will add $1 to $10 to the coin's value and is relatively common.

The classes are III-E-1, close double strike (both centered); III-E-2, rotated second over centered first strike; III-E-3, off-center second over centered first; III-E-4, off-center second over off-centered first; III-E-5, saddle strike; III-E-6, multiple strike; III-E-7, obverse over reverse; III-E-8, struck over different denomination or series; III-E-9, U.S. over foreign; III-E-10, foreign over U.S.; III-E-11, foreign over foreign; III-E-12, chain

III-E-3          III-E-5          III-E-6

**Chain strike (III-E-12)**

strike; III-E-13, flat-field doubling (proof); III-E-14, second strike loose die (proof); III-E-15, second strike loose die (screw press); and III-E-16, first strike broadstrike, second strike off-center; III-E-17, second strike centered over off-center first strike (open collar); III-E-18, double strike on scrap or junk; III-E-19, struck on struck token or medal.

| | III-E-1 | III-E-2 | III-E-3 | III-E-4 | III-E-5 | III-E-6 | III-E-7 | III-E-8 | III-E-9 | III-E-10 | III-E-11 |
|---|---|---|---|---|---|---|---|---|---|---|---|
| Large cent 1793-1857 | 150. | 200. | 575. | — | — | — | 350. | 750. | — | — | — |
| Flying Eagle cent 1856-58 | 600. | 175. | 500. | — | — | 300. | 1500. | — | — | — | — |
| Indian cent 1859-1909 | 200. | 150. | 400. | — | — | — | 250. | 1000. | — | — | — |
| Lincoln cent 1909-1942 | 50. | 60. | 120. | — | — | — | 200. | 300. | — | — | — |
| Lincoln cent 1943 | 100. | 150. | 200. | — | — | — | 400. | 500. | — | — | — |
| Lincoln cent 1944-1958 | 50. | 55. | 60. | — | — | — | 100. | 250. | — | — | — |
| Lincoln cent 1959-1982 | 25. | 45. | 35. | — | — | — | 150. | 250. | — | — | — |
| Lincoln cent 1976 | 30. | 50. | 40. | — | — | — | 150. | 250. | — | — | — |
| Lincoln cent 1982- | 30. | 50. | 50. | — | — | — | 150. | 250. | — | — | — |
| Liberty nickel 1883-1912 | 250. | 350. | 850. | — | — | — | 350. | 500. | — | — | — |
| Buffalo nickel 1913-1938 | 325. | 125. | 500. | — | — | — | 225. | 800. | — | — | — |
| Jefferson nickel 1938- | 50. | 75. | 25. | — | — | — | 150. | 250. | — | — | — |
| Jefferson nickel 1942-1945 | 125. | 150. | 175. | — | — | — | 200. | 350. | — | — | — |
| Jefferson nickel 1976 | 60. | 100. | 35. | — | — | — | 150. | 250. | — | — | — |
| Half dime 1794-1873 | 500. | 200. | 650. | — | — | — | — | — | — | — | — |
| Dime 1798-1891 | 350. | 200. | 500. | — | — | — | — | 1250. | — | — | — |
| Barber dime 1892-1916 | 300. | 175. | 400. | — | — | — | — | 1200. | — | — | — |
| Mercury dime 1916-1945 | 200. | 125. | 350. | — | — | — | — | — | — | — | — |
| Roosevelt dime 1946-1964 | 50. | 120. | 100. | — | — | — | — | — | — | — | — |
| Roosevelt dime 1965- | 45. | 115. | 55. | — | — | — | — | — | — | — | — |
| Roosevelt dime 1976 | 50. | 125. | 60. | — | — | — | — | — | — | — | — |
| Quarter 1796-1891 | 600. | — | 750. | — | — | — | 500. | — | — | — | — |
| Barber quarter 1892-1916 | 400. | 200. | 800. | — | — | — | 500. | — | — | — | — |
| Standing Liberty quarter 1916-30 | | | | | | | | Rare in all classes | | | |
| Washington quarter 1932-64 | 120. | 120. | 140. | — | — | — | 350. | 500. | — | — | — |
| Washington quarter 1965- | 75. | 100. | 50. | — | — | — | 250. | 400. | — | — | — |
| Washington quarter 1976 | 100. | 150. | 250. | — | — | — | Rare | Rare | — | — | — |
| Barber half 1891-1915 | 500. | 600. | 1000. | — | — | — | 750. | — | — | — | — |
| Walking Liberty 1916-47 | 450. | 500. | 600. | — | — | — | 700. | — | — | — | — |
| Franklin half 1948-1963 | 400. | 450. | 500. | — | — | — | 500. | 500. | — | — | — |
| Kennedy half 1964 | 400. | 450. | 500. | — | — | — | 500. | 500. | — | — | — |
| Kennedy half 1965-1970 | 275. | 300. | 400. | — | — | — | 300. | 450. | — | — | — |
| Kennedy half 1971- | 200. | 250. | 300. | — | — | — | 300. | 400. | — | — | — |
| Kennedy half 1976 | | | | | | | | Rare in all classes | | | |
| Morgan dollar 1878-1921 | | | | | | | | Rare in all classes | | | |
| Peace dollar 1921-1935 | | | | | | | | Rare in all classes | | | |
| Ike dollar 1971-78 | | | | | | | | Rare in all classes | | | |
| Anthony dollar 1979-81 | | | | | | | | Rare in all classes | | | |

### III-F: Collar varieties

The collar is often referred to as the "third die" and is involved in a number of forms of misstrikes. The collar normally rises around the planchet, preventing it from squeezing sideways between the dies and at the same time forming the reeding on reeded-edge coins. If the collar is out of position or tilted, a form of partial collar results. If completely missing, it causes a broadstrike; if the planchet is not entirely between the dies, an off-center strike results.

The classes are III-F-1, flanged partial collar; III-F-2, tilted partial collar; III-F-3, centered broadstrike; III-F-4, uncentered broadstrike; III-F-5, off-center 10 percent to 30 percent; III-F-6, off-center 31 percent to 70 percent; III-F-7, off-center 71 percent and over; III-F-8, reversed partial collar; III-F-9, strike clip; III-F-10, reverse broadstrike; and III-F-11, rotated multisided planchet; III-F-12, collar too high; III-F-13, wire edge; III-F-14, split-off reeding; and III-F-15, reedless coin.

III-F-1

III-F-5          III-F-6          III-F-7

| | III-F-1 | III-F-2 | III-F-3 | III-F-4 | III-F-5 | III-F-6 | III-F-7 | III-F-8 | III-F-9 | III-F-10 | III-F-11 |
|---|---|---|---|---|---|---|---|---|---|---|---|
| Half cent 1793-1857 | — | — | — | — | 450. | 600. | — | — | — | — | — |
| Large cent 1793-1857 | — | — | — | — | 350. | 700. | 600. | — | — | — | — |
| Flying Eagle cent 1856-58 | — | — | — | — | 175. | 1000. | 500. | — | — | — | — |
| Indian cent 1859-1909 | 20. | 15. | 20. | — | 125. | 650. | 425. | — | — | — | — |
| Lincoln cent 1909-1942 | 15. | 10. | 15. | — | 25. | 75. | 35. | — | — | — | — |
| Lincoln cent 1943 | 50. | 25. | 50. | — | 55. | 100. | 75. | — | — | — | — |
| Lincoln cent 1944-1958 | 5. | 3. | 5. | — | 2. | 5. | 3. | — | — | — | — |
| Lincoln cent 1959-1982 | 4. | 3. | 4. | — | 2. | 4.* | 2. | — | — | — | — |
| Lincoln cent 1976 | 10. | 5. | 10. | — | 5. | 15. | 3. | — | — | — | — |
| Lincoln cent 1982- | 15. | 10. | 15. | — | 5. | 15. | 10. | — | — | — | — |
| Shield nickel 1866-83 | 50. | 25. | 50. | — | 275. | 600. | 400. | — | — | — | — |
| Liberty nickel 1883-1912 | 50. | 25. | 50. | — | 175. | 450. | 400. | — | — | — | — |
| Buffalo nickel 1913-1938 | 40. | 20. | 40. | — | 150. | 425. | 600. | — | — | — | — |
| Jefferson nickel 1938- | 15. | 10. | 10. | — | 10. | 15. | 5. | — | — | — | — |
| Jefferson nickel 1942-1945 | 30. | 20. | 25. | — | 50. | 100. | 35. | — | — | — | — |
| Jefferson nickel 1976 | 20. | 25. | 20. | — | 35. | 50. | 15. | — | — | — | — |
| Mercury dime 1916-1945 | 30. | 20. | 30. | — | 50. | 200. | 175. | — | — | — | — |
| Roosevelt dime 1946-1964 | 20. | 15. | 15. | — | 15. | 35. | 25. | — | — | — | — |
| Roosevelt dime 1965- | 10. | 5. | 5. | — | 4. | 10. | 6. | — | — | — | — |
| Roosevelt dime 1976 | 15. | 10. | 10. | — | 15. | 35. | 10. | — | — | — | — |
| Standing Liberty 1916-30 | — | — | — | — | — | 2500. | — | — | — | — | — |
| Washington quarter 1932-64 | 35. | 25. | 25. | — | 150. | 300. | 200. | — | — | — | — |
| Washington quarter 1965- | 10. | 7. | 7. | — | 4. | 15. | 10. | — | — | — | — |
| Washington quarter 1976 | 25. | 20. | 20. | — | 20. | 100. | 75. | — | — | — | — |
| Walking Liberty 1916-47 | — | — | — | — | 400. | 600. | 300. | — | — | — | — |
| Franklin half 1948-1963 | 50. | 30. | 100. | — | 275. | 600. | 200. | — | — | — | — |
| Kennedy half 1964 | 50. | 30. | 50. | — | 175. | 250. | 100. | — | — | — | — |
| Kennedy half 1965-1970 | 50. | 25. | 40. | — | 200. | 400. | 375. | — | — | — | — |
| Kennedy half 1971- | 40. | 15. | 30. | — | 100. | 175. | 50. | — | — | — | — |
| Kennedy half 1976 | 75. | 45. | 70. | — | 25. | 350. | 250. | — | — | — | — |
| Morgan dollar 1878-1921 | 250. | 200. | 300. | — | 1200. | 2500. | 800. | — | — | — | — |
| Peace dollar 1921-1935 | 225. | 200. | 350. | — | 1250. | 3000. | 800. | — | — | — | — |
| Ike dollar 1971-1978 | 350. | 250. | Rare | — | 125. | 950. | 300. | — | — | —1800.up | |
| Anthony dollar 1979-81 | 150. | 100. | 100. | — | 150. | 850. | 950. | — | — | — to Rare | |

* Note: 1973-S off-center cents bring up to $125, 1974-S up to $175.

## III-G: Misaligned and rotated (die) strikes

**Misaligned die (III-G-1)**

**Normal**              **90 degrees**    **135 degrees**

One (rarely both) of the dies may be offset misaligned — off to one side — or may be tilted (vertically misaligned) to one side. It may have been installed so that it is turned in relation to the other die, or may turn in the holder, or the shank may break, allowing the die face to rotate in relation to the opposing die. Values for offset misalignment range from $5 to $50, depending on the denomination. Vertical misaligned dies are rarely found and, like rotated dies, find only limited collector interest. Ninety- and 180-degree rotations are the most popular, bringing premiums of $5 to $400, again depending on the coin. Rotations of 14 degrees or less have no value.

The 1989-D Congress dollar is found with a nearly 180-degree rotated reverse and currently retails for around $2,000. A total of 30 have been reported.

The classes are III-G-1, offset misalignment; III-G-2, vertical misalignment; III-G-3, rotated 15 to 45 degrees; III-G-4, rotated 46 to 135 degrees; and III-G-5, rotated 136 to 180 degrees.

## III-H: Lettered- and design-edge varieties

**III-H-2**

Some early U.S. coins and a number of foreign coins have lettered edges or designs on the edges. These are applied to the planchet before it is struck by the dies. Missing edge letters on early U.S. half dollars will add $10; overlapping edge letters will add $25 to the coin's value. Malfunctions of the application of the motto or design to the edge fall in this section.

The classes are III-H-1, overlapping edge letters or design; III-H-2, wrong edge motto or design; III-H-3, missing edge motto or design; III-H-4, jammed edge die; III-H-5, misplaced segment of edge die; and III-H-6, double-struck edge motto or design.

### III-I: Defective strikes, mismatched dies, and die changes

The final section of the striking division covers coins not properly struck for reasons other than those in previous classes, coins struck with mismatched ("muled") dies, and those where it is possible to determine that a die was removed and a different die substituted. The mismatched-die varieties must be taken on a case-by-case basis, and the other two classes presently have little collector demand or premium. Some coins are struck with transposed dies (reverse die as hammer die), but this rarely affects value.

The classes are III-I-1, defective strikes; III-I-2, mismatched die; III-I-3, die substitutions; III-I-4, single strike proof; III-I-5, single die proof; and III-I-6, transposed dies.

# Division IV: Official mint modifications

Several mint-produced varieties occur after the coin has been struck, resulting in the addition of a fourth division to the original PDS system. Since most of these coins are either unique or special varieties, each one must be taken on a case-by-case basis.

### IV-A: Matte proofs

To provide a cataloging system, we have listed matte proofs (IV-A), including IV-A-1, matte proof; IV-A-II, matte proof on one side; and IV-A-3, sandblasted proofs.

## IV-B: Additional engraving

IV-B-1                                    IV-B-3

Classes consist of IV-B-1, punched or engraved lettering; IV-B-2, countermark; and IV-B-3, counterstamp.

## IV-C: Restrikes

IV-C-7

Restrikes consist of IV-C-1, restrike on same denomination; IV-C-2, restrike on different denomination; IV-C-3, restrike on foreign coin; IV-C-4, restrike on token or medal; IV-C-5, restrike with original dies; IV-C-6, restrike with mismatched dies; IV-C-7, restrike with new dies; and IV-C-8, fantasy strike.

## IV-D: Adjustment marks

Adjustment marks are one of the principal means of correcting a coin's weight. Such marks rarely add value to a coin but deserve mention.

## IV-D: Machine doubling damage

The commonest form of doubling that occurs on coins is machine doubling damage, formerly called ejection doubling and by a variety of other names by other authors and writers, including "shift," shelf doubling, and micro doubling. It is important that the collector recognize it to avoid wasting time collecting it. Machine doubling has a number of causes, including loose or worn parts in the coin press, which allow the die to contact the coin after it is struck, damaging it in a manner that causes parts of the design to appear doubled.

Machine doubling will usually be found on only one side of the design elements, appearing as a shelf above the field and never reaching the field. It never displays the notching that punching or hubbing varieties cause between the overlapping images and commonly will affect the date and mintmark, something that can't happen with a hubbing variety because the mintmark is added after the hubbing process. When you find doubling affecting only a small portion of the design on one side of a coin, always suspect machine doubling damage.

Since it is not a part of the strike and is, in fact, damage to the already struck coin, it has no collector value.

# Canada

## Large cents

**1858-1910**                    **1911-1920**

### BRONZE

| KM# | Date | Mintage | VG-8 | F-12 | VF-20 | XF-40 | MS-60 | MS-63 |
|---|---|---|---|---|---|---|---|---|
| 1 | 1858 | 421,000 | 35.00 | 40.00 | 55.00 | 75.00 | 190.00 | 475.00 |
| | 1859/8 wide 9 | I.A. | 20.00 | 25.00 | 35.00 | 50.00 | 125.00 | 250.00 |
| | 1859 narrow 9 | 9,579,000 | 1.25 | 2.00 | 3.00 | 5.00 | 20.00 | 120.00 |
| | 1859 double punched narrow 9 Type I | | | | | | | |
| | | I.A. | 170.00 | 240.00 | 325.00 | 500.00 | 1000. | 1800. |
| | 1859 double punched narrow 9 Type II | | | | | | | |
| | | I.A. | 25.00 | 35.00 | 55.00 | 75.00 | 150.00 | 325.00 |
| 7 | 1876H | 4,000,000 | 1.25 | 2.00 | 3.00 | 5.00 | 40.00 | 180.00 |
| | 1881H | 2,000,000 | 2.25 | 3.25 | 4.75 | 10.00 | 50.00 | 200.00 |
| | 1882H | 4,000,000 | 1.25 | 2.00 | 3.00 | 6.00 | 27.00 | 120.00 |
| | 1884 | 2,500,000 | 2.00 | 3.00 | 4.00 | 7.50 | 40.00 | 160.00 |
| | 1886 | 1,500,000 | 3.25 | 4.50 | 6.00 | 11.50 | 60.00 | 210.00 |
| | 1887 | 1,500,000 | 2.25 | 3.25 | 5.00 | 8.00 | 40.00 | 170.00 |
| | 1888 | 4,000,000 | 1.25 | 2.00 | 2.75 | 4.50 | 27.00 | 100.00 |
| | 1890H | 1,000,000 | 3.75 | 6.50 | 11.50 | 20.00 | 100.00 | 300.00 |
| | 1891 lg. date | 1,452,000 | 4.50 | 7.50 | 11.50 | 18.50 | .90.00 | 275.00 |
| | 1891 S.D.L.L. | I.A. | 40.00 | 60.00 | 70.00 | 100.00 | 275.00 | 750.00 |
| | 1891 S.D.S.L. | I.A. | 30.00 | 45.00 | 60.00 | 75.00 | 200.00 | 550.00 |
| | 1892 | 1,200,000 | 2.50 | 4.50 | 6.00 | 10.00 | 35.00 | 120.00 |
| | 1893 | 2,000,000 | 1.50 | 2.50 | 4.00 | 7.00 | 30.00 | 100.00 |
| | 1894 | 1,000,000 | 4.50 | 7.50 | 12.00 | 20.00 | 85.00 | 215.00 |
| | 1895 | 1,200,000 | 3.00 | 5.00 | 7.00 | 10.00 | 50.00 | 160.00 |
| | 1896 | 2,000,000 | 1.50 | 2.00 | 3.00 | 5.50 | 30.00 | 100.00 |
| | 1897 | 1,500,000 | 1.50 | 2.50 | 3.50 | 6.00 | 30.00 | 110.00 |
| | 1898H | 1,000,000 | 3.50 | 5.50 | 8.00 | 11.00 | 50.00 | 200.00 |
| | 1899 | 2,400,000 | 1.50 | 2.00 | 3.00 | 5.00 | 30.00 | 100.00 |
| | 1900 | 1,000,000 | 4.00 | 8.00 | 12.00 | 20.00 | 65.00 | 185.00 |
| | 1900H | 2,600,000 | 1.25 | 2.75 | 3.50 | 5.00 | 22.00 | 70.00 |
| | 1901 | 4,100,000 | 1.25 | 2.00 | 2.75 | 4.50 | 22.00 | 60.00 |
| 8 | 1902 | 3,000,000 | 1.00 | 1.50 | 2.00 | 4.00 | 15.00 | 40.00 |
| | 1903 | 4,000,000 | 1.00 | 1.50 | 2.00 | 4.00 | 20.00 | 50.00 |
| | 1904 | 2,500,000 | 1.50 | 2.00 | 3.25 | 5.00 | 25.00 | 75.00 |
| | 1905 | 2,000,000 | 2.50 | 4.00 | 6.00 | 8.50 | 35.00 | 95.00 |
| | 1906 | 4,100,000 | 1.00 | 1.50 | 2.00 | 4.00 | 20.00 | 50.00 |
| | 1907 | 2,400,000 | 1.50 | 2.50 | 3.50 | 5.00 | 30.00 | 85.00 |
| | 1907H | 800,000 | 7.00 | 9.00 | 14.00 | 20.00 | 85.00 | 275.00 |
| | 1908 | 2,401,506 | 2.00 | 3.50 | 4.50 | 6.00 | 26.00 | 80.00 |
| | 1909 | 3,973,339 | 1.00 | 1.50 | 2.00 | 4.00 | 20.00 | 50.00 |
| | 1910 | 5,146,487 | 1.00 | 1.25 | 1.75 | 3.00 | 20.00 | 50.00 |
| 15 | 1911 | 4,663,486 | 1.00 | 1.25 | 1.75 | 3.50 | 20.00 | 65.00 |
| 21 | 1912 | 5,107,642 | .75 | 1.00 | 1.50 | 2.50 | 15.00 | 45.00 |
| | 1913 | 5,735,405 | .75 | 1.00 | 1.50 | 2.50 | 15.00 | 45.00 |
| | 1914 | 3,405,958 | 1.15 | 1.40 | 2.00 | 3.50 | 28.00 | 90.00 |
| | 1915 | 4,932,134 | .75 | 1.00 | 1.75 | 2.75 | 16.50 | 60.00 |
| | 1916 | 11,022,367 | .45 | .65 | .90 | 2.00 | 12.00 | 45.00 |
| | 1917 | 11,899,254 | .45 | .65 | .90 | 1.50 | 8.00 | 30.00 |
| | 1918 | 12,970,798 | .45 | .65 | .90 | 1.50 | 8.00 | 30.00 |
| | 1919 | 11,279,634 | .45 | .65 | .90 | 1.50 | 8.00 | 30.00 |
| | 1920 | 6,762,247 | .50 | .75 | 1.00 | 2.00 | 10.00 | 40.00 |

# Small cents

Dot

**BRONZE**

| KM# | Date | Mintage | VG-8 | F-12 | VF-20 | XF-40 | MS-60 | MS-63 |
|-----|------|---------|------|------|-------|-------|-------|-------|
| 28 | 1920 | 15,483,923 | .15 | .30 | .90 | 2.00 | 9.00 | 35.00 |
| | 1921 | 7,601,627 | .40 | .75 | 1.75 | 4.00 | 14.00 | 55.00 |
| | 1922 | 1,243,635 | 8.00 | 10.00 | 14.00 | 22.50 | 100.00 | 275.00 |
| | 1923 | 1,019,002 | 14.00 | 18.00 | 24.00 | 34.00 | 160.00 | 500.00 |
| | 1924 | 1,593,195 | 3.50 | 5.00 | 7.50 | 11.00 | 75.00 | 190.00 |
| | 1925 | 1,000,622 | 11.00 | 13.00 | 20.00 | 28.00 | 135.00 | 400.00 |
| | 1926 | 2,143,372 | 1.75 | 2.25 | 4.00 | 8.00 | 55.00 | 175.00 |
| | 1927 | 3,553,928 | .75 | 1.00 | 2.25 | 4.00 | 24.00 | 90.00 |
| | 1928 | 9,144,860 | .15 | .25 | .65 | 1.50 | 10.00 | 35.00 |
| | 1929 | 12,159,840 | .15 | .25 | .65 | 1.50 | 10.00 | 35.00 |
| | 1930 | 2,538,613 | 1.60 | 1.80 | 3.00 | 5.00 | 27.00 | 90.00 |
| | 1931 | 3,842,776 | .60 | 1.00 | 1.75 | 3.50 | 20.00 | 70.00 |
| | 1932 | 21,316,190 | .15 | .25 | .60 | 1.50 | 9.00 | 30.00 |
| | 1933 | 12,079,310 | .15 | .25 | .60 | 1.50 | 9.00 | 30.00 |
| | 1934 | 7,042,358 | .15 | .25 | .60 | 1.50 | 9.00 | 30.00 |
| | 1935 | 7,526,400 | .15 | .25 | .60 · | 1.50 | 9.00 | 30.00 |
| | 1936 | 8,768,769 | .15 | .25 | .60 | 1.50 | 8.00 | 27.50 |
| | 1936 dot below dt | 678,823 | — | — | — | — | Unique | — |
| | 1936 dot below dt | 4 known | — | — | — | — | Specimen | — |

Maple Leaf

| KM# | Date | Mintage | VG-8 | F-12 | VF-20 | XF-40 | MS-60 | MS-63 |
|-----|------|---------|------|------|-------|-------|-------|-------|
| 32 | 1937 | 10,040,231 | .20 | .30 | .60 | 1.20 | 2.00 | 5.00 |
| | 1938 | 18,365,608 | .15 | .20 | .30 | .60 | 2.00 | 7.00 |
| | 1939 | 21,600,319 | .15 | .20 | .30 | .60 | 2.00 | 6.00 |
| | 1940 | 85,740,532 | — | .10 | .20 | .40 | 1.50 | 4.50 |
| | 1941 | 56,336,011 | — | .10 | .25 | .70 | 8.00 | 35.00 |
| | 1942 | 76,113,708 | — | .10 | .20 | .70 | 7.00 | 25.00 |
| | 1943 | 89,111,969 | — | .10 | .20 | .40 | 3.00 | 10.00 |
| | 1944 | 44,131,216 | .15 | .20 | .25 | 1.00 | 9.00 | 30.00 |
| | 1945 | 77,268,591 | — | .10 | .20 | .35 | 1.25 | 4.00 |
| | 1946 | 56,662,071 | — | .20 | .30 | .60 | 1.50 | 4.50 |
| | 1947 | 31,093,901 | — | .10 | .20 | .35 | 1.50 | 5.00 |
| | 1947ML | 47,855,448 | — | .10 | .20 | .35 | 1.25 | 3.50 |

**Modified Obverse Legend**

| KM# | Date | Mintage | VG-8 | F-12 | VF-20 | XF-40 | MS-60 | MS-63 |
|-----|------|---------|------|------|-------|-------|-------|-------|
| 41 | 1948 | 25,767,779 | .10 | .20 | .35 | .60 | 2.00 | 7.00 |
| | 1949 | 33,128,933 | — | .10 | .15 | .25 | 1.25 | 3.00 |
| | 1950 | 60,444,992 | — | .10 | .15 | .25 | 1.25 | 3.00 |
| | 1951 | 80,430,379 | — | .10 | .15 | .25 | 1.00 | 2.75 |
| | 1952 | 67,631,736 | — | .10 | .15 | .25 | 1.00 | 2.75 |

**Elizabeth II Effigy**

| KM# | Date | Mintage | VG-8 | F-12 | VF-20 | XF-40 | MS-60 | MS-63 |
|-----|------|---------|------|------|-------|-------|-------|-------|
| 49 | 1953 w/o strap | 67,806,016 | — | .10 | .15 | .25 | .60 | 2.00 |
| | 1953 w/strap | Inc. Ab. | .50 | 1.00 | 1.50 | 3.00 | 12.00 | 30.00 |
| | 1954 w/strap | 22,181,760 | .10 | .15 | .30 | .50 | 2.00 | 4.50 |
| | 1954 w/o strap | Inc. Ab. | | Proof-Like Only | | — | 150.00 | 250.00 |
| | 1955 w/strap | 56,403,193 | — | .10 | .15 | .20 | .50 | 1.00 |
| | 1955 w/o strap | Inc. Ab. | 75.00 | 125.00 | 185.00 | 225.00 | 475.00 | 900.00 |
| | 1956 | 78,658,535 | — | — | — | .10 | .50 | .80 |
| | 1957 | 100,601,792 | — | — | — | .10 | .30 | .70 |
| | 1958 | 59,385,679 | — | — | — | .10 | .30 | .70 |
| | 1959 | 83,615,343 | — | — | — | .10 | .25 | .60 |
| | 1960 | 75,772,775 | — | — | — | .10 | .25 | .60 |
| | 1961 | 139,598,404 | — | — | — | — | .15 | .40 |
| | 1962 | 227,244,069 | — | — | — | — | .10 | .25 |
| | 1963 | 279,076,334 | — | — | — | — | .10 | .25 |
| | 1964 | 484,655,322 | — | — | — | — | .10 | .25 |

| KM# | Date | Mintage | New Elizabeth II Effigy VG-8 | F-12 | VF-20 | XF-40 | MS-60 | MS-63 |
|---|---|---|---|---|---|---|---|---|
| 59.1 | 1965 sm. beads, pointed 5 | | | | | | | |
| | | 304,441,082 | — | — | — | .10 | .45 | 1.00 |
| | 1965 sm. beads, blunt 5 | I.A. | — | — | — | — | .10 | .25 |
| | 1965 lg. beads, pointed 5 | I.A. | — | — | 1.50 | 4.00 | 15.00 | 30.00 |
| | 1965 lg. beads, blunt 5 | I.A. | — | — | — | .10 | .20 | .35 |
| | 1966 | 184,151,087 | — | — | — | — | .10 | .20 |
| | 1968 | 329,695,772 | — | — | — | — | .10 | .20 |
| | 1969 | 335,240,929 | — | — | — | — | .10 | .20 |
| | 1970 | 311,145,010 | — | — | — | — | .10 | .20 |
| | 1971 | 298,228,936 | — | — | — | — | .10 | .20 |
| | 1972 | 451,304,591 | — | — | — | — | .10 | .20 |
| | 1973 | 457,059,852 | — | — | — | — | .10 | .20 |
| | 1974 | 692,058,489 | — | — | — | — | .10 | .20 |
| | 1975 | 642,318,000 | — | — | — | — | .10 | .20 |
| | 1976 | 701,122,890 | — | — | — | — | .10 | .20 |
| | 1977 | 453,762,670 | — | — | — | — | .10 | .20 |
| | 1978 | 911,170,647 | — | — | — | — | .10 | .20 |

|  |  | **Smaller Bust** |  |  |  |  |  |  |
|---|---|---|---|---|---|---|---|---|
| 59.2 | 1979 | 754,394,064 | — | — | — | — | .10 | .20 |

|  |  | **Reduced Weight** |  |  |  |  |  |  |
|---|---|---|---|---|---|---|---|---|
| 127 | 1980 | 912,052,318 | — | — | — | — | .10 | .15 |
| | 1981 | 1,209,468,500 | — | — | — | — | .10 | .15 |
| | 1981 | 199,000 | — | — | — | — | Proof | 1.00 |

| KM# | Date | Mintage | New Elizabeth II Effigy VG-8 | F-12 | VF-20 | XF-40 | MS-60 | MS-63 |
|---|---|---|---|---|---|---|---|---|
| 132 | 1982 | 911,001,000 | — | — | — | — | .10 | .15 |
| | 1982 | 180,908 | — | — | — | — | Proof | 1.00 |
| | 1983 | 975,510,000 | — | — | — | — | .10 | .15 |
| | 1983 | 168,000 | — | — | — | — | Proof | 1.00 |
| | 1984 | 838,225,000 | — | — | — | — | .10 | .15 |
| | 1984 | 161,602 | — | — | — | — | Proof | 1.00 |
| | 1985 | 126,618,000 | — | — | — | — | .10 | .15 |
| | 1985 | 157,037 | — | — | — | — | Proof | 1.00 |
| | 1986 | 740,335,000 | — | — | — | — | .10 | .15 |
| | 1986 | 175,745 | — | — | — | — | Proof | 1.00 |
| | 1987 | 774,549,000 | — | — | — | — | .10 | .15 |
| | 1987 | 179,004 | — | — | — | — | Proof | 1.00 |
| | 1988 | 482,676,752 | — | — | — | — | .10 | .15 |
| | 1988 | 175,259 | — | — | — | — | Proof | 1.00 |
| | 1989 | 1,077,347,200 | — | — | — | — | .10 | .15 |
| | 1989 | 170,928 | — | — | — | — | Proof | 1.00 |

| KM# | Date | Mintage | New Elizabeth II Effigy VG-8 | F-12 | VF-20 | XF-40 | MS-60 | MS-63 |
|---|---|---|---|---|---|---|---|---|
| 181 | 1990 | 218,035,000 | — | — | — | — | .10 | .15 |
| | 1990 | 140,649 | — | — | — | — | Proof | 1.00 |
| | 1991 | 696,629,000 | — | — | — | — | .10 | .15 |
| | 1991 | — | — | — | — | — | Proof | 1.00 |
| | 1993 | — | — | — | — | — | .10 | .15 |
| | 1993 | — | — | — | — | — | Proof | 1.00 |

# Commemorative cents

**BRONZE**

| KM# | Date | Mintage | VG-8 | F-12 | VF-20 | XF-40 | MS-60 | MS-63 |
|-----|------|---------|------|------|-------|-------|-------|-------|
| 65 | 1967 Confederation Centennial | | | | | | | |
| | | 345,140,645 | — | — | — | — | .10 | .20 |
| 204 | 1992 Confederation 125 | | | | | | | |
| | | | — | — | — | — | .10 | .15 |
| | | — | — | — | — | — | Proof | 1.00 |

# Five cents

Round 0's          Oval 0's

| KM# | Date | Mintage | 1.1620 g, .925 SILVER, .0346 oz ASW VG-8 | F-12 | VF-20 | XF-40 | MS-60 | MS-63 |
|-----|------|---------|------|------|-------|-------|-------|-------|
| 2 | 1858 sm. date | 1,500,000 | 8.00 | 12.00 | 18.00 | 35.00 | 225.00 | 425.00 |
| | 1858 lg. date over sm. date | | | | | | | |
| | | Inc. Ab. | 85.00 | 135.00 | 225.00 | 325.00 | 700.00 | 2000. |
| | 1870 flat rim | 2,800,000 | 6.50 | 10.00 | 20.00 | 40.00 | 175.00 | 435.00 |
| | 1870 wire rim | Inc. Ab. | 7.00 | 11.00 | 22.50 | 45.00 | 200.00 | 450.00 |
| | 1871 | 1,400,000 | 7.00 | 10.00 | 18.00 | 35.00 | 165.00 | 430.00 |
| | 1872H | 2,000,000 | 5.00 | 9.00 | 15.00 | 30.00 | 185.00 | 450.00 |
| | 1874H plain 4 | 800,000 | 12.00 | 20.00 | 40.00 | 75.00 | 400.00 | 875.00 |
| | 1874H crosslet 4 | Inc. Ab. | 8.00 | 12.00 | 25.00 | 50.00 | 300.00 | 700.00 |
| | 1875H lg. date | 1,000,000 | 90.00 | 150.00 | 275.00 | 450.00 | 1600. | 3750. |
| | 1875H sm. date | Inc. Ab. | 70.00 | 110.00 | 210.00 | 350.00 | 1350. | 2750. |
| | 1880H | 3,000,000 | 3.00 | 6.00 | 12.00 | 25.00 | 125.00 | 400.00 |
| | 1881H | 1,500,000 | 3.50 | 7.00 | 15.00 | 30.00 | 160.00 | 450.00 |
| | 1882H | 1,000,000 | 4.25 | 8.50 | 16.50 | 32.50 | 180.00 | 525.00 |
| 2 | 1883H | 600,000 | 10.00 | 20.00 | 40.00 | 65.00 | 400.00 | 900.00 |
| | 1884 | 200,000 | 60.00 | 100.00 | 150.00 | 350.00 | 1850. | 5500. |
| | 1885 sm. 5 | 1,000,000 | 4.75 | 9.50 | 17.50 | 40.00 | 300.00 | 600.00 |
| | 1885 lg. 5 | Inc. Ab. | 7.00 | 17.50 | 35.00 | 60.00 | 375.00 | 800.00 |
| | 1885 lg. 5 over sm. 5 | | | | | | | |
| | | Inc. Ab. | 30.00 | 50.00 | 135.00 | 400.00 | 1000. | 1900. |
| | 1886 sm. 6 | 1,700,000 | 3.75 | 7.00 | 14.00 | 27.50 | 225.00 | 500.00 |
| | 1886 lg. 6 | Inc. Ab. | 6.00 | .9.00 | 17.50 | 37.50 | 275.00 | 550.00 |
| | 1887 | 500,000 | 12.00 | 20.00 | 35.00 | 60.00 | 275.00 | 675.00 |
| | 1888 | 1,000,000 | 3.00 | 5.00 | 10.00 | 20.00 | 125.00 | 300.00 |
| | 1889 | 1,200,000 | 14.00 | 26.00 | 45.00 | 90.00 | 400.00 | 1000. |
| | 1890H | 1,000,000 | 3.50 | 6.00 | 16.00 | 30.00 | 165.00 | 400.00 |
| | 1891 | 1,800,000 | 2.50 | 4.00 | 8.00 | 16.00 | 100.00 | 235.00 |
| | 1892 | 860,000 | 3.50 | 6.00 | 12.00 | 30.00 | 175.00 | 400.00 |
| | 1893 | 1,700,000 | 2.50 | 4.00 | 8.00 | 16.00 | 110.00 | 235.00 |
| | 1894 | 500,000 | 9.00 | 18.00 | 32.00 | 65.00 | 325.00 | 750.00 |
| | 1896 | 1,500,000 | 3.00 | 6.00 | 11.00 | 20.00 | 125.00 | 250.00 |
| | 1897 | 1,319,283 | 3.00 | 5.00 | 10.00 | 20.00 | 120.00 | 225.00 |
| | 1898 | 580,717 | 6.50 | 12.00 | 30.00 | 45.00 | 175.00 | 400.00 |
| | 1899 | 3,000,000 | 2.00 | 3.50 | 7.00 | 16.00 | 90.00 | 210.00 |
| | 1900 oval 0's | 1,800,000 | 2.50 | 4.00 | 7.00 | 16.00 | 100.00 | 235.00 |
| | 1900 round 0's | Inc. Ab. | 12.50 | 25.00 | 40.00 | 80.00 | 285.00 | 750.00 |
| | 1901 | 2,000,000 | 2.00 | 3.50 | 7.00 | 16.00 | 95.00 | 220.00 |
| 9 | 1902 | 2,120,000 | 1.50 | 2.00 | 3.00 | 6.50 | 35.00 | 60.00 |
| | 1902 lg. broad H | 2,200,000 | 2.00 | 2.75 | 4.50 | 8.00 | 45.00 | 70.00 |
| | 1902 sm. narrow H | Inc. Ab. | 7.50 | 12.50 | 22.50 | 45.00 | 150.00 | 225.00 |
| 13 | 1903 | 1,000,000 | 4.00 | 6.00 | 12.50 | 25.00 | 185.00 | 400.00 |
| | 1903H | 2,640,000 | 1.75 | 3.00 | 6.00 | 13.00 | 80.00 | 200.00 |
| | 1904 | 2,400,000 | 1.75 | 3.00 | 6.00 | 14.00 | 100.00 | 325.00 |
| | 1905 | 2,600,000 | 1.75 | 3.00 | 6.00 | 12.00 | 85.00 | 200.00 |
| | 1906 | 3,100,000 | 1.50 | 2.00 | 4.00 | 7.00 | 70.00 | 150.00 |
| | 1907 | 5,200,000 | 1.50 | 2.00 | 4.00 | 7.00 | 65.00 | 125.00 |
| | 1908 | 1,220,524 | 4.00 | 6.50 | 12.00 | 25.00 | 95.00 | 200.00 |
| | 1909 round leaves | 1,983,725 | 1.75 | 2.25 | 6.00 | 12.00 | 125.00 | 325.00 |
| | 1909 pointed leaves | Inc. Ab. | 8.00 | 11.00 | 27.50 | 55.00 | 250.00 | 700.00 |
| | 1910 pointed leaves | 3,850,325 | 1.25 | 1.75 | 3.00 | 6.00 | 45.00 | 85.00 |
| | 1910 round leaves | Inc. Ab. | 10.00 | 15.00 | 30.00 | 70.00 | 290.00 | 900.00 |
| 16 | 1911 | 3,692,350 | 1.75 | 2.50 | 5.00 | 11.00 | 90.00 | 175.00 |
| 22 | 1912 | 5,863,170 | 1.50 | 2.00 | 3.00 | 6.00 | 45.00 | 110.00 |
| | 1913 | 5,488,048 | 1.25 | 2.00 | 3.00 | 5.00 | 30.00 | 60.00 |
| | 1914 | 4,202,179 | 1.50 | 2.20 | 3.50 | 7.00 | 55.00 | 125.00 |
| | 1915 | 1,172,258 | 7.00 | 12.00 | 22.00 | 40.00 | 250.00 | 475.00 |
| | 1916 | 2,481,675 | 2.75 | 4.00 | 6.50 | 15.00 | 95.00 | 225.00 |
| | 1917 | 5,521,373 | 1.25 | 1.75 | 2.50 | 4.00 | 40.00 | 75.00 |
| | 1918 | 6,052,298 | 1.25 | 1.75 | 2.50 | 4.00 | 30.00 | 65.00 |
| | 1919 | 7,835,400 | 1.25 | 1.75 | 2.50 | 4.00 | 35.00 | 65.00 |

### 1.1664 g, .800 SILVER, .0300 oz ASW

| KM# | Date | Mintage | VG-8 | F-12 | VF-20 | XF-40 | MS-60 | MS-63 |
|-----|------|---------|------|------|-------|-------|-------|-------|
| 22a | 1920 | 10,649,851 | 1.25 | 1.75 | 2.50 | 4.00 | 30.00 | 60.00 |
|     | 1921 | 2,582,495 | 1250. | 1850. | 2550. | 4750. | 11,000. | 20,000. |

NOTE: Approximately 460 known, balance remelted.
NOTE: Stack's A.G. Carter Jr. Sale 12-89 Choice BU finest known realized $57,200.

Near 6                          Far 6

### NICKEL

| KM# | Date | Mintage | VG-8 | F-12 | VF-20 | XF-40 | MS-60 | MS-63 |
|-----|------|---------|------|------|-------|-------|-------|-------|
| 29 | 1922 | 4,794,119 | .25 | .75 | 2.00 | 7.00 | 40.00 | 75.00 |
|    | 1923 | 2,502,279 | .40 | 1.25 | 3.50 | 10.00 | 100.00 | 225.00 |
|    | 1924 | 3,105,839 | .30 | .70 | 2.50 | 7.00 | 75.00 | 160.00 |
|    | 1925 | 201,921 | 25.00 | 32.50 | 55.00 | 150.00 | 750.00 | 1650. |
|    | 1926 near 6 | 938,162 | 2.50 | 5.50 | 12.00 | 40.00 | 240.00 | 600.00 |
|    | 1926 far 6 | Inc. Ab. | 50.00 | 90.00 | 150.00 | 300.00 | 1200. | 2200. |
|    | 1927 | 5,285,627 | .20 | .60 | 2.00 | 5.00 | 45.00 | 120.00 |
|    | 1928 | 4,577,712 | .20 | .60 | 2.00 | 5.00 | 40.00 | 80.00 |
|    | 1929 | 5,611,911 | .20 | .60 | 2.00 | 5.00 | 45.00 | 120.00 |
|    | 1930 | 3,704,673 | .20 | .60 | 2.00 | 5.00 | 70.00 | 150.00 |
|    | 1931 | 5,100,830 | .20 | .60 | 2.00 | 5.00 | 70.00 | 150.00 |
|    | 1932 | 3,198,566 | .20 | .60 | 2.25 | 6.00 | 75.00 | 150.00 |
|    | 1933 | 2,597,867 | .40 | 1.00 | 3.00 | 8.00 | 110.00 | 300.00 |
|    | 1934 | 3,827,304 | .20 | .60 | 2.00 | 5.00 | 80.00 | 200.00 |
|    | 1935 | 3,900,000 | .20 | .60 | 2.00 | 5.00 | 70.00 | 160.00 |
|    | 1936 | 4,400,450 | .20 | .60 | 2.00 | 5.00 | 40.00 | 85.00 |

| KM# | Date | Mintage | VG-8 | F-12 | VF-20 | XF-40 | MS-60 | MS-63 |
|-----|------|---------|------|------|-------|-------|-------|-------|
| 33 | 1937 dot | 4,593,263 | .20 | .35 | 1.75 | 3.00 | 10.00 | 25.00 |
|    | 1938 | 3,898,974 | .15 | .75 | 1.75 | 7.00 | 65.00 | 150.00 |
|    | 1939 | 5,661,123 | .20 | .50 | 1.75 | 4.50 | 40.00 | 70.00 |
|    | 1940 | 13,920,197 | .15 | .30 | 1.00 | 2.00 | 14.00 | 40.00 |
|    | 1941 | 8,681,785 | .10 | .25 | 1.00 | 2.50 | 17.00 | 42.00 |
|    | 1942 round | 6,847,544 | .10 | .30 | 1.00 | 2.50 | 14.00 | 40.00 |

### Tombac (BRASS)

| KM# | Date | Mintage | VG-8 | F-12 | VF-20 | XF-40 | MS-60 | MS-63 |
|-----|------|---------|------|------|-------|-------|-------|-------|
| 39 | 1942 - 12 sided | 3,396,234 | .30 | .60 | 1.00 | 1.50 | 3.00 | 9.00 |

Dot                          Maple leaf

### NICKEL

| KM# | Date | Mintage | VG-8 | F-12 | VF-20 | XF-40 | MS-60 | MS-63 |
|-----|------|---------|------|------|-------|-------|-------|-------|
| 39a | 1946 | 6,952,684 | .15 | .25 | .50 | 2.00 | 10.00 | 22.50 |
|     | 1947 | 7,603,724 | .15 | .25 | .50 | 1.00 | 6.00 | 14.00 |
|     | 1947 dot | Inc. Ab. | 10.00 | 12.50 | 20.00 | 40.00 | 220.00 | 600.00 |
|     | 1947 maple leaf | 9,595,124 | .15 | .25 | .50 | 1.00 | 6.00 | 12.00 |

### Modified Obverse Legend

| KM# | Date | Mintage | VG-8 | F-12 | VF-20 | XF-40 | MS-60 | MS-63 |
|-----|------|---------|------|------|-------|-------|-------|-------|
| 42 | 1948 | 1,810,789 | .50 | .80 | 1.00 | 2.00 | 15.00 | 25.00 |
|    | 1949 | 13,037,090 | .15 | .15 | .20 | .60 | 4.00 | 7.00 |
|    | 1950 | 11,970,521 | .15 | .15 | .20 | .60 | 4.00 | 7.00 |

**CHROMIUM-PLATED STEEL**

| KM# | Date | Mintage | VG-8 | F-12 | VF-20 | XF-40 | MS-60 | MS-63 |
|---|---|---|---|---|---|---|---|---|
| 42a | 1951 low relief* | 4,313,410 | .15 | .20 | .50 | 1.00 | 2.50 | 4.50 |
| | 1951 high relief* * | Inc. Ab. | 200.00 | 325.00 | 500.00 | 750.00 | 1150. | 2000. |
| | 1952 | 10,891,148 | .15 | .20 | .50 | 1.00 | 3.00 | 5.00 |

**\*NOTE:** A in GRATIA points between denticles.
**\* \*NOTE:** A in GRATIA points to a denticle.

**Elizabeth II Effigy - 12 Sided Coinage**

| KM# | Date | Mintage | VG-8 | F-12 | VF-20 | XF-40 | MS-60 | MS-63 |
|---|---|---|---|---|---|---|---|---|
| 50 | 1953 w/o strap | 16,635,552 | .15 | .25 | .40 | .75 | 3.00 | 4.50 |
| | 1953 w/strap | Inc.Ab. | .15 | .25 | .45 | 1.00 | 3.50 | 7.00 |
| | 1954 | 6,998,662 | .15 | .25 | .50 | 1.00 | 4.50 | 7.50 |

**NICKEL**

| KM# | Date | Mintage | VG-8 | F-12 | VF-20 | XF-40 | MS-60 | MS-63 |
|---|---|---|---|---|---|---|---|---|
| 50a | 1955 | 5,355,028 | .15 | .20 | .25 | .75 | 3.00 | 4.50 |
| | 1956 | 9,399,854 | — | .20 | .30 | .45 | 1.75 | 3.00 |
| | 1957 | 7,387,703 | — | — | .25 | .30 | 1.25 | 2.75 |
| | 1958 | 7,607,521 | — | — | .25 | .30 | 1.25 | 2.75 |
| | 1959 | 11,552,523 | — | — | — | .20 | .65 | 1.25 |
| | 1960 | 37,157,433 | — | — | — | .15 | .25 | .75 |
| | 1961 | 47,889,051 | — | — | — | — | .20 | .40 |
| | 1962 | 46,307,305 | — | — | — | — | .20 | .40 |

**Round Coinage**

| KM# | Date | Mintage | VG-8 | F-12 | VF-20 | XF-40 | MS-60 | MS-63 |
|---|---|---|---|---|---|---|---|---|
| 57 | 1963 | 43,970,320 | — | — | — | — | .20 | .40 |
| | 1964 | 78,075,068 | — | — | — | — | ,20 | .40 |
| | 1964 XWL | — | 6.00 | 8.00 | 10.00 | 12.50 | 22.00 | 35.00 |

**New Elizabeth II Effigy**

| KM# | Date | Mintage | VG-8 | F-12 | VF-20 | XF-40 | MS-60 | MS-63 |
|---|---|---|---|---|---|---|---|---|
| 60.1 | 1965 | 84,876,018 | — | — | — | — | .20 | .30 |
| | 1966 | 27,976,648 | — | — | — | — | .20 | .30 |
| | 1968 | 101,930,379 | — | — | — | — | .20 | .30 |
| | 1969 | 27,830,229 | — | — | — | — | .20 | .30 |
| | 1970 | 5,726,010 | — | — | — | .25 | .55 | .75 |
| | 1971 | 27,312,609 | — | — | — | — | .20 | .30 |
| | 1972 | 62,417,387 | — | — | — | — | .20 | .30 |
| | 1973 | 53,507,435 | — | — | — | — | .20 | .30 |
| | 1974 | 94,704,645 | — | — | — | — | .20 | .30 |
| | 1975 | 138,882,000 | — | — | — | — | .20 | .30 |
| | 1976 | 55,140,213 | — | — | — | — | .20 | .30 |
| | 1977 | 89,120,791 | — | — | — | — | .20 | .30 |
| | 1978 | 137,079,273 | — | — | — | — | .20 | .30 |

**Smaller bust**

| KM# | Date | Mintage | VG-8 | F-12 | VF-20 | XF-40 | MS-60 | MS-63 |
|---|---|---|---|---|---|---|---|---|
| 60.2 | 1979 | 186,295,825 | — | — | — | — | .20 | .30 |
| | 1980 | 134,878,000 | — | — | — | — | .20 | .30 |
| | 1981 | 99,107,900 | — | — | — | — | .20 | .30 |
| | 1981 | 199,000 | — | — | — | — | Proof | 1.00 |

**COPPER-NICKEL**

| KM# | Date | Mintage | VG-8 | F-12 | VF-20 | XF-40 | MS-60 | MS-63 |
|---|---|---|---|---|---|---|---|---|
| 60.2a | 1982 | 64,924,400 | — | — | — | — | .20 | .30 |
| | 1982 | 180,908 | — | — | — | — | Proof | 1.00 |
| | 1983 | 72,596,000 | — | — | — | — | .20 | .30 |
| | 1983 | 168,000 | — | — | — | — | Proof | 1.00 |
| | 1984 | 84,088,000 | — | — | — | — | .20 | .30 |
| | 1984 | 161,602 | — | — | — | — | Proof | 1.00 |
| | 1985 | 126,618,000 | — | — | — | — | .20 | .30 |
| | 1985 | 157,037 | — | — | — | — | Proof | 1.00 |
| | 1986 | 156,104,000 | — | — | — | — | .20 | .30 |
| | 1986 | 175,745 | — | — | — | — | Proof | 1.00 |
| | 1987 | 106,299,000 | — | .20 | — | — | .10 | .15 |
| | 1987 | 179,004 | — | — | — | — | Proof | 1.00 |
| | 1988 | 75,025,000 | — | — | — | — | .10 | .15 |
| | 1988 | 175,259 | — | — | — | — | Proof | 1.00 |
| | 1989 | 141,570,538 | — | — | — | — | .10 | .15 |
| | 1989 | 170,928 | — | — | — | — | Proof | 1.00 |

**New Elizabeth II Effigy**

| KM# | Date | Mintage | VG-8 | F-12 | VF-20 | XF-40 | MS-60 | MS-63 |
|---|---|---|---|---|---|---|---|---|
| 182 | 1990 | 42,537,000 | — | — | — | — | .10 | .15 |
| | 1990 | 140,649 | — | — | — | — | Proof | 1.00 |
| | 1991 | 10,931,000 | — | — | — | — | .10 | .35 |
| | 1991 | — | — | — | — | — | Proof | 1.00 |
| | 1993 | — | — | — | — | — | .10 | .15 |
| | 1993 | — | — | — | — | — | Proof | 1.00 |

# Commemorative five cents

| KM# | Date | Mintage | VG-8 | F-12 | VF-20 | XF-40 | MS-60 | MS-63 |
|---|---|---|---|---|---|---|---|---|
| 40 | 1943 Victory, Tombac (Brass) | | | | | | | |
| | | 24,760,256 | .15 | .25 | .35 | 1.00 | 2.00 | 6.00 |
| | | **CHROMIUM-PLATED STEEL** | | | | | | |
| 40a | 1944 | 11,532,784 | .15 | .25 | .50 | 1.00 | 2.00 | 4.50 |
| | 1945 | 18,893,216, | .15 | .25 | .50 | 1.00 | 2.00 | 4.50 |

| KM# | Date | Mintage | VG-8 | F-12 | VF-20 | XF-40 | MS-60 | MS-63 |
|---|---|---|---|---|---|---|---|---|
| 48 | 1951 Nickel Bicentennial, Nickel | | | | | | | |
| | | 9,028,507 | .15 | .20 | .25 | .50 | 1.75 | 3.00 |

| KM# | Date | Mintage | VG-8 | F-12 | VF-20 | XF-40 | MS-60 | MS-63 |
|---|---|---|---|---|---|---|---|---|
| 66 | 1967 Confederation Centennial | | | | | | | |
| | | 36,876,574 | — | — | — | — | .20 | .30 |
| 205 | 1992 Confederation 125 | | | | | | | |
| | | — | — | — | — | — | .10 | .15 |
| | | — | — | — | — | — | Proof | 1.00 |

# Ten cents

**1858-1901**                    **1902-1910**

| | | | 2.3240 g, .925 SILVER, .0691 oz ASW | | | | | |
|---|---|---|---|---|---|---|---|---|
| KM# | Date | Mintage | VG-8 | F-12 | VF-20 | XF-40 | MS-60 | MS-63 |
| 3 | 1858/5 | Inc. Below | — | — | — | — | Rare | — |
| | 1858 | 1,250,000 | 12.00 | 22.00 | 40.00 | 70.00 | 275.00 | 700.00 |
| | 1870 narrow 0 | 1,600,000 | 10.00 | 18.00 | 40.00 | 75.00 | 285.00 | 725.00 |
| | 1870 wide 0 | Inc. Ab. | 15.00 | 25.00 | 50.00 | 100.00 | 350.00 | 775.00 |
| | 1871 | 800,000 | 13.50 | 25.00 | 45.00 | 100.00 | 325.00 | 800.00 |
| | 1871H | 1,870,000 | 16.00 | 27.00 | 60.00 | 120.00 | 450.00 | 900.00 |
| | 1872H | 1,000,000 | 50.00 | 90.00 | 165.00 | 350.00 | 950.00 | 2400. |
| | 1874H | 600,000 | 6.00 | 12.00 | 25.00 | 60.00 | 275.00 | 750.00 |
| | 1875H | 1,000,000 | 175.00 | 300.00 | 500.00 | 1050. | 3000. | 7000. |
| | 1880H | 1,500,000 | 5.00 | 10.00 | 20.00 | 50.00 | 250.00 | 600.00 |
| | 1881H | 950,000 | 7.00 | 15.00 | 32.50 | 75.00 | 275.00 | 700.00 |

| KM# | Date | Mintage | VG-8 | F-12 | VF-20 | XF-40 | MS-60 | MS-63 |
|---|---|---|---|---|---|---|---|---|
| 3 | 1882H | 1,000,000 | 6.00 | 12.00 | 25.00 | 60.00 | 300.00 | 700.00 |
| | 1883H | 300,000 | 20.00 | 40.00 | 75.00 | 165.00 | 800.00 | 1800. |
| | 1884 | 150,000 | 130.00 | 250.00 | 500.00 | 1250. | 3750. | 8000. |
| | 1885 | 400,000 | 12.00 | 25.00 | 65.00 | 145.00 | 900.00 | 2500. |
| | 1886 sm. 6 | 800,000 | 9.00 | 18.00 | 40.00 | 80.00 | 375.00 | 900.00 |
| | 1886 lg. 6 | Inc. Ab. | 12.00 | 22.00 | 55.00 | 125.00 | 475.00 | 1000. |
| | 1887 | 350,000 | 17.00 | 35.00 | 90.00 | 200.00 | 1150. | 2750. |
| | 1888 | 500,000 | 5.00 | 9.00 | 22.00 | 50.00 | 235.00 | 550.00 |
| | 1889 | 600,000 | 350.00 | 600.00 | 1300. | 2000. | 5000. | 10,000. |
| | 1890H | 450,000 | 9.00 | 17.50 | 40.00 | 85.00 | 325.00 | 725.00 |
| | 1891 21 leaves | 800,000 | 10.00 | 20.00 | 45.00 | 90.00 | 375.00 | 825.00 |
| | 1891 22 leaves | Inc. Ab. | 9.00 | 17.50 | 40.00 | 90.00 | 350.00 | 825.00 |
| | 1892/1 | 520,000 | 85.00 | 150.00 | 220.00 | — | — | — |
| | 1892 | Inc. Ab. | 7.00 | 15.00 | 30.00 | 70.00 | 350.00 | 800.00 |
| | 1893 flat top 3 | 500,000 | 12.00 | 25.00 | 60.00 | 120.00 | 450.00 | 1250. |
| | 1893 rd. top 3 | Inc. Ab. | 325.00 | 750.00 | 1450. | 2850. | 6000. | 12,500. |
| | 1894 | 500,000 | 9.00 | 20.00 | 45.00 | 90.00 | 350.00 | 1000. |
| | 1896 | 650,000 | 5.00 | 10.00 | 20.00 | 50.00 | 250.00 | 550.00 |
| | 1898 | 720,000 | 5.00 | 12.00 | 22.00 | 55.00 | 275.00 | 600.00 |
| | 1899 sm. 9's | 1,200,000 | 4.00 | 8.00 | 20.00 | 45.00 | 210.00 | 575.00 |
| | 1899 lg. 9's | Inc. Ab. | 7.00 | 15.00 | 30.00 | 75.00 | 300.00 | 850.00 |
| | 1900 | 1,100,000 | 2.50 | 5.00 | 14.00 | 30.00 | 150.00 | 370.00 |
| | 1901 | 1,200,000 | 2.50 | 5.00 | 14.00 | 30.00 | 150.00 | 370.00 |
| 10 | 1902 | 720,000 | 3.00 | 7.00 | 15.00 | 40.00 | 160.00 | 450.00 |
| | 1902H | 1,100,000 | 2.00 | 4.25 | 10.00 | 25.00 | 100.00 | 235.00 |
| | 1903 | 500,000 | 7.00 | 15.00 | 40.00 | 100.00 | 700.00 | 1850. |
| | 1903H | 1,320,000 | 2.25 | 5.00 | 12.00 | 40.00 | 185.00 | 450.00 |
| | 1904 | 1,000,000 | 4.00 | 8.00 | 18.00 | 60.00 | 240.00 | 500.00 |
| | 1905 | 1,000,000 | 3.00 | 6.00 | 15.00 | 50.00 | 275.00 | 575.00 |
| | 1906 | 1,700,000 | 1.75 | 4.00 | 10.00 | 32.50 | 175.00 | 400.00 |
| | 1907 | 2,620,000 | 1.75 | 4.00 | 9.00 | 27.50 | 150.00 | 350.00 |
| | 1908 | 776,666 | 4.50 | 9.00 | 25.00 | 60.00 | 225.00 | 425.00 |
| | 1909 Victorian leaves, similar to 1902-1908 coinage | | | | | | | |
| | | 1,697,200 | 3.00 | 7.00 | 15.00 | 40.00 | 275.00 | 650.00 |
| | 1909 broad leaves similar to 1910-1912 coinage | | | | | | | |
| | | Inc. Ab. | 4.50 | 9.00 | 25.00 | 65.00 | 375.00 | 750.00 |
| | 1910 | 4,468,331 | 1.75 | 4.00 | 8.00 | 20.00 | 125.00 | 275.00 |
| 17 | 1911 | 2,737,584 | 4.00 | 9.00 | 15.00 | 44.00 | 140.00 | 325.00 |

Small leaves

Broad leaves

| KM# | Date | Mintage | VG-8 | F-12 | VF-20 | XF-40 | MS-60 | MS-63 |
|---|---|---|---|---|---|---|---|---|
| 23 | 1912 | 3,235,557 | 1.75 | 2.50 | 6.00 | 18.00 | 150.00 | 375.00 |
| | 1913 sm. leaves | 3,613,937 | 1.50 | 2.25 | 5.00 | 15.00 | 145.00 | 375.00 |
| | 1913 lg. leaves | Inc. Ab. | 90.00 | 160.00 | 285.00 | 600.00 | 3250. | 6500. |
| | 1914 | 2,549,811 | 1.50 | 2.50 | 5.50 | 16.00 | 150.00 | 400.00 |
| | 1915 | 688,057 | 4.00 | 9.00 | 22.00 | 80.00 | 400.00 | 750.00 |
| | 1916 | 4,218,114 | 1.00 | 1.50 | 4.00 | 9.00 | 90.00 | 225.00 |
| | 1917 | 5,011,988 | .75 | 1.25 | 3.00 | 7.00 | 60.00 | 125.00 |
| | 1918 | 5,133,602 | .75 | 1.25 | 3.00 | 7.00 | 50.00 | 90.00 |
| | 1919 | 7,877,722 | .75 | 1.25 | 3.00 | 7.00 | 50.00 | 90.00 |
| | **2.3328 g, .800 SILVER, .0600 oz ASW** | | | | | | | |
| 23a | 1920 | 6,305,345 | .75 | 1.25 | 3.00 | 6.50 | 50.00 | 100.00 |
| | 1921 | 2,469,562 | 1.25 | 2.00 | 4.00 | 10.00 | 60.00 | 155.00 |
| | 1928 | 2,458,602 | 1.00 | 1.75 | 4.00 | 9.00 | 55.00 | 140.00 |
| | 1929 | 3,253,888 | 1.00 | 1.50 | 3.50 | 8.50 | 55.00 | 130.00 |
| | 1930 | 1,831,043 | 1.50 | 2.50 | 4.50 | 12.00 | 60.00 | 150.00 |
| | 1931 | 2,067,421 | 1.00 | 2.00 | 4.25 | 9.00 | 55.00 | 125.00 |
| | 1932 | 1,154,317 | 1.50 | 2.50 | 5.50 | 15.00 | 80.00 | 175.00 |
| | 1933 | 672,368 | 2.00 | 3.50 | 8.00 | 25.00 | 175.00 | 400.00 |
| | 1934 | 409,067 | 3.50 | 6.00 | 16.00 | 50.00 | 375.00 | 1250. |
| | 1935 | 384,056 | 4.00 | 6.50 | 18.00 | 60.00 | 275.00 | 600.00 |
| | 1936 | 2,460,871 | .60 | 1.25 | 3.00 | 7.00 | 40.00 | 80.00 |
| | 1936 dot on rev. | 4 known | — | — | — | Specimen | | — |

Maple Leaf

| KM# | Date | Mintage | VG-8 | F-12 | VF-20 | XF-40 | MS-60 | MS-63 |
|---|---|---|---|---|---|---|---|---|
| 34 | 1937 | 2,500,095 | 1.00 | 1.50 | 3.00 | 5.00 | 14.00 | 24.00 |
| | 1938 | 4,197,323 | 1.25 | 2.50 | 3.50 | 8.00 | 40.00 | 80.00 |
| | 1939 | 5,501,748 | 1.00 | 1.75 | 2.50 | 8.00 | 40.00 | 80.00 |
| | 1940 | 16,526,470 | BV | 1.00 | 1.75 | 4.00 | 15.00 | 30.00 |
| | 1941 | 8,716,386 | BV | 1.25 | 3.00 | 7.00 | 40.00 | 85.00 |
| | 1942 | 10,214,011 | BV | 1.00 | 2.00 | 4.00 | 30.00 | 45.00 |
| | 1943 | 21,143,229 | BV | 1.00 | 2.00 | 4.00 | 14.00 | 30.00 |
| | 1944 | 9,383,582 | BV | 1.00 | 2.00 | 5.00 | 25.00 | 45.00 |
| | 1945 | 10,979,570 | BV | 1.00 | 2.00 | 4.00 | 15.00 | 25.00 |
| | 1946 | 6,300,066 | BV | 1.00 | 2.25 | 5.00 | 25.00 | 45.00 |
| | 1947 | 4,431,926 | BV | 1.50 | 3.00 | 7.00 | 35.00 | 50.00 |
| | 1947 maple leaf | 9,638,793 | BV | 1.00 | 2.00 | 3.50 | 10.00 | 18.00 |

**Modified Obverse Legend**

| KM# | Date | Mintage | VG-8 | F-12 | VF-20 | XF-40 | MS-60 | MS-63 |
|---|---|---|---|---|---|---|---|---|
| 43 | 1948 | 422,741 | 2.50 | 4.50 | 8.00 | 17.00 | 45.00 | 90.00 |
| | 1949 | 11,336,172 | — | BV | 1.50 | 2.50 | 8.00 | 14.00 |
| | 1950 | 17,823,075 | — | BV | 1.25 | 2.00 | 7.00 | 12.00 |
| | 1951 | 15,079,265 | — | BV | 1.00 | 2.00 | 6.00 | 9.00 |
| | 1952 | 10,474,455 | — | BV | 1.00 | 2.00 | 6.00 | 9.00 |

**Elizabeth II Effigy**

| KM# | Date | Mintage | VG-8 | F-12 | VF-20 | XF-40 | MS-60 | MS-63 |
|---|---|---|---|---|---|---|---|---|
| 51 | 1953 w/o straps | 17,706,395 | — | BV | 1.00 | 1.50 | 3.50 | 6.00 |
| | 1953 w/straps | Inc. Ab. | — | BV | 1.00 | 1.75 | 5.00 | 6.50 |
| | 1954 | 4,493,150 | — | BV | 1.00 | 1.75 | 7.00 | 12.00 |
| | 1955 | 12,237,294 | — | BV | .75 | 1.00 | 3.50 | 5.00 |
| | 1956 | 16,732,844 | — | BV | .75 | 1.00 | 2.75 | 4.00 |
| | 1956 dot below date | Inc. Ab. | 2.00 | 3.00 | 5.00 | 6.00 | 12.00 | 16.00 |
| | 1957 | 16,110,229 | — | — | BV | .60 | 1.50 | 2.00 |
| | 1958 | 10,621,236 | — | — | BV | .60 | 1.50 | 2.00 |
| | 1959 | 19,691,433 | — | — | BV | .50 | 1.25 | 2.00 |
| | 1960 | 45,446,835 | — | — | — | BV | .75 | 1.00 |
| | 1961 | 26,850,859 | — | — | — | BV | .75 | 1.00 |
| | 1962 | 41,864,335 | — | — | — | BV | .75 | 1.00 |
| | 1963 | 41,916,208 | — | — | — | BV | .75 | 1.00 |
| | 1964 | 49,518,549 | — | — | — | BV | .75 | 1.00 |

**New Elizabeth II Effigy**

| KM# | Date | Mintage | VG-8 | F-12 | VF-20 | XF-40 | MS-60 | MS-63 |
|---|---|---|---|---|---|---|---|---|
| 61 | 1965 | 56,965,392 | — | — | — | BV | .75 | 1.00 |
| | 1966 | 34,567,898 | — | — | — | BV | .75 | 1.00 |

Reeding

| KM# | Date | Mintage | VG-8 | F-12 | VF-20 | XF-40 | MS-60 | MS-63 |
|---|---|---|---|---|---|---|---|---|
| | **OTTAWA** | | | | | **PHILADELPHIA** | | |
| 72 | 1968 Ottawa, .500 Silver | | | | | | | |
| | | 70,460,000 | — | — | — | BV | .60 | .75 |
| 72a | 1968 Ottawa, Nickel | | | | | | | |
| | | 87,412,930 | — | — | — | .15 | .25 | .40 |
| 73 | 1968 Philadelphia, Nickel | | | | | | | |
| | | 85,170,000 | — | — | — | .15 | .25 | .40 |
| | 1969 lg.date, lg.ship | 4 known | — | — | 6500. | — | — | — |

**Redesigned Smaller Ship**

| KM# | Date | Mintage | VG-8 | F-12 | VF-20 | XF-40 | MS-60 | MS-63 |
|---|---|---|---|---|---|---|---|---|
| 77.1 | 1969 | 55,833,929 | — | — | — | .15 | .25 | .40 |
| | 1970 | 5,249,296 | — | — | — | .25 | .65 | .95 |
| | 1971 | 41,016,968 | — | — | — | .15 | .25 | .40 |
| | 1972 | 60,169,387 | — | — | — | .15 | .25 | .40 |
| | 1973 | 167,715,435 | — | — | — | .15 | .25 | .40 |
| | 1974 | 201,566,565 | — | — | — | .15 | .25 | .40 |
| | 1975 | 207,680,000 | — | — | — | .15 | .25 | .40 |
| | 1976 | 95,018,533 | — | — | — | .15 | .25 | .40 |
| | 1977 | 128,452,206 | — | — | — | .15 | .25 | .40 |
| | 1978 | 170,366,431 | — | — | — | .15 | .25 | .40 |

**Smaller bust**

| KM# | Date | Mintage | VG-8 | F-12 | VF-20 | XF-40 | MS-60 | MS-63 |
|---|---|---|---|---|---|---|---|---|
| 77.2 | 1979 | 237,321,321 | — | — | — | .15 | .25 | .40 |
| | 1980 | 170,111,533 | — | — | — | .15 | .25 | .40 |
| | 1981 | 123,912,900 | — | — | — | .15 | .25 | .40 |
| | 1981 | 199,000 | — | — | — | — | Proof | 1.50 |
| | 1982 | 93,475,000 | — | — | — | .15 | .25 | .40 |
| | 1982 | 180,908 | — | — | — | — | Proof | 1.50 |
| | 1983 | 111,065,000 | — | — | — | .15 | .25 | .40 |
| | 1983 | 168,000 | — | — | — | — | Proof | 1.50 |
| | 1984 | 121,690,000 | — | — | — | .15 | .25 | .40 |
| | 1984 | 161,602 | — | — | — | — | Proof | 1.50 |

| KM# | Date | Mintage | VG-8 | F-12 | VF-20 | XF-40 | MS-60 | MS-63 |
|-----|------|---------|------|------|-------|-------|-------|-------|
| 77.2 | 1985 | 143,025,000 | — | — | — | .15 | .25 | .40 |
| | 1985 | 157,037 | — | — | — | — | Proof | 1.50 |
| | 1986 | 168,620,000 | — | — | — | .15 | .25 | .40 |
| | 1986 | 175,745 | — | — | — | — | Proof | 1.50 |
| | 1987 | 147,309,000 | — | — | — | .15 | .25 | .40 |
| | 1987 | 179,004 | — | — | — | — | Proof | 1.50 |
| | 1988 | 162,998,558 | — | — | — | .15 | .25 | .40 |
| | 1988 | 175,259 | — | — | — | — | Proof | 1.50 |
| | 1989 | 199,104,414 | — | — | — | .15 | .25 | .40 |
| | 1989 | 170,528 | — | — | — | — | Proof | 1.50 |

**New Elizabeth II Effigy**

| KM# | Date | Mintage | VG-8 | F-12 | VF-20 | XF-40 | MS-60 | MS-63 |
|-----|------|---------|------|------|-------|-------|-------|-------|
| 183 | 1990 | 75,023,000 | — | — | — | .15 | .25 | .40 |
| | 1990 | 140,649 | — | — | — | — | Proof | 1.50 |
| | 1991 | 46,693,000 | — | — | — | .15 | .25 | .40 |
| | 1991 | — | — | — | — | — | Proof | 1.50 |
| | 1993 | — | — | — | — | .15 | .25 | .40 |
| | 1993 | — | — | — | — | — | Proof | 1.50 |

# Commemorative ten cents

| KM# | Date | Mintage | VG-8 | F-12 | VF-20 | XF-40 | MS-60 | MS-63 |
|-----|------|---------|------|------|-------|-------|-------|-------|
| 67 | 1967 Confederation Centennial, .800 Silver | | | | | | | |
| | | 62,998,215 | — | — | — | BV | .75 | 1.00 |
| 67a | 1967 Confederation Centennial, .500 Silver | | | | | | | |
| | | Inc. Ab. | — | — | — | BV | .75 | 1.00 |
| 206 | 1992 Confederation 125 | | | | | | | |
| | | — | — | — | — | .15 | .25 | .40 |
| | | — | — | — | — | — | Proof | 1.50 |

# Twenty cents

**4.6480 g, .925 SILVER, .1382 oz ASW**

| KM# | Date | Mintage | VG-8 | F-12 | VF-20 | XF-40 | MS-60 | MS-63 |
|-----|------|---------|------|------|-------|-------|-------|-------|
| 4 | 1858 | 750,000 | 45.00 | 65.00 | 100.00 | 175.00 | 800.00 | 1600. |

# Twenty-five cents

**1870-1901**

**5.8100 g, .925 SILVER, .1728 oz ASW**

| KM# | Date | Mintage | VG-8 | F-12 | VF-20 | XF-40 | MS-60 | MS-63 |
|-----|------|---------|------|------|-------|-------|-------|-------|
| 5 | 1870 | 900,000 | 9.00 | 16.00 | 40.00 | 90.00 | 550.00 | 1250. |
| | 1871 | 400,000 | 12.00 | 20.00 | 60.00 | 150.00 | 600.00 | 1750. |
| | 1871H | 748,000 | 14.00 | 22.00 | 65.00 | 170.00 | 600.00 | 1450. |
| | 1872H | 2,240,000 | 6.00 | 8.00 | 22.50 | 65.00 | 325.00 | 850.00 |
| | 1874H | 1,600,000 | 6.00 | 8.00 | 22.50 | 65.00 | 350.00 | 900.00 |

| KM# | Date | Mintage | VG-8 | F-12 | VF-20 | XF-40 | MS-60 | MS-63 |
|---|---|---|---|---|---|---|---|---|
| 5 | 1875H | 1,000,000 | 200.00 | 400.00 | 1000. | 2000. | 4750. | 10,000. |
| | 1880H narrow 0 | 400,000 | 27.50 | 55.00 | 150.00 | 300.00 | 850.00 | 2000. |
| | 1880H wide 0 | Inc. Ab. | 80.00 | 150.00 | 325.00 | 625.00 | 1800. | 4000. |
| | 1880H wide/narrow 0 | Inc. Ab. | 90.00 | 160.00 | 350.00 | 600.00 | — | — |
| | 1881H | 820,000 | 10.00 | 20.00 | 45.00 | 115.00 | 550.00 | 1300. |
| | 1882H | 600,000 | 12.50 | 25.00 | 55.00 | 160.00 | 650.00 | 1450. |
| | 1883H | 960,000 | 9.00 | 15.00 | 37.50 | 110.00 | 650.00 | 1450. |
| | 1885 | 192,000 | 70.00 | 130.00 | 300.00 | 600.00 | 2750. | 5500. |
| | 1886/3 | 540,000 | 10.00 | 20.00 | 60.00 | 175.00 | 900.00 | 2000. |
| | 1886 | Inc. Ab. | 9.00 | 18.00 | 50.00 | 160.00 | 775.00 | 1750. |
| | 1887 | 100,000 | 65.00 | 130.00 | 300.00 | 600.00 | 2750. | 5500. |
| | 1888 | 400,000 | 9.00 | 16.00 | 45.00 | 110.00 | 500.00 | 1100. |
| | 1889 | 66,324 | 75.00 | 165.00 | 325.00 | 725.00 | 3200. | 6500. |
| | 1890H | 200,000 | 15.00 | 25.00 | 65.00 | 165.00 | 900.00 | 2250. |
| | 1891 | 120,000 | 40.00 | 75.00 | 175.00 | 350.00 | 1100. | 2400. |
| | 1892 | 510,000 | 8.00 | 15.00 | 40.00 | 120.00 | 500.00 | 1400. |
| | 1893 | 100,000 | 65.00 | 110.00 | 250.00 | 475.00 | 1450. | 3000. |
| | 1894 | 220,000 | 12.50 | 25.00 | 60.00 | 170.00 | 725.00 | 1600. |
| | 1899 | 415,580 | 5.00 | 8.00 | 22.50 | 70.00 | 400.00 | 900.00 |
| | 1900 | 1,320,000 | 4.00 | 7.00 | 20.00 | 60.00 | 325.00 | 750.00 |
| | 1901 | 640,000 | 4.00 | 7.00 | 20.00 | 60.00 | 325.00 | 750.00 |
| 11 | 1902 | 464,000 | 5.00 | 8.00 | 27.50 | 80.00 | 475.00 | 1350. |
| | 1902H | 800,000 | 3.00 | 5.00 | 20.00 | 50.00 | 200.00 | 450.00 |
| | 1903 | 846,150 | 4.00 | 7.00 | 25.00 | 75.00 | 400.00 | 950.00 |
| | 1904 | 400,000 | 8.00 | 20.00 | 65.00 | 200.00 | 1000. | 2250. |
| | 1905 | 800,000 | 5.00 | 10.00 | 35.00 | 115.00 | 850.00 | 2000. |
| | 1906 lg. crown | 1,237,843 | 3.50 | 6.50 | 20.00 | 65.00 | 300.00 | 950.00 |
| | 1906 sm. crown | Inc. Ab. | — | — | — | — | Rare | — |
| | 1907 | 2,088,000 | 3.00 | 6.50 | 20.00 | 65.00 | 300.00 | 900.00 |
| | 1908 | 495,016 | 5.00 | 10.00 | 35.00 | 110.00 | 375.00 | 850.00 |
| | 1909 | 1,335,929 | 4.00 | 8.00 | 25.00 | 85.00 | 475.00 | 1250. |
| | 1910 | 3,577,569 | 3.00 | 6.00 | 18.00 | 50.00 | 200.00 | 450.00 |
| 18 | 1911 | 1,721,341 | 7.00 | 16.00 | 30.00 | 75.00 | 375.00 | 750.00 |
| 24 | 1912 | 2,544,199 | 2.50 | 4.00 | 9.00 | 30.00 | 275.00 | 850.00 |
| | 1913 | 2,213,595 | 2.50 | 4.00 | 9.00 | 27.50 | 250.00 | 800.00 |
| | 1914 | 1,215,397 | 3.50 | 5.00 | 12.00 | 35.00 | 500.00 | 1250. |
| | 1915 | 242,382 | 10.00 | 22.00 | 100.00 | 275.00 | 1800. | 3750. |
| | 1916 | 1,462,566 | 2.00 | 4.00 | 9.00 | 20.00 | 200.00 | 500.00 |
| | 1917 | 3,365,644 | 1.75 | 3.50 | 9.00 | 18.00 | 100.00 | 175.00 |
| | 1918 | 4,175,649 | 1.75 | 3.50 | 9.00 | 18.00 | 70.00 | 175.00 |
| | 1919 | 5,852,262 | 1.75 | 3.50 | 9.00 | 18.00 | 70.00 | 175.00 |

| KM# | Date | Mintage | VG-8 | F-12 | VF-20 | XF-40 | MS-60 | MS-63 |
|---|---|---|---|---|---|---|---|---|
| | | | **5.8319 g, .800 SILVER, .1500 oz ASW** | | | | | |
| 24a | 1920 | 1,975,278 | 1.75 | 2.75 | 9.00 | 22.00 | 120.00 | 400.00 |
| | 1921 | 597,337 | 9.00 | 20.00 | 65.00 | 160.00 | 900.00 | 2200. |
| | 1927 | 468,096 | 20.00 | 35.00 | 80.00 | 200.00 | 900.00 | 1800. |
| | 1928 | 2,114,178 | 2.00 | 3.00 | 8.00 | 22.00 | 100.00 | 300.00 |
| | 1929 | 2,690,562 | 1.75 | 2.75 | 7.50 | 20.00 | 100.00 | 300.00 |
| | 1930 | 968,748 | 2.00 | 3.50 | 10.00 | 25.00 | 175.00 | 475.00 |
| | 1931 | 537,815 | 2.00 | 3.50 | 10.00 | 25.00 | 225.00 | 600.00 |
| | 1932 | 537,994 | 2.25 | 4.00 | 12.00 | 30.00 | 190.00 | 475.00 |
| | 1933 | 421,282 | 3.50 | 6.50 | 16.50 | 40.00 | 180.00 | 400.00 |
| | 1934 | 384,350 | 4.00 | 8.00 | 22.00 | 60.00 | 250.00 | 425.00 |
| | 1935 | 537,772 | 3.50 | 7.00 | 17.50 | 42.00 | 200.00 | 450.00 |
| | 1936 | 972,094 | 2.00 | 3.00 | 9.00 | 22.00 | 90.00 | 200.00 |

| KM# | Date | Mintage | VG-8 | F-12 | VF-20 | XF-40 | MS-60 | MS-63 |
|---|---|---|---|---|---|---|---|---|
| 24a | 1936 dot | 153,322 | 25.00 | 60.00 | 135.00 | 275.00 | 900.00 | 2000. |

Maple Leaf Variety

| KM# | Date | Mintage | VG-8 | F-12 | VF-20 | XF-40 | MS-60 | MS-63 |
|---|---|---|---|---|---|---|---|---|
| 35 | 1937 | 2,690,176 | 1.50 | 2.50 | 4.50 | 6.00 | 14.00 | 32.00 |
| | 1938 | 3,149,245 | 1.50 | 3.00 | 6.00 | 9.00 | 70.00 | 155.00 |
| | 1939 | 3,532,495 | 1.50 | 2.50 | 5.00 | 7.00 | 60.00 | 125.00 |
| | 1940 | 9,583,650 | BV | 1.75 | 3.50 | 5.00 | 13.00 | 30.00 |
| | 1941 | 6,654,672 | BV | 1.75 | 3.50 | 5.00 | 18.00 | 37.50 |
| | 1942 | 6,935,871 | BV | 1.75 | 3.50 | 5.00 | 18.00 | 37.50 |
| | 1943 | 13,559,575 | BV | 1.25 | 2.75 | 3.75 | 16.00 | 35.00 |
| | 1944 | 7,216,237 | BV | 1.25 | 2.75 | 4.00 | 30.00 | 70.00 |
| | 1945 | 5,296,495 | BV | 1.25 | 2.75 | 4.00 | 14.00 | 30.00 |
| | 1946 | 2,210,810 | 1.50 | 2.25 | 3.25 | 6.50 | 40.00 | 70.00 |
| | 1947 | 1,524,554 | 1.50 | 2.25 | 3.50 | 7.00 | 55.00 | 100.00 |
| | 1947 dot after 7 | Inc. Ab. | 30.00 | 50.00 | 70.00 | 125.00 | 300.00 | 600.00 |
| | 1947 maple leaf | 4,393,938 | BV | 1.50 | 2.75 | 5.00 | 18.00 | 30.00 |

**Modified Obverse Legend**

| KM# | Date | Mintage | VG-8 | F-12 | VF-20 | XF-40 | MS-60 | MS-63 |
|---|---|---|---|---|---|---|---|---|
| 44 | 1948 | 2,564,424 | 1.50 | 2.25 | 3.25 | 6.00 | 50.00 | 120.00 |
| | 1949 | 7,988,830 | — | BV | 1.25 | 2.25 | 10.00 | 22.00 |
| | 1950 | 9,673,335 | — | BV | 1.25 | 2.25 | 9.00 | 17.50 |
| | 1951 | 8,290,719 | — | BV | 1.25 | 2.25 | 7.00 | 14.00 |
| | 1952 | 8,859,642 | — | BV | 1.25 | 2.25 | 7.00 | 14.00 |

**Elizabeth II Effigy**

| KM# | Date | Mintage | VG-8 | F-12 | VF-20 | XF-40 | MS-60 | MS-63 |
|---|---|---|---|---|---|---|---|---|
| 52 | 1953 NSS | 10,546,769 | — | BV | 1.75 | 2.25 | 5.00 | 7.00 |
| | 1953 SS | Inc. Ab. | — | BV | 1.75 | 2.25 | 8.00 | 14.00 |
| | 1954 | 2,318,891 | 1.75 | 2.50 | 3.50 | 7.00 | 25.00 | 35.00 |
| 52 | 1955 | 9,552,505 | — | — | BV | 1.50 | 4.00 | 7.00 |
| | 1956 | 11,269,353 | — | — | BV | 1.25 | 3.50 | 5.00 |
| | 1957 | 12,770,190 | — | — | BV | 1.00 | 2.25 | 4.00 |
| | 1958 | 9,336,910 | — | — | BV | 1.00 | 2.25 | 4.00 |
| | 1959 | 13,503,461 | — | — | — | BV | 2.00 | 3.00 |
| | 1960 | 22,835,327 | — | — | — | BV | 2.00 | 3.00 |
| | 1961 | 18,164,368 | — | — | — | BV | 2.00 | 3.00 |
| | 1962 | 29,559,266 | — | — | — | BV | 2.00 | 2.25 |
| | 1963 | 21,180,652 | — | — | — | BV | 1.75 | 2.25 |
| | 1964 | 36,479,343 | — | — | — | BV | 1.75 | 2.25 |

**Machin Portrait**

| KM# | Date | Mintage | VG-8 | F-12 | VF-20 | XF-40 | MS-60 | MS-63 |
|---|---|---|---|---|---|---|---|---|
| 62 | 1965 | 44,708,869 | — | — | — | BV | 1.75 | 2.25 |
| | 1966 | 25,626,315 | — | — | — | BV | 1.75 | 2.25 |

**5.8319 g, .500 SILVER, .0937 oz ASW**

| KM# | Date | Mintage | VG-8 | F-12 | VF-20 | XF-40 | MS-60 | MS-63 |
|---|---|---|---|---|---|---|---|---|
| 62a | 1968 | 71,464,000 | — | — | — | BV | 1.50 | 2.25 |

**NICKEL**

| KM# | Date | Mintage | VG-8 | F-12 | VF-20 | XF-40 | MS-60 | MS-63 |
|---|---|---|---|---|---|---|---|---|
| 74.1 | 1968 | 88,686,931 | — | — | — | .30 | .50 | .75 |
| | 1969 | 133,037,929 | — | — | — | .30 | .50 | .75 |
| | 1970 | 10,302,010 | — | — | — | .30 | 1.00 | 1.50 |
| | 1971 | 48,170,428 | — | — | — | .30 | .50 | .75 |
| | 1972 | 43,743,387 | — | — | — | .30 | .50 | .75 |
| | 1974 | 192,360,598 | — | — | — | .30 | .50 | .75 |
| | 1975 | 141,148,000 | — | — | — | .30 | .50 | .75 |
| | 1976 | 86,898,261 | — | — | — | .30 | .50 | .75 |
| | 1977 | 99,634,555 | — | — | — | .30 | .50 | .75 |
| | 1978 | 176,475,408 | — | — | — | .30 | .50 | .75 |

**Smaller bust**

| KM# | Date | Mintage | VG-8 | F-12 | VF-20 | XF-40 | MS-60 | MS-63 |
|---|---|---|---|---|---|---|---|---|
| 74.2 | 1979 | 131,042,905 | — | — | — | .30 | .50 | .75 |
| | 1980 | 76,178,000 | — | — | — | .30 | .50 | .75 |
| | 1981 | 131,580,272 | — | — | — | .30 | .50 | .75 |
| | 1981 | 199,000 | — | — | — | — | Proof | 2.00 |
| | 1982 | 171,926,000 | — | — | — | .30 | .50 | .75 |
| | 1982 | 180,908 | — | — | — | — | Proof | 2.00 |
| | 1983 | 13,162,000 | — | — | — | .30 | .75 | 1.50 |
| | 1983 | 168,000 | — | — | — | — | Proof | 2.00 |
| | 1984 | 121,668,000 | — | — | — | .30 | .50 | .75 |
| | 1984 | 161,602 | — | — | — | — | Proof | 2.00 |
| | 1985 | 158,734,000 | — | — | — | .30 | .50 | .75 |
| | 1985 | 157,037 | — | — | — | — | Proof | 2.00 |
| | 1986 | 132,220,000 | — | — | — | .30 | .50 | .75 |
| | 1986 | 175,745 | — | — | — | — | Proof | 2.00 |
| | 1987 | 53,408,000 | — | — | — | .30 | .75 | 1.50 |
| | 1987 | 179,004 | — | — | — | — | Proof | 2.00 |
| | 1988 | 80,368,473 | — | — | — | .30 | .75 | 1.50 |

**Smaller bust**

| KM# | Date | Mintage | VG-8 | F-12 | VF-20 | XF-40 | MS-60 | MS-63 |
|-----|------|---------|------|------|-------|-------|-------|-------|
| 74.2 | 1988 | 175,259 | — | — | — | — | Proof | 2.00 |
| | 1989 | 119,796,307 | — | — | — | .30 | .50 | .75 |
| | 1989 | 170,928 | — | — | — | — | Proof | 2.00 |

**New Elizabeth II Effigy**

| KM# | Date | Mintage | VG-8 | F-12 | VF-20 | XF-40 | MS-60 | MS-63 |
|-----|------|---------|------|------|-------|-------|-------|-------|
| 184 | 1990 | 31,258,000 | — | — | — | .30 | .75 | 1.50 |
| | 1990 | 140,649 | — | — | — | — | Proof | 2.00 |
| | 1991 | 459,000 | — | — | 2.00 | 5.00 | 9.00 | 12.00 |
| | 1991 | — | — | — | — | — | Proof | 15.00 |
| | 1993 | — | — | — | — | .30 | .75 | 1.50 |
| | 1993 | — | — | — | — | — | Proof | 2.00 |

# Commemorative twenty-five cents

| KM# | Date | Mintage | VG-8 | F-12 | VF-20 | XF-40 | MS-60 | MS-63 |
|-----|------|---------|------|------|-------|-------|-------|-------|
| 68 | 1967 Confederation Centennial, .800 Silver | | | | | | | |
| | | 48,855,500 | — | — | — | BV | 1.50 | 2.25 |
| 68a | 1967 Confederation Centennial, .500 Silver | | | | | | | |
| | | Inc. Ab. | — | — | — | BV | 1.50 | 2.25 |

| KM# | Date | Mintage | VG-8 | F-12 | VF-20 | XF-40 | MS-60 | MS-63 |
|-----|------|---------|------|------|-------|-------|-------|-------|
| 81.1 | 1973 RCMP Centennial, 120 beads, Nickel | | | | | | | |
| | | 134,958,587 | — | — | — | .30 | .50 | .75 |
| 81.2 | 1973 RCMP Centennial, 132 beads, Nickel | | | | | | | |
| | | Inc. Ab. | 15.00 | 25.00 | 35.00 | 55.00 | 85.00 | 120. |
| 207 | 1992 Confederation 125, Nickel | | | | | | | |
| | | — | — | — | — | — | — | 1.00 |
| | | — | — | — | — | — | Proof | 2.50 |

**125th Anniversary of Confederation**

| KM# | Date | Mintage | VG-8 | F-12 | VF-20 | XF-40 | MS-60 | MS-63 |
|-----|------|---------|------|------|-------|-------|-------|-------|
| 203 | 1992 New Brunswick, Nickel | | | | | | | |
| | | 12,174,000 | — | — | — | — | — | .75 |
| 203a | 1992 New Brunswick, .925 Silver | | | | | | | |
| | | — | — | — | — | — | Proof | 11.50 |

| KM# | Date | Mintage | VG-8 | F-12 | VF-20 | XF-40 | MS-60 | MS-63 |
|---|---|---|---|---|---|---|---|---|
| 212 | 1992 North West Territories, Nickel | | | | | | | |
| | | 12,582,000 | — | — | — | — | — | .75 |
| 212a | 1992 North West Territories, .925 Silver | | | | | | | |
| | | | — | — | — | — | Proof | 11.50 |
| 213 | 1992 Newfoundland, Nickel | | | | | | | |
| | | 11,405,000 | — | — | — | — | — | .75 |
| 213a | 1992 Newfoundland, .925 Silver | | | | | | | |
| | | | — | — | — | — | Proof | 11.50 |

| KM# | Date | Mintage | VG-8 | F-12 | VF-20 | XF-40 | MS-60 | MS-63 |
|---|---|---|---|---|---|---|---|---|
| 214 | 1992 Manitoba, Nickel | | | | | | | |
| | | 11,349,000 | — | — | — | — | — | .75 |
| 214a | 1992 Manitoba, .925 Silver | | | | | | | |
| | | | — | — | — | — | Proof | 10.00 |
| 220 | 1992 Yukon, Nickel | | | | | | | |
| | | 10,388,000 | — | — | — | — | — | .75 |
| 220a | 1992 Yukon, .925 Silver | | | | | | | |
| | | | — | — | — | — | Proof | 11.50 |

| KM# | Date | Mintage | VG-8 | F-12 | VF-20 | XF-40 | MS-60 | MS-63 |
|---|---|---|---|---|---|---|---|---|
| 221 | 1992 Alberta, Nickel | | | | | | | |
| | | 12,133,000 | — | — | — | — | — | .75 |
| 221a | 1992 Alberta, .925 Silver | | | | | | | |
| | | | — | — | — | — | Proof | 11.50 |
| 222 | 1992 Prince Edward Island, Nickel | | | | | | | |
| | | 13,001,000 | — | — | — | — | — | .75 |
| 222a | 1992 Prince Edward Island, .925 Silver | | | | | | | |
| | | | — | — | — | — | Proof | 11.50 |

| KM# | Date | Mintage | VG-8 | F-12 | VF-20 | XF-40 | MS-60 | MS-63 |
|---|---|---|---|---|---|---|---|---|
| 223 | 1992 Ontario, Nickel | | | | | | | |
| | | 14,263,000 | — | — | — | — | — | .75 |
| 223a | 1992 Ontario, .925 Silver | | | | | | | |
| | | | — | — | — | — | Proof | 11.50 |
| 231 | 1992 Nova Scotia, Nickel | | | | | | | |
| | | 13,600,000 | — | — | — | — | — | .75 |
| 231a | 1992 Nova Scotia, .925 Silver | | | | | | | |
| | | | — | — | — | — | Proof | 11.50 |

| KM# | Date | Mintage | VG-8 | F-12 | VF-20 | XF-40 | MS-60 | MS-63 |
|---|---|---|---|---|---|---|---|---|
| 232 | 1992 British Columbia, Nickel | | | | | | | |
| | | 14,001,000 | — | — | — | — | — | .75 |
| 232a | 1992 British Columbia, .925 Silver | | | | | | | |
| | | — | — | — | — | — | Proof | 11.50 |
| 233 | 1992 Saskatchewan, Nickel | | | | | | | |
| | | 14,165,000 | — | — | — | — | — | .75 |
| 233a | 1992 Saskatchewan, .925 Silver | | | | | | | |
| | | — | — | — | — | — | Proof | 11.50 |

| KM# | Date | Mintage | VG-8 | F-12 | VF-20 | XF-40 | MS-60 | MS-63 |
|---|---|---|---|---|---|---|---|---|
| 234 | 1992 Quebec, Nickel | | | | | | | |
| | | 13,607,000 | — | — | — | — | — | .75 |
| 234a | 1992 Quebec, .925 Silver | | | | | | | |
| | | — | — | — | — | — | Proof | 11.50 |

# Fifty cents

1870-1901

11.6200 g, .925 SILVER, .3456 oz ASW

| KM# | Date | Mintage | VG-8 | F-12 | VF-20 | XF-40 | MS-60 | MS-63 |
|---|---|---|---|---|---|---|---|---|
| 6 | 1870 | 450,000 | 500.00 | 1000. | 2000. | 3300. | 10,000. | 17,000. |
| | 1870 LCW | Inc. Ab. | 40.00 | 65.00 | 140.00 | 325.00 | 3500. | 6750. |
| | 1871 | 200,000 | 45.00 | 95.00 | 220.00 | 500.00 | 4500. | 7500. |
| | 1871H | 45,000 | 65.00 | 145.00 | 300.00 | 725.00 | 5750. | 9500. |
| | 1872H | 80,000 | 30.00 | 65.00 | 170.00 | 275.00 | 4000. | 7500. |
| | 1872H inverted A for V in VICTORIA | | | | | | | |
| | | Inc. Ab. | 85.00 | 175.00 | 375.00 | 800.00 | — | — |
| | 1881H | 150,000 | 40.00 | 80.00 | 175.00 | 300.00 | 3750. | 7250. |
| | 1888 | 60,000 | 90.00 | 200.00 | 400.00 | 900.00 | 5750. | 10,000. |
| | 1890H | 20,000 | 600.00 | 1100. | 2000. | 3500. | 12,000. | 22,000. |
| | 1892 | 151,000 | 40.00 | 90.00 | 200.00 | 400.00 | 5000. | 9500. |
| | 1894 | 29,036 | 200.00 | 400.00 | 950.00 | 1800. | 8500. | 16,000. |
| | 1898 | 100,000 | 40.00 | 90.00 | 200.00 | 400.00 | 4500. | 9000. |
| | 1899 | 50,000 | 80.00 | 165.00 | 350.00 | 900.00 | 6000. | 12,500. |
| | 1900 | 118,000 | 30.00 | 55.00 | 150.00 | 250.00 | 4500. | 8000. |
| | 1901 | 80,000 | 35.00 | 60.00 | 150.00 | 250.00 | 4500. | 7750. |

Victorian Leaves                    Edwardian Leaves

| KM# | Date | Mintage | VG-8 | F-12 | VF-20 | XF-40 | MS-60 | MS-63 |
|---|---|---|---|---|---|---|---|---|
| 12 | 1902 | 120,000 | 10.00 | 22.00 | 70.00 | 150.00 | 1000. | 3000. |
| | 1903H | 140,000 | 18.00 | 35.00 | 110.00 | 225.00 | 1400. | 3900. |
| | 1904 | 60,000 | 70.00 | 140.00 | 275.00 | 600.00 | 3100. | 7000. |
| | 1905 | 40,000 | 90.00 | 200.00 | 400.00 | 900.00 | 5500. | 11,000. |
| | 1906 | 350,000 | 10.00 | 22.00 | 65.00 | 160.00 | 1100. | 3500. |
| | 1907 | 300,000 | 10.00 | 20.00 | 55.00 | 140.00 | 1100. | 3500. |
| | 1908 | 128,119 | 20.00 | 45.00 | 125.00 | 300.00 | 1200. | 2750. |
| | 1909 | 302,118 | 12.50 | 35.00 | 90.00 | 250.00 | 1750. | 3600. |
| | 1910 Victorian lvs. | 649,521 | 9.00 | 18.00 | 50.00 | 125.00 | 1000. | 3000. |
| | 1910 Edwardian lvs. | Inc. Ab. | 9.00 | 18.00 | 50.00 | 125.00 | 1000. | 3000. |
| | **Modified Obverse Legend** | | | | | | | |
| 19 | 1911 | 209,972 | 9.00 | 55.00 | 225.00 | 475.00 | 1300. | 2900. |
| | **Modified Obverse Legend** | | | | | | | |
| 25 | 1912 | 285,867 | 4.50 | 16.00 | 70.00 | 175.00 | 1200. | 2500. |
| | 1913 | 265,889 | 5.00 | 16.00 | 70.00 | 175.00 | 1400. | 3200. |
| | 1914 | 160,128 | 15.00 | 45.00 | 160.00 | 400.00 | 2000. | 4250. |
| | 1916 | 459,070 | 3.00 | 14.00 | 50.00 | 125.00 | 750.00 | 1800. |
| | 1917 | 752,213 | 3.00 | 14.00 | 35.00 | 90.00 | 500.00 | 1400. |
| | 1918 | 754,989 | 3.00 | 8.00 | 22.00 | 70.00 | 400.00 | 1000. |
| | 1919 | 1,113,429 | 3.00 | 8.00 | 22.00 | 70.00 | 400.00 | 1000. |

### 1902-1936
### 11.6638 g, .800 SILVER, .3000 oz ASW

| KM# | Date | Mintage | VG-8 | F-12 | VF-20 | XF-40 | MS-60 | MS-63 |
|---|---|---|---|---|---|---|---|---|
| 25a | 1920 | 584,691 | 5.00 | 10.00 | 35.00 | 125.00 | 600.00 | 1400. |
| | 1921 | 75 to 100 pcs.known | 10,000. | 13,000. | 18,000. | 24,000. | 37,500. | 63,800. |
| NOTE: Bowers and Merena Victoria Sale 9-89 MS-65 realized $110,000. | | | | | | | | |
| | 1929 | 228,328 | 3.00 | 10.00 | 35.00 | 110.00 | 550.00 | 1400. |
| | 1931 | 57,581 | 7.00 | 20.00 | 60.00 | 175.00 | 1200. | 2400. |
| | 1932 | 19,213 | 30.00 | 90.00 | 200.00 | 475.00 | 2000. | 4000. |
| | 1934 | 39,539 | 10.00 | 25.00 | 75.00 | 200.00 | 900.00 | 1800. |
| | 1936 | 38,550 | 9.00 | 20.00 | 65.00 | 175.00 | 600.00 | 1200. |
| 36 | 1937 | 192,016 | 2.50 | 4.00 | 7.00 | 10.00 | 30.00 | 70.00 |
| | 1938 | 192,018 | 4.00 | 8.00 | 15.00 | 30.00 | 140.00 | 350.00 |
| | 1939 | 287,976 | 3.00 | 5.00 | 8.00 | 18.00 | 100.00 | 275.00 |
| | 1940 | 1,996,566 | BV | 3.00 | 3.50 | 6.00 | 25.00 | 70.00 |
| | 1941 | 1,714,874 | BV | 2.25 | 3.50 | 6.00 | 25.00 | 70.00 |
| | 1942 | 1,974,164 | BV | 2.25 | 3.50 | 6.00 | 25.00 | 70.00 |
| | 1943 | 3,109,583 | BV | 2.25 | 3.50 | 6.00 | 25.00 | 70.00 |
| | 1944 | 2,460,205 | BV | 2.25 | 3.50 | 6.00 | 25.00 | 70.00 |
| | 1945 | 1,959,528 | BV | 2.25 | 3.50 | 6.00 | 25.00 | 70.00 |
| | 1946 | 950,235 | BV | 5.00 | 6.50 | 9.00 | 75.00 | 120.00 |
| | 1946 hoof in 6 | Inc. Ab. | 15.00 | 22.50 | 40.00 | 110.00 | 900.00 | 1750. |
| | 1947 straight 7 | 424,885 | 3.00 | 4.00 | 6.00 | 14.00 | 90.00 | 175.00 |
| | 1947 curved 7 | Inc. Ab. | 2.00 | 3.50 | 7.00 | 14.00 | 90.00 | 190.00 |
| | 1947ML straight 7 | 38,433 | 12.00 | 16.00 | 30.00 | 50.00 | 150.00 | 300.00 |
| | 1947ML curved 7 | Inc. Ab. | 750.00 | 1250. | 1700. | 2000. | 3200. | 4750. |

### Modified Obverse Legend

| KM# | Date | Mintage | VG-8 | F-12 | VF-20 | XF-40 | MS-60 | MS-63 |
|---|---|---|---|---|---|---|---|---|
| 45 | 1948 | 37,784 | 35.00 | 45.00 | 60.00 | 90.00 | 180.00 | 275.00 |
| | 1949 | 858,991 | 2.25 | 3.00 | 6.50 | 10.00 | 40.00 | 100.00 |
| | 1949 hoof over 9 | Inc. Ab. | 8.00 | 12.50 | 30.00 | 65.00 | 350.00 | 700.00 |
| | 1950 | 2,384,179 | 3.00 | 6.00 | 9.00 | 20.00 | 175.00 | 300.00 |
| | 1950 lines in 0 | Inc. Ab. | BV | 2.50 | 3.00 | 4.00 | 12.00 | 20.00 |
| | 1951 | 2,421,730 | BV | 2.00 | 2.50 | 3.75 | 8.00 | 18.00 |
| | 1952 | 2,596,465 | BV | 2.50 | 3.00 | 3.75 | 8.00 | 18.00 |

### Elizabeth II Effigy

| KM# | Date | Mintage | VG-8 | F-12 | VF-20 | XF-40 | MS-60 | MS-63 |
|---|---|---|---|---|---|---|---|---|
| 53 | 1953 sm. date | 1,630,429 | BV | 2.50 | 3.00 | 3.50 | 8.00 | 14.00 |
| | 1953 lg.dt,straps | Inc. Ab. | BV | 2.50 | 3.50 | 6.00 | 24.00 | 35.00 |
| | 1953 lg.dt,w/o straps | I.A. | 3.00 | 5.00 | 6.00 | 14.00 | 90.00 | 150.00 |
| | 1954 | 506,305 | 2.25 | 3.25 | 4.75 | 7.00 | 25.00 | 35.00 |
| | 1955 | 753,511 | BV | 3.00 | 4.00 | 5.00 | 14.00 | 24.00 |
| | 1956 | 1,379,499 | — | BV | 2.00 | 3.50 | 6.00 | 10.00 |
| | 1957 | 2,171,689 | — | — | BV | 2.00 | 4.00 | 7.00 |
| | 1958 | 2,957,266 | — | — | BV | 2.00 | 2.75 | 6.00 |

| KM# | Date | Mintage | VG-8 | F-12 | VF-20 | XF-40 | MS-60 | MS-63 |
|---|---|---|---|---|---|---|---|---|
| 56 | 1959 | 3,095,535 | — | — | BV | 2.00 | 3.00 | 5.00 |
| | 1960 | 3,488,897 | — | — | — | BV | 2.50 | 3.50 |
| | 1961 | 3,584,417 | — | — | — | BV | 2.25 | 3.25 |
| | 1962 | 5,208,030 | — | — | — | BV | 2.25 | 3.25 |
| | 1963 | 8,348,871 | — | — | — | BV | 2.25 | 3.25 |
| | 1964 | 9,377,676 | — | — | — | BV | 2.25 | 3.25 |

### New Elizabeth II Effigy

| KM# | Date | Mintage | VG-8 | F-12 | VF-20 | XF-40 | MS-60 | MS-63 |
|---|---|---|---|---|---|---|---|---|
| 63 | 1965 | 12,629,974 | — | — | — | BV | 2.25 | 3.25 |
| | 1966 | 7,920,496 | — | — | — | BV | 2.25 | 3.25 |

### NICKEL

| KM# | Date | Mintage | VG-8 | F-12 | VF-20 | XF-40 | MS-60 | MS-63 |
|---|---|---|---|---|---|---|---|---|
| 75.1 | 1968 | 3,966,932 | — | — | — | .50 | .65 | 1.00 |
| | 1969 | 7,113,929 | — | — | — | .50 | .65 | 1.00 |
| | 1970 | 2,429,526 | — | — | — | .50 | .65 | 1.00 |
| | 1971 | 2,166,444 | — | — | — | .50 | .65 | 1.00 |
| | 1972 | 2,515,632 | — | — | — | .50 | .65 | 1.00 |
| | 1973 | 2,546,096 | — | — | — | .50 | .65 | 1.00 |
| | 1974 | 3,436,650 | — | — | — | .50 | .65 | 1.00 |
| | 1975 | 3,710,000 | — | — | — | .50 | .65 | 1.00 |
| | 1976 | 2,940,719 | — | — | — | .50 | .65 | 1.00 |

**Smaller bust**

| KM# | Date | Mintage | VG-8 | F-12 | VF-20 | XF-40 | MS-60 | MS-63 |
|-----|------|---------|------|------|-------|-------|-------|-------|
| 75.2 | 1977 | 709,839 | — | — | .50 | .75 | 1.50 | 2.00 |

| KM# | Date | Mintage | VG-8 | F-12 | VF-20 | XF-40 | MS-60 | MS-63 |
|-----|------|---------|------|------|-------|-------|-------|-------|
| 75.3 | 1978 square jewels | 3,341,892 | — | — | — | .50 | .75 | 1.00 |
| | 1978 round jewels | Inc. Ab. | — | — | .50 | 2.50 | 3.00 | 4.00 |
| | 1979 | 3,425,000 | — | — | — | .50 | .65 | 1.00 |
| | 1980 | 1,574,000 | — | — | — | .50 | .65 | 1.00 |
| | 1981 | 2,690,272 | — | — | — | .50 | .65 | 1.00 |
| | 1981 | 199,000 | — | — | — | — | Proof | 3.00 |
| | 1982 small beads | 2,236,674 | — | — | — | .50 | .65 | 1.00 |
| | 1982 small beads | 180,908 | — | — | — | — | Proof | 3.00 |
| | 1982 large beads | Inc. Ab. | — | — | — | .50 | .65 | 1.00 |
| | 1983 | 1,177,000 | — | — | — | .50 | .65 | 1.00 |
| | 1983 | 168,000 | — | — | — | — | Proof | 3.00 |
| | 1984 | 1,502,989 | — | — | — | .50 | .65 | 1.00 |
| | 1984 | 161,602 | — | — | — | — | Proof | 3.00 |
| | 1985 | 2,188,374 | — | — | — | .50 | .65 | 1.00 |
| | 1985 | 157,037 | — | — | — | — | Proof | 3.00 |
| | 1986 | 781,400 | — | — | — | .50 | .85 | 1.25 |
| | 1986 | 175,745 | — | — | — | — | Proof | 3.00 |
| | 1987 | 373,000 | — | — | — | .50 | .85 | 1.25 |
| | 1987 | 179,004 | — | — | — | — | Proof | 3.00 |
| | 1988 | 220,000 | — | — | — | .50 | .85 | 1.25 |
| | 1988 | 175,259 | — | — | — | — | Proof | 3.00 |
| | 1989 | 266,419 | — | — | — | .50 | .85 | 1.25 |
| | 1989 | 170,928 | — | — | — | — | Proof | 3.00 |
| | **New Elizabeth II Effigy** | | | | | | | |
| 185 | 1990 | 207,000 | — | — | — | .50 | 1.25 | 2.50 |
| | 1990 | 140,649 | — | — | — | — | Proof | 3.00 |
| | 1991 | 490,000 | — | — | — | .50 | 1.00 | 1.75 |
| | 1991 | | — | — | — | — | Proof | 3.00 |
| | 1993 | | — | — | — | .50 | 1.00 | 1.75 |
| | 1993 | | — | — | — | — | Proof | 3.00 |

# Commemorative fifty cents

| KM# | Date | Mintage | VG-8 | F-12 | VF-20 | XF-40 | MS-60 | MS-63 |
|-----|------|---------|------|------|-------|-------|-------|-------|
| 69 | 1967 Confederation Centennial, .800 Silver | | | | | | | |
| | | 4,211,392 | — | — | — | BV | 3.00 | 4.00 |
| 208 | 1992 Confederation 125, Nickel | | | | | | | |
| | | | — | — | — | .50 | .85 | 1.75 |
| | | | — | — | — | — | Proof | 3.00 |

# Voyageur dollars

**23.3276 g, .800 SILVER, .6000 oz ASW**

| KM# | Date | Mintage | F-12 | VF-20 | XF-40 | AU-50 | MS-60 | MS-63 |
|-----|------|---------|------|-------|-------|-------|-------|-------|
| 31 | 1936 | 339,600 | 10.00 | 15.00 | 20.00 | 27.50 | 50.00 | 80.00 |

|  | Pointed 7 | | Blunt 7 | | Maple Leaf (blunt 7 only) | | |

| KM# | Date | Mintage | F-12 | VF-20 | XF-40 | AU-50 | MS-60 | MS-63 |
|-----|------|---------|------|-------|-------|-------|-------|-------|
| 37 | 1937 | 207,406 | 10.00 | 12.00 | 14.00 | 17.50 | 35.00 | 75.00 |
|  | 1937 | 1,295 | — | — | — | Proof | — | 800.00 |
|  | 1937 | I.A. | — | — | — | Matte Proof | — | 400.00 |
|  | 1938 | 90,304 | 20.00 | 30.00 | 40.00 | 50.00 | 85.00 | 250.00 |
|  | 1945 | 38,391 | 65.00 | 110.00 | 135.00 | 160.00 | 225.00 | 550.00 |
|  | 1945 | — | — | — | — | Specimen | — | 2750. |
|  | 1946 | 93,055 | 12.50 | 20.00 | 28.00 | 35.00 | 80.00 | 270.00 |
|  | 1947 pointed 7 | Inc. Bl. | 60.00 | 90.00 | 120.00 | 175.00 | 350.00 | 1000. |
|  | 1947 blunt 7 | 65,595 | 30.00 | 50.00 | 65.00 | 80.00 | 120.00 | 275.00 |
|  | 1947 maple leaf | 21,135 | 100.00 | 130.00 | 160.00 | 200.00 | 275.00 | 600.00 |
| 46 | 1948 | 18,780 | 425.00 | 525.00 | 675.00 | 750.00 | 900. | 1250. |
|  | 1950 w/4 water lines | 261,002 | 5.00 | 6.00 | 8.00 | 12.50 | 16.50 | 35.00 |
|  | 1950 w/4 water lines, (1 known) |  | — | — | — | Matte Proof | — | — |
|  | 1950 Arnprior w/1-1/2 w.l. | I.A. | 8.00 | 10.00 | 15.00 | 25.00 | 45.00 | 125.00 |
|  | 1951 w/4 water lines | 416,395 | 5.00 | 7.00 | 8.00 | 9.00 | 12.50 | 30.00 |
|  | 1951 w/4 water lines | — | — | — | — | — | Proof | 400.00 |
|  | 1951 Arnprior w/1-1/2 w.l. | I.A. | 22.00 | 35.00 | 45.00 | 70.00 | 120.00 | 350.00 |
|  | 1952 w/4 water lines | 406,148 | 5.00 | 6.00 | 7.00 | 8.00 | 12.00 | 30.00 |
|  | 1952 Arnprior | I.A. | 35.00 | 55.00 | 70.00 | 120.00 | 175.00 | 375.00 |
|  | 1952 Arnprior | — | — | — | — | — | Proof | Rare |
|  | 1952 w/o water lines | I.A. | 6.00 | 7.00 | 8.00 | 10.00 | 13.50 | 40.00 |

| KM# | Date | Mintage | VF-20 | XF-40 | AU-50 | MS-60 | MS-63 |
|-----|------|---------|-------|-------|-------|-------|-------|
| 54 | 1953 w/o strap, wire rim | 1,074,578 | 4.00 | 5.00 | 6.00 | 7.00 | 18.00 |
|  | 1953 w/strap, flat rim | Inc. Ab. | 4.00 | 5.00 | 6.00 | 7.00 | 20.00 |
|  | 1954 | 246,606 | 5.00 | 6.00 | 9.00 | 16.00 | 35.00 |
|  | 1955 w/4 water lines | 268,105 | 5.00 | 6.00 | 8.00 | 14.00 | 30.00 |
|  | 1955 Arnprior w/1-1/2 w.l.* | I.A. | 70.00 | 90.00 | 100.00 | 125.00 | 200.00 |
|  | 1956 | 209,092 | 10.00 | 12.00 | 14.00 | 18.00 | 45.00 |
|  | 1957 w/4 water lines | 496,389 | BV | 6.00 | 8.00 | 10.00 | 20.00 |
|  | 1957 w/1 water line | I.A. | 7.50 | 10.00 | 15.00 | 20.00 | 30.00 |
|  | 1959 | 1,443,502 | — | BV | 5.00 | 6.00 | 8.00 |
|  | 1960 | 1,420,486 | — | BV | 6.00 | 7.00 | 8.00 |
|  | 1961 | 1,262,231 | — | BV | 6.00 | 7.00 | 8.00 |
|  | 1962 | 1,884,789 | — | BV | 6.00 | 7.00 | 8.00 |
|  | 1963 | 4,179,981 | — | BV | 6.00 | 7.00 | 8.00 |

**\*NOTE:** All genuine circulation strike 1955 Arnprior dollars have a die break running along the top of TI in the word GRATIA on the obverse.

|  | Small Beads | | Medium Beads | | Large Beads | | |

**New Elizabeth II Effigy**

| KM# | Date | Mintage | VF-20 | XF-40 | AU-50 | MS-60 | MS-63 |
|-----|------|---------|-------|-------|-------|-------|-------|
| 64.1 | 1965 sm. beads, pointed 5 | 10,768,569 | — | BV | 6.00 | 7.00 | 8.00 |
|  | 1965 sm. beads, blunt 5 | Inc. Ab. | — | BV | 6.00 | 7.00 | 8.00 |
|  | 1965 lg. beads, blunt 5 | Inc. Ab. | — | BV | 6.00 | 7.00 | 8.00 |

| KM# | Date | Mintage | VF-20 | XF-40 | AU-50 | MS-60 | MS-63 |
|---|---|---|---|---|---|---|---|
| 64.1 | 1965 lg. beads, pointed 5 | Inc. Ab. | BV | 4.00 | 4.25 | 5.00 | 8.00 |
| | 1965 med. beads, pointed 5 | Inc. Ab. | 4.00 | 6.00 | 7.00 | 10.00 | 25.00 |
| | 1966 lg. beads | 9,912,178 | — | BV | 6.00 | 7.00 | 8.00 |
| | 1966 sm. beads | *485 pcs. | — | 600. | 1000. | 1200. | 1500. |

**23.3276 g, .500 SILVER, .3750 oz ASW, 36mm**

| KM# | Date | Mintage | Smaller bust MS-63 | Mintage | P/L | Spec. |
|---|---|---|---|---|---|---|
| 64.2a | 1972 | — | — | 341,598 | — | 16.00 |

**NICKEL, 32mm**

| KM# | Date | Mintage | Large bust MS-63 | Mintage | P/L | Spec. |
|---|---|---|---|---|---|---|
| 76.1 | 1968 | 5,579,714 | 1.50 | 1,408,143 | 2.50 | — |
| | 1969 | 4,809,313 | 1.50 | 594,258 | 2.50 | — |
| | 1972 | 2,676,041 | 2.00 | 405,865 | 2.50 | — |

| KM# | Date | Mintage | Smaller bust MS-63 | Mintage | P/L | Spec. |
|---|---|---|---|---|---|---|
| 76.2 | 1975 | 3,256,000 | 2.00 | 322,325 | 3.25 | — |
| | 1976 | 2,498,204 | 2.50 | 274,106 | 4.00 | — |
| 76.3 | 1975 mule w/1976 obv. | Inc. Ab. | — | — | * | — |

*NOTE: Only known in proof-like sets w/1976 obv. slightly modified.

| KM# | Date | Mintage | VF-20 | | | MS-60 | Spec. |
|---|---|---|---|---|---|---|---|
| 117 | 1977 | 1,393,745 | 2.50 | | — | 4.50 | — |
| 120 | 1978 | 2,948,488 | 2.00 | | — | 3.50 | — |
| | 1979 | 2,954,842 | 2.00 | | — | 5.50 | — |
| | 1980 | 3,291,221 | 2.00 | | — | 9.00 | — |
| | 1981 | 2,778,900 | 2.00 | | — | 5.00 | 6.50 |
| | 1982 | 1,098,500 | 2.00 | | — | 5.50 | 10.00 |
| | 1983 | 2,267,525 | 2.00 | | — | 6.00 | 15.00 |
| | 1984 | 1,223,486 | 2.00 | | — | 6.00 | — |
| | 1984 | 161,602 | — | | — | — | 15.00 |
| | 1985 | 3,104,092 | 2.00 | | — | 7.00 | — |
| | 1985 | 157,037 | — | | — | — | 35.00 |
| | 1986 | 3,089,225 | 2.00 | | — | 12.00 | — |
| | 1986 | 175,259 | — | | — | — | 30.00 |
| | 1987 | 287,330 | 2.00 | | — | 8.00 | — |
| | 1987 | 179,004 | — | | — | — | 30.00 |

# Loon dollars

| KM# | Date | AUREATE NICKEL Mintage | MS-63 | P/L | Proof |
|---|---|---|---|---|---|
| 157 | 1987 | 205,405,000 | 3.00 | — | — |
| | 1987 | 178,120 | — | — | 15.00 |
| | 1988 | 138,893,539 | 2.00 | 7.50 | — |
| | 1988 | 175,259 | — | — | 16.50 |
| | 1989 | 184,773,902 | 2.00 | 7.50 | — |
| | 1989 | 170,928 | — | — | 16.50 |

| KM# | Date | New Elizabeth II Effigy Mintage | MS-63 | P/L | Proof |
|---|---|---|---|---|---|
| 186 | 1990 | 68,402,000 | 2.00 | 7.50 | — |
| | 1990 | 140,649 | — | — | 18.00 |
| | 1991 | 23,156,000 | 3.00 | 8.50 | — |
| | 1991 | — | — | — | 20.00 |
| | 1993 | — | 2.00 | 7.50 | — |
| | 1993 | — | — | — | 20.00 |

# Commemorative dollars

**23.3276 g, .800 SILVER, .6000 oz ASW**

| KM# | Date | Mintage | F-12 | VF-20 | XF-40 | AU-50 | MS-60 | MS-63 |
|-----|------|---------|------|-------|-------|-------|-------|-------|
| 30 | 1935 Jubilee | 428,707 | 15.00 | 25.00 | 35.00 | 45.00 | 60.00 | 120.00 |

| KM# | Date | Mintage | F-12 | VF-20 | XF-40 | AU-50 | MS-60 | MS-63 |
|-----|------|---------|------|-------|-------|-------|-------|-------|
| 38 | 1939 Royal Visit | 1,363,816 | 6.00 | 8.00 | 10.00 | 15.00 | 18.00 | 30.00 |
| | 1939 Royal Visit | — | — | — | — | — | Specimen | 600.00 |
| | 1939 Royal Visit | — | — | — | — | — | Proof | 2500. |
| 47 | 1949 Newfoundland | 672,218 | 9.00 | 15.00 | 25.00 | 30.00 | 40.00 | 55.00 |
| | 1949 Newfoundland | — | — | — | — | — | Specimen | 425.00 |

| KM# | Date | Mintage | F-12 | VF-20 | XF-40 | AU-50 | MS-60 | MS-63 |
|-----|------|---------|------|-------|-------|-------|-------|-------|
| 55 | 1958 Br. Columbia | 3,039,630 | BV | 4.00 | 5.00 | 6.00 | 7.00 | 14.00 |

| KM# | Date | Mintage | F-12 | VF-20 | XF-40 | AU-50 | MS-60 | MS-63 |
|-----|------|---------|------|-------|-------|-------|-------|-------|
| 58 | 1964 Charlottetown | 7,296,832 | — | BV | 5.00 | 6.00 | 7.00 | 11.50 |

| KM# | Date | Mintage | MS-63 | P/L | Spec. |
|-----|------|---------|-------|-----|-------|
| 70 | 1967 Goose,Confederation Centennial | 6,767,496 | 8.00 | 11.50 | 450.00 |

| KM# | Date | Mintage | MS-63 | P/L | Spec. |
|-----|------|---------|-------|-----|-------|
| 78 | 1970 Manitoba (Nickel, 32mm) | 4,140,058 | 2.00 | — | — |
|  |  | 645,869 | — | 3.25 | — |

| KM# | Date | Mintage | MS-63 | P/L | Spec. |
|-----|------|---------|-------|-----|-------|
| 79 | 1971 Br. Columbia (Nickel, 32mm) | 4,260,781 | 2.00 | 3.00 | — |
|  |  | 468,729 | — | (c) 2.50 | — |

| KM# | Date | Mintage | MS-63 | P/L | Spec. |
|-----|------|---------|-------|-----|-------|
|  | **23.3276 g, .500 SILVER, .3750 oz ASW*** |  |  |  |  |
| 80 | 1971 Br. Columbia (.500 Silver, 36mm) | 585,674 | — | — | 14.50 |

*NOTE: All silver dollars dated 1971 to date are minted to this standard.

| KM# | Date | Mintage | MS-63 | P/L | Spec. |
|-----|------|---------|-------|-----|-------|
| 82 | 1973 Pr. Edward Island (Nickel, 32mm) | 3,196,452 | 2.50 | — | — |
| | | 466,881 | — | (c) 3.25 | — |

| KM# | Date | Mintage | MS-63 | P/L | Spec. |
|-----|------|---------|-------|-----|-------|
| 83 | 1973 Mountie (.500 Silver, 36mm) | 1,031,271 | — | — | 15.00 |
| 83v | 1973 Mountie, with metal crest on case | Inc. Ab. | — | — | 17.00 |

| KM# | Date | Mintage | MS-63 | P/L | Spec. |
|-----|------|---------|-------|-----|-------|
| 88 | 1974 Winnipeg (Nickel, 32mm) | 2,799,363 | 3.00 | — | — |
| | | 363,786 | — | (c) 5.00 | — |
| 88a | 1974 Winnipeg (.500 Silver, 36mm) | 728,947 | — | — | 14.50 |

| KM# | Date | Mintage | MS-63 | P/L | Spec. |
|-----|------|---------|-------|-----|-------|
| 97 | 1975 Calgary (.500 Silver, 36mm) | 930,956 | — | — | 9.00 |

| KM# | Date | Mintage | MS-63 | P/L | Spec. |
|---|---|---|---|---|---|
| 106 | 1976 Parliament Library (.500 Silver, 36mm) | 578,708 | — | — | 22.50 |

| KM# | Date | Mintage | MS-63 | P/L | Spec. |
|---|---|---|---|---|---|
| 118 | 1977 Silver Jubilee | 744,848 | — | — | 15.50 |

| KM# | Date | Mintage | MS-63 | P/L | Spec. |
|---|---|---|---|---|---|
| 121 | 1978 XI Games (.500 Silver, 36mm) | 709,602 | — | — | 15.50 |

| KM# | Date | Mintage | MS-63 | P/L | Spec. |
|---|---|---|---|---|---|
| 124 | 1979 Griffon (.500 Silver, 36mm) | 826,695 | — | — | 26.00 |

| KM# | Date | Mintage | MS-63 | P/L | Spec. |
|---|---|---|---|---|---|
| 128 | 1980 Arctic Territories | | | | |
| | (.500 Silver, 36mm) | 539,617 | — | — | 65.00 |

| KM# | Date | Mintage | MS-63 | P/L | Proof |
|---|---|---|---|---|---|
| 130 | 1981 Railroad (.500 Silver, 36mm) | 699,494 | 50.00 | — | 35.00 |

| KM# | Date | Mintage | MS-63 | P/L | Proof |
|---|---|---|---|---|---|
| 133 | 1982 Regina | 144,930 | 37.50 | — | |
| | (.500 Silver, 36mm) | 758,958 | — | — | 8.00 |

| KM# | Date | Mintage | MS-63 | P/L | Proof |
|---|---|---|---|---|---|
| 134 | 1982 Constitution (Nickel, 32mm) | 9,709,422 | 2.00 | — | 7.00 |

| KM# | Date | Mintage | MS-63 | P/L | Proof |
|-----|------|---------|-------|-----|-------|
| 138 | 1983 Edmonton University Games | 159,450 | 32.50 | — | — |
|  | (.500 Silver, 36mm) | 506,847 | — | — | 16.50 |

| KM# | Date | Mintage | MS-63 | P/L | Proof |
|-----|------|---------|-------|-----|-------|
| 140 | 1984 Toronto Sesquicentennial | 133,610 | 37.50 | — | — |
|  | (.500 Silver, 36mm) | 732,542 | — | — | 10.00 |

| KM# | Date | Mintage | MS-63 | P/L | Proof |
|-----|------|---------|-------|-----|-------|
| 141 | 1984 Cartier (Nickel, 32mm) | 7,009,323 | 2.25 | — | — |
|  |  | 87,760 | — | — | 7.00 |

| KM# | Date | Mintage | MS-63 | P/L | Proof |
|-----|------|---------|-------|-----|-------|
| 143 | 1985 National Parks -Moose | 163,314 | 35.00 | — | — |
|  | (.500 Silver, 36mm) | 733,354 | — | — | 10.00 |

| KM# | Date | Mintage | MS-63 | P/L | Proof |
|---|---|---|---|---|---|
| 149 | 1986 Vancouver | 125,949 | 40.00 | — | — |
| | (.500 Silver, 36mm) | 680,004 | — | — | 15.50 |

| KM# | Date | Mintage | MS-63 | P/L | Proof |
|---|---|---|---|---|---|
| 154 | 1987 John Davis | 118,722 | 37.50 | — | — |
| | (.500 Silver, 36mm) | 602,374 | — | — | 22.00 |

| KM# | Date | Mintage | MS-63 | P/L | Proof |
|---|---|---|---|---|---|
| 161 | 1988 Ironworks | 106,872 | 45.00 | — | — |
| | (.500 Silver, 36mm) | 255,013 | — | — | 50.00 |

| KM# | Date | Mintage | MS-63 | P/L | Proof |
|---|---|---|---|---|---|
| 168 | 1989 MacKenzie River | 99,774 | 27.50 | — | — |
| | (.500 Silver, 36mm) | 244,062 | — | — | 50.00 |

| KM# | Date | Mintage | MS-63 | P/L | Proof |
|---|---|---|---|---|---|
| 170 | 1990 Henry Kelsey | 99,455 | 22.50 | — | — |
|  | (.500 Silver, 36mm) | 254,959 | — | — | 23.50 |

| KM# | Date | Mintage | MS-63 | P/L | Proof |
|---|---|---|---|---|---|
| 179 | 1991 S.S. Frontenac | 73,843 | 17.50 | — | — |
|  | (.500 Silver, 36mm) | 195,424 | — | — | 25.00 |

| KM# | Date | Mintage | MS-63 | P/L | Proof |
|---|---|---|---|---|---|
| 210 | 1992 Stagecoach Service | — | 16.50 | — | 22.00 |
|  | (.925 Silver, 36mm) |  |  |  |  |

| KM# | Date | Mintage | MS-63 | P/L | Proof |
|---|---|---|---|---|---|
| 235 | 1993 Stanley Cup Hockey | — | 15.00 | — | — |
|  | (.925 Silver, 36mm) | 281,664 | — | — | 20.00 |

| KM# | Date | Mintage | MS-63 | P/L | Proof |
|---|---|---|---|---|---|
| 248 | 1994 War Memorial | 15.000 | 2.00 | — | — |
| | Aureate, 26mm | Inc. Ab. | — | — | 25.00 |

| 251 | 1994 Last RCMP Sled Dog Patrol | — | 15.25 | — | — |
|---|---|---|---|---|---|
| | (.925 Silver, 36mm) | — | — | — | 21.00 |

### 125th Anniversary of the Confederation

| KM# | Date | Mintage | MS-63 | P/L | Proof |
|---|---|---|---|---|---|
| 209 | 1992 Loon, Aureate | — | 2.00 | — | 20.00 |

| 218 | 1992 Parliament, Aureate | 23,915,000 | 2.00 | — | — |
|---|---|---|---|---|---|
| | Aureate | — | — | — | 18.00 |

**NOTE:** (c) Individually cased Proof-likes (P/L), Proofs or Specimens are from broken up Proof-like or specimen sets.

# 5 DOLLARS

| | | 8.3592 g, .900 GOLD, .2419 oz AGW | | | | | |
|---|---|---|---|---|---|---|---|
| KM# | Date | Mintage | F-12 | VF-20 | XF-40 | AU-50 | MS-60 | MS-63 |
| 26 | 1912 | 165,680 | 120.00 | 140.00 | 165.00 | 220.00 | 325.00 | 600.00 |
| | 1913 | 98,832 | 120.00 | 140.00 | 165.00 | 220.00 | 325.00 | 600.00 |
| | 1914 | 31,122 | 200.00 | 300.00 | 375.00 | 500.00 | 750.00 | 1550. |

Olympic Commemoratives

24.3000 g, .925 SILVER, .7227 oz ASW

Series I

| KM# | Date | Mintage | MS-63 | Proof |
|-----|------|---------|-------|-------|
| 84 | 1973 Sailboats (Kingston) | — | 5.50 | — |
| | | 165,203 | — | 7.25 |

| KM# | Date | Mintage | MS-63 | Proof |
|-----|------|---------|-------|-------|
| 85 | 1973 North America Map | — | 5.50 | — |
| | | 165,203 | — | 7.25 |

| KM# | Date | Mintage | MS-63 | Proof |
|-----|------|---------|-------|-------|
| 89 | 1974 Olympic Rings | — | 5.50 | — |
| | | 97,431 | — | 7.25 |

Series II

| KM# | Date | Mintage | MS-63 | Proof |
|-----|------|---------|-------|-------|
| 90 | 1974 Athlete with torch | — | 5.50 | — |
| | | 97,431 | — | 7.25 |

**Series III**

| KM# | Date | Mintage | MS-63 | Proof |
|-----|------|---------|-------|-------|
| 91 | 1974 Rowing | — | 5.50 | — |
| | | 104,684 | — | 7.25 |

| KM# | Date | Mintage | MS-63 | Proof |
|-----|------|---------|-------|-------|
| 92 | 1974 Canoeing | — | 5.50 | — |
| | | 104,684 | — | 7.25 |

**Series IV**

| KM# | Date | Mintage | MS-63 | Proof |
|-----|------|---------|-------|-------|
| 98 | 1975 Marathon | — | 5.50 | — |
| | | 89,155 | — | 7.25 |

| KM# | Date | Mintage | MS-63 | Proof |
|-----|------|---------|-------|-------|
| 99 | 1975 Ladies' javelin | — | 5.50 | — |
| | | 89,155 | — | 7.25 |

**Series V**

| KM# | Date | Mintage | MS-63 | Proof |
|-----|------|---------|-------|-------|
| 100 | 1975 Swimmer | | 5.50 | — |
| | | 89,155 | — | 7.25 |

| KM# | Date | Mintage | MS-63 | Proof |
|-----|------|---------|-------|-------|
| 101 | 1975 Diver | — | 5.50 | — |
| | | 89,155 | — | 7.25 |

**Series VI**

| KM# | Date | Mintage | MS-63 | Proof |
|-----|------|---------|-------|-------|
| 107 | 1976 Fencing | — | 5.50 | — |
| | | 82,302 | — | 10.00 |

| KM# | Date | Mintage | MS-63 | Proof |
|-----|------|---------|-------|-------|
| 108 | 1976 Boxing | — | 5.50 | — |
| | | 82,302 | — | 10.00 |

**Series VII**

| KM# | Date | Mintage | MS-63 | Proof |
|-----|------|---------|-------|-------|
| 109 | 1976 Olympic Village | — | 5.50 | — |
| | | 76,908 | — | 11.50 |

| KM# | Date | Mintage | MS-63 | Proof |
|-----|------|---------|-------|-------|
| 110 | 1976 Olympic flame | — | 5.50 | — |
| | | 79,102 | — | 11.50 |

# 10 dollars

| | | 16.7185 g, .900 GOLD, .4838 oz AGW | | | | | |
|-----|------|---------|------|-------|-------|-------|-------|
| KM# | Date | Mintage | F-12 | VF-20 | XF-40 | AU-50 | MS-60 | MS-63 |
| 27 | 1912 | 74,759 | 200.00 | 300.00 | 380.00 | 500.00 | 750.00 | 1500. |
| | 1913 | 149,232 | 200.00 | 300.00 | 380.00 | 500.00 | 775.00 | 1550. |
| | 1914 | 140,068 | 210.00 | 320.00 | 425.00 | 625.00 | 975.00 | 1950. |

Olympic Commemoratives

**48.6000 g, .925 SILVER, 1.4454 oz ASW**

Series I

| KM# | Date | Mintage | MS-63 | Proof |
|---|---|---|---|---|
| 86.1 | 1973 World Map | 103,426 | 11.50 | — |
| | | 165,203 | — | 14.00 |
| 86.2 | 1974 World Map (Error-Mule) | 320 pcs. | 315.00 | — |

| KM# | Date | Mintage | MS-63 | Proof |
|---|---|---|---|---|
| 87 | 1973 Montreal Skyline | — | 11.00 | — |
| | | 165,203 | — | 14.00 |

| | | Series II | Mintage | MS-63 | Proof |
|---|---|---|---|---|---|
| KM# | Date | | | | |
| 93 | 1974 Head of Zeus | | — | 11.00 | — |
| | | | 104,684 | — | 14.00 |

| KM# | Date | Mintage | MS-63 | Proof |
|---|---|---|---|---|
| 94 | 1974 Temple of Zeus | — | 11.00 | — |
| | | 104,684 | — | 14.00 |

Series III

| KM# | Date | Mintage | MS-63 | Proof |
|---|---|---|---|---|
| 95 | 1974 Cycling | — | 11.00 | — |
| | | 97,431 | — | 14.00 |

| KM# | Date | Mintage | MS-63 | Proof |
|---|---|---|---|---|
| 96 | 1974 Lacrosse | — | 11.00 | — |
| | | 97,431 | — | 14.00 |

**Series IV**

| KM# | Date | Mintage | MS-63 | Proof |
|---|---|---|---|---|
| 102 | 1975 Men's hurdles | — | 11.00 | — |
|  |  | 82,302 | — | 14.00 |

| KM# | Date | Mintage | MS-63 | Proof |
|---|---|---|---|---|
| 103 | 1975 Ladies' shot put | — | 11.00 | — |
|  |  | 82,302 | — | 14.00 |

**Series V**

| KM# | Date | Mintage | MS-63 | Proof |
|---|---|---|---|---|
| 104 | 1975 Sailing | — | 11.00 | — |
|  |  | 89,155 | — | 14.00 |

| KM# | Date | Mintage | MS-63 | Proof |
|-----|------|---------|-------|-------|
| 105 | 1975 Paddler | — | 11.00 | — |
|     |              | 89,155 | — | 14.00 |

**Series VI**

| KM# | Date | Mintage | MS-63 | Proof |
|-----|------|---------|-------|-------|
| 111 | 1976 Football | — | 11.00 | — |
|     |               | 76,908 | — | 17.50 |

| KM# | Date | Mintage | MS-63 | Proof |
|-----|------|---------|-------|-------|
| 112 | 1976 Field Hockey | — | 11.00 | — |
|     |                   | 76,908 | — | 17.50 |

**Series VII**

| KM# | Date | Mintage | MS-63 | Proof |
|-----|------|---------|-------|-------|
| 113 | 1976 Olympic Stadium | — | 11.00 | — |
|     |      | 79,102 | — | 18.50 |

| KM# | Date | Mintage | MS-63 | Proof |
|-----|------|---------|-------|-------|
| 114 | 1976 Olympic Velodrome | — | 11.00 | — |
|     |      | 79,102 | — | 18.50 |

# 15 dollars
Olympic Commemoratives

|     |      | 33.6300 g, .925 SILVER, 1.0000 oz ASW | | |
|-----|------|---------|-------|-------|
| KM# | Date | Mintage | MS-63 | Proof |
| 215 | 1992 Coaching Track | *275,000 | — | 42.50 |

| KM# | Date | Mintage | MS-63 | Proof |
|---|---|---|---|---|
| 216 | 1992 High Jump, Rings, Speed Skating | *275,000 | — | 42.50 |

# 20 dollars

**18.2733 g, .900 GOLD, .5288 oz AGW**

| KM# | Date | Mintage | MS-63 | Proof |
|---|---|---|---|---|
| 71 | 1967 Centennial | 337,688 | — | 215.00 |

Olympic Commemoratives

**33.6300 g, .925 SILVER, 1.0000 oz ASW**

| KM# | Date | Mintage | MS-63 | Proof |
|---|---|---|---|---|
| 145 | 1985 Winter Olympics, Downhill Skier, lettered edge | | | |
| | | 406,360 | — | 27.50 |
| | 1985 Plain edge | Inc. Ab. | — | 425.00 |

| KM# | Date | Mintage | MS-63 | Proof |
|-----|------|---------|-------|-------|
| 146 | 1985 Winter Olympics, Speed Skater, lettered edge | | | |
| | | 354,222 | — | 27.50 |
| | 1985 Plain edge | Inc. Ab. | — | 340.00 |

| KM# | Date | Mintage | MS-63 | Proof |
|-----|------|---------|-------|-------|
| 147 | 1986 Winter Olympics, Biathlon, lettered edge | | | |
| | | 308,086 | — | 27.50 |
| | 1986 Plain edge | Inc. Ab. | — | 340.00 |

| KM# | Date | Mintage | MS-63 | Proof |
|-----|------|---------|-------|-------|
| 148 | 1986 Winter Olympics, Hockey, lettered edge | | | |
| | | 396,602 | — | 27.50 |
| | 1986 Plain edge | Inc. Ab. | — | 340.00 |

| KM# | Date | Mintage | MS-63 | Proof |
|-----|------|---------|-------|-------|
| 150 | 1986 Winter Olympics, Cross Country Skier | 303,199 | — | 27.50 |

| KM# | Date | Mintage | MS-63 | Proof |
|-----|------|---------|-------|-------|
| 151 | 1986 Winter Olympics, Free Style Skier, lettered edge | | | |
| | | 294,322 | — | 27.50 |
| | 1986 Plain edge | Inc. Ab. | — | 340.00 |

**34.1070 g, .925 SILVER, 1.0000 oz ASW**

| KM# | Date | Mintage | MS-63 | Proof |
|-----|------|---------|-------|-------|
| 155 | 1987 Winter Olympics, Figure Skater | 334,875 | — | 27.50 |

| KM# | Date | Mintage | MS-63 | Proof |
|-----|------|---------|-------|-------|
| 156 | 1987 Winter Olympics, Curling | 286,457 | — | 27.50 |

| KM# | Date | Mintage | MS-63 | Proof |
|-----|------|---------|-------|-------|
| 159 | 1987 Winter Olympics, Ski Jumper | 290,954 | — | 27.50 |

| KM# | Date | Mintage | MS-63 | Proof |
|-----|------|---------|-------|-------|
| 160 | 1987 Winter Olympics, Bobsled | 274,326 | — | 27.50 |

### Aviation Commemoratives

31.1030 g, .925 SILVER w/1.0000 GOLD Cameo, 1.0000 oz ASW

| KM# | Date | Mintage | MS-63 | Proof |
|-----|------|---------|-------|-------|
| 172 | 1990 Lancaster/Fauquier | 43,596 | — | 65.00 |

| KM# | Date | Mintage | MS-63 | Proof |
|-----|------|---------|-------|-------|
| 173 | 1990 Anson and Harvard | 41,844 | — | 75.00 |

31.1030 g, .925 SILVER, .9743 oz ASW

| KM# | Date | Mintage | MS-63 | Proof |
|-----|------|---------|-------|-------|
| 196 | 1991 Silver Dart | 28,791 | — | 47.50 |

| KM# | Date | Mintage | MS-63 | Proof |
|-----|------|---------|-------|-------|
| 197 | 1991 de Haviland "Beaver" | 29,399 | — | 47.50 |

| KM# | Date | Mintage | MS-63 | Proof |
|-----|------|---------|-------|-------|
| 224 | 1992 Curtiss JN-4 Canuck ("Jenny") | *50,000 | — | 47.50 |

| KM# | Date | Mintage | MS-63 | Proof |
|-----|------|---------|-------|-------|
| 225 | 1992 de Haviland Gypsy Moth | *50,000 | — | 47.50 |

| KM# | Date | Mintage | MS-63 | Proof |
|-----|------|---------|-------|-------|
| 236 | 1993 Fairchild 71C Float plane | *50,000 | — | 47.50 |

| KM# | Date | Mintage | MS-63 | Proof |
|------|------|---------|-------|-------|
| 237 | 1993 Lockheed 14 | *50,000 | — | 47.50 |

| KM# | Date | Mintage | MS-63 | Proof |
|------|------|---------|-------|-------|
| 246 | 1994 Curtiss HS-26 Seaplane | *50,000 | — | 47.00 |

| KM# | Date | Mintage | MS-63 | Proof |
|------|------|---------|-------|-------|
| 247 | 1994 Vickers Vedette | *50,000 | — | 47.00 |

# 100 dollars

| KM# | Date | Mintage | MS-63 | Proof |
|------|------|---------|-------|-------|
| | **13.3375 g, .583 GOLD, .2500 oz AGW** | | | |
| 115 | 1976 Olympics, beaded borders, 27mm | 650,000 | 105.00 | — |
| | **16.9655 g, .917 GOLD, .5000 oz AGW** | | | |
| 116 | 1976 Olympics, reduced size, 25mm, plain borders | 337,342 | — | 200.00 |

| KM# | Date | Mintage | MS-63 | Proof |
|-----|------|---------|-------|-------|
| 119 | 1977 Queen's Silver Jubilee | 180,396 | — | 220.00 |
| 122 | 1978 Canadian Unification | 200,000 | — | 210.00 |

| KM# | Date | Mintage | MS-63 | Proof |
|-----|------|---------|-------|-------|
| 126 | 1979 Year of the Child | 250,000 | — | 200.00 |
| 129 | 1980 Arctic Territories | 300,000 | — | 215.00 |

| KM# | Date | Mintage | MS-63 | Proof |
|-----|------|---------|-------|-------|
| 131 | 1981 National Anthem | 102,000 | — | 225.00 |
| 137 | 1982 New Constitution | 121,708 | — | 215.00 |

| KM# | Date | Mintage | MS-63 | Proof |
|-----|------|---------|-------|-------|
| 139 | 1983 St. John's, Newfoundland | 83,128 | — | 220.00 |
| 142 | 1984 Jacques Cartier | 67,662 | — | 220.00 |

| KM# | Date | Mintage | MS-63 | Proof |
|-----|------|---------|-------|-------|
| 144 | 1985 National Parks - Big horn sheep | 61,332 | — | 230.00 |
| 152 | 1986 Peace | 76,409 | — | 220.00 |

**13.3375 g, .583 GOLD, .2500 oz AGW**

| KM# | Date | Mintage | MS-63 | Proof |
|-----|------|---------|-------|-------|
| 158 | 1987 1988 Olympics - Torch and logo, lettered edge | 142,750 | — | 120.00 |
| | 1987 Plain edge | Inc. Ab. | — | — |
| 162 | 1988 Whales | 52,594 | — | 240.00 |

| KM# | Date | Mintage | MS-63 | Proof |
|-----|------|---------|-------|-------|
| 169 | 1989 Sainte-Marie | 59,657 | — | 135.00 |
| 171 | 1990 Intl. Literacy Year | 49,940 | — | 150.00 |

| KM# | Date | Mintage | MS-63 | Proof |
|-----|------|---------|-------|-------|
| 180 | 1991 S.S. Empress of India | *33,966 | — | 240.00 |
| 211 | 1992 Montreal | —. | — | 210.00 |

| KM# | Date | Mintage | MS-63 | Proof |
|-----|------|---------|-------|-------|
| 245 | 1993 Antique automobiles | 25,790 | — | 205.00 |
| 249 | 1994 WWII Home Front | *35,000 | — | 210.00 |

# 175 dollars

**16.9700 g, .917 GOLD, .5000 oz AGW**

| KM# | Date | Mintage | MS-63 | Proof |
|-----|------|---------|-------|-------|
| 217 | 1992 Olympics - Passing the Torch | *35,000 | — | 370.00 |

# 200 dollars

**17.1060 g, .917 GOLD, .5042 oz AGW**

| KM# | Date | Mintage | MS-63 | Proof |
|-----|------|---------|-------|-------|
| 178 | 1990 Canada Flag Silver Jubilee | 20,980 | — | 275.00 |
| 202 | 1991 Hockey | 8,741 | — | 320.00 |
| 230 | 1992 Niagara Falls | *25,000 | — | 320.00 |

**17.1350 g, .917 GOLD, .5500 oz AGW**

| KM# | Date | Mintage | MS-63 | Proof |
|-----|------|---------|-------|-------|
| 244 | 1993 Mounted police | *25,000 | — | 335.00 |
| 250 | 1994 Novel: Anne of Green Gables | *15,000 | — | 345.00 |

# Sovereign

| | **1908-1910** | | **7.9881 g, .917 GOLD, .2354 oz AGW** | | | | **1911-1919** | |
|---|---|---|---|---|---|---|---|---|
| | | | **C mint mark below horse's rear hooves** | | | | | |
| **KM#** | **Date** | **Mintage** | **F-12** | **VF-20** | **XF-40** | **AU-50** | **MS-60** | **MS-63** |
| 14 | 1908C | 636 pcs. | 1000. | 1700. | 2300. | 2800. | 3300. | 4100. |
| | 1909C | 16,273 | 175.00 | 250.00 | 325.00 | 550.00 | 875.00 | 1400. |
| | 1910C | 28,012 | 125.00 | 175.00 | 250.00 | 400.00 | 600.00 | 1200. |
| | | | | | | | | |
| 20 | 1911C | 256,946 | 110.00 | 120.00 | 130.00 | 170.00 | 250.00 | 300.00 |
| | 1911C | — | — | — | — | | Specimen | 6500. |
| | 1913C | 3,715 | 400.00 | 550.00 | 750.00 | 1000. | 1650. | 2750. |
| | 1914C | 14,871 | 175.00 | 250.00 | 325.00 | 550.00 | 875.00 | 1400. |
| | 1916C | Rare | | *About 20 known | | 20,000. | 25,000. | 35,000. |

**NOTE:** Stacks's A.G. Carter Jr. Sale 12-89 Gem BU realized $82,500.

| | | | | | | | | |
|---|---|---|---|---|---|---|---|---|
| | 1917C | 58,845 | 110.00 | 120.00 | 130.00 | 170.00 | 250.00 | 325.00 |
| | 1918C | 106,516 | 110.00 | 120.00 | 130.00 | 170.00 | 250.00 | 325.00 |
| | 1919C | 135,889 | 110.00 | 120.00 | 130.00 | 170.00 | 250.00 | 325.00 |

# Silver bullion issues
# 5 dollars

| | | **31.1000 g, .9999 SILVER, 1.0000 oz ASW** | | |
|---|---|---|---|---|
| **KM#** | **Date** | **Mintage** | **MS-63** | **Proof** |
| 163 | 1988 Maple leaf | 1,155,931 | 7.00 | — |
| | 1989 Maple leaf | — | 7.00 | — |
| | 1989 Maple leaf | 43,965 | — | 75.00 |

**New Elizabeth II Effigy**

| **KM#** | **Date** | **Mintage** | **MS-63** | **Proof** |
|---|---|---|---|---|
| 187 | 1990 Maple leaf | 1,708,800 | 7.00 | — |
| | 1991 Maple leaf | 644,300 | 15.00 | — |
| | 1992 Maple leaf | — | 10.00 | — |
| | 1993 Maple leaf | — | 7.00 | — |
| | 1994 Maple leaf | — | 7.00 | — |

# Gold bullion issues
# 1 dollar

**1.5551 g, .9999 GOLD, .0500 oz AGW**

| KM# | Date | Mintage | MS-63 | Proof |
|-----|------|---------|-------|-------|
| 238 | 1993 Maple Leaf | — | *BV + 20 %* | — |

# 5 dollars

**3.1200 g, .9999 GOLD, .1000 oz AGW**

| KM# | Date | Mintage | MS-63 | Proof |
|-----|------|---------|-------|-------|
| 135 | 1982 Maple leaf | 246,000 | *BV + 15%* | — |
|  | 1983 Maple leaf | 304,000 | *BV + 15%* | — |
|  | 1984 Maple leaf | 262,000 | *BV + 15%* | — |
|  | 1985 Maple leaf | 398,000 | *BV + 15%* | — |
|  | 1986 Maple leaf | 529,516 | *BV + 15%* | — |
|  | 1987 Maple leaf | 459,000 | *BV + 15%* | — |
|  | 1988 Maple leaf | 506,500 | *BV + 15%* | — |
|  | 1989 Maple leaf | — | *BV + 15%* | — |
|  | 1989 Maple leaf | 16,992 | — | 100.00 |

**New Elizabeth II Effigy**

| KM# | Date | Mintage | MS-63 | Proof |
|-----|------|---------|-------|-------|
| 188 | 1990 Maple leaf | 47,600 | *BV + 15%* | — |
|  | 1991 Maple leaf | 32,200 | *BV + 15%* | — |
|  | 1992 Maple leaf | — | *BV + 15%* | — |
|  | 1993 Maple leaf | — | *BV + 15%* | — |

# 10 dollars

**7.7850 g, .9999 GOLD, .2500 oz AGW**

| KM# | Date | Mintage | MS-63 | Proof |
|-----|------|---------|-------|-------|
| 136 | 1982 Maple leaf | 184,000 | *BV + 11 %* | — |
|  | 1983 Maple leaf | 308,800 | *BV + 11 %* | — |
|  | 1984 Maple leaf | 242,400 | *BV + 11 %* | — |
|  | 1985 Maple leaf | 620,000 | *BV + 11 %* | — |
|  | 1986 Maple leaf | 915,200 | *BV + 11 %* | — |
|  | 1987 Maple leaf | 376,000 | *BV + 11 %* | — |
|  | 1988 Maple leaf | 436,000 | *BV + 11%* | — |
|  | 1989 Maple leaf | — | *BV + 11%* | — |
|  | 1989 Maple leaf | 6,998 | — | 220.00 |

**New Elizabeth II Effigy**

| KM# | Date | Mintage | MS-63 | Proof |
|-----|------|---------|-------|-------|
| 189 | 1990 Maple leaf | 63,400 | *BV + 11%* | — |
|  | 1991 Maple leaf | 41,600 | *BV + 11%* | — |
|  | 1992 Maple leaf | — | *BV + 11%* | — |
|  | 1993 Maple leaf | — | *BV + 11%* | — |

# 20 dollars

**15.5515 g, .9999 GOLD, .5000 oz AGW**

| KM# | Date | Mintage | MS-63 | Proof |
|-----|------|---------|-------|-------|
| 153 | 1986 Maple leaf | 529,200 | BV + 7% | — |
| | 1987 Maple leaf | 332,800 | BV + 7% | — |
| | 1988 Maple leaf | 538,400 | BV + 7% | — |
| | 1989 Maple leaf | — | BV + 7% | — |
| | 1989 Maple leaf | 6,998 | — | 365.00 |

**New Elizabeth II Effigy**

| KM# | Date | Mintage | MS-63 | Proof |
|-----|------|---------|-------|-------|
| 190 | 1990 Maple leaf | 87,200 | BV + 7% | — |
| | 1991 Maple leaf | 48,100 | BV + 7% | — |
| | 1992 Maple leaf | — | BV + 7% | — |
| | 1993 Maple leaf | — | BV + 7% | — |

# 50 dollars

31.1030 g, .999 GOLD, 1.0000 oz AGW
Rev: 999. Maple Leaf. 999.

| KM# | Date | Mintage | MS-63 | Proof |
|-----|------|---------|-------|-------|
| 125.1 | 1979 Maple leaf | 1,000,000 | BV + 5% | — |
| | 1980 Maple leaf | 1,251,500 | BV + 5% | — |
| | 1981 Maple leaf | 863,000 | BV + 5% | — |
| | 1982 Maple leaf | 883,000 | BV + 5% | — |

31.1030 g, .9999 GOLD, 1.0000 oz AGW
Rev: 9999 Maple Leaf 9999

| KM# | Date | Mintage | MS-63 | Proof |
|-----|------|---------|-------|-------|
| 125.2 | 1983 Maple leaf | 843,000 | BV + 5% | — |
| | 1984 Maple leaf | 1,067,500 | BV + 5% | — |
| | 1985 Maple leaf | 1,908,000 | BV + 5% | — |
| | 1986 Maple leaf | 779,115 | BV + 5% | — |
| | 1987 Maple leaf | 978,000 | BV + 5% | — |
| | 1988 Maple leaf | 826,500 | BV + 5% | — |
| | 1989 Maple leaf | — | BV + 5% | — |
| | 1989 Maple leaf | 17,781 | — | 700.00 |

**New Elizabeth II Effigy**

| KM# | Date | Mintage | MS-63 | Proof |
|-----|------|---------|-------|-------|
| 191 | 1990 Maple leaf | 815,000 | BV + 5% | — |
| | 1991 Maple leaf | 290,000 | BV + 5% | — |
| | 1992 Maple leaf | — | BV + 5% | — |
| | 1993 Maple leaf | — | BV + 5% | — |

# Platinum bullion issues
# 1 dollar

1.5552 g, .9995 PLATINUM, .0500 oz APW

| KM# | Date | Mintage | MS-63 | Proof |
|-----|------|---------|-------|-------|
| 239 | 1993 Maple Leaf | — | BV + 22 % | — |

# 5 dollars

3.1203 g, .9995 PLATINUM, .1000 oz APW

| KM# | Date | Mintage | MS-63 | Proof |
|-----|------|---------|-------|-------|
| 164 | 1988 Maple leaf | 74,000 | BV + 17% | — |
| | 1989 Maple leaf | — | BV + 17% | — |
| | 1989 Maple leaf | 11,999 | — | 125.00 |

**New Elizabeth II Effigy**

| KM# | Date | Mintage | MS-63 | Proof |
|-----|------|---------|-------|-------|
| 192 | 1990 Maple leaf | 900 pcs. | BV + 17% | — |
| | 1991 Maple leaf | 1,300 | BV + 17% | — |
| | 1992 Maple leaf | — | BV + 17% | — |

# 10 dollars

**7.7857 g, .9995 PLATINUM, .2500 oz APW**

| KM# | Date | Mintage | MS-63 | Proof |
|---|---|---|---|---|
| 165 | 1988 Maple leaf | 93,600 | BV + 12% | — |
| | 1989 Maple leaf | — | BV + 12% | — |
| | 1989 Maple leaf | 1,999 | — | 300.00 |
| | **New Elizabeth II Effigy** | | | |
| 193 | 1990 Maple leaf | 400 pcs. | BV + 12% | — |
| | 1991 Maple leaf | 1,800 | BV + 12% | — |
| | 1992 Maple leaf | — | BV + 12% | — |

# 20 dollars

**15.5519 g, .9995 PLATINUM, .5000 oz APW**

| KM# | Date | Mintage | MS-63 | Proof |
|---|---|---|---|---|
| 166 | 1988 Maple leaf | 23,600 | BV + 8% | — |
| | 1989 Maple leaf | — | BV + 8% | — |
| | 1989 Maple leaf | 1,999 | — | 550.00 |
| | **New Elizabeth II Effigy** | | | |
| 194 | 1990 Maple leaf | 1,300 | BV + 8% | — |
| | 1991 Maple leaf | 2,800 | BV + 8% | — |
| | 1992 Maple leaf | — | BV + 8% | — |

# 30 dollars

**3.1100 g, .999 PLATINUM, .1000 oz APW**

| KM# | Date | Mintage | MS-63 | Proof |
|---|---|---|---|---|
| 174 | 1990 Polar bear swimming | 1,928 | Proof | 80.00 |
| 198 | 1991 Owls | *3,500 | Proof | 90.00 |
| 226 | 1992 Cougar head and shoulders | *3,500 | Proof | 100.00 |
| 240 | 1993 Arctic fox head and shoulders | *3,500 | Proof | 90.00 |

# 50 dollars

**31.1030 g, .9995 PLATINUM, 1.0000 oz APW**

| KM# | Date | Mintage | MS-63 | Proof |
|---|---|---|---|---|
| 167 | 1988 Maple leaf | 37,500 | BV + 6% | — |
| | 1989 Maple leaf | 1,500 | BV + 6% | — |
| | 1989 Maple leaf | 5,965 | — | 1000. |
| | **New Elizabeth II Effigy** | | | |
| 195 | 1990 Maple leaf | 15,100 | BV + 6% | — |
| | 1991 Maple leaf | 31,900 | BV + 6% | — |
| | 1992 Maple leaf | — | BV + 6% | — |

# 75 dollars

**7.7760 g, .999 PLATINUM, .2500 oz APW**

| KM# | Date | Mintage | MS-63 | Proof |
|---|---|---|---|---|
| 175 | 1990 Polar bear resting | 1,928 | Proof | 220.00 |
| 199 | 1991 Owls perched on branch | *3,500 | Proof | 240.00 |
| 227 | 1992 Cougar prowling | *3,500 | Proof | 250.00 |
| 241 | 1993 2 Arctic foxes | *3,500 | Proof | 240.00 |

# 150 dollars

**15.5520 g, .999 PLATINUM, .5000 oz APW**

| KM# | Date | Mintage | MS-63 | Proof |
|---|---|---|---|---|
| 176 | 1990 Polar bear walking | 1,928 | Proof | 400.00 |
| 200 | 1991 Owl flying | *3,500 | Proof | 425.00 |
| 228 | 1992 Cougar mother and cub | *3,500 | Proof | 450.00 |
| 242 | 1993 Arctic fox overlooking lake | *3,500 | Proof | 425.00 |

# 300 dollars

**31.1035 g, .999 PLATINUM, 1.0000 oz APW**

| KM# | Date | Mintage | MS-63 | Proof |
|---|---|---|---|---|
| 177 | 1990 Polar bear mother and cub | 1,928 | Proof | 800.00 |
| 201 | 1991 Owl w/chicks | *3,500 | Proof | 850.00 |

| KM# | Date | Mintage | MS-63 | Proof |
|---|---|---|---|---|
| 229 | 1992 Cougar resting in tree | *3,500 | Proof | 875.00 |
| 243 | 1993 Mother Arctic fox and 3 kits | *3,500 | Proof | 850.00 |

# Proof-like dollars

### 23.3276 g, .800 SILVER, .6000 oz ASW

| KM# | Date | Mintage | Identification | Issue Price | Mkt Value |
|---|---|---|---|---|---|
| D3 | 1953 | 1,200 | KM54, Canoe w/shoulder fold | — | 500.00 |
| D4 | 1954 | 5,300 | KM54, Canoe | 1.25 | 190.00 |
| D5 | 1955 | 7,950 | KM54, Canoe | 1.25 | 165.00 |
| D5a | 1955 | Inc. Ab. | KM54, Arnprior | 1.25 | 320.00 |
| D6 | 1956 | 10,212 | KM54, Canoe | 1.25 | 120.00 |
| D7 | 1957 | 16,241 | KM54, Canoe | 1.25 | 50.00 |
| D8 | 1958 | 33,237 | KM55, British Columbia | 1.25 | 35.00 |
| D9 | 1959 | 45,160 | KM54, Canoe | 1.25 | 16.50 |
| D10 | 1960 | 82,728 | KM54, Canoe | 1.25 | 15.00 |
| D11 | 1961 | 120,928 | KM54, Canoe | 1.25 | 13.50 |
| D12 | 1962 | 248,901 | KM54, Canoe | 1.25 | 12.00 |
| D13 | 1963 | 963,525 | KM54, Canoe | 1.25 | 11.00 |
| D14 | 1964 | 2,862,441 | KM58, Charlottetown | 1.25 | 11.00 |
| D15 | 1965 | 2,904,352 | KM64, Canoe | — | 11.00 |
| D16 | 1966 | 672,514 | KM64, Canoe | — | 12.00 |
| D17 | 1967 | 1,036,176 | KM70, Confederation | — | 17.00 |

# Mint sets

### Olympic Commemoratives

| KM# | Date | Mintage | Identification | Issue Price | Mkt Value |
|---|---|---|---|---|---|
| MS1 | 1973(4) | — | KM84-87, Series I | 45.00 | 32.00 |
| MS2 | 1974(4) | — | KM89-90,93-94, Series II | 48.00 | 32.00 |
| MS3 | 1974(4) | — | KM91-92,95-96, Series III | 48.00 | 32.00 |
| MS4 | 1975(4) | — | KM98-99,102-103, Series IV | 48.00 | 32.00 |
| MS5 | 1975(4) | — | KM100-101,104-105, Series V | 60.00 | 32.00 |
| MS6 | 1976(4) | — | KM107-108,111-112, Series VI | 60.00 | 32.00 |
| MS7 | 1976(4) | — | KM109-110,113-114, Series VII | 60.00 | 35.00 |

# Specimen sets

NOTE: Some authorities list these as proof sets. However, the Canadian Mint does not. The coins are double struck with higher than usual pressure, but are considered to have the same quality as proof issue from the Royal Mint, London.

| KM# | Date | Mintage | Identification | Issue Price | Mkt Value |
|---|---|---|---|---|---|
| SS1 | 1858(4) | — | KM1-4 Reeded Edge | — | 6000. |
| SS2 | 1858(4) | — | KM1-4 Plain Edge | — | 6000. |
| SS3 | 1858(8) | — | KM1-4 Double Set | — | 12,500. |
| SS4 | 1858(8) | — | KM1(overdate),2-4 Double Set | — | 14,000. |
| SS5 | 1870(4) | 100* | KM2,3,5,6 (reeded edges) | — | 12,500. |
| SS6 | 1870(8) | — | KM2,3,5,6 Double Set (plain edges) | — | 25,000. |
| SS7 | 1872H(4) | — | KM2,3,5,6 | — | 12,500. |
| SS8 | 1875H(3) | — | KM2(Large Date),3,5 | — | 20,000. |
| SS9 | 1880H(3) | — | KM2,3,5(Narrow 0) | — | 7000. |
| SS10 | 1881H(5) | — | KM7,2,3,5,6 | — | 12,000. |
| SS11 | 1892(2) | — | KM3,5 | — | 10,000. |
| SS12 | 1902(5) | 100* | KM8-12 | — | 10,000. |
| SS13 | 1902H(3) | — | KM9(Large H),10,11 | — | 6500. |
| SS14 | 1903H(3) | — | KM10,12,13 | — | 7000. |

NOTE: A 1903H double set has been reported on display in Bombay, India.

| KM# | Date | Mintage | Identification | Issue Price | Mkt Value |
|-----|------|---------|----------------|-------------|-----------|
| SS15 | 1908(5) | 1,000* | KM8,10-13 | — | 2800. |
| SS16 | 1911(5) | 1,000* | KM15-19 | — | 5500. |
| SS17 | 1911/12(8) | 5 | KM15-20,26-27 | — | 52,250. |
| SS18 | 1921(5) | — | KM22-25,28 | — | 80,000. |
| SS19 | 1922(2) | — | KM28,29 | — | 800.00 |
| SS20 | 1923(2) | — | KM28,29 | — | 800.00 |
| SS21 | 1924(2) | — | KM28,29 | — | 800.00 |
| SS22 | 1925(2) | — | KM28,29 | — | 1800. |
| SS23 | 1926(2) | — | KM28,29 (Near 6) | — | 1800. |
| SS24 | 1927(3) | — | KM24a,28,29 | — | 3200. |
| SS25 | 1928(4) | — | KM23a,24a,28,29 | — | 2800. |
| SS26 | 1929(5) | — | KM23a-25a,28,29 | — | 10,000. |
| SS27 | 1930(4) | — | KM23a,24a,28,29 | — | 6500. |
| SS28 | 1931(5) | — | KM23a-25a,28,29 | — | 8500. |
| SS29 | 1932(5) | — | KM23a-25a,28,29 | — | 10,000. |
| SS30 | 1934(5) | — | KM23-25,28,29 | — | 8500. |
| SS31 | 1936(5) | — | KM23-25,28,29 | — | 8500. |
| SS32 | 1936(6) | — | KM23a(dot),24a(dot),25a,28(dot),29,30 | — | Rare |
| SS33 | 1937(6) | 1025* | KM32-37 Matte Finish | — | 850.00 |
| SS34 | 1937(4) | — | KM32-35 Mirror Fields | — | 500.00 |
| SS35 | 1937(6) | 75* | KM32-37 Mirror Fields | — | 2000. |
| SS36 | 1938(6) | — | KM32-37 | — | 25,000. |
| SS-A36 | 1939(6) | — | KM32-35,38 Matte Finish | — | — |
| SS-B36 | 1939(6) | — | KM32-35,38 Mirror Fields | — | — |
| SS-C36 | 1942(2) | — | KM32,33 | — | 300.00 |
| SS-D36 | 1943(2) | — | KM32,40 | — | 300.00 |
| SS37 | 1944(5) | 3 | KM32,34-37,40a | — | 20,000. |
| SS-A37 | 1944(2) | — | KM32,40a | — | 300.00 |
| SS38 | 1945(6) | 6 | KM32,34-37,40a | — | 6500. |
| SS-A38 | 1945(2) | — | KM32,40a | — | 300.00 |
| SS39 | 1946(6) | 15 | KM32,34-37,39a | — | 4000. |
| SS40 | 1947(6) | — | KM32,34-36(7 curved),37(pointed 7),39a | — | 6000. |
| SS41 | 1947(6) | — | KM32,34-36(7 curved),37(blunt 7),39a | — | 6000. |
| SS42 | 1947ML(6) | — | KM32,34-36(7 curved right),37,39a | — | 6000. |
| SS43 | 1948(6) | 30 | KM41-46 | — | 5000. |
| SS44 | 1949(6) | 20 | KM41-45,47 | — | 2000. |
| SS44A | 1949(2) | — | KM47 | — | 1000. |
| SS45 | 1950(6) | 12 | KM41-46 | — | 2100. |
| SS46 | 1950(6) | — | KM41-45,46(Arnprior) | — | 2300. |
| SS47 | 1951(7) | 12 | KM41,48,42a,43-46 (w/water lines) | — | 3750. |
| SS48 | 1952(6) | 2,317 | KM41,42a,43-46 (water lines) | — | 4500 |
| SS48A | 1952(6) | — | KM41,42a,43-46 (w/o water lines) | — | 4500. |
| SS49 | 1953(6) | 28 | KM49 w/o straps,50-54 | — | 1800. |
| SS50 | 1953(6) | — | KM49 w/straps,50-54 | — | 1800. |
| SS51 | 1964(6) | — | KM49,51,52,56-58 | — | 450.00 |
| SS52 | 1965(6) | — | KM59.1-60.1.61-63.64.1 | — | 450.00 |

## Double Dollar Prestige Sets

| KM# | Date | Mintage | Identification | Issue Price | Mkt Value |
|-----|------|---------|----------------|-------------|-----------|
| SS56 | 1971(7) | 66,860 | KM59.1-60.1,74.1-75.1,77.1,79(2 pcs.) | 12.00 | 15.00 |
| SS57 | 1972(7) | 36,349 | KM59.1-60.1,74.1-75.1,76.1,(2 pcs.),77.1 | 12.00 | 35.00 |
| SS58 | 1973(7) | 119,819 | KM59.1-60.1,75.1,77.1,81.1,82,83 | 12.00 | 20.00 |
| SS59 | 1973(7) | Inc. Ab. | KM59.1-60.1,75.1,77.1,81.2,82,83 | — | 150.00 |
| SS60 | 1974(7) | 85,230 | KM59.1-60.1,74.1-75.1,77.1,88,88a | 15.00 | 22.00 |
| SS61 | 1975(7) | 97,263 | KM59.1-60.1,74.1-75.1,76.2,77.1,97 | 15.00 | 15.50 |
| SS62 | 1976(7) | 87,744 | KM59.1-60.1,74.1-75.1,76.2,77.1,106 | 16.00 | 30.00 |
| SS63 | 1977(7) | 142,577 | KM59.1-60.1,74.1,75.2,77.1,117.1,118 | 16.50 | 21.50 |
| SS64 | 1978(7) | 147,000 | KM59.1-60.1,74.1,75.3,77.1,120,121 | 16.50 | 21.50 |
| SS65 | 1979(7) | 155,698 | KM59.2-60.2,74.2,75.3,77.2,120,124 | 18.50 | 36.50 |
| SS66 | 1980(7) | 162,875 | KM60.2,74.2,75.3,77.2,120,127,128 | 30.50 | 70.00 |

## Regular Specimen Sets Resumed

| KM# | Date | Mintage | Identification | Issue Price | Mkt Value |
|-----|------|---------|----------------|-------------|-----------|
| SS67 | 1981(6) | 71,300 | KM60.2,74.2,75.3,77.2,120,123 | 10.00 | 10.00 |
| SS68 | 1982(6) | 62,298 | KM60.2a,74.2,75.3,77.2,120,123 | 11.50 | 10.00 |
| SS69 | 1983(6) | 60,329 | KM60.2a,74.2,75.3,77.2,120,132 | 12.75 | 10.00 |
| SS70 | 1984(6) | 60,400 | KM60.2a,74.2,75.3,77.2,120,132 | 10.00 | 10.00 |
| SS71 | 1985(6) | 61,553 | KM60.2a,74.2,75.3,77.2,120,132 | 10.00 | 10.00 |
| SS73 | 1986(6) | 67,152 | KM60.2a,74.2,75.3,77.2,120,132 | 10.00 | 12.50 |
| SS72 | 1987(6) | 75,194 | KM60.2a,74.2,75.3,77.2,120,132 | 11.00 | 14.00 |
| SS73 | 1988(6) | 70,205 | KM60.2a,74.2,75.3,77.2,132,157 | 12.30 | 15.00 |
| SS74 | 1989(6) | 75,306 | KM60.2a,74.2,75.3,77.2,132,157 | 14.50 | 20.00 |
| SS75 | 1990(6) | 76,611 | KM181-186 | 15.50 | 20.00 |
| SS76 | 1991(6) | 54,462 | KM181-186 | 15.50 | 40.00 |
| SS77 | 1992(6) | — | KM204-209 | 16.25 | 25.00 |
| SS78 | 1993(6) | — | KM181-186 | 16.25 | 9.00 |
| SS79 | 1994(6) | — | KM181-186 | *16.50 | — |

NOTE: stimated.

Regular Specimen Sets Resumed

# V.I.P. specimen sets

**NOTE:** A very limited number of cased Specimen sets were produced by the Mint beginning in 1969 for presentation to dignitaries visiting the Royal Canadian Mint or other parts of Canada. (A small quantity of 1970 cased Specimen sets were sold to the public for $13.00 each.) The coins, 1¢ to $1.00 were cased in long narrow leather cases (black and other colors).

| KM# | Date | Mintage | Identification | Issue Price | Mkt Value |
|---|---|---|---|---|---|
| VS1 | 1969 | 4 known | — | — | 1700. |
| VS2 | 1970 | 100 | KM59.1-60.1,74.1-75.1,77.1,78 | — | 475.00 |
| VS3 | 1971 | 69 | KM59.1-60.1,74.1-75.1,77.1,79(2 pcs.) | — | 375.00 |
| VS4 | 1972 | 25 | KM59.1-60.1,74.1-75.1,76.1,(2 pcs.),77.1 | — | 435.00 |
| VS5 | 1973 | 26 | KM59.1-60.1,75.1,77.1,81.1,82,83 | — | 435.00 |
| VS6 | 1974 | 72 | KM59.1-60.1,74.1-75.1,77.1,88,88a | — | 375.00 |
| VS7 | 1975 | 94 | KM59.1-60.1,74.1-75.1,76.2,77.1,97 | — | 375.00 |
| VS8 | 1976 | — | KM59.1-60.1,74.1-75.1,76.2,77.1,106 | — | 375.00 |

# Proof-like sets

**NOTE:** These sets do not have the quality of the Proof or Specimen Set, but are specially produced and packaged.

| KM# | Date | Mintage | Identification | Issue Price | Mkt Value |
|---|---|---|---|---|---|
| PL1 | 1953(6) | 1,200 | KM49 w/o straps, 50-54 | 2.20 | 1250. |
| PL2 | 1953(6) | Inc. Ab. | KM49-54 | 2.20 | 750.00 |
| PL3 | 1954(6) | 3,000 | KM49-54 | 2.50 | 280.00 |
| PL4 | 1954(6) | Inc. Ab. | KM49 w/o straps, 50-54 | 2.50 | 460.00 |
| PL5 | 1955(6) | 6,300 | KM49,50a,51-54 | 2.50 | 190.00 |
| PL6 | 1955(6) | Inc. Ab. | KM49,50a,51-54,Arnprior | 2.50 | 280.00 |
| PL7 | 1956(6) | 6,500 | KM49,50a,51-54 | 2.50 | 110.00 |
| PL8 | 1957(6) | 11,862 | KM49,50a,51-54 | 2.50 | 65.00 |
| PL9 | 1958(6) | 18,259 | KM49,50a,51-53,55 | 2.50 | 55.00 |
| PL10 | 1959(6) | 31,577 | KM49,50a,51,52,54,56 | 2.50 | 25.00 |
| PL11 | 1960(6) | 64,097 | KM49,50a,51,52,54,56 | 3.00 | 17.50 |
| PL12 | 1961(6) | 98,373 | KM49,50a,51,52,54,56 | 3.00 | 15.00 |
| PL13 | 1962(6) | 200,950 | KM49,50a,51,52,54,56 | 3.00 | 10.00 |
| PL14 | 1963(6) | 673,006 | KM49,51,52,54,56,57 | 3.00 | 8.00 |
| PL15 | 1964(6) | 1,653,162 | KM49,51,52,56-58 | 3.00 | 8.00 |
| PL16 | 1965(6) | 2,904,352 | KM59.1-60.1,61-63,64.1 | 4.00 | 8.00 |
| PL17 | 1966(6) | 672,514 | KM59.1-60.1,61-63,64.1 | 4.00 | 8.00 |

| KM# | Date | Mintage | Identification | Issue Price | Mkt Value |
|---|---|---|---|---|---|
| PL18 | 1967(6) | 961,887 | KM65-70 (pliofilm flat pack) | 4.00 | 15.00 |
| PL18A | 1967(6) | 70,583 | KM65-70 and Silver Medal | | |
| | | | (red box) | 12.00 | 18.00 |
| PL18B | 1967(7) | 337,688 | KM65-71 (black box) | 40.00 | 275.00 |
| PL19 | 1968(6) | 521,641 | KM59.1-60.1,72a,74.1-76.1 | 4.00 | 2.85 |
| PL20 | 1969(6) | 326,203 | KM59.1-60.1,74.1-77.1 | 4.00 | 3.10 |
| PL21 | 1970(6) | 349,120 | KM59.1-60.1,74.1-75.1,77.1,78 | 4.00 | 4.80 |

| KM# | Date | Mintage | Identification | Issue Price | Mkt Value |
|---|---|---|---|---|---|
| PL22 | 1971(6) | 253,311 | KM59.1-60.1,74.1-75.1,77.1,79 | 4.00 | 3.85 |
| PL23 | 1972(6) | 224,275 | KM59.1-60.1,74.1-77.1 | 4.00 | 3.50 |
| PL24 | 1973(6) | 243,695 | KM59.1-60.1,74.1-75.1 obv. 120 beads, 77.1,81.1,82 | 4.00 | 4.25 |
| PL25 | 1973(6) | Inc. Ab. | KM59.1-60.1,74.1-75.1 obv. 132 beads, 77.1,81.2,82 | 4.00 | 145.00 |
| PL26 | 1974(6) | 213,589 | KM59.1-60.1,74.1-75.1,77.1,88 | 5.00 | 4.25 |
| PL27.1 | 1975(6) | 197,372 | KM59.1,60.1,74.1-77.1 | 5.00 | 3.85 |
| PL27.2 | 1975(6) | Inc. Ab. | KM59.1,60.1,74.1-75.1,76.2,77.1 | 5.00 | — |
| PL28 | 1976(6) | 171,737 | KM59.1,60.1,74.1-75.1,76.2,77.1 | 5.15 | 5.50 |
| PL29 | 1977(6) | 225,307 | KM59.1,60.1,74.1,75.2,77.1,117.1 | 5.15 | 4.50 |
| PL30 | 1978(6) | 260,000 | KM59.1-60.1,74.1,75.3,77.1,120 | 5.25 | 3.50 |
| PL31 | 1979(6) | 187,624 | KM59.2-60.2,74.2,75.3,77.2,120 | 6.25 | 4.50 |
| PL32 | 1980(6) | 410,842 | KM60.2,74.2,75.3,77.2,120,127 | 6.50 | 7.00 |
| PL33 | 1981(6) | 186,250 | KM60.2,74.2,75.3,77.2,120,123 | 5.00 | 5.50 |
| PL34 | 1982(6) | 203,287 | KM60.2,74.2,75.3,77.2,120,123 | 6.00 | 4.25 |
| PL36 | 1983(6) | 190,838 | KM60.2a,74.2,75.3,77.2,120,132 | 5.00 | 10.50 |
| PL37 | 1984(6) | 181,249 | KM60.2a,74.2,75.3,77.2,120,132 | 5.25 | 9.25 |
| PL38 | 1985(6) | 173,924 | KM60.2a,74.2,75.3,77.2,120,132 | 5.25 | 9.25 |
| PL40 | 1986(6) | 167,338 | KM60.2a,74.2,75.3,77.2,120,132 | 5.25 | 12.75 |
| PL39 | 1987(6) | 212,136 | KM60.2a,74.2,75.3,77.2,120,132 | 5.25 | 7.75 |
| PL41 | 1988(6) | 182,048 | KM60.2a,74.2,75.3,77.2,132,157 | 6.05 | 9.25 |
| PL42 | 1989(6) | 173,622 | KM60.2a,74.2,75.3,77.2,132,157 | 6.60 | 14.50 |
| PL43 | 1990(6) | 170,791 | KM181-186 | 7.40 | 14.50 |
| PL44 | 1991(6) | 130,867 | KM181-186 | 7.40 | 35.00 |
| PL45 | 1992(6) | — | KM204-209 | 8.25 | 19.50 |
| PL46 | 1993(6) | — | KM181-186 | 8.25 | 9.00 |
| PL47 | 1994(6) | — | KM181-186 | *8.50 | — |

## Custom proof-like sets

| KM# | Date | Mintage | Identification | Issue Price | Mkt Value |
|---|---|---|---|---|---|
| Each set contains two 1 cent pieces. |||||| 
| CPL1 | 1971(7) | 33,517 | KM59.1(2 pcs.),60.1,74.1-75.1,77.1,79 | 6.50 | 6.00 |
| CPL2 | 1972(7) | 38,198 | KM59.1(2 pcs.),60.1,74.1-77.1 | 6.50 | 6.00 |
| CPL3 | 1973(7) | 35,676 | KM59.1(2 pcs.),60.1,75.1, 77.1,81.1 obv. 120 beads, 82 | 6.50 | 5.75 |
| CPL4 | 1973(7) | Inc. Ab. | KM59.1(2 pcs.),60.1,75.1, 77.1,81.1 obv. 132 beads,82 | 6.50 | 160.00 |
| CPL5 | 1974(7) | 44,296 | KM59.1(2 pcs.),60.1,74.1-75.1,77.1,88 | 8.00 | 5.75 |
| CPL6 | 1975(7) | 36,851 | KM59.1(2 pcs.),60.1,74.1-75.1,76.2,77.1 | 8.00 | 6.00 |
| CPL7 | 1976(7) | 28,162 | KM59.1(2 pcs.),60.1,74.1-75.1,76.2,77.1 | 8.00 | 8.75 |
| CPL8 | 1977(7) | 44,198 | KM59.1(2 pcs.),60.1,74.1,75.2,77.1,117 | 8.15 | 10.00 |
| CPL9 | 1978(7) | 41,000 | KM59.1(2 pcs.),60.1,74.1,75.3,77.1,120 | — | 6.00 |
| CPL10 | 1979(7) | 31,174 | KM59.2(2 pcs.),60.2,74.2,75.3,77.2,120 | 10.75 | 8.75 |
| CPL11 | 1980(7) | 41,447 | KM60.2,74.2,75.3,77.2,120,127(2 pcs.) | 10.75 | 11.50 |

## Proof sets

| KM# | Date | Mintage | Identification | Issue Price | Mkt Value |
|---|---|---|---|---|---|
| PS1 | 1981(7) | 199,000 | KM60.2,74.2,75.3,77.2,120,123,130 | 36.00 | 38.00 |
| PS2 | 1982(7) | 180,908 | KM60.2a,74.2,75.3,77.2,120,123,133 | 36.00 | 15.00 |
| PS3 | 1983(7) | 166,779 | KM60.2a,74.2,75.3,77.2,120,132,138 | 36.00 | 24.00 |
| PS4 | 1984(7) | 161,602 | KM60.2a,74.2,75.3,77.2,120,132,140 | 30.00 | 17.50 |
| PS5 | 1985(7) | 157,037 | KM60.2a,74.2,75.3,77.2,120,132,143 | 30.00 | 18.50 |
| PS6 | 1986(7) | 175,745 | KM60.2a,74.2,75.3,77.2,120,132,149 | 30.00 | 21.50 |
| PS7 | 1987(7) | 179,004 | KM60.2a,74.2,75.3,77.2,120,132,154 | 34.00 | 28.00 |
| PS8 | 1988(7) | 175,259 | KM60.2a,74.2,75.3,77.2,132,157,161 | 37.50 | 63.50 |
| PS9 | 1989(7) | 170,928 | KM60.2a,74.2,75.3,77.2,132,157,168 | 40.00 | 63.50 |
| PS10 | 1989(4) | 6,823 | KM125.2,135-136,153 | 1190. | 1250. |
| PS11 | 1989(4) | 1,995 | KM164-167 | 1700. | 1975. |
| PS12 | 1989(3) | 2,550 | KM125.2,163,167 | 1530. | 1625. |
| PS13 | 1989(3) | 9,979 | KM135,163-164 | 165.00 | 225. |
| PS14 | 1990(7) | 158,068 | KM170,181-186 | 41.00 | 60.00 |
| PS15 | 1990(4) | 2,629 | KM174-177 | 1720. | 1500. |
| PS16 | 1991(7) | 14,629 | KM179,181-186 | — | 135.00 |
| PS17 | 1991(4) | 873 | KM198-201 | 1760. | 1680. |
| PS18 | 1992(7) | — | KM204-210 | 42.75 | 85.00 |
| PS19 | 1992 (4) | *3,500 | KM226-229 | 1680. | 1680. |
| PS20 | 1993(7) | — | KM181-186,235 | 42.75 | 45.00 |
| PS21 | 1994(7) | — | KM181-186,251 | *43.00 | — |

### Olympic Commemoratives (OCP)

| KM# | Date | Mintage | Identification | Issue Price | Mkt Value |
|---|---|---|---|---|---|
| OCP1 | 1973(4) | — | KM84-87,Series I | 78.50 | 42.50 |
| OCP2 | 1974(4) | — | KM89,90,93,94,Series II | 88.50 | 42.50 |
| OCP3 | 1974(4) | — | KM91,92,95,96,Series III | 88.50 | 42.50 |
| OCP4 | 1975(4) | — | KM98,99,102,103,Series IV | 88.50 | 42.50 |
| OCP5 | 1975(4) | — | KM100,101,104,105,Series V | 88.50 | 42.50 |
| OCP6 | 1976(4) | — | KM107,108,111,112, Series VI | 88.50 | 55.00 |
| OCP7 | 1976(4) | — | KM109,110,113,114,Series VII | 88.50 | 60.00 |

# Newfoundland

## Large cents

**1865-1896**

**1904-1936**

| KM# | Date | Mintage | VG-8 | BRONZE F-12 | VF-20 | XF-40 | MS-60 | MS-63 |
|---|---|---|---|---|---|---|---|---|
| 1 | 1865 | 240,000 | 1.50 | 2.75 | 5.00 | 11.00 | 100.00 | 275.00 |
| | 1872H | 200,000 | 1.75 | 2.75 | 5.00 | 11.00 | 65.00 | 160.00 |
| | 1872H | — | — | — | — | — | Proof | 600.00 |
| | 1873 | 200,025 | 2.00 | 3.50 | 7.50 | 18.00 | 175.00 | 550.00 |
| | 1873 | — | — | — | — | — | Proof | 600.00 |
| | 1876H | 200,000 | 1.75 | 2.75 | 5.00 | 12.50 | 150.00 | 450.00 |
| | 1876H | — | — | — | — | — | Proof | 600.00 |
| | 1880 round O, even date | | | | | | | |
| | | 400,000 | 1.50 | 2.50 | 5.00 | 11.00 | 100.00 | 275.00 |
| | 1880 round O, low O | Inc. Ab. | 1.75 | 3.00 | 6.00 | 15.00 | 125.00 | 375.00 |
| | 1880 oval 0 | Inc. Ab. | 55.00 | 80.00 | 120.00 | 200.00 | 550.00 | 1200. |
| | 1885 | 40,000 | 15.00 | 22.00 | 30.00 | 70.00 | 300.00 | 900.00 |
| | 1888 | 50,000 | 14.00 | 18.00 | 25.00 | 60.00 | 275.00 | 850.00 |
| | 1890 | 200,000 | 1.75 | 2.75 | 4.25 | 9.00 | 100.00 | 250.00 |
| | 1894 | 200,000 | 1.75 | 2.75 | 4.25 | 9.00 | 100.00 | 250.00 |
| | 1896 | 200,000 | 1.75 | 2.75 | 4.25 | 9.00 | 100.00 | 250.00 |
| | | | | | | | | |
| 9 | 1904H | 100,000 | 4.50 | 7.50 | 13.50 | 18.00 | 200.00 | 600.00 |
| | 1907 | 200,000 | 1.00 | 2.00 | 3.00 | 8.00 | 110.00 | 250.00 |
| | 1909 | 200,000 | 1.00 | 2.00 | 3.00 | 8.00 | 100.00 | 200.00 |
| | 1909 | — | — | — | — | — | Proof | 400.00 |
| | | | | | | | | |
| 16 | 1913 | 400,000 | .75 | 1.50 | 2.00 | 4.00 | 40.00 | 100.00 |
| | 1917C | 702,350 | .75 | 1.50 | 2.00 | 4.00 | 50.00 | 175.00 |
| | 1919C | 300,000 | .75 | 1.50 | 2.25 | 5.00 | 75.00 | 225.00 |
| | 1919C | — | — | — | — | — | Proof | 150.00 |
| | 1920C | 302,184 | .75 | 1.50 | 3.00 | 7.00 | 85.00 | 250.00 |
| | 1929 | 300,000 | .75 | 1.50 | 2.00 | 4.00 | 50.00 | 160.00 |
| | 1929 | — | — | — | — | — | Proof | 125.00 |
| | 1936 | 300,000 | .75 | 1.25 | 1.75 | 3.00 | 25.00 | 70.00 |
| | 1936 | — | — | — | — | — | Proof | 250.00 |

## Small cents

| KM# | Date | Mintage | VG-8 | BRONZE F-12 | VF-20 | XF-40 | MS-60 | MS-63 |
|---|---|---|---|---|---|---|---|---|
| 18 | 1938 | 500,000 | .50 | 1.00 | 1.50 | 2.50 | 16.00 | 35.00 |
| | 1938 | — | — | — | — | — | Proof | 65.00 |
| | 1940 | 300,000 | 1.75 | 2.50 | 4.00 | 7.00 | 35.00 | 120.00 |
| | 1940 re-engraved date | — | 15.00 | 27.50 | 35.00 | 45.00 | 175.00 | 375.00 |
| | 1941C | 827,662 | .35 | .65 | 1.00 | 1.50 | 13.50 | 40.00 |
| | 1941C re-engraved date | — | 12.50 | 20.00 | 27.50 | 40.00 | 150.00 | 400.00 |
| | 1942 | 1,996,889 | .35 | .65 | 1.00 | 1.50 | 13.50 | 40.00 |
| | 1943C | 1,239,732 | .35 | .65 | 1.00 | 1.50 | 13.50 | 40.00 |
| | 1944C | 1,328,776 | 1.00 | 2.00 | 3.00 | 4.50 | 35.00 | 100.00 |
| | 1947C | 313,772 | 1.00 | 2.00 | 3.00 | 4.50 | 40.00 | 140.00 |

## Five cents

| KM# | Date | Mintage | 1.1782 g, .925 SILVER, .0350 oz ASW VG-8 | F-12 | VF-20 | XF-40 | MS-60 | MS-63 |
|---|---|---|---|---|---|---|---|---|
| 2 | 1865 | 80,000 | 20.00 | 32.50 | 60.00 | 125.00 | 775.00 | 1500. |
| | 1870 | 40,000 | 35.00 | 50.00 | 90.00 | 175.00 | 1100. | 1800. |
| | 1870 | — | — | — | — | — | Proof | 3900. |
| | 1872H | 40,000 | 22.00 | 32.00 | 55.00 | 135.00 | 600.00 | 1200. |
| | 1873 | 44,260 | 35.00 | 45.00 | 100.00 | 225.00 | 1150. | 2000. |
| | 1873H | Inc. Ab. | 700.00 | 1150. | 1750. | 2100. | 3750. | — |

| KM# | Date | Mintage | VG-8 | F-12 | VF-20 | XF-40 | MS-60 | MS-63 |
|---|---|---|---|---|---|---|---|---|
| 2 | 1876H | 20,000 | 70.00 | 100.00 | 175.00 | 350.00 | 1600. | 3000. |
| | 1880 | 40,000 | 22.00 | 35.00 | 75.00 | 150.00 | 1000. | 1750. |
| | 1881 | 40,000 | 15.00 | 30.00 | 45.00 | 110.00 | 750.00 | 1500. |
| | 1882H | 60,000 | 12.50 | 22.50 | 40.00 | 100.00 | 650.00 | 1300. |
| | 1882H | — | — | — | — | — | Proof | 2800. |
| | 1885 | 16,000 | 60.00 | 100.00 | 180.00 | 300.00 | 2000. | 4250. |
| | 1888 | 40,000 | 20.00 | 30.00 | 50.00 | 125.00 | 700.00 | 1200. |
| | 1890 | 160,000 | 6.00 | 12.00 | 30.00 | 70.00 | 500.00 | 1100. |
| | 1890 | — | — | — | — | — | Proof | 2100. |
| | 1894 | 160,000 | 7.00 | 12.50 | 30.00 | 75.00 | 500.00 | 1100. |
| | 1896 | 400,000 | 4.00 | 8.00 | 20.00 | 35.00 | 400.00 | 1000. |
| 7 | 1903 | 100,000 | 3.00 | 6.00 | 18.00 | 45.00 | 450.00 | 1000. |
| | 1904H | 100,000 | 2.00 | 5.00 | 14.00 | 35.00 | 245.00 | 500.00 |
| | 1908 | 400,000 | 1.75 | 3.50 | 11.50 | 25.00 | 200.00 | 425.00 |
| 13 | 1912 | 300,000 | 1.50 | 2.50 | 5.00 | 16.00 | 175.00 | 300.00 |
| | 1917C | 300,319 | 1.00 | 1.75 | 4.00 | 14.00 | 175.00 | 400.00 |
| | 1919C | 100,844 | 2.00 | 3.00 | 12.00 | 30.00 | 350.00 | 700.00 |
| | 1929 | 300,000 | 1.00 | 1.75 | 3.25 | 12.00 | 150.00 | 300.00 |
| | 1929 | — | — | — | — | — | Proof | 750.00 |
| 19 | 1938 | 100,000 | 1.00 | 1.50 | 2.00 | 4.00 | 75.00 | 190.00 |
| | 1938 | — | — | — | — | — | Proof | 350.00 |
| | 1940C | 200,000 | 1.00 | 1.50 | 2.00 | 4.00 | 45.00 | 140.00 |
| | 1941C | 621,641 | .75 | 1.50 | 2.00 | 3.00 | 18.00 | 27.50 |
| | 1942C | 298,348 | 1.00 | 1.50 | 2.50 | 3.00 | 30.00 | 55.00 |
| | 1943C | 351,666 | .75 | 1.50 | 2.00 | 3.00 | 18.00 | 27.50 |
| | **1.1664 g, .800 SILVER, .0300 oz ASW** | | | | | | | |
| 19a | 1944C | 286,504 | 1.00 | 1.75 | 2.50 | 3.00 | 30.00 | 90.00 |
| | 1945C | 203,828 | .75 | 1.50 | 2.00 | 3.00 | 18.00 | 15.00 |
| | 1945C | — | — | — | — | — | Proof | 250.00 |
| | 1946C | 2,041 | 150.00 | 200.00 | 275.00 | 400.00 | 1500. | 2150. |
| | 1946C | — | — | — | — | — | Proof | 4000. |
| | 1947C | 38,400 | 4.00 | 6.00 | 9.00 | 15.00 | 60.00 | 125.00 |
| | 1947C | — | — | — | — | — | Proof | 400.00 |

# Ten cents

| | | | **1865-1896** | | | | | |
|---|---|---|---|---|---|---|---|---|
| | | | **2.3564 g, .925 SILVER, .0701 oz ASW** | | | | | |
| KM# | Date | Mintage | VG-8 | F-12 | VF-20 | XF-40 | MS-60 | MS-63 |
| 3 | 1865 | 80,000 | 15.00 | 22.50 | 60.00 | 175.00 | 1200. | 2500. |
| | 1865 plain edge | — | — | — | — | — | Proof | 5500. |
| | 1870 | 30,000 | 120.00 | 175.00 | 325.00 | 700.00 | 3000. | 6500. |
| | 1872H | 40,000 | 15.00 | 22.50 | 55.00 | 150.00 | 900.00 | 1900. |
| | 1873 flat 3 | 23,614 | 16.00 | 30.00 | 75.00 | 200.00 | 1850. | 3200. |
| | 1873 round 3 | Inc. Ab. | 16.00 | 30.00 | 75.00 | 200.00 | 1850. | 3200. |
| | 1876H | 10,000 | 22.50 | 40.00 | 80.00 | 275.00 | 2000. | 3250. |
| | 1880/70 | 10,000 | 22.50 | 40.00 | 90.00 | 300.00 | 2250. | 3250. |
| | 1882H | 20,000 | 12.50 | 25.00 | 60.00 | 125.00 | 1200. | 2000. |
| | 1882H | — | — | — | — | — | Proof | 3400. |
| | 1885 | 8,000 | 55.00 | 100.00 | 220.00 | 500.00 | 2500. | 4500. |
| | 1888 | 30,000 | 12.50 | 22.00 | 55.00 | 150.00 | 1300. | 2600. |
| | 1890 | 100,000 | 6.00 | 12.00 | 22.00 | 70.00 | 750.00 | 1500. |
| | 1890 | — | — | — | — | — | Proof | 3200. |
| | 1894 | 100,000 | 6.00 | 12.00 | 22.00 | 70.00 | 750.00 | 1500. |
| | 1894 | — | — | — | — | — | Proof | 1750. |
| | 1896 | 230,000 | 4.00 | 10.00 | 20.00 | 65.00 | 600.00 | 1400. |

| | | | **1903-1947** | | | | | |
|---|---|---|---|---|---|---|---|---|
| 8 | 1903 | 100,000 | 4.00 | 10.00 | 27.50 | 75.00 | 750.00 | 1600. |
| | 1904H | 100,000 | 3.00 | 7.00 | 20.00 | 55.00 | 325.00 | 550.00 |

| KM# | Date | Mintage | VG-8 | F-12 | VF-20 | XF-40 | MS-60 | MS-63 |
|---|---|---|---|---|---|---|---|---|
| 14 | 1912 | 150,000 | 1.50 | 3.00 | 9.00 | 30.00 | 325.00 | 550.00 |
| | 1917C | 250,805 | 1.25 | 2.00 | 6.00 | 20.00 | 375.00 | 900.00 |
| | 1919C | 54,342 | 1.50 | 3.00 | 9.00 | 28.00 | 190.00 | 350.00 |
| 20 | 1938 | 100,000 | 1.00 | 1.50 | 2.50 | 7.00 | 100.00 | 250.00 |
| | 1938 | — | — | — | — | — | Proof | 500.00 |
| | 1940 | 100,000 | .50 | 1.00 | 2.00 | 5.00 | 90.00 | 250.00 |
| | 1941C | 483,630 | .50 | 1.00 | 2.00 | 4.00 | 35.00 | 95.00 |
| | 1942C | 293,736 | .50 | 1.00 | 2.00 | 4.00 | 35.00 | 100.00 |
| | 1943C | 104,706 | .50 | 1.00 | 2.00 | 4.00 | 40.00 | 125.00 |

| | | 2.3328 g, .800 SILVER, .0600 oz ASW | | | | | | |
|---|---|---|---|---|---|---|---|---|
| 20a | 1944C | 151,471 | 1.00 | 1.25 | 2.00 | 5.00 | 55.00 | 190.00 |
| | 1945C | 175,833 | .60 | 1.00 | 2.00 | 4.00 | 35.00 | 100.00 |
| | 1946C | 38,400 | 3.00 | 5.00 | 10.00 | 20.00 | 70.00 | 300.00 |
| | 1947C | 61,988 | 1.75 | 3.00 | 7.00 | 12.00 | 90.00 | 220.00 |

# Twenty cents

**1865-1900**
**4.7127 g, .925 SILVER, .1401 oz ASW**

| KM# | Date | Mintage | VG-8 | F-12 | VF-20 | XF-40 | MS-60 | MS-63 |
|---|---|---|---|---|---|---|---|---|
| 4 | 1865 | 100,000 | 8.00 | 14.00 | 40.00 | 110.00 | 950.00 | 2000. |
| | 1865 plain edge | — | — | — | — | — | Proof | 4500. |
| | 1870 | 50,000 | 11.00 | 18.00 | 60.00 | 140.00 | 1250. | 2500. |
| | 1872H | 90,000 | 7.00 | 12.00 | 30.00 | 90.00 | 750.00 | 1800. |
| | 1873 | 45,797 | 9.00 | 15.00 | 40.00 | 120.00 | 1300. | 2600. |
| | 1876H | 50,000 | 10.00 | 16.00 | 45.00 | 125.00 | 1350. | 2700. |
| | 1880/70 | 30,000 | 15.00 | 25.00 | 60.00 | 150.00 | 1350. | 3000. |
| | 1881 | 60,000 | 4.00 | 10.00 | 25.00 | 75.00 | 800.00 | 1800. |
| | 1882H | 100,000 | 5.00 | 12.00 | 27.50 | 80.00 | 800.00 | 1800. |
| | 1882H | — | — | — | — | — | Proof | 3700. |
| | 1885 | 40,000 | 8.00 | 12.50 | 30.00 | 100.00 | 1300. | 2600. |
| | 1888 | 75,000 | 4.00 | 9.00 | 27.00 | 90.00 | 800.00 | 1750. |
| | 1890 | 100,000 | 3.00 | 6.00 | 20.00 | 55.00 | 550.00 | 1500. |
| | 1890 | — | — | — | — | — | Proof | 2750. |
| | 1894 | 100,000 | 3.00 | 6.00 | 20.00 | 55.00 | 550.00 | 1600. |
| | 1896 small 96 | 125,000 | 3.00 | 6.00 | 16.00 | 50.00 | 550.00 | 1500. |
| | 1896 large 96 | Inc. Ab. | 3.50 | 9.00 | 20.00 | 70.00 | 600.00 | 1550. |
| | 1899 small 99 | 125,000 | 6.00 | 14.00 | 30.00 | 90.00 | 750.00 | 1750. |
| | 1899 large 99 | Inc. Ab. | 2.50 | 6.00 | 15.00 | 50.00 | 600.00 | 1750. |
| | 1900 | 125,000 | 2.50 | 5.00 | 14.00 | 45.00 | 600.00 | 1750. |

**1904-1912**

| KM# | Date | Mintage | VG-8 | F-12 | VF-20 | XF-40 | MS-60 | MS-63 |
|---|---|---|---|---|---|---|---|---|
| 10 | 1904H | 75,000 | 9.00 | 15.00 | 50.00 | 125.00 | 1100. | 2500. |
| | 1904H | — | — | — | — | — | Proof | 4150. |
| 15 | 1912 | 350,000 | 2.00 | 3.00 | 10.00 | 35.00 | 350.00 | 1000. |

# Twenty-five cents

| KM# | Date | Mintage | 5.8319 g, .925 SILVER, .1734 oz ASW VG-8 | F-12 | VF-20 | XF-40 | MS-60 | MS-63 |
|-----|------|---------|------|------|-------|-------|-------|-------|
| 17 | 1917C | 464,779 | 1.50 | 2.00 | 4.00 | 8.00 | 110.00 | 250.00 |
|  | 1919C | 163,939 | 1.50 | 2.25 | 4.25 | 12.00 | 150.00 | 400.00 |

# Fifty cents

1870-1900

1904-1919

| KM# | Date | Mintage | 11.7818 g, .925 SILVER, .3504 oz ASW VG-8 | F-12 | VF-20 | XF-40 | MS-60 | MS-63 |
|-----|------|---------|------|------|-------|-------|-------|-------|
| 6 | 1870 | 50,000 | 10.00 | 15.00 | 40.00 | 150.00 | 1250. | 2500. |
|  | 1870 plain edge | — | — | — | — | — | Proof | 5500. |
|  | 1872H | 48,000 | 10.00 | 15.00 | 40.00 | 150.00 | 1250. | 2500. |
|  | 1873 | 37,675 | 22.00 | 45.00 | 90.00 | 350.00 | 2400. | 5000. |
|  | 1874 | 80,000 | 12.00 | 20.00 | 65.00 | 300.00 | 2400. | 5000. |
|  | 1876H | 28,000 | 18.00 | 30.00 | 75.00 | 275.00 | 2250. | 5250. |
|  | 1880 | 24,000 | 18.00 | 27.50 | 75.00 | 275.00 | 2250. | 5250. |
|  | 1881 | 50,000 | 10.00 | 18.00 | 55.00 | 200.00 | 2000. | 5250. |
|  | 1882H | 100,000 | 8.00 | 12.50 | 30.00 | 130.00 | 1500. | 3500. |
|  | 1882H | — | — | — | — | — | Proof | 5500. |
|  | 1885 | 40,000 | 10.00 | 18.00 | 55.00 | 225.00 | 2000. | 5000. |
|  | 1888 | 20,000 | 15.00 | 25.00 | 70.00 | 300.00 | 2200. | 5200. |
|  | 1894 | 40,000 | 5.00 | 8.00 | 35.00 | 130.00 | 1600. | 2750. |
|  | 1896 | 60,000 | 4.00 | 7.00 | 25.00 | 110.00 | 1400. | 2500. |
|  | 1898 | 76,607 | 4.00 | 7.00 | 26.00 | 120.00 | 1400. | 2400. |
|  | 1899 wide 9's | 150,000 | 4.00 | 7.00 | 25.00 | 100.00 | 1400. | 2400. |
|  | 1899 narrow 9's | Inc. Ab. | 4.00 | 7.00 | 25.00 | 100.00 | 1400. | 2400. |
|  | 1900 | 150,000 | 4.00 | 7.00 | 22.50 | 100.00 | 1400. | 2400. |
| 11 | 1904H | 140,000 | 3.00 | 5.00 | 16.00 | 40.00 | 350.00 | 900.00 |
|  | 1907 | 100,000 | 5.00 | 7.00 | 20.00 | 45.00 | 375.00 | 1000. |
|  | 1908 | 160,000 | 2.50 | 4.50 | 12.50 | 25.00 | 175.00 | 550.00 |
|  | 1909 | 200,000 | 2.50 | 4.50 | 12.50 | 25.00 | 175.00 | 550.00 |
| 12 | 1911 | 200,000 | 2.00 | 3.00 | 8.00 | 20.00 | 250.00 | 600.00 |
|  | 1917C | 375,560 | 2.00 | 3.00 | 6.00 | 15.00 | 140.00 | 350.00 |
|  | 1918C | 294,824 | 2.00 | 3.00 | 6.00 | 15.00 | 140.00 | 350.00 |
|  | 1919C | 306,267 | 2.00 | 3.00 | 6.00 | 15.00 | 140.00 | 350.00 |

# Two dollars

### 3.3284 g, .917 GOLD, .0981 oz AGW

| KM# | Date | Mintage | F-12 | VF-20 | XF-40 | AU-50 | MS-60 | MS-63 |
|---|---|---|---|---|---|---|---|---|
| 5 | 1865 | 10,000 | 175.00 | 225.00 | 350.00 | 600.00 | 1250. | 2800. |
| | 1865 plain edge | about 10 known | — | — | — | — | Proof | 10,000. |
| | 1870 | 10,000 | 175.00 | 225.00 | 350.00 | 600.00 | 1250. | 3000. |
| | 1870 plain edge | — | — | — | — | — | Proof | 10,000. |
| | 1872 | 6,050 | 200.00 | 275.00 | 400.00 | 750.00 | 2500. | 5250. |
| | 1880 | 2,500 | 1000. | 1400. | 1800. | 2200. | 3500. | 9000. |
| | 1880 | — | — | — | — | — | Proof | 18,500. |
| | 1881 | 10,000 | 120.00 | 190.00 | 235.00 | 350.00 | 750.00 | 1450. |
| | 1882H | 25,000 | 100.00 | 150.00 | 185.00 | 260.00 | 450.00 | 1000. |
| | 1882H | — | — | — | — | — | Proof | 6000. |
| | 1885 | 10,000 | 120.00 | 190.00 | 235.00 | 350.00 | 750.00 | 1450. |
| | 1888 | 25,000 | 100.00 | 150.00 | 185.00 | 260.00 | 450.00 | 1000. |

# New Brunswick
# Half penny token

| KM# | Date | Mintage | VG-8 | COPPER F-12 | VF-20 | XF-40 | MS-60 | MS-63 |
|---|---|---|---|---|---|---|---|---|
| 1 | 1843 | 480,000 | 3.00 | 6.00 | 12.00 | 25.00 | 95.00 | 250.00 |
| | 1843 | — | — | — | — | — | Proof | 750.00 |

| KM# | Date | Mintage | VG-8 | F-12 | VF-20 | XF-40 | MS-60 | MS-63 |
|---|---|---|---|---|---|---|---|---|
| 3 | 1854 | 864,000 | 3.00 | 6.00 | 12.00 | 25.00 | 95.00 | 250.00 |

# One penny token

| | | | | COPPER | | | | |
|---|---|---|---|---|---|---|---|---|
| KM# | Date | Mintage | VG-8 | F-12 | VF-20 | XF-40 | MS-60 | MS-63 |
| 2 | 1843 | 480,000 | 3.00 | 6.00 | 12.00 | 30.00 | 150.00 | 300.00 |
| | 1843 | — | — | — | — | — | Proof | 800.00 |

| KM# | Date | Mintage | VG-8 | F-12 | VF-20 | XF-40 | MS-60 | MS-63 |
|---|---|---|---|---|---|---|---|---|
| 4 | 1854 | 432,000 | 3.00 | 6.00 | 12.00 | 35.00 | 160.00 | 320.00 |

# Decimal coinage
# Half cent

| | | | | BRONZE | | | | |
|---|---|---|---|---|---|---|---|---|
| KM# | Date | Mintage | VG-8 | F-12 | VF-20 | XF-40 | MS-60 | MS-63 |
| 5 | 1861 | 222,800 | 45.00 | 70.00 | 100.00 | 150.00 | 350.00 | 850.00 |
| | 1861 | — | — | — | — | — | Proof | 2200. |

# One cent

| | | | | BRONZE | | | | |
|---|---|---|---|---|---|---|---|---|
| KM# | Date | Mintage | VG-8 | F-12 | VF-20 | XF-40 | MS-60 | MS-63 |
| 6 | 1861 | 1,000,000 | 1.50 | 2.50 | 4.00 | 7.50 | 60.00 | 170.00 |
| | 1861 | — | — | — | — | — | Proof | 450.00 |
| | 1864 short 6 | 1,000,000 | 1.50 | 2.50 | 4.00 | 7.50 | 60.00 | 175.00 |
| | 1864 long 6 | Inc. Ab. | 1.50 | 2.50 | 4.00 | 7.50 | 60.00 | 165.00 |

# Five cents

**1.1620 g, .925 SILVER, .0346 oz ASW**

| KM# | Date | Mintage | VG-8 | F-12 | VF-20 | XF-40 | MS-60 | MS-63 |
|-----|------|---------|------|------|-------|-------|-------|-------|
| 7 | 1862 | 100,000 | 20.00 | 40.00 | 90.00 | 170.00 | 900.00 | 1800. |
|   | 1862 | — | — | — | — | — | Proof | 2500. |
|   | 1864 small 6 | 100,000 | 20.00 | 40.00 | 90.00 | 170.00 | 900.00 | 1900. |
|   | 1864 large 6 | Inc. Ab. | 20.00 | 40.00 | 90.00 | 170.00 | 900.00 | 1800. |

# Ten cents

**2.3240 g, .925 SILVER, .0691 oz ASW**

| KM# | Date | Mintage | VG-8 | F-12 | VF-20 | XF-40 | MS-60 | MS-63 |
|-----|------|---------|------|------|-------|-------|-------|-------|
| 8 | 1862 | 150,000 | 22.00 | 40.00 | 90.00 | 170.00 | 750.00 | 1600. |
|   | 1862 recut 2 | Inc. Ab. | 22.00 | 40.00 | 90.00 | 170.00 | 750.00 | 1600. |
|   | 1862 | — | — | — | — | — | Proof | 2200. |
|   | 1864 | 100,000 | 22.00 | 40.00 | 90.00 | 170.00 | 750.00 | 1600. |

# Twenty cents

**4.6480 g, .925 SILVER, .1382 oz ASW**

| KM# | Date | Mintage | VG-8 | F-12 | VF-20 | XF-40 | MS-60 | MS-63 |
|-----|------|---------|------|------|-------|-------|-------|-------|
| 9 | 1862 | 150,000 | 12.00 | 17.00 | 30.00 | 100.00 | 750.00 | 1600. |
|   | 1862 | — | — | — | — | — | Proof | 2200. |
|   | 1864 | 150,000 | 12.00 | 17.00 | 30.00 | 100.00 | 750.00 | 1600. |

# Nova Scotia  Sterling coinage
# Half penny token

**COPPER**

| KM# | Date | Mintage | VG-8 | F-12 | VF-20 | XF-40 | MS-60 | MS-63 |
|-----|------|---------|------|------|-------|-------|-------|-------|
| 1 | 1823 | 400,000 | 2.00 | 4.00 | 8.00 | 15.00 | 65.00 | 150.00 |
|   | 1823 w/o hyphen | Inc. Ab. | 5.00 | 10.00 | 20.00 | 35.00 | 170.00 | 350.00 |
|   | 1824 | 118,636 | 2.50 | 5.00 | 12.50 | 22.50 | 100.00 | 225.00 |
|   | 1832 | 800,000 | 1.50 | 3.00 | 7.50 | 12.50 | 55.00 | 150.00 |

| KM# | Date | Mintage | VG-8 | F-12 | VF-20 | XF-40 | MS-60 | MS-63 |
|---|---|---|---|---|---|---|---|---|
| 1a | 1382(error) | — | 150.00 | 300.00 | 550.00 | — | — | — |
| | 1832/1382 | — | 500.00 | 700.00 | — | — | — | — |
| | 1832 (imitation) | — | 3.25 | 5.00 | 8.00 | 12.50 | 50.00 | 100.00 |

| KM# | Date | Mintage | VG-8 | F-12 | VF-20 | XF-40 | MS-60 | MS-63 |
|---|---|---|---|---|---|---|---|---|
| 3 | 1840 small 0 | 300,000 | 3.50 | 5.00 | 8.50 | 12.50 | 55.00 | 165.00 |
| | 1840 medium 0 | Inc. Ab. | 2.50 | 4.00 | 6.50 | 11.00 | 45.00 | 125.00 |
| | 1840 large 0 | Inc. Ab. | 4.00 | 6.00 | 10.00 | 16.00 | 60.00 | 185.00 |
| | 1843 | 300,000 | 3.00 | 5.00 | 8.00 | 12.00 | 50.00 | 160.00 |

| KM# | Date | Mintage | VG-8 | F-12 | VF-20 | XF-40 | MS-60 | MS-63 |
|---|---|---|---|---|---|---|---|---|
| 5 | 1856 w/o LCW | 720,000 | 2.00 | 4.00 | 7.50 | 12.50 | 55.00 | 175.00 |
| | 1856 w/o LCW | — | — | — | — | — | Proof | 600.00 |
| | 1856 w/o LCW, inverted A for V in PROVINCE | | | — | — | Proof | 600.00 |

**BRONZE**

| | | | | | | | | |
|---|---|---|---|---|---|---|---|---|
| 5a | 1856 w/LCW | — | — | — | — | — | Proof | 600.00 |

# One penny token

**COPPER**

| KM# | Date | Mintage | VG-8 | F-12 | VF-20 | XF-40 | MS-60 | MS-63 |
|---|---|---|---|---|---|---|---|---|
| 2 | 1824 | 217,776 | 3.00 | 6.00 | 10.00 | 22.50 | 100.00 | 250.00 |
| | 1832 | 200,000 | 2.00 | 4.00 | 7.50 | 18.00 | 80.00 | 230.00 |
| 2a | 1832 (imitation) | — | 5.50 | 16.00 | 24.00 | 40.00 | — | — |

| KM# | Date | Mintage | VG-8 | F-12 | VF-20 | XF-40 | MS-60 | MS-63 |
|---|---|---|---|---|---|---|---|---|
| 4 | 1840 | 150,000 | 2.00 | 4.00 | 7.00 | 15.00 | 60.00 | 175.00 |
| | 1843/0 | 150,000 | 9.00 | 12.50 | 18.00 | 30.00 | 85.00 | — |
| | 1843 | Inc. Ab. | 3.00 | 6.00 | 10.00 | 20.00 | 75.00 | 200.00 |

| KM# | Date | Mintage | VG-8 | F-12 | VF-20 | XF-40 | MS-60 | MS-63 |
|---|---|---|---|---|---|---|---|---|
| 6 | 1856 w/o LCW | 360,000 | 2.50 | 4.50 | 8.50 | 12.00 | 55.00 | 135.00 |
| | 1856 w/LCW | Inc. Ab. | 2.00 | 4.00 | 7.00 | 10.00 | 45.00 | 115.00 |

**BRONZE**

| KM# | Date | | | | | | | |
|---|---|---|---|---|---|---|---|---|
| 6a | 1856 | — | — | — | — | — | Proof | 400.00 |

# Decimal coinage
# Half cent

**BRONZE**

| KM# | Date | Mintage | VG-8 | F-12 | VF-20 | XF-40 | MS-60 | MS-63 |
|---|---|---|---|---|---|---|---|---|
| 7 | 1861 | 400,000 | 3.00 | 5.00 | 8.00 | 12.00 | 55.00 | 130.00 |
| | 1864 | 400,000 | 3.00 | 5.00 | 8.00 | 12.00 | 55.00 | 130.00 |
| | 1864 | — | — | — | — | — | Proof | 300.00 |

# One cent

**BRONZE**

| KM# | Date | Mintage | VG-8 | F-12 | VF-20 | XF-40 | MS-60 | MS-63 |
|---|---|---|---|---|---|---|---|---|
| 8 | 1861 | 800,000 | 1.50 | 2.25 | 4.50 | 8.00 | 60.00 | 150.00 |
| | 1862 | (Est.) 100,000 | 20.00 | 30.00 | 50.00 | 100.00 | 350.00 | 750.00 |
| | 1864 | 800,000 | 1.50 | 2.25 | 4.50 | 8.00 | 60.00 | 160.00 |

NOTE: The Royal Mint Report records mintage of 1,000,000 for 1862 which is considered incorrect.

# Prince Edward Island
# One cent

| KM# | Date | Mintage | VG-8 | BRONZE F-12 | VF-20 | XF-40 | MS-60 | MS-63 |
|---|---|---|---|---|---|---|---|---|
| 4 | 1871 | 2,000,000 | 1.25 | 2.00 | 3.50 | 8.00 | 70.00 | 175.00 |
|  | 1871 | — | — | — | — | — | Proof | 2000. |

# Mexico

## COLONIAL COB COINAGE

### RULERS
Philip V, 1700-1724, 1724-1746
Luis I, 1724

### MINT MARKS
Mo, MXo - Mexico City Mint

### ASSAYERS INITIALS

| Letter | Date | Name |
|---|---|---|
| L | 1678-1703 | Martin Lopez |
| J | 1708-1723 | Jose E. de Leon |
| D | 1724-1727 | ? |
| R | 1729-1730 | Nicolas de Roxas |
| G | 1730 | — |
| F | 1730-1733 | Felipe Rivas de Angulo |
| F | 1733-1784 | Francisco de la Pena |
| M | 1733-1763 | Manuel de la Pena |

## 1/2 REAL

**.931 SILVER, 1.69 g**
**Philip V**
Obv: Legend around crowned PHILIPVS monogram.
Rev: Legend around cross, lions and castles.

| KM# | Date | Good | VG | Fine | VF |
|---|---|---|---|---|---|
| 24 | 1701 L | 30.00 | 40.00 | 55.00 | 90.00 |
| | 1702 L | 25.00 | 35.00 | 50.00 | 65.00 |
| | 1703 L | 25.00 | 35.00 | 50.00 | 65.00 |
| | 1704 L | 30.00 | 42.50 | 65.00 | 85.00 |
| | 1705 L | 30.00 | 42.50 | 65.00 | 85.00 |
| | 1706 L | 30.00 | 42.50 | 65.00 | 85.00 |
| | 1707 L | 30.00 | 42.50 | 65.00 | 85.00 |
| | 1708 J | 35.00 | 50.00 | 70.00 | 110.00 |
| | 1709 J | 30.00 | 42.50 | 65.00 | 85.00 |
| | 1710 J | 30.00 | 42.50 | 65.00 | 85.00 |
| | 1711 J | 30.00 | 42.50 | 65.00 | 85.00 |
| | 1712 J | 30.00 | 42.50 | 65.00 | 85.00 |
| | 1714 J | 30.00 | 42.50 | 65.00 | 85.00 |
| | 1715 J | 30.00 | 42.50 | 65.00 | 85.00 |
| | 1716 J | 30.00 | 42.50 | 65.00 | 85.00 |
| | 1717 J | 30.00 | 42.50 | 65.00 | 85.00 |
| | 1718 J | 30.00 | 42.50 | 65.00 | 85.00 |
| | 1719 J | 30.00 | 42.50 | 65.00 | 85.00 |
| | 1720 J | 30.00 | 42.50 | 65.00 | 85.00 |
| | 1721 J | 30.00 | 42.50 | 65.00 | 85.00 |
| | 1722 J | 42.50 | 55.00 | 80.00 | 125.00 |
| | 1723 J | 42.50 | 55.00 | 80.00 | 125.00 |
| | 1724 J | 50.00 | 65.00 | 85.00 | 140.00 |
| | 1724 D | 50.00 | 65.00 | 85.00 | 140.00 |
| | 1725 D | 50.00 | 65.00 | 85.00 | 140.00 |
| | 1726 D | 35.00 | 50.00 | 70.00 | 110.00 |
| | 1727 D | 35.00 | 50.00 | 70.00 | 110.00 |
| | 1728 D | 35.00 | 50.00 | 70.00 | 110.00 |

**.916 SILVER, 1.69 g**

| KM# | Date | Good | VG | Fine | VF |
|---|---|---|---|---|---|
| 24a | 1729 D | 35.00 | 50.00 | 70.00 | 110.00 |
| | 1730 G | 35.00 | 50.00 | 70.00 | 110.00 |
| | 1730 D | 35.00 | 50.00 | 70.00 | 110.00 |
| | 1731 F | 35.00 | 50.00 | 70.00 | 110.00 |
| | 1732 F | 35.00 | 50.00 | 70.00 | 110.00 |
| | 1733 F | 35.00 | 50.00 | 70.00 | 110.00 |
| | Date off flan | 15.00 | 20.00 | 25.00 | 30.00 |

**.931 SILVER, 1.69 g**
**Luis I**
Obv: Legend around crowned LVDOVICVS monogram.
Rev: Legend around cross, lions and castles.

| KM# | Date | Good | VG | Fine | VF |
|---|---|---|---|---|---|
| 25 | 1724 D | 225.00 | 350.00 | 500.00 | 600.00 |
| | 1725 D | 225.00 | 350.00 | 500.00 | 600.00 |
| | 1726 D | 250.00 | 370.00 | 550.00 | 650.00 |
| | Date off flan | 100.00 | 200.00 | 250.00 | 300.00 |

## REAL

### ROYAL STRIKES

**Philip V**

Full struck sample specimens referred to as "Royal" strikes are seldom encountered and are considered rare.

### CIRCULATION STRIKES

**.931 SILVER, 3.38 g**
Obv. leg: PHILIPVS V DEI G and date around crowned arms.

| KM# | Date | Good | VG | Fine | VF |
|---|---|---|---|---|---|
| 30 | 1701 L | 45.00 | 60.00 | 70.00 | 115.00 |
| | 1702 L | 45.00 | 60.00 | 70.00 | 115.00 |
| | 1703 L | 45.00 | 60.00 | 70.00 | 115.00 |
| | 1703 L | 45.00 | 60.00 | 70.00 | 115.00 |
| | 1704 L | 45.00 | 60.00 | 70.00 | 115.00 |
| | 1705 L | 45.00 | 60.00 | 70.00 | 115.00 |
| | 1706 L | 45.00 | 60.00 | 70.00 | 115.00 |
| | 1707 L | 45.00 | 60.00 | 70.00 | 115.00 |
| | 1708 J | 45.00 | 60.00 | 70.00 | 115.00 |
| | 1709 J | 45.00 | 60.00 | 70.00 | 115.00 |
| | 1710 J | 45.00 | 60.00 | 70.00 | 115.00 |
| | 1711 J | 45.00 | 60.00 | 70.00 | 115.00 |
| | 1712 J | 45.00 | 60.00 | 70.00 | 115.00 |
| | 1713 J | 35.00 | 45.00 | 57.50 | 85.00 |
| | 1714 J | 35.00 | 45.00 | 57.50 | 85.00 |
| | 1715 J | 45.00 | 60.00 | 70.00 | 100.00 |
| | 1716 J | 45.00 | 60.00 | 70.00 | 100.00 |
| | 1717 J | 45.00 | 60.00 | 70.00 | 100.00 |
| | 1718 J | 45.00 | 60.00 | 70.00 | 100.00 |
| | 1719 J | 45.00 | 60.00 | 70.00 | 100.00 |
| | 1720 J | 45.00 | 60.00 | 70.00 | 100.00 |
| | 1721 J | 45.00 | 60.00 | 70.00 | 100.00 |
| | 1722 J | 45.00 | 60.00 | 70.00 | 100.00 |
| | 1723 J | 45.00 | 60.00 | 70.00 | 100.00 |
| | 1724 J | 45.00 | 60.00 | 70.00 | 100.00 |
| | 1726 D | 45.00 | 60.00 | 70.00 | 100.00 |
| | 1727 D | 45.00 | 60.00 | 70.00 | 100.00 |
| | 1728 D | 45.00 | 60.00 | 70.00 | 100.00 |
| | 1729 F | 45.00 | 60.00 | 70.00 | 100.00 |

**.916 SILVER**

| KM# | Date | Good | VG | Fine | VF |
|---|---|---|---|---|---|
| 30a | 1729 R | 45.00 | 60.00 | 70.00 | 100.00 |
| | 1730 R | 45.00 | 60.00 | 70.00 | 100.00 |
| | 1730 F | 45.00 | 60.00 | 70.00 | 100.00 |
| | 1730 G | 45.00 | 60.00 | 70.00 | 100.00 |
| | 1731 F | 45.00 | 60.00 | 70.00 | 100.00 |
| | Date off flan | 10.00 | 15.00 | 20.00 | 30.00 |

## 2 REALES

### ROYAL STRIKES

**Philip V**

Fully struck sample specimens referred to as "Royal" strikes are seldom encountered and are considered rare.

### CIRCULATION STRIKES

**.931 SILVER, 6.77 g**
Obv. leg: PHILIPVS V DEI G and date around crowned arms.

| KM# | Date | Good | VG | Fine | VF |
|---|---|---|---|---|---|
| 35 | 1701 L | 25.00 | 40.00 | 50.00 | 75.00 |
| | 1702 L | 25.00 | 40.00 | 50.00 | 75.00 |
| | 1703 L | 25.00 | 40.00 | 50.00 | 75.00 |
| | 1704 L | 35.00 | 75.00 | 150.00 | 250.00 |
| | 1705 L | 25.00 | 40.00 | 50.00 | 75.00 |
| | 1706 L | 25.00 | 40.00 | 50.00 | 75.00 |
| | 1707 L | 35.00 | 75.00 | 150.00 | 250.00 |
| | 1708 J | 25.00 | 40.00 | 50.00 | 75.00 |
| | 1710 J | 25.00 | 40.00 | 50.00 | 75.00 |
| | 1711 J | 25.00 | 40.00 | 50.00 | 75.00 |
| | 1712 J | 25.00 | 40.00 | 50.00 | 75.00 |
| | 1713 J | 25.00 | 40.00 | 50.00 | 75.00 |
| | 1714 J | 25.00 | 40.00 | 50.00 | 80.00 |
| | 1715 J | 25.00 | 40.00 | 50.00 | 80.00 |
| | 1716 J | 25.00 | 40.00 | 50.00 | 75.00 |
| | 1717 J | 25.00 | 40.00 | 50.00 | 75.00 |
| | 1718 J | 25.00 | 40.00 | 50.00 | 75.00 |
| | 1719 J | 25.00 | 40.00 | 50.00 | 75.00 |
| | 1720 J | 25.00 | 40.00 | 50.00 | 75.00 |
| | 1721 J | 25.00 | 40.00 | 60.00 | 100.00 |
| | 1722 J | 25.00 | 40.00 | 50.00 | 75.00 |
| 35 | 1723 J | 25.00 | 40.00 | 50.00 | 75.00 |
| | 1724 J | 36.00 | 50.00 | 60.00 | 100.00 |
| | 1725 D | 36.00 | 57.50 | 75.00 | 125.00 |
| | 1725 R | 36.00 | 40.00 | 50.00 | 100.00 |
| | 1726 D | 36.00 | 57.50 | 75.00 | 125.00 |
| | 1727 D | 36.00 | 57.50 | 75.00 | 125.00 |
| | 1728 D | 28.00 | 37.50 | 75.00 | 125.00 |

**.916 SILVER**

| KM# | Date | Good | VG | Fine | VF |
|---|---|---|---|---|---|
| 35a | 1729 R | 28.00 | 37.50 | 75.00 | 125.00 |
| | 1730 R | 28.00 | 37.50 | 75.00 | 125.00 |
| | 1731 MF | 25.00 | 30.00 | 40.00 | 60.00 |
| | 1731/0 J | 25.00 | 30.00 | 40.00 | 60.00 |
| | 1733 F | 25.00 | 40.00 | 80.00 | 150.00 |
| | Date off flan | 10.00 | 20.00 | 30.00 | 40.00 |

## 4 REALES

### ROYAL STRIKES

**Philip V**

Fully struck sample specimens referred to as "Royal" strikes are seldom encountered and are considered rare.

### CIRCULATION STRIKES

**.931 SILVER, 13.54 g**
Obv. leg: PHILIPVS V DEI G and date around crowned arms.

| KM# | Date | Good | VG | Fine | VF |
|---|---|---|---|---|---|
| 40 | 1701 L | 80.00 | 125.00 | 225.00 | 375.00 |
| | 1702 L | 80.00 | 125.00 | 225.00 | 375.00 |
| | 1703 L | 45.00 | 90.00 | 150.00 | 250.00 |
| | 1704 L | 80.00 | 125.00 | 225.00 | 375.00 |
| | 1705 L | 65.00 | 100.00 | 200.00 | 300.00 |
| | 1706 L | 65.00 | 100.00 | 200.00 | 300.00 |
| | 1707 L | 65.00 | 100.00 | 200.00 | 300.00 |
| | 1708 J | 30.00 | 70.00 | 120.00 | 200.00 |
| | 1709 J | 65.00 | 100.00 | 200.00 | 300.00 |
| | 1710 J | 50.00 | 90.00 | 175.00 | 250.00 |
| | 1711 J | 50.00 | 90.00 | 175.00 | 250.00 |
| | 1712 J | 80.00 | 125.00 | 225.00 | 375.00 |
| | 1713 J | 80.00 | 125.00 | 225.00 | 375.00 |
| | 1714 J | 65.00 | 100.00 | 200.00 | 300.00 |
| | 1715 J | 80.00 | 125.00 | 225.00 | 375.00 |
| | 1716 J | 65.00 | 100.00 | 200.00 | 300.00 |
| | 1717 J | 80.00 | 125.00 | 225.00 | 375.00 |
| | 1718 J | 80.00 | 125.00 | 225.00 | 375.00 |
| | 1719 J | 65.00 | 100.00 | 200.00 | 300.00 |
| | 1720 J | 65.00 | 100.00 | 200.00 | 300.00 |
| | 1721 J | 65.00 | 100.00 | 200.00 | 300.00 |
| | 1722 J | 90.00 | 150.00 | 300.00 | 500.00 |
| | 1723 J | 90.00 | 150.00 | 300.00 | 500.00 |
| | 1725 D | 90.00 | 150.00 | 300.00 | 500.00 |
| | 1726 D | 90.00 | 150.00 | 300.00 | 500.00 |
| | 1727 D | 90.00 | 150.00 | 300.00 | 500.00 |
| | 1728 D | 80.00 | 125.00 | 225.00 | 375.00 |

**.916 SILVER, 13.54 g**

| KM# | Date | Good | VG | Fine | VF |
|---|---|---|---|---|---|
| 40a | 1729 D | 90.00 | 150.00 | 300.00 | 500.00 |
| | 1730 R | 90.00 | 150.00 | 300.00 | 500.00 |
| | 1730 G | 90.00 | 150.00 | 300.00 | 500.00 |
| | 1731 F | 90.00 | 150.00 | 300.00 | 500.00 |
| | 1731 F | 90.00 | 150.00 | 300.00 | 500.00 |
| | 1732/1 F | 75.00 | 120.00 | 240.00 | 360.00 |
| | 1732 F | 65.00 | 100.00 | 200.00 | 300.00 |
| | 1733 F | 65.00 | 100.00 | 200.00 | 300.00 |
| | 1734 F | 65.00 | 100.00 | 200.00 | 300.00 |
| | Date off flan | 40.00 | 50.00 | 70.00 | 100.00 |

Similar to KM#40a but 'klippe' planchet.

| KM# | Date | Good | VG | Fine | VF |
|---|---|---|---|---|---|
| 41 | 1733 MF | 200.00 | 250.00 | 300.00 | 400.00 |
| | 1734 MF | 250.00 | 300.00 | 400.00 | 500.00 |
| | 1734/3 MF | 225.00 | 250.00 | 300.00 | 400.00 |
| | 1740/30 MF | 250.00 | 275.00 | 350.00 | 450.00 |
| | 1742/32 MF | — | — | — | — |
| | 1743/33 MF | — | — | — | — |

**.931 SILVER, 13.54 g**
Luis I
Obv. leg: LVDOVICVS I DEI G around crowned arms.

| KM# | Date | Good | VG | Fine | VF |
|---|---|---|---|---|---|
| 42 | 1724 D | 650.00 | 1000. | 1500. | 2500. |
| | 1725 D | 750.00 | 1200. | 2000. | 3000. |
| | Date off flan | 225.00 | 350.00 | 500.00 | 850.00 |

# 8 REALES
## ROYAL STRIKES

**Philip V**

Fully struck sample specimens referred to as "Royal" strikes are seldom encountered and are considered rare.

## CIRCULATION STRIKES

**.931 SILVER, 27.07 g**
**Obv. leg: PHILIPVS V DEI G and date**
**around crowned arms.**

| KM# | Date | Good | VG | Fine | VF |
|---|---|---|---|---|---|
| 47 | 1701 L | 100.00 | 175.00 | 275.00 | 400.00 |
| | 1702 L | 125.00 | 200.00 | 300.00 | 450.00 |
| | 1703 L | 125.00 | 200.00 | 300.00 | 450.00 |
| | 1704 L | 150.00 | 250.00 | 400.00 | 600.00 |
| | 1706 L | 150.00 | 250.00 | 400.00 | 600.00 |
| | 1707 L | 150.00 | 250.00 | 400.00 | 600.00 |
| | 1707 J | 150.00 | 250.00 | 400.00 | 600.00 |
| | 1708 J | 125.00 | 200.00 | 300.00 | 450.00 |
| | 1709 J | 100.00 | 175.00 | 275.00 | 400.00 |
| | 1710 J | 150.00 | 250.00 | 400.00 | 600.00 |
| | 1711 J | 100.00 | 175.00 | 275.00 | 400.00 |
| | 1712 J | 125.00 | 200.00 | 300.00 | 450.00 |

| KM# | Date | Good | VG | Fine | VF |
|---|---|---|---|---|---|
| 47 | 1713 J | 60.00 | 100.00 | 165.00 | 250.00 |
| | 1714 J | 60.00 | 100.00 | 165.00 | 250.00 |
| | 1715 J | 100.00 | 175.00 | 275.00 | 400.00 |
| | 1716 J | 100.00 | 175.00 | 275.00 | 400.00 |
| | 1717 J | 100.00 | 175.00 | 275.00 | 400.00 |
| | 1718 J | 100.00 | 175.00 | 275.00 | 400.00 |
| | 1719 J | 100.00 | 175.00 | 275.00 | 400.00 |
| | 1720 J | 100.00 | 175.00 | 275.00 | 400.00 |
| | 1721 J | 125.00 | 200.00 | 300.00 | 450.00 |
| | 1722 J | 100.00 | 175.00 | 275.00 | 400.00 |
| | 1723 J | 125.00 | 200.00 | 300.00 | 450.00 |
| | 1724 D | 125.00 | 200.00 | 300.00 | 450.00 |
| | 1725 D | 180.00 | 350.00 | 500.00 | 900.00 |
| | 1726 D | 180.00 | 350.00 | 500.00 | 900.00 |
| | 1727 D | 180.00 | 350.00 | 500.00 | 900.00 |
| | 1728 D | 200.00 | 400.00 | 600.00 | 1000. |
| | Date off flan | 25.00 | 50.00 | 85.00 | 125.00 |
| | **.916 SILVER** | | | | |
| 47a | 1729 R | 75.00 | 150.00 | 250.00 | 375.00 |
| | 1730 R | 75.00 | 150.00 | 250.00 | 375.00 |
| | 1730 G | 100.00 | 175.00 | 275.00 | 400.00 |
| | 1730 F | 75.00 | 150.00 | 250.00 | 375.00 |
| | 1731/0 F | 250.00 | 450.00 | 650.00 | 1200. |
| | 1731 F | 75.00 | 150.00 | 250.00 | 375.00 |
| | 1732 F | 75.00 | 150.00 | 250.00 | 375.00 |
| | 1733 F | 75.00 | 150.00 | 250.00 | 400.00 |
| | Date off flan | 25.00 | 50.00 | 85.00 | 125.00 |

**Similar to KM#47a but 'klippe' planchet.**

| KM# | Date | Good | VG | Fine | VF |
|---|---|---|---|---|---|
| 48 | 1733 F | 150.00 | 250.00 | 375.00 | 600.00 |
| | 1733 MF | 100.00 | 150.00 | 250.00 | 375.00 |
| | 1734/3 MF | 100.00 | 175.00 | 275.00 | 400.00 |
| | 1734 MF | 100.00 | 175.00 | 275.00 | 400.00 |
| | Date off flan | 25.00 | 50.00 | 85.00 | 125.00 |

.931 SILVER, 27.07 g
Luis I
Obv. leg: LVDOVICVS I DEI G.

| KM# | Date | Good | VG | Fine | VF |
|---|---|---|---|---|---|
| 49 | 1724 D | 1500. | 2000. | 2500. | 3000. |
| | 1725 D | 1500. | 2000. | 2500. | 3000. |
| | Date off flan | 400.00 | 600.00 | 1000. | 1500. |

# ESCUDO

## ROYAL STRIKES

### Philip V

Fully struck sample specimens referred to as "Royal" strikes are seldom encountered and are considered rare.

## CIRCULATION STRIKES

3.3800 g, .917 GOLD, .0997 oz AGW
Mint mark: MXo
Obv. leg: PHILIPVS V DEI G and date
around crowned arms.

| KM# | Date | Good | VG | Fine | VF |
|---|---|---|---|---|---|
| 51.1 | 1702 L | 350.00 | 400.00 | 450.00 | 700.00 |
| | 1703 L | 350.00 | 400.00 | 450.00 | 700.00 |
| | 1704 L | 350.00 | 400.00 | 450.00 | 700.00 |
| | 1706 M | 350.00 | 400.00 | 450.00 | 700.00 |
| | 1707 L | 350.00 | 400.00 | 450.00 | 700.00 |
| | 1708 L | 350.00 | 400.00 | 450.00 | 700.00 |
| | 1709 J | 350.00 | 400.00 | 450.00 | 700.00 |
| | 1710 J | 350.00 | 400.00 | 450.00 | 700.00 |
| | 1711 J | 350.00 | 400.00 | 450.00 | 700.00 |
| | 1712 J | 350.00 | 400.00 | 450.00 | 700.00 |
| | Date off flan | 250.00 | 300.00 | 350.00 | 450.00 |

Mint mark: Mo

| KM# | Date | Good | VG | Fine | VF |
|---|---|---|---|---|---|
| 51.2 | 1713 J | 300.00 | 400.00 | 450.00 | 700.00 |
| | 1714 J | 300.00 | 375.00 | 400.00 | 550.00 |
| | Date off flan | 250.00 | 300.00 | 350.00 | 450.00 |

# 2 ESCUDOS

6.7700 g, .917 GOLD, .1996 oz AGW
Mint mark: MXo
Obv. leg: CAROLVS II DEI G and date
around crowned arms.
Rev: Legend around cross.

| | | Good | VG | Fine | VF |
|---|---|---|---|---|---|
| 52 | 1701 L | 600.00 | 750.00 | 900.00 | 1200. |
| | Date off flan | 375.00 | 400.00 | 450.00 | 750.00 |

NOTE: Earlier dates (1690-1699) exist for this type.

## ROYAL STRIKES

### Philip V

Fully struck sample specimens referred to as "Royal" strikes are seldom encountered and are considered rare.

## CIRCULATION STRIKES

6.7700 g, .917 GOLD, .1996 oz AGW
Mint mark: MXo
Obv. leg: PHILIPVS V DEI G and date
around crowned arms.

| | | Good | VG | Fine | VF |
|---|---|---|---|---|---|
| 53.1 | 1704 L | 400.00 | 500.00 | 650.00 | 850.00 |
| | 1705 L | 400.00 | 500.00 | 650.00 | 850.00 |
| | 1707 L | 400.00 | 500.00 | 650.00 | 850.00 |
| | 1708 J | 400.00 | 500.00 | 650.00 | 850.00 |
| | 1709 J | 400.00 | 500.00 | 650.00 | 850.00 |
| | 1710 J | 400.00 | 500.00 | 650.00 | 850.00 |
| | 1711 J | 400.00 | 500.00 | 600.00 | 850.00 |
| | 1712 J | 400.00 | 500.00 | 600.00 | 850.00 |
| | 1713 J | 400.00 | 500.00 | 600.00 | 850.00 |
| | Date off flan | 300.00 | 350.00 | 400.00 | 550.00 |

Mint mark: Mo

| KM# | Date | Good | VG | Fine | VF |
|---|---|---|---|---|---|
| 53.2 | 1714 J | 350.00 | 400.00 | 600.00 | 750.00 |
| | 1717 J | 350.00 | 400.00 | 600.00 | 750.00 |
| | 1722 J | 350.00 | 400.00 | 600.00 | 800.00 |
| | 1723 J | 350.00 | 400.00 | 600.00 | 800.00 |
| | 1729 R | 350.00 | 400.00 | 600.00 | 800.00 |
| | 1731 F | 350.00 | 400.00 | 600.00 | 700.00 |
| | Date off flan | 300.00 | 350.00 | 400.00 | 450.00 |

Luis I

| | | | | | |
|---|---|---|---|---|---|
| A54 | ND D | 500.00 | 1000. | 2000. | 3000. |

# 4 ESCUDOS
## ROYAL STRIKES

**Philip V**

Fully struck sample specimens referred to as "Royal" strikes are seldom encountered and are considered rare.

## CIRCULATION STRIKES

**13.5400 g, .917 GOLD, .3992 oz AGW**
**Mint mark: MXo**
Obv. leg: PHILIPVS V DEI G and date
around crowned arms.
Rev: Legend around cross.

| KM# | Date | Good | VG | Fine | VF |
|-----|------|------|------|------|------|
| 55.1 | 1701 L | 700.00 | 800.00 | 1000. | 1500. |
| | 1702 L | 700.00 | 800.00 | 1000. | 1500. |
| | 1703 L | 700.00 | 800.00 | 1000. | 1500. |
| | 1704 L | 700.00 | 800.00 | 1000. | 1500. |
| | 1705 L | 700.00 | 800.00 | 1000. | 1500. |
| | 1706 L | 700.00 | 800.00 | 1000. | 1500. |
| | 1707 L | 700.00 | 800.00 | 1000. | 1500. |
| | 1708 J | 700.00 | 800.00 | 1000. | 1500. |
| | 1709 J | 700.00 | 800.00 | 1000. | 1500. |
| | 1710 J | 700.00 | 800.00 | 1000. | 1500. |
| | 1711 J | 700.00 | 800.00 | 1000. | 1500. |
| | 1712 J | 700.00 | 800.00 | 1000. | 1500. |
| | 1713 J | 700.00 | 800.00 | 1000. | 1500. |
| | Date off flan | 500.00 | 600.00 | 700.00 | 1000. |

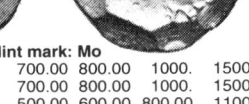

**Mint mark: Mo**

| KM# | Date | Good | VG | Fine | VF |
|-----|------|------|------|------|------|
| 55.2 | 1714 J | 700.00 | 800.00 | 1000. | 1500. |
| | 1720 J | 700.00 | 800.00 | 1000. | 1500. |
| | Date off flan | 500.00 | 600.00 | 800.00 | 1100. |

# 8 ESCUDOS
## ROYAL STRIKES

## ROYAL STRIKES

**Philip V**

Fully struck sample specimens referred to as "Royal" strikes are seldom encountered and are considered rare.

## CIRCULATION STRIKES

**27.0700 g, .917 GOLD, .7980 oz AGW**
**Mint mark: MXo**
Obv. leg: PHILIPVS V DEI G and date
around crowned arms.
Rev: Legend around cross.

| KM# | Date | Good | VG | Fine | VF |
|-----|------|------|------|------|------|
| 57.1 | 1701 L | 1000. | 1500. | 2000. | 2500. |
| | 1702 L | 1000. | 1500. | 2000. | 2500. |
| | 1703 L | 1000. | 1500. | 2000. | 2500. |
| | 1704 L | 1000. | 1500. | 2000. | 2500. |
| | 1705 L | 1000. | 1500. | 2000. | 2500. |
| | 1706 L | 1000. | 1500. | 2000. | 2500. |
| | 1707 L | 1000. | 1500. | 2000. | 2500. |
| | 1708 J | 1000. | 1500. | 2000. | 2500. |
| | 1709 J | 1000. | 1500. | 2000. | 2500. |
| | 1710 J | 1000. | 1500. | 2000. | 2500. |
| | 1711 J | 1000. | 1200. | 1800. | 2500. |
| | 1712 J | 1000. | 1200. | 1800. | 2500. |
| | 1713 J | 600.00 | 900.00 | 1200. | 1800. |
| | Date off flan | 500.00 | 800.00 | 1000. | 1500. |

## ROYAL STRIKES

Fully struck sample specimens referred to as "Royal" strikes are seldom encountered and are considered rare.

## CIRCULATION STRIKES

**Mint mark: Mo**

| KM# | Date | Good | VG | Fine | VF |
|---|---|---|---|---|---|
| 57.2 | 1714 J | 750.00 | 1000. | 1600. | 2250. |
| | 1714 J date on rev. | | | | |
| | | 750.00 | 1000. | 1600. | 2250. |
| | 1715 J | 750.00 | 1000. | 1600. | 2250. |
| | 1717 J | 800.00 | 1200. | 2000. | 3000. |
| | 1718 J | 800.00 | 1200. | 2000. | 3000. |
| | 1720 J | 800.00 | 1200. | 2000. | 3000. |
| | 1723 J | 800.00 | 1200. | 2000. | 3000. |
| | 1728 D | 800.00 | 1200. | 2000. | 3000. |
| | 1729 R | 800.00 | 1200. | 2000. | 3000. |
| | 1730 R | 800.00 | 1200. | 2000. | 3000. |
| | 1730 F | 800.00 | 1200. | 2000. | 3000. |
| | 1731 F | 800.00 | 1200. | 2000. | 3000. |
| | 1732 F | 800.00 | 1200. | 2000. | 3000. |
| | Date off flan | 650.00 | 850.00 | 1100. | 1500. |

**Obv. leg: LVDOVICVS I DEI G and date
around crowned arms.
Rev: Legend around cross.**

| KM# | Date | Good | VG | Fine | VF |
|---|---|---|---|---|---|
| 58 | 1725 D | 3000. | 5000. | 7500. | 12,000. |
| | Date off flan | 1500. | 2500. | 3500. | 5000. |

# COLONIAL MILLED COINAGE

## RULERS

Philip V, 1700-1746
Ferdinand VI, 1746-1759
Charles III, 1760-1788
Charles IV, 1788-1808
Ferdinand VII, 1808-1821

## MINT MARKS

Mo - Mexico City Mint

## ASSAYERS INITIALS

| Letter | Date | Name |
|---|---|---|
| F | 1733-1784 | Francisco de la Pena |
| M | 1733-1763 | Manuel de la Pena |
| M | 1754-1770 | Manuel Assorin |
| F | 1762-1770 | Francisco de Rivera |
| M | 1770-1777 | Manuel de Rivera |
| F | 1777-1803 | Francisco Arance Cobos |
| M | 1784-1801 | Mariano Rodriguez |
| T | 1801-1810 | Tomas Butron Miranda |
| H | 1803-1814 | Henrique Buenaventura Azorin |
| J | 1809-1833 | Joaquin Davila Madrid |
| J | 1812-1833 | Jose Garcia Ansaldo |

## MONETARY SYSTEM

16 Pilones = 1 Real
8 Tlaco = 1 Real
16 Reales = 1 Escudo

## 1/8 (PILON)

(1/16 Real)

**COPPER
Obv: Crowned F VII monogram.
Rev: Castles and lions in wreath.**

| KM# | Date | VG | Fine | VF | XF |
|---|---|---|---|---|---|
| 59 | 1814 | 8.00 | 15.00 | 30.00 | 100.00 |
| | 1815 | 8.00 | 15.00 | 30.00 | 100.00 |

## 1/4 (TLACO)

(1/8 Real)

**COPPER
Obv. leg: FERDIN. VII. . around crowned F.VII.**

| KM# | Date | VG | Fine | VF | XF |
|---|---|---|---|---|---|
| 63 | 1814 | 10.00 | 20.00 | 40.00 | 125.00 |
| | 1815 | 10.00 | 20.00 | 40.00 | 125.00 |
| | 1816 | 10.00 | 20.00 | 40.00 | 125.00 |

## 2/4 (2 TLACO)

(1/4 Real)

**COPPER
Obv. leg: FERDIN. VII. . around crowned F.VII.**

| KM# | Date | VG | Fine | VF | XF |
|---|---|---|---|---|---|
| 64 | 1814 | 6.00 | 12.00 | 25.00 | 100.00 |
| | 1815/4 | 8.00 | 15.00 | 35.00 | 125.00 |
| | 1815 | 6.00 | 12.00 | 25.00 | 100.00 |
| | 1816 | 6.00 | 12.00 | 25.00 | 100.00 |
| | 1821 | 15.00 | 30.00 | 50.00 | 175.00 |

## 1/4 REAL

**.8450 g, .903 SILVER, .0245 oz ASW
Obv: Castle. Rev: Lion.**

| KM# | Date | VG | Fine | VF | XF |
|---|---|---|---|---|---|
| 62 | 1796 | 10.00 | 20.00 | 40.00 | 80.00 |
| | 1797 | 10.00 | 25.00 | 40.00 | 80.00 |
| | 1798 | 12.50 | 20.00 | 35.00 | 60.00 |
| | 1799/8 | 12.50 | 17.50 | 35.00 | 65.00 |
| | 1799 | 10.00 | 15.00 | 27.50 | 60.00 |
| | 1800 | 10.00 | 25.00 | 35.00 | 80.00 |
| | 1801 | 10.00 | 15.00 | 27.50 | 60.00 |
| | 1802 | 12.50 | 20.00 | 27.50 | 60.00 |
| | 1803 | 12.50 | 20.00 | 27.50 | 60.00 |
| | 1804 | 10.00 | 20.00 | 27.50 | 70.00 |
| | 1805/4 | 12.50 | 22.50 | 40.00 | 65.00 |
| | 1805 | 10.00 | 20.00 | 35.00 | 60.00 |
| | 1806 | 10.00 | 20.00 | 35.00 | 70.00 |
| | 1807/797 | 15.00 | 30.00 | 40.00 | 75.00 |
| | 1807 | 12.50 | 25.00 | 35.00 | 70.00 |
| | 1808 | 12.50 | 25.00 | 35.00 | 70.00 |
| | 1809/8 | 12.50 | 25.00 | 35.00 | 70.00 |
| | 1809 | 12.50 | 25.00 | 35.00 | 70.00 |
| | 1810 | 12.50 | 25.00 | 35.00 | 60.00 |
| | 1811 | 12.50 | 25.00 | 35.00 | 60.00 |
| | 1812 | 12.50 | 25.00 | 35.00 | 60.00 |
| | 1813 | 10.00 | 20.00 | 27.50 | 60.00 |
| | 1815 | 10.00 | 20.00 | 35.00 | 60.00 |
| | 1816 | 10.00 | 20.00 | 30.00 | 50.00 |

## 1/2 REAL

**1.6900 g, .917 SILVER, .0498 oz ASW**
**Obv. leg: PHILIP.V.D.G. HISPAN.ET IND. REX.**

| KM# | Date | VG | Fine | VF | XF |
|---|---|---|---|---|---|
| 65 | 1732 | — | — | Rare | — |
| | 1732 F | 500.00 | 800.00 | 1200. | 2000. |
| | 1733 F(MX) | 375.00 | 600.00 | 1000. | 1500. |
| | 1733 MF(MX) | | | | |
| | | 400.00 | 600.00 | 1000. | 1500. |
| | 1733 F | 200.00 | 325.00 | 550.00 | 800.00 |
| | 1733 MF | 300.00 | 400.00 | 600.00 | 800.00 |
| | 1734/3 MF | 10.00 | 25.00 | 35.00 | 60.00 |
| | 1734 MF | 10.00 | 25.00 | 35.00 | 60.00 |
| | 1735/4 MF | 7.50 | 20.00 | 35.00 | 60.00 |
| | 1735 MF | 7.50 | 20.00 | 35.00 | 60.00 |
| | 1736/5 MF | 7.50 | 20.00 | 35.00 | 60.00 |
| | 1736 MF | 7.50 | 20.00 | 35.00 | 60.00 |
| | 1737/6 MF | 7.50 | 20.00 | 35.00 | 60.00 |
| | 1737 MF | 7.50 | 20.00 | 35.00 | 60.00 |
| | 1738/7 MF | 7.50 | 20.00 | 35.00 | 60.00 |
| | 1738 MF | 7.50 | 20.00 | 35.00 | 60.00 |
| | 1739 MF | 7.50 | 20.00 | 35.00 | 60.00 |
| | 1740/30MF | 5.00 | 10.00 | 20.00 | 45.00 |
| | 1740/39MF | 5.00 | 10.00 | 20.00 | 45.00 |
| | 1740 MF | 5.00 | 10.00 | 20.00 | 45.00 |
| | 1741/39MF | 5.00 | 10.00 | 20.00 | 45.00 |
| | 1741/0MF | 5.00 | 10.00 | 20.00 | 45.00 |
| | 1741 MF | 5.00 | 10.00 | 20.00 | 45.00 |

**Obv. leg:.PHS.V.D.G. HISP.ET IND.R.**

| KM# | Date | VG | Fine | VF | XF |
|---|---|---|---|---|---|
| 66 | 1742 M | 5.00 | 10.00 | 20.00 | 45.00 |
| | 1743 M | 5.00 | 10.00 | 20.00 | 45.00 |
| | 1744/3 M | 5.00 | 10.00 | 20.00 | 45.00 |
| | 1744 M | 5.00 | 10.00 | 20.00 | 45.00 |
| | 1745 M | 5.00 | 10.00 | 20.00 | 45.00 |
| | 1746 M | 5.00 | 10.00 | 20.00 | 45.00 |
| | 1747 M | 5.00 | 10.00 | 20.00 | 45.00 |

**Obv. leg: FRD.VI.D.G.HISP.ET IND.R.**

| KM# | Date | VG | Fine | VF | XF |
|---|---|---|---|---|---|
| 67 | 1747/6 M | — | — | — | — |
| | 1747 M | 6.00 | 12.00 | 25.00 | 50.00 |
| | 1748/7 M | 6.00 | 12.00 | 25.00 | 50.00 |
| | 1748 M | 6.00 | 12.00 | 25.00 | 50.00 |
| | 1749 M | 6.00 | 12.00 | 25.00 | 50.00 |
| | 1750 M | 6.00 | 12.00 | 25.00 | 50.00 |
| | 1751 M | 6.00 | 12.00 | 30.00 | 60.00 |
| | 1752 M | 6.00 | 12.00 | 25.00 | 50.00 |
| | 1753 M | 6.00 | 12.00 | 25.00 | 50.00 |
| | 1754 M | 7.50 | 15.00 | 40.00 | 100.00 |
| | 1755/6 M | 6.00 | 12.00 | 25.00 | 50.00 |
| | 1755 M | 6.00 | 12.00 | 25.00 | 50.00 |
| | 1756/5 M | 6.00 | 12.00 | 25.00 | 50.00 |
| | 1756 M | 6.00 | 12.00 | 25.00 | 50.00 |
| | 1757/6 M | 6.00 | 12.00 | 25.00 | 50.00 |
| | 1757 M | 6.00 | 12.00 | 25.00 | 50.00 |
| | 1758/7 M | 6.00 | 12.00 | 25.00 | 50.00 |
| | 1758 M | 6.00 | 12.00 | 25.00 | 50.00 |
| | 1759 M | 6.00 | 12.00 | 25.00 | 50.00 |
| | 1760 M | 7.50 | 15.00 | 30.00 | 60.00 |

**Obv. leg: CAR.III.D.G.HISP.ET IND.R.**

| KM# | Date | VG | Fine | VF | XF |
|---|---|---|---|---|---|
| 68 | 1760 M | 5.00 | 7.50 | 12.50 | 50.00 |
| | 1761 M | 5.00 | 7.50 | 12.50 | 50.00 |
| | 1762 M | 4.00 | 6.00 | 10.00 | 50.00 |
| | 1763/2 M | 5.00 | 7.50 | 12.50 | 55.00 |
| | 1763 M | 4.00 | 6.00 | 10.00 | 50.00 |
| | 1764 M | 5.00 | 7.50 | 12.50 | 50.00 |
| | 1765 M | 5.00 | 7.50 | 12.50 | 50.00 |
| | 1766 M | 5.00 | 7.50 | 12.50 | 50.00 |
| | 1767 M | 7.50 | 13.50 | 27.50 | 65.00 |
| | 1768/6 M | 6.00 | 10.00 | 18.00 | 60.00 |
| | 1768 M | 4.00 | 6.00 | 12.50 | 50.00 |
| | 1769 M | 6.00 | 10.00 | 20.00 | 50.00 |
| | 1770 M | 6.00 | 10.00 | 20.00 | 50.00 |
| | 1770 F | 10.00 | 15.00 | 30.00 | 75.00 |
| | 1771 F | 6.00 | 10.00 | 20.00 | 50.00 |

**1.6900 g, .903 SILVER, .0490 oz ASW**
**Obv. leg: CAROLUS.III.DEI.GRATIA.**
**Rev: Inverted FM and mint mark.**

| KM# | Date | VG | Fine | VF | XF |
|---|---|---|---|---|---|
| 69.1 | 1772 FM | 3.00 | 6.50 | 12.50 | 60.00 |
| | 1773 FM | 3.00 | 5.00 | 10.00 | 50.00 |

**Rev: Normal initials and mint mark.**

| KM# | Date | VG | Fine | VF | XF |
|---|---|---|---|---|---|
| 69.2 | 1772 FF | 6.00 | 10.00 | 20.00 | 75.00 |
| | 1773 FM | 3.00 | 5.00 | 10.00 | 50.00 |
| | 1773 FM (error) CAROLS | | | | |
| | | 300.00 | — | — | — |
| | 1774 FM | 3.00 | 5.00 | 10.00 | 50.00 |
| | 1775 FM | 3.00 | 5.00 | 10.00 | 50.00 |
| | 1776 FM | 3.00 | 5.00 | 10.00 | 50.00 |
| | 1777 FM | 6.00 | 10.00 | 20.00 | 60.00 |
| | 1778 FF | 4.50 | 9.00 | 18.50 | 50.00 |
| | 1779 FF | 3.00 | 5.00 | 10.00 | 50.00 |
| | 1780/g FF | 3.00 | 5.00 | 10.00 | 50.00 |
| | 1780 FF | 3.00 | 5.00 | 10.00 | 50.00 |
| | 1781 FF | 2.50 | 4.00 | 8.50 | 50.00 |
| | 1782/1 FF | 5.00 | 10.00 | 20.00 | 75.00 |
| | 1782 FF | 3.00 | 5.00 | 10.00 | 50.00 |
| | 1783 FF | 3.00 | 5.00 | 10.00 | 50.00 |
| | 1783 FM | 125.00 | 300.00 | 450.00 | — |
| | 1784 FF | 3.00 | 5.00 | 10.00 | 50.00 |
| | 1784 FM | 6.00 | 10.00 | 20.00 | 75.00 |
| | 1785 FM | 3.50 | 6.00 | 13.50 | 50.00 |
| | 1786 FM | 3.00 | 5.00 | 10.00 | 50.00 |
| | 1787 FM | 3.00 | 5.00 | 10.00 | 50.00 |
| | 1788 FM | 3.00 | 5.00 | 10.00 | 50.00 |
| | 1789 FM | 6.00 | 10.00 | 30.00 | 100.00 |

**Obv: Armored bust of Charles III, leg: .CAROLUS.IV.**

| KM# | Date | VG | Fine | VF | XF |
|---|---|---|---|---|---|
| 70 | 1789 FM | 6.00 | 10.00 | 20.00 | 90.00 |
| | 1790 FM | 6.00 | 10.00 | 20.00 | 90.00 |

**Obv: Armored bust of Charles III, leg: .CAROLUS.IIII.**

| KM# | Date | VG | Fine | VF | XF |
|---|---|---|---|---|---|
| 71 | 1790 FM | 6.00 | 10.00 | 20.00 | 90.00 |

## 1/2 REAL

**Obv: Armored bust of Charles IIII.**
**Rev: Pillars and arms.**

| KM# | Date | VG | Fine | VF | XF |
|---|---|---|---|---|---|
| 72 | 1792 FM | 6.00 | 10.00 | 20.00 | 45.00 |
| | 1793 FM | 6.00 | 10.00 | 20.00 | 45.00 |
| | 1794/3 FM | 7.50 | 12.50 | 25.00 | 75.00 |
| | 1794 FM | 5.00 | 6.00 | 10.00 | 45.00 |
| | 1795 FM | 4.00 | 6.00 | 10.00 | 45.00 |
| | 1796 FM | 4.00 | 6.00 | 10.00 | 45.00 |
| | 1797 FM | 4.00 | 6.00 | 10.00 | 45.00 |
| | 1798/7 FM | 4.50 | 6.50 | 11.50 | 50.00 |
| | 1798 FM | 4.00 | 6.00 | 10.00 | 45.00 |
| | 1799 FM | 4.00 | 6.00 | 10.00 | 45.00 |
| | 1800/799 FM | 4.50 | 7.50 | 10.00 | 50.00 |
| | 1800 FM | 4.00 | 6.50 | 7.50 | 45.00 |
| | 1800 FT | — | — | — | — |

**Obv: Armored bust of Charles IIII.**
**Rev: Pillars and arms.**

| KM# | Date | VG | Fine | VF | XF |
|---|---|---|---|---|---|
| 72 | 1801 FM | 6.50 | 10.00 | 20.00 | 75.00 |
| | 1801 FT | 4.00 | 6.00 | 10.00 | 45.00 |
| | 1802 FT | 4.00 | 6.00 | 10.00 | 45.00 |
| | 1803 FT | 5.00 | 9.00 | 15.00 | 45.00 |
| | 1804 TH | 4.00 | 6.00 | 10.00 | 45.00 |
| | 1805 TH | 4.00 | 6.00 | 10.00 | 45.00 |
| | 1806 TH | 4.00 | 6.00 | 10.00 | 45.00 |
| | 1807/6 TH | 4.50 | 6.50 | 11.50 | 50.00 |
| | 1807 TH | 4.00 | 6.00 | 10.00 | 45.00 |
| | 1808/7 TH | 4.50 | 6.50 | 11.50 | 50.00 |
| | 1808 TH | 4.00 | 6.00 | 10.00 | 45.00 |

**Obv: Armored bust of Ferdinand VII.**

| KM# | Date | VG | Fine | VF | XF |
|---|---|---|---|---|---|
| 73 | 1808 TH | 3.00 | 5.00 | 10.00 | 30.00 |
| | 1809 TH | 3.00 | 5.00 | 10.00 | 30.00 |
| | 1810 TH | 5.00 | 8.00 | 12.00 | 35.00 |
| | 1810 HJ | 3.00 | 5.00 | 10.00 | 30.00 |
| | 1811 HJ | 3.00 | 5.00 | 10.00 | 30.00 |
| | 1812 HJ | 3.00 | 5.00 | 10.00 | 30.00 |
| | 1813 TH | 3.50 | 6.00 | 10.00 | 30.00 |
| | 1813 JJ | 10.00 | 20.00 | 40.00 | 100.00 |
| | 1813 HJ | 7.50 | 15.00 | 30.00 | 90.00 |
| | 1814 JJ | 5.00 | 8.00 | 12.00 | 35.00 |

**Obv: Draped bust of Ferdinand VII.**

| KM# | Date | VG | Fine | VF | XF |
|---|---|---|---|---|---|
| 74 | 1814 JJ | 3.00 | 5.00 | 12.00 | 45.00 |
| | 1815 JJ | 3.00 | 5.00 | 10.00 | 40.00 |
| | 1816 JJ | 3.00 | 5.00 | 10.00 | 40.00 |
| | 1817/6 JJ | — | — | — | — |
| | 1817 JJ | 3.00 | 5.00 | 12.00 | 45.00 |
| | 1818/7 JJ | 3.00 | 5.00 | 15.00 | 50.00 |
| | 1818 JJ | 3.00 | 5.00 | 15.00 | 50.00 |
| | 1819 JJ | 3.00 | 5.00 | 10.00 | 40.00 |
| | 1820 JJ | 3.00 | 5.00 | 15.00 | 50.00 |
| | 1821 JJ | 3.00 | 5.00 | 10.00 | 40.00 |

## REAL

**3.3800 g, .917 SILVER, .0996 oz ASW**
**Obv. leg: PHILIP.V.D.G.HISPAN.ET IND.REX.**

| KM# | Date | VG | Fine | VF | XF |
|---|---|---|---|---|---|
| 75.1 | 1732 | — | — | Rare | — |
| (75) | 1732 F | 125.00 | 225.00 | 350.00 | 500.00 |
| | 1733 F(MX) | 150.00 | 300.00 | 425.00 | 600.00 |
| | 1733/2 MF(MX) | | | | |
| | | 150.00 | 350.00 | 425.00 | 600.00 |
| | 1733 MF(MX) | 150.00 | 350.00 | 425.00 | 600.00 |
| | 1733 F | — | — | Rare | — |
| | 1733 MF | 85.00 | 150.00 | 225.00 | 325.00 |
| | 1734/3 MF | 15.00 | 30.00 | 60.00 | 125.00 |
| | 1734 MF | 12.00 | 25.00 | 50.00 | 150.00 |
| | 1735 MF | 12.00 | 25.00 | 50.00 | 150.00 |
| | 1736 MF | 12.00 | 20.00 | 50.00 | 150.00 |
| | 1737 MF | 12.00 | 20.00 | 50.00 | 150.00 |
| | 1738 MF | 12.00 | 20.00 | 50.00 | 150.00 |
| | 1739 MF | 12.00 | 20.00 | 50.00 | 150.00 |
| | 1740 MF | 12.00 | 20.00 | 50.00 | 150.00 |
| | 1741 MF | 12.00 | 20.00 | 50.00 | 150.00 |

**Obv. leg: PHS.V.D.G.HISP.ET.IND.R.**

| KM# | Date | VG | Fine | VF | XF |
|---|---|---|---|---|---|
| 75.2 | 1742 M | 8.00 | 15.00 | 30.00 | 60.00 |
| (75.1) | 1743 M | 8.00 | 15.00 | 30.00 | 90.00 |
| | 1744/3 M | 8.00 | 15.00 | 30.00 | 90.00 |
| | 1744 M | 8.00 | 15.00 | 30.00 | 90.00 |
| | 1745 M | 8.00 | 15.00 | 30.00 | 60.00 |
| | 1746/5 M | 10.00 | 20.00 | 60.00 | 200.00 |
| | 1746 M | 10.00 | 20.00 | 60.00 | 200.00 |
| | 1747 M | 8.00 | 15.00 | 35.00 | 90.00 |

**Obv. leg: .FRD.VI.D.G.HISP.ET IND.R.**

| KM# | Date | VG | Fine | VF | XF |
|---|---|---|---|---|---|
| 76 | 1747 M | 8.00 | 15.00 | 30.00 | 60.00 |
| | 1748/7 M | 8.00 | 15.00 | 30.00 | 60.00 |
| | 1748 M | 8.00 | 15.00 | 30.00 | 60.00 |
| | 1749/8 M | 8.00 | 15.00 | 30.00 | 60.00 |
| | 1749 M | 8.00 | 15.00 | 30.00 | 60.00 |
| | 1750/49 M | 8.00 | 15.00 | 30.00 | 60.00 |
| | 1750 M | 8.00 | 15.00 | 30.00 | 60.00 |
| | 1751 M | 10.00 | 20.00 | 40.00 | 80.00 |
| | 1752 M | 8.00 | 15.00 | 30.00 | 60.00 |
| | 1753 M | 8.00 | 15.00 | 30.00 | 60.00 |
| | 1754 M | 10.00 | 20.00 | 40.00 | 80.00 |
| | 1755/4 M | 8.00 | 15.00 | 30.00 | 60.00 |
| | 1755 M | 8.00 | 15.00 | 30.00 | 60.00 |
| | 1756 M | 10.00 | 20.00 | 40.00 | 80.00 |
| | 1757 M | 10.00 | 20.00 | 40.00 | 80.00 |
| | 1758/5 M | 8.00 | 15.00 | 30.00 | 60.00 |
| | 1758 M | 8.00 | 15.00 | 30.00 | 60.00 |
| | 1759 M | 10.00 | 20.00 | 40.00 | 80.00 |
| | 1760 M | 10.00 | 20.00 | 40.00 | 80.00 |

**Obv. leg: CAR.III.D.G.HISP.ET IND.R.**

| KM# | Date | VG | Fine | VF | XF |
|---|---|---|---|---|---|
| 77 | 1760 M | 8.00 | 12.00 | 20.00 | 60.00 |
| | 1761 M | 6.00 | 9.00 | 17.50 | 50.00 |
| | 1762 M | 6.00 | 9.00 | 17.50 | 50.00 |
| | 1763/2 M | 7.00 | 10.00 | 17.50 | 50.00 |
| | 1763 M | 6.00 | 9.00 | 17.50 | 50.00 |
| | 1764 M | 10.00 | 15.00 | 50.00 | 100.00 |
| | 1765 M | 10.00 | 15.00 | 50.00 | 100.00 |
| | 1766 M | 6.00 | 9.00 | 17.50 | 50.00 |
| | 1767 M | 10.00 | 15.00 | 50.00 | 100.00 |
| | 1768 M | 6.00 | 9.00 | 17.50 | 50.00 |
| | 1769 M | 6.00 | 9.00 | 17.50 | 50.00 |
| | 1770/69M | 6.00 | 9.00 | 15.00 | 80.00 |
| | 1770 M | 6.00 | 9.00 | 15.00 | 80.00 |
| | 1770 F | 20.00 | 40.00 | 90.00 | 250.00 |
| | 1771 F | 20.00 | 40.00 | 90.00 | 250.00 |

**3.3800 g, .903 SILVER, .0981 oz ASW**
**Obv. leg: CAROLUS.III.DEI.GRATIA.**
**Rev: Inverted FM and mint mark.**

| KM# | Date | VG | Fine | VF | XF |
|---|---|---|---|---|---|
| 78.1 | 1772 FM | 3.00 | 7.50 | 12.50 | 60.00 |
|  | 1773 FM | 3.00 | 7.50 | 12.50 | 60.00 |

**Rev: Normal initials and mint mark.**

| KM# | Date | VG | Fine | VF | XF |
|---|---|---|---|---|---|
| 78.2 | 1773 FM | 6.50 | 12.50 | 30.00 | 90.00 |
|  | 1774 FM | 3.00 | 7.50 | 12.50 | 60.00 |
|  | 1775 FM | 3.00 | 7.50 | 12.50 | 60.00 |
|  | 1776 FM | 3.00 | 7.50 | 12.50 | 60.00 |
|  | 1777 FM | 3.00 | 7.50 | 12.50 | 60.00 |
|  | 1778 FF | 3.00 | 7.50 | 12.50 | 60.00 |
|  | 1779 FF | 3.00 | 8.50 | 15.50 | 60.00 |
|  | 1780 FF | 3.00 | 7.50 | 12.50 | 60.00 |
|  | 1781 FF | 3.00 | 7.50 | 12.50 | 60.00 |
|  | 1782 FF | 3.00 | 7.50 | 12.50 | 60.00 |
|  | 1783 FF | 3.00 | 8.50 | 15.00 | 60.00 |
|  | 1784 FF | 3.00 | 8.50 | 15.00 | 60.00 |
|  | 1785 FM | 3.00 | 7.50 | 12.50 | 60.00 |
|  | 1785 FF | 3.00 | 8.50 | 13.50 | 60.00 |
|  | 1786 FM | 3.00 | 7.50 | 12.50 | 60.00 |
|  | 1787 FM | 12.00 | 25.00 | 50.00 | 125.00 |
|  | 1787 FF | 10.00 | 20.00 | 40.00 | 100.00 |
|  | 1788 FM | 3.00 | 9.00 | 15.00 | 60.00 |
|  | 1788 FF | 3.00 | 7.50 | 12.50 | 60.00 |
|  | 1789 FM | 5.00 | 10.00 | 20.00 | 75.00 |

**Obv: Armored bust of Charles III, leg: CAROLUS.IV. .**

| KM# | Date | VG | Fine | VF | XF |
|---|---|---|---|---|---|
| 79 | 1789 FM | 8.00 | 15.00 | 25.00 | 100.00 |
|  | 1790 FM | 8.00 | 15.00 | 25.00 | 100.00 |

**Obv: Armored bust of Charles III; leg: CAROLUS.IIII.**

| KM# | Date | VG | Fine | VF | XF |
|---|---|---|---|---|---|
| 80 | 1790 FM | 10.00 | 20.00 | 35.00 | 125.00 |

**Obv: Armored bust of Charles IIII.**

| KM# | Date | VG | Fine | VF | XF |
|---|---|---|---|---|---|
| 81 | 1792 FM | 10.00 | 20.00 | 30.00 | 90.00 |
|  | 1793 FM | 15.00 | 30.00 | 50.00 | 150.00 |
|  | 1794 FM | 25.00 | 50.00 | 90.00 | 250.00 |
|  | 1795 FM | 15.00 | 30.00 | 50.00 | 150.00 |
|  | 1796 FM | 3.50 | 8.50 | 13.50 | 65.00 |
|  | 1797/6 FM | 5.00 | 10.00 | 20.00 | 80.00 |
|  | 1797 FM | 3.00 | 7.50 | 12.50 | 60.00 |
|  | 1798/7 FM | 3.50 | 8.50 | 13.50 | 65.00 |
|  | 1798 FM | 3.00 | 7.50 | 12.50 | 60.00 |
|  | 1799 FM | 3.00 | 7.50 | 13.50 | 60.00 |
|  | 1800 FM | 3.00 | 7.50 | 13.50 | 60.00 |

| KM# | Date | VG | Fine | VF | XF |
|---|---|---|---|---|---|
| 81 | 1801 FM | 8.00 | 15.00 | 25.00 | 80.00 |
|  | 1801 FT | 3.00 | 8.50 | 16.50 | 60.00 |
|  | 1802 FM | 3.00 | 8.50 | 16.50 | 60.00 |
|  | 1802 FT | 3.00 | 7.50 | 12.50 | 60.00 |
|  | 1803 FT | 3.00 | 8.50 | 16.50 | 60.00 |
|  | 1804 TH | 3.00 | 7.50 | 12.50 | 60.00 |
|  | 1805 TH | 3.00 | 8.50 | 16.50 | 60.00 |
|  | 1806 TH | 3.00 | 7.50 | 12.50 | 60.00 |
|  | 1807/6 TH | 3.50 | 8.50 | 13.50 | 65.00 |
|  | 1807 TH | 3.00 | 7.50 | 12.50 | 60.00 |
|  | 1808/7 TH | 3.50 | 8.50 | 13.50 | 65.00 |
|  | 1808 TH | 3.00 | 7.50 | 12.50 | 60.00 |

| KM# | Date | VG | Fine | VF | XF |
|---|---|---|---|---|---|
| 82 | 1809 TH | 4.00 | 7.50 | 15.00 | 100.00 |
|  | 1810/09 TH | 4.00 | 7.50 | 15.00 | 100.00 |
|  | 1810 TH | 4.00 | 7.50 | 15.00 | 100.00 |
|  | 1810 HJ | 6.00 | 10.00 | 20.00 | 125.00 |
|  | 1811 HJ | 4.00 | 7.50 | 15.00 | 100.00 |
|  | 1811 TH | 25.00 | 35.00 | 60.00 | 250.00 |
|  | 1812 HJ | 4.00 | 7.50 | 15.00 | 80.00 |
|  | 1812 JJ | 6.00 | 10.00 | 20.00 | 125.00 |
|  | 1813 HJ | 5.50 | 8.50 | 17.50 | 125.00 |
|  | 1813 JJ | 50.00 | 100.00 | 150.00 | 250.00 |
|  | 1814 HJ | 50.00 | 100.00 | 175.00 | 300.00 |
|  | 1814 JJ | 50.00 | 100.00 | 175.00 | 300.00 |

**Obv: Draped bust of Ferdinand VII.**

| KM# | Date | VG | Fine | VF | XF |
|---|---|---|---|---|---|
| 83 | 1814 JJ | 25.00 | 50.00 | 100.00 | 350.00 |
|  | 1815 JJ | 5.50 | 8.50 | 17.50 | 125.00 |
|  | 1815 HJ | 15.00 | 30.00 | 60.00 | 150.00 |
|  | 1816 JJ | 4.00 | 7.50 | 12.50 | 75.00 |
|  | 1817 JJ | 4.00 | 7.50 | 12.50 | 75.00 |
|  | 1818 JJ | 30.00 | 60.00 | 125.00 | 500.00 |
|  | 1819 JJ | 5.50 | 8.50 | 17.50 | 75.00 |
|  | 1820 JJ | 5.00 | 8.50 | 17.50 | 75.00 |
|  | 1821/0 JJ | 7.50 | 12.50 | 27.50 | 110.00 |
|  | 1821 JJ | 5.00 | 8.50 | 12.50 | 50.00 |

## 2 REALES

**6.7700 g, .917 SILVER, .1996 oz ASW**
**Obv. leg: PHILIP.V.D.G.HISPAN.ET IND. REX.**

| KM# | Date | VG | Fine | VF | XF |
|---|---|---|---|---|---|
| 84 | 1732 F | 800.00 | 1200. | 1600. | 2500. |
|  | 1733 F(MX) | 500.00 | 750.00 | 1200. | 2000. |
|  | 1733 F | 500.00 | 675.00 | 1000. | 1750. |
|  | 1733 MF(MX) |  |  |  |  |
|  |  | 350.00 | 600.00 | 1000. | 1500. |
|  | 1733 MF | 500.00 | 750.00 | 1200. | 2000. |
|  | 1734/3 MF | 20.00 | 40.00 | 80.00 | 150.00 |
|  | 1734 MF | 20.00 | 40.00 | 80.00 | 150.00 |
|  | 1735/3 MF | 10.00 | 20.00 | 40.00 | 90.00 |
|  | 1735/4 MF | 10.00 | 20.00 | 40.00 | 90.00 |
|  | 1735 MF | 10.00 | 20.00 | 40.00 | 90.00 |
|  | 1736/3 MF | 15.00 | 30.00 | 60.00 | 125.00 |
|  | 1736/4 MF | 15.00 | 30.00 | 60.00 | 125.00 |

| KM# | Date | VG | Fine | VF | XF |
|-----|------|-----|------|-----|-----|
| 84 | 1736/5 MF | 15.00 | 30.00 | 60.00 | 125.00 |
| | 1736 MF | 15.00 | 30.00 | 60.00 | 125.00 |
| | 1737/3 MF | 15.00 | 30.00 | 60.00 | 125.00 |
| | 1737 MF | 15.00 | 30.00 | 60.00 | 125.00 |
| | 1738/7 MF | 15.00 | 30.00 | 60.00 | 125.00 |
| | 1738 MF | 15.00 | 30.00 | 60.00 | 125.00 |
| | 1739 MF | 15.00 | 30.00 | 60.00 | 125.00 |
| | 1740/30 MF | 15.00 | 30.00 | 60.00 | 125.00 |
| | 1740 MF | 15.00 | 30.00 | 60.00 | 125.00 |
| | 1741 MF | 15.00 | 30.00 | 60.00 | 125.00 |

**Obv. leg: PHS.V.D.G.HISP.ET IND.R.**

| KM# | Date | VG | Fine | VF | XF |
|-----|------|-----|------|-----|-----|
| 85 | 1742 M | 10.00 | 20.00 | 50.00 | 100.00 |
| | 1743/2 M | 10.00 | 20.00 | 50.00 | 100.00 |
| | 1743 M | 10.00 | 20.00 | 50.00 | 100.00 |
| | 1744/2 M | 10.00 | 20.00 | 50.00 | 100.00 |
| | 1744/3 M | 10.00 | 20.00 | 50.00 | 100.00 |
| | 1744 M | 10.00 | 20.00 | 50.00 | 100.00 |
| | 1745/4 M | 10.00 | 20.00 | 50.00 | 100.00 |
| | 1745 M | 10.00 | 20.00 | 50.00 | 100.00 |
| | 1746 M | 10.00 | 20.00 | 50.00 | 100.00 |
| | 1747 M | 10.00 | 20.00 | 50.00 | 100.00 |
| | 1749 M | 150.00 | 225.00 | 300.00 | 600.00 |
| | 1750 M | 150.00 | 225.00 | 300.00 | 600.00 |

**Obv. leg: FRD.VI.D.G.HISP.ET IND.R.**

| KM# | Date | VG | Fine | VF | XF |
|-----|------|-----|------|-----|-----|
| 86 | 1747 M | 12.00 | 25.00 | 45.00 | 125.00 |
| | 1748/7 M | 12.00 | 25.00 | 45.00 | 125.00 |
| | 1748 M | 10.00 | 20.00 | 30.00 | 100.00 |
| | 1749 M | 10.00 | 20.00 | 30.00 | 100.00 |
| | 1750 M | 10.00 | 20.00 | 30.00 | 100.00 |
| | 1751/41 M | 12.00 | 25.00 | 45.00 | 125.00 |
| | 1751 M | 10.00 | 20.00 | 30.00 | 100.00 |
| | 1752 M | 10.00 | 20.00 | 30.00 | 100.00 |
| | 1753/2 M | 12.00 | 25.00 | 60.00 | 150.00 |
| | 1753 M | 12.00 | 25.00 | 60.00 | 150.00 |
| | 1754 M | 12.00 | 25.00 | 60.00 | 150.00 |
| | 1755 M | 12.00 | 25.00 | 60.00 | 150.00 |
| | 1756 M | 12.00 | 25.00 | 60.00 | 150.00 |
| | 1757/6 M | 10.00 | 20.00 | 30.00 | 100.00 |
| | 1757 M | 10.00 | 20.00 | 30.00 | 100.00 |
| | 1758 M | 10.00 | 20.00 | 30.00 | 100.00 |
| | 1759/8 M | 10.00 | 20.00 | 30.00 | 100.00 |
| | 1759 M | 10.00 | 20.00 | 30.00 | 100.00 |
| | 1760 M | 15.00 | 25.00 | 45.00 | 100.00 |

**Obv. leg: CAR.III.D.G.HISP.ET IND.R.**

| KM# | Date | VG | Fine | VF | XF |
|-----|------|-----|------|-----|-----|
| 87 | 1760 M | 10.00 | 20.00 | 50.00 | 100.00 |
| | 1761 M | 10.00 | 20.00 | 50.00 | 100.00 |

| KM# | Date | VG | Fine | VF | XF |
|-----|------|-----|------|-----|-----|
| 87 | 1762 M | 10.00 | 20.00 | 50.00 | 100.00 |
| | 1763/2 M | 10.00 | 20.00 | 50.00 | 100.00 |
| | 1763 M | 10.00 | 20.00 | 50.00 | 100.00 |
| | 1764 M | 10.00 | 20.00 | 50.00 | 100.00 |
| | 1765 M | 10.00 | 20.00 | 50.00 | 100.00 |
| | 1766 M | 12.00 | 25.00 | 70.00 | 150.00 |
| | 1767 M | 7.50 | 15.00 | 30.00 | 100.00 |
| | 1768/6 M | 7.50 | 15.00 | 30.00 | 80.00 |
| | 1768 M | 7.50 | 15.00 | 30.00 | 80.00 |
| | 1769 M | 7.50 | 15.00 | 35.00 | 100.00 |
| | 1770 M | — | — | Rare | — |
| | 1770 F | — | — | Rare | — |
| | 1771 F | 7.50 | 15.00 | 30.00 | 80.00 |

**6.7700 g, .903 SILVER, .1965 oz ASW**
**Obv. leg: CAROLUS.III.DEI.GRATIA.**
**Rev: Inverted FM and mint mark.**

| KM# | Date | VG | Fine | VF | XF |
|-----|------|-----|------|-----|-----|
| 88.1 | 1772 FM | 5.00 | 10.00 | 15.00 | 100.00 |
| | 1773 FM | 5.00 | 10.00 | 15.00 | 100.00 |

**Rev: Normal initials and mint mark.**

| KM# | Date | VG | Fine | VF | XF |
|-----|------|-----|------|-----|-----|
| 88.2 | 1773 FM | 5.00 | 10.00 | 15.00 | 100.00 |
| | 1774 FM | 5.00 | 10.00 | 15.00 | 100.00 |
| | 1775 FM | 5.00 | 10.00 | 15.00 | 100.00 |
| | 1776 FM | 5.00 | 10.00 | 15.00 | 100.00 |
| | 1777 FM | 5.00 | 10.00 | 15.00 | 100.00 |
| | 1778 FF | 5.00 | 10.00 | 15.00 | 100.00 |
| | 1779 FF | 5.00 | 10.00 | 15.00 | 100.00 |
| | 1780 FF | 5.00 | 10.00 | 15.00 | 100.00 |
| | 1781 FF | 5.00 | 10.00 | 15.00 | 100.00 |
| | 1782 FF | 5.00 | 10.00 | 15.00 | 100.00 |
| | 1783 FF | 5.00 | 10.00 | 15.00 | 100.00 |
| | 1784 FF | 5.00 | 10.00 | 15.00 | 100.00 |
| | 1784 FF (error) DEI GRTIA | | | | |
| | | 100.00 | 150.00 | 250.00 | 600.00 |
| | 1784 FM | 100.00 | 150.00 | 250.00 | 600.00 |
| | 1785 FM | 5.00 | 10.00 | 15.00 | 100.00 |
| | 1786 FM | 5.00 | 10.00 | 15.00 | 100.00 |
| | 1786 FF | 100.00 | 150.00 | 250.00 | 600.00 |
| | 1787 FM | 5.00 | 10.00 | 15.00 | 100.00 |
| | 1788 FM | 5.00 | 10.00 | 15.00 | 100.00 |
| | 1789 FM | 11.50 | 25.00 | 40.00 | 150.00 |

**Obv: Armored bust of Charles III; leg: CAROLUS.IV. .**

| KM# | Date | VG | Fine | VF | XF |
|-----|------|-----|------|-----|-----|
| 89 | 1789 FM | 11.50 | 25.00 | 40.00 | 150.00 |
| | 1790 FM | 11.50 | 25.00 | 40.00 | 150.00 |

**Obv: Armored bust of Charles III, leg: CAROLUS.IIII.**

| KM# | Date | VG | Fine | VF | XF |
|-----|------|-----|------|-----|-----|
| 90 | 1790 FM | 12.50 | 27.50 | 60.00 | 200.00 |

**6.7700 g, .903 SILVER, .1965 oz ASW**
**Obv: Armored bust of Carolus IIII.**

| KM# | Date | VG | Fine | VF | XF |
|---|---|---|---|---|---|
| 91 | 1792 FM | 15.00 | 30.00 | 60.00 | 200.00 |
| | 1793 FM | 15.00 | 30.00 | 60.00 | 200.00 |
| | 1794/3 FM | 50.00 | 100.00 | 200.00 | 450.00 |
| | 1794 FM | 40.00 | 75.00 | 150.00 | 400.00 |
| | 1795 FM | 5.00 | 10.00 | 15.00 | 100.00 |
| | 1796 FM | 5.00 | 10.00 | 15.00 | 100.00 |
| | 1797 FM | 5.00 | 10.00 | 15.00 | 100.00 |
| | 1798 FM | 5.00 | 10.00 | 15.00 | 100.00 |
| | 1799/8 FM | 5.50 | 11.50 | 16.50 | 110.00 |
| | 1799 FM | 5.00 | 10.00 | 15.00 | 100.00 |
| | 1800 FM | 5.00 | 10.00 | 15.00 | 100.00 |
| | 1801 FT | 5.00 | 10.00 | 15.00 | 100.00 |
| | 1801 FM | 20.00 | 40.00 | 75.00 | 250.00 |
| | 1802 FT | 5.00 | 10.00 | 15.00 | 100.00 |
| | 1803 FT | 5.00 | 10.00 | 15.00 | 100.00 |
| | 1804 TH | 5.00 | 10.00 | 15.00 | 100.00 |
| | 1805 TH | 5.00 | 10.00 | 15.00 | 100.00 |
| | 1806/5 TH | 5.50 | 11.50 | 16.50 | 110.00 |
| | 1806 TH | 5.00 | 10.00 | 15.00 | 100.00 |
| | 1807/5 TH | 5.50 | 11.50 | 16.50 | 110.00 |
| | 1807/6 TH | 15.00 | 30.00 | 60.00 | 200.00 |
| | 1807 TH | 5.00 | 10.00 | 15.00 | 100.00 |
| | 1808/7 TH | 5.50 | 11.5Q | 16.50 | 110.00 |
| | 1808 TH | 5.00 | 10.00 | 15.00 | 100.00 |

**Obv: Armored bust of Ferdinand VII.**

| | | | | | |
|---|---|---|---|---|---|
| 92 | 1809 TH | 6.50 | 12.50 | 45.00 | 150.00 |
| | 1810 TH | 6.50 | 12.50 | 45.00 | 150.00 |
| | 1810 HJ | 6.50 | 12.50 | 45.00 | 150.00 |
| | 1811 HJ | 6.50 | 12.50 | 45.00 | 150.00 |
| | 1811 HJ/TH | 40.00 | 80.00 | 150.00 | 300.00 |
| | 1811 TH | 100.00 | 200.00 | 300.00 | 750.00 |

**Obv: Draped bust of Ferdinand VII.**

| | | | | | |
|---|---|---|---|---|---|
| 93 | 1812 HJ | 15.00 | 30.00 | 100.00 | 300.00 |
| | 1812 TH | 60.00 | 125.00 | 250.00 | 500.00 |
| | 1812 JJ | 10.00 | 20.00 | 60.00 | 200.00 |
| | 1813 HJ | 40.00 | 100.00 | 200.00 | 500.00 |
| | 1813 JJ | 20.00 | 60.00 | 125.00 | 350.00 |
| | 1813 TH | 15.00 | 30.00 | 100.00 | 400.00 |
| | 1814/13 JJ | 15.00 | 30.00 | 100.00 | 400.00 |
| | 1814 JJ | 15.00 | 30.00 | 100.00 | 400.00 |
| | 1815 JJ | 5.00 | 10.00 | 30.00 | 100.00 |
| | 1816 JJ | 5.00 | 10.00 | 30.00 | 100.00 |
| | 1817 JJ | 5.00 | 10.00 | 30.00 | 100.00 |
| | 1818 JJ | 5.00 | 10.00 | 30.00 | 100.00 |

| KM# | Date | VG | Fine | VF | XF |
|---|---|---|---|---|---|
| 93 | 1819 JJ | 5.00 | 10.00 | 30.00 | 100.00 |
| | 1820 JJ | 125.00 | — | — | — |
| | 1821/0 JJ | 5.00 | 10.00 | 30.00 | 110.00 |
| | 1821 JJ | 5.00 | 10.00 | 30.00 | 100.00 |

# 4 REALES

**13.5400 g, .917 SILVER, .3992 oz ASW**
**Obv. leg: PHILLIP.V.D.G.HISPAN.ET IND.REX**

| | | | | | |
|---|---|---|---|---|---|
| 94 | 1732 | — | — | Rare Specimen | |
| | 1732 F | 2000. | 3000. | 5000. | 10,000. |
| | 1733 F | 1500. | 2000. | 4000. | 6000. |
| | 1733 MF | 1200. | 1800. | 2500. | 4000. |
| | 1733 MF(MX) | 1500. | 2200. | 3250. | 5000. |
| | 1733 F(MX) | 1500. | 2500. | 3500. | 6000. |
| | 1734/3 MF | 150.00 | 300.00 | 600.00 | 1200. |
| | 1734 MF | 150.00 | 300.00 | 600.00 | 1200. |
| | 1735 MF | 100.00 | 200.00 | 300.00 | 500.00 |
| | 1736 MF | 100.00 | 200.00 | 300.00 | 500.00 |
| | 1737 MF | 100.00 | 200.00 | 300.00 | 500.00 |
| | 1738/7 MF | 100.00 | 200.00 | 300.00 | 500.00 |
| | 1738 MF | 100.00 | 200.00 | 300.00 | 500.00 |
| | 1739 MF | 100.00 | 200.00 | 300.00 | 500.00 |
| | 1740/30 MF | 100.00 | 200.00 | 300.00 | 600.00 |
| | 1740 MF | 100.00 | 200.00 | 300.00 | 500.00 |
| | 1741 MF | 100.00 | 200.00 | 300.00 | 500.00 |
| | 1742/1 MF | 100.00 | 200.00 | 300.00 | 500.00 |
| | 1742 MF | 100.00 | 200.00 | 300.00 | 500.00 |
| | 1743 MF | 100.00 | 200.00 | 300.00 | 500.00 |
| | 1744/3 MF | 100.00 | 200.00 | 300.00 | 600.00 |
| | 1744 MF | 100.00 | 200.00 | 300.00 | 500.00 |
| | 1745 MF | 100.00 | 200.00 | 300.00 | 500.00 |
| | 1746 MP | 100.00 | 200.00 | 300.00 | 500.00 |
| | 1747 MF | 150.00 | 275.00 | 400.00 | 650.00 |

**Obv. leg: FERDND.VI.D.G.HISPAN.ET IND.REX**

| | | | | | |
|---|---|---|---|---|---|
| 95 | 1747 MF | 100.00 | 150.00 | 300.00 | 500.00 |
| | 1748/7 MF | 100.00 | 150.00 | 300.00 | 500.00 |
| | 1748 MF | 100.00 | 125.00 | 250.00 | 450.00 |
| | 1749 MF | 150.00 | 225.00 | 350.00 | 650.00 |
| | 1750/40 MF | 100.00 | 125.00 | 250.00 | 400.00 |
| | 1750 MF | 100.00 | 125.00 | 250.00 | 450.00 |
| | 1751 MF | 100.00 | 125.00 | 250.00 | 450.00 |
| | 1752 MF | 100.00 | 125.00 | 250.00 | 450.00 |
| | 1753 MF | 100.00 | 125.00 | 300.00 | 500.00 |
| | 1754 MM | 250.00 | 375.00 | 500.00 | 850.00 |
| | 1754 MF | 250.00 | 375.00 | 500.00 | 850.00 |
| | 1755 MM | 100.00 | 125.00 | 225.00 | 400.00 |
| | 1756 MM | 100.00 | 150.00 | 300.00 | 500.00 |
| | 1757 MM | 100.00 | 150.00 | 250.00 | 450.00 |
| | 1758 MM | 100.00 | 125.00 | 225.00 | 400.00 |
| | 1759 MM | 100.00 | 125.00 | 225.00 | 400.00 |
| | 1760/59 MM | 100.00 | 175.00 | 350.00 | 550.00 |
| | 1760 MM | 100.00 | 175.00 | 350.00 | 550.00 |

**Rev: Normal initials and mint mark.**

| KM# | Date | VG | Fine | VF | XF |
|---|---|---|---|---|---|
| 97.2 | 1773 MF | 200.00 | 300.00 | 400.00 | 800.00 |
| | 1774 FM | 25.00 | 40.00 | 75.00 | 350.00 |
| | 1775 FM | 25.00 | 40.00 | 75.00 | 350.00 |
| | 1776 FM | 25.00 | 40.00 | 75.00 | 350.00 |
| | 1777 FM | 25.00 | 40.00 | 75.00 | 350.00 |
| | 1778 FF | 25.00 | 40.00 | 75.00 | 350.00 |
| | 1779 FF | 25.00 | 40.00 | 75.00 | 350.00 |
| | 1780 FF | 25.00 | 40.00 | 75.00 | 350.00 |
| | 1781 FF | 250.00 | 350.00 | 500.00 | 1000. |
| | 1782 FF | 35.00 | 65.00 | 150.00 | 450.00 |
| | 1783 FF | 25.00 | 40.00 | 75.00 | 350.00 |
| | 1784 FF | 25.00 | 40.00 | 75.00 | 350.00 |
| | 1784 FM | 100.00 | 200.00 | 350.00 | 600.00 |
| | 1785 FM | 100.00 | 200.00 | 350.00 | 600.00 |
| | 1786 FM | 25.00 | 40.00 | 75.00 | 350.00 |
| | 1787 FM | 25.00 | 40.00 | 75.00 | 350.00 |
| | 1788 FM | 25.00 | 40.00 | 75.00 | 350.00 |
| | 1789 FM | 50.00 | 100.00 | 150.00 | 400.00 |

**Obv. leg: CAROLVS.III.D.G.HISPAN.ET IND.REX**

| KM# | Date | VG | Fine | VF | XF |
|---|---|---|---|---|---|
| 96 | 1760 MM | 100.00 | 150.00 | 250.00 | 900.00 |
| | 1761 MM | 100.00 | 150.00 | 250.00 | 900.00 |
| | 1761 MM cross between H and I | | | | |
| | | 100.00 | 150.00 | 250.00 | 900.00 |
| | 1762 MM | 75.00 | 100.00 | 150.00 | 450.00 |
| | 1762 MF | 100.00 | 150.00 | 300.00 | 600.00 |
| | 1763/1 MM | 100.00 | 150.00 | 300.00 | 600.00 |
| | 1763/2 MF | 100.00 | 150.00 | 300.00 | 600.00 |
| | 1763 MM | 100.00 | 150.00 | 300.00 | 600.00 |
| | 1763 MF | 100.00 | 200.00 | 350.00 | 800.00 |
| | 1764 MM | 400.00 | 600.00 | 1000. | 2000. |
| | 1764 MF | 350.00 | 500.00 | 1000. | 2000. |
| | 1765 MF | 350.00 | 500.00 | 1000. | 2000. |
| | 1766 MF | 250.00 | 350.00 | 500.00 | 1250. |
| | 1767 MF | 100.00 | 150.00 | 300.00 | 600.00 |
| | 1768 MF | 75.00 | 100.00 | 150.00 | 450.00 |
| | 1769 MF | 75.00 | 100.00 | 150.00 | 450.00 |
| | 1770 MF | 75.00 | 100.00 | 150.00 | 450.00 |
| | 1771 MF | 125.00 | 200.00 | 300.00 | 700.00 |
| | 1771 FM | 150.00 | 275.00 | 400.00 | 900.00 |

**Obv: Armored bust of Charles III, leg: CAROLUS.IV. .**

| | | | | | |
|---|---|---|---|---|---|
| 98 | 1789 FM | 60.00 | 100.00 | 150.00 | 400.00 |
| | 1790 FM | 25.00 | 50.00 | 100.00 | 350.00 |

**13.5400 g, .903 SILVER, .3931 oz ASW**
**Obv. leg: CAROLUS.III.DEI.GRATIA.**
**Rev: Inverted FM and mint mark.**

| | | | | | |
|---|---|---|---|---|---|
| 97.1 | 1772 FM | 90.00 | 125.00 | 200.00 | 450.00 |
| | 1773 FM | 100.00 | 175.00 | 300.00 | 650.00 |

**Obv: Armored bust of Charles III, leg: CAROLUS.IIII.**

| | | | | | |
|---|---|---|---|---|---|
| 99 | 1790 FM | 30.00 | 60.00 | 175.00 | 500.00 |

13.5400 g, .903 SILVER, .3931 oz ASW
Obv: Armored bust of Charles IIII.
Rev: Pillars, arms.

| KM# | Date | VG | Fine | VF | XF |
|---|---|---|---|---|---|
| 100 | 1792 FM | 25.00 | 40.00 | 75.00 | 350.00 |
| | 1793 FM | 75.00 | 125.00 | 200.00 | 500.00 |
| | 1794/3 FM | 25.00 | 40.00 | 80.00 | 375.00 |
| | 1794 FM | 25.00 | 40.00 | 80.00 | 350.00 |
| | 1795 FM | 25.00 | 40.00 | 80.00 | 350.00 |
| | 1796 FM | 150.00 | 250.00 | 400.00 | 800.00 |
| | 1797 FM | 40.00 | 75.00 | 150.00 | 500.00 |
| | 1798/7 FM | 25.00 | 40.00 | 80.00 | 375.00 |
| | 1798 FM | 25.00 | 40.00 | 80.00 | 350.00 |
| | 1799 FM | 25.00 | 40.00 | 80.00 | 350.00 |
| | 1800 FM | 25.00 | 40.00 | 80.00 | 350.00 |
| | 1801 FM | 25.00 | 40.00 | 80.00 | 350.00 |
| | 1801 FT | 60.00 | 100.00 | 150.00 | 500.00 |
| | 1802 FT | 200.00 | 300.00 | 500.00 | 1000. |
| | 1803 FT | 60.00 | 125.00 | 200.00 | 550.00 |
| | 1803 FM | 350.00 | 450.00 | 650.00 | 1250. |
| | 1804 TH | 25.00 | 50.00 | 150.00 | 450.00 |
| | 1805 TH | 25.00 | 40.00 | 80.00 | 350.00 |
| | 1806 TH | 25.00 | 40.00 | 80.00 | 350.00 |
| | 1807 TH | 25.00 | 40.00 | 80.00 | 350.00 |
| | 1808/7 TH | 25.00 | 50.00 | 150.00 | 450.00 |
| | 1808 TH | 25.00 | 50.00 | 150.00 | 450.00 |

Obv: Armored bust of Ferdinand VII.

| KM# | Date | VG | Fine | VF | XF |
|---|---|---|---|---|---|
| 101 | 1809 HJ | 75.00 | 125.00 | 175.00 | 450.00 |
| | 1810 TH | 75.00 | 125.00 | 175.00 | 450.00 |
| | 1810 HJ | 75.00 | 125.00 | 175.00 | 450.00 |
| | 1811 HJ | 75.00 | 125.00 | 175.00 | 450.00 |
| | 1812 HJ | 500.00 | 750.00 | 1000. | 2000. |

Obv: Draped bust of Ferdinand VII.

| KM# | Date | VG | Fine | VF | XF |
|---|---|---|---|---|---|
| 102 | 1816 JJ | 150.00 | 200.00 | 350.00 | 600.00 |
| | 1817 JJ | 250.00 | 400.00 | 500.00 | 1000. |
| | 1818/7 JJ | 250.00 | 400.00 | 500.00 | 1000. |
| | 1818 JJ | 250.00 | 400.00 | 500.00 | 1000. |
| | 1819 JJ | 175.00 | 250.00 | 350.00 | 700.00 |
| | 1820 JJ | 175.00 | 250.00 | 350.00 | 700.00 |
| | 1821 JJ | 75.00 | 125.00 | 200.00 | 425.00 |

# 8 REALES

27.0700 g, .917 SILVER, .7982 oz ASW
Obv. leg: PHILIP.V.D.G.HISPAN.ET IND.REX

| KM# | Date | VG | Fine | VF | XF |
|---|---|---|---|---|---|
| 103 | 1732 F | — | — | Rare | — |
| | 1733/2 F(MX) | — | — | Rare | — |
| | 1733 F | — | — | Rare | — |
| | 1733 F(MX) | — | — | Rare | — |
| | 1733 MF(MX) | — | — | Rare | — |
| | 1733 MF | 700.00 | 1500. | 2500. | 4000. |
| | 1734/3 MF | 100.00 | 150.00 | 250.00 | 550.00 |
| | 1734 MF | 100.00 | 150.00 | 250.00 | 500.00 |
| | 1735 MF | 100.00 | 150.00 | 250.00 | 500.00 |
| | 1736 MF | 100.00 | 150.00 | 250.00 | 500.00 |
| | 1737 MF | 65.00 | 100.00 | 150.00 | 350.00 |
| | 1738/6 MF | 65.00 | 100.00 | 150.00 | 350.00 |
| | 1738/7 MF | 65.00 | 100.00 | 150.00 | 350.00 |
| | 1738 MF | 65.00 | 100.00 | 150.00 | 350.00 |
| | 1739/6 MF | 65.00 | 100.00 | 150.00 | 350.00 |
| | 1739/8 MF | 65.00 | 100.00 | 150.00 | 350.00 |
| | 1739 MF | 65.00 | 100.00 | 150.00 | 350.00 |
| | 1740/30 MF | 65.00 | 100.00 | 150.00 | 350.00 |
| | 1740/39 MF | 65.00 | 100.00 | 150.00 | 350.00 |
| | 1740 MF | 65.00 | 100.00 | 150.00 | 350.00 |

| KM# | Date | VG | Fine | VF | XF |
|---|---|---|---|---|---|
| 103 | 1741/31 MF | 65.00 | 100.00 | 150.00 | 350.00 |
| | 1741 MF | 65.00 | 100.00 | 150.00 | 350.00 |
| | 1742/32 MF | 75.00 | 125.00 | 200.00 | 450.00 |
| | 1742/1 MF | 65.00 | 100.00 | 150.00 | 350.00 |
| | 1742 MF | 65.00 | 100.00 | 150.00 | 350.00 |
| | 1743/2 MF | 65.00 | 100.00 | 150.00 | 350.00 |
| | 1743 MF | 65.00 | 100.00 | 150.00 | 350.00 |
| | 1744/34 MF | 65.00 | 100.00 | 150.00 | 350.00 |
| | 1744/3 MF | 65.00 | 100.00 | 150.00 | 350.00 |
| | 1744 MF | 65.00 | 100.00 | 150.00 | 350.00 |
| | 1745 MF | 65.00 | 100.00 | 150.00 | 350.00 |
| | 1746/5 MF | 65.00 | 100.00 | 150.00 | 350.00 |
| | 1746 MF | 65.00 | 100.00 | 150.00 | 350.00 |
| | 1747 MF | 65.00 | 100.00 | 150.00 | 350.00 |

**NOTE:** Ponterio AMAT sale 3-91 AU 1732 F realized $28,000., XF 1733/2 F (MX) realized $27,000., XF 1733 F realized $11,500., XF 1733 MF (MX) realized $35,000.

**Obv. leg: FERDND.VI.D.G.HISPAN.ET IND.REX**
**Rev: W/Royal crown on left pillar.**

| | Date | VG | Fine | VF | XF |
|---|---|---|---|---|---|
| 104.1 | 1747 MF | 50.00 | 100.00 | 175.00 | 300.00 |
| | 1748/7 MF | 50.00 | 80.00 | 150.00 | 250.00 |
| | 1748 MF | 50.00 | 75.00 | 100.00 | 200.00 |
| | 1749 MF | 50.00 | 75.00 | 100.00 | 200.00 |
| | 1750 MF | 50.00 | 75.00 | 100.00 | 200.00 |
| | 1751/0 MF | 50.00 | 75.00 | 100.00 | 200.00 |
| | 1751 MF | 50.00 | 75.00 | 100.00 | 200.00 |
| | 1752/1 MF | 50.00 | 75.00 | 100.00 | 200.00 |
| | 1752 MF | 50.00 | 75.00 | 100.00 | 200.00 |
| | 1753/2 MF | 50.00 | 75.00 | 100.00 | 200.00 |
| | 1753 MF | 50.00 | 75.00 | 100.00 | 200.00 |
| | 1754/3 MF | 50.00 | 75.00 | 120.00 | 225.00 |
| | 1754 MF | 50.00 | 75.00 | 100.00 | 200.00 |
| | 1754 MM/MF | | | | |
| | | 250.00 | 600.00 | 1250. | 2500. |
| | 1754 MM | 250.00 | 600.00 | 1250. | 2500. |
| | 1755/4 MM | 50.00 | 80.00 | 150.00 | 250.00 |
| | 1755 MM | 50.00 | 75.00 | 100.00 | 200.00 |
| | 1756/5 MM | 50.00 | 75.00 | 100.00 | 200.00 |
| | 1756 MM | 50.00 | 75.00 | 100.00 | 200.00 |
| | 1757/6 MM | 50.00 | 75.00 | 100.00 | 200.00 |
| | 1757 MM | 50.00 | 75.00 | 100.00 | 200.00 |
| | 1758 MM | 50.00 | 75.00 | 100.00 | 200.00 |
| | 1759 MM | 60.00 | 100.00 | 150.00 | 250.00 |
| | 1760/59 MM | 60.00 | 100.00 | 150.00 | 250.00 |
| | 1760 MM | 60.00 | 100.00 | 150.00 | 250.00 |

**Rev: Imperial crown.**

| | Date | VG | Fine | VF | XF |
|---|---|---|---|---|---|
| 104.2 | 1754 MM | 75.00 | 125.00 | 200.00 | 400.00 |
| | 1754 MF | 150.00 | 300.00 | 500.00 | 800.00 |

**Obv. leg: CAROLUS.III.D.G.HISPAN.ET IND.REX**

| KM# | Date | VG | Fine | VF | XF |
|---|---|---|---|---|---|
| 105 | 1760/59 MM CAROLUS.III/Ferdin.Vi | — | — | — | — |
| | 1760 MM CAROLUS.III/FERDIN. VI. recut die | 60.00 | 100.00 | 150.00 | 325.00 |
| | 1760 MM | 60.00 | 100.00 | 150.00 | 300.00 |
| | 1761/50 MM tip of cross between I and S in leg. | 65.00 | 110.00 | 165.00 | 325.00 |
| | 1761/51 MM tip of cross between I and S in leg. | 65.00 | 110.00 | 165.00 | 325.00 |
| | 1761/0 MM tip of cross between H and I in leg. | 65.00 | 110.00 | 165.00 | 300.00 |
| | 1761 MM tip of cross between H and I in leg. | 60.00 | 100.00 | 150.00 | 275.00 |
| | 1761 MM tip of cross between I and S in leg. | 60.00 | 100.00 | 150.00 | 300.00 |
| 105 | 1762/1 MM tip of cross between H and I in leg. | 70.00 | 120.00 | 175.00 | 450.00 |
| | 1762/1 MM | 70.00 | 120.00 | 175.00 | 450.00 |
| | 1762 MM tip of cross between H and I in leg. | 50.00 | 75.00 | 100.00 | 200.00 |
| | 1762 MM tip of cross between I and S in leg. | 50.00 | 75.00 | 100.00 | 200.00 |
| | 1762 MF | 500.00 | 750.00 | 1000. | 1500. |
| | 1763/53 MF | 50.00 | 75.00 | 100.00 | 250.00 |
| | 1763/1 MF | 50.00 | 75.00 | 100.00 | 250.00 |
| | 1763/2 MM | 300.00 | 450.00 | 750.00 | 1500. |
| | 1763/2 MF | 50.00 | 75.00 | 100.00 | 250.00 |
| | 1763/72 MF | 50.00 | 75.00 | 100.00 | 250.00 |
| | 1763 MM | 450.00 | 650.00 | 1150. | 2500. |
| | 1763 MF | 50.00 | 75.00 | 100.00 | 250.00 |
| | 1764/54 MF | 50.00 | 75.00 | 100.00 | 250.00 |
| | 1764/54 MF CAR/CRA | 50.00 | 75.00 | 100.00 | 250.00 |
| | 1764/1 MF | 50.00 | 75.00 | 100.00 | 250.00 |
| | 1764/3 MF | 50.00 | 75.00 | 100.00 | 250.00 |
| | 1764 MF | 50.00 | 75.00 | 100.00 | 250.00 |
| | 1765 MF | 50.00 | 75.00 | 100.00 | 250.00 |
| | 1766/5 MF | 50.00 | 75.00 | 100.00 | 250.00 |
| | 1766 MF | 50.00 | 75.00 | 100.00 | 250.00 |
| | 1767/17 MF | 50.00 | 75.00 | 100.00 | 250.00 |
| | 1767/6 MF | 50.00 | 75.00 | 100.00 | 250.00 |
| | 1767 MF | 50.00 | 75.00 | 100.00 | 250.00 |
| | 1768/6 MF | 50.00 | 75.00 | 100.00 | 250.00 |
| | 1768/7 MF | 50.00 | 75.00 | 100.00 | 250.00 |
| | 1768 MF | 50.00 | 75.00 | 100.00 | 250.00 |
| | 1769 MF | 50.00 | 75.00 | 100.00 | 250.00 |
| | 1770/60 MF | 50.00 | 75.00 | 100.00 | 250.00 |
| | 1770/60 FM | 50.00 | 75.00 | 100.00 | 250.00 |
| | 1770/69 FM | 50.00 | 75.00 | 100.00 | 250.00 |
| | 1770 MF | 50.00 | 75.00 | 100.00 | 250.00 |
| | 1770 FM/F | 50.00 | 75.00 | 100.00 | 250.00 |
| | 1770 FM | 50.00 | 75.00 | 100.00 | 250.00 |

| KM# | Date | VG | Fine | VF | XF |
|---|---|---|---|---|---|
| 105 | 1771/0 FM | 50.00 | 75.00 | 100.00 | 250.00 |
| | 1771 FM | 50.00 | 75.00 | 100.00 | 250.00 |
| | 1772 FM | — | — | Rare | — |

**27.0700 g, .903 SILVER, .7859 oz ASW**
MF (error) inverted

FM (normal)

**Obv. leg: CAROLUS.III.DEI.GRATIA.**
**Rev: Inverted FM or MF and mint mark**

| KM# | Date | VG | Fine | VF | XF |
|---|---|---|---|---|---|
| 106.1 | 1772 FM | 25.00 | 50.00 | 90.00 | 250.00 |
| | 1772 MF inverted MF (error) | | | | |
| | | 150.00 | 350.00 | 750.00 | 1250. |
| | 1773 FM | 25.00 | 50.00 | 80.00 | 175.00 |

**Rev: Normal initials and mint mark.**

| | | | | | |
|---|---|---|---|---|---|
| 106.2 | 1773 FM | 25.00 | 50.00 | 75.00 | 150.00 |
| | 1774 FM | 25.00 | 45.00 | 60.00 | 135.00 |
| | 1775 FM | 25.00 | 45.00 | 60.00 | 135.00 |
| | 1776 FM | 25.00 | 45.00 | 60.00 | 135.00 |
| | 1777/6 FM | 35.00 | 55.00 | 90.00 | 300.00 |
| | 1777 FM | 25.00 | 45.00 | 60.00 | 135.00 |
| | 1777 FF | 35.00 | 50.00 | 80.00 | 250.00 |
| | 1778 FM | — | — | *Rare | — |
| | 1778/7FF | 25.00 | 45.00 | 60.00 | 135.00 |

| KM# | Date | VG | Fine | VF | XF |
|---|---|---|---|---|---|
| 106.2 | 1778 FF | 25.00 | 45.00 | 60.00 | 135.00 |
| | 1779 FF | 25.00 | 45.00 | 60.00 | 135.00 |
| | 1780 FF | 25.00 | 45.00 | 60.00 | 135.00 |
| | 1781 FF | 25.00 | 45.00 | 60.00 | 135.00 |
| | 1782 FF | 25.00 | 45.00 | 60.00 | 135.00 |
| | 1783 FF | 25.00 | 45.00 | 60.00 | 135.00 |
| | 1783 FM | 4000. | 6000. | 9000. | — |
| | 1784 FF | 150.00 | 300.00 | 500.00 | 1250. |
| | 1784 FM | 25.00 | 45.00 | 60.00 | 135.00 |
| | 1785 FM | 25.00 | 45.00 | 60.00 | 135.00 |
| | 1786/5 FM | 25.00 | 45.00 | 60.00 | 135.00 |
| | 1786 FM | 25.00 | 45.00 | 60.00 | 135.00 |
| | 1787/6 FM | 100.00 | 250.00 | 450.00 | 1200. |
| | 1787 FM | 25.00 | 45.00 | 60.00 | 135.00 |
| | 1788 FM | 25.00 | 45.00 | 60.00 | 135.00 |
| | 1789 FM | 50.00 | 100.00 | 150.00 | 225.00 |

**NOTE:** Superior Casterline sale 5-89 VF realized $17,600.

**Obv: Armored bust of Charles III, leg: CAROLUS.IV. .**

| 107 | 1789 FM | 40.00 | 65.00 | 100.00 | 200.00 |
|---|---|---|---|---|---|
| | 1790 FM | 30.00 | 50.00 | 80.00 | 190.00 |

**Obv: Armored bust of Charles III, leg: CAROLUS.IIII.**

| 108 | 1790 FM | 30.00 | 50.00 | 75.00 | 175.00 |
|---|---|---|---|---|---|

**Obv: Armored bust of Ferdinand VII.**

| KM# | Date | VG | Fine | VF | XF |
|---|---|---|---|---|---|
| 110 | 1808 TH | 25.00 | 40.00 | 65.00 | 125.00 |
| | 1809/8 TH | 25.00 | 40.00 | 65.00 | 125.00 |
| | 1809 HJ | 25.00 | 40.00 | 65.00 | 125.00 |
| | 1809 HJ/TH | 20.00 | 40.00 | 50.00 | 100.00 |
| | 1809 TH/JH | 20.00 | 40.00 | 50.00 | 100.00 |
| | 1809 TH | 20.00 | 40.00 | 50.00 | 100.00 |
| | 1810/09 HJ | 25.00 | 40.00 | 65.00 | 125.00 |
| | 1810 HJ | 25.00 | 40.00 | 65.00 | 125.00 |
| | 1810 HJ/TH | 25.00 | 40.00 | 65.00 | 125.00 |
| | 1810 TH | 75.00 | 150.00 | 300.00 | 600.00 |
| | 1811/0 HJ | 20.00 | 40.00 | 50.00 | 100.00 |
| | 1811 HJ | 20.00 | 40.00 | 50.00 | 100.00 |

**Obv: Armored bust of Charles IIII.**

| KM# | Date | VG | Fine | VF | XF |
|---|---|---|---|---|---|
| 109 | 1791 FM | 20.00 | 40.00 | 50.00 | 100.00 |
| | 1792 FM | 20.00 | 40.00 | 50.00 | 100.00 |
| | 1793 FM | 20.00 | 40.00 | 50.00 | 100.00 |
| | 1794 FM | 20.00 | 40.00 | 50.00 | 100.00 |
| | 1795/4 FM | 20.00 | 40.00 | 50.00 | 100.00 |
| | 1795 FM | 20.00 | 40.00 | 50.00 | 100.00 |
| | 1796 FM | 20.00 | 40.00 | 50.00 | 100.00 |
| | 1797 FM | 20.00 | 40.00 | 50.00 | 100.00 |
| | 1798 FM | 20.00 | 40.00 | 50.00 | 100.00 |
| | 1799 FM | 20.00 | 40.00 | 50.00 | 100.00 |
| | 1800/700 FM | 20.00 | 40.00 | 50.00 | 100.00 |
| | 1800 FM | 20.00 | 40.00 | 50.00 | 100.00 |
| | 1801/791 FM | 35.00 | 60.00 | 100.00 | 250.00 |
| | 1801/0 FM | 35.00 | 60.00 | 100.00 | 250.00 |
| | 1801/0 FT/FM | | | | |
| | | 20.00 | 40.00 | 50.00 | 100.00 |
| | 1801 FM | 20.00 | 40.00 | 100.00 | 250.00 |
| | 1801 FT/M | 35.00 | 60.00 | 100.00 | 250.00 |
| | 1801 FT | 20.00 | 40.00 | 50.00 | 100.00 |
| | 1802/1 FT | 35.00 | 60.00 | 100.00 | 250.00 |
| | 1802 FT | 20.00 | 40.00 | 50.00 | 100.00 |
| | 1802 FT/FM | 20.00 | 40.00 | 50.00 | 100.00 |
| | 1803 FT | 20.00 | 40.00 | 50.00 | 110.00 |
| | 1803 FM | 600.00 | 900.00 | — | — |
| | 1803 FT/FM | 20.00 | 40.00 | 50.00 | 100.00 |
| | 1803 TH | 75.00 | 150.00 | 250.00 | 500.00 |
| | 1804/3 TH | 35.00 | 60.00 | 100.00 | 250.00 |
| | 1804 TH | 20.00 | 40.00 | 50.00 | 100.00 |
| | 1805/4 TH | 40.00 | 80.00 | 125.00 | 275.00 |
| | 1805 TH | 20.00 | 40.00 | 50.00 | 100.00 |
| | 1806 TH | 20.00 | 40.00 | 50.00 | 100.00 |
| | 1807/6 TH | 150.00 | 250.00 | 350.00 | 700.00 |
| | 1807 TH | 20.00 | 40.00 | 50.00 | 100.00 |
| | 1870 TH(error 1807) | | | | |
| | | 150.00 | 250.00 | 350.00 | 700.00 |
| | 1808/7 TH | 20.00 | 40.00 | 50.00 | 100.00 |
| | 1808 TH | 20.00 | 40.00 | 50.00 | 100.00 |

**Obv: Draped bust of Ferdinand VII.**

| | Date | VG | Fine | VF | XF |
|---|---|---|---|---|---|
| 111 | 1811 HJ | 20.00 | 40.00 | 60.00 | 125.00 |
| | 1812 HJ | 50.00 | 75.00 | 125.00 | 250.00 |
| | 1812 JJ/HJ | 20.00 | 40.00 | 50.00 | 90.00 |
| | 1812 JJ | 20.00 | 40.00 | 50.00 | 90.00 |
| | 1813 HJ | 50.00 | 75.00 | 125.00 | 250.00 |
| | 1813 JJ | 20.00 | 40.00 | 50.00 | 90.00 |
| | 1814/3 HJ | 1200. | 2500. | 5000. | — |
| | 1814/3 JJ/HJ | | | | |
| | | 20.00 | 40.00 | 50.00 | 90.00 |
| | 1814/3 JJ | 20.00 | 40.00 | 50.00 | 90.00 |
| | 1814 JJ | 20.00 | 40.00 | 50.00 | 90.00 |
| | 1814 HJ | 500.00 | 800.00 | 1500. | 3000. |
| | 1815/4 JJ | 20.00 | 40.00 | 50.00 | 90.00 |
| | 1815 JJ | 20.00 | 40.00 | 50.00 | 90.00 |
| | 1816/5 JJ | 20.00 | 40.00 | 50.00 | 85.00 |
| | 1816 JJ | 20.00 | 40.00 | 50.00 | 85.00 |
| | 1817 JJ | 20.00 | 40.00 | 50.00 | 85.00 |
| | 1818 JJ | 20.00 | 40.00 | 50.00 | 85.00 |
| | 1819 JJ | 20.00 | 40.00 | 50.00 | 85.00 |
| | 1820 JJ | 20.00 | 40.00 | 50.00 | 85.00 |
| | 1821 JJ | 20.00 | 40.00 | 50.00 | 85.00 |

## 1/2 ESCUDO

**1.6900 g, .875 GOLD, .0475 oz AGW**
**Obv. leg: FERD.VII.D.G.HISP.ET IND.**

| KM# | Date | VG | Fine | VF | XF |
|---|---|---|---|---|---|
| 112 | 1814 JJ | 250.00 | 350.00 | 450.00 | 600.00 |
| | 1815/4 JJ | 150.00 | 200.00 | 250.00 | 350.00 |
| | 1815 JJ | 150.00 | 200.00 | 250.00 | 350.00 |
| | 1816 JJ | 100.00 | 150.00 | 200.00 | 300.00 |
| | 1817 JJ | 150.00 | 200.00 | 250.00 | 350.00 |
| | 1818 JJ | 150.00 | 200.00 | 250.00 | 350.00 |
| | 1819 JJ | 150.00 | 200.00 | 250.00 | 350.00 |
| | 1820 JJ | 200.00 | 300.00 | 450.00 | 600.00 |

## ESCUDO

**3.3800 g, .917 GOLD, .0996 oz AGW**
**Obv. leg: PHILIP.V.D.G.HISPAN.ET IND.REX**

| | Date | VG | Fine | VF | XF |
|---|---|---|---|---|---|
| 113 | 1732 F | 1000. | 2000. | 3000. | 4000. |
| | 1733/2 F | 1000. | 2000. | 3000. | 4000. |
| | 1733 F | 1000. | 2000. | 3000. | 4000. |
| | 1734/3 MF | 150.00 | 250.00 | 400.00 | 950.00 |
| | 1734 MF | 150.00 | 250.00 | 400.00 | 950.00 |
| | 1735/4 MF | 150.00 | 250.00 | 400.00 | 950.00 |
| | 1735 MF | 150.00 | 250.00 | 400.00 | 950.00 |
| | 1736/5 MF | 150.00 | 250.00 | 400.00 | 950.00 |
| | 1736 MF | 150.00 | 250.00 | 400.00 | 950.00 |
| | 1737 MF | 200.00 | 300.00 | 600.00 | 1200. |
| | 1738/7 MF | 200.00 | 300.00 | 600.00 | 1200. |
| | 1738 MF | 200.00 | 300.00 | 600.00 | 1200. |
| | 1739 MF | 200.00 | 300.00 | 600.00 | 1200. |
| | 1740 MF | 200.00 | 300.00 | 600.00 | 1200. |
| | 1741 MF | 200.00 | 300.00 | 600.00 | 1200. |
| | 1742 MF | 200.00 | 300.00 | 600.00 | 1200. |
| | 1743/2 MF | 150.00 | 275.00 | 450.00 | 900.00 |
| | 1743 MF | 150.00 | 250.00 | 400.00 | 800.00 |
| | 1744 MF | 150.00 | 250.00 | 400.00 | 800.00 |
| | 1745 MF | 150.00 | 250.00 | 400.00 | 800.00 |
| | 1746 MF | 150.00 | 250.00 | 400.00 | 800.00 |
| | 1747 MF | — | — | Rare | — |

**Obv: Long bust; leg: FERD.VI.D.G.HISPAN.ET IND.REX.**

| 114 | 1747 MF | 600.00 | 900.00 | 1500. | 2250. |
|---|---|---|---|---|---|

**Obv: Short bust**

| 115.1 | 1748 MF | 250.00 | 350.00 | 550.00 | 950.00 |
|---|---|---|---|---|---|
| | 1749 MF | 300.00 | 450.00 | 700.00 | 1150. |
| | 1750 MF | 200.00 | 300.00 | 450.00 | 800.00 |
| | 1751 MF | 200.00 | 300.00 | 450.00 | 800.00 |

**Rev: W/o 1 S by arms.**

| KM# | Date | VG | Fine | VF | XF |
|---|---|---|---|---|---|
| 115.2 | 1752 MF | 150.00 | 250.00 | 400.00 | 750.00 |
| | 1753/2 MF | 200.00 | 300.00 | 450.00 | 800.00 |
| | 1753 MF | 200.00 | 300.00 | 450.00 | 800.00 |
| | 1754 MF | 200.00 | 300.00 | 450.00 | 800.00 |
| | 1755 MM | 200.00 | 300.00 | 450.00 | 800.00 |
| | 1756 MF | 200.00 | 300.00 | 450.00 | 800.00 |
| | 1756 MM | 200.00 | 300.00 | 450.00 | 800.00 |

**Obv: Armored bust.**

| A116 | 1757 MM | 200.00 | 300.00 | 450.00 | 800.00 |
|---|---|---|---|---|---|
| | 1758 MM | 200.00 | 300.00 | 450.00 | 800.00 |
| | 1759 MM | 200.00 | 300.00 | 450.00 | 800.00 |

**Obv. leg: CAROLVS.III.D.G.HISPAN.ET IND.REX**
**Rev. leg: NOMINA MAGNA SEQUOR**

| 116 | 1760 MM | 500.00 | 1000. | 1750. | 2500. |
|---|---|---|---|---|---|
| | 1761/0 MM | 500.00 | 1000. | 1750. | 2500. |
| | 1761 MM | 500.00 | 1000. | 1750. | 2500. |

**Obv: Large bust, leg: CAR.III.D.G.HISP.ET IND.R.**
**Rev. leg: IN.UTROQ. FELIX.**

| 117 | 1762 MF | 250.00 | 375.00 | 600.00 | 1100. |
|---|---|---|---|---|---|
| | 1762 MM | 250.00 | 375.00 | 600.00 | 1100. |
| | 1763 MF | 250.00 | 375.00 | 600.00 | 1100. |
| | 1763 MM | 275.00 | 425.00 | 700.00 | 1200. |
| | 1764 MM | 250.00 | 375.00 | 600.00 | 1100. |
| | 1765 MF | 250.00 | 375.00 | 600.00 | 1100. |
| | 1766 MF | 250.00 | 375.00 | 600.00 | 1100. |
| | 1767 MF | 250.00 | 375.00 | 600.00 | 1100. |
| | 1768 MF | 250.00 | 375.00 | 600.00 | 1100. |
| | 1769 MF | 250.00 | 375.00 | 600.00 | 1100. |
| | 1770 MF | 250.00 | 375.00 | 600.00 | 1100. |
| | 1771 MF | 250.00 | 375.00 | 600.00 | 1100. |

**3.3800 g, .901 GOLD, .0979 oz AGW**
**Obv. leg: CAROL.III.D.G. HISPAN.ET IND.R.**
**Rev. leg: . . . . .FELIX.A.D.; FM and mint mark upright.**

| 118.1 | 1772 FM | 125.00 | 200.00 | 300.00 | 600.00 |
|---|---|---|---|---|---|
| | 1773 FM | 125.00 | 200.00 | 300.00 | 600.00 |

**Rev: Initial letters and mint mark inverted.**

| KM# | Date | VG | Fine | VF | XF |
|-----|------|-----|------|-----|-----|
| 118.2 | 1772 FM | 125.00 | 200.00 | 300.00 | 600.00 |
| | 1773 FM | 125.00 | 200.00 | 300.00 | 600.00 |
| | 1774 FM | 125.00 | 200.00 | 300.00 | 600.00 |
| | 1775 FM | 125.00 | 200.00 | 300.00 | 600.00 |
| | 1776 FM | 125.00 | 200.00 | 300.00 | 600.00 |

**3.3800 g, .875 GOLD, .0950 oz AGW**

| KM# | Date | VG | Fine | VF | XF |
|-----|------|-----|------|-----|-----|
| 118.2a | 1777 FM | 125.00 | 200.00 | 300.00 | 600.00 |
| | 1778 FF | 125.00 | 200.00 | 300.00 | 600.00 |
| | 1779 FF | 125.00 | 200.00 | 300.00 | 600.00 |
| | 1780 FF | 125.00 | 200.00 | 300.00 | 600.00 |
| | 1781 FF | 125.00 | 200.00 | 300.00 | 600.00 |
| | 1782 FF | 125.00 | 200.00 | 300.00 | 600.00 |
| | 1783/2 FF | 125.00 | 200.00 | 300.00 | 600.00 |
| | 1783 FF | 125.00 | 200.00 | 300.00 | 600.00 |
| | 1784 FF | 125.00 | 200.00 | 300.00 | 600.00 |
| | 1784 FM | 125.00 | 200.00 | 300.00 | 600.00 |
| | 1785 FM | 125.00 | 200.00 | 300.00 | 600.00 |
| | 1786 FM | 125.00 | 200.00 | 300.00 | 600.00 |
| | 1787 FM | 125.00 | 200.00 | 300.00 | 600.00 |
| | 1788 FM | 125.00 | 200.00 | 300.00 | 600.00 |

**Rev: Initial letters and mint mark upright.**

| KM# | Date | VG | Fine | VF | XF |
|-----|------|-----|------|-----|-----|
| 118.1a | 1787 FM | 125.00 | 200.00 | 300.00 | 600.00 |
| | 1788 FM | 125.00 | 200.00 | 300.00 | 600.00 |

**Obv: Bust of Charles III, leg: CAROLUS.IV.D.G. .**

| KM# | Date | VG | Fine | VF | XF |
|-----|------|-----|------|-----|-----|
| 119 | 1789 FM | 125.00 | 200.00 | 300.00 | 600.00 |
| | 1790 FM | 125.00 | 200.00 | 300.00 | 600.00 |

**Obv: Armored bust of Charles IV.**

| KM# | Date | VG | Fine | VF | XF |
|-----|------|-----|------|-----|-----|
| 120 | 1792 MF | 125.00 | 200.00 | 250.00 | 375.00 |
| | 1793 FM | 125.00 | 200.00 | 250.00 | 375.00 |
| | 1794 FM | 125.00 | 200.00 | 250.00 | 375.00 |
| | 1795 FM | 125.00 | 200.00 | 250.00 | 375.00 |
| | 1796 FM | 125.00 | 200.00 | 250.00 | 375.00 |
| | 1797 FM | 125.00 | 200.00 | 250.00 | 375.00 |
| | 1798 FM | 125.00 | 200.00 | 250.00 | 375.00 |
| | 1799 FM | 125.00 | 200.00 | 250.00 | 375.00 |
| | 1800 FM | 125.00 | 200.00 | 250.00 | 350.00 |

**3.3800 g, .875 GOLD, .0950 oz AGW**
**Obv: Armored bust of Charles IV.**

| KM# | Date | VG | Fine | VF | XF |
|-----|------|-----|------|-----|-----|
| 120 | 1801 FT | 125.00 | 200.00 | 250.00 | 350.00 |
| | 1801 FM | 125.00 | 200.00 | 250.00 | 350.00 |
| | 1802 FT | 125.00 | 200.00 | 250.00 | 350.00 |
| | 1803 FT | 125.00 | 200.00 | 250.00 | 350.00 |
| | 1804/3 TH | 125.00 | 200.00 | 250.00 | 350.00 |
| | 1804 TH | 125.00 | 200.00 | 250.00 | 350.00 |
| | 1805 TH | 125.00 | 200.00 | 250.00 | 350.00 |
| | 1806 TH | 125.00 | 200.00 | 250.00 | 350.00 |
| | 1807 TH | 125.00 | 200.00 | 250.00 | 350.00 |
| | 1808 TH | 125.00 | 200.00 | 250.00 | 350.00 |

**Obv: Armored bust of Ferdinand VII.**

| KM# | Date | VG | Fine | VF | XF |
|-----|------|-----|------|-----|-----|
| 121 | 1809 HJ | 125.00 | 200.00 | 250.00 | 400.00 |
| | 1810 HJ | 125.00 | .200.00 | 250.00 | 400.00 |
| | 1811 HJ | 125.00 | 200.00 | 250.00 | 400.00 |
| | 1812 HJ | 150.00 | 250.00 | 300.00 | 500.00 |

**Obv: Undraped bust of Ferdinand VII.**

| KM# | Date | VG | Fine | VF | XF |
|-----|------|-----|------|-----|-----|
| 122 | 1814 HJ | 100.00 | 150.00 | 225.00 | 400.00 |
| | 1815 JJ | 100.00 | 150.00 | 225.00 | 400.00 |
| | 1815 HJ | 100.00 | 150.00 | 225.00 | 400.00 |
| | 1816 JJ | 125.00 | 175.00 | 275.00 | 500.00 |
| | 1817 JJ | 100.00 | 150.00 | 225.00 | 400.00 |
| | 1818 JJ | 100.00 | 150.00 | 225.00 | 400.00 |
| | 1819 JJ | 100.00 | 150.00 | 225.00 | 400.00 |
| | 1820 JJ | 100.00 | 150.00 | 225.00 | 400.00 |

# 2 ESCUDOS

**6.7700 g, .917 GOLD, .1996 oz AGW**
**Obv. leg: PHILIP.V.D.G.HISPAN.ET IND.REX**
**Rev. leg: INITIUM SAPIENTIAE TIMOR DOMINI**

| KM# | Date | VG | Fine | VF | XF |
|-----|------|-----|------|-----|-----|
| 124 | 1732 F | 1000. | 1500. | 2000. | 3000. |
| | 1733 F | 750.00 | 1000. | 1500. | 2500. |
| | 1734 MF | 400.00 | 500.00 | 700.00 | 1300. |
| | 1735 MF | 400.00 | 500.00 | 700.00 | 1300. |
| | 1736/5 MF | 400.00 | 500.00 | 700.00 | 1300. |
| | 1736 MF | 400.00 | 500.00 | 700.00 | 1300. |
| | 1737 MF | 400.00 | 500.00 | 700.00 | 1300. |
| | 1738/7 MF | 400.00 | 500.00 | 700.00 | 1300. |
| | 1738 MF | 400.00 | 500.00 | 700.00 | 1300. |
| | 1739 MF | 400.00 | 500.00 | 700.00 | 1300. |
| | 1740 MF | 400.00 | 500.00 | 700.00 | 1300. |
| | 1741 MF | 400.00 | 500.00 | 700.00 | 1300. |
| | 1742 MF | 400.00 | 500.00 | 700.00 | 1300. |
| | 1743 MF | 400.00 | 500.00 | 700.00 | 1300. |
| | 1744/3 MF | 350.00 | 450.00 | 600.00 | 1200. |
| | 1744 MF | 400.00 | 500.00 | 700.00 | 1300. |
| | 1745 MF | 400.00 | 500.00 | 700.00 | 1300. |
| | 1746 MF | 400.00 | 500.00 | 700.00 | 1300. |
| | 1747 MF | 400.00 | 500.00 | 700.00 | 1300. |

**Obv: Large bust; leg: FERD.VI.D.G. .**
**Rev. leg: INITIUM. .**

| KM# | Date | VG | Fine | VF | XF |
|-----|------|-----|------|-----|-----|
| 125 | 1747 MF | 1500. | 2000. | 3000. | 4500. |

**Obv: Small young bust; leg: FERD.VI.D.G. . .**
**Rev. leg: NOMINA MAGNA SEQUOR**

| KM# | Date | VG | Fine | VF | XF |
|-----|------|-----|------|-----|-----|
| 126.1 | 1748 MF | 450.00 | 550.00 | 700.00 | 1250. |
| | 1749/8 MF | 450.00 | 550.00 | 700.00 | 1250. |
| | 1749 MF | 600.00 | 800.00 | 1000. | 1800. |
| | 1750 MF | 400.00 | 500.00 | 600.00 | 1100. |
| | 1751 MF | 400.00 | 500.00 | 600.00 | 1100. |

**Rev: W/o 2 S by arms.**

| KM# | Date | VG | Fine | VF | XF |
|-----|------|-----|------|-----|-----|
| 126.2 | 1752 MF | 400.00 | 500.00 | 600.00 | 1100. |
| | 1753 MF | 400.00 | 500.00 | 600.00 | 1100. |
| | 1754 MF | 600.00 | 800.00 | 1000. | 1800. |
| | 1755 MM | 400.00 | 500.00 | 600.00 | 1100. |
| | 1756 MM | 600.00 | 800.00 | 1000. | 1800. |
| | 1756 MF | 450.00 | 550.00 | 700.00 | 1250. |

**Obv: Armored bust; leg: FERDND.VI.D.G. .**

| | | VG | Fine | VF | XF |
|-----|------|-----|------|-----|-----|
| 127 | 1757 MM | 500.00 | 800.00 | 1300. | 2200. |
| | 1758 MM | 500.00 | 800.00 | 1300. | 2200. |
| | 1759 MM | 500.00 | 800.00 | 1300. | 2200. |

**Obv: Young bust, leg: CAROLVS.III.D.G. .**

| | | VG | Fine | VF | XF |
|-----|------|-----|------|-----|-----|
| 128 | 1760 MM | 550.00 | 900.00 | 1500. | 2500. |
| | 1761 MM | 550.00 | 900.00 | 1500. | 2500. |

**Obv: Large young bust, leg: CAROLUS.III.D.G. .**
**Rev. leg: IN.UTROQ.FELIX.AUSPICE.DEO**

| | | VG | Fine | VF | XF |
|-----|------|-----|------|-----|-----|
| 129 | 1762 MF | 500.00 | 600.00 | 800.00 | 1500. |
| | 1763 MF | 500.00 | 600.00 | 800.00 | 1500. |
| | 1764 MF | 500.00 | 600.00 | 800.00 | 1500. |
| | 1764 MM | 500.00 | 600.00 | 800.00 | 1500. |
| | 1765 MF | 500.00 | 600.00 | 800.00 | 1500. |
| | 1766 MF | 500.00 | 600.00 | 800.00 | 1500. |
| | 1767 MF | 500.00 | 600.00 | 800.00 | 1500. |
| | 1768 MF | 500.00 | 600.00 | 800.00 | 1500. |
| | 1769 MF | 500.00 | 600.00 | 800.00 | 1500. |
| | 1770 MF | 500.00 | 600.00 | 1000. | 1800. |
| | 1771 MF | 500.00 | 600.00 | 800.00 | 1500. |

**6.7700 g, .901 GOLD, .1961 oz AGW**
**Obv: Older bust, leg: CAROLUS.III.D.G. .**
**Rev: FM and mint mark upright.**

| | | VG | Fine | VF | XF |
|-----|------|-----|------|-----|-----|
| 130.1 | 1772 FM | 300.00 | 450.00 | 600.00 | 1000. |
| | 1773 FM | 300.00 | 450.00 | 600.00 | 1000. |

**Rev: Initial letters and mint mark inverted.**

| | | VG | Fine | VF | XF |
|-----|------|-----|------|-----|-----|
| 130.2 | 1773 FM | 300.00 | 450.00 | 600.00 | 1000. |
| | 1774 FM | 300.00 | 450.00 | 600.00 | 1000. |
| | 1775 FM | 300.00 | 450.00 | 600.00 | 1000. |
| | 1776 FM | 300.00 | 450.00 | 600.00 | 1000. |

**6.7700 g, .875 GOLD, .1904 oz AGW**

| KM# | Date | VG | Fine | VF | XF |
|-----|------|-----|------|-----|-----|
| 130.2a | 1777 FM | 300.00 | 400.00 | 500.00 | 800.00 |
| | 1778 FF | 300.00 | 400.00 | 500.00 | 800.00 |
| | 1779 FF | 300.00 | 400.00 | 500.00 | 800.00 |
| | 1780 FF | 300.00 | 400.00 | 500.00 | 800.00 |
| | 1781 FF/FM | 300.00 | 400.00 | 500.00 | 800.00 |
| | 1781 FF | 300.00 | 400.00 | 500.00 | 800.00 |
| | 1782 FF | 300.00 | 400.00 | 500.00 | 800.00 |
| | 1783 FF | 300.00 | 400.00 | 500.00 | 800.00 |
| | 1784 FF | 300.00 | 400.00 | 500.00 | 800.00 |
| | 1784 FM | 500.00 | 750.00 | 1000. | 1500. |
| | 1785 FM | 300.00 | 400.00 | 500.00 | 800.00 |
| | 1786 FM | 300.00 | 400.00 | 500.00 | 800.00 |
| | 1787 FM | 300.00 | 400.00 | 500.00 | 800.00 |
| | 1788 FM | 300.00 | 400.00 | 500.00 | 800.00 |

**Rev: Initial letters and mint mark upright.**

| | | VG | Fine | VF | XF |
|-----|------|-----|------|-----|-----|
| 130.1a | 1788 FM | 300.00 | 400.00 | 500.00 | 800.00 |

**Obv: Bust of Charles III, leg: CAROL.IV.D.G. .**

| | | VG | Fine | VF | XF |
|-----|------|-----|------|-----|-----|
| 131 | 1789 FM | 300.00 | 400.00 | 650.00 | 1000. |
| | 1790 FM | 300.00 | 400.00 | 650.00 | 1000. |

**Obv: Armored bust of Charles IV.**

| | | VG | Fine | VF | XF |
|-----|------|-----|------|-----|-----|
| 132 | 1791 FM | 300.00 | 400.00 | 650.00 | 1000. |
| | 1792 FM | 125.00 | 250.00 | 350.00 | 600.00 |
| | 1793 FM | 125.00 | 250.00 | 350.00 | 600.00 |
| | 1794 FM | 125.00 | 250.00 | 350.00 | 600.00 |
| | 1795 FM | 125.00 | 250.00 | 350.00 | 600.00 |
| | 1796 FM | 125.00 | 250.00 | 350.00 | 600.00 |
| | 1797 FM | 125.00 | 250.00 | 400.00 | 750.00 |
| | 1798 FM | 125.00 | 250.00 | 350.00 | 600.00 |
| | 1799 FM | 125.00 | 250.00 | 350.00 | 600.00 |
| | 1800 FM | 125.00 | 250.00 | 350.00 | 600.00 |

**6.7700 g, .875 GOLD, .1904 oz AGW**
**Obv: Armored bust of Charles IV.**

| | | VG | Fine | VF | XF |
|-----|------|-----|------|-----|-----|
| 132 | 1801 FM | 125.00 | 250.00 | 350.00 | 600.00 |
| | 1802 FT | 125.00 | 250.00 | 350.00 | 600.00 |
| | 1803 FT | 125.00 | 250.00 | 350.00 | 600.00 |
| | 1804 TH | 125.00 | 250.00 | 350.00 | 600.00 |
| | 1805 TH | 125.00 | 250.00 | 350.00 | 600.00 |
| | 1806 TH | 125.00 | 250.00 | 350.00 | 600.00 |
| | 1807 TH | 125.00 | 250.00 | 350.00 | 600.00 |
| | 1808 TH | 125.00 | 250.00 | 350.00 | 600.00 |

**Obv: Undraped bust of Ferdinand VII.**

| | | VG | Fine | VF | XF |
|-----|------|-----|------|-----|-----|
| 134 | 1814 HJ | 250.00 | 400.00 | 650.00 | 1200. |
| | 1814 JJ | 250.00 | 400.00 | 650.00 | 1200. |
| | 1815 JJ | 250.00 | 400.00 | 650.00 | 1200. |
| | 1816 JJ | 250.00 | 400.00 | 650.00 | 1200. |
| | 1817 JJ | 250.00 | 400.00 | 650.00 | 1200. |
| | 1818 JJ | 250.00 | 400.00 | 650.00 | 1200. |
| | 1819 JJ | 250.00 | 400.00 | 650.00 | 1200. |
| | 1820 JJ | 250.00 | 400.00 | 650.00 | 1200. |

# 4 ESCUDOS

**13.5400 g, .917 GOLD, .3992 oz AGW**
**Obv. leg: PHILIP.V.D.G.HISPAN.ET IND.REX**
**Rev. leg: INITIUM SAPIENTIAE TIMOR DOMINI**

| KM# | Date | VG | Fine | VF | XF |
|-----|------|-----|------|-----|-----|
| 135 | 1732 | — | — | Rare | — |
| | 1732 F | — | — | Rare | — |
| | 1733 F | — | — | Rare | — |
| | 1734/3 F | 1000. | 1500. | 2000. | 3500. |
| | 1734 MF | 800.00 | 1200. | 1750. | 3000. |
| | 1735 MF | 800.00 | 1200. | 1750. | 3000. |
| | 1736 MF | 800.00 | 1200. | 1750. | 3000. |
| | 1737 MF | 600.00 | 1000. | 1500. | 2750. |
| | 1738 MF | 600.00 | 1000. | 1500. | 2750. |
| | 1739 MF | 600.00 | 1000. | 1500. | 2750. |
| | 1740/30 | 600.00 | 1000. | 1500. | 2750. |
| | 1740 MF | 600.00 | 1000. | 1500. | 2750. |
| | 1741 MF | 600.00 | 1000. | 1500. | 2750. |
| | 1742 MF | 600.00 | 1000. | 1500. | 2750. |
| | 1743 MF | 600.00 | 1000. | 1500. | 2750. |
| | 1744 MD | 600.00 | 1000. | 1500. | 2750. |
| | 1745 MF | 600.00 | 1000. | 1500. | 2750. |
| | 1746 MF | 600.00 | 1000. | 1500. | 2750. |
| | 1747 MF | 600.00 | 1000. | 1500. | 2750. |

**Obv: Large bust; leg: FERDND.VI.D.G. .**

| 136 | 1747 MF | — | — | Rare | — |
|-----|---------|---|---|------|---|

**Obv: Small bust; leg: FERDND.VI.D.G. .**
**Rev. leg: NOMINA MAGNA SEQUOR, 4S by arms.**

| 137 | 1748 MF | 1500. | 3000. | 5000. | 7000. |
|-----|---------|-------|-------|-------|-------|
| | 1749 MF | 1500. | 3000. | 5000. | 7000. |
| | 1750 MF | 1500. | 3000. | 5000. | 7000. |
| | 1751 MF | 1500. | 3000. | 5000. | 7000. |

**Rev: Without 4 S by arms.**

| KM# | Date | VG | Fine | VF | XF |
|-----|------|-----|------|-----|-----|
| 138 | 1752 MF | 800.00 | 1500. | 2750. | 4000. |
| | 1753 MF | 800.00 | 1500. | 2750. | 4000. |
| | 1754 MF | 800.00 | 1500. | 2750. | 4000. |
| | 1755 MM | 800.00 | 1500. | 2750. | 4000. |
| | 1756 MM | 800.00 | 1500. | 2750. | 4000. |

**Obv: Large full bust; leg: FERDND.VI.D.G. .**

| 139 | 1757 MM | 1250. | 2500. | 4500. | 6500. |
|-----|---------|-------|-------|-------|-------|
| | 1758 MM | 1250. | 2500. | 4500. | 6500. |
| | 1759 MM | 1250. | 2500. | 4500. | 6500. |

**Obv: Young bust, leg: CAROLVS.III.D.G. .**
**Rev. leg: NOMINA MAGNA SEQUOR**

| 140 | 1760 MM | 2500. | 5000. | 7000. | 10,000. |
|-----|---------|-------|-------|-------|---------|
| | 1761 MM | 2500. | 5000. | 7000. | 10,000. |

**Obv: Large young bust, leg: CAROLUS.III.D.G. .**
**Rev. leg: IN.UTROQ.FELIX.AUSPICE.DEO.**

| 141 | 1762 MF | 800.00 | 1200. | 1800. | 3000. |
|-----|---------|--------|-------|-------|-------|
| | 1763 MF | 800.00 | 1200. | 1800. | 3000. |
| | 1764 MF | — | — | Rare | — |
| | 1765 MF | 800.00 | 1200. | 1800. | 3000. |
| | 1766 MF | 800.00 | 1200. | 1800. | 3000. |
| | 1767 MF | 800.00 | 1200. | 1800. | 3000. |
| | 1768 MF | 800.00 | 1200. | 1800. | 3000. |
| | 1769 MF | 800.00 | 1200. | 1800. | 3000. |
| | 1770 MF | 800.00 | 1200. | 1800. | 3000. |
| | 1771 MF | 800.00 | 1200. | 1800. | 3000. |

**13.5400 g, .901 GOLD, .3922 oz AGW**
**Obv. leg: CAROL.III.D.G. .**
**Rev: FM and mint mark upright.**

| KM# | Date | VG | Fine | VF | XF |
|---|---|---|---|---|---|
| 142.1 | 1772 FM | 400.00 | 650.00 | 1000. | 1850. |
| | 1773 FM | 400.00 | 650.00 | 1000. | 1850. |

**Rev: Initial letters and mint mark inverted.**

| | | | | | |
|---|---|---|---|---|---|
| 142.2 | 1773 FM | 400.00 | 600.00 | 900.00 | 1600. |
| | 1774 FM | 400.00 | 600.00 | 900.00 | 1600. |
| | 1775 FM | 400.00 | 600.00 | 900.00 | 1600. |
| | 1776 FM | 400.00 | 600.00 | 900.00 | 1600. |

**13.5400 g, .875 GOLD, .3809 oz AGW**

| | | | | | |
|---|---|---|---|---|---|
| 142.2a | 1777 FM | 400.00 | 600.00 | 900.00 | 1600. |
| | 1778 FF | 400.00 | 600.00 | 900.00 | 1600. |
| | 1779 FF | 400.00 | 600.00 | 900.00 | 1600. |
| | 1780 FF | 400.00 | 600.00 | 900.00 | 1600. |
| | 1781 FF | 400.00 | 600.00 | 900.00 | 1600. |
| | 1782 FF | 400.00 | 600.00 | 900.00 | 1600. |
| | 1783 FF | 400.00 | 600.00 | 900.00 | 1600. |
| | 1784 FF | 400.00 | 600.00 | 900.00 | 1600. |
| | 1784 FM | 400.00 | 600.00 | 900.00 | 1600. |
| | 1785 FM | 400.00 | 600.00 | 900.00 | 1600. |
| | 1786 FM | 400.00 | 600.00 | 900.00 | 1600. |
| | 1787 FM | 400.00 | 600.00 | 900.00 | 1600. |
| | 1788 FM | 400.00 | 600.00 | 900.00 | 1600. |
| | 1789 FM | 400.00 | 600.00 | 900.00 | 1600. |

**Rev: Initial letters and mint mark upright.**

| | | | | | |
|---|---|---|---|---|---|
| 142.1a | 1788 FM | 400.00 | 650.00 | 1000. | 1850. |

**Obv: Bust of Charles III, leg: CAROL.IV.D.G. .**

| | | | | | |
|---|---|---|---|---|---|
| 143.1 | 1789 FM | 500.00 | 700.00 | 1000. | 1750. |
| | 1790 FM | 500.00 | 700.00 | 1000. | 1750. |

**Obv: Bust of Charles III, leg: CAROL. IIII D.G. . . .**

| | | | | | |
|---|---|---|---|---|---|
| 143.2 | 1790 FM | 600.00 | 1000. | 1800. | 3000. |

**Obv: Armored bust of Charles IIII.**

| | | | | | |
|---|---|---|---|---|---|
| 144 | 1792 FM | 300.00 | 500.00 | 750.00 | 1400. |
| | 1793 FM | 300.00 | 500.00 | 750.00 | 1400. |
| | 1794/3 FM | 300.00 | 500.00 | 750.00 | 1400. |
| | 1794 FM | 300.00 | 500.00 | 750.00 | 1400. |
| | 1795 FM | 300.00 | 500.00 | 750.00 | 1400. |
| | 1796 FM | 300.00 | 500.00 | 750.00 | 1400. |
| | 1797 FM | 300.00 | 500.00 | 750.00 | 1400. |
| | 1798/7 FM | 300.00 | 500.00 | 750.00 | 1400. |
| | 1798 FM | 300.00 | 500.00 | 750.00 | 1400. |
| | 1799 FM | 300.00 | 500.00 | 750.00 | 1400. |
| | 1800 FM | 300.00 | 500.00 | 750.00 | 1400. |

**13.5400 g, .875 GOLD, .3809 oz AGW**
**Obv: Armored bust of Charles IIII.**

| | | | | | |
|---|---|---|---|---|---|
| | 1801 FM | 300.00 | 500.00 | 750.00 | 1400. |
| | 1801 FT | 300.00 | 500.00 | 750.00 | 1400. |
| | 1802 FT | 300.00 | 500.00 | 750.00 | 1400. |
| | 1803 FT | 300.00 | 500.00 | 750.00 | 1400. |
| | 1804/3 TH | 300.00 | 500.00 | 750.00 | 1400. |
| | 1804 TH | 300.00 | 500.00 | 750.00 | 1400. |
| | 1805 TH | 300.00 | 500.00 | 750.00 | 1400. |

| KM# | Date | VG | Fine | VF | XF |
|---|---|---|---|---|---|
| 144 | 1806/5 TH | 300.00 | 500.00 | 750.00 | 1400. |
| | 1806 TH | 300.00 | 500.00 | 750.00 | 1400. |
| | 1807 TH | 300.00 | 500.00 | 750.00 | 1400. |
| | 1808/0 TH | 300.00 | 500.00 | 750.00 | 1400. |
| | 1808 TH | 300.00 | 500.00 | 750.00 | 1400. |

**Obv: Armored bust of Ferdinand VII.**

| | | | | | |
|---|---|---|---|---|---|
| 145 | 1810 HJ | 450.00 | 600.00 | 950.00 | 1600. |
| | 1811 HJ | 350.00 | 500.00 | 850.00 | 1400. |
| | 1812 HJ | 350.00 | 500.00 | 850.00 | 1400. |

**Obv: Undraped bust of Ferdinand VII.**

| | | | | | |
|---|---|---|---|---|---|
| 146 | 1814 HJ | 400.00 | 650.00 | 900.00 | 1600. |
| | 1815 HJ | 400.00 | 650.00 | 900.00 | 1600. |
| | 1815 JJ | 400.00 | 650.00 | 900.00 | 1600. |
| | 1816 JJ | 400.00 | 650.00 | 900.00 | 1600. |
| | 1817 JJ | 400.00 | 650.00 | 900.00 | 1600. |
| | 1818 JJ | 400.00 | 650.00 | 900.00 | 1600. |
| | 1819 JJ | 400.00 | 650.00 | 900.00 | 1600. |
| | 1820 JJ | 400.00 | 650.00 | 900.00 | 1600. |

# 8 ESCUDOS

**27.0700 g, .917 GOLD, .7981 oz AGW**
**Obv. leg: PHILIP.V.D.G.HISPAN.ET IND.REX**
**Rev. leg: INITIUM SAPIENTIAE TIMOR DOMINI**

| KM# | Date | VG | Fine | VF | XF |
|---|---|---|---|---|---|
| 148 | 1732 | — | — | Rare | — |
| | 1732 F | — | — | Rare | — |
| | 1733 F | — | — | Rare | — |
| | 1734 MF | 1000. | 1600. | 2600. | 3750. |
| | 1735 MF | 1000. | 1500. | 2250. | 3250. |
| | 1736 MF | 1000. | 1500. | 2250. | 3250. |
| | 1737 MF | 1000. | 1500. | 2250. | 3250. |
| | 1738/7 MF | 1000. | 1500. | 2250. | 3250. |
| | 1738 MF | 1000. | 1500. | 2250. | 3250. |
| | 1739 MF | 1000. | 1500. | 2250. | 3250. |
| | 1740 MF | 1000. | 1500. | 2250. | 3250. |
| | 1741 MF | 1000. | 1500. | 2250. | 3250. |
| | 1742 MF | 1000. | 1500. | 2250. | 3250. |
| | 1743 MF | 1000. | 1500. | 2250. | 3250. |
| | 1744 MF | 1000. | 1500. | 2250. | 3250. |
| | 1745 MF | 1000. | 1500. | 2250. | 3250. |
| | 1746 MF | 1000. | 1500. | 2250. | 3250. |
| | 1747 MF | 2000. | 3000. | 2250. | 3250. |

Obv: Large bust; leg: FERDND.VI.D.G. .
Rev: W/o 8 S by arms.

| KM# | Date | VG | Fine | VF | XF |
|---|---|---|---|---|---|
| 151 | 1752 MF | 1000. | 1500. | 2500. | 4000. |
| | 1753 MF | 1000. | 1500. | 2500. | 4000. |
| | 1754 MF | 1000. | 1500. | 2500. | 4000. |
| | 1755 MM | 1000. | 1500. | 2500. | 4000. |
| | 1756 MM | 1000. | 1500. | 2500. | 4000. |

Obv: Medium, full bust; leg: FERDND.VI.D.G. . .

| | | | | | |
|---|---|---|---|---|---|
| 152 | 1757 MM | 1200. | 2000. | 3000. | 4000. |
| | 1758 MM | 1200. | 2000. | 3000. | 4000. |
| | 1759 MM | 1200. | 2000. | 3000. | 4000. |

Obv: Young bust, leg: CAROLVS.III.D.G. .
w/Order of the Golden Fleece at date.

| | | | | | |
|---|---|---|---|---|---|
| 153 | 1760 MM | 1500. | 2500. | 4250. | 7000. |
| | 1761 MM | 1750. | 3000. | 5000. | 8000. |

Obv: Young bust; leg: FERDND.VI.D.G. .

| | | | | | |
|---|---|---|---|---|---|
| 149 | 1747 MF | 3000. | 4000. | 6500. | 12,500. |

Obv: Small bust; leg: FERDND.VI.D.G. .
Rev. leg: NOMINA MAGNA SEQUOR

| | | | | | |
|---|---|---|---|---|---|
| 150 | 1748 MF | 1000. | 1500. | 2500. | 4000. |
| | 1749/8 MF | 1000. | 1500. | 2500. | 4000. |
| | 1749 MF | 1000. | 1500. | 2500. | 4000. |
| | 1750 MF | 1000. | 1500. | 2500. | 4000. |
| | 1751 MF | 1000. | 1500. | 2500. | 4000. |

Obv: Young bust, leg: CAROLVS.III.D.G. .
w/Order of the Golden Fleece on chest.

| | | | | | |
|---|---|---|---|---|---|
| 154 | 1761 MM | 1500. | 2750. | 4500. | 7500. |

Obv: Large bust, leg: CAROLUS.III.D.G. .
Rev. leg: IN.UTROQ.FELIX.AUSPICE

| KM# | Date | VG | Fine | VF | XF |
|---|---|---|---|---|---|
| 155 | 1762 MF | 1000. | 1500. | 2750. | 5000. |
| | 1762 MM | 1000. | 1500. | 2750. | 5000. |
| | 1763 MF | 1000. | 1500. | 2750. | 5000. |
| | 1763 MM | 1000. | 1500. | 2750. | 5000. |
| | 1764 MF | 1500. | 3000. | 4000. | 6000. |
| | 1764 MM | 1500. | 3000. | 4000. | 6000. |
| | 1765/4 MF | 1500. | 3000. | 4000. | 6000. |
| | 1765 MF | 1500. | 3000. | 4000. | 6000. |
| | 1765 MM | 1000. | 1500. | 2500. | 4000. |
| | 1766 MF | 1000. | 1500. | 2500. | 4000. |
| | 1767 MF | 1000. | 1500. | 2500. | 4000. |
| | 1768 MF | 1000. | 1500. | 2500. | 4000. |
| | 1769 MF | 1000. | 1500. | 2500. | 4000. |
| | 1770 MF | 1000. | 1500. | 2500. | 4000. |
| | 1771 MF | 1500. | 3000. | 4000. | 6000. |

**27.0700 g, .901 GOLD, .7841 oz AGW**
Obv: Mature bust, leg: CAROL.III.D.G. .
Rev. leg: . . . . .AUSPICE.DEO.; FM and mint mark upright.

| 156.1 | 1772 FM | 500.00 | 750.00 | 1250. | 2000. |
|---|---|---|---|---|---|
| | 1773 FM | 550.00 | 850.00 | 1350. | 2250. |

**Rev: Initial letters and mint mark inverted.**

| 156.2 | 1773 FM | 500.00 | 700.00 | 1150. | 1750. |
|---|---|---|---|---|---|
| | 1774 FM | 500.00 | 700.00 | 1150. | 1750. |
| | 1775 FM | 500.00 | 700.00 | 1150. | 1750. |
| | 1776 FM | 500.00 | 700.00 | 1150. | 1750. |

**27.0700 g, .875 GOLD, .7616 oz AGW**

| KM# | Date | VG | Fine | VF | XF |
|---|---|---|---|---|---|
| 156.2a | 1777/6 FM | 500.00 | 700.00 | 1150. | 1750. |
| | 1777 FM | 500.00 | 700.00 | 1150. | 1750. |
| | 1778 FF | 500.00 | 700.00 | 1150. | 1750. |
| | 1779 FF | 500.00 | 700.00 | 1150. | 1750. |
| | 1780 FF | 500.00 | 700.00 | 1150. | 1750. |
| | 1781 FF | 500.00 | 700.00 | 1150. | 1750. |
| | 1782 FF | 500.00 | 700.00 | 1150. | 1750. |
| | 1783 FF | 500.00 | 700.00 | 1150. | 1750. |
| | 1784 FF | 500.00 | 700.00 | 1150. | 1750. |
| | 1784 FM | 500.00 | 700.00 | 1150. | 1750. |
| | 1785 FM | 500.00 | 700.00 | 1150. | 1750. |
| | 1786 FM | 500.00 | 700.00 | 1150. | 1750. |
| | 1787 FM | 500.00 | 700.00 | 1150. | 1750. |
| | 1788 FM | 500.00 | 700.00 | 1150. | 1750. |

**Rev: Initial letters and mint mark upright.**

| 156.1a | 1788 FM | 600.00 | 900.00 | 1500. | 2500. |
|---|---|---|---|---|---|

Obv: Bust of Charles III, leg: CAROL.IV.D.G. .
Rev: IN UTROQ. . .a.d., arms, order chain.

| 157 | 1789 FM | 500.00 | 750.00 | 1500. | 3000. |
|---|---|---|---|---|---|
| | 1790 FM | 500.00 | 750.00 | 1500. | 3000. |

Obv: Bust of Charles III, leg: CAROL.IIII.D.G. .

| 158 | 1790 FM | 500.00 | 750.00 | 1500. | 3000. |
|---|---|---|---|---|---|

Obv: Armored bust of Charles IIII.
Rev. leg: IN UTROQ. FELIX., arms, order chain.

| 159 | 1791 FM | 375.00 | 475.00 | 650.00 | 900.00 |
|---|---|---|---|---|---|
| | 1792 FM | 375.00 | 475.00 | 650.00 | 900.00 |
| | 1793 FM | 375.00 | 475.00 | 650.00 | 900.00 |
| | 1794 FM | 375.00 | 475.00 | 650.00 | 900.00 |
| | 1795 FM | 375.00 | 475.00 | 650.00 | 900.00 |
| | 1796/5 FM | 400.00 | 500.00 | 700.00 | 1000. |
| | 1796 FM | 375.00 | 475.00 | 650.00 | 900.00 |

| KM# | Date | VG | Fine | VF | XF |
|---|---|---|---|---|---|
| 159 | 1797 FM | 375.00 | 475.00 | 650.00 | 900.00 |
| | 1798 FM | 375.00 | 475.00 | 650.00 | 900.00 |
| | 1799 FM | 375.00 | 475.00 | 650.00 | 900.00 |
| | 1800 FM | 375.00 | 475.00 | 650.00 | 900.00 |
| | 1801/0 FT | 400.00 | 500.00 | 700.00 | 1000. |
| | 1801 FM | 375.00 | 475.00 | 650.00 | 900.00 |
| | 1801 FT | 375.00 | 475.00 | 650.00 | 900.00 |
| | 1802 FT | 375.00 | 475.00 | 650.00 | 900.00 |
| | 1803 FT | 375.00 | 475.00 | 650.00 | 900.00 |
| | 1804/3 TH | 400.00 | 500.00 | 700.00 | 1000. |
| | 1804 TH | 375.00 | 475.00 | 650.00 | 900.00 |
| | 1805 TH | 375.00 | 475.00 | 650.00 | 900.00 |
| | 1806 TH | 375.00 | 475.00 | 650.00 | 900.00 |
| | 1807/6 TH | 400.00 | 500.00 | 700.00 | 1000. |
| | 1807 TH | 450.00 | 550.00 | 750.00 | 1000. |
| | 1808 TH | 450.00 | 600.00 | 800.00 | 1100. |

**Obv: Armored bust of Ferdinand VII.**

| | Date | VG | Fine | VF | XF |
|---|---|---|---|---|---|
| 160 | 1808 TH | 400.00 | 500.00 | 750.00 | 1000. |
| | 1809 HJ | 400.00 | 500.00 | 750.00 | 1000. |
| | 1810 HJ | 375.00 | 475.00 | 650.00 | 875.00 |
| | 1811/0 HJ | 400.00 | 500.00 | 750.00 | 1000. |
| | 1811 HJ | 400.00 | 500.00 | 750.00 | 1000. |
| | 1811 JJ | 375.00 | 475.00 | 650.00 | 875.00 |
| | 1812 JJ | 375.00 | 475.00 | 650.00 | 875.00 |

**Obv: Undraped bust of Ferdinand VII.**

| KM# | Date | VG | Fine | VF | XF |
|---|---|---|---|---|---|
| 161 | 1814 JJ | 375.00 | 475.00 | 650.00 | 850.00 |
| | 1815/4 JJ | 400.00 | 500.00 | 700.00 | 1000. |
| | 1815/4 HJ | 400.00 | 500.00 | 700.00 | 1000. |
| | 1815 JJ | 375.00 | 475.00 | 650.00 | 850.00 |
| | 1815 HJ | 375.00 | 475.00 | 650.00 | 850.00 |
| | 1816/5 JJ | 400.00 | 500.00 | 700.00 | 1000. |
| | 1816 JJ | 375.00 | 475.00 | 650.00 | 850.00 |
| | 1817 JJ | 375.00 | 475.00 | 650.00 | 850.00 |
| | 1818/7 JJ | 375.00 | 475.00 | 650.00 | 850.00 |
| | 1818 JJ | 375.00 | 475.00 | 650.00 | 850.00 |
| | 1819 JJ | 375.00 | 475.00 | 650.00 | 850.00 |
| | 1820 JJ | 375.00 | 475.00 | 650.00 | 850.00 |
| | 1821 JJ | 400.00 | 500.00 | 700.00 | 1000. |

# PROCLAMATION MEDALLIC ISSUES (Q)

The 'Q' used in the following listings refer to STAN-
DARD CATALOG OF MEXICAN COINS, PAPER
MONEY, STOCKS, BONDS and MEDALS, Krause Pub-
lications, Inc., copyright 1981.

## Chiapa
### REAL

**SILVER**
**Obv: Crowned arms between pillars, IR below,
leg: FERNANDO VII REY DE ESPANA Y DE SUS
INDIAS. Rev: Legend in 5 lines within wreath,
PROCLA/MADO/ENCIUD/R.DECHIAPPA/1808.**

| KM# | Date | | Fine | VF | XF | Unc |
|---|---|---|---|---|---|---|
| Q8 | 1808 | | 22.50 | 35.00 | 50.00 | — |

### 2 REALES

**SILVER**
**Obv. leg: FERNANDO VII REY DE ESPANA Y DE
SUS INDIAS.**

| | | | | | | |
|---|---|---|---|---|---|---|
| Q10 | 1808 | | 50.00 | 70.00 | 100.00 | — |

## Mexico City
### 1/2 REAL

**SILVER, 1.60 g**
**Obv. leg: A CARLOS IV REY DE ESPANA Y DE LAS
YNDIAS.**
**Rev. leg: PROCLAMADO EN MEXICO ANO DE 1789.**

| KM# | Date | Fine | VF | XF | Unc |
|---|---|---|---|---|---|
| Q22 | 1789 | 20.00 | 28.50 | 40.00 | — |

**BRONZE, 18mm**

| Q22a | 1789 | 22.50 | 35.00 | 50.00 | — |
|---|---|---|---|---|---|

**SILVER, 17mm**
**Obv: Crowned arms in double-lined circle.**

| Q23 | 1789 | 20.00 | 28.50 | 40.00 | — |
|---|---|---|---|---|---|

**BRONZE**

| Q23a | 1789 | 22.50 | 35.00 | 50.00 | — |
|---|---|---|---|---|---|

# REAL

**SILVER**

| KM# | Date | Fine | VF | XF | Unc |
|-----|------|------|-----|-----|-----|
| Q24 | 1789 | 20.00 | 28.50 | 40.00 | — |

**BRONZE, 21mm**

| | | | | | |
|-----|------|------|-----|-----|-----|
| Q24a | 1789 | 22.50 | 35.00 | 50.00 | — |

**SILVER**
**Obv: Crowned arms in double-lined circle.**

| | | | | | |
|-----|------|------|-----|-----|-----|
| Q-A24 | 1789 | 20.00 | 28.50 | 40.00 | — |

**COPPER**

| | | | | | |
|-----|------|------|-----|-----|-----|
| Q-A24a | 1789 | 22.50 | 35.00 | 50.00 | — |

**SILVER, 27.00 g**

| KM# | Date | Fine | VF | XF | Unc |
|-----|------|------|-----|-----|-----|
| Q28 | 1789 | 200.00 | 275.00 | 400.00 | — |

**BRONZE**

| | | | | | |
|-----|------|------|-----|-----|-----|
| Q28a | 1789 | 70.00 | 100.00 | 150.00 | — |

# 2 REALES

**SILVER, 6.70 g**

| | | | | | |
|-----|------|------|-----|-----|-----|
| Q25 | 1789 | 35.00 | 50.00 | 75.00 | — |

**BRONZE**

| | | | | | |
|-----|------|------|-----|-----|-----|
| Q25a | 1789 | 30.00 | 45.00 | 60.00 | — |

# Queretaro
## 2 REALES

**SILVER**
**Obv. leg: FERNANDO VII REY DE ESPANA.**

| | | | | | |
|-----|------|------|-----|-----|-----|
| Q64 | 1808 | 35.00 | 50.00 | 75.00 | — |

# 4 REALES

**SILVER, 13.60 g**

| | | | | | |
|-----|------|------|-----|-----|-----|
| Q27 | 1789 | 100.00 | 150.00 | 225.00 | — |

**BRONZE**

| | | | | | |
|-----|------|------|-----|-----|-----|
| Q27a | 1789 | 70.00 | 100.00 | 150.00 | — |

# 4 REALES

**SILVER**

| | | | | | |
|-----|------|------|-----|-----|-----|
| Q-A66 | 1808 | 140.00 | 200.00 | 300.00 | — |

# 8 REALES

# 8 REALES

**SILVER**

| KM# | Date | Fine | VF | XF | Unc |
|-----|------|------|-----|-----|-----|
| Q68 | 1808 | 300.00 | 425.00 | 600.00 | — |

# WAR OF INDEPENDENCE
## ROYALIST ISSUES
(1810-1821)
### Provisional Mints
#### RULER

Ferdinand VII, 1808-1821

#### MINT MARKS

CA - Chihuahua
D - Durango
GA - Guadalajara
GO - Guanajuato
ZS - Zacatecas

#### MONETARY SYSTEM

16 Reales = 1 Escudo

## CHIHUAHUA

The Chihuahua Mint was established by a decree of October 8, 1810 as a temporary mint. Their first coins were cast 8 reales using Mexico City coins as patterns and obliterating/changing the mint mark and moneyer initials. Two c/m were placed on the obverse - on the left, a T designating its having been received by the Royal Treasurer and on the right crowned pillars of Hercules with pomegranate beneath; the symbol of the comptroller.

In 1814 standard dies were available and from 1814 to 1822 standard 8 reales were struck. Only the one denomination was made at this mint.

#### MINT MARK: CA

## 8 REALES

**CAST SILVER**
**Obv: Imaginary bust of Ferdinand VII;**
**leg: FERDIN.VII.DEI.GRATIA.**
**c/m: 'T' at left and pomegranate**
**pillars at right.**

| KM# | Date | Good | VG | Fine | VF |
|-----|------|------|-----|------|-----|
| 123 | 1810 RP | — | — | Rare | — |
| | 1811 RP | 45.00 | 60.00 | 100.00 | 150.00 |
| | 1812 RP | 30.00 | 40.00 | 60.00 | 90.00 |
| | 1813/2 RP | 32.50 | 45.00 | 70.00 | 100.00 |
| | 1813 RP | 30.00 | 40.00 | 60.00 | 90.00 |

**27.0700 g, .903 SILVER, .7860 oz ASW**
**Obv: Draped bust of Ferdinand VII.**
**Rev: Similar to KM#123.**

| KM# | Date | VG | Fine | VF | XF |
|-----|------|-----|------|-----|-----|
| 111.1 | 1813 RP | — | Reported, not confirmed | | |
| | 1814 RP | — | Reported, not confirmed | | |
| | 1815 RP | 200.00 | 275.00 | 350.00 | 500.00 |
| | 1816 RP | 80.00 | 125.00 | 150.00 | 275.00 |
| | 1817 RP | 100.00 | 150.00 | 185.00 | 275.00 |
| | 1818 RP | 100.00 | 150.00 | 185.00 | 275.00 |
| | 1819 RP | 125.00 | 175.00 | 250.00 | 350.00 |
| | 1820 RP | 200.00 | 275.00 | 350.00 | 500.00 |
| | 1821 RP | 200.00 | 275.00 | 350.00 | 500.00 |
| | 1822 RP | 400.00 | 600.00 | 800.00 | 1100. |

**NOTE:** KM#111.1 is normally found counterstamped over earlier cast 8 Reales, KM#123.

## DURANGO

The Durango mint was authorized as a temporary mint at the same time as the Chihuahua Mint, October 8, 1810. The mint opened sometime in 1811 and made coins of 6 denominations - 5 silver and 1 copper - during the period 1811 to 1822.

#### MINT MARK: D

### 1/8 REAL

## COPPER
**Obv: Crown above double F7 monogram.**
**Rev: EN DURANGO, value, date.**

| KM# | Date | VG | Fine | VF | XF |
|---|---|---|---|---|---|
| 60 | 1812 | 35.00 | 75.00 | 125.00 | 225.00 |
| | 1813 | — | — | Rare | — |
| | 1814 | — | — | Rare | — |

**Rev: Spray added above date.**

| | | | | | |
|---|---|---|---|---|---|
| 61 | 1814 | 15.00 | 25.00 | 50.00 | 85.00 |
| | 1815 | 15.00 | 25.00 | 50.00 | 85.00 |
| | 1816 | 15.00 | 25.00 | 50.00 | 85.00 |
| | 1817 | 15.00 | 25.00 | 50.00 | 80.00 |
| | 1818 | 15.00 | 25.00 | 50.00 | 80.00 |
| | 1818 OCTAVO DD REAL (error) | | | | |
| | | 45.00 | 75.00 | — | — |

## 1/2 REAL

**1.6900 g, .903 SILVER, .0491 oz ASW**
**Obv: Draped bust of Ferdinand VII.**

| | | | | | |
|---|---|---|---|---|---|
| 74.1 | 1813 RM | 250.00 | 350.00 | 600.00 | 1500. |
| | 1814 MZ | 250.00 | 350.00 | 600.00 | 1500. |
| | 1816 MZ | 250.00 | 350.00 | 600.00 | 1500. |

## REAL

**3.3800 g, .903 SILVER, .0981 oz ASW**
**Obv: Draped bust of Ferdinand VII.**

| | | | | | |
|---|---|---|---|---|---|
| 83.1 | 1813 RM | 250.00 | 350.00 | 500.00 | 1250. |
| | 1814 MZ | 250.00 | 350.00 | 500.00 | 1250. |
| | 1815 MZ | 250.00 | 300.00 | 500.00 | 1250. |

## 2 REALES

**6.7700 g, .903 SILVER, .1966 oz ASW**
**Obv: Armored bust of Ferdinand VII.**

| | | | | | |
|---|---|---|---|---|---|
| 92.2 | 1811 RM | 200.00 | 300.00 | 400.00 | 1500. |
| | 1812 RM | — | — | Rare | — |

**Obv: Draped bust of Ferdinand VII.**

| | | | | | |
|---|---|---|---|---|---|
| 93.1 | 1812 MZ | 200.00 | 300.00 | 400.00 | 1500. |
| | 1812 RM | — | — | Rare | — |
| | 1813 MZ | 300.00 | 500.00 | 800.00 | 2500. |
| | 1813 RM | 300.00 | 500.00 | 800.00 | 2500. |
| | 1814 MZ | 300.00 | 500.00 | 800.00 | 2500. |
| | 1815 MZ | 300.00 | 500.00 | 800.00 | 2500. |
| | 1816 MZ | 300.00 | 500.00 | 800.00 | 2500. |
| | 1817 MZ | 300.00 | 500.00 | 800.00 | 2500. |

## 4 REALES

**13.5400 g, .903 SILVER, .3931 oz ASW**
**Obv: Draped bust of Ferdinand VII.**

| | | | | | |
|---|---|---|---|---|---|
| 102.1 | 1814 MZ | 500.00 | 1000. | 1500. | 4000. |
| | 1816 MZ | 400.00 | 800.00 | 1200. | 3000. |
| | 1817 MZ | 400.00 | 800.00 | 1200. | 3000. |

## 8 REALES

**27.0700 g, .903 SILVER, .7860 oz ASW**
**Obv: Armored bust of Ferdinand VII.**

| | | | | | |
|---|---|---|---|---|---|
| 110.1 | 1811 RM | 500.00 | 800.00 | 1200. | 4000. |
| | 1812 RM | 300.00 | 500.00 | 800.00 | 3000. |
| | 1813 MZ | 300.00 | 500.00 | 800.00 | 3000. |
| | 1814 MZ | 300.00 | 500.00 | 800.00 | 3000. |

**Obv: Draped bust of Ferdinand VII.**

| KM# | Date | VG | Fine | VF | XF |
|---|---|---|---|---|---|
| 111.2 | 1812 MZ | 300.00 | 400.00 | 600.00 | 1500. |
| | 1812 RM | 125.00 | 175.00 | 275.00 | 800.00 |
| | 1813 RM | 150.00 | 200.00 | 325.00 | 850.00 |
| | 1813 MZ | 125.00 | 175.00 | 275.00 | 750.00 |
| | 1814 MZ | 150.00 | 225.00 | 275.00 | 750.00 |
| | 1815 MZ | 75.00 | 125.00 | 225.00 | 600.00 |
| | 1816 MZ | 50.00 | 75.00 | 125.00 | 325.00 |
| | 1817 MZ | 30.00 | 50.00 | 90.00 | 250.00 |
| | 1818 MZ | 50.00 | 75.00 | 125.00 | 350.00 |
| | 1818 RM | 50.00 | 75.00 | 125.00 | 325.00 |
| | 1818 CG/RM | | | | |
| | | 100.00 | 125.00 | 150.00 | 350.00 |
| | 1818 CG | 50.00 | 75.00 | 125.00 | 325.00 |
| | 1819 CG/RM | 50.00 | 100.00 | 150.00 | 300.00 |
| | 1819 CG | 30.00 | 60.00 | 100.00 | 250.00 |
| | 1820 CG | 30.00 | 60.00 | 100.00 | 250.00 |
| | 1821 CG | 30.00 | 40.00 | 50.00 | 150.00 |
| | 1822 CG | 30.00 | 50.00 | 75.00 | 160.00 |

**NOTE:** Occasionally these are found struck over Guadalajara 8 reales and are very rare in general, specimens dated prior to 1816 are rather weakly struck.

## GUADALAJARA

The Guadalajara Mint made its first coins in 1812 and the mint operated until April 30, 1815. It was to reopen in 1818 and continue operations until 1822. It was the only Royalist mint to strike gold coins, both 4 and 8 escudos. In addition to these it struck the standard 5 denominations in silver.

**MINT MARK: GA**

## 1/2 REAL

**1.6900 g, .903 SILVER, .0491 oz ASW**
**Obv: Draped bust of Ferdinand VII.**

| | | | | | |
|---|---|---|---|---|---|
| 74.2 | 1812 MR | — | — | Rare | — |
| | 1814 MR | 40.00 | 100.00 | 200.00 | 300.00 |
| | 1815 MR | 200.00 | 350.00 | 500.00 | 1000. |

## REAL

**3.3800 g, .903 SILVER, .0981 oz ASW**
**Obv: Draped bust of Ferdinand VII.**

| KM# | Date | VG | Fine | VF | XF |
|---|---|---|---|---|---|
| 83.2 | 1814 MR | 125.00 | 175.00 | 275.00 | 600.00 |
| | 1815 MR | — | — | Rare | — |

## 2 REALES

**6.7700 g, .903 SILVER, .1966 oz ASW**
**Obv: Draped bust of Ferdinand VII.**

| | | | | | |
|---|---|---|---|---|---|
| 93.2 | 1812 MR | 300.00 | 500.00 | 800.00 | 2500. |
| | 1814 MR | 75.00 | 125.00 | 200.00 | 600.00 |
| | 1815/4 MR | 425.00 | 725.00 | 1100. | 3600. |
| | 1815 MR | 400.00 | 700.00 | 1000. | 3500. |
| | 1821 FS | 200.00 | 250.00 | 350.00 | 900.00 |

## 4 REALES

**13.5400 g, .903 SILVER, .3931 oz ASW**
**Obv: Draped bust of Ferdinand VII.**

| | | | | | |
|---|---|---|---|---|---|
| 102.2 | 1814 MR | 40.00 | 65.00 | 150.00 | 250.00 |
| | 1815 MR | 80.00 | 150.00 | 300.00 | 500.00 |

**Obv: Large bust.**

| | | | | | |
|---|---|---|---|---|---|
| 102.3 | 1814 MR | 50.00 | 100.00 | 200.00 | 400.00 |

**Obv: Large bust w/berries in laurel.**

| | | | | | |
|---|---|---|---|---|---|
| 102.4 | 1814 MR | — | — | Rare | — |

## 8 REALES

**27.0700 g, .903 SILVER, .7860 oz ASW**
**Obv: Draped bust of Ferdinand VII.**

| KM# | Date | VG | Fine | VF | XF |
|---|---|---|---|---|---|
| 111.3 | 1812 MR | 1000. | 1500. | 3000. | 4500. |
| | 1813/2 MR | 60.00 | 100.00 | 150.00 | 400.00 |
| | 1813 MR | 60.00 | 100.00 | 150.00 | 400.00 |
| | 1814 MR | 20.00 | 30.00 | 50.00 | 175.00 |
| | 1815 MR | 150.00 | 200.00 | 250.00 | 750.00 |
| | 1818 FS | 30.00 | 50.00 | 65.00 | 200.00 |
| | 1821/18 FS | 30.00 | 50.00 | 75.00 | 200.00 |
| | 1821 FS | 25.00 | 35.00 | 50.00 | 150.00 |
| | 1822/1 FS | 30.00 | 50.00 | 75.00 | 200.00 |
| | 1822 FS | 30.00 | 50.00 | 75.00 | 200.00 |

**NOTE:** Die varieties exist. Early dates are also encountered struck over other types.

## 4 ESCUDOS

**13.5400 g, .875 GOLD, .3809 oz ASW**
**Obv: Uniformed bust of Ferdinand VII.**

| | | | | | |
|---|---|---|---|---|---|
| 147 | 1812 MR | — | — | Rare | — |

## 8 ESCUDOS

**27.0700 g, .875 GOLD, .7616 oz AGW**
**Obv: Large uniformed bust of Ferdinand VII.**

| | | | | |
|---|---|---|---|---|
| 162 | 1812 MR | — | Reported, not confirmed | |
| | 1813 MR | 4000. | 7000. | 10,000. | 18,000. |

Obv: Small uniformed bust of Ferdinand VII.

| KM# | Date | VG | Fine | VF | XF |
|---|---|---|---|---|---|
| 163 | 1813 MR | 7000. | 10,000. | 15,000. | 22,000. |

Obv: Undraped bust of Ferdinand VII.

| 161.1 | 1821 FS | 1500. | 2500. | 4500. | 7500. |

Obv: Draped bust of Ferdinand VII.

| 164 | 1821 FS | 6000. | 8500. | 12,500. | 20,000. |

# GUANAJUATO

Guanajuato Mint was authorized December 24, 1812 and started production shortly thereafter. For unknown reasons it closed on May 15, 1813. The mint was reopened in April of 1821 by the insurgent forces. They continued to make coins of the Spanish design to pay their army. After independence coins were made into the year 1822. Only the 2 and 8 reales coins were made.

MINT MARK: Go

## 2 REALES

6.7700 g, .903 SILVER, .1966 oz ASW
Obv: Draped bust of Ferdinand VII.

| KM# | Date | VG | Fine | VF | XF |
|---|---|---|---|---|---|
| 93.3 | 1821 JM | 30.00 | 60.00 | 90.00 | 175.00 |
| | 1822 JM | 25.00 | 45.00 | 65.00 | 125.00 |

## 8 REALES

27.0700 g, .903 SILVER, .7860 oz ASW
Obv: Draped bust of Ferdinand VII.

| | | | | | |
|---|---|---|---|---|---|
| 111.4 | 1812 JJ | 750.00 | 1250. | 1750. | 2500. |
| | 1813 JJ | 125.00 | 175.00 | 275.00 | 600.00 |
| | 1821 JM | 25.00 | 50.00 | 75.00 | 200.00 |
| | 1822/0 JM | 40.00 | 100.00 | 150.00 | 300.00 |
| | 1822 JM | 20.00 | 30.00 | 50.00 | 175.00 |

# NUEVA VISCAYA

(Later became Durango State)

This 8 reales, intended for the province of Nueva Viscaya was minted in the newly opened Durango Mint during the months of February and March of 1811 before the regular coinage of Durango was started.

## 8 REALES

.903 SILVER
Obv. leg: MON.PROV. DE NUEV.VIZCAYA,
arms of Durango. Rev: Royal arms.

| KM# | Date | Good | VG | Fine | VF |
|---|---|---|---|---|---|
| 181 | 1811 RM | 1250. | 2000. | 2750. | 4500. |

NOTE: Several varieties exist.

# OAXACA

The city of Oaxaca was in the midst of a coin shortage when it became apparent the city would be taken by insurgent forces. The Royalist forces under Lt. Gen. Saravia had some coins made. They were cast in a blacksmith shop and were made in 3 denominations - 1/2, 1 and 8 reales. They were made only briefly in 1812 before the city fell to the opposing forces.

## 1/2 REAL

**.903 SILVER**
**Obv: Cross separating castle, lion, F,7O.**
**Rev. leg: OAXACA around shield.**

| KM# | Date | Good | VG | Fine | VF |
|-----|------|------|------|------|------|
| 166 | 1812 | 1000. | 1500. | 2500. | 3500. |

## REAL

**.903 SILVER**

| KM# | Date | Good | VG | Fine | VF |
|-----|------|------|------|------|------|
| 167 | 1812 | 300.00 | 600.00 | 1000. | 2000. |

## 8 REALES

**.903 SILVER**

| KM# | Date | Good | VG | Fine | VF |
|-----|------|------|------|------|------|
| 168 | 1812 c/m:A | 1200. | 1800. | 3000. | 4500. |
| | 1812 c/m:B | 1200. | 1800. | 3000. | 4500. |
| | 1812 c/m:C | 1200. | 1800. | 3000. | 4500. |
| | 1812 c/m:D | 1200. | 1800. | 3000. | 4500. |
| | 1812 c/m:K | 1200. | 1800. | 3000. | 4500. |
| | 1812 c/m:L | 1200. | 1800. | 3000. | 4500. |
| | 1812 c/m:Mo | 1200. | 1800. | 3000. | 4500. |
| | 1812 c/m:N | 1200. | 1800. | 3000. | 4500. |
| | 1812 c/m:O | 1200. | 1800. | 3000. | 4500. |
| | 1812 c/m:R | 1200. | 1800. | 3000. | 4500. |
| | 1812 c/m:V | 1200. | 1800. | 3000. | 4500. |
| | 1812 c/m:Z | 1200. | 1800. | 3000. | 4500. |

**NOTE:** The above issue usually has a second c/m: O between crowned pillars.

# REAL DEL CATORCE

(City in San Luis Potosi)

Real del Catorce is an important mining center in the state of San Luis Potosi. In 1811 an 8 reales coin was issued under very tedious conditions while the city was still in Royalist hands. Few survive.

## 8 REALES

**.903 SILVER**
**Obv. leg: EL R.D. CATORC. POR FERNA. VII.**
**Rev. leg: MONEDA. PROVISIONAL.VALE.8R.**

| KM# | Date | VG | Fine | VF | XF |
|-----|------|------|------|------|------|
| 169 | 1811 | 2000. | 4000. | 7500. | 15,000. |

# SAN FERNAN-DO DE BEXAR

Struck by Jose Antonio de la Garza, the 'jolas' are the only known coins issued under Spanish rule in the continental United States of America.

## 1/8 REAL

**COPPER**

| KM# | Date | Mintage | Good | VG | Fine | VF |
|-----|------|---------|------|------|------|------|
| 170 | 1818 | 8,000 | 500.00 | 750.00 | 1200. | 1600. |

| KM# | Date | Mintage | Good | VG | Fine | VF |
|-----|------|---------|------|------|------|------|
| 171 | 1818 | Inc. Ab. | 500.00 | 750.00 | 1200. | 1600. |

# SAN LUIS POTOSI

## Sierra De Pinos

Villa

## 1/4 REAL

**COPPER**

| KM# | Date | Good | VG | Fine | VF |
|-----|------|------|-----|------|-----|
| A172 | 1814 | 85.00 | 125.00 | 185.00 | 250.00 |

**SILVER**

| KM# | Date | Good | VG | Fine | VF |
|-----|------|------|-----|------|-----|
| A172a | 1814 | — | — | Rare | — |

# SOMBRERETE
## (Under Royalist Vargas)

The Sombrerete Mint opened on October 8, 1810 in an area that boasted some of the richest mines in Mexico. The mint operated until July 16, 1811 when it closed only to reopen in 1812 and finally to close for good at the end of 1812. The man in charge of the mines, Fernando Vargas, was also in charge of the coinage. All of the coins bear his name.

## 1/2 REAL

**.903 SILVER**
**Obv. leg: FERDIN.VII.SOMBRERETE. . .,**
**around crowned globes.**
**Rev. leg: VARGAS above lys in oval, sprays.**

| | | | | | |
|-----|------|------|-----|------|-----|
| 172 | 1811 | 35.00 | 60.00 | 100.00 | 175.00 |
| | 1812 | 50.00 | 90.00 | 150.00 | 225.00 |

## REAL

**.903 SILVER**
**Obv. leg: FERDIN.VII.SOMBRERETE. .,**
**around crowned globes.**
**Rev. leg: VARGAS above lys in oval, sprays.**

| | | | | | |
|-----|------|------|-----|------|-----|
| 173 | 1811 | 40.00 | 60.00 | 100.00 | 160.00 |
| | 1812 | 30.00 | 40.00 | 80.00 | 125.00 |

## 2 REALES

**.903 SILVER**
**Obv: R.CAXA.DE.SOMBRERETE, royal arms.**
**Rev. c/m: VARGAS, 1811, S between crowned pillars.**

| | | | | | |
|-----|--------|-------|--------|--------|--------|
| 174 | 1811 SE | 65.00 | 200.00 | 400.00 | 650.00 |

## 4 REALES

**.903 SILVER**
**Obv. leg: R.CAXA.DE.SOMBRERETE, royal arms.**
**Rev. leg: Small VARGAS/1811.**

| KM# | Date | Good | VG | Fine | VF |
|-----|------|------|-----|------|-----|
| 175.1 | 1811 | 100.00 | 200.00 | 400.00 | 750.00 |

**Rev: Large VARGAS/1812.**

| | | | | | |
|-------|------|-------|--------|--------|--------|
| 175.2 | 1812 | 50.00 | 150.00 | 250.00 | 400.00 |

## 8 REALES

**.903 SILVER**
**Obv. leg: R.CAXA. DE SOMBRERETE.**
**Rev. c/m: VARGAS, date, S between crowned pillars.**

| | | | | | |
|-----|------|--------|--------|--------|--------|
| 176 | 1810 | 1000. | 1500. | 2500. | 3500. |
| | 1811 | 200.00 | 300.00 | 400.00 | 500.00 |

**Obv. leg: R.CAXA. DE SOMBRETE, crowned arms.**
**Rev. leg: VARGAS/date/3**

| | | | | | |
|-----|------|--------|--------|--------|--------|
| 177 | 1811 | 100.00 | 150.00 | 200.00 | 300.00 |
| | 1812 | 100.00 | 150.00 | 200.00 | 300.00 |

# VALLADOLID MICHOACAN

## (Now Morelia)

Valladolid, capitol of Michoacan province, was a strategically important center for military thrusts into the adjoining provinces. The Royalists made every effort to retain the position. In 1813, with the advance of the insurgent forces, it became apparent that to maintain the position would be very difficult. During 1813 it was necessary to make coins in the city due to lack of traffic with other areas. These were made only briefly before the city fell and were also used by the insurgents with appropriate countermarks.

## 8 REALES

.903 SILVER
Obv: Royal arms in wreath, value at sides.
Rev: PROVISIONAL/DE VALLADOLID/1813.

| KM# | Date | Good | VG | Fine | VF |
|---|---|---|---|---|---|
| 178 | 1813 | 1000. | 2000. | 3000. | 5000. |

Obv: Bust, leg: FERDIN. VII.
Rev: Arms, pillars.

| KM# | Date | Good | VG | Fine | VF |
|---|---|---|---|---|---|
| 179 | 1813 | 1500. | 2500. | 3500. | 5500. |

# ZACATECAS

The city of Zacatecas, in a rich mining area, has a long history of providing silver for the world. From the mid-1500's silver poured from its mines. On November 14, 1810 a mint began production for the Royalist cause. Zacatecas was the most prolific of the mints during the War of Independence. The 4 silver denominations were made here. The first type was a local type with the mountains of silver shown on the coins. These were made only in 1810 and 1811. Some of the 1811 were made by the insurgents after the town fell on April 15, 1811. The town was retaken by the Royalists on May 21, 1811. From then until 1822 the standard bust type of Ferdinand VII was made.

## MINT MARKS: Z, ZS, Zs

## 1/2 REAL

.903 SILVER
Similar to KM#181 but w/local arms.
Flowers 1 and 4, castles 2 and 3.

| KM# | Date | Good | VG | Fine | VF |
|---|---|---|---|---|---|
| 180 | 1810 | 75.00 | 125.00 | 200.00 | 400.00 |
| | 1181 (error 1811) | | | | |
| | | 30.00 | 50.00 | 75.00 | 150.00 |

Obv: Royal arms.
Rev. leg: MONEDA PROVISIONAL DE ZACATECAS., mountain.

| KM# | Date | Good | VG | Fine | VF |
|---|---|---|---|---|---|
| 181 | 1811 | 30.00 | 50.00 | 75.00 | 100.00 |

Obv: Provincial bust FERDIN. VII.
Rev. leg: MONEDA PROVISIONAL DE ZACATECAS.

| KM# | Date | Good | VG | Fine | VF |
|---|---|---|---|---|---|
| 182 | 1811 | 30.00 | 40.00 | 60.00 | 80.00 |
| | 1812 | 25.00 | 35.00 | 50.00 | 70.00 |

1.6900 g, .903 SILVER, .0491 oz ASW
Obv: Armored bust of Ferdinand VII.

| KM# | Date | Good | VG | Fine | VF |
|---|---|---|---|---|---|
| 73.1 | 1813 FP | 30.00 | 60.00 | 100.00 | 175.00 |
| | 1813 AG | 20.00 | 40.00 | 60.00 | 100.00 |
| | 1814 AG | 15.00 | 30.00 | 60.00 | 100.00 |
| | 1815 AG | 12.50 | 25.00 | 40.00 | 60.00 |
| | 1816 AG | 10.00 | 15.00 | 25.00 | 50.00 |
| | 1817 AG | 10.00 | 15.00 | 25.00 | 50.00 |
| | 1818 AG | 10.00 | 15.00 | 25.00 | 50.00 |
| | 1819 AG | 10.00 | 15.00 | 25.00 | 50.00 |

Obv: Draped bust Ferdinand VII.

| KM# | Date | VG | Fine | VF | XF |
|---|---|---|---|---|---|
| 74.3 | 1819 AG | 8.00 | 12.00 | 25.00 | 50.00 |
| | 1820 AG | 8.00 | 12.00 | 25.00 | 50.00 |
| | 1820 RG | 5.00 | 10.00 | 20.00 | 45.00 |
| | 1821 AG | 50.00 | 100.00 | 150.00 | 250.00 |
| | 1821 RG | 5.00 | 10.00 | 20.00 | 45.00 |

## REAL

.903 SILVER
Obv: Local arms w/flowers and castles.

| | Date | Good | VG | Fine | VF |
|---|---|---|---|---|---|
| 183 | 1810 | 100.00 | 150.00 | 300.00 | 500.00 |
| | 1181 (error 1811) | | | | |
| | | 20.00 | 40.00 | 75.00 | 125.00 |

Obv: Royal arms.
Rev. leg: MONEDA PROVISIONAL DE ZACATECAS., mountain.

| | Date | Good | VG | Fine | VF |
|---|---|---|---|---|---|
| 184 | 1811 | 15.00 | 30.00 | 50.00 | 100.00 |

Obv: Provincial bust, leg: FERDIN. VII.
Rev. leg: MONEDA PROVISIONAL DE ZACATECAS, arms, pillars.

| | Date | Good | VG | Fine | VF |
|---|---|---|---|---|---|
| 185 | 1811 | 45.00 | 75.00 | 100.00 | 175.00 |
| | 1812 | 45.00 | 75.00 | 100.00 | 175.00 |

3.3800 g, .903 SILVER, .0981 oz ASW
Obv: Armored bust of Ferdinand VII.

| | Date | Good | VG | Fine | VF |
|---|---|---|---|---|---|
| 82.1 | 1813 FP | 50.00 | 100.00 | 150.00 | 250.00 |
| | 1814 FP | 20.00 | 35.00 | 50.00 | 75.00 |
| | 1814 AG | 20.00 | 35.00 | 50.00 | 75.00 |
| | 1815 AG | 20.00 | 35.00 | 50.00 | 75.00 |
| | 1816 AG | 10.00 | 20.00 | 30.00 | 60.00 |
| | 1817 AG | 6.50 | 12.50 | 20.00 | 40.00 |
| | 1818 AG | 6.50 | 12.50 | 20.00 | 40.00 |
| | 1819 AG | 5.00 | 9.00 | 15.00 | 30.00 |
| | 1820 AG | 4.00 | 7.50 | 12.50 | 25.00 |

Obv: Draped bust of Ferdinand VII.

| KM# | Date | VG | Fine | VF | XF |
|---|---|---|---|---|---|
| 83.3 | 1820 AG | 5.00 | 10.00 | 17.50 | 40.00 |
| | 1820 RG | 5.00 | 10.00 | 17.50 | 40.00 |
| | 1821 AG | 15.00 | 30.00 | 45.00 | 75.00 |
| | 1821 AZ | 10.00 | 20.00 | 30.00 | 60.00 |
| | 1821 RG | 6.00 | 12.00 | 17.50 | 45.00 |
| | 1822 AZ | 6.00 | 12.00 | 17.50 | 45.00 |
| | 1822 RG | 15.00 | 30.00 | 45.00 | 75.00 |

| KM# | Date | Good | VG | Fine | VF |
|---|---|---|---|---|---|
| 92.1 | 1813 FP | 37.50 | 50.00 | 75.00 | 125.00 |
| | 1814 FP | 37.50 | 50.00 | 75.00 | 125.00 |
| | 1814 AG | 37.50 | 50.00 | 75.00 | 125.00 |
| | 1815 AG | 6.50 | 12.50 | 25.00 | 50.00 |
| | 1816 AG | 6.50 | 12.50 | 25.00 | 50.00 |
| | 1817 AG | 6.50 | 12.50 | 25.00 | 50.00 |
| | 1818 AG | 6.50 | 12.50 | 25.00 | 50.00 |

# 2 REALES

**.903 SILVER**
**Obv: Local arms w/flowers and castles.**

| KM# | Date | Good | VG | Fine | VF |
|---|---|---|---|---|---|
| 186 | 1810 | — | — | Rare | — |
| | 1181 (error 1811) | | | | |
| | | 25.00 | 40.00 | 60.00 | 100.00 |

**Obv: Royal arms.**
**Rev. leg: MONEDA PROVISIONAL DE ZACATECAS.,**
**mountain above L.V.O.**

| | | | | | |
|---|---|---|---|---|---|
| 187 | 1811 | 15.00 | 30.00 | 50.00 | 75.00 |

**Obv: Armored bust, leg: FERDIN. VII.**
**Rev. leg: MONEDA PROVISIONAL DE**
**ZACATECAS, crowned arms, pillars.**

| | | | | | |
|---|---|---|---|---|---|
| 188 | 1811 | 40.00 | 75.00 | 150.00 | 225.00 |
| | 1812 | 30.00 | 60.00 | 125.00 | 200.00 |

**6.7700 g, .903 SILVER, .1966 oz ASW**
**Obv: Large armored bust of Ferdinand VII.**

**Obv: Small armored bust of Ferdinand VII.**

| | | | | | |
|---|---|---|---|---|---|
| A92 | 1819 AG | 25.00 | 50.00 | 100.00 | 200.00 |

**Obv: Draped bust of Ferdinand VII.**

| KM# | Date | VG | Fine | VF | XF |
|---|---|---|---|---|---|
| 93.4 | 1818 AG | 6.50 | 12.50 | 20.00 | 40.00 |
| | 1819 AG | 10.00 | 20.00 | 40.00 | 75.00 |
| | 1820 AG | 10.00 | 20.00 | 40.00 | 75.00 |
| | 1820 RG | 10.00 | 20.00 | 40.00 | 75.00 |
| | 1821 AG | 10.00 | 20.00 | 40.00 | 75.00 |
| | 1821 AZ/RG | 10.00 | 20.00 | 40.00 | 75.00 |
| | 1821 AZ | 10.00 | 20.00 | 40.00 | 75.00 |
| | 1821 RG | 10.00 | 20.00 | 40.00 | 75.00 |
| | 1822 AG | 10.00 | 20.00 | 40.00 | 75.00 |
| | 1822 AZ | 15.00 | 30.00 | 60.00 | 120.00 |
| | 1822 RG | 10.00 | 20.00 | 40.00 | 75.00 |

# 8 REALES

**.903 SILVER**
**Obv: Local arm w/flowers and castles.**
**Rev: Similar to KM#190.**

| KM# | Date | Good | VG | Fine | VF |
|---|---|---|---|---|---|
| 189 | 1810 | 300.00 | 450.00 | 600.00 | 800.00 |
| | 1181 (error 1811) | | | | |
| | | 100.00 | 150.00 | 225.00 | 300.00 |

**NOTE:** Also exists with incomplete date.

27.0700 g, .903 SILVER, .7860 oz ASW
Obv: Draped bust of Ferdinand VII.

| KM# | Date | VG | Fine | VF | XF |
|-----|------|-----|------|-----|-----|
| 111.5 | 1813 AG | 125.00 | 200.00 | 250.00 | 350.00 |
| | 1813 FP | 75.00 | 125.00 | 175.00 | 275.00 |
| | 1814 AG | 100.00 | 150.00 | 200.00 | 300.00 |
| | 1814 AG D over horizontal D in IND | | | | |
| | | 125.00 | 175.00 | 225.00 | 325.00 |
| | 1814 AG/FP | 100.00 | 150.00 | 200.00 | 300.00 |
| | 1814 FP | 150.00 | 250.00 | 350.00 | 450.00 |
| | 1815 AG | 50.00 | 100.00 | 150.00 | 250.00 |
| | 1816 AG | 35.00 | 50.00 | 65.00 | 125.00 |
| | 1817 AG | 35.00 | 50.00 | 65.00 | 125.00 |
| | 1818 AG | 30.00 | 40.00 | 50.00 | 100.00 |
| | 1819 AG | 30.00 | 40.00 | 50.00 | 100.00 |
| | 1820 AG | 30.00 | 40.00 | 50.00 | 100.00 |
| | 1820 RG | 30.00 | 40.00 | 50.00 | 100.00 |
| | 1821/81 RG | 75.00 | 150.00 | 225.00 | 300.00 |
| | 1821 RG | 15.00 | 25.00 | 35.00 | 65.00 |
| | 1821 AZ | 50.00 | 100.00 | 150.00 | 200.00 |
| | 1822 RG | 40.00 | 60.00 | 100.00 | 175.00 |

Obv. leg: FERDIN.VII.DEI. ., royal arms.
Rev. leg: MONEDA PROVISIONAL DE
ZACATECAS, mountain above L.V.O.

| KM# | Date | Good | VG | Fine | VF |
|-----|------|------|-----|------|-----|
| 190 | 1811 | 75.00 | 125.00 | 150.00 | 225.00 |

Rev: Crown with lower rear arc.

| | | | | | |
|-----|------|------|-----|------|-----|
| 111.6 | 1821 RG | 160.00 | 320.00 | 550.00 | 750.00 |

# COUNTERMARKED COINAGE
## Crown and Flag
(Refer to Multiple Countermarks)
## LCM - La Comandancia Militar
**NOTE:** This countermark exists in 15 various sizes.

### 2 REALES

.903 SILVER
c/m: LCM on Mexico KM#92.

Obv: Armored bust of Ferdinand VII.
Rev. leg: MONEDA PROVISIONAL DE ZACATECAS,
crowned arms, pillars.

| 191 | 1811 | 35.00 | 50.00 | 100.00 | 150.00 |
|-----|------|-------|-------|--------|--------|
| | 1812 | 35.00 | 50.00 | 100.00 | 150.00 |

Obv: Draped bust of Ferdinand VII.
Rev. leg: MONEDA PROVISIONAL DE ZACATECAS,
crowned arms, pillars.

| 192 | 1812 | 50.00 | 75.00 | 125.00 | 200.00 |
|-----|------|-------|-------|--------|--------|

| KM# | Date | Good | VG | Fine | VF |
|---|---|---|---|---|---|
| 193.1 | ND(1809) TH | 100.00 | 150.00 | 200.00 | 275.00 |

**c/m: LCM on Zacatecas KM#187.**

| KM# | Date | Good | VG | Fine | VF |
|---|---|---|---|---|---|
| 193.2 | ND(1811) | 100.00 | 150.00 | 200.00 | 275.00 |

## 8 REALES

**CAST SILVER**
**c/m: LCM on Chihuahua KM#123.**

| KM# | Date | Good | VG | Fine | VF |
|---|---|---|---|---|---|
| 194.1 | ND(1811) RP | 100.00 | 200.00 | 300.00 | 450.00 |
| | ND(1812) RP | 100.00 | 200.00 | 300.00 | 450.00 |

**.903 SILVER**
**c/m: LCM on Chihuahua KM#111.1 struck over KM#123.**

| KM# | Date | Good | VG | Fine | VF |
|---|---|---|---|---|---|
| 194.2 | ND(1815) RP | 200.00 | 275.00 | 400.00 | 550.00 |
| | ND(1817) RP | 125.00 | 175.00 | 225.00 | 300.00 |
| | ND(1820) RP | 125.00 | 175.00 | 225.00 | 300.00 |
| | ND(1821) RP | 125.00 | 175.00 | 225.00 | 300.00 |

**c/m: LCM on Durango KM#111.2.**

| KM# | Date | Good | VG | Fine | VF |
|---|---|---|---|---|---|
| 194.3 | ND(1812) RM | 70.00 | 125.00 | 190.00 | 250.00 |
| | ND(1821) CG | 70.00 | 125.00 | 190.00 | 250.00 |

**c/m: LCM on Guadalajara KM#111.3.**

| KM# | Date | Good | VG | Fine | VF |
|---|---|---|---|---|---|
| 194.4 | ND(1813) MR | 150.00 | 225.00 | 300.00 | 475.00 |
| | ND(1820) FS | — | — | Rare | — |

**c/m: LCM on Guanajuato KM#111.4.**

| KM# | Date | Good | VG | Fine | VF |
|---|---|---|---|---|---|
| 194.5 | ND(1813) JM | 225.00 | 350.00 | 475.00 | 650.00 |

**c/m: LCM on Nueva Vizcaya KM#165.**

| KM# | Date | Good | VG | Fine | VF |
|---|---|---|---|---|---|
| 194.6 | ND(1811) RM | — | — | Rare | — |

**c/m: LCM on Mexico KM#111.**

| KM# | Date | Good | VG | Fine | VF |
|---|---|---|---|---|---|
| 194.7 | ND(1811) HJ | 125.00 | 225.00 | 350.00 | 600.00 |
| | ND(1812) JJ | 110.00 | 135.00 | 190.00 | 325.00 |
| | ND(1817) JJ | 50.00 | 65.00 | 85.00 | 125.00 |
| | ND(1818) JJ | 50.00 | 65.00 | 85.00 | 125.00 |
| | ND(1820) JJ | — | — | — | — |

**c/m: LCM on Sombrerete KM#176.**

| KM# | Date | Good | VG | Fine | VF |
|---|---|---|---|---|---|
| 194.8 | ND(1811) | — | — | Rare | — |
| | ND(1812) | —. | — | Rare | — |

**c/m: LCM on Zacatecas KM#190.**

| KM# | Date | Good | VG | Fine | VF |
|---|---|---|---|---|---|
| 194.9 | ND(1811) | 225.00 | 350.00 | 450.00 | — |

**c/m: LCM on Zacatecas KM#111.5.**

| KM# | Date | Good | VG | Fine | VF |
|---|---|---|---|---|---|
| 194.10 | ND(1813) FP | — | — | — | — |
| | ND(1814) AG | — | — | — | — |
| | ND(1822) RG | — | — | — | — |

## LCV - Las Cajas de Veracruz

(The Royal Treasury
of the City of Veracruz)

## 7 REALES

**SILVER**
**c/m: LCV and 7 on underweight 8 Reales.**

| KM# | Date | Good | VG | Fine | VF |
|---|---|---|---|---|---|
| 195 | ND(-) | — | — | Rare | — |

## 7-1/4 REALES

**SILVER**
**c/m: LCV and 7-1/4 on underweight 8 Reales.**

| KM# | Date | Good | VG | Fine | VF |
|---|---|---|---|---|---|
| 196 | ND(-) | — | — | Rare | — |

## 7-1/2 REALES

**SILVER**
**c/m: LCV and 7-1/2 on underweight 8 Reales.**

| KM# | Date | Good | VG | Fine | VF |
|---|---|---|---|---|---|
| 197 | ND(-) | — | — | Rare | — |

## 7-3/4 REALES

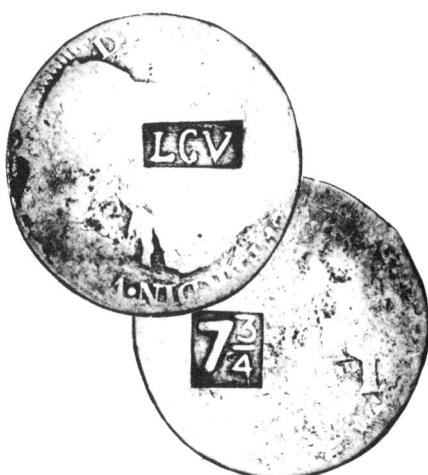

**SILVER**
c/m: LCV and 7-3/4 on underweight 8 Reales.

| KM# | Date | Good | VG | Fine | VF |
|-----|------|------|-----|------|-----|
| 198 | ND(-) | 300.00 | 375.00 | 450.00 | 600.00 |

## 8 REALES
**CAST SILVER**
c/m: LCV on Chihuahua KM#123.

| A198 | ND(1811) RP | 150.00 | 250.00 | 400.00 | 500.00 |
|------|-------------|--------|--------|--------|--------|

**SILVER**
c/m: LCV on Zacatecas KM#191.

| 199 | ND(1811) | 175.00 | 225.00 | 275.00 | 350.00 |
|-----|----------|--------|--------|--------|--------|
|     | ND(1812) | 175.00 | 225.00 | 275.00 | 350.00 |

## MS (Monogram) - Manuel Salcedo

## 8 REALES

**SILVER**
c/m: MS monogram on Mexico KM#110.

| KM# | Date | Good | VG | Fine | VF |
|-----|------|------|-----|------|-----|
| 200 | ND(1809) TH | 150.00 | 250.00 | 400.00 | 500.00 |
|     | ND(1810) HJ | 150.00 | 250.00 | 400.00 | 500.00 |
|     | ND(1811) HJ | 150.00 | 250.00 | 400.00 | 500.00 |

## MVA - Monclova

## 8 REALES
**SILVER**
c/m: MVA/1811 on Chihuahua KM#111.1; struck over cast Mexico KM#110.

| 201 | ND(1809) | — | — | Rare | — |
|-----|----------|---|---|------|---|
|     | ND(1816) RP | — | — | Rare | — |
|     | ND(1821) RP | — | — | Rare | — |

c/m: MVA/1812 on Chihuahua KM#111.1; struck over cast Mexico KM#109.

| 202.1 | 1812(1810) | 125.00 | 175.00 | 250.00 | 350.00 |
|-------|------------|--------|--------|--------|--------|

c/m: MVA/1812 on cast Mexico KM#109.

| 202.2 | 1812(1798) FM | 100.00 | 150.00 | 250.00 | 350.00 |
|-------|---------------|--------|--------|--------|--------|
|       | 1812(1802) FT | 100.00 | 150.00 | 250.00 | 350.00 |

c/m: MVA/1812 on cast Mexico KM#110.

| KM# | Date | Good | VG | Fine | VF |
|---|---|---|---|---|---|
| 202.3 | 1812(1809) HJ | 100.00 | 150.00 | 250.00 | 350.00 |
| | 1812(1809) TH | 100.00 | 150.00 | 250.00 | 350.00 |
| | 1812(1810) HJ | 100.00 | 150.00 | 250.00 | 350.00 |

c/m: MVA/1812 on Zacatecas KM#189.

| KM# | Date | Good | VG | Fine | VF |
|---|---|---|---|---|---|
| 202.5 | 1812(1813) | 300.00 | 350.00 | 450.00 | 550.00 |

## PDV - Provisional de Valladolid
## VTIL - (Util = useful)
(Refer to Multiple countermarks)

# INSURGENT COINAGE
## Supreme National Congress
## Of America
### 1/2 REAL

**COPPER**
Obv. leg: FERDIN. VII DEI GRATIA, eagle on bridge.
Rev. leg: S.P.CONG.NAT.IND.
GUV.T., value, bow, quiver, etc.

| KM# | Date | Good | VG | Fine | VF |
|---|---|---|---|---|---|
| 203 | 1811 | 30.00 | 45.00 | 60.00 | 100.00 |

### REAL

**SILVER**
Similar to 1/2 Real, KM#203.

| KM# | Date | Good | VG | Fine | VF |
|---|---|---|---|---|---|
| 204 | 1811 | 50.00 | 75.00 | 125.00 | 200.00 |

### 2 REALES

**SILVER**

| KM# | Date | Good | VG | Fine | VF |
|---|---|---|---|---|---|
| 205 | 1812 | 250.00 | 350.00 | 500.00 | 700.00 |

### 8 REALES

**CAST SILVER**

| KM# | Date | Good | VG | Fine | VF |
|---|---|---|---|---|---|
| 206 | 1811 | 150.00 | 250.00 | 350.00 | 500.00 |
| | 1812 | 150.00 | 250.00 | 350.00 | 500.00 |

**STRUCK SILVER**

| KM# | Date | Good | VG | Fine | VF |
|---|---|---|---|---|---|
| 207 | 1811 | — | Rare | — | — |
| | 1812 | 300.00 | 600.00 | 1000. | 1500. |

**COPPER**
Obv. leg: FERDIN.VII. . . ., eagle on bridge.
Rev. leg: PROVICIONAL POR LA SUPREMA JUNTA
DE AMERICA, bow, sword and quiver.

| KM# | Date | Good | VG | Fine | VF |
|---|---|---|---|---|---|
| 208 | 1811 | 100.00 | 150.00 | 225.00 | 450.00 |
| | 1812 | 100.00 | 150.00 | 225.00 | 450.00 |

## National Congress
### 1/2 REAL

**COPPER**
Obv. leg: VICE FERD. VII DEI GRATIA ET,
eagle on bridge.
Rev. leg: S. P. CONG. NAT. IND.
GUV. T., value, bow, quiver, etc.

| KM# | Date | Good | VG | Fine | VF |
|---|---|---|---|---|---|
| 209 | 1811 | 50.00 | 100.00 | 150.00 | 200.00 |
| | 1812 | 30.00 | 60.00 | 100.00 | 150.00 |
| | 1813 | 30.00 | 60.00 | 100.00 | 150.00 |
| | 1814 | 50.00 | 100.00 | 150.00 | 200.00 |

**.903 SILVER**

| KM# | Date | Good | VG | Fine | VF |
|---|---|---|---|---|---|
| 210 | 1812 | 30.00 | 60.00 | 100.00 | 150.00 |
| | 1813 | 50.00 | 100.00 | 175.00 | 275.00 |

**NOTE:** 1812 exists with the date reading inwards and outwards.

## REAL

**.903 SILVER**

| KM# | Date | | | | |
|---|---|---|---|---|---|
| 211 | 1812 | 25.00 | 45.00 | 65.00 | 100.00 |
| | 1813 | 25.00 | 45.00 | 65.00 | 100.00 |

**NOTE:** 1812 exists with the date reading either inward or outward.

## 2 REALES

**COPPER**

| KM# | Date | | | | |
|---|---|---|---|---|---|
| 212 | 1812 | 100.00 | 150.00 | 200.00 | 250.00 |
| | 1813 | 25.00 | 50.00 | 75.00 | 100.00 |
| | 1814 | 35.00 | 75.00 | 110.00 | 150.00 |

**.903 SILVER**

| KM# | Date | | | | |
|---|---|---|---|---|---|
| 213 | 1813 | 125.00 | 250.00 | 300.00 | 400.00 |

**NOTE:** These dies were believed to be intended for the striking of 2 Escudos.

## 4 REALES

**.903 SILVER**
**Mint: Mexico City**

| KM# | Date | | | | |
|---|---|---|---|---|---|
| 214 | 1813 | 500.00 | 1000. | 2000. | 3000. |

## 8 REALES

**.903 SILVER**
**Mint: Mexico City**
**Obv: Small crowned eagle.**

| KM# | Date | Good | VG | Fine | VF |
|---|---|---|---|---|---|
| 215.1 | 1812 | 500.00 | 1000. | 2000. | 3500. |

**Obv: Large crowned eagle.**

| | | | | | |
|---|---|---|---|---|---|
| 215.2 | 1813 | 500.00 | 1000. | 2000. | 3500. |

## American Congress
## REAL

**.903 SILVER**
**Obv: Eagle on cactus,**
**leg: CONGRESO AMERICANO.**
**Rev: F.7 on spread mantle,**
**leg: DEPOSIT D.L.AUCTORI J.**

| KM# | Date | | | | |
|---|---|---|---|---|---|
| 216 | ND (1813) | 35.00 | 65.00 | 100.00 | 150.00 |

**Obv: Eagle on cactus, leg: CONGR.AMER.**
**Rev: F.7 on spread mantle,**
**leg: DEPOS.D.L.AUT.D.**

| | | | | | |
|---|---|---|---|---|---|
| 217 | ND(1813) | 35.00 | 65.00 | 100.00 | 150.00 |

# NUEVA GALICIA
### (Later became Jalisco State)

Nueva Galicia was a province in early colonial times that was similar to modern Zacatecas, etc. The name was adopted again during the War of Independence. The only issue was an 1812 2 reales of rather enigmatic origin.

**PRICING SECTION**

## 2 REALES

**.903 SILVER**
Obv. leg: PROVYCIONAL. . . . ., N.G. in center, date.

| KM# | Date | Good | VG | Fine | VF |
|---|---|---|---|---|---|
| 218 | 1813 | 1000. | 3000. | 6000. | 10,000. |

### OAXACA

Oaxaca was the hub of insurgent activity in the south. The issues of Oaxaca represent various episodic strikings of coins, usually under dire circumstances, by various individuals. The copper coins were made because of urgency and were to be redeemed at its face value in gold or silver. The silver coins were made after the copper coins when silver was available to the insurgent forces. Coinage started in July, 1811 and ran until October 1814.

## SUD
(Under General Morelos)
### 1/2 REAL

**COPPER**
Obv: Bow, SUD.
Rev: Morelos monogram Mo, date.

| KM# | Date | Good | VG | Fine | VF |
|---|---|---|---|---|---|
| 219 | 1811 | 7.50 | 12.50 | 20.00 | 30.00 |
| | 1812 | 7.50 | 12.50 | 20.00 | 30.00 |
| | 1813 | 6.00 | 10.00 | 17.50 | 25.00 |
| | 1814 | 10.00 | 17.50 | 25.00 | 35.00 |

**NOTE:** Uniface strikes exist of #219.

**STRUCK SILVER**

| | | | | | |
|---|---|---|---|---|---|
| 220.1 | 1811 | — | — | — | — |
| | 1812 | — | — | — | — |
| | 1813 | — | — | — | — |

**CAST SILVER**

| | | | | | |
|---|---|---|---|---|---|
| 220.2 | 1811 | — | — | — | — |
| | 1812 | — | — | — | — |
| | 1813 | 25.00 | 50.00 | 100.00 | 150.00 |

**NOTE:** Most silver specimens available on today's market are considered spurious.

**SILVER**
Obv. leg: PROVICIONAL DE OAXACA, bow, arrow.
Rev. leg: AMERICA MORELOS, lion.

| KM# | Date | Good | VG | Fine | VF |
|---|---|---|---|---|---|
| 221 | 1812 | 35.00 | 60.00 | 100.00 | 150.00 |
| | 1813 | 35.00 | 60.00 | 100.00 | 150.00 |
| | **COPPER** | | | | |
| 221a | 1812 | 27.50 | 42.50 | 70.00 | 100.00 |
| | 1813 | 20.00 | 35.00 | 60.00 | 85.00 |

**Obv: Similar to KM#220.**
**Rev: Similar to KM#221 but w/1/2 at left of lion.**

| | | | | | |
|---|---|---|---|---|---|
| A222 | 1813 | 27.50 | 42.50 | 70.00 | 100.00 |

## REAL

**COPPER**

| | | | | | |
|---|---|---|---|---|---|
| 222 | 1811 | 5.00 | 10.00 | 20.00 | 40.00 |
| | 1812 | 4.00 | 8.00 | 15.00 | 30.00 |
| | 1813 | 4.00 | 8.00 | 15.00 | 30.00 |
| | **STRUCK SILVER** | | | | |
| 222a | 1812 | — | — | — | — |
| | 1813 | — | — | — | — |

**CAST SILVER**

| | | | | | |
|---|---|---|---|---|---|
| 223 | 1812 | — | — | — | — |
| | 1813 | 40.00 | 76.00 | 125.00 | 175.00 |

**NOTE:** Most silver specimens available on today's market are considered spurious.

**COPPER**
Obv: Bow, arrow/SUD.
Rev. leg: AMERICA MORELOS, lion.

| | | | | | |
|---|---|---|---|---|---|
| 224 | 1813 | 27.50 | 42.50 | 75.00 | 110.00 |
| | **SILVER** | | | | |
| 225 | 1813 | — | — | Rare | — |

## 2 REALES

**COPPER**

| | | | | | |
|---|---|---|---|---|---|
| 226.1 | 1811 | 12.50 | 25.00 | 50.00 | 100.00 |
| | 1812 | 2.50 | 3.75 | 5.00 | 10.00 |
| | 1813 | 2.50 | 3.75 | 5.00 | 10.00 |

**Obv: 3 large stars added.**

| KM# | Date | Good | VG | Fine | VF |
|-----|------|------|-----|------|-----|
| 226.2 | . 1814 | 10.00 | 20.00 | 40.00 | 60.00 |

**Obv. leg: SUD-OXA, bow, arrow.**
**Rev: Morelos monogram, value, date.**

| | | | | | |
|-----|------|------|------|------|------|
| 227 | 1813 | 60.00 | 100.00 | 200.00 | 300.00 |
| | 1814 | 60.00 | 100.00 | 200.00 | 300.00 |

**Obv. leg: SUD. OAXACA**

| | | | | | |
|-----|------|------|------|------|------|
| 228 | 1814 | 60.00 | 100.00 | 200.00 | 325.00 |

**CAST SILVER**

| | | | | | |
|-----|------|------|------|------|------|
| 229 | 1812 | 60.00 | 100.00 | 150.00 | 225.00 |
| | 1812 filled D in SUD | | | | |
| | | 60.00 | 100.00 | 150.00 | 225.00 |

**NOTE:** Most silver specimens available on today's market are spurious.

## 4 REALES

**NOTE:** All known examples are modern fabrications.

**CAST SILVER**

| | | | | | |
|-----|------|------|------|------|------|
| 230 | 1811 | — | — | — | — |
| | 1812 | — | — | — | — |

**Obv. leg: SUD-OXA, bow, arrow.**
**Rev: Morelos monogram.**

| | | | | | |
|-----|------|------|------|------|------|
| 231 | . 1813 | 125.00 | 250.00 | 400.00 | 800.00 |

**COPPER**
**Obv. leg: SUD-OXA, bow, arrow.**
**Rev: Morelos monogram.**

| | | | | | |
|-----|------|------|------|------|------|
| 232 | 1814 | 100.00 | 150.00 | 200.00 | 400.00 |

## 8 REALES

**COPPER**
**Plain fields**

| KM# | Date | Good | VG | Fine | VF |
|-----|------|------|-----|------|-----|
| 233.1 | 1812 | 15.00 | 30.00 | 60.00 | 90.00 |

| | | | | | |
|-----|------|------|------|------|------|
| 233.2 | 1812 | 6.00 | 8.00 | 12.00 | 15.00 |
| | 1813 | 6.00 | 8.00 | 12.00 | 15.00 |
| | 1814 | 10.00 | 12.00 | 15.00 | 20.00 |

**Similar to KM#233.4 but lines below bow slant left.**

| | | | | | |
|-----|------|------|------|------|------|
| 233.3 | 1813 | 10.00 | 17.50 | 30.00 | 50.00 |

**Obv: Lines below bow slant right.**

| | | | | | |
|-----|------|------|------|------|------|
| 233.4 | 1813 | 10.00 | 17.50 | 30.00 | 50.00 |

**Ornate flowery fields**

| | | | | | |
|-----|------|------|------|------|------|
| 234 | 1811 | 75.00 | 125.00 | 150.00 | 225.00 |
| | 1812 | 4.00 | 5.00 | 7.50 | 15.00 |
| | 1813 | 4.00 | 5.00 | 7.50 | 15.00 |
| | 1814 | 10.00 | 15.00 | 25.00 | 50.00 |

## Huautla
### 8 REALES

### CAST SILVER

| KM# | Date | Good | VG | Fine | VF |
|-----|------|------|-----|------|-----|
| 235 | 1811 | — | — | — | — |
|     | 1812 | 100.00 | 200.00 | 300.00 | 400.00 |
|     | 1813 | 75.00 | 150.00 | 250.00 | 350.00 |
|     | 1814 | — | — | — | — |

NOTE: Most silver specimens available on today's market are considered spurious.

**.903 SILVER, struck**
**Obv: PROV. D. OAXACA, M monogram.**
**Rev: Lion shield w/or w/o bow above.**

| 236 | 1812 | — | — | Rare | — |
|-----|------|-----|-----|------|-----|

**Obv: W/o leg.**

| 237 | 1813 | — | — | Rare | — |
|-----|------|-----|-----|------|-----|

**Obv: Bow/M/SUD. .**
**Rev: PROV. DE, . . . . ., arms.**

| 238 | 1813 | — | — | Rare | — |
|-----|------|-----|-----|------|-----|

**CAST SILVER**
**Similar to 4 Reales, KM#231.**

| 239 | 1814 | — | — | Rare | — |
|-----|------|-----|-----|------|-----|

**COPPER**

| 240 | 1814 | 30.00 | 60.00 | 125.00 | 200.00 |
|-----|------|-------|-------|--------|--------|

**OAXACA spelled out**

| 241 | 1814 | — | — | Rare | — |
|-----|------|-----|-----|------|-----|

**COPPER**
**Obv. leg: MONEDA PROVI.CIONAL PS.ES.**
**around bow, arrow/SUD.**
**Rev. leg: FABRICADO EN HUAUTLA**

| KM# | Date | Good | VG | Fine | VF |
|-----|------|------|-----|------|-----|
| 242 | 1812 | 500.00 | 800.00 | 1200. | 1750. |

## Tierra Caliente
(Hot Country)
**Under General Morelos**

### 1/2 REAL

**COPPER**
**Obv: Bow, T.C., SUD.**
**Rev: Morelos monogram, value, date.**

| 243 | 1813 | 40.00 | 70.00 | 125.00 | 200.00 |
|-----|------|-------|-------|--------|--------|

### REAL
**COPPER**
**Similar to 1/2 Real, KM#243.**

| 244 | 1813 | 15.00 | 30.00 | 50.00 | 80.00 |
|-----|------|-------|-------|-------|-------|

### 2 REALES
**COPPER**
**Similar to 1/2 Real, KM#243.**

| 245 | 1813 | 10.00 | 25.00 | 35.00 | 50.00 |
|-----|------|-------|-------|-------|-------|

| 246 | 1814 | 25.00 | 50.00 | 100.00 | 175.00 |
|-----|------|-------|-------|--------|--------|

**CAST SILVER**

| 247 | 1814 | — | — | Rare | — |
|-----|------|-----|-----|------|-----|

## 8 REALES

### COPPER

| KM# | Date | Good | VG | Fine | VF |
|---|---|---|---|---|---|
| 248 | 1813 | 10.00 | 20.00 | 40.00 | 75.00 |

### CAST SILVER

| | | | | | |
|---|---|---|---|---|---|
| 249 | 1813 | — | — | — | — |

**NOTE:** Most specimens available on todays market are considered spurious.

## PUEBLA

The coins of Puebla emanated from Zacatlan, the head-quarters of the hit-and-run insurgent leader Osorno. The mint opened in April of 1812 and operated until the end of 1813. The coins were 2 reales in silver and 1 and 1/2 reales in copper.

## Zacatlan

(Struck by General Osorno)

### 1/2 REAL

### COPPER
**Obv: Osorno monogram, ZACATLAN, date.**
**Rev: Crossed arrows, wreath, value.**

| | | | | | |
|---|---|---|---|---|---|
| 250 | 1813 | — | — | Rare | — |

### REAL

### COPPER

| | | | | | |
|---|---|---|---|---|---|
| 251 | 1813 | 100.00 | 150.00 | 250.00 | 450.00 |

### 2 REALES

### COPPER

| | | | | | |
|---|---|---|---|---|---|
| 252 | 1813 | 125.00 | 200.00 | 325.00 | 550.00 |

## VERACRUZ

Veracruz was the province that housed the town of Zongolica. In this town 2 priests and a lawyer decided to raise an army to fight for independence. Because of their isolation from other insurgent forces they decided to make coins for their area. Records show that they planned to or did mint coins of 1/2, 1, 2, 4, and 8 reales denominations. Extant specimens are known for only the three higher values.

## Zongolica

### 2 REALES

**.903 SILVER**
**Obv. leg: VIVA FERNANDO VII Y AMERICA,**
**bow and arrow.**
**Rev. leg: ZONGOLICA, value, crossed palm branch,**
**sword, date.**

| KM# | Date | Good | VG | Fine | VF |
|---|---|---|---|---|---|
| 253 | 1812 | 100.00 | 200.00 | 300.00 | 600.00 |

### 4 REALES

**.903 SILVER**
**Similar to 2 Reales, KM#253.**

| | | | | | |
|---|---|---|---|---|---|
| 254 | 1812 | 600.00 | 800.00 | 1200. | 2000. |

### 8 REALES

**.903 SILVER**

| | | | | | |
|---|---|---|---|---|---|
| 255 | 1812 | 1200. | 1600. | 3000. | 6000. |

## COUNTERMARKED COINAGE

### Congress Of Chilpanzingo

**Type A: Hand holding bow and arrow between quiver**
**w/arrows, sword and bow.**

Type B: Crowned eagle on bridge.

## 1/2 REAL

**SILVER**
**c/m: Type A on cast Mexico City KM#72.**

| KM# | Date | Good | VG | Fine | VF |
|-----|------|------|----|----|------|
| 256.1 | ND(1812) | 45.00 | 70.00 | 90.00 | 120.00 |

**c/m: Type A on Zacatecas KM#181.**

| | | | | | |
|-----|------|------|----|----|------|
| 256.2 | ND(1811) | 55.00 | 75.00 | 100.00 | 125.00 |

## REAL

**SILVER**
**c/m: Type A on cast Mexico City KM#81.**

| | | | | | |
|-----|------|------|----|----|------|
| A257 | ND(1803) | 20.00 | 30.00 | 50.00 | 80.00 |

## 2 REALES

**SILVER**
**c/m: Type B on 1/4 cut of 8 Reales.**

| | | | | |
|-----|------|------|----|----|
| 257.1 | ND | — | — Unique | — |

**c/m: Type B on Zacatecas KM#186.**

| | | | | |
|-----|------|------|----|----|
| 257.2 | ND(1811) | — | — Unique | — |

## 8 REALES

**SILVER**
**c/m: Type A on cast Mexico City KM#109.**

| KM# | Date | Good | VG | Fine | VF |
|-----|------|------|----|----|------|
| 258.1 | ND(1805) TH | 45.00 | 65.00 | 85.00 | 125.00 |

**c/m: Type A on cast Mexico City KM#110.**

| | | | | | |
|-----|------|------|----|----|------|
| 258.2 | ND(1810) HJ | 50.00 | 75.00 | 100.00 | 150.00 |

**c/m: Type A on cast Mexico City KM#111.**

| | | | | | |
|-----|------|------|----|----|------|
| 258.3 | ND(1811) HJ | 45.00 | 65.00 | 85.00 | 125.00 |
| | ND(1812) HJ | 100.00 | 125.00 | 175.00 | 275.00 |

**c/m: Type B on Chihuahua KM#111.1.**

| | | | | | |
|-----|------|------|----|----|------|
| 259.1 | ND(1816) RP | 200.00 | 250.00 | 300.00 | 350.00 |

**c/m: Type B on cast Mexico City KM#111.**

| | | | | | |
|-----|------|------|----|----|------|
| 259.2 | ND(1811) HJ | 130.00 | 140.00 | 150.00 | 175.00 |

**c/m: Type B on Valladolid KM#178.**

| | | | | | |
|-----|------|------|----|----|------|
| 259.3 | ND(1813) | 1000. | 2000. | 3000. | 5000. |

**c/m: Type B on Zacatecas KM#190.**

| | | | | | |
|-----|------|------|----|----|------|
| 259.4 | ND(1810) | 400.00 | 500.00 | 600.00 | 750.00 |

## Ensaie
## 8 REALES

**SILVER**
**c/m: Eagle over ENSAIE on Mexico City KM#110.**

| | | | | | |
|-----|------|------|----|----|------|
| 260.1 | ND(1811) HJ | 150.00 | 200.00 | 275.00 | 350.00 |

**c/m: Eagle over ENSAIE crude sling below on Zacatecas KM#189.**

| KM# | Date | Good | VG | Fine | VF |
|-----|------|------|----|----|------|
| 260.2 | ND(1811) | 200.00 | 400.00 | 600.00 | 800.00 |

**c/m: Eagle over ENSAIE, crude sling below on Zacatecas KM#190.**

| KM# | Date | Good | VG | Fine | VF |
|---|---|---|---|---|---|
| 260.3 | ND(1810) | — | — | — | — |
| | ND(1811) | 100.00 | 150.00 | 200.00 | 300.00 |

**c/m: Eagle over ENSAIE, crude sling below on Zacatecas KM#191.**

| | | | | | |
|---|---|---|---|---|---|
| 260.4 | ND(1810) | 500.00 | 700.00 | 900.00 | 1200. |
| | ND(1811) | 275.00 | 325.00 | 400.00 | 500.00 |
| | ND(1812) | 225.00 | 275.00 | 300.00 | 400.00 |

## Jose Maria Liceaga

**J.M.L. with banner on cross, crossed olive branches.
(J.M.L./V., D.s, S.M.,S.Y.S.L., Ve, A.P.,
s.r.a., Sea, P.G.,S.,S.M.,E.)**

### 1/2 REAL

SILVER
**c/m: JML/SM on cast Mexico City 1/2 Real.**

| A260 | ND | 100.00 | 150.00 | 200.00 | 275.00 |
|---|---|---|---|---|---|

### 2 REALES

SILVER
**c/m: J.M.L./Ve on 1/4 cut of 8 Reales.**

| 261.1 | ND | 175.00 | 225.00 | 300.00 | — |
|---|---|---|---|---|---|

**c/m: J.M.L./V. on Zacatecas KM#186-187.**

| 261.2 | ND(1811) | 200.00 | 225.00 | 250.00 | 300.00 |
|---|---|---|---|---|---|

**c/m: J.M.L./DS on Zacatecas KM#186-187.**

| KM# | Date | Good | VG | Fine | VF |
|---|---|---|---|---|---|
| 261.3 | ND(1811) | 200.00 | 235.00 | 275.00 | 325.00 |

**c/m: J.M.L./S.M. on Zacatecas KM#186-187.**

| 261.4 | ND(1811) | 200.00 | 235.00 | 275.00 | 325.00 |
|---|---|---|---|---|---|

**c/m: J.M.L./S.Y. on Zacatecas KM#186-187.**

| 261.5 | ND(1811) | 200.00 | 235.00 | 275.00 | 325.00 |
|---|---|---|---|---|---|

### 8 REALES

SILVER
**c/m: J.M.L./D.S. on Zacatecas KM#189-190.**

| 262.1 | ND(1811) | 250.00 | 325.00 | 425.00 | 550.00 |
|---|---|---|---|---|---|

**c/m: J.M.L./E on Zacatecas KM#189-190.**

| 262.2 | ND(1811) | 225.00 | 300.00 | 400.00 | 550.00 |
|---|---|---|---|---|---|

**c/m: J.M.L./P.G. on Durango KM#111.2.**

| 262.3 | ND(1813) RM | 200.00 | 275.00 | 375.00 | 525.00 |
|---|---|---|---|---|---|

**c/m: J.M.L./S.F. on Zacatecas KM#189-190.**

| 262.4 | ND(1811) | 200.00 | 275.00 | 375.00 | 525.00 |
|---|---|---|---|---|---|

**c/m: J.M.L./S.M. on Zacatecas KM#189-190.**

| 262.5 | ND(1811) | 200.00 | 275.00 | 375.00 | 525.00 |
|---|---|---|---|---|---|

**c/m: J.M.L./V.E. on Zacatecas KM#189-190.**

| KM# | Date | Good | VG | Fine | VF |
|---|---|---|---|---|---|
| 262.6 | ND(1811) | 200.00 | 275.00 | 375.00 | 525.00 |

## Don Jose Maria De Linares

## 8 REALES

**SILVER**
**c/m: LINA/RES\* on Mexico City KM#110.**
263.1  ND(1808) TH    300.00  350.00  425.00  525.00

**c/m: LINA/RES \* on Zacatecas KM#189-190.**
263.2  ND(1811)         350.00  425.00  500.00  600.00

**c/m: LINA/RES\* on Zacatecas, KM#191-192.**
263.3  ND(1812)         300.00  350.00  425.00  525.00

## L.V.S. - Labor Vincit Semper

**NOTE:** Some authorities believe L.V.S. is for 'La Villa de Sombrerete'.

## 8 REALES

**CAST SILVER**
**c/m: L.V.S. on Chihuahua KM#123.**

| KM# | Date | Good | VG | Fine | VF |
|---|---|---|---|---|---|
| 264.1 | ND(1811) RP | 275.00 | 350.00 | 450.00 | 550.00 |
|  | ND(1812) RP | 200.00 | 250.00 | 300.00 | 375.00 |

**c/m: L.V.S. on Chihuahua KM#111.1 overstruck on KM#123.**

| | | | | | |
|---|---|---|---|---|---|
| 264.2 | ND(1816) RP | 250.00 | 300.00 | 325.00 | 375.00 |
|  | ND(1817) RP | 250.00 | 300.00 | 325.00 | 375.00 |
|  | ND(1818) RP | 250.00 | 300.00 | 325.00 | 375.00 |
|  | ND(1819) RP | 400.00 | 450.00 | 500.00 | 600.00 |
|  | ND(1820) RP | 450.00 | 500.00 | 550.00 | 650.00 |

**c/m: L.V.S. on Guadalajara KM#111.3.**
264.3  ND(1817)      185.00  220.00  250.00  310.00

**c/m: L.V.S. on Nueva Vizcaya KM#165.**
264.4  ND(1811) RM   1150.   3150.   5250.   8250.

**c/m: L.V.S. on Sombrerete KM#177.**

| | | | | | |
|---|---|---|---|---|---|
| 264.5 | ND(1811) | 300.00 | 350.00 | 450.00 | 550.00 |
|  | ND(1812) | 300.00 | 350.00 | 450.00 | 550.00 |

**c/m: L.V.S. on Zacatecas KM#189-190.**
264.6  ND(1811)      350.00  400.00  450.00  550.00

**c/m: L.V.S. on Zacatecas KM#192.**
264.7  ND(1813)      350.00  400.00  450.00  550.00

# Morelos
### Morelos monogram

Type A: Stars above and below monogram in circle.

Type B: Dots above and below monogram in oval.

**Type C: Monogram in rectangle.**
NOTE: Many specimens of Type C available in today's market are considered spurious.

## 2 REALES

**COPPER**
**c/m: Type A on Oaxaca Sud, KM#226.1.**

| KM# | Date | Good | VG | Fine | VF |
|---|---|---|---|---|---|
| A265 | 1812 | — | — | — | — |

## 8 REALES

**SILVER**
**c/m: Type A on cast Mexico City KM#109.**

| | | | | | |
|---|---|---|---|---|---|
| 265.1 | ND(1797) FM | 45.00 | 50.00 | 55.00 | 75.00 |
| | ND(1798) FM | 45.00 | 50.00 | 55.00 | 75.00 |
| | ND(1800) FM | 45.00 | 50.00 | 55.00 | 75.00 |
| | ND(1807) TH | 45.00 | 50.00 | 55.00 | 75.00 |

**c/m: Type A on Mexico City KM#110.**

| KM# | Date | Good | VG | Fine | VF |
|---|---|---|---|---|---|
| 265.2 | ND(1809) TH | 55.00 | 65.00 | 75.00 | 100.00 |
| | ND(1811) HJ | 55.00 | 65.00 | 75.00 | 100.00 |

**c/m: Type A on Mexico City KM#111.**

| | | | | | |
|---|---|---|---|---|---|
| 265.3 | ND(1812) JJ | 50.00 | 55.00 | 60.00 | 70.00 |

**COPPER**
**c/m: Type A on Oaxaca Sud KM#233.**

| | | | | | |
|---|---|---|---|---|---|
| 265.4 | ND(1811) | 12.50 | 17.50 | 25.00 | 35.00 |
| | ND(1812) | 12.50 | 17.50 | 25.00 | 35.00 |
| | ND(1813) | 12.50 | 17.50 | 25.00 | 35.00 |
| | ND(1814) | 12.50 | 17.50 | 25.00 | 35.00 |

**CAST SILVER**
**c/m: Type A on Supreme National Congress KM#206.**

| | | | | | |
|---|---|---|---|---|---|
| 265.5 | ND(1811) | 200.00 | 250.00 | 300.00 | 450.00 |

**SILVER**
**c/m: Type A on Zacatecas KM#189-190.**

| | | | | | |
|---|---|---|---|---|---|
| 265.6 | ND(1811) | 200.00 | 250.00 | 350.00 | 450.00 |

**c/m: Type A on Zacatecas KM#191.**

| | | | | | |
|---|---|---|---|---|---|
| 265.7 | ND(1811) | 200.00 | 250.00 | 350.00 | 450.00 |

**c/m: Type B on Guatemala 8 Reales, C#67.**

| | | | | | |
|---|---|---|---|---|---|
| 266.1 | ND(1810) M | — | — | Rare | — |

**c/m: Type B on Mexico City KM#110.**

| | | | | | |
|---|---|---|---|---|---|
| 266.2 | ND(1809) TH | 45.00 | 55.00 | 65.00 | 90.00 |

c/m: Type C on Zacatecas KM#189-190.

| KM# | Date | Good | VG | Fine | VF |
|---|---|---|---|---|---|
| 267 | ND(1811) | 300.00 | 350.00 | 400.00 | 500.00 |

# Norte

Issued by the Supreme National Congress
and the Army of the North.

c/m: Eagle on cactus; star to left; NORTE below.

c/m: On Guanajuato KM#111.4.

| KM# | Date | Good | VG | Fine | VF |
|---|---|---|---|---|---|
| 270.2 | ND(1813) JM | 400.00 | 550.00 | 700.00 | 800.00 |

## 1/2 REAL

SILVER
c/m: On Zacatecas KM#180.

| KM# | Date | Good | VG | Fine | VF |
|---|---|---|---|---|---|
| 268 | ND(1811) | 250.00 | 300.00 | 375.00 | 450.00 |

## 2 REALES

c/m: On Zacatecas KM#189-190.

| | | | | | |
|---|---|---|---|---|---|
| 270.3 | ND(1811) | 300.00 | 400.00 | 500.00 | 650.00 |

SILVER
c/m: On Zacatecas KM#187.

| | | | | | |
|---|---|---|---|---|---|
| 269 | ND(1811) | 225.00 | 275.00 | 325.00 | 400.00 |

c/m: On Zacatecas KM#188.

| | | | | | |
|---|---|---|---|---|---|
| A269 | ND(1812) | — | — | — | — |

## 4 REALES

SILVER
c/m: On Sombrerete KM#175.

| | | | | | |
|---|---|---|---|---|---|
| B269 | ND(1812) | 100.00 | 150.00 | 200.00 | 275.00 |

## 8 REALES

SILVER
c/m: On Chihuahua KM#111.1.

| | | | | | |
|---|---|---|---|---|---|
| 270.1 | ND(1813) RP | 250.00 | 350.00 | 450.00 | 550.00 |

c/m: On Zacatecas KM#191.

| | | | | | |
|---|---|---|---|---|---|
| 270.4 | ND(1811) | 200.00 | 300.00 | 400.00 | 550.00 |
| | ND(1812) | 200.00 | 300.00 | 400.00 | 550.00 |

## Osorno

c/m: Osorno monogram.
(Jose Francisco Osorno)

### 1/2 REAL

**SILVER**
**c/m: On Mexico City KM#72.**

| KM# | Date | Good | VG | Fine | VF |
|---|---|---|---|---|---|
| 271.1 | ND(1798) FM | 65.00 | 100.00 | 150.00 | 200.00 |
| | ND(1802) FT | 65.00 | 100.00 | 150.00 | 200.00 |
| | ND(1806) | 65.00 | 100.00 | 150.00 | 200.00 |

**c/m: On Mexico City KM#73.**

| | | | | | |
|---|---|---|---|---|---|
| 271.2 | ND(1809) | 65.00 | 100.00 | 150.00 | 200.00 |

### REAL

**SILVER**
**c/m: On Mexico City KM#81.**

| | | | | | |
|---|---|---|---|---|---|
| 272.1 | ND(1803) FT | 65.00 | 100.00 | 150.00 | 200.00 |
| | ND(1803) FT | 65.00 | 100.00 | 150.00 | 200.00 |

**c/m: On Potosi Real.**

| | | | | | |
|---|---|---|---|---|---|
| 272.2 | ND | 65.00 | 100.00 | 150.00 | 200.00 |

### 2 REALES

**SILVER**
**c/m: On cast Mexico City KM#92.**

| | | | | | |
|---|---|---|---|---|---|
| A272.1 | ND(1809) TH | 75.00 | 125.00 | 175.00 | 250.00 |

**c/m: On Zacatlan KM#252.**

| | | | | | |
|---|---|---|---|---|---|
| A272.2 | ND(1813) | | 150.00 | 200.00 | 300.00 | 400.00 |

### 4 REALES

**SILVER**
**c/m: On Mexico City KM#97.**

| | | | | | |
|---|---|---|---|---|---|
| 273 | ND(1782) FF | — | — | — | — |

## 8 REALES

**SILVER**
**c/m: On Lima 8 Reales, C#101.**

| KM# | Date | Good | VG | Fine | VF |
|---|---|---|---|---|---|
| 274.1 | ND(1811) JP | 200.00 | 225.00 | 250.00 | 300.00 |

**c/m: On Mexico City KM#110.**

| | | | | | |
|---|---|---|---|---|---|
| 274.2 | ND(1809) TH | 125.00 | 150.00 | 225.00 | 300.00 |
| | ND(1810) HJ | 125.00 | 150.00 | 225.00 | 300.00 |
| | ND(1811) HJ | 125.00 | 150.00 | 225.00 | 300.00 |

## S.J.N.G. - Suprema Junta National Gubernativa

(Refer to Multiple countermarks)

## VILLA/GRAN

(Julian Villagran)

### 2 REALES

**SILVER**
**c/m: On cast Mexico City KM#91.**

| | | | | | |
|---|---|---|---|---|---|
| 298 | ND(1799) FM | 150.00 | 200.00 | 250.00 | 350.00 |
| | ND(1802) FT | 150.00 | 200.00 | 250.00 | 350.00 |

## 8 REALES

**SILVER**
**c/m: VILLA/GRAN on cast Mexico City KM#109.**

| KM# | Date | Good | VG | Fine | VF |
|-----|------|------|-----|------|-----|
| 275 | ND(1796) FM | 200.00 | 250.00 | 300.00 | 350.00 |
| | ND(1806) TH | 200.00 | 250.00 | 300.00 | 350.00 |

# UNCLASSIFIED COUNTERMARKS

## General Vicente Guerrero

The countermark of an eagle facing left within a pearled oval has been attributed by some authors as that of General Vicente Guerrero, a leader of the insurgents in the south, 1816-1821.

### 1/2 REAL

**SILVER**
**c/m: Eagle on Mexico City 1/2 Real.**

| | | | | | |
|-----|------|------|-----|------|-----|
| 276 | ND | | 40.00 | 60.00 | 80.00 | 175.00 |

### REAL

**SILVER**
**c/m: Eagle on Mexico City KM#78.**

| KM# | Date | Good | VG | Fine | VF |
|-----|------|------|-----|------|-----|
| 277 | ND(1772) FM | 35.00 | 50.00 | 75.00 | 150.00 |

### 2 REALES

**SILVER**
**c/m: Eagle on Mexico City KM#88.**

| | | | | | |
|-----|------|------|-----|------|-----|
| 278.1 | ND(1784) FM | 50.00 | 75.00 | 125.00 | 250.00 |

**c/m: Eagle on Mexico City KM#91.**

| | | | | | |
|-----|------|------|-----|------|-----|
| 278.2 | ND(1807) PJ | 35.00 | 65.00 | 85.00 | 200.00 |

## 8 REALES

**SILVER**
**c/m: Eagle on Zacatecas KM#191.**

| KM# | Date | Good | VG | Fine | VF |
|-----|------|------|-----|------|-----|
| 279 | ND(1811) | 100.00 | 150.00 | 200.00 | 350.00 |

## ZMY

### 8 REALES

**SILVER**
**c/m: ZMY on Zacatecas KM#191.**

| | | | | | |
|-----|------|------|-----|------|-----|
| 286 | ND(1812) | 100.00 | 150.00 | 210.00 | 275.00 |

# MULTIPLE COUNTERMARKS

Many combinations of Royalist and Insurgent countermarks are found usually on the cast copies produced by the Chihuahua and Mexico City Mints and also the crude provisional mint issues of this period. Struck Mexico Mint coins were used for molds to cast necessity coinage and were countermarked to show issuing authority. Some were marked again by opposing forces or by friendly forces to allow circulation in their area of occupation. Some countermarks are only obtainable with companion markings.

## Chilpanzingo Crown and Flag

### 8 REALES

**SILVER**
**c/m: Chilpanzingo Type B and crown and flag on Zacatecas KM#189-190.**

| | | | | | |
|-----|------|------|-----|------|-----|
| 280 | ND(1811) | — | — | — | — |

## Chilpanzingo/LVA
### 8 REALES

SILVER
c/m: Chilpanzingo Type A and LVA on Mexico City
KM#109.

| KM# | Date | Good | VG | Fine | VF |
|---|---|---|---|---|---|
| 297 | ND(1805) TH | — | — | — | — |

## Chilpanzingo/LVS
### 8 REALES

SILVER
c/m: Chilpanzingo Type A and
script LVS on cast Mexico City KM#110.

| | | | | | |
|---|---|---|---|---|---|
| 281 | ND(1809) HJ | 50.00 | 75.00 | 150.00 | 250.00 |

## Chilpanzingo/Morelos
### 8 REALES

SILVER
c/m: Chilpanzingo Type A and Morelos
monogram Type A on cast Mexico City KM#109.

| KM# | Date | Good | VG | Fine | VF |
|---|---|---|---|---|---|
| 284 | ND(1806) TH | 35.00 | 45.00 | 55.00 | 150.00 |
| | ND(1807) TH | — | — | — | — |

c/m: Chilpanzingo Type A and Morelos monogram
Type A on struck Mexico City KM#110.

| | | | | | |
|---|---|---|---|---|---|
| 285.1 | ND(1809) TH | 35.00 | 50.00 | 100.00 | 250.00 |

c/m: Chilpanzingo Type A and Morelos monogram
Type A on cast Mexico City KM#110.

| | | | | | |
|---|---|---|---|---|---|
| 285.2 | ND(1810) HJ | 35.00 | 45.00 | 55.00 | 150.00 |
| | ND(1811) HJ | | | | |

c/m: Chilpanzingo Type A and Morelos monogram
Type A on cast Mexico City KM#111.

| | | | | | |
|---|---|---|---|---|---|
| 285.3 | ND(1811) HJ | — | — | — | — |

## Chilpanzingo/Morelos/LVS
### 8 REALES

SILVER
c/m: Chilpanzingo Type A, Morelos Type A and
LVS monogram on cast Mexico City KM#110.

| | | | | | |
|---|---|---|---|---|---|
| 286 | ND(1809) HJ | 35.00 | 50.00 | 75.00 | 200.00 |

## Chilpanzingo/P.D.V.
### 8 REALES

**SILVER**
c/m: Chilpanzingo Type B and P.D.V. (Provisional
De Valladolid) on Valladolid KM#178.

| KM# | Date | Good | VG | Fine | VF |
|-----|------|------|-----|------|-----|
| 287 | ND(1813) | — | — | — | — |

**SILVER**
c/m: ENSAIE and J.M.L. on Zacatecas, KM#190.

| KM# | Date | Good | VG | Fine | VF |
|-----|------|------|-----|------|-----|
| A290 | ND(1811) | — | — | — | — |

## Chilpanzingo/S.J.N.G.
### 8 REALES

**SILVER**
c/m: Chilpanzingo Type B and S.J.N.G.
(Suprema Junta Nacional Gubernativa)
on Zacatecas KM#189-190.

| | | | | | |
|-----|------|------|-----|------|-----|
| 288 | ND(1811) | — | — | — | — |

## ENSAIE/VTIL
### 8 REALES

**SILVER**
c/m: ENSAIE and VTIL on Zacatecas KM#189-190.

| | | | | | |
|-----|------|------|-----|------|-----|
| 290 | ND(1811) | — | — | — | — |

## C.M.S./S.C.M.
### 2 REALES

**SILVER**
c/m: C.M.S. (Comandancia Militar Suriana) and
eagle w/S.C.M. (Soberano Congreso Mexicano)
on Mexico City 2 Reales.

| | | | | | |
|-----|------|------|-----|------|-----|
| 289 | ND | — | — | — | — |

## ENSAIE/J.M.L.
### 8 REALES

## J.M.L./VTIL
### 2 REALES

**SILVER**
c/m: J.M.L./D.S. and VTIL on Zacatecas, KM#186.

| | | Good | VG | Fine | VF |
|------|------|------|-----|------|-----|
| A286 | ND(1811) | 75.00 | 125.00 | 175.00 | 250.00 |

c/m: J.M.L./V.E. and VTIL on Zacatecas KM#186.

| | | Good | VG | Fine | VF |
|------|------|------|-----|------|-----|
| B286 | ND(1810) | 75.00 | 125.00 | 175.00 | 250.00 |
| | ND(1811) | 75.00 | 125.00 | 175.00 | 250.00 |

## 8 REALES

**SILVER**
c/m: J.M.L./D.S. and VTIL on Mexico City KM#110.

| KM# | Date | Good | VG | Fine | VF |
|-----|------|------|-----|------|-----|
| 291 | ND(1810) HJ | — | — | — | — |

## L.C.M./Morelos
### 8 REALES

**SILVER**
c/m: LCM and Morelos monogram
Type A on cast Mexico City KM#109.

| | | | | | |
|-----|------|------|-----|------|-----|
| 282 | ND(1792) FM | — | — | — | — |

## Morelos/Morelos
### 8 REALES

**SILVER**
c/m: Morelos Type A and C on cast
Mexico City KM#109.

| | | | | | |
|-----|------|------|-----|------|-----|
| 283 | ND(1806) TH | — | — | — | — |

## LCM/MVA-1812
### 8 REALES

**SILVER**
c/m: LCM and MVA/1812 on Chihuahua KM#123.

| KM# | Date | Good | VG | Fine | VF |
|-----|------|------|-----|------|-----|
| 292 | 1812(1810) RP | — | — | — | — |

c/m: LCM and MVA 1812 on Chihuahua KM#110.

| | | | | | |
|-----|------|------|-----|------|-----|
| A293 | 1812(1810) HJ | — | — | — | — |

c/m: LCM and MVA/1812 on Chihuahua KM#111.1.

| | | | | | |
|-----|------|------|-----|------|-----|
| 293 | 1812(1818) | 200.00 | 300.00 | 450.00 | 700.00 |

## L.V.A./Morelos
### 8 REALES

**SILVER**
c/m: Script LVA and Morelos monogram Type A
on cast Mexico City KM#110.

| | | | | | |
|-----|------|------|-----|------|-----|
| 294 | ND(-) HJ | — | — | — | — |

## M.d.S./S.C.M.

### 2 REALES

**SILVER**
c/m: M.d.S. (Militar del Sur) and eagle
w/S.C.M. (Soberano Congreso Mexicano)
on Mexico City 2 Reales.

| KM# | Date | Good | VG | Fine | VF |
|-----|------|------|-----|------|-----|
| 295 | ND | — | — | — | — |

## OSORNO/VILLAGRAN

### 8 REALES

**SILVER**
c/m: Osorno monogram and VILLA/GRAN on cast
Mexico City KM#110.

| KM# | Date | | | | |
|-----|------|---|---|---|---|
| 296 | ND(1809) TH | — | — | — | — |

## S.J.N.G./VTIL

### 8 REALES

**SILVER**
c/m: S.J.N.G. and VTIL on Zacatecas KM#191.

| KM# | Date | Good | VG | Fine | VF |
|-----|------|------|-----|------|-----|
| 297 | ND | 35.00 | 50.00 | 75.00 | 200.00 |

# EMPIRE OF ITURBIDE

### RULERS

Augustin I Iturbide, 1822-1823

### MINT MARKS

Mo - Mexico City Mint

### ASSAYERS INITIALS

JA - Jose Garcia Ansaldo, 1812-1833
JM - Joaquin Davila Madrid,
1809-1833

## 1/8 REAL

**COPPER**
**Mint: Nueva Viscaya**

| KM# | Date | Mintage | Good | VG | Fine | VF |
|-----|------|---------|------|-----|------|-----|
| 299 | 1821 | — | 25.00 | 50.00 | 85.00 | 150.00 |
| | 1822 | — | 7.50 | 12.50 | 25.00 | 45.00 |
| | 1823 | — | 7.50 | 12.50 | 25.00 | 45.00 |

## 1/4 REAL

**COPPER**
**Mint: Nueva Viscaya**

| KM# | Date | Mintage | Good | VG | Fine | VF |
|-----|------|---------|------|-----|------|-----|
| 300 | 1822 | — | 175.00 | 275.00 | 425.00 | 500.00 |

## 1/2 REAL

**.903 SILVER**
**Mint mark: Mo**

| KM# | Date | Mintage | Fine | VF | XF | Unc |
|-----|------|---------|------|-----|-----|-----|
| 301 | 1822 JM | — | 17.50 | 30.00 | 60.00 | 310.00 |
| | 1823 JM | — | 12.50 | 25.00 | 50.00 | 285.00 |

## REAL

**.903 SILVER**
**Mint mark: Mo**

| KM# | Date | Mintage | Fine | VF | XF | Unc |
|-----|------|---------|------|-----|-----|-----|
| 302 | 1822 JM | — | 50.00 | 110.00 | 225.00 | 750.00 |

## 2 REALES

**.903 SILVER**
**Mint mark: Mo**

| KM# | Date | Mintage | Fine | VF | XF | Unc |
|-----|------|---------|------|-----|-----|-----|
| 303 | 1822 JM | — | 25.00 | 55.00 | 225.00 | 800.00 |
| | 1823 JM | — | 20.00 | 45.00 | 175.00 | 750.00 |

## 8 REALES

**.903 SILVER**
**Mint mark: Mo**

| KM# | Date | Mintage | Fine | VF | XF | Unc |
|-----|------|---------|------|-----|-----|-----|
| 304 | 1822 JM | — | 45.00 | 95.00 | 250.00 | 850.00 |

**Obv: Bust similar to 8 Escudos, KM#313.**
**Rev: Similar to KM#304.**

| KM# | Date | Mintage | Fine | VF | XF | Unc |
|-----|------|---------|------|-----|-----|-----|
| 305 | 1822 JM | — | — | — | Rare | — |

**Type IV. Obv: Similar to KM#308.**
**Rev: Similar to KM#310.**

| KM# | Date | Mintage | Fine | VF | XF | Unc |
|-----|------|---------|------|-----|-----|-----|
| 309 | 1822 JM | — | 50.00 | 125.00 | 225.00 | 800.00 |

**Type I. Obv: Leg. divided. Rev: 8 R.J.M. at upper left of eagle.**

| | | | | | | |
|-----|------|---------|------|-----|-----|-----|
| 306.1 | 1822 JM | — | 60.00 | 145.00 | 350.00 | 1250. |

**Rev: Cross on crown.**

| | | | | | | |
|-----|------|---------|------|-----|-----|-----|
| 306.2 | 1822 JM | — | — | — | Rare | — |

**Type II. Obv: Similar to KM#306.**
**Rev: Similar to KM#310.**

| | | | | | | |
|-----|------|---------|------|-----|-----|-----|
| 307 | 1822 JM | — | 135.00 | 325.00 | 550.00 | 2150. |

**Type V. Obv. continuous leg. w/short irregular truncation. Rev: 8 R.J.M. below eagle.**

| | | | | | | |
|-----|------|---------|------|-----|-----|-----|
| 310 | 1822 JM | — | 50.00 | 125.00 | 200.00 | 750.00 |
| | 1823 JM | — | 50.00 | 125.00 | 200.00 | 750.00 |

**Type VI. Obv: Bust w/long truncation.**
**Rev: Similar to KM#310.**

| | | | | | | |
|-----|------|---------|------|-----|-----|-----|
| 311 | 1822 JM | — | — | — | Rare | — |

# 4 SCUDOS

**Type III. Obv: Continuous leg. w/long smooth truncation. Rev: Similar to KM#306.**

| | | | | | | |
|-----|------|---------|------|-----|-----|-----|
| 308 | 1822 JM | — | 175.00 | 500.00 | 950.00 | 1400. |

**NOTE:** Variety with long, straight truncation is valued at $5,000. in uncirculated condition.

**.875 GOLD**
**Mint mark: Mo**

| | | | | | | |
|-----|------|---------|------|-----|-----|-----|
| 312 | 1823 JM | — | 1000. | 1750. | 2500. | 4500. |

## 8 SCUDOS

.875 GOLD
Mint mark: Mo
Obv. leg: AUGUSTINUS.

| KM# | Date | Mintage | Fine | VF | XF | Unc |
|---|---|---|---|---|---|---|
| 313.1 | 1822 JM | — | 1200. | 2000. | 3500. | — |

**NOTE:** Superior Casterline sale 5-89 choice AU realized $11,000.

Obv. leg: AUGSTINUS (error).

| | | | | | | |
|---|---|---|---|---|---|---|
| 313.2 | 1822 JM | — | 1250. | 2250. | 4000. | — |

| | | | | | | |
|---|---|---|---|---|---|---|
| 314 | 1823 JM | — | 1000. | 1800. | 3000. | 5000. |

# REPUBLIC
## MINT MARKS
A, AS - Alamos
CE - Real de Catorce
CA,CH - Chihuahua
C, Cn, Gn(error) - Culiacan
D, Do - Durango
EoMo - Estado de Mexico
Ga - Guadalajara
GC - Guadalupe y Calvo
G, Go - Guanajuato
H, Ho - Hermosillo
M, Mo - Mexico City
O, OA - Oaxaca
SLP, PI, P, I/P - San Luis Potosi
Z, Zs - Zacatecas

## ASSAYERS INITIALS
### ALAMOS MINT

| Initials | Years | Mintmaster |
|---|---|---|
| PG | 1862-1868 | Pascual Gaxiola |
| DL, L | 1866-1879 | Domingo Larraguibel |
| AM | 1872-1874 | Antonio Moreno |
| ML, L | 1878-1895 | Manuel Larraguibel |

### REAL DE CATORCE MINT

| Initials | Years | Mintmaster |
|---|---|---|
| ML | 1863 | Mariano Leon |

### CHIHUAHUA MINT

| | | |
|---|---|---|
| MR | 1831-1834 | Mariano Cristobal Ramirez |
| AM | 1833-1839 | Jose Antonio Mucharraz |
| MJ | 1832 | Jose Mariano Jimenez |
| RG | 1839-1856 | Rodrigo Garcia |
| JC | 1856-1865 | Joaquin Campa |
| BA | 1858 | Bruno Arriada |
| FP | 1866 | Francisco Potts |
| JG | 1866-1868 | Jose Maria Gomez del Campo |
| MM, M | 1868-1895 | Manuel Merino |
| AV | 1873-1880 | Antonio Valero |
| EA | 1877 | Eduardo Avila |
| JM | 1877 | Jacobo Mucharraz |
| GR | 1877 | Guadalupe Rocha |
| MG | 1880-1882 | Manuel Gameros |

### CULIACAN MINT

| | | |
|---|---|---|
| CE | 1846-1870 | Clemente Espinosa de los Monteros |
| C | 1870 | ??? |
| PV | 1860-1861 | Pablo Viruega |
| MP, P | 1871-1876 | Manuel Onofre Parodi |
| GP | 1876 | Celso Gaxiola & Manuel Onofre Parodi |
| CG, G | 1876-1878 | Celso Gaxiola |
| JD, D | 1878-1882 | Juan Dominguez |
| AM, M | 1882-1899 | Antonio Moreno |
| F | 1870 | Fernando Ferrari |
| JQ, Q | 1899-1903 | Jesus S. Quiroz |
| FV, V | 1903 | Francisco Valdez |
| MH, H | 1904 | Merced Hernandez |
| RP, P | 1904-1905 | Ramon Ponce de Leon |

### DURANGO MINT

| | | |
|---|---|---|
| RL | 1825-1832 | ??? |
| RM | 1830-1848 | Ramon Mascarenas |
| OMC | 1840 | Octavio Martinez de Castro |
| CM | 1848-1876 | Clemente Moron |
| JMR | 1849-1852, | Jose Maria Ramirez |
| CP, P | 1853-1864, 1867-1873 | Carlos Leon de la Pena |
| LT | 1864-1865 | ??? |
| JMP, P | 1877 | Carlos Miguel de la Palma |
| PE, E | 1878 | Pedro Espejo |
| TB, B | 1878-1880 | Trinidad Barrera |
| JP | 1880-1894 | J. Miguel Palma |
| MC, C | 1882-1890 | Manuel M. Canseco or Melchor Calderon |

| Initials | Years | Mintmaster |
|---|---|---|
| JB | 1885 | Jacobo Blanco |
| ND, D | 1892-1895 | Norberto Dominguez |

### ESTADO DE MEXICO MINT

| | | |
|---|---|---|
| L | 1828-1830 | Luis Valazquez de la Cadena |
| F | 1828-1830 | Francisco Parodi |

### GUADALAJARA MINT

| | | |
|---|---|---|
| FS | 1818-1835 | Francisco Suarez |
| JM | 1830-1832 | ??? |
| JG | 1836-1839 1842-1867 | Juan de Dios Guzman |
| MC | 1839-1846 | Manuel Cueras |
| JM | 1867-1869 | Jesus P. Manzano |
| IC, C | 1869-1877 | Ignacio Canizo y Soto |
| MC | 1874-1875 | Manuel Contreras |
| JA, A | 1877-1881 | Julio Arancivia |
| FS, S | 1880-1882 | Fernando Sayago |
| TB, B | 1883-1884 | Trinidad Barrera |
| AH, H | 1884-1885 | Antonio Hernandez y Prado |
| JS, S | 1885-1895 | Jose S. Schiafino |

### GUADALUPE Y CALVO MINT

| | | |
|---|---|---|
| MP | 1844-1852 | Manuel Onofre Parodi |

### GUANAJUATO MINT

| | | |
|---|---|---|
| JJ | 1825-1826 | Jose Mariano Jimenez |
| MJ, MR, JM, PG, PJ, PF | | ??? |
| PM | 1841-1848, 1853-1861 | Patrick Murphy |
| YF | 1862-1868 | Yldefonso Flores |
| YE | 1862-1863 | Ynocencio Espinoza |
| FR | 1870-1878 | Faustino Ramirez |
| SB, RR | ??? | |
| RS | 1891-1900 | Rosendo Sandoval |

### HERMOSILLO MINT

| | | |
|---|---|---|
| PP | 1835-1836 | Pedro Peimbert |
| FM | 1871-1876 | Florencio Monteverde |
| MP | 1866 | Manuel Onofre Parodi |
| PR | 1866-1875 | Pablo Rubio |
| R | 1874-1875 | Pablo Rubio |
| GR | 1877 | Guadalupe Rocha |
| AF, F | 1876-1877 | Alejandro Fourcade |
| JA, A | 1877-1883 | Jesus Acosta |
| FM, M | 1883-1886 | Fernando Mendez |
| FG, G | 1886-1895 | Fausto Gaxiola |

### MEXICO CITY MINT

Because of the great number of assayers for this mint (Mexico City is a much larger mint than any of the others) there is much confusion as to which initial stands for which assayer at any one time. Therefore we feel that it would be of no value to list the assayers.

### OAXACA MINT

| | | |
|---|---|---|
| AE | 1859-1891 | Agustin Endner |
| E | 1889-1890 | Agustin Endner |
| FR | 1861-1864 | Francisco de la Rosa |
| EN | 1890 | Eduardo Navarro Luna |
| N | 1890 | Eduardo Navarro Luna |

### POTOSI MINT

| | | |
|---|---|---|
| JS | 1827-1842 | Juan Sanabria |
| AM | 1838,1843-1849 | Jose Antonio Mucharraz |
| PS | 1842-1843,1848-1849, 1857-1861,1867-1870 | Pompaso Sanabria |
| S | 1869-1870 | Pomposo Sanabria |
| MC | 1849-1859 | Mariano Catano |
| RO | 1859-1865 | Romualdo Obregon |
| MH, H | 1870-1885 | Manuel Herrera Razo |
| O | 1870-1873 | Juan R. Ochoa |
| CA, G | 1867-1870 | Carlos Aguirre Gomez |
| BE, E | 1879-1881 | Blas Escontria |
| LC, C | 1885-1886 | Luis Cuevas |
| MR, R | 1886-1893 | Mariano Reyes |

### ZACATECAS MINT

| Initials | Years | Mintmaster |
|---|---|---|
| A | 1825-1829 | Adalco |
| Z | 1825-1826 | Mariano Zaldivar |
| V | 1824-1831 | Jose Mariano Vela |
| O | 1829-1867 | Manuel Ochoa |
| M | 1831-1867 | Manuel Miner |
| VL | 1860-1866 | Vicente Larranaga |
| JS | 1867-1868, 1876-1886 | J.S. de Santa Ana |
| YH | 1868-1874 | Ygnacio Hierro |
| JA | 1874-1876 | Juan H. Acuna |
| FZ | 1886-1905 | Francisco de P. Zarate |
| FM | 1904-1905 | Francisco Mateos |

## State and Federal Issues
### 1/16 REAL
(Medio Octavo)

**COPPER**
**Mint: Jalisco**
**Obv. leg: DEPARTAMENTO DE JALISCO**

| KM# | Date | Mintage | Good | VG | Fine | VF |
|---|---|---|---|---|---|---|
| 316 | 1860 | — | 3.00 | 5.00 | 10.00 | 50.00 |

**Obv. leg: ESTADO LIBRE DE JALISCO**

| | | | | | | |
|---|---|---|---|---|---|---|
| 317 | 1861 | — | 3.00 | 5.00 | 10.00 | 50.00 |

**Mint: Mexico City**
**Obv. leg: REPUBLICA MEXICANA**

| KM# | Date | Mintage | VG | Fine | VF | XF |
|---|---|---|---|---|---|---|
| 315 | 1831 | — | 10.00 | 15.00 | 35.00 | 100.00 |
| | 1832/1 | — | 12.00 | 17.50 | 35.00 | 125.00 |
| | 1832 | — | 10.00 | 15.00 | 35.00 | 100.00 |
| | 1833 | — | 10.00 | 15.00 | 35.00 | 100.00 |

**BRASS**

| | | | | | | |
|---|---|---|---|---|---|---|
| 315a | 1832 | — | 15.00 | 22.50 | 60.00 | 150.00 |
| | 1833 | — | 12.00 | 17.50 | 50.00 | 100.00 |
| | 1835 | — | 400.00 | 800.00 | 1250. | 2300. |

### 1/8 REAL
(Octavo Real)
**COPPER**
**Mint: Chihuahua**
**Obv. leg: ESTADO SOBERANO DE CHIHUAHUA**

| KM# | Date | Mintage | Good | VG | Fine | VF |
|---|---|---|---|---|---|---|
| 318 | 1833 | — | — | — | Rare | — |
| | 1834 | — | — | — | Rare | — |
| | 1835/3 | — | — | — | Rare | — |

**Obv. leg: ESTADO DE CHIHUAHUA**

| | | | | | | |
|---|---|---|---|---|---|---|
| 319 | 1855 | — | 3.50 | 5.00 | 18.00 | 60.00 |

### Mint: Durango
#### Rev. leg: LIBERTAD

| KM# | Date | Mintage | Good | VG | Fine | VF |
|---|---|---|---|---|---|---|
| 320 | 1824 | — | 5.00 | 10.00 | 35.00 | 100.00 |
| | 1828 | — | 150.00 | 250.00 | 400.00 | 900.00 |

NOTE: These pieces were frequently struck over 1/8 Real, dated 1821-23 of Nueva Vizcaya. All known examples are collectable contemporary counterfeits.

#### Rev. leg: OCTo.DE.R.DE DO., date.

| | | | | | | |
|---|---|---|---|---|---|---|
| 321 | 1828 | — | 6.00 | 15.00 | 35.00 | 100.00 |

#### Obv. leg: ESTADO DE DURANGO

| | | | | | | |
|---|---|---|---|---|---|---|
| 322 | 1833 | — | — | — | Rare | — |

#### Obv. leg: REPUBLICA MEXICANA

| | | | | | | |
|---|---|---|---|---|---|---|
| 323 | 1842/33 | — | 15.00 | 20.00 | 40.00 | 125.00 |
| | 1842 | — | 10.00 | 15.00 | 30.00 | 100.00 |

#### Obv. leg: REPUBLICA MEXICANA
#### Rev. leg: DEPARTAMENTO DE DURANGO

| | | | | | | |
|---|---|---|---|---|---|---|
| 324 | 1845 | — | 25.00 | 50.00 | 100.00 | 250.00 |
| | 1846 | — | — | — | Rare | — |
| | 1847 | — | 3.00 | 5.00 | 8.00 | 35.00 |

#### Obv. leg: REPUBLICA MEXICANA
#### Rev. leg: ESTADO DE DURANGO

| | | | | | | |
|---|---|---|---|---|---|---|
| 325 | 1851 | — | 3.00 | 5.00 | 8.00 | 30.00 |
| | 1852/1 | — | 3.00 | 5.00 | 8.00 | 30.00 |
| | 1852 | — | 3.00 | 5.00 | 8.00 | 30.00 |
| | 1854 | — | 6.00 | 10.00 | 17.50 | 65.00 |

### Mint: Guanajuato
#### Obv. leg: ESTADO LIBRE DE GUANAJUATO

| KM# | Date | Mintage | Good | VG | Fine | VF |
|---|---|---|---|---|---|---|
| 326 | 1829 | — | 3.00 | 5.00 | 10.00 | 30.00 |
| | 1829 error w/GUANJUATO | | | | | |
| | | — | 3.00 | 5.00 | 10.00 | 30.00 |
| | 1830 | — | 8.00 | 12.00 | 20.00 | 75.00 |

#### BRASS

| | | | | | | |
|---|---|---|---|---|---|---|
| 327 | 1856 | — | 8.00 | 12.00 | 20.00 | 75.00 |

#### 25mm

| | | | | | | |
|---|---|---|---|---|---|---|
| 328 | 1856 | — | 4.00 | 6.00 | 10.00 | 30.00 |
| | 1857 | — | 4.00 | 6.00 | 10.00 | 30.00 |

#### COPPER

| | | | | | | |
|---|---|---|---|---|---|---|
| 328a | 1857 | — | 10.00 | 20.00 | 35.00 | 60.00 |

### Mint: Jalisco
#### Obv. leg: ESTADO LIBRE DE JALISCO

| | | | | | | |
|---|---|---|---|---|---|---|
| 329 | 1828 | — | 3.00 | 5.00 | 8.00 | 25.00 |
| | 1831 | — | 100.00 | 200.00 | 300.00 | 400.00 |
| | 1832/28 | — | 3.00 | 5.00 | 8.00 | 25.00 |
| | 1832 | — | 3.00 | 5.00 | 8.00 | 25.00 |
| | 1833 | — | 3.00 | 5.00 | 8.00 | 25.00 |
| | 1834 | — | 50.00 | 100.00 | 175.00 | 300.00 |

| | | | | | | |
|---|---|---|---|---|---|---|
| 330 | 1856 | — | 4.00 | 7.00 | 10.00 | 25.00 |
| | 1857 | — | 4.00 | 7.00 | 10.00 | 25.00 |

| KM# | Date | Mintage | Good | VG | Fine | VF |
|---|---|---|---|---|---|---|
| 330 | 1858 | — | 4.00 | 7.00 | 10.00 | 25.00 |
| | 1861 | — | 100.00 | 200.00 | 300.00 | 400.00 |
| | 1862/1 | — | 4.00 | 7.00 | 10.00 | 25.00 |
| | 1862 | — | 4.00 | 7.00 | 10.00 | 25.00 |

**Obv. leg: DEPARTAMENTO DE JALISCO**

| KM# | Date | Mintage | Good | VG | Fine | VF |
|---|---|---|---|---|---|---|
| 331 | 1858 | — | 3.00 | 5.00 | 8.00 | 20.00 |
| | 1859 | — | 3.00 | 5.00 | 8.00 | 20.00 |
| | 1860/59 | — | 3.00 | 5.00 | 8.00 | 20.00 |
| | 1860 | — | 3.00 | 5.00 | 8.00 | 20.00 |
| | 1862 | — | 6.00 | 10.00 | 20.00 | 60.00 |

**Mint: Mexico City**
**27mm**
**Obv. leg: REPUBLICA MEXICANA**

| KM# | Date | Mintage | VG | Fine | VF | XF |
|---|---|---|---|---|---|---|
| 332 | 1829 | — | 450.00 | 900.00 | 1500. | 2500. |

**21mm**
**Obv. leg: REPUBLICA MEXICANA**

| KM# | Date | Mintage | Good | VG | Fine | VF |
|---|---|---|---|---|---|---|
| 333 | 1829 | — | 10.00 | 15.00 | 30.00 | 60.00 |
| | 1830 | — | 2.00 | 3.00 | 5.00 | 15.00 |
| | 1831 | — | 2.00 | 4.00 | 6.00 | 20.00 |
| | 1832 | — | 2.00 | 4.00 | 6.00 | 20.00 |
| | 1833/2 | — | 2.00 | 4.00 | 6.00 | 20.00 |
| | 1833 | — | 2.00 | 3.00 | 5.00 | 15.00 |
| | 1834 | — | 2.00 | 3.00 | 5.00 | 15.00 |
| | 1835/4 | — | 2.25 | 4.00 | 6.00 | 20.00 |
| | 1835 | — | 2.00 | 3.00 | 5.00 | 15.00 |

**Obv. leg: LIBERTAD**

| KM# | Date | Mintage | Good | VG | Fine | VF |
|---|---|---|---|---|---|---|
| 334 | 1841 | — | 7.00 | 15.00 | 30.00 | 75.00 |
| | 1842 | — | 3.00 | 5.00 | 10.00 | 30.00 |
| | 1850 | — | 15.00 | 20.00 | 30.00 | 80.00 |
| | 1861 | — | 8.00 | 12.00 | 25.00 | 70.00 |

**Mint: Occidente**
**Obv. leg: ESTADO DE OCCIDENTE**

| KM# | Date | Mintage | Good | VG | Fine | VF |
|---|---|---|---|---|---|---|
| 335 | 1828 reverse S | | | | | |
| | | — | 15.00 | 30.00 | 45.00 | 100.00 |
| | 1829 | — | 15.00 | 30.00 | 45.00 | 100.00 |

**Mint: Potosi**
**Obv. leg: ESTADO LIBRE DE SAN LUIS POTOSI**

| | | | | | | |
|---|---|---|---|---|---|---|
| 336 | 1829 | — | 6.00 | 9.00 | 15.00 | 50.00 |
| | 1830 | — | 8.00 | 12.00 | 20.00 | 60.00 |
| | 1831 | — | 5.00 | 8.00 | 12.00 | 40.00 |
| | 1859 | — | 5.00 | 8.00 | 12.00 | 40.00 |

**Mint: Sonora**
**Obv. leg: ESTO LIBE Y SOBO DE SONORA, 28mm.**

| | | | | | | |
|---|---|---|---|---|---|---|
| 337 | 1859 | — | — | Rare | — | — |

**Mint: Zacatecas**
**Obv. leg: ESTo LIBe FEDo DE ZACATECAS**

| | | | | | | |
|---|---|---|---|---|---|---|
| 338 | 1825 | — | 3.00 | 5.00 | 10.00 | 25.00 |
| | 1827 | — | 3.00 | 5.00 | 10.00 | 25.00 |
| | 1827 inverted A for V in OCTAVO | | | | | |
| | | — | 12.00 | 20.00 | 40.00 | 100.00 |
| | 1829 | — | — | — | Rare | — |
| | 1830 | — | 3.00 | 5.00 | 8.00 | 20.00 |
| | 1831 | — | 4.00 | 6.00 | 10.00 | 25.00 |
| | 1832 | — | 3.00 | 5.00 | 8.00 | 20.00 |
| | 1833 | — | 3.00 | 5.00 | 8.00 | 20.00 |
| | 1835 | — | 4.00 | 6.00 | 10.00 | 25.00 |
| | 1846 | — | 4.00 | 6.00 | 10.00 | 25.00 |
| | 1851 | — | 125.00 | 175.00 | 250.00 | 350.00 |
| | 1852 | — | 4.00 | 6.00 | 10.00 | 25.00 |
| | 1858 | — | 3.00 | 5.00 | 8.00 | 20.00 |
| | 1859 | — | 3.00 | 5.00 | 8.00 | 20.00 |
| | 1862 | — | 3.00 | 5.00 | 8.00 | 20.00 |
| | 1863 reversed 6 in date | | | | | |
| | | — | 3.00 | 5.00 | 8.00 | 20.00 |

**Obv. leg: DEPARTAMENTO DE ZACATECAS**

| | | | | | | |
|---|---|---|---|---|---|---|
| 339 | 1836 | — | 4.00 | 8.00 | 15.00 | 40.00 |
| | 1845 | — | 6.00 | 10.00 | 20.00 | 50.00 |
| | 1846 | — | 4.00 | 8.00 | 15.00 | 40.00 |

# 1/4 REAL
(Un Quarto/Una Quartilla)
**(Copper/Brass Series)**

### COPPER
### Mint: Chihuahua
### Obv. leg: ESTADO SOBERANO DE CHIHUAHUA

| KM# | Date | Mintage | Good | VG | Fine | VF |
|---|---|---|---|---|---|---|
| 340 | 1833 | — | 8.00 | 12.00 | 35.00 | 75.00 |
| | 1834 | — | 5.00 | 8.00 | 12.00 | 50.00 |
| | 1835 | — | 5.00 | 8.00 | 12.00 | 50.00 |

### Obv. leg: ESTADO LIBRE DE CHIHUAHUA

| KM# | Date | Mintage | Good | VG | Fine | VF |
|---|---|---|---|---|---|---|
| 341 | 1846 | — | 4.00 | 6.00 | 12.00 | 50.00 |

**NOTE:** Varieties with or without fraction bar.

### Obv. leg: ESTADO DE CHIHUAHUA

| KM# | Date | Mintage | Good | VG | Fine | VF |
|---|---|---|---|---|---|---|
| 342 | 1855 | — | 3.00 | 5.00 | 10.00 | 50.00 |
| | 1856 | — | 3.00 | 5.00 | 10.00 | 50.00 |

### Obv. leg: DEPARTAMENTO DE CHIHUAHUA

| KM# | Date | Mintage | Good | VG | Fine | VF |
|---|---|---|---|---|---|---|
| 343 | 1855 | — | 3.00 | 5.00 | 10.00 | 50.00 |
| | 1855 DE/reversed D and E | | | | | |
| | | — | 3.00 | 5.00 | 10.00 | 50.00 |

### Obv. leg: E. CHIHA LIBERTAD

| KM# | Date | Mintage | Good | VG | Fine | VF |
|---|---|---|---|---|---|---|
| 344 | 1860 | — | 2.00 | 4.00 | 8.00 | 25.00 |
| | 1861 | — | 2.00 | 4.00 | 8.00 | 25.00 |
| | 1865/1 | — | 2.50 | 5.50 | 10.00 | 30.00 |
| | 1865 | — | 10.00 | 20.00 | 35.00 | 95.00 |
| | 1866/5 | — | 10.00 | 20.00 | 35.00 | 95.00 |
| | 1866 | — | 2.00 | 4.00 | 8.00 | 25.00 |

### Mint: Durango
### Obv. leg: REPUBLICA MEXICANA

| KM# | Date | Mintage | Good | VG | Fine | VF |
|---|---|---|---|---|---|---|
| 345 | 1845 | — | — | — | Rare | — |

### Obv. leg: REPUBLICA MEXICANA
### Rev: DURANGO, date, value.

| KM# | Date | Mintage | Good | VG | Fine | VF |
|---|---|---|---|---|---|---|
| 346 | 1858 | — | — | — | Rare | — |

### Obv. leg: ESTADO DE DURANGO
### Rev. leg: CONSTITUCION

| KM# | Date | Mintage | Good | VG | Fine | VF |
|---|---|---|---|---|---|---|
| 347 | 1858 | — | 3.00 | 6.00 | 12.00 | 50.00 |

**NOTE:** Variety exists in brass.

### Obv. leg: DEPARTAMENTO DE DURANGO
### Rev. leg: LIBERTAD EN EL ORDEN.

| KM# | Date | Mintage | Good | VG | Fine | VF |
|---|---|---|---|---|---|---|
| 348 | 1860 | — | 2.00 | 5.00 | 15.00 | 45.00 |
| | 1866 | — | 2.00 | 5.00 | 15.00 | 45.00 |

### Obv. leg: ESTADO DE DURANGO
### Rev. leg: INDEPENDENCIA Y LIBERTAD

| KM# | Date | Mintage | Good | VG | Fine | VF |
|---|---|---|---|---|---|---|
| 349 | 1866 | — | 3.00 | 5.00 | 12.00 | 45.00 |

### Rev. leg: SUFRAGIO LIBRE

| KM# | Date | Mintage | Good | VG | Fine | VF |
|---|---|---|---|---|---|---|
| 350 | 1872 | — | 2.00 | 4.00 | 10.00 | 20.00 |

**NOTE:** Variety exists in brass.

### Mint: Guanajuato
#### Obv. leg: ESTADO LIBRE DE GUANAJUATO

| KM# | Date | Mintage | Good | VG | Fine | VF |
|---|---|---|---|---|---|---|
| 351 | 1828 | — | 4.00 | 7.00 | 10.00 | 45.00 |
| | 1828 error w/GUANJUATO | | | | | |
| | | — | 4.00 | 7.00 | 10.00 | 45.00 |
| | 1829 | — | 4.00 | 7.00 | 10.00 | 45.00 |

#### Obv. leg: EST. LIB. DE GUANAXUATO
#### Rev. leg: OMNIA VINCIT LABOR

| | | | | | | |
|---|---|---|---|---|---|---|
| 352 | 1856 | — | 12.00 | 25.00 | 50.00 | 100.00 |
| | 1857 | — | 6.00 | 9.00 | 15.00 | 45.00 |

#### BRASS

| | | | | | | |
|---|---|---|---|---|---|---|
| 352a | 1856 | — | 4.00 | 7.00 | 10.00 | 30.00 |
| | 1857 | — | 4.00 | 7.00 | 10.00 | 30.00 |

### COPPER
### Mint: Jalisco
#### Obv. leg: ESTADO LIBRE DE JALISCO

| | | | | | | |
|---|---|---|---|---|---|---|
| 353 | 1828 | — | 4.00 | 6.00 | 12.00 | 35.00 |
| | 1829/8 | — | 3.00 | 5.00 | 8.00 | 35.00 |
| | 1829 | — | 3.00 | 5.00 | 8.00 | 35.00 |
| | 1830/20 | — | 3.00 | 5.00 | 8.00 | 30.00 |
| | 1830/29 | — | 3.00 | 5.00 | 8.00 | 30.00 |
| | 1830 | — | 3.00 | 5.00 | 8.00 | 30.00 |
| | 1831 | — | — | — | Rare | — |
| | 1832/20 | — | 3.00 | 5.00 | 8.00 | 30.00 |
| | 1832/28 | — | 3.00 | 5.00 | 8.00 | 30.00 |
| | 1832 | — | 3.00 | 5.00 | 8.00 | 30.00 |
| | 1833/2 | — | 3.00 | 5.00 | 8.00 | 30.00 |
| | 1834 | — | 3.00 | 5.00 | 8.00 | 30.00 |
| | 1835/3 | — | 3.00 | 5.00 | 8.00 | 30.00 |
| | 1835 | — | 3.00 | 5.00 | 8.00 | 30.00 |
| | 1836 | — | — | — | Rare | — |

#### Obv. leg: DEPARTAMENTO DE JALISCO

| KM# | Date | Mintage | VG | Fine | VF | XF |
|---|---|---|---|---|---|---|
| 354 | 1836 | — | — | — | Rare | — |

#### Obv. leg: ESTADO LIBRE DE JALISCO

| | | | | | | |
|---|---|---|---|---|---|---|
| 355 | 1858 | — | 3.00 | 5.00 | 8.00 | 20.00 |
| | 1861 | — | 3.00 | 5.00 | 10.00 | 25.00 |
| | 1862 | — | 3.00 | 5.00 | 8.00 | 20.00 |

#### Obv. leg: DEPARTAMENTO DE JALISCO

| | | | | | | |
|---|---|---|---|---|---|---|
| 356 | 1858 | — | 3.00 | 5.00 | 8.00 | 20.00 |
| | 1859/8 | — | 3.00 | 5.00 | 8.00 | 20.00 |
| | 1859 | — | 3.00 | 5.00 | 8.00 | 20.00 |
| | 1860 | — | 3.00 | 5.00 | 8.00 | 20.00 |

### Mint: Mexico City
#### Obv. leg: REPUBLICA MEXICANA.

| | | | | | | |
|---|---|---|---|---|---|---|
| 357 | 1829 | — | 8.00 | 20.00 | 60.00 | 150.00 |

#### Reduced size.

| | | | | | | |
|---|---|---|---|---|---|---|
| 358 | 1829 | — | 12.00 | 25.00 | 50.00 | 150.00 |
| | 1830 | — | 2.00 | 3.00 | 4.00 | 10.00 |
| | 1831 | — | 2.00 | 3.00 | 4.00 | 10.00 |
| | 1832 | — | 5.50 | 10.00 | 20.00 | 35.00 |
| | 1833 | — | 2.00 | 3.00 | 4.00 | 10.00 |
| | 1834/3 | — | 2.00 | 3.00 | 4.00 | 10.00 |
| | 1834 | — | 2.00 | 3.00 | 4.00 | 10.00 |
| | 1835 | — | 2.00 | 3.00 | 4.00 | 10.00 |
| | 1836 | — | 2.00 | 3.00 | 4.00 | 10.00 |
| | 1837 | — | 5.00 | 10.00 | 20.00 | 40.00 |

#### BRASS
#### c/m: JM

| | | | | | | |
|---|---|---|---|---|---|---|
| 358a.1 | 1831 | — | 8.00 | 15.00 | 35.00 | 75.00 |

#### W/o countermark

| | | | | | | |
|---|---|---|---|---|---|---|
| 358a.2 | 1831 | — | — | — | — | — |

**COPPER**
**Mint: Potosi**
**Obv. leg: ESTADO LIBRE DE SAN LUIS POTOSI**
**Rev. leg: MEXICO LIBRE**

| KM# | Date | Mintage | Good | VG | Fine | VF |
|-----|------|---------|------|-----|------|-----|
| 359 | 1828 | — | 3.00 | 4.00 | 6.00 | 15.00 |
| | 1829 | — | 3.00 | 4.00 | 6.00 | 15.00 |
| | 1830 | — | 3.00 | 4.00 | 6.00 | 15.00 |
| | 1832 | — | 3.00 | 4.00 | 6.00 | 15.00 |
| | 1859 large LIBRE | | | | | |
| | | — | 3.00 | 4.00 | 6.00 | 15.00 |
| | 1859 small LIBRE | | | | | |
| | | — | 3.00 | 4.00 | 6.00 | 15.00 |
| | 1860 | — | 3.00 | 4.00 | 6.00 | 15.00 |

**Rev. leg: REPUBLICA MEXICANA**

| | | | | | | |
|-----|------|---------|------|-----|------|-----|
| 360 | 1862 | 1,367 | 3.00 | 4.00 | 6.00 | 10.00 |
| | 1862 LIBR | | | | | |
| | | Inc. Ab. | 3.00 | 4.00 | 6.00 | 10.00 |

**Milled edge**
**Obv. leg: ESTADO LIBRE Y SOBERANO DE**
**S.L. POTOSI**
**Rev. leg: LIBERTAD Y REFORMA**

| | | | | | | |
|-----|------|---------|------|-----|------|-----|
| 361 | 1867 | 3.177 | 3.00 | 4.00 | 7.00 | 20.00 |
| | 1867 AFG I.A. | | 3.00 | 4.00 | 7.00 | 20.00 |

**Plain edge**

| | | | | | | |
|-----|------|---------|------|-----|------|-----|
| 362 | 1867 | Inc. Ab. | 3.00 | 4.00 | 7.00 | 20.00 |
| | 1867 AFG I.A. | | 3.00 | 4.00 | 7.00 | 20.00 |

**Mint: Sinaloa**
**Obv. leg: ESTADO LIBRE Y SOBERANO**
**DE SINALOA**

| KM# | Date | Mintage | Good | VG | Fine | VF |
|-----|------|---------|------|-----|------|-----|
| 363 | 1847 | — | 3.00 | 5.00 | 8.00 | 20.00 |
| | 1848 | — | 3.00 | 5.00 | 8.00 | 20.00 |
| | 1859 | — | 2.00 | 3.00 | 4.00 | 9.00 |
| | 1861 | — | 2.00 | 3.00 | 4.00 | 9.00 |
| | 1862 | — | 2.00 | 3.00 | 4.00 | 9.00 |
| | 1863 | — | 2.50 | 3.50 | 5.00 | 10.00 |
| | 1864/3 | — | 2.50 | 3.50 | 5.00 | 10.00 |
| | 1864 | — | 2.00 | 3.00 | 4.00 | 9.00 |
| | 1865 | — | 2.00 | 3.00 | 4.00 | 9.00 |
| | 1866/5 | 7.401 | 2.50 | 3.50 | 5.00 | 10.00 |
| | 1866 | Inc. Ab. | 2.00 | 3.00 | 4.00 | 9.00 |

**BRASS**

| | | | | | | |
|-----|------|---------|------|-----|------|-----|
| 363a | 1847 | — | 5.00 | 10.00 | 20.00 | 50.00 |

**COPPER**
**Mint: Sonora**
**Obv. leg: EST.D.SONORA UNA CUART**

| | | | | | | |
|-----|------|---------|------|-----|------|-----|
| 364 | 1831 | — | — | — | Rare | — |
| | 1832 | — | 3.00 | 5.00 | 9.00 | 50.00 |
| | 1833/2 | — | 2.50 | 4.00 | 7.00 | 40.00 |
| | 1833 | — | 2.50 | 4.00 | 7.00 | 40.00 |
| | 1834 | — | 2.50 | 4.00 | 7.00 | 40.00 |
| | 1835/3 | — | 2.50 | 4.00 | 7.00 | 40.00 |
| | 1835 | — | 2.50 | 4.00 | 7.00 | 40.00 |
| | 1836 | — | 2.50 | 4.00 | 7.00 | 40.00 |

**Obv. leg: ESTO.LIBE.Y SOBO.DE SONORA**

| | | | | | | |
|-----|------|---------|------|-----|------|-----|
| 365 | 1859 | — | 3.00 | 5.00 | 8.00 | 20.00 |
| | 1861/59 | — | 4.00 | 6.50 | 11.00 | 25.00 |
| | 1861 | — | 3.00 | 5.00 | 8.00 | 20.00 |
| | 1862 | — | 3.00 | 5.00 | 8.00 | 20.00 |
| | 1863/2 | — | 7.00 | 15.00 | 30.00 | 50.00 |

**BRASS**
**Mint: Zacatecas**
**Obv. leg: ESTO LIBE FEDO DE ZACATECAS**

| | | | | | | |
|-----|------|---------|------|-----|------|-----|
| 366 | 1824 | — | — | — | Rare | — |
| | 1825 | — | 3.00 | 5.00 | 8.00 | 20.00 |
| | 1826 | — | 100.00 | 150.00 | 200.00 | 300.00 |
| | 1827/17 | — | 3.00 | 5.00 | 8.00 | 20.00 |
| | 1829 | — | 3.00 | 5.00 | 8.00 | 20.00 |
| | 1830 | — | 3.00 | 5.00 | 8.00 | 20.00 |
| | 1831 | — | 50.00 | 100.00 | 125.00 | 250.00 |
| | 1832 | — | 3.00 | 5.00 | 8.00 | 20.00 |
| | 1833 | — | 3.00 | 5.00 | 8.00 | 20.00 |
| | 1834 | — | — | — | Rare | — |
| | 1835 | — | 3.00 | 5.00 | 8.00 | 20.00 |
| | 1846 | — | 3.00 | 5.00 | 8.00 | 20.00 |

| KM# | Date | Mintage | Good | VG | Fine | VF |
|---|---|---|---|---|---|---|
| 366 | 1847 | — | 3.00 | 5.00 | 8.00 | 20.00 |
| | 1852 | — | 3.00 | 5.00 | 8.00 | 20.00 |
| | 1853 | — | 3.00 | 5.00 | 8.00 | 20.00 |
| | 1855 | — | 5.00 | 10.00 | 20.00 | 65.00 |
| | 1858 | — | 3.00 | 5.00 | 8.00 | 20.00 |
| | 1859 | — | 3.00 | 5.00 | 8.00 | 20.00 |
| | 1860 | — | 100.00 | 150.00 | 200.00 | 300.00 |
| | 1862/57 | — | 3.50 | 5.00 | 8.00 | 20.00 |
| | 1862/59/7 | — | 10.00 | 20.00 | 40.00 | 80.00 |
| | 1862 | — | 3.00 | 5.00 | 8.00 | 20.00 |
| | 1863/2 | — | 3.00 | 5.00 | 8.00 | 20.00 |
| | 1863 | — | 3.00 | 5.00 | 8.00 | 20.00 |
| | 1864/58 | — | 5.00 | 10.00 | 25.00 | 60.00 |

**COPPER**
Obv. leg: DEPARTAMENTO DE ZACATECAS

| 367 | 1836 | — | 5.00 | 8.00 | 12.00 | 25.00 |
|---|---|---|---|---|---|---|
| | 1845 | — | — | — | Rare | — |
| | 1846 | — | 3.00 | 5.00 | 8.00 | 20.00 |

**SILVER SERIES**

0.8450 g, .903 SILVER, .0245 oz ASW
Mint mark: CA

| KM# | Date | Mintage | VG | Fine | VF | XF |
|---|---|---|---|---|---|---|
| 368 | 1843 RG | — | 75.00 | 125.00 | 300.00 | 500.00 |

Mint mark: C
| 368.1 | 1855 LR | — | 50.00 | 100.00 | 200.00 | 400.00 |

Mint mark: Do
| 368.2 | 1842 LR | — | 12.00 | 20.00 | 40.00 | 125.00 |
| | 1843 LR | — | 20.00 | 25.00 | 60.00 | 150.00 |

Mint mark: Ga
| 368.3 | 1842 JG | — | 2.50 | 5.50 | 8.00 | 20.00 |
| | 1843/2 JG | — | — | — | — | — |
| | 1843 JG | — | 6.00 | 9.00 | 12.50 | 30.00 |
| | 1843 MC | — | 4.00 | 6.50 | 9.00 | 25.00 |
| | 1844 MC | — | 4.00 | 6.50 | 9.00 | 25.00 |
| | 1844 LR | — | 2.50 | 5.00 | 7.50 | 15.00 |
| | 1845 LR | — | 2.50 | 4.50 | 7.50 | 15.00 |
| | 1846 LR | — | 5.00 | 8.00 | 10.00 | 25.00 |
| | 1847 LR | — | 4.00 | 6.50 | 9.00 | 25.00 |
| | 1848 LR | — | — | — | Rare | — |
| | 1850 LR | — | — | — | Rare | — |
| | 1851 LR | — | 6.00 | 10.00 | 20.00 | 50.00 |
| | 1852 LR | — | 50.00 | 100.00 | 135.00 | 200.00 |
| | 1854/3 LR | — | 50.00 | 100.00 | 135.00 | 200.00 |
| | 1854 LR | — | 5.00 | 10.00 | 12.50 | 30.00 |
| | 1855 LR | — | 5.00 | 8.00 | 10.00 | 30.00 |
| | 1857 LR | — | 6.50 | 10.00 | 15.00 | 27.50 |
| | 1862 LR | — | 5.50 | 10.00 | 15.00 | 30.00 |

Mint mark: GC
| 368.4 | 1844 LR | — | 50.00 | 75.00 | 125.00 | 200.00 |

Mint mark: Go
| 368.5 | 1842 PM | — | 4.00 | 6.00 | 10.00 | 20.00 |
| | 1842 LR | — | 2.00 | 4.00 | 8.00 | 15.00 |
| | 1843/2 LR | — | 4.00 | 6.00 | 10.00 | 20.00 |
| | 1843 LR | — | 2.00 | 4.00 | 8.00 | 15.00 |
| | 1844/3 LR | — | — | — | — | — |
| | 1844 LR | — | 2.00 | 4.00 | 8.00 | 15.00 |
| | 1845 LR | — | 8.00 | 15.00 | 30.00 | 60.00 |
| | 1846/5 LR | — | — | — | — | — |
| | 1846 LR | — | 4.00 | 6.00 | 10.00 | 20.00 |
| | 1847 LR | — | 2.00 | 4.00 | 8.00 | 15.00 |

| KM# | Date | Mintage | VG | Fine | VF | XF |
|---|---|---|---|---|---|---|
| 368.5 | 1848/7 LR | — | 2.00 | 4.00 | 8.00 | 15.00 |
| | 1848 LR | — | 2.00 | 4.00 | 8.00 | 15.00 |
| | 1849/7 LR | — | 8.00 | 15.00 | 30.00 | 60.00 |
| | 1849 LR | — | 2.00 | 4.00 | 8.00 | 15.00 |
| | 1850 LR | — | 2.00 | 4.00 | 8.00 | 15.00 |
| | 1851 LR | — | 2.00 | 4.00 | 8.00 | 15.00 |
| | 1852 LR | — | 2.00 | 4.00 | 8.00 | 15.00 |
| | 1853 LR | — | 2.00 | 4.00 | 8.00 | 15.00 |
| | 1855 LR | — | 4.00 | 8.00 | 15.00 | 30.00 |
| | 1856/4 LR | — | — | — | — | — |
| | 1856 LR | — | 5.00 | 10.00 | 20.00 | 35.00 |
| | 1862/1 LR | — | 3.00 | 5.00 | 10.00 | 20.00 |
| | 1862 LR | — | 2.00 | 4.00 | 8.00 | 15.00 |
| | 1863 LR | — | 2.00 | 4.00 | 8.00 | 15.00 |

Mint mark: Mo
| 368.6 | 1842 LR | — | 2.00 | 4.00 | 8.00 | 15.00 |
| | 1843 LR | — | 2.00 | 4.00 | 8.00 | 15.00 |
| | 1844/3 LR | — | 8.00 | 12.00 | 20.00 | 40.00 |
| | 1844 LR | — | 4.00 | 6.00 | 10.00 | 20.00 |
| | 1845 LR | — | 4.00 | 6.00 | 10.00 | 20.00 |
| | 1846 LR | — | 2.00 | 4.00 | 8.00 | 15.00 |
| | 1850 LR | — | 5.00 | 10.00 | 20.00 | 35.00 |
| | 1858 LR | — | 4.00 | 8.00 | 15.00 | 30.00 |
| | 1859 LR | — | 4.00 | 6.00 | 10.00 | 20.00 |
| | 1860 LR | — | 4.00 | 6.00 | 10.00 | 20.00 |
| | 1861 LR | — | 4.00 | 6.00 | 10.00 | 20.00 |
| | 1862 LR | — | 4.00 | 6.00 | 10.00 | 20.00 |
| | 1863/53 LR | — | — | — | — | — |
| | 1863 LR | — | 4.00 | 6.00 | 10.00 | 20.00 |

Mint mark: S.L.Pi
| 368.7 | 1842 | — | 2.00 | 4.00 | 8.00 | 15.00 |
| | 1843/2 | — | 4.00 | 6.00 | 10.00 | 20.00 |
| | 1843 | — | 2.00 | 4.00 | 8.00 | 15.00 |
| | 1844 | — | 2.00 | 4.00 | 8.00 | 15.00 |
| | 1845/3 | — | 4.00 | 6.00 | 10.00 | 25.00 |
| | 1845/4 | — | 4.00 | 6.00 | 10.00 | 25.00 |
| | 1845 | — | 2.00 | 4.00 | 8.00 | 15.00 |
| | 1847/5 | — | 4.00 | 6.00 | 10.00 | 20.00 |
| | 1847 | — | 2.00 | 4.00 | 8.00 | 15.00 |
| | 1851/47 | — | 4.00 | 8.00 | 15.00 | 30.00 |
| | 1854 | — | 125.00 | 200.00 | 275.00 | 400.00 |
| | 1856 | — | 4.00 | 8.00 | 15.00 | 30.00 |
| | 1857 | — | 5.00 | 10.00 | 20.00 | 35.00 |
| | 1862/57 | — | 10.00 | 20.00 | 40.00 | 85.00 |

Mint mark: Zs
| 368.8 | 1842/1 LR | — | 4.00 | 8.00 | 15.00 | 30.00 |
| | 1842 LR | — | 4.00 | 6.00 | 10.00 | 20.00 |

## 1/2 REAL

1.6900 g, .903 SILVER, .0490 oz ASW
Mint mark: Mo
Obv: Hooked neck eagle

| KM# | Date | Mintage | Fine | VF | XF | Unc |
|---|---|---|---|---|---|---|
| 369 | 1824 JM | — | 40.00 | 60.00 | 125.00 | 500.00 |

Mint mark: A
| 370 | 1862 PG | — | — | — | Rare | — |

Mint mark: Ca
Obv: Facing eagle
| 370.1 | 1844 RG | — | 75.00 | 125.00 | 175.00 | 275.00 |
| | 1845 RG | — | 75.00 | 125.00 | 150.00 | 250.00 |

Mint mark: C, Co
| 370.2 | 1846 CE | — | 30.00 | 50.00 | 75.00 | 150.00 |
| | 1848/7 CE | — | 15.00 | 25.00 | 45.00 | 90.00 |
| | 1849/8 CE | — | 15.00 | 25.00 | 45.00 | 90.00 |

| KM# | Date Mintage | Fine | VF | XF | Unc |
|---|---|---|---|---|---|
| 370.2 | 1849 CE — | — | — | — | — |
| | 1852 CE — | 12.50 | 20.00 | 40.00 | 80.00 |
| | 1853/1 CE — | 12.50 | 20.00 | 40.00 | 80.00 |
| | 1854 CE — | 20.00 | 35.00 | 50.00 | 100.00 |
| | 1856 CE — | 12.50 | 20.00 | 40.00 | 80.00 |
| | 1857/6 CE — | 20.00 | 35.00 | 50.00 | 100.00 |
| | 1857 CE — | 15.00 | 25.00 | 45.00 | 90.00 |
| | 1858 CE (error 1 for 1/2) | | | | |
| | — | 12.50 | 20.00 | 40.00 | 80.00 |
| | 1860/59 PV — | 20.00 | 35.00 | 50.00 | 100.00 |
| | 1860 PV — | 12.50 | 20.00 | 40.00 | 80.00 |
| | 1861 PV — | 12.50 | 20.00 | 40.00 | 80.00 |
| | 1863 CE (error 1 for 1/2) | | | | |
| | — | 15.00 | 25.00 | 45.00 | 90.00 |
| | 1867 CE — | 12.50 | 20.00 | 40.00 | 80.00 |
| | 1869 CE (error 1 for 1/2) | | | | |
| | — | 12.50 | 20.00 | 40.00 | 80.00 |

**Mint mark: D, Do**

| KM# | Date Mintage | Fine | VF | XF | Unc |
|---|---|---|---|---|---|
| 370.3 | 1832 RM — | 125.00 | 225.00 | 350.00 | 600.00 |
| | 1832 RM/L — | — | — | — | — |
| | 1833/2 RM/L | | | | |
| | — | 75.00 | 100.00 | 150.00 | 225.00 |
| | 1833/1 RM/L | | | | |
| | — | 12.50 | 20.00 | 40.00 | 80.00 |
| | 1833 RM — | 25.00 | 40.00 | 75.00 | 150.00 |
| | 1834/1 RM — | 25.00 | 40.00 | 75.00 | 150.00 |
| | 1834 RM — | 12.50 | 20.00 | 40.00 | 80.00 |
| | 1837/1 RM — | 12.50 | 20.00 | 40.00 | 80.00 |
| | 1837/4 RM — | 12.50 | 20.00 | 40.00 | 80.00 |
| | 1837/6 RM — | 12.50 | 20.00 | 40.00 | 80.00 |
| | 1841/33 RM — | 15.00 | 25.00 | 50.00 | 100.00 |
| | 1842/32 RM — | 12.50 | 20.00 | 40.00 | 80.00 |
| | 1842 RM — | 12.50 | 20.00 | 40.00 | 80.00 |
| | 1842 RM 8R (error) | | | | |
| | — | 12.50 | 20.00 | 40.00 | 80.00 |
| | 1842 RM 1/2/8R | | | | |
| | — | 12.50 | 20.00 | 40.00 | 80.00 |
| | 1843/33 RM — | 15.00 | 25.00 | 50.00 | 100.00 |
| | 1843 RM — | — | — | — | — |
| | 1845/31 RM — | 12.50 | 20.00 | 40.00 | 80.00 |
| | 1845/34 RM — | 12.50 | 20.00 | 40.00 | 80.00 |
| | 1845/35 RM — | 12.50 | 20.00 | 40.00 | 80.00 |
| | 1845 RM — | 15.00 | 25.00 | 50.00 | 100.00 |
| | 1846 RM — | 30.00 | 50.00 | 80.00 | 200.00 |
| | 1848/5 RM — | 35.00 | 55.00 | 110.00 | 250.00 |
| | 1848/36 RM — | 25.00 | 40.00 | 75.00 | 200.00 |
| | 1849 JMR — | 25.00 | 40.00 | 75.00 | 200.00 |
| | 1850 RM — | — | — | Rare | — |
| | 1850 JMR — | 25.00 | 40.00 | 75.00 | 200.00 |
| | 1851 JMR — | 20.00 | 35.00 | 50.00 | 100.00 |
| | 1852/1 JMR — | 65.00 | 125.00 | 250.00 | 600.00 |
| | 1852 JMR — | 30.00 | 50.00 | 80.00 | 200.00 |
| | 1853 CP — | 12.50 | 20.00 | 40.00 | 80.00 |
| | 1854 CP — | 25.00 | 40.00 | 75.00 | 200.00 |
| | 1855 CP — | 25.00 | 40.00 | 60.00 | 150.00 |
| | 1856/5 CP — | 20.00 | 35.00 | 50.00 | 100.00 |
| | 1857 CP — | 20.00 | 35.00 | 50.00 | 100.00 |
| | 1858/7 CP — | 20.00 | 35.00 | 50.00 | 100.00 |
| | 1859 CP — | 20.00 | 35.00 | 50.00 | 100.00 |
| | 1860/59 CP — | 40.00 | 65.00 | 135.00 | 300.00 |
| | 1861 CP — | 125.00 | 200.00 | 300.00 | 600.00 |
| | 1862 CP — | 25.00 | 40.00 | 60.00 | 125.00 |
| | 1864 LT — | 50.00 | 100.00 | 200.00 | 450.00 |
| | 1869 CP — | 40.00 | 65.00 | 125.00 | 275.00 |

**Mint mark: EoMo**

| KM# | Date Mintage | Fine | VF | XF | Unc |
|---|---|---|---|---|---|
| 370.4 | 1829 LF — | 175.00 | 300.00 | 450.00 | 1300. |

**Mint mark: Ga**

| KM# | Date Mintage | Fine | VF | XF | Unc |
|---|---|---|---|---|---|
| 370.5 | 1825 FS — | 25.00 | 40.00 | 75.00 | 150.00 |
| | 1826 FS — | 10.00 | 15.00 | 35.00 | 70.00 |
| | 1828/7 FS — | 12.50 | 20.00 | 40.00 | 80.00 |
| | 1829 FS — | 7.50 | 15.00 | 30.00 | 60.00 |
| | 1830/29 FS — | 40.00 | 60.00 | 100.00 | 200.00 |
| | 1831 LP — | — | — | Rare | — |
| | 1832 FS — | 10.00 | 20.00 | 35.00 | 70.00 |
| | 1834/3 FS — | 65.00 | 100.00 | 175.00 | 250.00 |
| | 1834 FS — | 10.00 | 20.00 | 35.00 | 70.00 |
| | 1835/4/3 FS/LP | | | | |
| | — | 15.00 | 25.00 | 40.00 | 80.00 |
| | 1837/6 JG — | 50.00 | 100.00 | 150.00 | 250.00 |
| | 1838/7 JG — | 15.00 | 25.00 | 40.00 | 80.00 |
| | 1839/8 JG/FS | | | | |
| | — | 35.00 | 75.00 | 150.00 | 250.00 |

| KM# | Date Mintage | Fine | VF | XF | Unc |
|---|---|---|---|---|---|
| 370.5 | 1839 MC — | 10.00 | 20.00 | 35.00 | 70.00 |
| | 1840/39 MC/JG | | | | |
| | — | — | — | — | — |
| | 1840 MC — | 15.00 | 25.00 | 40.00 | 80.00 |
| | 1841 MC — | 20.00 | 35.00 | 50.00 | 100.00 |
| | 1842/1 JG — | 15.00 | 25.00 | 40.00 | 80.00 |
| | 1842 JG — | 10.00 | 20.00 | 35.00 | 70.00 |
| | 1843/2 JG — | 15.00 | 30.00 | 50.00 | 100.00 |
| | 1843 JG — | 10.00 | 20.00 | 35.00 | 70.00 |
| | 1843 MC/JG — | 10.00 | 20.00 | 35.00 | 70.00 |
| | 1843 MC — | 10.00 | 20.00 | 35.00 | 70.00 |
| | 1844 MC — | 10.00 | 20.00 | 35.00 | 70.00 |
| | 1845 MC — | 10.00 | 20.00 | 35.00 | 70.00 |
| | 1845 JG — | 10.00 | 20.00 | 35.00 | 70.00 |
| | 1846 MC — | 10.00 | 20.00 | 35.00 | 70.00 |
| | 1846 JG — | 10.00 | 20.00 | 35.00 | 70.00 |
| | 1847 JG — | 10.00 | 20.00 | 35.00 | 70.00 |
| | 1848/7 JG — | 10.00 | 20.00 | 35.00 | 70.00 |
| | 1849 JG — | 10.00 | 20.00 | 35.00 | 70.00 |
| | 1850/49 JG — | — | — | — | — |
| | 1850 JG — | 10.00 | 20.00 | 35.00 | 70.00 |
| | 1851/0 JG — | 10.00 | 20.00 | 35.00 | 70.00 |
| | 1852 JG — | 10.00 | 20.00 | 35.00 | 70.00 |
| | 1853 JG — | 10.00 | 20.00 | 35.00 | 70.00 |
| | 1854 JG — | 10.00 | 20.00 | 35.00 | 70.00 |
| | 1855/4 JG — | 10.00 | 20.00 | 35.00 | 70.00 |
| | 1855 JG — | 10.00 | 20.00 | 35.00 | 70.00 |
| | 1856 JG — | 10.00 | 20.00 | 35.00 | 70.00 |
| | 1857 JG — | 10.00 | 20.00 | 35.00 | 70.00 |
| | 1858/7 JG — | 10.00 | 20.00 | 35.00 | 70.00 |
| | 1858 JG — | 10.00 | 20.00 | 35.00 | 70.00 |
| | 1859/7 JG — | 10.00 | 20.00 | 35.00 | 70.00 |
| | 1860/59 JG — | 10.00 | 20.00 | 35.00 | 70.00 |
| | 1861 JG — | 5.00 | 12.50 | 25.00 | 50.00 |
| | 1862/1 JG — | 15.00 | 25.00 | 40.00 | 80.00 |

**Mint mark: GC**

| KM# | Date Mintage | Fine | VF | XF | Unc |
|---|---|---|---|---|---|
| 370.6 | 1844 MP — | 50.00 | 100.00 | 150.00 | 350.00 |
| | 1845 MP — | 25.00 | 50.00 | 100.00 | 200.00 |
| | 1846 MP — | 25.00 | 50.00 | 100.00 | 200.00 |
| | 1847 MP — | 20.00 | 40.00 | 75.00 | 150.00 |
| | 1848 MP — | 25.00 | 50.00 | 100.00 | 200.00 |
| | 1849 MP — | 25.00 | 50.00 | 100.00 | 200.00 |
| | 1850 MP — | 30.00 | 60.00 | 125.00 | 250.00 |
| | 1851 MP — | 25.00 | 50.00 | 100.00 | 200.00 |

**Mint mark: Go**

| KM# | Date Mintage | Fine | VF | XF | Unc |
|---|---|---|---|---|---|
| 370.7 | 1826 MJ — | 125.00 | 250.00 | 400.00 | 1000. |
| | 1827/6 MJ — | 7.50 | 15.00 | 30.00 | 75.00 |
| | 1828/7 MJ — | 7.50 | 15.00 | 30.00 | 75.00 |
| | 1828 MJ denomination 2/1 | | | | |
| | — | — | — | — | — |
| | 1828 JG — | — | — | — | — |
| | 1828 MR — | 50.00 | 100.00 | 150.00 | 250.00 |
| | 1829/8 MJ — | 5.00 | 10.00 | 25.00 | 50.00 |
| | 1829 MJ — | 5.00 | 10.00 | 25.00 | 50.00 |
| | 1829 MJ reversed N in MEXICANA | | | | |
| | — | 5.00 | 10.00 | 25.00 | 50.00 |
| | 1830 MJ — | 5.00 | 10.00 | 25.00 | 50.00 |
| | 1831/29 MJ — | 15.00 | 30.00 | 60.00 | 150.00 |
| | 1831 MJ — | 10.00 | 20.00 | 40.00 | 80.00 |
| | 1832/1 MJ — | 7.50 | 15.00 | 30.00 | 75.00 |
| | 1832 MJ — | 7.50 | 15.00 | 30.00 | 75.00 |
| | 1833 MJ round top 3 | | | | |
| | — | 10.00 | 20.00 | 40.00 | 80.00 |
| | 1833 MJ flat top 3 | | | | |
| | — | 10.00 | 20.00 | 40.00 | 80.00 |
| | 1834 PJ — | 5.00 | 10.00 | 25.00 | 50.00 |
| | 1835 PJ — | 5.00 | 10.00 | 25.00 | 50.00 |
| | 1836/5 PJ — | 7.50 | 15.00 | 30.00 | 75.00 |
| | 1836 PJ — | 5.00 | 10.00 | 25.00 | 50.00 |
| | 1837 PJ — | 5.00 | 10.00 | 25.00 | 50.00 |
| | 1838/7 PJ — | 5.00 | 10.00 | 25.00 | 50.00 |
| | 1839 PJ — | 5.00 | 10.00 | 25.00 | 50.00 |
| | 1839 PJ (error: REPUBLIGA) | | | | |
| | — | 5.00 | 10.00 | 25.00 | 50.00 |
| | 1840/39 PJ — | 7.50 | 10.00 | 25.00 | 75.00 |
| | 1840 PJ straight J | | | | |
| | — | 5.00 | 10.00 | 25.00 | 50.00 |
| | 1840 PJ curved J | | | | |
| | — | 5.00 | 10.00 | 25.00 | 50.00 |
| | 1841/31 PJ — | 5.00 | 10.00 | 25.00 | 50.00 |
| | 1841 PJ — | 5.00 | 10.00 | 25.00 | 50.00 |
| | 1842/1 PJ — | 5.00 | 10.00 | 25.00 | 50.00 |
| | 1842/1 PM — | 5.00 | 10.00 | 25.00 | 50.00 |

| KM# | Date Mintage | Fine | VF | XF | Unc |
|---|---|---|---|---|---|
| 370.7 | 1842 PM/J — | 5.00 | 10.00 | 25.00 | 50.00 |
| | 1842 PJ — | 5.00 | 10.00 | 25.00 | 50.00 |
| | 1842 PM — | 5.00 | 10.00 | 25.00 | 50.00 |
| | 1843/33 PM 1/2 over 8 | | | | |
| | — | 5.00 | 10.00 | 25.00 | 50.00 |
| | 1843 PM convex wings | | | | |
| | — | 5.00 | 10.00 | 25.00 | 50.00 |
| | 1843 PM concave wings | | | | |
| | — | 5.00 | 10.00 | 25.00 | 50.00 |
| | 1844/3 PM — | 5.00 | 10.00 | 25.00 | 50.00 |
| | 1844 PM — | 10.00 | 20.00 | 40.00 | 90.00 |
| | 1845/4 PM — | 5.00 | 10.00 | 25.00 | 50.00 |
| | 1845 PM — | 5.00 | 10.00 | 25.00 | 50.00 |
| | 1846/4 PM — | 5.00 | 10.00 | 25.00 | 50.00 |
| | 1846/5 PM — | 5.00 | 10.00 | 25.00 | 50.00 |
| | 1846 PM — | 5.00 | 10.00 | 25.00 | 50.00 |
| | 1847/6 PM — | 7.50 | 15.00 | 30.00 | 60.00 |
| | 1847 PM — | 7.50 | 15.00 | 30.00 | 60.00 |
| | 1848/35 PM — | 5.00 | 10.00 | 25.00 | 50.00 |
| | 1848 PM — | 5.00 | 10.00 | 25.00 | 50.00 |
| | 1848 PF/M — | 5.00 | 10.00 | 25.00 | 50.00 |
| | 1849/39 PF — | 5.00 | 10.00 | 25.00 | 50.00 |
| | 1849 PF — | 5.00 | 10.00 | 25.00 | 50.00 |
| | 1849 PF (error: MEXCANA) | | | | |
| | — | 5.00 | 10.00 | 25.00 | 50.00 |
| | 1850 PF — | 5.00 | 10.00 | 25.00 | 50.00 |
| | 1851 PF — | 5.00 | 10.00 | 25.00 | 50.00 |
| | 1852/1 PF — | 5.00 | 10.00 | 25.00 | 50.00 |
| | 1852 PF — | 2.50 | 7.50 | 17.50 | 40.00 |
| | 1853 PF/R — | 5.00 | 10.00 | 25.00 | 50.00 |
| | 1853 PF — | 5.00 | 10.00 | 25.00 | 50.00 |
| | 1854 PF — | 5.00 | 10.00 | 25.00 | 50.00 |
| | 1855 PF — | 5.00 | 10.00 | 25.00 | 50.00 |
| | 1856/4 PF — | 5.00 | 10.00 | 25.00 | 50.00 |
| | 1856/5 PF — | 5.00 | 10.00 | 25.00 | 50.00 |
| | 1856 PF — | 5.00 | 10.00 | 25.00 | 50.00 |
| | 1857/6 PF — | 5.00 | 10.00 | 25.00 | 50.00 |
| | 1857 PF — | 5.00 | 10.00 | 25.00 | 50.00 |
| | 1858/7 PF — | 7.50 | 15.00 | 30.00 | 60.00 |
| | 1858 PF — | 5.00 | 10.00 | 25.00 | 50.00 |
| | 1859 PF — | 5.00 | 10.00 | 25.00 | 50.00 |
| | 1860 PF small 1/2 | | | | |
| | 1860 PF large 1/2 | | | | |
| | — | 5.00 | 10.00 | 25.00 | 50.00 |
| | 1860/59 PF — | 5.00 | 10.00 | 25.00 | 50.00 |
| | 1861 PF small 1/2 | | | | |
| | — | 5.00 | 10.00 | 25.00 | 50.00 |
| | 1861 PF large 1/2 | | | | |
| | — | 5.00 | 10.00 | 25.00 | 50.00 |
| | 1862/1 YE — | 5.00 | 10.00 | 25.00 | 50.00 |
| | 1862 YE — | 2.50 | 7.50 | 17.50 | 40.00 |
| | 1862 YF — | 5.00 | 10.00 | 25.00 | 50.00 |
| | 1867 YF — | 2.50 | 7.50 | 17.50 | 40.00 |
| | 1868 YF — | 2.50 | 7.50 | 17.50 | 40.00 |

NOTE: Varieties exist.

**Mint mark: Ho**

| KM# | Date Mintage | Fine | VF | XF | Unc |
|---|---|---|---|---|---|
| 370.8 | 1839 PP — | — | — | Unique | — |
| | 1862 FM — | 65.00 | 125.00 | 200.00 | 400.00 |
| | 1867 PR/FM 6/inverted 6, & 7/1 | | | | |
| | — | 100.00 | 175.00 | 250.00 | 450.00 |

**Mint mark: Mo**

| KM# | Date Mintage | Fine | VF | XF | Unc |
|---|---|---|---|---|---|
| 370.9 | 1825 JM — | 10.00 | 20.00 | 40.00 | 80.00 |
| | 1826/5 JM — | 10.00 | 20.00 | 40.00 | 80.00 |
| | 1826 JM — | 5.00 | 10.00 | 20.00 | 60.00 |
| | 1827/6 JM — | 5.00 | 10.00 | 20.00 | 60.00 |
| | 1827 JM — | 5.00 | 10.00 | 20.00 | 60.00 |
| | 1828/7 JM — | 7.50 | 15.00 | 25.00 | 75.00 |
| | 1828 JM — | 10.00 | 20.00 | 40.00 | 80.00 |
| | 1829 JM — | 7.50 | 15.00 | 25.00 | 75.00 |
| | 1830 JM — | 5.00 | 10.00 | 20.00 | 60.00 |
| | 1831 JM — | 5.00 | 10.00 | 20.00 | 60.00 |
| | 1832 JM — | 7.50 | 12.50 | 27.50 | 60.00 |
| | 1833 MJ — | 7.50 | 12.50 | 27.50 | 60.00 |
| | 1834 ML — | 5.00 | 10.00 | 20.00 | 60.00 |
| | 1835 ML — | 5.00 | 10.00 | 20.00 | 60.00 |
| | 1836/5 ML/MF | | | | |
| | — | 7.50 | 15.00 | 25.00 | 65.00 |
| | 1836 ML — | 7.50 | 15.00 | 25.00 | 65.00 |
| | 1838 ML — | 5.00 | 10.00 | 20.00 | 60.00 |
| | 1839/8 ML — | 5.00 | 10.00 | 25.00 | 65.00 |
| | 1839 ML — | 5.00 | 10.00 | 20.00 | 50.00 |
| | 1840 ML — | 5.00 | 10.00 | 20.00 | 50.00 |

| KM# | Date Mintage | Fine | VF | XF | Unc |
|---|---|---|---|---|---|
| 370.9 | 1841 ML — | 5.00 | 10.00 | 20.00 | 50.00 |
| | 1842 ML — | 5.00 | 10.00 | 20.00 | 50.00 |
| | 1842 MM — | 5.00 | 10.00 | 20.00 | 50.00 |
| | 1843 MM — | 10.00 | 20.00 | 40.00 | 80.00 |
| | 1844 MF — | 5.00 | 10.00 | 20.00 | 50.00 |
| | 1845/4 MF — | 5.00 | 10.00 | 25.00 | 60.00 |
| | 1845 MF — | 5.00 | 10.00 | 20.00 | 50.00 |
| | 1846 MF — | 5.00 | 10.00 | 20.00 | 50.00 |
| | 1847 RC — | 10.00 | 20.00 | 40.00 | 80.00 |
| | 1848/7 GC/RC | | | | |
| | — | 5.00 | 10.00 | 20.00 | 50.00 |
| | 1849 GC — | 5.00 | 10.00 | 20.00 | 50.00 |
| | 1850 GC — | 5.00 | 10.00 | 20.00 | 50.00 |
| | 1851 GC — | 5.00 | 10.00 | 20.00 | 50.00 |
| | 1852 GC — | 5.00 | 10.00 | 20.00 | 50.00 |
| | 1853 GC — | 5.00 | 10.00 | 20.00 | 50.00 |
| | 1854 GC — | 5.00 | 10.00 | 20.00 | 50.00 |
| | 1855 GC — | 5.00 | 10.00 | 20.00 | 50.00 |
| | 1855 GF/GC — | 7.50 | 12.50 | 25.00 | 65.00 |
| | 1856/5 GF — | 7.50 | 12.50 | 25.00 | 65.00 |
| | 1857 GF — | 5.00 | 10.00 | 20.00 | 50.00 |
| | 1858 FH — | 3.00 | 5.00 | 12.50 | 40.00 |
| | 1858/9 FH — | 5.00 | 10.00 | 20.00 | 50.00 |
| | 1859 FH — | 3.00 | 6.00 | 15.00 | 50.00 |
| | 1860 FH/GC | | | | |
| | — | 5.00 | 10.00 | 20.00 | 50.00 |
| | 1860/59 FH — | 7.50 | 12.50 | 25.00 | 65.00 |
| | 1860 FH — | 3.00 | 6.00 | 15.00 | 50.00 |
| | 1860 TH — | 5.00 | 10.00 | 20.00 | 50.00 |
| | 1861 CH — | 3.00 | 6.00 | 15.00 | 45.00 |
| | 1862/52 CH — | 5.00 | 10.00 | 20.00 | 50.00 |
| | 1862 CH — | 3.00 | 6.00 | 15.00 | 45.00 |
| | 1863/55 TH/GC | | | | |
| | — | 5.00 | 10.00 | 20.00 | 50.00 |
| | 1863 CH/GC — | 5.00 | 10.00 | 20.00 | 50.00 |
| | 1863 CH — | 3.00 | 6.00 | 15.00 | 45.00 |

**Mint mark: Pi**

| KM# | Date Mintage | Fine | VF | XF | Unc |
|---|---|---|---|---|---|
| 370.10 | 1831 JS — | 7.50 | 12.50 | 25.00 | 65.00 |
| | 1841/36 JS — | 20.00 | 40.00 | 75.00 | 125.00 |
| | 1842/1 PS — | 20.00 | 40.00 | 75.00 | 125.00 |
| | 1842/1 PS P/J | | | | |
| | — | 60.00 | 80.00 | 150.00 | 300.00 |
| | 1842 PS/JS — | 50.00 | 75.00 | 125.00 | 250.00 |
| | 1842 JS — | 20.00 | 40.00 | 75.00 | 125.00 |
| | 1843/2 PS — | 17.50 | 25.00 | 40.00 | 80.00 |
| | 1843 PS — | 15.00 | 25.00 | 35.00 | 70.00 |
| | 1843 AM — | 10.00 | 15.00 | 25.00 | 60.00 |
| | 1844 AM — | 10.00 | 15.00 | 30.00 | 65.00 |
| | 1845 AM — | 250.00 | 375.00 | 500.00 | 1500. |
| | 1846/5 AM — | 40.00 | 75.00 | 125.00 | 200.00 |
| | 1847/6 AM — | 15.00 | 25.00 | 40.00 | 80.00 |
| | 1848 AM — | 15.00 | 25.00 | 40.00 | 80.00 |
| | 1849 MC/AM — | 15.00 | 25.00 | 40.00 | 80.00 |
| | 1849 MC — | 12.50 | 20.00 | 35.00 | 70.00 |
| | 1850/49 MC — | — | — | | |
| | 1850Pi MC — | 10.00 | 15.00 | 25.00 | 60.00 |
| | 1850P MC — | — | — | | |
| | 1851 MC — | 10.00 | 15.00 | 25.00 | 60.00 |
| | 1852 MC — | 10.00 | 20.00 | 30.00 | 65.00 |
| | 1853 MC — | 7.50 | 12.50 | 20.00 | 60.00 |
| | 1854 MC — | 7.50 | 12.50 | 20.00 | 60.00 |
| | 1855 MC — | 15.00 | 20.00 | 35.00 | 70.00 |
| | 1856 MC — | 15.00 | 25.00 | 50.00 | 100.00 |
| | 1857 MC — | 7.50 | 12.50 | 20.00 | 60.00 |
| | 1857 PS — | 10.00 | 15.00 | 30.00 | 65.00 |
| | 1858 MC — | 12.50 | 20.00 | 35.00 | 70.00 |
| | 1858 PS — | 12.50 | 20.00 | 35.00 | 70.00 |
| | 1859 MC — | — | — | Rare | — |
| | 1860/59 PS — | 12.50 | 20.00 | 35.00 | 70.00 |
| | 1861 RO — | 10.00 | 15.00 | 30.00 | 60.00 |
| | 1862/1 RO — | 15.00 | 25.00 | 50.00 | 125.00 |
| | 1862 RO — | 15.00 | 25.00 | 50.00 | 125.00 |
| | 1863/2 RO — | 15.00 | 25.00 | 45.00 | 100.00 |

**Mint mark: Z, Zs**

| KM# | Date Mintage | Fine | VF | XF | Unc |
|---|---|---|---|---|---|
| 370.11 | 1826 AZ — | 5.00 | 10.00 | 20.00 | 60.00 |
| | 1826 AO — | 5.00 | 10.00 | 20.00 | 60.00 |
| | 1827 AO — | 5.00 | 10.00 | 20.00 | 60.00 |
| | 1828/7 AO — | 5.00 | 10.00 | 20.00 | 60.00 |
| | 1829 AO — | 5.00 | 10.00 | 20.00 | 60.00 |
| | 1830 OV — | 5.00 | 10.00 | 20.00 | 60.00 |

| KM# | Date Mintage | Fine | VF | XF | Unc |
|---|---|---|---|---|---|
| 370.11 | 1831 OV — | 25.00 | 50.00 | 75.00 | 150.00 |
| | 1831 OM — | 5.00 | 10.00 | 20.00 | 60.00 |
| | 1832 OM — | 5.00 | 10.00 | 20.00 | 60.00 |
| | 1833 OM — | 5.00 | 10.00 | 20.00 | 60.00 |
| | 1834 OM — | 5.00 | 10.00 | 20.00 | 60.00 |
| | 1835/4 OM — | 5.00 | 10.00 | 20.00 | 60.00 |
| | 1835 OM — | 5.00 | 10.00 | 20.00 | 60.00 |
| | 1836 OM — | 5.00 | 10.00 | 20.00 | 60.00 |
| | 1837 OM — | 10.00 | 20.00 | 40.00 | 80.00 |
| | 1838 OM — | 5.00 | 10.00 | 20.00 | 60.00 |
| | 1839 OM — | 7.50 | 15.00 | 30.00 | 65.00 |
| | 1840 OM — | 10.00 | 25.00 | 45.00 | 90.00 |
| | 1841 OM — | 10.00 | 25.00 | 45.00 | 90.00 |
| | 1842/1 OM — | 5.00 | 10.00 | 20.00 | 60.00 |
| | 1842 OM — | 5.00 | 10.00 | 20.00 | 60.00 |
| | 1843 OM — | 40.00 | 75.00 | 115.00 | 250.00 |
| | 1844 OM — | 5.00 | 10.00 | 20.00 | 60.00 |
| | 1845 OM — | 5.00 | 10.00 | 20.00 | 60.00 |
| | 1846 OM — | 7.50 | 15.00 | 30.00 | 65.00 |
| | 1847 OM — | 5.00 | 10.00 | 20.00 | 50.00 |
| | 1848 OM — | 5.00 | 10.00 | 20.00 | 50.00 |
| | 1849 OM — | 5.00 | 10.00 | 20.00 | 50.00 |
| | 1850 OM — | 5.00 | 10.00 | 20.00 | 50.00 |
| | 1851 OM — | 5.00 | 10.00 | 20.00 | 50.00 |
| | 1852 OM — | 5.00 | 10.00 | 20.00 | 50.00 |
| | 1853 OM — | 5.00 | 10.00 | 20.00 | 50.00 |
| | 1854/3 OM — | 5.00 | 10.00 | 20.00 | 50.00 |
| | 1854 OM — | 5.00 | 10.00 | 20.00 | 50.00 |
| | 1855/3 OM — | 7.50 | 15.00 | 30.00 | 65.00 |
| | 1855 OM — | 5.00 | 10.00 | 20.00 | 50.00 |
| | 1856 OM — | 5.00 | 10.00 | 20.00 | 50.00 |
| | 1857 MO — | 5.00 | 10.00 | 20.00 | 50.00 |
| | 1858 MO — | 5.00 | 10.00 | 20.00 | 50.00 |
| | 1859 MO — | 6.00 | 8.50 | 17.50 | 35.00 |
| | 1859 VL — | 6.00 | 8.50 | 17.50 | 40.00 |
| | 1860/50 VL inverted A for V | | | | |
| | — | 5.00 | 10.00 | 20.00 | 50.00 |
| | 1860/59 VL inverted A for V | | | | |
| | | 5.00 | 10.00 | 20.00 | 50.00 |
| | 1860 MO — | 5.00 | 10.00 | 20.00 | 50.00 |
| | 1860 VL — | 5.00 | 10.00 | 20.00 | 50.00 |
| | 1861/0 VL inverted A for V | | | | |
| | — | 7.50 | 15.00 | 30.00 | 65.00 |
| | 1861 VL inverted A for V | | | | |
| | — | 5.00 | 10.00 | 20.00 | 50.00 |
| | 1862 VL inverted A for V | | | | |
| | — | 5.00 | 10.00 | 20.00 | 50.00 |
| | 1863/1 VL inverted A for V | | | | |
| | — | 7.50 | 15.00 | 30.00 | 65.00 |
| | 1863 VL inverted A for V | | | | |
| | — | 5.00 | 10.00 | 20.00 | 50.00 |
| | 1869 YH — | 5.00 | 10.00 | 20.00 | 50.00 |

## REAL

**3.3800 g, .903 SILVER, .0981 oz ASW**
**Mint mark: Do**

| KM# | Date Mintage | Fine | VF | XF | Unc |
|---|---|---|---|---|---|
| 371 | 1824 RL — | 2750. | 3250. | 4000. | 5500. |

**Mint mark: Ca**

| KM# | Date Mintage | Fine | VF | XF | Unc |
|---|---|---|---|---|---|
| 372 | 1844 RG — | 500.00 | 1000. | 1500. | 2750. |
| | 1845 RG — | 500.00 | 1000. | 1500. | 2750. |
| | 1855 RG — | 100.00 | 150.00 | 225.00 | 450.00 |

**Mint mark: C**

| KM# | Date Mintage | Fine | VF | XF | Unc |
|---|---|---|---|---|---|
| 372.1 | 1846 CE — | 12.50 | 25.00 | 40.00 | 110.00 |
| | 1848 CE — | 12.50 | 25.00 | 40.00 | 110.00 |
| | 1850 CE — | 12.50 | 25.00 | 40.00 | 110.00 |
| | 1851/0 CE — | 12.50 | 25.00 | 40.00 | 110.00 |
| | 1852/1 CE — | 7.50 | 15.00 | 30.00 | 100.00 |
| | 1853/2 CE — | 7.50 | 15.00 | 30.00 | 100.00 |
| | 1854 CE — | 7.50 | 15.00 | 30.00 | 100.00 |
| | 1856 CE — | 40.00 | 65.00 | 100.00 | 225.00 |
| | 1857/4 CE — | 10.00 | 20.00 | 35.00 | 100.00 |
| | 1857/6 CE — | 10.00 | 20.00 | 35.00 | 100.00 |
| | 1858 CE — | 5.00 | 7.50 | 15.00 | 100.00 |
| | 1859 CE — | — | — | — | — |
| | 1860 PV — | 5.00 | 7.50 | 15.00 | 100.00 |
| | 1861 PV — | 5.00 | 7.50 | 15.00 | 100.00 |
| | 1863 CE | | | | |
| | 3 known — | — | 1650. | 2250. | |
| | 1869 CE — | 5.00 | 7.50 | 15.00 | 100.00 |

**Mint mark: Do**

| KM# | Date Mintage | Fine | VF | XF | Unc |
|---|---|---|---|---|---|
| 372.2 | 1832/1 RM — | 5.00 | 10.00 | 20.00 | 90.00 |
| | 1832 RM/RL — | 10.00 | 15.00 | 30.00 | 100.00 |
| | 1832 RM — | 5.00 | 10.00 | 20.00 | 100.00 |
| | 1834/24 RM/RL | | | | |
| | — | 15.00 | 25.00 | 50.00 | 150.00 |
| | 1834/3 RM/RL | | | | |
| | — | 15.00 | 25.00 | 50.00 | 150.00 |
| | 1834 RM — | 10.00 | 20.00 | 40.00 | 110.00 |
| | 1836/4 RM — | 5.00 | 7.50 | 15.00 | 100.00 |
| | 1836 RM — | 5.00 | 7.50 | 15.00 | 100.00 |
| | 1837 RM — | 12.50 | 20.00 | 40.00 | 110.00 |
| | 1841 RM — | 7.50 | 15.00 | 30.00 | 100.00 |
| | 1842/32 RM — | 10.00 | 20.00 | 40.00 | 110.00 |
| | 1842 RM — | 7.50 | 15.00 | 30.00 | 100.00 |
| | 1843 RM — | 5.00 | 7.50 | 15.00 | 100.00 |
| | 1844/34 RM — | 15.00 | 25.00 | 45.00 | 125.00 |
| | 1845 RM — | 5.00 | 7.50 | 15.00 | 100.00 |
| | 1846 RM — | 7.50 | 15.00 | 30.00 | 100.00 |
| | 1847 RM — | 10.00 | 15.00 | 35.00 | 100.00 |
| | 1848/31 RM — | 10.00 | 15.00 | 35.00 | 100.00 |
| | 1848/33 RM — | 10.00 | 15.00 | 35.00 | 100.00 |
| | 1848/5 RM — | 10.00 | 15.00 | 35.00 | 100.00 |
| | 1848 RM — | 7.50 | 12.50 | 20.00 | 100.00 |
| | 1849/8 CM — | 10.00 | 15.00 | 30.00 | 100.00 |
| | 1850 JMR — | 15.00 | 25.00 | 45.00 | 125.00 |
| | 1851 JMR — | 15.00 | 25.00 | 45.00 | 120.00 |
| | 1852 JMR — | 15.00 | 25.00 | 45.00 | 120.00 |
| | 1853 CP — | 12.50 | 20.00 | 35.00 | 100.00 |
| | 1854/1 CP — | 10.00 | 15.00 | 25.00 | 100.00 |
| | 1854 CP — | 7.50 | 12.50 | 20.00 | 100.00 |
| | 1855 CP — | 10.00 | 15.00 | 25.00 | 100.00 |
| | 1856 CP — | 12.50 | 20.00 | 35.00 | 100.00 |
| | 1857 CP — | 12.50 | 20.00 | 35.00 | 100.00 |
| | 1858 CP — | 12.50 | 20.00 | 35.00 | 100.00 |
| | 1859 CP — | 7.50 | 12.50 | 20.00 | 100.00 |
| | 1860/59 CP — | 10.00 | 15.00 | 25.00 | 100.00 |
| | 1861 CP — | 15.00 | 25.00 | 40.00 | 110.00 |
| | 1862/1 CP — | 225.00 | 300.00 | 450.00 | 1250. |
| | 1864 LT — | 15.00 | 25.00 | 40.00 | 110.00 |

**Mint mark: EoMo**

| KM# | Date Mintage | Fine | VF | XF | Unc |
|---|---|---|---|---|---|
| 372.3 | 1828 LF — | 200.00 | 300.00 | 450.00 | 1500. |

**Mint mark: Ga**

| KM# | Date Mintage | Fine | VF | XF | Unc |
|---|---|---|---|---|---|
| 372.4 | 1826 FS — | 15.00 | 30.00 | 50.00 | 125.00 |
| | 1828/7 FS — | 15.00 | 30.00 | 50.00 | 125.00 |
| | 1829/8/7 FS — | — | — | — | — |
| | 1829 FS — | 15.00 | 30.00 | 50.00 | 125.00 |
| | 1830 FS — | 250.00 | 350.00 | 500.00 | — |
| | 1831 LP — | 15.00 | 30.00 | 50.00 | 125.00 |
| | 1831 LP/FS — | 300.00 | 450.00 | 600.00 | — |
| | 1832 FS — | 250.00 | 350.00 | 500.00 | — |
| | 1833/2 G FS — | 100.00 | 150.00 | 275.00 | 550.00 |
| | 1833 FS — | 75.00 | 125.00 | 225.00 | 500.00 |
| | 1834/3 FS — | 75.00 | 125.00 | 225.00 | 500.00 |
| | 1835 FS — | — | — | — | — |
| | 1837/6 JG/FS | | | | |
| | — | 12.50 | 20.00 | 35.00 | 100.00 |
| | 1838/7 JG/FS | | | | |
| | — | 12.50 | 20.00 | 35.00 | 100.00 |
| | 1839 JG — | 250.00 | 350.00 | 500.00 | — |
| | 1840 JG — | 12.50 | 20.00 | 35.00 | 100.00 |

| KM# | Date | Mintage | Fine | VF | XF | Unc |
|---|---|---|---|---|---|---|
| 372.4 | 1840 MC | — | 7.50 | 12.50 | 25.00 | 70.00 |
| | 1841 MC | — | 50.00 | 75.00 | 125.00 | 250.00 |
| | 1842/0 JG/MC | — | 10.00 | 15.00 | 30.00 | 100.00 |
| | 1842 JG | — | 7.50 | 12.50 | 20.00 | 100.00 |
| | 1843 JG | — | 150.00 | 200.00 | 300.00 | 750.00 |
| | 1843 MC | — | 5.00 | 7.50 | 15.00 | 100.00 |
| | 1844 MC | — | 7.50 | 12.50 | 20.00 | 100.00 |
| | 1845 MC | — | 10.00 | 15.00 | 25.00 | 100.00 |
| | 1845 JG | — | 5.00 | 7.50 | 20.00 | 100.00 |
| | 1846 JG | — | 12.50 | 20.00 | 35.00 | 100.00 |
| | 1847/6 JG | — | 10.00 | 15.00 | 25.00 | 100.00 |
| | 1847 JG | — | 10.00 | 15.00 | 25.00 | 100.00 |
| | 1848 JG | — | 400.00 | 550.00 | 700.00 | — |
| | 1849 JG | — | 7.50 | 12.50 | 20.00 | 100.00 |
| | 1850 JG | — | 175.00 | 275.00 | 400.00 | — |
| | 1851 JG | — | 10.00 | 15.00 | 25.00 | 100.00 |
| | 1852 JG | — | 10.00 | 15.00 | 25.00 | 100.00 |
| | 1853/2 JG | — | 10.00 | 15.00 | 25.00 | 100.00 |
| | 1854 JG | — | 10.00 | 15.00 | 25.00 | 100.00 |
| | 1855 JG | — | 15.00 | 25.00 | 40.00 | 100.00 |
| | 1856 JG | — | 7.50 | 12.50 | 20.00 | 100.00 |
| | 1857/6 JG | — | 12.50 | 20.00 | 35.00 | 100.00 |
| | 1858/7 JG | — | 15.00 | 25.00 | 40.00 | 110.00 |
| | 1859/8 JG | — | 25.00 | 50.00 | 75.00 | 150.00 |
| | 1860/59 JG | — | 30.00 | 60.00 | 90.00 | 225.00 |
| | 1861/0 JG | — | 20.00 | 30.00 | 50.00 | 125.00 |
| | 1861 JG | — | 25.00 | 50.00 | 100.00 | 250.00 |
| | 1862 JG | — | 7.50 | 12.50 | 20.00 | 100.00 |

**Mint mark: GC**

| KM# | Date | Mintage | Fine | VF | XF | Unc |
|---|---|---|---|---|---|---|
| 372.5 | 1844 MP | — | 40.00 | 60.00 | 100.00 | 250.00 |
| | 1845 MP | — | 40.00 | 60.00 | 100.00 | 250.00 |
| | 1846 MP | — | 40.00 | 60.00 | 100.00 | 250.00 |
| | 1847 MP | — | 40.00 | 60.00 | 100.00 | 250.00 |
| | 1848 MP | — | 40.00 | 60.00 | 100.00 | 250.00 |
| | 1849/7 MP | — | 40.00 | 60.00 | 100.00 | 250.00 |
| | 1849/8 MP | — | 40.00 | 60.00 | 100.00 | 250.00 |
| | 1849 MP | — | 40.00 | 60.00 | 100.00 | 250.00 |
| | 1850 MP | — | 40.00 | 60.00 | 100.00 | 250.00 |
| | 1851 MP | — | 40.00 | 60.00 | 100.00 | 250.00 |

**Mint mark: Go**

| KM# | Date | Mintage | Fine | VF | XF | Unc |
|---|---|---|---|---|---|---|
| 372.6 | 1826/5 JJ | — | 5.00 | 7.50 | 15.00 | 85.00 |
| | 1826 MJ | — | 4.00 | 6.00 | 15.00 | 85.00 |
| | 1827 MJ | — | 4.00 | 6.00 | 15.00 | 65.00 |
| | 1827 JM | — | 10.00 | 15.00 | 25.00 | 75.00 |
| | 1828/7 MR | — | 4.00 | 6.00 | 15.00 | 85.00 |
| | 1828 MJ, straight J, small 8 | — | 4.00 | 6.00 | 15.00 | 85.00 |
| | 1828Go MJ, full J, large 8 | — | 4.00 | 6.00 | 15.00 | 85.00 |
| | 1828G MJ, full J, large 8 | — | 4.00 | 6.00 | 15.00 | 85.00 |
| | 1828 MR | — | 4.00 | 6.00 | 15.00 | 85.00 |
| | 1829/8 MG small eagle | — | 4.00 | 6.00 | 15.00 | 85.00 |
| | 1829 MJ small eagle | — | 4.00 | 6.00 | 15.00 | 85.00 |
| | 1829 MJ large eagle | — | 4.00 | 6.00 | 15.00 | 85.00 |
| | 1830 MJ small initials | — | 4.00 | 6.00 | 15.00 | 85.00 |
| | 1830 MJ medium initials | — | 4.00 | 6.00 | 15.00 | 85.00 |
| | 1830 MJ large initials | — | 4.00 | 6.00 | 15.00 | 85.00 |
| | 1830 MJ reversed N in MEXICANA | — | 4.00 | 6.00 | 15.00 | 85.00 |
| | 1831/0 MJ reversed N in MEXICANA | — | 4.00 | 6.00 | 15.00 | 85.00 |
| | 1831 MJ | — | 4.00 | 6.00 | 15.00 | 85.00 |
| | 1832/1 MJ | — | 15.00 | 30.00 | 50.00 | 125.00 |
| | 1832 MJ | — | 15.00 | 30.00 | 50.00 | 125.00 |
| | 1833 MJ top of 3 round | — | 4.00 | 6.00 | 15.00 | 85.00 |
| | 1833 MJ top of 3 flat | — | 4.00 | 6.00 | 15.00 | 85.00 |
| | 1834 PJ | — | 4.00 | 6.00 | 15.00 | 85.00 |
| | 1835 PJ | — | 7.50 | 12.50 | 20.00 | 85.00 |
| | 1836 PJ | — | 4.00 | 6.00 | 15.00 | 85.00 |
| | 1837 PJ | — | 15.00 | 30.00 | 50.00 | 125.00 |
| | 1838/7 PJ | — | 10.00 | 20.00 | 35.00 | 85.00 |
| | 1839 PJ | — | 4.00 | 6.00 | 15.00 | 85.00 |
| | 1840/39 PJ | — | 4.00 | 6.00 | 15.00 | 85.00 |
| 372.6 | 1840 PJ | — | 4.00 | 6.00 | 15.00 | 85.00 |
| | 1841/31 PJ | — | 10.00 | 20.00 | 35.00 | 85.00 |
| | 1841 PJ | — | 4.00 | 6.00 | 15.00 | 85.00 |
| | 1842 PJ | — | 4.00 | 6.00 | 15.00 | 85.00 |
| | 1842 PM | — | 4.00 | 6.00 | 15.00 | 85.00 |
| | 1843 PM convex wings | — | 4.00 | 6.00 | 15.00 | 85.00 |
| | 1843 PM concave wings | — | 4.00 | 6.00 | 15.00 | 85.00 |
| | 1844 PM | — | 4.00 | 6.00 | 15.00 | 85.00 |
| | 1845/4 PM | — | 4.00 | 6.00 | 15.00 | 85.00 |
| | 1845 PM | — | 4.00 | 6.00 | 15.00 | 85.00 |
| | 1846/5 PM | — | 7.50 | 12.50 | 20.00 | 85.00 |
| | 1846 PM | — | 4.00 | 6.00 | 15.00 | 85.00 |
| | 1847/6 PM | — | 4.00 | 6.00 | 15.00 | 85.00 |
| | 1847 PM | — | 4.00 | 6.00 | 15.00 | 85.00 |
| | 1848 PM | — | 4.00 | 6.00 | 15.00 | 85.00 |
| | 1849 PF | — | 10.00 | 20.00 | 35.00 | 85.00 |
| | 1850 PF | — | 4.00 | 6.00 | 15.00 | 85.00 |
| | 1851 PF | — | 10.00 | 20.00 | 35.00 | 100.00 |
| | 1853/2 PF | — | 7.50 | 12.50 | 20.00 | 75.00 |
| | 1853 PF | — | 4.00 | 6.00 | 15.00 | 75.00 |
| | 1854/3 PF | — | 4.00 | 6.00 | 15.00 | 75.00 |
| | 1854 PF large eagle | — | 4.00 | 6.00 | 15.00 | 75.00 |
| | 1854 PF small eagle | — | 4.00 | 6.00 | 15.00 | 75.00 |
| | 1855/3 PF | — | 4.00 | 6.00 | 15.00 | 75.00 |
| | 1855/4 PF | — | 4.00 | 6.00 | 15.00 | 75.00 |
| | 1855 PF | — | 4.00 | 6.00 | 15.00 | 75.00 |
| | 1856/5 PF | — | 4.00 | 6.00 | 15.00 | 75.00 |
| | 1856 PF | — | 4.00 | 6.00 | 15.00 | 75.00 |
| | 1857/6 PF | — | 4.00 | 6.00 | 15.00 | 75.00 |
| | 1857 PF | — | 4.00 | 6.00 | 15.00 | 75.00 |
| | 1858 PF | — | 4.00 | 6.00 | 15.00 | 75.00 |
| | 1859 PF | — | 4.00 | 6.00 | 15.00 | 75.00 |
| | 1860/50 PF | — | 4.00 | 6.00 | 15.00 | 75.00 |
| | 1860 PF | — | 4.00 | 6.00 | 15.00 | 75.00 |
| | 1861 PF | — | 4.00 | 6.00 | 15.00 | 75.00 |
| | 1862 YE | — | 4.00 | 6.00 | 15.00 | 75.00 |
| | 1862/1 YF | — | 7.50 | 12.50 | 20.00 | 75.00 |
| | 1862 YF | — | 4.00 | 6.00 | 15.00 | 75.00 |
| | 1867 YF | — | 4.00 | 6.00 | 15.00 | 75.00 |
| | 1868/7 YF | — | 4.00 | 6.00 | 15.00 | 75.00 |

**Mint mark: Ho**

| KM# | Date | Mintage | Fine | VF | XF | Unc |
|---|---|---|---|---|---|---|
| 372.7 | 1867 small 7/1 PR | — | 50.00 | 65.00 | 100.00 | 250.00 |
| | 1867 large 7/small 7 PR | — | 50.00 | 65.00 | 100.00 | 250.00 |
| | 1868 PR | — | 50.00 | 65.00 | 100.00 | 250.00 |

**Mint mark: Mo**

| KM# | Date | Mintage | Fine | VF | XF | Unc |
|---|---|---|---|---|---|---|
| 372.8 | 1825 JM | — | 10.00 | 20.00 | 40.00 | 110.00 |
| | 1826 JM | — | 7.50 | 15.00 | 30.00 | 100.00 |
| | 1827/6 JM | — | 7.50 | 15.00 | 30.00 | 75.00 |
| | 1827 JM | — | 5.00 | 10.00 | 20.00 | 70.00 |
| | 1828 JM | — | 7.50 | 15.00 | 30.00 | 100.00 |
| | 1830/29 JM | — | 5.00 | 10.00 | 20.00 | 100.00 |
| | 1830 JM | — | 5.00 | 12.50 | 25.00 | 100.00 |
| | 1831 JM | — | 100.00 | 200.00 | 300.00 | 750.00 |
| | 1832 JM | — | 5.00 | 10.00 | 20.00 | 100.00 |
| | 1833/2 MJ | — | 5.00 | 10.00 | 20.00 | 100.00 |
| | 1850 GC | — | 5.00 | 10.00 | 20.00 | 100.00 |
| | 1852 GC | — | 275.00 | 425.00 | 575.00 | — |
| | 1854 GC | — | 10.00 | 20.00 | 40.00 | 100.00 |
| | 1855 GF | — | 5.00 | 10.00 | 20.00 | 80.00 |
| | 1856 GF | — | 5.00 | 10.00 | 20.00 | 80.00 |
| | 1857 GF | — | 5.00 | 10.00 | 20.00 | 80.00 |
| | 1858 FH | — | 5.00 | 10.00 | 20.00 | 80.00 |
| | 1859 FH | — | 5.00 | 10.00 | 20.00 | 80.00 |
| | 1861 CH | — | 5.00 | 10.00 | 20.00 | 80.00 |
| | 1862 CH | — | 5.00 | 10.00 | 20.00 | 80.00 |
| | 1863/2 CH | — | 7.50 | 12.50 | 25.00 | 80.00 |

**Mint mark: Pi**

| KM# | Date | Mintage | Fine | VF | XF | Unc |
|---|---|---|---|---|---|---|
| 372.9 | 1831 JS | — | 5.00 | 10.00 | 20.00 | 125.00 |
| | 1837 JS | — | 750.00 | 850.00 | 1000. | — |
| | 1838/7 JS | — | 250.00 | 300.00 | 375.00 | — |
| | 1838 JS | — | 20.00 | 35.00 | 60.00 | 125.00 |
| | 1840/39 JS | — | 7.50 | 15.00 | 30.00 | 125.00 |
| | 1840 JS | — | 7.50 | 15.00 | 30.00 | 125.00 |
| | 1841 JS | — | 7.50 | 15.00 | 30.00 | 125.00 |
| | 1842 JS | — | 15.00 | 30.00 | 55.00 | 150.00 |

| KM# | Date | Mintage | Fine | VF | XF | Unc |
|---|---|---|---|---|---|---|
| 372.9 | 1842 PS | — | 5.00 | 10.00 | 20.00 | 125.00 |
| | 1843 PS | — | 12.50 | 20.00 | 35.00 | 125.00 |
| | 1843 AM | — | 40.00 | 60.00 | 80.00 | 150.00 |
| | 1844 AM | — | 40.00 | 60.00 | 80.00 | 150.00 |
| | 1845 AM | — | 7.50 | 15.00 | 30.00 | 125.00 |
| | 1846/5 AM | — | 7.50 | 15.00 | 30.00 | 125.00 |
| | 1847/6 AM | — | 7.50 | 15.00 | 30.00 | 125.00 |
| | 1847 AM | — | 7.50 | 15.00 | 30.00 | 125.00 |
| | 1848/7 AM | — | 7.50 | 15.00 | 30.00 | 125.00 |
| | 1849 PS | — | 7.50 | 15.00 | 30.00 | 125.00 |
| | 1849/8 SP | — | 60.00 | 100.00 | 150.00 | — |
| | 1849 SP | — | 15.00 | 25.00 | 40.00 | 125.00 |
| | 1850 MC | — | 5.00 | 10.00 | 20.00 | 125.00 |
| | 1851/0 MC | — | 7.50 | 15.00 | 30.00 | 125.00 |
| | 1851 MC | — | 7.50 | 15.00 | 30.00 | 125.00 |
| | 1852/1/0 MC | | | | | |
| | | — | 10.00 | 20.00 | 35.00 | 125.00 |
| | 1852 MC | — | 7.50 | 15.00 | 30.00 | 125.00 |
| | 1853/1 MC | — | 12.50 | 20.00 | 35.00 | 125.00 |
| | 1853 MC | — | 10.00 | 20.00 | 35.00 | 125.00 |
| | 1854/3 MC | — | 20.00 | 40.00 | 60.00 | 150.00 |
| | 1855/4 MC | — | 20.00 | 40.00 | 60.00 | 150.00 |
| | 1855 MC | — | 15.00 | 25.00 | 45.00 | 125.00 |
| | 1856 MC | — | 15.00 | 25.00 | 45.00 | 125.00 |
| | 1857 PS | — | 20.00 | 35.00 | 55.00 | 135.00 |
| | 1857 MC | — | 20.00 | 40.00 | 60.00 | 150.00 |
| | 1858 MC | — | 12.50 | 20.00 | 35.00 | 125.00 |
| | 1859 PS | — | 10.00 | 15.00 | 30.00 | 125.00 |
| | 1860/59 PS | — | 10.00 | 15.00 | 30.00 | 125.00 |
| | 1861 PS | — | 7.50 | 12.50 | 20.00 | 125.00 |
| | 1861 RO | — | 12.50 | 20.00 | 35.00 | 125.00 |
| | 1862/1 RO | — | 12.50 | 20.00 | 35.00 | 90.00 |
| | 1862 RO | — | 7.50 | 12.50 | 20.00 | 125.00 |
| | **Mint mark: Zs** | | | | | |
| 372.10 | 1826 AZ | — | 5.00 | 12.50 | 35.00 | 120.00 |
| | 1826 AO | — | 5.00 | 12.50 | 35.00 | 120.00 |
| | 1827 AO | — | 5.00 | 12.50 | 35.00 | 120.00 |
| | 1828/7 AO | — | 5.00 | 12.50 | 35.00 | 120.00 |
| | 1828 AO | — | 5.00 | 12.50 | 35.00 | 120.00 |
| | 1828 AO inverted V for A | | | | | |
| | | — | 5.00 | 12.50 | 35.00 | 120.00 |
| | 1829 AO | — | 5.00 | 12.50 | 35.00 | 120.00 |
| | 1830 ZsOV | — | 5.00 | 12.50 | 35.00 | 120.00 |
| | 1830 ZOV | — | 5.00 | 12.50 | 35.00 | 120.00 |
| | 1831 OV | — | 5.00 | 12.50 | 35.00 | 120.00 |
| | 1831 OM | — | 5.00 | 12.50 | 30.00 | 120.00 |
| | 1832 OM | — | 5.00 | 12.50 | 30.00 | 120.00 |
| | 1833/2 OM | — | 5.00 | 12.50 | 30.00 | 120.00 |
| | 1833 OM | — | 5.00 | 12.50 | 30.00 | 120.00 |
| | 1834/3 OM | — | 5.00 | 12.50 | 30.00 | 120.00 |
| | 1834 OM | — | 5.00 | 12.50 | 30.00 | 120.00 |
| | 1835/4 OM | — | 20.00 | 35.00 | 60.00 | 150.00 |
| | 1835 OM | — | 4.00 | 8.00 | 20.00 | 65.00 |
| | 1836/5 OM | — | 4.00 | 8.00 | 20.00 | 85.00 |
| | 1836 OM | — | 4.00 | 8.00 | 20.00 | 85.00 |
| | 1837 OM | — | 4.00 | 8.00 | 20.00 | 85.00 |
| | 1838 OM | — | 4.00 | 8.00 | 20.00 | 85.00 |
| | 1839 OM | — | 4.00 | 8.00 | 20.00 | 85.00 |
| | 1840 OM | — | 4.00 | 8.00 | 20.00 | 85.00 |
| | 1841 OM | — | 20.00 | 40.00 | 60.00 | 150.00 |
| | 1842/1 OM | — | 4.00 | 8.00 | 20.00 | 85.00 |
| | 1842 OM | — | 4.00 | 8.00 | 20.00 | 85.00 |
| | 1843 OM | — | 4.00 | 8.00 | 20.00 | 85.00 |
| | 1844 OM | — | 4.00 | 8.00 | 20.00 | 85.00 |
| | 1845/4 OM | — | 5.00 | 12.50 | 30.00 | 100.00 |
| | 1845 OM | — | 4.00 | 8.00 | 20.00 | 85.00 |
| | 1846 OM old font and obv. | | | | | |
| | | — | 4.00 | 8.00 | 20.00 | 85.00 |
| | 1846 OM new font and obv. | | | | | |
| | | — | 4.00 | 8.00 | 20.00 | 85.00 |
| | 1847 OM | — | 4.00 | 8.00 | 20.00 | 85.00 |
| | 1848 OM | — | 4.00 | 8.00 | 20.00 | 85.00 |
| | 1849 OM | — | 10.00 | 25.00 | 50.00 | 125.00 |
| | 1850 OM | — | 4.00 | 6.00 | 15.00 | 85.00 |
| | 1851 OM | — | 4.00 | 6.00 | 15.00 | 85.00 |
| | 1852 OM | — | 4.00 | 6.00 | 15.00 | 85.00 |
| | 1853 OM | — | 4.00 | 6.00 | 15.00 | 85.00 |
| | 1854/2 OM | — | 4.00 | 6.00 | 15.00 | 85.00 |
| | 1854/3 OM | — | 4.00 | 6.00 | 15.00 | 85.00 |
| | 1854 OM | — | 4.00 | 6.00 | 15.00 | 85.00 |
| | 1855/4 OM | — | 4.00 | 6.00 | 15.00 | 85.00 |
| | 1855 OM | — | 4.00 | 6.00 | 15.00 | 85.00 |
| | 1855 MO | — | 4.00 | 6.00 | 15.00 | 85.00 |
| | 1856 MO | — | 4.00 | 6.00 | 15.00 | 85.00 |

| KM# | Date | Mintage | Fine | VF | XF | Unc |
|---|---|---|---|---|---|---|
| 372.10 | 1856 MO/OM | — | 4.00 | 6.00 | 15.00 | 85.00 |
| | 1857 MO | — | 4.00 | 6.00 | 15.00 | 85.00 |
| | 1858 MO | — | 4.00 | 6.00 | 15.00 | 85.00 |
| | 1859 MO | — | 4.00 | 6.00 | 15.00 | 75.00 |
| | 1860 VL | — | 4.00 | 6.00 | 15.00 | 75.00 |
| | 1861 VL | — | 4.00 | 6.00 | 15.00 | 75.00 |
| | 1862 VL | — | 5.00 | 12.50 | 30.00 | 100.00 |
| | 1868 JS | — | 25.00 | 45.00 | 90.00 | 175.00 |
| | 1869 YH | — | 4.00 | 8.00 | 20.00 | 75.00 |

## 2 REALES

**6.7600 g, .903 SILVER, .1962 oz ASW**
**Mint mark: D, Do**
**Obv: Hooked-neck eagle.**

| KM# | Date | Mintage | Fine | VF | XF | Unc |
|---|---|---|---|---|---|---|
| 373 | 1824 Do RL | — | 50.00 | 125.00 | 300.00 | 850.00 |
| | 1824 D RL | — | 100.00 | 200.00 | 500.00 | 1650. |
| | **Mint mark: Mo** | | | | | |
| 373.1 | 1824 JM | — | 20.00 | 50.00 | 100.00 | 350.00 |

**Mint mark: A**
**Obv: Facing eagle, reeded edge.**

| KM# | Date | Mintage | Fine | VF | XF | Unc |
|---|---|---|---|---|---|---|
| 374 | 1872 AM | .015 | 40.00 | 100.00 | 200.00 | 500.00 |
| | **Mint mark: Ce** | | | | | |
| 374.1 | 1863 ML | — | 125.00 | 200.00 | 325.00 | 675.00 |
| | **Mint mark: Ca** | | | | | |
| 374.2 | 1832 MR | — | 30.00 | 60.00 | 100.00 | 200.00 |
| | 1833 MR | — | 30.00 | 60.00 | 125.00 | 500.00 |
| | 1834 MR | — | 35.00 | 75.00 | 125.00 | 500.00 |
| | 1834 AM | — | 35.00 | 75.00 | 125.00 | 500.00 |
| | 1835 AM | — | 35.00 | 75.00 | 125.00 | 500.00 |
| | 1836 AM | — | 20.00 | 40.00 | 80.00 | 200.00 |
| | 1844 RG | — | — | — | Unique | — |
| | 1845 RG | — | 20.00 | 40.00 | 80.00 | 200.00 |
| | 1855 RG | — | 20.00 | 40.00 | 80.00 | 200.00 |
| | **Mint mark: C** | | | | | |
| 374.3 | 1846/1146 CE | | | | | |
| | | — | 25.00 | 50.00 | 100.00 | 225.00 |
| | 1847 CE | — | 12.50 | 20.00 | 40.00 | 200.00 |
| | 1848 CE | — | 12.50 | 20.00 | 40.00 | 200.00 |
| | 1850 CE | — | 25.00 | 50.00 | 75.00 | 200.00 |
| | 1851 CE | — | 12.50 | 20.00 | 40.00 | 200.00 |
| | 1852/1 CE | — | 12.50 | 20.00 | 40.00 | 200.00 |
| | 1853/2 CE | — | 12.50 | 20.00 | 40.00 | 200.00 |
| | 1854 CE | — | 15.00 | 30.00 | 50.00 | 200.00 |
| | 1856 CE | — | 20.00 | 35.00 | 70.00 | 200.00 |
| | 1857 CE | — | 12.50 | 20.00 | 40.00 | 200.00 |
| | 1860 PV | — | 12.50 | 20.00 | 40.00 | 200.00 |
| | 1861 PV | — | 12.50 | 20.00 | 40.00 | 200.00 |
| | 1869 CE | — | 12.50 | 20.00 | 40.00 | 200.00 |
| | **Mint mark: Do** | | | | | |
| 374.4 | 1826 RL | — | 20.00 | 40.00 | 60.00 | 200.00 |
| | 1832 RM style of pre-1832 | | | | | |
| | | — | 20.00 | 40.00 | 60.00 | 200.00 |
| | 1832 RM style of post-1832 | | | | | |
| | | — | 20.00 | 40.00 | 60.00 | 200.00 |
| | 1834/2 RM | — | 20.00 | 40.00 | 60.00 | 200.00 |
| | 1834/3 RM | — | 20.00 | 40.00 | 60.00 | 200.00 |

| KM# | Date | Mintage | Fine | VF | XF | Unc |
|---|---|---|---|---|---|---|
| 374.4 | 1835/4 RM/RL | | | | | |
| | | — | 200.00 | 300.00 | 500.00 | — |
| | 1841/31 RM | — | 50.00 | 75.00 | 125.00 | 250.00 |
| | 1841 RM | — | 50.00 | 75.00 | 125.00 | 250.00 |
| | 1842/32 RM | — | 12.50 | 20.00 | 40.00 | 200.00 |
| | 1843 RM/RL | — | 12.50 | 20.00 | 40.00 | 200.00 |
| | 1844 RM | — | 35.00 | 50.00 | 80.00 | 200.00 |
| | 1845/34 RM/RL | | | | | |
| | | — | 12.50 | 20.00 | 40.00 | 200.00 |
| | 1846/36 RM | — | 100.00 | 150.00 | 200.00 | 350.00 |
| | 1848/36 RM | — | 12.50 | 20.00 | 40.00 | 200.00 |
| | 1848/37 RM | — | 12.50 | 20.00 | 40.00 | 200.00 |
| | 1848/7 RM | — | 12.50 | 20.00 | 40.00 | 200.00 |
| | 1848 RM | — | 12.50 | 20.00 | 40.00 | 200.00 |
| | 1849 CM/RM | — | 12.50 | 20.00 | 40.00 | 200.00 |
| | 1849 CM | — | 12.50 | 20.00 | 40.00 | 200.00 |
| | 1851 JMR/RL | | | | | |
| | | — | 12.50 | 20.00 | 40.00 | 200.00 |
| | 1852 JMR | — | 12.50 | 20.00 | 40.00 | 200.00 |
| | 1854 CP/CR | — | 30.00 | 50.00 | 80.00 | 200.00 |
| | 1855 CP | — | 250.00 | 350.00 | 500.00 | — |
| | 1856 CP | — | 100.00 | 150.00 | 250.00 | 500.00 |
| | 1858 CP | — | 12.50 | 20.00 | 40.00 | 200.00 |
| | 1859/8 CP | — | 12.50 | 20.00 | 40.00 | 200.00 |
| | 1861 CP | — | 12.50 | 20.00 | 40.00 | 200.00 |

**Mint mark: EoMo**

| KM# | Date | Mintage | Fine | VF | XF | Unc |
|---|---|---|---|---|---|---|
| 374.5 | 1828 LF | — | 325.00 | 525.00 | 900.00 | 2500. |

**Mint mark: Ga**

| KM# | Date | Mintage | Fine | VF | XF | Unc |
|---|---|---|---|---|---|---|
| 374.6 | 1825 FS | — | 20.00 | 40.00 | 80.00 | 200.00 |
| | 1826 FS | — | 20.00 | 40.00 | 80.00 | 200.00 |
| | 1828/7 FS | — | 100.00 | 150.00 | 225.00 | 400.00 |
| | 1829 FS | — | — | | Rare | — |
| | 1832/0 FS/LP | | | | | |
| | | — | 100.00 | 150.00 | 225.00 | 350.00 |
| | 1832 FS | — | 12.50 | 20.00 | 40.00 | 200.00 |
| | 1833/2 FS/LP | | | | | |
| | | — | 12.50 | 20.00 | 40.00 | 200.00 |
| | 1834/27 FS | — | — | — | Rare | — |
| | 1834 FS | — | 12.50 | 20.00 | 40.00 | 200.00 |
| | 1835 FS | — | 2100. | — | — | — |
| | 1837 JG | — | 12.50 | 20.00 | 40.00 | 200.00 |
| | 1838 JG | — | 12.50 | 20.00 | 40.00 | 200.00 |
| | 1840/30 MC | — | 12.50 | 20.00 | 40.00 | 200.00 |
| | 1841 MC | — | 12.50 | 20.00 | 40.00 | 200.00 |
| | 1842/32 JG/MC | | | | | |
| | | — | 35.00 | 50.00 | 100.00 | 200.00 |
| | 1842 JG | — | 20.00 | 40.00 | 80.00 | 200.00 |
| | 1843 JG | — | 12.50 | 20.00 | 40.00 | 200.00 |
| | 1843 MC/JG | — | 12.50 | 20.00 | 40.00 | 200.00 |
| | 1844 MC | — | 12.50 | 20.00 | 40.00 | 200.00 |
| | 1845/3 MC/JG | | | | | |
| | | — | 12.50 | 20.00 | 40.00 | 200.00 |
| | 1845/4 MC/JG | | | | | |
| | | — | 12.50 | 20.00 | 40.00 | 200.00 |
| | 1845 JG | — | 12.50 | 20.00 | 40.00 | 200.00 |
| | 1846 JG | — | 12.50 | 20.00 | 40.00 | 200.00 |
| | 1847/6 JG | — | 25.00 | 40.00 | 80.00 | 200.00 |
| | 1848/7 JG | — | 12.50 | 20.00 | 40.00 | 200.00 |
| | 1849 JG | — | 12.50 | 20.00 | 40.00 | 200.00 |
| | 1850/40 JG | — | 12.50 | 20.00 | 40.00 | 200.00 |
| | 1851 JG | — | 250.00 | 350.00 | 500.00 | — |
| | 1852 JG | — | 12.50 | 20.00 | 40.00 | 200.00 |
| | 1853/1 JG | — | 12.50 | 20.00 | 40.00 | 200.00 |
| | 1854/3 JG | — | 250.00 | 350.00 | 500.00 | — |
| | 1855 JG | — | 35.00 | 50.00 | 80.00 | 200.00 |
| | 1856 JG | — | 12.50 | 20.00 | 40.00 | 200.00 |
| | 1857 JG | — | 250.00 | 350.00 | 500.00 | — |
| | 1859/8 JG | — | 12.50 | 20.00 | 40.00 | 200.00 |
| | 1859 JG | — | 12.50 | 20.00 | 40.00 | 200.00 |
| | 1862/1 JG | — | 12.50 | 20.00 | 40.00 | 200.00 |

**Mint mark: GC**

| KM# | Date | Mintage | Fine | VF | XF | Unc |
|---|---|---|---|---|---|---|
| 374.7 | 1844 MP | — | 40.00 | 60.00 | 125.00 | 275.00 |
| | 1845 MP | — | 40.00 | 60.00 | 125.00 | 275.00 |
| | 1846 MP | — | 50.00 | 100.00 | 150.00 | 300.00 |
| | 1847 MP | — | 35.00 | 50.00 | 100.00 | 250.00 |
| | 1848 MP | — | 50.00 | 100.00 | 150.00 | 300.00 |
| | 1849 MP | — | 50.00 | 100.00 | 150.00 | 300.00 |
| | 1850 MP | — | 50.00 | 100.00 | 150.00 | 300.00 |
| | 1851/0 MP | — | 50.00 | 100.00 | 150.00 | 300.00 |
| | 1851 MP | — | 50.00 | 100.00 | 150.00 | 300.00 |

**Mint mark: Go**

| KM# | Date | Mintage | Fine | VF | XF | Unc |
|---|---|---|---|---|---|---|
| 374.8 | 1825 JJ | — | 7.50 | 15.00 | 30.00 | 150.00 |
| | 1826/5 JJ | — | 7.50 | 15.00 | 30.00 | 150.00 |
| | 1826 JJ | — | 7.50 | 10.00 | 25.00 | 150.00 |
| | 1826 MJ | — | 7.50 | 10.00 | 25.00 | 150.00 |
| | 1827/6 MJ | — | 7.50 | 10.00 | 25.00 | 150.00 |
| | 1827 MJ | — | 7.50 | 10.00 | 25.00 | 150.00 |
| | 1828/7 MR | — | 7.50 | 15.00 | 30.00 | 150.00 |
| | 1828 MJ | — | 7.50 | 10.00 | 20.00 | 150.00 |
| | 1828 JM | — | 7.50 | 10.00 | 20.00 | 150.00 |
| | 1829 MJ | — | 7.50 | 10.00 | 20.00 | 150.00 |
| | 1831 MJ | — | 7.50 | 10.00 | 20.00 | 150.00 |
| | 1832 MJ | — | 7.50 | 10.00 | 20.00 | 150.00 |
| | 1833 MJ | — | 7.50 | 10.00 | 20.00 | 150.00 |
| | 1834 PJ | — | 7.50 | 10.00 | 20.00 | 150.00 |
| | 1835/4 PJ | — | 7.50 | 15.00 | 30.00 | 150.00 |
| | 1835 PJ | — | 7.50 | 10.00 | 20.00 | 150.00 |
| | 1836 PJ | — | 7.50 | 10.00 | 20.00 | 150.00 |
| | 1837/6 PJ | — | 7.50 | 10.00 | 20.00 | 150.00 |
| | 1837 PJ | — | 7.50 | 10.00 | 20.00 | 150.00 |
| | 1838/7 PJ | — | 7.50 | 10.00 | 20.00 | 150.00 |
| | 1838 PJ | — | 7.50 | 10.00 | 20.00 | 150.00 |
| 374.8 | 1839/8 PJ | — | 7.50 | 15.00 | 30.00 | 150.00 |
| | 1839 PJ | — | 7.50 | 10.00 | 20.00 | 150.00 |
| | 1840 PJ | — | 7.50 | 10.00 | 20.00 | 150.00 |
| | 1841 PJ | — | 7.50 | 10.00 | 20.00 | 150.00 |
| | 1842 PJ | — | 7.50 | 10.00 | 20.00 | 150.00 |
| | 1842 PM/PJ | — | 7.50 | 10.00 | 20.00 | 150.00 |
| | 1842 PM | — | 7.50 | 10.00 | 20.00 | 150.00 |
| | 1843/2 PM concave wings, thin rays, sm. letters | | | | | |
| | | — | 7.50 | 10.00 | 20.00 | 150.00 |
| | 1843 PM convex wings, thick rays, lg. letters | | | | | |
| | | — | 7.50 | 10.00 | 20.00 | 150.00 |
| | 1844 PM | — | 7.50 | 10.00 | 20.00 | 150.00 |
| | 1845/4 PM | — | 7.50 | 10.00 | 20.00 | 150.00 |
| | 1845 PM | — | 7.50 | 10.00 | 20.00 | 150.00 |
| | 1846/5 PM | — | 10.00 | 15.00 | 35.00 | 150.00 |
| | 1846 PM | — | 7.50 | 10.00 | 20.00 | 150.00 |
| | 1847 PM | — | 7.50 | 10.00 | 20.00 | 150.00 |
| | 1848/7 PM | — | 7.50 | 15.00 | 30.00 | 150.00 |
| | 1848 PM | — | 7.50 | 15.00 | 30.00 | 150.00 |
| | 1848 PF | — | 100.00 | 150.00 | 250.00 | 500.00 |
| | 1849/8 PF/PM | | | | | |
| | | — | 7.50 | 10.00 | 20.00 | 150.00 |
| | 1849 PF | — | 7.50 | 10.00 | 20.00 | 150.00 |
| | 1850/40 PF | — | 7.50 | 10.00 | 20.00 | 150.00 |
| | 1850 PF | — | 7.50 | 10.00 | 20.00 | 150.00 |
| | 1851 PF | — | 7.50 | 10.00 | 20.00 | 150.00 |
| | 1852/1 PF | — | 7.50 | 10.00 | 20.00 | 150.00 |
| | 1852 PF | — | 7.50 | 10.00 | 20.00 | 150.00 |
| | 1853 PF | — | 7.50 | 10.00 | 20.00 | 150.00 |
| | 1854/3 PF | — | 7.50 | 10.00 | 20.00 | 150.00 |
| | 1854 PF old font and obv. | | | | | |
| | | — | 7.50 | 10.00 | 20.00 | 150.00 |
| | 1854 PF new font and obv. | | | | | |
| | | — | 7.50 | 10.00 | 20.00 | 150.00 |
| | 1855 PF | — | 7.50 | 10.00 | 20.00 | 150.00 |
| | 1855 PF star in G of mint mark | | | | | |
| | | — | 7.50 | 10.00 | 20.00 | 150.00 |
| | 1856/5 PF | — | 10.00 | 15.00 | 35.00 | 150.00 |
| | 1856 PF | — | 10.00 | 15.00 | 25.00 | 150.00 |
| | 1857/6 PF | — | 7.50 | 10.00 | 20.00 | 150.00 |
| | 1857 PF | — | 7.50 | 10.00 | 20.00 | 150.00 |
| | 1858/7 PF | — | 7.50 | 10.00 | 20.00 | 150.00 |
| | 1858 PF | — | 7.50 | 10.00 | 20.00 | 150.00 |
| | 1859/7 PF | — | 7.50 | 10.00 | 20.00 | 150.00 |
| | 1859 PF | — | 7.50 | 10.00 | 20.00 | 150.00 |
| | 1860/50 PF | — | 7.50 | 10.00 | 20.00 | 150.00 |
| | 1860/59 PF | — | 7.50 | 10.00 | 20.00 | 150.00 |
| | 1860 PF | — | 7.50 | 10.00 | 20.00 | 150.00 |
| | 1861/51 PF | — | 7.50 | 10.00 | 20.00 | 150.00 |
| | 1861/57 PF | — | 7.50 | 10.00 | 20.00 | 150.00 |
| | 1861/0 PF | — | 7.50 | 10.00 | 20.00 | 150.00 |
| | 1861 PF | — | 7.50 | 10.00 | 20.00 | 150.00 |
| | 1862/1 YE | — | 7.50 | 10.00 | 20.00 | 125.00 |
| | 1862 YE | — | 7.50 | 10.00 | 20.00 | 125.00 |
| | 1862/57 YE | — | 7.50 | 10.00 | 20.00 | 125.00 |
| | 1862 YE/PF | — | 7.50 | 10.00 | 20.00 | 125.00 |
| | 1862 YF | — | 7.50 | 10.00 | 20.00 | 125.00 |
| | 1863/52 YF | — | 7.50 | 10.00 | 20.00 | 125.00 |
| | 1863 YF | — | 7.50 | 10.00 | 20.00 | 125.00 |
| | 1867/57 YF | — | 7.50 | 10.00 | 20.00 | 125.00 |
| | 1868/57 YF | — | 10.00 | 15.00 | 25.00 | 125.00 |

**NOTE:** Varieties exist.

**PRICING SECTION**

### Mint mark: Ho

| KM# | Date | Mintage | Fine | VF | XF | Unc |
|---|---|---|---|---|---|---|
| 374.9 | 1861 FM | — | 200.00 | 300.00 | 400.00 | 650.00 |
| | 1862/52 Ho FM/C. CE | | | | | |
| | | — | 250.00 | 350.00 | 500.00 | — |
| | 1867/1 PR/FM | | | | | |
| | | — | 75.00 | 150.00 | 250.00 | 500.00 |

### Mint mark: Mo

| KM# | Date | Mintage | Fine | VF | XF | Unc |
|---|---|---|---|---|---|---|
| 374.10 | 1825 JM | — | 10.00 | 15.00 | 30.00 | 175.00 |
| | 1826 JM | — | 10.00 | 15.00 | 30.00 | 175.00 |
| | 1827 JM | — | 10.00 | 15.00 | 30.00 | 175.00 |
| | 1828 JM | — | 10.00 | 15.00 | 30.00 | 175.00 |
| | 1829/8 JM | — | 10.00 | 15.00 | 30.00 | 175.00 |
| | 1829 JM | — | 10.00 | 15.00 | 30.00 | 175.00 |
| | 1830 JM | — | 40.00 | 60.00 | 125.00 | 250.00 |
| | 1831 JM | — | 10.00 | 15.00 | 30.00 | 175.00 |
| | 1832 JM | — | 100.00 | 200.00 | 400.00 | — |
| | 1833/2 MJ/JM | | | | | |
| | | — | 10.00 | 15.00 | 30.00 | 175.00 |
| | 1834 ML | — | 50.00 | 100.00 | 200.00 | 400.00 |
| | 1836 ML | — | Reported, not confirmed | | | |
| | 1836 MF | — | 10.00 | 15.00 | 30.00 | 175.00 |
| | 1837 ML | — | 10.00 | 15.00 | 30.00 | 175.00 |
| | 1840 ML | — | 150.00 | 225.00 | 350.00 | — |
| | 1841 ML | — | 10.00 | 15.00 | 30.00 | 175.00 |
| | 1842 ML | — | — | — | Rare | — |
| | 1847 RC | — | 10.00 | 15.00 | 30.00 | 175.00 |
| | 1848 GC | — | 10.00 | 15.00 | 30.00 | 175.00 |
| | 1849 GC | — | 10.00 | 15.00 | 30.00 | 175.00 |
| | 1850 GC | — | 10.00 | 15.00 | 30.00 | 175.00 |
| | 1851 GC | — | 40.00 | 60.00 | 125.00 | 250.00 |
| | 1852 GC | — | 10.00 | 15.00 | 30.00 | 175.00 |
| | 1853 GC | — | 10.00 | 15.00 | 30.00 | 175.00 |
| | 1854/44 GC | — | 10.00 | 15.00 | 30.00 | 175.00 |
| | 1855 GC | — | 10.00 | 15.00 | 30.00 | 175.00 |
| | 1855 GF/GC | — | 10.00 | 15.00 | 30.00 | 175.00 |
| | 1855 GF | — | 10.00 | 15.00 | 30.00 | 175.00 |
| | 1856/5 GF/GC | | | | | |
| | | — | 10.00 | 15.00 | 30.00 | 175.00 |
| | 1857 GF | — | 10.00 | 15.00 | 30.00 | 175.00 |
| | 1858 FH | — | 7.50 | 12.50 | 25.00 | 150.00 |
| | 1858 FH/GF | — | 7.50 | 12.50 | 25.00 | 150.00 |
| | 1859 FH | — | 7.50 | 12.50 | 25.00 | 150.00 |
| | 1860 FH | — | 7.50 | 12.50 | 25.00 | 150.00 |
| | 1860 TH | — | 7.50 | 12.50 | 25.00 | 150.00 |
| | 1861 TH | — | — | Reported, not confirmed | | |
| | 1861 CH | — | 7.50 | 12.50 | 25.00 | 150.00 |
| | 1862 CH | — | 7.50 | 12.50 | 25.00 | 150.00 |
| | 1863 CH | — | 7.50 | 12.50 | 25.00 | 150.00 |
| | 1863 TH | — | 7.50 | 12.50 | 25.00 | 150.00 |
| | 1867 CH | — | 7.50 | 12.50 | 25.00 | 150.00 |
| | 1868 CH | — | 10.00 | 15.00 | 30.00 | 150.00 |
| | 1868 PH | — | 7.50 | 12.50 | 25.00 | 150.00 |

**NOTE:** Varieties exist.

### Mint mark: Pi

| KM# | Date | Mintage | Fine | VF | XF | Unc |
|---|---|---|---|---|---|---|
| 374.11 | 1829 JS | — | 10.00 | 15.00 | 30.00 | 200.00 |
| | 1830/20 JS | — | 20.00 | 30.00 | 60.00 | 200.00 |
| | 1837 JS | — | 10.00 | 15.00 | 30.00 | 200.00 |
| | 1841 JS | — | 10.00 | 15.00 | 30.00 | 200.00 |
| | 1842/1 JS | — | 10.00 | 15.00 | 30.00 | 200.00 |
| | 1842 JS | — | 10.00 | 15.00 | 30.00 | 200.00 |
| | 1842 PS | — | 20.00 | 35.00 | 60.00 | 200.00 |
| | 1843 PS | — | 12.50 | 20.00 | 40.00 | 200.00 |
| | 1843 AM | — | 10.00 | 15.00 | 30.00 | 200.00 |
| | 1844 AM | — | 10.00 | 15.00 | 30.00 | 200.00 |
| | 1845 AM | — | 10.00 | 15.00 | 30.00 | 200.00 |
| | 1846 AM | — | 10.00 | 15.00 | 30.00 | 200.00 |
| | 1849 MC | — | 10.00 | 15.00 | 30.00 | 200.00 |
| | 1850 MC | — | 10.00 | 15.00 | 30.00 | 200.00 |
| | 1856 MC | — | 40.00 | 60.00 | 125.00 | 250.00 |
| | 1857 MC | — | — | — | — | — |
| | 1858 MC | — | 12.50 | 20.00 | 40.00 | 200.00 |
| | 1859 MC | — | 50.00 | 70.00 | 100.00 | 200.00 |
| | 1861 PS | — | 10.00 | 15.00 | 30.00 | 200.00 |
| | 1862 RO | — | 12.50 | 20.00 | 40.00 | 200.00 |
| | 1863 RO | — | 100.00 | 250.00 | 350.00 | 500.00 |
| | 1868 PS | — | 10.00 | 15.00 | 30.00 | 200.00 |

| KM# | Date | Mintage | Fine | VF | XF | Unc |
|---|---|---|---|---|---|---|
| 374.11 | 1869/8 PS | — | 10.00 | 15.00 | 30.00 | 200.00 |
| | 1869 PS | — | 10.00 | 15.00 | 30.00 | 200.00 |

### Mint mark: Zs

| KM# | Date | Mintage | Fine | VF | XF | Unc |
|---|---|---|---|---|---|---|
| 374.12 | 1825 AZ | — | 10.00 | 15.00 | 30.00 | 150.00 |
| | 1826 AV (A is inverted V) | | | | | |
| | | — | 7.50 | 10.00 | 25.00 | 150.00 |
| | 1826 AZ (A is inverted V) | | | | | |
| | | — | 7.50 | 10.00 | 25.00 | 150.00 |
| | 1826 AO | — | 10.00 | 15.00 | 30.00 | 150.00 |
| | 1827 AO (A is inverted V) | | | | | |
| | | — | 6.00 | 8.00 | 12.00 | 150.00 |
| | 1828/7 AO | — | 15.00 | 30.00 | 60.00 | 175.00 |
| | 1828 AO | — | 7.50 | 10.00 | 25.00 | 100.00 |
| | 1828 AO (A is inverted V) | | | | | |
| | | — | 7.50 | 10.00 | 25.00 | 150.00 |
| | 1829 AO | — | 7.50 | 10.00 | 25.00 | 150.00 |
| | 1829 OV | — | 7.50 | 10.00 | 25.00 | 150.00 |
| | 1830 OV | — | 7.50 | 10.00 | 25.00 | 150.00 |
| | 1831 OV | — | 7.50 | 10.00 | 25.00 | 150.00 |
| | 1831 OM/OV | — | 7.50 | 10.00 | 25.00 | 150.00 |
| | 1831 OM | — | 7.50 | 10.00 | 25.00 | 150.00 |
| | 1832/1 OM | — | 15.00 | 30.00 | 60.00 | 150.00 |
| | 1832 OM | — | 7.50 | 10.00 | 25.00 | 150.00 |
| | 1833/27 OM | — | 7.50 | 10.00 | 25.00 | 150.00 |
| | 1833/2 OM | — | 7.50 | 10.00 | 25.00 | 150.00 |
| | 1833 OM | — | 7.50 | 10.00 | 25.00 | 150.00 |
| | 1834 OM | — | 40.00 | 60.00 | 125.00 | 200.00 |
| | 1835 OM | — | 7.50 | 10.00 | 25.00 | 150.00 |
| | 1836 OM | — | 7.50 | 10.00 | 25.00 | 150.00 |
| | 1837 OM | — | 7.50 | 10.00 | 25.00 | 150.00 |
| | 1838 OM | — | 15.00 | 30.00 | 60.00 | 150.00 |
| | 1839 OM | — | 7.50 | 10.00 | 25.00 | 150.00 |
| | 1840 OM | — | 7.50 | 10.00 | 20.00 | 150.00 |
| | 1841/0 OM | — | 7.50 | 10.00 | 20.00 | 150.00 |
| | 1841 OM | — | 7.50 | 10.00 | 20.00 | 150.00 |
| | 1842 OM | — | 7.50 | 10.00 | 20.00 | 150.00 |
| | 1843 OM | — | 7.50 | 10.00 | 20.00 | 150.00 |
| | 1844 OM | — | 7.50 | 10.00 | 20.00 | 150.00 |
| | 1845 OM small letters and leaves | | | | | |
| | | — | 7.50 | 10.00 | 20.00 | 150.00 |
| | 1845 OM large letters and leaves | | | | | |
| | | — | 7.50 | 10.00 | 20.00 | 150.00 |
| | 1846 OM | — | 7.50 | 10.00 | 20.00 | 150.00 |
| | 1847 OM | — | 7.50 | 10.00 | 20.00 | 150.00 |
| | 1848 OM | — | 7.50 | 10.00 | 20.00 | 150.00 |
| | 1849 OM | — | 7.50 | 10.00 | 20.00 | 150.00 |
| | 1850 OM | — | 7.50 | 10.00 | 20.00 | 150.00 |
| | 1851 OM | — | 7.50 | 10.00 | 20.00 | 150.00 |
| | 1852 OM | — | 7.50 | 10.00 | 20.00 | 150.00 |
| | 1853 OM | — | 7.50 | 10.00 | 20.00 | 150.00 |
| | 1854/3 OM | — | 7.50 | 10.00 | 20.00 | 150.00 |
| | 1854 OM | — | 7.50 | 10.00 | 20.00 | 150.00 |
| | 1855/4 OM | — | 7.50 | 10.00 | 20.00 | 150.00 |
| | 1855 OM | — | 7.50 | 10.00 | 20.00 | 150.00 |
| | 1855 MO | — | 7.50 | 10.00 | 20.00 | 150.00 |
| | 1856/5 MO | — | 7.50 | 10.00 | 20.00 | 150.00 |
| | 1856 MO | — | 7.50 | 10.00 | 20.00 | 150.00 |
| | 1857 MO | — | 7.50 | 10.00 | 20.00 | 150.00 |
| | 1858 MO | — | 7.50 | 10.00 | 20.00 | 150.00 |
| | 1859 MO | — | 7.50 | 10.00 | 20.00 | 150.00 |
| | 1860/59 MO | — | 7.50 | 10.00 | 20.00 | 150.00 |
| | 1860 MO | — | 7.50 | 10.00 | 20.00 | 100.00 |
| | 1860 VL | — | 7.50 | 10.00 | 20.00 | 150.00 |
| | 1861 VL | — | 7.50 | 10.00 | 20.00 | 150.00 |
| | 1862 VL | — | 7.50 | 10.00 | 20.00 | 100.00 |
| | 1863 MO | — | 12.50 | 20.00 | 40.00 | 150.00 |
| | 1863 VL | — | 7.50 | 10.00 | 20.00 | 150.00 |
| | 1864 MO | — | 7.50 | 10.00 | 20.00 | 150.00 |
| | 1864 VL | — | 7.50 | 10.00 | 20.00 | 150.00 |
| | 1865 MO | — | 7.50 | 10.00 | 20.00 | 150.00 |
| | 1867 JS | — | 7.50 | 10.00 | 20.00 | 150.00 |
| | 1868 JS | — | 10.00 | 15.00 | 35.00 | 150.00 |
| | 1868 YH | — | 7.50 | 10.00 | 20.00 | 150.00 |
| | 1869 YH | — | 7.50 | 10.00 | 20.00 | 150.00 |
| | 1870 YH | — | 7.50 | 10.00 | 20.00 | 150.00 |

**NOTE:** Varieties exist.

## 4 REALES

**13.5400 g, .903 SILVER, .3925 oz ASW**
**Mint mark: Ce**
**Obv: Facing eagle.**

| KM# | Date | Mintage | Fine | VF | XF | Unc |
|---|---|---|---|---|---|---|
| 375 | 1863 ML large C | | | | | |
| | | — | 200.00 | 500.00 | 850.00 | 4000. |
| | 1863 ML small C | | | | | |
| | | — | 350.00 | 650.00 | 1250. | 4750. |

**Mint mark: C**

| KM# | Date | Mintage | Fine | VF | XF | Unc |
|---|---|---|---|---|---|---|
| 375.1 | 1846 CE | — | 400.00 | 550.00 | 900.00 | — |
| | 1850 CE | — | 75.00 | 125.00 | 250.00 | 600.00 |
| | 1852 CE | — | 200.00 | 300.00 | 500.00 | 1250. |
| | 1857 CE | — | — | — | Rare | — |
| | 1858 CE | — | 100.00 | 200.00 | 350.00 | 1000. |
| | 1860 PV | — | 25.00 | 50.00 | 125.00 | 600.00 |

**Mint mark: Ga**

| KM# | Date | Mintage | Fine | VF | XF | Unc |
|---|---|---|---|---|---|---|
| 375.2 | 1842/1 JG | — | — | Reported, not confirmed | | |
| | 1842 JG | — | — | Reported, not confirmed | | |
| | 1843 MC | — | 20.00 | 40.00 | 80.00 | 400.00 |
| | 1844/3 MC | — | 30.00 | 60.00 | 125.00 | 400.00 |
| | 1844 MC | — | 20.00 | 40.00 | 80.00 | 400.00 |
| | 1845 MC | — | 20.00 | 40.00 | 80.00 | 400.00 |
| | 1845 JG | — | 20.00 | 40.00 | 80.00 | 400.00 |
| | 1846 JG | — | 20.00 | 40.00 | 80.00 | 400.00 |
| | 1847 JG | — | 40.00 | 80.00 | 150.00 | 400.00 |
| | 1848/7 JG | — | 40.00 | 80.00 | 150.00 | 400.00 |
| | 1849 JG | — | 40.00 | 80.00 | 150.00 | 400.00 |
| | 1850 JG | — | 65.00 | 125.00 | 250.00 | 550.00 |
| | 1852 JG | — | — | — | Rare | — |
| | 1854 JG | — | — | — | Rare | — |
| | 1855 JG | — | 100.00 | 200.00 | 400.00 | 1250. |
| | 1856 JG | — | — | — | Rare | — |
| | 1857/6 JG | — | 65.00 | 125.00 | 250.00 | 550.00 |
| | 1858 JG | — | 125.00 | 250.00 | 450.00 | 1250. |
| | 1859/8 JG | — | 125.00 | 250.00 | 450.00 | 1250. |
| | 1860 JG | — | — | — | Rare | — |
| | 1863/2 JG | — | 150.00 | 300.00 | 1250. | 6000. |
| | 1863 JG | — | 150.00 | 300.00 | 1250. | 6000. |

**Mint mark: GC**

| KM# | Date | Mintage | Fine | VF | XF | Unc |
|---|---|---|---|---|---|---|
| 375.3 | 1844 MP | — | 1000. | 2000. | 3000. | — |
| | 1845 MP | — | 3000. | 4000. | 5000. | 9000. |
| | 1846 MP | — | 1700. | 2800. | — | — |
| | 1847 MP | — | 1500. | 2500. | — | — |
| | 1849 MP | — | 2000. | 3000. | — | — |
| | 1850 MP | — | 500.00 | 1000. | — | — |

**Mint mark: Go**

| KM# | Date | Mintage | Fine | VF | XF | Unc |
|---|---|---|---|---|---|---|
| 375.4 | 1835 PJ | — | 12.50 | 25.00 | 60.00 | 350.00 |
| | 1836/5 PJ | — | 15.00 | 30.00 | 75.00 | 350.00 |
| | 1836 PJ | — | 15.00 | 30.00 | 75.00 | 350.00 |
| | 1837 PJ | — | 12.50 | 25.00 | 60.00 | 350.00 |
| | 1838/7 PJ | — | 15.00 | 30.00 | 75.00 | 350.00 |
| | 1838 PJ | — | 12.50 | 30.00 | 75.00 | 350.00 |
| | 1839 PJ | — | 12.50 | 25.00 | 60.00 | 350.00 |
| | 1840/30 PJ | — | 20.00 | 50.00 | 100.00 | 350.00 |
| | 1841/31 PJ | — | 150.00 | 250.00 | 450.00 | 1250. |
| | 1842 PJ | — | — | — | Rare | — |
| | 1842 PM | — | 15.00 | 30.00 | 75.00 | 350.00 |
| | 1843/2 PM eagle w/convex wings, thick rays | | | | | |
| | | — | 12.50 | 25.00 | 60.00 | 350.00 |
| | 1843 PM eagle w/concave wings, thin rays | | | | | |
| | | — | 12.50 | 25.00 | 60.00 | 350.00 |
| | 1844/3 PM | — | 15.00 | 30.00 | 75.00 | 350.00 |
| | 1844 PM | — | 20.00 | 50.00 | 100.00 | 350.00 |
| | 1845/4 PM | — | 20.00 | 50.00 | 100.00 | 350.00 |
| | 1845 PM | — | 20.00 | 50.00 | 100.00 | 350.00 |

| KM# | Date | Mintage | Fine | VF | XF | Unc |
|---|---|---|---|---|---|---|
| 375.4 | 1846/5 PM | — | 15.00 | 30.00 | 75.00 | 350.00 |
| | 1846 PM | — | 15.00 | 30.00 | 75.00 | 350.00 |
| | 1847/6 PM | — | 15.00 | 30.00 | 75.00 | 350.00 |
| | 1847 PM | — | 15.00 | 30.00 | 75.00 | 350.00 |
| | 1848/7 PM | — | 20.00 | 50.00 | 100.00 | 350.00 |
| | 1848 PM | — | 20.00 | 50.00 | 100.00 | 350.00 |
| | 1849 PF | — | 20.00 | 50.00 | 100.00 | 350.00 |
| | 1850 PF | — | 12.50 | 25.00 | 60.00 | 350.00 |
| | 1851 PF | — | 12.50 | 25.00 | 60.00 | 350.00 |
| | 1852 PF | — | 15.00 | 30.00 | 75.00 | 350.00 |
| | 1853 PF | — | 15.00 | 30.00 | 75.00 | 350.00 |
| | 1854 PF large eagle | | | | | |
| | | — | 15.00 | 30.00 | 75.00 | 350.00 |
| | 1854 PF small eagle | | | | | |
| | | — | 15.00 | 30.00 | 75.00 | 350.00 |
| | 1855/4 PF | — | 15.00 | 30.00 | 75.00 | 350.00 |
| | 1855 PF | — | 12.50 | 25.00 | 60.00 | 350.00 |
| | 1856 PF | — | 12.50 | 25.00 | 60.00 | 350.00 |
| | 1857 PF | — | 20.00 | 50.00 | 100.00 | 350.00 |
| | 1858 PF | — | 20.00 | 50.00 | 100.00 | 350.00 |
| | 1859 PF | — | 20.00 | 50.00 | 100.00 | 350.00 |
| | 1860/59 PF | — | 15.00 | 30.00 | 75.00 | 350.00 |
| | 1860 PF | — | 15.00 | 30.00 | 75.00 | 350.00 |
| | 1861/51 PF | — | 15.00 | 30.00 | 75.00 | 350.00 |
| | 1861 PF | — | 20.00 | 50.00 | 100.00 | 350.00 |
| | 1862/1 YE | — | 15.00 | 30.00 | 75.00 | 350.00 |
| | 1862/1 YF | — | 15.00 | 30.00 | 75.00 | 350.00 |
| | 1862 YE/PF | — | 15.00 | 30.00 | 75.00 | 350.00 |
| | 1862 YE | — | 15.00 | 30.00 | 75.00 | 350.00 |
| | 1862 YF | — | 15.00 | 30.00 | 75.00 | 350.00 |
| | 1863/53 YF | — | 15.00 | 30.00 | 75.00 | 350.00 |
| | 1863 YF/PF | — | 15.00 | 30.00 | 75.00 | 350.00 |
| | 1863 YF | — | 15.00 | 30.00 | 75.00 | 350.00 |
| | 1867/57 YF/PF | | | | | |
| | | — | 15.00 | 30.00 | 75.00 | 350.00 |
| | 1868/58 YF/PF | | | | | |
| | | — | 15.00 | 30.00 | 75.00 | 350.00 |
| | 1870 FR | — | 15.00 | 30.00 | 75.00 | 350.00 |

**NOTE:** Varieties exist. Some 1862 dates appear to be 1869 because of weak dies.

**Mint mark: Ho**

| KM# | Date | Mintage | Fine | VF | XF | Unc |
|---|---|---|---|---|---|---|
| 375.5 | 1861 FM | — | 200.00 | 350.00 | 500.00 | 1850. |
| | 1867/1 PR/FM | | | | | |
| | | — | 150.00 | 275.00 | 400.00 | 1750. |

**Mint mark: Mo**

| KM# | Date | Mintage | Fine | VF | XF | Unc |
|---|---|---|---|---|---|---|
| 375.6 | 1827/6 JM | — | 200.00 | 400.00 | — | — |
| | 1850 GC | — | — | — | Rare | — |
| | 1852 GC | — | — | — | Rare | — |
| | 1854 GC | — | — | — | Rare | — |
| | 1855 GF/GC | — | 50.00 | 100.00 | 200.00 | 500.00 |
| | 1855 GF | — | 100.00 | 200.00 | 350.00 | 800.00 |
| | 1856 GF/GC | — | 20.00 | 50.00 | 100.00 | 350.00 |
| | 1856 GF | — | — | — | Rare | — |
| | 1859 FH | — | 20.00 | 50.00 | 100.00 | 350.00 |
| | 1861 CH | — | 15.00 | 30.00 | 75.00 | 300.00 |
| | 1862 CH | — | 20.00 | 50.00 | 100.00 | 350.00 |
| | 1863/2 CH | — | 20.00 | 50.00 | 100.00 | 350.00 |
| | 1863 CH | — | 75.00 | 150.00 | 300.00 | 650.00 |
| | 1867 CH | — | 20.00 | 50.00 | 100.00 | 350.00 |
| | 1868 CH/PH | — | 30.00 | 75.00 | 150.00 | 400.00 |
| | 1868 CH | — | 20.00 | 50.00 | 100.00 | 350.00 |
| | 1868 PH | — | 30.00 | 75.00 | 150.00 | 400.00 |

**Mint mark: O**

| KM# | Date | Mintage | Fine | VF | XF | Unc |
|---|---|---|---|---|---|---|
| 375.7 | 1861 FR ornamental edge | | | | | |
| | | — | 225.00 | 450.00 | 700.00 | 2500. |
| | 1861 FR herringbone edge | | | | | |
| | | — | 275.00 | 550.00 | 800.00 | 2500. |
| | 1861 FR obliquely reeded edge | | | | | |
| | | — | 200.00 | 400.00 | 650.00 | — |

**Mint mark: Pi**

| KM# | Date | Mintage | Fine | VF | XF | Unc |
|---|---|---|---|---|---|---|
| 375.8 | 1837 JS | — | — | — | Rare | — |
| | 1838 JS | — | 150.00 | 250.00 | 400.00 | 800.00 |
| | 1842 PS | — | 50.00 | 100.00 | 200.00 | 450.00 |
| | 1843/2 PS | — | 50.00 | 100.00 | 200.00 | 450.00 |
| | 1843/2 PS 3 cut from 8 punch | | | | | |
| | | — | 50.00 | 100.00 | 200.00 | 450.00 |
| | 1843 AM | — | 30.00 | 75.00 | 150.00 | 450.00 |
| | 1843 PS | — | 50.00 | 100.00 | 200.00 | 450.00 |
| | 1844 AM | — | 30.00 | 75.00 | 150.00 | 450.00 |
| | 1845/4 AM | — | 20.00 | 50.00 | 100.00 | 450.00 |
| | 1845 AM | — | 20.00 | 50.00 | 100.00 | 450.00 |

| KM# | Date | Mintage | Fine | VF | XF | Unc |
|---|---|---|---|---|---|---|
| 375.8 | 1846 AM | — | 20.00 | 50.00 | 100.00 | 450.00 |
| | 1847 AM | — | 75.00 | 150.00 | 250.00 | 550.00 |
| | 1848 AM | — | — | — | Rare | — |
| | 1849 MC/AM | — | 20.00 | 50.00 | 100.00 | 450.00 |
| | 1849 MC | — | 20.00 | 50.00 | 100.00 | 450.00 |
| | 1849 PS | — | 20.00 | 50.00 | 100.00 | 450.00 |
| | 1850 MC | — | 20.00 | 50.00 | 100.00 | 450.00 |
| | 1851 MC | — | 20.00 | 50.00 | 100.00 | 450.00 |
| | 1852 MC | — | 20.00 | 50.00 | 100.00 | 450.00 |
| | 1853 MC | — | 20.00 | 50.00 | 100.00 | 450.00 |
| | 1854 MC | — | 100.00 | 200.00 | 400.00 | 1100. |
| | 1855 MC | — | 200.00 | 350.00 | 500.00 | 1500. |
| | 1856 MC | — | 300.00 | 450.00 | 700.00 | — |
| | 1857 MC | — | — | — | Rare | — |
| | 1857 PS | — | — | — | Rare | — |
| | 1858 MC | — | 100.00 | 200.00 | 400.00 | 1000. |
| | 1859 MC | — | 2000. | 3000. | — | — |
| | 1860 PS | — | 300.00 | 450.00 | 700.00 | — |
| | 1861 PS | — | 30.00 | 75.00 | 150.00 | 450.00 |
| | 1861 RO/PS | — | 30.00 | 75.00 | 150.00 | 450.00 |
| | 1861 RO | — | 50.00 | 100.00 | 200.00 | 450.00 |
| | 1862 RO | — | 30.00 | 75.00 | 150.00 | 450.00 |
| | 1863 RO | — | 30.00 | 75.00 | 150.00 | 450.00 |
| | 1864 RO | — | 1600. | 2600. | — | — |
| | 1868 PS | — | 30.00 | 75.00 | 150.00 | 450.00 |
| | 1869/8 PS | — | 30.00 | 75.00 | 150.00 | 450.00 |
| | 1869 PS | — | 30.00 | 75.00 | 150.00 | 450.00 |

**Mint mark: Zs**

| KM# | Date | Mintage | Fine | VF | XF | Unc |
|---|---|---|---|---|---|---|
| 375.9 | 1830 OM | — | 20.00 | 50.00 | 100.00 | 350.00 |
| | 1831 OM | — | 15.00 | 30.00 | 75.00 | 350.00 |
| | 1832/1 OM | — | 20.00 | 50.00 | 100.00 | 350.00 |
| | 1832 OM | — | 20.00 | 50.00 | 100.00 | 350.00 |
| | 1833/2 OM | — | 20.00 | 50.00 | 100.00 | 350.00 |
| | 1833/27 OM | — | 15.00 | 30.00 | 75.00 | 350.00 |
| | 1833 OM | — | 15.00 | 30.00 | 75.00 | 350.00 |
| | 1834/3 OM | — | 20.00 | 50.00 | 100.00 | 350.00 |
| | 1834 OM | — | 15.00 | 30.00 | 75.00 | 350.00 |
| | 1835 OM | — | 15.00 | 30.00 | 75.00 | 350.00 |
| | 1836 OM | — | 15.00 | 30.00 | 75.00 | 350.00 |
| | 1837/5 OM | — | 20.00 | 50.00 | 100.00 | 350.00 |
| | 1837/6 OM | — | 20.00 | 50.00 | 100.00 | 350.00 |
| | 1837 OM | — | 20.00 | 50.00 | 100.00 | 350.00 |
| | 1838/7 OM | — | 15.00 | 30.00 | 75.00 | 350.00 |
| | 1839 OM | — | 250.00 | 375.00 | 500.00 | — |
| | 1840 OM | — | — | — | Rare | — |
| | 1841 OM | — | 15.00 | 30.00 | 75.00 | 350.00 |
| | 1842 OM small letters | — | 75.00 | 150.00 | 300.00 | 800.00 |
| | 1842 OM large letters | — | 15.00 | 30.00 | 75.00 | 350.00 |
| | 1843 OM | — | 15.00 | 30.00 | 75.00 | 350.00 |
| | 1844 OM | — | 20.00 | 50.00 | 100.00 | 350.00 |
| | 1845 OM | — | 20.00 | 50.00 | 100.00 | 350.00 |
| | 1846/5 OM | — | 25.00 | 60.00 | 125.00 | 350.00 |
| | 1846 OM | — | 20.00 | 50.00 | 100.00 | 350.00 |
| | 1847 OM | — | 15.00 | 30.00 | 75.00 | 350.00 |
| | 1848/6 OM | — | 50.00 | 75.00 | 125.00 | 350.00 |
| | 1848 OM | — | 20.00 | 50.00 | 100.00 | 350.00 |
| | 1849 OM | — | 20.00 | 50.00 | 100.00 | 350.00 |
| | 1850 OM | — | 20.00 | 50.00 | 100.00 | 350.00 |
| | 1851 OM | — | 15.00 | 30.00 | 75.00 | 350.00 |
| | 1852 OM | — | 15.00 | 30.00 | 75.00 | 350.00 |
| | 1853 OM | — | 20.00 | 50.00 | 100.00 | 350.00 |
| | 1854/3 OM | — | 30.00 | 75.00 | 150.00 | 350.00 |
| | 1855/4 OM | — | 20.00 | 50.00 | 100.00 | 350.00 |
| | 1855 OM | — | 15.00 | 30.00 | 75.00 | 350.00 |
| | 1856 OM | — | 15.00 | 30.00 | 75.00 | 350.00 |
| | 1856 MO | — | 20.00 | 50.00 | 100.00 | 350.00 |
| | 1857/5 MO | — | 20.00 | 50.00 | 100.00 | 350.00 |
| | 1857 O/M | — | 20.00 | 50.00 | 100.00 | 350.00 |
| | 1857 MO | — | 15.00 | 30.00 | 75.00 | 350.00 |
| | 1858 MO | — | 20.00 | 50.00 | 100.00 | 350.00 |
| | 1859 MO | — | 15.00 | 30.00 | 75.00 | 350.00 |
| | 1860/59 MO | — | 20.00 | 50.00 | 100.00 | 350.00 |
| | 1860 MO | — | 15.00 | 30.00 | 75.00 | 350.00 |
| | 1860 VL | — | 20.00 | 50.00 | 100.00 | 350.00 |
| | 1861/0 VL | — | 20.00 | 50.00 | 100.00 | 350.00 |
| | 1861 VL | — | 15.00 | 30.00 | 75.00 | 350.00 |
| | 1862/1 VL | — | 20.00 | 50.00 | 100.00 | 350.00 |
| | 1862 VL | — | 20.00 | 50.00 | 100.00 | 350.00 |
| | 1863 VL | — | 20.00 | 50.00 | 100.00 | 350.00 |
| | 1863 MO | — | 20.00 | 50.00 | 100.00 | 350.00 |
| | 1864 VL | — | 15.00 | 30.00 | 75.00 | 350.00 |
| | 1868 JS | — | 20.00 | 50.00 | 100.00 | 350.00 |

| KM# | Date | Mintage | Fine | VF | XF | Unc |
|---|---|---|---|---|---|---|
| 375.9 | 1868 YH | — | 15.00 | 30.00 | 75.00 | 350.00 |
| | 1869 YH | — | 15.00 | 30.00 | 75.00 | 350.00 |
| | 1870 YH | — | 15.00 | 30.00 | 75.00 | 350.00 |

# 8 REALES

**27.0700 g, .903 SILVER, .7859 oz ASW**
**Mint mark: Do**
**Obv: Hooked-neck eagle.**

| | | | | | | |
|---|---|---|---|---|---|---|
| 376 | 1824 RL | — | 200.00 | 350.00 | 1250. | 2750. |

**NOTE:** Varieties exist.

**Mint mark: Go**

| | | | | | | |
|---|---|---|---|---|---|---|
| 376.1 | 1824 JM | — | 200.00 | 325.00 | 1000. | 3500. |
| | 1825/4 JJ | — | 550.00 | 800.00 | 1500. | 6000. |
| | 1825 JJ | — | 500.00 | 750.00 | 1400. | 5500. |

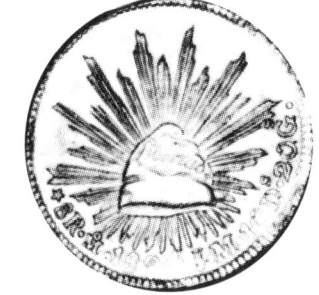

**Mint mark: Mo**

| | | | | | | |
|---|---|---|---|---|---|---|
| 376.2 | 1823 JM edge: circle and rectangle pattern | — | — | — | Rare | — |
| | 1823 JM edge: laurel leaves | — | 150.00 | 300.00 | 650.00 | 2500. |
| | 1824 JM | — | 125.00 | 250.00 | 450.00 | 2000. |
| | 1824 JM (error) REPULICA | — | — | — | Rare | — |

**NOTE:** These are rarely found with detail on the eagles breast and bring a premium if even slight feather detail is present there.

**Mint mark: A, As**

| KM# | Date | Mintage | Fine | VF | XF | Unc |
|---|---|---|---|---|---|---|
| 377 | 1864 PG | — | 650.00 | 900.00 | 1200. | — |
| | 1865/4 PG | — | — | — | Rare | — |
| | 1865 PG | — | 500.00 | 750.00 | 1000. | — |
| | 1866/5 PG | — | — | — | Rare | — |
| | 1866 PG | — | — | — | Rare | — |
| | 1866 DL | — | — | — | Rare | — |
| | 1867 DL | — | — | — | Rare | — |
| | 1868 DL | — | 50.00 | 90.00 | 150.00 | 300.00 |
| | 1869/8 DL | — | 50.00 | 90.00 | 150.00 | — |
| | 1869 DL | — | 50.00 | 80.00 | 120.00 | 300.00 |
| | 1870 DL | — | 30.00 | 60.00 | 120.00 | 300.00 |
| | 1871 DL | — | 20.00 | 35.00 | 75.00 | 200.00 |
| | 1872 AM/DL | — | 25.00 | 50.00 | 100.00 | 300.00 |
| | 1872 AM | — | 25.00 | 50.00 | 100.00 | 250.00 |
| | 1873 AM | .509 | 15.00 | 25.00 | 50.00 | 150.00 |
| | 1874 DL | — | 15.00 | 25.00 | 50.00 | 150.00 |
| | 1875A DL 7/7 | — | 40.00 | 80.00 | 120.00 | 300.00 |
| | 1875A DL | — | 15.00 | 25.00 | 50.00 | 150.00 |
| | 1875AsDL | — | 30.00 | 60.00 | 110.00 | 250.00 |
| | 1876 DL | — | 15.00 | 25.00 | 50.00 | 150.00 |
| | 1877 DL | .515 | 15.00 | 25.00 | 50.00 | 150.00 |
| | 1878 DL | .513 | 15.00 | 25.00 | 50.00 | 150.00 |
| | 1879 DL | — | 20.00 | 35.00 | 75.00 | 175.00 |
| | 1879 ML | — | 30.00 | 60.00 | 125.00 | 300.00 |
| | 1880 ML | — | 12.00 | 15.00 | 30.00 | 140.00 |
| | 1881 ML | .966 | 12.00 | 15.00 | 30.00 | 140.00 |
| | 1882 ML | .480 | 12.00 | 15.00 | 30.00 | 140.00 |
| | 1883 ML | .464 | 12.00 | 15.00 | 30.00 | 140.00 |
| | 1884 ML | — | 12.00 | 15.00 | 30.00 | 140.00 |
| | 1885 ML | .280 | 12.00 | 15.00 | 30.00 | 140.00 |
| | 1886 ML | .857 | 12.00 | 15.00 | 25.00 | 110.00 |
| | 1886/0 As/Cn ML/JD | | | | | |
| | | I.A. | 15.00 | 20.00 | 35.00 | 160.00 |
| | 1887 ML | .650 | 12.00 | 15.00 | 25.00 | 110.00 |
| | 1888/7 ML | .508 | 30.00 | 60.00 | 100.00 | 400.00 |
| | 1888 ML | I.A. | 12.00 | 15.00 | 25.00 | 110.00 |
| | 1889 ML | .427 | 12.00 | 15.00 | 25.00 | 110.00 |
| | 1890 ML | .450 | 12.00 | 15.00 | 25.00 | 110.00 |
| | 1891 ML | .533 | 12.00 | 15.00 | 25.00 | 110.00 |
| | 1892 ML | .465 | 12.00 | 15.00 | 25.00 | 110.00 |
| | 1893 ML | .734 | 10.00 | 12.00 | 20.00 | 80.00 |
| | 1894 ML | .725 | 10.00 | 12.00 | 20.00 | 80.00 |
| | 1895 ML | .477 | 10.00 | 12.00 | 20.00 | 80.00 |

**NOTE:** Varieties exist.

**Mint mark: Ce**

| KM# | Date | Mintage | Fine | VF | XF | Unc |
|---|---|---|---|---|---|---|
| 377.1 | 1863 ML | — | 375.00 | 625.00 | 1000. | 2250. |
| | 1863 CeML/PiMC | | | | | |
| | | — | 375.00 | 650.00 | 1100. | 2750. |

**Mint mark: Ca**

| KM# | Date | Mintage | Fine | VF | XF | Unc |
|---|---|---|---|---|---|---|
| 377.2 | 1831 MR | — | 1000. | 1750. | 2250. | 3250. |
| | 1832 MR | — | 125.00 | 200.00 | 300.00 | 600.00 |
| | 1833 MR | — | 500.00 | 750.00 | 1250. | |
| | 1834 MR | — | — | — | Rare | — |
| | 1834 AM | — | — | — | Rare | — |
| | 1835 AM | — | 150.00 | 250.00 | 400.00 | 800.00 |
| | 1836 AM | — | 100.00 | 150.00 | 225.00 | 450.00 |
| | 1837 AM | — | — | — | Rare | — |
| | 1838 AM | — | 100.00 | 200.00 | 300.00 | 600.00 |
| | 1839 RG | — | 1250. | 2500. | — | — |
| | 1840 RG 1 dot after date | | | | | |
| | | — | 400.00 | 600.00 | 800.00 | 1500. |
| | 1840 RG 3 dots after date | | | | | |
| | | — | 400.00 | 600.00 | 800.00 | 1500. |
| | 1841 RG | — | 50.00 | 100.00 | 150.00 | 300.00 |
| | 1842 RG | — | 25.00 | 40.00 | 65.00 | 125.00 |
| | 1843 RG | — | 40.00 | 80.00 | 125.00 | 250.00 |
| | 1844/1 RG | — | 35.00 | 70.00 | 100.00 | 200.00 |
| | 1844 RG | — | 25.00 | 40.00 | 65.00 | 125.00 |
| | 1845 RG | — | 25.00 | 40.00 | 65.00 | 125.00 |
| | 1846 RG | — | 30.00 | 60.00 | 100.00 | 250.00 |
| | 1847 RG | — | 40.00 | 80.00 | 125.00 | 250.00 |
| | 1848 RG | — | 30.00 | 60.00 | 100.00 | 200.00 |
| | 1849 RG | — | 30.00 | 60.00 | 100.00 | 200.00 |
| | 1850/40 RG | — | 40.00 | 80.00 | 125.00 | 250.00 |
| | 1850 RG | — | 30.00 | 60.00 | 100.00 | 200.00 |
| | 1851/41 RG | — | 100.00 | 200.00 | 300.00 | 500.00 |
| | 1851 RG | — | 150.00 | 250.00 | 400.00 | 750.00 |
| | 1852/42 RG | — | 150.00 | 250.00 | 400.00 | 750.00 |
| | 1852 RG | — | 150.00 | 250.00 | 400.00 | 750.00 |
| | 1853/43 RG | — | 150.00 | 250.00 | 400.00 | 750.00 |
| | 1853 RG | — | 150.00 | 250.00 | 400.00 | 750.00 |
| | 1854/44 RG | — | 100.00 | 200.00 | 300.00 | 500.00 |
| | 1854 RG | — | 50.00 | 100.00 | 150.00 | 300.00 |
| | 1855/45 RG | — | 100.00 | 200.00 | 350.00 | 650.00 |
| | 1855 RG | — | 75.00 | 125.00 | 200.00 | 400.00 |
| | 1856/45 RG | — | 200.00 | 400.00 | 600.00 | 1000. |
| | 1856/5 JC | — | 600.00 | 1000. | 1250. | 1750. |
| | 1857 JC/RG | — | 40.00 | 80.00 | 125.00 | 250.00 |
| | 1857 JC | — | 50.00 | 100.00 | 150.00 | 250.00 |
| | 1858 JC | — | 20.00 | 30.00 | 50.00 | 120.00 |
| | 1858 BA | — | — | — | Rare | — |
| | 1859 JC | — | 40.00 | 80.00 | 125.00 | 250.00 |
| | 1860 JC | — | 20.00 | 40.00 | 90.00 | 175.00 |
| | 1861 JC | — | 15.00 | 25.00 | 50.00 | 120.00 |
| | 1862 JC | — | 15.00 | 25.00 | 50.00 | 120.00 |
| | 1863 JC | — | 20.00 | 35.00 | 75.00 | 150.00 |
| | 1864 JC | — | 20.00 | 35.00 | 75.00 | 150.00 |
| | 1865 JC | — | 100.00 | 200.00 | 350.00 | 600.00 |
| | 1865 FP | — | — | — | Rare | — |
| | 1866 JC | — | — | — | Rare | — |
| | 1866 FP | — | — | — | Rare | — |
| | 1866 JG | — | — | — | Rare | — |
| | 1867 JG | — | 100.00 | 200.00 | 350.00 | 600.00 |
| | 1868 JG | — | 75.00 | 150.00 | 200.00 | 350.00 |
| | 1868 MM | — | 50.00 | 100.00 | 150.00 | 300.00 |
| | 1869 MM | — | 20.00 | 35.00 | 65.00 | 125.00 |
| | 1870 MM | — | 20.00 | 35.00 | 65.00 | 125.00 |
| | 1871/0 MM | — | 15.00 | 25.00 | 50.00 | 100.00 |
| | 1871 MM | — | 15.00 | 25.00 | 50.00 | 100.00 |
| | 1871 MM first M/inverted M | | | | | |
| | | — | 20.00 | 35.00 | 65.00 | 125.00 |
| | 1873 MM | — | 20.00 | 35.00 | 65.00 | 125.00 |
| | 1873 MM/T | | | | | |
| | | — | 15.00 | 25.00 | 50.00 | 100.00 |
| | 1874 MM | — | 12.00 | 15.00 | 30.00 | 100.00 |
| | 1875 MM | — | 12.00 | 15.00 | 30.00 | 100.00 |
| | 1876 MM | — | 12.00 | 15.00 | 30.00 | 100.00 |
| | 1877 EA | .472 | 12.00 | 15.00 | 30.00 | 100.00 |
| | 1877 GR | I.A. | 25.00 | 45.00 | 65.00 | 150.00 |
| | 1877 JM | I.A. | 12.00 | 15.00 | 30.00 | 100.00 |
| | 1877 AV | I.A. | 100.00 | 200.00 | 350.00 | 750.00 |
| | 1878 AV | .439 | 12.00 | 15.00 | 25.00 | 75.00 |
| | 1879 AV | — | 12.00 | 15.00 | 25.00 | 75.00 |
| | 1880 AV | — | 250.00 | 400.00 | 600.00 | 1200. |
| | 1880 PM | — | 500.00 | 750.00 | 1000. | 1500. |
| | 1880 MG normal initials | | | | | |
| | | — | 12.00 | 15.00 | 25.00 | 100.00 |
| | 1880 MG tall initials | | | | | |
| | | — | 12.00 | 15.00 | 25.00 | 100.00 |
| | 1880 MM | — | 12.00 | 15.00 | 25.00 | 100.00 |
| | 1881 MG | 1.085 | 10.00 | 12.00 | 20.00 | 60.00 |
| | 1882 MG | .779 | 10.00 | 12.00 | 20.00 | 60.00 |

| KM# | Date | Mintage | Fine | VF | XF | Unc |
|---|---|---|---|---|---|---|
| 377.2 | 1882 MM | I.A. | 10.00 | 12.00 | 20.00 | 60.00 |
| | 1882 MM M sideways | | | | | |
| | | Inc. Ab. | 20.00 | 40.00 | 90.00 | 150.00 |
| | 1883 sideways M MM | | | | | |
| | | .818 | — | — | — | — |
| | 1883 MM | I.A. | 10.00 | 12.00 | 20.00 | 60.00 |
| | 1884/3 MM | — | 12.00 | 15.00 | 30.00 | 75.00 |
| | 1884 MM | — | 10.00 | 12.00 | 20.00 | 60.00 |
| | 1885/4 MM | | | | | |
| | | 1.345 | 15.00 | 25.00 | 50.00 | 100.00 |
| | 1885/6 MM | I.A. | 15.00 | 25.00 | 50.00 | 100.00 |
| | 1885 MM | I.A. | 10.00 | 12.00 | 20.00 | 60.00 |
| | 1886 MM | 2.483 | 10.00 | 12.00 | 20.00 | 60.00 |
| | 1887 MM | 2.625 | 10.00 | 12.00 | 20.00 | 60.00 |
| | 1888/7 MM | | | | | |
| | | 2.434 | 15.00 | 25.00 | 50.00 | 100.00 |
| | 1888 MM | I.A. | 10.00 | 12.00 | 20.00 | 60.00 |
| | 1889 MM | 2.681 | 10.00 | 12.00 | 20.00 | 60.00 |
| | 1890 MM | 2.137 | 10.00 | 12.00 | 20.00 | 60.00 |
| | 1891/0 MM | | | | | |
| | | 2.268 | 15.00 | 25.00 | 50.00 | 100.00 |
| | 1891 MM | I.A. | 10.00 | 12.00 | 20.00 | 80.00 |
| | 1892 MM | 2.527 | 10.00 | 12.00 | 20.00 | 60.00 |
| | 1893 MM | 2.632 | 10.00 | 12.00 | 20.00 | 60.00 |
| | 1894 MM | 2.642 | 10.00 | 12.00 | 20.00 | 60.00 |
| | 1895 MM | 1.112 | 10.00 | 12.00 | 20.00 | 60.00 |

NOTE: Varieties exist.

### Mint mark: C, Cn

| KM# | Date | Mintage | Fine | VF | XF | Unc |
|---|---|---|---|---|---|---|
| 377.3 | 1846 CE | — | 150.00 | 300.00 | 800.00 | 1500. |
| | 1847 CE | — | 600.00 | 1000. | 1500. | — |
| | 1848 CE | — | 150.00 | 300.00 | 600.00 | 1000. |
| | 1849 CE | — | 75.00 | 125.00 | 200.00 | 400.00 |
| | 1850 CE | — | 75.00 | 125.00 | 200.00 | 400.00 |
| | 1851 CE | — | 125.00 | 250.00 | 450.00 | 1000. |
| | 1852/1 CE | — | 100.00 | 150.00 | 250.00 | 500.00 |
| | 1852 CE | — | 100.00 | 200.00 | 350.00 | 650.00 |
| | 1853/0 CE | — | 200.00 | 350.00 | 700.00 | 1300. |
| | 1853/2/0 | — | 200.00 | 400.00 | 750.00 | 1400. |
| | 1853 CE thick rays | | | | | |
| | | — | 100.00 | 175.00 | 300.00 | 600.00 |
| | 1853 CE (error:) MEXIGANA | | | | | |
| | | — | 200.00 | 350.00 | 650.00 | — |
| | 1854 CE | — | — | — | Rare | — |
| | 1854 CE large eagle & hat | | | | | |
| | | — | 150.00 | 300.00 | 600.00 | 1000. |
| | 1855/6 CE | — | 40.00 | 60.00 | 100.00 | 200.00 |
| | 1855 CE | — | 25.00 | 40.00 | 60.00 | 125.00 |
| | 1856 CE | — | 50.00 | 100.00 | 175.00 | 350.00 |
| | 1857 CE | — | 20.00 | 30.00 | 45.00 | 100.00 |
| | 1858 CE | — | 30.00 | 40.00 | 60.00 | 125.00 |
| | 1859 CE | — | 20.00 | 30.00 | 45.00 | 100.00 |
| | 1860/9 PV/CV | | | | | |
| | | — | 50.00 | 70.00 | 100.00 | 200.00 |
| | 1860/9 PV/E | — | 50.00 | 70.00 | 100.00 | 200.00 |
| | 1860 CE | — | 25.00 | 40.00 | 55.00 | 100.00 |
| | 1860 PV | — | 40.00 | 60.00 | 80.00 | 150.00 |
| | 1861/0 CE | — | 40.00 | 60.00 | 100.00 | 250.00 |
| | 1861 PV/CE | — | 75.00 | 125.00 | 200.00 | 350.00 |
| | 1861 CE | — | 20.00 | 35.00 | 50.00 | 150.00 |
| | 1862 CE | — | 20.00 | 35.00 | 50.00 | 150.00 |
| | 1863/2 CE | — | 30.00 | 50.00 | 75.00 | 200.00 |
| | 1863 CE | — | 20.00 | 30.00 | 50.00 | 150.00 |
| | 1864 CE | — | 30.00 | 60.00 | 100.00 | 300.00 |
| | 1865 CE | — | 125.00 | 200.00 | 325.00 | 650.00 |
| | 1866 CE | — | — | — | Rare | — |
| | 1867 CE | — | 125.00 | 200.00 | 375.00 | 750.00 |
| | 1868/7 CE | — | 30.00 | 40.00 | 75.00 | 150.00 |
| | 1868/8 | — | 50.00 | 100.00 | 150.00 | 300.00 |
| | 1868 CE | — | 30.00 | 40.00 | 75.00 | 150.00 |
| | 1869 CE | — | 30.00 | 40.00 | 75.00 | 175.00 |
| | 1870 CE | — | 35.00 | 50.00 | 90.00 | 200.00 |
| | 1873 MP | — | 50.00 | 100.00 | 150.00 | 300.00 |
| | 1874C MP | — | 20.00 | 30.00 | 45.00 | 100.00 |
| | 1874CN MP | — | 125.00 | 200.00 | 300.00 | 600.00 |
| | 1875 MP | — | 12.00 | 15.00 | 20.00 | 75.00 |
| | 1876 GP | — | 12.00 | 15.00 | 30.00 | 90.00 |
| | 1876 CG | — | 12.00 | 15.00 | 20.00 | 75.00 |
| | 1877 CG | .339 | 12.00 | 15.00 | 20.00 | 75.00 |
| | 1877 Gn CG (error) | | | | | |
| | | — | 65.00 | 125.00 | 200.00 | 400.00 |
| | 1877 JA | I.A. | 35.00 | 75.00 | 125.00 | 250.00 |
| | 1878/7 CG | .483 | 35.00 | 75.00 | 125.00 | 250.00 |
| | 1878 CG | I.A. | 15.00 | 25.00 | 35.00 | 125.00 |

| KM# | Date | Mintage | Fine | VF | XF | Unc |
|---|---|---|---|---|---|---|
| 377.3 | 1878 JD | I.A. | 15.00 | 20.00 | 30.00 | 125.00 |
| | 1878 JD D/retrograde D | | | | | |
| | | I.A. | 20.00 | 30.00 | 40.00 | 150.00 |
| | 1879 JD | — | 12.00 | 15.00 | 30.00 | 90.00 |
| | 1880/70 JD | — | 15.00 | 20.00 | 30.00 | 90.00 |
| | 1880 JD | — | 12.00 | 15.00 | 20.00 | 75.00 |
| | 1881/0 JD | | | | | |
| | | 1.032 | 15.00 | 20.00 | 30.00 | 90.00 |
| | 1881C JD | I.A. | 12.00 | 15.00 | 20.00 | 75.00 |
| | 1881CnJD | I.A. | 40.00 | 60.00 | 90.00 | 150.00 |
| | 1882 JD | .397 | 12.00 | 15.00 | 20.00 | 75.00 |
| | 1882 AM | I.A. | 12.00 | 15.00 | 20.00 | 75.00 |
| | 1883 AM | .333 | 12.00 | 15.00 | 20.00 | 125.00 |
| | 1884 AM | — | 12.00 | 15.00 | 20.00 | 75.00 |
| | 1885/6 AM | .227 | 20.00 | 30.00 | 45.00 | 100.00 |
| | 1885C AM | I.A. | 75.00 | 125.00 | 250.00 | 500.00 |
| | 1885CnAM | I.A. | 12.00 | 15.00 | 20.00 | 75.00 |
| | 1885GnAM (error) | | | | | |
| | | Inc. Ab. | 60.00 | 100.00 | 150.00 | 300.00 |
| | 1886 AM | .571 | 12.00 | 15.00 | 20.00 | 75.00 |
| | 1887 AM | .732 | 12.00 | 15.00 | 20.00 | 75.00 |
| | 1888 AM | .768 | 12.00 | 15.00 | 20.00 | 75.00 |
| | 1889 AM | 1.075 | 12.00 | 15.00 | 20.00 | 75.00 |
| | 1890 AM | .874 | 10.00 | 12.00 | 18.00 | 60.00 |
| | 1891 AM | .777 | 10.00 | 12.00 | 18.00 | 60.00 |
| | 1892 AM | .681 | 10.00 | 12.00 | 18.00 | 60.00 |
| | 1893 AM | 1.144 | 10.00 | 12.00 | 18.00 | 60.00 |
| | 1894 AM | 2.118 | 10.00 | 12.00 | 18.00 | 60.00 |
| | 1895 AM | 1.834 | 10.00 | 12.00 | 18.00 | 60.00 |
| | 1896 AM | 2.134 | 10.00 | 12.00 | 18.00 | 60.00 |
| | 1897 AM | 1.580 | 10.00 | 12.00 | 18.00 | 60.00 |

NOTE: Varieties exist.

### Mint mark: Do

| KM# | Date | Mintage | Fine | VF | XF | Unc |
|---|---|---|---|---|---|---|
| 377.4 | 1825 RL | — | 30.00 | 55.00 | 85.00 | 175.00 |
| | 1826 RL | — | 40.00 | 100.00 | 250.00 | 500.00 |
| | 1827/6 RL | — | 35.00 | 60.00 | 80.00 | 175.00 |
| | 1827 RL | — | 30.00 | 50.00 | 75.00 | 150.00 |
| | 1828/7 RL | — | 35.00 | 60.00 | 80.00 | 175.00 |
| | 1828 RL | — | 25.00 | 50.00 | 75.00 | 150.00 |
| | 1829 RL | — | 25.00 | 50.00 | 75.00 | 150.00 |
| | 1830 RM B on eagles claw | | | | | |
| | | — | 25.00 | 50.00 | 75.00 | 150.00 |
| | 1831 RM B on eagles claw | | | | | |
| | | — | 20.00 | 30.00 | 50.00 | 125.00 |
| | 1832 RM Mexican dies, B on eagles claw | | | | | |
| | | — | 25.00 | 50.00 | 100.00 | 200.00 |
| | 1832/1 RM/RL French dies | | | | | |
| | | — | 25.00 | 35.00 | 75.00 | 150.00 |
| | 1833/2 RM/RL | | | | | |
| | | — | 20.00 | 35.00 | 75.00 | 150.00 |
| | 1833 RM | — | 15.00 | 30.00 | 50.00 | 125.00 |
| | 1834/3/2 RM/RL | | | | | |
| | | — | 20.00 | 35.00 | 75.00 | 150.00 |
| | 1834 RM | — | 15.00 | 25.00 | 45.00 | 100.00 |
| | 1835/4 RM/RL | | | | | |
| | | — | 25.00 | 40.00 | 80.00 | 150.00 |
| | 1835 RM | — | 20.00 | 35.00 | 55.00 | 125.00 |
| | 1836/1 RM | — | 20.00 | 30.00 | 50.00 | 125.00 |
| | 1836/4 RM | — | 20.00 | 30.00 | 50.00 | 125.00 |
| | 1836/5/4 RM/RL | | | | | |
| | | — | 75.00 | 150.00 | 250.00 | 500.00 |
| | 1836 RM | — | 20.00 | 30.00 | 50.00 | 125.00 |
| | 1836 RM M on snake | | | | | |
| | | — | 20.00 | 30.00 | 50.00 | 125.00 |
| | 1837/1 RM | — | 20.00 | 30.00 | 50.00 | 125.00 |
| | 1837 RM | — | 20.00 | 30.00 | 50.00 | 125.00 |

| KM# | Date Mintage | Fine | VF | XF | Unc |
|---|---|---|---|---|---|
| 377.4 | 1838/1 RM | — | 20.00 | 30.00 | 50.00 | 125.00 |
| | 1838/7 RM | — | 20.00 | 30.00 | 50.00 | 125.00 |
| | 1838 RM | — | 20.00 | 30.00 | 50.00 | 125.00 |
| | 1839/1 RM/RL | — | 20.00 | 30.00 | 50.00 | 125.00 |
| | 1839/1 RM | — | 20.00 | 30.00 | 50.00 | 125.00 |
| | 1839 RM | — | 20.00 | 30.00 | 50.00 | 125.00 |
| | 1840/38/31 RM | — | 20.00 | 30.00 | 50.00 | 125.00 |
| | 1840/39 RM | — | 20.00 | 30.00 | 50.00 | 125.00 |
| | 1840 RM | — | 20.00 | 30.00 | 50.00 | 125.00 |
| | 1841/31 RM | — | 25.00 | 50.00 | 75.00 | 175.00 |
| | 1842/31 RM B below cactus | — | 125.00 | 250.00 | 400.00 | 750.00 |
| | 1842/31 RM | — | 40.00 | 80.00 | 125.00 | 250.00 |
| | 1842/32 RM | — | 40.00 | 80.00 | 125.00 | 250.00 |
| | 1842 RM eagle of 1832-41 | — | 20.00 | 30.00 | 50.00 | 125.00 |
| | 1842 RM pre 1832 eagle resumed | — | 20.00 | 30.00 | 50.00 | 125.00 |
| | 1842 RM | — | 40.00 | 80.00 | 125.00 | 250.00 |
| | 1843/33 RM | — | 50.00 | 90.00 | 150.00 | 250.00 |
| | 1844/34 RM | — | 100.00 | 200.00 | 300.00 | 500.00 |
| | 1844/35 RM | — | 100.00 | 200.00 | 300.00 | 500.00 |
| | 1845/31 RM | — | 35.00 | 75.00 | 125.00 | 250.00 |
| | 1845/34 RM | — | 35.00 | 75.00 | 125.00 | 250.00 |
| | 1845/35 RM | — | 35.00 | 75.00 | 125.00 | 250.00 |
| | 1845 RM | — | 20.00 | 30.00 | 50.00 | 125.00 |
| | 1846/31 RM | — | 20.00 | 30.00 | 50.00 | 125.00 |
| | 1846/36 RM | — | 20.00 | 30.00 | 50.00 | 125.00 |
| | 1846 RM | — | 20.00 | 30.00 | 50.00 | 125.00 |
| | 1847 RM | — | 25.00 | 50.00 | 75.00 | 150.00 |
| | 1848/7 RM | — | 125.00 | 250.00 | 400.00 | 750.00 |
| | 1848/7 CM/RM | — | 100.00 | 200.00 | 350.00 | 700.00 |
| | 1848 CM/RM | — | 100.00 | 200.00 | 350.00 | 700.00 |
| | 1848 RM | — | 100.00 | 200.00 | 300.00 | 600.00 |
| | 1848 CM | — | 50.00 | 100.00 | 200.00 | 400.00 |
| | 1849/39 CM | — | 100.00 | 200.00 | 350.00 | 700.00 |
| | 1849 CM | — | 100.00 | 200.00 | 350.00 | 700.00 |
| | 1849 JMR/CM oval 0 | — | 200.00 | 325.00 | 450.00 | 800.00 |
| | 1849 DoJMR oval O | — | 200.00 | 400.00 | 600.00 | 1000. |
| | 1849 DoJMR round O | — | 200.00 | 400.00 | 600.00 | 1000. |
| | 1850 JMR | — | 100.00 | 150.00 | 250.00 | 500.00 |
| | 1851/0 JMR | — | 100.00 | 150.00 | 250.00 | 500.00 |
| | 1851 JMR | — | 100.00 | 150.00 | 250.00 | 500.00 |
| | 1852 CP/JMR | — | — | — | Rare | — |
| | 1852 CP | — | — | — | Rare | — |
| | 1852 JMR | — | 175.00 | 250.00 | 375.00 | 550.00 |
| | 1853 CP/JMR | — | 175.00 | 275.00 | 400.00 | 700.00 |
| | 1853 CP | — | 200.00 | 350.00 | 600.00 | 1200. |
| | 1854 CP | — | 25.00 | 35.00 | 65.00 | 300.00 |
| | 1855 CP eagle type of 1854 | — | 50.00 | 100.00 | 175.00 | 350.00 |
| | 1855 CP eagle type of 1856 | — | 50.00 | 100.00 | 175.00 | 350.00 |
| | 1856 CP | — | 50.00 | 100.00 | 175.00 | 350.00 |
| | 1857 CP | — | 35.00 | 75.00 | 175.00 | 350.00 |
| | 1858/7 CP | — | 25.00 | 35.00 | 70.00 | 150.00 |
| | 1858 CP | — | 20.00 | 30.00 | 60.00 | 150.00 |
| | 1859 CP | — | 20.00 | 30.00 | 60.00 | 150.00 |
| | 1860/59 CP | — | 30.00 | 50.00 | 100.00 | 200.00 |
| | 1860 CP | — | 20.00 | 30.00 | 60.00 | 150.00 |
| | 1861/0 CP | — | 30.00 | 50.00 | 100.00 | 200.00 |
| | 1861 CP | — | 20.00 | 30.00 | 50.00 | 125.00 |
| | 1862/1 CP | — | 25.00 | 35.00 | 60.00 | 125.00 |
| | 1862 CP | — | 20.00 | 30.00 | 55.00 | 100.00 |
| | 1863/2 CP | — | 25.00 | 50.00 | 75.00 | 175.00 |
| | 1863/53 CP | — | 30.00 | 60.00 | 90.00 | 200.00 |
| | 1863 CP | — | 25.00 | 50.00 | 75.00 | 175.00 |
| | 1864 CP | — | 100.00 | 150.00 | 250.00 | 500.00 |
| | 1864 LT | — | 25.00 | 40.00 | 80.00 | 175.00 |
| | 1865 LT | — | — | — | Rare | — |
| | 1866 CM | — | — | — | Rare | — |
| | 1867 CM | — | — | — | Rare | — |
| | 1867/6 CP | — | 200.00 | 400.00 | 600.00 | 1200. |
| | 1867 CP | — | 175.00 | 300.00 | 500.00 | 1000. |
| | 1867 CP/CM | — | 175.00 | 300.00 | 500.00 | 1000. |
| | 1867 CP/LT | — | 175.00 | 300.00 | 500.00 | 1000. |

| KM# | Date Mintage | Fine | VF | XF | Unc |
|---|---|---|---|---|---|
| 377.4 | 1868 CP | — | 25.00 | 40.00 | 80.00 | 175.00 |
| | 1869 CP | — | 20.00 | 30.00 | 50.00 | 125.00 |
| | 1870/69 CP | — | 20.00 | 30.00 | 50.00 | 125.00 |
| | 1870/9 CP | — | 20.00 | 30.00 | 50.00 | 125.00 |
| | 1870 CP | — | 20.00 | 30.00 | 50.00 | 125.00 |
| | 1873 CP | — | 125.00 | 225.00 | 325.00 | 600.00 |
| | 1873 CM | — | 30.00 | 50.00 | 100.00 | 200.00 |
| | 1874/3 CM | — | 12.00 | 15.00 | 20.00 | 100.00 |
| | 1874 CM | — | 10.00 | 15.00 | 20.00 | 60.00 |
| | 1874 JH | — | — | — | Rare | — |
| | 1875 CM | — | 10.00 | 15.00 | 20.00 | 75.00 |
| | 1875 JH | — | 100.00 | 175.00 | 275.00 | 500.00 |
| | 1876 CM | — | 10.00 | 15.00 | 20.00 | 75.00 |
| | 1877 CM | .431 | — | — | Rare | — |
| | 1877 CP | I.A. | 10.00 | 15.00 | 20.00 | 75.00 |
| | 1877 JMP | I.A. | — | — | Rare | — |
| | 1878 PE | .409 | 15.00 | 25.00 | 40.00 | 90.00 |
| | 1878 TB | I.A. | 10.00 | 15.00 | 20.00 | 75.00 |
| | 1879 TB | — | 10.00 | 15.00 | 20.00 | 75.00 |
| | 1880/70 TB | — | 150.00 | 250.00 | 375.00 | 650.00 |
| | 1880/70 TB/JP | — | 150.00 | 250.00 | 375.00 | 650.00 |
| | 1880/70 JP | — | 15.00 | 25.00 | 40.00 | 90.00 |
| | 1880 TB | — | 150.00 | 250.00 | 375.00 | 650.00 |
| | 1880 JP | — | 10.00 | 15.00 | 20.00 | 75.00 |
| | 1881 JP | .928 | 10.00 | 15.00 | 20.00 | 75.00 |
| | 1882 JP | .414 | 10.00 | 15.00 | 20.00 | 75.00 |
| | 1882 MC/JP | Inc. Ab. | 30.00 | 60.00 | 100.00 | 200.00 |
| | 1882 MC | I.A. | 25.00 | 50.00 | 75.00 | 150.00 |
| | 1883/73 MC | .452 | 15.00 | 25.00 | 40.00 | 90.00 |
| | 1883 MC | I.A. | 10.00 | 15.00 | 20.00 | 75.00 |
| | 1884/3 MC | — | 20.00 | 30.00 | 60.00 | 110.00 |
| | 1884 MC | — | 10.00 | 15.00 | 20.00 | 75.00 |
| | 1885 MC | .547 | 10.00 | 12.00 | 18.00 | 65.00 |
| | 1885 JB | I.A. | 25.00 | 35.00 | 50.00 | 125.00 |
| | 1886/3 MC | .955 | 15.00 | 25.00 | 40.00 | 90.00 |
| | 1886 MC | I.A. | 10.00 | 12.00 | 18.00 | 65.00 |
| | 1887 MC | 1.004 | 10.00 | 12.00 | 18.00 | 65.00 |
| | 1888 MC | .996 | 10.00 | 12.00 | 18.00 | 65.00 |
| | 1889 MC | .874 | 10.00 | 12.00 | 18.00 | 65.00 |
| | 1890 MC | 1.119 | 10.00 | 12.00 | 18.00 | 65.00 |
| | 1890 JP | I.A. | 10.00 | 12.00 | 18.00 | 65.00 |
| | 1891 JP | 1.487 | 10.00 | 12.00 | 18.00 | 65.00 |
| | 1892 JP | 1.597 | 10.00 | 12.00 | 18.00 | 65.00 |
| | 1892 ND | I.A. | 25.00 | 50.00 | 100.00 | 200.00 |
| | 1893 ND | 1.617 | 10.00 | 12.00 | 18.00 | 65.00 |
| | 1894 ND | 1.537 | 10.00 | 12.00 | 18.00 | 65.00 |
| | 1895/3 ND | .761 | 15.00 | 25.00 | 40.00 | 90.00 |
| | 1895 ND | I.A. | 10.00 | 12.00 | 18.00 | 65.00 |

NOTE: Varieties exist.

**Mint mark: EoMo**

| KM# | Date Mintage | Fine | VF | XF | Unc |
|---|---|---|---|---|---|
| 377.5 | 1828 LF/LP | — | 500.00 | 1000. | 2500. | — |
| | 1828 LF | — | 500.00 | 1000. | 2500. | — |
| | 1829 LF | — | 400.00 | 800.00 | 1500. | — |
| | 1830/20 LF | — | — | — | Rare | — |
| | 1830 LF | — | 1000. | 2000. | 3000. | — |

**Mint mark: Ga**

| KM# | Date | Mintage | Fine | VF | XF | Unc |
|---|---|---|---|---|---|---|
| 377.6 | 1825 FS | — | 150.00 | 275.00 | 425.00 | 850.00 |
| | 1826/5 FS | — | 125.00 | 250.00 | 400.00 | 800.00 |
| | 1827/87 FS | — | 125.00 | 250.00 | 400.00 | 800.00 |
| | 1827 FS | — | 225.00 | 350.00 | 500.00 | 1000. |
| | 1287 FS (error) | 8500. | — | — | — | — |
| | 1828 FS | — | 200.00 | 375.00 | 550.00 | 1100. |
| | 1829/8 FS | — | 200.00 | 375.00 | 550.00 | 1100. |
| | 1829 FS | — | 175.00 | 325.00 | 475.00 | 950.00 |
| | 1830/29 FS | — | 175.00 | 300.00 | 450.00 | 900.00 |
| | 1830 FS | — | 100.00 | 175.00 | 300.00 | 600.00 |
| | 1830 LP/FS | — | — | — | Rare | — |
| | 1831 LP | — | 200.00 | 400.00 | 600.00 | 1200. |
| | 1831 FS/LP | — | 300.00 | 500.00 | 750.00 | 1500. |
| | 1831 FS | — | — | — | — | — |
| | 1832/1 FS | — | 50.00 | 100.00 | 175.00 | 300.00 |
| | 1832/1 FS/LP | — | 60.00 | 125.00 | 200.00 | 350.00 |
| | 1832 FS | — | 25.00 | 50.00 | 100.00 | 200.00 |
| | 1833/2/1 FS/LP | — | 45.00 | 75.00 | 125.00 | 250.00 |
| | 1833/2 FS | — | 25.00 | 50.00 | 100.00 | 200.00 |
| | 1834/2 FS | — | 60.00 | 125.00 | 200.00 | 350.00 |
| | 1834/3 FS | — | 60.00 | 125.00 | 200.00 | 350.00 |
| | 1834/0 FS | — | 60.00 | 125.00 | 200.00 | 350.00 |
| | 1834 FS | — | 50.00 | 100.00 | 150.00 | 300.00 |
| | 1835 FS | — | 25.00 | 50.00 | 100.00 | 200.00 |
| | 1836/1 JG/FS | — | 40.00 | 80.00 | 125.00 | 250.00 |
| | 1836 FS | — | — | — | Rare | — |
| | 1836 JG/FS | — | 25.00 | 50.00 | 100.00 | 200.00 |
| | 1836 JG | — | 25.00 | 50.00 | 100.00 | 200.00 |
| | 1837/6 JG/FS | — | 50.00 | 100.00 | 175.00 | 300.00 |
| | 1837 JG | — | 40.00 | 80.00 | 125.00 | 250.00 |
| | 1838/7 JG | — | 100.00 | 175.00 | 300.00 | 550.00 |
| | 1838 JG | — | 100.00 | 150.00 | 275.00 | 500.00 |
| | 1839 MC | — | 100.00 | 200.00 | 300.00 | 550.00 |
| | 1839 MC/JG | — | 100.00 | 200.00 | 300.00 | 550.00 |
| | 1839 JG | — | 60.00 | 125.00 | 200.00 | 350.00 |
| | 1840/30 MC | — | 50.00 | 75.00 | 150.00 | 275.00 |
| | 1840 MC | — | 30.00 | 60.00 | 125.00 | 250.00 |
| | 1841 MC | — | 30.00 | 60.00 | 125.00 | 250.00 |
| | 1842/1 JG/MG | — | 100.00 | 150.00 | 250.00 | 450.00 |
| | 1842/1 JG/MC | — | 100.00 | 150.00 | 250.00 | 450.00 |
| | 1842 JG | — | 25.00 | 50.00 | 100.00 | 200.00 |
| | 1842 JG/MG | — | 25.00 | 50.00 | 100.00 | 200.00 |
| | 1843/2 MC/JG | — | 25.00 | 50.00 | 100.00 | 200.00 |
| | 1843 MC/JG | — | 25.00 | 50.00 | 100.00 | 200.00 |
| | 1843 JG | — | 400.00 | 600.00 | 800.00 | 1500. |
| | 1843 MC | — | 50.00 | 100.00 | 150.00 | 300.00 |
| | 1844 MC | — | 50.00 | 100.00 | 150.00 | 300.00 |
| | 1845 MC | — | 75.00 | 150.00 | 250.00 | 450.00 |
| | 1845 JG | — | 600.00 | 1000. | 1500. | — |
| | 1846 JG | — | 40.00 | 80.00 | 150.00 | 300.00 |
| | 1847 JG | — | 100.00 | 150.00 | 225.00 | 400.00 |
| | 1848/7 JG | — | 55.00 | 85.00 | 125.00 | 250.00 |
| | 1848 JG | — | 50.00 | 75.00 | 100.00 | 200.00 |
| | 1849 JG | — | 90.00 | 125.00 | 175.00 | 300.00 |
| | 1850 JG | — | 50.00 | 100.00 | 150.00 | 300.00 |
| | 1851 JG | — | 125.00 | 200.00 | 350.00 | 650.00 |
| | 1852 JG | — | 100.00 | 150.00 | 250.00 | 450.00 |
| | 1853/2 JG | — | 125.00 | 175.00 | 250.00 | 475.00 |
| | 1853 JG | — | 90.00 | 125.00 | 175.00 | 300.00 |
| | 1854/3 JG | — | 65.00 | 90.00 | 125.00 | 250.00 |

| KM# | Date | Mintage | Fine | VF | XF | Unc |
|---|---|---|---|---|---|---|
| 377.6 | 1854 JG | — | 50.00 | 75.00 | 125.00 | 250.00 |
| | 1855/4 JG | — | 50.00 | 100.00 | 150.00 | 275.00 |
| | 1855 JG | — | 25.00 | 50.00 | 100.00 | 200.00 |
| | 1856/4 JG | — | 60.00 | 125.00 | 175.00 | 300.00 |
| | 1856/5 56 | — | 60.00 | 125.00 | 175.00 | 300.00 |
| | 1856 JG | — | 50.00 | 100.00 | 150.00 | 275.00 |
| | 1857 JG | — | 50.00 | 100.00 | 225.00 | 400.00 |
| | 1858 JG | — | 100.00 | 150.00 | 300.00 | 500.00 |
| | 1859/7 JG | — | 25.00 | 50.00 | 100.00 | 175.00 |
| | 1859/8 JG | — | 25.00 | 50.00 | 100.00 | 175.00 |
| | 1859 JG | — | 20.00 | 40.00 | 80.00 | 125.00 |
| | 1860 JG w/o dot | — | 400.00 | 800.00 | 1200. | 2000. |
| | 1860 JG dot in loop of eagles tail (base alloy) | — | — | — | Rare | — |
| | 1861 JG | — | — | — | Rare | — |
| | 1862 JG | — | — | — | Rare | — |
| | 1863/52 JG | — | — | — | — | — |
| | 1863/59 JG | — | 45.00 | 50.00 | 85.00 | 135.00 |
| | 1863/2 JG | — | 30.00 | 50.00 | 90.00 | 175.00 |
| | 1863/4 JG | — | 40.00 | 60.00 | 125.00 | 200.00 |
| | 1863 JG | — | 25.00 | 45.00 | 75.00 | 150.00 |
| | 1863 FV | — | — | — | Rare | — |
| | 1867 JM | — | — | — | Rare | — |
| | 1868/7 JM | — | 50.00 | 75.00 | 125.00 | 200.00 |
| | 1868 JM | — | 50.00 | 75.00 | 125.00 | 200.00 |
| | 1869 JM | — | 50.00 | 75.00 | 125.00 | 200.00 |
| | 1869 IC | — | 75.00 | 125.00 | 200.00 | 375.00 |
| | 1870/60 IC | — | 60.00 | 90.00 | 150.00 | 275.00 |
| | 1870 IC | — | 60.00 | 90.00 | 150.00 | 275.00 |
| | 1873 IC | — | 15.00 | 25.00 | 50.00 | 125.00 |
| | 1874 IC | — | 10.00 | 15.00 | 20.00 | 85.00 |
| | 1874 MC | — | 25.00 | 50.00 | 100.00 | 200.00 |
| | 1875 IC | — | 15.00 | 30.00 | 60.00 | 125.00 |
| | 1875 MC | — | 10.00 | 15.00 | 20.00 | 85.00 |
| | 1876 IC | .559 | 15.00 | 30.00 | 50.00 | 100.00 |
| | 1876 MC | I.A. | 125.00 | 175.00 | 250.00 | 375.00 |
| | 1877 IC | .928 | 10.00 | 15.00 | 20.00 | 85.00 |
| | 1877 JA | I.A. | 10.00 | 15.00 | 20.00 | 85.00 |
| | 1878 JA | .764 | 10.00 | 15.00 | 20.00 | 85.00 |
| | 1879 JA | — | 10.00 | 15.00 | 20.00 | 85.00 |
| | 1880/70 FS | — | 15.00 | 25.00 | 50.00 | 125.00 |
| | 1880 JA | — | 10.00 | 15.00 | 20.00 | 85.00 |
| | 1880 FS | — | 10.00 | 15.00 | 20.00 | 85.00 |
| | 1881 FS | 1.300 | 10.00 | 15.00 | 20.00 | 85.00 |
| | 1882/1 FS | .537 | 15.00 | 25.00 | 50.00 | 125.00 |
| | 1882 FS | I.A. | 10.00 | 15.00 | 20.00 | 85.00 |
| | 1882 TB/FS | I.A. | 75.00 | 150.00 | 250.00 | 450.00 |
| | 1882 TB | I.A. | 50.00 | 100.00 | 175.00 | 300.00 |
| | 1883 TB | .561 | 15.00 | 25.00 | 40.00 | 125.00 |
| | 1884 TB | — | 10.00 | 12.00 | 18.00 | 85.00 |
| | 1884 AH | — | 10.00 | 12.00 | 18.00 | 85.00 |
| | 1885 AH | .443 | 10.00 | 12.00 | 18.00 | 85.00 |
| | 1885 JS | I.A. | 30.00 | 60.00 | 100.00 | 200.00 |
| | 1886 JS | 1.039 | 10.00 | 12.00 | 18.00 | 85.00 |
| | 1887 JS | .878 | 10.00 | 12.00 | 18.00 | 85.00 |
| | 1888 JS | 1.159 | 10.00 | 12.00 | 18.00 | 85.00 |
| | 1889 JS | 1.583 | 10.00 | 12.00 | 18.00 | 85.00 |
| | 1890 JS | 1.658 | 10.00 | 12.00 | 18.00 | 85.00 |
| | 1891 JS | 1.507 | 10.00 | 12.00 | 18.00 | 85.00 |
| | 1892/1 JS | 1.627 | 15.00 | 25.00 | 50.00 | 125.00 |
| | 1892 JS | I.A. | 10.00 | 12.00 | 18.00 | 75.00 |
| | 1893 JS | 1.952 | 10.00 | 12.00 | 18.00 | 75.00 |
| | 1894 JS | 2.046 | 10.00 | 12.00 | 18.00 | 75.00 |
| | 1895 JS | 1.146 | 10.00 | 12.00 | 18.00 | 60.00 |

NOTE: Varieties exist. The 1830 LP/FS is currently only known with a Philippine countermark.

### Mint mark: GC

| KM# | Date | Mintage | Fine | VF | XF | Unc |
|---|---|---|---|---|---|---|
| 377.7 | 1844 MP | — | 350.00 | 500.00 | 1000. | 2000. |
| | 1844 MP (error) reversed S in Ds, Gs | | | | | |
| | | — | 400.00 | 600.00 | 1200. | 2250. |
| | 1845 MP eagle's tail square | | | | | |
| | | — | 125.00 | 225.00 | 300.00 | 600.00 |
| | 1845 MP eagle's tail round | | | | | |
| | | — | 225.00 | 450.00 | 650.00 | 1200. |
| | 1846 MP eagle's tail square | | | | | |
| | | — | 100.00 | 150.00 | 350.00 | 750.00 |
| | 1846 MP eagle's tail round | | | | | |
| | | — | 100.00 | 150.00 | 350.00 | 750.00 |
| | 1847 MP | — | 150.00 | 250.00 | 400.00 | 800.00 |
| | 1848 MP | — | 175.00 | 300.00 | 500.00 | 900.00 |
| | 1849 MP | — | 175.00 | 300.00 | 525.00 | 1000. |
| | 1850 MP | — | 175.00 | 300.00 | 575.00 | 1100. |
| | 1851 MP | — | 400.00 | 600.00 | 900.00 | 1600. |
| | 1852 MP | — | 500.00 | 800.00 | 1250. | 2250. |

### Mint mark: Go

| KM# | Date | Mintage | Fine | VF | XF | Unc |
|---|---|---|---|---|---|---|
| 377.8 | 1825 JJ | — | 40.00 | 70.00 | 150.00 | 300.00 |
| | 1826 JJ straight J's | | | | | |
| | | — | 40.00 | 80.00 | 175.00 | 350.00 |
| | 1826 JJ full J's | | | | | |
| | | — | 30.00 | 60.00 | 125.00 | 250.00 |
| | 1826 MJ | — | — | — | Rare | — |
| | 1827 MJ | — | 40.00 | 75.00 | 125.00 | 250.00 |
| | 1827 MJ/JJ | — | 40.00 | 75.00 | 125.00 | 250.00 |
| | 1827 MR | — | 100.00 | 200.00 | 350.00 | 600.00 |
| | 1828 MJ | — | 30.00 | 60.00 | 125.00 | 250.00 |
| | 1828/7 MR | — | 200.00 | 400.00 | 600.00 | 1200. |
| | 1828 MR | — | 200.00 | 400.00 | 600.00 | 1200. |
| | 1829 MJ | — | 20.00 | 35.00 | 55.00 | 150.00 |
| | 1830 MJ oblong beading and narrow J | | | | | |
| | | — | 20.00 | 30.00 | 55.00 | 150.00 |
| | 1830 MJ regular beading and wide J | | | | | |
| | | — | 20.00 | 30.00 | 55.00 | 150.00 |
| | 1831 MJ colon after date | | | | | |
| | | — | 12.00 | 20.00 | 30.00 | 100.00 |
| | 1831 MJ 2 stars after date | | | | | |
| | | — | 12.00 | 20.00 | 30.00 | 100.00 |
| | 1832 MJ | — | 12.00 | 20.00 | 30.00 | 100.00 |
| | 1832 MJ 1 of date over inverted 1 | | | | | |
| | | — | 20.00 | 35.00 | 65.00 | 125.00 |
| | 1833 MJ | — | 12.00 | 20.00 | 30.00 | 100.00 |
| | 1833 JM | — | 1000. | 1500. | 2000. | 2500. |
| | 1834 PJ | — | 12.00 | 20.00 | 30.00 | 100.00 |
| | 1835 PJ star on cap | | | | | |
| | | — | 12.00 | 20.00 | 30.00 | 100.00 |
| | 1835 PJ dot on cap | | | | | |
| | | — | 12.00 | 20.00 | 30.00 | 100.00 |
| | 1836 PJ | — | 12.00 | 20.00 | 30.00 | 100.00 |
| | 1837 PJ | — | 12.00 | 20.00 | 30.00 | 100.00 |
| | 1838 PJ | — | 12.00 | 20.00 | 30.00 | 100.00 |
| | 1839 PJ/JJ | — | 12.00 | 20.00 | 30.00 | 100.00 |
| | 1839 PJ | — | 12.00 | 20.00 | 30.00 | 100.00 |
| | 1840/30 PJ | — | 20.00 | 30.00 | 50.00 | 150.00 |
| | 1840 PJ | — | 12.00 | 20.00 | 30.00 | 125.00 |
| | 1841/31 PJ | — | 12.00 | 20.00 | 30.00 | 100.00 |
| | 1841 PJ | — | 12.00 | 20.00 | 30.00 | 100.00 |
| | 1842/31 PM/PJ | | | | | |
| | | — | 25.00 | 35.00 | 60.00 | 150.00 |
| | 1842 PJ | — | 20.00 | 30.00 | 50.00 | 125.00 |
| | 1842 PM/PJ | — | 12.00 | 20.00 | 30.00 | 100.00 |
| | 1842 PM | — | 12.00 | 20.00 | 30.00 | 100.00 |
| | 1843 PM dot after date | | | | | |
| | | — | 12.00 | 20.00 | 30.00 | 100.00 |

| KM# | Date | Mintage | Fine | VF | XF | Unc |
|---|---|---|---|---|---|---|
| 377.8 | 1843 PM triangle of dots after date | | | | | |
| | | — | 12.00 | 20.00 | 30.00 | 100.00 |
| | 1844 PM | — | 12.00 | 20.00 | 30.00 | 100.00 |
| | 1845 PM | — | 12.00 | 20.00 | 30.00 | 100.00 |
| | 1846/5 PM eagle type of 1845 | | | | | |
| | | — | 20.00 | 30.00 | 50.00 | 150.00 |
| | 1846 PM early type of 1847 | | | | | |
| | | — | 15.00 | 25.00 | 35.00 | 125.00 |
| | 1847 PM | — | 12.00 | 20.00 | 30.00 | 75.00 |
| | 1847/7 PM | — | 20.00 | 35.00 | 65.00 | 150.00 |
| | 1848 PM | — | 20.00 | 35.00 | 65.00 | 150.00 |
| | 1848 PF | — | 12.00 | 20.00 | 30.00 | 75.00 |
| | 1849 PF | — | 12.00 | 20.00 | 30.00 | 75.00 |
| | 1850 PF | — | 12.00 | 20.00 | 30.00 | 75.00 |
| | 1851/0 PF | — | 20.00 | 30.00 | 50.00 | 100.00 |
| | 1851 PF | — | 12.00 | 20.00 | 30.00 | 75.00 |
| | 1852/1 PF | — | 20.00 | 30.00 | 50.00 | 100.00 |
| | 1852 PF | — | 12.00 | 20.00 | 30.00 | 75.00 |
| | 1853/2 PF | — | 20.00 | 30.00 | 50.00 | 100.00 |
| | 1853 PF | — | 12.00 | 20.00 | 30.00 | 75.00 |
| | 1854 PF | — | 12.00 | 20.00 | 30.00 | 75.00 |
| | 1855 PF large letters | | | | | |
| | | — | 12.00 | 20.00 | 30.00 | 75.00 |
| | 1855 PF small letters | | | | | |
| | | — | 12.00 | 20.00 | 30.00 | 75.00 |
| | 1856/5 PF | — | 20.00 | 30.00 | 50.00 | 100.00 |
| | 1856 PF | — | 12.00 | 20.00 | 30.00 | 75.00 |
| | 1857/5 PF | — | 20.00 | 30.00 | 50.00 | 100.00 |
| | 1857/6 PF | — | 20.00 | 30.00 | 50.00 | 100.00 |
| | 1857 PF | — | 12.00 | 20.00 | 30.00 | 75.00 |
| | 1858 PF | — | 12.00 | 20.00 | 30.00 | 75.00 |
| | 1859/7 PF | — | 20.00 | 30.00 | 50.00 | 100.00 |
| | 1859/8 PF | — | 20.00 | 30.00 | 50.00 | 100.00 |
| | 1859 PF | — | 12.00 | 20.00 | 30.00 | 75.00 |
| | 1860/50 PF | — | 20.00 | 30.00 | 50.00 | 100.00 |
| | 1860/59 PF | — | 12.00 | 18.00 | 25.00 | 85.00 |
| | 1860 PF | — | 12.00 | 15.00 | 20.00 | 75.00 |
| | 1861/51 PF | — | 15.00 | 20.00 | 30.00 | 100.00 |
| | 1861/0 PF | — | 12.00 | 15.00 | 20.00 | 75.00 |
| | 1861 PF | — | 12.00 | 15.00 | 20.00 | 75.00 |
| | 1862 YE/PF | — | 12.00 | 15.00 | 20.00 | 75.00 |
| | 1862 YE | — | 12.00 | 15.00 | 20.00 | 75.00 |
| | 1862 YF | — | 12.00 | 15.00 | 20.00 | 75.00 |
| | 1862 YF/PF | — | 12.00 | 15.00 | 20.00 | 75.00 |
| | 1863/53 YF | — | 12.00 | 18.00 | 25.00 | 75.00 |
| | 1863/54 YF | — | 15.00 | 20.00 | 30.00 | 100.00 |
| | 1863 YE | — | — | — | Rare | — |
| | 1863 YF | — | 12.00 | 15.00 | 20.00 | 75.00 |
| | 1867/57 YF | — | 15.00 | 20.00 | 30.00 | 100.00 |
| | 1867 YF | — | 12.00 | 15.00 | 20.00 | 75.00 |
| | 1868/58 YF | — | 15.00 | 20.00 | 30.00 | 100.00 |
| | 1868 YF | — | 12.00 | 15.00 | 20.00 | 75.00 |
| | 1870/60 FR | — | 20.00 | 30.00 | 50.00 | 150.00 |
| | 1870 YF | — | — | — | Rare | — |
| | 1870 FR/YF | — | 12.00 | 18.00 | 25.00 | 85.00 |
| | 1870 FR | — | 12.00 | 15.00 | 20.00 | 75.00 |
| | 1873 FR | — | 12.00 | 15.00 | 20.00 | 75.00 |
| | 1874/3 FR | — | 15.00 | 20.00 | 30.00 | 85.00 |
| | 1874 FR | — | 15.00 | 25.00 | 35.00 | 100.00 |
| | 1875/6 FR | — | 15.00 | 20.00 | 30.00 | 85.00 |
| | 1875 FR small circle w/dot on eagle | | | | | |
| | | — | 12.00 | 15.00 | 20.00 | 75.00 |
| | 1876/5 FR | — | 15.00 | 20.00 | 30.00 | 85.00 |
| | 1876 FR | — | 12.00 | 15.00 | 20.00 | 60.00 |
| | 1877 FR | 2.477 | 12.00 | 15.00 | 20.00 | 60.00 |
| | 1878/7 FR | | | | | |
| | | 2.273 | 15.00 | 20.00 | 30.00 | 75.00 |
| | 1878/7 SM | — | 15.00 | 20.00 | 30.00 | 75.00 |
| | 1878 FR | I.A. | 12.00 | 15.00 | 20.00 | 65.00 |
| | 1878 SM,S/F | — | 15.00 | 20.00 | 25.00 | 70.00 |
| | 1878 SM | — | 12.00 | 15.00 | 20.00 | 65.00 |
| | 1879/7 SM | — | 15.00 | 20.00 | 30.00 | 75.00 |
| | 1879/8 SM | — | 15.00 | 20.00 | 30.00 | 75.00 |
| | 1879/8 SM/FR | | | | | |
| | | — | 15.00 | 20.00 | 30.00 | 75.00 |
| | 1879 SM | — | 12.00 | 15.00 | 20.00 | 65.00 |
| | 1879 SM/FR | — | 15.00 | 20.00 | 30.00 | 75.00 |

| KM# | Date | Mintage | Fine | VF | XF | Unc |
|---|---|---|---|---|---|---|
| 377.8 | 1880/70 SB | — | 15.00 | 20.00 | 30.00 | 75.00 |
| | 1880 SB/SM | — | 12.00 | 15.00 | 20.00 | 65.00 |
| | 1881/71 SB | — | | | | |
| | | 3.974 | 15.00 | 20.00 | 30.00 | 75.00 |
| | 1881/0 SB | I.A. | 15.00 | 20.00 | 30.00 | 75.00 |
| | 1881 SB | I.A. | 12.00 | 15.00 | 20.00 | 65.00 |
| | 1882 SB | 2.015 | 12.00 | 15.00 | 20.00 | 75.00 |
| | 1883 SB | 2.100 | 35.00 | 75.00 | 125.00 | 250.00 |
| | 1883 BR | I.A. | 12.00 | 15.00 | 20.00 | 65.00 |
| | 1883 BR/SR | — | 12.00 | 15.00 | 20.00 | 65.00 |
| | 1883 BR/SB | | | | | |
| | | Inc. Ab. | 12.00 | 15.00 | 20.00 | 65.00 |
| | 1884/73 BR | — | 20.00 | 30.00 | 40.00 | 100.00 |
| | 1884/74 BR | — | 20.00 | 30.00 | 40.00 | 100.00 |
| | 1884/3 BR | — | 20.00 | 30.00 | 40.00 | 100.00 |
| | 1884 BR | — | 12.00 | 15.00 | 20.00 | 65.00 |
| | 1884/74 RR | — | 50.00 | 100.00 | 175.00 | 350.00 |
| | 1884 RR | — | 50.00 | 100.00 | 175.00 | 350.00 |
| | 1885/75 RR | | | | | |
| | | 2.363 | 15.00 | 20.00 | 30.00 | 75.00 |
| | 1885 RR | I.A. | 12.00 | 15.00 | 20.00 | 65.00 |
| | 1886/75 RR | | | | | |
| | | 4.127 | 15.00 | 20.00 | 25.00 | 70.00 |
| | 1886/76 RR | | | | | |
| | | Inc. Ab. | 12.00 | 15.00 | 20.00 | 65.00 |
| | 1886/5 RR/BR | | | | | |
| | | Inc. Ab. | 12.00 | 15.00 | 20.00 | 65.00 |
| | 1886 RR | I.A. | 12.00 | 15.00 | 20.00 | 65.00 |
| | 1887 RR | 4.205 | 10.00 | 15.00 | 20.00 | 65.00 |
| | 1888 RR | 3.985 | 10.00 | 15.00 | 20.00 | 65.00 |
| | 1889 RR | 3.646 | 10.00 | 15.00 | 20.00 | 65.00 |
| | 1890 RR | 3.615 | 10.00 | 15.00 | 20.00 | 65.00 |
| | 1891 RS | 3.197 | 10.00 | 15.00 | 20.00 | 65.00 |
| | 1891 RR | — | | Contemporary counterfeit | | |
| | 1892 RS | 3.672 | 10.00 | 15.00 | 20.00 | 65.00 |
| | 1893 RS | 3.854 | 10.00 | 15.00 | 20.00 | 65.00 |
| | 1894 RS | 4.127 | 10.00 | 15.00 | 20.00 | 65.00 |
| | 1895/1 RS | | | | | |
| | | 3.768 | 15.00 | 20.00 | 25.00 | 75.00 |
| | 1895/3 RS | I.A. | 15.00 | 20.00 | 25.00 | 75.00 |
| | 1895 RS | I.A. | 10.00 | 15.00 | 20.00 | 65.00 |
| | 1896/1 Go/As RS/ML | | | | | |
| | | 5.229 | 15.00 | 20.00 | 25.00 | 75.00 |
| | 1896/1 RS | I.A. | 12.00 | 15.00 | 20.00 | 65.00 |
| | 1896 Go/Ga RS | | | | | |
| | | Inc. Ab. | — | — | — | — |
| | 1896 RS | I.A. | 10.00 | 12.00 | 18.00 | 60.00 |
| | 1897 RS | 4.344 | 10.00 | 12.00 | 18.00 | 60.00 |

**NOTE:** Varieties exist.

| KM# | Date | Mintage | Fine | VF | XF | Unc |
|---|---|---|---|---|---|---|
| 377.9 | 1866 FM | — | — | — | Rare | — |
| | 1866 MP | — | — | — | Rare | — |
| | 1867 PR | — | 100.00 | 175.00 | 275.00 | 500.00 |
| | 1868 PR | — | 20.00 | 35.00 | 65.00 | 175.00 |
| | 1869 PR | — | 40.00 | 60.00 | 125.00 | 250.00 |
| | 1870 PR | — | 50.00 | 80.00 | 150.00 | 300.00 |
| | 1871/0 PR | — | 50.00 | 75.00 | 125.00 | 250.00 |
| | 1871 PR | — | 30.00 | 50.00 | 90.00 | 200.00 |
| | 1872/1 PR | — | 35.00 | 60.00 | 90.00 | 200.00 |
| | 1872 PR | — | 30.00 | 50.00 | 75.00 | 175.00 |
| | 1873 PR | .351 | 30.00 | 50.00 | 85.00 | 150.00 |
| | 1874 PR | — | 15.00 | 20.00 | 40.00 | 125.00 |
| | 1875 PR | — | 15.00 | 20.00 | 40.00 | 125.00 |
| | 1876 AF | — | 15.00 | 20.00 | 40.00 | 125.00 |
| | 1877 AF | .410 | 20.00 | 30.00 | 50.00 | 150.00 |
| | 1877 GR | I.A. | 100.00 | 150.00 | 225.00 | 400.00 |
| | 1877 JA | I.A. | 25.00 | 50.00 | 85.00 | 175.00 |
| | 1878 JA | .451 | 15.00 | 20.00 | 40.00 | 100.00 |
| | 1879 JA | — | 15.00 | 20.00 | 40.00 | 100.00 |
| | 1880 JA | — | 15.00 | 20.00 | 40.00 | 100.00 |
| | 1881 JA | .586 | 15.00 | 20.00 | 40.00 | 100.00 |
| | 1882 HoJA | O above H | | | | |
| | | .240 | 25.00 | 40.00 | 65.00 | 125.00 |
| | 1882 HoJA | O after H | | | | |
| | | I.A. | 25.00 | 40.00 | 65.00 | 125.00 |
| | 1883/2 JA | .204 | 225.00 | 375.00 | 550.00 | 1000. |
| | 1883/2 FM/JA | | | | | |
| | | I.A. | 25.00 | 40.00 | 75.00 | 150.00 |
| | 1883 FM | I.A. | 20.00 | 30.00 | 60.00 | 125.00 |
| | 1883 JA | I.A. | 200.00 | 350.00 | 500.00 | 1000. |
| | 1884/3 FM | — | 20.00 | 25.00 | 50.00 | 125.00 |
| | 1884 FM | — | 15.00 | 20.00 | 40.00 | 100.00 |
| | 1885 FM | .132 | 15.00 | 20.00 | 40.00 | 100.00 |
| | 1886 FM | .225 | 20.00 | 30.00 | 45.00 | 125.00 |
| | 1886 FG | I.A. | 20.00 | 30.00 | 45.00 | 125.00 |
| | 1887 FG | .150 | 20.00 | 35.00 | 65.00 | 150.00 |
| | 1888 FG | .364 | 12.00 | 18.00 | 25.00 | 100.00 |
| | 1889 FG | .490 | 12.00 | 18.00 | 25.00 | 100.00 |
| | 1890 FG | .565 | 12.00 | 18.00 | 25.00 | 100.00 |
| | 1891 FG | .738 | 12.00 | 18.00 | 25.00 | 100.00 |
| | 1892 FG | .643 | 12.00 | 18.00 | 25.00 | 100.00 |
| | 1893 FG | .518 | 12.00 | 18.00 | 25.00 | 100.00 |
| | 1894 FG | .504 | 12.00 | 18.00 | 25.00 | 100.00 |
| | 1895 FG | .320 | 12.00 | 18.00 | 25.00 | 100.00 |

**NOTE:** Varieties exist.

**Mint mark: Mo**

| KM# | Date | Mintage | Fine | VF | XF | Unc |
|---|---|---|---|---|---|---|
| 377.10 | 1824 JM round tail | | | | | |
| | | — | 75.00 | 125.00 | 250.00 | 500.00 |
| | 1824 JM square tail | | | | | |
| | | — | 75.00 | 125.00 | 250.00 | 500.00 |
| | 1825 JM | — | 25.00 | 35.00 | 50.00 | 150.00 |
| | 1826/5 JM | — | 25.00 | 40.00 | 75.00 | 150.00 |
| | 1826 JM | — | 20.00 | 30.00 | 50.00 | 125.00 |
| | 1827 JM medal alignment | | | | | |
| | | — | 25.00 | 35.00 | 50.00 | 125.00 |
| | 1827 JM coin alignment | | | | | |
| | | — | 25.00 | 35.00 | 50.00 | 125.00 |
| | 1828 JM | — | 30.00 | 60.00 | 100.00 | 200.00 |
| | 1829 JM | — | 20.00 | 30.00 | 50.00 | 125.00 |
| | 1830/20 JM | — | 35.00 | 55.00 | 100.00 | 200.00 |
| | 1830 JM | — | 30.00 | 50.00 | 90.00 | 175.00 |
| | 1831 JM | — | 30.00 | 50.00 | 100.00 | 200.00 |
| | 1832/1 JM | — | 25.00 | 40.00 | 60.00 | 125.00 |
| | 1832 JM | — | 20.00 | 30.00 | 40.00 | 100.00 |
| | 1833 MJ | — | 25.00 | 40.00 | 80.00 | 175.00 |
| | 1833 ML | — | 500.00 | 750.00 | 950.00 | 2000. |

**Mint mark: Ho**

| KM# | Date | Mintage | Fine | VF | XF | Unc |
|---|---|---|---|---|---|---|
| 377.9 | 1835 PP | — | — | — | — | — |
| | 1836 PP | — | — | — | Unique | — |
| | 1839 PR | — | — | — | Unique | — |
| | 1861 FM | — | — | — | Rare | — |
| | 1862 FM | — | — | — | Rare | — |
| | 1862 FM reeded edge | | | | | |
| | | — | — | — | Rare | — |
| | 1863 FM | — | 150.00 | 300.00 | 800.00 | — |
| | 1864 FM | — | — | — | Rare | — |
| | 1864 PR | — | — | — | Rare | — |
| | 1865 FM | — | 250.00 | 500.00 | 950.00 | — |

| KM# | Date | Mintage | Fine | VF | XF | Unc |
|---|---|---|---|---|---|---|
| 377.10 | 1834/3 ML | — | 25.00 | 35.00 | 50.00 | 125.00 |
| | 1834 ML | — | 20.00 | 30.00 | 40.00 | 100.00 |
| | 1835 ML | — | 20.00 | 30.00 | 40.00 | 125.00 |
| | 1836 ML | — | 50.00 | 100.00 | 150.00 | 300.00 |
| | 1836 ML/MF | — | 50.00 | 100.00 | 150.00 | 300.00 |
| | 1836 MF | — | 30.00 | 50.00 | 80.00 | 175.00 |
| | 1836 MF/ML | — | 35.00 | 60.00 | 90.00 | 200.00 |
| | 1837/6 ML | — | 30.00 | 50.00 | 75.00 | 150.00 |
| | 1837/6 MM | — | 30.00 | 50.00 | 75.00 | 150.00 |
| | 1837/6 MM/ML | — | 30.00 | 50.00 | 75.00 | 150.00 |
| | 1837/6 MM/MF | — | 30.00 | 50.00 | 75.00 | 150.00 |
| | 1837 ML | — | 30.00 | 50.00 | 75.00 | 150.00 |
| | 1837 MM | — | 75.00 | 125.00 | 175.00 | 325.00 |
| | 1838 MM | — | 30.00 | 50.00 | 75.00 | 150.00 |
| | 1838 ML | — | 20.00 | 35.00 | 60.00 | 125.00 |
| | 1838 ML/MM | — | 20.00 | 35.00 | 60.00 | 125.00 |
| | 1839 ML | — | 15.00 | 25.00 | 35.00 | 100.00 |
| | 1840 ML | — | 15.00 | 25.00 | 35.00 | 100.00 |
| | 1841 ML | — | 15.00 | 25.00 | 35.00 | 75.00 |
| | 1842 ML | — | 15.00 | 25.00 | 35.00 | 75.00 |
| | 1842 MM | — | 15.00 | 25.00 | 35.00 | 75.00 |
| | 1843 MM | — | 15.00 | 25.00 | 35.00 | 75.00 |
| | 1844 MF/MM | — | — | — | — | — |
| | 1844 MF | — | 15.00 | 25.00 | 35.00 | 75.00 |
| | 1845/4 MF | — | 15.00 | 25.00 | 35.00 | 75.00 |
| | 1845 MF | — | 15.00 | 25.00 | 35.00 | 75.00 |
| | 1846/5 MF | — | 15.00 | 25.00 | 35.00 | 100.00 |
| | 1846 MF | — | 15.00 | 25.00 | 35.00 | 100.00 |
| | 1847/6 MF | — | — | — | Rare | — |
| | 1847 MF | — | — | — | Rare | — |
| | 1847 RC | — | 20.00 | 30.00 | 40.00 | 100.00 |
| | 1847 RC/MF | — | 15.00 | 25.00 | 35.00 | 75.00 |
| | 1848 GC | — | 15.00 | 25.00 | 35.00 | 75.00 |
| | 1849/8 GC | — | 20.00 | 35.00 | 50.00 | 100.00 |
| | 1849 GC | — | 15.00 | 25.00 | 35.00 | 75.00 |
| | 1850/40 GC | — | 25.00 | 50.00 | 100.00 | 200.00 |
| | 1850/49 GC | — | 25.00 | 50.00 | 100.00 | 200.00 |
| | 1850 GC | — | 20.00 | 40.00 | 75.00 | 150.00 |
| | 1851 GC | — | 20.00 | 40.00 | 60.00 | 125.00 |
| | 1852 GC | — | 15.00 | 30.00 | 45.00 | 100.00 |
| | 1853 GC | — | 15.00 | 25.00 | 40.00 | 100.00 |
| | 1854 GC | — | 15.00 | 25.00 | 40.00 | 100.00 |
| | 1855 GC | — | 20.00 | 35.00 | 65.00 | 125.00 |
| | 1855 GF | — | 12.00 | 15.00 | 20.00 | 75.00 |
| | 1855 GF/GC | — | 12.00 | 15.00 | 20.00 | 75.00 |
| | 1856/4 GF | — | 15.00 | 25.00 | 40.00 | 100.00 |
| | 1856/5 GF | — | 15.00 | 25.00 | 40.00 | 100.00 |
| | 1856 GF | — | 12.00 | 15.00 | 20.00 | 75.00 |
| | 1857 GF | — | 10.00 | 15.00 | 20.00 | 75.00 |
| | 1858/7 FH/GF | — | 10.00 | 15.00 | 20.00 | 75.00 |
| | 1858 FH | — | 10.00 | 15.00 | 20.00 | 75.00 |
| | 1859 FH | — | 10.00 | 15.00 | 20.00 | 75.00 |
| | 1860/59 FH | — | 15.00 | 20.00 | 25.00 | 75.00 |
| | 1860 FH | — | 10.00 | 15.00 | 20.00 | 65.00 |
| | 1860 TH | — | 12.00 | 18.00 | 30.00 | 100.00 |
| | 1861 TH | — | 10.00 | 15.00 | 20.00 | 75.00 |
| | 1861 CH | — | 10.00 | 15.00 | 20.00 | 75.00 |
| | 1862 CH | — | 10.00 | 15.00 | 20.00 | 75.00 |
| | 1863 CH | — | 10.00 | 15.00 | 20.00 | 75.00 |
| | 1863 CH/TH | — | 10.00 | 15.00 | 20.00 | 75.00 |
| | 1863 TH | — | 10.00 | 15.00 | 20.00 | 75.00 |
| | 1867 CH | — | 10.00 | 15.00 | 20.00 | 65.00 |
| | 1868 CH | — | 10.00 | 15.00 | 20.00 | 65.00 |
| | 1868 CH/PH | — | 10.00 | 15.00 | 20.00 | 65.00 |
| | 1868 PH | — | 10.00 | 15.00 | 20.00 | 65.00 |
| | 1869 CH | — | 10.00 | 15.00 | 20.00 | 65.00 |
| | 1873 MH | — | 10.00 | 15.00 | 20.00 | 65.00 |
| | 1873 MH/HH | — | 12.00 | 18.00 | 25.00 | 75.00 |
| | 1874/69 MH | — | 15.00 | 25.00 | 45.00 | 100.00 |
| | 1874 MH | — | 12.00 | 18.00 | 25.00 | 75.00 |
| | 1874 BH/MH | — | 12.00 | 15.00 | 20.00 | 65.00 |
| | 1874 BH | — | 10.00 | 15.00 | 20.00 | 65.00 |
| | 1875 BH | — | 10.00 | 15.00 | 20.00 | 65.00 |
| | 1876/4 BH | — | 12.00 | 18.00 | 25.00 | 75.00 |
| | 1876/5 BH | — | 12.00 | 18.00 | 25.00 | 75.00 |
| | 1876 BH | — | 10.00 | 15.00 | 20.00 | 65.00 |
| | 1877 MH | .898 | 10.00 | 15.00 | 20.00 | 65.00 |
| | 1877 MH/BH Inc. Ab. | | 12.00 | 18.00 | 25.00 | 75.00 |
| | 1878 MH | 2.154 | 10.00 | 15.00 | 20.00 | 65.00 |
| | 1879/8 MH | — | 10.00 | 15.00 | 20.00 | 75.00 |

| KM# | Date | Mintage | Fine | VF | XF | Unc |
|---|---|---|---|---|---|---|
| 377.10 | 1879 MH | — | 10.00 | 15.00 | 20.00 | 65.00 |
| | 1880/79 MH | — | 15.00 | 20.00 | 30.00 | 75.00 |
| | 1880 MH | — | 10.00 | 15.00 | 20.00 | 75.00 |
| | 1881 MH | 5.712 | 10.00 | 15.00 | 20.00 | 65.00 |
| | 1882/1 MH | 2.746 | 12.00 | 15.00 | 20.00 | 75.00 |
| | 1882 MH | I.A. | 10.00 | 15.00 | 20.00 | 65.00 |
| | 1883/2 MH | 2.726 | 12.00 | 18.00 | 25.00 | 85.00 |
| | 1883 MH | I.A. | 10.00 | 15.00 | 20.00 | 65.00 |
| | 1884/3 MH | — | 15.00 | 20.00 | 30.00 | 75.00 |
| | 1884 MH | — | 10.00 | 15.00 | 20.00 | 65.00 |
| | 1885 MH | 3.649 | 10.00 | 15.00 | 20.00 | 65.00 |
| | 1886 MH | 7.558 | 10.00 | 12.00 | 18.00 | 60.00 |
| | 1887 MH | 7.681 | 10.00 | 12.00 | 18.00 | 60.00 |
| | 1888 MH | 7.179 | 10.00 | 12.00 | 18.00 | 60.00 |
| | 1889 MH | 7.332 | 10.00 | 15.00 | 20.00 | 65.00 |
| | 1890 MH | 7.412 | 10.00 | 12.00 | 18.00 | 60.00 |
| | 1890 AM | I.A. | 10.00 | 12.00 | 18.00 | 60.00 |
| | 1891 AM | 8.076 | 10.00 | 12.00 | 18.00 | 60.00 |
| | 1892 AM | 9.392 | 10.00 | 12.00 | 18.00 | 60.00 |
| | 1893 AM | 10.773 | 10.00 | 12.00 | 18.00 | 55.00 |
| | 1894 AM | 12.394 | 10.00 | 12.00 | 18.00 | 45.00 |
| | 1895 AM | 10.474 | 10.00 | 12.00 | 18.00 | 45.00 |
| | 1895 AB | I.A. | 10.00 | 12.00 | 18.00 | 60.00 |
| | 1896 MH | 9.327 | 10.00 | 12.00 | 18.00 | 60.00 |
| | 1896 AM | I.A. | 10.00 | 12.00 | 18.00 | 60.00 |
| | 1897 AM | 8.621 | 10.00 | 12.00 | 18.00 | 60.00 |

NOTE: Varieties exist. 1874 CP is a die struck counterfeit.

**Mint mark: O, Oa**

| KM# | Date | Mintage | Fine | VF | XF | Unc |
|---|---|---|---|---|---|---|
| 377.11 | 1858O AE | — | — | — | Rare | — |
| | 1858OaAE | — | — | — | Rare | — |
| | 1859 AE A in O of mm | — | 250.00 | 550.00 | 1000. | — |
| | 1860 AE A in O of mm | — | 200.00 | 400.00 | 600.00 | — |
| | 1861 O FR | — | 125.00 | 250.00 | 500.00 | 1000. |
| | 1861OaFR | — | 200.00 | 400.00 | 600.00 | — |
| | 1862O FR | — | 40.00 | 80.00 | 200.00 | 375.00 |
| | 1862OaFR | — | 65.00 | 125.00 | 250.00 | 450.00 |
| | 1863O FR | — | 30.00 | 60.00 | 100.00 | 250.00 |
| | 1863O AE | — | 30.00 | 60.00 | 100.00 | 250.00 |
| | 1863OaAE A in O of mm | — | 100.00 | 150.00 | 250.00 | 450.00 |
| | 1863OaAE A above O in mm | — | — | — | Rare | — |
| | 1864 FR | — | 25.00 | 50.00 | 75.00 | 200.00 |
| | 1867 AE | — | 40.00 | 80.00 | 150.00 | 400.00 |
| | 1868 AE | — | 25.00 | 50.00 | 100.00 | 250.00 |
| | 1869 AE | — | 30.00 | 60.00 | 100.00 | 250.00 |
| | 1873 AE | — | 200.00 | 300.00 | 600.00 | 1250. |
| | 1874 AE | .142 | 15.00 | 30.00 | 50.00 | 200.00 |
| | 1875/4 AE | .131 | 25.00 | 50.00 | 75.00 | 200.00 |
| | 1875 AE | I.A. | 15.00 | 30.00 | 40.00 | 125.00 |
| | 1876 AE | .140 | 20.00 | 35.00 | 55.00 | 200.00 |
| | 1877 AE | .139 | 20.00 | 30.00 | 50.00 | 200.00 |
| | 1878 AE | .125 | 15.00 | 25.00 | 50.00 | 200.00 |
| | 1879 AE | .153 | 15.00 | 30.00 | 45.00 | 150.00 |
| | 1880 AE | .143 | 15.00 | 30.00 | 45.00 | 150.00 |
| | 1881 AE | .134 | 20.00 | 35.00 | 60.00 | 150.00 |
| | 1882 AE | .100 | 20.00 | 35.00 | 60.00 | 150.00 |
| | 1883 AE | .122 | 15.00 | 30.00 | 45.00 | 150.00 |
| | 1884 AE | .142 | 15.00 | 30.00 | 50.00 | 150.00 |
| | 1885 AE | .158 | 15.00 | 25.00 | 40.00 | 125.00 |
| | 1886 AE | .120 | 15.00 | 30.00 | 45.00 | 150.00 |

| KM# | Date | Mintage | Fine | VF | XF | Unc |
|---|---|---|---|---|---|---|
| 377.11 | 1887/6 AE | .115 | 25.00 | 50.00 | 80.00 | 200.00 |
| | 1887 AE | I.A. | 15.00 | 25.00 | 40.00 | 125.00 |
| | 1888 AE | .145 | 15.00 | 25.00 | 40.00 | 125.00 |
| | 1889 AE | .150 | 20.00 | 30.00 | 60.00 | 175.00 |
| | 1890 AE | .181 | 20.00 | 30.00 | 60.00 | 175.00 |
| | 1891 EN | .160 | 15.00 | 25.00 | 40.00 | 125.00 |
| | 1892 EN | .120 | 15.00 | 25.00 | 40.00 | 125.00 |
| | 1893 EN | .066 | 45.00 | 75.00 | 115.00 | 225.00 |

NOTE: Varieties exist.

**Mint mark: Pi**

| KM# | Date | Mintage | Fine | VF | XF | Unc |
|---|---|---|---|---|---|---|
| 377.12 | 1827 JS | — | — | — | Rare | — |
| | 1828/7 JS | — | 250.00 | 400.00 | 600.00 | 1200. |
| | 1828 JS | — | 200.00 | 350.00 | 500.00 | 1000. |
| | 1829 JS | — | 35.00 | 65.00 | 125.00 | 250.00 |
| | 1830 JS | — | 30.00 | 50.00 | 100.00 | 200.00 |
| | 1831/0 JS | — | 30.00 | 60.00 | 125.00 | 250.00 |
| | 1831 JS | — | 25.00 | 35.00 | 65.00 | 200.00 |
| | 1832/22 JS | — | 25.00 | 35.00 | 55.00 | 150.00 |
| | 1832 JS | — | 25.00 | 35.00 | 55.00 | 150.00 |
| | 1833/2 JS | — | 30.00 | 40.00 | 50.00 | 150.00 |
| | 1833 JS | — | 20.00 | 30.00 | 40.00 | 125.00 |
| | 1834/3 JS | — | 25.00 | 35.00 | 50.00 | 125.00 |
| | 1834 JS | — | 15.00 | 25.00 | 40.00 | 125.00 |
| | 1835 JS denomination 8R | | | | | |
| | | — | 20.00 | 30.00 | 60.00 | 150.00 |
| | 1835 JS denomination 8Rs | | | | | |
| | | — | 15.00 | 25.00 | 40.00 | 125.00 |
| | 1836 JS | — | 20.00 | 30.00 | 45.00 | 125.00 |
| | 1837 JS | — | 30.00 | 50.00 | 80.00 | 175.00 |
| | 1838 JS | — | 20.00 | 30.00 | 45.00 | 125.00 |
| | 1839 JS | — | 20.00 | 40.00 | 60.00 | 125.00 |
| | 1840 JS | — | 20.00 | 30.00 | 50.00 | 125.00 |
| | 1841PiJS | — | 25.00 | 40.00 | 80.00 | 175.00 |
| | 1841iPJS (error) | | | | | |
| | | — | 50.00 | 100.00 | 200.00 | 400.00 |
| | 1842/1 JS | — | 40.00 | 60.00 | 90.00 | 175.00 |
| | 1842/1 PS/JS | | | | | |
| | | — | 35.00 | 55.00 | 85.00 | 175.00 |
| | 1842 JS eagle type of 1843 | | | | | |
| | | — | 30.00 | 50.00 | 75.00 | 150.00 |
| | 1842 PS | — | 30.00 | 50.00 | 75.00 | 150.00 |
| | 1842 PS/JS eagle type of 1841 | | | | | |
| | | — | 30.00 | 50.00 | 75.00 | 150.00 |
| | 1843/2 PS round top 3 | | | | | |
| | | — | 50.00 | 75.00 | 150.00 | 250.00 |
| | 1843 PS flat top 3 | | | | | |
| | | — | 30.00 | 60.00 | 125.00 | 225.00 |
| | 1843 AM round top 3 | | | | | |
| | | — | 20.00 | 30.00 | 50.00 | 125.00 |
| | 1843 AM flat top 3 | | | | | |
| | 1844 AM | — | 20.00 | 30.00 | 50.00 | 125.00 |
| | 1845/4 AM | — | 25.00 | 50.00 | 100.00 | 225.00 |
| | 1845 AM | — | 25.00 | 50.00 | 100.00 | 225.00 |
| | 1846/5 AM | — | 25.00 | 35.00 | 50.00 | 125.00 |
| | 1846 AM | — | 15.00 | 25.00 | 40.00 | 125.00 |
| | 1847 AM | — | 30.00 | 50.00 | 80.00 | 150.00 |
| | 1848/7 AM | — | 30.00 | 60.00 | 90.00 | 175.00 |
| | 1848 AM | — | 30.00 | 50.00 | 80.00 | 150.00 |
| | 1849/8 PS/AM | | | | | |
| | | — | — | — | Rare | — |
| | 1849 PS/AM | — | — | — | Rare | — |
| | 1849 MC/PS | — | 60.00 | 125.00 | 250.00 | 500.00 |

| KM# | Date | Mintage | Fine | VF | XF | Unc |
|---|---|---|---|---|---|---|
| 377.12 | 1849 AM | — | — | — | Rare | — |
| | 1849 MC | — | 60.00 | 125.00 | 250.00 | 500.00 |
| | 1850 MC | — | 40.00 | 80.00 | 150.00 | 300.00 |
| | 1851 MC | — | 125.00 | 200.00 | 300.00 | 600.00 |
| | 1852 MC | — | 75.00 | 125.00 | 200.00 | 400.00 |
| | 1853 MC | — | 125.00 | 175.00 | 300.00 | 600.00 |
| | 1854 MC | — | 100.00 | 150.00 | 250.00 | 500.00 |
| | 1855 MC | — | 100.00 | 150.00 | 250.00 | 500.00 |
| | 1856 MC | — | 65.00 | 100.00 | 200.00 | 400.00 |
| | 1857 MC | — | — | — | Rare | — |
| | 1857 PS/MC | — | 150.00 | 225.00 | 375.00 | 700.00 |
| | 1857 PS | — | 125.00 | 200.00 | 350.00 | 650.00 |
| | 1858 MC/PS | — | 250.00 | 400.00 | 650.00 | 1200. |
| | 1858 MC | — | 250.00 | 400.00 | 650.00 | 1200. |
| | 1858 PS | — | — | — | Rare | — |
| | 1859/8 MC/PS | | | | | |
| | | — | — | — | Rare | — |
| | 1859 MC/PS | — | — | — | Rare | — |
| | 1859 PS/PC | — | — | — | Rare | — |
| | 1859 PS | — | — | — | Rare | — |
| | 1860 FC | — | 2000. | 4000. | 6500. | — |
| | 1860 FE | — | — | — | Rare | — |
| | 1860 MC | — | 2000. | 4000. | 6500. | — |
| | 1860 PS | — | 400.00 | 600.00 | 900.00 | 1750. |
| | 1861 PS | — | 30.00 | 60.00 | 90.00 | 175.00 |
| | 1861 RO | — | 25.00 | 35.00 | 55.00 | 125.00 |
| | 1862/1 RO | — | 20.00 | 25.00 | 50.00 | 125.00 |
| | 1862 RO | — | 15.00 | 20.00 | 40.00 | 100.00 |
| | 1862 RO oval O in RO | | | | | |
| | | — | 15.00 | 20.00 | 40.00 | 100.00 |
| | 1862 RO round O in RO, 6 is inverted 9 | | | | | |
| | | — | 20.00 | 30.00 | 50.00 | 125.00 |
| | 1863/2 RO | — | 25.00 | 35.00 | 65.00 | 150.00 |
| | 1863 RO | — | 15.00 | 20.00 | 40.00 | 125.00 |
| | 1863 6/inverted 6 | | | | | |
| | | — | 25.00 | 35.00 | 55.00 | 125.00 |
| | 1863 FC | — | — | — | Rare | — |
| | 1864 RO | — | — | — | Rare | — |
| | 1867 CA | — | — | — | Rare | — |
| | 1867 LR | — | — | — | Rare | — |
| | 1867 PS | — | 30.00 | 60.00 | 125.00 | 275.00 |
| | 1868/7 PS | — | 30.00 | 60.00 | 125.00 | 250.00 |
| | 1868 PS | — | 20.00 | 30.00 | 50.00 | 125.00 |
| | 1869/8 PS | — | 20.00 | 25.00 | 45.00 | 125.00 |
| | 1869 PS | — | 15.00 | 20.00 | 40.00 | 125.00 |
| | 1870/69 PS | — | — | — | Rare | — |
| | 1870 PS | — | — | — | Rare | — |
| | 1873 MH | — | 15.00 | 20.00 | 40.00 | 135.00 |
| | 1874/3 MH | — | 15.00 | 20.00 | 30.00 | 125.00 |
| | 1874 MH | — | 10.00 | 12.00 | 18.00 | 100.00 |
| | 1875 MH | — | 10.00 | 12.00 | 18.00 | 100.00 |
| | 1876/5 MH | — | 15.00 | 20.00 | 30.00 | 125.00 |
| | 1876 MH | — | 10.00 | 12.00 | 18.00 | 100.00 |
| | 1877 MH | 1.018 | 10.00 | 12.00 | 18.00 | 100.00 |
| | 1878 MH | 1.046 | 12.00 | 15.00 | 25.00 | 125.00 |
| | 1879/8 MH | — | 15.00 | 20.00 | 30.00 | 125.00 |
| | 1879 MH | — | 10.00 | 12.00 | 18.00 | 100.00 |
| | 1879 BE | — | 25.00 | 50.00 | 75.00 | 150.00 |
| | 1879 MR | — | 30.00 | 50.00 | 100.00 | 200.00 |
| | 1880 MR | — | 250.00 | 400.00 | 800.00 | — |
| | 1880 MH | — | 10.00 | 12.00 | 18.00 | 100.00 |
| | 1881 MH | 2.100 | 10.00 | 12.00 | 18.00 | 100.00 |
| | 1882/1 MH | | | | | |
| | | 1.602 | 15.00 | 20.00 | 30.00 | 125.00 |
| | 1882 MH | I.A. | 10.00 | 12.00 | 18.00 | 100.00 |
| | 1883 MH | 1.545 | 10.00 | 12.00 | 18.00 | 100.00 |
| | 1884/3 MH | — | 15.00 | 20.00 | 30.00 | 125.00 |
| | 1884 MH/MM | | | | | |
| | | — | 12.00 | 15.00 | 20.00 | 85.00 |
| | 1884 MH | — | 10.00 | 12.00 | 18.00 | 75.00 |
| | 1885/4 MH | | | | | |
| | | 1.736 | 15.00 | 20.00 | 30.00 | 125.00 |
| | 1885/8 MH | I.A. | 15.00 | 20.00 | 30.00 | 125.00 |
| | 1885 MH | I.A. | 10.00 | 12.00 | 18.00 | 75.00 |
| | 1885 LC | I.A. | 12.00 | 18.00 | 25.00 | 100.00 |
| | 1886 LC | 3.347 | 10.00 | 12.00 | 18.00 | 75.00 |
| | 1886 MR | I.A. | 10.00 | 12.00 | 18.00 | 75.00 |
| | 1887 MR | 2.922 | 10.00 | 12.00 | 18.00 | 75.00 |
| | 1888 MR | 2.438 | 10.00 | 12.00 | 18.00 | 75.00 |
| | 1889 MR | 2.103 | 10.00 | 12.00 | 18.00 | 75.00 |
| | 1890 MR | 1.562 | 10.00 | 12.00 | 18.00 | 65.00 |
| | 1891 MR | 1.184 | 10.00 | 12.00 | 18.00 | 65.00 |
| | 1892 MR | 1.336 | 10.00 | 12.00 | 18.00 | 65.00 |
| | 1893 MR | .530 | 10.00 | 12.00 | 18.00 | 75.00 |

NOTE: Varieties exist.

## Right column (top)

| KM# | Date | Mintage | Fine | VF | XF | Unc |
|---|---|---|---|---|---|---|
| 377.13 | 1861/0 VL/MO | — | 10.00 | 12.00 | 18.00 | 75.00 |
| | 1861/0 VL | — | 10.00 | 12.00 | 18.00 | 75.00 |
| | 1861 VL | — | 10.00 | 12.00 | 18.00 | 75.00 |
| | 1862/1 VL | — | 15.00 | 20.00 | 30.00 | 100.00 |
| | 1862 VL | — | 10.00 | 12.00 | 18.00 | 75.00 |
| | 1863 VL | — | 10.00 | 12.00 | 18.00 | 75.00 |
| | 1863 MO | — | 10.00 | 12.00 | 18.00 | 75.00 |
| | 1864/3 VL | — | 15.00 | 20.00 | 30.00 | 100.00 |
| | 1864 VL | — | 10.00 | 12.00 | 18.00 | 75.00 |
| | 1864 MO | — | 15.00 | 20.00 | 30.00 | 100.00 |
| | 1865/4 MO | — | 200.00 | 450.00 | 700.00 | 1500. |
| | 1865 MO | — | 175.00 | 400.00 | 600.00 | 1250. |
| | 1866 VL | — | | Contemporary counterfeit | | |
| | 1867 JS | — | — | — | Rare | — |
| | 1868 JS | — | 10.00 | 12.00 | 18.00 | 75.00 |
| | 1868 YH | — | 10.00 | 12.00 | 18.00 | 75.00 |
| | 1869 YH | — | 10.00 | 12.00 | 18.00 | 75.00 |
| | 1870 YH | — | — | — | Rare | — |
| | 1873 YH | — | 10.00 | 12.00 | 18.00 | 75.00 |
| | 1874 YH | — | 10.00 | 12.00 | 18.00 | 75.00 |
| | 1874 JA/YA | — | 10.00 | 12.00 | 18.00 | 75.00 |
| | 1874 JA | — | 10.00 | 12.00 | 18.00 | 75.00 |
| | 1875 JA | — | 10.00 | 12.00 | 18.00 | 75.00 |
| | 1876 JA | — | 10.00 | 12.00 | 18.00 | 75.00 |
| | 1876 JS | — | 10.00 | 12.00 | 18.00 | 75.00 |
| | 1877 JS | 2.700 | 10.00 | 12.00 | 18.00 | 75.00 |
| | 1878 JS | 2.310 | 10.00 | 12.00 | 18.00 | 75.00 |
| | 1879/8 JS | — | 15.00 | 20.00 | 30.00 | 100.00 |
| | 1879 JS | — | 10.00 | 12.00 | 18.00 | 75.00 |
| | 1880 JS | — | 10.00 | 12.00 | 18.00 | 75.00 |
| | 1881 JS | 5.592 | 10.00 | 12.00 | 18.00 | 75.00 |
| | 1882/1 JS | 2.485 | 15.00 | 20.00 | 30.00 | 100.00 |
| | 1882 JS straight J | Inc. Ab. | 10.00 | 12.00 | 18.00 | 60.00 |
| | 1882 JS full J | Inc. Ab. | 10.00 | 12.00 | 18.00 | 60.00 |
| | 1883/2 JS | 2.563 | 15.00 | 20.00 | 30.00 | 100.00 |
| | 1883 JS | I.A. | 10.00 | 12.00 | 18.00 | 75.00 |
| | 1884 JS | — | 10.00 | 12.00 | 18.00 | 75.00 |
| | 1885 JS | 2.252 | 10.00 | 12.00 | 18.00 | 60.00 |
| | 1886/5 JS | 5.303 | 15.00 | 20.00 | 30.00 | 100.00 |
| | 1886/8 JS | I.A. | 15.00 | 20.00 | 30.00 | 100.00 |
| | 1886 JS | I.A. | 10.00 | 12.00 | 18.00 | 60.00 |
| | 1886 FZ | I.A. | 10.00 | 12.00 | 18.00 | 60.00 |
| | 1887ZsFZ | 4.733 | 10.00 | 12.00 | 18.00 | 60.00 |
| | 1887Z FZ | I.A. | 20.00 | 30.00 | 50.00 | 100.00 |
| | 1888/7 FZ | 5.132 | 12.00 | 15.00 | 25.00 | 75.00 |
| | 1888 FZ | I.A. | 10.00 | 12.00 | 18.00 | 60.00 |
| | 1889 FZ | 4.344 | 10.00 | 12.00 | 18.00 | 60.00 |
| | 1890 FZ | 3.887 | 10.00 | 12.00 | 18.00 | 60.00 |
| | 1891 FZ | 4.114 | 10.00 | 12.00 | 18.00 | 60.00 |
| | 1892/1 FZ | 4.238 | 12.00 | 15.00 | 25.00 | 75.00 |
| | 1892 FZ | I.A. | 10.00 | 12.00 | 18.00 | 60.00 |
| | 1893 FZ | 3.872 | 10.00 | 12.00 | 18.00 | 60.00 |
| | 1894 FZ | 3.081 | 10.00 | 12.00 | 18.00 | 60.00 |
| | 1895 FZ | 4.718 | 10.00 | 12.00 | 18.00 | 60.00 |
| | 1896 FZ | 4.226 | 10.00 | 12.00 | 18.00 | 50.00 |
| | 1897 FZ | 4.877 | 10.00 | 12.00 | 18.00 | 50.00 |

NOTE: Varieties exist.

**Mint mark: Zs**

| KM# | Date | Mintage | Fine | VF | XF | Unc |
|---|---|---|---|---|---|---|
| 377.13 | 1825 AZ | — | 25.00 | 35.00 | 60.00 | 150.00 |
| | 1826/5 AZ | — | 25.00 | 45.00 | 75.00 | 175.00 |
| | 1826 AZ | — | 20.00 | 35.00 | 60.00 | 150.00 |
| | 1826 AV | — | 225.00 | 450.00 | 700.00 | 1500. |
| | 1826 AO | — | 350.00 | 650.00 | 1000. | 2000. |
| | 1827 AO/AZ | — | 35.00 | 50.00 | 125.00 | 250.00 |
| | 1827 AO | — | 25.00 | 45.00 | 85.00 | 175.00 |
| | 1828 AO | — | 15.00 | 20.00 | 40.00 | 125.00 |
| | 1829 AO | — | 15.00 | 20.00 | 40.00 | 125.00 |
| | 1829 OV | — | 50.00 | 90.00 | 150.00 | 300.00 |
| | 1830 OV | — | 15.00 | 20.00 | 40.00 | 125.00 |
| | 1831 OV | — | 25.00 | 50.00 | 90.00 | 175.00 |
| | 1831 OM | — | 15.00 | 25.00 | 50.00 | 125.00 |
| | 1832/1 OM | — | 20.00 | 25.00 | 40.00 | 125.00 |
| | 1832 OM | — | 15.00 | 20.00 | 35.00 | 100.00 |
| | 1833/2 OM | — | 20.00 | 30.00 | 40.00 | 125.00 |
| | 1833 OM/MM | — | 15.00 | 25.00 | 35.00 | 100.00 |
| | 1833 OM | — | 15.00 | 20.00 | 30.00 | 100.00 |
| | 1834 OM | — | 15.00 | 20.00 | 30.00 | 100.00 |
| | 1835 OM | — | 15.00 | 20.00 | 35.00 | 100.00 |
| | 1836/4 OM | — | 20.00 | 30.00 | 45.00 | 125.00 |
| | 1836/5 OM | — | 20.00 | 30.00 | 45.00 | 125.00 |
| | 1836 OM | — | 15.00 | 20.00 | 30.00 | 100.00 |
| | 1837 OM | — | 15.00 | 20.00 | 30.00 | 100.00 |
| | 1838/7 OM | — | 20.00 | 30.00 | 40.00 | 125.00 |
| | 1838 OM | — | 15.00 | 20.00 | 30.00 | 100.00 |
| | 1839 OM | — | 15.00 | 20.00 | 30.00 | 100.00 |
| | 1840 OM | — | 15.00 | 20.00 | 30.00 | 100.00 |
| | 1841 OM | — | 15.00 | 20.00 | 30.00 | 100.00 |
| | 1842 OM eagle type of 1841 | — | 15.00 | 20.00 | 30.00 | 100.00 |
| | 1842 OM eagle type of 1843 | — | 15.00 | 20.00 | 30.00 | 100.00 |
| | 1843 OM | — | 15.00 | 20.00 | 30.00 | 100.00 |
| | 1844 OM | — | 15.00 | 20.00 | 30.00 | 100.00 |
| | 1845 OM | — | 15.00 | 20.00 | 30.00 | 100.00 |
| | 1846 OM | — | 15.00 | 20.00 | 30.00 | 100.00 |
| | 1847 OM | — | 15.00 | 20.00 | 30.00 | 100.00 |
| | 1848/7 OM | — | 20.00 | 30.00 | 40.00 | 125.00 |
| | 1848 OM | — | 15.00 | 20.00 | 30.00 | 100.00 |
| | 1849 OM | — | 15.00 | 20.00 | 30.00 | 100.00 |
| | 1850 OM | — | 15.00 | 20.00 | 30.00 | 100.00 |
| | 1851 OM | — | 15.00 | 20.00 | 30.00 | 100.00 |
| | 1852 OM | — | 15.00 | 20.00 | 30.00 | 100.00 |
| | 1853 OM | — | 30.00 | 45.00 | 65.00 | 200.00 |
| | 1854/3 OM | — | 20.00 | 30.00 | 50.00 | 150.00 |
| | 1854 OM | — | 15.00 | 25.00 | 40.00 | 125.00 |
| | 1855 OM | — | 20.00 | 30.00 | 60.00 | 125.00 |
| | 1855 MO | — | 30.00 | 60.00 | 90.00 | 175.00 |
| | 1856/5 MO | — | 20.00 | 30.00 | 40.00 | 125.00 |
| | 1856 MO | — | 15.00 | 20.00 | 30.00 | 100.00 |
| | 1857/5 MO | — | 20.00 | 30.00 | 40.00 | 125.00 |
| | 1857 MO | — | 15.00 | 20.00 | 30.00 | 100.00 |
| | 1858/7 MO | — | 15.00 | 20.00 | 30.00 | 100.00 |
| | 1858 MO | — | 15.00 | 20.00 | 30.00 | 100.00 |
| | 1859/8 MO | — | 15.00 | 20.00 | 30.00 | 100.00 |
| | 1859 MO | — | 15.00 | 20.00 | 30.00 | 100.00 |
| | 1859 VL/MO | — | 25.00 | 50.00 | 75.00 | 150.00 |
| | 1859 VL | — | 20.00 | 40.00 | 60.00 | 125.00 |
| | 1860/50 MO | — | 10.00 | 12.00 | 18.00 | 75.00 |
| | 1860/59 MO | — | 10.00 | 12.00 | 18.00 | 75.00 |
| | 1860 MO | — | 10.00 | 12.00 | 18.00 | 75.00 |
| | 1860 VL/MO | — | 10.00 | 12.00 | 18.00 | 75.00 |
| | 1860 VL | — | 10.00 | 12.00 | 18.00 | 75.00 |

## 1/2 ESCUDO

**1.6900 g, .875 GOLD, .0475 oz AGW**
**Mint mark: C**
**Obv: Facing eagle.**

| KM# | Date | Mintage | VG | Fine | VF | XF |
|---|---|---|---|---|---|---|
| 378 | 1848 CE | — | 35.00 | 50.00 | 75.00 | 150.00 |
| | 1853 CE | — | 35.00 | 50.00 | 75.00 | 150.00 |
| | 1854 CE | — | 35.00 | 50.00 | 75.00 | 150.00 |
| | 1856 CE | — | 50.00 | 100.00 | 150.00 | 250.00 |

| KM# | Date Mintage | VG | Fine | VF | XF |
|---|---|---|---|---|---|
| 378 | 1857 CE — | 35.00 | 50.00 | 75.00 | 150.00 |
| | 1859 CE — | 35.00 | 50.00 | 75.00 | 150.00 |
| | 1860 CE — | 35.00 | 50.00 | 75.00 | 150.00 |
| | 1862 CE — | 35.00 | 50.00 | 75.00 | 125.00 |
| | 1863 CE — | 35.00 | 50.00 | 75.00 | 125.00 |
| | 1866 CE — | 35.00 | 50.00 | 75.00 | 125.00 |
| | 1867 CE — | 35.00 | 50.00 | 75.00 | 125.00 |
| | 1870 CE — | — | — | — | — |

**Mint mark: Do**

| KM# | Date Mintage | VG | Fine | VF | XF |
|---|---|---|---|---|---|
| 378.1 | 1833 RM/RL — | 35.00 | 50.00 | 75.00 | 150.00 |
| | 1834/3 RM — | 35.00 | 50.00 | 75.00 | 150.00 |
| | 1835/3 RM — | 35.00 | 50.00 | 75.00 | 150.00 |
| | 1836/4 RM — | 35.00 | 50.00 | 75.00 | 150.00 |
| | 1837 RM — | 35.00 | 50.00 | 75.00 | 150.00 |
| | 1838 RM — | 40.00 | 60.00 | 100.00 | 175.00 |
| | 1843 RM — | 40.00 | 60.00 | 100.00 | 175.00 |
| | 1844/33 RM — | 40.00 | 60.00 | 100.00 | 175.00 |
| | 1844/33 RM/RL | | | | |
| | — | 40.00 | 60.00 | 100.00 | 175.00 |
| | 1846 RM — | 40.00 | 60.00 | 100.00 | 175.00 |
| | 1848 RM — | 40.00 | 60.00 | 100.00 | 175.00 |
| | 1850/33 JMR — | 40.00 | 60.00 | 100.00 | 175.00 |
| | 1851 JMR — | 40.00 | 60.00 | 100.00 | 200.00 |
| | 1852 JMR — | 40.00 | 60.00 | 100.00 | 175.00 |
| | 1853/33 CP — | 75.00 | 150.00 | 300.00 | 500.00 |
| | 1853 CP — | 35.00 | 50.00 | 75.00 | 150.00 |
| | 1854 CP — | 35.00 | 50.00 | 75.00 | 150.00 |
| | 1855 CP — | 35.00 | 50.00 | 75.00 | 150.00 |
| | 1859 CP — | 35.00 | 50.00 | 75.00 | 150.00 |
| | 1861 CP — | 35.00 | 50.00 | 75.00 | 150.00 |
| | 1864 LT — | 75.00 | 125.00 | 250.00 | 400.00 |

**Mint mark: Ga**

| KM# | Date Mintage | VG | Fine | VF | XF |
|---|---|---|---|---|---|
| 378.2 | 1825 FS — | 40.00 | 60.00 | 100.00 | 175.00 |
| | 1829 FS — | 40.00 | 60.00 | 100.00 | 175.00 |
| | 1831 FS — | 40.00 | 60.00 | 100.00 | 175.00 |
| | 1834 FS — | 40.00 | 60.00 | 100.00 | 175.00 |
| | 1835 FS — | 40.00 | 60.00 | 100.00 | 175.00 |
| | 1837 JG — | 40.00 | 60.00 | 100.00 | 175.00 |
| | 1838 JG — | 40.00 | 60.00 | 100.00 | 175.00 |
| | 1839 JG — | 40.00 | 60.00 | 100.00 | 175.00 |
| | 1842 JG — | 40.00 | 60.00 | 100.00 | 175.00 |
| | 1847 JG — | 40.00 | 60.00 | 100.00 | 175.00 |
| | 1850 JG — | 35.00 | 50.00 | 75.00 | 150.00 |
| | 1852 JG — | 35.00 | 50.00 | 75.00 | 150.00 |
| | 1859 JG — | 40.00 | 60.00 | 100.00 | 175.00 |
| | 1861 JG — | 35.00 | 50.00 | 75.00 | 150.00 |

**Mint mark: GC**

| KM# | Date Mintage | VG | Fine | VF | XF |
|---|---|---|---|---|---|
| 378.3 | 1846 MP — | 50.00 | 75.00 | 100.00 | 175.00 |
| | 1847 MP — | 50.00 | 75.00 | 100.00 | 175.00 |
| | 1848/7 MP — | 50.00 | 75.00 | 100.00 | 200.00 |
| | 1851 MP — | 50.00 | 75.00 | 100.00 | 175.00 |

**Mint mark: Go**

| KM# | Date Mintage | VG | Fine | VF | XF |
|---|---|---|---|---|---|
| 378.4 | 1845 PM — | 30.00 | 40.00 | 65.00 | 125.00 |
| | 1849 PF — | 30.00 | 40.00 | 65.00 | 125.00 |
| | 1851/41 PF — | 30.00 | 40.00 | 65.00 | 125.00 |
| | 1851 PF — | 30.00 | 40.00 | 65.00 | 125.00 |
| | 1852 PF — | 30.00 | 40.00 | 65.00 | 125.00 |
| | 1853 PF — | 30.00 | 40.00 | 65.00 | 125.00 |
| | 1855 PF — | 30.00 | 50.00 | 80.00 | 150.00 |
| | 1857 PF — | 30.00 | 40.00 | 65.00 | 125.00 |
| | 1858/7 PF — | 30.00 | 40.00 | 65.00 | 125.00 |
| | 1859 PF — | 30.00 | 40.00 | 65.00 | 125.00 |
| | 1860 PF — | 30.00 | 40.00 | 65.00 | 125.00 |
| | 1861 PF — | 30.00 | 40.00 | 65.00 | 125.00 |
| | 1862/1 YE — | 30.00 | 40.00 | 65.00 | 125.00 |
| | 1863 YF — | 30.00 | 40.00 | 65.00 | 125.00 |

**Mint mark: Mo**

| KM# | Date Mintage | VG | Fine | VF | XF |
|---|---|---|---|---|---|
| 378.5 | 1825/1 JM — | 50.00 | 75.00 | 125.00 | 200.00 |
| | 1825/4 JM — | 50.00 | 75.00 | 125.00 | 200.00 |
| | 1825 JM — | 30.00 | 40.00 | 80.00 | 150.00 |
| | 1827/6 JM — | 30.00 | 40.00 | 80.00 | 150.00 |
| | 1827 JM — | 30.00 | 40.00 | 80.00 | 150.00 |
| | 1829 JM — | 30.00 | 40.00 | 80.00 | 150.00 |
| | 1831/0 JM — | 30.00 | 40.00 | 80.00 | 150.00 |
| | 1831 JM — | 30.00 | 40.00 | 60.00 | 125.00 |
| | 1832 JM — | 30.00 | 40.00 | 60.00 | 125.00 |
| | 1833 MJ olive & oak branches reversed | | | | |
| | — | 30.00 | 50.00 | 90.00 | 175.00 |
| | 1834 ML — | 30.00 | 40.00 | 60.00 | 125.00 |
| | 1835 ML — | 30.00 | 40.00 | 80.00 | 150.00 |
| | 1838 ML — | 30.00 | 50.00 | 90.00 | 175.00 |
| | 1839 ML — | 30.00 | 50.00 | 90.00 | 175.00 |

| KM# | Date Mintage | VG | Fine | VF | XF |
|---|---|---|---|---|---|
| 378.5 | 1840 ML — | 30.00 | 40.00 | 60.00 | 125.00 |
| | 1841 ML — | 30.00 | 40.00 | 60.00 | 125.00 |
| | 1842 ML — | 30.00 | 40.00 | 80.00 | 150.00 |
| | 1842 MM — | 30.00 | 40.00 | 80.00 | 150.00 |
| | 1843 MM — | 30.00 | 40.00 | 60.00 | 125.00 |
| | 1844 MF — | 30.00 | 40.00 | 60.00 | 125.00 |
| | 1845 MF — | 30.00 | 40.00 | 60.00 | 125.00 |
| | 1846/5 MF — | 30.00 | 40.00 | 60.00 | 125.00 |
| | 1846 MF — | 30.00 | 40.00 | 60.00 | 125.00 |
| | 1848 GC — | 30.00 | 40.00 | 60.00 | 125.00 |
| | 1850 GC — | 30.00 | 40.00 | 60.00 | 125.00 |
| | 1851 GC — | 30.00 | 40.00 | 60.00 | 125.00 |
| | 1852 GC — | 30.00 | 40.00 | 60.00 | 125.00 |
| | 1853 GC — | 30.00 | 40.00 | 60.00 | 125.00 |
| | 1854 GC — | 30.00 | 40.00 | 60.00 | 125.00 |
| | 1855 GF — | 30.00 | 40.00 | 60.00 | 125.00 |
| | 1856/4 GF — | 30.00 | 40.00 | 60.00 | 125.00 |
| | 1857 GF — | 30.00 | 40.00 | 60.00 | 125.00 |
| | 1858/7 FH/GF | | | | |
| | — | 35.00 | 50.00 | 75.00 | 150.00 |
| | 1858 FH — | 30.00 | 40.00 | 60.00 | 125.00 |
| | 1859 FH — | 30.00 | 40.00 | 60.00 | 125.00 |
| | 1860/59 FH — | 30.00 | 40.00 | 60.00 | 125.00 |
| | 1861 CH/FH — | 30.00 | 40.00 | 80.00 | 150.00 |
| | 1862 CH — | 30.00 | 40.00 | 60.00 | 125.00 |
| | 1863/57 CH/GF | | | | |
| | — | 30.00 | 40.00 | 60.00 | 125.00 |
| | 1868/58 PH — | 30.00 | 40.00 | 80.00 | 150.00 |
| | 1869/59 CH — | 30.00 | 40.00 | 80.00 | 150.00 |

**Mint mark: Zs**

| KM# | Date Mintage | VG | Fine | VF | XF |
|---|---|---|---|---|---|
| 378.6 | 1860 VL — | 35.00 | 50.00 | 75.00 | 150.00 |
| | 1862/1 VL — | 35.00 | 50.00 | 75.00 | 150.00 |
| | 1862 VL — | 30.00 | 40.00 | 65.00 | 125.00 |

# ESCUDO

**3.3800 g, .875 GOLD, .0950 oz AGW**
**Mint mark: C**
**Obv: Facing eagle.**

| KM# | Date Mintage | VG | Fine | VF | XF |
|---|---|---|---|---|---|
| 379 | 1846 CE — | 75.00 | 100.00 | 200.00 | 350.00 |
| | 1847 CE — | 50.00 | 75.00 | 125.00 | 175.00 |
| | 1848 CE — | 50.00 | 75.00 | 125.00 | 175.00 |
| | 1849/8 CE — | 60.00 | 100.00 | 150.00 | 225.00 |
| | 1850 CE — | 50.00 | 75.00 | 125.00 | 175.00 |
| | 1851 CE — | 60.00 | 100.00 | 150.00 | 225.00 |
| | 1853/1 CE — | 60.00 | 100.00 | 150.00 | 225.00 |
| | 1854 CE — | 50.00 | 75.00 | 125.00 | 175.00 |
| | 1856/5/4 CE — | 60.00 | 100.00 | 150.00 | 225.00 |
| | 1856 CE — | 50.00 | 75.00 | 125.00 | 175.00 |
| | 1857/1 CE — | 60.00 | 100.00 | 150.00 | 225.00 |
| | 1857 CE — | 50.00 | 75.00 | 125.00 | 175.00 |
| | 1861 PV — | 50.00 | 75.00 | 125.00 | 175.00 |
| | 1862 CE — | 50.00 | 75.00 | 125.00 | 175.00 |
| | 1863 CE — | 50.00 | 75.00 | 125.00 | 175.00 |
| | 1866 CE — | 50.00 | 75.00 | 125.00 | 175.00 |
| | 1870 CE — | 50.00 | 75.00 | 125.00 | 175.00 |

**Mint mark: Do**

| KM# | Date Mintage | VG | Fine | VF | XF |
|---|---|---|---|---|---|
| 379.1 | 1833/2 RM/RL | | | | |
| | — | 75.00 | 125.00 | 200.00 | 300.00 |
| | 1834 RM — | 60.00 | 100.00 | 150.00 | 200.00 |
| | 1835 RM — | — | — | — | — |
| | 1836 RM/RL — | 60.00 | 100.00 | 150.00 | 200.00 |
| | 1838 RM — | 60.00 | 100.00 | 150.00 | 200.00 |
| | 1846/38 RM — | 75.00 | 125.00 | 200.00 | 300.00 |
| | 1850 JMR — | 75.00 | 125.00 | 175.00 | 225.00 |
| | 1851/31 JMR | | | | |
| | — | 75.00 | 125.00 | 200.00 | 300.00 |
| | 1851 JMR — | 75.00 | 125.00 | 175.00 | 225.00 |
| | 1853 CP — | 75.00 | 125.00 | 175.00 | 225.00 |
| | 1854/34 CP — | 75.00 | 125.00 | 175.00 | 225.00 |
| | 1854/44 CP/RP | | | | |
| | — | 75.00 | 125.00 | 175.00 | 225.00 |
| | 1855 CP — | 75.00 | 125.00 | 175.00 | 225.00 |
| | 1859 CP — | 75.00 | 125.00 | 175.00 | 225.00 |
| | 1861 CP — | 75.00 | 125.00 | 175.00 | 225.00 |
| | 1864 LT/CP — | 75.00 | 125.00 | 175.00 | 225.00 |

**Mint mark: Ga**

| KM# | Date | Mintage | VG | Fine | VF | XF |
|---|---|---|---|---|---|---|
| 379.2 | 1825 FS | — | 60.00 | 90.00 | 125.00 | 200.00 |
| | 1826 FS | — | 60.00 | 90.00 | 125.00 | 200.00 |
| | 1829 FS | — | — | — | — | — |
| | 1831 FS | — | 60.00 | 90.00 | 125.00 | 200.00 |
| | 1834 FS | — | 60.00 | 90.00 | 125.00 | 200.00 |
| | 1835 JG | — | 60.00 | 90.00 | 125.00 | 200.00 |
| | 1842 JG/MC | — | 60.00 | 90.00 | 125.00 | 200.00 |
| | 1843 MC | — | 60.00 | 90.00 | 125.00 | 200.00 |
| | 1847 JG | — | 60.00 | 90.00 | 125.00 | 200.00 |
| | 1848/7 JG | — | 60.00 | 90.00 | 125.00 | 200.00 |
| | 1849 JG | — | 60.00 | 90.00 | 125.00 | 200.00 |
| | 1850/40 JG | — | 60.00 | 125.00 | 225.00 | 325.00 |
| | 1850 JG | — | 60.00 | 90.00 | 125.00 | 200.00 |
| | 1852/1 JG | — | 60.00 | 90.00 | 125.00 | 200.00 |
| | 1856 JG | — | 60.00 | 90.00 | 125.00 | 200.00 |
| | 1857 JG | — | 60.00 | 90.00 | 125.00 | 200.00 |
| | 1859/7 JG | — | 60.00 | 90.00 | 125.00 | 200.00 |
| | 1860/59 JG | — | 60.00 | 90.00 | 125.00 | 200.00 |
| | 1860 JG | — | 60.00 | 90.00 | 125.00 | 200.00 |

**Mint mark: GC**

| KM# | Date | Mintage | VG | Fine | VF | XF |
|---|---|---|---|---|---|---|
| 379.3 | 1844 MP | — | 75.00 | 100.00 | 175.00 | 250.00 |
| | 1845 MP | — | 75.00 | 100.00 | 175.00 | 250.00 |
| | 1846 MP | — | 75.00 | 100.00 | 175.00 | 250.00 |
| | 1847 MP | — | 75.00 | 100.00 | 175.00 | 250.00 |
| | 1848 MP | — | 75.00 | 100.00 | 175.00 | 250.00 |
| | 1849 MP | — | 75.00 | 100.00 | 175.00 | 250.00 |
| | 1850 MP | — | 75.00 | 100.00 | 175.00 | 250.00 |
| | 1851 MP | — | 75.00 | 100.00 | 175.00 | 250.00 |

**Mint mark: Go**

| KM# | Date | Mintage | VG | Fine | VF | XF |
|---|---|---|---|---|---|---|
| 379.4 | 1845 PM | — | 60.00 | 75.00 | 125.00 | 200.00 |
| | 1849 PF | — | 60.00 | 75.00 | 125.00 | 200.00 |
| | 1851 PF | — | 60.00 | 75.00 | 125.00 | 200.00 |
| | 1853 PF | — | 60.00 | 75.00 | 125.00 | 200.00 |
| | 1860 PF | — | 75.00 | 125.00 | 200.00 | 300.00 |
| | 1862 YE | — | 60.00 | 75.00 | 125.00 | 200.00 |

**Mint mark: Mo**

| KM# | Date | Mintage | VG | Fine | VF | XF |
|---|---|---|---|---|---|---|
| 379.5 | 1825 JM | — | 50.00 | 70.00 | 100.00 | 150.00 |
| | 1827/6 JM | — | 50.00 | 70.00 | 100.00 | 150.00 |
| | 1827 JM | — | 50.00 | 70.00 | 100.00 | 150.00 |
| | 1830/29 JM | — | 50.00 | 70.00 | 100.00 | 150.00 |
| | 1831 JM | — | 50.00 | 70.00 | 100.00 | 150.00 |
| | 1832 JM | — | 50.00 | 70.00 | 100.00 | 175.00 |
| | 1833 MJ | — | 50.00 | 70.00 | 100.00 | 150.00 |
| | 1834 ML | — | 50.00 | 70.00 | 125.00 | 175.00 |
| | 1841 ML | — | 50.00 | 70.00 | 125.00 | 175.00 |
| | 1843 MM | — | 50.00 | 70.00 | 100.00 | 150.00 |
| | 1845 MF | — | 50.00 | 70.00 | 100.00 | 150.00 |
| | 1846/5 MF | — | 50.00 | 70.00 | 100.00 | 150.00 |
| | 1848 GC | — | 50.00 | 70.00 | 125.00 | 175.00 |
| | 1850 GC | — | 50.00 | 70.00 | 125.00 | 175.00 |
| | 1856/4 GF | — | 50.00 | 70.00 | 100.00 | 150.00 |
| | 1856/5 GF | — | 50.00 | 70.00 | 100.00 | 150.00 |
| | 1856 GF | — | 50.00 | 70.00 | 100.00 | 150.00 |
| | 1858 FH | — | 50.00 | 70.00 | 125.00 | 175.00 |
| | 1859 FH | — | 50.00 | 70.00 | 100.00 | 150.00 |
| | 1860 TH | — | 50.00 | 70.00 | 125.00 | 175.00 |
| | 1861 CH | — | 50.00 | 70.00 | 100.00 | 150.00 |
| | 1862 CH | — | 50.00 | 70.00 | 125.00 | 175.00 |
| | 1863 TH | — | 50.00 | 70.00 | 100.00 | 150.00 |
| | 1869 CH | — | 50.00 | 70.00 | 100.00 | 150.00 |

**Mint mark: Zs**

| KM# | Date | Mintage | VG | Fine | VF | XF |
|---|---|---|---|---|---|---|
| 379.6 | 1853 OM | — | 100.00 | 125.00 | 200.00 | 300.00 |
| | 1860/59 VL V is inverted A | — | 75.00 | 100.00 | 200.00 | 350.00 |
| | 1860 VL | — | 75.00 | 100.00 | 150.00 | 200.00 |
| | 1862 VL | — | 75.00 | 100.00 | 150.00 | 200.00 |

## 2 ESCUDOS

6.7700 g, .875 GOLD, .1904 oz AGW
Mint mark: C
Obv: Facing eagle.

| KM# | Date | Mintage | VG | Fine | VF | XF |
|---|---|---|---|---|---|---|
| 380 | 1846 CE | — | 100.00 | 150.00 | 225.00 | 325.00 |
| | 1847 CE | — | 100.00 | 150.00 | 225.00 | 325.00 |
| | 1848 CE | — | 100.00 | 150.00 | 225.00 | 325.00 |
| | 1852 CE | — | 100.00 | 150.00 | 225.00 | 325.00 |
| | 1854 CE | — | 100.00 | 175.00 | 250.00 | 375.00 |
| | 1856/4 CE | — | 100.00 | 175.00 | 250.00 | 375.00 |
| | 1857 CE | — | 100.00 | 150.00 | 225.00 | 325.00 |

**Mint mark: Do**

| KM# | Date | Mintage | VG | Fine | VF | XF |
|---|---|---|---|---|---|---|
| 380.1 | 1833 RM | — | 300.00 | 450.00 | 700.00 | 1200. |
| | 1837/4 RM | — | — | — | — | — |
| | 1837 RM | — | — | — | — | — |
| | 1844 RM | — | 275.00 | 400.00 | 600.00 | 1000. |

**Mint mark: EoMo**

| KM# | Date | Mintage | VG | Fine | VF | XF |
|---|---|---|---|---|---|---|
| 380.2 | 1828 LF | — | 700.00 | 1000. | 1750. | 2500. |

**Mint mark: Ga**

| KM# | Date | Mintage | VG | Fine | VF | XF |
|---|---|---|---|---|---|---|
| 380.3 | 1835 FS | — | 100.00 | 150.00 | 225.00 | 325.00 |
| | 1836/5 JG | — | 100.00 | 150.00 | 225.00 | 300.00 |
| | 1839/5 JG | — | — | — | — | — |
| | 1839 JG | — | 100.00 | 150.00 | 200.00 | 275.00 |
| | 1840 MC | — | 100.00 | 150.00 | 200.00 | 275.00 |
| | 1841 MC | — | 100.00 | 150.00 | 250.00 | 400.00 |
| | 1847/6 JG | — | 100.00 | 150.00 | 225.00 | 300.00 |
| | 1848/7 JG | — | 100.00 | 150.00 | 225.00 | 300.00 |
| | 1850/40 JG | — | 100.00 | 150.00 | 200.00 | 250.00 |
| | 1851 JG | — | 100.00 | 150.00 | 200.00 | 275.00 |
| | 1852 JG | — | 100.00 | 150.00 | 225.00 | 325.00 |
| | 1853 JG | — | 100.00 | 150.00 | 200.00 | 275.00 |
| | 1854/2 JG | — | — | — | — | — |
| | 1858 JG | — | 100.00 | 150.00 | 200.00 | 275.00 |
| | 1859/8 JG | — | 100.00 | 150.00 | 225.00 | 300.00 |
| | 1859 JG | — | 100.00 | 150.00 | 200.00 | 275.00 |
| | 1860/50 JG | — | 100.00 | 150.00 | 225.00 | 300.00 |
| | 1860 JG | — | 100.00 | 150.00 | 225.00 | 300.00 |
| | 1861/59 JG | — | 100.00 | 150.00 | 200.00 | 275.00 |
| | 1861/0 JG | — | 100.00 | 150.00 | 200.00 | 275.00 |
| | 1863/1 JG | — | 100.00 | 150.00 | 200.00 | 275.00 |
| | 1870 IC | — | 100.00 | 150.00 | 200.00 | 275.00 |

**Mint mark: GC**

| KM# | Date | Mintage | VG | Fine | VF | XF |
|---|---|---|---|---|---|---|
| 380.4 | 1844 MP | — | 150.00 | 200.00 | 275.00 | 400.00 |
| | 1845 MP | — | 750.00 | 1250. | 2000. | 3000. |
| | 1846 MP | — | 750.00 | 1250. | 2000. | 3000. |
| | 1847 MP | — | 125.00 | 175.00 | 350.00 | 500.00 |
| | 1848 MP | — | 150.00 | 200.00 | 350.00 | 450.00 |
| | 1849 MP | — | 150.00 | 200.00 | 300.00 | 400.00 |
| | 1850 MP | — | 150.00 | 200.00 | 300.00 | 400.00 |

**Mint mark: Go**

| KM# | Date | Mintage | VG | Fine | VF | XF |
|---|---|---|---|---|---|---|
| 380.5 | 1845 PM | — | 100.00 | 150.00 | 250.00 | 400.00 |
| | 1849 PF | — | 100.00 | 150.00 | 250.00 | 400.00 |
| | 1853 PF | — | 100.00 | 150.00 | 250.00 | 400.00 |
| | 1856 PF | — | 100.00 | 150.00 | 250.00 | 400.00 |
| | 1859 PF | — | 100.00 | 150.00 | 250.00 | 400.00 |
| | 1860/59 PF | — | 100.00 | 150.00 | 250.00 | 400.00 |
| | 1860 PF | — | 100.00 | 150.00 | 250.00 | 400.00 |
| | 1862 YE | — | 100.00 | 150.00 | 250.00 | 400.00 |

**Mint mark: Ho**

| KM# | Date | Mintage | VG | Fine | VF | XF |
|---|---|---|---|---|---|---|
| 380.6 | 1861 FM | — | 500.00 | 1000. | 1500. | 2000. |

**Mint mark: Mo**

| KM# | Date | Mintage | VG | Fine | VF | XF |
|---|---|---|---|---|---|---|
| 380.7 | 1825 JM | — | 100.00 | 150.00 | 200.00 | 275.00 |
| | 1827/6 JM | — | 100.00 | 150.00 | 200.00 | 275.00 |
| | 1827 JM | — | 100.00 | 150.00 | 200.00 | 275.00 |
| | 1830/29 JM | — | 100.00 | 150.00 | 200.00 | 275.00 |
| | 1831 JM | — | 100.00 | 150.00 | 200.00 | 275.00 |
| | 1833 ML | — | 100.00 | 150.00 | 200.00 | 275.00 |
| | 1841 ML | — | 100.00 | 150.00 | 200.00 | 275.00 |
| | 1844 MF | — | 100.00 | 150.00 | 200.00 | 275.00 |
| | 1845 MF | — | 100.00 | 150.00 | 200.00 | 275.00 |
| | 1846 MF | — | 125.00 | 200.00 | 400.00 | 600.00 |
| | 1848 GC | — | 100.00 | 150.00 | 200.00 | 275.00 |
| | 1850 GC | — | 100.00 | 150.00 | 200.00 | 275.00 |
| | 1856/5 GF | — | 100.00 | 150.00 | 200.00 | 275.00 |
| | 1856 GF | — | 100.00 | 150.00 | 200.00 | 275.00 |
| | 1858 FH | — | 100.00 | 150.00 | 200.00 | 275.00 |
| | 1859 FH | — | 100.00 | 150.00 | 200.00 | 275.00 |
| | 1861 TH | — | 100.00 | 150.00 | 200.00 | 275.00 |
| | 1861 CH | — | 100.00 | 150.00 | 200.00 | 300.00 |
| | 1862 CH | — | 100.00 | 150.00 | 200.00 | 300.00 |
| | 1863 TH | — | 100.00 | 150.00 | 200.00 | 300.00 |
| | 1868 PH | — | 100.00 | 150.00 | 200.00 | 300.00 |
| | 1869 CH | — | 100.00 | 150.00 | 200.00 | 300.00 |

**Mint mark: Zs**

| KM# | Date | Mintage | VG | Fine | VF | XF |
|---|---|---|---|---|---|---|
| 380.8 | 1860 VL | — | 150.00 | 300.00 | 600.00 | 1200. |
| | 1862 VL | — | 250.00 | 500.00 | 800.00 | 1200. |
| | 1864 MO | — | 150.00 | 300.00 | 600.00 | 1200. |

## 4 ESCUDOS

**13.5400 g, .875 GOLD, .3809 oz AGW**
**Mint mark: C**
**Facing eagle**

| KM# | Date | Mintage | VG | Fine | VF | XF |
|---|---|---|---|---|---|---|
| 381 | 1846 CE | — | 1200. | 1700. | — | — |
| | 1847 CE | — | 400.00 | 650.00 | 850.00 | 1250. |
| | 1848 CE | — | 600.00 | 900.00 | 1250. | 1750. |

**Mint mark: Do**

| | | | | | | |
|---|---|---|---|---|---|---|
| 381.1 | 1832 RM/LR | — | — | — | Rare | — |
| | 1832 RM | — | 600.00 | 900.00 | 1250. | 1750. |
| | 1833 RM/RL | — | — | — | Rare | — |
| | 1852 JMR | — | — | — | Rare | — |

**Mint mark: Ga**

| | | | | | | |
|---|---|---|---|---|---|---|
| 381.2 | 1844 MC | — | 500.00 | 750.00 | 1000. | 1500. |
| | 1844 JG | — | 400.00 | 650.00 | 850.00 | 1250. |

**Mint mark: GC**

| | | | | | | |
|---|---|---|---|---|---|---|
| 381.3 | 1844 MP | — | 400.00 | 650.00 | 850.00 | 1250. |
| | 1845 MP | — | 350.00 | 500.00 | 700.00 | 1000. |
| | 1846 MP | — | 400.00 | 650.00 | 850.00 | 1250. |
| | 1848 MP | — | 400.00 | 650.00 | 850.00 | 1250. |
| | 1850 MP | — | 500.00 | 750.00 | 1000. | 1500. |

**Mint mark: Go**

| | | | | | | |
|---|---|---|---|---|---|---|
| 381.4 | 1829/8 MJ | — | 250.00 | 400.00 | 550.00 | 750.00 |
| | 1829 JM | — | 250.00 | 400.00 | 550.00 | 750.00 |
| | 1829 MJ | — | 250.00 | 400.00 | 550.00 | 750.00 |
| | 1831 MJ | — | 250.00 | 400.00 | 550.00 | 750.00 |
| | 1832 MJ | — | 250.00 | 400.00 | 550.00 | 750.00 |
| | 1833 MJ | — | 250.00 | 400.00 | 600.00 | 850.00 |
| | 1834 PJ | — | 300.00 | 500.00 | 700.00 | 1000. |
| | 1835 PJ | — | 300.00 | 500.00 | 700.00 | 1000. |
| | 1836 PJ | — | 250.00 | 400.00 | 600.00 | 850.00 |
| | 1837 PJ | — | 250.00 | 400.00 | 600.00 | 850.00 |
| | 1838 PJ | — | 250.00 | 400.00 | 600.00 | 850.00 |
| | 1839 PJ | — | 300.00 | 500.00 | 700.00 | 1000. |
| | 1840 PJ | — | 250.00 | 400.00 | 600.00 | 850.00 |
| | 1841 PJ | — | 300.00 | 500.00 | 700.00 | 1000. |
| | 1845 PM | — | 250.00 | 400.00 | 600.00 | 850.00 |
| | 1847/5 YE | — | 300.00 | 500.00 | 700.00 | 1000. |
| | 1847 PM | — | 300.00 | 500.00 | 700.00 | 1000. |
| | 1849 PF | — | 300.00 | 500.00 | 700.00 | 1000. |
| | 1851 PF | — | 300.00 | 500.00 | 700.00 | 1000. |
| | 1852 PF | — | 250.00 | 400.00 | 600.00 | 850.00 |
| | 1855 PF | — | 250.00 | 400.00 | 600.00 | 850.00 |
| | 1857/5 PF | — | 250.00 | 400.00 | 600.00 | 850.00 |
| | 1858/7 PF | — | 250.00 | 400.00 | 600.00 | 850.00 |
| | 1858 PF | — | 250.00 | 400.00 | 600.00 | 850.00 |
| | 1859/7 PF | — | 300.00 | 500.00 | 700.00 | 1000. |
| | 1860 PF | — | 300.00 | 500.00 | 800.00 | 1200. |
| | 1862 YE | — | 250.00 | 400.00 | 600.00 | 850.00 |
| | 1863 YF | — | 250.00 | 400.00 | 600.00 | 850.00 |

**Mint mark: Ho**

| | | | | | | |
|---|---|---|---|---|---|---|
| 381.5 | 1861 FM | — | 1000. | 1500. | 2500. | 4000. |

**Mint mark: Mo**

| | | | | | | |
|---|---|---|---|---|---|---|
| 381.6 | 1825 JM | — | 250.00 | 400.00 | 600.00 | 900.00 |
| | 1827/6 JM | — | 250.00 | 400.00 | 550.00 | 850.00 |
| | 1829 JM | — | 250.00 | 450.00 | 700.00 | 1000. |
| | 1831 JM | — | 250.00 | 450.00 | 700.00 | 1000. |

| KM# | Date | Mintage | VG | Fine | VF | XF |
|---|---|---|---|---|---|---|
| 381.6 | 1832 JM | — | 300.00 | 500.00 | 800.00 | 1200. |
| | 1844 MF | — | 250.00 | 450.00 | 700.00 | 1000. |
| | 1850 GC | — | 250.00 | 450.00 | 700.00 | 1000. |
| | 1856 GF | — | 250.00 | 400.00 | 550.00 | 850.00 |
| | 1857/6 GF | — | 250.00 | 400.00 | 550.00 | 850.00 |
| | 1857 GF | — | 250.00 | 400.00 | 550.00 | 850.00 |
| | 1858 FH | — | 250.00 | 450.00 | 700.00 | 1000. |
| | 1859/8 FH | — | 250.00 | 450.00 | 700.00 | 1000. |
| | 1861 CH | — | 400.00 | 800.00 | 1200. | 1600. |
| | 1863 CH | — | 250.00 | 450.00 | 700.00 | 1000. |
| | 1868 PH | — | 250.00 | 400.00 | 550.00 | 850.00 |
| | 1869 CH | — | 250.00 | 400.00 | 500.00 | 800.00 |

**Mint mark: O, Oa**

| | | | | | | |
|---|---|---|---|---|---|---|
| 381.7 | 1861 FR | — | 1500. | 2500. | 4000. | 7000. |

**Mint mark: Zs**

| | | | | | | |
|---|---|---|---|---|---|---|
| 381.8 | 1862 VL | — | 750.00 | 1250. | 2250. | 3500. |

## 8 ESCUDOS

**Tail Curved**　　　　**Tail Looped**

**27.0700 g, .875 GOLD, .7616 oz AGW**
**Mint mark: Mo**
**Obv: Hooked-neck eagle.**

| KM# | Date | Mintage | Fine | VF | XF | Unc |
|---|---|---|---|---|---|---|
| 382.1 | 1823 JM snake's tail curved | — | 3500. | 6500. | 10,000. | — |

**NOTE:** Superior Casterline sale 5-89 choice AU realized $18,700.

| | | | | | | |
|---|---|---|---|---|---|---|
| 382.2 | 1823 JM snake's tail looped | — | 3500. | 6500. | 10,000. | — |

**Mint mark: A**
**Obv: Facing eagle.**

| KM# | Date | Mintage | Fine | VF | XF | Unc |
|---|---|---|---|---|---|---|
| 383 | 1864 PG | — | 650.00 | 1250. | 2250. | — |
| | 1866 DL | — | — | — | 7500. | — |
| | 1868/7 DL | — | 1500. | 2250. | 3250. | — |
| | 1869 DL | — | 650.00 | 1250. | 2250. | — |
| | 1870 DL | — | 1500. | 2250. | 3250. | — |
| | 1872 AM | — | — | — | Rare | — |

**Mint mark: Ca**

| KM# | Date | Mintage | Fine | VF | XF | Unc |
|---|---|---|---|---|---|---|
| 383.1 | 1841 RG | — | 400.00 | 750.00 | 1250. | 1750. |
| | 1842 RG | — | 375.00 | 500.00 | 1000. | 1500. |
| | 1843 RG | — | 375.00 | 500.00 | 1000. | 1500. |
| | 1844 RG | — | 350.00 | 500.00 | 1000. | 1500. |
| | 1845 RG | — | 350.00 | 500.00 | 1000. | 1500. |
| | 1846 RG | — | 500.00 | 1250. | 1500. | 2000. |
| | 1847 RG | — | 1000. | 2500. | — | — |
| | 1848 RG | — | 350.00 | 500.00 | 1000. | 1500. |
| | 1849 RG | — | 350.00 | 500.00 | 1000. | 1500. |
| | 1850/40 RG | — | 350.00 | 500.00 | 1000. | 1500. |
| | 1851/41 RG | — | 350.00 | 500.00 | 1000. | 1500. |
| | 1852/42 RG | — | 350.00 | 500.00 | 1000. | 1500. |
| | 1853/43 RG | — | 350.00 | 500.00 | 1000. | 1500. |
| | 1854/44 RG | — | 350.00 | 500.00 | 1000. | 1500. |
| | 1855/43 RG | — | 400.00 | 650.00 | 1250. | 1750. |
| | 1856/46 RG | — | 350.00 | 500.00 | 750.00 | 1250. |
| | 1857 JC/RG | — | 350.00 | 500.00 | 750.00 | 1250. |
| | 1858 JC | — | 350.00 | 500.00 | 750.00 | 1250. |
| | 1858 BA/RG | — | 350.00 | 500.00 | 750.00 | 1250. |
| | 1859 JC/RG | — | 350.00 | 500.00 | 750.00 | 1250. |
| | 1860 JC/RG | — | 350.00 | 500.00 | 1000. | 1500. |
| | 1861 JC | — | 375.00 | 500.00 | 750.00 | 1250. |
| | 1862 JC | — | 375.00 | 500.00 | 750.00 | 1250. |
| | 1863 JC | — | 500.00 | 1000. | 1750. | 2250. |
| | 1864 JC | — | 400.00 | 750.00 | 1250. | 1750. |
| | 1865 JC | — | 750.00 | 1500. | 2500. | 3500. |
| | 1866 JC | — | 375.00 | 500.00 | 1000. | 1500. |
| | 1866 FP | — | 600.00 | 1250. | 2000. | 2500. |
| | 1866 JG | — | 375.00 | 500.00 | 1000. | 1500. |
| | 1867 JG | — | 375.00 | 500.00 | 750.00 | 1250. |
| | 1868 JG concave wings | | | | | |
| | | — | 375.00 | 500.00 | 750.00 | 1250. |
| | 1869 MM regular eagle | | | | | |
| | | — | 375.00 | 500.00 | 750.00 | 1250. |
| | 1870/60 MM | — | 375.00 | 500.00 | 750.00 | 1250. |
| | 1871/61 MM | — | 375.00 | 500.00 | 1000. | 1500. |

**Mint mark: C**

| KM# | Date | Mintage | Fine | VF | XF | Unc |
|---|---|---|---|---|---|---|
| 383.2 | 1846 CE | — | 375.00 | 500.00 | 1000. | 1750. |
| | 1847 CE | — | 375.00 | 500.00 | 800.00 | 1250. |
| | 1848 CE | — | 375.00 | 500.00 | 1000. | 1750. |
| | 1849 CE | — | 375.00 | 450.00 | 700.00 | 1250. |
| | 1850 CE | — | 375.00 | 450.00 | 700.00 | 1250. |
| | 1851 CE | — | 375.00 | 500.00 | 800.00 | 1250. |
| | 1852 CE | — | 375.00 | 500.00 | 800.00 | 1250. |
| | 1853/1 CE | — | 375.00 | 450.00 | 700.00 | 1250. |
| | 1854 CE | — | 375.00 | 450.00 | 700.00 | 1250. |
| | 1855/4 CE | — | 375.00 | 500.00 | 1000. | 1750. |
| | 1855 CE | — | 375.00 | 500.00 | 800.00 | 1250. |
| | 1856 CE | — | 375.00 | 450.00 | 700.00 | 1250. |
| | 1857 CE | — | 375.00 | 450.00 | 700.00 | 1250. |
| | 1857 CE w/o periods after C's | | | | | |
| | | — | — | — | — | — |
| | 1858 CE | — | 375.00 | 450.00 | 700.00 | 1250. |
| | 1859 CE | — | 375.00 | 450.00 | 700.00 | 1250. |
| | 1860/58 CE | — | 375.00 | 500.00 | 800.00 | 1250. |
| | 1860 CE | — | 375.00 | 500.00 | 800.00 | 1250. |
| | 1860 PV | — | 375.00 | 450.00 | 700.00 | 1250. |
| | 1861 PV | — | 375.00 | 500.00 | 800.00 | 1250. |

| KM# | Date | Mintage | Fine | VF | XF | Unc |
|---|---|---|---|---|---|---|
| 383.2 | 1861 CE | — | 375.00 | 500.00 | 800.00 | 1250. |
| | 1862 CE | — | 375.00 | 500.00 | 800.00 | 1250. |
| | 1863 CE | — | 375.00 | 500.00 | 800.00 | 1250. |
| | 1864 CE | — | 375.00 | 450.00 | 700.00 | 1250. |
| | 1865 CE | — | 375.00 | 500.00 | 800.00 | 1250. |
| | 1866/5 CE | — | 375.00 | 450.00 | 700.00 | 1250. |
| | 1866 CE | — | 375.00 | 450.00 | 700.00 | 1250. |
| | 1867 CB (error) | | | | | |
| | | — | 375.00 | 450.00 | 700.00 | 1250. |
| | 1867 CE/CB | — | 375.00 | 450.00 | 700.00 | 1250. |
| | 1868 CB (error) | | | | | |
| | | — | 375.00 | 500.00 | 800.00 | 1250. |
| | 1869 CE | — | 375.00 | 500.00 | 800.00 | 1250. |
| | 1870 CE | — | 375.00 | 500.00 | 800.00 | 1250. |

**Mint mark: Do**

| KM# | Date | Mintage | Fine | VF | XF | Unc |
|---|---|---|---|---|---|---|
| 383.3 | 1832 RM | — | 850.00 | 1750. | 2000. | 3000. |
| | 1833 RM/RL | — | 375.00 | 500.00 | 800.00 | 1250. |
| | 1834 RM | — | 375.00 | 500.00 | 800.00 | 1250. |
| | 1835 RM | — | 375.00 | 500.00 | 800.00 | 1250. |
| | 1836 RM/RL | — | 375.00 | 500.00 | 800.00 | 1250. |
| | 1836 RM M on snake | | | | | |
| | | — | 375.00 | 500.00 | 800.00 | 1250. |
| | 1837 RM | — | 375.00 | 500.00 | 800.00 | 1250. |
| | 1838/6 RM | — | 375.00 | 500.00 | 800.00 | 1250. |
| | 1838 RM | — | 375.00 | 500.00 | 800.00 | 1250. |
| | 1839 RM | — | 375.00 | 450.00 | 700.00 | 1250. |
| | 1840/30 RM/RL | | | | | |
| | | — | 400.00 | 600.00 | 1000. | 1750. |
| | 1841/30 RM | — | 550.00 | 750.00 | 1250. | 2000. |
| | 1841/31 RM | — | 375.00 | 500.00 | 800.00 | 1250. |
| | 1841/34 RM | — | 375.00 | 500.00 | 800.00 | 1250. |
| | 1841 RM/RL | — | 375.00 | 500.00 | 800.00 | 1250. |
| | 1842/32 RM | — | 375.00 | 500.00 | 800.00 | 1250. |
| | 1843/33 RM | — | 550.00 | 750.00 | 1250. | 2000. |
| | 1843/1 RM | — | 375.00 | 500.00 | 800.00 | 1250. |
| | 1843 RM | — | 375.00 | 500.00 | 800.00 | 1250. |
| | 1844/34 RM/RL | | | | | |
| | | — | 500.00 | 1000. | 1500. | 2500. |
| | 1844 RM | — | 450.00 | 800.00 | 1250. | 2000. |
| | 1845/36 RM | — | 400.00 | 600.00 | 1000. | 1750. |
| | 1845 RM | — | 400.00 | 600.00 | 1000. | 1750. |
| | 1846 RM | — | 375.00 | 500.00 | 800.00 | 1250. |
| | 1847/37 RM | — | 375.00 | 500.00 | 800.00 | 1250. |
| | 1848/37 RM | — | — | — | — | — |
| | 1848/38 CM | — | 375.00 | 500.00 | 800.00 | 1250. |
| | 1849/39 CM | — | 375.00 | 500.00 | 800.00 | 1250. |
| | 1849 JMR | — | 400.00 | 750.00 | 1250. | 2000. |
| | 1850 JMR | — | 400.00 | 750.00 | 1250. | 2000. |
| | 1851 JMR | — | 400.00 | 750.00 | 1250. | 2000. |
| | 1852/1 JMR | — | 450.00 | 800.00 | 1250. | 2000. |
| | 1852 CP | — | 450.00 | 800.00 | 1250. | 2000. |
| | 1853 CP | — | 450.00 | 800.00 | 1250. | 2000. |
| | 1854 CP | — | 400.00 | 600.00 | 1000. | 1750. |
| | 1855/4 CP | — | 375.00 | 500.00 | 800.00 | 1250. |
| | 1855 CP | — | 375.00 | 500.00 | 800.00 | 1250. |
| | 1856 CP | — | 400.00 | 600.00 | 1000. | 1750. |
| | 1857 CP French style eagle, 1832-57 | | | | | |
| | | — | 375.00 | 500.00 | 800.00 | 1250. |
| | 1857 CP Mexican style eagle | | | | | |
| | | — | 375.00 | 500.00 | 800.00 | 1250. |
| | 1858 CP | — | 375.00 | 500.00 | 800.00 | 1250. |
| | 1859 CP | — | 375.00 | 500.00 | 800.00 | 1250. |
| | 1860/59 CP | — | 450.00 | 700.00 | 1250. | 2200. |
| | 1861/0 CP | — | 400.00 | 600.00 | 1000. | 1750. |
| | 1862/52 CP | — | 375.00 | 500.00 | 800.00 | 1250. |
| | 1862/1 CP | — | 375.00 | 500.00 | 800.00 | 1250. |
| | 1862 CP | — | 375.00 | 500.00 | 800.00 | 1250. |

| KM# | Date | Mintage | Fine | VF | XF | Unc |
|---|---|---|---|---|---|---|
| 383.3 | 1863/53 CP | — | 375.00 | 500.00 | 800.00 | 1250. |
| | 1864 LT | — | 375.00 | 500.00 | 800.00 | 1250. |
| | 1865/4 LT | — | 500.00 | 1000. | 1650. | 2750. |
| | 1866/4 CM | — | 1250. | 2000. | 2500. | — |
| | 1866 CM | — | 400.00 | 600.00 | 1000. | 1750. |
| | 1867/56 CP | — | 400.00 | 600.00 | 1000. | 1750. |
| | 1867/4 CP | — | 375.00 | 500.00 | 800.00 | 1250. |
| | 1868/4 CP/LT | | | | | |
| | | — | — | — | — | — |
| | 1869 CP | — | 500.00 | 1250. | 1750. | 2750. |
| | 1870 CP | — | 400.00 | 600.00 | 1000. | 1750. |

**Mint mark: EoMo**

| KM# | Date | Mintage | Fine | VF | XF | Unc |
|---|---|---|---|---|---|---|
| 383.4 | 1828 LF | — | 2500. | 4500. | 7500. | — |
| | 1829 LF | — | 2500. | 4500. | 7500. | — |

**Mint mark: Ga**

| KM# | Date | Mintage | Fine | VF | XF | Unc |
|---|---|---|---|---|---|---|
| 383.5 | 1825 FS | — | 500.00 | 1000. | 1250. | 1750. |
| | 1826 FS | — | 500.00 | 1000. | 1250. | 1750. |
| | 1830 FS | — | 500.00 | 1000. | 1250. | 1750. |
| | 1836 FS | — | 750.00 | 1500. | 2000. | 3000. |
| | 1836 JG | — | 1000. | 2500. | 3500. | — |
| | 1837 JG | — | 1000. | 2500. | 3500. | — |
| | 1840 MC | — | 750.00 | 1500. | 2000. | 3000. |
| | 1841/31 MC | — | 1000. | 2500. | | — |
| | 1841 MC | — | 850.00 | 1650. | 2250. | — |
| | 1842 JG | — | — | — | — | — |
| | 1843 MC | — | — | — | — | — |
| | 1845 MC | — | 400.00 | 750.00 | 1000. | 1500. |
| | 1847 JG | — | 2250. | — | — | — |
| | 1849 JG | — | 500.00 | 1000. | 1250. | 1750. |
| | 1850 JG | — | 400.00 | 750.00 | 1000. | 1500. |
| | 1851 JG | — | 400.00 | 750.00 | 1000. | 1500. |
| | 1852/1 JG | — | 500.00 | 1000. | 1250. | 1750. |
| | 1855 JG | — | 1000. | 2500. | 3500. | — |
| | 1856 JG | — | 400.00 | 750.00 | 1000. | 1500. |
| | 1857 JG | — | 400.00 | 750.00 | 1000. | 1500. |
| | 1861/0 JG | — | 500.00 | 1000. | 1250. | 1750. |
| | 1861 JG | — | 400.00 | 600.00 | 1000. | 1750. |
| | 1863/1 JG | — | 500.00 | 1000. | 1250. | 1750. |
| | 1866 JG | — | 400.00 | 750.00 | 1000. | 1500. |

**Mint mark: GC**

| KM# | Date | Mintage | Fine | VF | XF | Unc |
|---|---|---|---|---|---|---|
| 383.6 | 1844 MP | — | 550.00 | 750.00 | 1250. | 2000. |
| | 1845 MP eagle's tail square | | | | | |
| | | — | 550.00 | 750.00 | 1250. | 2000. |
| | 1845 MP eagle's tail round | | | | | |
| | | — | 550.00 | 750.00 | 1250. | 2000. |
| | 1846 MP eagle's tail square | | | | | |
| | | — | 450.00 | 650.00 | 1000. | 1750. |
| | 1846 MP eagle's tail round | | | | | |
| | | — | 450.00 | 650.00 | 1000. | 1750. |
| | 1847 MP | — | 450.00 | 650.00 | 1000. | 1750. |
| | 1848 MP | — | 550.00 | 750.00 | 1250. | 2000. |
| | 1849 MP | — | 550.00 | 750.00 | 1250. | 2000. |
| | 1850 MP | — | 450.00 | 650.00 | 1000. | 1750. |
| | 1851 MP | — | 450.00 | 650.00 | 1000. | 1750. |
| | 1852 MP | — | 550.00 | 750.00 | 1250. | 2000. |

**Mint mark: Go**

| KM# | Date | Mintage | Fine | VF | XF | Unc |
|---|---|---|---|---|---|---|
| 383.7 | 1828 MJ | — | 700.00 | 1750. | 2250. | 3000. |
| | 1829 MJ | — | 600.00 | 1500. | 2000. | 2750. |
| | 1830 MJ | — | 375.00 | 500.00 | 750.00 | 1000. |
| | 1831 MJ | — | 600.00 | 1500. | 2000. | 2750. |
| | 1832 MJ | — | 500.00 | 1250. | 1750. | 2500. |
| | 1833 MJ | — | 375.00 | 500.00 | 750.00 | 1000. |
| | 1834 PJ | — | 375.00 | 500.00 | 750.00 | 1000. |
| | 1835 PJ | — | 375.00 | 500.00 | 750.00 | 1000. |
| | 1836 PJ | — | 400.00 | 650.00 | 900.00 | 1250. |
| | 1837 PJ | — | 400.00 | 650.00 | 900.00 | 1250. |

**Mint mark: Go**

| KM# | Date | Mintage | Fine | VF | XF | Unc |
|---|---|---|---|---|---|---|
| 383.7 | 1838/7 PJ | — | 375.00 | 500.00 | 750.00 | 1000. |
| | 1838 PJ | — | 375.00 | 500.00 | 800.00 | 1200. |
| | 1839/8 PJ | — | 375.00 | 500.00 | 750.00 | 1000. |
| | 1839 PJ regular eagle | | | | | |
| | | — | 375.00 | 500.00 | 800.00 | 1200. |
| | 1840 PJ concave wings | | | | | |
| | | — | 375.00 | 500.00 | 750.00 | 1000. |
| | 1841 PJ | — | 375.00 | 500.00 | 750.00 | 1000. |
| | 1842 PJ | — | 375.00 | 475.00 | 650.00 | 1000. |
| | 1842 PM | — | 375.00 | 500.00 | 750.00 | 1000. |
| | 1843 PM small eagle | | | | | |
| | | — | 375.00 | 500.00 | 750.00 | 1000. |
| | 1844/3 PM | — | 400.00 | 650.00 | 900.00 | 1250. |
| | 1844 PM | — | 375.00 | 500.00 | 750.00 | 1000. |
| | 1845 PM | — | 375.00 | 500.00 | 750.00 | 1000. |
| | 1846/5 PM | — | 375.00 | 500.00 | 800.00 | 1200. |
| | 1846 PM | — | 375.00 | 500.00 | 750.00 | 1000. |
| | 1847 PM | — | 400.00 | 650.00 | 900.00 | 1250. |
| | 1848/7 PM | — | 375.00 | 500.00 | 750.00 | 1000. |
| | 1848 PM | — | 375.00 | 500.00 | 750.00 | 1000. |
| | 1848 PF | — | 375.00 | 500.00 | 750.00 | 1000. |
| | 1849 PF | — | 375.00 | 425.00 | 650.00 | 900.00 |
| | 1850 PF | — | 375.00 | 425.00 | 650.00 | 900.00 |
| | 1851 PF | — | 375.00 | 500.00 | 750.00 | 1000. |
| | 1852 PF | — | 375.00 | 500.00 | 750.00 | 1000. |
| | 1853 PF | — | 375.00 | 425.00 | 650.00 | 900.00 |
| | 1854 PF eagle of 1853 | | | | | |
| | | — | 375.00 | 500.00 | 750.00 | 1000. |
| | 1854 PF eagle of 1855 | | | | | |
| | | — | 375.00 | 500.00 | 750.00 | 1000. |
| | 1855/4 PF | — | 400.00 | 650.00 | 900.00 | 1250. |
| | 1855 PF | — | 375.00 | 500.00 | 750.00 | 1000. |
| | 1856 PF | — | 375.00 | 500.00 | 750.00 | 1000. |
| | 1857 PF | — | 375.00 | 500.00 | 750.00 | 1000. |
| | 1858 PF | — | 375.00 | 500.00 | 750.00 | 1000. |
| | 1859 PF | — | 375.00 | 400.00 | 550.00 | 750.00 |
| | 1860/50 PF | — | 375.00 | 425.00 | 650.00 | 900.00 |
| | 1860/59 PF | — | 400.00 | 650.00 | 900.00 | 1250. |
| | 1860 PF | — | 375.00 | 500.00 | 750.00 | 1100. |
| | 1861/0 PF | — | 375.00 | 400.00 | 500.00 | 750.00 |
| | 1861 PF | — | 375.00 | 400.00 | 500.00 | 750.00 |
| | 1862/1 YE | — | 375.00 | 500.00 | 750.00 | 1000. |
| | 1862 YE | — | 375.00 | 500.00 | 750.00 | 1000. |
| | 1862 YF | — | — | — | — | — |
| | 1863/53 YF | — | 375.00 | 500.00 | 750.00 | 1000. |
| | 1863 PF | — | 375.00 | 500.00 | 750.00 | 1000. |
| | 1867/57 YF/PF | | | | | |
| | | — | 375.00 | 500.00 | 750.00 | 1000. |
| | 1867 YF | — | 375.00 | 500.00 | 750.00 | 1000. |
| | 1868/58 YF | — | 375.00 | 500.00 | 750.00 | 1000. |
| | 1870 FR | — | 375.00 | 425.00 | 650.00 | 900.00 |

**Mint mark: Ho**

| KM# | Date | Mintage | Fine | VF | XF | Unc |
|---|---|---|---|---|---|---|
| 383.8 | 1863 FM | — | 400.00 | 650.00 | 1000. | 2000. |
| | 1864 FM | — | 600.00 | 1250. | 1750. | 2750. |
| | 1864 PR/FM | — | 400.00 | 650.00 | 1000. | 2000. |
| | 1865 FM/PR | — | 500.00 | 800.00 | 1250. | 2500. |
| | 1867/57 PR | — | 400.00 | 650.00 | 1000. | 2000. |
| | 1868 PR | — | 500.00 | 800.00 | 1250. | 2500. |
| | 1868 PR/FM | — | 500.00 | 800.00 | 1250. | 2500. |
| | 1869 PR/FM | — | 400.00 | 650.00 | 1000. | 2000. |
| | 1869 PR | — | 400.00 | 650.00 | 1000. | 2000. |
| | 1870 PR | — | 400.00 | 650.00 | 1000. | 2000. |
| | 1871/0 PR | — | 500.00 | 800.00 | 1250. | 2500. |
| | 1871 PR | — | 500.00 | 800.00 | 1250. | 2500. |
| | 1872/1 PR | — | 600.00 | 1250. | 1750. | 2750. |
| | 1873 PR | — | 400.00 | 650.00 | 1000. | 2000. |

Large book.

| KM# | Date | Mintage | Fine | VF | XF | Unc |
|---|---|---|---|---|---|---|
| 383.9 | 1855 GF | — | 375.00 | 450.00 | 600.00 | 900.00 |
| | 1856/5 GF | — | 375.00 | 450.00 | 600.00 | 900.00 |
| | 1856 GF | — | 375.00 | 450.00 | 600.00 | 900.00 |
| | 1857 GF | — | 375.00 | 450.00 | 600.00 | 900.00 |
| | 1858 FH | — | 375.00 | 450.00 | 600.00 | 900.00 |
| | 1859 FH | — | 400.00 | 750.00 | 1000. | 1500. |
| | 1860 FH | — | 375.00 | 450.00 | 600.00 | 900.00 |
| | 1860 TH | — | 375.00 | 450.00 | 600.00 | 900.00 |
| | 1861/51 CH | — | 375.00 | 450.00 | 600.00 | 900.00 |
| | 1862 CH | — | 375.00 | 450.00 | 600.00 | 900.00 |
| | 1863/53 CH | — | 375.00 | 450.00 | 600.00 | 900.00 |
| | 1863/53 TH | — | 375.00 | 450.00 | 600.00 | 900.00 |
| | 1867 CH | — | 375.00 | 450.00 | 600.00 | 900.00 |
| | 1868 CH | — | 375.00 | 450.00 | 600.00 | 900.00 |
| | 1868 PH | — | 375.00 | 450.00 | 600.00 | 900.00 |
| | 1869 CH | — | 375.00 | 450.00 | 600.00 | 900.00 |

NOTE: Formerly reported 1825/3 JM is merely a reworked 5.

Small book.
Mint mark: Mo

| KM# | Date | Mintage | Fine | VF | XF | Unc |
|---|---|---|---|---|---|---|
| 383.9 | 1824 JM lg. book reverse | | | | | |
| | | — | 500.00 | 1000. | 1250. | 2000. |
| | 1825 JM sm. book reverse | | | | | |
| | | — | 375.00 | 450.00 | 600.00 | 1000. |
| | 1826/5 JM | — | 700.00 | 1750. | 2250. | 3000. |
| | 1827 JM | — | 375.00 | 600.00 | 725.00 | 1000. |
| | 1828 JM | — | 375.00 | 600.00 | 725.00 | 1000. |
| | 1829 JM | — | 375.00 | 600.00 | 725.00 | 1000. |
| | 1830 JM | — | 375.00 | 600.00 | 725.00 | 1000. |
| | 1831 JM | — | 375.00 | 600.00 | 725.00 | 1000. |
| | 1832/1 JM | — | 375.00 | 600.00 | 725.00 | 1000. |
| | 1832 JM | — | 375.00 | 600.00 | 725.00 | 1000. |
| | 1833 MJ | — | 400.00 | 750.00 | 1000. | 1500. |
| | 1833 ML | — | 375.00 | 450.00 | 600.00 | 900.00 |
| | 1834 ML | — | 375.00 | 450.00 | 600.00 | 900.00 |
| | 1835/4 ML | — | 500.00 | 1000. | 1250. | 2000. |
| | 1836 ML | — | 375.00 | 450.00 | 600.00 | 900.00 |
| | 1836 MF | — | 500.00 | 700.00 | 1200. | 2000. |
| | 1837/6 ML | — | 375.00 | 450.00 | 600.00 | 900.00 |
| | 1838 ML | — | 375.00 | 450.00 | 600.00 | 900.00 |
| | 1839 ML | — | 375.00 | 450.00 | 600.00 | 900.00 |
| | 1840 ML | — | 375.00 | 450.00 | 600.00 | 900.00 |
| | 1841 ML | — | 375.00 | 450.00 | 600.00 | 900.00 |
| | 1842/1 ML | — | — | — | — | — |
| | 1842 ML | — | 375.00 | 450.00 | 600.00 | 900.00 |
| | 1842 MM | — | — | — | — | — |
| | 1843 MM | — | 375.00 | 450.00 | 600.00 | 900.00 |
| | 1844 MF | — | 375.00 | 450.00 | 600.00 | 900.00 |
| | 1845 MF | — | 375.00 | 450.00 | 600.00 | 900.00 |
| | 1846 MF | — | 500.00 | 1000. | 1250. | 2000. |
| | 1847 MF | — | 950.00 | 2250. | — | — |
| | 1847 RC | — | 375.00 | 500.00 | 800.00 | 1250. |
| | 1848 GC | — | 375.00 | 450.00 | 600.00 | 900.00 |
| | 1849 GC | — | 375.00 | 450.00 | 600.00 | 900.00 |
| | 1850 GC | — | 375.00 | 450.00 | 600.00 | 900.00 |
| | 1851 GC | — | 375.00 | 450.00 | 600.00 | 900.00 |
| | 1852 GC | — | 375.00 | 450.00 | 600.00 | 900.00 |
| | 1853 GC | — | 375.00 | 450.00 | 600.00 | 900.00 |
| | 1854/44 GC | — | 375.00 | 450.00 | 600.00 | 900.00 |
| | 1854/3 GC | — | 375.00 | 450.00 | 600.00 | 900.00 |

Mint mark: O

| KM# | Date | Mintage | Fine | VF | XF | Unc |
|---|---|---|---|---|---|---|
| 383.10 | 1858 AE | — | 2000. | 3000. | 4000. | 6000. |
| | 1859 AE | — | 1000. | 2500. | 3750. | 5500. |
| | 1860 AE | — | 1000. | 2500. | 3750. | 5500. |
| | 1861 FR | — | 450.00 | 900.00 | 1500. | 2750. |
| | 1862 FR | — | 450.00 | 900.00 | 1500. | 2750. |
| | 1863 FR | — | 450.00 | 900.00 | 1500. | 2750. |
| | 1864 FR | — | 500.00 | 900.00 | 1500. | 2750. |
| | 1867 AE | — | 450.00 | 900.00 | 1500. | 2750. |
| | 1868 AE | — | 450.00 | 900.00 | 1500. | 2750. |
| | 1869 AE | — | 450.00 | 900.00 | 1500. | 2750. |

Mint mark: Zs

| KM# | Date | Mintage | Fine | VF | XF | Unc |
|---|---|---|---|---|---|---|
| 383.11 | 1858 MO | — | 400.00 | 750.00 | 1000. | 2000. |
| | 1859 MO | — | 375.00 | 450.00 | 650.00 | 900.00 |
| | 1860/59 VL/MO | | | | | |
| | | — | 2000. | 3000. | 4000. | — |
| | 1860/9 MO | — | 400.00 | 750.00 | 1000. | 2000. |
| | 1860 MO | — | 375.00 | 500.00 | 700.00 | 1000. |
| | 1861/0 VL | — | 375.00 | 500.00 | 700.00 | 1000. |
| | 1861 VL | — | 375.00 | 500.00 | 700.00 | 1000. |
| | 1862 VL | — | 375.00 | 500.00 | 700.00 | 1100. |
| | 1863 VL | — | 375.00 | 500.00 | 700.00 | 1000. |
| | 1863 MO | — | 375.00 | 500.00 | 700.00 | 1000. |
| | 1864 MO | — | 750.00 | 1000. | 1500. | 3000. |
| | 1865 MO | — | 375.00 | 500.00 | 700.00 | 1000. |
| | 1865 MP | — | Contemporary counterfeit | | | |
| | 1868 JS | — | 400.00 | 600.00 | 800.00 | 1250. |
| | 1868 YH | — | 400.00 | 600.00 | 800.00 | 1250. |
| | 1869 YH | — | 400.00 | 600.00 | 800.00 | 1250. |
| | 1870 YH | — | 400.00 | 600.00 | 800.00 | 1250. |
| | 1871 YH | — | 400.00 | 600.00 | 800.00 | 1250. |

# EMPIRE OF MAXIMILIAN

## RULER
Maximilian, Emperor, 1864-1867

## MINT MARKS
Refer To Republic Coinage

## MONETARY SYSTEM
100 Centavos = 1 Peso (8 Reales)

## CENTAVO

COPPER
Mint mark: M

| KM# | Date | Mintage | Fine | VF | XF | Unc |
|-----|------|---------|------|-----|-----|-----|
| 384 | 1864 | — | 35.00 | 60.00 | 150.00 | 900.00 |

## 5 CENTAVOS

1.3537 g, .903 SILVER, .0393 oz ASW
Mint mark: G

| KM# | Date | Mintage | Fine | VF | XF | Unc |
|-----|------|---------|------|-----|-----|-----|
| 385 | 1864 | .090 | 17.50 | 35.00 | 65.00 | 225.00 |
| | 1865 | — | 20.00 | 30.00 | 50.00 | 200.00 |
| | 1866 | — | 65.00 | 140.00 | 300.00 | 1800. |

Mint mark: M

| | | | | | | |
|-----|------|---------|------|-----|-----|-----|
| 385.1 | 1864 | — | 12.50 | 20.00 | 40.00 | 200.00 |
| | 1866/4 | — | 25.00 | 40.00 | 75.00 | 365.00 |
| | 1866 | — | 20.00 | 35.00 | 65.00 | 350.00 |

Mint mark: P

| | | | | | | |
|-----|------|---------|------|-----|-----|-----|
| 385.2 | 1864 | — | 100.00 | 215.00 | 950.00 | 2000. |

Mint mark: Z

| | | | | | | |
|-----|------|---------|------|-----|-----|-----|
| 385.3 | 1865 | — | 20.00 | 30.00 | 100.00 | 300.00 |

## 10 CENTAVOS

2.7073 g, .903 SILVER, .0786 oz ASW
Mint mark: G

| KM# | Date | Mintage | Fine | VF | XF | Unc |
|-----|------|---------|------|-----|-----|-----|
| 386 | 1864 | .045 | 17.50 | 35.00 | 65.00 | 225.00 |
| | 1865 | — | 25.00 | 40.00 | 80.00 | 275.00 |

Mint mark: M

| | | | | | | |
|-----|------|---------|------|-----|-----|-----|
| 386.1 | 1864 | — | 12.50 | 20.00 | 40.00 | 200.00 |
| | 1866/4 | — | 20.00 | 30.00 | 55.00 | 275.00 |
| | 1866/5 | — | 20.00 | 30.00 | 65.00 | 300.00 |
| | 1866 | — | 20.00 | 30.00 | 65.00 | 300.00 |

Mint mark: P

| | | | | | | |
|-----|------|---------|------|-----|-----|-----|
| 386.2 | 1864 | — | 60.00 | 110.00 | 200.00 | 550.00 |

Mint mark: Z

| | | | | | | |
|-----|------|---------|------|-----|-----|-----|
| 386.3 | 1865 | — | 25.00 | 50.00 | 120.00 | 450.00 |

## 50 CENTAVOS

13.5365 g, .903 SILVER, .3929 oz ASW
Mint mark: Mo

| KM# | Date | Mintage | Fine | VF | XF | Unc |
|-----|------|---------|------|-----|-----|-----|
| 387 | 1866 | .031 | 30.00 | 50.00 | 100.00 | 550.00 |

## PESO

27.0700 g, .903 SILVER, .7857 oz ASW
Mint mark: Go

| KM# | Date | Mintage | Fine | VF | XF | Unc |
|-----|------|---------|------|-----|-----|-----|
| 388 | 1866 | — | 300.00 | 425.00 | 650.00 | 2250. |

Mint mark: Mo

| | | | | | | |
|-----|------|---------|------|-----|-----|-----|
| 388.1 | 1866 | 2.148 | 25.00 | 40.00 | 80.00 | 325.00 |
| | 1867 | 1.238 | 35.00 | 60.00 | 120.00 | 400.00 |

Mint mark: Pi

| | | | | | | |
|-----|------|---------|------|-----|-----|-----|
| 388.2 | 1866 | — | 40.00 | 80.00 | 150.00 | 600.00 |

## 20 PESOS

33.8400 g, .875 GOLD, .9520 oz AGW
Mint mark: Mo

| KM# | Date | Mintage | Fine | VF | XF | Unc |
|-----|------|---------|------|-----|-----|-----|
| 389 | 1866 | 8,274 | 500.00 | 850.00 | 1150. | 2250. |

## GOLD PESO FANTASIES

Modern gold 'Peso' fantasies of Maximilian exist. Five varieties exist, some dated 1865. One has an eagle in a plain field above a wreath on the reverse. On the second type a numeral '1' appears to either side of the eagle, and the metallic content is designated below: LEY-ORO-K22.

## TRIAL STRIKES (TS)

| KM# | Date | Mintage | Identification | Mkt.Val. |
|-----|------|---------|----------------|----------|
| TS1 | 1866 Mo | — | 20 Pesos, Copper | — |

# REPUBLIC
# DECIMAL COINAGE

100 Centavos = 1 Peso

# UN (1) CENTAVO

**COPPER**
**Mint mark: Mo**
**Obv: Seated Liberty.**

| KM# | Date | Mintage | Fine | VF | XF | Unc |
|---|---|---|---|---|---|---|
| 390 | 1863 round top 3, reeded edge | | | | | |
| | | — | 10.00 | 15.00 | 30.00 | 150.00 |
| | 1863 round top 3, plain edge | | | | | |
| | | — | 10.00 | 15.00 | 30.00 | 150.00 |
| | 1863 flat top 3 | | | | | |
| | | — | 8.00 | 12.50 | 25.00 | 150.00 |

**Mint mark: SLP**

| KM# | Date | Mintage | Fine | VF | XF | Unc |
|---|---|---|---|---|---|---|
| 390.1 | 1863 | 1.025 | 10.00 | 25.00 | 50.00 | 300.00 |

**Mint mark: As**
**Obv: Standing eagle.**

| KM# | Date | Mintage | Fine | VF | XF | Unc |
|---|---|---|---|---|---|---|
| 391 | 1875 | — | — | — | Rare | — |
| | 1876 | .050 | 100.00 | 200.00 | 300.00 | 650.00 |
| | 1880 | — | 25.00 | 50.00 | 100.00 | 400.00 |
| | 1881 | — | 30.00 | 60.00 | 125.00 | 250.00 |

**Mint mark: Cn**

| KM# | Date | Mintage | Fine | VF | XF | Unc |
|---|---|---|---|---|---|---|
| 391.1 | 1874 | .266 | 12.50 | 17.50 | 35.00 | 150.00 |
| | 1875/4 | .153 | 15.00 | 20.00 | 45.00 | 150.00 |
| | 1875 | Inc. Ab. | 10.00 | 15.00 | 25.00 | 150.00 |
| 391.1 | 1876 | .154 | 5.00 | 8.00 | 15.00 | 150.00 |
| | 1877/6 | .993 | 7.50 | 11.50 | 17.50 | 175.00 |
| | 1877 | Inc. Ab. | 6.00 | 9.00 | 15.00 | 150.00 |
| | 1880 | .142 | 7.50 | 10.00 | 12.50 | 150.00 |
| | 1881 | .167 | 7.50 | 10.00 | 25.00 | 175.00 |
| | 1897 large N in mm. | | | | | |
| | | .300 | 2.50 | 5.00 | 12.00 | 50.00 |
| | 1897 small N in mm. | | | | | |
| | | Inc. Ab. | 2.50 | 5.00 | 9.00 | 45.00 |

**Mint mark: Do**

| KM# | Date | Mintage | Fine | VF | XF | Unc |
|---|---|---|---|---|---|---|
| 391.2 | 1879 | .110 | 10.00 | 17.50 | 35.00 | 150.00 |
| | 1880 | .069 | 40.00 | 90.00 | 175.00 | 500.00 |
| | 1891 | — | 8.00 | 11.00 | 30.00 | 150.00 |
| | 1891 Do/Mo | — | 8.00 | 11.00 | 30.00 | 150.00 |

**Mint mark: Ga**

| KM# | Date | Mintage | Fine | VF | XF | Unc |
|---|---|---|---|---|---|---|
| 391.3 | 1872 | .263 | 15.00 | 30.00 | 60.00 | 200.00 |
| | 1873 | .333 | 6.00 | 9.00 | 25.00 | 150.00 |
| | 1874 | .076 | 15.00 | 25.00 | 50.00 | 175.00 |
| | 1875 | — | 10.00 | 15.00 | 30.00 | 150.00 |
| | 1876 | .303 | 3.00 | 6.00 | 17.50 | 150.00 |
| | 1877 | .108 | 4.00 | 6.00 | 20.00 | 150.00 |
| | 1878 | .543 | 4.00 | 6.00 | 15.00 | 150.00 |
| | 1881/71 | .975 | 7.00 | 9.00 | 20.00 | 175.00 |
| | 1881 | Inc. Ab. | 7.00 | 9.00 | 20.00 | 175.00 |
| | 1889 Ga/Mo | — | 3.50 | 5.00 | 25.00 | 125.00 |
| | 1890 | — | 4.00 | 7.50 | 20.00 | 100.00 |

**Mint mark: Go**

| KM# | Date | Mintage | Fine | VF | XF | Unc |
|---|---|---|---|---|---|---|
| 391.4 | 1874 | — | 20.00 | 40.00 | 80.00 | 250.00 |
| | 1875 | .190 | 11.50 | 20.00 | 60.00 | 200.00 |
| | 1876 | — | 125.00 | 200.00 | 350.00 | 750.00 |
| | 1877 | — | — | — | Rare | — |
| | 1878 | .576 | 8.00 | 11.00 | 30.00 | 175.00 |
| | 1880 | .890 | 6.00 | 10.00 | 25.00 | 175.00 |

**Mint mark: Ho**

| KM# | Date | Mintage | Fine | VF | XF | Unc |
|---|---|---|---|---|---|---|
| 391.5 | 1875 | 3,500 | 450.00 | — | — | — |
| | 1876 | 8,508 | 50.00 | 100.00 | 225.00 | 500.00 |
| | 1880 short H, round O | | | | | |
| | | .102 | 7.50 | 15.00 | 35.00 | 150.00 |
| | 1880 tall H, oval O | | | | | |
| | | Inc. Ab. | 7.50 | 15.00 | 35.00 | 150.00 |
| | 1881 | .459 | 5.00 | 10.00 | 25.00 | 150.00 |

**Mint mark: Mo**

| KM# | Date | Mintage | Fine | VF | XF | Unc |
|---|---|---|---|---|---|---|
| 391.6 | 1869 | 1.874 | 7.50 | 25.00 | 60.00 | 200.00 |
| | 1870/69 | 1.200 | 10.00 | 25.00 | 60.00 | 225.00 |
| | 1870 | Inc. Ab. | 8.00 | 20.00 | 50.00 | 200.00 |
| | 1871 | .918 | 8.00 | 15.00 | 40.00 | 200.00 |
| | 1872/1 | 1.625 | 6.50 | 10.00 | 30.00 | 200.00 |
| | 1872 | Inc. Ab. | 6.00 | 9.00 | 25.00 | 200.00 |
| | 1873 | 1.605 | 4.00 | 7.50 | 20.00 | 200.00 |
| | 1874/3 | 1.700 | 5.00 | 7.00 | 15.00 | 100.00 |
| | 1874 | Inc. Ab. | 3.00 | 5.50 | 15.00 | 100.00 |
| | 1874. | Inc. Ab. | 5.00 | 10.00 | 25.00 | 200.00 |
| | 1875 | 1.495 | 6.00 | 8.00 | 30.00 | 100.00 |
| | 1876 | 1.600 | 3.00 | 5.50 | 12.50 | 100.00 |
| | 1877 | 1.270 | 3.00 | 5.50 | 13.50 | 100.00 |
| | 1878/5 | 1.900 | 7.50 | 11.00 | 22.50 | 125.00 |
| | 1878/6 | Inc. Ab. | 7.50 | 11.00 | 22.50 | 125.00 |
| | 1878/7 | Inc. Ab. | 7.50 | 11.00 | 20.00 | 125.00 |
| | 1878 | Inc. Ab. | 6.00 | 9.00 | 13.50 | 100.00 |
| | 1879/8 | 1.505 | 4.50 | 6.50 | 13.50 | 100.00 |
| | 1879 | Inc. Ab. | 3.00 | 5.50 | 11.50 | 75.00 |
| | 1880/70 | 1.130 | 5.50 | 7.50 | 15.00 | 100.00 |
| | 1880/72 | I.A. | 20.00 | 50.00 | 100.00 | 250.00 |
| | 1880/79 | I.A. | 15.00 | 35.00 | 75.00 | 175.00 |
| | 1880 | Inc. Ab. | 4.25 | 6.00 | 12.50 | 75.00 |
| | 1881 | 1.060 | 4.50 | 7.00 | 15.00 | 75.00 |
| | 1886 | 12.687 | 1.50 | 2.00 | 8.50 | 40.00 |
| | 1887 | 7.292 | 1.50 | 2.00 | 5.00 | 35.00 |
| | 1888/78 | 9.984 | 2.50 | 3.00 | 10.00 | 30.00 |
| | 1888/7 | Inc. Ab. | 2.50 | 3.00 | 10.00 | 30.00 |
| | 1888 | Inc. Ab. | 1.50 | 2.00 | 8.50 | 30.00 |
| | 1889 | 19.970 | 2.00 | 3.00 | 8.00 | 30.00 |
| | 1890/89 | | | | | |
| | | 18.726 | 2.50 | 3.00 | 10.00 | 40.00 |
| | 1890/990 | I.A. | 2.50 | 3.00 | 10.00 | 40.00 |
| | 1890 | Inc. Ab. | 1.50 | 2.00 | 8.50 | 30.00 |
| | 1891 | 14.544 | 1.50 | 2.00 | 8.50 | 30.00 |
| | 1892 | 12.908 | 1.50 | 2.00 | 8.50 | 30.00 |
| | 1893/2 | 5.078 | 2.50 | 3.00 | 10.00 | 35.00 |
| | 1893 | Inc. Ab. | 1.50 | 2.00 | 8.50 | 30.00 |
| | 1894/3 | 1.896 | 3.00 | 6.00 | 15.00 | 50.00 |
| | 1894 | Inc. Ab. | 2.00 | 3.00 | 10.00 | 35.00 |
| | 1895/3 | 3.453 | 3.00 | 4.50 | 12.50 | 35.00 |
| | 1895/85 | I.A. | 3.00 | 6.00 | 15.00 | 50.00 |
| | 1895 | Inc. Ab. | 2.00 | 3.00 | 8.50 | 25.00 |
| | 1896 | 3.075 | 2.00 | 3.00 | 8.50 | 25.00 |
| | 1897 | 4.150 | 1.50 | 2.00 | 8.50 | 25.00 |

**NOTE:** Varieties exist.

**Mint mark: Oa**

| KM# | Date | Mintage | Fine | VF | XF | Unc |
|---|---|---|---|---|---|---|
| 391.7 | 1872 | .016 | 300.00 | 500.00 | 1200. | — |
| | 1873 | .011 | 350.00 | 600.00 | — | — |
| | 1874 | 4,835 | 450.00 | — | — | — |
| | 1875 | 2,860 | 500.00 | — | — | — |

**Mint mark: Pi**

| KM# | Date | Mintage | Fine | VF | XF | Unc |
|---|---|---|---|---|---|---|
| 391.8 | 1871 | — | — | — | Rare | — |
| | 1877 | .249 | — | — | Rare | — |
| | 1878 | .751 | 12.50 | 25.00 | 50.00 | 200.00 |
| | 1891 Pi/Mo | — | 10.00 | 17.50 | 35.00 | 150.00 |
| | 1891 | — | 8.00 | 15.00 | 30.00 | 150.00 |

**Mint mark: Zs**

| KM# | Date | Mintage | Fine | VF | XF | Unc |
|---|---|---|---|---|---|---|
| 391.9 | 1872 | .055 | 22.50 | 30.00 | 100.00 | 300.00 |
| | 1873 | 1.460 | 4.00 | 8.00 | 25.00 | 150.00 |
| | 1874/3 | .685 | 5.50 | 11.00 | 30.00 | 250.00 |
| | 1874 | Inc. Ab. | 4.00 | 8.00 | 25.00 | 200.00 |
| | 1875/4 | .200 | 8.50 | 17.00 | 45.00 | 250.00 |
| | 1875 | Inc. Ab. | 7.00 | 14.00 | 35.00 | 200.00 |
| | 1876 | — | 5.00 | 10.00 | 25.00 | 200.00 |
| | 1877 | — | 50.00 | 125.00 | 300.00 | 750.00 |
| | 1878 | — | 4.50 | 9.00 | 25.00 | 200.00 |
| | 1880 | .100 | 5.00 | 10.00 | 30.00 | 200.00 |
| | 1881 | 1.200 | 4.25 | 8.00 | 25.00 | 150.00 |

## COPPER-NICKEL
### Mint: Mexico City

| KM# | Date | Mintage | Fine | VF | XF | Unc |
|---|---|---|---|---|---|---|
| 392 | 1882 | 99.955 | 7.50 | 12.50 | 17.50 | 35.00 |
| | 1883 | Inc. Ab. | .50 | .75 | 1.00 | 1.50 |

### Obv: Restyled eagle.

| 393 | 1898 | 1.529 | 4.00 | 6.00 | 15.00 | 40.00 |
|---|---|---|---|---|---|---|

NOTE: Varieties exist.

### Mint mark: C
### Reduced size

| 394 | 1901 | .220 | 15.00 | 22.50 | 35.00 | 65.00 |
|---|---|---|---|---|---|---|
| | 1902 | .320 | 15.00 | 22.50 | 45.00 | 90.00 |
| | 1903 | .536 | 7.50 | 12.50 | 20.00 | 45.00 |
| | 1904/3 | .148 | 35.00 | 50.00 | 75.00 | 125.00 |
| | 1905 | .110 | 100.00 | 150.00 | 300.00 | 550.00 |

NOTE: Varieties exist.

### Mint mark: M,Mo

| 394.1 | 1899 | .051 | 150.00 | 175.00 | 300.00 | 800.00 |
|---|---|---|---|---|---|---|
| | 1900 wide date | | | | | |
| | | 4.010 | 2.50 | 4.00 | 7.50 | 25.00 |
| | 1900 narrow date | | | | | |
| | | Inc. Ab. | 2.50 | 4.00 | 7.50 | 25.00 |
| | 1901 | 1.494 | 3.00 | 8.00 | 17.50 | 50.00 |
| | 1902/899 | | | | | |
| | | 2.090 | 30.00 | 60.00 | 100.00 | 175.00 |
| | 1902 | Inc. Ab. | 2.25 | 4.00 | 10.00 | 35.00 |
| | 1903 | 8.400 | 1.50 | 2.25 | 4.00 | 20.00 |
| | 1904 | 10.250 | 1.50 | 2.00 | 4.00 | 20.00 |
| | 1905 | 3.643 | 2.25 | 4.00 | 10.00 | 40.00 |

NOTE: Varieties exist.

## 2 CENTAVOS

### COPPER-NICKEL
### Mint: Mexico City

| 395 | 1882 | 50.023 | 2.00 | 3.00 | 7.50 | 15.00 |
|---|---|---|---|---|---|---|
| | 1883/2 | Inc. Ab. | 2.00 | 3.00 | 7.50 | 15.00 |
| | 1883 | Inc. Ab. | .50 | .75 | 1.00 | 2.50 |

## 5 CENTAVOS

| KM# | Date | Mintage | Fine | VF | XF | Unc |
|---|---|---|---|---|---|---|

### 1.3530 g, .903 SILVER, .0392 oz ASW
### Mint mark: Ca
### Obv: Facing eagle. Rev: Denomination in wreath.

| 396 | 1868 | — | 40.00 | 65.00 | 125.00 | 400.00 |
|---|---|---|---|---|---|---|
| | 1869 | *.030 | 25.00 | 40.00 | 100.00 | 350.00 |
| | 1870 | .035 | 30.00 | 50.00 | 100.00 | 350.00 |

### Mint mark: SLP

| 396.1 | 1863 | — | 75.00 | 125.00 | 350.00 | 1200. |
|---|---|---|---|---|---|---|

### Mint mark: Mo
### Rev: Cap and rays.

| 397 | 1867/3 | — | 25.00 | 50.00 | 125.00 | 275.00 |
|---|---|---|---|---|---|---|
| | 1867 | — | 20.00 | 40.00 | 100.00 | 250.00 |
| | 1868/7 | — | 25.00 | 50.00 | 150.00 | 325.00 |
| | 1868 | — | 20.00 | 40.00 | 100.00 | 250.00 |

NOTE: Varieties exist.

### Mint mark: P

| 397.1 | 1868/7 | .034 | 25.00 | 50.00 | 125.00 | 300.00 |
|---|---|---|---|---|---|---|
| | 1868 | Inc. Ab. | 20.00 | 45.00 | 100.00 | 250.00 |
| | 1869 | .014 | 200.00 | 300.00 | 600.00 | — |

### Mint mark: As
### Obv: Standing eagle.

| 398 | 1874 DL | — | 10.00 | 20.00 | 40.00 | 150.00 |
|---|---|---|---|---|---|---|
| | 1875 DL | — | 10.00 | 20.00 | 40.00 | 150.00 |
| | 1876 L | — | 22.00 | 45.00 | 70.00 | 160.00 |
| | 1878 L mule, gold peso obverse | | | | | |
| | | — | 250.00 | 350.00 | 650.00 | — |
| | 1879 L mule, gold peso obverse | | | | | |
| | | — | 40.00 | 65.00 | 120.00 | 275.00 |
| | 1880 L mule, gold peso obverse | | | | | |
| | | .012 | 55.00 | 85.00 | 165.00 | 325.00 |
| | 1886 L | .043 | 12.00 | 25.00 | 50.00 | 165.00 |
| | 1886 L mule, gold peso obverse | | | | | |
| | | Inc. Ab. | 55.00 | 85.00 | 165.00 | 300.00 |
| | 1887 L | .020 | 25.00 | 50.00 | 75.00 | 165.00 |
| | 1888 L | .032 | 12.00 | 25.00 | 50.00 | 125.00 |
| | 1889 L | .016 | 25.00 | 50.00 | 100.00 | 200.00 |
| | 1890 L | .030 | 25.00 | 50.00 | 85.00 | 175.00 |
| | 1891 L | 8,000 | 65.00 | 125.00 | 200.00 | 400.00 |
| | 1892 L | .013 | 20.00 | 40.00 | 60.00 | 125.00 |
| | 1893 L | .024 | 10.00 | 20.00 | 45.00 | 90.00 |
| | 1895 L | .020 | 10.00 | 20.00 | 45.00 | 90.00 |

### Mint mark: CH, Ca

| 398.1 | 1871 M | .014 | 20.00 | 40.00 | 100.00 | 250.00 |
|---|---|---|---|---|---|---|
| | 1873 M crude date | | | | | |
| | | — | 100.00 | 150.00 | 250.00 | 500.00 |
| | 1874 M crude date | | | | | |
| | | — | 25.00 | 50.00 | 75.00 | 150.00 |
| | 1886 M | .025 | 7.50 | 15.00 | 30.00 | 100.00 |
| | 1887 M | .037 | 7.50 | 15.00 | 30.00 | 100.00 |
| | 1887 Ca/MoM | | | | | |
| | | Inc. Ab. | 10.00 | 20.00 | 40.00 | 125.00 |
| | 1888 M | .145 | 1.50 | 3.00 | 6.00 | 25.00 |
| | 1889 M | .044 | 5.00 | 10.00 | 20.00 | 50.00 |
| | 1890 M | .102 | 1.50 | 3.00 | 6.00 | 25.00 |
| | 1891 M | .164 | 1.50 | 3.00 | 6.00 | 25.00 |
| | 1892 M | .085 | 1.50 | 3.00 | 6.00 | 25.00 |
| | 1892 M 9/inverted 9 | | | | | |
| | | Inc. Ab. | 2.00 | 4.00 | 7.50 | 30.00 |
| | 1893 M | .133 | 1.50 | 3.00 | 6.00 | 25.00 |
| | 1894 M | .108 | 1.50 | 3.00 | 6.00 | 25.00 |
| | 1895 M | .074 | 2.00 | 4.00 | 7.50 | 30.00 |

### Mint mark: Cn

| 398.2 | 1871 P | — | 125.00 | 200.00 | 350.00 | — |
|---|---|---|---|---|---|---|
| | 1873 P | 4,992 | 50.00 | 100.00 | 200.00 | 400.00 |
| | 1874 P | — | 25.00 | 50.00 | 100.00 | 200.00 |
| | 1875 P | — | — | — | Rare | — |

| KM# | Date | Mintage | Fine | VF | XF | Unc |
|---|---|---|---|---|---|---|
| 398.2 | 1876 P | — | 25.00 | 50.00 | 100.00 | 200.00 |
| | 1886 M | .010 | 25.00 | 50.00 | 100.00 | 200.00 |
| | 1887 M | .010 | 25.00 | 50.00 | 100.00 | 200.00 |
| | 1888 M | .119 | 1.50 | 3.00 | 6.00 | 30.00 |
| | 1889 M | .066 | 4.00 | 7.50 | 15.00 | 50.00 |
| | 1890 M | .180 | 1.50 | 3.00 | 6.00 | 25.00 |
| | 1890 D (error) | | | | | |
| | Inc. Ab. | 125.00 | 175.00 | 250.00 | | — |
| | 1891 M | .087 | 2.00 | 4.00 | 7.50 | 25.00 |
| | 1894 M | .024 | 4.00 | 7.50 | 15.00 | 40.00 |
| | 1896 M | .016 | 7.50 | 12.50 | 25.00 | 75.00 |
| | 1897 M | .223 | 1.50 | 2.50 | 5.00 | 20.00 |

**Mint mark: Do**

| KM# | Date | Mintage | Fine | VF | XF | Unc |
|---|---|---|---|---|---|---|
| 398.3 | 1874 M | — | 100.00 | 150.00 | 225.00 | 500.00 |
| | 1877 P | 4,795 | 75.00 | 125.00 | 225.00 | 450.00 |
| | 1878/7 E/P | | | | | |
| | | 4,300 | 200.00 | 300.00 | 450.00 | — |
| | 1879 B | — | 125.00 | 200.00 | 350.00 | — |
| | 1880 B | — | — | — | Rare | — |
| | 1881 P | 3,020 | 300.00 | 500.00 | 800.00 | — |
| | 1887 C | .042 | 5.00 | 8.00 | 17.50 | 60.00 |
| | 1888/9 C | .091 | 6.00 | 10.00 | 20.00 | 70.00 |
| | 1888 C Inc. Ab. | | 4.00 | 7.50 | 15.00 | 55.00 |
| | 1889 C | .049 | 3.50 | 6.00 | 12.50 | 50.00 |
| | 1890 C | .136 | 4.00 | 7.50 | 15.00 | 55.00 |
| | 1890 P Inc. Ab. | | 5.00 | 8.00 | 17.50 | 60.00 |
| | 1891/0 P | .048 | 3.50 | 6.00 | 12.50 | 50.00 |
| | 1891 P Inc. Ab. | | 3.00 | 5.00 | 10.00 | 45.00 |
| | 1894 D | .038 | 3.50 | 6.00 | 12.50 | 50.00 |

**Mint mark: Ga**

| KM# | Date | Mintage | Fine | VF | XF | Unc |
|---|---|---|---|---|---|---|
| 398.4 | 1877 A | — | 15.00 | 30.00 | 60.00 | 150.00 |
| | 1881 S | .156 | 4.00 | 7.50 | 15.00 | 60.00 |
| | 1886 S | .087 | 2.00 | 4.00 | 7.50 | 25.00 |
| | 1888 S lg.G | | | | | |
| | | .262 | 2.00 | 4.00 | 10.00 | 30.00 |
| | 1888 S sm.g | | | | | |
| | Inc. Ab. | | 2.00 | 4.00 | 10.00 | 30.00 |
| | 1889 S | .178 | 1.50 | 3.00 | 7.50 | 25.00 |
| | 1890 S | .068 | 4.00 | 7.50 | 12.50 | 35.00 |
| | 1891 S | .050 | 4.00 | 6.50 | 10.00 | 35.00 |
| | 1892 S | .078 | 2.00 | 4.00 | 7.50 | 25.00 |
| | 1893 S | .044 | 4.00 | 4.00 | 15.00 | 45.00 |

**Mint mark: Go**

| KM# | Date | Mintage | Fine | VF | XF | Unc |
|---|---|---|---|---|---|---|
| 398.5 | 1869 S | .080 | 15.00 | 30.00 | 75.00 | 175.00 |
| | 1871 S | .100 | 5.00 | 10.00 | 25.00 | 75.00 |
| | 1872 S | .030 | 30.00 | 60.00 | 125.00 | 250.00 |
| | 1873 S | .040 | 30.00 | 60.00 | 125.00 | 250.00 |
| | 1874 S | — | 7.00 | 12.00 | 25.00 | 75.00 |
| | 1875 S | — | 8.00 | 15.00 | 30.00 | 75.00 |
| | 1876 S | — | 8.00 | 15.00 | 30.00 | 75.00 |
| | 1877 S | — | 7.00 | 12.00 | 20.00 | 75.00 |
| | 1878/7 S | .020 | 8.00 | 15.00 | 25.00 | 75.00 |
| | 1879 S | — | 8.00 | 15.00 | 25.00 | 75.00 |
| | 1880 S | .055 | 15.00 | 30.00 | 60.00 | 200.00 |
| | 1881/0 S | .160 | 5.00 | 8.00 | 17.50 | 60.00 |
| | 1881 S Inc. Ab. | | 4.00 | 6.00 | 12.00 | 45.00 |
| | 1886 R | .230 | 1.50 | 3.00 | 6.00 | 30.00 |
| | 1887 R | .230 | 1.50 | 2.50 | 5.00 | 30.00 |
| | 1888 R | .320 | 1.50 | 2.50 | 5.00 | 20.00 |
| | 1889 R | .060 | 4.00 | 6.00 | 12.00 | 45.00 |
| | 1890 R | .250 | 1.50 | 2.50 | 5.00 | 20.00 |
| | 1891/0 R | .168 | 1.80 | 3.00 | 6.00 | 30.00 |
| | 1891 R Inc. Ab. | | 1.50 | 2.50 | 5.00 | 20.00 |
| | 1892 R | .138 | 1.50 | 3.00 | 6.00 | 25.00 |
| | 1893 R | .200 | 1.25 | 2.50 | 5.00 | 20.00 |
| | 1894 R | .200 | 1.25 | 2.50 | 5.00 | 20.00 |
| | 1896 R | .525 | 1.25 | 2.00 | 4.00 | 15.00 |
| | 1897 R | .596 | 1.50 | 2.00 | 4.00 | 15.00 |

**Mint mark: Ho**

| KM# | Date | Mintage | Fine | VF | XF | Unc |
|---|---|---|---|---|---|---|
| 398.6 | 1874/69 R | — | 125.00 | 225.00 | 350.00 | — |
| | 1874 R | — | 100.00 | 200.00 | 325.00 | — |
| | 1878/7 A | .022 | — | — | Rare | — |
| | 1878 A Inc. Ab. | | 20.00 | 40.00 | 80.00 | 175.00 |
| | 1878 A mule, gold peso obverse | | | | | |
| | Inc. Ab. | | 40.00 | 80.00 | 150.00 | 300.00 |
| | 1880 A | .043 | 7.50 | 15.00 | 30.00 | 75.00 |
| | 1886 G | .044 | 5.00 | 10.00 | 20.00 | 75.00 |
| | 1887 G | .020 | 5.00 | 10.00 | 20.00 | 75.00 |
| | 1888 G | .012 | 7.50 | 15.00 | 30.00 | 85.00 |
| | 1889 G | .067 | 3.00 | 6.00 | 12.50 | 40.00 |
| | 1890 G | .050 | 3.00 | 6.00 | 12.50 | 40.00 |

| KM# | Date | Mintage | Fine | VF | XF | Unc |
|---|---|---|---|---|---|---|
| 398.6 | 1891 G | .046 | 3.00 | 6.00 | 12.50 | 40.00 |
| | 1893 G | .084 | 2.50 | 5.00 | 10.00 | 30.00 |
| | 1894 G | .068 | 2.00 | 4.00 | 10.00 | 30.00 |

**Mint mark: Mo**

| KM# | Date | Mintage | Fine | VF | XF | Unc |
|---|---|---|---|---|---|---|
| 398.7 | 1869/8 C | .040 | 8.00 | 15.00 | 40.00 | 120.00 |
| | 1870 C | .140 | 4.00 | 7.00 | 20.00 | 60.00 |
| | 1871 C | .103 | 9.00 | 20.00 | 40.00 | 100.00 |
| | 1871 M Inc. Ab. | | 7.50 | 12.50 | 25.00 | 60.00 |
| | 1872 M | .266 | 5.00 | 8.00 | 20.00 | 55.00 |
| | 1873 M | .020 | 40.00 | 60.00 | 100.00 | 225.00 |
| | 1874/69 M | — | 7.50 | 15.00 | 30.00 | 75.00 |
| | 1874 M | — | 4.00 | 7.00 | 17.50 | 50.00 |
| | 1874/3 B | — | 5.00 | 8.00 | 22.50 | 55.00 |
| | 1874 B | — | 5.00 | 8.00 | 22.50 | 55.00 |
| | 1875 B | — | 4.00 | 7.00 | 15.00 | 50.00 |
| | 1875 B/M | — | 6.00 | 9.00 | 17.50 | 60.00 |
| | 1876/5 B | — | 4.00 | 7.00 | 15.00 | 50.00 |
| | 1876 B | — | 4.00 | 7.00 | 12.50 | 50.00 |
| | 1877/6 M | .080 | 4.00 | 7.00 | 15.00 | 60.00 |
| | 1877 M Inc. Ab. | | 4.00 | 7.00 | 12.50 | 60.00 |
| | 1878/7 M | .100 | 4.00 | 7.00 | 15.00 | 55.00 |
| | 1878 M Inc. Ab. | | 2.50 | 5.00 | 12.50 | 45.00 |
| | 1879/8 M | — | 8.00 | 12.50 | 22.50 | 55.00 |
| | 1879 M | — | 4.50 | 7.00 | 15.00 | 50.00 |
| | 1879 M 9/inverted 9 | | | | | |
| | | — | 10.00 | 15.00 | 25.00 | 75.00 |
| | 1880/76 M/B | | | | | |
| | | — | 5.00 | 7.50 | 15.00 | 50.00 |
| | 1880/76 M | — | 5.00 | 7.50 | 15.00 | 50.00 |
| | 1880 M | — | 4.00 | 6.00 | 12.00 | 40.00 |
| | 1881/0 M | .180 | 4.00 | 6.00 | 10.00 | 35.00 |
| | 1881 M Inc. Ab. | | 3.00 | 4.50 | 9.00 | 35.00 |
| | 1886/0 M | .398 | 2.00 | 2.75 | 7.50 | 25.00 |
| | 1886/1 M | I.A. | 2.00 | 2.75 | 7.50 | 25.00 |
| | 1886 M Inc. Ab. | | 1.75 | 2.25 | 6.00 | 20.00 |
| | 1887 m | .720 | 1.75 | 2.00 | 5.00 | 20.00 |
| | 1887 M/m | I.A. | 1.75 | 2.00 | 6.00 | 20.00 |
| | 1888/7 M | 1.360 | 2.25 | 2.50 | 6.00 | 20.00 |
| | 1888 M Inc. Ab. | | 1.75 | 2.00 | 5.00 | 20.00 |
| | 1889/8 M | 1.242 | 2.25 | 2.50 | 6.00 | 20.00 |
| | 1889 M Inc. Ab. | | 1.75 | 2.00 | 5.00 | 20.00 |
| | 1890/00 M | | | | | |
| | | 1.694 | 1.75 | 2.75 | 6.00 | 20.00 |
| | 1890 M Inc. Ab. | | 1.50 | 2.00 | 5.00 | 20.00 |
| | 1891 M | 1.030 | 1.75 | 2.00 | 5.00 | 20.00 |
| | 1892 M | 1.400 | 1.75 | 2.00 | 5.00 | 20.00 |
| | 1892 M 9/inverted 9 | | | | | |
| | Inc. Ab. | | 2.00 | 2.75 | 7.50 | 20.00 |
| | 1893 M | .220 | 1.75 | 2.00 | 5.00 | 15.00 |
| | 1894 M | .320 | 1.75 | 2.00 | 5.00 | 15.00 |
| | 1895 M | .078 | 3.00 | 5.00 | 8.00 | 25.00 |
| | 1896 B | .080 | 1.75 | 2.00 | 5.00 | 20.00 |
| | 1897 M | .160 | 1.75 | 2.00 | 5.00 | 15.00 |

**NOTE:** Varieties exist.

**Mint mark: Oa**

| KM# | Date | Mintage | Fine | VF | XF | Unc |
|---|---|---|---|---|---|---|
| 398.8 | 1890 E | .048 | — | — | Rare | — |
| | 1890 N Inc. Ab. | | 65.00 | 125.00 | 200.00 | 350.00 |

**Mint mark: Pi**

| KM# | Date | Mintage | Fine | VF | XF | Unc |
|---|---|---|---|---|---|---|
| 398.9 | 1869 S | — | 300.00 | 400.00 | 500.00 | — |
| | 1870 G/MoC | | | | | |
| | | .020 | — | — | Rare | — |
| | 1870 O Inc. Ab. | | 200.00 | 300.00 | 400.00 | — |
| | 1871 O | 5,400 | — | — | Rare | — |
| | 1872 O | — | 75.00 | 100.00 | 175.00 | 400.00 |
| | 1873 | 5,000 | — | — | Rare | — |
| | 1874 H | — | 30.00 | 50.00 | 100.00 | 225.00 |
| | 1875 H | — | 7.50 | 12.50 | 30.00 | 75.00 |
| | 1876 H | — | 10.00 | 20.00 | 45.00 | 100.00 |
| | 1877 H | — | 7.50 | 12.50 | 20.00 | 60.00 |
| | 1878/7 H | — | — | — | Rare | — |
| | 1878 H | — | 60.00 | 90.00 | 150.00 | 300.00 |
| | 1880 H | 6,200 | — | — | Rare | — |
| | 1881 H | 4,500 | — | — | Rare | — |
| | 1886 R | .033 | 12.50 | 25.00 | 50.00 | 125.00 |
| | 1887/0 R | .169 | 4.00 | 7.50 | 15.00 | 45.00 |
| | 1887 R Inc. Ab. | | 3.00 | 5.00 | 10.00 | 32.00 |
| | 1888 R | .210 | 2.00 | 4.00 | 9.00 | 30.00 |
| | 1889/7 R | .197 | 2.50 | 5.00 | 10.00 | 32.00 |
| | 1889 R Inc. Ab. | | 2.00 | 4.00 | 9.00 | 30.00 |
| | 1890 R | .221 | 2.00 | 3.00 | 6.00 | 25.00 |
| | 1891/89 R/B | | | | | |
| | | .176 | 2.00 | 4.00 | 8.00 | 25.00 |
| | 1891 R Inc. Ab. | | 2.00 | 3.00 | 6.00 | 20.00 |

| KM# | Date | Mintage | Fine | VF | XF | Unc |
|---|---|---|---|---|---|---|
| 398.9 | 1892/89 R | .182 | 2.00 | 4.00 | 8.00 | 25.00 |
| | 1892/0.R | I.A. | 2.00 | 4.00 | 8.00 | 25.00 |
| | 1892 R | Inc. Ab. | 2.00 | 3.00 | 6.00 | 20.00 |
| | 1893 R | .041 | 5.00 | 10.00 | 20.00 | 60.00 |

NOTE: Varieties exist.

**Mint mark: Zs**

| KM# | Date | Mintage | Fine | VF | XF | Unc |
|---|---|---|---|---|---|---|
| 398.10 | 1870 H | .040 | 12.50 | 25.00 | 50.00 | 125.00 |
| | 1871 H | .040 | 12.50 | 25.00 | 50.00 | 125.00 |
| | 1872 H | .040 | 12.50 | 25.00 | 50.00 | 125.00 |
| | 1873/2 H | .020 | 35.00 | 65.00 | 125.00 | 275.00 |
| | 1873 H | Inc. Ab. | 25.00 | 50.00 | 100.00 | 250.00 |
| | 1874 H | — | 7.50 | 12.50 | 25.00 | 75.00 |
| | 1874 A | — | 40.00 | 75.00 | 150.00 | 300.00 |
| | 1875 A | — | 7.50 | 12.50 | 25.00 | 75.00 |
| | 1876 A | — | 50.00 | 75.00 | 100.00 | 200.00 |
| | 1876 S | — | 12.50 | 25.00 | 50.00 | 125.00 |
| | 1877 S | — | 3.00 | 6.00 | 12.00 | 40.00 |
| | 1878 S | .060 | 3.00 | 6.00 | 12.00 | 40.00 |
| | 1879/8 S | — | 3.00 | 6.00 | 15.00 | 50.00 |
| | 1879 S | — | 3.00 | 6.00 | 12.00 | 40.00 |
| | 1880/79 S | .130 | 6.00 | 10.00 | 20.00 | 60.00 |
| | 1880 S | Inc. Ab. | 5.00 | 8.00 | 16.00 | 45.00 |
| | 1881 S | .210 | 2.50 | 5.00 | 10.00 | 35.00 |
| | 1886/4 S | .360 | 6.00 | 10.00 | 20.00 | 60.00 |
| | 1886 S | Inc. Ab. | 2.00 | 3.00 | 6.00 | 20.00 |
| | 1886 Z | Inc. Ab. | 5.00 | 10.00 | 25.00 | 65.00 |
| | 1887 Z | .400 | 2.00 | 3.00 | 6.00 | 25.00 |
| | 1888/7 Z | .500 | 2.00 | 3.00 | 6.00 | 25.00 |
| | 1888 Z | Inc. Ab. | 2.00 | 3.00 | 6.00 | 25.00 |
| | 1889 Z | .520 | 2.00 | 3.00 | 6.00 | 25.00 |
| | 1889 Z 9/inverted 9 | | | | | |
| | | Inc. Ab. | 2.00 | 3.00 | 6.00 | 25.00 |
| | 1889 ZsZ/MoM | | | | | |
| | | Inc. Ab. | 2.00 | 3.00 | 6.00 | 25.00 |
| | 1890 Z | .580 | 1.75 | 2.50 | 5.00 | 20.00 |
| | 1890 ZsZ/MoM | | | | | |
| | | Inc. Ab. | 2.00 | 3.00 | 6.00 | 25.00 |
| | 1891 Z | .420 | 1.75 | 2.50 | 5.00 | 20.00 |
| | 1892 Z | .346 | 1.75 | 2.50 | 5.00 | 20.00 |
| | 1893 Z | .258 | 1.75 | 2.50 | 5.00 | 20.00 |
| | 1894 Z | .228 | 1.75 | 2.50 | 5.00 | 20.00 |
| | 1894 ZoZ (error) | | | | | |
| | | Inc. Ab. | 2.00 | 4.00 | 8.00 | 30.00 |
| | 1895 Z | .260 | 1.75 | 2.50 | 5.00 | 20.00 |
| | 1896 Z | .200 | 1.75 | 2.50 | 5.00 | 20.00 |
| | 1896 6/inverted 6 | | | | | |
| | | Inc. Ab. | 2.00 | 3.00 | 6.00 | 25.00 |
| | 1897/6 Z | .200 | 2.00 | 3.00 | 6.00 | 25.00 |
| | 1897 Z | Inc. Ab. | 1.75 | 2.50 | 5.00 | 20.00 |

**COPPER-NICKEL**
**Mint: Mexico City**

| | | | | | | |
|---|---|---|---|---|---|---|
| 399 | 1882 | Inc. Ab. | .50 | 1.00 | 2.50 | 7.50 |
| | 1883 | Inc. Ab. | 25.00 | 50.00 | 80.00 | 250.00 |

**.903 SILVER**
**Mint mark: Cn**
**Obv: Restyled eagle.**

| | | | | | | |
|---|---|---|---|---|---|---|
| 400 | 1898 M | .044 | 1.75 | 4.00 | 8.00 | 20.00 |
| | 1899 M | .111 | 5.50 | 8.50 | 20.00 | 50.00 |
| | 1899 Q | Inc. Ab. | 1.75 | 2.25 | 4.50 | 12.50 |
| | 1900/800 Q | | | | | |
| | | .239 | 3.50 | 5.00 | 12.50 | 30.00 |
| | 1900 Q round Q, single tail | | | | | |
| | | Inc. Ab. | 1.75 | 2.50 | 6.00 | 15.00 |
| | 1900 Q narrow C, oval Q | | | | | |
| | | Inc. Ab. | 1.75 | 2.50 | 6.00 | 15.00 |
| | 1900 Q wide C, oval Q | | | | | |
| | | Inc. Ab. | 1.75 | 2.50 | 6.00 | 15.00 |

| KM# | Date | Mintage | Fine | VF | XF | Unc |
|---|---|---|---|---|---|---|
| 400 | 1901 Q | ⁻.148 | 1.75 | 2.25 | 4.50 | 12.50 |
| | 1902 Q narrow C, heavy serifs | | | | | |
| | | .262 | 1.75 | 2.50 | 6.00 | 15.00 |
| | 1902 Q wide C, light serifs | | | | | |
| | | Inc. Ab. | 1.75 | 2.50 | 6.00 | 15.00 |
| | 1903/1 Q | .331 | 2.00 | 2.50 | 6.00 | 15.00 |
| | 1903 Q | Inc. Ab. | 1.75 | 2.25 | 4.50 | 12.50 |
| | 1903/1898 V | | | | | |
| | | Inc. Ab. | 3.50 | 4.50 | 9.00 | 22.50 |
| | 1903 V | Inc. Ab. | 1.75 | 2.25 | 4.50 | 12.50 |
| | 1904 H | .352 | 1.75 | 2.25 | 5.00 | 15.00 |

NOTE: Varieties exist.

**Mint mark: Go**

| | | | | | | |
|---|---|---|---|---|---|---|
| 400.1 | 1898 R mule, gold peso obverse | | | | | |
| | | .180 | 7.50 | 15.00 | 30.00 | 75.00 |
| | 1899 R | .260 | 1.75 | 2.25 | 4.50 | 12.50 |
| | 1900 R | .200 | 1.75 | 2.25 | 4.50 | 12.50 |

NOTE: Varieties exist.

**Mint mark: Mo**

| | | | | | | |
|---|---|---|---|---|---|---|
| 400.2 | 1898 M | .080 | 2.00 | 4.00 | 7.00 | 25.00 |
| | 1899 M | .168 | 1.75 | 2.25 | 4.50 | 12.50 |
| | 1900/800 M | | | | | |
| | | .300 | 4.50 | 6.50 | 10.00 | 30.00 |
| | 1900 M | Inc. Ab. | 1.75 | 2.25 | 4.50 | 12.50 |
| | 1901 M | .100 | 1.75 | 2.25 | 4.50 | 12.50 |
| | 1902 M | .144 | 1.25 | 2.00 | 3.75 | 10.00 |
| | 1903 M | .500 | 1.25 | 2.00 | 3.75 | 10.00 |
| | 1904/804 M | | | | | |
| | | 1.090 | 1.75 | 2.50 | 6.00 | 15.00 |
| | 1904/94 M | I.A. | 1.75 | 2.50 | 6.00 | 15.00 |
| | 1904 M | Inc. Ab. | 1.25 | 2.00 | 6.00 | 12.50 |
| | 1905 M | .344 | 1.75 | 3.75 | 7.50 | 17.50 |

**Mint mark: Zs**

| | | | | | | |
|---|---|---|---|---|---|---|
| 400.3 | 1898 Z | .100 | 1.75 | 2.25 | 4.50 | 12.50 |
| | 1899 Z | .050 | 2.00 | 3.00 | 7.00 | 20.00 |
| | 1900 Z | .055 | 1.75 | 2.50 | 5.00 | 15.00 |
| | 1901 Z | .040 | 1.75 | 2.50 | 5.00 | 15.00 |
| | 1902/1 Z | .034 | 2.00 | 4.50 | 9.00 | 22.50 |
| | 1902 Z | Inc. Ab. | 1.75 | 3.75 | 7.50 | 17.50 |
| | 1903 Z | .217 | 1.25 | 2.00 | 5.00 | 12.50 |
| | 1904 Z | .191 | 1.75 | 2.50 | 5.00 | 12.50 |
| | 1904 M | Inc. Ab. | 1.75 | 2.50 | 6.00 | 15.00 |
| | 1905 M | .046 | 2.00 | 4.50 | 9.00 | 22.50 |

## 10 CENTAVOS

**2.7070 g, .903 SILVER, .0785 oz ASW**
**Mint mark: Ca**
**Obv: Eagle. Rev: Value within wreath.**

| | | | | | | |
|---|---|---|---|---|---|---|
| 401 | 1868/7 | — | 30.00 | 60.00 | 150.00 | 550.00 |
| | 1868 | — | 30.00 | 60.00 | 150.00 | 550.00 |
| | 1869 | .015 | 25.00 | 50.00 | 125.00 | 600.00 |
| | 1870 | .017 | 22.50 | 45.00 | 100.00 | 550.00 |

**Mint mark: SLP**

| | | | | | | |
|---|---|---|---|---|---|---|
| 401.2 | 1863 | — | 75.00 | 150.00 | 275.00 | 900.00 |

**Mint mark: Mo**

| | | | | | | |
|---|---|---|---|---|---|---|
| 402 | 1867/3 | — | 50.00 | 100.00 | 150.00 | 450.00 |
| | 1867 | — | 20.00 | 40.00 | 60.00 | 250.00 |
| | 1868/7 | — | 20.00 | 40.00 | 80.00 | 275.00 |
| | 1868 | — | 20.00 | 45.00 | 75.00 | 250.00 |

**Mint mark: P**

| | | | | | | |
|---|---|---|---|---|---|---|
| 402.1 | 1868/7 | .038 | 45.00 | 90.00 | 175.00 | 650.00 |
| | 1868 | Inc. Ab. | 20.00 | 40.00 | 100.00 | 550.00 |
| | 1869/7 | 4,900 | 55.00 | 125.00 | 250.00 | 800.00 |

### Mint mark: As

| KM# | Date | Mintage | Fine | VF | XF | Unc |
|-----|------|---------|------|-----|-----|-----|
| 403 | 1874 DL | — | 20.00 | 40.00 | 80.00 | 175.00 |
| | 1875 L | — | 5.00 | 10.00 | 25.00 | 90.00 |
| | 1876 L | — | 10.00 | 18.00 | 40.00 | 110.00 |
| | 1878/7 L | — | 10.00 | 18.00 | 45.00 | 120.00 |
| | 1878 L | — | 5.00 | 10.00 | 30.00 | 100.00 |
| | 1879 L | — | 10.00 | 18.00 | 40.00 | 110.00 |
| | 1880 L | .013 | 10.00 | 18.00 | 40.00 | 110.00 |
| | 1882 L | .022 | 10.00 | 18.00 | 40.00 | 110.00 |
| | 1883 L | 8,520 | 25.00 | 50.00 | 100.00 | 225.00 |
| | 1884 L | — | 7.50 | 12.50 | 35.00 | 100.00 |
| | 1885 L | .015 | 7.50 | 12.50 | 35.00 | 100.00 |
| | 1886 L | .045 | 7.50 | 12.50 | 35.00 | 100.00 |
| | 1887 L | .015 | 7.50 | 12.50 | 35.00 | 100.00 |
| | 1888 L | .038 | 7.50 | 12.50 | 35.00 | 100.00 |
| | 1889 L | .020 | 7.50 | 12.50 | 35.00 | 100.00 |
| | 1890 L | .040 | 7.50 | 12.50 | 35.00 | 100.00 |
| | 1891 L | .038 | 7.50 | 12.50 | 35.00 | 100.00 |
| | 1892 L | .057 | 5.00 | 10.00 | 25.00 | 90.00 |
| | 1893 L | .070 | 10.00 | 18.00 | 40.00 | 110.00 |

NOTE: Varieties exist.

### Mint mark: CH,Ca

| KM# | Date | Mintage | Fine | VF | XF | Unc |
|-----|------|---------|------|-----|-----|-----|
| 403.1 | 1871 M | 8,150 | 15.00 | 30.00 | 60.00 | 150.00 |
| | 1873 M crude date | | | | | |
| | | — | 35.00 | 75.00 | 125.00 | 175.00 |
| | 1874 M | — | 10.00 | 17.50 | 35.00 | 100.00 |
| | 1880/70 G | | | | | |
| | | 7,620 | 20.00 | 40.00 | 80.00 | 175.00 |
| | 1880 G/g | I.A. | 15.00 | 25.00 | 50.00 | 125.00 |
| | 1881 | 340 pcs. | — | — | Rare | — |
| | 1883 M | 9,000 | 10.00 | 20.00 | 40.00 | 125.00 |
| | 1884 M | — | 10.00 | 20.00 | 40.00 | 125.00 |
| | 1886 M | .045 | 7.50 | 12.50 | 30.00 | 100.00 |
| | 1887/3 M/G | | | | | |
| | | .096 | 5.00 | 10.00 | 20.00 | 75.00 |
| | 1887 M | Inc. Ab. | 2.00 | 4.00 | 8.00 | 75.00 |
| | 1888 M | .299 | 1.50 | 2.50 | 5.00 | 75.00 |
| | 1888 Ca/Mo | | | | | |
| | | Inc. Ab. | 1.50 | 2.50 | 5.00 | 75.00 |
| | 1889/8 M | .115 | 2.00 | 4.00 | 8.00 | 75.00 |
| | 1889 M small 89 (5 Centavo font) | | | | | |
| | | Inc. Ab. | 2.00 | 4.00 | 8.00 | 75.00 |
| | 1890/80 M | .140 | 2.00 | 4.00 | 8.00 | 75.00 |
| | 1890/89 M | I.A. | 2.00 | 4.00 | 8.00 | 75.00 |
| | 1890 M | Inc. Ab. | 1.50 | 3.00 | 7.00 | 75.00 |
| | 1891 M | .163 | 1.50 | 3.00 | 7.00 | 75.00 |
| | 1892 M | .169 | 1.50 | 3.00 | 7.00 | 75.00 |
| | 1892 M 9/inverted 9 | | | | | |
| | | Inc. Ab. | 2.00 | 4.00 | 8.00 | 75.00 |
| | 1893 M | .246 | 1.50 | 3.00 | 7.00 | 75.00 |
| | 1894 M | .163 | 1.50 | 3.00 | 7.00 | 75.00 |
| | 1895 M | .127 | 1.50 | 3.00 | 7.00 | 75.00 |

NOTE: Varieties exist.

### Mint mark: Cn

| KM# | Date | Mintage | Fine | VF | XF | Unc |
|-----|------|---------|------|-----|-----|-----|
| 403.2 | 1871 P | — | — | — | Rare | — |
| | 1873 P | 8,732 | 20.00 | 50.00 | 100.00 | 225.00 |
| | 1881 D | 9,440 | 75.00 | 175.00 | 325.00 | 500.00 |
| | 1882 D | .012 | 75.00 | 125.00 | 200.00 | 400.00 |
| | 1885 M mule gold 2-1/2 Peso obv. | | | | | |
| | | .018 | 25.00 | 50.00 | 100.00 | 200.00 |
| | 1886 M mule, gold 2-1/2 Peso obv. | | | | | |
| | | .013 | 50.00 | 100.00 | 150.00 | 300.00 |
| | 1887 M | .011 | 20.00 | 40.00 | 75.00 | 175.00 |
| | 1888 M | .056 | 5.00 | 10.00 | 25.00 | 125.00 |
| | 1889 M | .042 | 5.00 | 10.00 | 20.00 | 75.00 |
| | 1890 M | .132 | 2.00 | 4.00 | 7.50 | 75.00 |
| | 1891 M | .084 | 5.00 | 10.00 | 20.00 | 75.00 |
| | 1892/1 M | .037 | 4.00 | 8.00 | 15.00 | 75.00 |
| | 1892 M | Inc. Ab. | 2.50 | 5.00 | 10.00 | 75.00 |
| | 1894 M | .043 | 2.50 | 5.00 | 10.00 | 75.00 |
| | 1895 M | .023 | 2.50 | 5.00 | 10.00 | 60.00 |
| | 1896 M | .121 | 1.50 | 2.50 | 5.00 | 50.00 |

### Mint mark: Do

| KM# | Date | Mintage | Fine | VF | XF | Unc |
|-----|------|---------|------|-----|-----|-----|
| 403.3 | 1878 E | 2,500 | 100.00 | 175.00 | 300.00 | 600.00 |
| | 1879 B | — | — | — | Rare | — |
| | 1880/70 B | — | — | — | Rare | — |
| | 1880/79 B | — | — | — | Rare | — |
| | 1884 C | — | 30.00 | 60.00 | 100.00 | 225.00 |
| | 1886 C | .013 | 75.00 | 150.00 | 300.00 | 500.00 |
| | 1887 C | .081 | 4.00 | 8.00 | 15.00 | 100.00 |
| | 1888 C | .031 | 6.00 | 12.00 | 30.00 | 100.00 |
| | 1889 C | .055 | 4.00 | 8.00 | 15.00 | 100.00 |
| | 1890 C | .050 | 4.00 | 8.00 | 15.00 | 100.00 |
| | 1891 P | .139 | 2.00 | 4.00 | 8.00 | 80.00 |
| | 1892 P | .212 | 2.00 | 4.00 | 8.00 | 80.00 |
| | 1892 D | Inc. Ab. | 2.00 | 4.00 | 8.00 | 80.00 |
| | 1893 D | .258 | 2.00 | 4.00 | 8.00 | 80.00 |
| | 1893 D/C | I.A. | 2.50 | 5.00 | 10.00 | 80.00 |
| | 1894 D | .184 | 1.50 | 3.00 | 6.00 | 80.00 |
| | 1894 D/C | I.A. | 2.00 | 4.00 | 8.00 | 80.00 |
| | 1895 D | .142 | 1.50 | 3.00 | 6.00 | 80.00 |

### Mint mark: Ga

| KM# | Date | Mintage | Fine | VF | XF | Unc |
|-----|------|---------|------|-----|-----|-----|
| 403.4 | 1871 C | 4,734 | 75.00 | 125.00 | 200.00 | 500.00 |
| | 1873/1 C | .025 | 10.00 | 15.00 | 35.00 | 150.00 |
| | 1873 C | Inc.Ab. | 10.00 | 15.00 | 35.00 | 150.00 |
| | 1874 C | — | 10.00 | 15.00 | 35.00 | 150.00 |
| | 1877 A | — | 10.00 | 15.00 | 30.00 | 150.00 |
| | 1881 S | .115 | 5.00 | 10.00 | 25.00 | 150.00 |
| | 1883 B | .090 | 4.00 | 8.00 | 15.00 | 90.00 |
| | 1884 B | — | 5.00 | 10.00 | 20.00 | 90.00 |
| | 1884 B/S | — | 6.00 | 12.50 | 25.00 | 90.00 |
| | 1884 H | — | 3.00 | 5.00 | 10.00 | 90.00 |
| | 1885 H | .093 | 3.00 | 5.00 | 10.00 | 90.00 |
| | 1886 S | .151 | 2.50 | 4.00 | 9.00 | 90.00 |
| | 1887 S | .162 | 1.50 | 3.00 | 6.00 | 90.00 |
| | 1888 S | .225 | 1.50 | 3.00 | 6.00 | 90.00 |
| | 1888 GaS/HoG | | | | | |
| | | Inc. Ab. | 1.50 | 3.00 | 6.00 | 90.00 |
| | 1889 S | .310 | 1.50 | 3.00 | 6.00 | 40.00 |
| | 1890 S | .303 | 1.50 | 3.00 | 6.00 | 40.00 |
| | 1891 S | .199 | 5.00 | 10.00 | 20.00 | 45.00 |
| | 1892 S | .329 | 1.50 | 3.00 | 6.00 | 40.00 |
| | 1893 S | .225 | 1.50 | 3.00 | 6.00 | 40.00 |
| | 1894 S | .243 | 3.00 | 6.00 | 12.00 | 40.00 |
| | 1895 S | .080 | 1.50 | 3.00 | 6.00 | 40.00 |

NOTE: Varieties exist.

### Mint mark: Go

| KM# | Date | Mintage | Fine | VF | XF | Unc |
|-----|------|---------|------|-----|-----|-----|
| 403.5 | 1869 S | 7,000 | 20.00 | 40.00 | 80.00 | 200.00 |
| | 1871/0 S | .060 | 15.00 | 25.00 | 50.00 | 125.00 |
| | 1872 S | .060 | 15.00 | 25.00 | 50.00 | 125.00 |
| | 1873 S | .050 | 15.00 | 25.00 | 50.00 | 125.00 |
| | 1874 S | — | 15.00 | 25.00 | 50.00 | 125.00 |
| | 1875 S | — | 250.00 | 350.00 | 500.00 | 800.00 |
| | 1876 S | — | 10.00 | 20.00 | 40.00 | 100.00 |
| | 1877 S | — | 80.00 | 120.00 | 200.00 | 400.00 |
| | 1878/7 S | .010 | 10.00 | 20.00 | 45.00 | 110.00 |
| | 1878 S | Inc. Ab. | 7.50 | 12.00 | 20.00 | 75.00 |
| | 1879 S | — | 7.50 | 12.00 | 20.00 | 75.00 |
| | 1880 S | — | 100.00 | 200.00 | 300.00 | 450.00 |
| | 1881/71 S | .100 | 3.00 | 5.00 | 10.00 | 75.00 |
| | 1881/0 S | I.A. | 3.50 | 5.00 | 10.00 | 75.00 |
| | 1881 S | Inc. Ab. | 3.00 | 5.00 | 10.00 | 75.00 |
| | 1882/1 S | .040 | 3.00 | 6.00 | 12.00 | 75.00 |
| | 1883 B | — | 3.00 | 5.00 | 10.00 | 75.00 |
| | 1884 B | — | 1.50 | 3.00 | 6.00 | 75.00 |
| | 1884 S | — | 6.00 | 12.50 | 25.00 | 90.00 |
| | 1885 R | .100 | 1.50 | 3.00 | 6.00 | 75.00 |
| | 1886 R | .095 | 3.00 | 5.00 | 10.00 | 75.00 |
| | 1887 R | .330 | 2.50 | 5.00 | 10.00 | 75.00 |
| | 1888 R | .270 | 1.50 | 3.00 | 6.00 | 75.00 |
| | 1889 R | .205 | 2.00 | 4.00 | 8.00 | 75.00 |
| | 1889 GoR/HoG | | | | | |
| | | Inc. Ab. | 3.00 | 5.00 | 10.00 | 75.00 |
| | 1890 R | .270 | 1.50 | 3.00 | 6.00 | 35.00 |
| | 1890 GoR/Cn M | | | | | |
| | | Inc. Ab. | 1.50 | 3.00 | 6.00 | 35.00 |
| | 1891 R | .523 | 1.50 | 3.00 | 6.00 | 35.00 |
| | 1891 GoR/HoG | | | | | |
| | | Inc. Ab. | 1.50 | 3.00 | 6.00 | 35.00 |
| | 1892 R | .440 | 1.50 | 3.00 | 6.00 | 35.00 |
| | 1893/1 R | .389 | 3.00 | 5.00 | 10.00 | 35.00 |
| | 1893 R | Inc. Ab. | 1.50 | 3.00 | 6.00 | 35.00 |
| | 1894 R | .400 | 1.50 | 2.50 | 5.00 | 35.00 |
| | 1895 R | .355 | 1.50 | 2.50 | 5.00 | 35.00 |

| KM# | Date | Mintage | Fine | VF | XF | Unc |
|---|---|---|---|---|---|---|
| 403.5 | 1896 R | .190 | 1.50 | 2.50 | 5.00 | 35.00 |
| | 1897 R | .205 | 1.50 | 2.50 | 5.00 | 35.00 |

NOTE: Varieties exist.

### Mint mark: Ho

| KM# | Date | Mintage | Fine | VF | XF | Unc |
|---|---|---|---|---|---|---|
| 403.6 | 1874 R | — | 30.00 | 60.00 | 100.00 | 200.00 |
| | 1876 F | 3,140 | 200.00 | 300.00 | 450.00 | 750.00 |
| | 1878 A | — | 5.00 | 10.00 | 15.00 | 85.00 |
| | 1879 A | — | 25.00 | 50.00 | 90.00 | 175.00 |
| | 1880 A | — | 3.00 | 6.00 | 12.50 | 85.00 |
| | 1881 A | .028 | 4.00 | 7.00 | 15.00 | 85.00 |
| | 1882/1 A | .025 | 5.00 | 10.00 | 20.00 | 85.00 |
| | 1882/1 a | I.A. | 6.00 | 12.50 | 25.00 | 85.00 |
| | 1882 A Inc. Ab. | | 4.00 | 7.00 | 15.00 | 85.00 |
| | 1883 | 7,000 | 65.00 | 100.00 | 200.00 | 400.00 |
| | 1884 A | — | 35.00 | 75.00 | 150.00 | 300.00 |
| | 1884 M | — | 7.50 | 15.00 | 30.00 | 85.00 |
| | 1885 M | .021 | 12.50 | 25.00 | 50.00 | 100.00 |
| | 1886 M | .010 | — | — | Rare | — |
| | 1886 G Inc. Ab. | | 7.50 | 12.50 | 25.00 | 85.00 |
| | 1887 G | — | 25.00 | 50.00 | 75.00 | 150.00 |
| | 1888 G | .025 | 6.00 | 12.50 | 25.00 | 85.00 |
| | 1889 G | .042 | 3.00 | 6.00 | 10.00 | 85.00 |
| | 1890 G | .048 | 3.00 | 6.00 | 10.00 | 85.00 |
| | 1891/80 G | .136 | 3.00 | 6.00 | 10.00 | 85.00 |
| | 1891/0 G | I.A. | 3.00 | 6.00 | 10.00 | 85.00 |
| | 1891 G Inc. Ab. | | 3.00 | 6.00 | 10.00 | 85.00 |
| | 1892 G | .067 | 3.00 | 6.00 | 10.00 | 85.00 |
| | 1893 G | .067 | 3.00 | 6.00 | 10.00 | 85.00 |

### Mint mark: Mo

| KM# | Date | Mintage | Fine | VF | XF | Unc |
|---|---|---|---|---|---|---|
| 403.7 | 1869/8 C | .030 | 10.00 | 20.00 | 40.00 | 100.00 |
| | 1869 C Inc. Ab. | | 8.00 | 17.50 | 35.00 | 90.00 |
| | 1870 C | .110 | 3.00 | 7.50 | 15.00 | 50.00 |
| | 1871 C | .084 | 50.00 | 75.00 | 125.00 | 250.00 |
| | 1871 M Inc. Ab. | | 12.00 | 17.50 | 45.00 | 125.00 |
| | 1872/69 M | .198 | 10.00 | 20.00 | 35.00 | 100.00 |
| | 1872 M Inc. Ab. | | 3.00 | 7.50 | 15.00 | 65.00 |
| | 1873 M | .040 | 10.00 | 15.00 | 30.00 | 75.00 |
| | 1874 M | — | 5.00 | 10.00 | 20.00 | 65.00 |
| | 1874/64 B | — | 5.00 | 10.00 | 20.00 | 65.00 |
| | 1874 B/M | — | 20.00 | 40.00 | 60.00 | 125.00 |
| | 1874 B | — | 5.00 | 10.00 | 15.00 | 65.00 |
| | 1875 B | — | 20.00 | 40.00 | 60.00 | 125.00 |
| | 1876/5 B | — | 3.00 | 5.00 | 9.00 | 65.00 |
| | 1876/5 B/M | — | 3.00 | 5.00 | 9.00 | 65.00 |
| | 1877/6 M | — | 3.00 | 5.00 | 9.00 | 65.00 |
| | 1877/6 M/B | — | 3.00 | 5.00 | 9.00 | 65.00 |
| | 1877 M | — | 3.00 | 5.00 | 9.00 | 65.00 |
| | 1878/7 M | .100 | 3.00 | 5.00 | 9.00 | 65.00 |
| | 1878 M Inc. Ab. | | 3.00 | 5.00 | 9.00 | 65.00 |
| | 1879/69 M | — | 3.00 | 5.00 | 9.00 | 65.00 |
| | 1879 M/C | — | 3.00 | 5.00 | 9.00 | 65.00 |
| | 1880/79 M | — | 3.00 | 5.00 | 9.00 | 65.00 |
| | 1881/0 M | .510 | 3.00 | 5.00 | 9.00 | 35.00 |
| | 1881 M Inc. Ab. | | 3.00 | 5.00 | 9.00 | 35.00 |
| | 1882/1 M | .550 | 3.00 | 5.00 | 9.00 | 35.00 |
| | 1882 M Inc. Ab. | | 3.00 | 5.00 | 9.00 | 35.00 |
| | 1883/2 M | .250 | 3.00 | 5.00 | 9.00 | 35.00 |
| | 1884 M | — | 3.00 | 5.00 | 9.00 | 35.00 |
| | 1885 M | .470 | 3.00 | 5.00 | 9.00 | 35.00 |
| | 1886 M | .603 | 3.00 | 5.00 | 9.00 | 35.00 |
| | 1887 M | .580 | 3.00 | 5.00 | 9.00 | 35.00 |
| | 1888/7 MoM | .710 | 3.00 | 5.00 | 9.00 | 35.00 |
| | 1888 MoM | I.A. | 3.00 | 5.00 | 9.00 | 35.00 |
| | 1888 MOM | I.A. | 3.00 | 5.00 | 9.00 | 35.00 |
| | 1889/8 M | .622 | 3.00 | 5.00 | 9.00 | 35.00 |
| | 1889 M Inc. Ab. | | 3.00 | 5.00 | 9.00 | 35.00 |
| | 1890/89 M | .815 | 3.00 | 5.00 | 9.00 | 35.00 |
| | 1890 M Inc. Ab. | | 3.00 | 5.00 | 9.00 | 35.00 |
| | 1891 M | .859 | 1.50 | 2.50 | 7.00 | 25.00 |
| | 1892 M | 1.030 | 1.50 | 2.50 | 7.00 | 25.00 |
| | 1893 M | .310 | 1.50 | 2.50 | 7.00 | 25.00 |
| | 1893 M/C | I.A. | 1.50 | 2.50 | 7.00 | 25.00 |
| | 1894 M | .350 | 5.00 | 10.00 | 20.00 | 60.00 |
| | 1895 M | .320 | 1.50 | 2.50 | 7.00 | 25.00 |
| | 1896 B/G | .340 | 1.50 | 2.50 | 7.00 | 25.00 |
| | 1896 M Inc. Ab. | | 35.00 | 70.00 | 100.00 | 150.00 |
| | 1897 M | .170 | 1.50 | 2.50 | 5.00 | 20.00 |

NOTE: Varieties exist.

### Mint mark: Oa

| KM# | Date | Mintage | Fine | VF | XF | Unc |
|---|---|---|---|---|---|---|
| 403.8 | 1889 E | .021 | 200.00 | 400.00 | 600.00 | — |
| | 1890 E | .031 | 100.00 | 150.00 | 250.00 | 500.00 |
| | 1890 N Inc. Ab. | | — | — | Rare | — |

### Mint mark: Pi

| KM# | Date | Mintage | Fine | VF | XF | Unc |
|---|---|---|---|---|---|---|
| 403.9 | 1869/8 S | 4,000 | — | — | Rare | — |
| | 1870/69 O | .018 | — | — | Rare | — |
| | 1870 G Inc. Ab. | | 125.00 | 200.00 | 325.00 | 600.00 |
| | 1871 O | .021 | 50.00 | 100.00 | 150.00 | 300.00 |
| | 1872 O | .016 | 150.00 | 225.00 | 350.00 | 650.00 |
| | 1873 O | 4,750 | — | — | Rare | — |
| | 1874 H | — | 25.00 | 50.00 | 100.00 | 200.00 |
| | 1875 H | — | 75.00 | 125.00 | 200.00 | 400.00 |
| | 1876 H | — | 75.00 | 125.00 | 200.00 | 400.00 |
| | 1877 H | — | 75.00 | 125.00 | 200.00 | 400.00 |
| | 1878 H | — | 250.00 | 500.00 | 750.00 | — |
| | 1879 H | — | — | — | — | — |
| | 1880 H | — | 150.00 | 250.00 | 350.00 | — |
| | 1881 H | 7,600 | 250.00 | 350.00 | 500.00 | — |
| | 1882 H | 4,000 | — | — | Rare | — |
| | 1883 H | — | 125.00 | 200.00 | 300.00 | 500.00 |
| | 1884 H | — | 25.00 | 50.00 | 100.00 | 200.00 |
| | 1885 H | .051 | 25.00 | 50.00 | 100.00 | 200.00 |
| | 1885 C Inc. Ab. | | — | — | Rare | — |
| | 1886 C | .052 | 15.00 | 30.00 | 60.00 | 150.00 |
| | 1886 R Inc. Ab. | | 5.00 | 10.00 | 20.00 | 65.00 |
| | 1887 R | .118 | 2.50 | 5.00 | 10.00 | 50.00 |
| | 1888 R | .136 | 2.50 | 5.00 | 10.00 | 50.00 |
| | 1889/7 R | .131 | 7.50 | 12.50 | 20.00 | 60.00 |
| | 1890 R | .204 | 1.50 | 3.00 | 7.50 | 40.00 |
| | 1891/89 R | .163 | 2.50 | 5.00 | 10.00 | 40.00 |
| | 1891 R Inc. Ab. | | 1.50 | 3.50 | 6.00 | 30.00 |
| | 1892/0 R | .200 | 2.00 | 4.00 | 8.00 | 40.00 |
| | 1892 R Inc. Ab. | | 1.50 | 2.50 | 5.00 | 40.00 |
| | 1893 R | .048 | 7.50 | 10.00 | 17.50 | 60.00 |

NOTE: Varieties exist.

### Mint mark: Zs

| KM# | Date | Mintage | Fine | VF | XF | Unc |
|---|---|---|---|---|---|---|
| 403.10 | 1870 H | .020 | 100.00 | 150.00 | 200.00 | 400.00 |
| | 1871/0 H | .010 | — | — | — | — |
| | 1871 H Inc. Ab. | | — | — | — | — |
| | 1872 H | .010 | 150.00 | 200.00 | 275.00 | 500.00 |
| | 1873 H | .010 | 250.00 | 350.00 | 600.00 | — |
| | 1874/3 H | — | 50.00 | 75.00 | 150.00 | 300.00 |
| | 1874 A | — | 200.00 | 300.00 | 500.00 | — |
| | 1875 A | — | 5.00 | 10.00 | 25.00 | 100.00 |
| | 1876 A | — | 5.00 | 10.00 | 25.00 | 100.00 |
| | 1876 S | — | 100.00 | 200.00 | 300.00 | 500.00 |
| | 1877 S small S | — | 7.50 | 12.50 | 25.00 | 100.00 |
| | 1877 S regular S | — | 7.50 | 12.50 | 25.00 | 100.00 |
| | 1878/7 S | .030 | 5.00 | 10.00 | 20.00 | 80.00 |
| | 1878 S Inc. Ab. | | 5.00 | 10.00 | 20.00 | 80.00 |
| | 1879 S | — | 5.00 | 10.00 | 20.00 | 80.00 |
| | 1880 S | — | 5.00 | 10.00 | 20.00 | 80.00 |
| | 1881/0 S | .120 | 3.00 | 6.00 | 12.50 | 50.00 |
| | 1881 S Inc. Ab. | | 3.00 | 6.00 | 12.50 | 50.00 |
| | 1882/1 S | .064 | 12.50 | 25.00 | 50.00 | 125.00 |
| | 1882 S Inc. Ab. | | 12.50 | 25.00 | 50.00 | 125.00 |
| | 1883/73 S | .102 | 2.00 | 4.00 | 8.00 | 50.00 |
| | 1883 S Inc. Ab. | | 2.00 | 4.00 | 8.00 | 50.00 |
| | 1884/3 S | — | 2.00 | 4.00 | 8.00 | 50.00 |
| | 1884 S | — | 2.00 | 4.00 | 8.00 | 50.00 |
| | 1885 S | .297 | 1.50 | 2.50 | 5.00 | 50.00 |
| | 1885 S small S in mint mark Inc. Ab. | | 2.50 | 4.00 | 8.00 | 50.00 |
| | 1885 Z w/o assayers initial (error) Inc. Ab. | | 3.50 | 7.50 | 15.00 | 65.00 |
| | 1886 S | .274 | 1.50 | 2.50 | 5.00 | 30.00 |
| | 1886 Z | I.A. | 12.50 | 25.00 | 50.00 | 125.00 |
| | 1887 ZsZ | .233 | 1.50 | 2.50 | 5.00 | 30.00 |
| | 1887 Z Z (error) Inc. Ab. | | 3.50 | 7.50 | 15.00 | 50.00 |
| | 1888 ZsZ | .270 | 1.50 | 2.50 | 5.00 | 30.00 |
| | 1888 Z Z (error) Inc. Ab. | | 3.50 | 7.50 | 15.00 | 40.00 |
| | 1889/7 Z/S | .240 | 4.00 | 8.00 | 12.50 | 40.00 |
| | 1889 Z/S | I.A. | 1.50 | 4.00 | 8.00 | 30.00 |
| | 1889 Z Inc. Ab. | | 1.50 | 2.50 | 5.00 | 30.00 |
| | 1890 ZsZ | .410 | 1.50 | 2.50 | 5.00 | 30.00 |
| | 1890 Z Z (error) Inc. Ab. | | 3.75 | 7.50 | 15.00 | 40.00 |
| | 1891 Z | 1.105 | 1.50 | 2.50 | 5.00 | 30.00 |
| | 1891 ZsZ double s Inc. Ab. | | 2.00 | 4.00 | 7.00 | 30.00 |
| | 1892 Z | 1.102 | 1.50 | 2.50 | 5.00 | 30.00 |
| | 1893 Z | 1.011 | 1.50 | 2.50 | 5.00 | 25.00 |

| KM# | Date | Mintage | Fine | VF | XF | Unc |
|---|---|---|---|---|---|---|
| 403.10 | 1894 Z | .892 | 1.50 | 2.50 | 5.00 | 30.00 |
| | 1895 Z | .920 | 1.50 | 2.50 | 5.00 | 30.00 |
| | 1896/5 ZsZ | .700 | 1.50 | 2.50 | 5.00 | 30.00 |
| | 1896 ZsZ | I.A. | 1.50 | 2.50 | 5.00 | 30.00 |
| | 1896 Z Z (error) | | | | | |
| | | Inc. Ab. | 3.75 | 7.50 | 15.00 | 40.00 |
| | 1897/6 ZsZ | .900 | 2.00 | 5.00 | 10.00 | 30.00 |
| | 1897/6 Z Z (error) | | | | | |
| | | Inc. Ab. | 3.75 | 7.50 | 15.00 | 40.00 |
| | 1897 Z | Inc. Ab. | 1.50 | 2.50 | 5.00 | 30.00 |

NOTE: Varieties exist.

**Mint mark: Cn**
**Obv: Restyled eagle.**

| KM# | Date | Mintage | Fine | VF | XF | Unc |
|---|---|---|---|---|---|---|
| 404 | 1898 M | 9,870 | 50.00 | 100.00 | 150.00 | 300.00 |
| | 1899 Q round Q, single tail | | | | | |
| | | .080 | 5.00 | 7.50 | 15.00 | 40.00 |
| | 1899 Q oval Q, double tail | | | | | |
| | | Inc. Ab. | 5.00 | 7.50 | 15.00 | 40.00 |
| | 1900 Q | .160 | 1.50 | 2.50 | 5.00 | 20.00 |
| | 1901 Q | .235 | 1.50 | 2.50 | 5.00 | 20.00 |
| | 1902 Q | .186 | 1.50 | 2.50 | 5.00 | 20.00 |
| | 1903 Q | .256 | 1.50 | 2.50 | 6.00 | 20.00 |
| | 1903 V | Inc. Ab. | 1.50 | 2.50 | 5.00 | 15.00 |
| | 1904 H | .307 | 1.50 | 2.50 | 5.00 | 15.00 |

NOTE: Varieties exist.

**Mint mark: Go**

| KM# | Date | Mintage | Fine | VF | XF | Unc |
|---|---|---|---|---|---|---|
| 404.1 | 1898 R | .435 | 1.50 | 2.50 | 5.00 | 20.00 |
| | 1899 R | .270 | 1.50 | 2.50 | 5.00 | 25.00 |
| | 1900 R | .130 | 7.50 | 12.50 | 25.00 | 60.00 |

**Mint mark: Mo**

| KM# | Date | Mintage | Fine | VF | XF | Unc |
|---|---|---|---|---|---|---|
| 404.2 | 1898 M | .130 | 1.50 | 2.50 | 5.00 | 17.50 |
| | 1899 M | .190 | 1.50 | 2.50 | 5.00 | 17.50 |
| | 1900 M | .311 | 1.50 | 2.50 | 5.00 | 17.50 |
| | 1901 M | .080 | 2.50 | 3.50 | 7.00 | 20.00 |
| | 1902 M | .181 | 1.50 | 2.50 | 5.00 | 17.50 |
| | 1903 M | .581 | 1.50 | 2.50 | 5.00 | 17.50 |
| | 1904 M | 1.266 | 1.25 | 2.00 | 4.50 | 15.00 |
| | 1904 MM (error) | | | | | |
| | | Inc. Ab. | 2.50 | 5.00 | 10.00 | 25.00 |
| | 1905 M | .266 | 2.00 | 3.75 | 7.50 | 20.00 |

**Mint mark: Zs**

| KM# | Date | Mintage | Fine | VF | XF | Unc |
|---|---|---|---|---|---|---|
| 404.3 | 1898 Z | .240 | 1.50 | 2.50 | 7.50 | 20.00 |
| | 1899 Z | .105 | 1.50 | 3.00 | 10.00 | 22.00 |
| | 1900 Z | .219 | 7.50 | 10.00 | 20.00 | 45.00 |
| | 1901 Z | .070 | 2.50 | 5.00 | 10.00 | 25.00 |
| | 1902 Z | .120 | 2.50 | 5.00 | 10.00 | 25.00 |
| | 1903 Z | .228 | 1.50 | 3.00 | 10.00 | 20.00 |
| | 1904 Z | .368 | 1.50 | 3.00 | 10.00 | 20.00 |
| | 1904 M | Inc. Ab. | 1.50 | 3.00 | 10.00 | 25.00 |
| | 1905 M | .066 | 7.50 | 15.00 | 30.00 | 60.00 |

## 20 CENTAVOS

**5.4150 g, .903 SILVER, .1572 oz ASW**
**Mint mark: Cn**
**Obv: Restyled eagle.**

| KM# | Date | Mintage | Fine | VF | XF | Unc |
|---|---|---|---|---|---|---|
| 405 | 1898 M | .114 | 5.00 | 12.50 | 35.00 | 140.00 |
| | 1899 M | .044 | 12.00 | 20.00 | 45.00 | 225.00 |
| | 1899 Q | Inc. Ab. | 20.00 | 35.00 | 100.00 | 250.00 |
| | 1900 Q | .068 | 6.50 | 12.50 | 35.00 | 140.00 |
| | 1901 Q | .185 | 5.00 | 10.00 | 30.00 | 120.00 |
| | 1902/802 Q | | | | | |
| | | .098 | 6.00 | 10.00 | 30.00 | 120.00 |
| | 1902 Q | Inc. Ab. | 4.00 | 9.00 | 30.00 | 120.00 |

| KM# | Date | Mintage | Fine | VF | XF | Unc |
|---|---|---|---|---|---|---|
| 405 | 1903 Q | .093 | 4.00 | 9.00 | 30.00 | 120.00 |
| | 1904/3 H | .258 | — | — | — | — |
| | 1904 H | Inc. Ab. | 5.00 | 10.00 | 30.00 | 120.00 |

**Mint mark: Go**

| KM# | Date | Mintage | Fine | VF | XF | Unc |
|---|---|---|---|---|---|---|
| 405.1 | 1898 R | .135 | 4.00 | 8.00 | 20.00 | 100.00 |
| | 1899 R | .215 | 4.00 | 8.00 | 20.00 | 100.00 |
| | 1900/800 R | | | | | |
| | | .038 | 10.00 | 20.00 | 50.00 | 150.00 |

**Mint mark: Mo**

| KM# | Date | Mintage | Fine | VF | XF | Unc |
|---|---|---|---|---|---|---|
| 405.2 | 1898 M | .150 | 4.00 | 8.00 | 20.00 | 85.00 |
| | 1899 M | .425 | 4.00 | 8.00 | 20.00 | 85.00 |
| | 1900/800 M | | | | | |
| | | .295 | 4.00 | 8.00 | 20.00 | 85.00 |
| | 1901 M | .110 | 4.00 | 8.00 | 20.00 | 85.00 |
| | 1902 M | .120 | 4.00 | 8.00 | 20.00 | 85.00 |
| | 1903 M | .213 | 4.00 | 8.00 | 20.00 | 85.00 |
| | 1904 M | .276 | 4.00 | 8.00 | 20.00 | 85.00 |
| | 1905 M | .117 | 6.50 | 20.00 | 50.00 | 150.00 |

NOTE: Varieties exist.

**Mint mark: Zs**

| KM# | Date | Mintage | Fine | VF | XF | Unc |
|---|---|---|---|---|---|---|
| 405.3 | 1898 Z | .195 | 5.00 | 10.00 | 20.00 | 100.00 |
| | 1899 Z | .210 | 5.00 | 10.00 | 20.00 | 100.00 |
| | 1900/800 Z | | | | | |
| | | .097 | 5.00 | 10.00 | 20.00 | 100.00 |
| | 1901/0 Z | .130 | 25.00 | 50.00 | 100.00 | 250.00 |
| | 1901 Z | Inc. Ab. | 5.00 | 10.00 | 20.00 | 100.00 |
| | 1902 Z | .105 | 5.00 | 10.00 | 20.00 | 100.00 |
| | 1903 Z | .143 | 5.00 | 10.00 | 20.00 | 100.00 |
| | 1904 Z | .246 | 5.00 | 10.00 | 20.00 | 100.00 |
| | 1904 M | Inc. Ab. | 5.00 | 10.00 | 20.00 | 100.00 |
| | 1905 M | .059 | 10.00 | 20.00 | 50.00 | 150.00 |

## 25 CENTAVOS

**6.7680 g, .903 SILVER, .1965 oz ASW**
**Mint mark: A,As**

| KM# | Date | Mintage | Fine | VF | XF | Unc |
|---|---|---|---|---|---|---|
| 406 | 1874 L | — | 20.00 | 40.00 | 90.00 | 200.00 |
| | 1875 L | — | 15.00 | 30.00 | 70.00 | 200.00 |
| | 1876 L | — | 30.00 | 50.00 | 100.00 | 200.00 |
| | 1877 L | .011 | 200.00 | 300.00 | 500.00 | — |
| | 1877. | Inc. Ab. | 10.00 | 25.00 | 60.00 | 200.00 |
| | 1878 L | .025 | 10.00 | 25.00 | 60.00 | 200.00 |
| | 1879 L | — | 10.00 | 25.00 | 60.00 | 200.00 |
| | 1880 L | — | 10.00 | 25.00 | 60.00 | 200.00 |
| | 1880.L | — | 10.00 | 25.00 | 60.00 | 200.00 |
| | 1881 L | 8,800 | 500.00 | 700.00 | — | — |
| | 1882 L | 7,777 | 15.00 | 35.00 | 80.00 | 200.00 |
| | 1883 L | .028 | 10.00 | 25.00 | 60.00 | 200.00 |
| | 1884 L | — | 10.00 | 25.00 | 60.00 | 200.00 |
| | 1885 L | — | 20.00 | 40.00 | 90.00 | 200.00 |
| | 1886 L | .046 | 15.00 | 30.00 | 70.00 | 200.00 |
| | 1887 L | .012 | 12.50 | 27.50 | 65.00 | 200.00 |
| | 1888 L | .020 | 12.50 | 27.50 | 65.00 | 200.00 |
| | 1889 L | .014 | 12.50 | 27.50 | 65.00 | 200.00 |
| | 1890 L | .023 | 10.00 | 25.00 | 60.00 | 200.00 |

**Mint mark: CA,CH,Ca**

| KM# | Date | Mintage | Fine | VF | XF | Unc |
|---|---|---|---|---|---|---|
| 406.1 | 1871 M | .018 | 25.00 | 50.00 | 100.00 | 200.00 |
| | 1872 M very crude date | | | | | |
| | | .024 | 50.00 | 100.00 | 150.00 | 300.00 |
| | 1883 M | .012 | 10.00 | 25.00 | 50.00 | 175.00 |
| | 1885/3 M | .035 | 10.00 | 25.00 | 50.00 | 175.00 |
| | 1885 M | Inc.Ab. | 10.00 | 25.00 | 50.00 | 175.00 |
| | 1886 M | .022 | 10.00 | 25.00 | 50.00 | 175.00 |
| | 1887/6 M | .026 | 10.00 | 15.00 | 30.00 | 175.00 |
| | 1887 M | Inc. Ab. | 10.00 | 15.00 | 30.00 | 175.00 |
| | 1888 M | .014 | 10.00 | 25.00 | 50.00 | 175.00 |
| | 1889 M | .050 | 10.00 | 15.00 | 30.00 | 175.00 |

### Mint mark: Cn

| KM# | Date | Mintage | Fine | VF | XF | Unc |
|---|---|---|---|---|---|---|
| 406.2 | 1871 P | — | 250.00 | 500.00 | 750.00 | — |
| | 1872 P | 2,780 | 300.00 | 550.00 | 800.00 | — |
| | 1873 P | .020 | 100.00 | 150.00 | 250.00 | 500.00 |
| | 1874 P | —' | 20.00 | 50.00 | 125.00 | 250.00 |
| | 1875 P | — | 250.00 | 500.00 | 750.00 | — |
| | 1876 P | — | — | — | Rare | — |
| | 1878/7 D/S | — | 100.00 | 150.00 | 250.00 | 500.00 |
| | 1878 D | — | 100.00 | 150.00 | 250.00 | 500.00 |
| | 1879 D | — | 15.00 | 35.00 | 70.00 | 175.00 |
| | 1880 D | — | 250.00 | 500.00 | 750.00 | — |
| | 1881/0 D | .018 | 15.00 | 30.00 | 60.00 | 175.00 |
| | 1882 D | — | 200.00 | 350.00 | 600.00 | — |
| | 1882 M | — | — | — | Rare | — |
| | 1883 M | .015 | 50.00 | 100.00 | 150.00 | 300.00 |
| | 1884 M | — | 20.00 | 40.00 | 80.00 | 175.00 |
| | 1885/4 M | .019 | 20.00 | 40.00 | 80.00 | 175.00 |
| | 1886 M | .022 | 12.50 | 20.00 | 50.00 | 175.00 |
| | 1887 M | .032 | 12.50 | 20.00 | 50.00 | 175.00 |
| | 1888 M | .086 | 7.50 | 15.00 | 30.00 | 175.00 |
| | 1889 M | .050 | 10.00 | 25.00 | 50.00 | 175.00 |
| | 1890 M | .091 | 7.50 | 17.50 | 40.00 | 175.00 |
| | 1892/0 M | .016 | 20.00 | 40.00 | 80.00 | 200.00 |
| | 1892 M | Inc. Ab. | 20.00 | 40.00 | 80.00 | 200.00 |

### Mint mark: Do

| KM# | Date | Mintage | Fine | VF | XF | Unc |
|---|---|---|---|---|---|---|
| 406.3 | 1873 P | 892 pcs. | — | — | Rare | — |
| | 1877 P | — | 25.00 | 50.00 | 100.00 | 200.00 |
| | 1878/7 E | — | 250.00 | 500.00 | 750.00 | — |
| | 1878 B | — | — | — | Rare | — |
| | 1879 B | — | 50.00 | 75.00 | 125.00 | 250.00 |
| | 1880 B | — | — | — | Rare | — |
| | 1882 C | .017 | 25.00 | 50.00 | 100.00 | 225.00 |
| | 1884/3 C | — | 25.00 | 50.00 | 100.00 | 200.00 |
| | 1885 C | .015 | 20.00 | 40.00 | 80.00 | 200.00 |
| | 1886 C | .033 | 15.00 | 30.00 | 60.00 | 200.00 |
| | 1887 C | .027 | 10.00 | 20.00 | 50.00 | 200.00 |
| | 1888 C | .025 | 10.00 | 20.00 | 50.00 | 200.00 |
| | 1889 C | .029 | 10.00 | 20.00 | 50.00 | 200.00 |
| | 1890 C | .068 | 7.50 | 15.00 | 40.00 | 200.00 |

### Mint mark: Ga

| KM# | Date | Mintage | Fine | VF | XF | Unc |
|---|---|---|---|---|---|---|
| 406.4 | 1880 A | .038 | 25.00 | 50.00 | 100.00 | 200.00 |
| | 1881/0 S | .039 | 25.00 | 50.00 | 100.00 | 200.00 |
| | 1881 S | Inc. Ab. | 25.00 | 50.00 | 100.00 | 200.00 |
| | 1882 S | .018 | 25.00 | 50.00 | 100.00 | 200.00 |
| | 1883/2 B/S | — | 50.00 | 100.00 | 150.00 | 300.00 |
| | 1884 B | — | 20.00 | 40.00 | 80.00 | 150.00 |
| | 1889 S | .030 | 20.00 | 40.00 | 80.00 | 150.00 |

### Mint mark: Go

| KM# | Date | Mintage | Fine | VF | XF | Unc |
|---|---|---|---|---|---|---|
| 406.5 | 1870 S | .128 | 10.00 | 20.00 | 50.00 | 125.00 |
| | 1871 S | .172 | 10.00 | 20.00 | 50.00 | 125.00 |
| | 1872/1 S | .178 | 10.00 | 20.00 | 50.00 | 125.00 |
| | 1872 S | Inc. Ab. | 10.00 | 20.00 | 50.00 | 125.00 |
| | 1873 S | .120 | 10.00 | 20.00 | 50.00 | 125.00 |
| | 1874 S | — | 15.00 | 30.00 | 60.00 | 150.00 |
| | 1875/4 S | — | 15.00 | 30.00 | 60.00 | 150.00 |
| | 1875 S | — | 10.00 | 20.00 | 50.00 | 125.00 |
| | 1876 S | — | 20.00 | 40.00 | 80.00 | 175.00 |
| | 1877 S | .124 | 10.00 | 20.00 | 50.00 | 125.00 |
| | 1878 S | .146 | 10.00 | 20.00 | 50.00 | 125.00 |
| | 1879 S | — | 10.00 | 20.00 | 50.00 | 125.00 |
| | 1880 S | — | 20.00 | 40.00 | 80.00 | 175.00 |
| | 1881 S | .408 | 7.50 | 17.50 | 45.00 | 125.00 |
| | 1882 S | .204 | 7.50 | 17.50 | 45.00 | 125.00 |
| | 1883 B | .168 | 7.50 | 17.50 | 45.00 | 125.00 |
| | 1884/69 B | — | 7.50 | 17.50 | 45.00 | 125.00 |
| | 1884/3 B | — | 7.50 | 17.50 | 45.00 | 125.00 |
| | 1884 B | — | 7.50 | 17.50 | 45.00 | 125.00 |
| | 1885/65 R | .300 | 7.50 | 17.50 | 45.00 | 125.00 |
| | 1885/69 R | I.A. | 7.50 | 17.50 | 45.00 | 125.00 |
| | 1885 R | Inc. Ab. | 7.50 | 17.50 | 45.00 | 125.00 |
| | 1886/66 R | .322 | 7.50 | 17.50 | 45.00 | 125.00 |
| | 1886/69 R/S | Inc. Ab. | 7.50 | 17.50 | 45.00 | 125.00 |
| | 1886/5/69R | Inc. Ab. | 7.50 | 15.00 | 45.00 | 125.00 |
| | 1886 R | Inc. Ab. | 7.50 | 15.00 | 45.00 | 125.00 |
| | 1887 R | .254 | 7.50 | 15.00 | 45.00 | 125.00 |
| | 1887 Go/Cn R/D | Inc. Ab. | 7.50 | 15.00 | 45.00 | 125.00 |
| | 1888 R | .312 | 7.50 | 15.00 | 45.00 | 125.00 |
| | 1889/8 R | .304 | 7.50 | 15.00 | 45.00 | 125.00 |

| KM# | Date | Mintage | Fine | VF | XF | Unc |
|---|---|---|---|---|---|---|
| 406.5 | 1889/8 Go/Cn R/D | Inc. Ab. | 7.50 | 15.00 | 45.00 | 125.00 |
| | 1889 R | Inc. Ab. | 7.50 | 15.00 | 45.00 | 125.00 |
| | 1890 R | .236 | 7.50 | 15.00 | 45.00 | 125.00 |

**NOTE:** Varieties exist.

### Mint mark: Ho

| KM# | Date | Mintage | Fine | VF | XF | Unc |
|---|---|---|---|---|---|---|
| 406.6 | 1874 R | .023 | 10.00 | 20.00 | 40.00 | 125.00 |
| | 1874/64 R | I.A. | 10.00 | 20.00 | 40.00 | 125.00 |
| | 1875 R | — | — | — | Rare | — |
| | 1876/4 F/R | .034 | 10.00 | 20.00 | 50.00 | 150.00 |
| | 1876 F/R | I.A. | 10.00 | 25.00 | 60.00 | 150.00 |
| | 1876 F | Inc. Ab. | 10.00 | 25.00 | 55.00 | 135.00 |
| | 1877 F | — | 10.00 | 20.00 | 50.00 | 125.00 |
| | 1878 A | .023 | 10.00 | 20.00 | 50.00 | 125.00 |
| | 1879 A | — | 10.00 | 20.00 | 50.00 | 125.00 |
| | 1880 A | — | 15.00 | 30.00 | 60.00 | 125.00 |
| | 1881 A | .019 | 15.00 | 30.00 | 60.00 | 125.00 |
| | 1882 A | 8,120 | 20.00 | 40.00 | 80.00 | 150.00 |
| | 1883 M | 2,000 | 100.00 | 200.00 | 300.00 | 600.00 |
| | 1884 M | — | 12.50 | 25.00 | 50.00 | 125.00 |
| | 1885 M | — | 10.00 | 20.00 | 50.00 | 125.00 |
| | 1886 G | 6,400 | 30.00 | 60.00 | 125.00 | 250.00 |
| | 1887 G | .012 | 10.00 | 20.00 | 40.00 | 125.00 |
| | 1888 G | .020 | 10.00 | 20.00 | 40.00 | 125.00 |
| | 1889 G | .028 | 10.00 | 20.00 | 40.00 | 125.00 |
| | 1890/80 G | .018 | 25.00 | 50.00 | 100.00 | 125.00 |
| | 1890 G | Inc. Ab. | 25.00 | 50.00 | 100.00 | 125.00 |

**NOTE:** Varieties exist.

### Mint mark: Mo

| KM# | Date | Mintage | Fine | VF | XF | Unc |
|---|---|---|---|---|---|---|
| 406.7 | 1869 C | .076 | 10.00 | 25.00 | 50.00 | 125.00 |
| | 1870/9 C | .136 | 6.00 | 12.00 | 30.00 | 125.00 |
| | 1870 C | Inc. Ab. | 6.00 | 12.00 | 30.00 | 125.00 |
| | 1871 M | .138 | 6.00 | 12.00 | 30.00 | 125.00 |
| | 1872 M | .220 | 6.00 | 12.00 | 30.00 | 125.00 |
| | 1873/1 M | .048 | 10.00 | 25.00 | 50.00 | 125.00 |
| | 1873 M | Inc. Ab. | 10.00 | 25.00 | 50.00 | 125.00 |
| | 1874/69 B/M | — | 10.00 | 25.00 | 50.00 | 125.00 |
| | 1874/3 M | — | 10.00 | 25.00 | 50.00 | 125.00 |
| | 1874/3 B | — | 10.00 | 25.00 | 50.00 | 125.00 |
| | 1874 M | — | 6.00 | 12.00 | 30.00 | 125.00 |
| | 1874 B/M | — | 10.00 | 25.00 | 50.00 | 125.00 |
| | 1875 B | — | 6.00 | 12.00 | 30.00 | 125.00 |
| | 1876/5 B | — | 7.50 | 15.00 | 40.00 | 125.00 |
| | 1876 B | — | 6.00 | 12.00 | 30.00 | 125.00 |
| | 1877 M | .056 | 10.00 | 25.00 | 50.00 | 125.00 |
| | 1878/1 M | .120 | 10.00 | 25.00 | 50.00 | 125.00 |
| | 1878/7 M | I.A. | 10.00 | 25.00 | 50.00 | 125.00 |
| | 1878 M | Inc. Ab. | 6.00 | 12.00 | 30.00 | 125.00 |
| | 1879 M | — | 10.00 | 20.00 | 40.00 | 125.00 |
| | 1880 M | — | 7.50 | 15.00 | 35.00 | 125.00 |
| | 1881/0 M | .300 | 10.00 | 25.00 | 50.00 | 125.00 |
| | 1881 M | Inc. Ab. | 10.00 | 25.00 | 50.00 | 125.00 |
| | 1882 M | .212 | 7.50 | 15.00 | 35.00 | 125.00 |
| | 1883 M | .108 | 7.50 | 15.00 | 35.00 | 125.00 |
| | 1884 M | — | 10.00 | 20.00 | 40.00 | 125.00 |
| | 1885 M | .216 | 10.00 | 20.00 | 50.00 | 125.00 |
| | 1886/5 M | .436 | 7.50 | 15.00 | 35.00 | 125.00 |
| | 1886 M | Inc. Ab. | 7.50 | 15.00 | 35.00 | 125.00 |
| | 1887 M | .376 | 7.50 | 15.00 | 35.00 | 125.00 |
| | 1888 M | .192 | 7.50 | 15.00 | 35.00 | 125.00 |
| | 1889 M | .132 | 7.50 | 15.00 | 35.00 | 125.00 |
| | 1890 M | .060 | 10.00 | 20.00 | 40.00 | 125.00 |

**NOTE:** Varieties exist.

### Mint mark: Pi

| KM# | Date | Mintage | Fine | VF | XF | Unc |
|---|---|---|---|---|---|---|
| 406.8 | 1869 S | — | 25.00 | 75.00 | 150.00 | 300.00 |
| | 1870 G | .050 | 10.00 | 30.00 | 75.00 | 150.00 |
| | 1870 O | Inc. Ab. | 15.00 | 35.00 | 85.00 | 175.00 |
| | 1871 O | .030 | 10.00 | 30.00 | 75.00 | 150.00 |
| | 1872 O | .046 | 10.00 | 30.00 | 75.00 | 150.00 |
| | 1873 O | .013 | 15.00 | 40.00 | 90.00 | 175.00 |
| | 1874 H | — | 15.00 | 40.00 | 90.00 | 200.00 |
| | 1875 H | — | 10.00 | 20.00 | 60.00 | 150.00 |
| | 1876/5 H | — | 15.00 | 30.00 | 80.00 | 175.00 |
| | 1876 H | — | 10.00 | 25.00 | 65.00 | 150.00 |
| | 1877 H | .019 | 10.00 | 25.00 | 65.00 | 150.00 |
| | 1878 H | — | 15.00 | 30.00 | 60.00 | 150.00 |
| | 1879/8 H | — | 10.00 | 25.00 | 60.00 | 150.00 |
| | 1879 H | — | 10.00 | 25.00 | 60.00 | 150.00 |
| | 1879 E | — | 100.00 | 200.00 | 300.00 | 600.00 |
| | 1880 H | — | 20.00 | 40.00 | 100.00 | 200.00 |

| KM# | Date | Mintage | Fine | VF | XF | Unc |
|---|---|---|---|---|---|---|
| 406.8 | 1881 H | .050 | 20.00 | 40.00 | 80.00 | 175.00 |
| | 1881 E | Inc. Ab. | — | — | Rare | — |
| | 1882 H | .020 | 10.00 | 20.00 | 60.00 | 150.00 |
| | 1883 H | .017 | 10.00 | 25.00 | 65.00 | 150.00 |
| | 1884 H | — | 10.00 | 25.00 | 65.00 | 150.00 |
| | 1885 H | .043 | 10.00 | 20.00 | 60.00 | 150.00 |
| | 1886 C | .078 | 10.00 | 25.00 | 65.00 | 150.00 |
| | 1886 R | Inc. Ab. | 7.50 | 20.00 | 50.00 | 150.00 |
| | 1886 R 6/inverted 6 | | | | | |
| | | Inc. Ab. | 7.50 | 20.00 | 50.00 | 150.00 |
| | 1887 Pi/ZsR | | | | | |
| | | .092 | 7.50 | 20.00 | 50.00 | 150.00 |
| | 1887 Pi/ZsB | | | | | |
| | | Inc. Ab. | 100.00 | 150.00 | 300.00 | 500.00 |
| | 1888 R | .106 | 7.50 | 20.00 | 50.00 | 150.00 |
| | 1888 Pi/ZsR | | | | | |
| | | Inc. Ab. | 10.00 | 20.00 | 50.00 | 150.00 |
| | 1888 R/B | I.A. | 10.00 | 20.00 | 50.00 | 150.00 |
| | 1889 R | .115 | 7.50 | 15.00 | 40.00 | 150.00 |
| | 1889 Pi/ZsR | | | | | |
| | | Inc. Ab. | 10.00 | 20.00 | 50.00 | 150.00 |
| | 1889 R/B | I.A. | 10.00 | 20.00 | 50.00 | 150.00 |
| | 1890 R | .064 | 10.00 | 20.00 | 50.00 | 150.00 |
| | 1890 Pi/ZsR/B | | | | | |
| | | Inc. Ab. | 7.50 | 15.00 | 40.00 | 150.00 |
| | 1890 R/B | I.A. | 10.00 | 20.00 | 50.00 | 150.00 |

NOTE: Varieties exist.

### Mint mark: Zs

| KM# | Date | Mintage | Fine | VF | XF | Unc |
|---|---|---|---|---|---|---|
| 406.9 | 1870 H | .152 | 6.00 | 15.00 | 50.00 | 125.00 |
| | 1871 H | .250 | 6.00 | 15.00 | 50.00 | 125.00 |
| | 1872 H | .260 | 6.00 | 15.00 | 50.00 | 125.00 |
| | 1873 H | .132 | 6.00 | 15.00 | 50.00 | 125.00 |
| | 1874 H | — | 10.00 | 20.00 | 60.00 | 125.00 |
| | 1874 A | — | 10.00 | 20.00 | 60.00 | 125.00 |
| | 1875 A | — | 7.00 | 20.00 | 60.00 | 125.00 |
| | 1876 A | — | 6.00 | 15.00 | 50.00 | 125.00 |
| | 1876 S | — | 6.00 | 15.00 | 50.00 | 125.00 |
| | 1877 S | .350 | 6.00 | 15.00 | 50.00 | 125.00 |
| | 1878 S | .252 | 6.00 | 15.00 | 50.00 | 125.00 |
| | 1879 S | — | 6.00 | 15.00 | 50.00 | 125.00 |
| | 1880 S | — | 6.00 | 15.00 | 50.00 | 125.00 |
| | 1881/0 S | .570 | 6.00 | 15.00 | 50.00 | 125.00 |
| | 1881 S | Inc. Ab. | 6.00 | 15.00 | 50.00 | 125.00 |
| | 1882/1 S | .300 | 10.00 | 17.50 | 55.00 | 125.00 |
| | 1882 S | Inc. Ab. | 6.00 | 15.00 | 50.00 | 125.00 |
| | 1883/2 S | .193 | 10.00 | 17.50 | 55.00 | 125.00 |
| | 1883 S | Inc. Ab. | 6.00 | 15.00 | 50.00 | 125.00 |
| | 1884/3 S | — | 10.00 | 17.50 | 55.00 | 125.00 |
| | 1884 S | — | 6.00 | 15.00 | 50.00 | 125.00 |
| | 1885 S | .309 | 6.00 | 15.00 | 50.00 | 125.00 |
| | 1886/5 S | .613 | 6.00 | 15.00 | 50.00 | 125.00 |
| | 1886 S | Inc. Ab. | 6.00 | 15.00 | 50.00 | 125.00 |
| | 1886 Z | Inc. Ab. | 6.00 | 15.00 | 55.00 | 125.00 |
| | 1887 Z | .389 | 6.00 | 15.00 | 50.00 | 125.00 |
| | 1888 Z | .408 | 6.00 | 15.00 | 50.00 | 125.00 |
| | 1889 Z | .400 | 6.00 | 15.00 | 50.00 | 125.00 |
| | 1890 Z | .269 | 6.00 | 15.00 | 50.00 | 125.00 |

NOTE: Varieties exist.

## 50 CENTAVOS

**13.5360 g, .903 SILVER, .3930 oz ASW**
**Mint mark: A, As**
**Rev: Balance scale.**

| KM# | Date | Mintage | Fine | VF | XF | Unc |
|---|---|---|---|---|---|---|
| 407 | 1875 L | — | 12.00 | 25.00 | 70.00 | 400.00 |
| | 1876/5 L | — | 25.00 | 50.00 | 120.00 | 450.00 |
| | 1876 L | — | 12.00 | 25.00 | 70.00 | 400.00 |
| | 1876.L | — | — | — | — | — |
| | 1877 L | .026 | 15.00 | 30.00 | 85.00 | 450.00 |
| | 1878 L | — | 12.00 | 25.00 | 70.00 | 400.00 |
| | 1879 L | — | 25.00 | 50.00 | 120.00 | 450.00 |

| KM# | Date | Mintage | Fine | VF | XF | Unc |
|---|---|---|---|---|---|---|
| 407 | 1880 L | .057 | 12.00 | 25.00 | 70.00 | 400.00 |
| | 1881 L | .018 | 15.00 | 30.00 | 80.00 | 450.00 |
| | 1884 L | 6,286 | 65.00 | 120.00 | 250.00 | 650.00 |
| | 1885 As/HoL | | | | | |
| | | .021 | 15.00 | 35.00 | 90.00 | 450.00 |
| | 1888 L | — | Contemporary counterfeits | | | |

### Mint mark: Ca, CHa

| | | | | | | |
|---|---|---|---|---|---|---|
| 407.1 | 1883 M | .012 | 30.00 | 60.00 | 125.00 | 500.00 |
| | 1884 M | — | 25.00 | 50.00 | 125.00 | 500.00 |
| | 1885 M | .013 | 15.00 | 35.00 | 90.00 | 400.00 |
| | 1886 M | .018 | 20.00 | 40.00 | 100.00 | 450.00 |
| | 1887 M | .026 | 25.00 | 65.00 | 150.00 | 500.00 |

### Mint mark: Cn

| | | | | | | |
|---|---|---|---|---|---|---|
| 407.2 | 1871 P | — | 400.00 | 550.00 | 750.00 | 1500. |
| | 1873 P | — | 400.00 | 550.00 | 750.00 | 1500. |
| | 1874 P | — | 200.00 | 300.00 | 500.00 | 1000. |
| | 1875/4 P | — | 20.00 | 40.00 | 75.00 | 450.00 |
| | 1875 P | — | 12.00 | 25.00 | 50.00 | 450.00 |
| | 1876 P | — | 15.00 | 30.00 | 60.00 | 450.00 |
| | 1877/6 G | — | 15.00 | 30.00 | 60.00 | 450.00 |
| | 1877 G | — | 12.00 | 25.00 | 50.00 | 450.00 |
| | 1878 G | .018 | 20.00 | 40.00 | 75.00 | 450.00 |
| | 1878 D Cn/Mo | | | | | |
| | | Inc. Ab. | 30.00 | 60.00 | 100.00 | 450.00 |
| | 1878 D | Inc. Ab. | 15.00 | 35.00 | 75.00 | 450.00 |
| | 1879 D | — | 12.00 | 25.00 | 50.00 | 450.00 |
| | 1879 D/G | — | 12.00 | 25.00 | 50.00 | 450.00 |
| | 1880 D | — | 15.00 | 30.00 | 60.00 | 450.00 |
| | 1881/0 D | .188 | 15.00 | 30.00 | 60.00 | 450.00 |
| | 1881 D | Inc. Ab. | 15.00 | 30.00 | 60.00 | 450.00 |
| | 1881 G | Inc. Ab. | 125.00 | 175.00 | 275.00 | 550.00 |
| | 1882 D | — | 175.00 | 225.00 | 325.00 | 1000. |
| | 1882 G | — | 100.00 | 250.00 | 300.00 | 1000. |
| | 1883 D | .019 | 25.00 | 50.00 | 100.00 | 500.00 |
| | 1885/3 CN/Pi M/H | | | | | |
| | | 9,254 | 30.00 | 60.00 | 100.00 | 500.00 |
| | 1886 M/G | 7,030 | 50.00 | 100.00 | 150.00 | 800.00 |
| | 1886 M | Inc. Ab. | 40.00 | 80.00 | 150.00 | 800.00 |
| | 1887 M | .076 | 20.00 | 40.00 | 100.00 | 450.00 |
| | 1888 M | — | Contemporary counterfeits | | | |
| | 1892 M | 8,200 | 40.00 | 80.00 | 150.00 | 800.00 |

### Mint mark: Do

| | | | | | | |
|---|---|---|---|---|---|---|
| 407.3 | 1871 P | 591 pcs. | — | — | Rare | — |
| | 1873 P | 4,010 | 150.00 | 250.00 | 500.00 | 1250. |
| | 1873 M/P | I.A. | 150.00 | 250.00 | 500.00 | 1250. |
| | 1874 M | — | 20.00 | 40.00 | 175.00 | 750.00 |
| | 1875 M | — | 20.00 | 40.00 | 80.00 | 350.00 |
| | 1875 H | — | 150.00 | 250.00 | 450.00 | 1000. |
| | 1876/5 M | — | 35.00 | 70.00 | 150.00 | 500.00 |
| | 1876 M | — | 35.00 | 70.00 | 150.00 | 500.00 |
| | 1877 P | 2,000 | 30.00 | 45.00 | 150.00 | 1250. |
| | 1878 B | — | — | — | Rare | — |
| | 1879 B | — | — | — | Rare | — |
| | 1880 P | — | 30.00 | 60.00 | 125.00 | 500.00 |
| | 1881 P | .010 | 40.00 | 80.00 | 150.00 | 550.00 |
| | 1882 C | 8,957 | 30.00 | 75.00 | 200.00 | 800.00 |
| | 1884/2 C | — | 20.00 | 50.00 | 125.00 | 600.00 |
| | 1884 C | — | — | — | — | — |
| | 1885 B | — | 15.00 | 40.00 | 100.00 | 500.00 |
| | 1886 C | .016 | 15.00 | 40.00 | 100.00 | 500.00 |
| | 1887 Do/MoC | | | | | |
| | | .028 | 15.00 | 40.00 | 100.00 | 500.00 |

### Mint mark: Go

| | | | | | | |
|---|---|---|---|---|---|---|
| 407.4 | 1869 S | — | 15.00 | 35.00 | 75.00 | 550.00 |
| | 1870 S | .166 | 12.00 | 25.00 | 50.00 | 450.00 |
| | 1871 S | .148 | 12.00 | 25.00 | 50.00 | 450.00 |
| | 1872/1 S | .144 | 15.00 | 30.00 | 60.00 | 500.00 |
| | 1872 S | Inc. Ab. | 12.00 | 25.00 | 50.00 | 450.00 |
| | 1873 S | .050 | 12.00 | 25.00 | 50.00 | 450.00 |
| | 1874 S | — | 12.00 | 25.00 | 50.00 | 450.00 |
| | 1875 S | — | 15.00 | 35.00 | 75.00 | 450.00 |
| | 1876/5 S | — | 12.00 | 25.00 | 50.00 | 450.00 |
| | 1877 S | .076 | 12.00 | 25.00 | 60.00 | 450.00 |
| | 1878 S | .037 | 15.00 | 30.00 | 75.00 | 550.00 |
| | 1879 S | — | 12.00 | 25.00 | 50.00 | 450.00 |
| | 1880 S | — | 12.00 | 25.00 | 50.00 | 450.00 |
| | 1881/79 S | .032 | 15.00 | 30.00 | 60.00 | 500.00 |
| | 1881 S | Inc. Ab. | 12.00 | 25.00 | 50.00 | 450.00 |
| | 1882 S | .018 | 12.00 | 25.00 | 50.00 | 450.00 |
| | 1883/2 B/S | — | 15.00 | 30.00 | 60.00 | 500.00 |
| | 1883 B | — | 12.00 | 25.00 | 50.00 | 450.00 |

| KM# | Date | Mintage | Fine | VF | XF | Unc |
|---|---|---|---|---|---|---|
| 407.4 | 1883 S | — | — | — | Rare | — |
| | 1884 B/S | — | 15.00 | 30.00 | 75.00 | 500.00 |
| | 1885 R | .053 | 12.00 | 25.00 | 50.00 | 450.00 |
| | 1886/5 R/B | | | | | |
| | | .059 | 15.00 | 30.00 | 60.00 | 500.00 |
| | 1886/5 R/S | | | | | |
| | | Inc. Ab. | 20.00 | 40.00 | 75.00 | 500.00 |
| | 1886 R | Inc. Ab. | 20.00 | 40.00 | 75.00 | 450.00 |
| | 1887 R | .018 | 20.00 | 40.00 | 75.00 | 550.00 |
| | 1888 R | — | Contemporary counterfeits | | | |

**NOTE:** Varieties exist.

### Mint mark: Ho

| KM# | Date | Mintage | Fine | VF | XF | Unc |
|---|---|---|---|---|---|---|
| 407.5 | 1874 R | — | 20.00 | 40.00 | 100.00 | 600.00 |
| | 1875/4 R | — | 20.00 | 50.00 | 125.00 | 600.00 |
| | 1875 R | — | 20.00 | 50.00 | 125.00 | 600.00 |
| | 1876/5 F/R | — | 15.00 | 35.00 | 100.00 | 550.00 |
| | 1876 F | — | 15.00 | 35.00 | 100.00 | 550.00 |
| | 1877 F | — | 50.00 | 75.00 | 150.00 | 650.00 |
| | 1880/70 A | — | 15.00 | 35.00 | 100.00 | 550.00 |
| | 1880 A | — | 15.00 | 35.00 | 100.00 | 550.00 |
| | 1881 A | .013 | 15.00 | 35.00 | 100.00 | 550.00 |
| | 1882 A | — | 75.00 | 150.00 | 250.00 | 750.00 |
| | 1888 G | — | Contemporary counterfeits | | | |
| | 1894 G | .059 | 15.00 | 30.00 | 100.00 | 450.00 |
| | 1895 G | 8,000 | 250.00 | 350.00 | 500.00 | 1250. |

**NOTE:** Varieties exist.

### Mint mark: Mo

| KM# | Date | Mintage | Fine | VF | XF | Unc |
|---|---|---|---|---|---|---|
| 407.6 | 1869 C | .046 | 15.00 | 35.00 | 95.00 | 600.00 |
| | 1870 C | .052 | 15.00 | 30.00 | 90.00 | 550.00 |
| | 1871 C | .014 | 40.00 | 75.00 | 150.00 | 650.00 |
| | 1871 M/C | I.A. | 35.00 | 75.00 | 150.00 | 600.00 |
| | 1872/1 M | .060 | 35.00 | 75.00 | 150.00 | 550.00 |
| | 1872 M | Inc. Ab. | 35.00 | 75.00 | 150.00 | 550.00 |
| | 1873 M | 6,000 | 35.00 | 75.00 | 150.00 | 600.00 |
| | 1874/3 M | — | 200.00 | 400.00 | 600.00 | 1250. |
| | 1874/2 B | — | 15.00 | 30.00 | 75.00 | 500.00 |
| | 1874/3 B/M | — | 15.00 | 30.00 | 75.00 | 500.00 |
| | 1874 B | — | 15.00 | 30.00 | 75.00 | 500.00 |
| | 1875 B | — | 15.00 | 30.00 | 75.00 | 550.00 |
| | 1876/5 B | — | 15.00 | 30.00 | 75.00 | 500.00 |
| | 1876 B | — | 12.00 | 25.00 | 75.00 | 500.00 |
| | 1877/2 M | — | 20.00 | 40.00 | 100.00 | 550.00 |
| | 1877 M | — | 15.00 | 30.00 | 90.00 | 500.00 |
| | 1878/7 M | | | | | |
| | | 8,000 | 25.00 | 50.00 | 125.00 | 600.00 |
| | 1878 M | Inc. Ab. | 15.00 | 35.00 | 100.00 | 550.00 |
| | 1879 M | — | 25.00 | 50.00 | 125.00 | 550.00 |
| | 1880 M | — | 100.00 | 150.00 | 250.00 | 750.00 |
| | 1881 M | .016 | 25.00 | 50.00 | 125.00 | 600.00 |
| | 1882/1 M | | | | | |
| | | 2,000 | 30.00 | 60.00 | 150.00 | 750.00 |
| | 1883/2 M | 4,000 | 150.00 | 225.00 | 350.00 | 1000. |
| | 1884 M | — | 150.00 | 225.00 | 350.00 | 1000. |
| | 1885 M | .012 | 30.00 | 60.00 | 150.00 | 600.00 |
| | 1886/5 M | .066 | 15.00 | 35.00 | 90.00 | 450.00 |
| | 1886 M | Inc. Ab. | 12.00 | 25.00 | 75.00 | 400.00 |
| | 1887/6 M | .088 | 15.00 | 35.00 | 90.00 | 450.00 |
| | 1887 M | Inc. Ab. | 15.00 | 35.00 | 75.00 | 450.00 |
| | 1888 M | — | Contemporary counterfeits | | | |

### Mint mark: Pi

| KM# | Date | Mintage | Fine | VF | XF | Unc |
|---|---|---|---|---|---|---|
| 407.7 | 1870/780 G | | | | | |
| | | .050 | 25.00 | 45.00 | 110.00 | 500.00 |
| | 1870 G | Inc. Ab. | 20.00 | 40.00 | 100.00 | 450.00 |
| | 1870 O | Inc. Ab. | 20.00 | 40.00 | 100.00 | 450.00 |
| | 1871 O/G | .064 | 15.00 | 30.00 | 80.00 | 400.00 |
| | 1872 O | .052 | 15.00 | 30.00 | 80.00 | 400.00 |
| | 1872 O/G | I.A. | 15.00 | 30.00 | 80.00 | 400.00 |
| | 1873 O | .032 | 20.00 | 40.00 | 100.00 | 450.00 |
| | 1873 H | Inc. Ab. | 25.00 | 50.00 | 125.00 | 550.00 |
| | 1874 H/O | — | 15.00 | 30.00 | 80.00 | 400.00 |
| | 1875 H | — | 15.00 | 30.00 | 80.00 | 400.00 |
| | 1876 H | — | 30.00 | 60.00 | 150.00 | 700.00 |
| | 1877 H | .034 | 20.00 | 40.00 | 100.00 | 450.00 |
| | 1878 H | 9,700 | 20.00 | 40.00 | 100.00 | 450.00 |
| | 1879/7 H | — | 15.00 | 35.00 | 90.00 | 450.00 |
| | 1879 H | — | 15.00 | 35.00 | 90.00 | 400.00 |
| | 1880 H | — | 20.00 | 40.00 | 100.00 | 450.00 |
| | 1881 H | .028 | 20.00 | 40.00 | 100.00 | 450.00 |
| | 1882 H | .022 | 15.00 | 30.00 | 80.00 | 400.00 |
| | 1883 H 8/8 | | | | | |
| | | .029 | 50.00 | 100.00 | 200.00 | 750.00 |
| | 1883 H | Inc. Ab. | 15.00 | 30.00 | 80.00 | 400.00 |

| KM# | Date | Mintage | Fine | VF | XF | Unc |
|---|---|---|---|---|---|---|
| 407.7 | 1884 H | — | 50.00 | 100.00 | 175.00 | 600.00 |
| | 1885/0 H | .045 | 20.00 | 40.00 | 100.00 | 450.00 |
| | 1885/4 H | I.A. | 20.00 | 40.00 | 100.00 | 450.00 |
| | 1885 H | Inc. Ab. | 25.00 | 50.00 | 125.00 | 450.00 |
| | 1885 C | Inc. Ab. | 15.00 | 30.00 | 80.00 | 400.00 |
| | 1886/1 R | .092 | 50.00 | 100.00 | 175.00 | 600.00 |
| | 1886 C | Inc. Ab. | 15.00 | 30.00 | 80.00 | 400.00 |
| | 1886 R | Inc. Ab. | 15.00 | 30.00 | 80.00 | 400.00 |
| | 1887 R | .032 | 15.00 | 30.00 | 90.00 | 450.00 |
| | 1888 R | — | Contemporary counterfeits | | | |

### Mint mark: Zs

| KM# | Date | Mintage | Fine | VF | XF | Unc |
|---|---|---|---|---|---|---|
| 407.8 | 1870 H | .086 | 12.00 | 25.00 | 60.00 | 450.00 |
| | 1871 H | .146 | 12.00 | 25.00 | 50.00 | 400.00 |
| | 1872 H | .132 | 12.00 | 25.00 | 50.00 | 400.00 |
| | 1873 H | .056 | 12.00 | 25.00 | 50.00 | 400.00 |
| | 1874 H | — | 12.00 | 25.00 | 50.00 | 400.00 |
| | 1874 A | — | — | — | Rare | — |
| | 1875 A | — | 12.00 | 25.00 | 50.00 | 400.00 |
| | 1876/5 A | — | 15.00 | 30.00 | 60.00 | 450.00 |
| | 1876 A | — | 12.00 | 25.00 | 50.00 | 400.00 |
| | 1876 S | — | 100.00 | 200.00 | 350.00 | 750.00 |
| | 1877 S | .100 | 12.00 | 25.00 | 50.00 | 400.00 |
| | 1878/7 S | .254 | 15.00 | 30.00 | 60.00 | 450.00 |
| | 1878 S | Inc. Ab. | 15.00 | 30.00 | 60.00 | 400.00 |
| | 1879 S | — | 12.00 | 25.00 | 50.00 | 400.00 |
| | 1880 S | — | 12.00 | 25.00 | 50.00 | 400.00 |
| | 1881 S | .201 | 12.00 | 25.00 | 50.00 | 400.00 |
| | 1882/1 S | 2,000 | 50.00 | 100.00 | 250.00 | 650.00 |
| | 1882 S | Inc. Ab. | 50.00 | 100.00 | 250.00 | 650.00 |
| | 1883 Zs/Za S | | | | | |
| | | .031 | 30.00 | 60.00 | 100.00 | 450.00 |
| | 1883 S | Inc. Ab. | 25.00 | 50.00 | 100.00 | 450.00 |
| | 1884/3 S | — | 15.00 | 30.00 | 60.00 | 450.00 |
| | 1884 S | — | 12.00 | 25.00 | 50.00 | 400.00 |
| | 1885/4 S | 2,000 | 25.00 | 50.00 | 125.00 | 450.00 |
| | 1885 S | Inc. Ab. | 25.00 | 50.00 | 125.00 | 450.00 |
| | 1886 Z | 2,000 | 150.00 | 275.00 | 400.00 | 1000. |
| | 1887 Z | .063 | 30.00 | 60.00 | 125.00 | 450.00 |

**NOTE:** Varieties exist.

## PESO

**27.0730 g, .903 SILVER, .7860 oz ASW**
**Mint mark: CH**
**Rev: Balance scale.**

| KM# | Date | Mintage | Fine | VF | XF | Unc |
|---|---|---|---|---|---|---|
| 408 | 1872 P/M | .747 | 750.00 | 1500. | 3500. | — |
| | 1872 P | Inc. Ab. | 350.00 | 700.00 | 1500. | — |
| | 1872/1 M | I.A. | 25.00 | 40.00 | 75.00 | 400.00 |
| | 1872 M | Inc. Ab. | 17.50 | 25.00 | 50.00 | 250.00 |
| | 1873 M | .320 | 20.00 | 30.00 | 60.00 | 250.00 |
| | 1873 M/P | I.A. | 25.00 | 40.00 | 75.00 | 350.00 |

### Mint mark: Cn

| KM# | Date | Mintage | Fine | VF | XF | Unc |
|-----|------|---------|------|-----|-----|-----|
| 408.1 | 1870 E | — | 40.00 | 80.00 | 150.00 | 500.00 |
| | 1871/11 P | .478 | 25.00 | 45.00 | 90.00 | 350.00 |
| | 1871 P | Inc. Ab. | 20.00 | 40.00 | 75.00 | 300.00 |
| | 1872 P | .209 | 20.00 | 40.00 | 75.00 | 300.00 |
| | 1873 P | .527 | 20.00 | 40.00 | 75.00 | 300.00 |

### Mint mark: Do

| KM# | Date | Mintage | Fine | VF | XF | Unc |
|-----|------|---------|------|-----|-----|-----|
| 408.2 | 1870 P | — | 50.00 | 100.00 | 175.00 | 450.00 |
| | 1871 P | .427 | 25.00 | 50.00 | 75.00 | 300.00 |
| | 1872 P | .296 | 20.00 | 40.00 | 75.00 | 350.00 |
| | 1872 PT | I.A. | 100.00 | 175.00 | 250.00 | 675.00 |
| | 1873 P | .203 | 25.00 | 45.00 | 85.00 | 350.00 |

### Mint mark: Ga

| KM# | Date | Mintage | Fine | VF | XF | Unc |
|-----|------|---------|------|-----|-----|-----|
| 408.3 | 1870 C | — | 650.00 | 850.00 | — | — |
| | 1871 C | .829 | 25.00 | 65.00 | 135.00 | 600.00 |
| | 1872 C | .485 | 40.00 | 90.00 | 175.00 | 650.00 |
| | 1873/2 C | .277 | 40.00 | 90.00 | 175.00 | 700.00 |
| | 1873 C | Inc. Ab. | 25.00 | 65.00 | 135.00 | 600.00 |

### Mint mark: Go

| KM# | Date | Mintage | Fine | VF | XF | Unc |
|-----|------|---------|------|-----|-----|-----|
| 408.4 | 1871/0 S | 3.946 | 30.00 | 50.00 | 90.00 | 350.00 |
| | 1871/3 S | I.A. | 20.00 | 35.00 | 70.00 | 250.00 |
| | 1871 S | Inc. Ab. | 12.00 | 20.00 | 40.00 | 200.00 |
| | 1872 S | 4.067 | 12.00 | 20.00 | 40.00 | 250.00 |
| | 1873/2 S | 1.560 | 15.00 | 25.00 | 50.00 | 250.00 |
| | 1873 S | Inc. Ab. | 12.00 | 20.00 | 45.00 | 200.00 |
| | 1873/Go/Mo/S/M | | | | | |
| | | Inc. Ab. | 12.00 | 20.00 | 45.00 | 250.00 |

### Mint mark: Mo

| KM# | Date | Mintage | Fine | VF | XF | Unc |
|-----|------|---------|------|-----|-----|-----|
| 408.5 | 1869 C | — | 35.00 | 65.00 | 135.00 | 450.00 |
| | 1870/69 C | | | | | |
| | | 5.115 | 15.00 | 25.00 | 50.00 | 275.00 |
| | 1870 C | Inc. Ab. | 12.00 | 20.00 | 40.00 | 250.00 |
| | 1870 M/C | I.A. | 18.00 | 30.00 | 50.00 | 275.00 |
| | 1870 M | Inc. Ab. | 18.00 | 30.00 | 50.00 | 275.00 |
| | 1871/0 M | | | | | |
| | | 6.974 | 15.00 | 25.00 | 50.00 | 275.00 |
| | 1871 M | Inc. Ab. | 12.00 | 20.00 | 40.00 | 250.00 |
| | 1872/1 M/C | | | | | |
| | | 4.801 | 15.00 | 25.00 | 50.00 | 275.00 |
| | 1872 M | Inc. Ab. | 12.00 | 20.00 | 40.00 | 250.00 |
| | 1873 M | 1.765 | 12.00 | 20.00 | 40.00 | 250.00 |

NOTE: The 1869 C with large LEY on the scroll is a pattern.

### Mint mark: Oa

| KM# | Date | Mintage | Fine | VF | XF | Unc |
|-----|------|---------|------|-----|-----|-----|
| 408.6 | 1869 E | — | 275.00 | 400.00 | 600.00 | 2000. |
| | 1870 OAE small A | | | | | |
| | | Inc. Ab. | 15.00 | 30.00 | 75.00 | 400.00 |
| | 1870 OA E large A | | | | | |
| | | Inc. Ab. | 100.00 | 150.00 | 300.00 | 900.00 |
| | 1871/69 E | .140 | 30.00 | 50.00 | 125.00 | 550.00 |
| | 1871 OaE small A | | | | | |
| | | Inc. Ab. | 15.00 | 30.00 | 60.00 | 300.00 |
| | 1871 OA E large A | | | | | |
| | | Inc. Ab. | 15.00 | 30.00 | 75.00 | 400.00 |
| | 1872 OaE small A | | | | | |
| | | .180 | 15.00 | 30.00 | 75.00 | 400.00 |
| | 1872 OA E large A | | | | | |
| | | Inc. Ab. | 50.00 | 100.00 | 200.00 | 450.00 |
| | 1873 E | .105 | 15.00 | 30.00 | 75.00 | 350.00 |

### Mint mark: Pi

| KM# | Date | Mintage | Fine | VF | XF | Unc |
|-----|------|---------|------|-----|-----|-----|
| 408.7 | 1870 S | 1.967 | 200.00 | 350.00 | 500.00 | 1000. |
| | 1870 S/A | I.A. | 200.00 | 350.00 | 500.00 | 1000. |
| | 1870 G | Inc. Ab. | 25.00 | 50.00 | 125.00 | 450.00 |
| | 1870 H | Inc. Ab. | | Contemporary counterfeit | | |
| | 1870 O/G | I.A. | 25.00 | 35.00 | 125.00 | 450.00 |
| | 1870 O | Inc. Ab. | 20.00 | 30.00 | 100.00 | 350.00 |
| | 1871/69 O | | | | | |
| | | 2.103 | 75.00 | 150.00 | 250.00 | 500.00 |
| | 1871 O/G | I.A. | 15.00 | 30.00 | 60.00 | 300.00 |
| | 1872 O | 1.873 | 15.00 | 30.00 | 60.00 | 300.00 |
| | 1873 O | .893 | 15.00 | 30.00 | 60.00 | 300.00 |
| | 1873 H | Inc. Ab. | 15.00 | 30.00 | 60.00 | 300.00 |

NOTE: Varieties exist.

### Mint mark: Zs

| KM# | Date | Mintage | Fine | VF | XF | Unc |
|-----|------|---------|------|-----|-----|-----|
| 408.8 | 1870 H | 4.519 | 12.00 | 30.00 | 40.00 | 200.00 |
| | 1871 H | 4.459 | 12.00 | 20.00 | 40.00 | 200.00 |
| | 1872 H | 4.039 | 12.00 | 20.00 | 40.00 | 200.00 |
| | 1873 H | 1.782 | 12.00 | 20.00 | 40.00 | 200.00 |

NOTE: Varieties exist.

### Mint mark: Cn
#### Liberty cap

| KM# | Date | Mintage | Fine | VF | XF | Unc |
|-----|------|---------|------|-----|-----|-----|
| 409 | 1898 AM | 1.720 | 10.00 | 15.00 | 30.00 | 65.00 |
| | 1898 Cn/MoAM | | | | | |
| | | I.A. | 15.00 | 30.00 | 90.00 | 150.00 |
| | 1899 AM | 1.722 | 25.00 | 50.00 | 90.00 | 175.00 |
| | 1899 JQ | I.A. | 10.00 | 15.00 | 50.00 | 125.00 |
| | 1900 JQ | 1.804 | 10.00 | 15.00 | 30.00 | 80.00 |
| | 1901 JQ | 1.473 | 10.00 | 15.00 | 30.00 | 80.00 |
| | 1902 JQ | 1.194 | 10.00 | 15.00 | 45.00 | 125.00 |
| | 1903 JQ | 1.514 | 10.00 | 15.00 | 30.00 | 80.00 |
| | 1903 FV | I.A. | 25.00 | 50.00 | 100.00 | 225.00 |
| | 1904 MH | 1.554 | 10.00 | 15.00 | 30.00 | 80.00 |
| | 1904 RP | I.A. | 45.00 | 85.00 | 125.00 | 300.00 |
| | 1905 RP | .598 | 20.00 | 40.00 | 75.00 | 225.00 |

### Mint mark: Go

| KM# | Date | Mintage | Fine | VF | XF | Unc |
|-----|------|---------|------|-----|-----|-----|
| 409.1 | 1898 RS | 4.256 | 10.00 | 15.00 | 35.00 | 75.00 |
| | 1898 Go/MoRS | | | | | |
| | | Inc. Ab. | 20.00 | 30.00 | 60.00 | 125.00 |
| | 1899 RS | 3.207 | 10.00 | 15.00 | 30.00 | 75.00 |
| | 1900 RS | 1.489 | 25.00 | 50.00 | 100.00 | 250.00 |

NOTE: Varieties exist.

### Mint mark: Mo

| KM# | Date | Mintage | Fine | VF | XF | Unc |
|-----|------|---------|------|-----|-----|-----|
| 409.2 | 1898 AM original strike - rev. w/139 Beads | | | | | |
| | | 10.156 | 7.50 | 10.00 | 17.50 | 60.00 |
| | 1898 AM restrike (1949) - rev. w/134 Beads | | | | | |
| | | 10.250 | 7.50 | 10.00 | 15.00 | 40.00 |
| | 1899 AM | 7.930 | 10.00 | 12.50 | 20.00 | 70.00 |
| | 1900 AM | 8.226 | 10.00 | 12.50 | 20.00 | 70.00 |
| | 1901 AM | 14.505 | 7.50 | 10.00 | 20.00 | 70.00 |
| | 1902/1 AM | | | | | |
| | | 16.224 | 150.00 | 300.00 | 500.00 | 950.00 |
| | 1902 AM | I.A. | 7.50 | 10.00 | 20.00 | 70.00 |
| | 1903 AM | | | | | |
| | | 22.396 | 7.50 | 10.00 | 20.00 | 70.00 |
| | 1903 MA (error) | | | | | |
| | | Inc. Ab. | 1500. | 2500. | 3500. | 7500. |
| | 1904 AM | 14.935 | 7.50 | 10.00 | 20.00 | 70.00 |
| | 1905 AM | 3.557 | 15.00 | 25.00 | 55.00 | 125.00 |
| | 1908 AM | 7.575 | 10.00 | 12.50 | 20.00 | 60.00 |
| | 1908 GV | I.A. | 10.00 | 12.50 | 17.50 | 40.00 |
| | 1909 GV | 2.924 | 10.00 | 12.50 | 17.50 | 45.00 |

NOTE: Varieties exist.

### Mint mark: Zs

| KM# | Date | Mintage | Fine | VF | XF | Unc |
|-----|------|---------|------|-----|-----|-----|
| 409.3 | 1898 FZ | 5.714 | 10.00 | 12.50 | 20.00 | 60.00 |
| | 1899 FZ | 5.618 | 10.00 | 12.50 | 20.00 | 65.00 |
| | 1900 FZ | 5.357 | 10.00 | 12.50 | 20.00 | 65.00 |
| | 1901 AZ | 5.706 | 4000. | 6500. | 10,000. | — |
| | 1901 FZ | I.A. | 10.00 | 12.50 | 20.00 | 60.00 |
| | 1902 FZ | 7.134 | 10.00 | 12.50 | 20.00 | 60.00 |
| | 1903/2 FZ | | | | | |
| | | 3.080 | 12.50 | 15.00 | 50.00 | 125.00 |
| | 1903 FZ | I.A. | 10.00 | 12.50 | 20.00 | 65.00 |
| | 1904 FZ | 2.423 | 10.00 | 15.00 | 25.00 | 70.00 |
| | 1904 FM | I.A. | 10.00 | 15.00 | 25.00 | 85.00 |
| | 1905 FM | .995 | 20.00 | 40.00 | 60.00 | 150.00 |

NOTE: Varieties exist.

**1.6920 g, .875 GOLD, .0476 oz AGW**
**Mint mark: As**

| KM# | Date | Mintage | Fine | VF | XF | Unc |
|---|---|---|---|---|---|---|
| 410 | 1888 L | — | — | — | Rare | — |
| | 1888 AsL/MoM | | | | | |
| | | — | — | — | Rare | — |

**Mint mark: Ca**

| KM# | Date | Mintage | Fine | VF | XF | Unc |
|---|---|---|---|---|---|---|
| 410.1 | 1888 Ca/MoM | | | | | |
| | | 104 pcs. | — | — | Rare | — |

**Mint mark: Cn**

| KM# | Date | Mintage | Fine | VF | XF | Unc |
|---|---|---|---|---|---|---|
| 410.2 | 1873 P | 1,221 | 75.00 | 100.00 | 150.00 | 250.00 |
| | 1875 P | — | 85.00 | 125.00 | 150.00 | 250.00 |
| | 1878 G | | | | | |
| | | 248 pcs. | 100.00 | 175.00 | 225.00 | 450.00 |
| | 1879 D | — | 100.00 | 150.00 | 175.00 | 275.00 |
| | 1881/0 D | | | | | |
| | | 338 pcs. | 100.00 | 150.00 | 175.00 | 275.00 |
| | 1882 D | | | | | |
| | | 340 pcs. | 100.00 | 150.00 | 175.00 | 275.00 |
| | 1883 D | — | 100.00 | 150.00 | 175.00 | 275.00 |
| | 1884 M | — | 100.00 | 150.00 | 175.00 | 275.00 |
| | 1886/4 M | | | | | |
| | | 277 pcs. | 100.00 | 150.00 | 225.00 | 450.00 |
| | 1888/7 M | 2,586 | 100.00 | 175.00 | 225.00 | 450.00 |
| | 1888 M Inc. Ab. | | 65.00 | 100.00 | 150.00 | 250.00 |
| | 1889 M | — | — | — | Rare | — |
| | 1891/89 M | | | | | |
| | | 969 pcs. | 75.00 | 100.00 | 150.00 | 250.00 |
| | 1892 M | | | | | |
| | | 780 pcs. | 75.00 | 100.00 | 150.00 | 250.00 |
| | 1893 M | | | | | |
| | | 498 pcs. | 85.00 | 125.00 | 150.00 | 250.00 |
| | 1894 M | | | | | |
| | | 493 pcs. | 80.00 | 125.00 | 150.00 | 250.00 |
| | 1895 M | 1,143 | 65.00 | 100.00 | 150.00 | 250.00 |
| | 1896/5 M | 1,028 | 65.00 | 100.00 | 150.00 | 250.00 |
| | 1897 M | | | | | |
| | | 785 pcs. | 65.00 | 100.00 | 150.00 | 250.00 |
| | 1898 M | 3,521 | 65.00 | 100.00 | 150.00 | 225.00 |
| | 1898 Cn/MoM | | | | | |
| | Inc. Ab. | | 65.00 | 100.00 | 150.00 | 250.00 |
| | 1899 Q | 2,000 | 65.00 | 100.00 | 150.00 | 225.00 |
| | 1901/0 Q | 2,350 | 65.00 | 100.00 | 150.00 | 225.00 |
| | 1902 Q | 2,480 | 65.00 | 100.00 | 150.00 | 225.00 |
| | 1902 Cn/MoQ/C | | | | | |
| | Inc. Ab. | | 65.00 | 100.00 | 150.00 | 225.00 |
| | 1904 H | 3,614 | 65.00 | 100.00 | 150.00 | 225.00 |
| | 1904 Cn/Mo/ H | | | | | |
| | Inc. Ab. | | 65.00 | 100.00 | 150.00 | 250.00 |
| | 1905 P | 1,000 | — | Reported, not confirmed | | |

**Mint mark: Go**

| KM# | Date | Mintage | Fine | VF | XF | Unc |
|---|---|---|---|---|---|---|
| 410.3 | 1870 S | — | 100.00 | 125.00 | 150.00 | 250.00 |
| | 1871 S | | | | | |
| | | 500 pcs. | 100.00 | 175.00 | 225.00 | 450.00 |
| | 1888 R | | | | | |
| | | 210 pcs. | 125.00 | 200.00 | 250.00 | 500.00 |
| | 1890 R | 1,916 | 75.00 | 100.00 | 150.00 | 250.00 |
| | 1892 R | | | | | |
| | | 533 pcs. | 100.00 | 150.00 | 175.00 | 325.00 |
| | 1894 R | | | | | |
| | | 180 pcs. | 150.00 | 200.00 | 250.00 | 500.00 |
| | 1895 R | | | | | |
| | | 676 pcs. | 100.00 | 150.00 | 175.00 | 300.00 |
| | 1896/5 R | 4,671 | 65.00 | 100.00 | 150.00 | 250.00 |
| | 1897/6 R | 4,280 | 65.00 | 100.00 | 150.00 | 250.00 |
| | 1897 R Inc. Ab. | | 65.00 | 100.00 | 150.00 | 250.00 |
| | 1898 R regular obv. | | | | | |
| | | 5,193 | 65.00 | 100.00 | 150.00 | 250.00 |
| | 1898 R mule, 5 Centavos obv., normal rev. | | | | | |
| | Inc. Ab. | | 75.00 | 100.00 | 150.00 | 250.00 |
| | 1899 R | 2,748 | 65.00 | 100.00 | 150.00 | 250.00 |
| | 1900/800 R | | | | | |
| | | 864 pcs. | 75.00 | 125.00 | 150.00 | 275.00 |

**Mint mark: Ho**

| KM# | Date | Mintage | Fine | VF | XF | Unc |
|---|---|---|---|---|---|---|
| 410.4 | 1875 R 310 pcs. | | — | — | Rare | — |
| | 1876 F | — | — | — | Rare | — |
| | 1888 G/MoM | — | — | — | Rare | — |

**Mint mark: Mo**

| KM# | Date | Mintage | Fine | VF | XF | Unc |
|---|---|---|---|---|---|---|
| 410.5 | 1870 C | 2,540 | 40.00 | 60.00 | 80.00 | 175.00 |
| | 1871 M/C | | | | | |
| | | 1,000 | 50.00 | 100.00 | 150.00 | 225.00 |
| | 1872 M/C | | | | | |
| | | 3,000 | 40.00 | 60.00 | 80.00 | 175.00 |

| KM# | Date | Mintage | Fine | VF | XF | Unc |
|---|---|---|---|---|---|---|
| 410.5 | 1873/1 M | | | | | |
| | | 2,900 | 40.00 | 60.00 | 80.00 | 175.00 |
| | 1873 M Inc. Ab. | | 40.00 | 60.00 | 80.00 | 175.00 |
| | 1874 M | — | 40.00 | 60.00 | 80.00 | 175.00 |
| | 1875 B/M | — | 40.00 | 60.00 | 80.00 | 175.00 |
| | 1876/5 B/M | — | 40.00 | 60.00 | 80.00 | 175.00 |
| | 1877 M | — | 40.00 | 60.00 | 80.00 | 175.00 |
| | 1878 M | 2,000 | 40.00 | 60.00 | 80.00 | 175.00 |
| | 1879 M | — | 40.00 | 60.00 | 80.00 | 175.00 |
| | 1880/70 M | — | 40.00 | 60.00 | 80.00 | 175.00 |
| | 1881/71 M | | | | | |
| | | 1,000 | 40.00 | 60.00 | 80.00 | 175.00 |
| | 1882/72 M | — | 40.00 | 60.00 | 80.00 | 175.00 |
| | 1883/72 M | — | 40.00 | 60.00 | 80.00 | 175.00 |
| | | 1,000 | 40.00 | 60.00 | 80.00 | 175.00 |
| | 1884 M | — | 40.00 | 60.00 | 80.00 | 175.00 |
| | 1885/71 M | — | 40.00 | 60.00 | 80.00 | 175.00 |
| | 1885 M | — | 40.00 | 60.00 | 80.00 | 175.00 |
| | 1886 M | 1,700 | 40.00 | 60.00 | 80.00 | 175.00 |
| | 1887 M | 2,200 | 40.00 | 60.00 | 80.00 | 175.00 |
| | 1888 M | 1,000 | 40.00 | 60.00 | 80.00 | 175.00 |
| | 1889 M | | | | | |
| | | 500 pcs. | 100.00 | 150.00 | 200.00 | 275.00 |
| | 1890 M | | | | | |
| | | 570 pcs. | 100.00 | 150.00 | 200.00 | 275.00 |
| | 1891 M | | | | | |
| | | 746 pcs. | 100.00 | 150.00 | 200.00 | 275.00 |
| | 1892/0 M | | | | | |
| | | 2,895 | 40.00 | 60.00 | 80.00 | 175.00 |
| | 1893 M | 5,917 | 40.00 | 60.00 | 80.00 | 175.00 |
| | 1894 M | 6,244 | 40.00 | 60.00 | 80.00 | 175.00 |
| | 1895 M | 8,994 | 40.00 | 60.00 | 80.00 | 175.00 |
| | 1895 B Inc. Ab. | | 40.00 | 60.00 | 80.00 | 175.00 |
| | 1896 B | 7,166 | 40.00 | 60.00 | 80.00 | 175.00 |
| | 1896 M Inc. Ab. | | 40.00 | 60.00 | 80.00 | 175.00 |
| | 1897 M | 5,131 | 40.00 | 60.00 | 80.00 | 175.00 |
| | 1898/7 M | 5,368 | 40.00 | 60.00 | 80.00 | 175.00 |
| | 1899 M | 9,515 | 40.00 | 60.00 | 80.00 | 175.00 |
| | 1900/800 M | | | | | |
| | | 9,301 | 40.00 | 60.00 | 80.00 | 175.00 |
| | 1900/880 M | | | | | |
| | Inc. Ab. | | 40.00 | 60.00 | 80.00 | 175.00 |
| | 1900/890 M | | | | | |
| | Inc. Ab. | | 40.00 | 60.00 | 80.00 | 175.00 |
| | 1900 M Inc. Ab. | | 40.00 | 60.00 | 80.00 | 175.00 |
| | 1901/801 M large date | | | | | |
| | | 8,293 | 40.00 | 60.00 | 80.00 | 175.00 |
| | 1901 M small date | | | | | |
| | Inc. Ab. | | 40.00 | 60.00 | 80.00 | 175.00 |
| | 1902 M large date | | | | | |
| | | .011 | 40.00 | 60.00 | 80.00 | 175.00 |
| | 1902 M small date | | | | | |
| | Inc. Ab. | | 40.00 | 60.00 | 80.00 | 175.00 |
| | 1903 M large date | | | | | |
| | | .010 | 40.00 | 60.00 | 80.00 | 175.00 |
| | 1903 M small date | | | | | |
| | Inc. Ab. | | 50.00 | 80.00 | 120.00 | 180.00 |
| | 1904 M | 9,845 | 40.00 | 60.00 | 80.00 | 175.00 |
| | 1905 M | 3,429 | 40.00 | 60.00 | 80.00 | 175.00 |

**Mint mark: Zs**

| KM# | Date | Mintage | Fine | VF | XF | Unc |
|---|---|---|---|---|---|---|
| 410.6 | 1872 H | 2,024 | 125.00 | 150.00 | 175.00 | 250.00 |
| | 1875/3 A | — | 125.00 | 150.00 | 200.00 | 300.00 |
| | 1878 S | — | 125.00 | 150.00 | 175.00 | 250.00 |
| | 1888 Z 280 pcs. | | 175.00 | 225.00 | 300.00 | 650.00 |
| | 1889 Z | 492 pcs. | 100.00 | 175.00 | 225.00 | 425.00 |
| | 1890 Z 738 pcs. | | 150.00 | 175.00 | 225.00 | 425.00 |

# 2-1/2 PESOS

**4.2300 g, .875 GOLD, .1190 oz AGW**

**Mint mark: As**

| KM# | Date | Mintage | Fine | VF | XF | Unc |
|---|---|---|---|---|---|---|
| 411 | 1888 As/MoL | — | — | — | Rare | — |

**Mint mark: Cn**

| KM# | Date | Mintage | Fine | VF | XF | Unc |
|---|---|---|---|---|---|---|
| 411.1 | 1893 M 141 pcs. | | 1500. | 2000. | 2500. | 3500. |

**Mint mark: Do**

| KM# | Date | Mintage | Fine | VF | XF | Unc |
|---|---|---|---|---|---|---|
| 411.2 | 1888 C | — | — | — | Rare | — |

**Mint mark: Go**

| KM# | Date | Mintage | Fine | VF | XF | Unc |
|---|---|---|---|---|---|---|
| 411.3 | 1871 S | 600 pcs. | 1250. | 2000. | 2500. | 3250. |
| | 1888 Go/MoR | 110 pcs. | 1750. | 2250. | 2750. | 3500. |

**Mint mark: Ho**

| KM# | Date | Mintage | Fine | VF | XF | Unc |
|---|---|---|---|---|---|---|
| 411.4 | 1874 R | — | — | — | Rare | — |
| | 1888 G | — | — | — | Rare | — |

**Mint mark: Mo**

| KM# | Date | Mintage | Fine | VF | XF | Unc |
|---|---|---|---|---|---|---|
| 411.5 | 1870 C | 820 pcs. | 150.00 | 250.00 | 350.00 | 650.00 |
| | 1872 M/C | 800 pcs. | 150.00 | 250.00 | 350.00 | 650.00 |
| | 1873/2 M | — | 200.00 | 350.00 | 750.00 | 1250. |
| | 1874 M | — | 200.00 | 350.00 | 750.00 | 1250. |
| | 1874 B/M | — | 200.00 | 350.00 | 750.00 | 1250. |
| | 1875 B | — | 200.00 | 350.00 | 750.00 | 1250. |
| | 1876 B | — | 250.00 | 500.00 | 1000. | 1500. |
| | 1877 M | — | 200.00 | 350.00 | 750.00 | 1250. |
| | 1878 M | 400 pcs. | 200.00 | 350.00 | 750.00 | 1250. |
| | 1879 M | — | 200.00 | 350.00 | 750.00 | 1250. |
| | 1880/79 M | — | 200.00 | 350.00 | 750.00 | 1250. |
| | 1881 M | 400 pcs. | 200.00 | 350.00 | 750.00 | 1250. |
| | 1882 M | — | 200.00 | 350.00 | 750.00 | 1250. |
| | 1883/73 M | 400 pcs. | 200.00 | 350.00 | 750.00 | 1250. |
| | 1884 M | — | 250.00 | 500.00 | 1000. | 1500. |
| | 1885 M | — | 200.00 | 350.00 | 750.00 | 1250. |
| | 1886 M | 400 pcs. | 200.00 | 350.00 | 750.00 | 1250. |
| | 1887 M | 400 pcs. | 200.00 | 350.00 | 750.00 | 1250. |
| | 1888 M | 540 pcs. | 200.00 | 350.00 | 750.00 | 1250. |
| | 1889 M | 240 pcs. | 150.00 | 300.00 | 525.00 | 850.00 |
| | 1890 M | 420 pcs. | 200.00 | 350.00 | 750.00 | 1250. |
| | 1891 M | 188 pcs. | 200.00 | 350.00 | 750.00 | 1250. |
| | 1892 M | 240 pcs. | 200.00 | 350.00 | 750.00 | 1250. |

**Mint mark: Zs**

| KM# | Date | Mintage | Fine | VF | XF | Unc |
|---|---|---|---|---|---|---|
| 411.6 | 1872 H | 1,300 | 200.00 | 350.00 | 500.00 | 1000. |
| | 1873 H | — | 175.00 | 325.00 | 450.00 | 700.00 |
| | 1875/3 A | — | 200.00 | 350.00 | 750.00 | 1250. |
| | 1877 S | — | 200.00 | 350.00 | 750.00 | 1250. |
| | 1878 S | 300 pcs. | 200.00 | 350.00 | 750.00 | 1250. |
| | 1888 Zs/MoS | 80 pcs. | 300.00 | 500.00 | 1000. | 1750. |
| | 1889 Zs/MoZ | 184 pcs. | 250.00 | 450.00 | 950.00 | 1500. |
| | 1890 Z | 326 pcs. | 200.00 | 350.00 | 750.00 | 1250. |

# CINCO (5) PESOS

**8.4600 g, .875 GOLD, .2380 oz AGW**

**Mint mark: As**

| KM# | Date | Mintage | Fine | VF | XF | Unc |
|---|---|---|---|---|---|---|
| 412 | 1875 L | — | — | — | — | — |
| | 1878 L | 383 pcs. | 900.00 | 1700. | 3000. | 4500. |

**Mint mark: Ca**

| KM# | Date | Mintage | Fine | VF | XF | Unc |
|---|---|---|---|---|---|---|
| 412.1 | 1888 M | 120 pcs. | — | — | Rare | — |

**Mint mark: Cn**

| KM# | Date | Mintage | Fine | VF | XF | Unc |
|---|---|---|---|---|---|---|
| 412.2 | 1873 P | — | 300.00 | 600.00 | 1000. | 1500. |
| | 1874 P | — | — | — | — | — |
| | 1875 P | — | 300.00 | 500.00 | 700.00 | 1250. |
| | 1876 P | — | 300.00 | 500.00 | 700.00 | 1250. |
| | 1877 G | — | 300.00 | 500.00 | 700.00 | 1250. |
| | 1882 | 174 pcs. | — | — | Rare | — |
| | 1888 M | — | 500.00 | 1000. | 1350. | 2000. |
| | 1890 M | 435 pcs. | 250.00 | 500.00 | 750.00 | 1250. |
| | 1891 M | 1,390 | 250.00 | 400.00 | 500.00 | 1000. |
| | 1894 M | 484 pcs. | 250.00 | 500.00 | 750.00 | 1600. |
| | 1895 M | 142 pcs. | 500.00 | 750.00 | 1500. | 2500. |
| | 1900 Q | 1,536 | 200.00 | 300.00 | 400.00 | 950.00 |
| | 1903 Q | 1,000 | 200.00 | 300.00 | 400.00 | 800.00 |

**Mintmark: Do**

| KM# | Date | Mintage | Fine | VF | XF | Unc |
|---|---|---|---|---|---|---|
| 412.3 | 1873/2 P | — | 700.00 | 1250. | 1800. | 3000. |
| | 1877 P | — | 700.00 | 1250. | 1800. | 3000. |
| | 1878 E | — | 700.00 | 1250. | 1800. | 3000. |
| | 1879/7 B | — | 700.00 | 1250. | 1800. | 3000. |
| | 1879 B | — | 700.00 | 1250. | 1800. | 3000. |

**Mint mark: Go**

| KM# | Date | Mintage | Fine | VF | XF | Unc |
|---|---|---|---|---|---|---|
| 412.4 | 1871 S | 1,600 | 400.00 | 800.00 | 1250. | 2500. |
| | 1887 R | 140 pcs. | 600.00 | 1200. | 1500. | 2750. |
| | 1888 R | 65 pcs. | — | — | Rare | — |
| | 1893 R | 16 pcs. | — | — | Rare | — |

**Mint mark: Ho**

| KM# | Date | Mintage | Fine | VF | XF | Unc |
|---|---|---|---|---|---|---|
| 412.5 | 1874 R | — | 1750. | 2500. | 3000. | 4500. |
| | 1877 R | 990 pcs. | 750.00 | 1250. | 2000. | 3000. |
| | 1877 A | Inc. Ab. | 650.00 | 1100. | 1750. | 2750. |
| | 1888G | — | — | — | Rare | — |

**Mint mark: Mo**

| KM# | Date | Mintage | Fine | VF | XF | Unc |
|---|---|---|---|---|---|---|
| 412.6 | 1870 C | 550 pcs. | 200.00 | 400.00 | 550.00 | 900.00 |
| | 1871/69 M | 1,600 | 175.00 | 350.00 | 475.00 | 750.00 |
| | 1871 M | Inc. Ab. | 175.00 | 350.00 | 475.00 | 750.00 |
| | 1872 M | 1,600 | 175.00 | 350.00 | 475.00 | 750.00 |
| | 1873/2 M | — | 200.00 | 400.00 | 550.00 | 850.00 |
| | 1874 M | — | 200.00 | 400.00 | 550.00 | 850.00 |
| | 1875/3 B/M | — | 200.00 | 400.00 | 550.00 | 950.00 |
| | 1875 B | — | 200.00 | 400.00 | 550.00 | 950.00 |
| | 1876/5 B/M | — | 200.00 | 400.00 | 550.00 | 1000. |
| | 1877 M | — | 250.00 | 450.00 | 750.00 | 1250. |
| | 1878/7 M | 400 pcs. | 200.00 | 400.00 | 550.00 | 1250. |
| | 1878 M | Inc. Ab. | 200.00 | 400.00 | 550.00 | 1250. |
| | 1879/8 M | — | 200.00 | 400.00 | 550.00 | 1250. |
| | 1880 M | — | 200.00 | 400.00 | 550.00 | 1250. |
| | 1881 M | — | 200.00 | 400.00 | 550.00 | 1250. |
| | 1882 M | 200 pcs. | 250.00 | 450.00 | 750.00 | 1250. |
| | 1883 M | 200 pcs. | 250.00 | 450.00 | 750.00 | 1250. |
| | 1884 M | — | 250.00 | 450.00 | 750.00 | 1250. |
| | 1886 M | 200 pcs. | 250.00 | 450.00 | 750.00 | 1250. |
| | 1887 M | 200 pcs. | 250.00 | 450.00 | 750.00 | 1250. |
| | 1888 M | 250 pcs. | 200.00 | 400.00 | 550.00 | 1250. |
| | 1889 M | 190 pcs. | 250.00 | 450.00 | 750.00 | 1250. |
| | 1890 M | 149 pcs. | 250.00 | 450.00 | 750.00 | 1250. |
| | 1891 M | 156 pcs. | 250.00 | 450.00 | 750.00 | 1250. |
| | 1892 M | 214 pcs. | 250.00 | 450.00 | 750.00 | 1250. |
| | 1893 M | 1,058 | 200.00 | 400.00 | 500.00 | 800.00 |
| | 1897 M | 370 pcs. | 200.00 | 400.00 | 550.00 | 1000. |
| | 1898 M | 376 pcs. | 200.00 | 400.00 | 550.00 | 1000. |
| | 1900 M | 1,014 | 175.00 | 350.00 | 450.00 | 750.00 |
| | 1901 M | 1,071 | 175.00 | 350.00 | 450.00 | 750.00 |
| | 1902 M | 1,478 | 175.00 | 350.00 | 450.00 | 750.00 |
| | 1903 M | 1,162 | 175.00 | 350.00 | 450.00 | 750.00 |
| | 1904 M | 1,415 | 175.00 | 350.00 | 450.00 | 750.00 |
| | 1905 M | 563 pcs. | 200.00 | 400.00 | 550.00 | 1500. |

PRICING SECTION

## Mint mark: Zs

| KM# | Date | Mintage | Fine | VF | XF | Unc |
|---|---|---|---|---|---|---|
| 412.7 | 1874 A | — | 200.00 | 400.00 | 500.00 | 750.00 |
| | 1875 A | — | 200.00 | 400.00 | 500.00 | 1000. |
| | 1877 S/A | — | 200.00 | 400.00 | 550.00 | 1000. |
| | 1878/7 S/A | — | 200.00 | 400.00 | 550.00 | 1000. |
| | 1883 S | — | 175.00 | 375.00 | 500.00 | 750.00 |
| | 1888 Z | 70 pcs. | 1000. | 1500. | 2000. | 3000. |
| | 1889 Z | | | | | |
| | | 373 pcs. | 200.00 | 300.00 | 500.00 | 850.00 |
| | 1892 Z | 1,229 | 200.00 | 300.00 | 450.00 | 750.00 |

## DIEZ (10) PESOS

**16.9200 g, .875 GOLD, .4760 oz AGW**
**Mint mark: As**
**Rev: Balance scale.**

| KM# | Date | Mintage | Fine | VF | XF | Unc |
|---|---|---|---|---|---|---|
| 413 | 1874 DL | — | — | — | Rare | — |
| | 1875 L | 642 pcs. | 600.00 | 1250. | 2500. | 3500. |
| | 1878 L | 977 pcs. | 500.00 | 1000. | 2000. | 3000. |
| | 1879 L | 1,078 | 500.00 | 1000. | 2000. | 3000. |
| | 1880 L | 2,629 | 500.00 | 1000. | 2000. | 3000. |
| | 1881 L | 2,574 | 500.00 | 1000. | 2000. | 3000. |
| | 1882 L | 3,403 | 500.00 | 1000. | 2000. | 3000. |
| | 1883 L | 3,597 | 500.00 | 1000. | 2000. | 3000. |
| | 1884 L | — | — | — | Rare | — |
| | 1885 L | 4,562 | 500.00 | 1000. | 2000. | 3000. |
| | 1886 L | 4,643 | 500.00 | 1000. | 2000. | 3000. |
| | 1887 L | 3,667 | 500.00 | 1000. | 2000. | 3000. |
| | 1888 L | 4,521 | 500.00 | 1000. | 2000. | 3000. |
| | 1889 L | 5,615 | 500.00 | 1000. | 2000. | 3000. |
| | 1890 L | 4,920 | 500.00 | 1000. | 2000. | 3000. |
| | 1891 L | 568 pcs. | 500.00 | 1000. | 2000. | 3000. |
| | 1892 L | — | — | — | — | — |
| | 1893 L | 817 pcs. | 500.00 | 1000. | 2000. | 3000. |
| | 1894/3 L | 1,658 | — | — | — | — |
| | 1894 L | Inc. Ab. | 500.00 | 1000. | 2000. | 3000. |
| | 1895 L | 1,237 | 500.00 | 1000. | 2000. | 3000. |

## Mint mark: Ca

| KM# | Date | Mintage | Fine | VF | XF | Unc |
|---|---|---|---|---|---|---|
| 413.1 | 1888 M | 175 pcs. | — | — | 7500. | — |

## Mint mark: Cn

| KM# | Date | Mintage | Fine | VF | XF | Unc |
|---|---|---|---|---|---|---|
| 413.2 | 1881 D | — | 400.00 | 600.00 | 1000. | 1750. |
| | 1882 D | | | | | |
| | | 874 pcs. | 400.00 | 600.00 | 1000. | 1750. |
| | 1882 E | Inc. Ab. | 400.00 | 600.00 | 1000. | 1750. |
| | 1883 D | | | | | |
| | | 221 pcs. | — | — | — | — |
| | 1883 M | Inc. Ab. | 400.00 | 600.00 | 1000. | 1750. |
| | 1884 D | — | 400.00 | 600.00 | 1000. | 1750. |
| | 1884 M | — | 400.00 | 600.00 | 1000. | 1750. |
| | 1885 M | 1,235 | 400.00 | 600.00 | 1000. | 1750. |
| | 1886 M | | | | | |
| | | 981 pcs. | 400.00 | 600.00 | 1000. | 1750. |
| | 1887 M | 2,289 | 400.00 | 600.00 | 1000. | 1750. |
| | 1888 M | | | | | |
| | | 767 pcs. | 400.00 | 600.00 | 1000. | 1750. |
| | 1889 M | | | | | |
| | | 859 pcs. | 400.00 | 600.00 | 1000. | 1750. |
| | 1890 M | 1,427 | 400.00 | 600.00 | 1000. | 1750. |
| | 1891 M | | | | | |
| | | 670 pcs. | 400.00 | 600.00 | 1000. | 1750. |
| | 1892 M | | | | | |
| | | 379 pcs. | 400.00 | 600.00 | 1000. | 1750. |
| | 1893 M | 1,806 | 400.00 | 600.00 | 1000. | 1750. |
| | 1895 M | | | | | |
| | | 179 pcs. | 500.00 | 1000. | 1500. | 2500. |
| | 1903 Q | | | | | |
| | | 774 pcs. | 400.00 | 600.00 | 1000. | 1750. |

## Mint mark: Do

| KM# | Date | Mintage | Fine | VF | XF | Unc |
|---|---|---|---|---|---|---|
| 413.3 | 1872 P | 1,755 | 350.00 | 550.00 | 850.00 | 1250. |
| | 1873/2 P | 1,091 | 350.00 | 550.00 | 900.00 | 1500. |
| | 1873/2 M/P | | | | | |
| | | Inc. Ab. | 350.00 | 550.00 | 900.00 | 1500. |
| | 1874 M | — | 350.00 | 550.00 | 900.00 | 1500. |
| | 1875 M | — | 350.00 | 550.00 | 900.00 | 1500. |
| | 1876 M | — | 450.00 | 750.00 | 1250. | 2000. |
| | 1877 P | — | 350.00 | 550.00 | 900.00 | 1500. |
| | 1878 E | | | | | |
| | | 582 pcs. | 350.00 | 550.00 | 900.00 | 1500. |
| | 1879/8 B | — | 350.00 | 550.00 | 900.00 | 1500. |
| | 1879 B | — | 350.00 | 550.00 | 900.00 | 1500. |
| | 1880 P | 2,030 | 350.00 | 550.00 | 900.00 | 1500. |
| | 1881/79 P | | | | | |
| | | 2,617 | 350.00 | 550.00 | 900.00 | 1500. |
| | 1882 P | 1,528 | — | — | Rare | — |
| | 1882 C | Inc. Ab. | 350.00 | 550.00 | 900.00 | 1500. |
| | 1883 C | | | | | |
| | | 793 pcs. | 450.00 | 750.00 | 1250. | 2000. |
| | 1884 C | | | | | |
| | | 108 pcs. | 450.00 | 750.00 | 1250. | 2000. |

## Mint mark: Ga

| KM# | Date | Mintage | Fine | VF | XF | Unc |
|---|---|---|---|---|---|---|
| 413.4 | 1870 C | | | | | |
| | | 490 pcs. | 500.00 | 800.00 | 1000. | 1500. |
| | 1871 C | 1,910 | 400.00 | 800.00 | 1500. | 2250. |
| | 1872 C | | | | | |
| | | 780 pcs. | 500.00 | 1000. | 2000. | 2500. |
| | 1873 C | | | | | |
| | | 422 pcs. | 500.00 | 1000. | 2000. | 3000. |
| | 1874/3 C | | | | | |
| | | 477 pcs. | 500.00 | 1000. | 2000. | 3000. |
| | 1875 C | | | | | |
| | | 710 pcs. | 500.00 | 1000. | 2000. | 3000. |
| | 1878 A | | | | | |
| | | 183 pcs. | 600.00 | 1200. | 2500. | 3500. |
| | 1879 A | | | | | |
| | | 200 pcs. | 600.00 | 1200. | 2500. | 3500. |
| | 1880 S | | | | | |
| | | 404 pcs. | 500.00 | 1000. | 2000. | 3000. |
| | 1881 S | | | | | |
| | | 239 pcs. | 600.00 | 1200. | 2500. | 3500. |
| | 1891 S | | | | | |
| | | 196 pcs. | 600.00 | 1200. | 2500. | 3500. |

## Mint mark: Go

| KM# | Date | Mintage | Fine | VF | XF | Unc |
|---|---|---|---|---|---|---|
| 413.5 | 1872 S | 1,400 | 800.00 | 1500. | 2000. | 3000. |
| | 1887 R | 80 pcs. | 1250. | 2000. | 2500. | 3500. |
| | 1888 R | 68 pcs. | 1500. | 2500. | 3000. | 4000. |

## Mint mark: Ho

| KM# | Date | Mintage | Fine | VF | XF | Unc |
|---|---|---|---|---|---|---|
| 413.6 | 1874 R | — | — | — | Rare | — |
| | 1876 F | | | | | |
| | | 357 pcs. | — | — | Rare | — |
| | 1878 A | | | | | |
| | | 814 pcs. | 1750. | 3000. | 3500. | 5500. |
| | 1879 A | — | 1000. | 2000. | 2500. | 4000. |
| | 1880 A | — | 1000. | 2000. | 2500. | 4000. |
| | 1881 A | — | — | — | Rare | — |

## Mint mark: Mo

| KM# | Date | Mintage | Fine | VF | XF | Unc |
|---|---|---|---|---|---|---|
| 413.7 | 1870 C | | | | | |
| | | 480 pcs. | 500.00 | 900.00 | 1200. | 2000. |
| | 1872/1 M/C | | | | | |
| | | 2,100 | 350.00 | 550.00 | 900.00 | 1400. |
| | 1873 M | — | 400.00 | 600.00 | 950.00 | 1500. |
| | 1874/3 M | — | 400.00 | 600.00 | 950.00 | 1500. |
| | 1875 B/M | — | 400.00 | 600.00 | 950.00 | 1500. |
| | 1876 B | — | — | — | Rare | — |
| | 1878 M | | | | | |
| | | 300 pcs. | 400.00 | 600.00 | 950.00 | 1500. |
| | 1879 M | — | — | — | — | — |
| | 1881 M | | | | | |
| | | 100 pcs. | 500.00 | 1000. | 1600. | 2500. |
| | 1882 M | — | 400.00 | 600.00 | 950.00 | 1500. |
| | 1883 M | | | | | |
| | | 100 pcs. | 600.00 | 1000. | 1600. | 2500. |
| | 1884 M | — | 600.00 | 1000. | 1600. | 2500. |
| | 1885 M | — | 400.00 | 600.00 | 950.00 | 1500. |
| | 1886 M | | | | | |
| | | 100 pcs. | 600.00 | 1000. | 1600. | 2500. |
| | 1887 M | | | | | |
| | | 100 pcs. | 600.00 | 1000. | 1625. | 2750. |

| KM# | Date | Mintage | Fine | VF | XF | Unc |
|---|---|---|---|---|---|---|
| 413.7 | 1888 M | 144 pcs. | 450.00 | 750.00 | 1200. | 2000. |
| | 1889 M | 88 pcs. | 600.00 | 1000. | 1600. | 2500. |
| | 1890 M | 137 pcs. | 600.00 | 1000. | 1600. | 2500. |
| | 1891 M | 133 pcs. | 600.00 | 1000. | 1600. | 2500. |
| | 1892 M | 45 pcs. | 600.00 | 1000. | 1600. | 2500. |
| | 1893 M | 1,361 | 350.00 | 550.00 | 900.00 | 1400. |
| | 1897 M | 239 pcs. | 400.00 | 600.00 | 950.00 | 1500. |
| | 1898/7 M | 244 pcs. | 425.00 | 625.00 | 1000. | 1750. |
| | 1900 M | 733 pcs. | 400.00 | 600.00 | 950.00 | 1500. |
| | 1901 M | 562 pcs. | 350.00 | 500.00 | 800.00 | 1400. |
| | 1902 M | 719 pcs. | 350.00 | 500.00 | 800.00 | 1400. |
| | 1903 M | 713 pcs. | 350.00 | 500.00 | 800.00 | 1400. |
| | 1904 M | 694 pcs. | 350.00 | 500.00 | 800.00 | 1400. |
| | 1905 M | 401 pcs. | 400.00 | 600.00 | 950.00 | 1500. |

### Mint mark: Oa

| KM# | Date | Mintage | Fine | VF | XF | Unc |
|---|---|---|---|---|---|---|
| 413.8 | 1870 E | 4,614 | 400.00 | 600.00 | 900.00 | 1350. |
| | 1871 E | 2,705 | 400.00 | 600.00 | 900.00 | 1350. |
| | 1872 E | 5,897 | 400.00 | 600.00 | 900.00 | 1350. |
| | 1873 E | 3,537 | 400.00 | 600.00 | 950.00 | 1500. |
| | 1874 E | 2,205 | 400.00 | 600.00 | 1200. | 1800. |
| | 1875 E | 312 pcs. | 450.00 | 750.00 | 1400. | 2250. |
| | 1876 E | 766 pcs. | 450.00 | 750.00 | 1400. | 2250. |
| | 1877 E | 463 pcs. | 450.00 | 750.00 | 1400. | 2250. |
| | 1878 E | 229 pcs. | 450.00 | 750.00 | 1400. | 2250. |
| | 1879 E | 210 pcs. | 450.00 | 750.00 | 1400. | 2250. |
| | 1880 E | 238 pcs. | 450.00 | 750.00 | 1400. | 2250. |
| | 1881 E | 961 pcs. | 400.00 | 600.00 | 1200. | 2000. |
| | 1882 E | 170 pcs. | 600.00 | 1000. | 1500. | 2500. |
| | 1883 E | 111 pcs. | 600.00 | 1000. | 1500. | 2500. |
| | 1884 E | 325 pcs. | 450.00 | 750.00 | 1400. | 2250. |
| | 1885 E | 370 pcs. | 450.00 | 750.00 | 1400. | 2250. |
| | 1886 E | 400 pcs. | 450.00 | 750.00 | 1400. | 2250. |
| | 1887 E | — | 700.00 | 1250. | 2250. | 4000. |
| | 1888 E | — | — | — | — | — |

### Mint mark: Zs

| KM# | Date | Mintage | Fine | VF | XF | Unc |
|---|---|---|---|---|---|---|
| 413.9 | 1871 H | 2,000 | 350.00 | 550.00 | 850.00 | 1200. |
| | 1872 H | 3,092 | 300.00 | 500.00 | 700.00 | 1000. |
| | 1873 H | 936 pcs. | 400.00 | 600.00 | 950.00 | 1500. |
| | 1874 H | — | 400.00 | 600.00 | 950.00 | 1500. |
| | 1875/3 A | — | 400.00 | 600.00 | 1000. | 1750. |
| | 1876/5 S | — | 400.00 | 600.00 | 1000. | 1750. |
| | 1877 S/H | 506 pcs. | 400.00 | 600.00 | 1000. | 1750. |
| | 1878 S | 711 pcs. | 400.00 | 600.00 | 1000. | 1750. |
| | 1879/8 S | — | 450.00 | 750.00 | 1400. | 2250. |
| | 1879 S | —' | 450.00 | 750.00 | 1400. | 2250. |
| | 1880 S | 2,089 | 350.00 | 550.00 | 950.00 | 1500. |
| | 1881 S | 736 pcs. | 400.00 | 600.00 | 1000. | 1750. |
| | 1882 S | 1,599 | 350.00 | 550.00 | 950.00 | 1500. |
| | 1883/2 S | 256 pcs. | 400.00 | 600.00 | 1000. | 1750. |
| | 1884/3 S | — | 350.00 | 550.00 | 950.00 | 1600. |
| | 1884 S | — | 350.00 | 550.00 | 950.00 | 1600. |
| | 1885 S | 1,588 | 350.00 | 550.00 | 950.00 | 1500. |
| | 1886 S | 5,364 | 350.00 | 550.00 | 950.00 | 1500. |
| | 1887 Z | 2,330 | 350.00 | 550.00 | 950.00 | 1500. |
| | 1888 Z | 4,810 | 350.00 | 550.00 | 950.00 | 1500. |

| KM# | Date | Mintage | Fine | VF | XF | Unc |
|---|---|---|---|---|---|---|
| 413.9 | 1889 Z | 6,154 | 300.00 | 500.00 | 750.00 | 1350. |
| | 1890 Z | 1,321 | 350.00 | 550.00 | 950.00 | 1500. |
| | 1891 Z | 1,930 | 350.00 | 550.00 | 950.00 | 1500. |
| | 1892 Z | 1,882 | 350.00 | 550.00 | 950.00 | 1500. |
| | 1893 Z | 2,899 | 350.00 | 550.00 | 950.00 | 1500. |
| | 1894 Z | 2,501 | 350.00 | 550.00 | 950.00 | 1500. |
| | 1895 Z | 1,217 | 350.00 | 550.00 | 950.00 | 1500. |

## VEINTE (20) PESOS

33.8400 g, .875 GOLD, .9520 oz AGW
Mint mark: As
Rev: Balance scale.

| KM# | Date | Mintage | Fine | VF | XF | Unc |
|---|---|---|---|---|---|---|
| 414 | 1876 L | 276 pcs. | — | — | Rare | — |
| | 1877 L | 166 pcs. | — | — | Rare | — |
| | 1878 L | — | — | — | — | — |
| | 1888 L | — | — | — | Rare | — |

### Mint mark: CH,Ca

| KM# | Date | Mintage | Fine | VF | XF | Unc |
|---|---|---|---|---|---|---|
| 414.1 | 1872 M | 995 pcs. | 500.00 | 650.00 | 950.00 | 2500. |
| | 1873 M | 950 pcs. | 500.00 | 650.00 | 950.00 | 2500. |
| | 1874 M | 1,116 | 500.00 | 650.00 | 950.00 | 2500. |
| | 1875 M | 750 pcs. | 500.00 | 650.00 | 950.00 | 2500. |
| | 1876 M | 600 pcs. | 500.00 | 800.00 | 1250. | 2750. |
| | 1877 | 55 pcs. | — | — | Rare | — |
| | 1882 M | 1,758 | 500.00 | 650.00 | 950.00 | 2500. |
| | 1883 M | 161 pcs. | 600.00 | 1000. | 1500. | 3000. |
| | 1884 M | 496 pcs. | 500.00 | 650.00 | 950.00 | 2500. |
| | 1885 M | 122 pcs. | 600.00 | 1000. | 1500. | 3000. |
| | 1887 M | 550 pcs. | 500.00 | 650.00 | 950.00 | 2500. |
| | 1888 M | 351 pcs. | 500.00 | 650.00 | 950.00 | 2500. |
| | 1889 M | 464 pcs. | 500.00 | 650.00 | 950.00 | 2500. |
| | 1890 M | 1,209 | 500.00 | 650.00 | 950.00 | 2500. |
| | 1891 M | 2,004 | 500.00 | 600.00 | 900.00 | 2250. |
| | 1893 M | 418 pcs. | 500.00 | 650.00 | 950.00 | 2500. |
| | 1895 M | 133 pcs. | 600.00 | 1000. | 1500. | 3000. |

### Mint mark: Cn

| KM# | Date | Mintage | Fine | VF | XF | Unc |
|---|---|---|---|---|---|---|
| 414.2 | 1870 E | 3,749 | 500.00 | 650.00 | 950.00 | 2000. |
| | 1871 P | 3,046 | 500.00 | 650.00 | 950.00 | 2000. |
| | 1872 P | 972 pcs. | 500.00 | 650.00 | 950.00 | 2000. |
| | 1873 P | 1,317 | 500.00 | 650.00 | 950.00 | 2000. |
| | 1874 P | — | 500.00 | 650.00 | 950.00 | 2000. |
| | 1875 P | — | 600.00 | 1200. | 1800. | 2500. |
| | 1876 P | — | 500.00 | 650.00 | 950.00 | 2000. |
| | 1876 G | — | 500.00 | 650.00 | 950.00 | 2000. |
| | 1877 G | 167 pcs. | 600.00 | 1000. | 1500. | 3000. |
| | 1878 | 842 pcs. | — | — | Rare | — |
| | 1881/0 D | 2,039 | — | — | — | — |
| | 1881 D | Inc. Ab. | 500.00 | 650.00 | 950.00 | 2000. |
| | 1882/1 D | 736 pcs. | 500.00 | 650.00 | 950.00 | 2000. |
| | 1883 M | 1,836 | 500.00 | 650.00 | 950.00 | 2000. |
| | 1884 M | — | 500.00 | 650.00 | 950.00 | 2000. |
| | 1885 M | 544 pcs. | 500.00 | 650.00 | 950.00 | 2000. |

| KM# | Date | Mintage | Fine | VF | XF | Unc |
|---|---|---|---|---|---|---|
| 414.2 | 1886 M | 882 pcs. | 500.00 | 650.00 | 950.00 | 2000. |
| | 1887 M | 837 pcs. | 500.00 | 650.00 | 950.00 | 2000. |
| | 1888 M | 473 pcs. | 500.00 | 650.00 | 950.00 | 2000. |
| | 1889 M | 1,376 | 500.00 | 650.00 | 950.00 | 2000. |
| | 1890 M | — | 500.00 | 650.00 | 950.00 | 2000. |
| | 1891 M | 237 pcs. | 500.00 | 900.00 | 1200. | 2250. |
| | 1892 M | 526 pcs. | 500.00 | 650.00 | 950.00 | 2000. |
| | 1893 M | 2,062 | 500.00 | 650.00 | 950.00 | 2000. |
| | 1894 M | 4,516 | 500.00 | 650.00 | 950.00 | 2000. |
| | 1895 M | 3,193 | 500.00 | 650.00 | 950.00 | 2000. |
| | 1896 M | 4,072 | 500.00 | 650.00 | 950.00 | 2000. |
| | 1897/6 M | 959 pcs. | 500.00 | 650.00 | 950.00 | 2000. |
| | 1897 M | Inc. Ab. | 500.00 | 650.00 | 950.00 | 2000. |
| | 1898 M | 1,660 | 500.00 | 650.00 | 950.00 | 2000. |
| | 1899 M | 1,243 | 500.00 | 650.00 | 950.00 | 2000. |
| | 1899 Q | Inc. Ab. | 500.00 | 900.00 | 1200. | 2250. |
| | 1900 Q | 1,558 | 500.00 | 650.00 | 950.00 | 2000. |
| | 1901/0 Q | 1,496 | — | — | — | — |
| | 1901 Q | Inc. Ab. | 500.00 | 650.00 | 950.00 | 2000. |
| | 1902 Q | 1,059 | 500.00 | 650.00 | 950.00 | 2000. |
| | 1903 Q | 1,121 | 500.00 | 650.00 | 950.00 | 2000. |
| | 1904 H | 4,646 | 500.00 | 650.00 | 950.00 | 2000. |
| | 1905 P | 1,738 | 500.00 | 900.00 | 1200. | 2250. |

### Mint mark: Do

| KM# | Date | Mintage | Fine | VF | XF | Unc |
|---|---|---|---|---|---|---|
| 414.3 | 1870 P | 416 pcs. | 1000. | 1500. | 2000. | 2500. |
| | 1871/0 P | 1,073 | 1000. | 1750. | 2250. | 2750. |
| | 1871 P | Inc. Ab. | 1000. | 1500. | 2000. | 2500. |
| | 1872/1 PT | — | 1500. | 3000. | 4500. | 7000. |
| | 1876 M | — | 1000. | 1500. | 2000. | 2500. |
| | 1877 P | 94 pcs. | 1500. | 2250. | 2750. | 3250. |
| | 1878 | 258 pcs. | — | — | Rare | — |

### Mint mark: Go

| KM# | Date | Mintage | Fine | VF | XF | Unc |
|---|---|---|---|---|---|---|
| 414.4 | 1870 S | 3,250 | 500.00 | 650.00 | 900.00 | 1250. |
| | 1871 S | .020 | 500.00 | 650.00 | 900.00 | 1250. |
| | 1872 S | .018 | 500.00 | 650.00 | 900.00 | 1250. |
| | 1873 S | 7,000 | 500.00 | 650.00 | 900.00 | 1250. |
| | 1874 S | — | 500.00 | 650.00 | 900.00 | 1250. |
| | 1875 S | — | 500.00 | 650.00 | 900.00 | 1250. |
| | 1876 S | — | 500.00 | 650.00 | 900.00 | 1250. |
| | 1876 M/S | — | — | — | — | — |
| | 1877 M/S | .015 | — | — | Rare | — |
| | 1877 R | Inc. Ab. | 500.00 | 650.00 | 900.00 | 1250. |
| | 1877 S | Inc. Ab. | — | — | Rare | — |
| | 1878/7 M/S | .013 | 650.00 | 1250. | 2000. | 2500. |
| | 1878 M | Inc. Ab. | 650.00 | 1250. | 2000. | 2500. |
| | 1878 S | Inc. Ab. | 500.00 | 650.00 | 900.00 | 1250. |
| | 1879 S | 8,202 | 500.00 | 800.00 | 1200. | 2250. |
| | 1880 S | 7,375 | 500.00 | 650.00 | 900.00 | 1250. |
| | 1881 S | 4,909 | 500.00 | 650.00 | 900.00 | 1250. |
| | 1882 S | 4,020 | 500.00 | 650.00 | 900.00 | 1250. |
| | 1883/2 B | 3,705 | 550.00 | 750.00 | 1150. | 2000. |
| | 1883 B | Inc. Ab. | 500.00 | 650.00 | 900.00 | 1250. |
| | 1884 B | 1,798 | 500.00 | 650.00 | 900.00 | 1250. |
| | 1885 R | 2,660 | 500.00 | 650.00 | 900.00 | 1250. |
| | 1886 R | 1,090 | 500.00 | 800.00 | 1200. | 2000. |
| | 1887 R | 1,009 | 500.00 | 800.00 | 1200. | 2000. |
| | 1888 R | 1,011 | 500.00 | 800.00 | 1200. | 2000. |
| | 1889 R | 956 pcs. | 500.00 | 800.00 | 1200. | 2000. |
| | 1890 R | 879 pcs. | 500.00 | 800.00 | 1200. | 2000. |
| | 1891 R | 818 pcs. | 500.00 | 800.00 | 1200. | 2000. |
| | 1892 R | 730 pcs. | 500.00 | 800.00 | 1200. | 2000. |
| | 1893 R | 3,343 | 500.00 | 650.00 | 950.00 | 1600. |
| | 1894/3 R | 6,734 | 500.00 | 650.00 | 900.00 | 1250. |
| | 1894 R | I.A. | 500.00 | 650.00 | 900.00 | 1250. |

| KM# | Date | Mintage | Fine | VF | XF | Unc |
|---|---|---|---|---|---|---|
| 414.4 | 1895/3 R | 7,118 | 500.00 | 650.00 | 900.00 | 1250. |
| | 1895 R | I.A. | 500.00 | 650.00 | 900.00 | 1250. |
| | 1896 R | 9,219 | 500.00 | 650.00 | 900.00 | 1250. |
| | 1897/6 R | 6,781 | 500.00 | 650.00 | 900.00 | 1250. |
| | 1897 R | I.A. | 500.00 | 650.00 | 900.00 | 1250. |
| | 1898 R | 7,710 | 500.00 | 650.00 | 900.00 | 1250. |
| | 1899 R | 8,527 | 500.00 | 650.00 | 900.00 | 1250. |
| | 1900 R | 4,512 | 500.00 | 650.00 | 900.00 | 1250. |

### Mint mark: Ho

| KM# | Date | Mintage | Fine | VF | XF | Unc |
|---|---|---|---|---|---|---|
| 414.5 | 1874 R | — | — | — | Rare | — |
| | 1875 R | — | — | — | Rare | — |
| | 1876 F | — | — | — | Rare | — |
| | 1888 G | — | — | — | Rare | — |

### Mint mark: Mo

| KM# | Date | Mintage | Fine | VF | XF | Unc |
|---|---|---|---|---|---|---|
| 414.6 | 1870 C | .014 | 500.00 | 600.00 | 800.00 | 1300. |
| | 1871 M | .021 | 500.00 | 600.00 | 800.00 | 1300. |
| | 1872/1 M | .011 | 500.00 | 600.00 | 800.00 | 1600. |
| | 1872 M | I.A. | 500.00 | 600.00 | 800.00 | 1300. |
| | 1873 M | 5,600 | 500.00 | 600.00 | 800.00 | 1300. |
| | 1874/2 M | — | 500.00 | 600.00 | 800.00 | 1350. |
| | 1874/2 B | — | 500.00 | 700.00 | 1000. | 1600. |
| | 1875 B | — | 500.00 | 650.00 | 900.00 | 1500. |
| | 1876 B | — | 500.00 | 650.00 | 900.00 | 1500. |
| | 1876 M | — | | — Reported, not confirmed | | | |
| | 1877 M | 2,000 | 500.00 | 700.00 | 1100. | 2000. |
| | 1878 M | 7,000 | 500.00 | 600.00 | 900.00 | 1500. |
| | 1879 M | — | 500.00 | 650.00 | 900.00 | 1750. |
| | 1880 M | — | 500.00 | 650.00 | 900.00 | 1750. |
| | 1881/0 M | .011 | 500.00 | 600.00 | 800.00 | 1350. |
| | 1881 M | I.A. | 500.00 | 600.00 | 800.00 | 1350. |
| | 1882/1 M | 5,800 | 500.00 | 600.00 | 800.00 | 1350. |
| | 1882 M | I.A. | 500.00 | 600.00 | 800.00 | 1350. |
| | 1883/1 M | 4,000 | 500.00 | 600.00 | 800.00 | 1350. |
| | 1883 M | I.A. | 500.00 | 600.00 | 800.00 | 1250. |
| | 1884/3 M | — | 500.00 | 650.00 | 900.00 | 1400. |
| | 1884 M | — | 500.00 | 650.00 | 900.00 | 1400. |
| | 1885 M | 6,000 | 500.00 | 650.00 | 900.00 | 1750. |
| | 1886 M | .010 | 500.00 | 600.00 | 800.00 | 1500. |
| | 1887 M | .012 | 500.00 | 600.00 | 800.00 | 1500. |
| | 1888 M | 7,300 | 500.00 | 600.00 | 800.00 | 1500. |
| | 1889 M | 6,477 | 500.00 | 600.00 | 900.00 | 1650. |
| | 1890 M | 7,852 | 500.00 | 600.00 | 900.00 | 1500. |
| | 1891/0 M | 8,725 | 500.00 | 600.00 | 800.00 | 1500. |
| | 1891 M | I.A. | 500.00 | 600.00 | 800.00 | 1500. |
| | 1892 M | .011 | 500.00 | 600.00 | 800.00 | 1300. |
| | 1893 M | .015 | 500.00 | 600.00 | 800.00 | 1300. |
| | 1894 M | .014 | 500.00 | 600.00 | 800.00 | 1300. |
| | 1895 M | .013 | 500.00 | 600.00 | 800.00 | 1300. |
| | 1896 B | .014 | 500.00 | 600.00 | 800.00 | 1300. |
| | 1897/6 M | .012 | 500.00 | 600.00 | 800.00 | 1300. |
| | 1897 M | I.A. | 500.00 | 600.00 | 800.00 | 1300. |
| | 1898 M | .020 | 500.00 | 600.00 | 800.00 | 1300. |
| | 1899 M | .023 | 500.00 | 600.00 | 800.00 | 1300. |
| | 1900 M | .021 | 500.00 | 600.00 | 800.00 | 1300. |
| | 1901 M | .029 | 500.00 | 600.00 | 800.00 | 1300. |
| | 1902 M | .038 | 500.00 | 600.00 | 800.00 | 1300. |
| | 1903/2 M | .031 | 500.00 | 600.00 | 800.00 | 1300. |
| | 1903 M | I.A. | 500.00 | 600.00 | 800.00 | 1300. |
| | 1904 M | .052 | 500.00 | 600.00 | 800.00 | 1300. |
| | 1905 M | 9,757 | 500.00 | 600.00 | 800.00 | 1300. |

### Mint mark: Oa

| KM# | Date | Mintage | Fine | VF | XF | Unc |
|---|---|---|---|---|---|---|
| 414.7 | 1870 E | 1,131 | 750.00 | 1500. | 2500. | 5000. |
| | 1871 E | 1,591 | 750.00 | 1500. | 2500. | 5000. |
| | 1872 E | 255 pcs. | 1000. | 1750. | 3000. | 7000. |
| | 1888 E | 170 pcs. | 2000. | 3000. | 5000. | — |

### Mint mark: Zs

| KM# | Date | Mintage | Fine | VF | XF | Unc |
|---|---|---|---|---|---|---|
| 414.8 | 1871 H | 1,000 | 3500. | 6500. | 7000. | 9000. |
| | 1875 A | — | 4000. | 6000. | 7500. | 9500. |
| | 1878 S | 441 pcs. | 4000. | 6000. | 7500. | 9500. |
| | 1888 Z | 50 pcs. | — | — | Rare | — |
| | 1889 Z | 640 pcs. | 3500. | 5500. | 7000. | 9000. |

# United States of Mexico

**MINT MARK**

o
M - Mexico City

## CENTAVO

### BRONZE, 20mm

| KM# | Date | Mintage | Fine | VF | XF | Unc |
|---|---|---|---|---|---|---|
| 415 | 1905 | 6.040 | 3.50 | 6.50 | 13.50 | 90.00 |
| | 1906 narrow date | | | | | |
| | *67.505 | .50 | 1.00 | 1.75 | 14.00 |
| | 1906 wide date | | | | | |
| | Inc. Ab. | .80 | 1.50 | 2.75 | 17.00 |
| | 1910 | 8.700 | 2.00 | 3.00 | 7.50 | 80.00 |
| | 1911 | 16.450 | .75 | 1.25 | 2.50 | 20.00 |
| | 1912 | 12.650 | .90 | 1.50 | 3.50 | 32.00 |
| | 1913 | 12.850 | .85 | 1.25 | 3.00 | 35.00 |
| | 1914 | 17.350 | .75 | 1.00 | 2.50 | 12.50 |
| | 1915 | 2.277 | 11.50 | 25.50 | 72.50 | 300.00 |
| | 1916 | .500 | 50.00 | 80.00 | 220.00 | 1150. |
| | 1920 | 1.433 | 22.50 | 52.50 | 90.00 | 400.00 |
| | 1921 | 3.470 | 6.00 | 15.00 | 50.00 | 275.00 |
| | 1922 | 1.880 | 8.50 | 16.00 | 60.00 | 300.00 |
| | 1923 | 4.800 | .75 | 1.00 | 2.00 | 13.50 |
| | 1924/3 | 2.000 | 57.50 | 125.00 | 250.00 | 475.00 |
| 415 | 1924 | Inc. Ab. | 4.50 | 7.50 | 22.50 | 275.00 |
| | 1925 | 1.550 | 5.00 | 10.00 | 22.50 | 225.00 |
| | 1926 | 5.000 | 1.00 | 2.00 | 4.00 | 26.00 |
| | 1927/6 | 6.000 | 25.00 | 42.50 | 60.00 | 140.00 |
| | 1927 | Inc. Ab. | .65 | 2.75 | 4.50 | 32.50 |
| | 1928 | 5.000 | .50 | 1.00 | 3.00 | 17.50 |
| | 1929 | 4.500 | .75 | 1.00 | 2.00 | 18.50 |
| | 1930 | 7.000 | .55 | 1.00 | 2.65 | 19.50 |
| | 1933 | 10.000 | .25 | .35 | 1.25 | 16.00 |
| | 1934 | 7.500 | .40 | 1.00 | 3.50 | 35.00 |
| | 1935 | 12.400 | .15 | .25 | .40 | 11.50 |
| | 1936 | 20.100 | .15 | .20 | .30 | 9.00 |
| | 1937 | 20.000 | .15 | .25 | .35 | 3.50 |
| | 1938 | 10.000 | .10 | .15 | .30 | 2.50 |
| | 1939 | 30.000 | .10 | .15 | .30 | 1.25 |
| | 1940 | 10.000 | .20 | .30 | .60 | 6.50 |
| | 1941 | 15.800 | .15 | .25 | .35 | 2.50 |
| | 1942 | 30.400 | .15 | .20 | .30 | 1.25 |
| | 1943 | 4.310 | .30 | .50 | .75 | 9.00 |
| | 1944 | 5.645 | .15 | .25 | .50 | 7.50 |
| | 1945 | 26.375 | .10 | .15 | .25 | 1.00 |
| | 1946 | 42.135 | — | .10 | .15 | .45 |
| | 1947 | 13.445 | — | .10 | .15 | 1.00 |
| | 1948 | 20.040 | — | .10 | .15 | 1.00 |
| | 1949 | 6.235 | .10 | .20 | .30 | 1.25 |

*NOTE: 50,000,000 pcs. were struck at the Birmingham Mint.
NOTE: Varieties exist.

**Zapata Issue**
**Reduced size, 16mm**

| | | | | | | |
|---|---|---|---|---|---|---|
| 416 | 1915 | .179 | 10.00 | 25.00 | 42.00 | 75.00 |

### BRASS, 16mm

| KM# | Date | Mintage | VF | XF | Unc | BU |
|---|---|---|---|---|---|---|
| 417 | 1950 | 12.815 | .15 | .30 | 1.65 | 2.00 |
| | 1951 | 25.740 | .15 | .25 | .75 | 1.10 |
| | 1952 | 24.610 | .10 | .15 | .40 | .75 |
| | 1953 | 21.160 | .10 | .15 | .40 | .85 |
| | 1954 | 25.675 | .10 | .15 | .75 | 1.10 |
| | 1955 | 9.820 | .15 | .25 | .85 | 1.50 |
| | 1956 | 11.285 | .15 | .25 | .70 | 1.15 |
| | 1957 | 9.805 | .10 | .15 | .85 | 1.35 |
| | 1958 | 12.155 | .10 | .15 | .40 | .80 |
| | 1959 | 11.875 | .10 | .20 | .70 | 1.25 |
| | 1960 | 10.360 | — | .15 | .35 | .65 |
| | 1961 | 6.385 | — | .15 | .50 | .85 |
| | 1962 | 4.850 | — | .15 | .50 | .90 |
| | 1963 | 7.775 | — | .15 | .25 | .45 |
| | 1964 | 4.280 | — | .10 | .15 | .35 |
| | 1965 | 2.255 | — | .10 | .20 | .40 |
| | 1966 | 1.760 | .10 | .15 | .40 | .70 |
| | 1967 | 1.290 | .10 | .15 | .40 | .70 |
| | 1968 | 1.000 | .10 | .25 | .75 | 1.30 |
| | 1969 | 1.000 | .10 | .15 | .70 | 1.25 |

### Reduced size, 13mm.

| | | | | | | |
|---|---|---|---|---|---|---|
| 418 | 1970 | 1.000 | .20 | .35 | 1.25 | 1.70 |
| | 1972 | 1.000 | .25 | .40 | 1.50 | 1.90 |
| | 1973 | 1.000 | 1.50 | 3.00 | 7.50 | 12.00 |

## 2 CENTAVOS

### BRONZE, 25mm

| KM# | Date | Mintage | Fine | VF | XF | Unc |
|---|---|---|---|---|---|---|
| 419 | 1905 | .050 | 150.00 | 250.00 | 400.00 | 1000. |
| | 1906/inverted 6 | | | | | |
| | | 9.998 | 20.00 | 40.00 | 90.00 | 275.00 |
| | 1906 wide date | | | | | |
| | I.A. | .5.00 | 11.50 | 22.50 | 77.50 |
| | 1906 narrow date | | | | | |
| | *I.A. | 6.50 | 15.00 | 27.50 | 80.00 |
| | 1920 | 1.325 | 9.00 | 27.50 | 52.50 | 260.00 |
| | 1921 | 4.275 | 3.00 | 5.75 | 11.00 | 90.00 |
| | 1922 | — | 250.00 | 550.00 | 1500. | 4000. |
| | 1924 | .750 | 10.00 | 22.50 | 50.00 | 400.00 |
| | 1925 | 3.650 | 2.50 | 4.00 | 9.75 | 40.00 |
| | 1926 | 4.750 | 1.25 | 2.75 | 5.75 | 35.00 |
| | 1927 | 7.250 | .75 | 1.25 | 2.75 | 25.00 |
| | 1928 | 3.250 | 1.00 | 1.75 | 4.25 | 28.00 |
| | 1929 | .250 | 70.00 | 175.00 | 435.00 | 875.00 |
| | 1935 | 1.250 | 5.00 | 10.00 | 25.00 | 195.00 |
| | 1939 | 5.000 | .45 | .85 | 1.50 | 20.00 |
| | 1941 | 3.550 | .40 | .50 | 1.50 | 20.00 |

*NOTE: 5,000,000 pcs. were struck at the Birmingham Mint.

**Zapata Issue**
**Reduced size, 20mm**

| KM# | Date | Mintage | Fine | VF | XF | Unc |
|---|---|---|---|---|---|---|
| 420 | 1915 | .487 | 6.00 | 9.50 | 12.50 | 50.00 |

# 5 CENTAVOS

### NICKEL

| KM# | Date | Mintage | Fine | VF | XF | Unc |
|---|---|---|---|---|---|---|
| 421 | 1905 | 1.420 | 6.00 | 10.00 | 25.00 | 275.00 |
| | 1906/5 | 10.615 | 12.00 | 20.00 | 50.00 | 325.00 |
| | 1906 | *Inc. Ab. | .90 | 1.25 | 3.25 | 55.00 |
| | 1907 | 4.000 | 1.00 | 3.50 | 12.00 | 250.00 |
| | 1909 | 2.052 | 3.50 | 11.00 | 55.00 | 365.00 |
| | 1910 | 6.181 | .90 | 1.75 | 6.00 | 65.00 |
| | 1911 narrow date | | | | | |
| | | 4.487 | .75 | 1.50 | 5.00 | 75.00 |
| | 1911 wide date | | | | | |
| | | Inc. Ab. | 2.50 | 4.50 | 10.00 | 80.00 |
| | 1912 small mint mark | | | | | |
| | | .420 | 85.00 | 100.00 | 200.00 | 700.00 |
| | 1912 large mint mark | | | | | |
| | | Inc. Ab. | 70.00 | 95.00 | 175.00 | 550.00 |
| | 1913 | 2.035 | 2.00 | 4.50 | 10.00 | 85.00 |
| | 1914 | 2.000 | 1.50 | 2.00 | 4.00 | 65.00 |

**NOTE:** 5,000,000 pcs. appear to have been struck at the Birmingham Mint in 1914 and all of 1909-1911. The Mexican Mint report does not mention receiving the 1914 dated coins.
**NOTE:** Varieties exist.

### BRONZE

| KM# | Date | Mintage | Fine | VF | XF | Unc |
|---|---|---|---|---|---|---|
| 422 | 1914 | 2.500 | 10.00 | 24.00 | 45.00 | 225.00 |
| | 1915 | 11.424 | 1.50 | 5.00 | 16.00 | 150.00 |
| | 1916 | 2.860 | 16.00 | 35.00 | 180.00 | 675.00 |
| | 1917 | .800 | 75.00 | 175.00 | 375.00 | 800.00 |
| | 1918 | 1.332 | 37.50 | 90.00 | 225.00 | 600.00 |
| | 1919 | .400 | 140.00 | 225.00 | 375.00 | 900.00 |
| | 1920 | 5.920 | 3.50 | 9.00 | 45.00 | 200.00 |
| | 1921 | 2.080 | 11.00 | 25.00 | 75.00 | 300.00 |
| | 1924 | .780 | 40.00 | 90.00 | 250.00 | 600.00 |
| | 1925 | 4.040 | 5.00 | 12.00 | 45.00 | 195.00 |
| | 1926 | 3.160 | 6.00 | 12.00 | 45.00 | 215.00 |
| | 1927 | 3.600 | 4.00 | 8.00 | 30.00 | 190.00 |
| | 1928 large date | | | | | |
| | | 1.740 | 9.00 | 18.00 | 67.50 | 225.00 |
| | 1928 small date | | | | | |
| | | Inc. Ab. | 25.00 | 45.00 | 90.00 | 375.00 |
| | 1929 | 2.400 | 6.00 | 10.00 | 35.00 | 165.00 |
| | 1930 large oval 0 in date | | | | | |
| | | 2.600 | 5.00 | 9.00 | 35.00 | 180.00 |
| | 1930 small square 0 in date | | | | | |
| | | Inc. Ab. | 55.00 | 95.00 | 225.00 | 550.00 |

| KM# | Date | Mintage | Fine | VF | XF | Unc |
|---|---|---|---|---|---|---|
| 422 | 1931 | — | 500.00 | 700.00 | 1150. | 3000. |
| | 1933 | 8.000 | 1.25 | 2.00 | 3.00 | 25.00 |
| | 1934 | 10.000 | 1.25 | 1.75 | 2.50 | 22.50 |
| | 1935 | 21.980 | .90 | 1.25 | 3.00 | 18.50 |

### COPPER-NICKEL

| KM# | Date | Mintage | VF | XF | Unc | BU |
|---|---|---|---|---|---|---|
| 423 | 1936 | 46.700 | .50 | 1.00 | 6.50 | 9.00 |
| | 1937 | 49.060 | .40 | 1.00 | 5.75 | 8.00 |
| | 1938 | 3.340 | 5.50 | 11.50 | 62.00 | — |
| | 1940 | 22.800 | .90 | 1.50 | 7.00 | 10.00 |
| | 1942 | 7.100 | 1.50 | 2.50 | 25.00 | 32.50 |

### BRONZE
**'Josefa' Ortiz de Dominguez**

| KM# | Date | Mintage | VF | XF | Unc | BU |
|---|---|---|---|---|---|---|
| 424 | 1942 | .900 | 27.50 | 75.00 | 350.00 | 450.00 |
| | 1943 | 54.660 | .50 | .75 | 3.00 | 3.75 |
| | 1944 | 53.463 | .20 | .25 | .75 | 1.00 |
| | 1945 | 44.262 | .25 | .35 | .90 | 1.65 |
| | 1946 | 49.054 | .50 | .90 | 2.00 | 2.75 |
| | 1951 | 50.758 | .75 | 1.00 | 3.00 | 4.75 |
| | 1952 | 17.674 | 1.50 | 2.75 | 9.00 | 11.00 |
| | 1953 | 31.568 | .50 | 1.00 | 2.75 | 4.00 |
| | 1954 | 58.680 | .50 | 1.00 | 2.75 | 4.00 |
| | 1955 | 31.114 | 1.25 | 2.00 | 11.00 | 15.00 |

### COPPER-NICKEL
**'White Josefa'**

| | | | | | | |
|---|---|---|---|---|---|---|
| 425 | 1950 | 5.700 | .80 | 1.50 | 6.00 | 8.00 |

**NOTE:** 5,600,000 pieces struck at Connecticut melted.

### BRASS

| KM# | Date | Mintage | VF | XF | Unc | BU |
|---|---|---|---|---|---|---|
| 426 | 1954 dot | — | 11.00 | 30.00 | 230.00 | 250.00 |
| | 1954 w/o dot | — | 9.00 | 21.00 | 125.00 | 175.00 |
| | 1955 | 12.136 | .90 | 1.75 | 9.00 | 12.50 |
| | 1956 | 60.216 | .20 | .30 | .90 | 1.50 |
| | 1957 | 55.288 | .15 | .20 | .90 | 1.50 |
| | 1958 | 104.624 | .15 | .20 | .50 | 1.00 |
| | 1959 | 106.000 | .15 | .20 | .90 | 1.35 |
| | 1960 | 99.144 | .10 | .15 | .40 | .75 |
| | 1961 | 61.136 | .10 | .15 | .40 | .70 |
| | 1962 | 47.232 | .10 | .15 | .30 | .55 |
| | 1963 | 156.680 | — | .10 | .20 | .35 |
| | 1964 | 71.168 | — | .10 | .20 | .40 |
| | 1965 | 155.720 | — | .10 | .15 | .35 |
| | 1966 | 124.944 | — | .10 | .30 | .50 |
| | 1967 | 118.816 | — | .10 | .25 | .40 |
| | 1968 | 189.588 | — | .10 | .25 | .35 |
| | 1969 | 210.492 | — | .10 | .25 | .35 |

## COPPER-NICKEL

| KM# | Date | Mintage | VF | XF | Unc | BU |
|---|---|---|---|---|---|---|
| 426a | 1962 | 19 pcs. | 300.00 | — | — | — |

## BRASS
### Reduced size, 18mm.

| | | | | | |
|---|---|---|---|---|---|
| 427 | 1970 | 163.368 | — | .10 | .30 | .45 |
| | 1971 | 198.844 | — | .10 | .15 | .30 |
| | 1972 | 225.000 | — | .10 | .15 | .30 |
| | 1973 flat top 3 | | | | | |
| | | 595.070 | — | .10 | .25 | .40 |
| | 1973 round top 3 | | | | | |
| | | Inc. Ab. | — | .10 | .15 | .25 |
| | 1974 | 401.584 | — | .10 | .20 | .30 |
| | 1975 | 342.308 | — | .10 | .25 | .35 |
| | 1976 | 367.524 | — | .10 | .30 | .50 |

**NOTE:** Due to some minor alloy variations this type is often encounntered with a bronze color toning.

## 10 CENTAVOS

### 2.5000 g, .800 SILVER, .0643 oz ASW

| | | | | | | |
|---|---|---|---|---|---|---|
| 428 | 1905 | 3.920 | 6.25 | 8.00 | 35.00 | 47.50 |
| | 1906 | 8.410 | 6.00 | 7.25 | 25.00 | 32.50 |
| | 1907/6 | 5.950 | 50.00 | 125.00 | 250.00 | 350.00 |
| | 1907 | Inc. Ab. | 6.75 | 9.25 | 35.00 | 42.50 |
| | 1909 | 2.620 | 9.50 | 12.00 | 70.00 | 85.00 |
| | 1910/00 | 3.450 | 15.00 | 30.00 | 80.00 | 100.00 |
| | 1910 | Inc. Ab. | 9.50 | 12.50 | 20.00 | 25.00 |
| | 1911 | 2.550 | 7.50 | 10.00 | 42.50 | 50.00 |
| | 1912 | 1.350 | 9.75 | 14.00 | 110.00 | 140.00 |
| | 1913/2 | 1.990 | 10.00 | 20.00 | 40.00 | 65.00 |
| | 1913 | Inc. Ab. | 7.00 | 10.00 | 33.50 | 45.00 |
| | 1914 | 3.110 | 4.50 | 6.75 | 13.50 | 18.75 |

### 1.8125 g, .800 SILVER, .0466 oz ASW
### Reduced size, 15mm.

| | | | | | | |
|---|---|---|---|---|---|---|
| 429 | 1919 | 8.360 | 9.50 | 17.50 | 97.50 | 115.00 |

### BRONZE

| | | | | | | |
|---|---|---|---|---|---|---|
| 430 | 1919 | 1.232 | 25.00 | 60.00 | 410.00 | 495.00 |
| | 1920 | 6.612 | 15.00 | 45.00 | 400.00 | 475.00 |
| | 1921 | 2.255 | 35.00 | 75.00 | 800.00 | 1000. |
| | 1935 | 5.970 | 17.00 | 30.00 | 90.00 | 140.00 |

### 1.6600 g, .720 SILVER, .0384 oz ASW

| KM# | Date | Mintage | VF | XF | Unc | BU |
|---|---|---|---|---|---|---|
| 431 | 1925/15 | 5.350 | 20.00 | 50.00 | 100.00 | 120.00 |
| | 1925/3 | Inc. Ab. | 20.00 | 35.00 | 100.00 | 125.00 |
| | 1925 | Inc. Ab. | 2.50 | 4.75 | 30.00 | 40.00 |
| | 1926/16 | 2.650 | 30.00 | 60.00 | 150.00 | 170.00 |
| | 1926 | Inc. Ab. | 4.00 | 7.25 | 60.00 | 80.00 |
| | 1927 | 2.810 | 2.75 | 3.50 | 17.50 | 21.50 |
| | 1928 | 5.270 | 2.00 | 2.50 | 10.00 | 12.25 |
| | 1930 | 2.000 | 4.75 | 6.00 | 20.00 | 23.50 |
| | 1933 | 5.000 | 2.00 | 3.60 | 9.00 | 11.00 |
| | 1934 | 8.000 | 1.50 | 2.65 | 9.50 | 12.00 |
| | 1935 | 3.500 | 3.50 | 6.00 | 15.00 | 20.00 |

### COPPER-NICKEL

| | | | | | | |
|---|---|---|---|---|---|---|
| 432 | 1936 | 33.030 | .40 | .90 | 7.00 | 8.50 |
| | 1937 | 3.000 | 5.00 | 15.00 | 215.00 | 235.00 |
| | 1938 | 3.650 | 1.75 | 5.50 | 52.00 | 65.00 |
| | 1939 | 6.920 | 1.00 | 4.00 | 30.00 | 40.00 |
| | 1940 | 12.300 | .50 | 1.25 | 5.00 | 6.50 |
| | 1942 | 14.380 | .75 | 1.75 | 7.00 | 8.50 |
| | 1945 | 9.558 | .40 | .65 | 3.50 | 4.00 |
| | 1946 | 46.230 | .30 | .50 | 2.50 | 3.00 |

### BRONZE
### Benito Juarez

| | | | | | | |
|---|---|---|---|---|---|---|
| 433 | 1955 | 1.818 | 1.00 | 3.50 | 22.50 | 28.00 |
| | 1956 | 5.255 | .50 | 2.25 | 20.00 | 27.50 |
| | 1957 | 11.925 | .20 | .50 | 5.00 | 6.50 |
| | 1959 | 26.140 | .20 | .30 | .50 | .65 |
| | 1966 | 5.873 | .15 | .25 | .45 | .60 |
| | 1967 | 32.318 | .15 | .25 | .35 | .50 |

### COPPER-NICKEL
### Variety I
### Rev: 5 full rows of kernels, sharp stem, wide date.

| | | | | | | |
|---|---|---|---|---|---|---|
| 434.1 | 1974 | 6.000 | — | .10 | .35 | .45 |
| | 1975 | 5.550 | .10 | .15 | .45 | .55 |
| | 1976 | 7.680 | .10 | .20 | .30 | .40 |
| | 1977 | 144.650 | .50 | 2.00 | 2.50 | 3.50 |
| | 1978 | 271.870 | — | 2.00 | 2.50 | 3.50 |
| | 1979 | 375.660 | — | .10 | .30 | .40 |
| | 1980/79 | 21.290 | 2.25 | 3.75 | 6.00 | 7.00 |
| | 1980 | I.A. | 1.25 | 2.00 | 4.50 | 5.00 |

**PRICING SECTION**

### Variety II
Rev: 5 full, plus 1 partial row at left, blunt stem, narrow date.

| KM# | Date | Mintage | VF | XF | Unc | BU |
|---|---|---|---|---|---|---|
| 434.2 | 1977 | Inc. Ab. | — | .10 | .20 | .25 |
| | 1978 | Inc. Ab. | — | .10 | .20 | .30 |
| | 1979 | Inc. Ab. | .10 | .50 | 1.00 | 2.00 |
| | 1980 | Inc. Ab. | — | .10 | .20 | .30 |

## 20 CENTAVOS

**5.0000 g, .800 SILVER, .1286 oz ASW**

| 435 | 1905 | 2.565 | 10.00 | 17.50 | 150.00 | 175.00 |
|---|---|---|---|---|---|---|
| | 1906 | 6.860 | 7.00 | 12.00 | 55.00 | 70.00 |
| | 1907 straight 7 | | | | | — |
| | | 4.000 | 10.00 | 20.00 | 70.00 | 100.00 |
| | 1907 curved 7 | | | | | — |
| | | 5.435 | 9.50 | 16.00 | 55.00 | 75.00 |
| | 1908 | .350 | 85.00 | 160.00 | 1500. | — |
| | 1910 | 1.135 | 11.00 | 18.00 | 80.00 | 90.00 |
| | 1911 | 1.150 | 17.50 | 37.50 | 125.00 | 150.00 |
| | 1912 | .625 | 35.00 | 75.00 | 335.00 | 375.00 |
| | 1913 | 1.000 | 18.00 | 35.00 | 92.50 | 115.00 |
| | 1914 | 1.500 | 12.50 | 18.00 | 67.50 | 75.00 |

**3.6250 g, .800 SILVER, .0932 oz ASW**
**Reduced size, 19mm.**

| 436 | 1919 | 4.155 | 30.00 | 60.00 | 210.00 | 250.00 |
|---|---|---|---|---|---|---|

**BRONZE**

| 437 | 1920 | 4.835 | 37.50 | 95.00 | 400.00 | 475.00 |
|---|---|---|---|---|---|---|
| | 1935 | 20.000 | 6.50 | 9.00 | 65.00 | 100.00 |

**3.3333 g, .720 SILVER, .0772 oz ASW**

| KM# | Date | Mintage | VF | XF | Unc | BU |
|---|---|---|---|---|---|---|
| 438 | 1920 | 3.710 | 5.50 | 12.00 | 140.00 | 175.00 |
| | 1921 | 6.160 | 5.50 | 12.00 | 95.00 | 125.00 |
| | 1925 | 1.450 | 9.00 | 20.00 | 120.00 | 150.00 |
| | 1926/5 | 1.465 | 20.00 | 50.00 | 300.00 | — |
| | 1926 | Inc. Ab. | 5.50 | 12.00 | 90.00 | 130.00 |
| | 1927 | 1.405 | 4.50 | 7.50 | 80.00 | 115.00 |
| | 1928 | 3.630 | 3.00 | 5.50 | 15.00 | 18.00 |
| | 1930 | 1.000 | 3.50 | 7.00 | 25.00 | 27.50 |
| | 1933 | 2.500 | 2.75 | 3.25 | 10.00 | 12.00 |
| | 1934 | 2.500 | 2.50 | 3.25 | 12.00 | 14.00 |
| | 1935 | 2.460 | 2.75 | 3.25 | 10.00 | 12.00 |
| | 1937 | 10.000 | 2.50 | 3.00 | 4.50 | 5.50 |
| | 1939 | 8.800 | 2.00 | 2.50 | 4.00 | 4.50 |
| | 1940 | 3.000 | 2.00 | 2.50 | 4.00 | 4.50 |
| | 1941 | 5.740 | 2.00 | 2.50 | 3.00 | 3.75 |
| | 1942 | 12.460 | 2.00 | 2.25 | 3.00 | 3.75 |
| | 1943 | 3.955 | 1.50 | 2.00 | 3.50 | 4.25 |

**BRONZE**

| 439 | 1943 | 46.350 | .95 | 3.25 | 18.00 | 25.00 |
|---|---|---|---|---|---|---|
| | 1944 | 83.650 | .50 | .75 | 9.00 | 11.00 |
| | 1945 | 26.801 | 2.25 | 4.00 | 10.50 | 13.00 |
| | 1946 | 25.695 | 1.10 | 2.50 | 6.00 | 8.25 |
| | 1951 | 11.385 | 3.00 | 6.50 | 60.00 | 100.00 |
| | 1952 | 6.560 | 2.50 | 5.50 | 25.00 | 32.50 |
| | 1953 | 26.948 | .35 | .75 | 6.50 | 10.00 |
| | 1954 | 40.108 | .35 | .85 | 9.00 | 12.50 |
| | 1955 | 16.950 | 3.00 | 6.50 | 50.00 | 80.00 |

| 440 | 1955 | | | | | |
|---|---|---|---|---|---|---|
| | | Inc. KM439 | .75 | 1.75 | 15.00 | 20.00 |
| | 1956 | 22.431 | .30 | .35 | 3.00 | 4.00 |
| | 1957 | 13.455 | .50 | 1.50 | 9.00 | 12.00 |
| | 1959 | 6.017 | 5.00 | 9.00 | 55.00 | 90.00 |
| | 1960 | 39.756 | .15 | .20 | .90 | 1.25 |
| | 1963 | 14.869 | .20 | .30 | .90 | 1.25 |
| | 1964 | 28.654 | .15 | .25 | .75 | 1.10 |
| | 1965 | 74.162 | .15 | .25 | .85 | 1.20 |
| | 1966 | 43.745 | .15 | .25 | .90 | 1.30 |
| | 1967 | 46.487 | .15 | .25 | 1.10 | 1.50 |
| | 1968 | 15.477 | .15 | .30 | 1.10 | 1.65 |
| | 1969 | 63.647 | .15 | .25 | 1.00 | 1.50 |
| | 1970 | 76.287 | .15 | .20 | .90 | 1.30 |
| | 1971 | 49.892 | .30 | .35 | 1.25 | 1.75 |

| KM# | Date | Mintage | VF | XF | Unc | BU |
|---|---|---|---|---|---|---|
| 441 | 1971 | | | | | |
| | | Inc. KM440 | .15 | .35 | 1.50 | 2.00 |
| | 1973 | 78.398 | .15 | .25 | .95 | 1.50 |
| | 1974 | 34.200 | .25 | .35 | 1.25 | 1.75 |

### COPPER-NICKEL
### Francisco Madero

| KM# | Date | Mintage | VF | XF | Unc | BU |
|---|---|---|---|---|---|---|
| 442 | 1974 | 112.000 | — | .10 | .25 | .30 |
| | 1975 | 611.000 | .10 | .15 | .30 | .35 |
| | 1976 | 394.000 | .10 | .15 | .35 | .45 |
| | 1977 | 394.350 | .10 | .15 | .40 | .45 |
| | 1978 | 527.950 | .10 | .15 | .25 | .30 |
| | 1979 | 524.615 | — | .10 | .25 | .35 |
| | 1979 Doubled die obv. large/small letters | | | | | |
| | | — | 1.00 | 2.00 | 4.00 | 8.00 |
| | 1980 | 326.500 | .10 | .20 | .40 | .60 |
| | 1981 open 8 | | | | | |
| | | 106.205 | .25 | .50 | 1.75 | 2.25 |
| | 1981 closed 8, high date | | | | | |
| | | 248.500 | .25 | .50 | 1.50 | 2.00 |
| | 1981 closed 8, low date | | | | | |
| | | — | 1.00 | 1.50 | 2.00 | 3.00 |
| | 1981/1982 | — | 30.00 | 60.00 | 125.00 | 150.00 |
| | 1982 | 286.855 | .15 | .40 | .90 | 1.10 |
| | 1983 round top 3 | | | | | |
| | | 100.930 | .25 | .40 | 1.75 | 2.25 |
| | 1983 flat top 3 | | | | | |
| | | Inc. Ab. | .25 | .50 | 1.25 | 1.75 |
| | 1983 | 998 pcs. | — | — | Proof | 18.00 |

**NOTE:** The 1981/1982 overdate is often mistaken as 1982/1981.

### BRONZE
### Olmec Culture

| | Date | Mintage | VF | XF | Unc | BU |
|---|---|---|---|---|---|---|
| 491 | 1983 | 260.000 | .10 | .25 | .90 | 1.10 |
| | 1983 | 53 pcs. | — | — | Proof | 185.00 |
| | 1984 | 180.320 | .20 | .30 | 1.50 | 1.70 |

## 25 CENTAVOS

### 3.3330 g, .300 SILVER, .0321 oz ASW

| | Date | Mintage | VF | XF | Unc | BU |
|---|---|---|---|---|---|---|
| 443 | 1950 | 77.060 | .60 | .75 | 1.75 | 2.25 |
| | 1951 | 41.172 | .60 | .75 | 1.60 | 2.00 |
| | 1952 | 29.264 | .75 | 1.00 | 1.80 | 2.50 |
| | 1953 | 38.144 | .60 | .75 | 1.50 | 2.00 |

### COPPER-NICKEL
### Francisco Madero

| KM# | Date | Mintage | VF | XF | Unc | BU |
|---|---|---|---|---|---|---|
| 444 | 1964 | 20.686 | — | .15 | .25 | .40 |
| | 1966 closed beak | | | | | |
| | | .180 | .50 | 1.00 | 2.50 | 3.00 |
| | 1966 open beak | | | | | |
| | | Inc. Ab. | 1.00 | 3.50 | 10.00 | 14.00 |

## 50 CENTAVOS

### 12.5000 g, .800 SILVER, .3215 oz ASW

| | Date | Mintage | VF | XF | Unc | BU |
|---|---|---|---|---|---|---|
| 445 | 1905 | 2.446 | 17.50 | 25.00 | 150.00 | 175.00 |
| | 1906 | 16.966 | 6.00 | 10.00 | 30.00 | 40.00 |
| | 1907 straight 7 | | | | | |
| | | 18.920 | 5.75 | 8.50 | 25.00 | 28.50 |
| | 1907 curved 7 | | | | | |
| | | 14.841 | 5.00 | 7.50 | 23.00 | 25.00 |
| | 1908 | .488 | 75.00 | 170.00 | 525.00 | 600.00 |
| | 1912 | 3.736 | 10.00 | 15.00 | 45.00 | 60.00 |
| | 1913/07 | 10.510 | 35.00 | 75.00 | 200.00 | 250.00 |
| | 1913/2 | Inc. Ab. | 15.00 | 25.00 | 55.00 | 70.00 |
| | 1913 | Inc. Ab. | 7.00 | 10.00 | 25.00 | 30.00 |
| | 1914 | 7.710 | 8.50 | 15.50 | 30.00 | 36.00 |
| | 1916 | .480 | 60.00 | 90.00 | 225.00 | 275.00 |
| | 1917 | 37.112 | 5.00 | 7.00 | 18.00 | 20.00 |
| | 1918 | 1.320 | 85.00 | 135.00 | 250.00 | 300.00 |

### 9.0625 g, .800 SILVER, .2331 oz ASW
### Reduced size, 27mm.

| | Date | Mintage | VF | XF | Unc | BU |
|---|---|---|---|---|---|---|
| 446 | 1918/7 | 2.760 | — | 625.00 | 1250. | — |
| | 1918 | Inc. Ab. | 20.00 | 60.00 | 325.00 | 400.00 |
| | 1919 | 29.670 | 10.00 | 20.00 | 100.00 | 115.00 |

### 8.3333 g, .720 SILVER, .1929 oz ASW

| KM# | Date | Mintage | VF | XF | Unc | BU |
|---|---|---|---|---|---|---|
| 447 | 1919 | 10.200 | 10.00 | 20.00 | 90.00 | 110.00 |
| | 1920 | 27.166 | 7.50 | 10.00 | 72.50 | 85.00 |
| | 1921 | 21.864 | 7.75 | 10.50 | 85.00 | 110.00 |
| | 1925 | 3.280 | 15.00 | 30.00 | 130.00 | 155.00 |
| | 1937 | 20.000 | 4.00 | 6.00 | 7.50 | 8.50 |
| | 1938 | .100 | 50.00 | 100.00 | 300.00 | 350.00 |
| | 1939 | 10.440 | 4.00 | 8.00 | 12.00 | 15.00 |
| | 1942 | .800 | 4.00 | 6.00 | 12.50 | 17.00 |
| | 1943 | 41.512 | 3.75 | 4.50 | 5.50 | 6.50 |
| | 1944 | 55.806 | 3.75 | 4.50 | 5.50 | 6.50 |
| | 1945 | 56.766 | 4.00 | 4.75 | 6.00 | 7.00 |

**7.9730 g, .420 SILVER, .1076 oz ASW**

| | | | | | | |
|---|---|---|---|---|---|---|
| 448 | 1935 | 70.800 | 2.50 | 3.25 | 5.25 | 6.00 |

**Obv: Stylized eagle.**

| KM# | Date | Mintage | VF | XF | Unc | BU |
|---|---|---|---|---|---|---|
| 452 | 1970 | 76.236 | — | .20 | 1.00 | 1.30 |
| | 1971 | 125.288 | — | .15 | .90 | 1.30 |
| | 1972 | 16.000 | 1.00 | 2.00 | 3.50 | 4.75 |
| | 1975 Dots | | | | | |
| | | 177.958 | .60 | 1.25 | 3.50 | 5.25 |
| | 1975 No dots | | | | | |
| | | Inc. Ab. | .10 | .15 | .40 | .60 |
| | 1976 Dots | | | | | |
| | | 37,480 | .60 | 1.25 | 5.00 | 6.00 |
| | 1976 No dots | | | | | |
| | | Inc. Ab. | .15 | .20 | .50 | .65 |
| | 1977 | 12.410 | 6.00 | 10.00 | 32.50 | 42.50 |
| | 1978 | 85.400 | .15 | .25 | .50 | .65 |
| | 1979 round 2nd 9 in date | | | | | |
| | | 229.000 | .15 | .20 | .50 | .65 |
| | 1979 square 9's in date | | | | | |
| | | Inc. Ab. | .15 | .35 | 1.60 | 2.10 |
| | 1980 narrow date, square 9 | | | | | |
| | | 89.978 | .40 | .75 | 2.00 | 2.50 |
| | 1980 wide date, round 9 | | | | | |
| | | 178.188 | .15 | .25 | 1.00 | 1.15 |
| | 1981 rectangular 9, narrow date | | | | | |
| | | 142.212 | .60 | 1.25 | 3.50 | 7.50 |
| | 1981 round 9, wide date | | | | | |
| | | Inc. Ab. | .20 | .50 | 1.25 | 1.75 |
| | 1982 | 45.474 | .15 | .40 | 1.50 | 2.00 |
| | 1983 | 90.318 | .15 | .50 | 2.00 | 2.50 |
| | 1983 | 998 pcs. | — | — | Proof | 18.00 |

**NOTE:** Coins dated 1975 and 1976 exist with and without dots in centers of three circles on plumage on reverse. Edge varieties exist.

**6.6600 g, .300 SILVER, .0642 oz ASW**
**Cuauhtemoc**

| | | | | | | |
|---|---|---|---|---|---|---|
| 449 | 1950 | 13.570 | 1.75 | 2.25 | 3.50 | 4.00 |
| | 1951 | 3.650 | 2.00 | 2.75 | 3.75 | 5.00 |

**STAINLESS STEEL**
**Palenque Culture**

| | | | | | | |
|---|---|---|---|---|---|---|
| 492 | 1983 | 99.540 | — | .25 | .75 | 1.00 |
| | 1983 | 53 pcs. | — | — | Proof | 185.00 |

## UN (1) PESO

**BRONZE**

| | | | | | | |
|---|---|---|---|---|---|---|
| 450 | 1955 | 3.502 | 1.50 | 2.50 | 25.00 | 37.50 |
| | 1956 | 34.643 | .85 | 1.25 | 3.25 | 4.50 |
| | 1957 | 9.675 | .95 | 1.25 | 4.50 | 5.75 |
| | 1959 | 4.540 | .40 | .60 | 1.50 | 2.00 |

**COPPER-NICKEL**

| | | | | | | |
|---|---|---|---|---|---|---|
| 451 | 1964 | 43.806 | — | .15 | .30 | .40 |
| | 1965 | 14.326 | — | .10 | .30 | .45 |
| | 1966 | 1.726 | .20 | .40 | 1.30 | 1.75 |
| | 1967 | 55.144 | .15 | .20 | .50 | .60 |
| | 1968 | 80.438 | — | .15 | .50 | .60 |
| | 1969 | 87.640 | .15 | .25 | .75 | 1.00 |

**27.0700 g, .903 SILVER, .7859 oz ASW**
**'Caballito'**

| KM# | Date | Mintage | VF | XF | Unc | BU |
|---|---|---|---|---|---|---|
| 453 | 1910 | 3.814 | 35.00 | 50.00 | 170.00 | 200.00 |
| | 1911 long lower left ray on rev. | | | | | |
| | | 1.227 | 40.00 | 70.00 | 210.00 | 275.00 |
| | 1911 short lower left ray on rev. | | | | | |
| | | Inc. Ab. | 140.00 | 185.00 | 600.00 | 800.00 |
| | 1912 | .322 | 100.00 | 225.00 | 325.00 | 400.00 |
| | 1913/2 | 2.880 | 40.00 | 70.00 | 275.00 | 350.00 |
| | 1913 | Inc. Ab. | 40.00 | 70.00 | 180.00 | 210.00 |
| | 1914 | .120 | 525.00 | 950.00 | 2750. | — |

**18.1300 g, .800 SILVER, .4663 oz ASW**

| 454 | 1918 | 3.050 | 35.00 | 100.00 | 2500. | — |
|---|---|---|---|---|---|---|
| | 1919 | 6.151 | 22.50 | 50.00 | 1200. | 1800. |

**16.6600 g, .720 SILVER, .3856 oz ASW**

| 455 | 1920/10 | 8.830 | 40.00 | 80.00 | 300.00 | — |
|---|---|---|---|---|---|---|
| | 1920 | Inc. Ab. | 9.00 | 20.00 | 160.00 | 200.00 |
| | 1921 | 5.480 | 9.00 | 20.00 | 160.00 | 200.00 |
| | 1922 | 33.620 | 4.00 | 5.50 | 22.00 | 25.00 |
| | 1923 | 35.280 | 4.00 | 5.50 | 22.00 | 25.00 |
| | 1924 | 33.060 | 4.00 | 5.50 | 22.00 | 25.00 |
| | 1925 | 9.160 | 5.00 | 11.00 | 60.00 | 80.00 |
| | 1926 | 28.840 | 4.00 | 5.50 | 20.00 | 24.00 |
| | 1927 | 5.060 | 5.00 | 10.00 | 70.00 | 90.00 |
| | 1932 | 50.770 | 3.50 | 4.50 | 6.00 | 6.75 |
| | 1933/2 | 43.920 | 15.00 | 25.00 | 80.00 | — |
| | 1933 | Inc. Ab. | 3.50 | 4.50 | 6.00 | 6.75 |
| | 1934 | 22.070 | 4.00 | 5.00 | 10.00 | 12.50 |
| | 1935 | 8.050 | 4.50 | 6.25 | 12.00 | 13.50 |
| | 1938 | 30.000 | 3.50 | 4.00 | 7.00 | 8.25 |
| | 1940 | 20.000 | 3.25 | 3.75 | 5.50 | 6.25 |
| | 1943 | 47.662 | 3.50 | 3.75 | 5.00 | 5.50 |
| | 1944 | 39.522 | 3.50 | 3.75 | 5.00 | 5.50 |
| | 1945 | 37.300 | 3.50 | 3.75 | 5.00 | 5.50 |

**14.0000 g, .500 SILVER, .2250 oz ASW**
**Jose Morelos y Pavon**

| KM# | Date | Mintage | VF | XF | Unc | BU |
|---|---|---|---|---|---|---|
| 456 | 1947 | 61.460 | 2.50 | 3.00 | 5.00 | 5.50 |
| | 1948 | 22.915 | 3.00 | 4.50 | 6.00 | 7.00 |
| | 1949 | *4.000 | — | 1000. | 1850. | 2750. |
| | 1949 | — | — | — | Proof | 4000. |

**\*NOTE:** Not released for circulation.

**13.3300 g, .300 SILVER, .1285 oz ASW**
**Jose Morelos y Pavon**

| 457 | 1950 | 3.287 | 3.50 | 4.75 | 7.00 | 8.50 |
|---|---|---|---|---|---|---|

**16.0000 g, .100 SILVER, .0514 oz ASW**
**100th Anniversary of Constitution**

| 458 | 1957 | .500 | 4.50 | 6.00 | 14.00 | 16.50 |
|---|---|---|---|---|---|---|

**Jose Morelos y Pavon**

| 459 | 1957 | 28.273 | .75 | 1.00 | 2.50 | 3.00 |
|---|---|---|---|---|---|---|
| | 1958 | 41.899 | .75 | .95 | 1.85 | 2.60 |
| | 1959 | 27.369 | 1.60 | 2.00 | 5.50 | 7.00 |
| | 1960 | 26.259 | .75 | 1.10 | 3.25 | 4.00 |
| | 1961 | 52.601 | .60 | .90 | 2.25 | 3.00 |
| | 1962 | 61.094 | .60 | .90 | 2.25 | 2.75 |
| | 1963 | 26.394 | BV | .75 | 1.75 | 2.40 |
| | 1964 | 15.615 | BV | .75 | 1.90 | 2.20 |
| | 1965 | 5.004 | BV | .60 | 1.75 | 2.00 |
| | 1966 | 30.998 | BV | .60 | 1.75 | 2.00 |
| | 1967 | 9.308 | BV | .60 | 3.00 | 3.50 |

**COPPER-NICKEL**

### Jose Morelos y Pavon

| KM# | Date | Mintage | VF | XF | Unc | BU |
|---|---|---|---|---|---|---|
| 460 | 1970 narrow date | | | | | |
| | | 102.715 | .25 | .35 | .65 | .85 |
| | 1970 wide date | | | | | |
| | | Inc. Ab. | 1.25 | 2.50 | 8.00 | 9.75 |
| | 1971 | 426.222 | .20 | .25 | .50 | .65 |
| | 1972 | 120.000 | .20 | .25 | .40 | .65 |
| | 1974 | 63.700 | .20 | .25 | .65 | .90 |

| | | | | | | |
|---|---|---|---|---|---|---|
| | 1975 tall narrow date | | | | | |
| | | 205.979 | .25 | .35 | 1.00 | 1.35 |

| | | | | | | |
|---|---|---|---|---|---|---|
| | 1975 short wide date | | | | | |
| | | Inc. Ab. | .30 | .40 | .75 | 1.00 |
| | 1976 | 94.489 | .15 | .20 | .50 | .75 |
| | 1977 thick date | | | | | |
| | | 94.364 | .20 | .45 | 1.00 | 1.25 |
| | 1977 thin date | | | | | |
| | | Inc. Ab. | 1.00 | 2.75 | 10.00 | 15.00 |
| | 1978 closed 8 | | | | | |
| | | 208.300 | .20 | .30 | 1.00 | 1.15 |
| | 1978 open 8 | | | | | |
| | | 55.140 | .75 | 1.50 | 11.00 | 15.00 |
| | 1979 thin date | | | | | |
| | | 117.884 | .20 | .30 | .75 | 1.00 |
| | 1979 thick date | | | | | |
| | | Inc. Ab. | .40 | .50 | 1.30 | 1.90 |
| | 1980 closed 8 | | | | | |
| | | 318.800 | .25 | .35 | .80 | 1.00 |
| | 1980 open 8 | | | | | |
| | | 23.865 | .75 | 1.50 | 10.00 | 12.75 |
| | 1981 closed 8 | | | | | |
| | | 413.349 | .20 | .30 | .75 | 1.00 |
| | 1981 open 8 | | | | | |
| | | 58.616 | .50 | 1.25 | 7.00 | 8.50 |
| | 1982 | 235.000 | .25 | .50 | 2.25 | 2.50 |
| | 1983 wide date | | | | | |
| | | 100.000 | .20 | .30 | 3.00 | 3.50 |
| | 1983 narrow date | | | | | |
| | | Inc. Ab. | .25 | .45 | 1.20 | 1.50 |
| | 1983 | 1,051 | — | — | Proof | 18.00 |

### STAINLESS STEEL
### Jose Morelos y Pavon

| KM# | Date | Mintage | VF | XF | Unc | BU |
|---|---|---|---|---|---|---|
| 496 | 1984 | 722.802 | — | .25 | .80 | 1.00 |
| | 1985 | 985.000 | — | .15 | .50 | .75 |
| | 1986 | 740.000 | — | .15 | .50 | .75 |
| | 1987 | 250.000 | — | .15 | .50 | .80 |
| | 1988 | — | — | .25 | .80 | 1.00 |

## DOS (2) PESOS

**1.6666 g, .900 GOLD, .0482 oz AGW**

| KM# | Date | Mintage | Fine | VF | XF | Unc |
|---|---|---|---|---|---|---|
| 461 | 1919 | 1.670 | — | BV | 30.00 | 50.00 |
| | 1920 | 4.282 | — | BV | 30.00 | 50.00 |
| | 1944 | .010 | 27.50 | 35.00 | 45.00 | 70.00 |
| | 1945 | *.140 | — | — | | BV + 20% |
| | 1946 | .168 | 30.00 | 50.00 | 55.00 | 100.00 |
| | 1947 | .025 | 27.50 | 40.00 | 45.00 | 65.00 |
| | 1948 | .045 | — | no specimens known | | |

**\*NOTE:** During 1951-1972 a total of 4,590,493 pieces were restruck, most likely dated 1945.

**26.6667 g, .900 SILVER, .7717 oz ASW**
**Centennial of Independence**

| KM# | Date | Mintage | VF | XF | Unc | BU |
|---|---|---|---|---|---|---|
| 462 | 1921 | 1.278 | 35.00 | 60.00 | 325.00 | 450.00 |

## DOS Y MEDIO (2-1/2) PESOS

**2.0833 g, .900 GOLD, .0602 oz AGW**

| KM# | Date | Mintage | Fine | VF | XF | Unc |
|---|---|---|---|---|---|---|
| 463 | 1918 | 1.704 | — | BV | 35.00 | 60.00 |
| | 1919 | .984 | — | BV | 35.00 | 70.00 |
| | 1920/10 | .607 | — | BV | 65.00 | 120.00 |
| | 1920 | Inc. Ab. | — | BV | 35.00 | 60.00 |
| | 1944 | .020 | BV | 35.00 | 40.00 | 70.00 |
| | 1945 | *.180 | — | — | | BV + 18% |
| | 1946 | .163 | BV | 35.00 | 40.00 | 65.00 |
| | 1947 | .024 | 200.00 | 250.00 | 300.00 | 550.00 |
| | 1948 | .063 | BV | 35.00 | 40.00 | 65.00 |

**\*NOTE:** During 1951-1972 a total of 5,025,087 pieces were restruck, most likely dated 1945.

## CINCO (5) PESOS

**4.1666 g, .900 GOLD, .1205 oz AGW**

| KM# | Date | Mintage | Fine | VF | XF | Unc |
|---|---|---|---|---|---|---|
| 464 | 1905 | .018 | 100.00 | 150.00 | 200.00 | 600.00 |
| | 1906 | 4.638 | — | BV | 60.00 | 90.00 |
| | 1907 | 1.088 | — | BV | 60.00 | 90.00 |
| | 1910 | .100 | BV | 65.00 | 75.00 | 140.00 |
| | 1918/7 | .609 | 60.00 | 65.00 | 75.00 | 120.00 |
| | 1918 | Inc. Ab. | — | BV | 60.00 | 90.00 |
| | 1919 | .506 | — | BV | 60.00 | 90.00 |
| | 1920 | 2.385 | — | BV | 60.00 | 80.00 |
| | 1955 | *.048 | — | — | | BV + 11% |

**\*NOTE:** During 1955-1972 a total of 1,767,645 pieces were restruck, most likely dated 1955.

### Miguel Hidalgo y Costilla

| KM# | Date | Mintage | VF | XF | Unc | BU |
|---|---|---|---|---|---|---|
| 467 | 1951 | 4.958 | BV | 5.50 | 8.00 | 9.50 |
| | 1952 | 9.595 | BV | 5.50 | 8.00 | 9.50 |
| | 1953 | 20.376 | BV | 5.25 | 7.50 | 9.50 |
| | 1954 | .030 | 30.00 | 60.00 | 80.00 | 90.00 |

### 30.0000 g, .900 SILVER, .8681 oz ASW
### Cuauhtemoc

| KM# | Date | Mintage | VF | XF | Unc | BU |
|---|---|---|---|---|---|---|
| 465 | 1947 | 5.110 | BV | 6.50 | 9.00 | 10.00 |
| | 1948 | 26.740 | BV | 6.00 | 8.00 | 9.00 |

### 27.7800 g, .720 SILVER, .6431 oz ASW
### Opening of Southern Railroad

| | | | | | | |
|---|---|---|---|---|---|---|
| 466 | 1950 | .200 | 30.00 | 40.00 | 50.00 | 55.00 |

**NOTE:** It is recorded that 100,000 pieces were melted to be used for the 1968 Mexican Olympic 25 Pesos.

### Bicentennial of Hidalgo Birth

| | | | | | | |
|---|---|---|---|---|---|---|
| 468 | 1953 | 1.000 | BV | 6.50 | 9.00 | 11.00 |

### 18.0500 g, .720 SILVER, .4178 oz ASW
### Reduced size, 36mm.

| | | | | | | |
|---|---|---|---|---|---|---|
| 469 | 1955 | 4.271 | 4.00 | 5.00 | 6.00 | 7.00 |
| | 1956 | 4.596 | 4.00 | 5.00 | 6.00 | 7.00 |
| | 1957 | 3.464 | 4.00 | 5.00 | 6.00 | 7.00 |

**100th Anniversary of Constitution**

| KM# | Date | Mintage | VF | XF | Unc | BU |
|---|---|---|---|---|---|---|
| 470 | 1957 | .200 | 5.50 | 9.00 | 13.50 | 15.50 |

**Centennial of Carranza Birth**

| | | | | | | |
|---|---|---|---|---|---|---|
| 471 | 1959 | 1.000 | BV | 5.00 | 9.00 | 10.00 |

Small date        Large date

**COPPER-NICKEL**
**Vicente Guerrero**

| | | | | | | |
|---|---|---|---|---|---|---|
| 472 | 1971 | 28.457 | .50 | .75 | 2.50 | 3.25 |
| | 1972 | 75.000 | .50 | .75 | 2.00 | 2.25 |
| | 1973 | 19.405 | 1.20 | 1.50 | 6.00 | 7.50 |
| | 1974 | 34.500 | .35 | .80 | 1.75 | 2.25 |
| | 1976 small date | | | | | |
| | | 26.121 | .75 | 1.25 | 3.50 | 4.25 |
| | 1976 large date | | | | | |
| | | 121.550 | .10 | .50 | 1.50 | 1.75 |
| | 1977 | 102.000 | .50 | .75 | 1.50 | 2.00 |
| | 1978 | 25.700 | .50 | 1.50 | 5.50 | 6.75 |

**Quetzalcoatl**

| KM# | Date | Mintage | VF | XF | Unc | BU |
|---|---|---|---|---|---|---|
| 485 | 1980 | 266.900 | .20 | .50 | 1.75 | 2.25 |
| | 1981 | 30.500 | .35 | .50 | 2.00 | 3.25 |
| | 1982 | 20.000 | .50 | 1.50 | 3.50 | 5.25 |
| | 1982 | 1,051 | — | — | Proof | 24.00 |
| | 1983 | 7 known | — | — | Proof | — |
| | 1984 | 16.300 | 1.25 | 2.00 | 4.00 | 6.00 |
| | 1985 | 76.900 | 1.50 | 2.25 | 4.50 | 6.50 |

**BRASS**
**Circulation Coinage**

| | | | | | | |
|---|---|---|---|---|---|---|
| 502 | 1985 | 30.000 | — | .10 | .35 | .50 |
| | 1987 | 81.900 | 6.00 | 7.50 | 12.50 | 15.00 |
| | 1988 | 76.600 | — | .10 | .25 | .35 |

# DIEZ (10) PESOS

**8.3333 g, .900 GOLD, .2411 oz AGW**
**Miguel Hidalgo**

| KM# | Date | Mintage | Fine | VF | XF | Unc |
|---|---|---|---|---|---|---|
| 473 | 1905 | .039 | 120.00 | 135.00 | 150.00 | 225.00 |
| | 1906 | 2.949 | — | BV | 120.00 | 145.00 |
| | 1907 | 1.589 | — | BV | 120.00 | 145.00 |
| | 1908 | .890 | — | BV | 120.00 | 145.00 |
| | 1910 | .451 | — | BV | 120.00 | 145.00 |
| | 1916 | .026 | 120.00 | 135.00 | 160.00 | 325.00 |
| | 1917 | 1.967 | — | BV | 120.00 | 145.00 |
| | 1919 | .266 | — | BV | 120.00 | 145.00 |
| | 1920 | .012 | 175.00 | 300.00 | 500.00 | 750.00 |
| | 1959 | *.050 | — | — | | BV + 7% |

**\*NOTE:** During 1961-1972 a total of 954,983 pieces were restruck, most likely dated 1959.

**28.8800 g, .900 SILVER, .8357 oz ASW**
**Miguel Hidalgo**

| KM# | Date | Mintage | VF | XF | Unc | BU |
|---|---|---|---|---|---|---|
| 474 | 1955 | .585 | BV | 6.50 | 10.00 | 12.00 |
| | 1956 | 3.535 | BV | 5.50 | 8.50 | 11.00 |

| KM# | Date | Mintage | VF | XF | Unc | BU |
|---|---|---|---|---|---|---|
| 477.1 | 1974 | 3.900 | .50 | 1.75 | 3.25 | 4.00 |
| | 1974 | — | — | — | Proof | 600.00 |
| | 1975 | 1.000 | 1.00 | 3.50 | 10.00 | 17.50 |
| | 1976 | 74.500 | .25 | .75 | 1.75 | 2.25 |
| | 1977 | 79.620 | .50 | 1.00 | 2.00 | 3.00 |
| | **Thick flan, 2.3mm.** | | | | | |
| 477.2 | 1978 | 124.850 | .50 | 1.00 | 2.50 | 2.75 |
| | 1979 | 57.200 | .50 | 1.00 | 2.25 | 2.50 |
| | 1980 | 55.200 | .50 | 1.00 | 2.75 | 3.50 |
| | 1981 | 222.768 | .30 | .60 | 2.00 | 2.25 |
| | 1982 | 151.770 | .40 | .75 | 2.50 | 3.25 |
| | 1982 | 1,051 | — | — | Proof | 24.00 |
| | 1983 | 3 known | — | — | Proof | — |
| | 1985 | 58.000 | 1.25 | 1.75 | 6.00 | 7.50 |

### STAINLESS STEEL
### Miguel Hidalgo

| KM# | Date | Mintage | VF | XF | Unc | BU |
|---|---|---|---|---|---|---|
| 512 | 1985 | 257.000 | — | .15 | .65 | .85 |
| | 1986 | 392.000 | — | .15 | .65 | 1.50 |
| | 1987 | 305.000 | — | .10 | .50 | .65 |
| | 1988 | 500.300 | — | .10 | .35 | .40 |
| | 1989 | — | — | .25 | .75 | 1.25 |
| | 1990 | — | — | .25 | .75 | 1.25 |

**NOTE:** Date varieties exist.

#### 100th Anniversary of Constitution

| KM# | Date | Mintage | VF | XF | Unc | BU |
|---|---|---|---|---|---|---|
| 475 | 1957 | .100 | 12.00 | 25.00 | 42.00 | 47.50 |

# VEINTE (20) PESOS

#### 16.6666 g, .900 GOLD, .4823 oz AGW

| KM# | Date | Mintage | Fine | VF | XF | Unc |
|---|---|---|---|---|---|---|
| 478 | 1917 | .852 | — | BV | 230.00 | 265.00 |
| | 1918 | 2.831 | — | BV | 230.00 | 275.00 |
| | 1919 | 1.094 | — | BV | 230.00 | 265.00 |
| | 1920/10 | .462 | — | BV | 235.00 | 285.00 |
| | 1920 | Inc. Ab. | — | BV | 230.00 | 275.00 |
| | 1921/11 | .922 | — | BV | 240.00 | 300.00 |
| | 1921 | Inc. Ab. | — | BV | 230.00 | 265.00 |
| | 1959 | *.013 | — | — | | BV + 4% |

**\*NOTE:** During 1960-1971 a total of 1,158,414 pieces were restruck, most likely dated 1959.

#### 150th Anniversary of War of Independence

| | | | | | | |
|---|---|---|---|---|---|---|
| 476 | 1960 | 1.000 | BV | 7.00 | 10.00 | 12.50 |

### COPPER-NICKEL
### Miguel Hidalgo
### Thin flan, 1.6mm.

#### COPPER-NICKEL

| KM# | Date | Mintage | VF | XF | Unc | BU |
|---|---|---|---|---|---|---|
| 486 | 1980 | 84.900 | .35 | .70 | 2.75 | 3.50 |
| | 1981 | 250.573 | .35 | .70 | 2.50 | 3.25 |
| | 1982 | 236.892 | .35 | .70 | 2.75 | 3.50 |
| | 1982 | 1,051 | — | — | Proof | 25.00 |
| | 1983 | 3 known | — | — | Proof | — |
| | 1984 | 55.000 | 1.00 | 1.50 | 6.00 | 7.50 |

### BRASS
### Guadalupe Victoria, First President

| KM# | Date | Mintage | VF | XF | Unc | BU |
|---|---|---|---|---|---|---|
| 508 | 1985 wide date | | | | | |
| | | 25.000 | .10 | .20 | 1.00 | 1.25 |
| | 1985 narrow date | | | | | |
| | | Inc. Ab. | .10 | .25 | 1.50 | 2.00 |
| | 1986 | 10.000 | — | — | — | 5.00 |
| | 1988 | 355.200 | — | .10 | .40 | .50 |
| | 1989 | — | .15 | .30 | 1.50 | 2.00 |
| | 1990 | — | .15 | .30 | 1.50 | 2.50 |

## VEINTICINCO (25) PESOS

22.5000 g, .720 SILVER, .5209 oz ASW
Summer Olympics - Mexico City
Type I, rings aligned.

| KM# | Date | Mintage | VF | XF | Unc | BU |
|---|---|---|---|---|---|---|
| 479.1 | 1968 | 27.182 | BV | 3.75 | 5.00 | 5.50 |

### Benito Juarez

| KM# | Date | Mintage | VF | XF | Unc | BU |
|---|---|---|---|---|---|---|
| 480 | 1972 | 2.000 | BV | 4.00 | 6.00 | 7.50 |

7.7760 g, .720 SILVER, .1800 oz ASW, 24mm
1986 World Cup Soccer Games

| KM# | Date | Mintage | VF | XF | Unc | BU |
|---|---|---|---|---|---|---|
| 497 | 1985 | .354 | — | — | — | 8.00 |

8.4060 g, .925 SILVER, .2450 oz ASW
Rev: W/o fineness statement.

| KM# | Date | Mintage | VF | XF | Unc | BU |
|---|---|---|---|---|---|---|
| 497a | 1986 | — | — | — | Proof | 15.00 |

Type II, center ring low.

| KM# | Date | Mintage | VF | XF | Unc | BU |
|---|---|---|---|---|---|---|
| 479.2 | 1968 | Inc. Ab. | BV | 5.00 | 9.25 | 10.00 |

1986 World Cup Soccer Games

| KM# | Date | Mintage | VF | XF | Unc | BU |
|---|---|---|---|---|---|---|
| 503 | 1985 | .277 | — | — | Proof | 15.00 |

Normal tongue    Long curved tongue
Type III, center rings low.
Snake with long curved tongue.

| KM# | Date | Mintage | VF | XF | Unc | BU |
|---|---|---|---|---|---|---|
| 479.3 | 1968 | Inc. Ab. | BV | 6.00 | 10.00 | 12.00 |

1986 World Cup Soccer Games

| KM# | Date | Mintage | VF | XF | Unc | BU |
|---|---|---|---|---|---|---|
| 514 | 1985 | .234 | — | — | Proof | 15.00 |

### 1986 World Cup Soccer Games

| KM# | Date | Mintage | VF | XF | Unc | BU |
|-----|------|---------|-----|-----|-------|-------|
| 519 | 1986 | — | — | — | Proof | 15.00 |

## 50 PESOS

### 41.6666 g, .900 GOLD, 1.2057 oz AGW
### Centennial of Independence

| KM# | Date | Mintage | Fine | VF | XF | Unc |
|-----|------|---------|------|-----|-----|-----|
| 481 | 1921 | .180 | — | — | BV | 775.00 |
| | 1922 | .463 | — | — | BV | 575.00 |
| | 1923 | .432 | — | — | BV | 575.00 |
| | 1924 | .439 | — | — | BV | 575.00 |
| | 1925 | .716 | — | — | BV | 575.00 |
| | 1926 | .600 | — | — | BV | 575.00 |
| | 1927 | .606 | — | — | BV | 575.00 |
| | 1928 | .538 | — | — | BV | 575.00 |
| | 1929 | .458 | — | — | BV | 575.00 |
| | 1930 | .372 | — | — | BV | 575.00 |
| | 1931 | .137 | — | — | BV | 700.00 |
| | 1944 | .593 | — | — | BV | 575.00 |
| | 1945 | 1.012 | — | — | BV | 575.00 |
| | 1946 | 1.588 | — | — | BV | 575.00 |
| | 1947 | .309 | — | — | | BV + 3% |
| | 1947 | — | — | — | Specimen 6500. |

**NOTE:** During 1949-1972 a total of 3,975,654 pieces were restruck, most likely dated 1947.

### COPPER-NICKEL
### Coyolxauhqui

| KM# | Date | Mintage | VF | XF | Unc | BU |
|-----|------|---------|------|------|-------|-------|
| 490 | 1982 | 222.890 | .65 | .85 | 3.25 | 3.75 |
| | 1983 | 45.000 | 1.50 | 2.00 | 4.25 | 5.75 |
| | 1983 | 1,051 | — | — | Proof | 30.00 |
| | 1984 | 73.537 | 1.00 | 1.25 | 3.50 | 4.00 |
| | 1984 | 4 known | — | — | Proof | — |

**NOTE:** Doubled die examples of 1982 and 1983 dates exist.

### Benito Juarez

| KM# | Date | Mintage | VF | XF | Unc | BU |
|-----|------|---------|------|------|-------|-------|
| 495 | 1984 | 94.216 | .25 | 1.00 | 1.50 | 2.25 |
| | 1985 | 296.000 | .25 | .75 | 1.50 | 2.25 |
| | 1986 | 50.000 | 5.00 | 7.00 | 10.00 | 12.00 |
| | 1987 | 210.000 | — | — | 1.00 | 1.25 |
| | 1988 | 80.200 | 5.00 | 7.00 | 9.00 | 11.50 |

### STAINLESS STEEL

| | | | | | | |
|-----|------|---------|------|------|-------|-------|
| 495a | 1988 | 353.300 | — | .10 | .50 | .60 |
| | 1990 | — | — | .25 | 1.00 | 2.00 |
| | 1992 | — | — | .10 | .50 | .60 |

### 15.5520 g, .720 SILVER, .3601 oz ASW
### 1986 World Cup Soccer Games

| | | | | | | |
|-----|------|------|-----|-----|-----|-------|
| 498 | 1985 | .347 | — | — | — | 11.00 |

### 16.8310 g, .925 SILVER, .5000 oz ASW
### Rev: W/o fineness statement.

| | | | | | | |
|------|------|------|-----|-----|-------|-------|
| 498a | 1986 | .010 | — | — | Proof | 22.50 |

### 1986 World Cup Soccer Games

| | | | | | | |
|-----|------|------|-----|-----|-------|-------|
| 504 | 1985 | .347 | — | — | Proof | 22.50 |

**1986 World Cup Soccer Games**

| KM# | Date | Mintage | VF | XF | Unc | BU |
|---|---|---|---|---|---|---|
| 515 | 1985 | .234 | — | — | Proof | 22.50 |

**1986 World Cup Soccer Games**

| | | | | | | |
|---|---|---|---|---|---|---|
| 523 | 1986 | .190 | — | — | Proof | 22.50 |

**15.5500 g, .999 SILVER, .5000 oz ASW**
**50th Anniversary of Nationalization of Oil Industry**

| | | | | | | |
|---|---|---|---|---|---|---|
| 532 | 1988 | .030 | — | — | 12.00 | 15.00 |

## CIEN (100) PESOS

| | |
|---|---|
| Low 7's | High 7's |

**27.7700 g, .720 SILVER, .6429 oz ASW**
**Jose Morelos y Pavon**

| KM# | Date | Mintage | VF | XF | Unc | BU |
|---|---|---|---|---|---|---|
| 483 | 1977 low 7's, sloping shoulder | | | | | |
| | | 5.225 | BV | 5.00 | 7.00 | 10.00 |
| | 1977 high 7's, sloping shoulder | | | | | |
| | | Inc. Ab. | BV | 6.00 | 10.00 | 14.50 |

| 484 | 1977 date in line, redesigned | | | | | |
|---|---|---|---|---|---|---|
| | higher right shoulder | | | | | |
| | | Inc. KM483 | BV | 4.00 | 5.25 | 5.75 |
| | 1978 | 9.879 | BV | 4.50 | 7.00 | 8.50 |
| | 1979 | .784 | BV | 5.00 | 7.50 | 9.00 |
| | 1979 | — | — | — | Proof | 500.00 |

**ALUMINUM-BRONZE**
**Venustiano Carranza**

| 493 | 1984 | 227.809 | .20 | .50 | 2.50 | 4.00 |
|---|---|---|---|---|---|---|
| | 1985 | 377.423 | .15 | .40 | 2.00 | 3.00 |
| | 1986 | 43.000 | .75 | 1.25 | 4.00 | 6.00 |
| | 1987 | 165.000 | — | .20 | 1.50 | 2.00 |
| | 1988 | 433.100 | — | .20 | .75 | 1.50 |
| | 1989 | — | — | .20 | 1.00 | 1.75 |
| | 1990 | — | — | .20 | 1.00 | 2.50 |
| | 1991 | — | — | .20 | 1.00 | 2.50 |
| | 1992 | — | — | .75 | 1.50 | 3.00 |

**31.1030 g, .720 SILVER, .7201 oz ASW**
**1986 World Cup Soccer Games**

| KM# | Date | Mintage | VF | XF | Unc | BU |
|-----|------|---------|-----|-----|-----|-----|
| 499 | 1985 | .302 | — | — | — | 16.50 |

**1986 World Cup Soccer Games**
**Rev: W/o fineness statement.**

| KM# | Date | Mintage | VF | XF | Unc | BU |
|-----|------|---------|-----|-----|-------|------|
| 521 | 1986 | .208 | — | — | Proof | 32.50 |

**32.6250 g, .925 SILVER, 1.0000 oz ASW**
**Rev: W/o fineness statement.**

| 499a | 1985 | 9,006 | — | — | Proof | 32.50 |
|------|------|-------|---|---|-------|-------|

**1986 World Cup Soccer Games**
**Rev: W/o fineness statement.**

| 524 | 1986 | .190 | — | — | Proof | 32.50 |
|-----|------|------|---|---|-------|-------|

**1986 World Cup Soccer Games**
**Rev: W/o fineness statement.**

| 505 | 1985 | 9,006 | — | — | Proof | 32.50 |
|-----|------|-------|---|---|-------|-------|

**World Wildlife Fund - Monarch Butterflies**

| 537 | 1987 | *.030 | — | — | Proof | 50.00 |
|-----|------|-------|---|---|-------|-------|

**31.1030 g, .999 SILVER, 1.0000 oz ASW**
**50th Anniversary of Nationalization of Oil Industry**

| KM# | Date | Mintage | VF | XF | Unc | BU |
|-----|------|---------|-----|-----|------|------|
| 533 | 1988 | .010 | — | — | 22.00 | 30.00 |

**31.1030 g, .999 SILVER, 1.0000 oz ASW**
**Save the Whale**

| KM# | Date | Mintage | VF | XF | Unc | BU |
|-----|------|---------|-----|-----|------|------|
| 566 | 1992 | — | — | — | Proof | 65.00 |

## 200 PESOS

**33.6250 g, .925 SILVER, 1.0000 oz ASW**
**Save the Children**

| | | | | | | |
|-----|------|------|-----|-----|-------|-------|
| 539 | 1991 | .030 | — | — | Proof | 45.00 |

**COPPER-NICKEL**
**175th Anniversary of Independence**

| | | | | | | |
|-----|------|--------|-----|-----|------|------|
| 509 | 1985 | 75.000 | — | .25 | 3.00 | 4.00 |

**27.0000 g, .925 SILVER, .8029 oz ASW**
**Ibero - American Series - Pillars**

| | | | | | | |
|-----|------|------|-----|-----|-------|-------|
| 540 | 1991 | .050 | — | — | Proof | 42.50 |
| | 1992 | .075 | — | — | Proof | 42.50 |

**75th Anniversary of 1910 Revolution**

| | | | | | | |
|-----|------|--------|-----|-----|------|------|
| 510 | 1985 | 98.590 | — | .25 | 3.25 | 4.75 |

**1986 World Cup Soccer Games**

| | | | | | | |
|-----|------|--------|-----|-----|------|------|
| 525 | 1986 | 50.000 | — | .25 | 3.50 | 4.50 |

## 500 PESOS

**17.2800 g, .900 GOLD, .5000 oz AGW**
**1986 World Cup Soccer Games**
**Obv: Eagle facing left w/snake in beak.**

| KM# | Date | Mintage | VF | XF | Unc | BU |
|-----|------|---------|----|----|-----|-----|
| 501.1 | 1985 | .102 | — | — | — | 210.00 |
|  | 1986 | — | — | — | — | 210.00 |

**Rev: W/o fineness statement.**

| KM# | Date | Mintage | VF | XF | Unc | BU |
|-----|------|---------|----|----|-----|-----|
| 501.2 | 1985 | 5,506 | — | — | Proof | 225.00 |
|  | 1986 | — | — | — | Proof | 225.00 |

**1986 World Cup Soccer Games**

| KM# | Date | Mintage | VF | XF | Unc | BU |
|-----|------|---------|----|----|-----|-----|
| 507.1 | 1985 | — | — | — | — | 215.00 |

**Rev: W/o fineness statement.**

| KM# | Date | Mintage | VF | XF | Unc | BU |
|-----|------|---------|----|----|-----|-----|
| 507.2 | 1985 | — | — | — | Proof | 225.00 |

**62.2060 g, .999 SILVER, 2.0000 oz ASW**
**1986 World Cup Soccer Games**

| KM# | Date | Mintage | VF | XF | Unc | BU |
|-----|------|---------|----|----|-----|-----|
| 526 | 1986 | .050 | — | — | 30.00 | 50.00 |

## 250 PESOS

**8.6400 g, .900 GOLD, .2500 oz AGW**
**1986 World Cup Soccer Games**

| KM# | Date | Mintage | VF | XF | Unc | BU |
|-----|------|---------|----|----|-----|-----|
| 500.1 | 1985 | .100 | — | — | — | 110.00 |
|  | 1986 | — | — | — | — | 110.00 |

**Rev: W/o fineness statement.**

| KM# | Date | Mintage | VF | XF | Unc | BU |
|-----|------|---------|----|----|-----|-----|
| 500.2 | 1985 | 4,506 | — | — | Proof | 125.00 |
|  | 1986 | — | — | — | Proof | 125.00 |

**1986 World Cup Soccer Games**

| KM# | Date | Mintage | VF | XF | Unc | BU |
|-----|------|---------|----|----|-----|-----|
| 506.1 | 1985 | .088 | — | — | — | 115.00 |

**Rev: W/o fineness statement.**

| KM# | Date | Mintage | VF | XF | Unc | BU |
|-----|------|---------|----|----|-----|-----|
| 506.2 | 1985 | *.080 | — | — | Proof | 125.00 |

**33.4500 g, .925 SILVER, 1.0000 oz ASW**
**75th Anniversary of 1910 Revolution**

| KM# | Date | Mintage | VF | XF | Unc | BU |
|-----|------|---------|----|----|-----|-----|
| 511 | 1985 | .040 | — | — | Proof | 40.00 |

**COPPER-NICKEL**
**Francisco Madero**

| KM# | Date | Mintage | VF | XF | Unc | BU |
|-----|------|---------|-----|-----|------|------|
| 529 | 1986 | 20.000 | — | .75 | 1.75 | 2.50 |
| | 1987 | 180.000 | — | .75 | 1.75 | 2.50 |
| | 1988 | 230.000 | — | .50 | 1.50 | 2.00 |
| | 1989 | — | — | .50 | 1.50 | 2.00 |
| | 1990 | — | — | .50 | 1.50 | 2.00 |

**17.2800 g, .900 GOLD, .5000 oz AGW**
**50th Anniversary of Nationalization of Oil Industry**
**Similar to 5000 Pesos, KM#531.**

| | | | | | | |
|-----|------|---------|-----|-----|------|------|
| 534 | 1988 | — | — | — | — | 225.00 |

## 1000 PESOS

**17.2800 g, .900 GOLD, .5000 oz AGW**
**175th Anniversary of Independence**

| | | | | | | |
|-----|------|---------|-----|-----|------|------|
| 513 | 1985 | — | — | — | Proof | 275.00 |

**31.1030 g, .999 GOLD, 1.0000 oz AGW**
**1986 World Cup Soccer Games**

| | | | | | | |
|-----|------|---------|-----|-----|------|------|
| 527 | 1986 | — | — | — | — | 675.00 |

**34.5590 g, .900 GOLD, 1.0000 oz AGW**
**50th Anniversary of Nationalization of Oil Industry**
**Similar to 5000 Pesos, KM#531.**

| | | | | | | |
|-----|------|---------|-----|-----|------|------|
| 535 | 1988 | — | — | — | Proof | 550.00 |

**ALUMINUM-BRONZE**
**Juana de Asbaje**

| KM# | Date | Mintage | VF | XF | Unc | BU |
|-----|------|---------|-----|-----|------|------|
| 536 | 1988 | 229.300 | — | 1.00 | 2.00 | 2.75 |
| | 1989 | — | — | .75 | 1.75 | 2.50 |
| | 1990 | — | — | 1.00 | 2.00 | 2.75 |
| | 1992 | — | — | .75 | 1.75 | 2.50 |

## 2000 PESOS

**62.2000 g, .999 GOLD, 2.0000 oz AGW**
**1986 World Cup Soccer Games**

| | | | | | | |
|-----|------|---------|-----|-----|------|------|
| 528 | 1986 | — | — | — | — | 1250. |

## 5000 PESOS

**COPPER-NICKEL**
**50th Anniversary of Nationalization of Oil Industry**

| | | | | | | |
|-----|------|---------|-----|-----|------|------|
| 531 | 1988 | 50.000 | — | 2.75 | 4.75 | 6.00 |

# MONETARY REFORM

1 New Peso = 1000 Old Pesos

## 5 CENTAVOS

**STAINLESS STEEL**

| KM# | Date | Mintage | VF | XF | Unc |
|-----|------|---------|-----|-----|------|
| 546 | 1992 | — | — | — | .15 |

## 10 CENTAVOS

### STAINLESS STEEL

| KM# | Date | Mintage | VF | XF | Unc | BU |
|-----|------|---------|-----|-----|-----|-----|
| 547 | 1992 | — | — | — | — | .20 |
|     | 1993 | — | — | — | — | .20 |

## 20 CENTAVOS

### ALUMINUM-BRONZE

| 548 | 1992 | — | — | — | — | .30 |
|-----|------|---|---|---|---|-----|
|     | 1993 | — | — | — | — | .30 |

## 50 CENTAVOS

### ALUMINUM-BRONZE

| 549 | 1992 | — | — | — | — | .60 |
|-----|------|---|---|---|---|-----|

## NEW PESO

### STAINLESS STEEL RING, ALUMINUM-BRONZE CENTER

| KM# | Date | Mintage | VF | XF | Unc |
|-----|------|---------|-----|-----|-----|
| 550 | 1992 | — | — | — | 1.10 |
|     | 1994 | — | — | — | 1.10 |

## 2 NEW PESOS

### STAINLESS STEEL RING, ALUMINUM-BRONZE CENTER

| 551 | 1992 | — | — | — | 2.25 |
|-----|------|---|---|---|------|
|     | 1993 | — | — | — | 2.25 |

## 5 NEW PESOS

### STAINLESS STEEL RING, ALUMINUM-BRONZE CENTER

| KM# | Date | Mintage | VF | XF | Unc |
|-----|------|---------|-----|-----|-----|
| 552 | 1992 | — | — | — | 4.25 |
|     | 1993 | — | — | — | 4.25 |

## 10 NEW PESOS

### ALUMINUM-BRONZE RING, .925 SILVER CENTER

| 553 | 1992 | — | — | — | 6.50 |
|-----|------|---|---|---|------|
|     | 1993 | — | — | — | 6.50 |

## 20 NEW PESOS

### ALUMINUM-BRONZE RING, .925 SILVER CENTER

| 561 | 1993 | — | — | — | 9.50 |
|-----|------|---|---|---|------|

## 50 NEW PESOS

### BRASS RING, .925 SILVER CENTER
### Nino Heroes

| 571 | 1993 | — | — | — | 25.00 |
|-----|------|---|---|---|-------|

# SILVER BULLION ISSUES
## NEW PESO

**7.7580 g, .999 SILVER, .2498 oz ASW**
Bajorrelieve Del El Tajin

| KM# | Date | Mintage | VF | XF | Unc |
|-----|------|---------|-----|-----|-----|
| 567 | 1993 | — | — | — | 3.50 |

## 2 NEW PESOS

**15.5516 g, .999 SILVER, .4995 oz ASW**
Bajorrelieve Del El Tajin

| | | | | | |
|-----|------|---------|-----|-----|-----|
| 568 | 1993 | — | — | — | 5.50 |

## 5 NEW PESOS

**31.1035 g, .999 SILVER, .9991 oz ASW**
Bajorrelieve Del El Tajin

| | | | | | |
|-----|------|---------|-----|-----|-----|
| 569 | 1993 | — | — | — | 8.50 |

# 10 NEW PESOS

**155.5175 g, .999 SILVER, 4.9956 oz ASW**
Illustration reduced. Actual size: 64.9mm.
Piramide Del El Tajin

| KM# | Date | Mintage | VF | XF | Unc |
|-----|------|---------|-----|-----|-----|
| 570 | 1993 | — | — | — | 45.00 |

## 25 PESOS

**7.7758 g, .999 SILVER, .2500 oz ASW**
Eagle Warrior

| | | | | | |
|-----|------|---------|-----|-----|-----|
| 554 | 1992 | — | — | — | 3.50 |
| | 1992 | .010 | — | Proof | 25.00 |

## 50 PESOS

**15.5517 g, .999 SILVER, .5000 oz ASW**
**Eagle Warrior**

| KM# | Date | Mintage | VF | XF | Unc |
|-----|------|---------|----|----|----|
| 555 | 1992 | — | — | — | 5.50 |
| | 1992 | .010 | — | Proof | 30.00 |

**Xochipilli - The God of Joy, Music and Dance**

| KM# | Date | Mintage | VF | XF | Unc |
|-----|------|---------|----|----|----|
| 562 | 1992 | .030 | — | Proof | 37.50 |

## 100 PESOS

**31.1035 g, .999 SILVER, 1.0000 oz ASW**
**Eagle Warrior**

| | | | | | |
|-----|------|---------|----|----|----|
| 556 | 1992 | — | — | — | 10.00 |
| | 1992 | .030 | — | Proof | 37.50 |

**Brasero Efigie - The God of Rain**

| | | | | | |
|-----|------|---------|----|----|----|
| 563 | 1992 | .030 | — | Proof | 37.50 |

**Huehueteotl - The God of Fire**

| | | | | | |
|-----|------|---------|----|----|----|
| 564 | 1992 | .030 | — | Proof | 37.50 |

## 10000 PESOS

### 1/10 ONZA TROY de PLATA
(1/10 Troy Ounce of Silver)

**3.1103 g, .999 SILVER, .1000 oz ASW**

| KM# | Date | Mintage | VF | XF | Unc | BU |
|-----|------|---------|----|----|-----|-----|
| 543 | 1991 | .050 | — | — | — | 3.00 |
|     | 1992 | — | — | — | — | 2.25 |
|     | 1993 | — | — | — | — | 2.00 |

### 1/4 ONZA TROY de PLATA
(1/4 Troy Ounce of Silver)

**7.7758 g, .999 SILVER, .2500 oz ASW**

| | Date | Mintage | VF | XF | Unc | BU |
|-----|------|---------|----|----|-----|-----|
| 544 | 1991 | .050 | — | — | — | 4.00 |
|     | 1992 | — | — | — | — | 3.25 |
|     | 1993 | — | — | — | — | 3.00 |

### 1/2 ONZA TROY de PLATA
(1/2 Troy Ounce of Silver)

**15.5517 g, .999 SILVER, .5000 oz ASW**

| | Date | Mintage | VF | XF | Unc | BU |
|-----|------|---------|----|----|-----|-----|
| 545 | 1991 | .051 | — | — | — | 6.00 |
|     | 1992 | — | — | — | — | 5.00 |
|     | 1993 | — | — | — | — | 5.00 |

**155.5175 g, .999 SILVER, 5.0000 oz ASW**
**Illustration reduced. Actual size: 65mm.**
**Native Warriors Taking Female Captive**

| KM# | Date | Mintage | VF | XF | Unc |
|-----|------|---------|----|----|-----|
| 557 | 1992 | — | — | — | 45.00 |
|     | 1992 | .010 | — | Proof | 95.00 |

### ONZA TROY de PLATA
(Troy Ounce of Silver)

### 1/20 ONZA TROY de PLATA
(1/20 Troy Ounce of Silver)

**1.5551 g, .999 SILVER, .0500 oz ASW**

| KM# | Date | Mintage | VF | XF | Unc | BU |
|-----|------|---------|----|----|-----|-----|
| 542 | 1991 | .054 | — | — | — | 3.00 |
|     | 1992 | — | — | — | — | 2.00 |
|     | 1993 | — | — | — | — | 1.75 |

**33.6250 g, .925 SILVER, 1.0000 oz ASW**
**Obv: Mint mark above coin press.**

| KM# | Date | Mintage | VF | XF | Unc | BU |
|-----|------|---------|-----|-----|------|------|
| M49a | 1949 | 1.000 | 12.50 | 17.50 | 25.00 | 30.00 |

**Type 4. Rev: Left scale pan points between**
**U and N of UNA.**

| KM# | Date | Mintage | VF | XF | Unc | BU |
|-----|------|---------|-----|-----|------|------|
| M49b.4 | 1979 | Inc. Ab. | — | BV | 13.00 | 15.00 |

**Type 5.**

| | | | | | | |
|-----|------|---------|-----|-----|------|------|
| M49b.5 | 1980 | 6.104 | — | BV | 12.00 | 13.50 |
| | 1980/70 | I.A. | — | BV | 15.50 | 17.50 |

# LIBERTAD
(Onza Troy de Plata)

**Type 1. Obv: Wide spacing between DE MONEDA**
**Rev: Mint mark below balance scale.**

| | | | | | | |
|-----|------|------|-----|-----|------|------|
| M49b.1 | 1978 | .280 | BV | 8.00 | 16.00 | 20.00 |

**31.1000 g, .999 SILVER, 1.0000 oz ASW**
**Libertad**

| | | | | | | |
|------|------|---------|-----|-----|------|------|
| 494.1 | 1982 | 1.050 | — | BV | 7.00 | 9.00 |
| | 1983 | 1.268 | — | BV | 7.00 | 10.00 |
| | 1983 | 998 pcs. | — | — | Proof | 275.00 |
| | 1984 | 1.014 | — | BV | 7.00 | 10.00 |
| | 1985 | 2.017 | — | BV | 7.00 | 9.50 |
| | 1986 | 1.699 | — | BV | 10.00 | 12.50 |
| | 1986 | .030 | — | — | Proof | 22.00 |
| | 1987 | .500 | — | BV | 20.00 | 30.00 |
| | 1987 | .012 | — | — | Proof | 40.00 |
| | 1988 | 1.501 | — | BV | 16.00 | 27.50 |
| | 1988 | *8,000 | Proof Reported, not confirmed | | | |
| | 1989 | 1.397 | — | BV | 10.00 | 12.50 |
| | 1989 | 3,500 | — | — | Proof | 45.00 |

**Reeded edge.**

| | | | | | | |
|------|------|---------|-----|-----|------|------|
| 494.2 | 1988 | *2,000 | — | — | Proof | 100.00 |
| | 1990 | 1.200 | — | BV | 8.00 | 10.00 |
| | 1990 | — | — | — | Proof | 20.00 |
| | 1991 | 1.651 | — | BV | 8.00 | 10.00 |
| | 1991 | — | — | — | Proof | 25.00 |

**Type 2. Obv: Close spacing between DE MONEDA**

| | | | | | | |
|--------|------|----------|-----|-----|-------|-------|
| M49b.2 | 1978 | Inc. Ab. | — | BV | 13.00 | 18.00 |

**Type 3. Rev: Left scale pan points to U in UNA.**

| | | | | | | |
|--------|------|-------|-----|-----|-------|-------|
| M49b.3 | 1979 | 4.508 | — | BV | 15.50 | 17.50 |

**Obv: Eight dots below eagles left talons.**
**Rev: Revised design and lettering.**

| KM# | Date | Mintage | VF | XF | Unc | BU |
|-----|------|---------|-----|-----|-----|-----|
| 494.3 | 1991 | Inc. Ab. | — | BV | 10.00 | 15.00 |
| | 1992 | — | — | BV | 7.00 | 9.50 |
| | 1992 | — | — | — | Proof | 25.00 |

**Obv: Seven dots below eagles left talons,**
**dull claws on right talon, thick letters.**

| 494.4 | 1993 | — | — | BV | 7.00 | 9.00 |
|-------|------|---|---|-----|------|------|

# GOLD BULLION ISSUES
## 250 PESOS

**7.7758 g, .999 GOLD, .2500 oz AGW**
**Native Culture - Sculpture of Jaguar Head**

| KM# | Date | Mintage | VF | XF | Unc |
|-----|------|---------|-----|-----|-----|
| 558 | 1992 | — | — | — | 100.00 |
| | 1992 | .010 | — | Proof | 250.00 |

## 500 PESOS

**15.5517 g, .999 GOLD, .5000 oz AGW**
**Native Culture - Sculpture of Jaguar Head**

| KM# | Date | Mintage | VF | XF | Unc |
|-----|------|---------|-----|-----|-----|
| 559 | 1992 | — | — | — | 200.00 |
| | 1992 | .010 | — | Proof | 400.00 |

## 1000 PESOS

**31.1035 g, .999 GOLD, 1.0000 oz AGW**
**Native Culture - Sculpture of Jaguar Head**

| 560 | 1992 | — | — | — | 400.00 |
|-----|------|---|---|---|--------|
| | 1992 | .010 | — | Proof | 600.00 |

## 1/20 ONZA ORO PURO
(1/20 Ounce of Pure Gold)

**1.7500 g, .900 GOLD, .0500 oz AGW**
**Obv: Winged Victory. Rev: Calendar stone.**

| KM# | Date | Mintage | VF | XF | Unc | BU |
|-----|------|---------|-----|-----|-----|-----|
| 530 | 1987 | — | — | — | — | BV + 30% |
| | 1988 | — | — | — | — | BV + 30% |
| | 1991 | .010 | — | — | — | BV + 30% |
| | 1992 | — | — | — | — | BV + 30% |

## 1/10 ONZA ORO PURO
(1/10 Ounce of Pure Gold)

**3.5000 g, .900 GOLD, .1000 oz AGW**

| 541 | 1991 | .010 | — | — | — | BV + 20% |
|-----|------|------|---|---|---|----------|
| | 1992 | — | — | — | — | BV + 20% |

## 1/4 ONZA ORO PURO
(1/4 Ounce of Pure Gold)

**8.6396 g, .900 GOLD, .2500 oz AGW**

| 487 | 1981 | .313 | — | — | BV + 11% |
|-----|------|------|---|---|----------|
| | 1991 | .010 | — | — | BV + 11% |
| | 1992 | — | — | — | BV + 11% |

## 1/2 ONZA ORO PURO
### (1/2 Ounce of Pure Gold)

**17.2792 g, .900 GOLD, .5000 oz AGW**

| KM# | Date | Mintage | VF | XF | Unc | BU |
|-----|------|---------|----|----|-----|-----|
| 488 | 1981 | .193 | — | — | | *BV + 8%* |
| | 1989 | 3,500 | — | — | Proof 400.00 | |
| | 1991 | .010 | — | — | | *BV + 8%* |
| | 1992 | — | — | — | | *BV + 8%* |

## ONZA ORO PURO
### (1 Ounce of Pure Gold)

**34.5585 g, .900 GOLD, 1.0000 oz AGW**

| | 1981 | .596 | — | — | | *BV + 3%* |
|-----|------|---------|----|----|-----|-----|
| 489 | 1985 | — | — | — | | *BV + 3%* |
| | 1988 | — | — | — | | *BV + 3%* |
| | 1991 | .010 | — | — | | *BV + 3%* |
| | 1992 | — | — | — | | *BV + 3%* |

## (50 PESOS)

**41.6666 g, .900 GOLD, 1.2057 oz AGW**

| | | | | | | |
|-----|------|---------|----|----|-----|-----|
| 482 | 1943 | .089 | — | — | BV 525.00 | |

## PLATINUM BULLION ISSUES
### 1/4 ONZA
(1/4 ounce)

**7.7775 g, .999 PLATINUM, .2500 oz APW**

| KM# | Date | Mintage | VF | XF | Unc | BU |
|-----|------|---------|----|----|-----|-----|
| 538 | 1989 | 3,500 | — | — | Proof | 200.00 |

## MEDALLIC ISSUES (M)
### (10 PESOS)

**8.3333 g, .900 GOLD, .2411 oz AGW**
**200th Anniversary of Birth of Hidalgo**

| KM# | Date | Mintage | VF | XF | Unc | BU |
|-----|------|---------|----|----|-----|-----|
| M91a | 1953 | — | — | — | BV | 135.00 |

**Centennial of Constitution**

| | | | | | | |
|---|---|---|---|---|---|---|
| M123a | 1957 | *.073 | — | — | BV | 135.00 |

**\*NOTE:** Mintage includes #M122a.

### (20 PESOS)

**16.6666 g, .900 GOLD, .4823 oz AGW**
**200th Anniversary of Birth of Hidalgo**

| | | | | | | |
|---|---|---|---|---|---|---|
| M92a | 1953 | — | — | — | BV | 240.00 |

### (50 PESOS)

**41.6666 g, .900 GOLD, 1.2057 oz AGW**
**Centennial of Constitution**

| | | | | | | |
|---|---|---|---|---|---|---|
| M122a | 1957 | Inc. M123a | — | — | BV | 575.00 |

## MINT SETS (MS)

| KM# | Date | Mintage | Identification | Issue Price | Mkt. Val. |
|---|---|---|---|---|---|
| MS1 | 1977(16) | 500 | — | — | 600.00 |
| MSa2 | 1977(9) | — | 434.1,434.2,442,452, 460 thick date, 460 thin date,472,477.1,484,Type 2 for 3 ring binder | — | 125.00 |
| MS2 | 1978(9) | 500 | KM434.1,434.2,442,452, 460 open 8, 460 closed 8, 472,477,484,Type 1 flat pack | — | 200.00 |
| MS3 | 1978(9) | — | KM434.1,434.2,442,452, 460 open 8, 460 closed 8, 472,477.2,484,Type 2 for 3 ring binder | — | 100.00 |
| MS4 | 1979(8) | — | KM434.2,442,452 square 9, 452 round 9, 460(2), 472, 477.2,484, Type 1 flat pack | 11.00 | 12.00 |
| MS5 | 1979(8) | — | KM434.1,434.2,442,452 square 9, 452 round 9, 460,477,484, Type 2 for 3 ring binder | 11.00 | 11.00 |
| MS6 | 1980(9) | — | KM434.2, 442, 452 square 9, 452 round 9, 460 open 8, 460 closed 8, 477.2, 485-486 | 4.20 | 15.00 |
| MS7 | 1981(9) | — | KM442 open 8, 442 closed 8, 452 rectangular 9, 452 round 9, 460 open 8, 460 closed 8, 477.2, 485,486 | — | 18.50 |
| MS8 | 1982(7) | — | KM442,452,460,477,485, 486,490 | — | 16.50 |
| MS9 | 1983(11) | — | KM442(2), 452(2), 460(2), 490(1), 491(2), 492(2) | — | 15.00 |
| MS10 | 1983(9) | — | KM442(2),452(2),460(2), 490(1),491(2),492(2) for 3 ring binder | — | 13.50 |
| MS11 | 1984(8) | — | KM485-486,490-491,493, 495(2),496 | — | 20.00 |
| MS12 | 1985(12) | — | KM477.2,485,493(2), 495(2),496,502,508,509, 510,512 | — | 17.50 |
| MS13 | 1986(7) | — | KM493,495,496,508,512, 525,529 | — | 17.50 |
| MS14 | 1985/1986(7) | — | KM493,495-496,502,508 509,512 | — | — |
| MS15 | 1987(9) | — | KM493,495(2),496,502(2), 512, 529(2) | — | 40.00 |
| MS16 | 1988(8) | — | KM493,495a,502,508,512, 529,531,536 | — | 25.00 |

**NOTE:** The 1978 and 1979 sets were issued in 2 varieties of plastic holders, one of which has holes for insertion in an official 3 ring binder which was sold for $3.30.
**NOTE:** In 1989 The Banco de Mexico began preparing mint sets by year with coins dated from 1971 thru 1988, MSa2 is such a set.

## PROOF SETS (PS)

| PS1 | 1982/1983(8) | 998 | KM442,452,460,485, 477.2,486,490,494 | 495.00 | 425.00 |
|---|---|---|---|---|---|
| PS2 | 1982/1983(8) | *2 | KM460,477.2,485,486, 490,491,492,PnB169 (in white box with Mo. in gold) | — | — |
| PS3 | 1982/1983(7) | *23 | KM460,477.2,485,486, 490,491,492(in white box with Mo in gold) | — | 560.00 |
| PS4 | 1982/1983(7) | *17 | KM460,477.2,485,486, 490,491,492 (in white box) | — | 560.00 |
| PS5 | 1982/1983(7) | *8 | KM460,477.2,485,486, 490,491,492 (in white box) | — | 560.00 |
| PS6 | 1983(7) | 3 | KM460,477.2,485,486, 490,491,492 | — | — |
| PS7 | 1985/1986(12) | — | KM497a-499a,503-505, 514-515,519,521, 523-524 | — | 250.00 |
| PS8 | 1985(4) | — | KM500.2-501.2,506.2, 507.2 | — | 700.00 |
| PS9 | 1985(3) | — | KM499a,514,515 (in blue box) | — | 70.00 |
| PS10 | 1985(3) | — | KM503-505 (in blue box) | — | 70.00 |
| PS11 | 1985(2) | — | KM511,513 | — | 325.00 |
| PS12 | 1989(3) | 3,500 | KM488,494,538, Rainbow | 730.00 | 650.00 |

**\*NOTE:** KM#PS2, PS3, PS4 and PS5 are commonly referred to as pattern proof sets.

# LOCAL COINAGE

This representation of local coinage is not to be considered as complete. Correspondence is welcomed by our editorial staff on any new varieties.

## Ahualulco
### OCTAVO - 1/8 REAL

**COPPER, uniface**
**AHUALULCO and 1813 around 1/8 in circle.**

| KM# | Date | Good | VG | Fine | VF |
|---|---|---|---|---|---|
| L1 | 1813 | 17.50 | 25.00 | 35.00 | 50.00 |
| | | **Script AHO, 1/8 below.** | | | |
| L2 | ND | 12.50 | 17.50 | 25.00 | 35.00 |

## Ameca
### OCTAVO - 1/8 REAL

**COPPER, uniface**
**Church flanked by trees.**

| L6 | 1824 | 12.50 | 17.50 | 25.00 | 35.00 |
|---|---|---|---|---|---|

**TLACO DE AMECA around QTG monogram in circle.**

| L7 | ND | 12.50 | 17.50 | 25.00 | 35.00 |
|---|---|---|---|---|---|
| | | **AME/CA 1811 in circle.** | | | |
| L8 | 1811 | 17.50 | 25.00 | 35.00 | 50.00 |
| | | **Octagonal planchet.** | | | |
| L9 | 1811 | 17.50 | 25.00 | 35.00 | 50.00 |
| | | **F 1/8 Z within wavy circle.** | | | |
| L10 | ND | 17.50 | 25.00 | 35.00 | 50.00 |

**T.Z. AMECA 1833 around value.**

| L11 | 1833 | 12.50 | 17.50 | 25.00 | 35.00 |
|---|---|---|---|---|---|

**V.F AMECA 1858 below value.**

| L12 | 1858 | 12.50 | 17.50 | 25.00 | 35.00 |
|---|---|---|---|---|---|

## Amescua
### OCTAVO - 1/8 REAL

**COPPER, uniface**
**Mexican Eagle**

| KM# | Date | Good | VG | Fine | VF |
|-----|------|------|------|------|------|
| L15 | 1828 | 12.50 | 17.50 | 25.00 | 35.00 |

**Date below eagle.**

| | | | | | |
|-----|------|------|------|------|------|
| L16 | 1838 | 13.50 | 20.00 | 28.50 | 40.00 |

## Atencinco
### OCTAVO - 1/8 REAL

**COPPER, uniface**
**ATENCINCO in outer border, 8 leaved rosette**
**above branch in center.**

| | | | | | |
|-----|------|------|------|------|------|
| L19 | ND | 15.00 | 20.00 | 28.00 | 40.00 |

## Atotonilco
### OCTAVO - 1/8 REAL

**COPPER, uniface**
**ATOTONILCO ANO DE 1808 in outer border,**
**L.S.S./JUSU/ESES in circle.**

| | | | | | |
|-----|------|------|------|------|------|
| L22 | 1808 | 27.50 | 37.50 | 52.50 | 75.00 |

**Obv. leg: ATOTONILCO ANO DE in outer border,**
**1821 in center. Rev. leg:**
**E T P D Z around outer border.**

| | | | | | |
|-----|------|------|------|------|------|
| L23 | 1821 | 17.50 | 25.00 | 35.00 | 50.00 |

**Obv. leg: VILL ATOTONILCO in outer border, 1826 in**
**center. Rev. leg: 1/8 in center, stars in outer border.**

| | | | | | |
|-----|------|------|------|------|------|
| L24 | 1826 | 17.50 | 25.00 | 35.00 | 50.00 |

## Campeche
### CENTAVO

**BRASS**

| | | | | | |
|-----|------|------|------|------|------|
| L27 | 1861 | 8.50 | 12.50 | 20.00 | 28.00 |

## Catorce
### 1/4 REAL

**COPPER**
**Obv. leg: FONDOS PUBLICO around border,**
**1/4 below flower and raised rectangle.**
**Rev. leg: DE CATORCE 1822 around border,**
**eagle on cactus.**

| KM# | Date | Good | VG | Fine | VF |
|-----|------|------|------|------|------|
| L30 | 1822 | 13.50 | 22.50 | 30.00 | 40.00 |

## Celaya
### OCTAVO - 1/8 REAL

**COPPER**
**Obv. leg: EN/CELAYA/DE/1803.**
**Rev. leg: LUIS/VASQUE/S,**
**branches below, flower above.**

| | | | | | |
|-----|------|------|------|------|------|
| L33 | 1803 | 27.50 | 37.50 | 52.50 | 75.00 |

**COPPER, uniface**
**VINDERI/QUE/CELALLA/1808**

| | | | | | |
|-----|------|------|------|------|------|
| L34 | 1808 | 27.50 | 37.50 | 52.50 | 75.00 |

**VISCARA/CELAYA/1814 w/ornament above.**

| | | | | | |
|-----|------|------|------|------|------|
| L35 | 1814 | 17.50 | 25.00 | 35.00 | 50.00 |

## Chilchota
### OCTAVO - 1/8 REAL

**COPPER**
**Obv: Head to right, leg: CHILCHOTA UN OCTAVO,**
**date below. Rev: Wreath in center,**
**leg: RESPONSAVIDAD DE MURGVIA.**

| | | | | | |
|-----|------|------|------|------|------|
| L38 | 1858 | 17.50 | 25.00 | 35.00 | 50.00 |

## Colima
### OCTAVO - 1/8 REAL

**COPPER**
**Obv. leg: VILLA DE COLIMA around border as**
**continuous leg. Rev: Blank.**

| | | | | | |
|-----|------|------|------|------|------|
| L41 | 1813 | 12.50 | 17.50 | 25.00 | 37.50 |

**Obv. leg: VILLA DE COLIMA and date in 3 lines.**
**Rev: Blank.**

| | | | | | |
|-----|------|------|------|------|------|
| L42 | 1814 | 12.50 | 17.50 | 25.00 | 37.50 |

**Obv. leg: QUART COLIMA 1816 in 3 lines in wreath.**
**Rev: Colima monogram in wreath.**

| | | | | | |
|-----|------|------|------|------|------|
| L43 | 1816 | 12.50 | 17.50 | 25.00 | 37.50 |

| KM# | Date | Good | VG | Fine | VF |
|-----|------|------|-----|------|-----|
| L44 | 1819 | 15.00 | 22.50 | 30.00 | 45.00 |

Obv. leg: QUARTo DE COLIMA around border;
date in center circle.
Rev: Colima monogram in wreath.

| | | | | | |
|-----|------|------|-----|------|-----|
| L45 | 1824 | 15.00 | 22.50 | 30.00 | 45.00 |

Obv. leg: OCTO DE COLIMA around border,
date in center circle. Rev. leg: OCTAVO
within wreath, pellet in center.

| | | | | | |
|-----|------|------|-----|------|-----|
| L46 | 1824 | 15.00 | 22.50 | 30.00 | 45.00 |

Obv. leg: OCTO DE COLA in 3 lines.

| | | | | | |
|-----|------|------|-----|------|-----|
| L47 | 1824 | 15.00 | 22.50 | 30.00 | 45.00 |
| | 1828 | 15.00 | 22.50 | 30.00 | 45.00 |

Obv. leg: OCTO DE COLIMA in 3 lines.
Rev. leg: ANO DE 1830 in 3 lines.

| | | | | | |
|-----|------|------|-----|------|-----|
| L48 | 1830 | 15.00 | 22.50 | 30.00 | 45.00 |

## Cotija
### OCTAVO - 1/8 REAL

COPPER
Obv: Seated Liberty w/staff and liberty cap,
leg: DE.D.JOSE NUNES. Rev: Value and date
in wreath, leg: COMMERCIO. D. COTIJA.

| KM# | Date | Good | VG | Fine | VF |
|-----|------|------|-----|------|-----|
| L51 | ND | 13.50 | 20.00 | 28.50 | 40.00 |

## Cuido
### OCTAVO - 1/8 REAL

COPPER, uniface
"CUIDO" above "1/8" in spray.

| | | | | | |
|-----|------|------|-----|------|-----|
| L52 | ND | 13.50 | 20.00 | 28.50 | 40.00 |

## Guadalajara
### OCTAVO - 1/8 REAL

COPPER, uniface
Eagle w/wings spread, leg: GUADALAXARA.

| | | | | | |
|-----|------|------|-----|------|-----|
| L57 | ND | 27.50 | 37.50 | 52.50 | 75.00 |

## Lagos
### 1/4 REAL

BRONZE
Obv: 2 globes w/crown above, wreath and 1/4 below.
Rev: Coat of arms of Lagos.

| | | | | | |
|-----|------|------|-----|------|-----|
| L59 | ND | 100.00 | 150.00 | 200.00 | 250.00 |

SILVER

| | | | | | |
|-----|------|------|-----|------|-----|
| L59a | ND | 150.00 | 200.00 | 300.00 | 500.00 |

## Merida
### 1/2 GRANO

LEAD
Obv. leg: PART/DE LA SO/CIED in center.
MERIDADE YUCATAN around border,
1859 below. Rev. leg:
1/2/GRANO/DE PESO/FUERTE.

| | | | | | |
|-----|------|------|-----|------|-----|
| L60 | 1859 | 15.00 | 18.50 | 25.00 | 35.00 |

## Pazcuaro
### OCTAVO - 1/8 REAL

**COPPER**
Obv: Town at base of mountains, lake in foreground,
value 1/8 above. Rev: Woman
walking right, carrying bag, fish net and fish.

| KM# | Date | Good | VG | Fine | VF |
|---|---|---|---|---|---|
| L63 | ND | 12.50 | 17.50 | 25.00 | 35.00 |

NOTE: Also in brass and cast in bronze.

Obv: 1/8 PAZCUARO. Rev: Crude portrait?.

| | | | | | |
|---|---|---|---|---|---|
| L64 | ND | 12.50 | 17.50 | 25.00 | 35.00 |

## Progreso
### OCTAVO - 1/8 REAL

**COPPER**
Obv: Radiant star above open book.
Rev: Value 1/8 in double wreath.

| | | | | | |
|---|---|---|---|---|---|
| L66 | 1858 | 17.50 | 25.00 | 35.00 | 50.00 |

### CENTAVO
**LEAD**
Obv. leg: MUNICIPALIDAD DE PROGRESSO
UN CENT, 1873 in center.
Rev: Flank in oval band.

| | | | | | |
|---|---|---|---|---|---|
| L67 | 1873 | 13.50 | 20.00 | 27.50 | 40.00 |

## Quitupan
### OCTAVO - 1/8 REAL

**COPPER**
Obv: Bow and 2 arrows in center,
leg: QUITUPAN. .1854. Rev: 1/8 in center,
leg: IGNACIO BUENROSTO, monogram c/m.

| | | | | | |
|---|---|---|---|---|---|
| L69 | 1854 | 17.50 | 25.00 | 35.00 | 50.00 |

## Tacambaro
### OCTAVO - 1/8 REAL

**COPPER**
Obv: Winged caduceus in sprays.
Rev: Value 1/8 in sprays.

| KM# | Date | Good | VG | Fine | VF |
|---|---|---|---|---|---|
| L72 | ND | 13.50 | 20.00 | 28.50 | 40.00 |

## Taretan
### OCTAVO - 1/8 REAL

**COPPER**
Obv: Head of man right. Rev: Tree.

| | | | | | |
|---|---|---|---|---|---|
| L75 | 1858 | 16.00 | 28.00 | 42.50 | 60.00 |

## Tlazasalca
### OCTAVO - 1/8 REAL

**COPPER**
Obv: 2 mountains, date below.
Rev: Value 1/8 in wreath.

| | | | | | |
|---|---|---|---|---|---|
| L78 | 1853 | 17.50 | 25.00 | 35.00 | 50.00 |

## Xalostotitlan
### OCTAVO - 1/8 REAL

**COPPER**
Obv: Crown in center,
leg: AYVNTAMIENTO ILVSTRE.
Rev: 4 in center, leg: DE XALOSTOTITLAN. 1820.

| | | | | | |
|---|---|---|---|---|---|
| L54 | 1820 | 23.50 | 37.50 | 52.50 | 75.00 |

# Zamora
## OCTAVO - 1/8 REAL

**COPPER**

| KM# | Date | Good | VG | Fine | VF |
|-----|------|------|------|------|------|
| L80 | 1842 | 8.50 | 12.50 | 22.50 | 37.50 |
|  | 1848 | 8.50 | 12.50 | 22.50 | 37.50 |
|  | 1854 | 8.50 | 12.50 | 22.50 | 37.50 |
|  | 1858 | 8.50 | 12.50 | 22.50 | 37.50 |

**COPPER or BRONZE**
Obv: Eagle on cactus above sprays.
Rev: Liberty cap, bow and arrows above sprays.
W/or w/o various c/m.

| KM# | Date | Good | VG | Fine | VF |
|-----|------|------|------|------|------|
| L81 | 1852 | 8.50 | 12.50 | 22.50 | 37.50 |
|  | 1853 | 8.50 | 12.50 | 22.50 | 37.50 |
|  | 1856 | 8.50 | 12.50 | 22.50 | 37.50 |
|  | 1857 | 8.50 | 12.50 | 22.50 | 37.50 |
|  | 1858 | 8.50 | 12.50 | 22.50 | 37.50 |

**NOTE:** These pieces are also found with various countermarks. "Za" in a dentilated circle is the most common. "1/8" in a circular c/m is also encountered.

# Zapotlan
## OCTAVO - 1/8 REAL

**COPPER, uniface**
**ZAPO/TLAN/1813**

| | | Good | VG | Fine | VF |
|-----|------|------|------|------|------|
| L84 | 1813 | 18.50 | 30.00 | 42.50 | 60.00 |

**ZAPOTLAM/A.DE 1814**

| | | Good | VG | Fine | VF |
|-----|------|------|------|------|------|
| L85 | 1814 | 21.50 | 32.50 | 50.00 | 75.00 |

# NON-CIRCULATING ISSUES
(Privately produced)

## 1838 Liberty Head Series
### REPUBLIC OF MEXICO
#### UNA QUARTILLA
(1/4) REAL
CHIHUAHUA

**BRASS**

| KM# | Date | Mintage | VF | XF | Unc |
|---|---|---|---|---|---|
| NC1 | 1838 | — | 250.00 | 500.00 | 800.00 |
| | | **SILVER** | | | |
| NC1a | 1838 | — | 500.00 | 1000. | 1500. |

| | | **COPPER** | | | |
|---|---|---|---|---|---|
| NC2 | 1838 | — | 250.00 | 500.00 | 800.00 |
| | | **BRASS** | | | |
| NC2a | 1838 | — | 250.00 | 500.00 | 800.00 |

DURANGO

| | | **BRASS** | | | |
|---|---|---|---|---|---|
| NC3 | 1838 | — | 250.00 | 500.00 | 800.00 |

GUADALAJARA

| | | **BRASS** | | | |
|---|---|---|---|---|---|
| NC4 | 1838 | — | 250.00 | 500.00 | 800.00 |

GUANAJUATO

**BRASS**

| KM# | Date | Mintage | VF | XF | Unc |
|---|---|---|---|---|---|
| NC5 | 1838 | — | 250.00 | 500.00 | 800.00 |

MEXICO

| | | **BRASS** | | | |
|---|---|---|---|---|---|
| NC6 | 1838 | — | 175.00 | 350.00 | 750.00 |

| | | | | | |
|---|---|---|---|---|---|
| NC7 | 1838 | — | 175.00 | 350.00 | 750.00 |

Rev: Column w/flying eagle above in wreath.

| | | | | | |
|---|---|---|---|---|---|
| NC8 | 1838 | — | 250.00 | 500.00 | 800.00 |

POTOSI

| | | **BRASS** | | | |
|---|---|---|---|---|---|
| NC9 | 1838 | — | 250.00 | 500.00 | 800.00 |

TUXTLA

| | | **COPPER** | | | |
|---|---|---|---|---|---|
| NC10 | 1838 | — | 37.50 | 75.00 | 125.00 |

ZACATECAS

PUEBLA

### BRASS

| KM# | Date | Mintage | VF | XF | Unc |
|-----|------|---------|------|--------|--------|
| NC11 | 1838 | — | 250.00 | 500.00 | 800.00 |

### SILVER

| KM# | Date | Mintage | VF | XF | Unc |
|-----|------|---------|------|------|------|
| NC11a | 1838 | — | 500.00 | 1000. | 1500. |

### BRONZE

| KM# | Date | Mintage | VF | XF | Unc |
|------|------|---------|-------|--------|--------|
| NC16 | 1890 | — | 40.00 | 50.00 | 65.00 |

### COPPER-NICKEL

| KM# | Date | Mintage | VF | XF | Unc |
|-------|------|---------|-------|--------|--------|
| NC16a | 1890 | — | 50.00 | 100.00 | 150.00 |

# 1889 Liberty Head Series
Struck by the firm of L. Chr. Lauer, Nurnberg, Germany.

## 2 CENTAVOS
### CAMPECHE

### BRONZE

| | | | | | |
|------|------|---|-------|-------|-------|
| NC12 | 1890 | — | 25.00 | 50.00 | 65.00 |

### COPPER-NICKEL

| | | | | | |
|-------|------|---|-------|--------|--------|
| NC12a | 1890 | — | 50.00 | 100.00 | 150.00 |

### COAHUILA
### BRONZE
Similar to NC15.

| | | | | | |
|------|------|---|-------|-------|-------|
| NC13 | 1890 | — | 25.00 | 50.00 | 65.00 |

### COPPER-NICKEL

| | | | | | |
|-------|------|---|-------|--------|--------|
| NC13a | 1890 | — | 50.00 | 100.00 | 150.00 |

### MEXICO
### BRONZE
Similar to NC15.

| | | | | | |
|------|------|---|-------|-------|-------|
| NC14 | 1890 | — | 25.00 | 50.00 | 65.00 |

### COPPER-NICKEL

| | | | | | |
|-------|------|---|-------|--------|--------|
| NC14a | 1890 | — | 50.00 | 100.00 | 150.00 |

### NUEVO LEON

### BRONZE

| | | | | | |
|------|------|---|-------|-------|-------|
| NC15 | 1890 | — | 25.00 | 50.00 | 65.00 |

### COPPER-NICKEL

| | | | | | |
|-------|------|---|-------|--------|--------|
| NC15a | 1890 | — | 50.00 | 100.00 | 150.00 |

QUERETARO

### BRONZE
Similar to NC15.

| | | | | | |
|------|------|---|-------|-------|-------|
| NC17 | 1890 | — | 25.00 | 50.00 | 65.00 |

### COPPER-NICKEL

| | | | | | |
|-------|------|---|-------|--------|--------|
| NC17a | 1890 | — | 50.00 | 100.00 | 150.00 |

### SAN LUIS POTOSI

### BRONZE

| | | | | | |
|------|------|---|-------|-------|-------|
| NC18 | 1890 | — | 25.00 | 50.00 | 65.00 |

### COPPER-NICKEL

| | | | | | |
|-------|------|---|-------|--------|--------|
| NC18a | 1890 | — | 50.00 | 100.00 | 150.00 |

### TLAXCALA

### BRONZE

| | | | | | |
|------|------|---|-------|-------|-------|
| NC19 | 1890 | — | 25.00 | 50.00 | 65.00 |

| KM# | Date | COPPER-NICKEL Mintage | VF | XF | Unc |
|---|---|---|---|---|---|
| NC19a | 1890 | — | 50.00 | 100.00 | 150.00 |

## ZACATECAS

**BRONZE**
Similar to NC19.

| KM# | Date | Mintage | VF | XF | Unc |
|---|---|---|---|---|---|
| NC20 | 1890 | — | 25.00 | 50.00 | 65.00 |

**COPPER-NICKEL**

| NC20a | 1890 | — | 50.00 | 100.00 | 150.00 |

## MEDALLIC ISSUES
### (2 CENTAVOS)

**BRONZE**
80th Anniversary of Independence

| NC21 | 1890 | — | 50.00 | 100.00 | 125.00 |

| KM# | Date | SILVERED BRONZE Mintage | VF | XF | Unc |
|---|---|---|---|---|---|
| NC21a | 1890 | — | 75.00 | 150.00 | 200.00 |

**COPPER-NICKEL**

| NC21b | 1890 | — | 100.00 | 200.00 | 250.00 |

## REPUBLIC OF NORTH MEXICO
### 2 CENTS

**BRONZE**

| NC22 | 1890 | — | 75.00 | 150.00 | 225.00 |

## REPUBLIC OF THE RIO GRANDE
### 2 CENTS

**BRONZE**
Similar to NC22

| NC23 | 1890 | — | 100.00 | 200.00 | 300.00 |

# Bibliography

Boyd, Julian P. (Editor). *The Papers of Thomas Jefferson.* Vol. 7. New Jersey: Princeton University Press, 1953.

Bowers, Q. David. *The History of United States Coinage as Illustrated by the Garrett Collection.* Los Angeles: Bowers & Ruddy Galleries, 1979.

Breen, Walter. *Walter Breen's Complete Encyclopedia of U.S. and Colonial Coins.* New York: F.C.I. Press, Doubleday, 1988.

Bressett, Ken, and Kosoff, A. *Official A.N.A. Grading Standards for United States Coins,* Fourth Edition. Colorado Springs, Colo.: American Numismatic Association, 1991.

Brown, Martin R., and Dunn, John W. *A Guide to the Grading of United States Coins.* Fourth and Fifth Editions. Racine, Wis.: Whitman Publishing Co., 1964 and 1969.

Bullowa, David M. *Numismatic Notes and Monographs No. 83: The Commemorative Coinage of the United States 1892-1938.* New York, N.Y.: American Numismatic Society, 1938.

Evans, George G. *Illustrated History of the United States Mint.* Revised Edition. Philadelphia: George G. Evans, 1892.

Fitzpatrick, John C. (Editor). *The Writings of George Washington.* Vol. 28. Washington: U.S. Government Printing Office, 1938.

Heath, Dr. George. *The Numismatist,* September 1888 and February 1892.

Hepburn, A. Barton. *A History of Currency in the United States.* Revised Edition. New York: Sentry Press, 1967.

Krueger, Kurt R. "Grading: Bestial Pandemonium Unleashed." *The Numismatist,* January 1976. Colorado Springs, Colo.: American Numismatic Association, 1975.

Ruddy, James F. *Photograde.* Wolfeboro, N.H.: Bowers and Merena Galleries Inc., 1983.

Sheldon, William H. *Early American Cents.* New York: Harper & Row. 1949.

Syrett, Harold C. *The Papers of Alexander Hamilton.* Vol. 7. New York: Columbia University Press, 1963.

Taxay, Don. *The U.S. Mint and Coinage: An Illustrated History From 1776 to the Present.* Second Edition. New York: Arco Publishing Co., 1969.

U.S. Congress. Senate. *International Monetary Conference.* 1878. Senate Ex. Doc., 58. 45th Congress, Third Session. Washington, 1879.

U.S. Congress. Senate. *Coinage Laws of the United States 1792 to 1894 with an Appendix of Statistics Relating to Coins and Currency.* Fourth Edition. Washington, D.C.: Government Printing Office, 1894.

Van Allen, Leroy C., and Mallis, A. George. *Comprehensive Catalog and Encyclopedia of U.S. Morgan and Peace Silver Dollars.* New York: F.C.I. Press, 1976.

Willem, John M. *The United States Trade Dollar: America's Only Unwanted, Unhonored Coin.* New York: By the author, 1959; reprint edition, Racine, Wis.: Western Publishing Co., 1965.

Yeoman, R.S. *A Guidebook of United States Coins.* 45th Edition. Racine, Wis.: Western Publishing Co., 1991.